The Norton Reader

NINTH EDITION

The Norton Reader

An Anthology of Expository Prose

NINTH EDITION

Linda H. Peterson, General Editor
YALE UNIVERSITY

Joan E. Hartman
COLLEGE OF STATEN ISLAND,
CITY UNIVERSITY OF NEW YORK

John C. Brereton
UNIVERSITY OF MASSACHUSETTS, BOSTON

W • W • Norton & Company • *New York* • *London*

This book is composed in Electra
Composition by ComCom
Manufacturing by R.R. Donnelley
Book design by Antonina Krass
Cover illustration: Romare Bearden, *Eden Midnight* (1988). Used by permission of the Estate of Romare Bearden.

Library of Congress Cataloging-in-Publication Data

The Norton reader : an anthology of expository prose / Linda H. Peterson, general editor ; Joan E. Hartman, John C. Brereton.—9th ed.

p. cm.
Includes bibliographical references and index.
1. College readers. 2. Exposition (Rhetoric) I. Peterson, Linda H. II. Hartman, Joan E. III. Brereton, John C.
PE1122.N68 1995b
808.88′8—dc20 95-2934

ISBN 0-393-96826-X (pbk.)

W. W. Norton & Company, Inc., 500 Fifth Avenue, New York, N.Y. 10110

W. W. Norton & Company Ltd., 10 Coptic Street, London WC1A 1PU

1 2 3 4 5 6 7 8 9 0

Contents

[*Entries marked • are followed by questions.*]

PROSE FORMS: JOURNALS

PEOPLE, PLACES

HUMAN NATURE

CULTURAL CRITIQUE

EDUCATION

LANGUAGE AND COMMUNICATION

AN ALBUM OF STYLES

NATURE AND THE ENVIRONMENT

ETHICS

PROSE FORMS: APOTHEGMS

HISTORY

POLITICS AND GOVERNMENT

SCIENCE AND TECHNOLOGY

LITERATURE AND THE ARTS

PROSE FORMS: PARABLES

PHILOSOPHY AND RELIGION

Index of Rhetorical Modes

Narration

DESCRIPTION

EXPOSITION

Essays That Compare and Contrast

Essays That Classify and Divide

Essays That Define

PERSUASION/ARGUMENT

Preface

The ninth edition of *The Norton Reader* is, in many significant ways, new. It has a new editorial team that includes John C. Brereton, Joan E. Hartman, and Linda H. Peterson; it includes sixty-four new essays and fifty-four new writers; among the familiar sections is a new one called "Cultural Critique"; and new study questions appear after many of the essays, whether old or new.

We, the editors, are most excited by the new essays—many of which represent the work of important contemporary writers of American and Canadian nonfiction. New writers range from Nancy Mairs describing her life with multiple sclerosis, to Edward Rivera recalling his first communion in an East Harlem parish, to Patricia Williams analyzing a personal experience of racial discrimination and legal frustration, to Henry Petroski detailing the discovery of the now universal, invaluable Post-it. Some of the new essays come from distinguished, well-established practitioners of nonfiction: John McPhee's "Duty of Care," Cynthia Ozick's "The Seam of the Snail," and Michael Arlen's "The Tyranny of the Visual." Others represent new voices: Judith Ortiz Cofer's "More Room," Rita Moir's "Leave Taking," Elizabeth Wurtzel's "Parental Guidance Suggested," and Randall Balmer's "Adirondack Fundamentalism."

In assembling this edition, we have relied much on the advice of our users. Users' suggestions led to our forming a new section, "Cultural Critique," and to a cluster of short essays focusing on specific cultural phenomena: Roland Barthes on "Toys," Arthur Schopenhauer "On Noise," Fred Strebeigh on "Bicycles in China," and Henry Louis Gates, Jr., on hair in African-American culture. Users, too, encouraged us to rethink the section "Philosophy and Religion," and to include more essays that specifically address issues in contemporary American religious life; two of the new essays that move me most—one to laughter, the other to serious self-reflection—appear in this newly revised section. Users also suggested that we find more short essays that deal directly with students' interests and needs, and we have done so with selections such as Maggie Helwig's on anorexia, Barbara Huttmann's on euthanasia, Susan Allen Toth's on going to the movies, and Jewel Gomez's reminiscences of a swimming lesson that taught her more than swimming. Finally, it was users who suggested that we restore some superb essays from earlier editions—Alice Walker's "Beauty: When the Other Dancer Is the Self" and Robert Finch's "Very Like a Whale"—and that we remember our commitment to classic essayists. We have happily done so.

What is new in this edition is, we believe, continuous with what was excellent in past editions. Arthur Eastman, now General Editor Emeritus, always insisted that essays be selected for their achievement: "Excellence would be their pillar of smoke by day, of fire by night," he wrote in the preface to the eighth edition. All the new essays are, we think, superb pieces of writing. They raise and reflect on important issues—"timely, timeless, engaging," as the introduction "To Students" puts it. We trust that the new study questions will help readers recognize and respond to this excellence, but we also hope that the questions—whether in this edition or from the new instructor's guide—will prompt students to envision themselves as writers, fully engaged with the same issues that have prompted the "professionals" to write.

For their many contributions, therefore, and for their support we thank our users, reviewers, colleagues, and friends: Chris Anderson, Oregon State University; Margaret Bendroth, Andover-Newton Theological Seminary; Walter Blanco, Herbert H. Lehman College; Bernard Bomba, Sussex County Community College; Ginny Brereton, Tufts University; Roberta Layman Burgess, Auburn University; Shannon Cary, Auburn University; Roger D. Carlstrom, Yakima Valley Community College; Casey Confoy, Trenton State College; Beth Cooley, Gonzaga University; Kathleen Culver, Santa Fe Community College; Ann Diego, Cornell University; Dara Duggan, Auburn University; Errol Dean Erickson, North Dakota State College of Science; Bertha P. Fagan, Florida Institute of Technology; Lydia Fakundiny, Cornell University; Douglas Fetherling, M. B. Fiddler, DePaul University; Carol Fokine, Portland State University; Carol Franks, Portland State University; John J. Gallaher, Southwest Texas State University; Thomas B. P. Goetz, University of Virginia; Katherine Gotteschalk, Cornell University; Steven R. Gulick, University of Northern Iowa; Joel Haefner, Illinois State University; Keith Harrison, Carleton College; David Havel, The Weitzman Institute; Douglas D. Hesse, Illinois State University; John S. Hillman, Essex Community College; Lorena Horton, San Jacinto College—North; Peter C. John, Lower

Columbia College; Monica Johnstone, Loyola College; Alice Kracke, Auburn University; Richard Krause, Somerset Community College; Greg Lineweaver, La Grande College of Business; Nancy Lynch, Massachusetts Institute of Technology; Susan McGury, DePaul University; David E. Middleton, Nicholls State University; Colleen M. Minogue, DePaul University; Sharon Mollerus, San Diego State University; James Mulvihill, University of Alberta; Amy Muse, Auburn University; Van Muse, Auburn University; Nancy Naugle, Auburn University; Mary G. Newell, Santa Fe Community College; Elaine Posanka, Auburn University; James Postema, Concordia College; Jeanne M. Purdy, University of Minnesota—Morris; Ed Quinn, City University of New York; Marguerite Majitton Rhodes, Auburn University; Stephen Robitaille, Santa Fe Community College; Dawn Rodrigues, Kennesaw State College; Daniel H. Rosensweig, University of Virginia; Connie G. Rothwell, University of North Carolina—Charlotte; J. W. Scheideman, DePaul University; Margaret Schwindler, Auburn University; Steve Singleton, Auburn University; Susan Belasco Smith, California State University, Los Angeles; Brad Stiles, University of Illinois; Ann Folwell Stanford, DePaul University; Ben Tanner, Auburn University; Victor H. Thompson, Thomas Nelson Community College; Susan D. Tilka, Southwest Texas State University; Stewart Todd, Auburn University; Sybil Virshbo, Roosevelt University; Claudia Waizkers, Brandeis University; Fontaine Wallace, Florida Institute of Technology; S. E. Winkle, Santa Fe Community College; Carolyn A. Wood, Santa Fe Community College; Dorothy Wolfberg, School of Visual Arts; Donna Younger, DePaul University.

Finally, we thank the editors emeriti, especially Arthur Eastman, for trusting us with their book; Libby Miles Clawson for her work on the biographical sketches; our friends at Norton who helped in the production of the ninth edition, Marian Johnson, Kate Lovelady, Shelley Perron, and Diane O'Connor; and our editors there, Julia Reidhead and Carol Hollar-Zwick, for their advice and counsel. We could easily and justifiably list Carol as one of the exciting, new features of this ninth edition of *The Norton Reader*. She joined us at the start and has participated through every stage, from nominating and selecting essays to copyediting and reading the proofs. We have been grateful for her lively, yet patient, presence.

—Linda H. Peterson

To Students: Reading and Writing with *The Norton Reader*

We, the editors of *The Norton Reader*, have put together a selection of essays on a range of subjects, some familiar, others more specialized. You'll find the first kind in sections like "Personal Report" and "People, Places," the second in sections like "History" and "Science." "Personal Report" goes back to the earliest edition; "Nature and the Environment," was added to the previous edition, "Cultural Critique" to this one. Some essays—E. B. White's "Once More to the Lake," for example, and Jonathan Swift's "A Modest Proposal"—are constant choices. Other essays—about one-third—are new to this edition.

The editors read widely in order to include a variety of authors writing on a variety of topics in a variety of ways. We include male and female voices; American, British, and Canadian voices; African-American, Asian-American, Native American, and Latino voices. Some essays are calculatedly challenging, others relatively simple. Some are long, others short. Although most are contemporary, some are not; although most were originally written in English, a few are translated from other languages. What they have in common is excellence: three editors, without actually defining good writing to ourselves or for each other, have agreed on the inclusion of each. We find their authors, sometimes well known, sometimes less well known, speaking with authority and, often, seeing with a distinctive angle of vision. We find their subjects important, timely, timeless, engaging. We find their writing convincing and clear, their style lean when elaboration is not required and adequate to complexity.

Most of the essays exemplify what might be called "academic" or "college" writing: that is, they are coherently organized and carefully developed with appropriate evidence and detail. Others are more loosely organized, often by association; these appear most often in "Personal Report" and "People, Places." The regular edition (not the shorter) also contains specialized kinds of writing: journals, apothegms, and parables. And both editions contain, in "An Album of Styles," selections by earlier writers and notable stylists.

Both editions contain a large number of essays, more than any instructor will assign during a semester: this time the regular edition contains 204, the shorter 118. The first two sections, "Personal Report" and "People, Places," are organized by kinds of writing, that is, narration and description. The remaining sections are organized by topic: for example, "Human Nature," "Cultural Critique," "Education," "Language and Communication." We know that there are many kinds of college writing courses; we know that instructors link reading and writing in a variety of ways. Our aim in *The Norton Reader* is to accommodate all or most of them. We leave it to your instructors to direct you through the essays, to decide which ones to assign and how to use them.

Most of the essays in *The Norton Reader* originally appeared in publications read by informed and educated general readers. Putting them in a textbook, even one called a *Reader*, makes reading them artificial. They were written for and read by people who wanted to know—or know more—about their subjects, who knew—or knew of—their authors, or who were tempted to launch into unfamiliar subjects written about by authors they had never heard of, because they encountered these essays in publications they ordinarily read. Outside the classroom, readers bring their own interests and motives to reading; inside the classroom, you are left to generate your own in response to assignments.

As editors, we've tried to make available to you some of the choices available to the original readers of these essays. Information about them appears in two places, in footnotes at the beginning of each essay and in the section called "Authors" at the end of the volume. The footnotes describe when and where the essays first appeared and, if they began as talks, when and where they were delivered and to whom. Maya Angelou's "Graduation," for example, is a chapter from her autobiography, *I Know Why the Caged Bird Sings*, published in 1969; Francis Bacon's "Of Youth and Age" was published in a collection called, simply, *Essays*, first in 1612 and, revised, in 1625; Frances Fitz-

Gerald's "Rewriting American History" comes from her *America Revised*, published in *The New Yorker* and then as a book in 1979; Scott Russell Sanders's "Looking at Women" was published in a journal called the *Georgia Review* in 1989; Chief Seattle's "Address" (which is translated) was delivered in response to a treaty offered by the commissioner of Indian Affairs for the Washington Territory in 1854. We don't explain, however, the differences between *The New Yorker* and the *Georgia Review*; the former, a large-circulation commercial weekly magazine, has more readers than the latter, a small-circulation journal published three times a year by the University of Georgia. If more information about context than we provide helps situate you in relation to what you are reading, ask your instructors. As editors, we could swamp a smaller number of essays with additional information about their contexts, but we prefer to include more essays and keep contextual information spare.

The section called "Authors" provides biographical and bibliographical information about the authors whose essays we include. Outside the classroom, we may know something about the authors we read before we read them or we may encounter them as unknowns. We may decide to let them speak for themselves, to see what we can discover about them as they do. Sometimes knowing who they are and where their voices come from helps us to hear them and to grasp what they say—and sometimes it doesn't. Putting biographical information at the end provides, in a textbook, something like the choices ordinary readers have as to how much knowledge about authors they bring to their reading.

An index listing essays by title and by author also appears at the end of *The Norton Reader*. It's of course useful for locating essays; it's also useful for identifying multiple essays by the same author. This edition contains multiple selections by fifteen authors, among them, for example, Joan Didion, Annie Dillard, Stephen Jay Gould, and George Orwell. When you enjoy encountering particular authors, it's worth looking in the index to see if we've included additional essays by them; following authors is a choice that was available to the original readers of these essays.

In addition to information about contexts and authors, we also provide footnotes; footnotes that are part of the original essays we designate, in square brackets, "author's note." Our rules for footnotes go something like this. 1. *Don't* define words, except foreign words, that appear in standard collegiate dictionaries. You can go to yours or, often more sensibly, guess from context. If an unfamiliar word is central to the meaning of an essay, the author is likely to define it. 2. *Do* provide information about people, places, works, theories, unfamiliar things. For example, for Maya Angelou's "Graduation" we explain Gabriel Prosser, Nat Turner, and Harriet Tubman (but not Abraham Lincoln and Christopher Columbus); Stamps (it's an Arkansas town); and "Invictus" (it's a poem). For Frances FitzGerald's "Rewriting American History" we explain socialist realism and American nuclear bomb tests in the Pacific. As editors we don't always agree about what needs annotation or how much is sufficient. In this we're not unique: all annotators make assumptions about the information readers they don't fully know bring to their reading. Our experience in the classroom helps. But you can be sure that we'll fail in some places and annoy you in others by explaining what you find obvious. When we fail, ask your instructors for help; when we annoy you, take our efforts as well intentioned. Again, rather than swamping a smaller number of essays with annotation, we keep them spare.

Our last rule is the trickiest. 3. Explain, don't interpret; that is, provide information but leave readers to decide how authors frame and engage it and how it contributes to their meanings. Francis Bacon's "Of Youth and Age" requires extensive annotation. It is possible to guess that Julius Caesar and Septimus Severus succeeded later in life, after stormy youths; the note, in addition to translating the Latin quotation about Severus, confirms their late success by giving dates and explains that Severus, like Caesar, ruled Rome. Another note identifies Augustus Caesar, Cosmus, Duke of Florence, and Gaston de Foix and confirms their early success by giving dates. These notes and others, taken together, suggest a number of assumptions Bacon made about his audience: they read Latin easily, were familiar with ancient and what to them was contemporary European history, and were willing to take as illustrative examples of "youth" and "age," generally, particular male rulers and public figures. We give dates and facts but leave you to work out meanings engaged by Bacon's examples.

Finally, for many (but not all) of the essays, we provide, at the end, suggestions for both reading and writing.

READING

Readers actively make meaning when they read. The process is somewhat mysterious and so too is the product, comprehension. Inexperienced readers tend to be passive: as they move their eyes over the words on the page they expect meaning to overtake them. When it doesn't, they may become frustrated or irritated by what they are reading, as if the words on the page had designs on them or a life independent of them.

Experienced readers take responsibility for making meaning. They monitor themselves, noticing when they drift off or become distracted. They make predictions and revise them, ask questions and answer them. They connect words, phrases, sentences, paragraphs, and chapters; generalizations and particulars; what they bring to reading and what they read. They create sensory as well as visual images; they voice, using intonation and phrasing, silently most of the time but, when they are stuck, out loud. They have a repertory of strategies for reading and use them appropriately according to what they read and their purposes in reading it. They take the time reading takes or, when time is limited, use the time they have to advantage. They expect partial understandings on a first reading, fuller understandings when they reread.

Many of the suggestions for reading that follow the essays are directions to *do* something. When we tell you to locate, mark, or identify, we ask you to notice essays' structural features, the patterns that undergird and make manifest their meanings. Narrative, description, exposition, persuasion, and argument take conventional shapes—or distort them, and recognizing these shapes enhances comprehension. Other suggestions direct you to paraphrase meanings, that is, to express them in your own words; to extend meanings by providing additional examples; and to reframe meanings by connecting them with meanings in other essays. Still others ask you to notice rhetorical features that contribute to meanings: authors' presences (or personas); authors' authority (and how they earn it); authors' assumptions about audience (and the evidence for them); authors' choices of styles and forms of expression. We also ask you to consider their effects.

At least one of our suggestions asks you to write. These suggestions vary: ordinarily we ask you to demonstrate comprehension by an informed assent—that is, by bringing in something from your experience or reading that extends an essay—or by an informed dissent—that is, by bringing in something from your experience or reading that qualifies or calls it into question. Or we ask you to adapt one or more of an essay's rhetorical strategies to a topic of your own choosing.

Although reading is a somewhat mysterious enterprise, writing about reading helps to demystify it. Watch yourself as you read. Mark up an essay. Write queries and comments in its margins. Keep a reading journal in which you make notes about both what you read and your activities as a reader. Stop reading to look back over what you've written and write something about it; look ahead to make predictions and ask questions and write them down. Write a preliminary summary after your first reading of an essay; expand your summary after rereading the essay. Reread what you've written about an essay and respond to it. Notice what happens when you succeed in making meaning and when you fail, for failure can be as instructive as success. Ordinarily you are the sole judge of both. Short-answer tests elicit only superficial comprehension. Writing about what you read, in essay examinations or papers, tests your comprehension of large structures. But sentence to sentence, paragraph to paragraph, your comprehension is manifest only to you. Keeping a reading journal clarifies the process of reading.

Sharing reading journals in class also helps to demystify reading in a larger community than most of us ordinarily encounter. Discussion, in class as a whole or in groups, can elucidate features of our own and others' reading. What interests and motives do we, students and instructors, bring to particular essays? Do some interests and motives yield better readings than others? Can we borrow or steal others' interests, motives, and readings? What strategies do we employ when we read? Are there other, more useful ones? What meanings do we agree about, what meanings do we disagree about? Can we account for our differences? Can we persuade one another to agree about meanings? Should we try? What are responsive and responsible readings? What are irresponsible readings, and how do we decide? Can writers protect themselves against irresponsible readings?

Readers write, writers read, and these questions concern them both, for making meaning by writing is the flip side of making it by reading. In neither enterprise are meanings passed from hand to hand like nickels, dimes, and quarters.

WRITING

The process of making meaning by writing is less mysterious than the process of making it by reading and so too is its product, a text. Nowadays most instructors, however they choose to link reading and writing, emphasize process and multiple products, that is, the first drafts and revisions that precede final drafts. As students you will seldom have time for as many drafts as professional and experienced writers produce. But learning to distribute the time you have over several drafts rather than one will turn out to be the most efficient use of your time.

Experienced writers know they can't do everything at once: find or invent material, assess its usefulness, arrange it in paragraphs, and write it out in well-formed sentences. Student writers, however, often expect to do all these things in a single draft. If that's what you expect of yourself, then a writing course is a good place to change your expectations and cultivate more sensible and profitable practices. When you try to produce a single draft, you are likely to thin out your material and arrange it simply; lock yourself into arrangements you don't have time to change even if, in the course of writing, you begin to discover additional meanings; and write jumbled paragraphs and clumsy sentences that need to be reworked. In addition, writing a single draft, when you're hoping to produce something reasonably thoughtful and deserving of a respectable grade, is harder than writing several drafts and no quicker.

The process experienced writers go through when they write is something like this. They start with brainstorming, note taking, listing, freewriting, or whatever heuristic devices—that is, means of discovering what to write—that they have learned work for them. They try out what they have to say in rough drafts. As they shape their material they find what it means and what they want it to mean; as they find what it means and what they want it to mean they figure out how to shape it—shape and meaning are reciprocal. Large and small are also reciprocal: they work back and forth among wholes and parts, sections and paragraphs in longer drafts, paragraphs in shorter. As shape and meaning come together, they refine smaller elements, that is, sentences, phrases, even words. They qualify their assertions, complicate their generalizations, and tease out the implications of their examples. At some point they stop, not because there isn't more to be done but because they have other things to do.

This is the rough sequence of tasks experienced writers perform in overlapping stages. They revise at all stages, and their revisions are substantial. What inexperienced writers call revision—tinkering with surface features by rewording, pruning, and correcting—experienced writers call editing and proofreading. These they do at the end, when they are ready to stop revising and prepare what they call a final draft; if larger elements still need repair, it's too soon to work on smaller ones. Student writers should probably plan on at least three drafts: a first draft, a revised draft in which they rework larger elements, and a final draft in which they polish smaller ones.

Writers need readers: although they compose and revise by themselves, they need to try out the meanings they think they have made on responsive and responsible readers. Writing classes, at best, enable students to put less-than-final drafts into circulation and receive responses to them through group work and peer editing. When others read what you have written, you may know what you want to ask them; when you read what others have written, they may have specific questions for you. The questions below are all-purpose. They should probably be asked in the order they appear, since they go from larger elements to smaller ones.

Take introductions as promises and ask: "Does this essay keep the promises the introduction makes?" If it doesn't, either the introduction or the essay will have to be revised. Experienced writers ordinarily write rough introductions and revise them after their drafts take shape. But student writers may discover that they've wandered off topic and need to pull themselves back to the task at hand, especially if it's been assigned, through substantial revision of content and organization.

Then ask, "Does this essay include enough material, and is it interpreted adequately?" Experienced writers ordinarily include more material than student writers. You may find the essays in *The Norton Reader* dense and overspecific; your instructors, on the other hand, may find your essays skimpy and underspecific. Experienced writers thicken their writing with particulars to transmit their meanings and engage readers' recognition, understanding, and imagination. Because they are more in control of their writing than student writers, they are able to be more inclusive, to sustain multiple illustrative examples.

Experienced writers ordinarily specify the meanings they derive from their examples. Student writers are more likely to hope that they speak for themselves. A case in point is their use of quotations. How many are there? Experienced writers ordinarily use fewer than student writers. How necessary are they? Experienced writers paraphrase more than they quote. How well are they integrated? Experienced writers introduce quotations by explaining who is speaking, where the voice is coming from, and what to listen for; they finish off quotations by linking them to what follows.

All writers need to try out their interpretations before they produce a final draft. Slanted interpretations are the stock-in-trade of advertisers and hucksters. But, because the world itself is complex and open to multiple interpretations, examples that seem to one person clear-cut illustrations may seem to another forced. Experienced writers know how to handle qualified examples. Student writers may overstate, and responsive readers will point to interpretations that need qualification.

Then ask, "Is the material in this essay well arranged?" Writing puts readers in possession of interrelated material in a temporal order: readers, that is, read from start to finish. Sometimes material that appears near the end of an essay might better appear near the beginning; sometimes material that appears near the beginning might better be postponed. Transitions between paragraphs should be clear; when they are hard to specify, the difficulty may lie in the arrangement of the material.

Then ask, "Which sentences unfold smoothly and which sentences are likely to cause readers to stumble?" Readers who can point to what makes them stumble as they read your writing will teach you more about well-formed sentences than any set of rules for forming them.

Both reading and writing can and should be shared. Collaboration provides communities of readers to read the writing of professional and experienced writers in texts such as *The Norton Reader* as well as one another's writing. And learning to become a responsive and responsible reader of professional writing will teach you to respond helpfully to the writing of other students in your classes.

Personal Report

Maya Angelou

GRADUATION

The children in Stamps[1] trembled visibly with anticipation. Some adults were excited too, but to be certain the whole young population had come down with graduation epidemic. Large classes were graduating from both the grammar school and the high school. Even those who were years removed from their own day of glorious release were anxious to help with preparations as a kind of dry run. The junior students who were moving into the vacating classes' chairs were tradition-bound to show their talents for leadership and management. They strutted through the school and around the campus exerting pressure on the lower grades. Their authority was so new that occasionally if they pressed a little too hard it had to be overlooked. After all, next term was coming, and it never hurt a sixth grader to have a play sister in the eighth grade, or a tenth-year student to be able to call a twelfth grader Bubba. So all was endured in a spirit of shared understanding. But the graduating classes themselves were the nobility. Like travelers with exotic destinations on their minds, the graduates were remarkably forgetful. They came to school without their books, or tablets or even pencils. Volunteers fell over themselves to secure replacements for the missing equipment. When accepted, the willing workers might or might not be thanked, and it was of no importance to the pre-graduation rites. Even teachers were respectful of the now quiet and aging seniors, and tended to speak to them, if not as equals, as beings only slightly lower than themselves. After tests were returned and grades given, the student body, which acted like an extended family, knew who did well, who excelled, and what piteous ones had failed.

Unlike the white high school, Lafayette County Training School

From *I Know Why the Caged Bird Sings* (1970).

1. A town in Arkansas.

distinguished itself by having neither lawn, nor hedges, nor tennis court, nor climbing ivy. Its two buildings (main classrooms, the grade school and home economics) were set on a dirt hill with no fence to limit either its boundaries or those of bordering farms. There was a large expanse to the left of the school which was used alternately as a baseball diamond or basketball court. Rusty hoops on swaying poles represented the permanent recreational equipment, although bats and balls could be borrowed from the P.E. teacher if the borrower was qualified and if the diamond wasn't occupied.

Over this rocky area relieved by a few shady tall persimmon trees the graduating class walked. The girls often held hands and no longer bothered to speak to the lower students. There was a sadness about them, as if this old world was not their home and they were bound for higher ground. The boys, on the other hand, had become more friendly, more outgoing. A decided change from the closed attitude they projected while studying for finals. Now they seemed not ready to give up the old school, the familiar paths and classrooms. Only a small percentage would be continuing on to college—one of the South's A & M (agricultural and mechanical) schools, which trained Negro youths to be carpenters, farmers, handymen, masons, maids, cooks and baby nurses. Their future rode heavily on their shoulders, and blinded them to the collective joy that had pervaded the lives of the boys and girls in the grammar school graduating class.

Parents who could afford it had ordered new shoes and readymade clothes for themselves from Sears and Roebuck or Montgomery Ward. They also engaged the best seamstresses to make the floating graduating dresses and to cut down secondhand pants which would be pressed to a military slickness for the important event.

5 Oh, it was important, all right. Whitefolks would attend the ceremony, and two or three would speak of God and home, and the Southern way of life, and Mrs. Parsons, the principal's wife, would play the graduation march while the lower-grade graduates paraded down the aisles and took their seats below the platform. The high school seniors would wait in empty classrooms to make their dramatic entrance.

In the Store I was the person of the moment. The birthday girl. The center. Bailey[2] had graduated the year before, although to do so he had had to forfeit all pleasures to make up for his time lost in Baton Rouge.

My class was wearing butter-yellow piqué dresses, and Momma launched out on mine. She smocked the yoke into tiny crisscrossing puckers, then shirred the rest of the bodice. Her dark fingers ducked in

2. The author's brother.

and out of the lemony cloth as she embroidered raised daisies around the hem. Before she considered herself finished she had added a crocheted cuff on the puff sleeves, and a pointy crocheted collar.

I was going to be lovely. A walking model of all the various styles of fine hand sewing and it didn't worry me that I was only twelve years old and merely graduating from the eighth grade. Besides, many teachers in Arkansas Negro schools had only that diploma and were licensed to impart wisdom.

The days had become longer and more noticeable. The faded beige of former times had been replaced with strong and sure colors. I began to see my classmates' clothes, their skin tones, and the dust that waved off pussy willows. Clouds that lazed across the sky were objects of great concern to me. Their shiftier shapes might have held a message that in my new happiness and with a little bit of time I'd soon decipher. During that period I looked at the arch of heaven so religiously my neck kept a steady ache. I had taken to smiling more often, and my jaws hurt from the unaccustomed activity. Between the two physical sore spots, I suppose I could have been uncomfortable, but that was not the case. As a member of the winning team (the graduating class of 1940) I had outdistanced unpleasant sensations by miles. I was headed for the freedom of open fields.

10 Youth and social approval allied themselves with me and we trammeled memories of slights and insults. The wind of our swift passage remodeled my features. Lost tears were pounded to mud and then to dust. Years of withdrawal were brushed aside and left behind, as hanging ropes of parasitic moss.

My work alone had awarded me a top place and I was going to be one of the first called in the graduating ceremonies. On the classroom blackboard, as well as on the bulletin board in the auditorium, there were blue stars and white stars and red stars. No absences, no tardinesses, and my academic work was among the best of the year. I could say the preamble to the Constitution even faster than Bailey. We timed ourselves often: "We the people of the United States in order to form a more perfect union . . ." I had memorized the Presidents of the United States from Washington to Roosevelt in chronological as well as alphabetical order.

My hair pleased me too. Gradually the black mass had lengthened and thickened, so that it kept at last to its braided pattern, and I didn't have to yank my scalp off when I tried to comb it.

Louise and I had rehearsed the exercises until we tired out ourselves. Henry Reed was class valedictorian. He was a small, very black boy with hooded eyes, a long, broad nose and an oddly shaped head. I had admired him for years because each term he and I vied for the best grades in our class. Most often he bested me, but instead of being disappointed I was pleased that we shared top places between us. Like many Southern Black children, he lived with his grandmother, who was as strict as Momma and as kind as she knew how to be. He was courteous, respectful and soft-spoken to elders, but on the playground he chose to play the roughest games. I admired him. Anyone, I reckoned, sufficiently afraid or sufficiently dull could be polite. But to be able to operate at a top level with both adults and children was admirable.

His valedictory speech was entitled "To Be or Not to Be." The rigid tenth-grade teacher had helped him write it. He'd been working on the dramatic stresses for months.

15 The weeks until graduation were filled with heady activities. A group of small children were to be presented in a play about buttercups and daisies and bunny rabbits. They could be heard throughout the building practicing their hops and their little songs that sounded like silver bells. The older girls (nongraduates, of course) were assigned the task of making refreshments for the night's festivities. A tangy scent of ginger, cinnamon, nutmeg and chocolate wafted around the home economics building as the budding cooks made samples for themselves and their teachers.

In every corner of the workshop, axes and saws split fresh timber as the woodshop boys made sets and stage scenery. Only the graduates were left out of the general bustle. We were free to sit in the library at the back of the building or look in quite detachedly, naturally, on the measures being taken for our event.

Even the minister preached on graduation the Sunday before. His subject was, "Let your light so shine that men will see your good works and praise your Father, Who is in Heaven." Although the sermon was purported to be addressed to us, he used the occasion to speak to backsliders, gamblers and general ne'er-do-wells. But since he had called our names at the beginning of the service we were mollified.

Among Negroes the tradition was to give presents to children going only from one grade to another. How much more important this was when the person was graduating at the top of the class. Uncle Willie and Momma had sent away for a Mickey Mouse watch like Bailey's. Louise gave me four embroidered handkerchiefs. (I gave her crocheted doilies.) Mrs. Sneed, the minister's wife, made me an undershirt to wear for graduation, and nearly every customer gave me a nickel or maybe even a dime with the instruction "Keep on moving to higher ground," or some such encouragement.

Amazingly the great day finally dawned and I was out of bed before I knew it. I threw open the back door to see it more clearly, but Momma said, "Sister, come away from that door and put your robe on."

20 I hoped the memory of that morning would never leave me. Sunlight was itself young, and the day had none of the insistence maturity would bring it in a few hours. In my robe and barefoot in the backyard, under cover of going to see about my new beans, I gave myself up to the gentle warmth and thanked God that no matter what evil I had done in my life He had allowed me to live to see this day. Somewhere in my fatalism I had expected to die, accidentally, and never have the chance to walk up the stairs in the auditorium and gracefully receive my hard-earned diploma. Out of God's merciful bosom I had won reprieve.

Bailey came out in his robe and gave me a box wrapped in Christmas paper. He said he had saved his money for months to pay for it. It felt like a box of chocolates, but I knew Bailey wouldn't save money to buy candy when we had all we could want under our noses.

He was as proud of the gift as I. It was a soft-leather-bound copy of a collection of poems by Edgar Allan Poe, or, as Bailey and I called him, "Eap." I turned to "Annabel Lee" and we walked up and down the garden rows, the cool dirt between our toes, reciting the beautifully sad lines.

Momma made a Sunday breakfast although it was only Friday. After we finished the blessing, I opened my eyes to find the watch on my plate. It was a dream of a day. Everything went smoothly and to my credit. I didn't have to be reminded or scolded for anything. Near evening I was too jittery to attend to chores, so Bailey volunteered to do all before his bath.

Days before, we had made a sign for the Store, and as we turned out the lights Momma hung the cardboard over the doorknob. It read clearly: CLOSED. GRADUATION.

25 My dress fitted perfectly and everyone said that I looked like a sunbeam in it. On the hill, going toward the school, Bailey walked behind with Uncle Willie, who muttered, "Go on, Ju." He wanted him to walk ahead with us because it embarrassed him to have to walk so slowly. Bailey said he'd let the ladies walk together, and the men would bring up the rear. We all laughed, nicely.

Little children dashed by out of the dark like fireflies. Their crepe-paper dresses and butterfly wings were not made for running and we heard more than one rip, dryly, and the regretful "uh uh" that followed.

The school blazed without gaiety. The windows seemed cold and unfriendly from the lower hill. A sense of ill-fated timing crept over me, and if Momma hadn't reached for my hand I would have drifted back to Bailey and Uncle Willie, and possibly beyond. She made a few slow jokes about my feet getting cold, and tugged me along to the now-strange building.

Around the front steps, assurance came back. There were my fellow "greats," the graduating class. Hair brushed back, legs oiled, new dresses and pressed pleats, fresh pocket handkerchiefs and little handbags, all homesewn. Oh, we were up to snuff, all right. I joined my comrades and didn't even see my family go in to find seats in the crowded auditorium.

The school band struck up a march and all classes filed in as had been rehearsed. We stood in front of our seats, as assigned, and on a signal from the choir director, we sat. No sooner had this been accomplished than the band started to play the national anthem. We rose again and sang the song, after which we recited the pledge of allegiance. We remained standing for a brief minute before the choir director and the principal signaled to us, rather desperately I thought, to take our seats. The command was so unusual that our carefully rehearsed and smooth-running machine was thrown off. For a full minute we fumbled for our chairs and bumped into each other awkwardly. Habits change or solidify under pressure, so in our state of nervous tension we had been ready to follow our usual assembly pattern: the American national anthem, then the pledge of allegiance, then the song every Black person I knew called the Negro National Anthem. All done in the same key, with the same passion and most often standing on the same foot.

30 Finding my seat at last, I was overcome with a presentiment of worse things to come. Something unrehearsed, unplanned, was going to happen, and we were going to be made to look bad. I distinctly remember being explicit in the choice of pronoun. It was "we," the graduating class, the unit, that concerned me then.

The principal welcomed "parents and friends" and asked the Baptist minister to lead us in prayer. His invocation was brief and punchy, and for a second I thought we were getting on the high road to right action. When the principal came back to the dais, however, his voice had changed. Sounds always affected me profoundly and the principal's voice was one of my favorites. During assembly it melted and lowed weakly into the audience. It had not been in my plan to listen to him, but my curiosity was piqued and I straightened up to give him my attention.

He was talking about Booker T. Washington, our "late great leader," who said we can be as close as the fingers on the hand, etc. . . . Then he said a few vague things about friendship and the friendship of kindly people to those less fortunate than themselves. With that his voice nearly faded, thin, away. Like a river diminishing to a stream and then to a trickle. But he cleared his throat and said, "Our speaker tonight, who is also our friend, came from Texarkana to deliver the commencement address, but due to the irregularity of the train schedule, he's going to, as they say, 'speak and run.' " He said that we understood and wanted the man to know that we were most grateful for the time he was able to give us and then something about how we were willing always to adjust to another's program, and without more ado—"I give you Mr. Edward Donleavy."

Not one but two white men came through the door off-stage. The shorter one walked to the speaker's platform, and the tall one moved to the center seat and sat down. But that was our principal's seat, and already occupied. The dislodged gentleman bounced around for a long breath or two before the Baptist minister gave him his chair, then with more dignity than the situation deserved, the minister walked off the stage.

Donleavy looked at the audience once (on reflection, I'm sure that he wanted only to reassure himself that we were really there), adjusted his glasses and began to read from a sheaf of papers.

He was glad "to be here and to see the work going on just as it was in 35
the other schools."

At the first "Amen" from the audience I willed the offender to immediate death by choking on the word. But Amens and Yes, sir's began to fall around the room like rain through a ragged umbrella.

He told us of the wonderful changes we children in Stamps had in store. The Central School (naturally, the white school was Central) had already been granted improvements that would be in use in the fall. A well-known artist was coming from Little Rock to teach art to them. They were going to have the newest microscopes and chemistry equipment for their laboratory. Mr. Donleavy didn't leave us long in the dark over who made these improvements available to Central High. Nor were we to be ignored in the general betterment scheme he had in mind.

He said that he had pointed out to people at a very high level that one of the first-line football tacklers at Arkansas Agricultural and Mechanical College had graduated from good old Lafayette County Training School. Here fewer Amen's were heard. Those few that did break through lay dully in the air with the heaviness of habit.

He went on to praise us. He went on to say how he had bragged that "one of the best basketball players at Fisk sank his first ball right here at Lafayette County Training School."

The white kids were going to have a chance to become Galileos and 40
Madame Curies and Edisons and Gauguins, and our boys (the girls weren't even in on it) would try to be Jesse Owenses and Joe Louises.

Owens and the Brown Bomber were great heroes in our world, but what school official in the white-goddom of Little Rock had the right to decide that those two men must be our only heroes? Who decided that for Henry Reed to become a scientist he had to work like George

Washington Carver, as a bootblack, to buy a lousy microscope? Bailey was obviously always going to be too small to be an athlete, so which concrete angel glued to what country seat had decided that if my brother wanted to become a lawyer he had to first pay penance for his skin by picking cotton and hoeing corn and studying correspondence books at night for twenty years?

The man's dead words fell like bricks around the auditorium and too many settled in my belly. Constrained by hard-learned manners I couldn't look behind me, but to my left and right the proud graduating class of 1940 had dropped their heads. Every girl in my row had found something new to do with her handkerchief. Some folded the tiny squares into love knots, some into triangles, but most were wadding them, then pressing them flat on their yellow laps.

On the dais, the ancient tragedy was being replayed. Professor Parsons sat, a sculptor's reject, rigid. His large, heavy body seemed devoid of will or willingness, and his eyes said he was no longer with us. The other teachers examined the flag (which was draped stage right) or their notes, or the windows which opened on our now-famous playing diamond.

Graduation, the hush-hush magic time of frills and gifts and congratulations and diplomas, was finished for me before my name was called. The accomplishment was nothing. The meticulous maps, drawn in three colors of ink, learning and spelling decasyllabic words, memorizing the whole of *The Rape of Lucrece*[3]—it was for nothing. Donleavy had exposed us.

45 We were maids and farmers, handymen and washerwomen, and anything higher that we aspired to was farcical and presumptuous.

Then I wished that Gabriel Prosser and Nat Turner[4] had killed all whitefolks in their beds and that Abraham Lincoln had been assassinated before the signing of the Emancipation Proclamation, and that Harriet Tubman[5] had been killed by that blow on her head and Christopher Columbus had drowned in the *Santa Maria.*

It was awful to be a Negro and have no control over my life. It was brutal to be young and already trained to sit quietly and listen to charges brought against my color with no chance of defense. We should all be dead. I thought I should like to see us all dead, one on top

3. A narrative poem of 1,855 lines by Shakespeare, which recounts the story of the daughter of a Roman prefect. When she was defiled, she stabbed herself in the presence of her father and her husband.
4. Gabriel Prosser (c. 1776–1800) and Nat Turner (1800–1831), executed leaders of slave rebellions in Virginia.
5. Black abolitionist (c. 1820–1913), known for her work as a "conductor" on the Underground Railroad.

of the other. A pyramid of flesh with the whitefolks on the bottom, as the broad base, then the Indians with their silly tomahawks and teepees and wigwams and treaties, the Negroes with their mops and recipes and cotton sacks and spirituals sticking out of their mouths. The Dutch children should all stumble in their wooden shoes and break their necks. The French should choke to death on the Louisiana Purchase (1803) while silkworms ate all the Chinese with their stupid pigtails. As a species, we were an abomination. All of us.

Donleavy was running for election, and assured our parents that if he won we could count on having the only colored paved playing field in that part of Arkansas. Also—he never looked up to acknowledge the grunts of acceptance—also, we were bound to get some new equipment for the home economics building and the workshop.

He finished, and since there was no need to give any more than the most perfunctory thank-you's, he nodded to the men on the stage, and the tall white man who was never introduced joined him at the door. They left with the attitude that now they were off to something really important. (The graduation ceremonies at Lafayette County Training School had been a mere preliminary.)

The ugliness they left was palpable. An uninvited guest who 50
wouldn't leave. The choir was summoned and sang a modern arrangement of "Onward, Christian Soldiers," with new words pertaining to graduates seeking their place in the world. But it didn't work. Elouise, the daughter of the Baptist minister, recited "Invictus,"[6] and I could have cried at the impertinence of "I am the master of my fate, I am the captain of my soul."

My name had lost its ring of familiarity and I had to be nudged to go and receive my diploma. All my preparations had fled. I neither marched up to the stage like a conquering Amazon, nor did I look in the audience for Bailey's nod of approval. Marguerite Johnson, I heard the name again, my honors were read, there were noises in the audience of appreciation, and I took my place on the stage as rehearsed.

I thought about colors I hated: ecru, puce, lavender, beige and black.

There was shuffling and rustling around me, then Henry Reed was giving his valedictory address, "To Be or Not to Be." Hadn't he heard the whitefolks? We couldn't *be*, so the question was a waste of time. Henry's voice came out clear and strong. I feared to look at him. Hadn't he got the message? There was no "nobler in the mind" for Negroes because the world didn't think we had minds, and they let us

6. An inspirational poem by William Ernest Henley (1849–1903), once very popular for occasions such as this one.

know it. "Outrageous fortune"? Now, that was a joke. When the ceremony was over I had to tell Henry Reed some things. That is, if I still cared. Not "rub," Henry, "erase." "Ah, there's the erase." Us.

Henry had been a good student in elocution. His voice rose on tides of promise and fell on waves of warnings. The English teacher had helped him to create a sermon winging through Hamlet's soliloquy. To be a man, a doer, a builder, a leader, or to be a tool, an unfunny joke, a crusher of funky toadstools. I marveled that Henry could go through with the speech as if we had a choice.

55 I had been listening and silently rebutting each sentence with my eyes closed; then there was a hush, which in an audience warns that something unplanned is happening. I looked up and saw Henry Reed, the conservative, the proper, the A student, turn his back to the audience and turn to us (the proud graduating class of 1940) and sing, nearly speaking,

> "Lift ev'ry voice and sing
> Till earth and heaven ring
> Ring with the harmonies of Liberty . . ."

It was the poem written by James Weldon Johnson. It was the music composed by J. Rosamond Johnson. It was the Negro national anthem. Out of habit we were singing it.

Our mothers and fathers stood in the dark hall and joined the hymn of encouragement. A kindergarten teacher led the small children onto the stage and the buttercups and daisies and bunny rabbits marked time and tried to follow:

> "Stony the road we trod
> Bitter the chastening rod
> Felt in the days when hope, unborn, had died.
> Yet with a steady beat
> Have not our weary feet
> Come to the place for which our fathers sighed?"

Each child I knew had learned that song with his ABC's and along with "Jesus Loves Me This I Know." But I personally had never heard it before. Never heard the words, despite the thousands of times I had sung them. Never thought they had anything to do with me.

On the other hand, the words of Patrick Henry had made such an impression on me that I had been able to stretch myself tall and trembling and say, "I know not what course others may take, but as for me, give me liberty or give me death."

And now I heard, really for the first time:

> "We have come over a way that with tears
> has been watered,

> We have come, treading our path through
> the blood of the slaughtered."

While echoes of the song shivered in the air, Henry Reed bowed his 60
head, said "Thank you," and returned to his place in the line. The tears that slipped down many faces were not wiped away in shame.

We were on top again. As always, again. We survived. The depths had been icy and dark, but now a bright sun spoke to our souls. I was no longer simply a member of the proud graduating class of 1940; I was a proud member of the wonderful, beautiful Negro race.

Oh, Black known and unknown poets, how often have your auctioned pains sustained us? Who will compute the lonely nights made less lonely by your songs, or the empty pots made less tragic by your tales?

If we were a people much given to revealing secrets, we might raise monuments and sacrifice to the memories of our poets, but slavery cured us of that weakness. It may be enough, however, to have it said that we survive in exact relationship to the dedication of our poets (include preachers, musicians and blues singers).

Bruno Bettelheim

A VICTIM

Many students of discrimination are aware that the victim often reacts in ways as undesirable as the action of the aggressor. Less attention is paid to this because it is easier to excuse a defendant than an offender, and because they assume that once the aggression stops the victim's reactions will stop too. But I doubt if this is of real service to the persecuted. His main interest is that the persecution cease. But that is less apt to happen if he lacks a real understanding of the phenomenon of persecution, in which victim and persecutor are inseparably interlocked.

Let me illustrate with the following example: in the winter of 1938 a Polish Jew murdered the German attaché in Paris, vom Rath. The Gestapo used the event to step up anti-Semitic actions, and in the camp new hardships were inflicted on Jewish prisoners. One of these was an order barring them from the medical clinic unless the need for treatment had originated in work accident.

Nearly all prisoners suffered from frostbite which often led to gan-

From *The Informed Heart: Autonomy in a Mass Age* (1960).

grene and then amputation. Whether or not a Jewish prisoner was admitted to the clinic to prevent such a fate depended on the whim of an SS private. On reaching the clinic entrance, the prisoner explained the nature of his ailment to the SS man, who then decided if he should get treatment or not.

I too suffered from frostbite. At first I was discouraged from trying to get medical care by the fate of Jewish prisoners whose attempts had ended up in no treatment, only abuse. Finally things got worse and I was afraid that waiting longer would mean amputation. So I decided to make the effort.

5 When I got to the clinic, there were many prisoners lined up as usual, a score of them Jews suffering from severe frostbite. The main topic of discussion was one's chances of being admitted to the clinic. Most Jews had planned their procedure in detail. Some thought it best to stress their service in the German army during World War I: wounds received or decorations won. Others planned to stress the severity of their frostbite. A few decided it was best to tell some "tall story," such as that an SS officer had ordered them to report at the clinic.

Most of them seemed convinced that the SS man on duty would not see through their schemes. Eventually they asked me about my plans. Having no definite ones, I said I would go by the way the SS man dealt with other Jewish prisoners who had frostbite like me, and proceed accordingly. I doubted how wise it was to follow a preconceived plan, because it was hard to anticipate the reactions of a person you didn't know.

The prisoners reacted as they had at other times when I had voiced similar ideas on how to deal with the SS. They insisted that one SS man was like another, all equally vicious and stupid. As usual, any frustration was immediately discharged against the person who caused it, or was nearest at hand. So in abusive terms they accused me of not wanting to share my plan with them, or of intending to use one of theirs; it angered them that I was ready to meet the enemy unprepared.

No Jewish prisoner ahead of me in the line was admitted to the clinic. The more a prisoner pleaded, the more annoyed and violent the SS became. Expressions of pain amused him; stories of previous services rendered to Germany outraged him. He proudly remarked that *he* could not be taken in by Jews, that fortunately the time had passed when Jews could reach their goal by lamentations.

When my turn came he asked me in a screeching voice if I knew that work accidents were the only reason for admitting Jews to the clinic, and if I came because of such an accident. I replied that I knew the rules, but that I couldn't work unless my hands were freed of the dead flesh. Since prisoners were not allowed to have knives, I asked to have the dead flesh cut away. I tried to be matter-of-fact, avoiding pleading, deference, or arrogance. He replied: "If that's all you want, I'll tear the flesh off myself." And he started to pull at the festering skin. Because it did not come off as easily as he may have expected, or for some other reason, he waved me into the clinic.

10 Inside, he gave me a malevolent look and pushed me into the treatment room. There he told the prisoner orderly to attend to the wound. While this was being done, the guard watched me closely for signs of pain but I was able to suppress them. As soon as the cutting was over, I started to leave. He showed surprise and asked why I didn't wait for further treatment. I said I had gotten the service I asked for, at which he told the orderly to make an exception and treat my hand. After I had left the room, he called me back and gave me a card entitling me to further treatment, and admittance to the clinic without inspection at the entrance.

* * *

Because my behavior did not correspond to what he expected of Jewish prisoners on the basis of his projection, he could not use his prepared defenses against being touched by the prisoner's plight. Since I did not act as the dangerous Jew was expected to, I did not activate the anxieties that went with his stereotype. Still he did not altogether trust me, so he continued to watch while I received treatment.

Throughout these dealings, the SS felt uneasy with me, though he did not unload on me the annoyance his uneasiness aroused. Perhaps he watched me closely because he expected that sooner or later I would slip up and behave the way his projected image of the Jew was expected to act. This would have meant that his delusional creation had become real.

Wallace Stegner

THE TOWN DUMP

The town dump of Whitemud, Saskatchewan, could only have been a few years old when I knew it, for the village was born in 1913 and I left there in 1919. But I remember the dump better than I remember most things in that town, better than I remember most of the people. I spent more time with it, for one thing; it has more poetry and excitement in it than people did.

It lay in the southeast corner of town, in a section that was always

From *Wolf Willow* (1959).

full of adventure for me. Just there the Whitemud River left the hills, bent a little south, and started its long traverse across the prairie and international boundary to join the Milk. For all I knew, it might have been on its way to join the Alph:[1] simply, before my eyes, it disappeared into strangeness and wonder.

Also, where it passed below the dumpground, it ran through willowed bottoms that were a favorite campsite for passing teamsters, gypsies, sometimes Indians. The very straw scattered around those camps, the ashes of those strangers' campfires, the manure of their teams and saddle horses, were hot with adventurous possibilities.

It was as an extension, a living suburb, as it were, of the dumpground that we most valued those camps. We scoured them for artifacts of their migrant tenants as if they had been archaeological sites full of the secrets of ancient civilizations. I remember toting around for weeks the broken cheek strap of a bridle. Somehow or other its buckle looked as if it had been fashioned in a far place, a place where they were accustomed to flatten the tongues of buckles for reasons that could only be exciting, and where they made a habit of plating the silver with some valuable alloy, probably silver. In places where the silver was worn away the buckle underneath shone dull yellow: probably gold.

5 It seemed that excitement liked that end of town better than our end. Once old Mrs. Gustafson, deeply religious and a little raddled in the head, went over there with a buckboard full of trash, and as she was driving home along the river she looked and saw a spent catfish, washed in from Cypress Lake or some other part of the watershed, floating on the yellow water. He was two feet long, his whiskers hung down, his fins and tail were limp. He was a kind of fish that no one had seen in the Whitemud in the three or four years of the town's life, and a kind that none of us children had ever seen anywhere. Mrs. Gustafson had never seen one like him either; she perceived at once that he was the devil, and she whipped up the team and reported him at Hoffman's elevator.

We could hear her screeching as we legged it for the river to see for ourselves. Sure enough, there he was. He looked very tired, and he made no great effort to get away as we pushed out a half-sunken rowboat from below the flume, submerged it under him, and brought him ashore. When he died three days later we experimentally fed him to two half-wild cats, but they seemed to suffer no ill effects.

At that same end of town the irrigation flume crossed the river. It always seemed to me giddily high when I hung my chin over its plank edge and looked down, but it probably walked no more than twenty

1. The imaginary, mysterious river of Samuel Taylor Coleridge's poem "Kubla Khan."

feet above the water on its spidery legs. Ordinarily in summer it carried about six or eight inches of smooth water, and under the glassy hurrying of the little boxed stream the planks were coated with deep sun-warmed moss as slick as frogs' eggs. A boy could sit in the flume with the water walling up against his back, and grab a cross brace above him, and pull, shooting himself sledlike ahead until he could reach the next brace for another pull and another slide, and so on across the river in four scoots.

After ten minutes in the flume he would come out wearing a dozen or more limber black leeches, and could sit in the green shade where darning needles flashed blue, and dragonflies hummed and darted and stopped, and skaters dimpled slack and eddy with their delicate transitory footprints, and there stretch the leeches out one by one while their sucking ends clung and clung, until at last, stretched far out, they let go with a tiny wet *puk* and snapped together like rubber bands. The smell of the river and the flume and the clay cutbanks and the bars of that part of the river was the smell of wolf willow.

But nothing in that end of town was as good as the dumpground that scattered along a little runoff coulee[2] dipping down toward the river from the south bench. Through a historical process that went back, probably, to the roots of community sanitation and distaste for eyesores, but that in law dated from the Unincorporated Towns Ordinance of the territorial government, passed in 1888, the dump was one of the very first community enterprises, almost our town's first institution.

More than that, it contained relics of every individual who had ever 10
lived there, and of every phase of the town's history.

The bedsprings on which the town's first child was begotten might be there; the skeleton of a boy's pet colt; two or three volumes of Shakespeare bought in haste and error from a peddler, later loaned in carelessness, soaked with water and chemicals in a house fire, and finally thrown out to flap their stained eloquence in the prairie wind.

Broken dishes, rusty tinware, spoons that had been used to mix paint; once a box of percussion caps, sign and symbol of the carelessness that most of those people felt about all matters of personal or public safety. We put them on the railroad tracks and were anonymously denounced in the *Enterprise*. There were also old iron, old brass, for which we hunted assiduously, by night conning junkmen's catalogues and the pages of the *Enterprise* to find how much wartime value there might be in the geared insides of clocks or in a pound of tea lead[3] carefully wrapped in a ball whose weight astonished and de-

2. A gully.
3. An alloy used for lining the chests in which tea was stored and transported.

lighted us. Sometimes the unimaginable outside world reached in and laid a finger on us. I recall that, aged no more than seven, I wrote a St. Louis junk house asking if they preferred their tea lead and tinfoil wrapped in balls, or whether they would rather have it pressed flat in sheets, and I got back a typewritten letter in a window envelope instructing me that they would be happy to have it in any way that was convenient for me. They added that they valued my business and were mine very truly. Dazed, I carried that windowed grandeur around in my pocket until I wore it out, and for months I saved the letter as a souvenir of the wondering time when something strange and distinguished had singled me out.

We hunted old bottles in the dump, bottles caked with dirt and filth, half buried, full of cobwebs, and we washed them out at the horse trough by the elevator, putting in a handful of shot along with the water to knock the dirt loose; and when we had shaken them until our arms were tired, we hauled them off in somebody's coaster wagon and turned them in at Bill Anderson's pool hall, where the smell of lemon pop was so sweet on the dark pool-hall air that I am sometimes awakened by it in the night, even yet.

Smashed wheels of wagons and buggies, tangles of rusty barbed wire, the collapsed perambulator that the French wife of one of the town's doctors had once pushed proudly up the planked sidewalks and along the ditchbank paths. A welter of foul-smelling feathers and coyote-scattered carrion which was all that remained of somebody's dream of a chicken ranch. The chickens had all got some mysterious pip at the same time, and died as one, and the dream lay out there with the rest of the town's history to rustle to the empty sky on the border of the hills.

15 There was melted glass in curious forms, and the half-melted office safe left from the burning of Bill Day's Hotel. On very lucky days we might find a piece of the lead casing that had enclosed the wires of the town's first telephone system. The casing was just the right size for rings, and so soft that it could be whittled with a jackknife. It was a material that might have made artists of us. If we had been Indians of fifty years before, that bright soft metal would have enlisted our maximum patience and craft and come out as ring and metal and amulet inscribed with the symbols of our observed world. Perhaps there were too many ready-made alternatives in the local drug, hardware, and general stores; perhaps our feeble artistic response was a measure of the insufficiency of the challenge we felt. In any case I do not remember that we did any more with the metal than to shape it into crude seal rings with our initials or pierced hearts carved in them; and these, though they served a purpose in juvenile courtship, stopped something short of art.

The dump held very little wood, for in that country anything burnable got burned. But it had plenty of old iron, furniture, papers, mattresses that were the delight of field mice, and jugs and demijohns that were sometimes their bane, for they crawled into the necks and drowned in the rain water or redeye that was inside.

If the history of our town was not exactly written, it was at least hinted, in the dump. I think I had a pretty sound notion even at eight or nine of how significant was that first institution of our forming Canadian civilization. For rummaging through its foul purlieus I had several times been surprised and shocked to find relics of my own life tossed out there to rot or blow away.

The volumes of Shakespeare belonged to a set that my father had bought before I was born. It had been carried through successive moves from town to town in the Dakotas, and from Dakota to Seattle, and from Seattle to Bellingham, and Bellingham to Redmond, and from Redmond back to Iowa, and from there to Saskatchewan. Then, stained in a stranger's house fire, these volumes had suffered from a house-cleaning impulse and been thrown away for me to stumble upon in the dump. One of the Cratchet girls had borrowed them, a hatchet-faced, thin, eager, transplanted Cockney girl with a frenzy, almost a hysteria, for reading. And yet somehow, through her hands, they found the dump, to become a symbol of how much was lost, how much thrown aside, how much carelessly or of necessity given up, in the making of a new country. We had so few books that I was familiar with them all, had handled them, looked at their pictures, perhaps even read them. They were the lares and penates, part of the skimpy impedimenta of household gods we had brought with us into Latium.[4] Finding those three thrown away was a little like finding my own name on a gravestone.

And yet not the blow that something else was, something that impressed me even more with the dump's close reflection of the town's intimate life. The colt whose picked skeleton lay out there was mine. He had been incurably crippled when dogs chased our mare, Daisy, the morning after she foaled. I had labored for months to make him well; had fed him by hand, curried him, exercised him, adjusted the iron braces that I had talked my father into having made. And I had not known that he would have to be destroyed. One weekend I turned him over to the foreman of one of the ranches, presumably so that he could be cared for. A few days later I found his skinned body, with the braces still on his crippled front legs, lying on the dump.

4. In Virgil's *Aeneid*, the Trojans who escaped the fall of Troy carried their household gods (lares and penates) as they wandered the Mediterranean, finally settling in Latium, the region around Rome.

20 Not even that, I think, cured me of going there, though our parents all forbade us on pain of cholera or worse to do so. The place fascinated us, as it should have. For this was the kitchen midden of all the civilization we knew; it gave us the most tantalizing glimpses into our lives as well as into those of the neighbors. It gave us an aesthetic distance from which to know ourselves.

The dump was our poetry and our history. We took it home with us by the wagonload, bringing back into town the things the town had used and thrown away. Some little part of what we gathered, mainly bottles, we managed to bring back to usefulness, but most of our gleanings we left lying around barn or attic or cellar until in some renewed fury of spring cleanup our families carted them off to the dump again, to be rescued and briefly treasured by some other boy with schemes for making them useful. Occasionally something we really valued with a passion was snatched from us in horror and returned at once. That happened to the mounted head of a white mountain goat, somebody's trophy from old times and the far Rocky Mountains, that I brought home one day in transports of delight. My mother took one look and discovered that his beard was full of moths.

I remember that goat; I regret him yet. Poetry is seldom useful, but always memorable. I think I learned more from the town dump than I learned from school: more about people, more about how life is lived, not elsewhere but here, not in other times but now. If I were a sociologist anxious to study in detail the life of any community, I would go very early to its refuse piles. For a community may be as well judged by what it throws away—what it has to throw away and what it chooses to—as by any other evidence. For whole civilizations we have sometimes no more of the poetry and little more of the history than this.

QUESTIONS

1. *Through what details does Stegner portray the dump as a record of his childhood? And how is it also a record of the town's history? Is it also a record of the North American West? In what sense?*
2. *How seriously do you take Stegner's claim (paragraph 22) that "I learned more from the town dump than I learned from school"? He has been making allusions to Coleridge and Virgil; what kind of learning is he thinking of?*
3. *Describe a "treasure" someone found and held on to.*

Lars Eighner

ON DUMPSTER DIVING

Long before I began Dumpster diving I was impressed with Dumpsters, enough so that I wrote the Merriam-Webster[1] research service to discover what I could about the word *Dumpster.* I learned from them that it is a proprietary word belonging to the Dempster Dumpster company. Since then I have dutifully capitalized the word, although it was lowercased in almost all the citations Merriam-Webster photocopied for me. Dempster's word is too apt. I have never heard these things called anything but Dumpsters. I do not know anyone who knows the generic name for these objects. From time to time I have heard a wino or hobo give some corrupted credit to the original and call them Dipsy Dumpsters.

I began Dumpster diving about a year before I became homeless.

I prefer the word *scavenging* and use the word *scrounging* when I mean to be obscure. I have heard people, evidently meaning to be polite, use the word *foraging,* but I prefer to reserve that word for gathering nuts and berries and such, which I do also according to the season and the opportunity. *Dumpster diving* seems to me to be a little too cute and, in my case, inaccurate because I lack the athletic ability to lower myself into the Dumpsters as the true divers do, much to their increased profit.

I like the frankness of the word *scavenging,* which I can hardly think of without picturing a big black snail on an aquarium wall. I live from the refuse of others. I am a scavenger. I think it a sound and honorable niche, although if I could I would naturally prefer to live the comfortable consumer life, perhaps—and only perhaps—as a slightly less wasteful consumer, owing to what I have learned as a scavenger.

While Lizbeth[2] and I were still living in the shack on Avenue B as 5
my savings ran out, I put almost all my sporadic income into rent. The necessities of daily life I began to extract from Dumpsters. Yes, we ate from them. Except for jeans, all my clothes came from Dumpsters. Boom boxes, candles, bedding, toilet paper, a virgin male love doll, medicine, books, a typewriter, dishes, furnishings, and change, sometimes amounting to many dollars—I acquired many things from the Dumpsters.

From *Travels with Lizbeth* (1993).

1. A large publisher of dictionaries.
2. The author's dog.

I have learned much as a scavenger. I mean to put some of what I have learned down here, beginning with the practical art of Dumpster diving and proceeding to the abstract.

What is safe to eat?

After all, the finding of objects is becoming something of an urban art. Even respectable employed people will sometimes find something tempting sticking out of a Dumpster or standing beside one. Quite a number of people, not all of them of the bohemian type, are willing to brag that they found this or that piece in the trash. But eating from Dumpsters is what separates the dilettanti from the professionals. Eating safely from the Dumpsters involves three principles: using the senses and common sense to evaluate the condition of the found materials, knowing the Dumpsters of a given area and checking them regularly, and seeking always to answer the question "Why was this discarded?"

Perhaps everyone who has a kitchen and a regular supply of groceries has, at one time or another, made a sandwich and eaten half of it before discovering mold on the bread or got a mouthful of milk before realizing the milk had turned. Nothing of the sort is likely to happen to a Dumpster diver because he is constantly reminded that most food is discarded for a reason. Yet a lot of perfectly good food can be found in Dumpsters.

10 Canned goods, for example, turn up fairly often in the Dumpsters I frequent. All except the most phobic people would be willing to eat from a can, even if it came from a Dumpster. Canned goods are among the safest of foods to be found in Dumpsters but are not utterly foolproof.

Although very rare with modern canning methods, botulism is a possibility. Most other forms of food poisoning seldom do lasting harm to a healthy person, but botulism is almost certainly fatal and often the first symptom is death. Except for carbonated beverages, all canned goods should contain a slight vacuum and suck air when first punctured. Bulging, rusty, and dented cans and cans that spew when punctured should be avoided, especially when the contents are not very acidic or syrupy.

Heat can break down the botulin, but this requires much more cooking than most people do to canned goods. To the extent that botulism occurs at all, of course, it can occur in cans on pantry shelves as well as in cans from Dumpsters. Need I say that home-canned goods are simply too risky to be recommended.

From time to time one of my companions, aware of the source of my provisions, will ask, "Do you think these crackers are really safe to eat?" For some reason it is most often the crackers they ask about.

This question has always made me angry. Of course I would not offer my companion anything I had doubts about. But more than that, I wonder why he cannot evaluate the condition of the crackers for himself. I have no special knowledge and I have been wrong before. Since he knows where the food comes from, it seems to me he ought to assume some of the responsibility for deciding what he will put in his mouth. For myself I have few qualms about dry foods such as crackers, cookies, cereal, chips, and pasta as if they are free of visible contaminates and still dry and crisp. Most often such things are found in the original packaging, which is not so much a positive sign as it is the absence of a negative one.

Raw fruits and vegetables with intact skins seem perfectly safe to 15
me, excluding of course the obviously rotten. Many are discarded for minor imperfections that can be pared away. Leafy vegetables, grapes, cauliflower, broccoli, and similar things may be contaminated by liquids and may be impractical to wash.

Candy, especially hard candy, is usually safe if it has not drawn ants. Chocolate is often discarded only because it has become discolored as the cocoa butter de-emulsified. Candying, after all, is one method of food preservation because pathogens do not like very sugary substances.

All of these foods might be found in any Dumpster and can be evaluated with some confidence largely on the basis of appearance. Beyond these are foods that cannot be correctly evaluated without additional information.

I began scavenging by pulling pizzas out of the Dumpster behind a pizza delivery shop. In general, prepared food requires caution, but in this case I knew when the shop closed and went to the Dumpster as soon as the last of the help left.

Such shops often get prank orders; both the orders and the products made to fill them are called *bogus*. Because help seldom stays long at these places, pizzas are often made with the wrong topping, refused on delivery for being cold, or baked incorrectly. The products to be discarded are boxed up because inventory is kept by counting boxes: A boxed pizza can be written off; an unboxed pizza does not exist.

I never placed a bogus order to increase the supply of pizzas and I 20
believe no one else was scavenging in this Dumpster. But the people in the shop became suspicious and began to retain their garbage in the shop overnight. While it lasted I had a steady supply of fresh, sometimes warm pizza. Because I knew the Dumpster I knew the source of the pizza, and because I visited the Dumpster regularly I knew what was fresh and what was yesterday's.

The area I frequent is inhabited by many affluent college students. I am not here by chance; the Dumpsters in this area are very rich. Students throw out many good things, including food. In particular they tend to throw everything out when they move at the end of a semester, before and after breaks, and around midterm, when many of them despair of college. So I find it advantageous to keep an eye on the academic calendar.

Students throw food away around breaks because they do not know whether it has spoiled or will spoil before they return. A typical discard is a half jar of peanut butter. In fact, nonorganic peanut butter does not require refrigeration and is unlikely to spoil in any reasonable time. The student does not know that, and since it is Daddy's money, the student decides not to take a chance. Opened containers require caution and some attention to the question, "Why was this discarded?" But in the case of discards from student apartments, the answer may be that the item was thrown out through carelessness, ignorance, or wastefulness. This can sometimes be deduced when the item is found with many others, including some that are obviously perfectly good.

Some students, and others, approach defrosting a freezer by chucking out the whole lot. Not only do the circumstances of such a find tell the story, but also the mass of frozen goods stays cold for a long time and items may be found still frozen or freshly thawed.

Yogurt, cheese, and sour cream are items that are often thrown out while they are still good. Occasionally I find a cheese with a spot of mold, which of course I just pare off, and because it is obvious why such a cheese was discarded, I treat it with less suspicion than an apparently perfect cheese found in similar circumstances. Yogurt is often discarded, still sealed, only because the expiration date on the carton had passed. This is one of my favorite finds because yogurt will keep for several days, even in warm weather.

25 Students throw out canned goods and staples at the end of semesters and when they give up college at midterm. Drugs, pornography, spirits, and the like are often discarded when parents are expected—Dad's Day, for example. And spirits also turn up after big party weekends, presumably discarded by the newly reformed. Wine and spirits, of course, keep perfectly well even once opened, but the same cannot be said of beer.

My test for carbonated soft drinks is whether they still fizz vigorously. Many juices or other beverages are too acidic or too syrupy to cause much concern, provided they are not visibly contaminated. I have discovered nasty molds in vegetable juices, even when the product was found under its original seal; I recommend that such products be decanted slowly into a clear glass. Liquids always require some care. One hot day I found a large jug of Pat O'Brien's Hurricane mix. The jug had been opened but was still ice cold. I drank three large glasses before it became apparent to me that someone had added the rum to the mix, and not a little rum. I never tasted the rum, and by the time I began to feel the effects I had already ingested a very large quantity of the beverage. Some divers would have considered this a boon, but being suddenly intoxicated in a public place in the early afternoon is not my idea of a good time.

I have heard of people maliciously contaminating discarded food and even handouts, but mostly I have heard of this from people with vivid imaginations who have had no experience with the Dumpsters themselves. Just before the pizza shop stopped discarding its garbage at night, jalapeños began showing up on most of the thrown-out pizzas. If indeed this was meant to discourage me, it was a wasted effort because I am a native Texan.

For myself, I avoid game, poultry, pork, and egg-based foods, whether I find them raw or cooked. I seldom have the means to cook what I find, but when I do I avail myself of plentiful supplies of beef, which is often in very good condition. I suppose fish becomes disagreeable before it becomes dangerous. Lizbeth is happy to have any such thing that is past its prime and, in fact, does not recognize fish as food until it is quite strong.

Home leftovers, as opposed to surpluses from restaurants, are very often bad. Evidently, especially among students, there is a common type of personality that carefully wraps up even the smallest leftover and shoves it into the back of the refrigerator for six months or so before discarding it. Characteristic of this type are the reused jars and margarine tubs to which the remains are committed. I avoid ethnic foods I am unfamiliar with. If I do not know what it is supposed to look like when it is good, I cannot be certain I will be able to tell if it is bad.

No matter how careful I am I still get dysentery at least once a 30
month, oftener in warm weather. I do not want to paint too romantic a picture. Dumpster diving has serious drawbacks as a way of life.

I learned to scavenge gradually, on my own. Since then I have initiated several companions into the trade. I have learned that there is a predictable series of stages a person goes through in learning to scavenge.

At first the new scavenger is filled with disgust and self-loathing. He is ashamed of being seen and may lurk around, trying to duck behind things, or he may try to dive at night. (In fact, most people instinctively look away from a scavenger. By skulking around, the novice calls attention to himself and arouses suspicion. Diving at night is ineffective and needlessly messy.)

Every grain of rice seems to be a maggot. Everything seems to stink. He can wipe the egg yolk off the found can, but he cannot erase from his mind the stigma of eating garbage.

That stage passes with experience. The scavenger finds a pair of running shoes that fit and look and smell brand-new. He finds a pocket calculator in perfect working order. He finds pristine ice cream, still frozen, more than he can eat or keep. He begins to understand: People throw away perfectly good stuff, a lot of perfectly good stuff.

35 At this stage, Dumpster shyness begins to dissipate. The diver, after all, has the last laugh. He is finding all manner of good things that are his for the taking. Those who disparage his profession are the fools, not he.

He may begin to hang on to some perfectly good things for which he has neither a use nor a market. Then he begins to take note of the things that are not perfectly good but are nearly so. He mates a Walkman with broken earphones and one that is missing a battery cover. He picks up things that he can repair.

At this stage he may become lost and never recover. Dumpsters are full of things of some potential value to someone and also of things that never have much intrinsic value but are interesting. All the Dumpster divers I have known come to the point of trying to acquire everything they touch. Why not take it, they reason, since it is all free? This is, of course, hopeless. Most divers come to realize that they must restrict themselves to items of relatively immediate utility. But in some cases the diver simply cannot control himself. I have met several of these pack-rat types. Their ideas of the values of various pieces of junk verge on the psychotic. Every bit of glass may be a diamond, they think, and all that glisters, gold.

I tend to gain weight when I am scavenging. Partly this is because I always find far more pizza and doughnuts than water-packed tuna, nonfat yogurt, and fresh vegetables. Also I have not developed much faith in the reliability of Dumpsters as a food source, although it has been proven to me many times. I tend to eat as if I have no idea where my next meal is coming from. But mostly I just hate to see food go to waste and so I eat much more than I should. Something like this drives the obsession to collect junk.

As for collecting objects, I usually restrict myself to collecting one kind of small object at a time, such as pocket calculators, sunglasses, or campaign buttons. To live on the street I must anticipate my needs to a certain extent: I must pick up and save warm bedding I find in August because it will not be found in Dumpsters in November. As I have no access to health care, I often hoard essential drugs, such as antibiotics and antihistamines. (This course can be recommended only to those with some grounding in pharmacology. Antibiotics, for example, even when indicated are worse than useless if taken in insufficient amounts.) But even if I had a home with extensive storage space, I could not save everything that might be valuable in some contingency.

I have proprietary feelings about my Dumpsters. As I have men- 40
tioned, it is no accident that I scavenge from ones where good finds are common. But my limited experience with Dumpsters in other areas suggests to me that even in poorer areas, Dumpsters, if attended with sufficient diligence, can be made to yield a livelihood. The rich students discard perfectly good kiwifruit; poorer people discard perfectly good apples. Slacks and Polo shirts are found in the one place; jeans and T-shirts in the other. The population of competitors rather than the affluence of the dumpers most affects the feasibility of survival by scavenging. The large number of competitors is what puts me off the idea of trying to scavenge in places like Los Angeles.

Curiously, I do not mind my direct competition, other scavengers, so much as I hate the can scroungers.

People scrounge cans because they have to have a little cash. I have tried scrounging cans with an able-bodied companion. Afoot a can scrounger simply cannot make more than a few dollars a day. One can extract the necessities of life from the Dumpsters directly with far less effort than would be required to accumulate the equivalent value in cans. (These observations may not hold in places with container redemption laws.)

Can scroungers, then, are people who must have small amounts of cash. These are drug addicts and winos, mostly the latter because the amounts of cash are so small. Spirits and drugs do, like all other commodities, turn up in Dumpsters and the scavenger will from time to time have a half bottle of a rather good wine with his dinner. But the wino cannot survive on these occasional finds; he must have his daily dose to stave off the DTs. All the cans he can carry will buy about three bottles of Wild Irish Rose.

I do not begrudge them the cans, but can scroungers tend to tear up the Dumpsters, mixing the contents and littering the area. They become so specialized that they can see only cans. They earn my contempt by passing up change, canned goods, and readily hockable items.

There are precious few courtesies among scavengers. But it is com- 45
mon practice to set aside surplus items: pairs of shoes, clothing, canned goods, and such. A true scavenger hates to see good stuff go to waste, and what he cannot use he leaves in good condition in plain sight.

Can scroungers lay waste to everything in their path and will stir one of a pair of good shoes to the bottom of a Dumpster, to be lost or ruined in the muck. Can scroungers will even go through individual garbage cans, something I have never seen a scavenger do.

Individual garbage cans are set out on the public easement only on garbage days. On other days going through them requires trespassing close to a dwelling. Going through individual garbage cans without scattering litter is almost impossible. Litter is likely to reduce the public's tolerance of scavenging. Individual cans are simply not as productive as Dumpsters; people in houses and duplexes do not move so often and for some reason do not tend to discard as much useful material. Moreover, the time required to go through one garbage can that serves one household is not much less than the time required to go through a Dumpster that contains the refuse of twenty apartments.

But my strongest reservation about going through individual garbage cans is that this seems to me a very personal kind of invasion to which I would object if I were a householder. Although many things in Dumpsters are obviously meant never to come to light, a Dumpster is somehow less personal.

I avoid trying to draw conclusions about the people who dump in the Dumpsters I frequent. I think it would be unethical to do so, although I know many people will find the idea of scavenger ethics too funny for words.

50 Dumpsters contain bank statements, correspondence, and other documents, just as anyone might expect. But there are also less obvious sources of information. Pill bottles, for example. The labels bear the name of the patient, the name of the doctor, and the name of the drug. AIDS drugs and antipsychotic medicines, to name but two groups, are specific and are seldom prescribed for any other disorders. The plastic compacts for birth-control pills usually have complete label information.

Despite all of this sensitive information, I have had only one apartment resident object to my going through the Dumpster. In that case it turned out the resident was a university athlete who was taking bets and who was afraid I would turn up his wager slips.

Occasionally a find tells a story. I once found a small paper bag containing some unused condoms, several partial tubes of flavored sexual lubricants, a partially used compact of birth-control pills, and the torn pieces of a picture of a young man. Clearly she was through with him and planning to give up sex altogether.

Dumpster things are often sad—abandoned teddy bears, shredded wedding books, despaired-of sales kits. I find many pets lying in state in Dumpsters. Although I hope to get off the streets so that Lizbeth can have a long and comfortable old age, I know this hope is not very realistic. So I suppose when her time comes she too will go into a Dumpster. I will have no better place for her. And after all, it is fitting, since for most of her life her livelihood has come from the Dumpster. When she finds something I think is safe that has been spilled from a Dumpster, I let her have it. She already knows the route around the best ones. I like to think that if she survives me she will have a chance of evading the dog catcher and of finding her sustenance on the route.

Silly vanities also come to rest in the Dumpsters. I am a rather accomplished needleworker. I get a lot of material from the Dumpsters. Evidently sorority girls, hoping to impress someone, perhaps themselves, with their mastery of a womanly art, buy a lot of embroider-by-number kits, work a few stitches horribly, and eventually discard the whole mess. I pull out their stitches, turn the canvas over, and work an original design. Do not think I refrain from chuckling as I make gifts from these kits.

I find diaries and journals. I have often thought of compiling a book 55
of literary found objects. And perhaps I will one day. But what I find is hopelessly commonplace and bad without being, even unconsciously, camp. College students also discard their papers. I am horrified to discover the kind of paper that now merits an A in an undergraduate course. I am grateful, however, for the number of good books and magazines the students throw out.

In the area I know best I have never discovered vermin in the Dumpsters, but there are two kinds of kitty surprise. One is alley cats whom I meet as they leap, claws first, out of Dumpsters. This is especially thrilling when I have Lizbeth in tow. The other kind of kitty surprise is a plastic garbage bag filled with some ponderous, amorphous mass. This always proves to be used cat litter.

City bees harvest doughnut glaze and this makes the Dumpster at the doughnut shop more interesting. My faith in the instinctive wisdom of animals is always shaken whenever I see Lizbeth attempt to catch a bee in her mouth, which she does whenever bees are present. Evidently some birds find Dumpsters profitable, for birdie surprise is almost as common as kitty surprise of the first kind. In hunting season all kinds of small game turn up in Dumpsters, some of it, sadly, not entirely dead. Curiously, summer and winter, maggots are uncommon.

The worse of the living and near-living hazards of the Dumpsters are the fire ants. The food they claim is not much of a loss, but they are vicious and aggressive. It is very easy to brush against some surface of the Dumpster and pick up half a dozen or more fire ants, usually in some sensitive area such as the underarm. One advantage of bringing Lizbeth along as I make Dumpster rounds is that, for obvious reasons, she is very alert to ground-based fire ants. When Lizbeth recognizes a fire-ant infestation around our feet, she does the Dance of the Zillion Fire Ants. I have learned not to ignore this warning from Lizbeth, whether I perceive the tiny ants or not, but to remove ourselves at Lizbeth's first pas de bourée. All the more so because the ants are the worst in the summer months when I wear flip-flops if I have them.

(Perhaps someone will misunderstand this. Lizbeth does the Dance of the Zillion Fire Ants when she recognizes more fire ants than she cares to eat, not when she is being bitten. Since I have learned to react promptly, she does not get bitten at all. It is the isolated patrol of fire ants that falls in Lizbeth's range that deserves pity. She finds them quite tasty.)

By far the best way to go through a Dumpster is to lower yourself into it. Most of the good stuff tends to settle at the bottom because it is usually weightier than the rubbish. My more athletic companions have often demonstrated to me that they can extract much good material from a Dumpster I have already been over.

To those psychologically or physically unprepared to enter a Dumpster, I recommend a stout stick, preferably with some barb or hook at one end. The hook can be used to grab plastic garbage bags. When I find canned goods or other objects loose at the bottom of a Dumpster, I lower a bag into it, roll the desired object into the bag, and then hoist the bag out—a procedure more easily described than executed. Much Dumpster diving is a matter of experience for which nothing will do except practice.

Dumpster diving is outdoor work, often surprisingly pleasant. It is not entirely predictable; things of interest turn up every day and some days there are finds of great value. I am always very pleased when I can turn up exactly the thing I most wanted to find. Yet in spite of the element of chance, scavenging more than most other pursuits tends to yield returns in some proportion to the effort and intelligence brought to bear. It is very sweet to turn up a few dollars in change from a Dumpster that has just been gone over by a wino.

The land is now covered with cities. The cities are full of Dumpsters. If a member of the canine race is ever able to know what it is doing, then Lizbeth knows that when we go around to the Dumpsters, we are hunting. I think of scavenging as a modern form of self-reliance. In any event, after having survived nearly ten years of government service, where everything is geared to the lowest common denominator, I find it refreshing to have work that rewards initiative and effort. Certainly I would be happy to have a sinecure again, but I am no longer heartbroken that I left one.

I find from the experience of scavenging two rather deep lessons. The first is to take what you can use and let the rest go by. I have come to think that there is no value in the abstract. A thing I cannot use or make useful, perhaps by trading, has no value however rare or fine it may be. I mean useful in a broad sense—some art I would find useful and some otherwise.

I was shocked to realize that some things are not worth acquiring, but now I think it is so. Some material things are white elephants that eat up the possessor's substance. The second lesson is the transience of material being. This has not quite converted me to a dualist, but it has made some headway in that direction. I do not suppose that ideas are immortal, but certainly mental things are longer lived than other material things.

Once I was the sort of person who invests objects with sentimental 65
value. Now I no longer have those objects, but I have the sentiments yet.

Many times in our travels I have lost everything but the clothes I was wearing and Lizbeth. The things I find in Dumpsters, the love letters and rag dolls of so many lives, remind me of this lesson. Now I hardly pick up a thing without envisioning the time I will cast it aside. This I think is a healthy state of mind. Almost everything I have now has already been cast out at least once, proving that what I own is valueless to someone.

Anyway, I find my desire to grab for the gaudy bauble has been largely sated. I think this is an attitude I share with the very wealthy—we both know there is plenty more where what we have came from. Between us are the rat-race millions who nightly scavenge the cable channels looking for they know not what.

I am sorry for them.

QUESTIONS

1. *Describe how Eighner organizes his essay. What does such an organization imply?*
2. *Eighner's simple, understated tone suggests that anyone can adapt to Dumpster diving with a little practice. Why do you think he chose such a tone?*
3. *What shocked or surprised you most in this essay?*
4. *Write about someone who does what Eighner deplores in his closing paragraphs, "invests objects with sentimental value." Let your description reveal whether or not you agree with Eighner.*

Zora Neale Hurston

HOW IT FEELS TO BE COLORED ME

I am colored but I offer nothing in the way of extenuating circumstances except the fact that I am the only Negro in the United States whose grandfather on the mother's side was *not* an Indian chief.

I remember the very day that I became colored. Up to my thirteenth year I lived in the little Negro town of Eatonville, Florida. It is exclusively a colored town. The only white people I knew passed through the town going to or coming from Orlando. The native whites rode dusty horses, the Northern tourists chugged down the sandy village road in automobiles. The town knew the Southerners and never stopped cane chewing[1] when they passed. But the Northerners were something else again. They were peered at cautiously from behind curtains by the timid. The more venturesome would come out on the porch to watch them go past and got just as much pleasure out of the tourists as the tourists got out of the village.

The front porch might seem a daring place for the rest of the town, but it was a gallery seat for me. My favorite place was atop the gate-post. Proscenium box for a born first-nighter. Not only did I enjoy the show, but I didn't mind the actors knowing that I liked it. I usually spoke to them in passing. I'd wave at them and when they returned my salute, I would say something like this: "Howdy-do-well-I-thank-you-where-you-goin'?" Usually automobile or the horse paused at this, and after a queer exchange of compliments, I would probably "go a piece of the way" with them, as we say in farthest Florida. If one of my family happened to come to the front in time to see me, of course negotiations would be rudely broken off. But even so, it is clear that I was the first "welcome-to-our-state" Floridian, and I hope the Miami Chamber of Commerce will please take notice.

During this period, white people differed from colored to me only in that they rode through town and never lived there. They liked to hear me "speak pieces" and sing and wanted to see me dance the parse-me-la, and gave me generously of their small silver for doing these things, which seemed strange to me for I wanted to do them so much that I

Originally published in *The World Tomorrow* (Vol. 11, May 1928); reprinted in *I Love Myself When I am Laughing* (1975), a collection of Hurston's writings edited by Alice Walker.

1. Chewing sugar cane.

needed bribing to stop. Only they didn't know it. The colored people gave no dimes. They deplored any joyful tendencies in me, but I was their Zora nevertheless. I belonged to them, to the nearby hotels, to the county—everybody's Zora.

But changes came in the family when I was thirteen, and I was sent to school in Jacksonville. I left Eatonville, the town of the oleanders,[2] as Zora. When I disembarked from the river-boat at Jacksonville, she was no more. It seemed that I had suffered a sea change. I was not Zora of Orange County any more, I was now a little colored girl. I found it out in certain ways. In my heart as well as in the mirror, I became a fast brown—warranted not to rub nor run.

But I am not tragically colored. There is no great sorrow dammed up in my soul, nor lurking behind my eyes. I do not mind at all. I do not belong to the sobbing school of Negrohood who hold that nature somehow has given them a lowdown dirty deal and whose feelings are all hurt about it. Even in the helter-skelter skirmish that is my life, I have seen that the world is to the strong regardless of a little pigmentation more or less. No, I do not weep at the world—I am too busy sharpening my oyster knife.[3]

Someone is always at my elbow reminding me that I am the granddaughter of slaves. It fails to register depression with me. Slavery is sixty years in the past. The operation was successful and the patient is doing well, thank you. The terrible struggle[4] that made me an American out of a potential slave said "On the line!" The Reconstruction said "Get set!"; and the generation before said "Go!" I am off to a flying start and I must not halt in the stretch to look behind and weep. Slavery is the price I paid for civilization, and the choice was not with me. It is a bully adventure and worth all that I have paid through my ancestors for it. No one on earth ever had a greater chance for glory. The world to be won and nothing to be lost. It is thrilling to think—to know that for any act of mine, I shall get twice as much praise or twice as much blame. It is quite exciting to hold the center of the national stage, with the spectators not knowing whether to laugh or to weep.

The position of my white neighbor is much more difficult. No brown specter pulls up a chair beside me when I sit down to eat. No dark ghost thrusts its leg against mine in bed. The game of keeping what one has is never so exciting as the game of getting.

2. Fragrant tropical flowers.
3. Cf. the popular expression "The world is my oyster."
4. I.e., the Civil War. The Reconstruction was the period immediately following the war; one of its better effects was that northern educators came south to teach newly freed slaves.

I do not always feel colored. Even now I often achieve the unconscious Zora of Eatonville before the Hegira.[5] I feel most colored when I am thrown against a sharp white background.

For instance at Barnard.[6] "Beside the waters of the Hudson" I feel my race. Among the thousand white persons, I am a dark rock surged upon, and overswept, but through it all, I remain myself. When covered by the waters, I am; and the ebb but reveals me again.

Sometimes it is the other way around. A white person is set down in our midst, but the contrast is just as sharp for me. For instance, when I sit in the drafty basement that is The New World Cabaret with a white person, my color comes. We enter chatting about any little nothing that we have in common and are seated by the jazz waiters. In the abrupt way that jazz orchestras have, this one plunges into a number. It loses no time in circumlocutions, but gets right down to business. It constricts the thorax and splits the heart with its tempo and narcotic harmonies. This orchestra grows rambunctious, rears on its hind legs and attacks the tonal veil with primitive fury, rending it, clawing it until it breaks through to the jungle beyond. I follow those heathen—follow them exultingly. I dance wildly inside myself; I yell within, I whoop; I shake my assegai[7] above my head, I hurl it true to the mark *yeeeeooww!* I am in the jungle and living in the jungle way. My face is painted red and yellow and my body is painted blue. My pulse is throbbing like a war drum. I want to slaughter something—give paid, give death to what, I do not know. But the piece ends. The men of the orchestra wipe their lips and rest their fingers. I creep back slowly to the veneer we call civilization with the last tone and find the white friend sitting motionless in his seat, smoking calmly.

"Good music they have here," he remarks, drumming the table with his fingertips.

Music. The great blobs of purple and red emotion have not touched him. He has only heard what I felt. He is far away and I see him but dimly across the ocean and the continent that have fallen between us. He is so pale with his whiteness then and I am *so* colored.

At certain times I have no race, I am *me*. When I set my hat at a certain angle and saunter down Seventh Avenue, Harlem City, feeling as snooty as the lions in front of the Forty-Second Street Library, for instance. So far as my feelings are concerned, Peggy Hopkins Joyce on

5. I.e., a journey undertaken away from a dangerous situation into a more highly desirable one (literally, the flight of Mohammed from Mecca in A.D. 622).
6. American women's college in New York City, near the Hudson River (cf. the psalmist's "by the waters of Babylon").
7. South African hunting spear.

the Boule Mich[8] with her gorgeous raiment, stately carriage, knees knocking together in a most aristocratic manner, has nothing on me. The cosmic Zora emerges. I belong to no race nor time. I am the eternal feminine with its string of beads.

15 I have no separate feeling about being an American citizen and colored. I am merely a fragment of the Great Soul that surges within the boundaries. My country, right or wrong.

Sometimes, I feel discriminated against, but it does not make me angry. It merely astonishes me. How *can* any deny themselves the pleasure of my company? It's beyond me.

But in the main, I feel like a brown bag of miscellany propped against a wall. Against a wall in company with other bags, white, red and yellow. Pour out the contents, and there is discovered a jumble of small things priceless and worthless. A first-water diamond, an empty spool, bits of broken glass, lengths of string, a key to a door long since crumbled away, a rusty knife-blade, old shoes saved for a road that never was and never will be, a nail bent under the weight of things too heavy for any nail, a dried flower or two still a little fragrant. In your hand is the brown bag. On the ground before you is the jumble it held—so much like the jumble in the bags, could they be emptied, that all might be dumped in a single heap and the bags refilled without altering the content of any greatly. A bit of colored glass more or less would not matter. Perhaps that is how the Great Stuffer of Bags filled them in the first place—who knows?

8. The Boulevard Saint-Michel, a fashionable Parisian street. Peggy Hopkins Joyce, American beauty and fashion-setter of the twenties.

Nancy Mairs

ON BEING A CRIPPLE

To escape is nothing. Not to escape is nothing.

—LOUISE BOGAN

The other day I was thinking of writing an essay on being a cripple. I was thinking hard in one of the stalls of the women's room in my office building, as I was shoving my shirt into my jeans and tugging up my zipper. Preoccupied, I flushed, picked up my book bag, took my cane down from the hook, and unlatched the door. So many movements unbalanced me, and as I pulled the door open I fell over backward,

From *Plaintext* (1986).

landing fully clothed on the toilet seat with my legs splayed in front of me: the old beetle-on-its-back routine. Saturday afternoon, the building deserted, I was free to laugh aloud as I wriggled back to my feet, my voice bouncing off the yellowish tiles from all directions. Had anyone been there with me, I'd have been still and faint and hot with chagrin. I decided that it was high time to write the essay.

First, the matter of semantics. I am a cripple. I choose this word to name me. I choose from among several possibilities, the most common of which are "handicapped" and "disabled." I made the choice a number of years ago, without thinking, unaware of my motives for doing so. Even now, I'm not sure what those motives are, but I recognize that they are complex and not entirely flattering. People—crippled or not—wince at the word "cripple," as they do not at "handicapped" or "disabled." Perhaps I want them to wince. I want them to see me as a tough customer, one to whom the fates/gods/viruses have not been kind, but who can face the brutal truth of her existence squarely. As a cripple, I swagger.

But, to be fair to myself, a certain amount of honesty underlies my choice. "Cripple" seems to me a clean word, straightforward and precise. It has an honorable history, having made its first appearance in the Lindisfarne Gospel[1] in the tenth century. As a lover of words, I like the accuracy with which it describes my condition: I have lost the full use of my limbs. "Disabled," by contrast, suggests any incapacity, physical or mental. And I certainly don't like "handicapped," which implies that I have deliberately been put at a disadvantage, by whom I can't imagine (my God is not a Handicapper General), in order to equalize chances in the great race of life. These words seem to me to be moving away from my condition, to be widening the gap between word and reality. Most remote is the recently coined euphemism "differently abled," which partakes of the same semantic hopefulness that transformed countries from "undeveloped" to "underdeveloped," then to "less developed," and finally to "developing" nations. People have continued to starve in those countries during the shift. Some realities do not obey the dictates of language.

Mine is one of them. Whatever you call me, I remain crippled. But I don't care what you call me, so long as it isn't "differently abled," which strikes me as pure verbal garbage designed, by its ability to describe anyone, to describe no one. I subscribe to George Orwell's thesis that "the slovenliness of our language makes it easier for us to have foolish thoughts."[2] And I refuse to participate in the degeneration of

1. Illustrated manuscript of the New Testament done by Irish monks; English commentaries were added in the tenth century.
2. A quotation from "Politics and the English Language" (see p. 617), by Orwell (1903–1950), British essayist and novelist, famous for his political satires.

the language to the extent that I deny that I have lost anything in the course of this calamitous disease; I refuse to pretend that the only differences between you and me are the various ordinary ones that distinguish any one person from another. But call me "disabled" or "handicapped" if you like. I have long since grown accustomed to them; and if they are vague, at least they hint at the truth. Moreover, I use them myself. Society is no readier to accept crippledness than to accept death, war, sex, sweat, or wrinkles. I would never refer to another person as a cripple. It is the word I use to name only myself.

5 I haven't always been crippled, a fact for which I am soundly grateful. To be whole of limb is, I know from experience, infinitely more pleasant and useful than to be crippled; and if that knowledge leaves one open to bitterness at my loss, the physical soundness I once enjoyed (though I did not enjoy it half enough) is well worth the occasional stab of regret. Though never any good at sports, I was a normally active child and young adult. I climbed trees, played hopscotch, jumped rope, skated, swam, rode my bicycle, sailed. I despised team sports, spending some of the wretchedest afternoons of my life, sweaty and humiliated, behind a field-hockey stick and under a basketball hoop. I tramped alone for miles along the bridle paths that webbed the woods behind the house I grew up in. I swayed through countless dim hours in the arms of one man or another under the scattered shot of light from mirrored balls, and gyrated through countless more as Tab Hunter and Johnny Mathis[3] gave way to the Rolling Stones, Creedence Clearwater Revival, Cream. I walked down the aisle. I pushed baby carriages, changed tires in the rain, marched for peace.

When I was twenty-eight I started to trip and drop things. What at first seemed my natural clumsiness soon became too pronounced to shrug off. I consulted a neurologist, who told me that I had a brain tumor. A battery of tests, increasingly disagreeable, revealed no tumor. About a year and a half later I developed a blurred spot in one eye. I had, at last, the episodes "disseminated in space and time" requisite for a diagnosis: multiple sclerosis. I have never been sorry for the doctor's initial misdiagnosis, however. For almost a week, until the negative results of the tests were in, I thought that I was going to die right away. Every day for the past nearly ten years, then, has been a kind of gift. I accept all gifts.

Multiple sclerosis is a chronic degenerative disease of the central nervous system, in which the myelin that sheathes the nerves is somehow eaten away and scar tissue forms in its place, interrupting the nerves' signals. During its course, which is unpredictable and uncontrollable, one may lose vision, hearing, speech, the ability to walk, con-

3. American singer (b. 1935), popular in the 1950s and 1960s and well known for his love ballads. Tab Hunter (b. 1931), American actor and singer popular in the 1960s.

trol of bladder and/or bowels, strength in any or all extremities, sensitivity to touch, vibration, and/or pain, potency, coordination of movements—the list of possibilities is lengthy and, yes, horrifying. One may also lose one's sense of humor. That's the easiest to lose and the hardest to survive without.

In the past ten years, I have sustained some of these losses. Characteristic of MS are sudden attacks, called exacerbations, followed by remissions, and these I have not had. Instead, my disease had been slowly progressive. My left leg is now so weak that I walk with the aid of a brace and a cane; and for distances I use an Amigo, a variation on the electric wheelchair that looks rather like an electrified kiddie car. I no longer have much use of my left hand. Now my right side is weakening as well. I still have the blurred spot in my right eye. Overall, though, I've been lucky so far. My world has, of necessity, been circumscribed by my losses, but the terrain left me has been ample enough for me to continue many of the activities that absorb me: writing, teaching, raising children and cats and plants and snakes, reading, speaking publicly about MS and depression, even playing bridge with people patient and honorable enough to let me scatter cards every which way without sneaking a peek.

Lest I begin to sound like Pollyanna, however, let me say that I don't like having MS. I hate it. My life holds realities—harsh ones, some of them—that no right-minded human being ought to accept without grumbling. One of them is fatigue. I know of no one with MS who does not complain of bone-weariness; in a disease that presents an astonishing variety of symptoms, fatigue seems to be a common factor. I wake up in the morning feeling the way most people do at the end of a bad day, and I take it from there. As a result, I spend a lot of time *in extremis*[4] and, impatient with limitation, I tend to ignore my fatigue until my body breaks down in some way and forces rest. Then I miss picnics, dinner parties, poetry readings, the brief visits of old friends from out of town. The offspring of a puritanical tradition of exceptional venerability, I cannot view these lapses without shame. My life often seems a series of small failures to do as I ought.

10 I lead, on the whole, an ordinary life, probably rather like the one I would have led had I not had MS. I am lucky that my predilections were already solitary, sedentary, and bookish—unlike the world-famous French cellist I have read about,[5] or the young woman I talked with one long afternoon who wanted only to be a jockey. I had just begun graduate school when I found out something was wrong with

4. Latin for "in the last straits"—here it means "at the limits of endurance."

5. Jacqueline du Pre (1945–1987), a great cellist whose career was ended by MS.

me, and I have remained, interminably, a graduate student. Perhaps I would not have if I'd thought I had the stamina to return to a full-time job as a technical editor; but I've enjoyed my studies.

In addition to studying, I teach writing courses. I also teach medical students how to give neurological examinations. I pick up freelance editing jobs here and there. I have raised a foster son and sent him into the world, where he has made me two grandbabies, and I am still escorting my daughter and son through adolescence. I go to Mass every Saturday. I am a superb, if messy, cook. I am also an enthusiastic laundress, capable of sorting a hamper full of clothes into five subtly differentiated piles, but a terrible housekeeper. I can do italic writing and, in an emergency, bathe an oil-soaked cat. I play a fiendish game of Scrabble. When I have the time and the money, I like to sit on my front steps with my husband, drinking Amaretto and smoking a cigar, as we imagine our counterparts in Leningrad and make sure that the sun gets down once more behind the sharp childish scrawl of the Tuscon Mountains.

This lively plenty has its bleak complement, of course, in all the things I can no longer do. I will never run again, except in dreams, and one day I may have to write that I will never walk again. I like to go camping, but I can't follow George and the children along the trails that wander out of a campsite through the desert or into the mountains. In fact, even on the level I've learned never to check the weather or try to hold a coherent conversation: I need all my attention for my wayward feet. Of late, I have begun to catch myself wondering how people can propel themselves without canes. With only one usable hand, I have to select my clothing with care not so much for style as for ease of ingress and egress, and even so, dressing can be laborious. I can no longer do fine stitchery, pick up babies, play the piano, braid my hair. I am immobilized by acute attacks of depression, which may or may not be physiologically related to MS but are certainly its logical concomitant.

These two elements, the plenty and the privation, are never pure, nor are the delight and wretchedness that accompany them. Almost every pickle that I get into as a result of my weakness and clumsiness—and I get into plenty—is funny as well as maddening and sometimes painful. I recall one May afternoon when a friend and I were going out for a drink after finishing up at school. As we were climbing into opposite sides of my car, chatting, I tripped and fell, flat and hard, onto the asphalt parking lot, my abrupt departure interrupting him in mid-sentence. "Where'd you go?" he called as he came around the back of the car to find me hauling myself up by the door frame. "Are you all right?" Yes, I told him, I was fine, just a bit rattly, and we drove off to find a shady patio and some beer. When I got home an hour or so later, my daughter greeted me with "What have you done to yourself?" I looked down. One elbow of my white turtleneck with the green froggies, one knee of my white trousers, one white kneesock were bloodsoaked. We peeled off the clothes and inspected the damage, which was nasty enough but not alarming. That part wasn't funny: The abrasions took a long time to heal, and one got a little infected. Even so, when I think of my friend talking earnestly, suddenly, to the hot thin air while I dropped from his view as though through a trap door, I find the image as silly as something from a Marx Brothers movie.

I may find it easier than other cripples to amuse myself because I live propped by the acceptance and the assistance and, sometimes, the amusement of those around me. Grocery clerks tear my checks out of my checkbook for me, and sales clerks find chairs to put into dressing rooms when I want to try on clothes. The people I work with make sure I teach at times when I am least likely to be fatigued, in places I can get to, with the materials I need. My students, with one anonymous exception (in an end-of-the-semester evaluation), have been unperturbed by my disability. Some even like it. One was immensely cheered by the information that I paint my own fingernails; she decided, she told me, that if I could go to such trouble over fine details, she could keep on writing essays. I suppose I became some sort of bright-fingered muse. She wrote good essays, too.

15 The most important struts in the framework of my existence, of course, are my husband and children. Dismayingly few marriages survive the MS test, and why should they? Most twenty-two- and nineteen-year-olds, like George and me, can vow in clear conscience, after a childhood of chicken pox and summer colds, to keep one another in sickness and in health so long as they both shall live. Not many are equipped for catastrophe: the dismay, the depression, the extra work, the boredom that a degenerative disease can insinuate into a relationship. And our society, with its emphasis on fun and its association of fun with physical performance, offers little encouragement for a whole spouse to stay with a crippled partner. Children experience similar stresses when faced with a crippled parent, and they are more helpless, since parents and children can't usually get divorced. They hate, of course, to be different from their peers, and the child whose mother is tacking down the aisle of a school auditorium packed with proud parents like a Cape Cod dinghy in a stiff breeze jolly well stands out in a crowd. Deprived of legal divorce, the child can at least deny the mother's disability, even her existence, forgetting to tell her about recitals and PTA meetings, refusing to accompany her to stores or church or the movies, never inviting friends to the house. Many do.

But I've been limping along for ten years now, and so far George and the children are still at my left elbow, holding tight. Anne and Matthew vacuum floors and dust furniture and haul trash and rake up dog droppings and button my cuffs and bake lasagna and Toll House cookies with just enough grumbling so I know that they don't have brain fever. And far from hiding me, they're forever dragging me by racks of fancy clothes or through teeming school corridors, or welcoming gaggles of friends while I'm wandering through the house in Anne's filmy pink babydoll pajamas. George generally calls before he brings someone home, but he does just as many dumb thankless chores as the children. And they all yell at me, laugh at some of my jokes, write me funny letters when we're apart—in short, treat me as an ordinary human being for whom they have some use. I think they like me. Unless they're faking. . . .

Faking. There's the rub. Tugging at the fringes of my consciousness always is the terror that people are kind to me only because I'm a cripple. My mother almost shattered me once, with that instinct mothers have—blind, I think, in this case, but unerring nonetheless—for striking blows along the fault-lines of their children's hearts, by telling me, in an attack on my selfishness, "We all have to make allowances for you, of course, because of the way you are." From the distance of a couple of years, I have to admit that I haven't any idea just what she meant, and I'm not sure that she knew either. She was awfully angry. But at the time, as the words thudded home, I felt my worst fear, suddenly realized. I could bear being called selfish: I am. But I couldn't bear the corroboration that those around me were doing in fact what I'd always suspected them of doing, professing fondness while silently putting up with me because of the way I am. A cripple. I've been a little cracked ever since.

Along with this fear that people are secretly accepting shoddy goods comes a relentless pressure to please—to prove myself worth the burdens I impose, I guess, or to build a substantial account of goodwill against which I may write drafts in times of need. Part of the pressure arises from social expectations. In our society, anyone who deviates from the norm had better find some way to compensate. Like fat people, who are expected to be jolly, cripples must bear their lot meekly and cheerfully. A grumpy cripple isn't playing by the rules. And much of the pressure is self-generated. Early on I vowed that, if I had to have MS, by God I was going to do it well. This is a class act, ladies and gentlemen. No tears, no recriminations, no faint-heartedness.

One way and another, then, I wind up feeling like Tiny Tim,[6] peering over the edge of the table at the Christmas goose, waving my crutch, piping down God's blessing on us all. Only sometimes I don't

6. A crippled, frail young boy saved by Scrooge's eventual generosity in Charles Dickens's novel A *Christmas Carol*.

want to play Tiny Tim. I'd rather be Caliban,[7] a most scurvy monster. Fortunately, at home no one much cares whether I'm a good cripple or a bad cripple as long as I make vichyssoise with fair regularity. One evening several years ago, Anne was reading at the dining-room table while I cooked dinner. As I opened a can of tomatoes, the can slipped in my left hand and juice spattered me and the counter with bloody spots. Fatigued and infuriated, I bellowed, "I'm so sick of being crippled!" Anne glanced at me over the top of her book. "There now," she said, "do you feel better?" "Yes," I said, "yes, I do." She went back to her reading. I felt better. That's about all the attention my scurviness ever gets.

20 Because I hate being crippled, I sometimes hate myself for being a cripple. Over the years I have come to expect—even accept—attacks of violent self-loathing. Luckily, in general our society no longer connects deformity and disease directly with evil (though a charismatic once told me that I have MS because a devil is in me) and so I'm allowed to move largely at will, even among small children. But I'm not sure that this revision of attitude has been particularly helpful. Physical imperfection, even freed of moral disapprobation, still defies and violates the ideal, especially for women, whose confinement in their bodies as objects of desire is far from over. Each age, of course, has its ideal, and I doubt that ours is any better or worse than any other. Today's ideal woman, who lives on the glossy pages of dozens of magazines, seems to be between the ages of eighteen and twenty-five; her hair has body, her teeth flash white, her breath smells minty, her underarms are dry; she has a career but is still a fabulous cook, especially of meals that take less than twenty minutes to prepare; she does not ordinarily appear to have a husband or children; she is trim and deeply tanned; she jogs, swims, plays tennis, rides a bicycle, sails, but does not bowl; she travels widely, even to out-of-the-way places like Finland and Samoa, always in the company of the ideal man, who possesses a nearly identical set of characteristics. There are a few exceptions. Though usually white and often blonde, she may be black, Hispanic, Asian, or Native American, so long as she is unusually sleek. She may be old, provided she is selling a laxative or is Lauren Bacall. If she is selling a detergent, she may be married and have a flock of strikingly messy children. But she is never a cripple.

Like many women I know, I have always had an uneasy relationship with my body. I was not a popular child, largely, I think now, because I was peculiar: intelligent, intense, moody, shy, given to unexpected actions and inexplicable notions and emotions. But as I entered adolescence, I believed myself unpopular because I was homely: my breasts

7. The monstrous son of the witch Sycorax in Shakespeare's play *The Tempest*.

too flat, my mouth too wide, my hips too narrow, my clothing never quite right in fit or style. I was not, in fact, particularly ugly, old photographs inform me, though I was well off the ideal; but I carried this sense of self-alienation with me into adulthood, where it regenerated in response to the depredations of MS. Even with my brace I walk with a limp so pronounced that, seeing myself on the videotape of a television program on the disabled, I couldn't believe that anything but an inchworm could make progress humping along like that. My shoulders droop and my pelvis thrusts forward as I try to balance myself upright, throwing my frame into a bony S. As a result of contractures, one shoulder is higher than the other and I carry one arm bent in front of me, the fingers curled into a claw. My left arm and leg have wasted into pipe-stems, and I try always to keep them covered. When I think about how my body must look to others, especially to men, to whom I have been trained to display myself, I feel ludicrous, even loathsome.

At my age, however, I don't spend much time thinking about my appearance. The burning egocentricity of adolescence, which assures one that all the world is looking all the time, has passed, thank God, and I'm generally too caught up in what I'm doing to step back, as I used to, and watch myself as though upon a stage. I'm also too old to believe in the accuracy of self-image. I know that I'm not a hideous crone, that in fact, when I'm rested, well dressed, and well made up, I look fine. The self-loathing I feel is neither physically nor intellectually substantial. What I hate is not me but a disease.

I am not a disease.

And a disease is not—at least not singlehandedly—going to determine who I am, though at first it seemed to be going to. Adjusting to a chronic incurable illness, I have moved through a process similar to that outlined by Elizabeth Kübler-Ross in *On Death and Dying*. The major difference—and it is far more significant than most people recognize—is that I can't be sure of the outcome, as the terminally ill cancer patient can. Research studies indicate that, with proper medical care, I may achieve a "normal" life span. And in our society, with its vision of death as the ultimate evil, worse even than decrepitude, the response to such news is, "Oh well, at least you're not going to *die*." Are there worse things than dying? I think that there may be.

I think of two women I know, both with MS, both enough older 25
than I to have served me as models. One took to her bed several years ago and has been there ever since. Although she can sit in a high-backed wheelchair, because she is incontinent she refuses to go out at all, even though incontinence pants, which are readily available at any pharmacy, could protect her from embarrassment. Instead, she stays at home and insists that her husband, a small quiet man, a retired civil servant, stay there with her except for a quick weekly foray to the su-

permarket. The other woman, whose illness was diagnosed when she was eighteen, a nursing student engaged to a young doctor, finished her training, married her doctor, accompanied him to Germany when he was in the service, bore three sons and a daughter, now grown and gone. When she can, she travels with her husband; she plays bridge, embroiders, swims regularly; she works, like me, as a symptomatic-patient instructor of medical students in neurology. Guess which woman I hope to be.

At the beginning, I thought about having MS almost incessantly. And because of the unpredictable course of the disease, my thoughts were always terrified. Each night I'd get into bed wondering whether I'd get out again the next morning, whether I'd be able to see, to speak, to hold a pen between my fingers. Knowing that the day might come when I'd be physically incapable of killing myself, I thought perhaps I ought to do so right away, while I still had the strength. Gradually I came to understand that the Nancy who might one day lie inert under a bedsheet, arms and legs paralyzed, unable to feed or bathe herself, unable to reach out for a gun, a bottle of pills, was not the Nancy I was at present, and that I could not presume to make decisions for that future Nancy, who might well not want in the least to die. Now the only provision I've made for the future Nancy is that when the time comes—and it is likely to come in the form of pneumonia, friend to the weak and the old—I am not to be treated with machines and medications. If she is unable to communicate by then, I hope she will be satisfied with these terms.

Thinking all the time about having MS grew tiresome and intrusive, especially in the large and tragic mode in which I was accustomed to considering my plight. Months and even years went by without catastrophe (at least without one related to MS), and really I was awfully busy, what with George and children and snakes and students and poems, and I hadn't the time, let alone the inclination, to devote myself to being a disease. Too, the richer my life became, the funnier it seemed, as though there were some connection between largesse and laughter, and so my tragic stance began to waver until, even with the aid of a brace and a cane, I couldn't hold it for very long at a time.

After several years I was satisfied with my adjustment. I had suffered my grief and fury and terror, I thought, but now I was at ease with my lot. Then one summer day I set out with George and the children across the desert for a vacation in California. Part way to Yuma I became aware that my right leg felt funny. "I think I've had an exacerbation," I told George. "What shall we do?" he asked. "I think we'd better get the hell to California," I said, "because I don't know whether I'll ever make it again." So we went on to San Diego and then to Orange, up the Pacific Coast Highway to Santa Cruz, across to Yosemite, down to Sequoia and Joshua Tree, and so back over the desert to home. It was a fine two-week trip, filled with friends and fair weather, and I wouldn't have missed it for the world, though I did in fact make it back to California two years later. Nor would there have been any point in missing it, since in MS, once the symptoms have appeared, the neurological damage has been done, and there's no way to predict or prevent that damage.

The incident spoiled my self-satisfaction, however. It renewed my grief and fury and terror, and I learned that one never finishes adjusting to MS. I don't know now why I thought one would. One does not, after all, finish adjusting to life, and MS is simply a fact of my life—not my favorite fact, of course—but as ordinary as my nose and my tropical fish and my yellow Mazda station wagon. It may at any time get worse, but no amount of worry or anticipation can prepare me for a new loss. My life is a lesson in losses. I learn one at a time.

And I had best be patient in the learning, since I'll have to do it like it or not. As any rock fan knows, you can't always get what you want. Particularly when you have MS. You can't, for example, get cured. In recent years researchers and the organizations that fund research have started to pay MS some attention even though it isn't fatal; perhaps they have begun to see that life is something other than a quantitative phenomenon, that one may be very much alive for a very long time in a life that isn't worth living. The researchers have made some progress toward understanding the mechanism of the disease: It may well be an autoimmune reaction triggered by a slow-acting virus. But they are nowhere near its prevention, control, or cure. And most of us want to be cured. Some, unable to accept incurability, grasp at one treatment after another, no matter how bizarre: megavitamin therapy, gluten-free diet, injections of cobra venom, hypothermal suits, lymphocytopharesis, hyperbaric chambers. Many treatments are probably harmless enough, but none are curative.

The absence of a cure often makes MS patients bitter toward their doctors. Doctors are, after all, the priests of modern society, the new shamans, whose business is to heal, and many an MS patient roves from one to another, searching for the "good" doctor who will make him well. Doctors too think of themselves as healers, and for this reason many have trouble dealing with MS patients, whose disease in its intransigence defeats their aims and mocks their skills. Too few doctors, it is true, treat their patients as whole human beings, but the reverse is also true. I have always tried to be gentle with my doctors, who often have more at stake in terms of ego than I do. I may be frustrated, maddened, depressed by the incurability of my disease, but I am not diminished by it, and they are. When I push myself up from my seat in the waiting room and stumble toward them, I incarnate the limitation of their powers. The least I can do is refuse to press on their tenderest spots.

This gentleness is part of the reason that I'm not sorry to be a cripple. I didn't have it before. Perhaps I'd have developed it anyway—how could I know such a thing?—and I wish I had more of it, but I'm glad of what I have. It has opened and enriched my life enormously, this sense that my frailty and need must be mirrored in others, that in searching for and shaping a stable core in a life wrenched by change and loss, change and loss, I must recognize the same process, under individual conditions, in the lives around me. I do not deprecate such knowledge, however I've come by it.

All the same, if a cure were found, would I take it? In a minute. I may be a cripple, but I'm only occasionally a loony and never a saint. Anyway, in my brand of theology God doesn't give bonus points for a limp. I'd take a cure; I just don't need one. A friend who also has MS startled me once by asking, "Do you ever say to yourself, 'Why me, Lord?' " "No, Michael, I don't," I told him, "because whenever I try, the only response I can think of is 'Why not?' " If I could make a cosmic deal, who would I put in my place? What in my life would I give up in exchange for sound limbs and a thrilling rush of energy? No one. Nothing. I might as well do the job myself. Now that I'm getting the hang of it.

QUESTIONS

1. *How does Mairs organize her essay? What connects the different parts to each other?*
2. *What stereotypes of "disabled" people does Mairs expect us to believe in? How does she set out to counter them?*
3. *Mairs deliberately chooses to call herself a "cripple." Select a person or group that deliberately chooses its own name or description and explain the rationale behind the choice.*

Alice Walker

BEAUTY: WHEN THE OTHER DANCER IS THE SELF

It is a bright summer day in 1947. My father, a fat, funny man with beautiful eyes and a subversive wit, is trying to decide which of his eight children he will take with him to the county fair. My mother, of

From *In Search of Our Mothers' Gardens* (1983).

course, will not go. She is knocked out from getting most of us ready: I hold my neck stiff against the pressure of her knuckles as she hastily completes the braiding and then beribboning of my hair.

My father is the driver for the rich old white lady up the road. Her name is Miss Mey. She owns all the land for miles around, as well as the house in which we live. All I remember about her is that she once offered to pay my mother thirty-five cents for cleaning her house, raking up piles of her magnolia leaves, and washing her family's clothes, and that my mother—she of no money, eight children, and a chronic earache—refused it. But I do not think of this in 1947. I am two and a half years old. I want to go everywhere my daddy goes. I am excited at the prospect of riding in a car. Someone has told me fairs are fun. That there is room in the car for only three of us doesn't faze me at all. Whirling happily in my starchy frock, showing off my biscuit-polished patent-leather shoes and lavender socks, tossing my head in a way that makes my ribbons bounce, I stand, hands on hips, before my father. "Take me, Daddy," I say with assurance; "I'm the prettiest!"

Later, it does not surprise me to find myself in Miss Mey's shiny black car, sharing the back seat with the other lucky ones. Does not surprise me that I thoroughly enjoy the fair. At home that night I tell the unlucky ones all I can remember about the merry-go-round, the man who eats live chickens, and the teddy bears, until they say: that's enough, baby Alice. Shut up now, and go to sleep.

It is Easter Sunday, 1950. I am dressed in a green, flocked, scalloped-hem dress (handmade by my adoring sister, Ruth) that has its own smooth satin petticoat and tiny hot-pink roses tucked into each scallop. My shoes, new T-strap patent leather, again highly biscuit-polished. I am six years old and have learned one of the longest Easter speeches to be heard that day, totally unlike the speech I said when I was two: "Easter lilies/pure and white/blossom in/the morning light." When I rise to give my speech I do so on a great wave of love and pride and expectation. People in the church stop rustling their new crinolines. They seem to hold their breath. I can tell they admire my dress, but it is my spirit, bordering on sassiness (womanishness), they secretly applaud.

"That girl's a little *mess*," they whisper to each other, pleased. 5

Naturally I say my speech without stammer or pause, unlike those who stutter, stammer, or, worst of all, forget. This is before the word "beautiful" exists in people's vocabulary, but "Oh, isn't she the *cutest* thing!" frequently floats my way. "And got so much sense!" they gratefully add . . . for which thoughtful addition I thank them to this day.

It was great fun being cute. But then, one day, it ended.

I am eight years old and a tomboy. I have a cowboy hat, cowboy boots, checkered shirt and pants, all red. My playmates are my brothers, two and four years older than I. Their colors are black and green, the only difference in the way we are dressed. On Saturday nights we all go to the picture show, even my mother; Westerns are her favorite kind of movie. Back home, "on the ranch," we pretend we are Tom Mix, Hopalong Cassidy, Lash LaRue (we've even named one of our dogs Lash LaRue); we chase each other for hours rustling cattle, being outlaws, delivering damsels from distress. Then my parents decide to buy my brothers guns. These are not "real" guns. They shoot "BBs," copper pellets my brothers say will kill birds. Because I am a girl, I do not get a gun. Instantly I am relegated to the position of Indian. Now there appears a great distance between us. They shoot and shoot at everything with their new guns. I try to keep up with my bow and arrows.

One day while I am standing on top of our makeshift "garage"—pieces of tin nailed across some poles—holding my bow and arrow and looking out toward the fields, I feel an incredible blow in my right eye. I look down just in time to see my brother lower his gun.

10 Both brothers rush to my side. My eye stings, and I cover it with my hand. "If you tell," they say, "we will get a whipping. You don't want that to happen, do you?" I do not. "Here is a piece of wire," says the older brother, picking it up from the roof; "say you stepped on one end of it and the other flew up and hit you." The pain is beginning to start. "Yes," I say, "Yes, I will say that is what happened." If I do not say this is what happened, I know my brothers will find ways to make me wish I had. But now I will say anything that gets me to my mother.

Confronted by our parents we stick to the lie agreed upon. They place me on a bench on the porch and I close my left eye while they examine the right. There is a tree growing from underneath the porch that climbs past the railing to the roof. It is the last thing my right eye sees. I watch as its trunk, its branches, and then its leaves are blotted out by the rising blood.

I am in shock. First there is intense fever, which my father tries to break using lily leaves bound around my head. Then there are chills: my mother tries to get me to eat soup. Eventually, I do not know how, my parents learn what has happened. A week after the "accident" they take me to see a doctor. "Why did you wait so long to come?" he asks, looking into my eye and shaking his head. "Eyes are sympathetic," he says. "If one is blind, the other will likely become blind too."

This comment of the doctor's terrifies me. But it is really how I look that bothers me most. Where the BB pellet struck there is a glob of whitish scar tissue, a hideous cataract, on my eye. Now when I stare at people—a favorite pastime, up to now—they will stare back. Not at the "cute" little girl, but at her scar. For six years I do not stare at anyone, because I do not raise my head.

Years later, in the throes of a mid-life crisis, I ask my mother and sister whether I changed after the "accident." "No," they say, puzzled. "What do you mean?"

What do I mean? 15

I am eight, and, for the first time, doing poorly in school, where I have been something of a whiz since I was four. We have just moved to the place where the "accident" occurred. We do not know any of the people around us because this is a different county. The only time I see the friends I knew is when we go back to our old church. The new school is the former state penitentiary. It is a large stone building, cold and drafty, crammed to overflowing with boisterous, ill-disciplined children. On the third floor there is a huge circular imprint of some partition that has been torn out.

"What used to be here?" I ask a sullen girl next to me on our way past it to lunch.

"The electric chair," says she.

At night I have nightmares about the electric chair, and about all the people reputedly "fried" in it. I am afraid of the school, where all the students seem to be budding criminals.

"What's the matter with your eye?" they ask, critically. 20

When I don't answer (I cannot decide whether it was an "accident" or not), they shove me, insist on a fight.

My brother, the one who created the story about the wire, comes to my rescue. But then brags so much about "protecting" me, I become sick.

After months of torture at the school, my parents decide to send me back to our old community, to my old school. I live with my grandparents and the teacher they board. But there is no room for Phoebe, my cat. By the time my grandparents decide there *is* room, and I ask for my cat, she cannot be found. Miss Yarborough, the boarding teacher, takes me under her wing, and begins to teach me to play the piano. But soon she marries an African—a "prince," she says—and is whisked away to his continent.

At my old school there is at least one teacher who loves me. She is the teacher who "knew me before I was born" and bought my first baby clothes. It is she who makes life bearable. It is her presence that finally helps me turn on the one child at the school who continually calls me "one-eyed bitch." One day I simply grab him by his coat and beat him until I am satisfied. It is my teacher who tells me my mother is ill.

25 My mother is lying in bed in the middle of the day, something I have never seen. She is in too much pain to speak. She has an abscess in her ear. I stand looking down on her, knowing that if she dies, I cannot live. She is being treated with warm oils and hot bricks held against her cheek. Finally a doctor comes. But I must go back to my grandparents' house. The weeks pass but I am hardly aware of it. All I know is that my mother might die, my father is not so jolly, my brothers still have their guns, and I am the one sent away from home.

"You did not change," they say.

Did I imagine the anguish of never looking up?

I am twelve. When relatives come to visit I hide in my room. My cousin Brenda, just my age, whose father works in the post office and whose mother is a nurse, comes to find me. "Hello," she says. And then she asks, looking at my recent school picture, which I did not want taken, and on which the "glob," as I think of it, is clearly visible, "You still can't see out of that eye?"

"No," I say, and flop back on the bed over my book.

30 That night, as I do almost every night, I abuse my eye. I rant and rave at it, in front of the mirror. I plead with it to clear up before morning. I tell it I hate and despise it. I do not pray for sight. I pray for beauty.

"You did not change," they say.

I am fourteen and baby-sitting for my brother Bill, who lives in Boston. He is my favorite brother and there is a strong bond between us. Understanding my feelings of shame and ugliness he and his wife take me to a local hospital, where the "glob" is removed by a doctor named O. Henry. There is still a small bluish crater where the scar tissue was, but the ugly white stuff is gone. Almost immediately I become a different person from the girl who does not raise her head. Or so I think. Now that I've raised my head I win the boyfriend of my dreams. Now that I've raised my head I have plenty of friends. Now that I've raised my head classwork comes from my lips as faultlessly as Easter speeches did, and I leave high school as valedictorian, most popular student, and *queen*, hardly believing my luck. Ironically, the girl who was voted most beautiful in our class (and was) was later shot twice through the chest by a male companion, using a "real" gun, while she was pregnant. But that's another story in itself. Or is it?

"You did not change," they say.

It is now thirty years since the "accident." A beautiful journalist comes to visit and to interview me. She is going to write a cover story for her magazine that focuses on my latest book. "Decide how you want to look on the cover," she says. "Glamorous, or whatever."

Never mind "glamorous," it is the "whatever" that I hear. Suddenly 35
all I can think of is whether I will get enough sleep the night before the photography session: if I don't, my eye will be tired and wander, as blind eyes will.

At night in bed with my lover I think up reasons why I should not appear on the cover of a magazine. "My meanest critics will say I've sold out," I say. "My family will now realize I write scandalous books."

"But what's the real reason you don't want to do this?" he asks.

"Because in all probability," I say in a rush, "my eye won't be straight."

"It will be straight enough," he says. Then, "Besides, I thought you'd made your peace with that."

And I suddenly remember that I have. 40

I remember:

I am talking to my brother Jimmy, asking if he remembers anything unusual about the day I was shot. He does not know I consider that day the last time my father, with his sweet home remedy of cool lily leaves, chose me, and that I suffered and raged inside because of this. "Well," he says, "all I remember is standing by the side of the highway with Daddy, trying to flag down a car. A white man stopped, but when Daddy said he needed somebody to take his little girl to the doctor, he drove off."

I remember:

I am in the desert for the first time. I fall totally in love with it. I am so overwhelmed by its beauty, I confront for the first time, consciously, the meaning of the doctor's words years ago: "Eyes are sympathetic. If one is blind, the other will likely become blind too." I realize I have dashed about the world madly, looking at this, looking at that, storing up images against the fading of the light. *But I might have missed seeing the desert!* The shock of that possibility—and gratitude for over twenty-five years of sight—sends me literally to my knees. Poem after poem comes—which is perhaps how poets pray.

On Sight

I am so thankful I have seen
The Desert
And the creatures in the desert
And the desert Itself.

The desert has its own moon
Which I have seen
With my own eye.
There is no flag on it.

Trees of the desert have arms
All of which are always up
That is because the moon is up

The sun is up
Also the sky
The stars
Clouds
None with flags.

If there *were* flags, I doubt
the trees would point.
Would you?

45 *But mostly, I remember this:*

I am twenty-seven, and my baby daughter is almost three. Since her birth I have worried about her discovery that her mother's eyes are different from other people's. Will she be embarrassed? I think. What will she say? Every day she watches a television program called "Big Blue Marble." It begins with a picture of the earth as it appears from the moon. It is bluish, a little battered-looking, but full of light, with whitish clouds swirling around it. Every time I see it I weep with love, as if it is a picture of Grandma's house. One day when I am putting Rebecca down for her nap, she suddenly focues on my eye. Something inside me cringes, gets ready to try to protect myself. All children are cruel about physical differences, I know from experience, and that they don't always mean to be is another matter. I assume Rebecca will be the same.

But no-o-o-o. She studies my face intently as we stand, her inside and me outside her crib. She even holds my face maternally between her dimpled little hands. Then, looking every bit as serious and lawyer-like as her father, she says, as if it may just possibly have slipped my attention: "Mommy, there's a *world* in your eye." (As in, "Don't be alarmed, or do anything crazy.") And then, gently, but with great interest: "Mommy, where did you *get* that world in your eye?"

For the most part, the pain left then. (So what, if my brothers grew up to buy even more powerful pellet guns for their sons and to carry real guns themselves. So what, if a young "Morehouse man"[1] once nearly fell off the steps of Trevor Arnett Library because he thought my eyes were blue.) Crying and laughing I ran to the bathroom, while Rebecca mumbled and sang herself off to sleep. Yes indeed, I realized, looking into the mirror. There *was* a world in my eye. And I saw that it was possible to love it: that in fact, for all it had taught me of shame and anger and inner vision, I *did* love it. Even to see it drifting out of orbit in boredom, or rolling up out of fatigue, not to mention floating back at attention in excitement (bearing witness, a friend has called it), deeply suitable to my personality, and even characteristic of me.

1. A student at Morehouse College in Atlanta, Georgia.

That night I dream I am dancing to Stevie Wonder's song "Always" (the name of the song is really "As," but I hear it as "Always"). As I dance, whirling and joyous, happier than I've ever been in my life, another bright-faced dancer joins me. We dance and kiss each other and hold each other through the night. The other dancer has obviously come through all right, as I have done. She is beautiful, whole and free. And she is also me.

QUESTIONS

1. *Throughout her essay, Walker refers to the "accident." Why does she put the word in quotation marks? Has Walker made her peace with the "accident" and its consequences?*
2. *Walker writes her essay by selecting particular moments in her life. What does each moment show? How do these moments relate to Walker's theme?*
3. *What is the effect of ending the essay by recounting a dream? How does the dream relate to the essay's title?*
4. *Write an essay comparing and contrasting Walker's essay and Mairs's "On Being a Cripple." Consider especially their subjects and their attitudes toward those subjects.*

Dylan Thomas

MEMORIES OF CHRISTMAS

One Christmas was so much like another, in those years, around the sea-town corner now and out of all sound except the distant speaking of the voices I sometimes hear a moment before sleep, that I can never remember whether it snowed for six days and six nights when I was twelve or whether it snowed for twelve days and twelve nights when I was six; or whether the ice broke and the skating grocer vanished like a snowman through a white trap-door on that same Christmas Day that the mince-pies finished Uncle Arnold and we tobogganed down the seaward hill, all the afternoon, on the best tea-tray, and Mrs. Griffiths complained, and we threw a snowball at her niece, and my hands burned so, with the heat and the cold, when I held them in front of the fire, that I cried for twenty minutes and then had some jelly.

All the Christmases roll down the hill towards the Welsh-speaking sea, like a snowball growing whiter and bigger and rounder, like a cold

From *Quite Early One Morning* (1954).

and headlong moon bundling down the sky that was our street; and they stop at the rim of the ice-edged, fish-freezing waves, and I plunge my hands in the snow and bring out whatever I can find; holly or robins or pudding, squabbles and carols and oranges and tin whistles, and the fire in the front room, and bang go the crackers, and holy, holy, holy, ring the bells, and the glass bells shaking on the tree, and Mother Goose, and Struwelpeter[1]—oh! the baby-burning flames and the clacking scissorman!—Billy Bunter[2] and Black Beauty, Little Women and boys who have three helpings, Alice and Mrs. Potter's badgers,[3] penknives, teddy-bears—named after a Mr. Theodore Bear, their inventor, or father, who died recently in the United States—mouth-organs, tin-soldiers, and blancmange, and Auntie Bessie playing "Pop Goes the Weasel" and "Nuts in May" and "Oranges and Lemons" on the untuned piano in the parlor all through the thimble-hiding musical-chairing blind-man's-buffing party at the end of the never-to-be-forgotten day at the end of the unremembered year.

In goes my hand into that wool-white bell-tongued ball of holidays resting at the margin of the carol-singing sea, and out come Mrs. Prothero and the firemen.

It was on the afternoon of the day of Christmas Eve, and I was in Mrs. Prothero's garden, waiting for cats, with her son Jim. It was snowing. It was always snowing at Christmas; December, in my memory, is white as Lapland, though there were no reindeers. But there were cats. Patient, cold, and callous, our hands wrapped in socks, we waited to snowball the cats. Sleek and long as jaguars and terrible-whiskered, spitting and snarling they would slink and sidle over the white back-garden walls, and the lynx-eyed hunters, Jim and I, fur-capped and moccasined trappers from Hudson's Bay off Eversley Road, would hurl our deadly snowballs at the green of their eyes. The wise cats never appeared. We were so still, Eskimo-footed arctic marksmen in the muffling silence of the eternal snows—eternal, ever since Wednesday—that we never heard Mrs. Prothero's first cry from her igloo at the bottom of the garden. Or, if we heard it at all, it was, to us, like the far-off challenge of our enemy and prey, the neighbor's Polar Cat. But soon the voice grew louder. "Fire!" cried Mrs. Prothero, and she beat the dinner-gong. And we ran down the garden, with the snowballs in

1. The title character of *Struwelpeter (Slovenly Peter), or Merry Tales and Funny Pictures*, a children's book originally in German, by Dr. Heinrich Hoffmann, containing gaily grim admonitory narratives in verse about little Pauline, for example, who played with matches and got burned up; or the little boy who sucked his thumbs until the tall scissorman cut them off.
2. The humorous fat boy in Frank Richards' tales of English school life.
3. Beatrix Potter, creator of *Peter Rabbit* and other animal tales for children, among them *The Tale of Mr. Tod*, a badger.

our arms, towards the house, and smoke, indeed, was pouring out of the dining-room, and the gong was bombilating, and Mrs. Prothero was announcing ruin like a town-crier in Pompeii. This was better than all the cats in Wales standing on the wall in a row. We bounded into the house, laden with snowballs, and stopped at the open door of the smoke-filled room. Something was burning all right; perhaps it was Mr. Prothero, who always slept there after midday dinner with a newspaper over his face; but he was standing in the middle of the room, saying "A fine Christmas!" and smacking at the smoke with a slipper.

"Call the fire-brigade," cried Mrs. Prothero as she beat the gong.

"They won't be there," said Mr. Prothero, "it's Christmas."

There was no fire to be seen, only clouds of smoke and Mr. Prothero standing in the middle of them, waving his slipper as though he were conducting.

"Do something," he said.

And we threw all our snowballs into the smoke—I think we missed Mr. Prothero—and ran out of the house to the telephone-box.

"Let's call the police as well," Jim said.

"And the ambulance."

"And Ernie Jenkins, he likes fires."

But we only called the fire-brigade, and soon the fire-engine came and three tall men in helmets brought a hose into the house and Mr. Prothero got out just in time before they turned it on. Nobody could have had a noisier Christmas Eve. And when the firemen turned off the hose and were standing in the wet and smoky room, Jim's aunt, Miss Prothero, came downstairs and peered in at them. Jim and I waited, very quietly, to hear what she would say to them. She said the right thing, always. She looked at the three tall firemen in their shining helmets, standing among the smoke and cinders and dissolving snowballs, and she said: "Would you like something to read?"

Now out of that bright white snowball of Christmas gone comes the stocking, the stocking of stockings, that hung at the foot of the bed with the arm of a golliwog dangling over the top and small bells ringing in the toes. There was a company, gallant and scarlet but never nice to taste though I always tried when very young, of belted and busbied and musketed lead soldiers so soon to lose their heads and legs in the wars on the kitchen table after the tea-things, the mince-pies, and the cakes that I helped to make by stoning the raisins and eating them, had been cleared away; and a bag of moist and many-colored jelly-babies and a folded flag and a false nose and a tram-conductor's cap and a machine that punched tickets and rang a bell; never a catapult; once, by a mistake that no one could explain, a little hatchet; and a rubber buffalo, or it may have been a horse, with a yellow head and haphazard legs; and a celluloid duck that made, when you pressed it, a most unducklike noise, a mewing moo that an ambitious cat might make who wishes to be a cow; and a painting-book in which I could make the grass, the trees, the sea, and the animals any color I pleased: and still the dazzling sky-blue sheep are grazing in the red field under a flight of rainbow-beaked and pea-green birds.

15 Christmas morning was always over before you could say Jack Frost. And look! suddenly the pudding was burning! Bang the gong and call the fire-brigade and the book-loving firemen! Someone found the silver three-penny-bit with a currant on it; and the someone was always Uncle Arnold. The motto in my cracker read:

> Let's all have fun this Christmas Day,
> Let's play and sing and shout hooray!

and the grown-ups turned their eyes towards the ceiling, and Auntie Bessie, who had already been frightened, twice, by a clockwork mouse, whimpered at the sideboard and had some elderberry wine. And someone put a glass bowl full of nuts on the littered table, and my uncle said, as he said once every year: "I've got a shoe-nut here. Fetch me a shoehorn to open it, boy."

And dinner was ended.

And I remember that on the afternoon of Christmas Day, when the others sat around the fire and told each other that this was nothing, no, nothing, to the great snowbound and turkey-proud yule-log-crackling holly-berry-bedizined and kissing-under-the-mistletoe Christmas when *they* were children, I would go out, school-capped and gloved and mufflered, with my bright new boots squeaking, into the white world on to the seaward hill, to call on Jim and Dan and Jack and to walk with them through the silent snowscape of our town.

We went padding through the streets, leaving huge deep footprints in the snow, on the hidden pavements.

"I bet people'll think there's been hippoes."

20 "What would you do if you saw a hippo coming down Terrace Road?"

"I'd go like this, bang! I'd throw him over the railings and roll him down the hill and then I'd tickle him under the ear and he'd wag his tail . . ."

"What would you do if you saw *two* hippoes . . . ?"

Iron-flanked and bellowing he-hippoes clanked and blundered and battered through the scudding snow towards us as we passed by Mr. Daniel's house.

"Let's post Mr. Daniel a snowball through his letter box."

25 "Let's write things in the snow."

"Let's write 'Mr. Daniel looks like a spaniel' all over his lawn."

"Look," Jack said, "I'm eating snow-pie."

"What's it taste like?"

"Like snow-pie," Jack said.

Or we walked on the white shore. 30

"Can the fishes see it's snowing?"

"They think it's the sky falling down."

The silent one-clouded heavens drifted on to the sea.

"All the old dogs have gone."

Dogs of a hundred mingled makes yapped in the summer at the sea- 35
rim and yelped at the trespassing mountains of the waves.

"I bet St. Bernards would like it now."

And we were snowblind travelers lost on the north hills, and the great dewlapped dogs, with brandy-flasks round their necks, ambled and shambled up to us, baying "Excelsior."[4]

We returned home through the desolate poor sea-facing streets where only a few children fumbled with bare red fingers in the thick wheel-rutted snow and catcalled after us, their voices fading away, as we trudged uphill, into the cries of the dock-birds and the hooters of ships out in the white and whirling bay.

Bring out the tall tales now that we told by the fire as we roasted chestnuts and the gaslight bubbled low. Ghosts with their heads under their arms trailed their chains and said "whooo" like owls in the long nights when I dared not look over my shoulder; wild beasts lurked in the cubby-hole under the stairs where the gas-meter ticked. "Once upon a time," Jim said, "there were three boys, just like us, who got lost in the dark in the snow, near Bethesda Chapel, and this is what happened to them . . ." It was the most dreadful happening I had ever heard.

And I remember that we went singing carols once, a night or two 40
before Christmas Eve, when there wasn't the shaving of a moon to light the secret, white-flying streets. At the end of a long road was a drive that led to a large house, and we stumbled up the darkness of the drive that night, each one of us afraid, each one holding a stone in his hand in case, and all of us too brave to say a word. The wind made through the drive-trees noises as of old and unpleasant and maybe web-footed men wheezing in caves. We reached the black bulk of the house.

"What shall we give them?" Dan whispered.

" 'Hark the Herald'? 'Christmas comes but Once a Year' ?"

"No," Jack said: "We'll sing 'Good King Wenceslas.' I'll count three."

4. "Higher"—recalling Henry Wadsworth Longfellow's poem "Excelsior," in which a traveler who has adopted that word as his motto dies while climbing a dangerous, snowy mountain trail in the Alps.

One, two, three, and we began to sing, our voices high and seemingly distant in the snow-felted darkness round the house that was occupied by nobody we knew. We stood close together, near the dark door.

> Good King Wenceslas looked out
> On the Feast of Stephen.

45 And then a small, dry voice, like the voice of someone who has not spoken for a long time, suddenly joined our singing: a small, dry voice from the other side of the door: a small, dry voice through the keyhole. And when we stopped running we were outside *our* house; the front room was lovely and bright; the gramophone was playing; we saw the red and white balloons hanging from the gas-bracket; uncles and aunts sat by the fire; I thought I smelt our supper being fried in the kitchen. Everything was good again, and Christmas shone through all the familiar town.

"Perhaps it was a ghost," Jim said.

"Perhaps it was trolls," Dan said, who was always reading.

"Let's go in and see if there's any jelly left," Jack said. And we did that.

Joan Didion

ON GOING HOME

I am home for my daughter's first birthday. By "home" I do not mean the house in Los Angeles where my husband and I and the baby live, but the place where my family is, in the Central Valley of California. It is a vital although troublesome distinction. My husband likes my family but is uneasy in their house, because once there I fall into their ways, which are difficult, oblique, deliberately inarticulate, not my husband's ways. We live in dusty houses ("D-U-S-T," he once wrote with his finger on surfaces all over the house, but no one noticed it) filled with mementos quite without value to him (what could the Canton dessert plates mean to him? how could he have known about the assay scales, why should he care if he did know?), and we appear to talk exclusively about people we know who have been committed to mental hospitals, about people we know who have been booked on drunk-driving charges, and about property, particularly about property, land, price per acre and C-2 zoning and assessments and freeway

From *Slouching towards Bethlehem* (1966).

access. My brother does not understand my husband's inability to perceive the advantage in the rather common real-estate transaction known as "sale-leaseback," and my husband in turn does not understand why so many of the people he hears about in my father's house have recently been committed to mental hospitals or booked on drunk-driving charges. Nor does he understand that when we talk about sale-leasebacks and right-of-way condemnations we are talking in code about the things we like best, the yellow fields and the cottonwoods and the rivers rising and falling and the mountain roads closing when the heavy snow comes in. We miss each other's points, have another drink and regard the fire. My brother refers to my husband, in his presence, as "Joan's husband." Marriage is the classic betrayal.

Or perhaps it is not any more. Sometimes I think that those of us who are now in our thirties were born into the last generation to carry the burden of "home," to find in family life the source of all tension and drama. I had by all objective accounts a "normal" and a "happy" family situation, and yet I was almost thirty years old before I could talk to my family on the telephone without crying after I had hung up. We did not fight. Nothing was wrong. And yet some nameless anxiety colored the emotional charges between me and the place that I came from. The question of whether or not you could go home again was a very real part of the sentimental and largely literary baggage with which we left home in the fifties; I suspect that it is irrelevant to the children born of the fragmentation after World War II. A few weeks ago in a San Francisco bar I saw a pretty young girl on crystal take off her clothes and dance for the cash prize in an "amateur-topless" contest. There was no particular sense of moment about this, none of the effect of romantic degradation, of "dark journey," for which my generation strived so assiduously. What sense could that girl possibly make of, say, *Long Day's Journey into Night?*[1] Who is beside the point?

That I am trapped in this particular irrelevancy is never more apparent to me than when I am home. Paralyzed by the neurotic lassitude engendered by meeting one's past at every turn, around every corner, inside every cupboard, I go aimlessly from room to room. I decide to meet it head-on and clean out a drawer, and I spread the contents on the bed. A bathing suit I wore the summer I was seventeen. A letter of rejection from *The Nation*, an aerial photograph of the site for a shopping center my father did not build in 1954. Three teacups hand-painted with cabbage roses and signed "E.M.," my grandmother's initials. There is no final solution for letters of rejection from *The Nation* and teacups hand-painted in 1900. Nor is there any answer to snap-

1. Tragedy by playwright Eugene O'Neill (1888–1952), based on the shame and deception that haunted his own family.

shots of one's grandfather as a young man on skis, surveying around Donner Pass in the year 1910. I smooth out the snapshot and look into his face, and do and do not see my own. I close the drawer, and have another cup of coffee with my mother. We get along very well, veterans of a guerrilla war we never understood.

Days pass. I see no one. I come to dread my husband's evening call, not only because he is full of news of what by now seems to me our remote life in Los Angeles, people he has seen, letters which require attention, but because he asks what I have been doing, suggests uneasily that I get out, drive to San Francisco or Berkeley. Instead I drive across the river to a family graveyard. It has been vandalized since my last visit and the monuments are broken, overturned in the dry grass. Because I once saw a rattlesnake in the grass I stay in the car and listen to a country-and-Western station. Later I drive with my father to a ranch he has in the foothills. The man who runs his cattle on it asks us to the roundup, a week from Sunday, and although I know that I will be in Los Angeles I say, in the oblique way my family talks, that I will come. Once home I mention the broken monuments in the graveyard. My mother shrugs.

5 I go to visit my great-aunts. A few of them think now that I am my cousin, or their daughter who died young. We recall an anecdote about a relative last seen in 1948, and they ask if I still like living in New York City. I have lived in Los Angeles for three years, but I say that I do. The baby is offered a horehound drop, and I am slipped a dollar bill "to buy a treat." Questions trail off, answers are abandoned, the baby plays with the dust motes in a shaft of afternoon sun.

It is time for the baby's birthday party: a white cake, strawberry-marshmallow ice cream, a bottle of champagne saved from another party. In the evening, after she has gone to sleep, I kneel beside the crib and touch her face, where it is pressed against the slats, with mine. She is an open and trusting child, unprepared for and unaccustomed to the ambushes of family life, and perhaps it is just as well that I can offer her little of that life. I would like to give her more. I would like to promise her that she will grow up with a sense of her cousins and of rivers and of her great-grandmother's teacups, would like to pledge her a picnic on a river with fried chicken and her hair uncombed, would like to give her *home* for her birthday, but we live differently now and I can promise her nothing like that. I give her a xylophone and a sundress from Madeira, and promise to tell her a funny story.

QUESTIONS

1. *Didion speaks of herself at home as "paralyzed by the neurotic lassitude engendered by meeting one's past at every turn" (paragraph 3). What about the essay helps explain that feeling?*

2. *What does Didion mean by "the ambushes of family life"? (Besides "ambushes" note Didion's other highly charged language: e.g., "betrayal" in paragraph 1 and "guerrilla war" in paragraph 3.)*
3. *In paragraph 6 Didion says she would like to give her daughter "home for her birthday, but we live differently and I can promise her nothing like that." In an essay, show to what extent this statement holds true or false about people you know.*

Mordecai Richler

ST. URBAIN STREET THEN AND NOW

Bad news. They're closing Baron Byng High School. Our Baron Byng. I speak of a legendary Montreal school, founded in 1921, that resembles nothing so much as a Victorian workhouse. Architecturally, the loss will be minimal (the building's a blight), but emotionally . . . ah, that's something else. If the Battle of Waterloo was won on the playing fields of Eton,[1] then the character of Montreal's diminishing Jewish community was hammered into shape in the smelly classrooms of that big brown brick building.

Themistocles, Thermopylae,
  the Peloponnesian War,
X^2, Y^2, H_2SO_4,
  One, two, three, four,
Who are we for?
  Byng! Byng! Byng!

Today's Jewish community in Montreal is a group riddled with apprehension. Nobody is signing a long lease, every family has its own contingency plans. Once, however, many of us were at BBHS together. Everything possible. September 1944. Even as our elder brothers and cousins were thrusting into Holland, with the Canadian army battling on the Hitler Line, we stood in rows in the BBHS gym, raw and pimply, but shiny trousers freshly pressed. New boys we were. Rambunctious thirteen-year-olds, charged with hope. We were told, "I suppose most of you expect to go on to McGill University four years from now. Well, you will have to work hard. McGill entrance calls for a sixty-five per-

From *Home Sweet Home: My Canadian Album* (1984).

1. Eton was (and still is) a prestigious English boarding school. The Battle of Waterloo was fought in 1815 at Waterloo, Belgium; in it English troops under the duke of Wellington defeated Napoleon's army. Richler is here repeating a common nineteenth-century belief.

cent average in the matriculations, but Jewish boys seeking admission will require seventy-five percent."

Baron Byng was being shut down because its student body, now largely Greek in origin, numbered only 405, but once those classrooms reverberated with the ambition of 1,000 strivers. Scrappy, driving boys and girls who led the province of Quebec in matriculation results year after year.

Baron Byng lies right out there on St. Urbain Street in what used to be the heart of Montreal's swirling Jewish quarter. In my day, St. Urbain Street was the lowest rung on a ladder we were all hot to climb. No, St. Urbain wasn't the lowest rung, for one street below came Clark, where they had no lane and had to plunk their garbage out on the street. Parked right before the front door. Immediately below Clark there came the fabled Main or, more properly, Boulevard St. Laurent. Levitt's delicatessen. Moishe's steak house. Richstone's bakery. The editorial offices of the *Canadian Jewish Eagle*. The Canada, where you could take in three movies for a quarter, but sometimes felt gray squishy things nibbling at your ankles. The Roxy and the Crystal Palace, where they showed only two movies, but offered a live show as well. A forlorn parade of pulpy strippers. "Put on your glasses, boys," the MC would say, "for here come the Hubba-Hubba Girls." It was to the Main we repaired for zoot trousers, ducktail haircuts, and free auto parts calendars that showed leggy girls, their skirts blown high by the wind. If the calendar was vintage, the real stuff, you could just make out the girl's nipples *straining against her blouse*, as they wrote in the best stories that appeared in *True Detective*.

5 Our world was largely composed of the five streets that ran between Park Avenue and the Main: Jeanne Mance, Esplanade, Waverly, St. Urbain, and Clark. Standing tippy-toe on St. Urbain's next-to-the-bottom rung, you could just peer over Park Avenue—Park Avenue, the dividing line—into blessed Outremont, with its tree-lined streets and parks and skating rinks and (oh my God) furnished basements. Outremont, where the girls didn't wear shiny discount dresses and gaudy shell necklaces, but frocks that had been bought retail and pearls, yes, strands of pearls that had not been pilfered from Kresge's grab-all counter, but paid for at Birks maybe. Outremont fathers, in their three-piece suits and natty fedoras, were in property or sweaters or insurance or (the coming thing) plastics. They were learning how to golf. They thought nothing of driving down to New York to "take in the shows" or of renting a summer cottage on the lakeside in Ste.-Agathe-des-Monts. For the children's sake, they bought sets of *The Book of Knowledge*, sheltering them in a prominently displayed glass-doored bookcase. *King's Row* or *Forever Amber*, on the other hand, was kept in the bottom desk drawer. Locked.

Outremont, our heart's desire, was amazing. Kids our own age there didn't hang out at the corner cigar store or poolroom, they had their very own quarters. *Basement playrooms, Ping-Pong tables.* There were heated towel racks in the bathrooms. In each kitchen, a Mixmaster. No icebox, but a refrigerator. I had a school friend up there whose mother wore a *pince-nez,*[2] and had hired a maid to answer the door, and even the telephone.

We would ring the house again and again, crowding round the receiver, stifling giggles, if only to hear the maid chirp, "This is the Feigelbaum residence."

But on St. Urbain, our fathers worked as cutters or pressers or scrap dealers and drifted into cold-water flats, sitting down to supper in their freckled Penman's long winter underwear, clipping their nails at the table. Mothers organized bazaars, proceeds for the Jewish National Fund, and jockeyed for position on the ladies' auxiliary of the Talmud Torah or the Folkshule, both parochial schools. Visiting aunts charged into the parlor, armed with raffle books, ten cents a ticket. Win an RCA Victor radio. Win a three-volume *History of the Jews,* slipcover case included. The ladies had a favorite record. It was Jan Peerce, one of ours, singing "The Bluebird of Happiness." "The poet with his pen / The peasant with his plow / It's all the same somehow."

We preferred Artie Shaw's "Stardust," which gave us a chance to dance close, or any boogie-woogie, an opportunity to strut. After supper, I had to sift the ashes before stoking the furnace for the night, emerging prematurely gray from the shed. I attended parochial school (studying English, modern Hebrew, and French), and after classes, three afternoons a week, I knuckled down to the Talmud[3] with Mr. Yalofsky's class in the back room of the Young Israel Synagogue.

—If a man tumbles off the roof of an eight-story building and four stories down another man sticks a sword out of the window and stabs him, is that second man guilty of murder? Or not?

—Rabbi Menasha asks, did he fall or was he pushed off the roof?

—Rabbi Yedhua asks, was he already dead of heart failure before he was stabbed?

—Were the two men related?

—Enemies?

—Friends?

—Was the sword already sticking out of the window or was it thrust into the falling body?

—Would the man have died from the fall in any event?

Who cared? Concealed on our laps, below the table, at the risk of having our ears twisted by Mr. Yalofsky, was the *Herald,* opened at the sports pages. What concerned us, children of the new world, was

2. Eyeglasses that clip onto the bridge of the nose; literally, "pinch nose."
3. The sacred, multivolume work of Jewish law and learning.

would the Punch Line (Maurice "the Rocket" Richard, Elmer Lach, Toe Blake) finish one-two-three in the scoring race, and would the Canadiens thrash the dreaded Toronto Maple Leafs in the Stanley Cup Finals?

Our parents were counting on us—a scruffy lot, but, for all that, the first Canadian-born generation—to elbow our way into McGill, not so much Cardinal Newman's notion of a university[4] as the block and tackle that would hoist the family into blessed Outremont. Many of us, but certainly not all, made it not only into Outremont, which turned out to be no more than a way station, but into the once *judenfrei* Town of Mount Royal, and even Westmount. *Above the Boulevard.*

20 Bliss, yes, but at a price.

En route, Schneider was anglicized to Taylor; Putterschnit was born again Patterson; Krashinsky, Kane. Children were no longer named Hershl or Muttel or Malke or Zippora, but, instead, Stuart, Byron, Melinda, and Vanessa. Rather than play jacks under a winding outside staircase after school, the girls in their trainer bras from New York, New York, were driven to the nose-job doctor and ballet class and the orthodontist in Mommy's Mercedes. The boys, instead of delivering for the drugstore after classes, saving up for their very own CCM bike, took tennis lessons, which would help them to meet the right people.

And then (surprise, surprise) suddenly the old neighborhood, *the starting line*, became modish and some of the children, the ungrateful ones, the know-it-alls, moved back into those yucky moldering cold-water flats on St. Urbain, nudging out the new tenants: Greeks, Italians, Portuguese. And there, on St. Urbain, where it was whispered that they smoked pot and didn't even remove their Frye boots to screw on those filthy sheets, they filled the front windows not with rubber plants of the old days, but with protest posters. Those play-poor kids in designer jeans were against nukes, acid rain, and herpes, and for organically grown, good multiple orgasms and the Parti Québécois.

The Parti Québécois?

"You exploited the French," they lectured grandfathers who used to eke out a living bent over a sewing machine, fathers who remembered flying into street battles against the followers of Adrian Arcand,[5] armed with lengths of lead pipe.

25 "You've got to learn to identify with the real Québécois," they argued.

4. John Henry Cardinal Newman (1801–1890), an English clergyman who converted to Roman Catholicism, served for many years as rector of the Catholic University of Ireland, and wrote *The Idea of a University.*

5. Founder (1900–1967) of the fascist political party Parti National Social Chrétien.

"What, at my age, I should acquire a taste for Mae Wests[6] or sugar pie or french fries soaked in vinegar?"

"That's a racist remark."

"Listen, kid, they don't have to fast with me on Yom Kippur,[7] I don't need to march in the St.-Jean Baptiste[8] parade."

Red-letter days on St. Urbain.

Sent to Jack and Moe's barbershop, corner of Park Avenue and 30
Laurier, for my monthly haircut, a quarter clutched in my hand, I had grown accustomed to the humiliation of waiting for Moe to slide the board over the barber chair's arms, which raised me high enough to be shorn. But this day of glory, Moe merely jerked his head at me and snarled, "Siddown." There was no board. I was now tall enough to sit in the actual chair. On the St. Urbain Street standard, my manhood had been certified. From this day forward anything was possible.

Another day, at Baron Byng High School, I came of political age.

Ramsay MacDonald's number-one son Malcolm, the British colonial secretary, came to address us in the gym, but those of us who were members of the Labour Zionist Movement absolutely refused to stand up to sing "God Save the King." We greeted MacDonald with hostile silence. Why, that bastard had cut off immigration to Palestine. Leaking tubs overflowing with emaciated concentration-camp survivors were being turned back or led to Cyprus.

On St. Urbain, we were either very observant Orthodox Jews, dedicated Labour Zionists, or red-hot communists. There were a few suspected homosexuals in the neighborhood, that is to say, young men who read poetry and smoked cork-tipped cigarettes; there was at least one professional hooker that I knew of; but nobody, certainly, who would admit to being a member of the Conservative Party.

Communist conundrums on St. Urbain were sometimes resolved in a peculiar fashion.

A cousin of mine, then a communist firebrand but now a com- 35
puter consultant, canvassed votes door-to-door for Labour-Progressive Party MP Fred Rose. Standing on one supposedly communist doorstep, expounding on Marx and Engels,[9] the worker's sorry plight in Montreal, he was cut short by the irate housewife. "What

6. Pastries named for Mae West (1892–1980), American film star of the 1930s.
7. The Jewish day of atonement.
8. John the Baptist, the forerunner and baptizer of Jesus. The St.-Jean Baptiste day parade, held on June 24, is an occasion for the expression of Québécois nationalism and the desire to separate from English-speaking Canada.
9. Karl Marx (1818–1883), German philosopher, political economist, and founder of socialism; Friedrich Engels (1820–1895), German socialist and philosopher, coauthor with Marx of *The Communist Manifesto.*

you say may be true," she allowed, "but this time I don't vote for him, you can count on it."

"Why?"

"When his niece got married last April, we were invited to the ceremony but not to the dinner. The hell with him."

In my last year at Baron Byng High School, I worked nights in a Park Avenue bowling alley, spotting pins. A year later, enrolled at Sir George Williams College, I found work reporting on college events for the *Montreal Herald* on space rates. The bowling alley paid me three cents a line, the *Herald* only two, but I chucked being a pin boy and stuck with the *Herald*, revealing, I think, a precocious dedication to letters no matter what the cost.

St. Urbain.

40 Like many another old boy of my generation, I still wander down there on occasion, tramping through the lanes where we once played hockey—lanes still thick with garbage and abandoned mattresses bleeding stuffing. I make the obligatory stop at the Bagel Factory on St. Viateur near Park Avenue. In deference to the French Language Charter, Bill 101, it is now called La Maison du Bagel, Boulangerie.[1] The YMHA, on Mount Royal, where we used to box, hoping to qualify for the Golden Gloves, has become the Pavillon Mont-Royal of the Université de Montréal. My old parochial school, the Talmud Torah, where we once stumbled over Hebrew grammar, has happily maintained a connection of sorts with Zion. It is now École Primaire Nazareth. Only a block away, on Laurier, the Stuart Biscuit Company, where we used to be able to buy a bag of broken biscuits for two cents, is still there. But immediately across the street, my father's favorite old cigar & soda, Schacter's, has become an overpriced antique shop, haunted—I like to think—by the ghosts of gin rummy games past. Laurier, above Park Avenue, is no longer a tacky street of bicycle and auto-parts shops. It has been transmogrified into a street of elegant restaurants, boutiques, fine-food shops, and bookstores. My God, my God, these days, only two blocks away from hot bagel heaven and Mehadrin's Marché de Viande Kosher,[2] you can feast on hot croissants and espresso.

Jack and Moe's barbershop, where you could once also lay down two bucks on a horse, has been displaced by a more reliable investment house, a branch of the Banque Nationale de Grèce. The Young Israel synagogue is no longer on Park Avenue. The Regent Theatre—where I

1. French for "bakery."
2. French for "Kosher meat market."

sat through at least four double features in the balcony before I dared slip my arm (slowly, slowly) around Riva Tannenbaum's bony shoulders, my heart thumping as I actually kissed her cheek in the dark—has, given such a start, slid into undreamed-of depravity. It has become le Beaver, where you can now catch HOT LEGS, "The Ups and Downs of the Stocking and Garter Industry Fully Exposed!" The Rialto, on the corner of Bernard, has also become a porn palace, this one showing the hot stuff in Greek. Indeed, this familiar chunk of Park Avenue, a street where our mothers used to comparison shop for odd cups and saucers—an avenue where the nearest you could come to sin was to flip hastily through the latest *Esquire* at the corner newsstand, searching for the Vargas girl[3]—is now totally disreputable. Where once it was a scandal for a neighborhood girl to be seen out for a stroll, wearing a tight sweater, acknowledging what she had there, you can now drop into SECRET SUPER SEXE, *danseuses nues*, as well as EXPO SEXE, both establishments serving hamburgers for lunch. To go with, as they say. But for all that, Park Avenue is still a street of Hasidic rabbis and their progeny. Immediately around the corner from Park Avenue, on Jeanne Mance, the two-fisted followers of the Satmar rabbi are rooted, and also in the neighborhood there are still many adherents of the Lubavitcher rabbi.[4] Boys, wearing skullcaps and long sidecurls, who gather together to sing:

> "We only eat a kosher diet,
> Non-kosher food we'd never try it.
> To be healthy Jews is our main goal
> Non-kosher food is harmful for body and soul."

Nobody who was raised on St. Urbain ventures into the old neighborhood without stopping for a special at Wilensky's, corner of Clark and Fairmount. A special, I should point out, is made up of cuts of different kinds of salami, grilled in a delicious roll. Traditionally, it is washed down with a nonvintage cherry Coke, mixed at the fountain.

Wilensky's, which has been serving the neighborhood since 1931, is now presided over by Moe, son of the original proprietor. During World War II days, we gathered at the soda fountain for heated political disputes. Should the Allies OPEN UP A SECOND FRONT NOW, relieving pressure on the hard-pressed Russians but risking the life of many a St. Urbain urchin who had enlisted?

St. Urbain Street old boys, running into each other at Wilensky's forty years on, still talk politics, but now it isn't about the war over

3. Vargas was an American magazine artist known for his drawings of luxurious nudes.
4. Satmar and Lubavitcher are two opposing sects of Hasidic Jews.

there, on the other side of the ocean, but about the trouble right here: the Parti Québécois. The boys I grew up with, parents themselves now, counting cholesterol rather than batting averages, drift off to whisper in the corners. "And what about you, are you staying on in Montreal?"

45 "What should I do? Take the chicken run to Toronto and make new friends at my age?"

In the quarrel between the English and French in Montreal, the Jews feel they are caught in the middle. "Look here," an old friend told me, "I don't think for a minute that the Parti Québécois is anti-Semitic. My God, you look at the faces on the front bench in the Assembly and they shine with intelligence. In a way, they're Zionists at home. I can understand everything they want. I can understand it in my head. But here," he continued, pounding his gut, "here, you know what I feel? If they don't get everything they want—we're the ones who are going to be blamed."

And now there are also the Italians, the Greeks, and the Portuguese, post–World War II immigrants for the most part, the inheritors of St. Urbain, Main, and Park Avenue, many of them with something like the old Jewish appetite.

Take feisty Jimmy Essaris, for instance. Forty-nine years old, dark, handsome, with flashing black eyes. Jimmy, sprung from a farming village near Athens, arrived here penniless in 1951, walking up and down the streets banging on doors before he finally surfaced with a job as a dishwasher in a Greek short-order restaurant in suburban Lachine. At the time, he spoke no English, no French, but within five months he was a counterman and had convinced the proprietor to stay open twenty-four hours a day, more than tripling his take. Jimmy stayed on there for three years, earning $100 weekly in 1954. "Don't mis-me-understand," he told me, "it was a lot of money at the time." But a year later, Jimmy had left to buy his own restaurant from an elderly Greek couple. They wanted $4,000; Jimmy offered them all the money he had saved, $3,000. " 'You will take it,' " he said to the couple, " 'because you are a Greek and I am a Greek and if not I will buy the place next door.' I laid the cash on the counter and the guy is shaking now. And you will pay the notary, too, I told him," Jimmy added.

"Soon I'm doing very good, I make maybe two hundred dollars a week net, but I don't like the place, it's too small for me, and I sell it for nine thousand dollars. It's 1955 now, and I have a little car, it cost me three hundred dollars. One night this girl phones me and she wants to go to a movie in Montreal. I still don't know what it means Montreal. But she wants Montreal, so we go. I can't park here, I can't park there. I have to go to a parking lot. The old man in the lot, he says to me one dollar. *One dollar parking*. I'm so polite I gave him the dollar and in the meantime I'm counting the cars. My head is pounding. I sit on the sidewalk and I think, hey, this is some fantastic business. One dollar parking, and you don't have to make club sandwiches or wash up. I can't concentrate on the movie. I tell the girl, hey, I will pay you twenty-five dollars a week, all I want is you find me a parking lot."

Early in 1956, Jimmy found one downtown, on Stanley Street, and 50
rented it for $750 a month. But no sooner did he sign the papers in the landlord's office and stride down to the lot than the parking attendant said to him, welcome, sucker, you are the fifth man to rent this lot in two years. "The first night I made twenty dollars, the second, eighteen dollars. I multiply this by thirty and I see I can't even make the seven-hundred-fifty rent. Then one day I invite the cop on the street in for a coffee and I say to him, don't miss-me-understand, but now I will tell you a sad story. I am a poor Greek boy. I have nothing. I need help. Give tickets. Scare them. I can't do that, he says. But we become friendly, *very friendly*, and he says, I'm going to help you. First night, one hundred tickets. Now everybody gets the medicine. My third week, I'm full. I start to make money. I'm grossing seventeen hundred dollars a month."

Now Jimmy Essaris owns fifty parking lots in Montreal, Quebec City, and Toronto; he employs 300 people and grosses $12 million annually.

"I am against separatism," he said, "but I do not run. If I have to fight, I will fight. English is necessary. It is the language of business, and they have to accept that. But I would be disappointed if my kids did not speak French also. Poor Greek families on St. Urbain feel threatened. They work hard. They came here looking for stability, now there is a quarrel here, it is terrible. We went through enough from 1939 to 1951 in Greece. The way Lévesque[5] is running the economy, everybody is going to go bankrupt and they will have to close the doors."

5. René Lévesque (1922–1987), founder of the Parti Québéquois and prime minister of Québec from 1976 until 1985.

QUESTIONS

1. *Richler's essay is loaded with the names of neighborhoods, streets, shops, and buildings. Pick out what seem like the most important places and tell what social or emotional significance Richler ascribes to them.*
2. *If most of the essay deals with Montreal's Jewish community, why does Richler end with a lengthy description of Jimmy Essaris, a Greek immigrant?*
3. *Using your own or others' memories, describe a place that has changed over time. Or describe a local place that doesn't seem like*

much to most people but has special memories for a few who spent their formative years there.

Joyce Maynard

FOUR GENERATIONS

My mother called last week to tell me that my grandmother is dying. She has refused an operation that would postpone, but not prevent, her death from pancreatic cancer. She can't eat, she has been hemorrhaging, and she has severe jaundice. "I always prided myself on being different," she told my mother. "Now I *am* different. I'm yellow."

My mother, telling me this news, began to cry. So I became the mother for a moment, reminding her, reasonably, that my grandmother is eighty-seven, she's had a full life, she has all her faculties, and no one who knows her could wish that she live long enough to lose them. Lately my mother has been finding notes in my grandmother's drawers at the nursing home, reminding her, "Joyce's husband's name is Steve. Their daughter is Audrey." In the last few years she hadn't had the strength to cook or garden, and she's begun to say she's had enough of living.

My grandmother was born in Russia, in 1892—the oldest daughter in a large and prosperous Jewish family. But the prosperity didn't last. She tells stories of the pogroms and the cossacks who raped her when she was twelve. Soon after that, her family emigrated to Canada, where she met my grandfather.

Their children were the center of their life. The story I loved best, as a child, was of my grandfather opening every box of Cracker Jack in the general store he ran, in search of the particular tin toy my mother coveted. Though they never had much money, my grandmother saw to it that her daughter had elocution lessons and piano lessons, and assured her that she would go to college.

5 But while she was at college, my mother met my father, who was blue-eyed and blond-haired and not Jewish. When my father sent love letters to my mother, my grandmother would open and hide them, and when my mother told her parents she was going to marry this man, my grandmother said if that happened, it would kill her.

Not likely, of course. My grandmother is a woman who used to crack Brazil nuts open with her teeth, a woman who once lifted a car off the ground, when there was an accident and it had to be moved. She has

Originally appeared in *The New York Times* "Hers" column (Apr. 12, 1979).

been representing her death as imminent ever since I've known her—twenty-five years—and has discussed, at length, the distribution of her possessions and her lamb coat. Every time we said goodbye, after our annual visit to Winnipeg, she'd weep and say she'd never see us again. But in the meantime, while every other relative of her generation, and a good many of the younger ones, has died (nursed usually by her), she has kept making knishes, shopping for bargains, tending the healthiest plants I've ever seen.

After my grandfather died, my grandmother lived, more than ever, through her children. When she came to visit, I would hide my diary. She couldn't understand any desire for privacy. She couldn't bear it if my mother left the house without her.

This possessiveness is what made my mother furious (and then guilt-ridden that she felt that way, when of course she owed so much to her mother). So I harbored the resentment that my mother—the dutiful daughter—would not allow herself. I—who had always performed specially well for my grandmother, danced and sung for her, presented her with kisses and good report cards—stopped writing to her, ceased to visit.

But when I heard that she was dying, I realized I wanted to go to Winnipeg to see her one more time. Mostly to make my mother happy, I told myself (certain patterns being hard to break). But also, I was offering up one more particularly fine accomplishment: my own dark-eyed, dark-skinned, dark-haired daughter, whom my grandmother had never met.

I put on my daughter's best dress for our visit to Winnipeg, the way 10
the best dresses were always put on me, and I filled my pockets with animal crackers, in case Audrey started to cry. I scrubbed her face mercilessly. On the elevator going up to her room, I realized how much I was sweating.

Grandma was lying flat with an IV tube in her arm and her eyes shut, but she opened them when I leaned over to kiss her. "It's Fredelle's daughter, Joyce," I yelled, because she doesn't hear well anymore, but I could see that no explanation was necessary. "You came," she said. "You brought the baby."

Audrey is just one, but she has seen enough of the world to know that people in beds are not meant to be so still and yellow, and she looked frightened. I had never wanted, more, for her to smile.

Then Grandma waved at her—the same kind of slow, finger-flexing wave a baby makes—and Audrey waved back. I spread her toys out on my grandmother's bed and sat her down. There she stayed, most of the afternoon, playing and humming and sipping on her bottle, taking a nap at one point, leaning against my grandmother's leg. When I cranked her Snoopy guitar, Audrey stood up on the bed and danced. Grandma wouldn't talk much anymore, though every once in a while she would say how sorry she was that she wasn't having a better day. "I'm not always like this," she said.

Mostly she just watched Audrey. Sometimes Audrey would get off the bed, inspect the get-well cards, totter down the hall. "Where is she?" Grandma kept asking. "Who's looking after her?" I had the feeling, even then, that if I'd said, "Audrey's lighting matches," Grandma would have shot up to rescue her.

We were flying home that night, and I had dreaded telling her, remembering all those other tearful partings. But in the end, I was the one who cried. She had said she was ready to die. But as I leaned over to stroke her forehead, what she said was, "I wish I had your hair" and "I wish I was well."

On the plane flying home, with Audrey in my arms, I thought about mothers and daughters, and the four generations of the family that I know most intimately. Every one of those mothers loves and needs her daughter more than her daughter will love or need her some day, and we are, each of us, the only person on earth who is quite so consumingly interested in our child.

Sometimes I kiss and hug Audrey so much she starts crying—which is, in effect, what my grandmother was doing to my mother, all her life. And what makes my mother grieve right now, I think, is not simply that her mother will die in a day or two, but that, once her mother dies, there will never again be someone to love her in quite such an unreserved, unquestioning way. No one else who believes that, fifty years ago, she could have put Shirley Temple out of a job, no one else who remembers the moment of her birth. She will only be a mother, then, not a daughter anymore.

Audrey and I have stopped over for a night in Toronto, where my mother lives. Tomorrow she will go to a safe-deposit box at the bank and take out the receipt for my grandmother's burial plot. Then she will fly back to Winnipeg, where, for the first time in anybody's memory, there was waist-high snow on April Fool's Day. But tonight she is feeding me, as she always does when I come, and I am eating more than I do anywhere else. I admire the wedding china (once my grandmother's) that my mother has set on the table. She says (the way Grandma used to say to her, of the lamb coat), "Some day it will be yours."

QUESTIONS

1. *What family characteristics does Maynard suggest have been inherited by the generations of daughters?*
2. *Maynard's story both tells of her visit to her dying grandmother and shows how four generations of women develop. How else could she*

have written about those four generations? What would be the gains and losses if she hadn't framed her discussion with the story of the visit?

3. *Maynard writes, "Every one of those mothers loves and needs her daughter more than her daughter will love or need her some day" (paragraph 16). To what extent is this true for all families? Is it different across genders? Does it often apply to fathers and sons? Fathers and daughters? Mothers and sons?*

Loren Eiseley

THE BROWN WASPS

There is a corner in the waiting room of one of the great Eastern stations where women never sit. It is always in the shadow and overhung by rows of lockers. It is, however, always frequented—not so much by genuine travelers as by the dying. It is here that a certain element of the abandoned poor seeks a refuge out of the weather, clinging for a few hours longer to the city that has fathered them. In a precisely similar manner I have seen, on a sunny day in midwinter, a few old brown wasps creep slowly over an abandoned wasp nest in a thicket. Numbed and forgetful and frost-blackened, the hum of the spring hive still resounded faintly in their sodden tissues. Then the temperature would fall and they would drop away into the white oblivion of the snow. Here in the station it is in no way different save that the city is busy in its snows. But the old ones cling to their seats as though these were symbolic and could not be given up. Now and then they sleep, their gray old heads resting with painful awkwardness on the backs of the benches.

Also they are not at rest. For an hour they may sleep in the gasping exhaustion of the ill-nourished and aged who have to walk in the night. Then a policeman comes by on his round and nudges them upright.

"You can't sleep here," he growls.

A strange ritual then begins. An old man is difficult to waken. After a muttered conversation the policeman presses a coin into his hand and passes fiercely along the benches prodding and gesturing toward the door. In his wake, like birds rising and settling behind the passage of a farmer through a cornfield, the men totter up, move a few paces and subside once more upon the benches.

One man, after a slight, apologetic lurch, does not move at all. 5

From *The Night Country* (1971).

Tubercularly thin, he sleeps on steadily. The policeman does not look back. To him, too, this has become a ritual. He will not have to notice it again officially for another hour.

Once in a while one of the sleepers will not awake. Like the brown wasps, he will have had his wish to die in the great droning center of the hive rather than in some lonely room. It is not so bad here with the shuffle of footsteps and the knowledge that there are others who share the bad luck of the world. There are also the whistles and the sounds of everyone, everyone in the world, starting on journeys. Amidst so many journeys somebody is bound to come out all right. Somebody.

Maybe it was on a like thought that the brown wasps fell away from the old paper nest in the thicket. You hold till the last, even if it is only to a public seat in a railroad station. You want your place in the hive more than you want a room or a place where the aged can be eased gently out of the way. It is the place that matters, the place at the heart of things. It is life that you want, that bruises your gray old head with the hard chairs; a man has a right to his place.

But sometimes the place is lost in the years behind us. Or sometimes it is a thing of air, a kind of vaporous distortion above a heap of rubble. We cling to a time and place because without them man is lost, not only man but life. This is why the voices, real or unreal, which speak from the floating trumpets at spiritualist seances are so unnerving. They are voices out of nowhere whose only reality lies in their ability to stir the memory of a living person with some fragment of the past. Before the medium's cabinet both the dead and the living revolve endlessly about an episode, a place, an event that has already been engulfed by time.

This feeling runs deep in life; it brings stray cats running over endless miles, and birds homing from the ends of the earth. It is as though all living creatures, and particularly the more intelligent, can survive only by fixing or transforming a bit of time into space or by securing a bit of space with its objects immortalized and made permanent in time. For example, I once saw, on a flower pot in my own living room, the efforts of a field mouse to build a remembered field. I have lived to see this episode repeated in a thousand guises, and since I have spent a large portion of my life in the shade of a nonexistent tree, I think I am entitled to speak for the field mouse.

10 One day as I cut across the field which at that time extended on one side of our suburban shopping center, I found a giant slug feeding from a runnel of pink ice cream in an abandoned Dixie cup. I could see his eyes telescope and protrude in a kind of dim, uncertain ecstasy as his dark body bunched and elongated in the curve of the cup. Then, as I stood there at the edge of the concrete, contemplating the slug, I began to realize it was like standing on a shore where a different type of life creeps up and fumbles tentatively among the rocks and sea

wrack. It knows its place and will only creep so far until something changes. Little by little as I stood there I began to see more of this shore that surrounds the place of man. I looked with sudden care and attention at things I had been running over thoughtlessly for years. I even waded out a short way into the grass and the wild-rose thickets to see more. A huge black-belted bee went droning by and there were some indistinct scurryings in the underbrush.

Then I came to a sign which informed me that this field was to be the site of a new Wanamaker suburban store. Thousands of obscure lives were about to perish, the spores of puffballs would go smoking off to new fields, and the bodies of little white-footed mice would be crunched under the inexorable wheels of the bulldozers. Life disappears or modifies its appearances so fast that everything takes on an aspect of illusion—a momentary fizzing and boiling with smoke rings, like pouring dissident chemicals into a retort. Here man was advancing, but in a few years his plaster and bricks would be disappearing once more into the insatiable maw of the clover. Being of an archaeological cast of mind, I thought of this fact with an obscure sense of satisfaction and waded back through the rose thickets to the concrete parking lot. As I did so, a mouse scurried ahead of me, frightened of my steps if not of that ominous Wanamaker sign. I saw him vanish in the general direction of my apartment house, his little body quivering with fear in the great open sun on the blazing concrete. Blinded and confused, he was running straight away from his field. In another week scores would follow him.

I forgot the episode then and went home to the quiet of my living room. It was not until a week later, letting myself into the apartment, that I realized I had a visitor. I am fond of plants and had several ferns standing on the floor in pots to avoid the noon glare by the south window.

As I snapped on the light and glanced carelessly around the room, I saw a little heap of earth on the carpet and a scrabble of pebbles that had been kicked merrily over the edge of one of the flower pots. To my astonishment I discovered a full-fledged burrow delving downward among the fern roots. I waited silently. The creature who had made the burrow did not appear. I remembered the wild field then, and the flight of the mice. No house mouse, no *Mus domesticus*, had kicked up this little heap of earth or sought refuge under a fern root in a flower pot. I thought of the desperate little creature I had seen fleeing from the wild-rose thicket. Through intricacies of pipes and attics, he, or one of his fellows, had climbed to this high green solitary room. I could visualize what had occurred. He had an image in his head, a world of seed pods and quiet, of green sheltering leaves in the dim light among the weed stems. It was the only world he knew and it was gone.

Somehow in his flight he had found his way to this room with drawn shades where no one would come till nightfall. And here he had smelled green leaves and run quickly up the flower pot to dabble his paws in common earth. He had even struggled half the afternoon to carry his burrow deeper and had failed. I examined the hole, but no whiskered twitching face appeared. He was gone. I gathered up the earth and refilled the burrow. I did not expect to find traces of him again.

Yet for three nights thereafter I came home to the darkened room and my ferns to find the dirt kicked gaily about the rug and the burrow reopened, though I was never able to catch the field mouse within it. I dropped a little food about the mouth of the burrow, but it was never touched. I looked under beds or sat reading with one ear cocked for rustlings in the ferns. It was all in vain; I never saw him. Probably he ended in a trap in some other tenant's room.

But before he disappeared I had come to look hopefully for his evening burrow. About my ferns there had begun to linger the insubstantial vapor of an autumn field, the distilled essence, as it were, of a mouse brain in exile from its home. It was a small dream, like our dreams, carried a long and weary journey along pipes and through spider webs, past holes over which loomed the shadows of waiting cats, and finally, desperately, into this room where he had played in the shuttered daylight for an hour among the green ferns on the floor. Every day these invisible dreams pass us on the street, or rise from beneath our feet, or look out upon us from beneath a bush.

Some years ago the old elevated railway in Philadelphia was torn down and replaced by a subway system. This ancient El with its barnlike stations containing nut-vending machines and scattered food scraps had, for generations, been the favorite feeding ground of flocks of pigeons, generally one flock to a station along the route of the El. Hundreds of pigeons were dependent upon the system. They flapped in and out of its stanchions and steel work or gathered in watchful little audiences about the feet of anyone who rattled the peanut-vending machines. They even watched people who jingled change in their hands, and prospected for food under the feet of the crowds who gathered between trains. Probably very few among the waiting people who tossed a crumb to an eager pigeon realized that this El was like a food-bearing river, and that the life which haunted its banks was dependent upon the running of the trains with their human freight.

I saw the river stop.

The time came when the underground tubes were ready; the traffic was transferred to a realm unreachable by pigeons. It was like a great river subsiding suddenly into desert sands. For a day, for two days, pigeons continued to circle over the El or stand close to the red vending machines. They were patient birds, and surely this great river which had flowed through the lives of unnumbered generations was merely suffering from some momentary drought.

They listened for the familiar vibrations that had always heralded an 20
approaching train; they flapped hopefully about the head of an occasional workman walking along the steel runways. They passed from one empty station to another, all the while growing hungrier. Finally they flew away.

I thought I had seen the last of them about the El, but there was a revival and it provided a curious instance of the memory of living things for a way of life or a locality that has long been cherished. Some weeks after the El was abandoned workmen began to tear it down. I went to work every morning by one particular station, and the time came when the demolition crews reached this spot. Acetylene torches showered passersby with sparks, pneumatic drills hammered at the base of the structure, and a blind man who, like the pigeons, had clung with his cup to a stairway leading to the change booth, was forced to give up his place.

It was then, strangely, momentarily, one morning that I witnessed the return of a little band of the familiar pigeons. I even recognized one or two members of the flock that had lived around this particular station before they were dispersed into the streets. They flew bravely in and out among the sparks and the hammers and the shouting workmen. They had returned—and they had returned because the hubbub of the wreckers had convinced them that the river was about to flow once more. For several hours they flapped in and out through the empty windows, nodding their heads and watching the fall of girders with attentive little eyes. By the following morning the station was reduced to some burned-off stanchions in the street. My bird friends had gone. It was plain, however, that they retained a memory for an insubstantial structure now compounded of air and time. Even the blind man clung to it. Someone had provided him with a chair, and he sat at the same corner staring sightlessly at an invisible stairway where, so far as he was concerned, the crowds were still ascending to the trains.

I have said my life has been passed in the shade of a nonexistent tree, so that such sights do not offend me. Prematurely I am one of the brown wasps and I often sit with them in the great droning hive of the station, dreaming sometimes of a certain tree. It was planted sixty years ago by a boy with a bucket and a toy spade in a little Nebraska town. That boy was myself. It was a cottonwood sapling and the boy remembered it because of some words spoken by his father and because everyone died or moved away who was supposed to wait and grow old under its shade. The boy was passed from hand to hand, but the tree for some intangible reason had taken root in his mind. It was under its branches that he sheltered; it was from this tree that his memories, which are my memories, led away into the world.

After sixty years the mood of the brown wasps grows heavier upon one. During a long inward struggle I thought it would do me good to go and look upon that actual tree. I found a rational excuse in which to clothe this madness. I purchased a ticket and at the end of two thousand miles I walked another mile to an address that was still the same. The house had not been altered.

25 I came close to the white picket fence and reluctantly, with great effort, looked down the long vista of the yard. There was nothing there to see. For sixty years that cottonwood had been growing in my mind. Season by season its seeds had been floating farther on the hot prairie winds. We had planted it lovingly there, my father and I, because he had a great hunger for soil and live things growing, and because none of these things had long been ours to protect. We had planted the little sapling and watered it faithfully, and I remembered that I had run out with my small bucket to drench its roots the day we moved away. And all the years since it had been growing in my mind, a huge tree that somehow stood for my father and the love I bore him. I took a grasp on the picket fence and forced myself to look again.

A boy with the hard bird eye of youth pedaled a tricycle slowly up beside me.

"What'cha lookin' at?" he asked curiously.

"A tree," I said.

"What for?" he said.

30 "It isn't there," I said, to myself mostly, and began to walk away at a pace just slow enough not to seem to be running.

"What isn't there?" the boy asked. I didn't answer. It was obvious I was attached by a thread to a thing that had never been there, or certainly not for long. Something that had to be held in the air, or sustained in the mind, because it was part of my orientation in the universe and I could not survive without it. There was more than an animal's attachment to a place. There was something else, the attachment of the spirit to a grouping of events in time; it was part of our mortality.

So I had come home at last, driven by a memory in the brain as surely as the field mouse who had delved long ago into my flower pot or the pigeons flying forever amidst the rattle of nut-vending machines. These, the burrow under the greenery in my living room and the red-bellied bowls of peanuts now hovering in midair in the minds of pigeons, were all part of an elusive world that existed nowhere and yet everywhere. I looked once at the real world about me while the persistent boy pedaled at my heels.

It was without meaning, though my feet took a remembered path.

In sixty years the house and street had rotted out of my mind. But the tree, the tree that no longer was, that had perished in its first season, bloomed on in my individual mind, unblemished as my father's words. "We'll plant a tree here, son, and we're not going to move any more. And when you're an old, old man you can sit under it and think how we planted it here, you and me, together."

I began to outpace the boy on the tricycle.

"Do you live here, Mister?" he shouted after me suspiciously. I took 35
a firm grasp on airy nothing—to be precise, on the bole of a great tree. "I do," I said. I spoke for myself, one field mouse, and several pigeons. We were all out of touch but somehow permanent. It was the world that had changed.

QUESTIONS

1. *Eiseley writes of old men in train stations, brown wasps, a field mouse, pigeons near the El, and his own return to his boyhood home in Nebraska. What do these all have in common? Can you state the essay's theme?*
2. *Some psychologists study animal behavior in order to learn about human behavior, but others write about animals in a very different fashion. Do you think that Eiseley's way of relating the behavior of animals to human behavior makes sense?*
3. *From close observation of an animal's behavior, write two brief descriptions, one using animal-human comparisons and one simply sticking to what you see.*

Michael Lynch

LAST ONSETS: TEACHING WITH AIDS

Setting: An ordinary undergraduate classroom, seats regimented in tiers. During the lecture, a pixelboard displays the section titles. The lecturer, white, male, hair newly shorn to a brush cut, opts not to use a lecturn but to stand in front of the desk, resting his weight against it at the backside. His audience includes his students in English 250 (Introduction to American Literature).

From *Profession 90* (1990). All notes to this essay are the author's.

FAMOUS LAST WORDS

You will, of course, remember Emmeline Grangerford, the young "poetess" who so fascinates Huckleberry Finn. No? Then let me remind us:

> Buck said she could rattle off poetry like nothing. She didn't ever have to stop to think. He said she would slap down a line, and if she couldn't find anything to rhyme with it she would just scratch it out and slap down another one, and go ahead. She warn't particular, she could write about anything you choose to give her to write about, just so it was sadful. Every time a man died, or a woman died, or a child died, she would be on hand with her "tribute" before he was cold. She called them tributes. The neighbors said it was the doctor first, then Emmeline, then the undertaker—the undertaker never got in ahead of Emmeline but once, and then she hung fire on a rhyme for the dead person's name, which was Whistler. She warn't ever the same, after that; she never complained, but she kind of pined away and did not live long.

Emmeline, who died before she was fourteen, was also an artist of, to Huck, impressive achievement. How lovingly he describes her drawings, their titles ranging widely from *Shall I Never See Thee More Alas* to *I Shall Never Hear Thy Sweet Chirrup More Alas* to *And Art Thou Gone Yes Thou Art Gone Alas*. Of all Emmeline's "crayons," the one her survivors most treasure was begun at the time of her illness and left incomplete at her death. Huck has conned it with care.

> It was a picture of a young woman in a long white gown, standing on the rail of a bridge all ready to jump off, with her hair all down her back, and looking up to the moon, with the tears running down her face, and she had two arms folded across her breast, and two arms stretched out in front, and two more reaching up towards the moon—and the idea was, to see which pair would look best and then scratch out all the other arms; but, as I was saying, she died before she got her mind made up.

This corporeal irresolution unsettles him: "The young woman in the picture had a kind of a nice, sweet face, but there was so many arms it made her look too spidery, seemed to me."

5 Evoked indiscriminately by deathbeds, any deathbed, every deathbed, Emmeline's tributes come to an end only because of an unrhymable name. (I fantasize introducing her to my friend Bob Schisler, but perhaps rhyming two proper names, like rhyming homophones, is cheating.) If "Whistler" ends her writing career, the onset of illness spurs her career in drawing. Alas.

I don't know when Euro-American cultures began investing so much in undertakings incomplete at death. Was Bach's *Art of the Fugue* always held in the awe that it is now? or Mozart's *Requiem*? or Michelangelo's *Rondanini Pietá*? When did biographers fall in love with sentences such as "And here, Bach laid down his pen"?

Whenever this investment became culturally mandated, I am pretty sure that it was big in the bourgeois nineteenth and early twentieth centuries. A staple of sentimental art, such as Emmeline Grangerford's, and antisentimental art, such as Mark Twain's, the deathbed scene held sway over many a body. Richard Howard, in fact, has called it "an age of Interesting Deathbeds." For public figures, deathbeds often interrupt phases of greatest influence or productivity, but not before the dying have uttered their Famous Last Words to be recorded and remembered through the ages. Goethe, as you know, calls for "mehr Licht." Bonaparte cries out "tête d'armée." Their oracular words grant awesome expectations to those gathered round the bed.

This business of Famous Last Words makes an interesting study. Ever tried to find out just when Oscar Wilde said, "My wallpaper and I are fighting a duel to the death. One or the other of us has to go"? or when Gertrude Stein said, "In that case, what is the question"? The almost dead have the best editors, rearranging and polishing post-mortem. And if the actual Last Words fail to speak an ultimate truth that the culture desires, amnesia comes in. Walt Whitman had the longest deathbed of any iconic writer of the Euro-American nineteenth century. Horace Traubel jotted down his words every day for years, but who recalls Whitman's last recorded words?[1] Who, besides me, repeats the last words of my own father? "Bring me the bedpan, Dorothy," he said to my mother, "I've got to shit."

Why the valorization, the authorization, the editorialization to achieve Famous Last Words? As one who has been at more deathbeds during the past eight years than I care to inventory, I'll testify to other scenes. Deathbeds tend to be rather ordinary. Bodies in extremis may suffer; they may not. They may articulate; they may not. If words are uttered, they may in themselves be as ordinary as any other utterance of the mortal person. Few great truths get said on the deathbed, and fewer yet get said better than they would be said under nonterminal circumstances. Modern bourgeois terminal illness surrounds the body with such technology, indeed turns the body itself into such technology, that beeping IV monitors supplant words and visions, respirators outgasp the patient, tubes and drugs paralyze the vocal apparatus.

The great art: the Famous Last Words. Perhaps both are the prog- 10
eny of a specific Christian tradition, not uncurrent among the bourgeois. Perhaps the most eloquent prose account of that tradition and its commodification comes from Willa Cather in *Death Comes to the Archbishop*:

> In those days, even in European countries, death had a solemn social importance. It was not regarded as a moment when certain bodily organs

1. According to J. W. Wallace, they were "Warry, shift."

> ceased to function, but as a dramatic climax, a moment when the soul made its entrance into the next world, passing in full consciousness through a lowly door to an unimaginable scene. Among the watchers there was always the hope that the dying man might reveal something of what he alone could see; that his countenance, if not his lips, would speak, and on his features would fall some light or shadow from beyond. The "Last Words" of great men, Napoleon, Lord Byron, were still printed in gift-books, and the dying murmurs of every common man and woman were listened for and treasured by their neighbours and kinsfolk. These sayings, no matter how unimportant, were given oracular significance and pondered by those who must one day go the same road.[2]

Soul on the threshold: in the moment of passage, the soul of the Euro-American male is expected to gain access to the unimaginable scene—thus the oracular significance of lips or countenance.

In another account of the valorization of this moment, some deity drops by to receive the passing soul. A black folk song such as "Swing Low, Sweet Chariot" evokes this script, but it's the white deathbed that pulls watchers to it in hopes of getting a glimpse of that deity. For blacks, waiting for the sweet chariot's band of angels is not the spectator sport that it is within the white family. Emily Dickinson, who wrote more moment-of-death poems than Emmeline Grangerford wrote tributes, had many names for the visitant—names such as Death, He, the King. But if sentimental conventions would have the visitant *appear,* the *Finn* of Amherst finds his *nonappearance* the occasion for poetry. In this poem, the *I* is carefully nongendered:

> I heard a Fly buzz—when I died—
> The Stillness in the Room
> Was like the Stillness in the Air
> Between the Heaves of Storm—
>
> The Eyes Around—had wrung them Dry—
> And Breaths were gathering firm
> For that last Onset—when the King
> Be witnessed—in the Room—
>
> I willed my keepsakes—signed away
> What portion of me be
> Assignable—and then it was
> there interposed a Fly—
>
> With Blue—Uncertain—stumbling Buzz—
> Between the light—and me—

2. The passage appears in the account of Padre Lucero's death; the archbishop's deathbed culminates not in the unimaginable scene but in the remembered one: his bonding with Joseph to escape their native land.

And then the Windows failed—and then
I could not see to see—[3]

Mehr Licht? Less licht. The King be witnessed? Rather, a dazed buzzy fly. Bad entomology, but good poetry to see it as akin to Emmeline's arachnid "crayon."

We don't know whether Dickinson's watchers asked for their money back. All those tears, and still no King? It's even worse than sitting through a bad warmup band, and then Elvis doesn't show.

Who's Talking Here?

Emmeline does not speak her own narrative. The deathbed convention positions the reader, not the mortal subject, as vigilant, recorder, rememberer. Cather's Padre Lucero is not writing his autobiography. Huck, for all his transvestite proclivities, is not Emmeline; he tells us what Buck told him people who knew Emmeline said about her greatest poem. Dickinson, on the other hand, astonishes by positioning her speaker and her reader as the mortal person, in this case the postmortem person. This stance strains against the sentimental, devalorizes the importance of the uncompleted achievement ("what portion of me be Assignable"), and, by claiming speech that no vigilant could hear, throws utterly askew any anecdotal frame of Last Words.

Oracular Expectations

In my recent experience deathbeds aren't all they're made out, or made up, to be. What is bigger than I ever expected is the effect of saying, with the upright personal pronoun, "I have AIDS."[4] When one perceives oneself as someone with AIDS, or is so perceived by others, a good deal of the sentimental deathbed apparatus activates itself.

First, let me say what the sentence means in my case. It means that 15
a number of years ago—never mind how long precisely—I became infected by the human immunodeficiency virus, alias HIV. In 1987 a blood test registered positive, perhaps explaining some chronic but non-life-threatening symptoms such as extreme fatigue. In 1988, a first bout of pneumonocystis pneumonia shifted me, by some official categories, across the page, from HIV-positive to diagnosed as "full-

3. Reprinted from *The Manuscript Books of Emily Dickinson* with the permission of the publishers and of the Trustees of Amherst College.

4. The self-help books that currently lard the shelves with techniques for death and dying recognize speaking as difficult only for some of the people some of the time. Robert Buckman's *I Don't Know What to Say*, for example, bears the subtitle *How to Help and Support Someone Who Is Dying*. What to say is a question for vigilants, not for the invigilated.

blown AIDS." By a wide range of watchers, from friends to diagnostic personnel, I am seen as a person with high odds of dying from illness within the next few years. "I am dead, Horatio," says Hamlet, not yet dead; "I have AIDS" carries a ready translation into "I'm on the marge of deadduckdom."[5]

People (including me) watch this soon-to-be-deadduck ever so closely. We overdetermine everything about me: he's wearing a black shirt today; it's because he's going to die soon. Or, he's walking more slowly than he used to; he's going to die soon. Or, this alopecia at the tip of my nose; it's because I'm going to die soon. Every detail can become a marker not so much of mortality as of imminent mortality. Besides overdetermination, there's an awe, a drawing back from morbidity, an urge to say Important Things to me (as if I'll relay them to that band of angels about to swing low), tongue-clucking pity. Most striking are the varieties of Oracular Expectations. We expect me to be more visionary, lucid as the setting sun, more productive, more productive of great works and wisdom, vulnerable to the max.

Many of these bits are indeed related to my having HIV disease. Many are not. Many are and are not. When I withhold the avowal "I have AIDS," that's sometimes an attempt to escape the overdetermined reading of my body. When I say up front, "I have AIDS," that too is sometimes an attempt to resist overdetermination. Yet both the withholding and the giving may operate to further the overdetermination. Whether I say it, or I don't, Oracular Expectations escalate. Willy-nilly, my life becomes a sentimental, or antisentimental, deathbed.

CAVEAT EMPTOR

Before we proceed, let me disentangle the equation that having HIV disease marks imminent morbidity. Even in the absence of a cure, treatments have begun to make a big difference postdiagnosis, in both the length and quality of life. Since September 1988, when I was sure that a bed in Women's College Hospital was, that weekend, to be my deathbed, I've lived and traveled and worked and diddled around. I've learned a lot about monitoring for illnesses and how certain early interventions up the odds for living another two or three years. Today's diagnosis is not tomorrow's guillotine.

5. On 6 January 1990 the British actor Ian Charleson died of—as the press put it—"complications from AIDS." Nine weeks earlier he had been playing Hamlet at the National Theatre, even as he was receiving daily chemotherapy treatments. Hamlet turns up a lot in AIDS writing.

THE CLASSROOM AS DEATHBED

How clearly these cross forces show up when I'm doing the part of my job that brings me into an undergraduate classroom. By definition, a teacher is watched. Closely. By necessity, teaching—often thought of as simply giving information—is just as much a withholding of information. Some professional codes exclude the out-of-class life of the teacher from the classroom—a strategy I find not only impossible (where, after all, did even the most impersonal of lecturers learn that material?) but undesirable (whether in the microbiology lab or in the violin studio, we teach who we are).

Over the last few years my reluctance to tell my classes that I have 20
AIDS comes from no professional code. That body named Michael Lynch is already one of the most self-revealing on this campus, and I find the revealing itself animating, life-giving. But if I say, "I have AIDS," the Oracular Expectations kick in, and everyone seems to keep one eye on me looking for marks and the other eye on the door, looking for the King: "*RINNNNG. Coop Cabs, may we help you? Yes. Please send ONE sweet chariot over to room 2000, 7 King's College Circle.*"

The drive to speak out can only be intensified when I'm reading, with my students, such passages as I've quoted here from Twain, Dickinson, and Cather. How wasteful, I think, to deny whatever voice my experience has in enjoying and deconstructing those/my deathbeds. Slave narratives are ringed with death by violence; the *Pequod* is a three-year deathbed. And did you ever notice how often death and dying come up in comedy, from Mark Twain to, say, *Golden Girls?*

I've engaged several strategies. Last summer, I taught English 103 (Effective Writing) and said, during our round-robin of unique introductions, "I have AIDS." Silence of awe, of course. But in the next class one student raised his hand: "May I ask you something personal?" "Go ahead." "If you have AIDS, as I think you said last class, then why are you so happy?" Perhaps my answer should have been "mood elevators, 20 mg b.i.d.," but instead I gave my best Mr. Chips reply, with Miss Dove thrown in for the gender blend. Yet that's true too. Several students, as a result, felt freer to talk about ultimate matters such as the vulnerability of grief, the fear of infection, and so on. Toward the end of the course, one woman asked to see me after class to talk about the positive test results a friend had just received. Or that's what I thought she said. It turned out, as we spoke on the slope outside University College in the July dusk, that she was speaking of her own test results. Would she ever have spoken had I not spoken first? Was my offering good, or weak, pedagogy?

Another example. Last December, at the final meeting of the Willa Cather seminar, where I had flirted with and skirted the announcement all term, I wanted to say that I would be giving a talk on teaching with AIDS. But I could only bring myself to announce the first half of the title. How could I hit them with the second half, the AIDS-marker half, when they were just about to write their course evaluations? This concealing-revealing and hinting-coding may remind us not just of the basic structures of teaching but also of the structures of the closets that pervade our culture. In a culture of identities, the textures of withholding and revealing can become all-encompassing. So can the textures of wanting to guess—and of wanting above all not to see.

WHO'S TALKING HERE? PART 2

I'm hardly the first man to treat the classroom as deathbed. If Emmeline Grangerford slipped your mind, you surely have been remembering Socrates. In the *Phaedo,* where our philosopher, about to down his poison, holds forth about the philosopher and the deathbed, his watchers are his students, his last words a lecture. I cathect not at all on the dear gorgeous nonsense he speaks but on Plato's playsome construction of the scene. Some very odd goings-on go on.

First. Plato, who twice elsewhere says he was present at Socrates's deathbed, has Phaedo explain that Plato is not present. Further, that he is not there because of illness. This absence or presence of Plato's own body, his health or illness, playfully destabilizes the eyewitness report.[6]

Second. Socrates can babble on as he does because there was an unusually long time between his trial and his execution, so long that Phaedo is called to explain the delay. It has to do with Athens's annual ritual remembering King Minos's annual ritual murders of Athenian youths and maidens, which Theseus brought to an end by slaying the Minotaur. On the day before Socrates's trial, the ritual ship departed for Delos, and until its return his execution cannot take place, since a law requires the city to keep pure during the ship's absence. So Socrates, who must die for corrupting the Athenian young, cannot die just yet, because of a ritual recalling the murder of other Athenian young. Odder still, Socrates, who must die to purify corruption, must for a long while *not* die, so that the city will remain pure.

Third. Xanthippe is excluded from the deathbed dialogue because, as Phaedo explains, she says "the sort of thing that women usually say." And what is that? "Socrates," she says, "this is the last time your friends will talk to you and you to them." Because of that line, Socrates orders her taken away. Later, his sons and some women from his household are brought in briefly and then sent away. At the great sun-

6. A remark made by Elizabeth V. Spellman in a lecture suggested these observations on Socrates's body in the *Phaedo.*

set moment, when his student-watchers break into "noisy tears," Socrates upbraids them: "I sent the women away, to avoid such unseemliness . . . so keep quiet and control yourselves."

Fourth. While Socrates is in chains, his legs hurt, but he feels pleasure from stroking them when the chains are removed. To explain that one cannot feel pleasure and pain at the same time, the imagines an Aesopian fable about two creatures with one head—bodily pain and bodily pleasure are linked only at the somehow nonbodily head.

Fifth. Socrates on his deathbed has been visited by dreams that say to him, "Socrates, practice and cultivate the arts." He is indecisive about which arts to cultivate, shifting from philosophy to poetry and then to the versification of Aesop, much as Emmeline shifts from tributes to crayons.

Sixth. As Socrates argues for the immortality of the soul and the instability of the body and derives his philosopher's calm from talking through these concepts, Phaedo becomes distressed. Socrates heals his distress not by argumentation but by stroking the youth's hair. "He was in the habit," says Phaedo, "of playing with my hair."

Seventh. There follows some really curious stuff about haircutting, which I'll not go into here.

Eighth. The poisonmonger keeps sending word that Socrates should shut up, because if the condemned man babbles on like this it may take extra swigs to produce death.

Ninth. One of the last acts Socrates performs is to take a bath—"to save the women the trouble," he explains, of washing his corpse.

Tenth. . . .

But here, at midnight, 10 mg of Serax kicking in, Lynch turned off his computer. His great lecture remains incomplete; it's because he has AIDS, you know. But it will be continued in a talk entitled "The Bodies in the Classroom," planned for the English-Philosophy Symposium next month. That is, if I live that long.

E. B. White

ONCE MORE TO THE LAKE

One summer, along about 1904, my father rented a camp on a lake in Maine and took us all there for the month of August. We all got

Originally appeared in "One Man's Meat," White's column for *Harper's Magazine* (Oct. 1941).

ringworm from some kittens and had to rub Pond's Extract on our arms and legs night and morning, and my father rolled over in a canoe with all his clothes on; but outside of that the vacation was a success and from then on none of us ever thought there was any place in the world like that lake in Maine. We returned summer after summer—always on August 1st for one month. I have since become a salt-water man, but sometimes in summer there are days when the restlessness of the tides and the fearful cold of the sea water and the incessant wind which blows across the afternoon and into the evening make me wish for the placidity of a lake in the woods. A few weeks ago this feeling got so strong I bought myself a couple of bass hooks and a spinner and returned to the lake where we used to go, for a week's fishing and to revisit old haunts.

I took along my son, who had never had any fresh water up his nose and who had seen lily pads only from train windows. On the journey over to the lake I began to wonder what it would be like. I wondered how time would have marred this unique, this holy spot—the coves and streams, the hills that the sun set behind, the camps and the paths behind the camps. I was sure the tarred road would have found it out and I wondered in what other ways it would be desolated. It is strange how much you can remember about places like that once you allow your mind to return into the grooves which lead back. You remember one thing, and that suddenly reminds you of another thing. I guess I remembered clearest of all the early mornings, when the lake was cool and motionless, remembered how the bedroom smelled of the lumber it was made of and of the wet woods whose scent entered through the screen. The partitions in the camp were thin and did not extend clear to the top of the rooms, and as I was always the first up I would dress softly so as not to wake the others, and sneak out into the sweet outdoors and start out in the canoe, keeping close along the shore in the long shadows of the pines. I remembered being very careful never to rub my paddle against the gunwale for fear of disturbing the stillness of the cathedral.

The lake had never been what you would call a wild lake. There were cottages sprinkled around the shores, and it was in farming country although the shores of the lake were quite heavily wooded. Some of the cottages were owned by nearby farmers, and you would live at the shore and eat your meals at the farmhouse. That's what our family did. But although it wasn't wild, it was a fairly large and undisturbed lake and there were places in it which, to a child at least, seemed infinitely remote and primeval.

I was right about the tar: it led to within half a mile of the shore. But when I got back there, with my boy, and we settled into a camp near a farmhouse and into the kind of summertime I had known, I could tell that it was going to be pretty much the same as it had been before—I knew it, lying in bed the first morning, smelling the bedroom, and hearing the boy sneak quietly out and go off along the shore in a boat. I began to sustain the illusion that he was I, and therefore, by simple transposition, that I was my father. This sensation persisted, kept cropping up all the time we were there. It was not an entirely new feeling, but in this setting it grew much stronger. I seemed to be living a dual existence. I would be in the middle of some simple act, I would be picking up a bait box or laying down a table fork, or I would be saying something, and suddenly it would be not I but my father who was saying the words or making the gesture. It gave me a creepy sensation.

5 We went fishing the first morning. I felt the same damp moss covering the worms in the bait can, and saw the dragonfly alight on the tip of my rod as it hovered a few inches from the surface of the water. It was the arrival of this fly that convinced me beyond any doubt that everything was as it always had been, that the years were a mirage and there had been no years. The small waves were the same, chucking the rowboat under the chin as we fished at anchor, and the boat was the same boat, the same color green and the ribs broken in the same places, and under the floor-boards the same fresh-water leavings and débris—the dead helgramite,[1] the wisps of moss, the rusty discarded fishhook, the dried blood from yesterday's catch. We stared silently at the tips of our rods, at the dragonflies that came and went. I lowered the tip of mine into the water, tentatively, pensively dislodging the fly, which darted two feet away, poised, darted two feet back, and came to rest again a little farther up the rod. There had been no years between the ducking of this dragonfly and the other one—the one that was part of memory. I looked at the boy, who was silently watching his fly, and it was my hands that held his rod, my eyes watching. I felt dizzy and didn't know which rod I was at the end of.

We caught two bass, hauling them in briskly as though they were mackerel, pulling them over the side of the boat in a businesslike manner without any landing net, and stunning them with a blow on the back of the head. When we got back for a swim before lunch, the lake was exactly where we had left it, the same number of inches from the dock, and there was only the merest suggestion of a breeze. This seemed an utterly enchanted sea, this lake you could leave to its own devices for a few hours and come back to, and find that it had not stirred, this constant and trustworthy body of water. In the shallows, the dark, water-soaked sticks and twigs, smooth and old, were undulating in clusters on the bottom against the clean ribbed sand, and the track of the mussel was plain. A school of minnows swam by, each

1. The nymph of the mayfly, used as bait.

minnow with its small individual shadow, doubling the attendance, so clear and sharp in the sunlight. Some of the other campers were in swimming, along the shore, one of them with a cake of soap, and the water felt thin and clear and unsubstantial. Over the years there had been this person with the cake of soap, this cultist, and here he was. There had been no years.

Up to the farmhouse to dinner through the teeming, dusty field, the road under our sneakers was only a two-track road. The middle track was missing, the one with the marks of the hooves and the splotches of dried, flaky manure. There had always been three tracks to choose from in choosing which track to walk in; now the choice was narrowed down to two. For a moment I missed terribly the middle alternative. But the way led past the tennis court, and something about the way it lay there in the sun reassured me; the tape had loosened along the backline, the alleys were green with plantains and other weeds, and the net (installed in June and removed in September) sagged in the dry noon, and the whole place steamed with midday heat and hunger and emptiness. There was a choice of pie for dessert, and one was blueberry and one was apple, and the waitresses were the same country girls, there having been no passage of time, only the illusion of it as in a dropped curtain—the waitresses were still fifteen; their hair had been washed, that was the only difference—they had been to the movies and seen the pretty girls with the clean hair.

Summertime, oh summertime, pattern of life indelible, the fadeproof lake, the woods unshatterable, the pasture with the sweetfern and the juniper forever and ever, summer without end; this was the background, and the life along the shore was the design, the cottagers with their innocent and tranquil design, their tiny docks with the flagpole and the American flag floating against the white clouds in the blue sky, the little paths over the roots of the trees leading from camp to camp and the paths leading back to the outhouses and the can of lime for sprinkling, and at the souvenir counters at the store the miniature birch-bark canoes and the post cards that showed things looking a little better than they looked. This was the American family at play, escaping the city heat, wondering whether the newcomers in the camp at the head of the cove were "common" or "nice," wondering whether it was true that the people who drove up for Sunday dinner at the farmhouse were turned away because there wasn't enough chicken.

It seemed to me, as I kept remembering all this, that those times and those summers had been infinitely precious and worth saving. There had been jollity and peace and goodness. The arriving (at the beginning of August) had been so big a business in itself, at the railway station the farm wagon drawn up, the first smell of the pine-laden air, the first glimpse of the smiling farmer, and the great importance of the trunks and your father's enormous authority in such matters, and the feel of the wagon under you for the long ten-mile haul, and at the top of the last long hill catching the first view of the lake after eleven months of not seeing this cherished body of water. The shouts and cries of the other campers when they saw you, and the trunks to be unpacked, to give up their rich burden. (Arriving was less exciting nowadays, when you sneaked up in your car and parked it under a tree near the camp and took out the bags and in five minutes it was all over, no fuss, no loud wonderful fuss about trunks.)

10 Peace and goodness and jollity. The only thing that was wrong now, really, was the sound of the place, an unfamiliar nervous sound of the outboard motors. This was the note that jarred, the one thing that would sometimes break the illusion and set the years moving. In those other summertimes all motors were inboard; and when they were at a little distance, the noise they made was a sedative, an ingredient of summer sleep. They were one-cylinder and two-cylinder engines, and some were make-and-break and some were jump-spark,[2] but they all made a sleepy sound across the lake. The one-lungers throbbed and fluttered, and the twin-cylinder ones purred and purred, and that was a quiet sound too. But now the campers all had outboards. In the daytime, in the hot mornings, these motors made a petulant, irritable sound; at night, in the still evening when the afterglow lit the water, they whined about one's ears like mosquitoes. My boy loved our rented outboard, and his great desire was to achieve singlehanded mastery over it, and authority, and he soon learned the trick of choking it a little (but not too much), and the adjustment of the needle valve. Watching him I would remember the things you could do with the old one-cylinder engine with the heavy flywheel, how you could have it eating out of your hand if you got really close to it spiritually. Motor boats in those days didn't have clutches, and you would make a landing by shutting off the motor at the proper time and coasting in with a dead rudder. But there was a way of reversing them, if you learned the trick, by cutting the switch and putting it on again exactly on the final dying revolution of the flywheel, so that it would kick back against compression and begin reversing. Approaching a dock in a strong following breeze, it was difficult to slow up sufficiently by the ordinary coasting method, and if a boy felt he had complete mastery over his motor, he was tempted to keep it running beyond its time and then reverse it a few feet from the dock. It took a cool nerve, because if you threw the switch a twentieth of a second too soon you would catch the flywheel when it still had speed enough to go up past center, and the boat would leap ahead, charging bull-fashion at the dock.

2. Methods of ignition timing.

We had a good week at the camp. The bass were biting well and the sun shone endlessly, day after day. We would be tired at night and lie down in the accumulated heat of the little bedrooms after the long hot day and the breeze would stir almost imperceptibly outside and the smell of the swamp drift in through the rusty screens. Sleep would come easily and in the morning the red squirrel would be on the roof, tapping out his gay routine. I kept remembering everything, lying in bed in the mornings—the small steamboat that had a long rounded stern like the lip of a Ubangi, and how quietly she ran on the moonlight sails, when the older boys played their mandolins and the girls sang and we ate doughnuts dipped in sugar, and how sweet the music was on the water in the shining night, and what it had felt like to think about girls then. After breakfast we would go up to the store and the things were in the same place—the minnows in a bottle, the plugs and spinners disarranged and pawed over by the youngsters from the boys' camp, the fig newtons and the Beeman's gum. Outside, the road was tarred and cars stood in front of the store. Inside, all was just as it had always been, except there was more Coca-Cola and not so much Moxie and root beer and birch beer and sarsaparilla. We would walk out with a bottle of pop apiece and sometimes the pop would backfire up our noses and hurt. We explored the streams, quietly, where the turtles slid off the sunny logs and dug their way into the soft bottom; and we lay on the town wharf and fed worms to the tame bass. Everywhere we went I had trouble making out which was I, the one walking at my side, the one walking in my pants.

One afternoon while we were there at that lake a thunderstorm came up. It was like the revival of an old melodrama that I had seen long ago with childish awe. The second-act climax of the drama of the electrical disturbance over a lake in America had not changed in any important respect. This was the big scene, still the big scene. The whole thing was so familiar, the first feeling of oppression and heat and a general air around camp of not wanting to go very far away. In midafternoon (it was all the same) a curious darkening of the sky, and a lull in everything that had made life tick; and then the way the boats suddenly swung the other way at their moorings with the coming of a breeze out of the new quarter, and the premonitory rumble. Then the kettle drum, then the snare, then the bass drum and cymbals, then crackling light against the dark, and the gods grinning and licking their chops in the hills. Afterward the calm, the rain steadily rustling in the calm lake, the return of light and hope and spirits, and the campers running out in joy and relief to go swimming in the rain, their bright cries perpetuating the deathless joke about how they were getting simply drenched, and the children screaming with delight at the new sensation of bathing in the rain, and the joke about getting drenched linking the generations in a strong indestructible chain. And the comedian who waded in carrying an umbrella.

When the others went swimming my son said he was going in too. He pulled his dripping trunks from the line where they had hung all through the shower, and wrung them out. Languidly, and with no thought of going in, I watched him, his hard little body, skinny and bare, saw him wince slightly as he pulled up around his vitals the small, soggy, icy garment. As he buckled the swollen belt suddenly my groin felt the chill of death.

QUESTIONS

1. *What has guided White in his selection of the details he gives about the trip? Why, for example, does he talk about the road, the dragonfly, the boat's motor?*
2. *White speaks of the lake as a "holy spot." What about it was holy?*
3. *White's last sentence often surprises first-time readers. Go back through the essay and pick out sections or words or phrases that seem to prepare for the ending.*
4. *Write about revisiting a place with a special meaning.*

Prose Forms: Journals

Occasionally one catches oneself having said something aloud, obviously with no concern to be heard, even by oneself. And all of us have overheard, perhaps while walking, a solitary person muttering or laughing softly or exclaiming abruptly. Something floats up from the world within, forces itself to be expressed, takes no real account of the time or the place, and certainly intends no conscious communication.

With more self-consciousness, and yet without a specific audience, one sometimes speaks out at something from the world without. A sharp play at the ball game, the twist of a political speech, an old photograph—something from the outer world impresses the mind, stimulates it, focuses certain of its memories and values, interests and needs. Thus stimulated, one may wish to share an experience with another, to inform or amuse that person, to rouse him or her to action, or to persuade someone to a certain belief. Often, though, the person experiencing may want most to talk to himself or herself, to give a public shape in words to thoughts and feelings but for the sake of a kind of private dialogue. Communication to another may be an ultimate desire, but the immediate motive is to articulate the experience for oneself.

To articulate and shape experience in language for one's own sake, one may keep a journal. Literally a day-book, the journal enables one to write down something about the experiences of a day which for a great variety of reasons may have been especially memorable or impressive. The journal entry may be merely a few words to call to mind a thing done, a person seen, a meal enjoyed with friends. It may be concerned at length with a political crisis in the community or a personal crisis in the home. It may even be as noble as it was with some pious people in the past who used the journal to keep a record of their consciences, a periodic reckoning of their moral and spiritual accounts. In its most public aspect, the idea of a journal calls to mind the newspaper or a record of proceedings like the U.S. Congressional Record *and the* Canadian Hansard. *In its most closely private form, the journal becomes the diary.*

To keep a journal is to hold onto experiences through writing. But to get it down on paper begins another adventure. The journalist has to focus on what he or she has experienced, and to be able to say what, in fact, the experience is. What of it is new? What of it is remarkable because of associations in the memory it stirs up? Is this like anything I—or others—have experienced before? Is it a good or a bad thing to have happened? And why, specifically? The questions multiply themselves quickly, and as the journalist seeks to answer the appropriate ones, he or she begins to know what is being contemplated. As one tries to find the words that best represent this discovery, the experience becomes even more clear in its shape and meaning. We can imagine Emerson going to the ballet, being absorbed in the spectacle, thinking casually of this or that association the dancer and the movements suggest. When he writes about the experience in his journal, a good many questions, judgments, and speculations get tied up with the spectacle, and it is this complex of event and his relation to it that becomes the experience he records. The simple facts of time, place, people, and actions drop down into one's consciousness and set in motion ideas and feelings which give those facts their real meaning to oneself.

Once this consciousness of events is formulated in words, the journalist has it, not only in the sense of understanding what has been seen or felt or thought, but also in the sense of having it there to contemplate long after the event itself. When we read a carefully kept journal covering a long period and varied experiences, we have the pleasure of a small world re-created for us in the consciousness of one who experienced it. Even more, we feel the continuity, the wholeness, of the writer. Something of the same feeling is there for the person who kept the journal: a whole world of events preserved in the form of their experienced reality, and with it the persistent self in the midst of that world. That world and that self are always accessible on the page and ultimately, therefore, usably real.

Beyond the value of the journal as record, there is the instructive value of the habit of mind and hand journal keeping can assure. One begins to attend more carefully to what happens to and around oneself. One learns the resources of language as a means of representing what one sees, and gains skill and certainty in doing justice to experience and to one's own consciousness. And the journal represents a discipline. It brings together an individual and a complex environment in a relation that teaches the individual something of himself or herself, something of the world, and something of the meaning of their relation. There is scarcely a moment in life when one is not poised for the lesson. When it comes with the promise of special force, there is the almost irresistible temptation to catch the impulse, give it form, make it permanent, assert its meaning. And so one commits oneself to language. To have given up one's experience to words is to have begun marking out the limits and potential of its meaning. In the journal that meaning is developed and clarified to oneself primarily. When the whole intention of the development and the clarification is the consideration of another reader, the method of the journal redirects itself to become that of the essay.

Joan Didion: On Keeping a Notebook

" 'That woman Estelle,' " the note reads, " 'is partly the reason why George Sharp and I are separated today.' *Dirty crepe-de-Chine wrapper, hotel bar, Wilmington RR, 9:45 a.m. August Monday morning.*"

Since the note is in my notebook, it presumably has some meaning to me. I study it for a long while. At first I have only the most general notion of what I was doing on an August Monday morning in the bar of the hotel across from the Pennsylvania Railroad station in Wilmington, Delaware (waiting for a train? missing one? 1960? 1961? why Wilmington?), but I do remember being there. The woman in the dirty crepe-de-Chine wrapper had come down from her room for a beer, and the bartender had heard before the reason why George Sharp and she were separated today. "Sure," he said, and went on mopping the floor. "You told me." At the other end of the bar is a girl. She is talking, pointedly, not to the man beside her but to a cat lying in the triangle of sunlight cast through the open door. She is wearing a plaid silk dress from Peck & Peck, and the hem is coming down.

Here is what it is: the girl has been on the Eastern Shore, and now she is going back to the city, leaving the man beside her, and all she can see ahead are the viscous summer sidewalks and the 3 a.m. long-distance calls that will make her lie awake and then sleep drugged through all the steaming mornings left in August (1960? 1961?). Because she must go directly from the train to lunch in New York, she wishes that she had a safety pin for the hem of the plaid silk dress, and she also wishes that she could forget about the hem and the lunch and stay in the cool bar that smells of disinfectant and malt and make friends with the woman in the crepe-de-Chine wrapper. She is afflicted by a little self-pity, and she wants to compare Estelles. That is what that was all about.

Why did I write it down? In order to remember, of course, but exactly what was it I wanted to remember? How much of it actually happened? Did any of it? Why do I keep a notebook at all? It is easy to deceive oneself on all those scores. The impulse to write things down is a peculiarly compulsive one, inexplicable to those who do not share it, useful only accidentally, only secondarily, in the way that any compulsion tries to justify itself. I suppose that it begins or does not begin in the cradle. Although I have felt compelled to write things down since I was five years old, I doubt that my daughter ever will, for she is a singularly blessed and accepting child, delighted with life exactly as

From *Slouching towards Bethlehem* (1966).

life presents itself to her, unafraid to go to sleep and unafraid to wake up. Keepers of private notebooks are a different breed altogether, lonely and resistant rearrangers of things, anxious malcontents, children afflicted apparently at birth with some presentiment of loss.

5 My first notebook was a Big Five tablet, given to me by my mother with the sensible suggestion that I stop whining and learn to amuse myself by writing down my thoughts. She returned the tablet to me a few years ago; the first entry is an account of a woman who believed herself to be freezing to death in the Arctic night, only to find, when day broke, that she had stumbled onto the Sahara Desert, where she would die of the heat before lunch. I have no idea what turn of a five-year-old's mind could have prompted so insistently "ironic" and exotic a story, but it does reveal a certain predilection for the extreme which has dogged me into adult life; perhaps if I were analytically inclined I would find it a truer story than any I might have told about Donald Johnson's birthday party or the day my cousin Brenda put Kitty Litter in the aquarium.

So the point of my keeping a notebook has never been, nor is it now, to have an accurate factual record of what I have been doing or thinking. That would be a different impulse entirely, an instinct for reality which I sometimes envy but do not possess. At no point have I ever been able successfully to keep a diary; my approach to daily life ranges from the grossly negligent to the merely absent, and on those few occasions when I have tried dutifully to record a day's events, boredom has so overcome me that the results are mysterious at best. What is this business about "shopping, typing piece, dinner with E, depressed"? Shopping for what? Typing what piece? Who is E? Was this "E" depressed, or was I depressed? Who cares?

In fact I have abandoned altogether that kind of pointless entry; instead I tell what some would call lies. "That's simply not true," the members of my family frequently tell me when they come up against my memory of a shared event. "The party was *not* for you, the spider was *not* a black widow, *it wasn't that way at all.*" Very likely they are right, for not only have I always had trouble distinguishing between what happened and what merely might have happened, but I remain unconvinced that the distinction, for my purposes, matters. The cracked crab that I recall having for lunch the day my father came home from Detroit in 1945 must certainly be embroidery, worked into the day's pattern to lend verisimilitude; I was ten years old and would not now remember the cracked crab. The day's events did not turn on cracked crab. And yet it is precisely that fictitious crab that makes me see the afternoon all over again, a home movie run all too often, the father bearing gifts, the child weeping, an exercise in family love and guilt. Or that is what it was to me. Similarly, perhaps it never did snow that August in Vermont; perhaps there never were flurries in the night wind, and maybe no one else felt the ground hardening and summer already dead even as we pretended to bask in it, but that was how it felt to me, and it might as well have snowed, could have snowed, did snow.

How it felt to me: that is getting closer to the truth about a notebook. I sometimes delude myself about why I keep a notebook, imagine that some thrifty virtue derives from preserving everything observed. See enough and write it down, I tell myself, and then some morning when the world seems drained of wonder, some day when I am only going through the motions of doing what I am supposed to do, which is write—on that bankrupt morning I will simply open my notebook and there it will all be, a forgotten account with accumulated interest, paid passage back to the world out there: dialogue overheard in hotels and elevators and at the hatcheck counter in Pavillon (one middle-aged man shows his hat check to another and says, "That's my old football number"); impressions of Bettina Aptheker and Benjamin Sonnenberg and Teddy ("Mr. Acapulco") Stauffer; careful *aperçus* about tennis bums and failed fashion models and Greek shipping heiresses, one of whom taught me a significant lesson (a lesson I could have learned from F. Scott Fitzgerald, but perhaps we all must meet the very rich for ourselves) by asking, when I arrived to interview her in her orchid-filled sitting room on the second day of a paralyzing New York blizzard, whether it was snowing outside.

I imagine, in other words, that the notebook is about other people. But of course it is not. I have no real business with what one stranger said to another at the hat-check counter in Pavillon; in fact I suspect that the line "That's my old football number" touched not my own imagination at all, but merely some memory of something once read, probably "The Eighty-Yard Run." Nor is my concern with a woman in a dirty crepe-de-Chine wrapper in a Wilmington bar. My stake is always, of course, in the unmentioned girl in the plaid silk dress. *Remember what it was to be me:* that is always the point.

It is a difficult point to admit. We are brought up in the ethic that 10
others, any others, all others, are by definition more interesting than ourselves; taught to be diffident, just this side of self-effacing. ("You're the least important person in the room and don't forget it," Jessica Mitford's governess would hiss in her ear on the advent of any social occasion; I copied that into my notebook because it is only recently that I have been able to enter a room without hearing some such phrase in my inner ear.) Only the very young and the very old may recount their dreams at breakfast, dwell upon self, interrupt with

memories of beach picnics and favorite Liberty lawn dresses and the rainbow trout in a creek near Colorado Springs. The rest of us are expected, rightly, to affect absorption in other people's favorite dresses, other people's trout.

And so we do. But our notebooks give us away, for however dutifully we record what we see around us, the common denominator of all we see is always, transparently, shamelessly, the implacable "I." We are not talking here about the kind of notebook that is patently for public consumption, a structural conceit for binding together a series of graceful *pensées*;[1] we are talking about something private, about bits of the mind's string too short to use, an indiscriminate and erratic assemblage with meaning only for its maker.

And sometimes even the maker has difficulty with the meaning. There does not seem to be, for example, any point in my knowing for the rest of my life that, during 1964, 720 tons of soot fell on every square mile of New York City, yet there it is in my notebook, labeled "FACT." Nor do I really need to remember that Ambrose Bierce liked to spell Leland Stanford's[2] name "£eland $tanford" or that "smart women almost alwayswear black in Cuba," a fashion hint without much potential for practical application. And does not the relevance of these notes seem marginal at best?:

> In the basement museum of the Inyo County Courthouse in Independence, California, sign pinned to a mandarin coat: "This MANDARIN COAT was often worn by Mrs. Minnie S. Brooks when giving lectures on her TEAPOT COLLECTION."
>
> Redhead getting out of car in front of Beverly Wilshire Hotel, chinchilla stole, Vuitton bags with tags reading:
>
> MRS LOU FOX
> HOTEL SAHARA
> VEGAS

Well, perhaps not entirely marginal. As a matter of fact, Mrs. Minnie S. Brooks and her MANDARIN COAT pull me back into my own childhood, for although I never knew Mrs. Brooks and did not visit Inyo County until I was thirty, I grew up in just such a world, in houses cluttered with Indian relics and bits of gold ore and ambergris and the souvenirs my Aunt Mercy Farnsworth brought back from the Orient. It is a long way from that world to Mrs. Lou Fox's world, where we all live now, and is it not just as well to remember that? Might not Mrs. Minnie S. Brooks help me to remember what I am? Might not Mrs. Lou Fox help me to remember what I am not?

1. Thoughts, reflections.
2. A nineteenth-century American millionaire.

But sometimes the point is harder to discern. What exactly did I have in mind when I noted down that it cost the father of someone I know $650 a month to light the place on the Hudson in which he lived before the Crash?[3] What use was I planning to make of this line by Jimmy Hoffa: "I may have my faults, but being wrong ain't one of them"? And although I think it interesting to know where the girls who travel with the Syndicate have their hair done when they find themselves on the West Coast, will I ever make suitable use of it? Might I not be better off just passing it on to John O'Hara? What is a recipe for sauerkraut doing in my notebook? What kind of magpie keeps this notebook? *"He was born the night the Titanic went down."* That seems a nice enough line, and I even recall who said it, but is it not really a better line in life than it could ever be in fiction?

But of course that is exactly it: not that I should ever use the line, 15
but that I should remember the woman who said it and the afternoon I heard it. We were on her terrace by the sea, and we were finishing the wine left from lunch, trying to get what sun there was, a California winter sun. The woman whose husband was born the night the *Titanic* went down wanted to rent her house, wanted to go back to her children in Paris. I remember wishing that I could afford the house, which cost $1,000 a month. "Someday you will," she said lazily. "Someday it all comes." There in the sun on her terrace it seemed easy to believe in someday, but later I had a low-grade afternoon hangover and ran over a black snake on the way to the supermarket and was flooded with inexplicable fear when I heard the checkout clerk explaining to the man ahead of me why she was finally divorcing her husband. "He left me no choice," she said over and over as she punched the register. "He has a little seven-month-old baby by her, he left me no choice." I would like to believe that my dread then was for the human condition, but of course it was for me, because I wanted a baby and did not then have one and because I wanted to own the house that cost $1,000 a month to rent and because I had a hangover.

It all comes back. Perhaps it is difficult to see the value in having one's self back in that kind of mood, but I do see it; I think we are well advised to keep on nodding terms with the people we used to be whether we find them attractive company or not. Otherwise they turn up unannounced and surprise us, come hammering on the mind's door at 4 a.m. of a bad night and demand to know who deserted them, who betrayed them, who is going to make amends. We forget all too soon the things we thought we could never forget. We forget the loves and the betrayals alike, forget what we whispered and what we

3. The stock market crash of 1929.

screamed, forget who we were. I have already lost touch with a couple of people I used to be; one of them, a seventeen-year-old, presents little threat, although it would be of some interest to me to know again what it feels like to sit on a river levee drinking vodka-and-orange-juice and listening to Les Paul and Mary Ford and their echoes sing "How High the Moon" on the car radio. (You see I still have the scenes, but I no longer perceive myself among those present, no longer could even improvise the dialogue.) The other one, a twenty-three-year-old, bothers me more. She was always a good deal of trouble, and I suspect she will reappear when I least want to see her, skirts too long, shy to the point of aggravation, always the injured party, full of recriminations and little hurts and stories I do not want to hear again, at once saddening me and angering me with her vulnerability and ignorance, an apparition all the more insistent for being so long banished.

It is a good idea, then, to keep in touch, and I suppose that keeping in touch is what notebooks are all about. And we are all on our own when it comes to keeping those lines open to ourselves: your notebook will never help me, nor mine you. "*So what's new in the whiskey business?*" What could that possibly mean to you? To me it means a blonde in a Pucci bathing suit sitting with a couple of fat men by the pool at the Beverly Hills Hotel. Another man approaches, and they all regard one another in silence for a while. "So what's new in the whiskey business?" one of the fat men finally says by way of welcome, and the blonde stands up, arches one foot and dips it in the pool, looking all the while at the cabaña where Baby Pignatari is talking on the telephone. That is all there is to that, except that several years later I saw the blonde coming out of Saks Fifth Avenue in New York with her California complexion and a voluminous mink coat. In the harsh wind that day she looked old and irrevocably tired to me, and even the skins in the mink coat were not worked the way they were doing them that year, not the way she would have wanted them done, and there is the point of the story. For a while after that I did not like to look in the mirror, and my eyes would skim the newspapers and pick out only the deaths, the cancer victims, the premature coronaries, the suicides, and I stopped riding the Lexington Avenue IRT[4] because I noticed for the first time that all the strangers I had seen for years—the man with the seeing-eye dog, the spinster who read the classified pages every day, the fat girl who always got off with me at Grand Central—looked older than they once had.

It all comes back. Even that recipe for sauerkraut: even that brings it back. I was on Fire Island when I first made that sauerkraut, and it was raining, and we drank a lot of bourbon and ate the sauerkraut and

4. A New York City subway line; one of its stops is the Grand Central railway terminal.

went to bed at ten, and I listened to the rain and the Atlantic and felt safe. I made the sauerkraut again last night and it did not make me feel any safer, but that is, as they say, another story.

QUESTIONS

1. *What distinction does Didion make between a diary and a notebook? What uses does a notebook have for Didion?*
2. *Didion says she uses her notebook to "tell what some would call lies" (paragraph 7). Why does she do this? Would some people call these things truths? Why?*
3. *Didion says,* "How it felt to me: *that is getting closer to the truth about a notebook.*" *What writing strategies does she use to convey "how it felt"?*
4. *Try keeping a notebook for a week, jotting down the sort of things that Didion does. At the end of the week, take one or two of your entries and expand on them, as Didion does with the entries on Mrs. Minnie S. Brooks and Mrs. Lou Fox.*

Ralph Waldo Emerson: FROM JOURNAL

I like to have a man's knowledge comprehend more than one class of topics, one row of shelves. I like a man who likes to see a fine barn as well as a good tragedy. [1828]

The Religion that is afraid of science dishonors God and commits suicide. [1831]

The things taught in colleges and schools are not an education, but the means of education. [1831]

Don't tell me to get ready to die. I know not what shall be. The only preparation I can make is by fulfilling my present duties. This is the everlasting life. [1832]

My aunt [Mary Moody Emerson] had an eye that went through and 5
through you like a needle. "She was endowed," she said, "with the fatal gift of penetration." She disgusted everybody because she knew them too well. [1832]

I am sure of this, that by going much alone a man will get more of a noble courage in thought and word than from all the wisdom that is in books. [1833]

I fretted the other night at the hotel at the stranger who broke into my chamber after midnight, claiming to share it. But after his lamp had smoked the chamber full and I had turned round to the wall in despair, the man blew out his lamp, knelt down at his bedside, and made in low whisper a long earnest prayer. Then was the relation entirely changed between us. I fretted no more, but respected and liked him. [1835]

I believe I shall some time cease to be an individual, that the eternal tendency of the soul is to become Universal, to animate the last extremities of organization. [1837]

It is very hard to be simple enough to be good. [1837]

A man must have aunts and cousins, must buy carrots and turnips, must have barn and woodshed, must go to market and to the blacksmith's shop, must saunter and sleep and be inferior and silly. [1838]

How sad a spectacle, so frequent nowadays, to see a young man after ten years of college education come out, ready for his voyage of life—and to see that the entire ship is made of rotten timber, of rotten, honeycombed, traditional timber without so much as an inch of new plank in the hull. [1839]

A sleeping child gives me the impression of a traveler in a very far country. [1840]

In reading these letters of M.M.E. I acknowledge (with surprise that I could ever forget it) the debt of myself and my brothers to that old religion which, in those years, still dwelt like a Sabbath peace in the country population of New England, which taught privation, self-denial, and sorrow. A man was born, not for prosperity, but to suffer for the benefit of others, like the noble rock-maple tree which all around the villages bleeds for the service of man.[1] Not praise, not men's acceptance of our doing, but the Spirit's holy errand through us, absorbed the thought. How dignified is this! how all that is called talents and worth in Paris and in Washington dwindles before it! [1841]

All writing is by the grace of God. People do not deserve to have good writing, they are so pleased with bad. In these sentences that you show me, I can find no beauty, for I see death in every clause and every word. There is a fossil or a mummy character which pervades this

1. The sap of the rock or sugar maple is collected and made into maple syrup.

book. The best sepulchers, the vastest catacombs, Thebes and Cairo, Pyramids, are sepulchers to me. I like gardens and nurseries. Give me initiative, spermatic, prophesying, man-making words. [1841]

When summer opens, I see how fast it matures, and fear it will be short; but after the heats of July and August, I am reconciled, like one who has had his swing, to the cool of autumn. So will it be with the coming of death. [1846]

In England every man you meet is some man's son; in America, he may be some man's father. [1848]

Every poem must be made up of lines that are poems. [1848]

Love is necessary to the righting the estate of woman in this world. Otherwise nature itself seems to be in conspiracy against her dignity and welfare; for the cultivated, high-thoughted, beauty-loving, saintly woman finds herself unconsciously desired for her sex, and even enhancing the appetite of her savage pursuers by these fine ornaments she has piously laid on herself. She finds with indignation that she is herself a snare, and was made such. I do not wonder at her occasional protest, violent protest against nature, in fleeing to nunneries, and taking black veils. Love rights all this deep wrong. [1848]

Natural Aristocracy. It is a vulgar error to suppose that a gentleman must be ready to fight. The utmost that can be demanded of the gentleman is that he be incapable of a lie. There is a man who has good sense, is well informed, well-read, obliging, cultivated, capable, and has an absolute devotion to truth. He always means what he says, and says what he means, however courteously. You may spit upon him—nothing could induce him to spit upon you—no praises, and no possessions, no compulsion of public opinion. You may kick him—he will think it the kick of a brute—but he is not a brute, and will not kick you in return. But neither your knife and pistol, nor your gifts and courting will ever make the smallest impression on his vote or word; for he is the truth's man, and will speak and act the truth until he dies. [1849]

Love is temporary and ends with marriage. Marriage is the perfection which love aimed at, ignorant of what it sought. Marriage is a good known only to the parties—a relation of perfect understanding, aid, contentment, possession of themselves and of the world—which dwarfs love to green fruit. [1850]

I found when I had finished my new lecture that it was a very good house, only the architect had unfortunately omitted the stairs. [1851]

This filthy enactment [The Fugitive Slave Law[2]] was made in the nineteenth century, by people who could read and write. I will not obey it, by God. [1851]

Henry [Thoreau] is military. He seemed stubborn and implacable; always manly and wise, but rarely sweet. One would say that, as Webster could never speak without an antagonist, so Henry does not feel himself except in opposition. He wants a fallacy to expose, a blunder to pillory, requires a little sense of victory, a roll of the drums, to call his powers into full exercise. [1853]

Shall we judge the country by the majority or by the minority? Certainly, by the minority. The mass are animal, in state of pupilage, and nearer the chimpanzee. [1854]

All the thoughts of a turtle are turtle. [1854]

Resources or feats. I like people who can do things. When Edward and I struggled in vain to drag our big calf into the barn, the Irish girl put her finger into the calf's mouth, and led her in directly. [1862]

George Francis Train said in a public speech in New York, "Slavery is a divine institution." "So is hell," exclaimed an old man in the crowd. [1862]

You complain that the Negroes are a base class. Who makes and keeps the Jew or the Negro base, who but you, who exclude them from the rights which others enjoy? [1867]

2. A law enacted in 1850 to compel the arrest of runaway slaves and their return to their owners.

Henry David Thoreau: FROM JOURNAL

As the least drop of wine tinges the whole goblet, so the least particle of truth colors our whole life. It is never isolated, or simply added as treasure to our stock. When any real progress is made, we unlearn and learn anew what we thought we knew before. [1837]

Not by constraint or severity shall you have access to true wisdom, but by abandonment, and childlike mirthfulness. If you would know aught, be gay before it. [1840]

It is the man determines what is said, not the words. If a mean person uses a wise maxim, I bethink me how it can be interpreted so as to commend itself to his meanness; but if a wise man makes a commonplace remark, I consider what wider construction it will admit. [1840]

Nothing goes by luck in composition. It allows of no tricks. The best you can write will be the best you are. Every sentence is the result of a long probation. The author's character is read from title-page to end. Of this he never corrects the proofs. We read it as the essential character of a handwriting without regard to the flourishes. And so of the rest of our actions; it runs as straight as a ruled line through them all, no matter how many curvets about it. Our whole life is taxed for the least thing well done: it is its net result. How we eat, drink, sleep, and use our desultory hours, now in these indifferent days, with no eye to observe and no occasion [to] excite us, determines our authority and capacity for the time to come. [1841]

What does education often do? It makes a straight-cut ditch of a free, meandering brook. [1850]

All perception of truth is the detection of an analogy; we reason from our hands to our head. [1851]

To set down such choice experiences that my own writings may inspire me and at last I may make wholes of parts. Certainly it is a distinct profession to rescue from oblivion and to fix the sentiments and thoughts which visit all men more or less generally, that the contemplation of the unfinished picture may suggest its harmonious completion. Associate reverently and as much as you can with your loftiest thoughts. Each thought that is welcomed and recorded is a nest egg, by the side of which more will be laid. Thoughts accidentally thrown together become a frame in which more may be developed and exhibited. Perhaps this is the main value of a habit of writing, of keeping a journal—that so we remember our best hours and stimulate ourselves. My thoughts are my company. They have a certain individuality and separate existence, aye, personality. Having by chance recorded a few disconnected thoughts and then brought them into juxtaposition, they suggest a whole new field in which it was possible to labor and to think. Thought begat thought. [1852]

It is pardonable when we spurn the proprieties, even the sanctities, making them stepping-stones to something higher. [1858]

There is always some accident in the best things, whether thoughts or expressions or deeds. The memorable thought, the happy expression, the admirable deed are only partly ours. The thought came to us because we were in a fit mood; also we were unconscious and did not know that we had said or done a good thing. We must walk consciously only part way toward our goal, and then leap in the dark to our success. What we do best or most perfectly is what we have most thoroughly learned by the longest practice, and at length it falls from us without our notice, as a leaf from a tree. It is the *last* time we shall do it—our unconscious leavings. [1859]

The expression "a *liberal* education" originally meant one worthy of freemen. Such is education simply in a true and broad sense. But education ordinarily so called—the learning of trades and professions which is designed to enable men to earn their living, or to fit them for a particular station in life—is *servile.* [1859]

QUESTIONS

1. *Thoreau writes that "Nothing goes by luck in composition. . . . The best you can write will be the best you are." In what sense are his journal entries examples of this belief?*
2. *Both Thoreau and Emerson write journal entries on the subject of education, both using metaphorical language. Compare their beliefs on education, in part by comparing the metaphors they use.*
3. *Choose one journal entry from either Emerson or Thoreau and write an essay by expanding, amplifying, or showing exceptions to it.*

Walt Whitman: ABRAHAM LINCOLN

August 12th.—I see the President almost every day, as I happen to live where he passes to or from his lodgings out of town. He never sleeps at the White House during the hot season, but has quarters at a healthy location some three miles north of the city, the Soldiers' home, a United States military establishment. I saw him this morning about $8\frac{1}{2}$ coming in to business, riding on Vermont avenue, near L street. He always has a company of twenty-five or thirty cavalry, with sabres drawn and held upright over their shoulders. They say this guard was against his personal wish, but he let his counselors have their way. The party makes no great show in uniform or horses. Mr Lincoln on the saddle generally rides a good-sized, easy-going gray horse, is dress'd in plain black, somewhat rusty and dusty, wears a

From *Specimen Days* (first published in 1882).

black stiff hat, and looks about as ordinary in attire, &c., as the commonest man. A lieutenant, with yellow straps, rides at his left, and following behind, two by two, come the cavalry men, in their yellow-striped jackets. They are generally going at a slow trot, as that is the pace set them by the one they wait upon. The sabres and accoutrements clank, and the entirely unornamental *cortège* as it trots towards Lafayette square arouses no sensation, only some curious stranger stops and gazes. I see very plainly ABRAHAM LINCOLN'S dark brown face, with the deep-cut lines, the eyes, always to me with a deep latent sadness in the expression. We have got so that we exchange bows, and very cordial ones. Sometimes the President goes and comes in an open barouche. The cavalry always accompany him, with drawn sabres. Often I notice as he goes out evenings—and sometimes in the morning, when he returns early—he turns off and halts at the large and handsome residence of the Secretary of War, on K street, and holds conference there. If in his barouche, I can see from my window he does not alight, but sits in his vehicle, and Mr. Stanton comes out to attend him. Sometimes one of his sons, a boy of ten or twelve, accompanies him, riding at his right on a pony. Earlier in the summer I occasionally saw the President and his wife, toward the latter part of the afternoon, out in a barouche, on a pleasure ride through the city. Mrs. Lincoln was dress'd in complete black, with a long crape veil. The equipage is of the plainest kind, only two horses, and they nothing extra. They pass'd me once very close, and I saw the President in the face fully, as they were moving slowly, and his look, though abstracted, happen'd to be directed steadily in my eye. He bow'd and smiled, but far beneath his smile I noticed well the expression I have alluded to. None of the artists or pictures has caught the deep, though subtle and indirect expression of this man's face. There is something else there. One of the great portrait painters of two or three centuries ago is needed.

The Inauguration

March 4.—The President very quietly rode down to the capitol in his own carriage, by himself, on a sharp trot, about noon, either because he wish'd to be on hand to sign bills, or to get rid of marching in line with the absurd procession, the muslin temple of liberty, and pasteboard monitor. I saw him on his return, at three o'clock, after the performance was over. He was in his plain two-horse barouche, and look'd very much worn and tired; the lines, indeed, of vast responsibilities, intricate questions, and demands of life and death, cut deeper than ever upon his dark brown face; yet all the old goodness, tenderness, sadness, and canny shrewdness, underneath the furrows. (I never see that man without feeling that he is one to become personally attach'd to, for his combination of purest, heartiest tenderness, and native western form of manliness.) By his side sat his little boy, of ten years. There were no soldiers, only a lot of civilians on horseback, with huge yellow scarfs over their shoulders, riding around the carriage. (At the inauguration four years ago, he rode down and back again surrounded by a dense mass of arm'd cavalrymen eight deep, with drawn sabres; and there were sharpshooters station'd at every corner on the route.) I ought to make mention of the closing levee[1] of Saturday night last. Never before was such a compact jam in front of the White House—all the grounds fill'd, and away out to the spacious sidewalks. I was there, as I took anotion to go—was in the rush inside with the crowd—surged along the passage-ways, the blue and other rooms, and through the great east room. Crowds of country people, some very funny. Fine music from the Marine band, off in a side place. I saw Mr. Lincoln, drest all in black, with white kid gloves and a claw-hammer coat, receiving, as in duty bound, shaking hands, looking very disconsolate, and as if he would give anything to be somewhere else.

Death of President Lincoln

April 16, '65.—I find in my notes of the time, this passage on the death of Abraham Lincoln: He leaves for America's history and biography, so far, not only its most dramatic reminiscence—he leaves, in my opinion, the greatest, best, most characteristic, artistic, moral personality. Not but that he had faults, and show'd them in the Presidency; but honesty, goodness, shrewdness, conscience, and (a new virtue, unknown to other lands, and hardly yet really known here, but the foundation and tie of all, as the future will grandly develop,) UNIONISM, in its truest and amplest sense, form'd the hard-pan of his character. These he seal'd with his life. The tragic splendor of his death, purging, illuminating all, throws round his form, his head, an aureole that will remain and will grow brighter through time, while history lives, and love of country lasts. By many has this Union been help'd; but if one name, one man, must be pick'd out, he, most of all, is the conservator of it, to the future. He was assassinated—but the Union is not assassinated—*çaira!*[2] One falls, and another falls. The soldier drops, sinks like a wave—but the ranks of the ocean eternally press on. Death does its work, obliterates a hundred, a thousand—President, general, captain, private—but the Nation is immortal.

1. An occasion of state for the receiving of visits, ceremonial greetings, and interviews.
2. It goes on; it succeeds.

No Good Portrait of Lincoln

Probably the reader has seen physiognomies (often old farmers, sea-captains, and such) that, behind their homeliness, or even ugliness, held superior points so subtle, yet so palpable, making the real life of their faces almost as impossible to depict as a wild perfume or fruit-taste, or a passionate tone of the living voice—and such was Lincoln's face, the peculiar color, the lines of it, the eyes, mouth, expression. Of technical beauty it had nothing—but to the eye of a great artist it furnished a rare study, a feast and fascination. The current portraits are all failures—most of them caricatures.

QUESTIONS

1. *The first entries in Whitman's journal record his personal observances of Abraham Lincoln. Which details best give a sense of the president? Why?*
2. *The last entries in Whitman's journal give an assessment of Lincoln's character? How are these entries different from the first ones?*
3. *If you have an opportunity to observe a public figure up close, write a journal entry like the first of Whitman's, perhaps followed by an entry that reflects on the person's character.*

Susanna Moodie

A VISIT TO GROSSE ISLE

31 August, 1832. By daybreak all was hurry and confusion on board the *Anne.* I watched boat after boat depart for the island, full of people and goods, and envied them the glorious privilege of once more standing firmly on the earth after two long months of rocking and rolling at sea. How ardently we anticipate pleasure, which often ends in positive pain! Such was my case when at last indulged in the gratification so eagerly desired. As cabin passengers we were not included in the general order of purification, but were only obliged to send our servant, with the clothes and bedding we had used during the voyage, on shore, to be washed.

The ship was soon emptied of all her live cargo. My husband went off with the boats to reconnoitre the island, and I was left alone with my baby in the otherwise empty vessel. Even Oscar, the captain's

From *Roughing It in the Bush* (1852).

Scotch terrier, who had formed a devoted attachment to me during the voyage, forgot his allegiance, became possessed of the land mania, and was away with the rest. With the most intense desire to go on shore, I was doomed to look and long and envy every boatful of emigrants that glided past. Nor was this all; the ship was out of provisions, and I was condemned to undergo a rigid fast until the return of the boat, when the captain had promised a supply of fresh butter and bread. The vessel had been nine weeks at sea; the poor steerage passengers for the two last weeks had been out of food, and the captain had been obliged to feed them from the ship's stores. The promised bread was to be obtained from a small steamboat which plied daily between Quebec and the island, transporting convalescent emigrants and their goods in her upward trip and provisions for the sick on her return.

How I reckoned on once more tasting bread and butter! The very thought of the treat in store served to sharpen my appetite and render the long fast more irksome. I could now fully realize all Mrs. Bowdich's longings for English bread and butter, after her three years' travel through the burning African deserts with her talented husband.

"When we arrived at the hotel at Plymouth," said she, "and were asked what refreshment we chose—'Tea, and home-made bread and butter,' was my instant reply. 'Brown bread, if you please, and plenty of it.' I never enjoyed any luxury like it. I was positively ashamed of asking the waiter to refill the plate. After the execrable messes, and the hard ship-biscuit, imagine the luxury of a good slice of English bread and butter!"

At home, I laughed heartily at the lively energy with which that charming woman of genius related this little incident in her eventual history—but off Grosse Isle I realized it all.

As the sun rose above the horizon, all these matter-of-fact circumstances were gradually forgotten and merged in the surpassing grandeur of the scene that rose majestically before me. The previous day had been dark and stormy, and a heavy fog had concealed the mountain chain, which forms the stupendous background to this sublime view, entirely from our sight. As the clouds rolled away from their grey, bald brows, and cast into denser shadow the vast forest belt that girdled them round, they loomed out like mighty giants—Titans of the earth,[1] in all their rugged and awful beauty—a thrill of wonder and delight pervaded my mind. The spectacle floated dimly on my sight—my eyes were blinded with tears—blinded by the excess of beauty. I

1. In Greek mythology, a race of giants begotten by the union of Uranus (sky) and Gaia (earth). The Titans ruled the world in the primitive age until they were overthrown by the Olympian gods led by Zeus.

turned to the right and to the left, I looked up and down the glorious river; never had I beheld so many striking objects blended into one mighty whole! Nature had lavished all her noblest features in producing that enchanting scene.

The rocky isle in front, with its neat farmhouses at the eastern point, and its high bluff at the western extremity, crowned with the telegraph—the middle space occupied by tents and sheds for the cholera patients, and its wooded shores dotted over with motley groups—added greatly to the picturesque effect of the land scene. Then the broad glittering river, covered with boats darting to and fro, conveying passengers from twenty-five vessels, of various size and tonnage, which rode at anchor, with their flags flying from the masthead, gave an air of life and interest to the whole. Turning to the south side of the St. Lawrence, I was not less struck with its low fertile shores, white houses, and neat churches, whose slender spires and bright tin roofs shone like silver as they caught the first rays of the sun. As far as the eye could reach, a line of white buildings extended along the bank, their background formed by the purple hue of the dense, interminable forest. It was a scene unlike any I had ever beheld, and to which Britain contains no parallel. Mackenzie, an old Scotch dragoon, who was one of our passengers, when he rose in the morning and saw the parish of St. Thomas for the first time, exclaimed: "Weel, it beats a'! Can thae white clouts be a' houses? They look like claes hung out to drie!" There was some truth in this odd comparison, and for some minutes I could scarcely convince myself that the white patches scattered so thickly over the opposite shore could be the dwellings of a busy, lively population.

"What sublime views of the north side of the river those *habitants* of St. Thomas must enjoy," thought I. Perhaps familiarity with the scene has rendered them indifferent to its astonishing beauty.

Eastward, the view down the St. Lawrence towards the Gulf is the finest of all, scarcely surpassed by anything in the world. Your eye follows the long range of lofty mountains until their blue summits are blended and lost in the blue of the sky. Some of these, partially cleared round the base, are sprinkled over with neat cottages, and the green slopes that spread around them are covered with flocks and herds. The surface of the splendid river is diversified with islands of every size and shape, some in wood, others partially cleared, and adorned with orchards and white farmhouses. As the early sun streamed upon the most prominent of these, leaving the others in deep shade, the effect was strangely novel and imposing. In more remote regions, where the forest has never yet echoed to the woodman's axe, or received the impress of civilization, the first approach to the shore inspires a melancholy awe which becomes painful in its intensity.

And silence—awful silence broods
Profoundly o'er these solitudes;
Not but the lapsing of the floods
Breaks the deep stillness of the woods;
A sense of desolation reigns
O'er these unpeopled forest plains
Where sounds of life ne'er wake a tone
Of cheerful praise round Nature's throne,
Man finds himself with God—alone.

10 My daydreams were dispelled by the return of the boat, which brought my husband and the captain from the island.

"No bread," said the latter, shaking his head; "you must be content to starve a little longer. Provision ship not in till four o'clock." My husband smiled at the look of blank disappointment with which I received these unwelcome tidings. "Never mind, I have news which will comfort you. The officer who commands the station sent a note to me by an orderly, inviting us to spend the afternoon with him. He promises to show us everything worthy of notice on the island. Captain—— claims acquaintance with me; but I have not the least recollection of him. Would you like to go?"

"Oh, by all means. I long to see the lovely island. It looks a perfect paradise at this distance."

The rough sailor-captain screwed his mouth on one side, and gave me one of his comical looks; but he said nothing until he assisted in placing me and the baby in the boat.

"Don't be too sanguine, Mrs. Moodie; many things look well at a distance which are bad enough when near."

15 I scarcely regarded the old sailor's warning. So eager was I to go on shore—to put my foot upon the soil of the new world for the first time—I was in no humor to listen to any depreciation of what seemed so beautiful.

It was four o'clock when we landed on the rocks, which the rays of an intensely scorching sun had rendered so hot that I could scarcely place my foot upon them. How the people without shoes bore it I cannot imagine. Never shall I forget the extraordinary spectacle that met our sight the moment we passed the low range of bushes which formed a screen in front of the river. A crowd of many hundred Irish emigrants had been landed during the present and former day and all this motley crew—men, women, and children, who were not confined by sickness to the sheds (which greatly resembled cattle-pens)—were employed in washing clothes or spreading them out on the rocks and bushes to dry.

The men and boys were *in* the water, while the women, with their scanty garments tucked above their knees, were tramping their bedding in tubs or in holes in the rocks, which the retiring tide had left half full of water. Those who did not possess washing tubs, pails, or iron pots, or could not obtain access to a hole in the rocks, were running to and fro, screaming and scolding in no measured terms. The confusion of Babel[2] was among them. All talkers and no hearers—each shouting and yelling in his or her uncouth dialect, and all accompanying their vociferations with violent and extraordinary gestures, quite incomprehensible to the uninitiated. We were literally stunned by the strife of tongues. I shrank, with feelings almost akin to fear, from the hard-featured, sunburnt women as they elbowed rudely past me.

I had heard and read much of savages, and have since seen, during my long residence in the bush, somewhat of uncivilized life, but the Indian is one of Nature's gentlemen—he never says or does a rude or vulgar thing. The vicious, uneducated barbarians, who form the surplus of overpopulous European countries, are far behind the wild man in delicacy of feeling or natural courtesy. The people who covered the island appeared perfectly destitute of shame, or even a sense of common decency. Many were almost naked, still more but partially clothed. We turned in disgust from the revolting scene, but were unable to leave the spot until the captain had satisfied a noisy group of his own people, who were demanding a supply of stores.

2. In Genesis, it is told that the survivors of the Flood decided to build a city and a tower that would reach to heaven. To force them to disperse, God mixed up their languages so that they could no longer understand one another. The tower was named Babel, a play on the Hebrew verb "to mix."

May Sarton: FROM JOURNAL OF A SOLITUDE

September 17th. Cracking open the inner world again, writing even a couple of pages, threw me back into depression, not made easier by the weather, two gloomy days of darkness and rain. I was attacked by a storm of tears, those tears that appear to be related to frustration, to buried anger, and come upon me without warning. I woke yesterday so depressed that I did not get up till after eight.

I drove to Brattleboro[1] to read poems at the new Unitarian church

From *Journal of a Solitude* (1970–1971), published in 1973.

1. Brattleboro, Vermont.

there in a state of dread and exhaustion. How to summon the vitality needed? I had made an arrangement of religious poems, going back to early books and forward into the new book not yet published. I suppose it went all right—at least it was not a disaster—but I felt (perhaps I am wrong) that the kind, intelligent people gathered in a big room looking out on pine trees did not really want to think about God. His absence (many of the poems speak of that) or His presence. Both are too frightening.

On the way back I stopped to see Perley Cole, my dear old friend, who is dying, separated from his wife, and has just been moved from a Dickensian nursing home into what seems like a far better one. He grows more transparent every day, a skeleton or nearly. Clasping his hand, I fear to break a bone. Yet the only real communication between us now (he is very deaf) is a handclasp. I want to lift him in my arms and hold him like a baby. He is dying a terribly lonely death. Each time I see him he says, "It is rough" or "I did not think it would end like this."

Everywhere I look about this place I see his handiwork: the three small trees by a granite boulder that he pruned and trimmed so they pivot the whole meadow; the new shady border he dug out for me one of the last days he worked here; the pruned-out stone wall between my field and the church. The second field where he cut brush twice a year and cleared out to the stone wall is growing back to wilderness now. What is done here has to be done over and over and needs the dogged strength of a man like Perley. I could have never managed it alone. We cherished this piece of land together, and fought together to bring it to some semblance of order and beauty.

I like to think that this last effort of Perley's had a certain ease about it, a game compared to the hard work of his farming years, and a game where his expert knowledge and skill could be well used. How he enjoyed teasing me about my ignorance!

5 While he scythed and trimmed, I struggled in somewhat the same way at my desk here, and we were each aware of the companionship. We each looked forward to noon, when I could stop for the day and he sat on a high stool in the kitchen, drank a glass or two of sherry with me, said, "Court's in session!" and then told me some tall tale he had been cogitating all morning.

It was a strange relationship, for he knew next to nothing about my life, really; yet below all the talk we recognized each other as the same kind. He enjoyed my anger as much as I enjoyed his. Perhaps that was part of it. Deep down there was understanding, not of the facts of our lives so much as of our essential natures. Even now in his hard, lonely end he has immense dignity. But I wish there were some way to make it easier. I leave him with bitter resentment against the circumstances of this death. "I know. But I did not approve. And I am not resigned."

In the mail a letter from a twelve-year-old child, enclosing poems, her mother having pushed her to ask my opinion. The child does really look at things, and I can write something helpful, I think. But it is troubling how many people expect applause, recognition, when they have not even begun to learn an art or a craft. Instant success is the order of the day; "I want it *now!*" I wonder whether this is not part of our corruption by machines. Machines do things very quickly and outside the natural rhythm of life, and we are indignant if a car doesn't start at the first try. So the few things that we still do, such as cooking (though there are TV dinners!), knitting, gardening, anything at all that cannot be hurried, have a very particular value.

September 18th. The value of solitude—one of its values—is, of course, that there is nothing to *cushion* against attacks from within, just as there is nothing to help balance at times of particular stress or depression. A few moments of desultory conversation with dear Arnold Miner, when he comes to take the trash, may calm an inner storm. But the storm, painful as it is, might have had some truth in it. So sometimes one has simply to endure a period of depression for what it may hold of illumination if one can live through it, attentive to what it exposes or demands.

The reasons for depression are not so interesting as the way one handles it, simply to stay alive. This morning I woke at four and lay awake for an hour or so in a bad state. It is raining again. I got up finally and went about the daily chores, waiting for the sense of doom to lift—and what did it was watering the house plants. Suddenly joy came back because I was fulfilling a simple need, a living one. Dusting never has this effect (and that may be why I am such a poor housekeeper!), but feeding the cats when they are hungry, giving Punch clean water, makes me suddenly feel calm and happy.

Whatever peace I know rests in the natural world, in feeling myself 10
a part of it, even in a small way. Maybe the gaiety of the Warner family, their wisdom, comes from this, that they work close to nature all the time. As simple as that? But it is not simple. Their life requires patient understanding, imagination, the power to endure constant adversity—the weather, for example! To go with, not against the elements, an inexhaustible vitality summoned back each day to do the same tasks, to feed the animals, clean out barns and pens, keep that complex world alive.

October 6th. A day when I am expecting someone for lunch is quite unlike ordinary days. There is a reason to make the flowers look beautiful all over the house, and I know that Anne Woodson, who is coming today, will notice them, for she sees this house in a way that few of my friends do, perhaps because she has lived here without me, has lived her way into the place by pruning and weeding, and once even tidying the linen cupboard!

It is a mellow day, very gentle. The ash has lost its leaves and when I went out to get the mail and stopped to look up at it, I rejoiced to think that soon everything here will be honed down to structure. It is all a rich farewell now to leaves, to color. I think of the trees and how simply they let go, let fall the riches of a season, how without grief (it seems) they can let go and go deep into their roots for renewal and sleep. Eliot's statement comes back to me these days:

> Teach us to care and not to care
> Teach us to sit still.[2]

It is there in Mahler's *Der Abschied,* which I play again every autumn (Bruno Walter with Kathleen Ferrier).[3] But in Mahler it is a cry of loss, a long lyrical cry just *before* letting go, at least until those last long phrases that suggest peace, renunciation. But I think of it as the golden leaves and the brilliant small red maple that shone transparent against the shimmer of the lake yesterday when I went over to have a picnic with Helen Milbank.

Does anything in nature despair except man? An animal with a foot caught in a trap does not seem to despair. It is too busy trying to survive. It is all closed in, to a kind of still, intense waiting. Is this a key? Keep busy with survival. Imitate the trees. Learn to lose in order to recover, and remember that nothing stays the same for long, not even pain, psychic pain. Sit it out. Let it all pass. Let it go.

Yesterday I weeded out violets from the iris bed. The iris was being choked by thick bunches of roots, so much like fruit under the earth. I found one single very fragrant violet and some small autumn crocuses. Now, after an hour's work as the light failed and I drank in the damp smell of earth, it looks orderly again.

October 9th. Has it really happened at last? I feel released from the rack, set free, in touch with the deep source that is only *good,* where poetry lives. We have waited long this year for the glory, but suddenly the big maple is all gold and the beeches yellow with a touch of green that makes the yellow even more intense. There are still nasturtiums to be picked, and now I must get seriously to work to get the remaining bulbs in.

It has been stupidly difficult to let go, but that is what has been

2. From T. S. Eliot's *Ash Wednesday* (1930), lines 38–39.
3. A famous record of "The Farewell," by Gustav Mahler (1860–1911), evocative of the coming of winter and death. Mahler died before it could be performed, and the premiere was conducted by his disciple Bruno Walter. Kathleen Ferrier was to die within a few years of recording the song.

needed. I had allowed myself to get overanxious, clutching at what seemed sure to pass, and clutching is the surest way to murder love, as if it were a kitten, not to be squeezed so hard, or a flower to fade in a tight hand. Letting go, I have come back yesterday and today to a sense of my life here in all its riches, depth, freedom for soulmaking.

It's a real break-through. I have not written in sonnet form for a long time, but at every major crisis in my life when I reach a point of clarification, where pain is transcended by the quality of the experience itself, sonnets come. Whole lines run through my head and I cannot *stop* writing until whatever it is gets said.

Found three huge mushrooms when I went out before breakfast to fill the bird feeder. So far only jays come, but the word will get around.

October 11th. The joke is on me. I filled this weekend with friends 20
so that I would not go down into depression, not knowing that I should have turned the corner and be writing poems. It is the climactic moment of autumn, but already I feel like Sleeping Beauty as the carpet of leaves on the front lawn gets thicker and thicker. The avenue of beeches as I drive up the winding road along the brook is glorious beyond words, wall on wall of transparent gold. Laurie Armstrong came for roast beef Sunday dinner. Then I went out for two hours late in the afternoon and put in a hundred tulips. In itself that would not be a big job, but everywhere I have to clear space for them, weed, divide perennials, rescue iris that is being choked by violets. I really get to weeding only in spring and autumn, so I am working through a jungle now. Doing it I feel strenuously happy and at peace. At the end of the afternoon on a gray day, the light is sad and one feels the chill, but the bitter smell of earth is a tonic.

I can hardly believe that relief from the anguish of these past months is here to stay, but so far it does feel like a true change of mood—or rather, a change of *being* where I can stand alone. So much of my life here is precarious. I cannot always believe even in my work. But I have come in these last days to feel again the validity of my struggle here, that it is meaningful whether I ever "succeed" as a writer or not, and that even its failures, failures of nerve, failures due to a difficult temperament, can be meaningful. It is an age where more and more human beings are caught up in lives where fewer and fewer inward decisions can be made, where fewer and fewer real choices exist. The fact that a middle-aged, single woman, without any vestige of family left, lives in this house in a silent village and is responsible only to her own soul means something. The fact that she is a writer and can tell where she is and what it is like on the pilgrimage inward can be of comfort. It is comforting to know there are lighthouse keepers on rocky islands along the coast. Sometimes, when I have been for a walk after dark and see my house lighted up, looking so alive, I feel that my presence here is worth all the Hell.

I have time to think. That is the great, the greatest luxury. I have time to be. Therefore my responsibility is huge. To use time well and to be all that I can in whatever years are left to me. This does not dismay. The dismay comes when I lose the sense of my life as connected (as if by an aerial) to many, many other lives whom I do not even know and cannot ever know. The signals go out and come in all the time.

Why is it that poetry always seems to me so much more a true work of the soul than prose? I never feel elated after writing a page of prose, though I have written good things on concentrated will, and at least in a novel the imagination is fully engaged. Perhaps it is that prose is earned and poetry given. Both can be revised almost indefinitely. I do not mean to say that I do not work at poetry. When I am really inspired I can put a poem through a hundred drafts and keep my excitement. But this sustained battle is possible only when I am in a state of grace, when the deep channels are open, and when they are, when I am both profoundly stirred and balanced, then poetry comes as a gift from powers beyond my will.

I have often imagined that if I were in solitary confinement for an indefinite time and knew that no one would ever read what I wrote, I would still write poetry, but I would not write novels. Why? Perhaps because the poem is primarily a dialogue with the self and the novel a dialogue with others. They come from entirely different modes of being. I suppose I have written novels to find out what I *thought* about something and poems to find out what I *felt* about something.

January 7th. I have worked all morning—and it is now afternoon—to try to make by sheer art and craft an ending to the first stanza of a lyric that shot through my head intact. I should not feel so pressed for time, but I do, and I suppose I always shall. Yeats[4] speaks of spending a week on one stanza. The danger, of course, is overmanipulation, when one finds oneself manipulating *words*, not images or concepts. My problem was to make a transition viable between lovers in a snowstorm and the whiteness of a huge amaryllis I look at across the hall in the cosy room—seven huge flowers that make constant silent hosannas as I sit here.

In a period of happy and fruitful isolation such as this, any interruption, any intrusion of the social, any obligation breaks the thread on my loom, breaks the pattern. Two nights ago I was called at the last minute to attend the caucus of Town Meeting . . . and it threw me. But at least the companionship gave me one insight: a neighbor told

4. William Butler Yeats (1865–1939), Irish poet and dramatist.

me she had been in a small car accident and had managed to persuade the local paper to ignore her true age (as it appears on her license) and to print her age as thirty-nine! I was really astonished by this confidence. I am proud of being fifty-eight, and still alive and kicking, in love, more creative, balanced, and potent than I have ever been. I mind certain physical deteriorations, but not *really*. And not at all when I look at the marvelous photograph that Bill sent me of Isak Dinesen[5] just before she died. For after all we make our faces as we go along, and who when young could ever look as she does? The ineffable sweetness of the smile, the total acceptance and joy one receives from it, life, death, everything taken in and, as it were, savored—and let go.

Wrinkles here and there seem unimportant compared to *Gestalt* of the whole person I have become in this past year. Somewhere in *The Poet and the Donkey* Andy speaks for me when he says, "Do not deprive me of my age. I have earned it."

My neighbor's wish to be known forever as thirty-nine years old made me think again of what K said in her letter about the people in their thirties mourning their lost youth because we have given them no ethos that makes maturity appear an asset. Yet we have many examples before us. It looks as if T. S. Eliot came into a fully consummated happy marriage only when he was seventy. Yeats married when he was fifty or over. I am coming into the most fulfilled love of my life now. But for some reason Americans are terrified of the very idea of passionate love going on past middle age. Are they afraid of being alive? Do they want to be dead, i.e., *safe?* For of course one is never safe when in love. Growth is demanding and may seem dangerous, for there is loss as well as gain in growth. But why go on living if one has ceased to grow? And what more demanding atmosphere for growth than love in any form, than any relationship which can call out and requires of us our most secret and deepest selves?

My neighbor who wishes to remain thirty-nine indefinitely does so out of anxiety—she is afraid she will no longer be "attractive" if people know her age. But if one wants mature relationships, one will look for them among one's peers. I cannot imagine being in love with someone much younger than I because I have looked on love as an *éducation sentimentale.* About love I have little to learn from the young.

January 8th. Yesterday was a strange, hurried, uncentered day; yet I 30
did not have to go out, the sun shone. Today I feel centered and time is a friend instead of the old enemy. It was zero this morning. I have a fire burning in my study, yellow roses and mimosa on my desk. There

5. Modern Danish short-story writer who despite painful illness in her later years continued writing until her death at seventy-seven.

is an atmosphere of festival, of release, in the house. We are one, the house and I, and I am happy to be alone—time to think, time to be. This kind of open-ended time is the only luxury that really counts and I feel stupendously rich to have it. And for the moment I have a sense of fulfillment both about my life and about my work that I have rarely experienced until this year, or perhaps until these last weeks. I look to my left and the transparent blue sky behind a flame-colored cyclamen, lifting about thirty winged flowers to the light, makes an impression of stained glass, light-flooded. I have put the vast heap of unanswered letters into a box at my feet, so I don't see them. And now I am going to make one more try to get that poem right. The last line is still the problem.

Woody Allen: SELECTIONS FROM THE ALLEN NOTEBOOKS

Following are excerpts from the hitherto secret, private journal of Woody Allen, which will be published posthumously or after his death, whichever comes first.

Getting through the night is becoming harder and harder. Last evening, I had the uneasy feeling that some men were trying to break into my room to shampoo me. But why? I kept imagining I saw shadowy forms, and at 3 A.M. the underwear I had draped over a chair resembled the Kaiser on roller skates. When I finally did fall asleep, I had that same hideous nightmare in which a woodchuck is trying to claim my prize at a raffle. Despair.

I believe my consumption has grown worse. Also my asthma. The wheezing comes and goes, and I get dizzy more and more frequently. I have taken to violent choking and fainting. My room is damp and I have perpetual chills and palpitations of the heart. I noticed, too, that I am out of napkins. Will it never stop?

Idea for a story: A man awakens to find his parrot has been made Secretary of Agriculture. He is consumed with jealousy and shoots himself, but unfortunately the gun is the type with a little flag that pops out, with the word "Bang" on it. The flag pokes his eye out, and

From *Without Feathers* (1972).

he lives—a chastened human being who, for the first time, enjoys the simple pleasures of life, like farming or sitting on an air hose.

Thought: Why does man kill? He kills for food. And not only food: frequently there must be a beverage.

Should I marry W.? Not if she won't tell me the other letters in her name. And what about her career? How can I ask a woman of her beauty to give up the Roller Derby? Decisions . . .

Once again I tried committing suicide—this time by wetting my nose and inserting it into the light socket. Unfortunately, there was a short in the wiring, and I merely caromed off the icebox. Still obsessed by thoughts of death, I brood constantly. I keep wondering if there is an afterlife, and if there is will they be able to break a twenty?

I ran into my brother today at a funeral. We had not seen one another for fifteen years, but as usual he produced a pig bladder from his pocket and began hitting me on the head with it. Time has helped me understand him better. I finally realize his remark that I am "some loathsome vermin fit only for extermination" was said more out of compassion than anger. Let's face it: he was always much brighter than me—wittier, more cultured, better educated. Why he is still working at McDonald's is a mystery.

Idea for story: Some beavers take over Carnegie Hall and perform *Wozzeck.*[1] (Strong theme. What will be the structure?)

Good Lord, why am I so guilty? Is it because I hated my father? Probably it was the veal-parmigian' incident. Well, what *was* it doing in his wallet? If I had listened to him, I would be blocking hats for a living. I can hear him now: "To block hats—that is everything." I remember his reaction when I told him I wanted to write. "The only writing you'll do is in collaboration with an owl." I still have no idea what he meant. What a sad man! When my first play, *A Cyst for Gus,* was produced at the Lyceum, he attended opening night in tails and a gas mask.

Today I saw a red-and-yellow sunset and thought, How insignificant I am! Of course, I thought that yesterday, too, and it rained. I was

1. A lurid and dissonant opera by the modern composer Alban Berg (1885–1935). Carnegie Hall is a famous concert hall in New York City.

overcome with self-loathing and contemplated suicide again—this time by inhaling next to an insurance salesman.

Short story: A man awakens in the morning and finds himself transformed into his own arch supports (This idea can work on many levels. Psychologically, it is the quintessence of Kruger, Freud's disciple who discovered sexuality in bacon.)

How wrong Emily Dickinson was! Hope is not "the thing with feathers." The thing with feathers has turned out to be my nephew. I must take him to a specialist in Zurich.

I have decided to break off my engagement with W. She doesn't understand my writing, and said last night that my *Critique of Metaphysical Reality* reminded her of *Airport*. We quarreled, and she brought up the subject of children again, but I convinced her they would be too young.

Do I believe in God? I did until Mother's accident. She fell on some meat loaf, and it penetrated her spleen. She lay in a coma for months, unable to do anything but sing "Granada" to an imaginary herring. Why was this woman in the prime of life so afflicted—because in her youth she dared to defy convention and got married with a brown paper bag on her head? And how can I believe in God when just last week I got my tongue caught in the roller of an electric typewriter? I am plagued by doubts. What if everything is an illusion and nothing exists? In that case, I definitely overpaid for my carpet. If only God would give me some clear sign! Like making a large deposit in my name at a Swiss bank.

Had coffee with Melnick today. He talked to me about his idea of having all government officials dress like hens.

Play idea: A character based on my father, but without quite so prominent a big toe. He is sent to the Sorbonne[2] to study the harmonica. In the end, he dies, never realizing his one dream—to sit up to his waist in gravy. (I see a brilliant second-act curtain, where two midgets come upon a severed head in a shipment of volleyballs.)

While taking my noon walk today, I had more morbid thoughts. What *is* it about death that bothers me so much? Probably the hours.

2. The University of Paris.

Melnick says the soul is immortal and lives on after the body drops away, but if my soul exists without my body I am convinced all my clothes will be too loose-fitting. Oh, well . . .

Did not have to break off with W. after all, for as luck would have it, she ran off to Finland with a professional circus geek. All for the best, I suppose, although I had another of those attacks where I start coughing out of my ears.

Last night, I burned all my plays and poetry. Ironically as I was burning my masterpiece, *Dark Penguin,* the room caught fire, and I am now the object of a lawsuit by some men named Pinchunk and Schlosser. Kierkegaard was right.

People, Places

Thomas Jefferson

GEORGE WASHINGTON

I think I knew General Washington intimately and thoroughly; and were I called on to delineate his character, it should be in terms like these.

His mind was great and powerful, without being of the very first order; his penetration strong, though not so acute as that of a Newton, Bacon, or Locke; and as far as he saw, no judgment was ever sounder. It was slow in operation, being little aided by invention or imagination, but sure in conclusion. Hence the common remark of his officers, of the advantage he derived from councils of war, where hearing all suggestions, he selected whatever was best; and certainly no general ever planned his battles more judiciously. But if deranged during the course of the action, if any member of his plan was dislocated by sudden circumstances, he was slow in re-adjustment. The consequence was, that he often failed in the field, and rarely against an enemy in station, as at Boston and York. He was incapable of fear, meeting personal dangers with the calmest unconcern. Perhaps the strongest feature in his character was prudence, never acting until every circumstance, every consideration, was maturely weighed; refraining if he saw a doubt, but, when once decided, going through with his purpose, whatever obstacles opposed. His integrity was most pure, his justice the most inflexible I have ever known, no motives of interest or consanguinity, of friendship or hatred, being able to bias his decision. He was, indeed, in every sense of the words, a wise, a good, and a great man. His temper was naturally irritable and high toned; but reflection and resolution had obtained a firm and habitual ascendency over it. If ever, however, it broke its bonds, he was most tremendous in his wrath. In his expenses he was honorable, but exact; liberal in contribu-

From a letter written in 1814 to a Doctor Jones, who was writing a history and wanted to know about Washington's role in the Federalist-Republican controversy.

tions to whatever promised utility; but frowning and unyielding on all visionary projects, and all unworthy calls on his charity. His heart was not warm in its affections; but he exactly calculated every man's value, and gave him a solid esteem proportioned to it. His person, you know, was fine, his stature exactly what one would wish, his deportment easy, erect and noble; the best horseman of his age, and the most graceful figure that could be seen on horseback. Although in the circle of his friends, where he might be unreserved with safety, he took a free share in conversation, his colloquial talents were not above mediocrity, possessing neither copiousness of ideas, nor fluency of words. In public, when called on for a sudden opinion, he was unready, short and embarrassed. Yet he wrote readily, rather diffusely, in an easy and correct style. This he had acquired by conversation with the world, for his education was merely reading, writing and common arithmetic, to which he added surveying at a later day. His time was employed in action chiefly, reading little, and that only in agriculture and English history. His correspondence became necessarily extensive, and, with journalizing his agricultural proceedings, occupied most of his leisure hours within doors. On the whole, his character was, in its mass, perfect, in nothing bad, in few points indifferent; and it may truly be said, that never did nature and fortune combine more perfectly to make a man great, and to place him in the same constellation with whatever worthies have merited from man an everlasting remembrance. For his was the singular destiny and merit, of leading the armies of his country successfully through an arduous war, for the establishment of its independence; of conducting its councils through the birth of a government, new in its forms and principles, until it had settled down into a quiet and orderly train; and of scrupulously obeying the laws through the whole of his career, civil and military, of which the history of the world furnishes no other example.

* * * I am satisfied, the great body of republicans think of him as I do. We were, indeed, dissatisfied with him on his ratification of the British treaty. But this was short lived. We knew his honesty, the wiles with which he was encompassed, and that age had already begun to relax the firmness of his purposes; and I am convinced he is more deeply seated in the love and gratitude of the republicans, than in the Pharisaical homage of the federal monarchists.[1] For he was no monarchist from preference of his judgment. The soundness of that gave him correct views of the rights of man, and his severe justice devoted him to them. He has often declared to me that he considered our new Constitution as an experiment on the practicability of republican gov-

1. Jefferson here compares those who sought to make the new United States a kingdom, with Washington as king, to the biblical Pharisees, the haughty sect of ancient Israel.

ernment, and with what dose of liberty man could be trusted for his own good; that he was determined the experiment should have a fair trial, and would lose the last drop of his blood in support of it. And these declarations he repeated to me the oftener and more pointedly, because he knew my suspicions of Colonel Hamilton's views,[2] and probably had heard from him the same declarations which I had, to wit, "that the British constitution, with its unequal representation, corruption and other existing abuses, was the most perfect government which had ever been established on earth, and that a reformation of those abuses would make it an impracticable government." I do believe that General Washington had not a firm confidence in the durability of our government. He was naturally distrustful of men, and inclined to gloomy apprehensions; and I was ever persuaded that a belief that we must at length end in something like a British constitution, had some weight in his adoption of the ceremonies of levees,[3] birthdays, pompous meetings with Congress, and other forms of the same character, calculated to prepare us gradually for a change which he believed possible, and to let it come on with as little shock as might be to the public mind.

These are my opinions of General Washington which I would vouch at the judgment seat of God, having been formed on an acquaintance of thirty years. I served with him in the Virginia legislature from 1769 to the Revolutionary war, and again, a short time in Congress, until he left us to take command of the army. During the war and after it we corresponded occasionally, and in the four years of my continuance in the office of Secretary of State, our intercourse was daily, confidential and cordial. After I retired from that office, great and malignant pains were taken by our federal monarchists, and not entirely without effect, to make him view me as a theorist, holding French principles of government,[4] which would lead infallibly to licentiousness and anarchy. And to this he listened the more easily, from my known disapprobation of the British treaty. I never saw him afterwards, or these malignant insinuations should have been dissipated before his just judgment, as mists before the sun. I felt on his death, with my countrymen, that "verily a great man hath fallen this day in Israel."

2. Alexander Hamilton (1755–1804) advocated a strong central federal government, led by the "wealthy, good, and wise." His views were opposed by the relatively more democratic views of Jefferson.
3. Morning receptions held by a head of state to enable him to attend to public affairs while rising and dressing. The form was characteristic of European monarchs.
4. Radical political views advanced by extreme democrats in the course of the French Revolution.

QUESTIONS

1. *What, in Jefferson's view, are Washington's outstanding virtues? What are Washington's greatest defects? From what he writes about Washington, can you infer those qualities of character that Jefferson most admires?*
2. *Do we learn anything from Jefferson's portrait about what Washington looked like? About his family life? About his hobbies? About his religion? If not, are these important omissions in the characterization of a person in public life?*
3. *Write in the manner of Jefferson a characterization of an important figure in public life today. Consider whether this manner enables you to present what you think is essential truth, and whether the attempt brings to light any special problems concerning either the task itself or public life today.*

Nathaniel Hawthorne

ABRAHAM LINCOLN

Of course, there was one other personage, in the class of statesmen, whom I should have been truly mortified to leave Washington without seeing; since (temporarily, at least, and by force of circumstances) he was the man of men. But a private grief had built up a barrier about him, impeding the customary free intercourse of Americans with their chief magistrate; so that I might have come away without a glimpse of his very remarkable physiognomy, save for a semi-official opportunity of which I was glad to take advantage. The fact is, we were invited to annex ourselves, as supernumeraries, to a deputation that was about to wait upon the President, from a Massachusetts whip factory, with a present of a splendid whip.

Our immediate party consisted only of four or five (including Major Ben Perley Poore,[1] with his note-book and pencil), but we were joined by several other persons, who seemed to have been lounging about the precincts of the White House, under the spacious porch, or within the hall, and who swarmed in with us to take the chances of a presentation. Nine o'clock had been appointed as the time for receiving the

One of a series of sketches published in the *Atlantic Monthly*, "Abraham Lincoln" appeared in 1862.

1. American journalist and biographer.

deputation, and we were punctual to the moment; but not so the President, who sent us word that he was eating his breakfast, and would come as soon as he could. His appetite, we were glad to think, must have been a pretty fair one; for we waited about half an hour in one of the antechambers, and then were ushered into a reception-room, in one corner of which sat the Secretaries of War and of the Treasury, expecting, like ourselves, the termination of the Presidential breakfast. During this interval there were several new additions to our group, one or two of whom were in a working-garb, so that we formed a very miscellaneous collection of people, mostly unknown to each other, and without any common sponsor, but all with an equal right to look our head servant in the face.

By and by there was a little stir on the staircase and in the passage-way, and in lounged a tall, loose-jointed figure, of an exaggerated Yankee port and demeanor, whom (as being about the homeliest man I ever saw, yet by no means repulsive or disagreeable) it was impossible not to recognize as Uncle Abe.

Unquestionably, Western man though he be, and Kentuckian by birth, President Lincoln is the essential representative of all Yankees, and the veritable specimen, physically, of what the world seems determined to regard as our characteristic qualities. It is the strangest and yet the fittest thing in the jumble of human vicissitudes, that he, out of so many millions, unlooked for, unselected by any intelligible process that could be based upon his genuine qualities, unknown to those who chose him, and unsuspected of what endowments may adapt him for his tremendous responsibility, should have found the way open for him to fling his lank personality into the chair of state—where, I presume, it was his first impulse to throw his legs on the council-table, and tell the Cabinet Ministers a story. There is no describing his lengthy awkwardness, nor the uncouthness of his movement; and yet it seemed as if I had been in the habit of seeing him daily, and had shaken hands with him a thousand times in some village street; so true was he to the aspect of the pattern American, though with a certain extravagance which, possibly, I exaggerated still further by the delighted eagerness with which I took it in. If put to guess his calling and livelihood, I should have taken him for a country school-master as soon as anything else. He was dressed in a rusty black frock coat and pantaloons, unbrushed, and worn so faithfully that the suit had adapted itself to the curves and angularities of his figure, and had grown to be an outer skin of the man. His hair was black, still unmixed with gray, stiff, somewhat bushy, and had apparently been acquainted with neither brush nor comb that morning, after the disarrangement of the pillow; and as to a nightcap, Uncle Abe probably knows nothing of such effeminacies. His complexion is dark and sallow, betokening, I fear, a insalubrious atmosphere around the White House; he has thick black eyebrows and an impending brow; his nose is large, and the lines about his mouth are very strongly defined.

The whole physiognomy is as coarse a one as you would meet anywhere in the length and breadth of the States; but, withal, it is redeemed, illuminated, softened, and brightened by a kindly though serious look out of his eyes, and an expression of homely sagacity, that seems weighted with rich results of village experience. A great deal of native sense; no bookish cultivation, no refinement; honest at heart, and thoroughly so, and yet, in some sort, sly—at least, endowed with a sort of tact and wisdom that are akin to craft, and would impel him, I think, to take an antagonist in flank, rather than to make a bull-run at him right in front. But, on the whole, I like this sallow, queer, sagacious visage, with the homely human sympathies that warmed it; and, for my small share in the matter, would as lief have Uncle Abe for a ruler as any man whom it would have been practicable to put in his place.

Immediately on his entrance the President accosted our member of Congress, who had us in charge, and, with a comical twist of his face, made some jocular remark about the length of his breakfast. He then greeted us all round, not waiting for an introduction, but shaking and squeezing everybody's hand with the utmost cordiality, whether the individual's name was announced to him or not. His manner towards us was wholly without pretence, but yet had a kind of natural dignity, quite sufficient to keep the forwardest of us from clapping him on the shoulder and asking him for a story. A mutual acquaintance being established, our leader took the whip out of its case, and began to read the address of presentation. The whip was an exceedingly long one, its handle wrought in ivory (by some artist in the Massachusetts State Prison, I believe), and ornamented with a medallion of the President, and other equally beautiful devices; and along its whole length there was a succession of golden bands and ferrules. The address was shorter than the whip, but equally well made, consisting chiefly of an explanatory description of these artistic designs, and closing with a hint that the gift was a suggestive and emblematic one, and that the President would recognize the use to which such an instrument should be put.

This suggestion gave Uncle Abe rather a delicate task in his reply, because, slight as the matter seemed, it apparently called for some declaration, or intimation, or faint foreshadowing of policy in reference to the conduct of the war, and the final treatment of the Rebels. But the President's Yankee aptness and not-to-be-caughtness stood him in good stead, and he jerked or wiggled himself out of the dilemma with an uncouth dexterity that was entirely in character; although, without his gesticulation of eye and mouth—and especially the flourish of the whip, with which he imagined himself touching up a pair of fat horses—I doubt whether his words would be worth recording, even if I could remember them. The gist of the reply was, that he accepted the whip as an emblem of peace, not punishment; and, this great affair over, we retired out of the presence in high good humor, only regretting that we could not have seen the President sit down and fold up his legs (which is said to be a most extraordinary spectacle), or have heard him tell one of those delectable stories for which he is so celebrated. A good many of them are afloat upon the common talk of Washington, and are certainly the aptest, pithiest, and funniest little things imaginable; though, to be sure, they smack of the frontier freedom, and would not always bear repetition in a drawing-room, or on the immaculate page of the *Atlantic*.[2]

Good Heavens! what liberties have I been taking with one of the potentates of the earth, and the man on whose conduct more important consequences depend than on that of any other historical personage of the century! But with whom is an American citizen entitled to take a liberty, if not with his own chief magistrate? However, lest the above allusions to President Lincoln's little peculiarities (already well known to the country and to the world) should be misinterpreted, I deem it proper to say a word or two in regard to him, of unfeigned respect and measurable confidence. He is evidently a man of keen faculties, and, what is still more to the purpose, of powerful character. As to his integrity, the people have that intuition of it which is never deceived. Before he actually entered upon his great office, and for a considerable time afterwards, there is no reason to suppose that he adequately estimated the gigantic task about to be imposed on him, or, at least, had any distinct idea how it was to be managed; and I presume there may have been more than one veteran politician who proposed to himself to take the power out of President Lincoln's hands into his own, leaving our honest friend only the public responsibility for the good or ill success of the career. The extremely imperfect development of his statesmanly qualities, at that period, may have justified such designs. But the President is teachable by events, and has

2. This passage was one of those omitted from the article as originally published, and the following note was appended to explain the omission, which had been indicated by a line of points:

"We are compelled to omit two or three pages, in which the author describes the interview, and gives his idea of the personal appearance and deportment of the President. The sketch appears to have been written in a benign spirit, and perhaps conveys a not inaccurate impression of its august subject; but it lacks *reverence*, and it pains us to see a gentleman of ripe age, and who has spent years under the corrective influence of foreign institutions, falling into the characteristic and most ominous fault of Young America."

now spent a year in a very arduous course of education; he has a flexible mind, capable of much expansion, and convertible towards far loftier studies and activities than those of his early life; and if he came to Washington a backwoods humorist, he has already transformed himself into as good a statesman (to speak moderately) as his prime minister.[3]

3. Presumably the secretary of state, William H. Seward.

QUESTIONS

1. *In his final paragraph, Hawthorne seeks to prevent misunderstanding by stressing his respect for and confidence in Lincoln. Is there anything in the paragraph that runs counter to that expression? To what effect?*
2. *In the footnote to the seventh paragraph, the editor of the* Atlantic Monthly *explains his omission of the first seven paragraphs. On the evidence of this statement, what sort of person does the editor seem to be? Is there anything in the omitted paragraphs that would tend to justify his decision as editor? Is the full description superior to the last paragraph printed alone? Explain.*
3. *What is the basic pattern of the opening sentence of the fifth paragraph? Find other examples of this pattern. What is their total impact on Hawthorne's description?*
4. *Write a paragraph of description of someone you know, using the same pattern for the entire paragraph that you discovered in the previous question.*

Tom Wolfe

YEAGER

Anyone who travels very much on airlines in the United States soon gets to know the voice of *the airline pilot* . . . coming over the intercom . . . with a particular drawl, a particular folksiness, a particular down-home calmness that is so exaggerated it begins to parody itself (nevertheless!—it's reassuring) . . . the voice that tells you, as the airliner is caught in thunderheads and goes bolting up and down a thousand feet at a single gulp, to check your seat belts because "it might get a little choppy" . . . the voice that tells you (on a flight from Phoenix preparing for its final approach into Kennedy Airport, New York, just after dawn): "Now, folks, uh . . . this is the captain . . . ummmm . . . We've

From *The Right Stuff* (1979).

got a little ol' red light up here on the control panel that's tryin' to tell us that the *lan*din' gears're not . . . uh . . . *lock*in' into position when we lower 'em . . . Now . . . *I* don't believe that little ol' red light knows what it's *talk*in' about—I believe it's that little ol' red light that iddn' workin' right" . . . faint chuckle, long pause, as if to say, *I'm not even sure all this is really worth going into—still, it may amuse you* . . . "*But* . . . I guess to play it by the rules, we oughta *humor* that little ol' light . . . so we're gonna take her down to about, oh, two or three hundred feet over the runway at Kennedy, and the folks down there on the ground are gonna see if they caint give us a *vis*ual inspection of those ol' landin' gears"—with which he is obviously on intimate ol'-buddy terms, as with every other working part of this mighty ship—"and if I'm right . . . they're gonna tell us everything is copa*cet*ic all the way aroun' an' we'll jes take her on in" . . . and, after a couple of low passes over the field, the voice returns: "Well, folks, those folks down there on the ground—it must be too early for 'em or somethin'—I 'spect they still got the *sleep*ers in their eyes . . . 'cause they say they caint tell if those ol' landin' gears are all the way down or not . . . But, you know, up here in the cockpit we're convinced they're all the way down, so we're jes gonna take her on in . . . And oh" . . . *(I almost forgot)* . . . "while we take a little swing out over the ocean an' empty some of that surplus fuel we're not gonna be needin' anymore—that's what you might be seein' comin' out of the wings—our lovely little ladies . . . if they'll be so kind . . . they're gonna go up and down the aisles and show you how we do what we call 'assumin' the position' " . . . another faint chuckle *(We do this so often, and it's so much fun, we even have a funny little name for it)* . . . and the stewardesses, a bit grimmer, by the looks of them, than *that voice,* start telling the passengers to take their glasses off and take the ballpoint pens and other sharp objects out of their pockets, and they show them *the position,* with the head lowered . . . while down on the field at Kennedy the little yellow emergency trucks start roaring across the field—and even though in your pounding heart and your sweating palms and your broiling brainpan you *know* this is a critical moment in your life, you still can't quite bring yourself to be*lieve* it, because if it were . . . how could *the captain,* the man who knows the actual situation most intimately . . . how could he keep on drawlin' and chucklin' and driftin' and lollygaggin' in that particular voice of his—

Well!—who doesn't know that voice! And who can forget it!—even after he is proved right and the emergency is over.

That particular voice may sound vaguely Southern or Southwestern, but it is specifically Appalachian in origin. It originated in the mountains of West Virginia, in the coal country, in Lincoln County, so far up in the hollows that, as the saying went, "they had to pipe in daylight." In the late 1940's and early 1950's this up-hollow voice drifted down from on high, from over the high desert of California, down, down, down, from the upper reaches of the Brotherhood into all phases of American aviation. It was amazing. It was *Pygmalion*[1] in reverse. Military pilots and then, soon, airline pilots, pilots from Maine and Massachusetts and the Dakotas and Oregon and everywhere else, began to talk in that poker-hollow West Virginia drawl, or as close to it as they could bend their native accents. It was the drawl of the most righteous of all the possessors of the right stuff: Chuck Yeager.

Yeager had started out as the equivalent, in the Second World War, of the legendary Frank Luke of the 27th Aero Squadron in the First. Which is to say, he was the boondocker, the boy from the back country, with only a high-school education, no credentials, no cachet or polish of any sort, who took off the feed-store overalls and put on a uniform and climbed into an airplane and lit up the skies over Europe.

Yeager grew up in Hamlin, West Virginia, a town on the Mud River 5
not far from Nitro, Hurricane Whirlwind, Salt Rock, Mud, Sod, Crum, Leet, Dollie, Ruth, and Alum Creek. His father was a gas driller (drilling for natural gas in the coalfields), his older brother was a gas driller, and he would have been a gas driller had he not enlisted in the Army Air Force in 1941 at the age of eighteen. In 1943, at twenty, he became a flight officer, i.e., a non-com who was allowed to fly, and went to England to fly fighter planes over France and Germany. Even in the tumult of the war Yeager was somewhat puzzling to a lot of other pilots. He was a short, wiry, but muscular little guy with dark curly hair and a tough-looking face that seemed (to strangers) to be saying: "You best not be lookin' me in the eye, you peckerwood, or I'll put four more holes in your nose." But that wasn't what was puzzling. What was puzzling was the way Yeager talked. He seemed to talk with some older forms of English elocution, syntax, and conjugation that had been preserved uphollow in the Appalachians. There were people up there who never said they disapproved of anything, they said: "I don't hold with it." In the present tense they were willing to *help* out, like anyone else; but in the past tense they only *holped*. "H'it weren't nothin' I hold with, but I holped him out with it, anyways."

In his first eight missions, at the age of twenty, Yeager shot down two German fighters. On his ninth he was shot down over German-occupied French territory, suffering flak wounds; he bailed out, was picked up by the French underground, which smuggled him across the Pyrenees into Spain disguised as a peasant. In Spain he was jailed

1. An allusion to the play by George Bernard Shaw (1856–1950), in which a teacher of phonetics attempts to transform a Cockney flower girl into an elegant lady by means of transforming her speech.

briefly, then released, whereupon he made it back to England and returned to combat during the Allied invasion of France. On October 12, 1944, Yeager took on and shot down five German fighter planes in succession. On November 6, flying a propeller-driven P-51 Mustang, he shot down one of the new jet fighters the Germans had developed, the Messerschmitt-262, and damaged two more, and on November 20 he shot down four FW-190s. It was a true Frank Luke-style display of warrior fury and personal prowess. By the end of the war he had thirteen and a half kills. He was twenty-two years old.

In 1946 and 1947 Yeager was trained as a test pilot at Wright Field in Dayton. He amazed his instructors with his ability at stunt-team flying, not to mention the unofficial business of hassling. That plus his up-hollow drawl had everybody saying, "He's a natural-born stick 'n' rudder man." Nevertheless, there was something extraordinary about it when a man so young, with so little experience in flight test, was selected to go to Muroc Field in California for the XS-1 project.

Muroc was up in the high elevations of the Mojave Desert. It looked like some fossil landscape that had long since been left behind by the rest of terrestrial evolution. It was full of huge dry lake beds, the biggest being Rogers Lake. Other than sagebrush the only vegetation was Joshua trees, twisted freaks of the plant world that looked like a cross between cactus and Japanese bonsai. They had a dark petrified green color and horribly crippled branches. At dusk the Joshua trees stood out in silhouette on the fossil wasteland like some arthritic nightmare. In the summer the temperature went up to 110 degrees as a matter of course, and the dry lake beds were covered in sand, and there would be windstorms and sandstorms right out of a Foreign Legion movie. At night it would drop to near freezing, and in December it would start raining, and the dry lakes would fill up with a few inches of water, and some sort of putrid prehistoric shrimps would work their way up from out of the ooze, and sea gulls would come flying in a hundred miles or more from the ocean, over the mountains, to gobble up these squirming little throwbacks. A person had to see it to believe it: flocks of sea gulls wheeling around in the air out in the middle of the high desert in the dead of winter and grazing on antediluvian crustaceans in the primordial ooze.

When the wind blew the few inches of water back and forth across the lake beds, they became absolutely smooth and level. And when the water evaporated in the spring, and the sun baked the ground hard, the lake beds became the greatest natural landing fields ever discovered, and also the biggest, with miles of room for error. That was highly desirable, given the nature of the enterprise at Muroc.

10 Besides the wind, sand, tumbleweed, and Joshua trees, there was nothing at Muroc except for two quonset-style hangars, side by side, a

couple of gasoline pumps, a single concrete runway, a few tarpaper shacks, and some tents. The officers stayed in the shacks marked "barracks," and lesser souls stayed in the tents and froze all night and fried all day. Every road into the property had a guardhouse on it manned by soldiers. The enterprise the Army had undertaken in this godforsaken place was the development of supersonic jet and rocket planes.

At the end of the war the Army had discovered that the Germans not only had the world's first jet fighter but also a rocket plane that had gone 596 miles an hour in tests. Just after the war a British jet, the Gloster Meteor, jumped the official world speed record from 469 to 606 in a single day. The next great plateau would be Mach 1, the speed of sound, and the Army Air Force considered it crucial to achieve it first.

The speed of sound, Mach 1, was known (thanks to the work of the physicist Ernst Mach) to vary at different altitudes, temperatures, and wind speeds. On a calm 60-degree day at sea level it was about 760 miles an hour, while at 40,000 feet, where the temperature would be at least sixty below, it was about 660 miles an hour. Evil and baffling things happened in the transonic zone, which began at about .7 Mach. Wind tunnels choked out at such velocities. Pilots who approached the speed of sound in dives reported that the controls would lock or "freeze" or even alter their normal functions. Pilots had crashed and died because they couldn't budge the stick. Just last year Geoffrey de Havilland, son of the famous British aircraft designer and builder, had tried to take one of his father's DH 108s to Mach 1. The ship started buffeting and then disintegrated, and he was killed. This led engineers to speculate that the shock waves became so severe and unpredictable at Mach 1, no aircraft could survive them. They started talking about "the sonic wall" and "the sound barrier."

So this was the task that a handful of pilots, engineers, and mechanics had at Muroc. The place was utterly primitive, nothing but bare bones, bleached tarpaulins, and corrugated tin rippling in the heat with caloric waves; and for an ambitious young pilot it was perfect. Muroc seemed like an outpost on the dome of the world, open only to a righteous few, closed off to the rest of humanity, including even the Army Air Force brass of command control, which was at Wright Field. The commanding officer at Muroc was only a colonel, and his superiors at Wright did not relish junkets to the Muroc rat shacks in the first place. But to pilots this prehistoric throwback of an airfield became . . . shrimp heaven! the rat-shack plains of Olympus!

Low Rent Septic Tank Perfection . . . yes; and not excluding those traditional essentials for the blissful hot young pilot: Flying & Drinking and Drinking & Driving.

Just beyond the base, to the southwest, there was a rickety wind-blown 1930's-style establishment called Pancho's Fly Inn, owned, run, and bartended by a woman named Pancho Barnes. Pancho Barnes wore tight white sweaters and tight pants, after the mode of Barbara Stanwyck in *Double Indemnity*. She was only forty-one when Yeager arrived at Muroc, but her face was so weatherbeaten, had so many hard miles on it, that she looked older, especially to the young pilots at the base. She also shocked the pants off them with her vulcanized tongue. Everybody she didn't like was an old bastard or a sonofabitch. People she liked were old bastards and sonsabitches, too. "I tol' 'at ol' bastard to get 'is ass on over here and I'd g'im a drink." But Pancho Barnes was anything but Low Rent. She was the granddaughter of the man who designed the old Mount Lowe cable-car system, Thaddeus S. C. Lowe. Her maiden name was Florence Leontine Lowe. She was brought up in San Marino, which adjoined Pasadena and was one of Los Angeles' wealthiest suburbs, and her first husband—she was married four times—was the pastor of the Pasadena Episcopal Church, the Rev. C. Rankin Barnes. Mrs. Barnes seemed to have few of the conventional community interests of a Pasadena matron. In the late 1920's, by boat and plane, she ran guns for Mexican revolutionaries and picked up the nickname Pancho. In 1930 she broke Amelia Earhart's[2] air-speed record for women. Then she barnstormed around the country as the featured performer of "Pancho Barnes's Mystery Circus of the Air." She always greeted her public in jodhpurs and riding boots, a flight jacket, a white scarf, and a white sweater that showed off her terrific Barbara Stanwyck chest. Pancho's desert Fly Inn had an airstrip, a swimming pool, a dude ranch corral, plenty of acreage for horseback riding, a big old guest house for the lodgers, and a connecting building that was the bar and restaurant. In the barroom the floors, the tables, the chairs, the walls, the beams, the bar were of the sort known as extremely weatherbeaten, and the screen doors kept banging. Nobody putting together such a place for a movie about flying in the old days would ever dare make it as dilapidated and generally go-to-hell as it actually was. Behind the bar were many pictures of airplanes and pilots, lavishly autographed and inscribed, badly framed and crookedly hung. There was an old piano that had been dried out and cracked to the point of hopeless desiccation. On a good night a huddle of drunken aviators could be heard trying to bang, slosh, and navigate their way through old Cole Porter[3] tunes. On average nights the tunes were not that good to start with. When the screen door banged and a man walked through the door into the saloon, every eye

2. Pioneering aviator (1897–1937) who disappeared while attempting a world flight in 1937.
3. American composer of popular music (1891–1964), including Broadway show tunes.

in the place checked him out. If he wasn't known as somebody who had something to do with flying at Muroc, he would be eyed like some lame goddamned mouseshit sheepherder from *Shane.*

The plane the Air Force wanted to break the sound barrier with was 15
called the X-1 at the outset and later on simply the X-1. The Bell Aircraft Corporation had built it under an Army contract. The core of the ship was a rocket of the type first developed by a young Navy inventor, Robert Truax, during the war. The fuselage was shaped like a 50-caliber bullet—an object that was known to go supersonic smoothly. Military pilots seldom drew major test assignments; they went to highly paid civilians working for the aircraft corporations. The prime pilot for the X-1 was a man whom Bell regarded as the best of the breed. This man looked like a movie star. He looked like a pilot from out of *Hell's Angels.*[4] And on top of everything else there was his name: Slick Goodlin.

The idea in testing the X-1 was to nurse it carefully into the transonic zone, up to seven-tenths, eight-tenths, nine-tenths the speed of sound (.7 Mach, .8 Mach, .9 Mach) before attempting the speed of sound itself, Mach 1, even though Bell and the Army already knew the X-1 had the rocket power to go to Mach 1 and beyond, if there *was* any *beyond.* The consensus of aviators and engineers, after Geoffrey de Havilland's death, was that the speed of sound was an absolute, like the firmness of the earth. The sound barrier was a farm you could buy in the sky. So Slick Goodlin began to probe the transonic zone in the X-1, going up to .8 Mach. Every time he came down he'd have a riveting tale to tell. The buffeting, it was so fierce—and the listeners, their imaginations aflame, could practically see poor Geoffrey de Havilland disintegrating in midair. And the goddamned aerodynamics—and the listeners got a picture of a man in ballroom pumps skidding across a sheet of ice, pursued by bears. A controversy arose over just how much bonus Slick Goodlin should receive for assaulting the dread Mach 1 itself. Bonuses for contract test pilots were not unusual; but the figure of $150,000 was now bruited about. The Army balked, and Yeager got the job. He took it for $283 a month, or $3,396 a year; which is to say, his regular Army captain's pay.

The only trouble they had with Yeager was in holding him back. On his first powered flight in the X-1 he immediately executed an unauthorized zero-g roll with a full load of rocket fuel, then stood the ship on its tail and went up to .85 Mach in a vertical climb, also unauthorized. On subsequent flights, at speeds between .85 Mach and .9 Mach, Yeager ran into most known airfoil problems—loss of elevator, aileron, and rudder control, heavy trim pressures, Dutch rolls, pitching

4. A notorious group of motorcyclists.

and buffeting, the lot—yet was convinced, after edging over .9 Mach, that this would all get better, not worse, as you reached Mach 1. The attempt to push beyond Mach 1—"breaking the sound barrier"—was set for October 14, 1947. Not being an engineer, Yeager didn't believe the "barrier" existed.

October 14 was a Tuesday. On Sunday evening, October 12, Chuck Yeager dropped in at Pancho's, along with his wife. She was a brunette named Glennis, whom he had met in California while he was in training, and she was such a number, so striking, he had the inscription "Glamorous Glennis" written on the nose of his P-51 in Europe and, just a few weeks back, on the X-1 itself. Yeager didn't go to Pancho's and knock back a few because two days later the big test was coming up. Nor did he knock back a few because it was the weekend. No, he knocked back a few because night had come and he was a pilot at Muroc. In keeping with the military tradition of Flying & Drinking, that was what you did, for no other reason than that the sun had gone down. You went to Pancho's and knocked back a few and listened to the screen doors banging and to other aviators torturing the piano and the nation's repertoire of Familiar Favorites and to lonesome mouse-turd strangers wandering in through the banging doors and to Pancho classifying the whole bunch of them as old bastards and miserable peckerwoods. That was what you did if you were a pilot at Muroc and the sun went down.

So about eleven Yeager got the idea that it would be a hell of a kick if he and Glennis saddled up a couple of Pancho's dude-ranch horses and went for a romp, a little rat race, in the moonlight. This was in keeping with the military tradition of Flying & Drinking and Drinking & Driving, except that this was prehistoric Muroc and you rode horses. So Yeager and his wife set off on a little proficiency run at full gallop through the desert in the moonlight amid the arthritic silhouettes of the Joshua trees. Then they start racing back to the corral, with Yeager in the lead and heading for the gateway. Given the prevailing conditions, it being nighttime, at Pancho's, and his head being filled with a black sandstorm of many badly bawled songs and vulcanized oaths, he sees too late that the gate has been closed. Like many a hard-driving midnight pilot before him, he does not realize that he is not equally gifted in the control of all forms of locomotion. He and the horse hit the gate, and he goes flying off and lands on his right side. His side hurts like hell.

20 The next day, Monday, his side still hurts like hell. It hurts every time he moves. It hurts every time he breathes deep. It hurts every time he moves his right arm. He knows that if he goes to a doctor at Muroc or says anything to anybody even remotely connected with his superiors, he will be scrubbed from the flight on Tuesday. They might

even go so far as to put some other miserable peckerwood in his place. So he gets on his motorcycle, an old junker that Pancho had given him, and rides over to see a doctor in the town of Rosamond, near where he lives. Every time the goddamned motorcycle hits a pebble in the road, his side hurts like a sonofabitch. The doctor in Rosamond informs him he has two broken ribs and he tapes them up and tells him that if he'll just keep his right arm immobilized for a couple of weeks and avoid any physical exertion or sudden movements, he should be all right.

Yeager gets up before daybreak on Tuesday morning—which is supposed to be the day he tries to break the sound barrier—and his ribs still hurt like a sonofabitch. He gets his wife to drive him over to the field, and he has to keep his right arm pinned down to his side to keep his ribs from hurting so much. At dawn, on the day of a flight, you could hear the X-1 screaming long before you got there. The fuel for the X-1 was alcohol and liquid oxygen, oxygen converted from a gas to a liquid by lowering its temperature to 297 degrees below zero. And when the lox, as it was called, rolled out of the hoses and into the belly of the X-1, it started boiling off and the X-1 started steaming and screaming like a teakettle. There's quite a crowd on hand, by Muroc standards . . . perhaps nine or ten souls. They're still fueling the X-1 with the lox, and the beast is wailing.

The X-1 looked like a fat orange swallow with white markings. But it was really just a length of pipe with four rocket chambers in it. It had a tiny cockpit and a needle nose, two little straight blades (only three and a half inches thick at the thickest part) for wings, and a tail assembly set up high to avoid the "sonic wash" from the wings. Even though his side was throbbing and his right arm felt practically useless, Yeager figured he could grit his teeth and get through the flight—except for one specific move he had to make. In the rocket launches, the X-1, which held only two and a half minutes' worth of fuel, was carried up to twenty-six thousand feet underneath a B-29. At seven thousand feet, Yeager was to climb down a ladder from the bomb bay of the B-29 to the open doorway of the X-1, hook up to the oxygen system and the radio microphone and earphones, and put his crash helmet on and prepare for the launch, which would come at twenty-five thousand feet. This helmet was a homemade number. There had never been any such thing as a crash helmet before, except in stunt flying. Throughout the war pilots had used the old skin-tight leather helmet-and-goggles. But the X-1 had a way of throwing the pilot around so violently that there was danger of getting knocked out against the walls of the cockpit. So Yeager had bought a big leather football helmet—there were no plastic ones at the time—and he butchered it with a hunting knife until he carved the right kind of holes in it, so that it would fit down over his regular flying helmet and the earphones and the oxygen rig. Anyway, then his flight engineer, Jack Ridley, would climb down the ladder, out in the breeze, and shove into place the cockpit door, which had to be lowered out of the belly of the B-29 on a chain. Then Yeager had to push a handle to lock the door airtight. Since the X-1's cockpit was minute, you had to push the handle with your right hand. It took quite a shove. There was no way you could move into position to get enough leverage with your left hand.

Out in the hangar Yeager makes a few test shoves on the sly, and the pain is so incredible he realizes that there is no way a man with two broken ribs is going to get the door closed. It is time to confide in somebody, and the logical man is Jack Ridley. Ridley is not only the flight engineer but a pilot himself and a good old boy from Oklahoma to boot. He will understand about Flying & Drinking and Drinking & Driving through the goddamned Joshua trees. So Yeager takes Ridley off to the side in the tin hangar and says: Jack, I got me a little ol' problem here. Over at Pancho's the other night I sorta . . . dinged my goddamned ribs. Ridley says, Whattya mean . . . *dinged?* Yeager says, Well, I guess you might say I damned near like to . . . *broke* a coupla the sonsabitches. Whereupon Yeager sketches out the problem he foresees.

Not for nothing is Ridley the engineer on this project. He has an inspiration. He tells a janitor named Sam to cut him about nine inches off a broom handle. When nobody's looking, he slips the broomstick into the cockpit of the X-1 and gives Yeager a little advice and counsel.

So with that added bit of supersonic flight gear Yeager went aloft.

At seven thousand feet he climbed down the ladder into the X-1's cockpit, clipped on his hoses and lines, and managed to pull the pumpkin football helmet over his head. Then Ridley came down the ladder and lowered the door into place. As Ridley had instructed, Yeager now took the nine inches of broomstick and slipped it between the handle and the door. This gave him just enough mechanical advantage to reach over with his left hand and whang the thing shut. So he whanged the door shut with Ridley's broomstick and was ready to fly.

At 26,000 feet the B-29 went into a shallow dive, then pulled up and released Yeager and the X-1 as if it were a bomb. Like a bomb it dropped and shot forward (at the speed of the mother ship) at the same time. Yeager had been launched straight into the sun. It seemed to be no more than six feet in front of him, filling up the sky and blinding him. But he managed to get his bearings and set off the four rocket chambers one after the other. He then experienced something that became known as the ultimate sensation in flying: "booming and zooming." The surge of the rockets was so tremendous, forced him back into his seat so violently, he could hardly move his hands forward the few inches necessary to reach the controls. The X-1 seemed to shoot straight up in an absolutely perpendicular trajectory, as if determined to snap the hold of gravity via the most direct route possible. In fact, he was only climbing at the 45-degree angle called for in the flight plan. At about .87 Mach the buffeting started.

On the ground the engineers could no longer see Yeager. They could only hear . . . that poker-hollow West Virginia drawl.

"Had a mild buffet there . . . jes the usual instability . . ."

Jes the usual instability?

Then the X-1 reached the speed of .96 Mach, and that incredible caint-hardlyin' aw-shuckin' drawl said:

"Say, Ridley . . . make a note here, will ya?" *(if you ain't got nothin' better to do)* ". . . elevator effectiveness *re*gained."

Just as Yeager had predicted, as the X-1 approached Mach 1, the stability improved. Yeager had his eyes pinned on the machometer. The needle reached .96, fluctuated, and went off the scale.

And on the ground they heard . . . that voice:

"Say, Ridley . . . make another note, will ya?" *(if you ain't too bored yet)* ". . . there's somethin' wrong with this ol' machometer . . ." (faint chuckle) ". . . it's gone kinda screwy on me . . ."

And in that moment, on the ground, they heard a boom rock over the desert floor—just as the physicist Theodore von Kármán had predicted many years before.

Then they heard Ridley back in the B-29: "If it is, Chuck, we'll fix it. Personally I think you're seeing things."

Then they heard Yeager's poker-hollow drawl again:

"Well, I guess I am, Jack . . . And I'm still goin' upstairs like a bat."

The X-1 had gone through "the sonic wall" without so much as a bump. As the speed topped out at Mach 1.05, Yeager had the sensation of shooting straight through the top of the sky. The sky turned a deep purple and all at once the stars and the moon came out—and the sun shone at the same time. He had reached a layer of the upper atmosphere where the air was too thin to contain reflecting dust particles. He was simply looking out into space. As the X-1 nosed over at the top of the climb, Yeager now had seven minutes of . . . Pilot Heaven . . . ahead of him. He was going faster than any man in history, and it was almost silent up here, since he had exhausted his rocket fuel, and he was so high in such a vast space that there was no sensation of motion. He was master of the sky. His was a king's solitude, unique and inviolate, above the dome of the world. It would take him seven minutes to glide back down and land at Muroc. He spent the time doing victory rolls and wing-over-wing aerobatics while Rogers Lake and the High Sierras spun around below.

QUESTIONS

1. *Before recounting Yeager's personal history or the story of breaking the sound barrier, Wolfe begins with the voice of an airline pilot. Why does he begin this way? What connection does the first paragraph have with the rest of the essay?*
2. *Wolfe interweaves Yeager's personal history with a more public, official history of the space program. Make a flowchart or diagram to show how this interweaving works.*
3. *Write an essay that interweaves some part of your personal history with some larger, public story.*

Daniel Mark Epstein

THE CASE OF HARRY HOUDINI

When my grandfather was a boy he saw the wild-haired magician escape from a riveted boiler. He would remember that image as long as he lived, and how Harry Houdini, the rabbi's son, defeated the German Imperial Police at the beginning of the twentieth century. Hearing those tales and others even more incredible, sixty years after the magician's death we cannot help but wonder: What did the historical Houdini *really* do? And how on earth did he do it?

The newspaper accounts are voluminous, and consistent. The mere cataloguing of Houdini's escapes soon grows tedious, which they were not, to be sure, in the flesh. But quickly: the police stripped him naked and searched him thoroughly before binding his wrists and ankles with five pairs of irons. Then they would slam him into a cell and turn the key of a three-bond burglar-proof lock. He escaped, hundreds of times, from the most secure prisons in the world. He hung upside down in a straitjacket from the tallest buildings in America, and escaped in full view of the populace. He was chained hand and foot and nailed into a packing case weighted with lead; the packing case was dropped from a tugboat into New York's East River and ninety seconds later Houdini surfaced. The packing case was hauled up intact, with the manacles inside, still fastened. He was sealed into a paper bag and got out without disturbing the seal. He was sewn into a huge football, into the belly of a whale, and escaped. In California he was buried six feet underground, and clawed his way out. He did this, he did that. These are facts that cannot be exaggerated, for they were conceived as exaggera-

Originally appeared in *The New Criterion* (Oct. 1986).

tions. We know he did these things because his actions were more public than the proceedings of Congress, and most of them he performed over and over, so no one would miss the point.

How did he do such things? For all rational people who are curious, sixty years after the magician's death, there is good news and bad news. The good news is that we know how the vast majority of Houdini's tricks were done, and the explanations are as fascinating as the mystery was. Much of our knowledge comes from the magician's writings, for Houdini kept ahead of his imitators by exposing his cast-off tricks. We have additional information from technicians and theater historians. No magician will reveal Houdini's secrets—their code forbids it. But so much controversy has arisen concerning his powers—so much conjecture they may have been supernatural—that extraordinary measures have been taken to assure us Houdini was a *mortal* genius. Many secrets have leaked out, and others have been discovered from examining the props. So at last we know more about Houdini's technique than any other magician's.

The disturbing news is that, sixty years after his last performance, some of his more spectacular escapes remain unexplained. And while magicians such as Doug Henning are bound not to expose their colleagues, they are free to admit what mystifies them. They know how Houdini walked through the brick wall at Hammerstein's Roof Garden, in 1914, but they do not know how he made the elephant disappear in 1918. This trick he performed only for a few months in New York. And when people asked him why he did not continue he told them that Teddy Roosevelt, a great hunter, had begged him to stop before he exhausted the world's supply of pachyderms.

5 But before we grapple with the mysteries, let us begin with what we can understand. Let us begin with my grandfather's favorite story, the case of Harry Houdini versus the German Police. Houdini's first tour of Europe depended upon the good will and cooperation of the law. When he arrived in London in 1900 the twenty-six-year-old magician did not have a single booking. His news clippings eventually inspired an English agent, who had Houdini manacled to a pillar in Scotland Yard. Seeing that Houdini was securely fastened, Superintendent Melville of the Criminal Investigation Department said he would return in a couple of hours, when the escapist had worn himself out. By the time Melville got to the door the magician was free to open it for him.

The publicity surrounding his escape from the most prestigious police force in the world opened up many another door for the young magician. Booked at the Alhambra Theater in London, he performed his "Challenge" handcuff act, which had made him famous on the vaudeville circuit. After some card tricks and standard illusions, Houdini would stand before the proscenium and challenge the world to restrain him with ropes, straitjackets, handcuffs, whatever they could bring on, from lockshops, prisons, and museums. A single failure might have ruined him. There is no evidence that he ever failed, though in several cases he nearly died from the effort required to escape from sadistic shackles. The "Challenge" act filled the Alhambra Theater for two months. Houdini might have stayed there if Germany had not already booked him; the Germans could hardly wait to get a look at Houdini.

As he had done in America and England, Houdini began his tour of Germany with a visit to police headquarters. The Dresden officers were not enthusiastic, yet they could hardly refuse the magician's invitation to lock him up. That might suggest a crisis of confidence. And like their colleagues the world over, the Dresden police viewed Houdini's news clippings as so much paper in the balance with their locks and chains. Of course the Dresden police had no more success than those of Kansas City, or San Francisco, or Scotland Yard. Their manacles were paper to him. The police chief reluctantly signed the certificate Houdini demanded, but the newspapers gave him little coverage.

So on his opening night at Dresden's Central Theatre, Houdini arranged to be fettered in the leg irons and manacles of the Mathildegasse Prison. Some of the locks weighed forty pounds. The audience, packed to the walls, went wild over his escape, and the fact that he spoke their language further endeared him. If anything could have held him captive it would have been the adoring burghers of Dresden, who mobbed the theater for weeks. The manager wanted to buy out Houdini's contract with the Wintergarten of Berlin, so as to hold him over in Dresden, but the people of Berlin could not wait to see the magician.

Houdini arrived in Berlin in October of 1900. The first thing he did was march into the police station, strip stark naked, and challenge the jailors. They could not hold him. This time Count von Windheim, the highest ranking policeman in Germany, signed the certificate of Houdini's escape. The Wintergarten was overrun. The management appealed to the theater of Houdini's next engagement, in Vienna, so they might hold him over an extra month in Berlin. The Viennese finally yielded, demanding an indemnity equal to Houdini's salary for one month. When the magician, at long last, opened at the Olympic Theater in Paris, in December of 1901, he was the highest paid foreign entertainer in French history.

10 But meanwhile there was big trouble brewing in Germany. It seems the police there had little sense of humor about Houdini's peculiar gifts, and the Jew had quickly exhausted what little there was. In Dortmund he escaped from the irons that had bound Glowisky, a notorious

murderer, beheaded three days before. At Hanover the police chief, Count von Schwerin, plotted to disgrace Houdini, challenging him to escape from a special straitjacket reinforced with thick leather. Houdini agonized for one and a half hours while von Schwerin looked on, his jubilant smile melting in wonder, then rage, as the magician worked himself free.

The cumulative anger of the German police went public in July of 1901. Inspector Werner Graff witnessed Houdini's escape from all the manacles at the Cologne police station and vowed to end the humiliation. It was not a simple matter of pride. Graff, along with von Schwerin and other officials, feared Houdini was weakening their authority and inviting jailbreaks, if not other kinds of antisocial behavior. So Graff wrote a letter to Cologne's newspaper, the *Rheinische Zeitung*. The letter stated that Houdini had escaped from simple restraints at the police headquarters, by trickery; but his publicity boasted he could escape from restraints *of any kind*. Such a claim, Graff wrote, was a lie, and Houdini ought to be prosecuted for fraud.

Though he knew the letter was nonsense the magician could not ignore it, for it was dangerous nonsense. If the police began calling him a fraud in every town he visited, Houdini would lose his audience. So he demanded that Graff apologize and the newspaper publish a retraction. Graff refused, and other German dailies reprinted his letter. Should Harry Houdini sue the German policeman for libel? Consider the circumstances. Germany, even in 1901, was one of the most authoritarian states in the world. Houdini was an American, a Jew who embarrassed the police. A libel case against Graff would turn upon the magician's claim that he could escape from *any* restraint, and the courtroom would become an international theater. There a German judge and jury would try his skill, and, should they find it wanting, Houdini would be washed up, exiled to play beer halls and dime museums. Only an artist with colossal pride and total confidence in his methods would act as Houdini did. He hired the most prominent trial lawyer in Cologne, and ordered him to sue Werner Graff and the Imperial Police of Germany for criminal libel.

There was standing room only in the Cologne *Schöffengericht*. The judge allowed Werner Graff to seek out the most stubborn locks and chains he could find, and tangle Houdini in them, in full view of everyone. Here was a hitch, for Houdini did not wish to show the crowd his technique. He asked the judge to clear the courtroom, and in the ensuing turmoil the magician released himself so quickly no one knew how he had done it. The *Schöffengericht* fined the astonished policeman and ordered a public apology. So Graff's lawyer appealed the case.

Two months later Graff was better prepared. In the *Strafkammer*, or court of appeals, he presented thirty letters from legal authorities declaring that the escape artist could not justify his advertisements. And Graff had a shiny new pair of handcuffs. The premier locksmith of Germany had engineered the cuffs especially for the occasion. Werner Graff explained to the judge that the lock, once closed, could never be opened, even with its own key. Let Houdini try to get out of these.

This time the court permitted Houdini to work in privacy, and a guard led the magician to an adjacent chamber. Everyone else settled down for a long wait, in a chatter of anticipation. They were interrupted four minutes later by the entrance of Houdini, who tossed the manacles on the judge's bench. So the *Strafkammer* upheld the lower court's decision, as did the *Oberlandesgericht* in a "paper" appeal. The court fined Werner Graff thirty marks and ordered him to pay for the trials as well as a published apology. Houdini's next poster showed him in evening dress, his hands manacled, standing before the judge, jurors, and a battery of mustachioed policemen. Looking down on the scene is a bust of the Kaiser against a crimson background, and a scroll that reads: "The Imperial Police of Cologne slandered Harry Houdini . . . were compelled to advertise 'An Honorary Apology' and pay costs of the trials. By command of Kaiser Wilhelm II, Emperor of Germany."

Now this is surely a wondrous tale, like something out of the Arabian Nights, and it will seem no less wonderful when we understand the technique that made it come true. In 1901, when Houdini took on the Imperial Police, he was not whistling in the dark. By the time he left America at the end of the nineteenth century he had dissected every kind of lock he could find in the New World, and whatever he could import from the old one. Arriving in London Houdini could write that there were only a few kinds of British handcuffs, "seven or eight at the utmost," and these were some of the simplest he had ever seen. He searched the markets, antique shops, and locksmiths, buying up all the European locks he could find so he could dismantle and study them.

Then during his Berlin engagement he worked up to ten hours a day at Mueller's locksmith on the Mittelstrasse, studying restraints. He was the Bobby Fischer of locks. With a chessmaster's foresight Houdini devised a set of picks to release every lock in existence, as well as *any he could imagine.* Such tireless ingenuity produced the incandescent light bulb and the atom bomb. Houdini's creation of a theatrical metaphor made a comparable impact on the human spirit. He had a message which he delivered so forcefully it goes without mentioning in theater courses: humankind cannot be held in chains. The European middle class had reached an impressionable age, and the meaning of Houdini's theater was not lost upon them. Nor was he mistaken by the aristocracy, who stayed away in droves. The spectacle of this American Jew bursting from chains by dint of ingenuity did not amuse the rich. They wanted desperately to demythologize him.

It was not about to happen in the German courtroom. When Werner Graff snapped the "new" handcuffs on Houdini, they were not strange to the magician. He had already invented them, so to speak, as well as the pick to open them, and the pick was in his pocket. Only a locksmith whose knowledge surpassed Houdini's could stop him; diligent study assured him that, as of 1901, there could be no such locksmith on the face of the earth.

What else can we understand about the methods of Harry Houdini, born Ehrich Weiss? We know he was a superbly conditioned athlete who did not smoke or take a drop of alcohol. His straitjacket escapes he performed in full view of the world so they could see it was by main force and flexibility that he freed himself. He may or may not have been able to dislocate his shoulders at will—he said he could, and it seems no more marvelous than certain other skills he demonstrated. Friends reported that his toes could untie knots most of us could not manage with our fingers. And routinely the magician would hold his breath for as long as four minutes to work underwater escapes. To cheapen the supernatural claims of the fakir Rahman Bey, Houdini remained underwater in an iron box for ninety minutes, as against the Egyptian's sixty. Examining Houdini, a physician testified that the fifty-year-old wizard had halved his blood pressure while doubling his pulse. Of course, more wonderful than any of these skills was the courage allowing him to employ them, in predicaments where any normal person would panic.

These things are known about Houdini. The same tireless ingenu- 20
ity, when applied to locks and jails, packing cases and riveted boilers; the same athletic prowess, when applied at the bottom of the East River, or while dangling from a rope attached to the cornice of the Sun Building in Baltimore—these talents account for the vast majority of Houdini's exploits. As we have mentioned, theater historians, notably Raymund Fitzsimons in his *Death and the Magician*, have carefully exposed Houdini's ingenuity, knowing that nothing can tarnish the miracle of the man's existence. Their accounts are technical and we need not dwell on them, except to say they *mostly* support Houdini's oath that his effects were achieved by natural, or mechanical means. The Houdini problem arises from certain outrageous effects no one has ever been able to explain, though capable technicians have been trying for more than sixty years.

Let us briefly recall those effects. We have mentioned the Disappearing Elephant. On January 7, 1918, Houdini had a ten-thousand-pound elephant led onto the bright stage of the Hippodrome in New

York City. A trainer marched the elephant around a cabinet large enough for an elephant, proving there was space behind. There was no trapdoor in the floor of the Hippodrome, and the elephant could not fly. Houdini ushered the pachyderm into the cabinet and closed the curtains. Then he opened them, and where the elephant had stood there was nothing but empty space. Houdini went on with his program, which might have been making the Hippodrome disappear, for all the audience knew. A reporter for the *Brooklyn Eagle* noted: "The program says that the elephant vanished into thin air. The trick is performed fifteen feet from the backdrop and the cabinet is slightly elevated. That explanation is as good as any." After Houdini stopped making elephants disappear, nineteen weeks later, the trick would never be precisely duplicated.

That is the single "conventional" illusion of Houdini's repertoire that remains unexplained. He was not the greatest illusionist of his time, though he was among them. His expertise was the "escape" act, that specialty of magic furthest removed from theater, for its challenges are quite real and sometimes beyond the magician's control. It was the escapes, as his wife later wrote, that were truly dangerous, and Houdini privately admitted some anxieties about them. Give a wizard twenty years to build a cabinet which snuffs an elephant, and you will applaud his cleverness if he succeeds, in the controlled environment of his theater. But surrender the same man, stark naked, to the Russian police, who stake their honor upon detaining him in a convict van, and you may well suspect the intercession of angels should he get out.

And that is exactly what Houdini did, in one of the strangest and most celebrated escapes of his career. Strange, because it was Houdini's habit to escape only from barred jail cells where the locks were within easy reach, and then only after inspection, so he might hide picks in crannies, or excuse himself if he foresaw failure. But the Siberian Transport Cell made his blood boil. On May 11, 1903, the chief of the Russian secret police searched the naked Houdini inside and out. The revolt of 1905 was in its planning stages and the Imperial Police were understandably touchy. The magician's wrists were padlocked and his ankles fettered before the police locked him into the *carette.* Mounted on a wagon, the zinc-lined steel cell stood in the prison courtyard in view of chief Lebedoeff, his staff, and a number of civilians. Twenty-eight minutes later Houdini was walking around the courtyard, stretching. Nobody saw him get out, but he was out. The police ran to the door of the *carette.* The door was still locked and the shackles lay on the floor of the undamaged van. The police were so furious they would not sign the certificate of escape, but so many people had witnessed the event that the news was soon being shouted all over Moscow. Doug Henning has written: "It remains one of his escapes about which the real method is pure conjecture."

In the Houdini Museum at Niagara Falls, Canada, you may view the famous Mirror Handcuffs. If you are a scholar you can inspect them. In March of 1904 the London *Daily Mirror* discovered a blacksmith who had been working for five years to build a set of handcuffs no mortal man could pick. Examining the cuffs, the best locksmiths in London agreed they had never seen such an ingenious mechanism. The newspaper challenged Houdini to escape from them. On March 17, before a house of four thousand in the London Hippodrome, a journalist fastened the cuffs on Houdini's wrists and turned the key six times. The magician retired to his cabinet onstage, and the band struck up a march. He did not emerge for twenty minutes. When he did, it was to hold the lock up to the light. Remember that most "Challenge" handcuffs were regulation, and familiar to Houdini. He studied the lock in the light, and then went back into the cabinet, as the band played a waltz.

Ten minutes later Houdini stuck his head out, asking if he could 25
have a cushion to kneel on. He was denied. After almost an hour Houdini came out of the cabinet again, obviously worn out, and his audience groaned. He wanted the handcuffs to be unlocked for a moment so he could take off his coat, as he was sweating profusely. The journalist denied the request, since Houdini had never before seen the handcuffs unlocked, and that might give him an advantage. Whereupon Houdini, in full view of the four thousand, extracted a penknife from his pocket and opened it with his teeth. Turning the coat inside out over his head, he shredded it loose with the penknife, and returned to the cabinet. Someone called out that Houdini had been handcuffed for more than an hour. As the band played on, the journalists of the London *Daily Mirror* could taste the greatest scoop of the twentieth century. But ten minutes later there was a cry from the cabinet and Houdini leapt out of it, free, waving the handcuffs high in the air. While the crowd roared, several men from the audience carried Houdini on their shoulders around the theater. He was crying as if his heart would break.

For all his other talents Houdini was a notoriously wooden actor, and we may assume the rare tears were altogether real, the product of an uncounterfeitable emotion. It is as if the man himself had been overwhelmed by his escape. Eighty years of technological progress have shed no light upon it. We know how Houdini got out of other handcuffs, but not these. As far as anyone can tell, the Mirror Handcuffs remain as the blacksmith described them—a set of handcuffs no mortal man could pick. One is tempted to dismiss the whole affair as mass hypnosis.

In the same Canadian museum you may view the Chinese Water Torture Cell, in which the magician was hung upside down, in water, his ankles padlocked to the riveted roof. His escape from this cell was the crowning achievement of his stage career, and though he performed it on tour during the last ten years of his life, no one has the slightest notion how he did it. The gifted Doug Henning revived the act in 1975, on television. But he would be the first to tell you his was *not* Houdini's version, but his own, and he would not do it onstage before a live audience seven nights a week, with matinees on Wednesday and Saturday, because the trick would be unspeakably dangerous even if he could perform it there. When Houdini died he willed the contraption to his brother Hardeen, a fine magician in his own right. But Hardeen would not get in it either, and the instructions were to be burned upon his death. Again, as with the Vanishing Elephant, we are reviewing a stage illusion under controlled conditions, and may bow to a master's technical superiority, without fretting that he has used supernatural powers.

But the Mirror Handcuffs and the Siberian Van Escape are troublesome, as are certain of Houdini's escapes from reinforced straitjackets, and packing cases underwater. So is the fact that he was buried six feet underground, and clawed his way out. He only tried it once, and nearly died in the struggle, but the feat was attested, and you do not need a degree in physics to know it is as preposterous as rising from the dead. The weight of the earth is so crushing you could not lift it in the open air. Try doing this with no oxygen. The maestro himself misjudged the weight, and, realizing his folly, tried to signal his crew when the grave was not yet full. They could not hear him and kept right on shoveling as fast as they could, so as not to keep him waiting. Then they stood back, to watch. A while later they saw his bleeding hands appear above the ground.

If we find Houdini's record unsettling, imagine what our grandparents must have thought of him. They knew almost nothing of his technique. Where we remain troubled by a few of his illusions and escapes, our ancestors were horrified by most of them. The European journalists thought he was some kind of hobgoblin, a shapeshifter who could crawl through keyholes, or dematerialize and reappear at will. One can hardly blame them. Despite his constant reassurances that his effects were technical, and natural, the practical-minded layman could not believe it, and even fellow magicians were disturbed by his behavior.

30 So we come to the central issue in the case of Harry Houdini. It is an issue he carefully avoided in public, while studying it diligently in private. To wit: Can a magician, by the ultimate perfection of a technique, generate a force which, at critical moments, will achieve a supernatural result? Houdini's writings show this was the abiding concern of his intellectual life. It is, of course, the essential mystery of classical magic since before the Babylonians. Yet it remained a private

and professional concern until Houdini's career forced it upon the public.

With the same determination that opened the world's locks, Houdini searched for an answer. His own technique was so highly evolved that its practice might have satisfied him, but his curiosity was unquenchable. He amassed the world's largest collection of books pertaining to magic and the occult, and no less a scholar than Edmund Wilson honored Houdini's authority. The son of a rabbi, Houdini pursued his studies with rabbinic thoroughness. And, from the beginning of his career, he sought out the living legends of magic and badgered them in retirement, sometimes with tragicomic results.

As far back as 1895 it seemed to Houdini something peculiar was going on when he performed the Metamorphosis with his wife Bess. You have probably seen this classic illusion. Two friends of mine once acted it in my living room, as a birthday present. When the Houdinis performed the Metamorphosis, Bess whould handcuff Harry, tie him in a sack, and lock him in a trunk. She would draw a curtain hiding the trunk and then it would open, showing Houdini free upon the stage. Where was Bess? Inside the trunk, inside the sack, handcuffed—there was Bess. The method of this trick is only mysterious if you cannot pay for it. But the Houdinis' *timing* of the Metamorphosis got very mysterious indeed. They polished the act until it happened in less than three seconds—three rather blurred seconds in their own minds, to be sure. Believe me, you cannot get *in*to the trunk in less than three seconds. So when the Houdinis had done the trick they were often as stunned as their audience. It seemed a sure case of technique unleashing a supernatural force. Perplexed, Houdini planned to interview Hermann the Great, the preeminent conjuror in America in 1895, and ask Hermann what was up. But Hermann died as Houdini was about to ask him the question.

And Houdini shadowed the marvelous Harry Kellar, cross-examining him, and Alexander Heimburger, and the decrepit Ira Davenport, who had been a medium as well as a magician. But the great magicians flatly denied the psychic possibility, and Davenport would not answer to Houdini's satisfaction. In 1903 he discovered that Wiljalba Frikell, a seemingly mythic wizard of the nineteenth century, was still alive, in retirement near Dresden. When the ancient mage would not acknowledge his letters, Houdini grew convinced Wiljalba Frikell was the man to answer his question. He took the train to Dresden and knocked on Frikell's door. His wife sent Houdini away. On the road in Germany and Russia, Houdini continued to send letters and gifts to Frikell. And at last, six months after he had been turned away from Frikell's door, the reclusive magician agreed to see him.

Houdini rang the doorbell at 2:00 P.M. on October 8, 1903, the exact hour of his appointment. The door swung open. An hour earlier Wiljalba Frikell had dressed in his best suit, and laid out his scrapbooks, programs, and medals for Houdini to view. Houdini excitedly followed Frikell's wife into the room where the master sat surrounded by the mementos of his glorious career. But he would not be answering any of the questions that buzzed in Houdini's brain. The old man was stone dead.

35 Throughout his life Houdini categorically denied that any of his effects were achieved by supernatural means. He crusaded against mediums, clairvoyants, and all who claimed psychic power, advertising that he would reproduce any of their manifestations by mechanical means. In the face of spiritualists who accused *him* of being a physical medium, he protested that all his escapes and illusions were tricks. He was probably telling the truth, as he understood it. But Rabbi Drachman, who spoke at Houdini's funeral, and had been in a position to receive confidences, said: "Houdini possessed a wondrous power that he never understood, and which he never revealed to anyone in life."

Houdini was not Solomon; he was a vaudeville specialist. If he ever experienced a psychic power it surely humbled his understanding. And to admit such a power, in his position, would have been a monumental stupidity. Why? If for no other reason, Talmudic law forbids the performance of miracles, and Houdini was the obedient son of Rabbi Weiss. Also, in case he should forget the Jewish law, it is strictly against the magician's code to claim a supernatural power, for reasons impossible to ignore. Mediums made such claims, at their own risk. Two of the more famous mediums of the nineteenth century, Ira and William Davenport, achieved manifestations similar to Houdini's. Audiences in Liverpool, Leeds, and Paris rioted, stormed the stage, and ran the mediums out of town, crying their performances were an outrage against God and a danger to man. Whether or not the acts were supernatural is beside the point—billing them as such was bad business, and hazardous to life and limb. Yet the Davenports were no more than a sideshow, compared to Houdini. The man was blinding. There had not been such a public display of apparent miracles in nearly two thousand years. Had the Jew so much as hinted his powers were spiritual he might have expected no better treatment than the renegade Hebrew of Nazareth.

Houdini was the self-proclaimed avatar of nothing but good old American know-how, and that is how he wished to be remembered. His wife of thirty years, Beatrice Houdini (known as "Bess"), was loyal to him in this, as in all other things. Pestered for revelations about Houdini's magic long after his death, the widow swore by her husband's account. But against her best intentions, Bess clouded the issue by saying just a little more than was necessary. It was in a letter to Sir Arthur Conan Doyle, who had been a close friend of hers and Houdini's.

The friendship was an odd one. The author of Sherlock Holmes believed in Spiritualism, and championed the séance with all the fervor with which Houdini opposed it. There were two great mysteries in Doyle's life: the powers of Sherlock Holmes and Harry Houdini. Doyle knew the Houdinis intimately, and nothing the magician said could shake Sir Arthur's conviction that certain of Houdini's escapes were supernatural. Doyle never stopped trying to get Houdini to confess. In 1922 it was more than a personal issue. The séance had become big business in America, with millions of bereaved relatives paying to communicate with their dear departed. Spiritualism was a homegrown, persuasive religious movement, a bizarre reaction to American science and pragmatism. The great critic Edmund Wilson, who admired Houdini and understood his gifts, recognized that the magician had appeared at a critical moment in the history of Spiritualism. Houdini was the only man living who had the authority, and the competence, to expose the predatory mediums, and his success was decisive.

Yet Houdini's lecture-demonstrations, and exposures of false mediums, only fueled Doyle's suspicions that his friend was the real thing, a physical medium. In all fairness, Sir Arthur Conan Doyle was a credulous old gentleman, who knew nothing of Houdini's techniques. But his instinct was sound. Two months after Houdini died, Sir Arthur wrote to Bess in despair of ever learning the truth from the magician's lips, and she wrote Doyle a long letter. What concerns us here are a few sentences which, coming from the woman who shared his life and work, and maintained her loyalty to Houdini alive and dead, we must regard as altogether startling.

> I will never be offended by anything you say for him or about him, but that he possessed psychic powers—he never knew it. As I told Lady Doyle often he would get a difficult lock, I stood by the cabinet and I would hear him say, "This is beyond me," and after many minutes when the audience became restless I nervously would say "Harry, if there is anything in this belief in Spiritism,—why don't you call on them to assist you," and before many minutes had passed Houdini had mastered the lock.
>
> We never attributed this to psychic help. We just knew that that particular instrument was the one to open that lock, and so did all his tricks.

The tone of this letter penned so soon after her husband's death is 40
somber throughout, painfully sincere. This was not a subject for levity, this being the central issue in the life of Harry Houdini. So what on

earth is Bess trying to tell Sir Arthur when she testifies to the invocation of spirits in one sentence, and repudiates psychic help in the next? What kind of double-talk is this, when the widow refers to the summoning of spiritual aid as "that particular instrument," as if a spirit were no different from any other skeleton key? It sounds like sheer euphemism; it sounds like the Houdinis' lifetime of work had uncovered a power so terrifying they would not admit it to each other, let alone the world. Would that Albert Einstein had been so discreet in 1905.

So what if Harry Houdini, once in a while, "spirited" himself out of a Siberian Van, or a pair of Mirror Handcuffs, or a packing case at the bottom of the East River? It is perhaps no more remarkable than that an American Jew won a verdict against the German Police for criminal libel in 1901, or reversed a religious movement in America in 1922. Houdini died in Detroit on Halloween in 1926, of acute appendicitis. He was born in Budapest on March 24, 1874, but told the world he was born in Appleton, Wisconsin on April 6. Not until after World War II did Americans discover that their greatest magician was an alien. Houdini's work was no more miraculous than his life. His life was no more miraculous than the opening and closing of a flower.

QUESTIONS

1. *What, according to Epstein, was the message to mankind of Houdini's career? What details in the essay exemplify that message?*
2. *How important to this account of Houdini is the fact that he was a Jew? What are some of the implications of that fact? What might Epstein mean to imply by his account of the confrontations between Houdini and the German police?*
3. *At several points in his account of Houdini, Epstein creates an effect of suspense. How does he manage that effect? What purposes does it serve?*
4. *Epstein's account of Houdini leaves some unanswered questions in, for example, paragraphs 3, 19, 30, and elsewhere. What are they? Why are they unanswered? Choose one unanswered question and, through research or speculation, write an answer to it.*

Virginia Woolf

MY FATHER: LESLIE STEPHEN

By the time that his children were growing up, the great days of my father's life were over. His feats on the river and on the mountains had been won before they were born. Relics of them were to be found lying about the house—the silver cup on the study mantelpiece; the rusty alpenstocks that leaned against the bookcase in the corner; and to the end of his days he would speak of great climbers and explorers with a peculiar mixture of admiration and envy. But his own years of activity were over, and my father had to content himself with pottering about the Swiss valleys or taking a stroll across the Cornish moors.

That to potter and to stroll meant more on his lips than on other people's is becoming obvious now that some of his friends have given their own version of those expeditions. He would start off after breakfast alone, or with one companion. Shortly after dinner he would return. If the walk had been successful, he would have out his great map and commemorate a new short cut in red ink. And he was quite capable, it appears, of striding all day across the moors without speaking more than a word or two to his companion. By that time, too, he had written the *History of English Thought in the Eighteenth Century*, which is said by some to be his masterpiece; and the *Science of Ethics*—the book which interested him most; and *The Playground of Europe*, in which is to be found "The Sunset on Mont Blanc"—in his opinion the best thing he ever wrote. He still wrote daily and methodically, though never for long at a time.

In London he wrote in the large room with three long windows at the top of the house. He wrote lying almost recumbent in a low rocking chair which he tipped to and fro as he wrote, like a cradle, and as he wrote he smoked a short clay pipe, and he scattered books round him in a circle. The thud of a book dropped on the floor could be heard in the room beneath. And often as he mounted the stairs to his study with his firm, regular tread he would burst, not into song, for he was entirely unmusical, but into a strange rhythmical chant, for verse of all kinds, both "utter trash," as he called it, and the most sublime words of Milton and Wordsworth, stuck in his memory, and the act of walking or climbing seemed to inspire him to recite whichever it was that came uppermost or suited his mood.

But it was his dexterity with his fingers that delighted his children

First published in the *London Times* (Nov. 28, 1932) as "Leslie Stephen, the Philosopher at Home: A Daughter's Memories."

before they could potter along the lanes at his heels or read his books. He would twist a sheet of paper beneath a pair of scissors and out would drop an elephant, a stag, or a monkey, with trunks, horns, and tails delicately and exactly formed. Or, taking a pencil, he would draw beast after beast—an art that he practiced almost unconsciously as he read, so that the flyleaves of his books swarm with owls and donkeys as if to illustrate the "Oh, you ass!" or "Conceited dunce" that he was wont to scribble impatiently in the margin. Such brief comments, in which one may find the germ of the more temperate statements of his essays, recall some of the characteristics of his talk. He could be very silent, as his friends have testified. But his remarks, made suddenly in a low voice between the puffs of his pipe, were extremely effective. Sometimes with one word—but his one word was accompanied by a gesture of the hand—he would dispose of the tissue of exaggerations which his own sobriety seemed to provoke. "There are 40,000,000 unmarried women in London alone!" Lady Ritchie once informed him. "Oh, Annie, Annie!" my father exclaimed in tones of horrified but affectionate rebuke. But Lady Ritchie, as if she enjoyed being rebuked, would pile it up even higher next time she came.

5 The stories he told to amuse his children of adventures in the Alps—but accidents only happened, he would explain, if you were so foolish as to disobey your guides—or of those long walks, after one of which, from Cambridge to London on a hot day, "I drank, I am sorry to say, rather more than was good for me," were told very briefly, but with a curious power to impress the scene. The things that he did not say were always there in the background. So, too, though he seldom told anecdotes, and his memory for facts was bad, when he described a person—and he had known many people, both famous and obscure—he would convey exactly what he thought of him in two or three words. And what he thought might be the opposite of what other people thought. He had a way of upsetting established reputations and disregarding conventional values that could be disconcerting, and sometimes perhaps wounding, though no one was more respectful of any feeling that seemed to him genuine. But when, suddenly opening his bright blue eyes and rousing himself from what had seemed complete abstraction, he gave his opinion, it was difficult to disregard it. It was a habit, especially when deafness made him unaware that this opinion could be heard, that had its inconveniences.

"I am the most easily bored of men," he wrote, truthfully as usual; and when, as was inevitable in a large family, some visitor threatened to stay not merely for tea but also for dinner, my father would express his anguish at first by twisting and untwisting a certain lock of hair. Then he would burst out, half to himself, half to the powers above, but quite audibly, "Why can't he go? Why can't he go?" Yet such is the charm of simplicity—and did he not say, also truthfully, that "bores are the salt of the earth"?—that the bores seldom went, or, if they did, forgave him and came again.

Too much, perhaps, has been said of his silence; too much stress has been laid upon his reserve. He loved clear thinking; he hated sentimentality and gush; but this by no means meant that he was cold and unemotional, perpetually critical and condemnatory in daily life. On the contrary, it was his power of feeling strongly and of expressing his feeling with vigor that made him sometimes so alarming as a companion. A lady, for instance, complained of the wet summer that was spoiling her tour in Cornwall. But to my father, though he never called himself a democrat, the rain meant that the corn was being laid; some poor man was being ruined; and the energy with which he expressed his sympathy—not with the lady—left her discomfited. He had something of the same respect for farmers and fishermen that he had for climbers and explorers. So, too, he talked little of patriotism, but during the South African War—and all wars were hateful to him—he lay awake thinking that he heard the guns on the battlefield. Again, neither his reason nor his cold common sense helped to convince him that a child could be late for dinner without having been maimed or killed in an accident. And not all his mathematics together with a bank balance which he insisted must be ample in the extreme could persuade him, when it came to signing a check, that the whole family was not "shooting Niagara to ruin,"[1] as he put it. The pictures that he would draw of old age and the bankruptcy court, of ruined men of letters who have to support large families in small houses at Wimbledon (he owned a very small house at Wimbledon), might have convinced those who complain of his understatements that hyperbole was well within his reach had he chosen.

Yet the unreasonable mood was superficial, as the rapidity with which it vanished would prove. The checkbook was shut; Wimbledon and the workhouse were forgotten. Some thought of a humorous kind made him chuckle. Taking his hat and his stick, calling for his dog and his daughter, he would stride off into Kensington Gardens, where he had walked as a little boy, where his brother Fitzjames and he had made beautiful bows to young Queen Victoria and she had swept them a curtsy; and so, round the Serpentine, to Hyde Park Corner, where he had once saluted the great Duke himself; and so home. He was not then in the least "alarming"; he was very simple, very confiding; and his silence, though one might last unbroken from the Round Pond to the Marble Arch, was curiously full of meaning, as if he were thinking half aloud, about poetry and philosophy and people he had known.

He himself was the most abstemious of men. He smoked a pipe per-

1. The reference is to going over Niagara Falls in a boat.

petually, but never a cigar. He wore his clothes until they were too shabby to be tolerable; and he held old-fashioned and rather puritanical views as to the vice of luxury and the sin of idleness. The relations between parents and children today have a freedom that would have been impossible with my father. He expected a certain standard of behavior, even of ceremony, in family life. Yet if freedom means the right to think one's own thoughts and to follow one's own pursuits, then no one respected and indeed insisted upon freedom more completely than he did. His sons, with the exception of the Army and Navy, should follow whatever professions they chose; his daughters, though he cared little enough for the higher education of women, should have the same liberty. If at one moment he rebuked a daughter sharply for smoking a cigarette—smoking was not in his opinion a nice habit in the other sex—she had only to ask him if she might become a painter, and he assured her that so long as she took her work seriously he would give her all the help he could. He had no special love for painting; but he kept his word. Freedom of that sort was worth thousands of cigarettes.

10 It was the same with the perhaps more difficult problem of literature. Even today there may be parents who would doubt the wisdom of allowing a girl of fifteen the free run of a large and quite unexpurgated library. But my father allowed it. There were certain facts—very briefly, very shyly he referred to them. Yet "Read what you like," he said, and all his books, "mangy and worthless," as he called them, but certainly they were many and various, were to be had without asking. To read what one liked because one liked it, never to pretend to admire what one did not—that was his only lesson in the art of reading. To write in the fewest possible words, as clearly as possible, exactly what one meant—that was his only lesson in the art of writing. All the rest must be learned for oneself. Yet a child must have been childish in the extreme not to feel that such was the teaching of a man of great learning and wide experience, though he would never impose his own views or parade his own knowledge. For, as his tailor remarked when he saw my father walk past his shop up Bond Street, "There goes a gentleman that wears good clothes without knowing it."

In those last years, grown solitary and very deaf, he would sometimes call himself a failure as a writer; he had been "jack of all trades, and master of none." But whether he failed or succeeded as a writer, it is permissible to believe that he left a distinct impression of himself on the minds of his friends. Meredith[2] saw him as "Phoebus Apollo turned fasting friar" in his earlier days; Thomas Hardy, years later, looked at the "spare and desolate figure" of the Schreckhorn[3] and thought of

2. George Meredith (1828–1909), English novelist and poet.

him,
Who scaled its horn with ventured life and limb,
Drawn on by vague imaginings, maybe,
Of semblance to his personality
In its quaint glooms, keen lights, and rugged trim.

But the praise he would have valued most, for though he was an agnostic nobody believed more profoundly in the worth of human relationships, was Meredith's tribute after his death: "He was the one man to my knowledge worthy to have married your mother." And Lowell,[4] when he called him "L.S., the most lovable of men," has best described the quality that makes him, after all these years, unforgettable.

3. One of the peaks in the Swiss Alps.
4. James Russell Lowell (1819–1891), American poet, essayist, and editor.

QUESTIONS

1. *Would you like to have been Leslie Stephen's son or daughter? Why, or why not?*
2. *Giving praise can be a difficult rhetorical and social undertaking. How does Woolf avoid the pitfalls or try to?*
3. *In some of her other work, Woolf shows a deep and sensitive concern for women's experience and awareness. Do you find a feminist awareness here? In what way?*
4. *In her novel* To the Lighthouse, *Woolf creates the fictional character of Mr. Ramsay from recollections of her father. Compare the characterization in her essay with this passage from the novel: "What he said was true. It was always true. He was incapable of untruth; never tampered with a fact; never altered a disagreeable word to suit the pleasure or convenience of any mortal being, least of all of his own children, who, sprung from his loins, should be aware from childhood that life is difficult; facts uncompromising; and the passage to that fabled land where our brightest hopes are extinguished, our frail barks founder in darkness (here Mr. Ramsay would straighten his back and narrow his little blue eyes upon the horizon), one that needs, above all, courage, truth, and the power to endure."* (To the Lighthouse, *Harcourt, Brace & World, 1927; © 1955 Leonard Woolf, pp. 10–11.)*
5. *Write a sketch about a father, real or fictional, adopting a tone similar to Woolf's in this sketch.*

Scott Russell Sanders

UNDER THE INFLUENCE

My father drank. He drank as a gut-punched boxer gasps for breath, as a starving dog gobbles food—compulsively, secretly, in pain and trembling. I use the past tense not because he ever quit drinking but because he quit living. That is how the story ends for my father, age sixty-four, heart bursting, body cooling and forsaken on the linoleum of my brother's trailer. The story continues for my brother, my sister, my mother, and me, and will continue so long as memory holds.

In the perennial present of memory, I slip into the garage or barn to see my father tipping back the flat green bottles of wine, the brown cylinders of whiskey, the cans of beer disguised in paper bags. His Adam's apple bobs, the liquid gurgles, he wipes the sandy-haired back of a hand over his lips, and then, his bloodshot gaze bumping into me, he stashes the bottle or can inside his jacket, under the workbench, between two bales of hay, and we both pretend the moment has not occurred.

"What's up, buddy?" he says, thick-tongued and edgy.

"Sky's up," I answer, playing along.

5 "And don't forget prices," he grumbles. "Prices are always up. And taxes."

In memory, his white 1951 Pontiac with the stripes down the hood and the Indian head on the snout jounces to a stop in the driveway; or it is the 1956 Ford station wagon, or the 1963 Rambler shaped like a toad, or the sleek 1969 Bonneville that will do 120 miles per hour on straightaways; or it is the robin's-egg blue pickup, new in 1980, battered in 1981, the year of his death. He climbs out, grinning dangerously, unsteady on his legs, and we children interrupt our game of catch, our building of snow forts, our picking of plums, to watch in silence as he weaves past into the house, where he slumps into his overstuffed chair and falls asleep. Shaking her head, our mother stubs out the cigarette he has left smoldering in the ashtray. All evening, until our bedtimes, we tiptoe past him, as past a snoring dragon. Then we curl in our fearful sheets, listening. Eventually he wakes with a grunt, Mother slings accusations at him, he snarls back, she yells, he growls, their voices clashing. Before long, she retreats to their bedroom, sobbing—not from the blows of fists, for he never strikes her, but from the force of words.

Originally published in *Harper's Magazine* (Nov. 1989).

Left alone, our father prowls the house, thumping into furniture, rummaging in the kitchen, slamming doors, turning the pages of the newspaper with a savage crackle, muttering back at the late-night drivel from television. The roof might fly off, the walls might buckle from the pressure of his rage. Whatever my brother and sister and mother may be thinking on their own rumpled pillows, I lie there hating him, loving him, fearing him, knowing I have failed him. I tell myself he drinks to ease an ache that gnaws at his belly, an ache I must have caused by disappointing him somehow, a murderous ache I should be able to relieve by doing all my chores, earning A's in school, winning baseball games, fixing the broken washer and the burst pipes, bringing in money to fill his empty wallet. He would not hide the green bottles in his tool box, would not sneak off to the barn with a lump under his coat, would not fall asleep in the daylight, would not roar and fume, would not drink himself to death, if only I were perfect.

I am forty-two as I write these words, and I know full well now that my father was an alcoholic, a man consumed by disease rather than by disappointment. What had seemed to me a private grief is in fact a public scourge. In the United States alone some ten or fifteen million people share his ailment, and behind the doors they slam in fury or disgrace, countless other children tremble. I comfort myself with such knowledge, holding it against the throb of memory like an ice pack against a bruise. There are keener sources of grief: poverty, racism, rape, war. I do not wish to compete for a trophy in suffering. I am only trying to understand the corrosive mixture of helplessness, responsibility, and shame that I learned to feel as the son of an alcoholic. I realize now that I did not cause my father's illness, nor could I have cured it. Yet for all this grown-up knowledge, I am still ten years old, my own son's age, and as that boy I struggle in guilt and confusion to save my father from pain.

Consider a few of our synonyms for *drunk:* tipsy, tight, pickled, soused, and plowed; stoned and stewed, lubricated and inebriated, juiced and sluiced; three sheets to the wind, in your cups, out of your mind, under the table; lit up, tanked up, wiped out; besotted, blotto, bombed, and buzzed; plastered, polluted, putrified; loaded or looped, boozy, woozy, fuddled, or smashed; crocked and shit-faced, corked and pissed, snockered and sloshed.

It is a mostly humorous lexicon, as the lore that deals with drunks— 10
in jokes and cartoons, in plays, films, and television skits—is largely comic. Aunt Matilda nips elderberry wine from the sideboard and burps politely during supper. Uncle Fred slouches to the table glassy-eyed, wearing a lamp shade for a hat and murmuring, "Candy is dandy but liquor is quicker." Inspired by cocktails, Mrs. Somebody recounts

the events of her day in a fuzzy dialect, while Mr. Somebody nibbles her ear and croons a bawdy song. On the sofa with Boyfriend, Daughter giggles, licking gin from her lips, and loosens the bows in her hair. Junior knocks back some brews with his chums at the Leopard Lounge and stumbles home to the wrong house, wonders foggily why he cannot locate his pajamas, and crawls naked into bed with the ugliest girl in school. The family dog slurps from a neglected martini and wobbles to the nursery, where he vomits in Baby's shoe.

It is all great fun. But if in the audience you notice a few laughing faces turn grim when the drunk lurches on stage, don't be surprised, for these are the children of alcoholics. Over the grinning mask of Dionysus,[1] the leering mask of Bacchus,[2] these children cannot help seeing the bloated features of their own parents. Instead of laughing, they wince, they mourn. Instead of celebrating the drunk as one freed from constraints, they pity him as one enslaved. They refuse to believe *in vino veritas,*[3] having seen their befuddled parents skid away from truth toward folly and oblivion. And so these children bite their lips until the lush staggers into the wings.

My father, when drunk, was neither funny nor honest; he was pathetic, frightening, deceitful. There seemed to be a leak in him somewhere, and he poured in booze to keep from draining dry. Like a torture victim who refuses to squeal, he would never admit that he had touched a drop, not even in his last year, when he seemed to be dissolving in alcohol before our very eyes. I never knew him to lie about anything, ever, except about this one ruinous fact. Drowsy, clumsy, unable to fix a bicycle tire, throw a baseball, balance a grocery sack, or walk across the room, he was stripped of his true self by drink. In a matter of minutes, the contents of a bottle could transform a brave man into a coward, a buddy into a bully, a gifted athlete and skilled carpenter and shrewd businessman into a bumbler. No dictionary of synonyms for *drunk* would soften the anguish of watching our prince turn into a frog.

Father's drinking became the family secret. While growing up, we children never breathed a word of it beyond the four walls of our house. To this day, my brother and sister rarely mention it, and then only when I press them. I did not confess the ugly, bewildering fact to my wife until his wavering walk and slurred speech forced me to. Recently, on the seventh anniversary of my father's death, I asked my mother if she ever spoke of his drinking to friends. "No, no, never," she replied hastily. "I couldn't bear for anyone to know."

1. Greek god of wine and intoxication.
2. Roman god of wine and intoxication.
3. "In wine is truth."

The secret bores under the skin, gets in the blood, into the bone, and stays there. Long after you have supposedly been cured of malaria, the fever can flare up, the tremors can shake you. So it is with the fevers of shame. You swallow the bitter quinine[4] of knowledge, and you learn to feel pity and compassion toward the drinker. Yet the shame lingers in your marrow, and, because of the shame, anger.

15 For a long stretch of my childhood we lived on a military reservation in Ohio, an arsenal where bombs were stored underground in bunkers, vintage airplanes burst into flames, and unstable artillery shells boomed nightly at the dump. We had the feeling, as children, that we played in a mine field, where a heedless footfall could trigger an explosion. When Father was drinking, the house, too, became a mine field. The least bump could set off either parent.

The more he drank, the more obsessed Mother became with stopping him. She hunted for bottles, counted the cash in his wallet, sniffed at his breath. Without meaning to snoop, we children blundered left and right into damning evidence. On afternoons when he came home from work sober, we flung ourselves at him for hugs, and felt against our ribs the telltale lump in his coat. In the barn we tumbled on the hay and heard beneath our sneakers the crunch of buried glass. We tugged open a drawer in his workbench, looking for screwdrivers or crescent wrenches, and spied a gleaming six-pack among the tools. Playing tag, we darted around the house just in time to see him sway on the rear stoop and heave a finished bottle into the woods. In his good night kiss we smelled the cloying sweetness of Clorets, the mints he chewed to camouflage his dragon's breath.

I can summon up that kiss right now by recalling Theodore Roethke's[5] lines about his own father in "My Papa's Waltz":

The whiskey on your breath
Could make a small boy dizzy;
But I hung on like death:
Such waltzing was not easy.

Such waltzing was hard, terribly hard, for with a boy's scrawny arms I was trying to hold my tipsy father upright.

For years, the chief source of those incriminating bottles and cans was a grimy store a mile from us, a cinder block place called Sly's, with two gas pumps outside and a moth-eaten dog asleep in the window. A strip of flypaper, speckled the year round with black bodies, coiled in the doorway. Inside, on rusty metal shelves or in wheezing coolers, you could find pop and Popsicles, cigarettes, potato chips, canned soup,

4. Drug from the bark of the South American cinchona tree, used to treat malaria.
5. American poet (1908–1963) whose father also drank too much.

raunchy postcards, fishing gear, Twinkies, wine, and beer. When Father drove anywhere on errands, Mother would send us kids along as guards, warning us not to let him out of our sight. And so with one or more of us on board, Father would cruise up to Sly's, pump a dollar's worth of gas or plump the tires with air, and then, telling us to wait in the car, he would head for that fly-spangled doorway.

Dutiful and panicky, we cried, "Let us go in with you!"

20 "No," he answered. "I'll be back in two shakes."

"Please!"

"No!" he roared. "Don't you budge, or I'll jerk a knot in your tails!"

So we stayed put, kicking the seats, while he ducked inside. Often, when he had parked the car at a careless angle, we gazed in through the window and saw Mr. Sly fetching down from a shelf behind the cash register two green pints of Gallo wine. Father swigged one of them right there at the counter, stuffed the other in his pocket, and then out he came, a bulge in his coat, a flustered look on his red face.

Because the Mom and Pop who ran the dump were neighbors of ours, living just down the tar-blistered road, I hated them all the more for poisoning my father. I wanted to sneak in their store and smash the bottles and set fire to the place. I also hated the Gallo brothers, Ernest and Julio, whose jovial faces shone from the labels of their wine, labels I would find, torn and curled, when I burned the trash. I noted the Gallo brothers' address, in California, and I studied the road atlas to see how far that was from Ohio, because I meant to go out there and tell Ernest and Julio what they were doing to my father, and then, if they showed no mercy, I would kill them.

25 While growing up on the back roads and in the country schools and cramped Methodist churches of Ohio and Tennessee, I never heard the word *alcoholism*, never happened across it in books or magazines. In the nearby towns, there were no addiction treatment programs, no community mental health centers, no Alcoholics Anonymous chapters, no therapists. Left alone with our grievous secret, we had no way of understanding Father's drinking except as an act of will, a deliberate folly or cruelty, a moral weakness, a sin. He drank because he chose to, pure and simple. Why our father, so playful and competent and kind when sober, would choose to ruin himself and punish his family, we could not fathom.

Our neighborhood was high on the Bible, and the Bible was hard on drunkards. "Woe to those who are heroes at drinking wine, and valiant men in mixing strong drink," wrote Isaiah. "The priest and the prophet reel with strong drink, they are confused with wine, they err in vision, they stumble in giving judgment. For all tables are full of vomit, no place is without filthiness." We children had seen those fouled tables at the local truck stop where the notorious boozers hung out, our father occasionally among them. "Wine and new wine take away the understanding," declared the prophet Hosea. We had also seen evidence of that in our father, who could multiply seven-digit numbers in his head when sober, but when drunk could not help us with fourth-grade math. Proverbs warned: "Do not look at wine when it is red, when it sparkles in the cup and goes down smoothly. At the last it bites like a serpent, and stings like an adder. Your eyes will see strange things, and your mind utter perverse things." Woe, woe.

Dismayingly often, these biblical drunkards stirred up trouble for their own kids. Noah made fresh wine after the flood, drank too much of it, fell asleep without any clothes on, and was glimpsed in the buff by his son Ham, whom Noah promptly cursed. In one passage—it was so shocking we had to read it under our blankets with flashlights—the patriarch Lot fell down drunk and slept with his daughters. The sins of the fathers set their children's teeth on edge.

Our ministers were fond of quoting St. Paul's pronouncement that drunkards would not inherit the kingdom of God. These grave preachers assured us that the wine referred to during the Last Supper was in fact grape juice. Bible and sermons and hymns combined to give us the impression that Moses should have brought down from the mountain another stone tablet, bearing the Eleventh Commandment: Thou shalt not drink.

The scariest and most illuminating Bible story apropos of drunkards was the one about the lunatic and the swine. Matthew, Mark, and Luke each told a version of the tale. We knew it by heart: When Jesus climbed out of his boat one day, this lunatic came charging up from the graveyard, stark naked and filthy, frothing at the mouth, so violent that he broke the strongest chains. Nobody would go near him. Night and day for years this madman had been wailing among the tombs and bruising himself with stones. Jesus took one look at him and said, "Come out of the man, you unclean spirits!" for he could see that the lunatic was possessed by demons. Meanwhile, some hogs were conveniently rooting nearby. "If we have to come out," begged the demons, "at least let us go into those swine." Jesus agreed. The unclean spirits entered the hogs, and the hogs rushed straight off a cliff and plunged into a lake. Hearing the story in Sunday school, my friends thought mainly of the pigs. (How big a splash did they make? Who paid for the lost pork?) But I thought of the redeemed lunatic, who bathed himself and put on clothes and calmly sat at the feet of Jesus, restored—so the Bible said—to "his right mind."

When drunk, our father was clearly in his wrong mind. He became a 30
stranger, as fearful to us as any graveyard lunatic, not quite frothing at the mouth but fierce enough, quick-tempered, explosive; or else he

grew maudlin and weepy, which frightened us nearly as much. In my boyhood despair, I reasoned that maybe he wasn't to blame for turning into an ogre. Maybe, like the lunatic, he was possessed by demons. I found support for my theory when I heard liquor referred to as "spirits," when the newspapers reported that somebody had been arrested for "driving under the influence," and when church ladies railed against that "demon drink."

If my father was indeed possessed, who would exorcise him? If he was a sinner, who would save him? If he was ill, who would cure him? If he suffered, who would ease his pain? Not ministers or doctors, for we could not bring ourselves to confide in them; not the neighbors, for we pretended they had never seen him drunk; not Mother, who fussed and pleaded but could not budge him; not my brother and sister, who were only kids. That left me. It did not matter that I, too, was only a child, and a bewildered one at that. I could not excuse myself.

On first reading a description of delirium tremens—in a book on alcoholism I smuggled from the library—I thought immediately of the frothing lunatic and the frenzied swine. When I read stories or watched films about grisly metamorphoses—Dr. Jekyll becoming Mr. Hyde,[6] the mild husband changing into a werewolf, the kindly neighbor taken over by a brutal alien—I could not help seeing my own father's mutation from sober to drunk. Even today, knowing better, I am attracted by the demonic theory of drink, for when I recall my father's transformation, the emergence of his ugly second self, I find it easy to believe in possession by unclean spirits. We never knew which version of Father would come home from work, the true or the tainted, nor could we guess how far down the slope toward cruelty he would slide.

How far a man *could* slide we gauged by observing our back-road neighbors—the out-of-work miners who had dragged their families to our corner of Ohio from the desolate hollows of Appalachia, the tight-fisted farmers, the surly mechanics, the balked and broken men. There was, for example, whiskey-soaked Mr. Jenkins, who beat his wife and kids so hard we could hear their screams from the road. There was Mr. Lavo the wino, who fell asleep smoking time and again, until one night his disgusted wife bundled up the children and went outside and left him in his easy chair to burn; he awoke on his own, staggered out coughing into the yard, and pounded her flat while the children looked on and the shack turned to ash. There was the truck driver, Mr. Sampson, who tripped over his son's tricycle one night while drunk and got so mad that he jumped into his semi and drove away, shifting through the dozen gears, and never came back. We saw the bruised

6. London physician and his evil alter ego in Robert Louis Stevenson's novel.

children of these fathers clump onto our school bus, we saw the abandoned children huddle in the pews at church, we saw the stunned and battered mothers begging for help at our doors.

Our own father never beat us, and I don't think he ever beat Mother, but he threatened often. The Old Testament Yahweh was not more terrible in his wrath. Eyes blazing, voice booming, Father would pull out his belt and swear to give us a whipping, but he never followed through, never needed to, because we could imagine it so vividly. He shoved us, pawed us with the back of his hand, as an irked bear might smack a cub, not to injure, just to clear a space. I can see him grabbing Mother by the hair as she cowers on a chair during a nightly quarrel. He twists her neck back until she gapes up at him, and then he lifts over her skull a glass quart bottle of milk, the milk running down his forearm; and he yells at her, "Say just one more word, one goddamn word, and I'll shut you up!" I fear she will prick him with her sharp tongue, but she is terrified into silence, and so am I, and the leaking bottle quivers in the air, and milk slithers through the red hair of my father's uplifted arm, and the entire scene is there to this moment, the head jerked back, the club raised.

35 When the drink made him weepy, Father would pack a bag and kiss each of us children on the head, and announce from the front door that he was moving out. "Where to?" we demanded, fearful each time that he would leave for good, as Mr. Sampson had roared away for good in his diesel truck. "Someplace where I won't get hounded every minute," Father would answer, his jaw quivering. He stabbed a look at Mother, who might say, "Don't run into the ditch before you get there," or, "Good riddance," and then he would slink away. Mother watched him go with arms crossed over her chest, her face closed like the lid on a box of snakes. We children bawled. Where could he go? To the truck stop, that den of iniquity? To one of those dark, ratty flophouses in town? Would he wind up sleeping under a railroad bridge or on a park bench or in a cardboard box, mummied in rags, like the bums we had seen on our trips to Cleveland and Chicago? We bawled and bawled, wondering if he would ever come back.

He always did come back, a day or a week later, but each time there was a sliver less of him.

In Kafka's[7] *The Metamorphosis,* which opens famously with Gregor Samsa waking up from uneasy dreams to find himself transformed into an insect, Gregor's family keep reassuring themselves that things will be just fine again, "When he comes back to us." Each time alco-

7. Franz Kafka (1883–1924), Czechoslovakian-born novelist and short-story writer whose works raise puzzling moral, spiritual, and political dilemmas.

hol transformed our father, we held out the same hope, that he would really and truly come back to us, our authentic father, the tender and playful and competent man, and then all things would be fine. We had grounds for such hope. After his weepy departures and chapfallen returns, he would sometimes go weeks, even months without drinking. Those were glad times. Joy banged inside my ribs. Every day without the furtive glint of bottles, every meal without a fight, every bedtime without sobs encouraged us to believe that such bliss might go on forever.

Mother was fooled by just such a hope all during the forty-odd years she knew this Greeley Ray Sanders. Soon after she met him in a Chicago delicatessen on the eve of World War II and fell for his butter-melting Mississippi drawl and his wavy red hair, she learned that he drank heavily. But then so did a lot of men. She would soon coax or scold him into breaking the nasty habit. She would point out to him how ugly and foolish it was, this bleary drinking, and then he would quit. He refused to quit during their engagement, however, still refused during the first years of marriage, refused until my sister came along. The shock of fatherhood sobered him, and he remained sober through my birth at the end of the war and right on through until we moved in 1951 to the Ohio arsenal, that paradise of bombs. Like all places that make a business of death, the arsenal had more than its share of alcoholics and drug addicts and other varieties of escape artists. There I turned six and started school and woke into a child's flickering awareness, just in time to see my father begin sneaking swigs in the garage.

He sobered up again for most of a year at the height of the Korean War, to celebrate the birth of my brother. But aside from that dry spell, his only breaks from drinking before I graduated from high school were just long enough to raise and then dash our hopes. Then during the fall of my senior year—the time of the Cuban missile crisis, when it seemed that the nightly explosions at the munitions dump and the nightly rages in our household might spread to engulf the globe—Father collapsed. His liver, kidneys, and heart all conked out. The doctors saved him, but only by a hair. He stayed in the hospital for weeks, going through a withdrawal so terrible that Mother would not let us visit him. If he wanted to kill himself, the doctors solemnly warned him, all he had to do was hit the bottle again. One binge would finish him.

40 Father must have believed them, for he stayed dry the next fifteen years. It was an answer to prayer, Mother said, it was a miracle. I believe it was a reflex of fear, which he sustained over the years through courage and pride. He knew a man could die from drink, for his brother Roscoe had. We children never laid eyes on doomed Uncle

Roscoe, but in the stories Mother told us he became a fairy-tale figure, like a boy who took the wrong turning in the woods and was gobbled up by the wolf.

The fifteen-year dry spell came to an end with Father's retirement in the spring of 1978. Like many men, he gave up his identity along with his job. One day he was a boss at the factory, with a brass plate on his door and a reputation to uphold; the next day he was a nobody at home. He and Mother were leaving Ontario, the last of the many places to which his job had carried them, and they were moving to a new house in Mississippi, his childhood stomping grounds. As a boy in Mississippi, Father sold Coca-Cola during dances while the moonshiners peddled their brew in the parking lot; as a young blade, he fought in bars and in the ring, seeking a state Golden Gloves championship; he gambled at poker, hunted pheasants, raced motorcycles and cars, played semiprofessional baseball, and, along with all his buddies—in the Black Cat Saloon, behind the cotton gin, in the woods—he drank. It was a perilous youth to dream of recovering.

After his final day of work, Mother drove on ahead with a car full of begonias and violets, while Father stayed behind to oversee the packing. When the van was loaded, the sweaty movers broke open a six-pack and offered him a beer.

"Let's drink to retirement!" they crowed. "Let's drink to freedom! to fishing! hunting! loafing! Let's drink to a guy who's going home!"

At least I imagine some such words, for that is all I can do, imagine, and I see Father's hand trembling in midair as he thinks about the fifteen sober years and about the doctors' warning, and he tells himself *God damnit, I am a free man,* and *Why can't a free man drink one beer after a lifetime of hard work?* and I see his arm reaching, his fingers closing, the can tilting to his lips. I even supply a label for the beer, a swaggering brand that promises on television to deliver the essence of life. I watch the amber liquid pour down his throat, the alcohol steal into his blood, the key turn in his brain.

Soon after my parents moved back to Father's treacherous stomp- 45
ing ground, my wife and I visited them in Mississippi with our five-year-old daughter. Mother had been too distraught to warn me about the return of the demons. So when I climbed out of the car that bright July morning and saw my father napping in the hammock, I felt uneasy, for in all his sober years I had never known him to sleep in daylight. Then he lurched upright, blinked his bloodshot eyes, and greeted us in a syrupy voice. I was hurled back helpless into childhood.

"What's the matter with Papaw?" our daughter asked.

"Nothing," I said. "Nothing!"

Like a child again, I pretended not to see him in his stupor, and behind my phony smile I grieved. On that visit and on the few that remained before his death, once again I found bottles in the workbench, bottles in the woods. Again his hands shook too much for him to run a saw, to make his precious miniature furniture, to drive straight down back roads. Again he wound up in the ditch, in the hospital, in jail, in treatment centers. Again he shouted and wept. Again he lied. "I never touched a drop," he swore. "Your mother's making it up."

I no longer fancied I could reason with the men whose names I found on the bottles—Jim Beam, Jack Daniels—nor did I hope to save my father by burning down a store. I was able now to press the cold statistics about alcoholism against the ache of memory: ten million victims, fifteen million, twenty. And yet, in spite of my age, I reacted in the same blind way as I had in childhood, ignoring biology, forgetting numbers, vainly seeking to erase through my efforts whatever drove him to drink. I worked on their place twelve and sixteen hours a day, in the swelter of Mississippi summers, digging ditches, running electrical wires, planting trees, mowing grass, building sheds, as though what nagged at him was some list of chores, as though by taking his worries on my shoulders I could redeem him. I was flung back into boyhood, acting as though my father would not drink himself to death if only I were perfect.

50 I failed of perfection; he succeeded in dying. To the end, he considered himself not sick but sinful. "Do you want to kill yourself?" I asked him. "Why not?" he answered. "Why the hell not? What's there to save?" To the end, he would not speak about his feelings, would not or could not give a name to the beast that was devouring him.

In silence, he went rushing off the cliff. Unlike the biblical swine, however, he left behind a few of the demons to haunt his children. Life with him and the loss of him twisted us into shapes that will be familiar to other sons and daughters of alcoholics. My brother became a rebel, my sister retreated into shyness, I played the stalwart and dutiful son who would hold the family together. If my father was unstable, I would be a rock. If he squandered money on drink, I would pinch every penny. If he wept when drunk—and only when drunk—I would not let myself weep at all. If he roared at the Little League umpire for calling my pitches balls, I would throw nothing but strikes. Watching him flounder and rage, I came to dread the loss of control. I would go through life without making anyone mad. I vowed never to put in my mouth or veins any chemical that would banish my everyday self. I would never make a scene, never lash out at the ones I loved, never hurt a soul. Through hard work, relentless work, I would achieve something dazzling—in the classroom, on the basketball floor, in the science lab, in the pages of books—and my achievement would distract the world's eyes from his humiliation. I would become a worthy sacrifice, and the smoke of my burning would please God.

It is far easier to recognize these twists in my character than to undo them. Work has become an addiction for me, as drink was an addiction for my father. Knowing this, my daughter gave me a placard for the wall: WORKAHOLIC. The labor is endless and futile, for I can no more redeem myself through work than I could redeem my father. I still panic in the face of other people's anger, because his drunken temper was so terrible. I shrink from causing sadness or disappointment even to strangers, as though I were still concealing the family shame. I still notice every twitch of emotion in the faces around me, having learned as a child to read the weather in faces, and I blame myself for their least pang of unhappiness or anger. In certain moods I blame myself for everything. Guilt burns like acid in my veins.

I am moved to write these pages now because my own son, at the age of ten, is taking on himself the griefs of the world, and in particular the griefs of his father. He tells me that when I am gripped by sadness he feels responsible; he feels there must be something he can do to spring me from depression, to fix my life. And that crushing sense of responsibility is exactly what I felt at the age of ten in the face of my father's drinking. My son wonders if I, too, am possessed. I write, therefore, to drag into the light what eats at me—the fear, the guilt, the shame—so that my own children may be spared.

I still shy away from nightclubs, from bars, from parties where the solvent is alcohol. My friends puzzle over this, but it is no more peculiar than for a man to shy away from the lions' den after seeing his father torn apart. I took my own first drink at the age of twenty-one, half a glass of burgundy. I knew the odds of my becoming an alcoholic were four times higher than for the sons of nonalcoholic fathers. So I sipped warily.

I still do—once a week, perhaps, a glass of wine, a can of beer, nothing stronger, nothing more. I listen for the turning of a key in my brain. 55

QUESTIONS

1. *Sanders frequently punctuates his memories of his father with information from other sources—dictionaries, medical encyclopedias, poems and short stories, the Bible. What function do these sources perform? How do they enlarge and enrich Sanders's essay?*
2. *Why does Sanders include the final three paragraphs (53 to 55)? What effect do they create that would be lost without them?*
3. *Drawing on your memories of a friend or family member, write an essay about some problem that person had and its effect on your life.*

Annie Dillard

TERWILLIGER BUNTS ONE

One Sunday afternoon Mother wandered through our kitchen, where Father was making a sandwich and listening to the ball game. The Pirates were playing the New York Giants at Forbes Field. In those days, the Giants had a utility infielder named Wayne Terwilliger. Just as Mother passed through, the radio announcer cried—with undue drama—"Terwilliger bunts one!"

"Terwilliger bunts one?" Mother cried back, stopped short. She turned. "Is that English?"

"The player's name is Terwilliger," Father said. "He bunted."

"That's marvelous," Mother said. " 'Terwilliger bunts one.' No wonder you listen to baseball. 'Terwilliger bunts one.' "

5 For the next seven or eight years, Mother made this surprising string of syllables her own. Testing a microphone, she repeated, "Terwilliger bunts one"; testing a pen or a typewriter, she wrote it. If, as happened surprisingly often in the course of various improvised gags, she pretended to whisper something else in my ear, she actually whispered, "Terwilliger bunts one." Whenever someone used a French phrase, or a Latin one, she answered solemnly, "Terwilliger bunts one." If Mother had had, like Andrew Carnegie, the opportunity to cook up a motto for a coat of arms, hers would have read simply and tellingly, "Terwilliger bunts one." (Carnegie's was "Death to Privilege.")

She served us with other words and phrases. On a Florida trip, she repeated tremulously, "That . . . is a royal poinciana." I don't remember the tree; I remember the thrill in her voice. She pronounced it carefully, and spelled it. She also liked to say "portulaca."

The drama of the words "Tamiami Trail" stirred her, we learned on the same Florida trip. People built Tampa on one coast, and they built Miami on another. Then—the height of visionary ambition and folly—they piled a slow, tremendous road through the terrible Everglades to connect them. To build the road, men stood sunk in muck to their armpits. They fought off cottonmouth moccasins and six-foot alligators. They slept in boats, wet. They blasted muck with dynamite, cut jungle with machetes; they laid logs, dragged drilling machines, hauled dredges, heaped limestone. The road took fourteen years to build up by the shovelful, a Panama Canal in reverse, and cost hundreds of lives from tropical, mosquito-carried diseases. Then, capping it all, some genius thought of the word Tamiami: they called the road

From Part Two of *An American Childhood* (1987).

from Tampa to Miami, this very road under our spinning wheels, the Tamiami Trail. Some called it Alligator Alley. Anyone could drive over this road without a thought.

Hearing this, moved, I thought all the suffering of road building was worth it (it wasn't my suffering), now that we had this new thing to hang these new words on—Alligator Alley for those who liked things cute, and, for connoisseurs like Mother, for lovers of the human drama in all its boldness and terror, the Tamiami Trail.

Back home, Mother cut clips from reels of talk, as it were, and played them back at leisure. She noticed that many Pittsburghers confuse "leave" and "let." One kind relative brightened our morning by mentioning why she'd brought her son to visit: "He wanted to come with me, so I left him." Mother filled in Amy and me on locutions we missed. "I can't do it on Friday," her pretty sister told a crowded dinner party, "because Friday's the day I lay in the stores."

(All unconsciously, though, we ourselves used some pure Pittsburghisms. We said "tele pole," pronounced "telly pole," for that splintery sidewalk post I loved to climb. We said "slippy"—the sidewalks are "slippy." We said, "That's all the farther I could go." And we said, as Pittsburghers do say, "This glass needs washed," or "The dog needs walked"—a usage our father eschewed; he knew it was not standard English, nor even comprehensible English, but he never let on.)

"Spell 'poinsettia,' " Mother would throw out at me, smiling with pleasure. "Spell 'sherbet.' " The idea was not to make us whizzes, but, quite the contrary, to remind us—and I, especially, needed reminding—that we didn't know it all just yet.

"There's a deer standing in the front hall," she told me one quiet evening in the country.

"Really?"

"No. I just wanted to tell you something once without your saying, 'I know.' "

Supermarkets in the middle 1950s began luring, or bothering, customers by giving out Top Value Stamps or Green Stamps. When, shopping with Mother, we got to the head of the checkout line, the checker, always a young man, asked, "Save stamps?"

"No," Mother replied genially, week after week, "I build model airplanes." I believe she originated this line. It took me years to determine where the joke lay.

Anyone who met her verbal challenges she adored. She had surgery on one of her eyes. On the operating table, just before she conked out, she appealed feelingly to the surgeon, saying, as she had been planning to say for weeks, "Will I be able to play the piano?" "Not on me," the surgeon said. "You won't pull that old one on me."

It was, indeed, an old one. The surgeon was supposed to answer,

"Yes, my dear, brave woman, you will be able to play the piano after this operation," to which Mother intended to reply, "Oh, good, I've always wanted to play the piano." This pat scenario bored her; she loved having it interrupted. It must have galled her that usually her acquaintances were so predictably unalert; it must have galled her that, for the length of her life, she could surprise everyone so continually, so easily, when she had been the same all along. At any rate, she loved anyone who, as she put it, saw it coming, and called her on it.

She regarded the instructions on bureaucratic forms as straight lines. "Do you advocate the overthrow of the United States government by force or violence?" After some thought she wrote, "Force." She regarded children, even babies, as straight men. When Molly learned to crawl, Mother delighted in buying her gowns with drawstrings at the bottom, like Swee'pea's,[1] because, as she explained energetically, you could easily step on the drawstring without the baby's noticing, so that she crawled and crawled and crawled and never got anywhere except into a small ball at the gown's top.

20 When we children were young, she mothered us tenderly and dependably; as we got older, she resumed her career of anarchism. She collared us into her gags. If she answered the phone on a wrong number, she told the caller, "Just a minute," and dragged the receiver to Amy or me, saying, "Here, take this, your name is Cecile," or, worse, just, "It's for you." You had to think on your feet. But did you want to perform well as Cecile, or did you want to take pity on the wretched caller?

During a family trip to the Highland Park Zoo, Mother and I were alone for a minute. She approached a young couple holding hands on a bench by the seals, and addressed the young man in dripping tones: "Where have you been? Still got those baby-blue eyes; always did slay me. And this"—a swift nod at the dumbstruck young woman, who had removed her hand from the man's—"must be the one you were telling me about. She's not so bad, really, as you used to make out. But listen, you know how I miss you, you know where to reach me, same old place. And there's Ann over there—see how she's grown? See the blue eyes?"

And off she sashayed, taking me firmly by the hand, and leading us around briskly past the monkey house and away. She cocked an ear back, and both of us heard the desperate man begin, in a high-pitched wail, "I swear, I never saw her before in my life. . . ."

On a long, sloping beach by the ocean, she lay stretched out sunning with Father and friends, until the conversation gradually grew tedious,

1. The infant in the comic strip "Popeye" by Elzie Crisler Segar.

when without forethought she gave a little push with her heel and rolled away. People were stunned. She rolled deadpan and apparently effortlessly, arms and legs extended and tidy, down the beach to the distant water's edge, where she lay at ease just as she had been, but half in the surf, and well out of earshot.

She dearly loved to fluster people by throwing out a game's rules at whim—when she was getting bored, losing in a dull sort of way, and when everybody else was taking it too seriously. If you turned your back, she moved the checkers around on the board. When you got them all straightened out, she denied she'd touched them; the next time you turned your back, she lined them up on the rug or hid them under your chair. In a betting rummy game called Michigan, she routinely played out of turn, or called out a card she didn't hold, or counted backward, simply to amuse herself by causing an uproar and watching the rest of us do double takes and have fits. (Much later, when serious suitors came to call, Mother subjected them to this fast card game as a trial by ordeal; she used it as an intelligence test and a measure of spirit. If the poor man could stay a round without breaking down or running out, he got to marry one of us, if he still wanted to.)

She excelled at bridge, playing fast and boldly, but when the stakes 25
were low and the hands dull, she bid slams for the devilment of it, or raised her opponents' suit to bug them, or showed her hand, or tossed her cards in a handful behind her back in a characteristic swift motion accompanied by a vibrantly innocent look. It drove our stolid father crazy. The hand was over before it began, and the guests were appalled. How do you score it, who deals now, what do you do with a crazy person who is having so much fun? Or they were down seven, and the guests were appalled. "Pam!" "Dammit, Pam!" He groaned. What ails such people? What on earth possesses them? He rubbed his face.

She was an unstoppable force; she never let go. When we moved across town, she persuaded the U.S. Post Office to let her keep her old address—forever—because she'd had stationery printed. I don't know how she did it. Every new post office worker, over decades, needed to learn that although the Doaks' mail is addressed to here, it is delivered to there.

Mother's energy and intelligence suited her for a greater role in a larger arena—mayor of New York, say—than the one she had. She followed American politics closely; she had been known to vote for Democrats. She saw how things should be run, but she had nothing to run but our household. Even there, small minds bugged her; she was smarter than the people who designed the things she had to use all day for the length of her life.

"Look," she said. "Whoever designed this corkscrew never used one. Why would anyone sell it without trying it out?" So she invented a better one. She showed me a drawing of it. The spirit of American enterprise never faded in Mother. If capitalizing and tooling up had been as interesting as theorizing and thinking up, she would have fired up a new factory every week, and chaired several hundred corporations.

"It grieves me," she would say, "it grieves my heart," that the company that made one superior product packaged it poorly, or took the wrong tack in its advertising. She knew, as she held the thing mournfully in her two hands, that she'd never find another. She was right. We children wholly sympathized, and so did Father; what could she do, what could anyone do, about it? She was Samson in chains.[2] She paced.

30 She didn't like the taste of stamps so she didn't lick stamps; she licked the corner of the envelope instead. She glued sandpaper to the sides of kitchen drawers, and under kitchen cabinets, so she always had a handy place to strike a match. She designed, and hounded workmen to build against all norms, doubly wide kitchen counters and elevated bathroom sinks. To splint a finger, she stuck it in a lightweight cigar tube. Conversely, to protect a pack of cigarettes, she carried it in a Band-Aid box. She drew plans for an over-the-finger toothbrush for babies, an oven rack that slid up and down, and—the family favorite—Lendalarm. Lendalarm was a beeper you attached to books (or tools) you loaned friends. After ten days, the beeper sounded. Only the rightful owner could silence it.

She repeatedly reminded us of P. T. Barnum's dictum: You could sell anything to anybody if you marketed it right. The adman who thought of making Americans believe they needed underarm deodorant was a visionary. So, too, was the hero who made a success of a new product, Ivory soap. The executives were horrified, Mother told me, that a cake of this stuff floated. Soap wasn't supposed to float. Anyone would be able to tell it was mostly whipped-up air. Then some inspired adman made a leap: Advertise that it floats. Flaunt it. The rest is history.

She respected the rare few who broke through to new ways. "Look," she'd say, "here's an intelligent apron." She called upon us to admire intelligent control knobs and intelligent pan handles, intelligent andirons and picture frames and knife sharpeners. She questioned everything, every pair of scissors, every knitting needle, gardening glove, tape dispenser. Hers was a restless mental vigor that just about ignited the dumb household objects with its force.

2. The Israelite champion against the Philistines, to whom he was betrayed by Delilah (see Judges xiv–xvi).

Torpid conformity was a kind of sin; it was stupidity itself, the mighty stream against which Mother would never cease to struggle. If you held no minority opinions, or if you failed to risk total ostracism for them daily, the world would be a better place without you.

Always I heard Mother's emotional voice asking Amy and me the same few questions: Is that your own idea? Or somebody else's? "*Giant* is a good movie," I pronounced to the family at dinner. "Oh, really?" Mother warmed to these occasions. She all but rolled up her sleeves. She knew I hadn't seen it. "Is that your considered opinion?"

She herself held many unpopular, even fantastic, positions. She was scathingly sarcastic about the McCarthy hearings[3] while they took place, right on our living-room television; she frantically opposed Father's wait-and-see calm. "We don't know enough about it," he said. "I do," she said. "I know all I need to know."

She asserted, against all opposition, that people who lived in trailer parks were not bad but simply poor, and had as much right to settle on beautiful land, such as rural Ligonier, Pennsylvania, as did the oldest of families in the finest of hidden houses. Therefore, the people who owned trailer parks, and sought zoning changes to permit trailer parks, needed our help. Her profound belief that the country-club pool sweeper was a person, and that the department-store saleslady, the bus driver, telephone operator, and housepainter were people, and even in groups the steelworkers who carried pickets and the Christmas shoppers who clogged intersections were people—this was a conviction common enough in democratic Pittsburgh, but not altogether common among our friends' parents, or even, perhaps, among our parents' friends.

Opposition emboldened Mother, and she would take on anybody on any issue—the chairman of the board, at a cocktail party, on the current strike; she would fly at him in a flurry of passion, as a songbird selflessly attacks a big hawk.

"Eisenhower's going to win," I announced after school. She lowered her magazine and looked me in the eyes: "How do you know?" I was doomed. It was fatal to say, "Everyone says so." We all knew well what happened. "Do you consult this Everyone before you make your decisions? What if Everyone decided to round up all the Jews?" Mother knew there was no danger of cowing me. She simply tried to keep us all awake. And in fact it was always clear to Amy and me, and to Molly

3. The televised hearings in 1954 (the army accused Wisconsin Senator Joseph R. McCarthy [1908–1957] of improperly seeking preferential treatment for a former colleague then in the service; Senator McCarthy, widely known as a Communist-hunter, accused the army of covering up certain espionage action) led to the senator's loss of public favor and contributed to his "condemnation" by the Senate in December 1954.

when she grew old enough to listen, that if our classmates came to cruelty, just as much as if the neighborhood or the nation came to madness, we were expected to take, and would be each separately capable of taking, a stand.

June Jordan

For My American Family: A Belated Tribute to a Legacy of Gifted Intelligence and Guts

I would love to see pictures of the Statue of Liberty taken by my father. They would tell me so much about him that I wish I knew. He couldn't very well ask that lady to "hold that smile" or "put on a little something with red to brighten it up." He'd have to take her "as is," using a choice of angles or focus or distance as the means to his statement. And I imagine that my father would choose a long-shot, soft-focus, wide-angle lens: that would place Miss Liberty in her full formal setting, and yet suggest the tears that easily spilled from his eyes whenever he spoke about "this great country of ours: America."

A camera buff, not averse to wandering around the city with both a Rolleiflex and a Rolleicord at the ready, my father thought nothing of a two or three hours' "setup" for a couple of shots of anything he found beautiful. I remember one Saturday, late morning, when I watched my father push the "best" table in the house under the dining-room windows, fidget the venetian blinds in order to gain the most interesting, slatted light, and then bring the antique Chinese vase downstairs from the parlor, fill that with fresh roses from the backyard, and then run out to the corner store for several pieces of fruit to complete his still-life composition.

All of this took place in the 1940s. We lived in the Bedford-Stuyvesant neighborhood of Brooklyn, one of the largest urban Black communities in the world. Besides the fruit and the flowers of my father's aesthetic preoccupation, and just beyond those narrow brownstone dining-room windows, there was a burly mix of unpredictable street life that he could not control, despite incessant telephone calls, for example, to the Department of Sanitation: "Hello. This is a man by the name of Granville Ivanhoe Jordan, and I'm calling about garbage collection. What happened? Did you forget?!"

The unlikely elements of my father's name may summarize his his-

Originally published in *New York Newsday*, July 4, 1986.

tory and character rather well. Jordan is a fairly common surname on the island of Jamaica where he was born, one of perhaps twelve or thirteen children who foraged for food, and who never forgot, or forgave, the ridicule his ragged clothing provoked in school. Leaving the classroom long before the normal conclusion to an elementary education, my father later taught himself to read and, after that, he never stopped reading and reading everything he could find, from Burpee seed catalogues to Shakespeare to the *National Geographic* magazines to "Negro" poetry to liner notes for the record albums of classical music that he devoured. But he was also "the little bull"—someone who loved a good rough fight and who even volunteered to teach boxing to other young "Negroes" at the Harlem YMCA, where he frequently participated in political and militant "uplifting-the-race" meetings, on West 135th Street.

Except for weekends, my father pursued all of his studies in the long 5
early hours of the night, 3 or 4 A.M., after eight hours' standing up at the post office where he speed-sorted mail quite without the assistance of computers and zip codes which, of course, had yet to be invented. Exceptionally handsome and exceptionally vain, Mr. G. I. Jordan, immaculate in one of his innumerable, rooster-elegant suits, would readily hack open a coconut with a machete, or slice a grapefruit in half, throw his head back, and squeeze the juice into his mouth—carefully held a tricky foot away—all to my mother's head-shaking dismay: "Why now you have to act up like a monkey chaser, eh?"

It is a sad thing to consider that this country has given its least to those who have loved it the most. I am the daughter of West Indian immigrants. And perhaps there are other Americans as believing and as grateful and as loyal, but I doubt it. In general, the very word *immigrant* connotes somebody white, while *alien* denotes everybody else. But hundreds and hundreds of thousands of Americans are hardworking, naturalized Black citizens whose trust in the democratic promise of the mainland has never been reckoned with, fully, or truly reciprocated. For instance, I know that my parents would have wanted to say, "Thanks, America!" if only there had been some way, some public recognition and welcome of their presence, here, and then some really big shot to whom their gratitude might matter.

I have seen family snapshots of my mother pushing me in a baby carriage decorated with the single decal F.D.R., and I have listened to endless tall stories about what I did or didn't do when my father placed me in the lap of New York's mayor, Fiorello La Guardia, and, on top of the ornate wallpaper of our parlor floor there was a large color photograph of the archbishop of the Episcopal diocese of Long Island; my parents lived in America, full of faith.

When I visited the birthplace of my mother, twelve years ago, I was embarrassed by the shiny rented car that brought me there: even in 1974, there were no paved roads in Clonmel, a delicate dot of a mountain village in Jamaica. And despite the breathtaking altitude, you could not poke or peer yourself into a decent position for "a view": the vegetation was that dense, that lush, and that chaotic. On or close to the site of my mother's childhood home, I found a neat wood cabin, still without windowpanes or screens, a dirt floor, and a barefoot family of seven, quietly bustling about.

I was stunned. There was neither electricity nor running water. How did my parents even hear about America, more than a half century ago? In the middle of the Roaring Twenties, these eager Black immigrants came, by boat. Did they have to borrow shoes for the journey?

10 I know that my aunt and my mother buckled into domestic work, once they arrived, barely into their teens. I'm not sure how my father managed to feed himself before that fantastic 1933 afternoon when he simply ran all the way from midtown Manhattan up to our Harlem apartment, shouting out the news: A job! He had found a job!

And throughout my childhood I cannot recall even one utterance of disappointment, or bitterness with America. In fact, my parents hid away any newspaper or magazine article that dealt with "jim crow" or "lynchings" or "discrimination." These were terms of taboo status neither to be spoken nor explained to me. Instead I was given a child's biography of Abraham Lincoln and the Bible stories of Daniel and David, and, from my father, I learned about Marcus Garvey and George Washington Carver and Mary McLeod Bethune. The focus was relentlessly upbeat. Or, as Jimmy Cliff used to sing it, "You can make it if you really try."

My mother's emphasis was more religious, and more consistently race-conscious, and she was equally affirmative: God would take care of me. And, besides, there was ("C'mon, Joe! C'mon!") the Brown Bomber, Joe Louis, and then, incredibly, Jackie Robinson who, by himself, elevated the Brooklyn Dodgers into a sacred cult worshipped by apparently dauntless Black baseball fans.

We had a pretty rich life. Towards the end of the 1960s I was often amazed by facile references to Black communities as "breeding grounds of despair" or "culturally deprived" or "ghettos." That was not the truth. There are grounds for despair in the suburbs, evidently, and I more than suspect greater cultural deprivation in economically and racially and socially homogeneous Long Island commuter towns than anything I ever had to overcome!

In Bedford-Stuyvesant, I learned all about white history and white literature, but I lived and learned about my own, as well. My father marched me to the American Museum of Natural History and to the

Planetarium, at least twice a month, while my mother picked up "the slack" by riding me, by trolley car, to public libraries progressively farther and farther away from our house. In the meantime, on our own block of Hancock Street, between Reid and Patchen avenues, we had rice and peas and curried lamb or, upstairs, in my aunt and uncle's apartment, pigs' feet and greens. On the piano in the parlor there was boogie-woogie, blues, and Chopin. Across the street, there were cold-water flats that included the Gumbs family or, more precisely, Donnie Gumbs, whom I saw as the inarguable paragon of masculine cute. There were "American Negroes," and "West Indians." Some rented their housing, and some were buying their homes. There were Baptists, Holy Rollers, and Episcopalians, side by side.

On that same one block, Father Coleman, the minister of our 15
church, lived and worked as the first Black man on New York's Board of Higher Education. There was Mrs. Taylor, whose music studio was actually a torture chamber into which many of us were forced for piano lessons. And a Black policeman. And a mail carrier. And a doctor. And my beloved Uncle Teddy, with a Doctor of Law degree from Fordham University. And the tiny, exquisite arrow of my aunt, who became one of the first Black principals in the entire New York City public school system. And my mother, who had been president of the first Black class to graduate from the Lincoln School of Nursing, and my father, who earned the traditional gold watch as a retiring civil servant, and Nat King Cole and calypso and boyfriends and Sunday School and confirmation and choir and stickball and roller skates and handmade wooden scooters and marbles and make-believe tea parties and I cannot recall feeling underprivileged, or bored, in that "ghetto."

And from such "breeding grounds of despair," Negro men volunteered, in droves, for active duty in an army that did not want or honor them. And from such "limited" communities, Negro women, such as my mother, left their homes in every kind of weather, and at any hour, to tend to the ailing and heal the sick, regardless of their color, or ethnicity. And in such a "culturally deprived" house as that modest home created by my parents, I became an American poet.

And in the name of my mother and my father, I want to say thanks to America. And I want something more:

My aunt has survived the deaths of her husband and my parents in typical, if I may say so, West Indian fashion. Now in her seventies, and no longer principal of a New York City public school, she rises at 5 A.M., every morning, to prepare for another day of complicated duties as the volunteer principal of a small Black private academy. In the front yard of her home in the Crown Heights section of Brooklyn, the tulips and buttercups have begun to bloom already. Soon every passerby will see her azaleas and jonquils and irises blossoming under the Japanese maple tree and around the base of the Colorado blue spruce. She is in her seventies, and she tells me:

> I love the United States and I always will uphold it as a place of opportunity. This is not to say that you won't meet prejudice along the way but it's up to you to overcome it. And it can be overcome!

20 Well, I think back to Clonmel, Jamaica, and I visualize my aunt skipping along the goat tracks, fast as she can, before the darkness under the banana tree leaves becomes too scary for a nine-year-old. Or I think about her, struggling to fetch water from the river, in a pail. And I jump-cut to Orange High School, New Jersey, U.S.A., where my aunt maintained a 95 average, despite her extracurricular activities as a domestic, and where she was denied the valedictory because, as the English teacher declared, "You have an accent that the parents will not understand." And I stay quiet as my aunt explains, "I could have let that bother me, but I said, 'Naw, I'm not gone let this keep me down!' "

And what I want is to uphold this America, this beckoning and this shelter provided by my parents and my aunt. I want to say thank you to them, my faithful American family.

QUESTIONS

1. *Jordan's essay might be called an "appreciation"—of her parents, her aunt, and the community in which she grew up. What qualities in them does she appreciate? How does she make these qualities concrete for the reader?*
2. *Who is the "American family" referred to in Jordan's title? What do you think is Jordan's conception of a "family"?*
3. *Jordan quotes her aunt near the end of the essay. Why does Jordan present an important point through her aunt's words?*
4. *Write an essay of appreciation about some person or some group, taking into account Jordan's techniques for making personal qualities come alive through anecdote and action.*

Judith Ortiz Cofer

MORE ROOM

My grandmother's house is like a chambered nautilus; it has many rooms, yet it is not a mansion. Its proportions are small and its design simple. It is a house that has grown organically, according to the needs of its inhabitants. To all of us in the family it is known as *la casa de Mamá.*[1] It is the place of our origin; the stage for our memories and dreams of Island life.

I remember how in my childhood it sat on stilts; this was before it had a downstairs. It rested on its perch like a great blue bird, not a flying sort of bird, more like a nesting hen, but with spread wings. Grandfather had built it soon after their marriage. He was a painter and housebuilder by trade, a poet and meditative man by nature. As each of their eight children were born, new rooms were added. After a few years, the paint did not exactly match, nor the materials, so that there was a chronology to it, like the rings of a tree, and Mamá could tell you the history of each room in her *casa,* and thus the genealogy of the family along with it.

Her room is the heart of the house. Though I have seen it recently, and both woman and room have diminished in size, changed by the new perspective of my eyes, now capable of looking over countertops and tall beds, it is not this picture I carry in my memory of Mamá's *casa.* Instead, I see her room as a queen's chamber where a small woman loomed large, a throne-room with a massive four-poster bed in its center which stood taller than a child's head. It was on this bed where her own children had been born that the smallest grandchildren were allowed to take naps in the afternoons; here too was where Mamá secluded herself to dispense private advice to her daughters, sitting on the edge of the bed, looking down at whoever sat on the rocker where generations of babies had been sung to sleep. To me she looked like a wise empress right out of the fairy tales I was addicted to reading.

Though the room was dominated by the mahogany four-posters, it also contained all of Mamá's symbols of power. On her dresser instead of cosmetics there were jars filled with herbs: *yerba buena, yerba mala,*[2] the making of purgatives and teas to which we were all subjected during childhood crises. She had a steaming cup for anyone who could

From *Silent Dancing: A Partial Remembrance of a Puerto Rican Childhood* (1990).

1. Mama's house.
2. Good herbs, bad herbs.

not, or would not, get up to face life on any given day. If the acrid aftertaste of her cures for malingering did not get you out of bed, then it was time to call *el doctor*.

And there was the monstrous chifforobe she kept locked with a little golden key she did not hide. This was a test of her dominion over us; though my cousins and I wanted a look inside that massive wardrobe more than anything, we never reached for that little key lying on top of her Bible on the dresser. This was also where she placed her earrings and rosary at night. God's word was her security system. This chifforobe was the place where I imagined she kept jewels, satin slippers, and elegant sequined, silk gowns of hearth-breaking fineness. I lusted after those imaginary costumes. I had heard that Mamá had been a great beauty in her youth, and the belle of many balls. My cousins had other ideas as to what she kept in that wooden vault: its secret could be money (Mamá did not hand cash to strangers, banks were out of the question, so there were stories that her mattress was stuffed with dollar bills, and that she buried coins in jars in her garden under rosebushes, or kept them in her inviolate chifforobe); there might be that legendary gun salvaged from the Spanish-American conflict over the Island. We went wild over suspected treasures that we made up simply because children have to fill locked trunks with something wonderful.

On the wall above the bed hung a heavy silver crucifix. Christ's agonized head hung directly over Mamá's pillow. I avoided looking at this weapon suspended over where her head would lay; and on the rare occasions when I was allowed to sleep on that bed, I scooted down to the safe middle of the mattress, where her body's impression took me in like a mother's lap. Having taken care of the obligatory religious decoration with a crucifix, Mamá covered the other walls with objects sent to her over the years by her children in the States. *Los Nueva Yores*[3] were represented by, among other things, a postcard of Niagara Falls from her son Hernán, postmarked, Buffalo, N.Y. In a conspicuous gold frame hung a large color photograph of her daughter Nena, her husband and their five children at the entrance to Disneyland in California. From us she had gotten a black lace fan. Father had brought it to her from a tour of duty with the Navy in Europe (on Sundays she would remove it from its hook on the wall to fan herself at Sunday mass). Each year more items were added as the family grew and dispersed, and every object in the room had a story attached to it, a *cuento*[4] which Mamá would bestow on anyone who received the privilege of a day alone with her. It was almost worth pretending to be sick, though the bitter herb purgatives of the body were a big price to pay for the spirit revivals of her story-telling.

3. A Puerto Rican phrase for the United States.
4. Tale.

Mamá slept alone on her large bed, except for the times when a sick grandchild warranted the privilege, or when a heartbroken daughter came home in need of more than herbal teas. In the family there is a story about how this came to be.

When one of the daughters, my mother or one of her sisters, tells the *cuento* of how Mamá came to own her nights, it is usually preceded by the qualifications that Papá's exile from his wife's room was not a result of animosity between the couple, but that the act had been Mamá's famous bloodless coup for her personal freedom. Papá was the benevolent dictator of her body and her life who had had to be banished from her bed so that Mamá could better serve her family. Before the telling, we had to agree that the old man was not to blame. We all recognized that in the family Papá was as an *alma de Dios*, [5] a saintly, soft-spoken presence whose main pleasures in life, such as writing poetry and reading the Spanish large-type editions of *Reader's Digest*, always took place outside the vortex of Mamá's crowded realm. It was not his fault, after all, that every year or so he planted a baby-seed in Mamá's fertile body, keeping her from leading the active life she needed and desired. He loved her and the babies. Papá composed odes and lyrics to celebrate births and anniversaries and hired musicians to accompany him in singing them to his family and friends at extravagant pig-roasts he threw yearly. Mamá and the oldest girls worked for days preparing the food. Papá sat for hours in his painter's shed, also his study and library, composing the songs. At these celebrations he was also known to give long speeches in praise of God, his fecund wife, and his beloved island. As a middle child, my mother remembers these occasions as a time when the women sat in the kitchen and lamented their burdens, while the men feasted out in the patio, their rum-thickened voice rising in song and praise for each other, *compañeros* all. [6]

It was after the birth of her eighth child, after she had lost three at birth or in infancy, that Mamá made her decision. They say that Mamá had had a special way of letting her husband know that they were expecting, one that had begun when, at the beginning of their marriage, he had built her a house too confining for her taste. So, when she discovered her first pregnancy, she supposedly drew plans for another room, which he dutifully executed. Every time a child was due, she would demand, *more space, more space*. Papá acceded to her wishes, child after child, since he had learned early that Mamá's renowned temper was a thing that grew like a monster along with a new belly. In this way Mamá got the house that she wanted, but with each child she lost in heart and energy. She had knowledge of her body and perceived that if she had any more children, her dreams and her plans

5. Simpleton, thoroughly good person.
6. Companions.

would have to be permanently forgotten, because she would be a chronically ill woman, like Flora with her twelve children: asthma, no teeth, in bed more than on her feet.

10 And so, after my youngest uncle was born, she asked Papá to build a large room at the back of the house. He did so in joyful anticipation. Mamá had asked him special things this time: shelves on the walls, a private entrance. He thought that she meant this room to be a nursery where several children could sleep. He thought it was a wonderful idea. He painted it his favorite color, sky blue, and made large windows looking out over a green hill and the church spires beyond. But nothing happened. Mamá's belly did not grow, yet she seemed in a frenzy of activity over the house. Finally, an anxious Papá approached his wife to tell her that the new room was finished and ready to be occupied. And Mamá, they say, replied: "Good, it's for *you.*"

And so it was that Mamá discovered the only means of birth control available to a Catholic woman of her time: sacrifice. She gave up the comfort of Papá's sexual love for something she deemed greater: the right to own and control her body, so that she might live to meet her grandchildren—me among them—so that she could give more of herself to the ones already there, so that she could be more than a channel for other lives, so that even now that time has robbed her of the elasticity of her body and of her amazing reservoir of energy, she still emanates the kind of joy that can only be achieved by living according to the dictates of one's own heart.

QUESTIONS

1. *At the end of the essay, Cofer explains in fairly direct terms why her grandmother wanted "more room." Why do you think she uses narration as the primary mode in the rest of the essay? What does she gain by narrating first, then explaining?*
2. *Cofer uses many similes and metaphors—for example, in paragraph 1 she says that her grandmother's house was "like a chambered nautilus" or in paragraph 5 that grandmother's Bible was "her security system." Discuss the use of one or two such comparisons that you find particularly effective.*
3. *What are the possible meanings of the title?*
4. *Write about a favorite or mysterious place that you remember from childhood.*

Margaret Atwood

TRUE NORTH

Land of the silver birch,
Home of the beaver,
Where still the mighty moose
Wanders at will,
Blue lake and rocky shore,
I will return once more;
Boom-diddy-boom-boom
Boom-diddy-boom-boom
Boo-OO-oo-oo-oom.

—ARCHAIC SONG

We sang this once, squatting around the papier-mâché Magic Mushroom in the Brownie pack, while pretending to be wolves in Cub Scouts, or while watching our marshmallows turn to melted Styrofoam on the ends of our sticks at some well-run, fairly safe summer camp in the wilds of Muskoka, Haliburton, or Algonquin Park. Then we grew up and found it corny. By that time we were into Jean-Paul Sartre[1] and the lure of the nauseous. Finally, having reached the age of nostalgia, we rediscovered it on a cassette in The Children's Book Store, in a haunting version that invested it with all the emotional resonance we once thought it possessed, and bought it, under the pretense of giving our children a little ethnic musical background.

It brought tears to our eyes, not for simple reasons. Whales get to us that way too, and whooping cranes, and other things hovering on the verge of extinction but still maintaining a tenuous foothold in the world of the actual. The beavers are doing all right—we know this because they just decimated our poplars—but the mighty moose is having a slimmer time of it. As for the blueness of the lakes, we worry about it: too blue and you've got acid rain.

Will we return once more, or will we go to Portugal instead? It depends, we have to admit, partly on the exchange rate, and this makes us feel disloyal. I am, rather quixotically, in Alabama, teaching, even more quixotically, a course in Canadian literature. Right now we're considering Marian Engel's novel *Bear.* Since everything in Canada, outside Toronto, begins with geography, I've unfolded a large map of Ontario and traced the heroine's route north; I've located the mythical

From *Saturday Night* (Jan. 1987).

1. French existentialist philosopher, novelist, playwright, essayist, literary critic, and political activist (1905–1980).

house of the book somewhere on the actual shore of Georgian Bay, northern edge. I've superimposed a same-scale map of Alabama on this scheme, to give the students an idea of the distances. In the north, space is larger than you think, because the points of reference are farther apart.

"Are there any words you came across that puzzled you?" I ask.

5 *Blackfly* comes up. A large black fly is proposed. I explain blackflies, their smallness, their multitude, their evil habits. It gives me a certain kick to do this: I'm competing with the local water moccasins.

Mackinaw. A raincoat? Not quite. *Loon. Tamarack. Reindeer moss. Portage. Moose. Wendigo.*

"Why does she make Lucy the old Indian woman talk so funny?" they ask. Lucy, I point out, is not merely Indian but a *French-speaking* Indian. This, to them, is a weird concept.

The north is another country. It's also another language. Or languages.

Where is the north, exactly? It's not only a place but a direction, and as such its location is relative: to the Mexicans, the United States is the north, to Americans Toronto is, even though it's on roughly the same latitude as Boston.

10 Wherever it is for us, there's a lot of it. You stand in Windsor and imagine a line going north, all the way to the pole. The same line going south would end up in South America. That's the sort of map we grew up with, at the front of the classroom in Mercator projection, which made it look even bigger than it was, all that pink stretching on forever, with a few cities sprinkled along the bottom edge. It's not only geographical space, it's space related to body image. When we face south, as we often do, our conscious mind may be directed down there, towards crowds, bright lights, some Hollywood version of fame and fortune, but the north is at the back of our minds, always. There's something, not someone, looking over our shoulders; there's a chill at the nape of the neck.

The north focuses our anxieties. Turning to face north, face the north, we enter our own unconscious. Always, in retrospect, the journey north has the quality of dream.

Where does the north begin?

Every province, every city, has its own road north. From Toronto you go up the 400. Where you cross the border, from here to there, is a matter of opinion. Is it the Severn River, where the Shield granite appears suddenly out of the earth? Is it the sign announcing that you're halfway between the equator and the North Pole? Is it the first gift shop shaped like a wigwam, the first town—there are several—that proclaims itself The Gateway to the North?

As we proceed, the farms become fewer, rockier, more desperate-looking, the trees change their ratios, coniferous moving in on deciduous. More lakes appear, their shorelines scraggier. Our eyes narrow and we look at the clouds: the weather is important again.

One of us used to spend summers in a cottage in Muskoka, before the road went in, when you took the train, when there were big cruise ships there, and matronly motor launches, and tea dances at the hotels, and men in white flannels on the lawns, which there may still be. This was not just a cottage but a Muskoka cottage, with boathouse and maid's quarters. Rich people went north in the summers then, away from cities and crowds; that was before the cure for polio, which has made a difference. In this sort of north, they tried to duplicate the south, or perhaps some dream of country life in England. In the living room there were armchairs, glass-fronted bookcases, family photos in silver frames, stuffed birds under glass bells. The north, as I said, is relative.

For me, the north used to be completely in force by the Trout Creek planing mill. Those stacks of fresh-cut lumber were the true gateway to the north, and north of that was North Bay, which used to be, to be blunt, a bit of an armpit. It was beef-sandwich-on-white-bread-with-gravy-and-canned-peas country. But no more. North Bay now has shopping malls, and baskets of flowers hanging from lampposts above paving-stone sidewalks, downtown. It has a Granite Club. It has the new, swish, carpeted buildings of Laurentian University. It has gourmet restaurants. And in the airport, where southbound DC-9s dock side by side with northbound Twin Otters, there's a book rack in the coffee shop that features Graham Greene and Kierkegaard,[2] hardly standard airport fare.

The south is moving north.

We bypass North Bay, which now has a bypass, creeping southerliness, and do not go, this time, to the Dionne Quints Museum, where five little silhouettes in black play forever beside an old log cabin, complete with the basket where they were packed in cotton wool, the oven where they were warmed, the five prams, the five Communion dresses.

Beyond North Bay there is a brief flurry of eccentricity—lawns populated with whole flocks of wooden-goose windmills—and then we go for miles and miles past nothing but trees, meeting nothing but the occasional truck loaded with lumber. This area didn't used to be

2. Søren Kierkegaard (1813–1855), Danish clergyman and philosopher who criticized Christianity and set the stage for modern existentialism. Graham Greene (1904–1991), English novelist.

called anything. Now it's the Near North Travel Area. You can see signs telling you that. Near what, we wonder uneasily? We don't want to be near. We want to be far.

20 At last we see the Ottawa River, which is the border. There's a dam across it, two dams, and an island between them. If there were a customs house it would be here. A sign faces us saying *Bienvenue;* out the back window there's one saying *Welcome.* This was my first lesson in points of view.

And there, across the border in Québec, in Témiscaming, is an image straight from my childhood: a huge mountain made of sawdust. I always wanted to slide down this sawdust mountain until I finally did, and discovered it was not like sand, dry and slippery, but damp and sticky and hard to get out of your clothes. This was my first lesson in the nature of illusion.

Continue past the sawdust mountain, past the baseball diamond, up the hill, and you're in the centre of town, which is remarkable for at least three things: a blocks-long public rock garden, still flourishing after more than forty-five years; a pair of statues, one a fountain, that look as if they've come straight from Europe, which I think they did; and the excellent, amazingly low-priced hamburgers you can get at the Boulevard Restaurant, where the décor, featuring last year's cardboard Santa Claus and a stuffed twenty-three-pound pike, is decidedly northern. Ask the owner about the pike and he'll tell you about one twice as big, forty-five pounds in fact, that a fellow showed him strapped to the tailgate of his van, and that long, too.

You can have this conversation in either French or English: Témiscaming is a border town and a northern one, and the distinctions made here are as likely to be north-south as French-English. Up in these parts you'll hear as much grumbling, or more, about Québec City as you will about Ottawa, which is, after all, closer. Spit in the river and it gets to Ottawa, eh?

For the north, Témiscaming is old, settled, tidy, even a little prosperous-looking. But it's had its crises. Témiscaming is the resource economy personified. Not long ago it was a company town, and when the company shut down the mill, which would have shut down the town too, the workers took the unprecedented step of trying to buy it. With some help they succeeded, and the result was Tembec, still going strong. But Témiscaming is still a one-industry town, like many northern towns, and its existence is thus precarious.

25 Not so long ago, logging was a different sort of business. The men went into the woods in winter, across the ice, using horse-drawn sledges, and set up camp. (You still come across these logging camps now and then in your travels through the lakes, abandoned, already looking as ancient as Roman aqueducts; more ancient, since there's been no upkeep.) They'd cut selectively, tree by tree, using axes and

saws and the skills that were necessary to avoid being squashed or hacked. They'd skid the trees to the ice; in the spring, after the ice went out, there would be a run down the nearest fast river to the nearest sawmill.

Now it's done with bulldozers and trucks, and the result is too often a blitzed shambles; cut everything, leave a wreck of dead and, incidentally, easily flammable branches behind. Time is money. Don't touch the shoreline though, we need that for tourists. In some places, the forest is merely a scrim along the water. In behind it's been hollowed out.

Those who look on the positive side say it's good for the blueberries.

Sometimes we went the other way, across to Sudbury, the trees getting smaller and smaller and finally disappearing as you approached. Sudbury was another magic place of my childhood. It was like interplanetary travel, which we liked to imagine, which was still just imagination in those days. With its heaps of slag and its barren shoulders of stone, it looked like the moon. Back then, we tell the children, before there were washer-dryers and you used something called a wringer washer and hung the sheets out on something called a clothesline, when there weren't even coloured sheets but all sheets were white, when Rinso white and its happy little washday song were an item, and Whiter than White was a catch phrase and female status really did have something to do with your laundry, Sudbury was a housewife's nightmare. We knew people there; the windowsills in their houses were always grey.

Now the trees are beginning to come back because they built higher smokestacks. But where is all that stuff going now?

The Acid Rain Dinner, in Toronto's Sheraton Centre, in 1985. The 30
first of these fund-raising events was fairly small. But the movement has grown, and this dinner is huge. The leaders of all three provincial parties are here. So is the minister of the environment from the federal government. So are several labour leaders, and several high-ranking capitalists, and representatives of numerous northerly chambers of commerce, summer residents' associations, tourist-camp runners, outfitters. Wishy washy urban professionals who say "frankly" a lot bend elbows with huntin', shootin', fishin', and cussin' burnt necks who wouldn't be caught dead saying "frankly." This is not a good place to be overheard saying that actually acid rain isn't such a bad thing because it gets rid of all that brown scum and leeches in the lake, or who cares because you can water-ski anyway. Teddy Kennedy, looking like a bulky sweater, is the guest speaker. Everyone wears a little gold pin in the shape of a rain drop. It looks like a tear.

Why has acid rain become the collective Canadian nightmare?

Why is it—as a good cause—bigger than baby-seal bashing? The reasons aren't just economic, although there are lots of those, as the fishing-camp people and foresters will tell you. It's more than that, and cognate with the outrage aroused by the uninvited voyage of the American icebreaker *Polar Sea* through the Northwest Passage, where almost none of us ever goes. It's territorial, partly; partly a felt violation of some area in us that we hardly ever think about unless it's invaded or tampered with. It's the neighbours throwing guck into our yard. It's our childhood dying.

On location, in summer and far from the glass and brass of the Sheraton Centre, we nervously check our lakes. Leeches still in place? Have the crayfish, among the first to go, gone yet? (We think in terms of "yet.") Are the loons reproducing, have you seen any young? Any minnows? How about the lichen on the rocks? These inventories have now become routine, and that is why we're willing to fork out a hundred dollars a plate to support our acid-rain lobbyists in Washington. A summer without loons is unthinkable, but how do you tell that to people who don't know it because they've never had any to begin with?

We're driving through Glencoe, in the Highlands of Scotland. It's imposing, as a landscape: bleak, large, bald, apparently empty. We can see why the Scots took so well to Canada. Yet we know that the glens and crags round about are crawling with at least a thousand campers, rock climbers, and other seekers after nature; we also know that, at one end of this glen, the Campbells butchered the MacDonalds in the seventeenth century, thus propelling both of them into memorable history. Go walking here and you'll find things human: outlines of stone fences now overgrown, shards of abandoned crofts.

In Europe, every scrap of land has been claimed, owned, re-owned, fought over, captured, bled on. The roads are the only no-man's-land. In northern Canada, the roads are civilization, owned by the collective human *we*. Off the road is *other*. Try walking in it, and you'll soon find out why all the early traffic here was by water. "Impenetrable wilderness" is not just verbal.

And suppose you get off the road. Suppose you get lost. Getting lost, elsewhere and closer to town, is not knowing exactly where you are. You can always ask, even in a foreign country. In the north, getting lost is not knowing how to get out.

You can get lost on a lake, of course, but getting lost in the forest is worse. It's tangly in there, and dim, and one tree does begin to look remarkably like another. The leaves and needles blot up sound, and you begin to feel watched: not by anyone, not by an animal even, or anything you can put a name to, just watched. You begin to feel judged. It's as if something is keeping an eye on you just to see what you will do.

What will you do? Which side of the tree does moss grow on, and here, where there are ferns and the earth is damp, or where it's dry as tinder, it seems that moss grows everywhere, or does not grow at all. Snippets of Boy Scout lore or truisms learned at summer camp come back to you, but scrambled. You tell yourself not to panic: you can always live off the land.

Easier said than done, you'd soon find. The Canadian Shield is a relatively foodless area, which is why even the Indians tended to pass through it, did not form large settlements except where there was arable land, and remained limited in numbers. This is not the Mekong delta. If you had a gun you could shoot something, maybe, a red squirrel perhaps; but if you're lost you probably don't have a gun, or a fishing rod either. You could eat blueberries, or cattail stems, or crayfish, or other delicacies dimly remembered from stories about people who got lost in the woods and were found later in good health although somewhat thinner. You could cook some reindeer moss, if you had matches.

Thus you pass on to fantasies about how to start a fire with a magnifying glass—you don't have one—or by rubbing two bits of stick together, a feat at which you suspect you would prove remarkably inept.

The fact is that not very many of us know how to survive in the 40
north. Rumour has it that only one German prisoner of war ever made it out, although many made it out of the actual prisoner-of-war camps. The best piece of northern survival advice is: *Don't get lost.*

One way of looking at a landscape is to consider the typical ways of dying in it. Given the worst, what's the worst it could do? Will it be delirium from drinking salty water on the high seas, shrivelling in the desert, snakebite in the jungle, tidal waves on a Pacific isle, volcanic fumes? In the north, there are several hazards. Although you're probably a lot safer there than you are on the highway at rush hour, given the odds, you still have to be a little wary.

Like most lessons of this sort, those about the north are taught by precept and example, but also, more enjoyably, by cautionary nasty tale. There is death by blackfly, the one about the fellow who didn't have his shirt cuffs tight enough in the spring and undressed at night only to find he was running with blood, the ones about the lost travellers who bloated up from too many bites and who, when found, were twice the size, unrecognizable, and dead. There is death from starvation, death by animal, death by forest fire; there is death from something called "exposure," which used to confuse me when I heard about men who exposed themselves: why would they intentionally do anything that fatal? There's death by thunderstorm, not to be sneered at: on the open lake, in one of the excessive northern midsummer thunderstorms, a canoe or a bush plane is a vulnerable target. The north is full of Struwwelpeter-like[3] stories about people who didn't do as they were told and got struck by lightning. Above all, there are death by freezing and death by drowning. Your body's heat-loss rate in the water is twenty times that in air, and northern lakes are cold. Even in a life jacket, even holding on to the tipped canoe, you're at risk. Every summer the numbers pile up.

Every culture has its exemplary dead people, its hagiography of landscape martyrs, those unfortunates who, by their bad ends, seem to sum up in one grisly episode what may be lurking behind the next rock for all of us, all of us who enter the territory they once claimed as theirs. I'd say that two of the top northern landscape martyrs are Tom Thomson, the painter who was found mysteriously drowned near his overturned canoe with no provable cause in sight, and the Mad Trapper of Rat River, also mysterious, who became so thoroughly bushed that he killed a Mountie and shot two others during an amazing wintertime chase before being finally mowed down. In our retelling of these stories, mystery is a key element. So, strangely enough, is a presumed oneness with the landscape in question. The Mad Trapper knew his landscape so well he survived in it for weeks, living off the land and his own bootlaces, eluding capture. One of the hidden motifs in these stories is a warning: maybe it's not so good to get *too* close to Nature.

I remember a documentary on Tom Thomson that ended, rather ominously, with the statement that the north had taken him to herself. This was, of course, pathetic fallacy[4] gone to seed, but it was also a comment on our distrust of the natural world, a distrust that remains despite our protests, our studies in the ethics of ecology, our elevation of "the environment" to a numinous noun, our save-the-tree campaigns. The question is, would the trees save us, given the chance? Would the water, would the birds, would the rocks? In the north, we have our doubts.

45 A bunch of us are sitting around the table, at what is now a summer cottage in Georgian Bay. Once it was a house, built by a local man for his family, which finally totalled eleven children, after they'd outgrown this particular house and moved on to another. The original Findlay wood-burning cook stove is still in the house, but so also are some electric lights and a propane cooker, which have come since the end of the old days. In the old days, this man somehow managed to scrape a living from the land: a little of this, a little of that, some fish-

3. Like a person with long, thick, unkempt hair, from a character in a children's book by Heinrich Hoffman (1809–1894).
4. The attribution of human emotions to inanimate objects, often the landscape.

ing here, some lumbering there, some hunting in the fall. That was back when you shot to eat. "Scrape" is an appropriate word: there's not much here between the topsoil and the rock.

We sit around the table and eat, fish among other things, caught by the children. Someone mentions the clams: there are still a lot of them, but who knows what's in them any more? Mercury, lead, things like that. We pick at the fish. Someone tells me not to drink the tap water. I already have. "What will happen?" I ask. "Probably nothing," they reply. "Probably nothing" is a relatively recent phrase around here. In the old days, you ate what looked edible.

We are talking about the old days, as people often do once they're outside the cities. When exactly did the old days end? Because we know they did. The old days ended when the youngest of us was ten, fifteen, or twenty; the old days ended when the oldest of us was five, or twelve, or thirty. Plastic-hulled superboats are not old days, but ten-horse-power outboard motors, circa 1945, are. There's an icebox in the back porch, unused now, a simple utilitarian model from Eaton's, ice chamber in the top section, metal shelves in the bottom one. We all go and admire it. "I remember iceboxes," I say, and indeed I can dimly remember them, I must have been five. What bits of our daily junk—our toasters, our pocket computers—will soon become obsolete and therefore poignant? Who will stand around, peering at them and admiring their design and the work that went into them, as we do with this icebox? "So this was a *toilet seat*," we think, rehearsing the future. "Ah! A *light bulb*," the ancient syllables thick in our mouths.

The kids have decided some time ago that all this chat is boring, and have asked if they can go swimming off the dock. They can, though they have to watch it, as this is a narrow place and speedboats tend to swoosh through, not always slowing down. Waste of gas, in the old days. Nobody then went anywhere just for pleasure, it was the war and gas was rationed.

"Oh, *that* old days," says someone.

There goes a speedboat now, towing a man strapped in a kneeling 50
position to some kind of board, looking as if he's had a terrible accident, or is about to have one. This must be some newfangled variety of water-skiing.

"Remember Klim?" I say. The children come through, trailing towels. "What's Klim?" one asks, caught by the space-age sound of the word.

"Klim was 'milk' spelled backwards," I say. "It was powdered milk."

"Yuk," they say.

"Not the same as now," I say. "It was whole milk, not skim; it wasn't instant. You had to beat it with an eggbeater." And even then some of it wouldn't dissolve. One of the treats of childhood was the little nodules of pure dry Klim that floated on top of your milk.

55 "There was also Pream," says someone. How revolutionary it seemed.

The children go down to take their chances in the risky motorized water. Maybe, much later, they will remember us sitting around the table, eating fish they themselves had caught, back when you could still (what? Catch a fish? See a tree? What desolations lie in store, beyond the plasticized hulls and the knee-skiers?). By then we will be the old days, for them. Almost we are already.

A different part of the north. We're sitting around the table, by lamplight—it's still the old days here, no electricity—talking about bad hunters. Bad hunters, bad fishers, everyone has a story. You come upon a campsite, way in the back of beyond, no roads into the lake, they must have come in by float plane, and there it is, garbage all over the place, beer cans, blobs of human poop flagged by melting toilet paper, and twenty-two fine pickerel left rotting on a rock. Business executives who get themselves flown in during hunting season with their high-powered rifles, shoot a buck, cut off the head, fill their quota, see another one with a bigger spread of antlers, drop the first head, cut off the second. The woods are littered with discarded heads, and who cares about the bodies?

New way to shoot polar bear: you have the natives on the ground finding them for you, then they radio the location in to the base camp, the base camp phones New York, fellow gets on the plane, gets himself flown in, they've got the rifle and the clothing all ready for him, fly him to the bear, he pulls the trigger from the plane, doesn't even get out of the g.d. *plane,* they fly him back, cut off the head, skin it, send the lot down to New York.

These are the horror stories of the north, one brand. They've replaced the ones in which you got pounced upon by a wolverine or had your arm chewed off by a she-bear with cubs or got chased into the lake by a moose in rut, or even the ones in which your dog got porcupine quills or rolled in poison ivy and gave it to you. In the new stories, the enemies and the victims of old have done a switch. Nature is no longer implacable, dangerous, ready to jump you; it is on the run, pursued by a number of unfair bullies with the latest technology.

60 One of the key nouns in these stories is "float plane." These outrages, this banditry, would not be possible without them, for the bad hunters are notoriously weak-muscled and are deemed incapable of portaging a canoe, much less paddling one. Among their other badnesses, they are sissies. Another key motif is money. What money buys these days, among other things, is the privilege of no-risk slaughter.

As for us, the ones telling the stories, tsk-tsking by lamplight, we are the good hunters, or so we think. We've given up saying we only kill to eat; Kraft dinner and freeze-dried food have put paid to that one. Really there's no excuse for us. However, we do have some virtues left. We can still cast a fly. We don't cut off heads and hang them stuffed on the wall. We would never buy an ocelot coat. We paddle our own canoes.

We're sitting on the dock at night, shivering despite our sweaters, in mid-August, watching the sky. There are a few shooting stars, as there always are at this time in August, as the earth passes through the Perseids. We pride ourselves on knowing a few things like that, about the sky; we find the Dipper, the North Star, Cassiopeia's Chair, and talk about consulting a star chart, which we know we won't actually do. But this is the only place you can really *see* the stars, we tell each other. Cities are hopeless.

Suddenly, an odd light appears, going very fast. It spirals around like a newly dead firecracker, and then bursts, leaving a cloud of luminous dust, caught perhaps in the light from the sun, still up there somewhere. What could this be? Several days later, we hear that it was part of an extinct Soviet satellite, or that's what they say. That's what they would say, wouldn't they? It strikes us that we don't really know very much about the night sky at all any more. There's all kinds of junk up there: spy planes, old satellites, tin cans, man-made matter gone out of control. It also strikes us that we are totally dependent for knowledge of these things on a few people who don't tell us very much.

Once, we thought that if the balloon ever went up we'd head for the bush and hide out up there, living—we naively supposed—off the land. Now we know that if the two superpowers begin hurling things at each other through the sky, they're likely to do it across the Arctic, with big bangs and fallout all over the north. The wind blows everywhere. Survival gear and knowing which moss you can eat is not going to be a large help. The north is no longer a refuge.

Driving back towards Toronto from the Near North, a small reprise 65
runs through my head:

> Land of the septic tank,
> Home of the speedboat,
> Where still the four-wheel-drive
> Wanders at will,
> Blue lake and tacky shore,
> I will return once more:
> Vroom-diddy-vroom-vroom

Vroom-diddy-vroom-vroom
Vroo-OO-oo-oom.

Somehow, just as the drive north inspires saga and tragedy, the drive south inspires parody. And here it comes: the gift shops shaped like teepees, the maple-syrup emporiums that get themselves up like olde-tyme sugaring-off huts; and, farther south, the restaurants that pretend to offer wholesome farm fare, the stores that pretend to be general stores, selling quilts, soap shaped like hearts, high-priced fancy conserves done up in frilly cloth caps, the way Grandma (whoever she might be) was fondly supposed to have made them.

And then come the housing developments, acres of prime farmland turning overnight into Quality All-Brick Family Homes; and then come the Industrial Parks; and there, in full anti-bloom, is the city itself, looming like a mirage or a chemical warfare zone on the horizon. A browny-grey scuzz hovers above it, and we think, as we always do when facing re-entry, we're going into *that?* We're going to breathe *that?*

But we go forward, as we always do, into what is now to us the unknown. And once inside, we breathe the air, not much bad happens to us, we hardly notice. It's as if we've never been anywhere else. But that's what we think, too, when we're in the north.

QUESTIONS

1. *What context does Atwood set for the opening section? How does her need to explain to American Southerners in a college classroom help her communicate with the readers of this essay?*
2. *Beginning in paragraph 16, Atwood reenacts a journey to the "north." What does this journey, re-created for the reader, help her achieve?*
3. *Why does Atwood include a section about "typical ways of dying" in a northern landscape? What qualities about northern Canada can she present through this unusual approach?*
4. *Write an essay about a geographical region that appeals to you but that may be unknown or unappealing to others. Using techniques learned from Atwood or other writers in this section, try to communicate the region's appeal as you write.*

N. Scott Momaday

THE WAY TO RAINY MOUNTAIN

A single knoll rises out of the plain in Oklahoma, north and west of the Wichita Range. For my people, the Kiowas, it is an old landmark, and they gave it the name Rainy Mountain. The hardest weather in the world is there. Winter brings blizzards, hot tornadic winds arise in the spring, and in summer the prairie is an anvil's edge. The grass turns brittle and brown, and it cracks beneath your feet. There are green belts along the rivers and creeks, linear groves of hickory and pecan, willow and witch hazel. At a distance in July or August the steaming foliage seems almost to writhe in fire. Great green and yellow grasshoppers are everywhere in the tall grass, popping up like corn to sting the flesh, and tortoises crawl about on the red earth, going nowhere in the plenty of time. Loneliness is an aspect of the land. All things in the plain are isolate; there is no confusion of objects in the eye, but *one* hill or *one* tree or *one* man. To look upon that landscape in the early morning, with the sun at your back, is to lose the sense of proportion. Your imagination comes to life, and this, you think, is where Creation was begun.

I returned to Rainy Mountain in July. My grandmother had died in the spring, and I wanted to be at her grave. She had lived to be very old and at last infirm. Her only living daughter was with her when she died, and I was told that in death her face was that of a child.

I like to think of her as a child. When she was born, the Kiowas were living the last great moment of their history. For more than a hundred years they had controlled the open range from the Smoky Hill River to the Red, from the headwaters of the Canadian to the fork of the Arkansas and Cimarron. In alliance with the Comanches, they had ruled the whole of the southern Plains. War was their sacred business, and they were among the finest horsemen the world has ever known. But warfare for the Kiowas was preeminently a matter of disposition rather than of survival, and they never understood the grim, unrelenting advance of the U.S. Cavalry. When at last, divided and ill-provisioned, they were driven onto the Staked Plains in the cold rains of autumn, they fell into panic. In Palo Duro Canyon they abandoned their crucial stores to pillage and had nothing then but their lives. In order to save themselves, they surrendered to the soldiers at Fort Sill and were imprisoned in the old stone corral that now stands as a military museum.

From *The Way to Rainy Mountain* (1969).

My grandmother was spared the humiliation of those high gray walls by eight or ten years, but she must have known from birth the affliction of defeat, the dark brooding of old warriors.

Her name was Aho, and she belonged to the last culture to evolve in North America. Her forebears came down from the high country in western Montana nearly three centuries ago. They were a mountain people, a mysterious tribe of hunters whose language has never been positively classified in any major group. In the late seventeenth century they began a long migration to the south and east. It was a journey toward the dawn, and it led to a golden age. Along the way the Kiowas were befriended by the Crows, who gave them the culture and religion of the Plains. They acquired horses, and their ancient nomadic spirit was suddenly free of the ground. They acquired Tai-me, the sacred Sun Dance doll, from that moment the object and symbol of their worship, and so shared in the divinity of the sun. Not least, they acquired the sense of destiny, therefore courage and pride. When they entered upon the southern Plains they had been transformed. No longer were they slaves to the simple necessity of survival; they were a lordly and dangerous society of fighters and thieves, hunters and priests of the sun. According to their origin myth, they entered the world through a hollow log. From one point of view, their migration was the fruit of an old prophecy, for indeed they emerged from a sunless world.

5 Although my grandmother lived out her long life in the shadow of Rainy Mountain, the immense landscape of the continental interior lay like memory in her blood. She could tell of the Crows, whom she had never seen, and of the Black Hills, where she had never been. I wanted to see in reality what she had seen more perfectly in the mind's eye, and traveled fifteen hundred miles to begin my pilgrimage.

Yellowstone, it seemed to me, was the top of the world, a region of deep lakes and dark timber, canyons and waterfalls. But, beautiful as it is, one might have the sense of confinement there. The skyline in all directions is close at hand, the high wall of the woods and deep cleavages of shade. There is a perfect freedom in the mountains, but it belongs to the eagle and the elk, the badger and the bear. The Kiowas reckoned their stature by the distance they could see, and they were bent and blind in the wilderness.

Descending eastward, the highland meadows are a stairway to the plain. In July the inland slope of the Rockies is luxuriant with flax and buckwheat, stonecrop and larkspur. The earth unfolds and the limit of the land recedes. Clusters of trees, and animals grazing far in the distance, cause the vision to reach away and wonder to build upon the mind. The sun follows a longer course in the day, and the sky is immense beyond all comparison. The great billowing clouds that sail upon it are the shadows that move upon the grain like water, dividing light. Farther down, in the land of the Crows and Blackfeet, the plain is yellow. Sweet clover takes hold of the hills and bends upon itself to cover and seal the soil. There the Kiowas paused on their way; they had come to the place where they must change their lives. The sun is at home on the plains. Precisely there does it have the certain character of a god. When the Kiowas came to the land of the Crows, they could see the dark lees of the hills at dawn across the Bighorn River, the profusion of light on the grain shelves, the oldest deity ranging after the solstices. Not yet would they veer southward to the caldron of the land that lay below; they must wean their blood from the northern winter and hold the mountains a while longer in their view. They bore Tai-me in procession to the east.

A dark mist lay over the Black Hills, and the land was like iron. At the top of a ridge I caught sight of Devil's Tower upthrust against the gray sky as if in the birth of time the core of the earth had broken through its crust and the motion of the world was begun. There are things in nature that engender an awful quiet in the heart of man; Devil's Tower is one of them. Two centuries ago, because they could not do otherwise, the Kiowas made a legend at the base of the rock. My grandmother said:

> Eight children were there at play, seven sisters and their brother. Suddenly the boy was struck dumb; he trembled and began to run upon his hands and feet. His fingers became claws, and his body was covered with fur. Directly there was a bear where the boy had been. The sisters were terrified; they ran, and the bear after them. They came to the stump of a great tree, and the tree spoke to them. It bade them climb upon it, and as they did so it began to rise into the air. The bear came to kill them, but they were just beyond its reach. It reared against the tree and scored the bark all around with its claws. The seven sisters were borne into the sky, and they became the stars of the Big Dipper.

From that moment, and so long as the legend lives, the Kiowas have kinsmen in the night sky. Whatever they were in the mountains, they could be no more. However tenuous their well-being, however much they had suffered and would suffer again, they had found a way out of the wilderness.

My grandmother had a reverence for the sun, a holy regard that now is all but gone out of mankind. There was a wariness in her, and an ancient awe. She was a Christian in her later years, but she had come a long way about, and she never forgot her birthright. As a child she had been to the Sun Dances; she had taken part in those annual rites, and by them she had learned the restoration of her people in the presence of Tai-me. She was about seven when the last Kiowa Sun Dance was held in 1887 on the Washita River above Rainy Mountain Creek. The buffalo were gone. In order to consummate the ancient sacrifice—to impale the head of a buffalo bull upon the medicine tree—a delegation of old men journeyed into Texas, there to beg and barter for an animal from the Goodnight herd. She was ten when the Kiowas came together for the last time as a living Sun Dance culture. They could find no buffalo; they had to hang an old hide from the sacred tree. Before the dance could begin, a company of soldiers rode out from Fort Sill under orders to disperse the tribe. Forbidden without cause the essential act of their faith, having seen the wild herds slaughtered and left to rot upon the ground, the Kiowas backed away forever from the medicine tree. That was July 20, 1890, at the great bend of the Washita. My grandmother was there. Without bitterness, and for as long as she lived, she bore a vision of deicide.

10 Now that I can have her only in memory, I see my grandmother in the several postures that were peculiar to her: standing at the wood stove on a winter morning and turning meat in a great iron skillet; sitting at the south window, bent above her beadwork, and afterwards, when her vision failed, looking down for a long time into the fold of her hands; going out upon a cane, very slowly as she did when the weight of age came upon her; praying. I remember her most often at prayer. She made long, rambling prayers out of suffering and hope, having seen many things. I was never sure that I had the right to hear, so exclusive where they of all mere custom and company. The last time I saw her she prayed standing by the side of her bed at night, naked to the waist, the light of a kerosene lamp moving upon her dark skin. Her long, black hair, always drawn and braided in the day, lay upon her shoulders and against her breasts like a shawl. I do not speak Kiowa, and I never understood her prayers, but there was something inherently sad in the sound, some merest hesitation upon the syllables of sorrow. She began in a high and descending pitch, exhausting her breath to silence; then again and again—and always the same intensity of effort, of something that is, and is not, like urgency in the human voice. Transported so in the dancing light among the shadows of her room, she seemed beyond the reach of time. But that was illusion; I think I knew then that I should not see her again.

Houses are like sentinels in the plain, old keepers of the weather watch. There, in a very little while, wood takes on the appearance of great age. All colors wear soon away in the wind and rain, and then the wood is burned gray and the grain appears and the nails turn red with rust. The windowpanes are black and opaque; you imagine there is nothing within, and indeed there are many ghosts, bones given up to the land. They stand here and there against the sky, and you approach them for a longer time than you expect. They belong in the distance; it is their domain.

Once there was a lot of sound in my grandmother's house, a lot of coming and going, feasting and talk. The summers there were full of excitement and reunion. The Kiowas are a summer people; they abide the cold and keep to themselves, but when the season turns and the land becomes warm and vital they cannot hold still; an old love of going returns upon them. The aged visitors who came to my grandmother's house when I was a child were made of lean and leather, and they bore themselves upright. They wore great black hats and bright ample shirts that shook in the wind. They rubbed fat upon their hair and wound their braids with strips of colored cloth. Some of them painted their faces and carried the scars of old and cherished enmities. They were an old council of warlords, come to remind and be reminded of who they were. Their wives and daughters served them well. The women might indulge themselves; gossip was at once the mark and compensation of their servitude. They made loud and elaborate talk among themselves, full of jest and gesture, fright and false alarm. They went abroad in fringed and flowered shawls, bright beadwork and German silver. They were at home in the kitchen, and they prepared meals that were banquets.

There were frequent prayer meetings, and great nocturnal feasts. When I was a child I played with my cousins outside, where the lamplight fell upon the ground and the singing of the old people rose up around us and carried away into the darkness. There were a lot of good things to eat, a lot of laughter and surprise. And afterwards, when the quiet returned, I lay down with my grandmother and could hear the frogs away by the river and feel the motion of the air.

Now there is a funeral silence in the rooms, the endless wake of some final word. The walls have closed in upon my grandmother's house. When I returned to it in mourning, I saw for the first time in my life how small it was. It was late at night, and there was a white moon, nearly full. I sat for a long time on the stone steps by the kitchen door. From there I could see out across the land; I could see the long row of trees by the creek, the low light upon the rolling plains, and the stars of the Big Dipper. Once I looked at the moon and caught sight of a strange thing. A cricket had perched upon the handrail, only a few inches away from me. My line of vision was such that the creature filled the moon like a fossil. It had gone there, I thought, to live and die, for there, of all places, was its small definition made whole and eternal. A warm wind rose up and purled like the longing within me.

The next morning I awoke at dawn and went out on the dirt road to 15
Rainy Mountain. It was already hot, and the grasshoppers began to fill the air. Still, it was early in the morning, and the birds sang out of the shadows. The long yellow grass on the mountain shone in the bright light, and a scissortail hied above the land. There, where it ought to be,

at the end of a long and legendary way, was my grandmother's grave. Here and there on the dark stones were ancestral names. Looking back once, I saw the mountain and came away.

Charlotte Gray

THE TEMPLE OF HYGIENE

Some years ago, I bought a nineteenth-century Japanese print of a fight in a bathhouse. The snarling intensity of the naked, dishevelled women always intrigues me—it's so at odds with the impassive neatness of the ranks of workers, schoolchildren, or commuters featured in the standard documentaries about the Japanese "economic miracle." So when I arrived in Japan on a Japanese government programme for foreign journalists, I ranked a *sento* above a teahouse on the "preferred excursions" list I was told to prepare. I made my request to Mr. Kondo, head of the foreign ministry's international press division, who processed foreigners along the conveyor belt of Constructive Japanese Experience. He listened, stony-faced. Organized tours around factories, yes. Voyeurism in the temples of hygiene—well, even an official guest and her accompanying spouse would have to organize that for themselves.

I persisted. The hospitality service of the foreign ministry had provided George and me with an escort: pretty, thirty-year-old Kaoru. Beneath Kaoru's demure smile and dutiful attention to my every whim, there bubbled a nonconformist streak. She always drank coffee instead of green tea. She refused to wear a kimono at her cousin's wedding, even though the most Westernized women in her family stuck to the national dress for the rites of passage. Most seriously, she had already rejected three suitors selected by her parents because they were too traditional, and would not have permitted her to continue working after marriage. Now, Kaoru giggled, she was "Christmas cake"—Japanese shorthand for women beyond their twenty-fifth birthday, as unwanted as Christmas cake beyond December 25.

"Kaoru, please could you take us to a *sento?*" I asked. Her smile froze for a second, then she replied, "Do you mean a swimming pool?" The limits of Japanese nonconformity began to show. I insisted that I wanted to visit an authentic bathhouse—not a swimming pool, or a gussied-up version in which Westerners outnumbered residents. We sparred for five minutes, then Kaoru got out her little notebook. The

From *The Saturday Night Traveller*, ed. George Galt (Sept. 1989).

previous time the notebook had appeared was when I had asked to visit the gate of Tokyo's Imperial Palace so I could see the crowds of tiny, bent old women keeping a death watch on the occupant of the Chrysanthemum Throne. Kaoru had found that expedition a little tacky: foreign television cameras outnumbered well-wishers during most of my visit. Nevertheless, she had written down the request and taken me.

The bathhouse opportunity finally arose in Kyoto. The ancient capital of Japan is now a badly planned, crowded city. Buddhist temples, Zen gardens, and ancient palaces are pools of serenity amongst bleak modern buildings. We were staying in a *ryokan*—a Japanese inn where smiling women in kimonos served us an elaborate meal at the traditional knee-level table in our own room. "Maybe tonight we'll visit a *sento?*" Kaoru suggested out of the blue. I uncurled from a cartilage-cracking kneel with enthusiasm. Kaoru summoned a cab, which ferried us through the "night area" of Kyoto—an exuberant bustle of bars, nightclubs, and restaurants.

Through the cab windows we saw the same kinds of street scenes 5
that had fascinated us in Tokyo. Clutches of neatly groomed men, wearing navy suits and carrying briefcases, strolled along, often propping up one of their number who was swaying like a stage lush. These "sararimen" (salary-men) had been male-bonding over beer or Scotches before lurching home to their wives. I had spent an afternoon with a sarariman's wife in a Tokyo suburb. Mrs. Hama's life had horrified me: she was trapped at home with only a microwave, electric bread maker, electric rice steamer, and koto (long harplike instrument) for company. Her days appeared to be spent ferrying her twelve-year-old daughter and sixteen-year-old son between schools and cramming classes. Once a week, she joined a group of other housewives for a gym class. She never knew when her husband would come home.

Mrs. Hama obviously found my life equally horrifying—though the merest shadows of shock flitted across her permanent smile. Why did I need to work if my husband was a government sarariman? What was I doing, leaving my three little boys with someone who was looking after them only for money? Wasn't I worried that, in a country like Canada, they might marry somebody from a different background—even a different race? As Kaoru escorted me home after the visit, her self-control dissolved. "I thought she would choke when you ate a grape *whole,* without removing the skin," she giggled, overcome by the hilarious culture clash between two forty-year-old mothers. "And then, when you told her that your seven-year-old rarely has homework. . . ."

The cab finally dropped Kaoru, George, and me at the end of an unlit lane. Towels in hand, we walked past the back doors of noodle shops and brightly lit windows with metal grilles in front of them. The bathhouse looked like a shabby municipal office. People scurried in and out, some wearing baggy pyjamas. A lick of hot, damp air curled round the door as we entered—George to the right and Kaoru and I to the left. We walked straight into a large, tiled locker room, with the inevitable row of neatly paired shoes by the entrance. A curtain separated the men's and women's changing rooms. A watchful attendant in a navy apron was seated at a raised counter which straddled the changing rooms. We paid her our 240 yen (about two dollars) each and went over to a bank of lockers.

Through a glass wall directly in front of us, I could see naked figures moving in clouds of steam. Around me, six women were silently getting dressed or undressed; another was drying her hair at a long horizontal mirror. A naked septuagenarian[1] in a brown leather armchair grunted with concentration—the chair appeared to be some kind of La-Z-Boy back-massager and she was rhythmically squirming against a set of rollers behind her. On a high shelf stood a row of twenty-five plastic bowls, neatly tied up in pink, blue, or purple gauze scarves. These contained the washing equipment of the regulars. The whole place looked entirely functional—a human laundrette rather than a health spa.

On the way over, Kaoru admitted that she had visited a bathhouse only once before; her family had always had their own bathroom. Once, communal bathhouses had been the centre of community life. In feudal Japan, there was a clear bathhouse pecking order: the samurai families used the bathhouses in the mornings, when the water was cleanest; the merchants in the afternoon; the peasants, workers, and household servants in the evening after they had toiled in fields and kitchens. As recently as ten years ago, more households had colour televisions than had bathtubs. But a twentyfold increase in GNP since the war has allowed the Mrs. Hamas of this world to have baths as well as bread makers (and, inevitably, reinforced their isolation). Only the poor continue to rely on bathhouses. Most of the women around Kaoru and me in the changing room seemed to be students or grannies.

10 It was hard to take the scene in, however, because bathing meant business. Kaoru didn't waste a second as she stripped and scuttled towards the door into the inner sanctum—the bathhouse proper. I was so busy keeping up that I forgot to pick up my *oke*, or water scoop, on my way through. A lady who had appeared oblivious to my presence caught my arm as I opened the big door and handed me one. If this had been a fancy Tokyo bathhouse, now geared to tourists and joggers, it would have been a beautifully turned little pail made of cypress

1. Person who is seventy years old.

wood, bound with copper hoops. What I was handed, however, was a utilitarian blue plastic bowl.

There were four separate baths in the bathhouse: a large Jacuzzi that could accommodate about eight people; a whirlpool in which six people could sit; a smaller tub filled with freezing cold water; and another tub filled with hot water that I didn't immediately see anything special about. Each bath was sunk into the floor, close to the wall, and covered in white tile. At two-foot intervals along the wall between the baths, and along a low wall down the middle of the room, were taps about eighteen inches off the ground.

Over each tap was a mirror with an advertising slogan pasted across it, for soft drinks including Coca-Cola and one unfortunately named Sweat, for different kinds of soap, and for electrical equipment. I could recognize the brand names, which were in the Roman alphabet *(romaji)*, though the other words were all indecipherable to me. A few were in *kanji*, the elaborate Chinese pictographs that the Japanese adopted between the fourth and ninth centuries; most were in *hiragana*, the much simpler, abbreviated system of forty-eight phonetic symbols that the Japanese evolved from the ninth century onwards. (Japanese schoolchildren are expected to master all three scripts by the age of eight—a feat that makes the challenge of bilingualism look Mickey Mouse.) Painted on the tile of the end wall was a large landscape, filled with the familiar clichés of a Hokusai print: a lavender Mount Fuji hovered in the distance; black-jacketed peasants in coolie hats toiled on the left; foam-tipped waves curled over on the right.

Kaoru bustled over to a tap, squatted in front of it, and hid her self-consciousness in the ferocity of her ablutions. Occasionally she gave me a slightly conspiratorial smile, as I followed her example. We soaped all over, then scrubbed with the long cotton cloths we had brought with us, then poured bowls of hot water over ourselves. We repeated the ritual three times. The seven other women in the bathhouse appeared completely indifferent to us as we soaped, even though I was as inconspicuous as a yellow Labrador in a cluster of Siamese cats. After a while, I noticed suspicious glances reflected in the mirrors, so I rubbed with ostentatious fervour. Kaoru had warned me that Japanese people don't trust Westerners in their bathhouses: they find our predilection for wallowing in our own dirty water disgusting.

One woman sat in the Jacuzzi, her eyes closed, her knees bunched up, her chin resting on her fist. Two other women squatted by the central row of taps, holding an animated conversation while one energetically scrubbed the other's back pink with a bristle brush. Another washed her hair with furious energy, creating bowlfuls of lather which she sluiced off and down the drain that circled the room. One crouched figure stared intently at her face in a mirror. She appeared to be stroking her forehead and cheeks: after a few minutes I realized that she was methodically shaving every square inch of her face, except for her carefully outlined eyebrows.

All the bodies around me were virtually hairless (except for pubic hair). They were also far firmer than the bodies that surround me on Canadian beaches every summer. Not a ripple of cellulite ruffled the surface of thighs or buttocks—not even on a couple of thickset, middle-aged women. Western women would die for such marble-smooth agelessness. Yet nearly every body in a fashion magazine or face on a store mannequin was Occidental.[2] "Why don't I ever see Japanese women in commercials?" I asked Kaoru. "Because your people are more beautiful than us," she replied firmly.

After taking the top layer of my skin off with merciless scrubbing, I did the rounds of the baths. My gasp of shock when I moved from the heat of the Jacuzzi to the icy cold bath triggered smiles from fellow bathers. I was quite startled: by now I'd become accustomed to the studied indifference to foreigners that Japanese exhibit (partly through respect for privacy, partly through fear of "getting involved" and actually having to take responsibility for a stranger). The impenetrability of the language, combined with Japanese *enryo* (usually translated as reserve or restraint), often made me feel I was knocking against a locked and soundproofed glass door. But for a moment, the door opened. The Rodin[3] thinker in the Jacuzzi opened her eyes and asked Kaoru where I was from. When Kaoru replied "Canada," a few more faces turned towards me. One of the two back scrubbers nodded vigorously. "Ben Johnson,"[4] she sang out, and assumed an expression of condolence. There was a muted chorus of sympathetic "Aaahs," then everyone returned to her own bath business.

The real shock came in the fourth, "mystery" bath. It was rectangular in shape, and had yellow panels with pinholes in them on the two long sides. I slid in at one end, and cautiously stuck my foot into the hot water between the two panels. An electric shock immediately zapped my calf. The current seemed to vary: sometimes it just tingled, other times, especially when I stood between the panels, it was torture. It was the perfect therapy for muscles aching from all the unaccustomed kneeling in teahouses, private homes, and the *ryokan*.

We'd arranged to meet George outside at ten o'clock. I rose from the electric-shock bath, where I'd given my neck a last zap, and care-

2. Western.
3. Auguste Rodin (1840–1917), French sculptor. *The Thinker*, Rodin's most famous sculpture, portrays a man in deep thought with his chin resting on his hand.
4. Ben Johnson (b. 1962), Canadian sprinter who, after winning a gold medal in the 1988 Olympics, was disqualified for anabolic steroid use.

lessly draped myself in the nice fluffy towel I'd brought from the *ryokan,* as though I'd just finished swimming. Another breach of bathhouse etiquette—the patrons didn't go in for big fluffy towels. They patted themselves dry with the thin white cloth, then draped that in front of themselves, as their only concession to modesty when they left the bathhouse area.

Back in the changing room I watched with covert fascination as one woman dressed in three layers of underwear, including thermal long johns, before donning the regulation dark skirt and polyester blouse that is the universal attire of middle-aged women. No wonder domestic energy consumption in Japan is one-quarter the level in Canada. Underwear is their primary heating source.

George emerged a few minutes after us. His side of the bathhouse had been more crowded and sociable. Bull-shaped men had roared at each other across the waters, while a couple of crones moved around, cleaning the place. But the bathing had been equally purposeful and thorough. He had not exchanged a word with his fellow bathers, and they had studiously ignored him. Even in the steamy intimacy of the *sento,* we had been firmly kept at arm's length. Only a mention of our Olympic steroid-user, who had committed the unforgivable sin (in Japanese eyes) of disgracing his family and his nation, had broken through the *enryo.*

QUESTIONS

1. *Much of Gray's essay reflects on the differences between Canadian and Japanese cultures. List some of those differences and Gray's techniques for portraying them.*
2. *After reading the title of this essay, "The Temple of Hygiene," did the opening paragraph startle you? What different perspectives on the Japanese bathhouse are presented by the title versus Gray's description of the picture? Which one dominates the essay?*
3. *If you have visited another country, or a region in your own country different from the one in which you live, write about the experience of encountering cultural difference by, as Gray does, focusing on a* place.

David Guterson

ENCLOSED. ENCYCLOPEDIC. ENDURED: THE MALL OF AMERICA

Last April, on a visit to the new Mall of America near Minneapolis, I carried with me the public-relations press kit provided for the benefit of reporters. It included an assortment of "fun facts" about the mall: 140,000 hot dogs sold each week, 10,000 permanent jobs, 44 escalators and 17 elevators, 12,750 parking places, 13,300 short tons of steel, $1 million in cash disbursed weekly from 8 automatic-teller machines. Opened in the summer of 1992, the mall was built on the 78-acre site of the former Metropolitan Stadium, a five-minute drive from the Minneapolis–St. Paul International Airport. With 4.2 million square feet of floor space—including twenty-two times the retail footage of the average American shopping center—the Mall of America was "the largest fully enclosed combination retail and family entertainment complex in the United States."

Eleven thousand articles, the press kit warned me, had already been written on the mall. Four hundred trees had been planted in its gardens, $625 million had been spent to build it, 350 stores had been leased. Three thousand bus tours were anticipated each year along with a half-million Canadian visitors and 200,000 Japanese tourists. Sales were projected at $650 million for 1993 and at $1 billion for 1996. Donny and Marie Osmond had visited the mall, as had Janet Jackson and Sally Jesse Raphael, Arnold Schwarzenegger, and the 1994 Winter Olympic Committee. The mall was five times larger than Red Square and twenty times larger than St. Peter's Basilica; it incorporated 2.3 miles of hallways and almost twice as much steel as the Eiffel Tower. It was also home to the nation's largest indoor theme park, a place called Knott's Camp Snoopy.

On the night I arrived, a Saturday, the mall was spotlit dramatically in the manner of a Las Vegas casino. It resembled, from the outside, a castle or fort, the Emerald City or Never-Never Land, impossibly large and vaguely unreal, an unbroken, windowless multi-storied edifice the size of an airport terminal. Surrounded by parking lots and new freeway ramps, monolithic and imposing in the manner of a walled city, it loomed brightly against the Minnesota night sky with the disturbing magnetism of a mirage.

I knew already that the Mall of America had been imagined by its

Originally published in *Harper's Magazine* (Aug. 1993).

creators not merely as a marketplace but as a national tourist attraction, an immense zone of entertainments. Such a conceit raised provocative questions, for our architecture testifies to our view of ourselves and to the condition of our souls. Large buildings stand as markers in the lives of nations and in the stream of a people's history. Thus I could only ask myself: Here was a new structure that had cost more than half a billion dollars to erect—what might it tell us about ourselves? If the Mall of America was part of America, what was that going to mean?

I passed through one of the mall's enormous entranceways and took myself inside. Although from a distance the Mall of America had appeared menacing—excluding the ambience of a monstrous hallucination—within it turned out to be simply a shopping mall, certainly more vast than other malls but in tone and aspect, design and feel, not readily distinguishable from them. Its nuances were instantly familiar as the generic features of the American shopping mall at the tail end of the twentieth century: polished stone, polished tile, shiny chrome and brass, terrazzo floors, gazebos. From third-floor vistas, across vaulted spaces, the Mall of America felt endlessly textured—glass-enclosed elevators, neon-tube lighting, bridges, balconies, gas lamps, vaulted skylights—and densely crowded with hordes of people circumambulating in an endless promenade. Yet despite the mall's expansiveness, it elicited claustrophobia, sensory deprivation, and an unnerving disorientation. Everywhere I went I spied other pilgrims who had found, like me, that the straight way was lost and that the YOU ARE HERE landmarks on the map kiosks referred to nothing in particular.

Getting lost, feeling lost, being lost—these states of mind are intentional features of the mall's psychological terrain. There are, one notices, no clocks or windows, nothing to distract the shopper's psyche from the alternate reality the mall conjures. Here we are free to wander endlessly and to furtively watch our fellow wanderers, thousands upon thousands of milling strangers who have come with the intent of losing themselves in the mall's grand, stimulating design. For a few hours we share some common ground—a fantasy of infinite commodities and comforts—and then we drift apart forever. The mall exploits our acquisitive instincts without honoring our communal requirements, our eternal desire for discourse and intimacy, needs that until the twentieth century were traditionally met in our marketplaces but that are not met at all in giant shopping malls.

On this evening a few thousand young people had descended on the mall in pursuit of alcohol and entertainment. They had come to Gators, Hooters, and Knuckleheads, Puzzles, Fat Tuesday, and Ltl

Ditty's. At Players, a sports bar, the woman beside me introduced herself as "the pregnant wife of an Iowa pig farmer" and explained that she had driven five hours with friends to "do the mall party scene together." She left and was replaced by Kathleen from Minnetonka, who claimed to have "a real shopping thing—I can't go a week without buying new clothes. I'm not fulfilled until I buy something."

Later a woman named Laura arrived, with whom Kathleen was acquainted. "I *am* the mall," she announced ecstatically upon discovering I was a reporter. "I'd move in here if I could bring my dog," she added. "This place is heaven, it's a *mecca*."

"We egg each other on," explained Kathleen, calmly puffing on a cigarette. "It's like, sort of, an addiction."

"You want the truth?" Laura asked. "I'm constantly suffering from megamall withdrawal. I come here all the time."

10 Kathleen: "It's a sickness. It's like cocaine or something; it's a drug."

Laura: "Kathleen's got this thing about buying, but I just need to *be* here. If I buy something it's an added bonus."

Kathleen: "She buys stuff all the time; don't listen."

Laura: "Seriously, I feel sorry for other malls. They're so small and *boring*."

Kathleen seemed to think about this: "Richdale Mall," she blurted finally. She rolled her eyes and gestured with her cigarette. "Oh, my God, Laura. Why did we even *go* there?"

15 There is, of course, nothing naturally abhorrent in the human impulse to dwell in marketplaces or the urge to buy, sell, and trade. Rural Americans traditionally looked forward to the excitement and sensuality of market day; Native Americans traveled long distances to barter and trade at sprawling, festive encampments. In Persian bazaars and in the ancient Greek agoras the very soul of the community was preserved and could be seen, felt, heard, and smelled as it might be nowhere else. All over the planet the humblest of people have always gone to market with hope in their hearts and in expectation of something beyond mere goods—seeking a place where humanity is temporarily in ascendance, a palette for the senses, one another.

But the illicit possibilities of the marketplace also have long been acknowledged. The Persian bazaar was closed at sundown; the Greek agora was off-limits to those who had been charged with certain crimes. One myth of the Old West we still carry with us is that market day presupposes danger; the faithful were advised to make purchases quickly and repair without delay to the farm, lest their attraction to the pleasures of the marketplace erode their purity of spirit.

In our collective discourse the shopping mall appears with the tract house, the freeway, and the backyard barbecue as a product of the

American postwar years, a testament to contemporary necessities and desires and an invention not only peculiarly American but peculiarly of our own era too. Yet the mall's varied and far-flung predecessors—the covered bazaars of the Middle East, the stately arcades of Victorian England, Italy's vaulted and skylit gallerias, Asia's monsoon-protected urban markets—all suggest that the rituals of indoor shopping, although in their nuances not often like our own, are nevertheless broadly known. The late twentieth-century American contribution has been to transform the enclosed bazaar into an economic institution that is vastly profitable yet socially enervated, one that redefines in fundamental ways the human relationship to the marketplace. At the Mall of America—an extreme example—we discover ourselves thoroughly lost among strangers in a marketplace intentionally designed to serve no community needs.

In the strict sense the Mall of America is not a marketplace at all—the soul of a community expressed as a *place*—but rather a tourist attraction. Its promoters have peddled it to the world at large as something more profound than a local marketplace and as a destination with deep implications. "I believe we can make Mall of America stand for all of America," asserted the mall's general manager, John Wheeler, in a promotional video entitled *There's a Place for Fun in Your Life*. "I believe there's a shopper in all of us," added the director of marketing, Maureen Hooley. The mall has memorialized its opening-day proceedings by producing a celebratory videotape: Ray Charles singing "America the Beautiful," a laser show followed by fireworks, "The Star-Spangled Banner" and "The Stars and Stripes Forever," the Gatlin Brothers, and Peter Graves. "Mall of America . . . ," its narrator intoned. "The name alone conjures up images of greatness, of a retail complex so magnificent it could only happen in America."

Indeed, on the day the mall opened, Miss America visited. The mall's logo—a red, white, and blue star bisected by a red, white, and blue ribbon—decorated everything from the mall itself to coffee mugs and the flanks of buses. The idea, director of tourism Colleen Hayes told me, was to position America's largest mall as an institution on the scale of Disneyland or the Grand Canyon, a place simultaneously iconic and totemic, a revered symbol of the United States and a mecca to which the faithful would flock in pursuit of all things purchasable.

On Sunday I wandered the hallways of the pleasure dome with the 20
sensation that I had entered an M. C. Escher drawing—there was no such thing as up or down, and the escalators all ran backward. A 1993 Ford Probe GT was displayed as if popping out of a giant packing box; a full-size home, complete with artificial lawn, had been built in the

mall's rotunda. At the Michael Ricker Pewter Gallery I came across a miniature tableau of a pewter dog peeing on a pewter man's leg; at Hologram Land I pondered 3-D hallucinations of the Medusa and Marilyn Monroe. I passed a kiosk called The Sportsman's Wife; I stood beside a life-size statue of the Hamm's Bear, carved out of pine and available for $1,395 at a store called Minnesot-ah! At Pueblo Spirit I examined a "dream catcher"—a small hoop made from deer sinew and willow twigs and designed to be hung over its owner's bed as a tactic for filtering bad dreams. For a while I sat in front of Glamour Shots and watched while women were groomed and brushed for photo sessions yielding high-fashion self-portraits at $34.95 each. There was no stopping, no slowing down. I passed Mug Me, Queen for a Day, and Barnyard Buddies, and stood in the Brookstone store examining a catalogue: a gopher "eliminator" for $40 (it's a vibrating, anodized-aluminum stake), a "no-stoop" shoehorn for $10, a nose-hair trimmer for $18. At the arcade inside Knott's Camp Snoopy I watched while teenagers played Guardians of the 'Hood, Total Carnage, Final Fight, and Varth Operation Thunderstorm; a small crowd of them had gathered around a lean, cool character who stood calmly shooting video cowpokes in a game called Mad Dog McCree. Left thumb on his silver belt buckle, biceps pulsing, he banged away without remorse while dozens of his enemies crumpled and died in alleyways and dusty streets.

At Amazing Pictures a teenage boy had his photograph taken as a bodybuilder—his face smoothly grafted onto a rippling body—then proceeded to purchase this pleasing image on a poster, a sweatshirt, and a coffee mug. At Painted Tipi there was wild rice for sale, hand-harvested from Leech Lake, Minnesota. At Animalia I came across a polyresin figurine of a turtle retailing for $3,200. At Bloomingdale's I pondered a denim shirt with its sleeves ripped away, the sort of thing available at used-clothing stores (the "grunge look," a Bloomingdale's employee explained), on sale for $125. Finally, at a gift shop in Knott's Camp Snoopy, I came across a game called Electronic Mall Madness, put out by Milton Bradley. On the box, three twelve-year-old girls with good features happily vied to beat one another to the game-board mall's best sales.

At last I achieved an enforced self-arrest, anchoring myself against a bench while the mall tilted on its axis. Two pubescent girls in retainers and braces sat beside me sipping coffees topped with whipped cream and chocolate sprinkles, their shopping bags gathered tightly around their legs, their eyes fixed on the passing crowds. They came, they said, from Shakopee—"It's nowhere," one of them explained. The megamall, she added, was "a buzz at first, but now it seems pretty normal. 'Cept my parents are like Twenty Questions every time I want to come here. 'Specially since the shooting."

On a Sunday night, she elaborated, three people had been wounded when shots were fired in a dispute over a San Jose Sharks jacket. "In the *mall*," her friend reminded me. "Right here at megamall. A shooting."

"It's like nowhere's safe," the first added.

The sipped their coffees and explicated for me the plot of a film 25
they saw as relevant, a horror movie called *Dawn of the Dead*, which they had each viewed a half-dozen times. In the film, they explained, apocalypse had come, and the survivors had repaired to a shopping mall as the most likely place to make their last stand in a poisoned, impossible world. And this would have been perfectly all right, they insisted, except that the place had also attracted hordes of the infamous living dead—sentient corpses who had not relinquished their attraction to indoor shopping.

I moved on and contemplated a computerized cash register in the infant's section of the Nordstrom store: "The Answer Is Yes!!!" its monitor reminded clerks. "Customer Service Is Our Number One Priority!" Then back at Bloomingdale's I contemplated a bank of televisions playing incessantly an advertisement for Egoïste, a men's cologne from Chanel. In the ad a woman on a wrought-iron balcony tossed her black hair about and screamed long and passionately; then there were many women screaming passionately, too, and throwing balcony shutters open and closed, and this was all followed by a bottle of the cologne displayed where I could get a good look at it. The brief, strange drama repeated itself until I could no longer stand it.

America's first fully enclosed shopping center—Southdale Center, in Edina, Minnesota—is a ten-minute drive from the Mall of America and thirty-six years its senior. (It is no coincidence that the Twin Cities area is such a prominent player in mall history: Minnesota is subject to the sort of severe weather that makes climate-controlled shopping seductive.) Opened in 1956, Southdale spawned an era of fervid mall construction and generated a vast new industry. Shopping centers proliferated so rapidly that by the end of 1992, says the National Research Bureau, there were nearly 39,000 of them operating everywhere across the country. But while malls recorded a much-ballyhooed success in the America of the 1970s and early 1980s, they gradually became less profitable to run as the exhausted and overwhelmed American worker inevitably lost interest in leisure shopping. Pressed for time and short on money, shoppers turned to factory outlet centers, catalogue purchasing, and "category killers" (specialty stores such as Home Depot and Price Club) at the expense of shopping malls. The industry, unnerved, re-invented itself, relying on smaller and more convenient local centers—especially the familiar neighborhood strip mall—and building far fewer large regional malls in an effort to stay afloat through troubled times. With the advent of cable television's Home Shopping Network and the proliferation of specialty catalogue retailers (whose access to computerized market research has made them, in the Nineties, powerful competitors), the mall industry reeled yet further. According to the International Council of Shopping Centers, new mall construction in 1992 was a third of what it had been in 1989, and the value of mall-construction contracts dropped 60 percent in the same three-year period.

Anticipating a future in which millions of Americans will prefer to shop in the security of their living rooms—conveniently accessing on-line retail companies as a form of quiet evening entertainment—the mall industry, after less than forty years, experienced a full-blown mid-life crisis. It was necessary for the industry to re-invent itself once more, this time with greater attentiveness to the qualities that would allow it to endure relentless change. Anxiety-ridden and sapped of vitality, mall builders fell back on an ancient truth, one capable of sustaining them through troubled seasons: they discovered what humanity had always understood, that shopping and frivolity go hand in hand and are inherently symbiotic. *If you build it fun, they will come.*

The new bread-and-circuses approach to mall building was first ventured in 1985 by the four Ghermezian brothers—Raphael, Nader, Bahman, and Eskandar—builders of Canada's $750 million West Edmonton Mall, which included a water slide, an artificial lake, a miniature-golf course, a hockey rink, and forty-seven rides in an amusement park known as Fantasyland. The complex quickly generated sales revenues at twice the rate per square foot of retail space that could be squeezed from a conventional outlet mall, mostly by developing its own shopping synergy: people came for a variety of reasons and to do a variety of things. West Edmonton's carnival atmosphere, it gradually emerged, lubricated pocketbooks and inspired the sort of impulse buying on which malls everywhere thrive. To put the matter another way, it was time for a shopping-and-pleasure palace to be attempted in the United States.

30 After selling the Mall of America concept to Minnesotans in 1985, the Ghermezians joined forces with their American counterparts—Mel and Herb Simon of Indianapolis, owners of the NBA's Indiana Pacers and the nation's second-largest developers of shopping malls. The idea, in the beginning, was to outdo West Edmonton by building a mall far larger and more expensive—something visionary, a wonder of the world—and to include such attractions as fashionable hotels, an elaborate tour de force aquarium, and a monorail to the Minneapolis–St. Paul airport. Eventually the project was downscaled substantially: a million square feet of floor space was eliminated, the construction

budget was cut, and the aquarium and hotels were never built (reserved, said marketing director Maureen Hooley, for "phase two" of the mall's development). Japan's Mitsubishi Bank, Mitsui Trust, and Chuo Trust together put up a reported $400 million to finance the cost of construction, and Teachers Insurance and Annuity Association (the majority owner of the Mall of America) came through with another $225 million. At a total bill of $625 million, the mall was ultimately a less ambitious project than its forebear up north on the Canadian plains, and neither as large nor as gaudy. Reflecting the economy's downturn, the parent companies of three of the mall's anchor tenants—Sears, Macy's, and Bloomingdale's—were battling serious financial trouble and needed substantial transfusions from mall developers to have their stores ready by opening day.

The mall expects to spend millions on marketing itself during its initial year of operation and has lined up the usual corporate sponsors—Ford, Pepsi, US West—in an effort to build powerful alliances. Its public-relations representatives travel to towns such as Rapid City, South Dakota, and Sioux City, Iowa, in order to drum up interest within the Farm Belt. Northwest Airlines, another corporate sponsor, offers package deals from London and Tokyo and fare adjustments for those willing to come from Bismarck, North Dakota; Cedar Rapids, Iowa; and Kalamazoo or Grand Rapids, Michigan. Calling itself a "premier tourism destination," the mall draws from a primary tourist market that incorporates the eleven Midwest states (and two Canadian provinces) lying within a day's drive of its parking lots. It also estimates that in its first six months of operation, 5.3 million out of 16 million visitors came from beyond the Twin Cities metropolitan area.

The mall has forecast a much-doubted figure of 46 million annual visits by 1996—four times the number of annual visits to Disneyland, for example, and twelve times the visits to the Grand Canyon. The number, Maureen Hooley explained, seems far less absurd when one takes into account that mall pilgrims make far more repeat visits—as many as eighty in a single year—than visitors to theme parks such as Disneyland. Relentless advertising and shrewd promotion, abetted by the work of journalists like myself, assure the mall that visitors will come in droves—at least for the time being. The national media have comported themselves as if the new mall were a place of light and promise, full of hope and possibility. Meanwhile the Twin Cities' media have been shameless: on opening night Minneapolis's WCCO-TV aired a one-hour mall special, hosted by local news anchors Don Shelby and Colleen Needles, and the *St. Paul Pioneer Press* (which was named an "official" sponsor of the opening) dedicated both a phone line and a weekly column to answering esoteric mall questions. Not to be outdone, the *Minneapolis Star Tribune* developed a special graphic to draw readers to mall stories and printed a vast Sunday supplement before opening day under the heading A WHOLE NEW MALLGAME. By the following Wednesday all perspective was in eclipse: the local press reported that at 9:05 A.M., the mall's Victoria's Secret outlet had recorded its first sale, a pair of blue/green silk men's boxer shorts; that mall developers Mel and Herb Simon ate black-bean soup for lunch at 12:30 P.M.; that Kimberly Levis, four years old, constructed a rectangular column nineteen bricks high at the mall's Lego Imagination Center; and that mall officials had retained a plumber on standby in case difficulties arose with the mall's toilets.

From all of this coverage—and from the words you now read—the mall gains status as a phenomenon worthy of our time and consideration: place as celebrity. The media encourage us to visit our megamall in the obligatory fashion we flock to *Jurassic Park*—because it is there, all glitter and glow, a piece of the terrain, a season's diversion, an assumption on the cultural landscape. All of us will want to be in on the conversation and, despite ourselves, we will go.

Lost in the fun house I shopped till I dropped, but the scale of the mall eventually overwhelmed me and I was unable to make a purchase. Finally I met Chuck Brand on a bench in Knott's Camp Snoopy; he was seventy-two and, in his personal assessment of it, had lost at least 25 percent of his mind. "It's fun being a doozy," he confessed to me. "The security cops got me figured and keep their distance. I don't get hassled for hanging out, not shopping. Because the deal is, when you're seventy-two, man, you're just about all done shopping."

35 After forty-seven years of selling houses in Minneapolis, Chuck comes to the mall every day. He carries a business card with his picture on it, his company name and phone number deleted and replaced by his pager code. His wife drops him at the mall at 10:00 A.M. each morning and picks him up again at six; in between he sits and watches. "I can't sit home and do nothing," he insisted. When I stood to go he assured me he understood: I was young and had things I had to do. "Listen," he added, "thanks for talking to me, man. I've been sitting in this mall for four months now and nobody ever said nothing."

The next day I descended into the mall's enormous basement, where its business offices are located. "I'm sorry to have to bring this up," my prearranged mall guide, Michelle Biesiada, greeted me. "But you were seen talking to one of our housekeepers—one of the people who empty the garbage?—and really, you aren't supposed to do that."

Later we sat in the mall's security center, a subterranean computerized command post where two uniformed officers manned a bank of television screens. The Mall of America, it emerged, employed 109 surveillance cameras to monitor the various activities of its guests, and had plans to add yet more. There were cameras in the food courts and parking lots, in the hallways and in Knott's Camp Snoopy. From where we sat, it was possible to monitor thirty-six locations simultaneously; it was also possible, with the use of a zoom feature, to narrow in on an object as small as a hand, a license plate, or a wallet.

While we sat in the darkness of the security room, enjoying the voyeuristic pleasures it allowed (I, for one, felt a giddy sense of power), a security guard noted something of interest occurring in one of the parking lots. The guard engaged a camera's zoom feature, and soon we were given to understand that a couple of bored shoppers were enjoying themselves by fornicating in the front seat of a parked car. An officer was dispatched to knock on their door and discreetly suggest that they move themselves along; the Mall of America was no place for this. "If they want to have sex they'll have to go elsewhere," a security officer told me. "We don't have anything against sex, per se, but we don't want it happening in our parking lots."

I left soon afterward for a tour of the mall's basement, a place of perpetual concrete corridors and home to a much-touted recyclery. Declaring itself "the most environmentally conscious shopping center in the industry," the Mall of America claims to recycle up to 80 percent of its considerable refuse and points to its "state-of-the-art" recycling system as a symbol of its dedication to Mother Earth. Yet Rick Doering of Browning-Ferris Industries—the company contracted to manage the mall's 700 tons of monthly garbage—described the on-site facility as primarily a public-relations gambit that actually recycles only a third of the mall's tenant waste and little of what is discarded by its thousands of visitors; furthermore, he admitted, the venture is unprofitable to Browning-Ferris, which would find it far cheaper to recycle the mall's refuse somewhere other than in its basement.

A third-floor "RecycleNOW Center," located next to Macy's and 40
featuring educational exhibits, is designed to enhance the mall's self-styled image as a national recycling leader. Yet while the mall's developers gave Macy's $35 million to cover most of its "build-out" expenses (the cost of transforming the mall's basic structure into finished, customer-ready floor space), Browning-Ferris got nothing in build-out costs and operates the center at a total loss, paying rent equivalent to that paid by the mall's retailers. As a result, the company has had to look for ways to keep its costs to a minimum, and the mall's garbage is now sorted by developmentally disabled adults working a conveyor belt in the basement. Doering and I stood watching them as they picked at a stream of paper and plastic bottles; when I asked about their pay, he flinched and grimaced, then deflected me toward another supervisor, who said that wages were based on daily productivity. Did this mean that they made less than minimum wage? I inquired. The answer was yes.

Upstairs once again, I hoped for relief from the basement's oppressive, concrete gloom, but the mall felt densely crowded and with panicked urgency I made an effort to leave. I ended up instead at Knott's Camp Snoopy—the seven-acre theme park at the center of the complex—a place intended to alleviate claustrophobia by "bringing the outdoors indoors." Its interior landscape, the press kit claims, "was inspired by Minnesota's natural habitat—forests, meadows, river banks, and marshes . . ." And "everything you see, feel, smell and hear adds to the illusion that it's summertime, seventy degrees and you're outside enjoying the awesome splendor of the Minnesota woods."

Creators of this illusion had much to contend with, including sixteen carnival-style midway rides, such as the Pepsi Ripsaw, the Screaming Yellow Eagle, Paul Bunyan's Log Chute by Brawny, Tumbler, Truckin', and Huff 'n' Puff; fifteen places for visitors to eat, such as Funnel Cakes, Stick Dogs and Campfire Burgers, Taters, Pizza Oven, and Wilderness Barbecue; seven shops with names like Snoopy's Boutique, Joe Cool's Hot Shop, and Camp Snoopy Toys; and such assorted attractions as Pan for Gold, Hunter's Paradise Shooting Gallery, the Snoopy Fountain, and the video arcade that includes the game Mad Dog McCree.

As if all this were not enough to cast a serious pall over the Minnesota woods illusion, the theme park's designers had to contend with the fact that they could use few plants native to Minnesota. At a constant temperature of seventy degrees, the mall lends itself almost exclusively to tropical varieties—orange jasmine, black olive, oleander, hibiscus—and not at all to the conifers of Minnesota, which require a cold dormancy period. Deferring ineluctably to this troubling reality, Knott's Camp Snoopy brought in 526 tons of plants—tropical rhododendrons, willow figs, buddhist pines, azaleas—from such places as Florida, Georgia, and Mississippi.

Anne Pryor, a Camp Snoopy marketing representative, explained to me that these plants were cared for via something called "integrated pest management," which meant the use of predators such as ladybugs instead of pesticides. Yet every member of the landscape staff I spoke to described a campaign of late-night pesticide spraying as a means of controlling the theme park's enemies—mealybugs, aphids, and spider mites. Two said they had argued for integrated pest management as a more environmentally sound method of controlling insects but that to date it had not been tried.

45 Even granting that Camp Snoopy is what it claims to be—an authentic version of Minnesota's north woods tended by environmentally correct means—the question remains whether it makes sense to place a forest in the middle of the country's largest shopping complex. Isn't it true that if people want woods, they are better off not going to a mall?

On Valentine's Day last February—cashing in on the promotional scheme of a local radio station—ninety-two couples were married en masse in a ceremony at the Mall of America. They rode the roller coaster and the Screaming Yellow Eagle and were photographed beside a frolicking Snoopy, who wore an immaculate tuxedo. "As we stand here together at the Mall of America," presiding district judge Richard Spicer declared, "we are reminded that there is a place for fun in your life and you have found it in each other." Six months earlier, the Reverend Leith Anderson of the Wooddale Church in Eden Prairie conducted services in the mall's rotunda. Six thousand people had congregated by 10:00 A.M., and Reverend Anderson delivered a sermon entitled "The Unknown God of the Mall." Characterizing the mall as a "direct descendant" of the ancient Greek agoras, the reverend pointed out that, like the Greeks before us, we Americans have many gods. Afterward, of course, the flock went shopping, much to the chagrin of Reverend Delton Krueger, president of the Mall Area Religious Council, who told the *Minneapolis Star Tribune* that as a site for church services, the mall may trivialize religion. "A good many people in the churches," said Krueger, "feel a lot of the trouble in the world is because of materialism."

But a good many people in the mall business today apparently think the trouble lies elsewhere. They are moving forward aggressively on the premise that the dawning era of electronic shopping does not preclude the building of shopping-and-pleasure palaces all around the globe. Japanese developers, in a joint venture with the Ghermezians known as International Malls Incorporated, are planning a $400 million Mall of Japan, with an ice rink, a water park, a fantasy-theme hotel, three breweries, waterfalls, and a sports center. We might shortly predict, too, a Mall of Europe, a Mall of New England, a Mall of California, and perhaps even a Mall of the World. The concept of shopping in a frivolous atmosphere, concocted to loosen consumers' wallets, is poised to proliferate globally. We will soon see monster malls everywhere, rooted in the soil of every nation and offering a preposterous, impossible variety of commodities and entertainments.

The new malls will be planets unto themselves, closed off from this world in the manner of space stations or of science fiction's underground cities. Like the Mall of America and West Edmonton Mall—prototypes for a new generation of shopping centers—they will project a separate and distinct reality in which an "outdoor café" is not outdoors, a "bubbling brook" is a concrete watercourse, and a "serpentine street" is a hallway. Safe, surreal, and outside of time and space, they will offer the mind a potent dreamscape from which there is no present waking. This carefully controlled fantasy—now operable in Minnesota—is so powerful as to inspire psychological addiction or to elicit in visitors a catatonic obsession with the mall's various hallucinations. The new malls will be theatrical, high-tech illusions capable of attracting enormous crowds from distant points and foreign ports. Their psychology has not yet been tried pervasively on the scale of the Mall of America, nor has it been perfected. But in time our marketplaces, all over the world, will be in essential ways interchangeable, so thoroughly divorced from the communities in which they sit that they will appear to rest like permanently docked spaceships against the landscape, windowless and turned in upon their own affairs. The affluent will travel as tourists to each, visiting the holy sites and taking photographs in the catacombs of far-flung temples.

Just as Victorian England is acutely revealed beneath the grandiose domes of its overwrought train stations, so is contemporary America well understood from the upper vistas of its shopping malls, places without either windows or clocks where the temperature is forever seventy degrees. It is facile to believe, from this vantage point, that the endless circumambulations of tens of thousands of strangers—all loaded down with the detritus of commerce—resemble anything akin to community. The shopping mall is not, as the architecture critic Witold Rybczynski has concluded, "poised to become a real urban place" with "a variety of commercial and noncommercial functions." On the contrary, it is poised to multiply around the world as an institution offering only a desolate substitute for the rich, communal lifeblood of the traditional marketplace, which will not survive its onslaught.

50 Standing on the Mall of America's roof, where I had ventured to inspect its massive ventilation units, I finally achieved a full sense of its vastness, of how it overwhelmed the surrounding terrain—the last sheep farm in sight, the Mississippi River incidental in the distance. Then I peered through the skylights down into Camp Snoopy, where throngs of my fellow citizens caroused happily in the vast entrails of the beast.

Joseph Addison

THE ROYAL EXCHANGE

There is no Place in the Town which I so much love to frequent as the Royal-Exchange. It gives me a secret Satisfaction, and, in some measure, gratifies my Vanity, as I am an Englishman, to see so rich an

Originally published in *The Spectator* (May 19, 1711).

Assembly of Country-men and Foreigners consulting together upon the private Business of Mankind, and making this Metropolis a kind of Emporium for the whole Earth. I must confess I look upon High-Change[1] to be a great Council, in which all considerable Nations have their Representatives. Factors in the Trading World are what Ambassadors are in the Politick World; they negotiate Affairs, conclude Treaties, and maintain a good Correspondence between those wealthy Societies of Men that are divided from one another by Seas and Oceans, or live on the different Extremities of a Continent. I have often been pleased to hear Disputes adjusted between an Inhabitant of Japan and an Alderman of London, or to see a Subject of the Great Mogul entering into a League with one of the Czar of Muscovy. I am infinitely delighted in mixing with these several Ministers of Commerce, as they are distinguished by their different Walks and different Languages: Sometimes I am justled among a Body of Armenians.[2] Sometimes I am lost in a Crowd of Jews, and sometimes make one in a Groupe of Dutch-men. I am a Dane, Swede, or French-Man at different times, or rather fancy my self like the old Philosopher, who upon being asked what Country-man he was, replied, That he was a Citizen of the World.[3]

Though I very frequently visit this busie Multitude of People, I am known to no Body there but my Friend, Sir Andrew, who often smiles upon me as he sees me bustling in the Croud, but at the same time connives at my Presence without taking any further notice of me. There is indeed a Merchant of Egypt, who just knows me by sight, having formerly remitted me some Money to Grand Cairo; but as I am not versed in the Modern Coptick, our Conferences go no further than a Bow and a Grimace.[4]

This grand Scene of Business gives me an infinite Variety of solid and substantial Entertainments. As I am a great Lover of Mankind, my Heart naturally overflows with Pleasure at the sight of a prosperous and happy Multitude, insomuch that at many publick Solemnities I cannot forbear expressing my Joy with Tears that have stolen down my Cheeks. For this reason I am wonderfully delighted to see such a Body of Men thriving in their own private Fortunes, and at the same time promoting the Publick Stock; or in other Words, raising Estates for their own Families, by bringing into their Country whatever is wanting, and carrying out of it whatever is superfluous.

Nature seems to have taken a particular Care to disseminate her

1. The time of greatest activity on the Exchange.
2. The Armenian Walk was on the east side facing Swithin's Alley.
3. The old philosopher who gave this answer was Diogenes the Cynic (c. 400–325 B.C.).
4. "Grimace" meant a turn of the countenance that expressed acquaintance or civility.

Blessings among the different Regions of the World, with an Eye to this mutual Intercourse and Traffick among Mankind, that the Natives of the several Parts of the Globe might have a kind of Dependence upon one another, and be united together by their common Interest. Almost every Degree produces something peculiar to it. The Food often grows in one Country, and the Sauce in another. The Fruits of Portugal are corrected by the Products of Barbadoes: The Infusion of a China Plant sweetned with the Pith of an Indian Cane: The Philippick Islands give a Flavour to our European Bowls. The single Dress of a Woman of Quality is often the Product of an hundred Climates. The Muff and the Fan come together from the different Ends of the Earth. The Scarf is sent from the Torrid Zone, and the Tippet from beneath the Pole. The Brocade Petticoat rises out of the Mines of Peru, and the Diamond Necklace out of the Bowels of Indostan.

5 If we consider our own Country in its natural Prospect, without any of the Benefits and Advantages of Commerce, what a barren uncomfortable Spot of Earth falls to our Share! Natural Historians tell us, that no Fruit grows originally among us, besides Hips and Haws, Acorns and Pig-Nutts, with other Delicacies of the like Nature; That our Climate of it self, and without the Assistances of Art, can make no further Advances towards a Plumb than to a Sloe, and carries an Apple to no greater a Perfection than a Crab: That our Melons, our Peaches, our Figs, our Apricots, and Cherries, are Strangers among us, imported in different Ages, and naturalized in our English Gardens; and that they would all degenerate and fall away into the Trash of our own Country, if they were wholly neglected by the Planter, and left to the Mercy of our Sun and Soil. Nor has Traffick more enriched our Vegetable World, than it has improved the whole Face of Nature among us. Our Ships are laden with the Harvest of every Climate: Our Tables are stored with Spices, and Oils, and Wines: Our Rooms are filled with Pyramids of China, and adorned with the Workmanship of Japan: Our Morning's-Draught comes to us from the remotest Corners of the Earth: We repair our Bodies by the Drugs of America, and repose our selves under Indian Canopies. My Friend Sir Andrew calls the Vineyards of France our Gardens; the Spice-Islands our Hot-Beds; the Persians our Silk-Weavers, and the Chinese our Potters. Nature indeed furnishes us with the bare Necessaries of Life, but Traffick gives us a great Variety of what is Useful, and at the same time supplies us with every thing that is Convenient and Ornamental. Nor is it the least part of this our Happiness, that whilst we enjoy the remotest Products of the North and South, we are free from those Extremities of Weather which give them Birth; That our Eyes are refreshed with the green Fields of Britain, at the same time that our Palates are feasted with Fruits that rise between the Tropicks.

For these Reasons there are not more useful Members in a Commonwealth than Merchants. They knit Mankind together in a mutual Intercourse of good Offices, distribute the Gifts of Nature, find Work for the Poor, add Wealth to the Rich, and Magnificence to the Great. Our English Merchant converts the Tin of his own Country into Gold, and exchanges his Wooll for Rubies. The Mahometans are cloathed in our British Manufacture, and the Inhabitants of the Frozen Zone warmed with the Fleeces of our Sheep.

When I have been upon the 'Change I have often fancied one of our old Kings[5] standing in Person, where he is represented in Effigy, and looking down upon the wealthy Concourse of People with which that Place is every Day filled. In this Case, how would he be surprized to hear all the Languages of Europe spoken in this little Spot of his former Dominions, and to see so many private Men, who in his Time would have been the Vassals of some powerful Baron, Negotiating like Princes for greater Sums of Mony than were formerly to be met with in the Royal Treasury! Trade, without enlarging the British Territories, has given us a kind of additional Empire: It has multiplied the Number of the Rich, made our Landed Estates infinitely more Valuable than they were formerly, and added to them an Accession of other Estates as Valuable as the Lands themselves.

5. A statue carved by Caius Gabriel Cibber (1630–1700).

Hugh MacLennan

SCOTCHMAN'S RETURN

Whenever I stop to think about it, the knowledge that I am three-quarters Scotch, and Highland at that, seems like a kind of doom from which I am too Scotch even to think of praying for deliverance. I can thank my father for this last-ditch neurosis. He was entirely Scotch; he was a living specimen of a most curious heritage. In spite of his medical knowledge, which was large; in spite of his quick, nervous vitality and tireless energy, he was never able to lay to rest the beasties which went bump in his mind at three o'clock in the morning. It mattered nothing that he was a third-generation Canadian who had never seen the Highlands before he visited them on leave in the First World War. He never needed to go there to understand whence he came or what he was. He was neither a Scot nor yet was he Scottish; he never used those genteel appellations which now are supposed to be *de rigueur*.[1] He was simply Scotch. All the perplexity and doggedness of the race

From *Hugh MacLennan's Best* (1991).

1. Strictly obligatory.

was in him, its loneliness, tenderness, and affection, its deceptive vitality, its quick flashes of violence, its dog-whistle sensitivity to sounds to which Anglo-Saxons are stone-deaf, its incapacity to tell its heart to foreigners save in terms foreigners do not comprehend, its resigned indifference to whether they comprehend or not. "It's not easy being Scotch," he told me more than once. To which I suppose another Scotchman might say: "It wasn't meant to be."

So far as I could tell, my father found it almost impossible to believe that anyone not Scotch is entirely real. Yet, at the same time, buried in the fastnesses of his complex mind was the contradictory notion that if a Scotchman ever amounts to anything important, he will not be any too real, either, for some beastie will come along and spoil him. As engineers keeping the ships going, as captains serving the owners of the lines, as surgeons, teachers, clergymen, and the like, as loyal seconds-in-command—in these niches the Scotch might expect to fare well. But you seldom found them on the summit, and if by reason of an accident one of them got there, something bad was pretty sure to happen. When Ramsay MacDonald became the first man with a Mac in his name to become a British Prime Minister, my father shook his head gloomily over MacDonald's picture on the front page of the paper, and when I asked him why, he said: "He won't do." He had an overweening admiration for the English so long as they stayed in England, and for the Royal Navy above all other English institutions. Indeed, one of his motives for becoming a doctor was an idea in the back of his youthful mind that as a surgeon he might become an R.N. officer. But he was no light Anglophile. I well remember a summer afternoon in the mid-twenties when a British squadron paid Halifax a courtesy call, and better still do I remember that the two leading ships were HMS *Hood* and HMS *Repulse*. As my father at that time was doing some work in the military hospital, he was called to perform an emergency operation on an officer of the *Repulse*, and the Commander of the ship later invited him to tea in the wardroom. He took me along, and as I also was brought up to love the Royal Navy, this was a great thrill to me. It turned out to be an experience almost traumatic.

No sooner had we taken our seats in the wardroom than the officer-of-the-watch entered, resplendent in the dress of the day carrying his cocked hat under his arm. He laid the hat beside him on the table, nodded to a steward for his tea, glanced at us, and when he saw we were civilians and natives, his lips parted in an expression of disdain in which, to quote a famous English author who has noted such expressions as carefully as Shelley[2] the lips of Ozymandias,[3] delicacy had no

2. Percy Bysshe Shelley (1792–1822), English Romantic poet.
3. Pharaoh of Egypt during the Exodus of the Jews. His statue is the subject of a poem by Shelley.

part. Ignoring my father, this officer inclined his eyes vaguely in my direction and said: "D'you live here?" "Yes, sir," I replied. "Beastly place," was his comment and then he fell silent. So did everyone else.

After several minutes the silence was broken by the racket of an R.C.A.F. training biplane stunting over the harbour and the arrogant disdain on the face of the former officer-of-the-watch was replaced by something very like a flush of anger. "So you have those wretched things over here, too?" he asked my father accusingly. I noted with some pride that my father did not reply to this officer, but instead turned to another man, who had been embarrassed by his colleague's behaviour, and asked mildly if the development of aircraft had made it necessary for the Navy to alter its battle tactics. This officer was beginning to reply in some detail when the officer-of-the-watch interrupted: "Do you," he asked my father, "seriously believe that a wretched little gnat like that aircraft could possibly threaten a ship like this?"

No, it was not a successful tea party, nor did it last much longer. My 5
father rose as soon as he felt it courteous to do so, we were escorted to the ladder and handed down into the launch, and as the launch drove through the fog my father was informatively silent. After a while he said, as though excusing the officer's rudeness: "Of course, the weather has been depressing here and they've come up from New York." But before the launch touched the jetty he added: "All the same, he shouldn't have said that." I understood then that my father had not felt himself snubbed, but that the Scotch in him had been gravely concerned by the officer's *hubris*[4] concerning the Air Force. A beastie had been alerted to keep a special eye on that slim, powerful, but extremely vulnerable battle-cruiser which was the last brain-child of the ferocious Admiral Jackie Fisher, the ship which Winston Churchill[5] later described as having the brilliance and the fragility one is apt to associate with the children of very old men. Years later in the terrible December of 1941, when the news came from Malaya, I recalled that afternoon aboard *Repulse* with a thrill of sheer horror.

My father was also the reason why I never visited the Highlands when I was a student in the Old Country. Nor did he think I should have done so. "You'll see them one of these days," he said. And he added as an afterthought: "If you're spared and well." And he added as another afterthought: "When you do see them you'll understand." Naturally he did not tell me what I would understand, assuming I would know, but this comment did nothing to foment a desire in me to travel north of the Highland line.

But we can't escape ourselves forever, and more of ourselves than we choose to admit is the accumulated weight of our ancestors. As I grew

4. Excessive self-pride.
5. Churchill (1874–1965) was prime minister of Great Britain during World War II.

older the thought of the Highlands began to haunt me, and in the summer of 1958, after having lived for a long time under a great strain, I decided to get a change and sail to England on a freight ship. I landed in Manchester and of course went south, but after spending a week in London, I went north on the train to Edinburgh and on a Monday morning I found myself in a car-rental agency in the Haymarket making a deal for a Vauxhall.

Ahead of me was the only American I saw in the Old Country that year who behaved as Europeans desire Americans to behave abroad. After complaining about the tastelessness of British food, the harshness and skiddiness of British toilet paper, and the absurdity of driving on the left-hand side of the road, he finally came to the topic of the Edinburgh Sabbath which he had just survived.

"Do you realize," he said to the car dealer, "that in the United States there's not even a village as quiet as this town was yesterday?"

The Scotchman looked up at him, inwardly gratified but outwardly glum.

"Ay!" he said, and assumed incorrectly that the American understood that both himself and his country had been rebuked.

When he turned to me after the American had departed, and had identified my nationality by my driving licence, he allowed himself the luxury of an irrelevant comment.

"Ye appear to have deeficult neighbours," he said.

"Perhaps you have difficult neighbours, too?"

"Ay!" he said, and seemed pleased, for an instant later he said "Ay" again.

More or less secure in the Vauxhall I headed north for Stirling and the Highland Line, and after a night by Loch Katrine struck north by Balquhidder, mistook my road to Glencoe and went too far west, and soon found myself beside Loch Awe. I also found myself, with some surprise and mortification, unwilling to perceive any beauty in this region because Loch Awe is in Campbell country, and in the near past of several centuries ago, the Campbell chiefs had been an anathema to the less successful clans they pillaged.

The roads in the Highlands, as those will know who have travelled them, are not only so narrow that in most sections two baby Austins are unable to pass, they are also infested with livestock. Sheep fall asleep on their narrow shoulders and cars must stop again and again while bullocks make up their minds whether or not to move out of the way. The roads were built by some English general, I think his name was Wade, who had the eighteenth-century English notion that if he built roads the communications between the clans would improve. Only lately have General Wade's roads been hard-topped, and never have they been widened except at regular intervals where cars may turn out to allow approaching cars to pass. They are adequately marked if you are familiar with them, but I was not familiar with them and again I lost my way. I went into the pub of a hamlet to ask where I was and discovered behind the bar an elderly gentleman with white hair and the demeanour of a Presbyterian elder, and beside the bar three workmen silently sipping ale.

"What's the name of this place?" I asked the publican.

"The Heather and Bull," he said.

"I meant, what's this community?" 20

"Mostly Protestant," he said, "but in recent years wi' a small smattering of Roman Catholics." He turned to one of the workmen: "John, how many Catholics now?"

"About eighteen per cent. Going on for twenty."

"They're risin' fast," said a third man.

"Ay!" said the publican. And turning to me he asked when I had left Canada.

"How on earth did you guess I'm a Canadian?" 25

"You are not English, that is certain, and you are not American. You still have some of the voice." He put out his hand: "God bless you!"

We talked of Scotland, Canada, and theology and I forgot what I had intended to ask him. An hour later, when I shook his hand and received my directions, his noble face was as solemn as a memory from childhood.

"You will be disappointed," he warned me. "Scotland is full of nothing but Irish now. Och, we have no dignity left."

An Anglo-Saxon or an American might assume a racial situation from this remark, but it was the sort of thing I grew up with, the sort of remark I have made myself, in different connotations, all my life. Its meaning was clear to me if to nobody else. The old gentleman was unburdening himself of a beastie which had nothing whatever to do with the Catholics, the Irish, or with anything, possibly, that he himself could put into words.

The next day I was in the true north of Scotland among the sheep, 30
the heather, the whin, the mists, and the homes of the vanished races. Such sweeps of emptiness I never saw in Canada before I went to the Mackenzie River later in that same summer. But this Highland emptiness, only a few hundred miles above the massed population of England, is a far different thing from the emptiness of our own Northwest Territories. Above the sixtieth parallel in Canada you feel that nobody but God has ever been there before you, but in a deserted Highland glen you feel that everyone who ever mattered is dead and gone. Those glens are the most hauntingly lovely sights I have ever seen: they are vaster, more moving, more truly vacated than the southern abbeys ruined by Henry VIII.[6] They are haunted by the lost loves

6. Born in 1491; king of England from 1509 to his death in 1547.

and passions of a thousand years. Later that summer on the lower reaches of the Mackenzie, after talking to an Athabascan Indian with Celtic eyes and the name of McPherson, I remembered the wild loneliness of Lochaber and it occurred to me that only a man from a country as lonely and ghost-ridden as the Highlands could have had the insane determination to paddle a canoe through the Rocky Mountains and down La Grande Rivière-en-bas to the Beaufort Sea, and that nothing was more in the life-style of the Highlander than Alexander Mackenzie's feat in searching for the Northwest Passage in a canoe. After an achievement of incredible boldness and endurance, what, after all, did this Highlander find but nothing?

Yet, as a by-product, he and others like him surely found much of Canada, even though one of them, solitary on the Qu'Appelle or the Saskatchewan, admitting the grandeur of the woods and prairies of the New World, sang from a broken heart that he was an exile from his native land, and while making possible the existence of a country so vast that Scotland would be lost in it, regretted his inability to wield a claymore[7] in defence of a barren glen presided over by an imbecile chief. The exiled Irish never forgave their landlords, but the exiled Highlanders pined for the scoundrel Pretender, and even regretted the proprietors who preferred sheep to humanity, enclosed their own people and drove them starving across the western ocean with such an uncomprehended yearning in their souls that some of them ended up in log cabins along the Athabasca and on the shores of James Bay.

In the parish of Kintail, whence some of my own people were driven a century and a half ago, I was told there are now barely four hundred inhabitants. In my ancestors' days there were more than twelve thousand.

"Where are they?" the minister said when I asked him. "Where indeed but in Canada? And some in Australia and New Zealand of course, but most of them in Canada."

With them they brought—no doubt of this—that nameless haunting guilt they never understood, and the feeling of failure, and the loneliness of all the warm-hearted, not very intelligent folk so outmoded by the Anglo-Saxon success that they knew they were helpless unless they lived as the Anglo-Saxons did, failures unless they learned to feel (or not to feel at all) as the Anglo-Saxons ordained. Had my father been clairvoyant when he told me I would understand when I went to the Highlands?

I'm not sure that I do understand or ever will understand what he wanted me to know. But one evening, watching a rainbow form over Loch Leven, the mists drop down the hills into rain, then watching the

7. A Scottish two-edged broadsword.

sky rent open and such a tumult of golden light pour forth that the mountains themselves moved and were transfigured, still moved and then were lifted up until they ceased to be mountains and turned themselves into an abstraction of sheer glory and gold—watching this I realized, or thought I did, why these desperate people had endured so long against the civilization of the south. Unlike Ulysses,[8] they had failed to stop their ears when the Sirens sang, and the Sirens that sing in the Highlands, suddenly and when you least expect to hear them, have voices more dangerously beguiling than any in the Aegean Isles. Beauty is nearly the most dangerous thing on earth, and those who love her too much, or look too deeply into her eyes, pay the price for her, which often is an empty stomach and a life of misunderstanding.

So it was here, though an economist would point out that the land is barren and that in the early days the people lacked education and civilized techniques. But this practical attitude merely begs the question of why the people stayed so long: stayed, in fact, until they were driven out. These mountains are almost as useless to the cultivator as the upper reaches of the Laurentian Shield. The Gaelic[9] tongue sounds soft and lovely, but compared with English and French it is a primitive means of communication. The ancestors of almost a quarter of modern Canada never did, and in their native glens they never could, develop even the rudiments of an urban culture. When they made the acquaintance of the English this must have sorely troubled their conscience, for they were religious, they were Christianized after a fashion, and the parable that meant most to them was the Parable of the Talents. Only a few of their chiefs could possibly be called intelligent, and the conduct of the chiefs of their only really successful clan (it shall be nameless here, though every Highlander knows the one I have in mind) was of the crafty peasant sort, the more base because it exploited the loyalty of a people who were already enslaved by their own conception of honour. But though these chiefs did well for themselves, they only became rich and famous after they had conspired with the English enemy. No leader, not even a genius, could have raised in the terrain of the Highlands a civilization capable of competing with England's. Yet the Highlanders held on to the glens; incredibly they held on to them until the end of the eighteenth century. Often I have said to myself that my grandfathers three times removed lived in a culture as primitive as Homer's, and last summer in the Highlands I knew that they really had.

8. A Latin name for Odysseus, the king of Ithaca and hero of Homer's epic *The Odyssey*. Ulysses encounters numerous dangers, including the Sirens, who attempt to ensnare him with their lovely female voices.
9. The Celtic language of the Highlands of Scotland. The term is also used to refer to the general language and culture of both Scotland and Ireland.

Driving south through Glencoe where the Campbells massacred the Macdonalds, I remembered the first time I met Angus L. Macdonald, who then was Premier of Nova Scotia and previously had been Canada's Minister for the Navy. With a suddenness that would have been startling to anyone but another clansman, Mr. Macdonald turned to me in a company of people and from the depths of a mutual empathy he said: "To be a Celt is never to be far from tears."

But we Celts are withal a mercurial people also; our sorrowful moods pass like the mists on the braes and the sunlight strikes through when we least expect it. A week later I was in the most fatally civilized country in the world, Sweden, waiting for a Pan-American Clipper to take me home.

Just as I belong to the last Canadian generation raised with a Highland nostalgia, so also do I belong to the last which regards a transatlantic flight as a miracle. When I was a boy I saw the first tiny plane to fly the ocean, the American seaplane N.C. 4, which took a very long time moving by stages from Halifax to Sydney, to Bonavista Bay, to the Azores, and finally to Lisbon. Eight years later plane after plane set out on non-stop ventures and disappeared into the sea.

40 Now, eating a filet mignon and sipping champagne in the supreme luxury of this Pan-American aircraft, I looked down on the waste of seas which, together with the mountains of British Columbia, had divided the clansmen from their homes over a century ago. Sitting there idle I felt an unwarranted lift of joy and omnipotent power. The plane nuzzled into the stratospheric wind, she rolled as slowly and surely as a shark speeding through the water in which it was born, she went so fast that though she left Stockholm as late as 4:30 in the afternoon it was still bright daylight when she put down in a rainstorm in Keflavik. She took on fuel and set out again, I slept for an hour or two, wakened to a change in the propeller pitch, and learned we were circling Gander, which as usual was buried in fog. After an hour the pilot said over the intercom:

"The weather in Gander has deteriorated to zero-zero. We are now proceeding to New York. We will arrive in Idlewild at 7:40 Eastern Daylight Time. We will arrive on schedule."

Here, of course, was the supreme triumph of the civilization which, in wrecking the clansmen, had made it possible for me to think of Canada as home. The plane tore through the fog, the stewardess brought a delicious breakfast, and just as I was sipping my coffee the sun broke dazzlingly through the window into the cabin. I looked out and there, in a semicircle of sunshine, the only sunshine apparently in the whole northern hemisphere at that particular moment, lay Cape Breton Island. The plane sloped down to eight thousand feet and I saw beside the Bras d'Or lake the tiny speck which was the house where my mother and sister at that very moment lay asleep. We did reach New York on schedule and that same day I ate my lunch in the Medical Arts restaurant on the corner of Sherbrooke Street and Guy. The man next to me at the counter asked where I had been and I told him I had been in the Scottish Highlands.

"It must have been nice," he said.

"It was. But it's also nice to be home."

Am I wrong, or is it true that it is only now, after so many years of 45
not knowing who we were or wanted to be, that we Canadians of Scotch descent are truly at home in the northern half of North America?

Human Nature

William Golding

THINKING AS A HOBBY

While I was still a boy, I came to the conclusion that there were three grades of thinking; and since I was later to claim thinking as my hobby, I came to an even stranger conclusion—namely, that I myself could not think at all.

I must have been an unsatisfactory child for grownups to deal with. I remember how incomprehensible they appeared to me at first, but not, of course, how I appeared to them. It was the headmaster of my grammar school who first brought the subject of thinking before me—though neither in the way, nor with the result he intended. He had some statuettes in his study. They stood on a high cupboard behind his desk. One was a lady wearing nothing but a bath towel. She seemed frozen in an eternal panic lest the bath towel slip down any farther; and since she had no arms, she was in an unfortunate position to pull the towel up again. Next to her, crouched the statuette of a leopard, ready to spring down at the top drawer of a filing cabinet labeled A-AH. My innocence interpreted this as the victim's last, despairing cry. Beyond the leopard was a naked, muscular gentleman, who sat, looking down, with his chin on his fist and his elbow on his knee. He seemed utterly miserable.

Some time later, I learned about these statuettes. The headmaster had placed them where they would face delinquent children, because they symbolized to him the whole of life. The naked lady was the Venus of Milo. She was Love. She was not worried about the towel. She was just busy being beautiful. The leopard was Nature, and he was being natural. The naked, muscular gentleman was not miserable. He was Rodin's Thinker, an image of pure thought. It is easy to buy small plaster models of what you think life is like.

First published in *Holiday Magazine* (Aug. 1961).

I had better explain that I was a frequent visitor to the headmaster's study, because of the latest thing I had done or left undone. As we now say, I was not integrated. I was, if anything, disintegrated; and I was puzzled. Grownups never made sense. Whenever I found myself in a penal position before the headmaster's desk, with the statuettes glimmering whitely above him, I would sink my head, clasp my hands behind my back and writhe one shoe over the other.

The headmaster would look opaquely at me through flashing spectacles. 5

"What are we going to do with you?"

Well, what *were* they going to do with me? I would writhe my shoe some more and stare down at the worn rug.

"Look up, boy! Can't you look up?"

Then I would look up at the cupboard, where the naked lady was frozen in her panic and the muscular gentleman contemplated the hindquarters of the leopard in endless gloom. I had nothing to say to the headmaster. His spectacles caught the light so that you could see nothing human behind them. There was no possibility of communication.

"Don't you ever think at all?" 10

No, I didn't think, wasn't thinking, couldn't think—I was simply waiting in anguish for the interview to stop.

"Then you'd better learn—hadn't you?"

On one occasion the headmaster leaped to his feet, reached up and plonked Rodin's masterpiece on the desk before me.

"That's what a man looks like when he's really thinking."

I surveyed the gentleman without interest or comprehension. 15

"Go back to your class."

Clearly there was something missing in me. Nature had endowed the rest of the human race with a sixth sense and left me out. This must be so, I mused, on my way back to the class, since whether I had broken a window, or failed to remember Boyle's Law, or been late for school, my teachers produced me one, adult answer: "Why can't you think?"

As I saw the case, I had broken the window because I had tried to hit Jack Arney with a cricket ball and missed him; I could not remember Boyle's Law because I had never bothered to learn it; and I was late for school because I preferred looking over the bridge into the river. In fact, I was wicked. Were my teachers, perhaps, so good that they could not understand the depths of my depravity? Were they clear, untormented people who could direct their every action by this mysterious business of thinking? The whole thing was incomprehensible. In my earlier years, I found even the statuette of the Thinker confusing. I did not believe any of my teachers were naked, ever. Like someone born deaf, but bitterly determined to find out about sound, I watched my teachers to find out about thought.

There was Mr. Houghton. He was always telling me to think. With a modest satisfaction, he would tell me that he had thought a bit himself. Then why did he spend so much time drinking? Or was there more sense in drinking than there appeared to be? But if not, and if drinking were in fact ruinous to health—and Mr. Houghton was ruined, there was no doubt about that—why was he always talking about the clean life and the virtues of fresh air? He would spread his arms wide with the action of a man who habitually spent his time striding along mountain ridges.

20 "Open air does me good, boys—I know it!"

Sometimes, exalted by his own oratory, he would leap from his desk and hustle us outside into a hideous wind.

"Now, boys! Deep breaths! Feel it right down inside you—huge draughts of God's good air!"

He would stand before us, rejoicing in his perfect health, an open-air man. He would put his hands on his waist and take a tremendous breath. You could hear the wind, trapped in the cavern of his chest and struggling with all the unnatural impediments. His body would reel with shock and his ruined face go white at the unaccustomed visitation. He would stagger back to his desk and collapse there, useless for the rest of the morning.

Mr. Houghton was given to high-minded monologues about the good life, sexless and full of duty. Yet in the middle of one of these monologues, if a girl passed the window, tapping along on her neat little feet, he would interrupt his discourse, his neck would turn of itself and he would watch her out of sight. In this instance, he seemed to me ruled not by thought but by an invisible and irresistible spring in his nape.

25 His neck was an object of great interest to me. Normally it bulged a bit over his collar. But Mr. Houghton had fought in the First World War alongside both Americans and French, and had come—by who knows what illogic?—to a settled detestation of both countries. If either country happened to be prominent in current affairs, no argument could make Mr. Houghton think well of it. He would bang the desk, his neck would bulge still further and go red. "You can say what you like," he would cry, "but I've thought about this—and I know what I think!"

Mr. Houghton thought with his neck.

There was Miss Parsons. She assured us that her dearest wish was our welfare, but I knew even then, with the mysterious clairvoyance of childhood, that what she wanted most was the husband she never got. There was Mr. Hands—and so on.

I have dealt at length with my teachers because this was my introduction to the nature of what is commonly called thought. Through them I discovered that thought is often full of unconscious prejudice, ignorance and hypocrisy. It will lecture on disinterested purity while its neck is being remorselessly twisted toward a skirt. Technically, it is about as proficient as most businessmen's golf, as honest as most politicians' intentions, or—to come near my own preoccupation—as coherent as most books that get written. It is what I came to call grade-three thinking, though more properly, it is feeling, rather than thought.

True, often there is a kind of innocence in prejudices, but in those days I viewed grade-three thinking with an intolerant contempt and an incautious mockery. I delighted to confront a pious lady who hated the Germans with the proposition that we should love our enemies. She taught me a great truth in dealing with grade-three thinkers; because of her, I no longer dismiss lightly a mental process which for nine-tenths of the population is the nearest they will ever get to thought. They have immense solidarity. We had better respect them, for we are outnumbered and surrounded. A crowd of grade-three thinkers, all shouting the same thing, all warming their hands at the fire of their own prejudices, will not thank you for pointing out the contradictions in their beliefs. Man is a gregarious animal, and enjoys agreement as cows will graze all the same way on the side of a hill.

Grade-two thinking is the detection of contradictions. I reached grade two when I trapped the poor, pious lady. Grade-two thinkers do not stampede easily, though often they fall into the other fault and lap behind. Grade-two thinking is a withdrawal, with eyes and ears open. It became my hobby and brought satisfaction and loneliness in either hand. For grade-two thinking destroys without having the power to create. It set me watching the crowds cheering His Majesty and King and asking myself what all the fuss was about, without giving me anything positive to put in the place of that heady patriotism. But there were compensations. To hear people justify their habit of hunting foxes and tearing them to pieces by claiming that the foxes liked it. To hear our Prime Minister talk about the great benefit we conferred on India by jailing people like Pandit Nehru and Gandhi. To hear American politicians talk about peace in one sentence and refuse to join the League of Nations in the next. Yes, there were moments of delight.

But I was growing toward adolescence and had to admit that Mr. Houghton was not the only one with an irresistible spring in his neck. I, too, felt the compulsive hand of nature and began to find that pointing out contradiction could be costly as well as fun. There was Ruth, for example, a serious and attractive girl. I was an atheist at the time. Grade-two thinking is a menace to religion and knocks down sects like skittles. I put myself in a position to be converted by her with an hypocrisy worthy of grade three. She was a Methodist—or at least, her parents were, and Ruth had to follow suit. But, alas, instead of relying on the Holy Spirit to convert me, Ruth was foolish enough to open her pretty mouth in argument. She claimed that the Bible (King James Version) was literally inspired. I countered by saying that the Catholics believed in the literal inspiration of Saint Jerome's *Vulgate*,[1] and the two books were different. Argument flagged.

At last she remarked that there were an awful lot of Methodists, and they couldn't be wrong, could they—not all those millions? That was too easy, said I restively (for the nearer you were to Ruth, the nicer she was to be near to) since there were more Roman Catholics than Methodists anyway; and they couldn't be wrong, could they—not all those hundreds of millions? An awful flicker of doubt appeared in her eyes. I slid my arm around her waist and murmured breathlessly that if we were counting heads, the Buddhists were the boys for my money. But Ruth had *really* wanted to do me good, because I was so nice. She fled. The combination of my arm and those countless Buddhists was too much for her.

That night her father visited my father and left, red-cheeked and indignant. I was given the third degree to find out what had happened. It was lucky we were both of us only fourteen. I lost Ruth and gained an undeserved reputation as a potential libertine.

So grade-two thinking could be dangerous. It was in this knowledge, at the age of fifteen, that I remember making a comment from the heights of grade two, on the limitations of grade three. One evening I found myself alone in the school hall, preparing it for a party. The door of the headmaster's study was open. I went in. The headmaster had ceased to thump Rodin's Thinker down on the desk as an example to the young. Perhaps he had not found any more candidates, but the statuettes were still there, glimmering and gathering dust on top of the cupboard. I stood on a chair and rearranged them. I stood Venus in her bath towel on the filing cabinet, so that now the top drawer caught its breath in a gasp of sexy excitement. "A-ah!" The portentous Thinker I placed on the edge of the cupboard so that he looked down at the bath towel and waited for it to slip.

Grade-two thinking, though it filled life with fun and excitement, did not make for content. To find out the deficiencies of our elders bolsters the young ego but does not make for personal security. I found that grade two was not only the power to point out contradictions. It took the swimmer some distance from the shore and left him there,

1. The Latin Bible as revised in the fourth century A.D. by Jerome and used thereafter as the authoritative text for Roman Catholic ritual.

out of his depth. I decided that Pontius Pilate was a typical grade-two thinker. "What is truth?" he said, a very common grade-two thought, but one that is used always as the end of an argument instead of the beginning. There is still a higher grade of thought which says, "What is truth?" and sets out to find it.

But these grade-one thinkers were few and far between. They did not visit my grammar school in the flesh though they were there in books. I aspired to them, partly because I was ambitious and partly because I now saw my hobby as an unsatisfactory thing if it went no further. If you set out to climb a mountain, however high you climb, you have failed if you cannot reach the top.

I *did* meet an undeniably grade-one thinker in my first year at Oxford. I was looking over a small bridge in Magdalen Deer Park, and a tiny mustached and hatted figure came and stood by my side. He was a German who had just fled from the Nazis to Oxford as a temporary refuge. His name was Einstein.

But Professor Einstein knew no English at that time and I knew only two words of German. I beamed at him, trying wordlessly to convey by my bearing all the affection and respect that the English felt for him. It is possible—and I have to make the admission—that I felt here were two grade-one thinkers standing side by side; yet I doubt if my face conveyed more than a formless awe. I would have given my Greek and Latin and French and a good slice of my English for enough German to communicate. But we were divided; he was as inscrutable as my headmaster. For perhaps five minutes we stood together on the bridge, undeniable grade-one thinker and breathless aspirant. With true greatness, Professor Einstein realized that my contact was better than none. He pointed to a trout wavering in midstream.

He spoke: "*Fisch.*"

40 My brain reeled. Here I was, mingling with the great, and yet helpless as the veriest grade-three thinker. Desperately I sought for some sign by which I might convey that I, too, revered pure reason. I nodded vehemently. In a brilliant flash I used up half of my German vocabulary.

"*Fisch. Ja Ja.*"

For perhaps another five minutes we stood side by side. Then Professor Einstein, his whole figure still conveying good will and amiability, drifted away out of sight.

I, too, would be a grade-one thinker. I was irreverent at the best of times. Political and religious systems, social customs, loyalties and traditions, they all came tumbling down like so many rotten apples off a tree. This was a fine hobby and a sensible substitute for cricket, since you could play it all the year round. I came up in the end with what must always remain the justification for grade-one thinking, its sign, seal and charter. I devised a coherent system for living. It was a moral system, which was wholly logical. Of course, as I readily admitted, conversion of the world to my way of thinking might be difficult, since my system did away with a number of trifles, such as big business, centralized government, armies, marriage. . . .

It was Ruth all over again. I had some very good friends who stood by me, and still do. But my acquaintances vanished, taking the girls with them. Young women seemed oddly contented with the world as it was. They valued the meaningless ceremony with a ring. Young men, while willing to concede the chaining sordidness of marriage, were hesitant about abandoning the organizations which they hoped would give them a career. A young man on the first rung of the Royal Navy, while perfectly agreeable to doing away with big business and marriage, got as rednecked as Mr. Houghton when I proposed a world without any battleships in it.

45 Had the game gone too far? Was it a game any longer? In those prewar days, I stood to lose a great deal, for the sake of a hobby.

Now you are expecting me to describe how I saw the folly of my ways and came back to the warm nest, where prejudices are so often called loyalties, where pointless actions are hallowed into custom by repetition, where we are content to say we think when all we do is feel.

But you would be wrong. I dropped my hobby and turned professional.

If I were to go back to the headmaster's study and find the dusty statuettes still there, I would arrange them differently. I would dust Venus and put her aside, for I have come to love her and know her for the fair thing she is. But I would put the Thinker, sunk in his desperate thought, where there were shadows before him—and at his back, I would put the leopard, crouched and ready to spring.

Isaac Asimov

THE EUREKA PHENOMENON

In the old days, when I was writing a great deal of fiction, there would come, once in a while, moments when I was stymied. Suddenly, I would find I had written myself into a hole and could see no way out. To take care of that, I developed a technique which invariably worked.

It was simply this—I went to the movies. Not just any movie. I had to pick a movie which was loaded with action but which made no demands on the intellect. As I watched, I did my best to avoid any con-

From *The Left Hand of the Electron* (1972).

scious thinking concerning my problem, and when I came out of the movie I knew exactly what I would have to do to put the story back on the track.

It never failed.

In fact, when I was working on my doctoral dissertation, too many years ago, I suddenly came across a flaw in my logic that I had not noticed before and that knocked out everything I had done. In utter panic, I made my way to a Bob Hope movie—and came out with the necessary change in point of view.

It is my belief, you see, that thinking is a double phenomenon like 5
breathing.

You can control breathing by deliberate voluntary action: you can breathe deeply and quickly, or you can hold your breath altogether, regardless of the body's needs at the time. This, however, doesn't work well for very long. Your chest muscles grow tired, your body clamors for more oxygen, or less, and you relax. The automatic involuntary control of breathing takes over, adjusts it to the body's needs and unless you have some respiratory disorder, you can forget about the whole thing.

Well, you can think by deliberate voluntary action, too, and I don't think it is much more efficient on the whole than voluntary breath control is. You can deliberately force your mind through channels of deductions and associations in search of a solution to some problem and before long you have dug mental furrows for yourself and find yourself circling round and round the same limited pathways. If those pathways yield no solution, no amount of further conscious thought will help.

On the other hand, if you let go, then the thinking process comes under automatic involuntary control and is more apt to take new pathways and make erratic associations you would not think of consciously. The solution will then come while you *think* you are *not* thinking.

The trouble is, though, that conscious thought involves no muscular action and so there is no sensation of physical weariness that would force you to quit. What's more, the panic of necessity tends to force you to go on uselessly, with each added bit of useless effort adding to the panic in a vicious cycle.

It is my feeling that it helps to relax, deliberately, by subjecting your 10
mind to material complicated enough to occupy the voluntary faculty of thought, but superficial enough not to engage the deeper involuntary one. In my case, it is an action movie; in your case, it might be something else.

I suspect it is the involuntary faculty of thought that gives rise to what we call "a flash of intuition," something that I imagine must be merely the result of unnoticed thinking.

Perhaps the most famous flash of intuition in the history of science took place in the city of Syracuse in third-century B.C. Sicily. Bear with me and I will tell you the story—

About 250 B.C., the city of Syracuse was experiencing a kind of Golden Age. It was under the protection of the rising power of Rome, but it retained a king of its own and considerable self-government; it was prosperous; and it had a flourishing intellectual life.

The king was Hieron II, and he had commissioned a new golden crown from a goldsmith, to whom he had given an ingot of gold as raw material. Hieron, being a practical man, had carefully weighed the ingot and then weighed the crown he received back. The two weights were precisely equal. Good deal!

15 But then he sat and thought for a while. Suppose the goldsmith had subtracted a little bit of the gold, not too much, and had substituted an equal weight of the considerably less valuable copper. The resulting alloy would still have the appearance of pure gold, but the goldsmith would be plus a quantity of gold over and above his fee. He would be buying gold with copper, so to speak, and Hieron would be neatly cheated.

Hieron didn't like the thought of being cheated any more than you or I would, but he didn't know how to find out for sure if he had been. He could scarcely punish the goldsmith on mere suspicion. What to do?

Fortunately, Hieron had an advantage few rulers in the history of the world could boast. He had a relative of considerable talent. The relative was named Archimedes and he probably had the greatest intellect the world was to see prior to the birth of Newton.

Archimedes was called in and was posed the problem. He had to determine whether the crown Hieron showed him was pure gold, or was gold to which a small but significant quantity of copper had been added.

If we were to reconstruct Archimedes' reasoning, it might go as follows. Gold was the densest known substance (at that time). Its density in modern terms is 19.3 grams per cubic centimeter. This means that a given weight of gold takes up less volume than the same weight of anything else! In fact, a given weight of pure gold takes up less volume than the same weight of *any* kind of impure gold.

20 The density of copper is 8.92 grams per cubic centimeter, just about half that of gold. If we consider 100 grams of pure gold, for instance, it is easy to calculate it to have a volume of 5.18 cubic centimeters. But suppose that 100 grams of what looked like pure gold was really only 90 grams of gold and 10 grams of copper. The 90 grams of gold would have a volume of 4.66 cubic centimeters, while the 10 grams of copper would have a volume of 1.12 cubic centimeters; for a total value of 5.78 cubic centimeters.

The difference between 5.18 cubic centimeters and 5.78 cubic centimeters is quite a noticeable one, and would instantly tell if the crown were of pure gold, or if it contained 10 per cent copper (with the missing 10 per cent of gold tucked neatly in the goldsmith's strongbox).

All one had to do, then, was measure the volume of the crown and compare it with the volume of the same weight of pure gold.

The mathematics of the time made it easy to measure the volume of many simple shapes: a cube, a sphere, a cone, a cylinder, any flattened object of simple regular shape and known thickness, and so on.

We can imagine Archimedes saying, "All that is necessary, sire, is to pound that crown flat, shape it into a square of uniform thickness, and then I can have the answer for you in a moment."

Whereupon Hieron must certainly have snatched the crown away 25
and said, "No such thing. I can do that much without you; I've studied the principles of mathematics, too. This crown is a highly satisfactory work of art and I won't have it damaged. Just calculate its volume without in any way altering it."

But Greek mathematics had no way of determining the volume of anything with a shape as irregular as the crown, since integral calculus had not yet been invented (and wouldn't be for two thousand years, almost). Archimedes would have had to say, "There is no known way, sire, to carry through a non-destructive determination of volume."

"Then think of one," said Hieron testily.

And Archimedes must have set about thinking of one, and gotten nowhere. Nobody knows how long he thought, or how hard, or what hypotheses he considered and discarded, or any of the details.

What we do know is that, worn out with thinking, Archimedes decided to visit the public baths and relax. I think we are quite safe in saying that Archimedes had no intention of taking his problem to the baths with him. It would be ridiculous to imagine he would, for the public baths of a Greek metropolis weren't intended for that sort of thing.

The Greek baths were a place for relaxation. Half the social aristoc- 30
racy of the town would be there and there was a great deal more to do than wash. One steamed one's self, got a massage, exercised, and engaged in general socializing. We can be sure that Archimedes intended to forget the stupid crown for a while.

One can envisage him engaging in light talk, discussing the latest news from Alexandria and Carthage, the latest scandals in town, the latest funny jokes at the expense of the country-squire Romans—and then he lowered himself into a nice hot bath which some bumbling attendant had filled too full.

The water in the bath slopped over as Archimedes got in. Did Archimedes notice that at once, or did he sigh, sink back, and paddle his feet awhile before noting the water-slop. I guess the latter. But, whether soon or late, he noticed, and that one fact, added to all the chains of reasoning his brain had been working on during the period of relaxation when it was unhampered by the comparative stupidities (even in Archimedes) of voluntary thought, gave Archimedes his answer in one blinding flash of insight.

Jumping out of the bath, he proceeded to run home at top speed through the streets of Syracuse. He did *not* bother to put on his clothes. The thought of Archimedes running naked through Syracuse has titillated dozens of generations of youngsters who have heard this story, but I must explain that the ancient Greeks were quite lighthearted in their attitude toward nudity. They thought no more of seeing a naked man on the streets of Syracuse, than we would on the Broadway stage.

And as he ran, Archimedes shouted over and over, "I've got it! I've got it!" Of course, knowing no English, he was compelled to shout it in Greek, so it came out, "*Eureka! Eureka!*"

35 Archimedes' solution was so simple that anyone could understand it—once Archimedes explained it.

If an object that is not affected by water in any way, is immersed in water, it is bound to displace an amount of water equal to its own volume, since two objects cannot occupy the same space at the same time.

Suppose, then, you had a vessel large enough to hold the crown and suppose it had a small overflow spout set into the middle of its side. And suppose further that the vessel was filled with water exactly to the spout, so that if the water level were raised a bit higher, however slightly, some would overflow.

Next, suppose that you carefully lower the crown into the water. The water level would rise by an amount equal to the volume of the crown, and that volume of water would pour out the overflow and be caught in a small vessel. Next, a lump of gold, known to be pure and exactly equal in weight to the crown, is also immersed in the water and again the level rises and the overflow is caught in a second vessel.

If the crown were pure gold, the overflow would be exactly the same in each case, and the volume of water caught in the two small vessels would be equal. If, however, the crown were of alloy, it would produce a larger overflow than the pure gold would and this would be easily noticeable.

40 What's more, the crown would in no way be harmed, defaced, or even as much as scratched. More important, Archimedes had discovered the "principle of buoyancy."

And was the crown pure gold? I've heard that it turned out to be alloy and that the goldsmith was executed, but I wouldn't swear to it.

How often does this "Eureka phenomenon" happen? How often is there this flash of deep insight during a moment of relaxation, this triumphant cry of "I've got it! I've got it!" which must surely be a moment of the purest ecstasy this sorry world can afford?

I wish there were some way we could tell. I suspect that in the history of science it happens *often;* I suspect that very few significant discoveries are made by the pure technique of voluntary thought; I suspect that voluntary thought may possibly prepare the ground (if even that), but that the final touch, the real inspiration, comes when thinking is under involuntary control.

But the world is in a conspiracy to hide the fact. Scientists are wedded to reason, to the meticulous working out of consequences from assumptions to the careful organization of experiments designed to check those consequences. If a certain line of experiments ends nowhere, it is omitted from the final report. If an inspired guess turns out to be correct, it is *not* reported as an inspired guess. Instead, a solid line of voluntary thought is invented after the fact to lead up to the thought, and that is what is inserted in the final report.

The result is that anyone reading scientific papers would swear that 45
nothing took place but voluntary thought maintaining a steady clumping stride from origin to destination, and that just can't be true.

It's such a shame. Not only does it deprive science of much of its glamour (how much of the dramatic story in Watson's *Double Helix* do you suppose got into the final reports announcing the great discovery of the structure of DNA?[1]), but it hands over the important process of "insight," "inspiration," "revelation" to the mystic.

The scientist actually becomes ashamed of having what we might call a revelation, as though to have one is to betray reason—when actually what we call revelation in a man who has devoted his life to reasoned thought, is after all merely reasoned thought that is not under voluntary control.

Only once in a while in modern times do we ever get a glimpse into the workings of involuntary reasoning, and when we do, it is always fascinating. Consider, for instance, the case of Friedrich August Kekule von Stradonitz.

In Kekule's time, a century and a quarter ago, a subject of great interest to chemists was the structure of organic molecules (those associated with living tissue). Inorganic molecules were generally simple in the sense that they were made up of few atoms. Water molecules, for instance, are made up of two atoms of hydrogen and one of oxygen

1. I'll tell you, in case you're curious. None! [Asimov's note]. How Francis Crick and James Watson discovered the molecular structure of this vital substance is told in Watson's autobiographical book, *The Double Helix.*

(H_2O). Molecules of ordinary salt are made up of one atom of sodium and one of chlorine (NaCl), and so on.

Organic molecules, on the other hand, often contained a large number of atoms. Ethyl alcohol molecules have two carbon atoms, six hydrogen atoms, and an oxygen atom (C_2H_6O); the molecule of ordinary cane sugar is $C_{12}H_{22}O_{11}$, and other molecules are even more complex.

Then, too, it is sufficient, in the case of inorganic molecules generally, merely to know the kinds and numbers of atoms in the molecule; in organic molecules, more is necessary. Thus, dimethyl ether has the formula C_2H_6O, just as ethyl alcohol does, and yet the two are quite different in properties. Apparently, the atoms are arranged differently within the molecules—but how to determine the arrangements?

In 1852, an English chemist, Edward Frankland, had noticed that the atoms of a particular element tended to combine with a fixed number of other atoms. This combining number was called "valence." Kekule in 1858 reduced this notion to a system. The carbon atom, he decided (on the basis of plenty of chemical evidence) had a valence of four; the hydrogen atom, a valence of one; and the oxygen atom, a valence of two (and so on).

Why not represent the atoms as their symbols plus a number of attached dashes, that number being equal to the valence. Such atoms could then be put together as though they were so many Tinker Toy units and "structural formulas" could be built up.

It was possible to reason out that the structural formula of ethyl alcohol was

```
    H H
    | |
  H—C—C—O—H,
    | |
    H H
```

while that of dimethyl ether was

```
    H   H
    |   |
  H—C—O—C—H.
    |   |
    H   H
```

In each case, there were two carbon atoms, each with four dashes 55
attached; six hydrogen atoms, each with one dash attached; and an oxygen atom with two dashes attached. The molecules were built up of the same components, but in different arrangements.

Kekule's theory worked beautifully. It has been immensely deepened and elaborated since his day, but you can still find structures very much like Kekule's Tinker Toy formulas in any modern chemical textbook. They represent oversimplifications of the true situation, but they remain extremely useful in practice even so.

The Kekule structures were applied to many organic molecules in the years after 1858 and the similarities and contrasts in the structures neatly matched similarities and contrasts in properties. The key to the rationalization of organic chemistry had, it seemed, been found.

Yet there was one disturbing fact. The well-known chemical benzene wouldn't fit. It was known to have a molecule made up of equal numbers of carbon and hydrogen atoms. Its molecular weight was known to be 78 and a single carbon-hydrogen combination had a weight of 13. Therefore, the benzene molecule had to contain six carbon-hydrogen combinations and its formula had to be C_6H_6.

But that meant trouble. By the Kekule formulas, the hydrocarbons (molecules made up of carbon and hydrogen atoms only) could easily be envisioned as chains of carbon atoms with hydrogen atoms attached. If all the valences of the carbon atoms were filled with hydrogen atoms, as in "hexane," whose molecule looks like this—

```
  H H H H H H
  | | | | | |
H—C—C—C—C—C—C—H
  | | | | | |
  H H H H H H
```

the compound is said to be saturated. Such saturated hydrocarbons were found to have very little tendency to react with other substances.

If some of the valences were not filled, unused bonds were added to 60
those connecting the carbon atoms. Double bonds were formed as in "hexene"—

```
  H H H H H H
  | | | | | |
H—C—C—C=C—C—C—H
  | |     | |
  H H     H H
```

Hexene is unsaturated, for that double bond has a tendency to open up and add other atoms. Hexene is chemically active.

When six carbons are present in a molecule, it takes fourteen hydrogen atoms to occupy all the valence bonds and make it inert—as in hexane. In hexene, on the other hand, there are only twelve hydrogens. If there were still fewer hydrogen atoms, there would be more than one double bond; there might even be triple bonds, and the compound would be still more active than hexene.

Yet benzene, which is C_6H_6 and has eight fewer hydrogen atoms than hexane, is *less* active than hexene, which has only two fewer hydrogen atoms than hexane. In fact, benzene is even less active than hexane itself. The six hydrogen atoms in the benzene molecule seem to satisfy the six carbon atoms to a greater extent than do the fourteen hydrogen atoms in hexane.

For heaven's sake, why?

This might seem unimportant. The Kekule formulas were so beautifully suitable in the case of so many compounds that one might simply dismiss benzene as an exception to the general rule.

65 Science, however, is not English grammar. You can't just categorize something as an exception. If the exception doesn't fit into the general system, then the general system must be wrong.

Or, take the more positive approach. An exception can often be made to fit into a general system, provided the general system is broadened. Such broadening generally represents a great advance and for this reason, exceptions ought to be paid great attention.

For some seven years, Kekule faced the problem of benzene and tried to puzzle out how a chain of six carbon atoms could be completely satisfied with as few as six hydrogen atoms in benzene and yet be left unsatisfied with twelve hydrogen atoms in hexene.

Nothing came to him!

And then one day in 1865 (he tells the story himself) he was in Ghent, Belgium, and in order to get to some destination, he boarded a public bus. He was tired and, undoubtedly, the droning beat of the horses' hooves on the cobblestones, lulled him. He fell into a comatose half-sleep.

70 In that sleep, he seemed to see a vision of atoms attaching themselves to each other in chains that moved about. (Why not? It was the sort of thing that constantly occupied his waking thoughts.) But then one chain twisted in such a way that head and tail joined, forming a ring—and Kekule woke with a start.

To himself, he must surely have shouted "Eureka," for indeed he had it. The six carbon atoms of benzene formed a ring and not a chain, so that the structural formula looked like this:

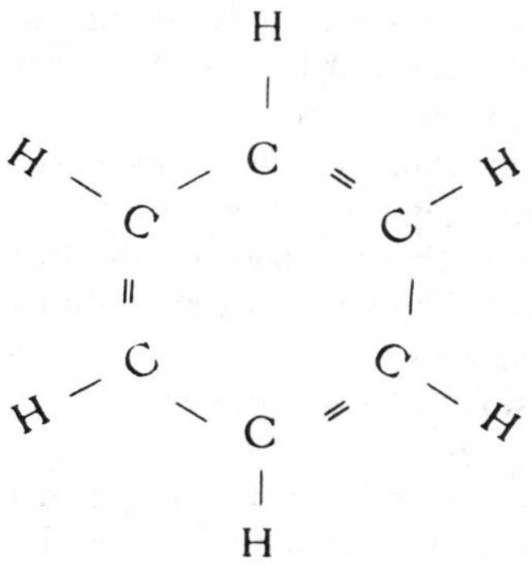

```
              H
              |
   H      /   C   =      H
     \             \   /
       C             C
       ||            |
       C             C
     /             \   \
   H      \   C   =      H
              |
              H
```

To be sure, there were still three double bonds, so you might think the molecule had to be very active—but now there was a difference. Atoms in a ring might be expected to have different properties from those in a chain and double bonds in one case might not have the properties of those in the other. At least, chemists could work on that assumption and see if it involved them in contradictions.

It didn't. The assumption worked excellently well. It turned out that organic molecules could be divided into two groups: aromatic and aliphatic. The former had the benzene ring (or certain other similar rings) as part of the structure and the latter did not. Allowing for different properties within each group, the Kekule structures worked very well.

For nearly seventy years, Kekule's vision held good in the hard field of actual chemical techniques, guiding the chemist through the jungle of reactions that led to the synthesis of more and more molecules. Then, in 1932, Linus Pauling applied quantum mechanics to chemical structure with sufficient subtlety to explain just why the benzene ring was so special and what had proven correct in practice proved correct in theory as well.

Other cases? Certainly. 75

In 1764, the Scottish engineer James Watt was working as an instrument maker for the University of Glasgow. The university gave him a model of a Newcomen steam engine, which didn't work well, and asked him to fix it. Watt fixed it without trouble, but even when it worked perfectly, it didn't work well. It was far too inefficient and consumed incredible quantities of fuel. Was there a way to improve that?

Thought didn't help; but a peaceful, relaxed walk on a Sunday afternoon did. Watt returned with the key notion in mind of using two separate chambers, one for steam only and one for cold water only, so that the same chamber did not have to be constantly cooled and reheated to the infinite waste of fuel.

The Irish mathematician William Rowan Hamilton worked up a theory of "quaternions" in 1843 but couldn't complete that theory until he grasped the fact that there were conditions under which $p \times q$ was *not* equal to $q \times p$. The necessary thought came to him in a flash one time when he was walking to town with his wife.

The German physiologist Otto Loewi was working on the mechanism of nerve action, in particular, on the chemicals produced by nerve endings. He awoke at 3 A.M. one night in 1921 with a perfectly clear notion of the type of experiment he would have to run to settle a key point that was puzzling him. He wrote it down and went back to sleep. When he woke in the morning, he found he couldn't remember what his inspiration had been. He remembered he had written it down, but he couldn't read his writing.

80 The next night, he woke again at 3 A.M. with the clear thought once more in mind. This time, he didn't fool around. He got up, dressed himself, went straight to the laboratory and began work. By 5 A.M. he had proved his point and the consequences of his findings became important enough in later years so that in 1936 he received a share in the Nobel prize in medicine and physiology.

How very often this sort of thing must happen, and what a shame that scientists are so devoted to their belief in conscious thought that they so consistently obscure the actual methods by which they obtain their results.

QUESTIONS

1. *Consider Asimov's narrative presentation of Archimedes' and Kekule's discoveries. What elements does he heighten and how? How does he include the scientific information necessary to understand them? How does he make (or attempt to make) this information accessible to nonscientists?*
2. *Scientists, Asimov concludes, "are so devoted to their belief in conscious thought that they . . . consistently obscure the actual methods by which they obtain their results" (paragraph 81). Consider your own experience in science courses and the way you have been taught to report it. Do you agree or disagree with Asimov? Why?*
3. *Have you ever had a "Eureka" experience? Does Asimov's account of the "Eureka phenomenon" help you to understand it? Write about your experience with reference to Asimov's essay.*

Jacob Bronowski

THE REACH OF IMAGINATION

For three thousand years, poets have been enchanted and moved and perplexed by the power of their own imagination. In a short and summary essay I can hope at most to lift one small corner of that mystery; and yet it is a critical corner. I shall ask, What goes on in the mind when we imagine? You will hear from me that one answer to this question is fairly specific: which is to say, that we can describe the working of the imagination. And when we describe it as I shall do, it becomes plain that imagination is a specifically *human* gift. To imagine is the characteristic act, not of the poet's mind, or the painter's, or the scientist's, but of the mind of man.

My stress here on the word *human* implies that there is a clear difference in this between the actions of men and those of other animals. Let me then start with a classical experiment with animals and children which Walter Hunter thought out in Chicago about 1910. That was the time when scientists were agog with the success of Ivan Pavlov in forming and changing the reflex actions of dogs, which Pavlov had first announced in 1903. Pavlov had been given a Nobel prize the next year, in 1904, although in fairness I should say that the award did not cite his work on the conditioned reflex, but on the digestive gland.

Hunter duly trained some dogs and other animals on Pavlov's lines. They were taught that when a light came on over one of three tunnels out of their cage, that tunnel would be open; they could escape down it, and were rewarded with food if they did. But once he had fixed that conditioned reflex, Hunter added to it a deeper idea: he gave the mechanical experiment a new dimension, literally—the dimension of time. Now he no longer let the dog go to the lighted tunnel at once; instead, he put out the light, and then kept the dog waiting a little while before he let him go. In this way Hunter timed how long an animal can remember where he has last seen the signal light to his escape route.

The results were and are staggering. A dog or a rat forgets which one of three tunnels has been lit up within a matter of seconds—in Hunter's experiment, ten seconds at most. If you want such an animal to do much better than this, you must make the task much simpler: you must face him with only two tunnels to choose from. Even so, the

From *Proceedings of the American Academy of Arts and Letters and National Institute of Arts and Letters* (2nd ser., No. 17, 1967).

best that Hunter could do was to have a dog remember for five minutes which one of two tunnels had been lit up.

I am not quoting these times as if they were exact and universal: they surely are not. Hunter's experiment, more than fifty years old now, had many faults of detail. For example, there were too few animals, they were oddly picked, and they did not all behave consistently. It may be unfair to test a dog for what he *saw*, when he commonly follows his nose rather than his eyes. It may be unfair to test any animal in the unnatural setting of a laboratory cage. And there are higher animals, such as chimpanzees and other primates, which certainly have longer memories than the animals that Hunter tried.

Yet when all these provisos have been made (and met, by more modern experiments) the facts are still startling and characteristic. An animal cannot recall a signal from the past for even a short fraction of the time that a man can—for even a short fraction of the time that a child can. Hunter made comparable tests with six-year-old children, and found, of course, that they were incomparably better than the best of his animals. There is a striking and basic difference between a man's ability to imagine something that he saw or experienced, and an animal's failure.

Animals make up for this by other and extraordinary gifts. The salmon and the carrier pigeon can find their way home as we cannot: they have, as it were, a practical memory that man cannot match. But their actions always depend on some form of habit: on instinct or on learning, which reproduce by rote a train of known responses. They do not depend, as human memory does, on calling to mind the recollection of absent things.

Where is it that the animal falls short? We get a clue to the answer, I think, when Hunter tells us how the animals in his experiment tried to fix their recollection. They most often pointed themselves at the light before it went out, as some gun dogs point rigidly at the game they scent—and get the name *pointer* from the posture. The animal makes ready to act by building the signal into its action. There is a primitive imagery in its stance, it seems to me; it is as if the animal were trying to fix the light on its mind by fixing it in its body. And indeed, how else can a dog mark and (as it were) name one of three tunnels, when he has no such words as *left* and *right*, and no such numbers as *one, two, three?* The directed gesture of attention and readiness is perhaps the only symbolic device that the dog commands to hold on to the past, and thereby to guide himself into the future.

I used the verb *to imagine* a moment ago, and now I have some ground for giving it a meaning. *To imagine* means to make images and to move them about inside one's head in new arrangements. When you and I recall the past, we imagine it in this direct and homely sense.

The tool that puts the human mind ahead of the animal is imagery. For us, memory does not demand the preoccupation that it demands in animals, and it lasts immensely longer, because we fix it in images or other substitute symbols. With the same symbolic vocabulary we spell out the future—not one but many futures, which we weigh one against another.

I am using the word *image* in a wide meaning, which does not re- 10
strict it to the mind's eye as a visual organ. An image in my usage is what Charles Peirce[1] called a *sign,* without regard for its sensory quality. Peirce distinguished between different forms of signs, but there is no reason to make his distinction here, for the imagination works equally with them all, and that is why I call them all images.

Indeed, the most important images for human beings are simply words, which are abstract symbols. Animals do not have words, in our sense: there is no specific center for language in the brain of any animal, as there is in the human being. In this respect at least we know that the human imagination depends on a configuration in the brain that has only evolved in the last one or two million years. In the same period, evolution has greatly enlarged the front lobes in the human brain, which govern the sense of the past and the future; and it is a fair guess that they are probably the seat of our other images. (Part of the evidence for this guess is that damage to the front lobes in primates reduces them to the state of Hunter's animals.) If the guess turns out to be right, we shall know why man has come to look like a highbrow or an egghead: because otherwise there would not be room in his head for his imagination.

The images play out for us events which are not present to our senses, and thereby guard the past and create the future—a future that does not yet exist, and may never come to exist in that form. By contrast, the lack of symbolic ideas, or their rudimentary poverty, cuts off an animal from the past and the future alike, and imprisons him in the present. Of all the distinctions between man and animal, the characteristic gift which makes us human is the power to work with symbolic images: the gift of imagination.

This is really a remarkable finding. When Philip Sidney[2] in 1580 defended poets (and all unconventional thinkers) from the Puritan charge that they were liars, he said that a maker must imagine things that are not. Halfway between Sidney and us, William Blake said, "What is now proved was once only imagined." About the same time, in 1796, Samuel Taylor Coleridge for the first time distinguished be-

1. American philosopher, physicist, and mathematician (1839–1914).
2. Sidney (1554–1586), Blake (1757–1827), Coleridge (1772–1834), Keats (1795–1821)—all English poets.

tween the passive fancy and the active imagination, "the living Power and prime Agent of all human Perception." Now we see that they were right, and precisely right: the human gift is the gift of imagination—and that is not just a literary phrase.

Nor is it just a literary gift; it is, I repeat, characteristically human. Almost everything that we do that is worth doing is done in the first place in the mind's eye. The richness of human life is that we have many lives; we live the events that do not happen (and some that cannot) as vividly as those that do; and if thereby we die a thousand deaths, that is the price we pay for living a thousand lives. (A cat, of course, has only nine.) Literature is alive to us because we live its images, but so is any play of the mind—so is chess: the lines of play that we foresee and try in our heads and dismiss are as much a part of the game as the moves that we make. John Keats said that the unheard melodies are sweeter, and all chess players sadly recall that the combinations that they planned and which never came to be played were the best.

15 I make this point to remind you, insistently, that imagination is the manipulation of images in one's head; and that the rational manipulation belongs to that, as well as the literary and artistic manipulation. When a child begins to play games with things that stand for other things, with chairs or chessmen, he enters the gateway to reason and imagination together. For the human reason discovers new relations between things not by deduction, but by that unpredictable blend of speculation and insight that scientists call induction, which—like other forms of imagination—cannot be formalized. We see it at work when Walter Hunter inquires into a child's memory, as much as when Blake and Coleridge do. Only a restless and original mind would have asked Hunter's questions and could have conceived his experiments, in a science that was dominated by Pavlov's reflex arcs and was heading toward the behaviorism of John Watson.[3]

Let me find a spectacular example for you from history. What is the most famous experiment that you had described to you as a child? I will hazard that it is the experiment that Galileo is said to have made in Sidney's age, in Pisa about 1590, by dropping two unequal balls from the Leaning Tower. There, we say, is a man in the modern mold, a man after our own hearts: he insisted on questioning the authority of Aristotle and St. Thomas Aquinas, and seeing with his own eyes whether (as they said) the heavy ball would reach the ground before the light one. Seeing is believing.

Yet seeing is also imagining. Galileo did challenge the authority of Aristotle, and he did look at his mechanics. But the eye that Galileo

3. Watson, a forerunner of B. F. Skinner, argued that all human behavior consists of conditioned reflexes in response to environmental stimuli.

used was the mind's eye. He did not drop balls from the Leaning Tower of Pisa—and if he had, he would have got a very doubtful answer. Instead, Galileo made an imaginary experiment in his head, which I will describe as he did years later in the book he wrote after the Holy Office silenced him: the *Discorsi . . . intorno a due nuove scienze,*[4] which was smuggled out to be printed in the Netherlands in 1638.

Suppose, said Galileo, that you drop two unequal balls from the tower at the same time. And suppose that Aristotle is right—suppose that the heavy ball falls faster, so that it steadily gains on the light ball, and hits the ground first. Very well. Now imagine the same experiment done again, with only one difference: this time the two unequal balls are joined by a string between them. The heavy ball will again move ahead, but now the light ball holds it back and acts as a drag or brake. So the light ball will be speeded up and the heavy ball will be slowed down; they must reach the ground together because they are tied together, but they cannot reach the ground as quickly as the heavy ball alone. Yet the string between them has turned the two balls into a single mass which is heavier than either ball—and surely (according to Aristotle) this mass should therefore move faster than either ball? Galileo's imaginary experiment has uncovered a contradiction; he says trenchantly, "You see how, from your assumption that a heavier body falls more rapidly than a lighter one, I infer that a (still) heavier body falls more slowly." There is only one way out of the contradiction: the heavy ball and the light ball must fall at the same rate, so that they go on falling at the same rate when they are tied together.

This argument is not conclusive, for nature might be more subtle (when the two balls are joined) than Galileo has allowed. And yet it is something more important: it is suggestive, it is stimulating, it opens a new view—in a word, it is imaginative. It cannot be settled without an actual experiment, because nothing that we imagine can become knowledge until we have translated it into, and backed it by, real experience. The test of imagination is experience. But then, that is as true of literature and the arts as it is of science. In science, the imaginary experiment is tested by confronting it with physical experience; and in literature, the imaginative conception is tested by confronting it with human experience. The superficial speculation in science is dismissed because it is found to falsify nature; and the shallow work of art is discarded because it is found to be untrue to our own nature. So when Ella Wheeler Wilcox[5] died in 1919, more people were reading her verses than Shakespeare's; yet in a few years her work was dead. It had

4. *Treatise . . . on Two New Sciences.* In 1630, after publishing his heretical theory that the earth moves around the sun, Galileo was forced by the Inquisition to recant it under threat of torture.

5. American poet (1850–1919).

been buried by its poverty of emotion and its trivialness of thought: which is to say that it had been proved to be as false to the nature of man as, say, Jean Baptiste Lamarck and Trofim Lysenko[6] were false to the nature of inheritance. The strength of the imagination, its enriching power and excitement, lies in its interplay with reality—physical and emotional.

I doubt if there is much to choose here between science and the arts: the imagination is not much more free, and not much less free, in one than in the other. All great scientists have used their imagination freely, and let it ride them to outrageous conclusions without crying "Halt!" Albert Einstein fiddled with imaginary experiments from boyhood, and was wonderfully ignorant of the facts that they were supposed to bear on. When he wrote the first of his beautiful papers on the random movement of atoms, he did not know that the Brownian motion which it predicted could be seen in any laboratory. He was sixteen when he invented the paradox that he resolved ten years later, in 1905, in the theory of relativity, and it bulked much larger in his mind than the experiment of Albert Michelson and Edward Morley[7] which had upset every other physicist since 1881. All his life Einstein loved to make up teasing puzzles like Galileo's, about falling lifts and the detection of gravity; and they carry the nub of the problems of general relativity on which he was working.

Indeed, it could not be otherwise. The power that man has over nature and himself, and that a dog lacks, lies in his command of imaginary experience. He alone has the symbols which fix the past and play with the future, possible and impossible. In the Renaissance, the symbolism of memory was thought to be mystical, and devices that were invented as mnemonics (by Giordano Bruno, for example, and by Robert Fludd)[8] were interpreted as magic signs. The symbol is the tool which gives man his power, and it is the same tool whether the symbols are images or words, mathematical signs or mesons. And the symbols have a reach and a roundness that goes beyond their literal and practical meaning. They are the rich concepts under which the

6. Lysenko (1898–1976), Russian biologist who has held that hereditary properties of organisms could be changed by manipulating the environment. Lamarck (1744–1829), French biologist who held that characteristics acquired by experience were biologically transmittable.
7. Physicists had believed space to be filled with an ether which made possible the propagation of light and magnetism; the Michelson-Morley experiment proved this untrue. Einstein, an outsider, always claimed not to have heard of the experiment until after he published his special theory of relativity, which not only accounted for the Michelson-Morley findings but resolved such paradoxes as the impossibility of distinguishing qualitatively between gravity and the pull caused by the acceleration of an elevator, or lift.
8. English philosopher (1574–1637). Bruno (1548?–1600), Italian philosopher.

mind gathers many particulars into one name, and many instances into one general induction. When a man says *left* and *right*, he is outdistancing the dog not only in looking for a light; he is setting in train all the shifts of meaning, the overtones and the ambiguities, between *gauche* and *adroit* and *dexterous*, between *sinister* and the sense of right. When a man counts *one, two, three*, he is not only doing mathematics; he is on the path to the mysticism of numbers in Pythagoras and Vitruvius and Kepler,[9] to the Trinity and the signs of the Zodiac.

I have described imagination as the ability to make images and to move them about inside one's head in new arrangements. This is the faculty that is specifically human, and it is the common root from which science and literature both spring and grow and flourish together. For they do flourish (and languish) together; the great ages of science are the great ages of all the arts, because in them powerful minds have taken fire from one another, breathless and higgledy-piggledy, without asking too nicely whether they ought to tie their imagination to falling balls or a haunted island. Galileo and Shakespeare, who were born in the same year, grew into greatness in the same age; when Galileo was looking through his telescope at the moon, Shakespeare was writing *The Tempest* and all Europe was in ferment, from Johannes Kepler to Peter Paul Rubens,[1] and from the first table of logarithms by John Napier to the Authorized Version of the Bible.

Let me end with a last and spirited example of the common inspiration of literature and science, because it is as much alive today as it was three hundred years ago. What I have in mind is man's ageless fantasy, to fly to the moon. I do not display this to you as a high scientific enterprise; on the contrary, I think we have more important discoveries to make here on earth than wait for us, beckoning, at the horned surface of the moon. Yet I cannot belittle the fascination which that ice-blue journey has had for the imagination of men, long before it drew us to our television screens to watch the tumbling astronauts. Plutarch and Lucian, Ariosto and Ben Jonson wrote about it, before the days of Jules Verne and H. G. Wells[2] and science fiction. The seventeenth century was heady with new dreams and fables about voyages to the moon. Kepler wrote one full of deep scientific ideas, which (alas) simply got his mother accused of witchcraft. In England,

9. Johannes Kepler (1571–1630), German astronomer. Pythagoras (5th century B.C.), early Greek philosopher. Marcus Vitruvius Pollio (1st century B.C.), Roman architect and engineer.

1. Flemish painter (1577–1640).

2. English novelist and historian (1866–1946). Plutarch (A.D. ?46–?120), Greek biographer and essayist. Lucian (A.D. 2nd century), Greek rhetorician and satirist. Ludovico Ariosto (1474–1533), Italian poet. Jonson (?1573–1637), English dramatist and poet. Verne (1828–1905), French author.

Francis Godwin wrote a wild and splendid work, *The Man in the Moone,* and the astronomer John Wilkins wrote a wild and learned one, *The Discovery of a New World.* They did not draw a line between science and fancy; for example, they all tried to guess just where in the journey the earth's gravity would stop. Only Kepler understood that gravity has no boundary, and put a law to it—which happened to be the wrong law.

All this was a few years before Isaac Newton was born, and it was all in his head that day in 1666 when he sat in his mother's garden, a young man of twenty-three, and thought about the reach of gravity. This was how he came to conceive his brilliant image, that the moon is like a ball which has been thrown so hard that it falls exactly as fast as the horizon, all the way round the earth. The image will do for any satellite, and Newton modestly calculated how long therefore an astronaut would take to fall round the earth once. He made it ninety minutes, and we have all seen now that he was right; but Newton had no way to check that. Instead he went on to calculate how long in that case the distant moon would take to round the earth, if indeed it behaves like a thrown ball that falls in the earth's gravity, and if gravity obeyed a law of inverse squares. He found that the answer would be twenty-eight days.

25 In that telling figure, the imagination that day chimed with nature, and made a harmony. We shall hear an echo of that harmony on the day when we land on the moon, because it will be not a technical but an imaginative triumph, that reaches back to the beginning of modern science and literature both. All great acts of imagination are like this, in the arts and in science, and convince us because they fill out reality with a deeper sense of rightness. We start with the simplest vocabulary of images, with *left* and *right* and *one, two, three,* and before we know how it happened the words and the numbers have conspired to make a match with nature: we catch in them the pattern of mind and matter as one.

QUESTIONS

1. "To imagine," *according to Bronowski, means* "to make images and to move them about inside one's head in new arrangements" (*paragraph* 9). *Mark his illustrations of imagination and then expand this definition to incorporate them.*
2. *Bronowski argues that imagination works similarly in artists and in scientists. List his illustrations and references in two columns, one for science and one for literature. Why do you think he demonstrates the working of the imagination in science more fully than in art?*
3. *Read Bronowski's* "The Nature of Scientific Reasoning" (*p. 1011*).

Write an essay in which you describe his illustrations from the work of Newton in both "The Reach of Imagination" and "The Nature of Scientific Reasoning." Could he have interchanged them? Why or why not?

Henry David Thoreau

OBSERVATION

There is no such thing as pure *objective* observation. Your observation, to be interesting, *i.e.* to be significant, must be *subjective*. The sum of what the writer of whatever class has to report is simply some human experience, whether he be poet or philosopher or man of science. The man of most science is the man most alive, whose life is the greatest event. Senses that take cognizance of outward things merely are of no avail. It matters not where or how far you travel—the farther commonly the worse—but how much alive you are. If it is possible to conceive of an event outside to humanity, it is not of the slightest significance, though it were the explosion of a planet. Every important worker will report what life there is in him. It makes no odds into what seeming deserts the poet is born. Though all his neighbors pronounce it a Sahara, it will be a paradise to him; for the desert which we see is the result of the barrenness of our experience. No mere willful activity whatever, whether in writing verses or collecting statistics, will produce true poetry or science. If you are really a sick man, it is indeed to be regretted, for you cannot accomplish so much as if you were well. All that a man has to say or do that can possibly concern mankind, is in some shape or other to tell the story of his love—to sing, and, if he is fortunate and keeps alive, he will be forever in love. This alone is to be alive to the extremities. It is a pity that this divine creature should ever suffer from cold feet; a still greater pity that the coldness so often reaches to his heart. I look over the report of the doings of a scientific association and am surprised that there is so little life to be reported; I am put off with a parcel of dry technical terms. Anything living is easily and naturally expressed in popular language. I cannot help suspecting that the life of these learned professors has been almost as inhuman and wooden as a rain-gauge or self-registering magnetic machine. They communicate no fact which rises to the temperature of blood-heat. It doesn't all amount to one rhyme.

Entry for May 6, 1854 from Thoreau's *Journal* (1837–59).

Desmond Morris

TERRITORIAL BEHAVIOR

A territory is a defended space. In the broadest sense, there are three kinds of human territory: tribal, family and personal.

It is rare for people to be driven to physical fighting in defense of these "owned" spaces, but fight they will, if pushed to the limit. The invading army encroaching on national territory, the gang moving into a rival district, the trespasser climbing into an orchard, the burglar breaking into a house, the bully pushing to the front of a queue, the driver trying to steal a parking space, all of these intruders are liable to be met with resistance varying from the vigorous to the savagely violent. Even if the law is on the side of the intruder, the urge to protect a territory may be so strong that otherwise peaceful citizens abandon all their usual controls and inhibitions. Attempts to evict families from their homes, no matter how socially valid the reasons, can lead to siege conditions reminiscent of the defense of a medieval fortress.

The fact that these upheavals are so rare is a measure of the success of Territorial Signals as a sytem of dispute prevention. It is sometimes cynically stated that "all property is theft," but in reality it is the opposite. Property, as owned space which is *displayed* as owned space, is a special kind of sharing system which reduces fighting much more than it causes it. Man is a co-operative species, but he is also competitive, and his struggle for dominance has to be structured in some way if chaos is to be avoided. The establishment of territorial rights is one such structure. It limits dominance geographically. I am dominant in my territory and you are dominant in yours. In other words, dominance is shared out spatially, and we all have some. Even if I am weak and unintelligent and you can dominate me when we meet on neutral ground, I can still enjoy a thoroughly dominant role as soon as I retreat to my private base. Be it ever so humble, there is no place like a home territory.

Of course, I can still be intimidated by a particularly dominant individual who enters my home base, but his encroachment will be dangerous for him and he will think twice about it, because he will know that here my urge to resist will be dramatically magnified and my usual subservience banished. Insulted at the heart of my own territory, I may easily explode into battle—either symbolic or real—with a result that may be damaging to both of us.

From *Manwatching: A Field Guide to Human Behavior* (1977).

In order for this to work, each territory has to be plainly advertised 5
as such. Just as a dog cocks its leg to deposit its personal scent on the trees in its locality, so the human animal cocks its leg symbolically all over his home base. But because we are predominantly visual animals we employ mostly visual signals, and it is worth asking how we do this at the three levels: tribal, family, and personal.

First: the Tribal Territory. We evolved as tribal animals, living in comparatively small groups, probably of less than a hundred, and we existed like that for millions of years. It is our basic social unit, a group in which everyone knows everyone else. Essentially, the tribal territory consisted of a home base surrounded by extended hunting grounds. Any neighboring tribe intruding on our social space would be repelled and driven away. As these early tribes swelled into agricultural super-tribes, and eventually into industrial nations, their territorial defense systems became increasingly elaborate. The tiny, ancient home base of the hunting tribe became the great capital city, the primitive warpaint became the flags, emblems, uniforms, and regalia of the specialized military, and the war-chants became national anthems, marching songs, and bugle calls. Territorial boundary-lines hardened into fixed borders, often conspicuously patrolled and punctuated with defensive structures—forts and lookout posts, checkpoints and great walls, and, today, customs barriers.

Today each nation flies its own flag, a symbolic embodiment of its territorial status. But patriotism is not enough. The ancient tribal hunter lurking inside each citizen finds himself unsatisfied by membership in such a vast conglomeration of individuals, most of whom are totally unknown to him personally. He does his best to feel that he shares a common territorial defense with them all, but the scale of the operation has become inhuman. It is hard to feel a sense of belonging with a tribe of fifty million or more. His answer is to form sub-groups, nearer to his ancient pattern, smaller, and more personally known to him—the local club, the teenage gang, the union, the specialist society, the sports association, the political party, the college fraternity, the social clique, the protest group, and the rest. Rare indeed is the individual who does not belong to at least one of these splinter groups, and take from it a sense of tribal allegiance and brotherhood. Typical of all these groups is the development of Territorial Signals—badges, costumes, headquarters, banners, slogans, and all the other displays of group identity. This is where the action is, in terms of tribal territorialism, and only when a major war breaks out does the emphasis shift upwards to the higher group level of the nations.

Each of these modern pseudo-tribes sets up its own special kind of home base. In extreme cases non-members are totally excluded, in others they are allowed in as visitors with limited rights and under a control system of special rules. In many ways they are like miniature nations, with their own flags and emblems and their own border guards. The exclusive club has its own "customs barrier": the doorman who checks your "passport" (your membership card) and prevents strangers from passing in unchallenged. There is a government: the club committee; and often special displays of the tribal elders: the photographs or portraits of previous officials on the walls. At the heart of the specialized territories there is a powerful feeling of security and importance, a sense of shared defense against the outside world. Much of the club chatter, both serious and joking, directs itself against the rottenness of everything outside the club boundaries—in that "other world" beyond the protected portals.

In social organizations which embody a strong class system, such as military units and large business concerns, there are many territorial rules, often unspoken, which interfere with the official hierarchy. High-status individuals, such as officers or managers, could in theory enter any of the regions occupied by the lower levels in the peck order, but they limit this power in a striking way. An officer seldom enters a sergeant's mess or a barrack room unless it is for a formal inspection. He respects those regions as alien territories even though he has the power to go there by virtue of his dominant role. And in businesses, part of the appeal of unions, over and above their obvious functions, is that with their officials, headquarters, and meetings they add a sense of territorial power for the staff workers. It is almost as if each military organization and business concern consists of two warring tribes: the officers versus the other ranks, and the management versus the workers. Each has its special home base within the system, and the territorial defense pattern thrusts itself into what, on the surface, is a pure social hierarchy. Negotiations between managements and unions are tribal battles fought out over the neutral ground of a boardroom table, and are as much concerned with territorial display as they are with resolving problems of wages and conditions. Indeed, if one side gives in too quickly and accepts the other's demands, the victors feel strangely cheated and deeply suspicious that it may be a trick. What they are missing is the protracted sequence of ritual and counter-ritual that keeps alive their group territorial identity.

10 Likewise, many of the hostile displays of sports fans and teenage gangs are primarily concerned with displaying their group image to rival fan-clubs and gangs. Except in rare cases, they do not attack one another's headquarters, drive out the occupants, and reduce them to a submissive, subordinate condition. It is enough to have scuffles on the borderlands between the two rival territories. This is particularly clear at football matches, where the fan-club headquarters becomes temporarily shifted from the club-house to a section of the stands, and where

minor fighting breaks out at the unofficial boundary line between the massed groups of rival supporters. Newspaper reports play up the few accidents and injuries which do occur on such occasions, but when these are studied in relation to the total numbers of displaying fans involved it is clear that the serious incidents represent only a tiny fraction of the overall group behavior. For every actual punch or kick there are a thousand war-cries, war dances, chants, and gestures.

Second: the Family Territory. Essentially, the family is a breeding unit and the family territory is a breeding ground. At the center of this space, there is the nest—the bedroom—where, tucked up in bed, we feel at our most territorially secure. In a typical house the bedroom is upstairs, where a safe nest should be. This puts it farther away from the entrance hall, the area where contact is made, intermittently, with the outside world. The less private reception rooms, where intruders are allowed access, are the next line of defense. Beyond them, outside the walls of the building, there is often a symbolic remnant of the ancient feeding grounds—a garden. Its symbolism often extends to the plants and animals it contains, which cease to be nutritional and become merely decorative—flowers and pets. But like a true territorial space it has a conspicuously displayed boundary-line, the garden fence, wall, or railings. Often no more than a token barrier, this is the outer territorial demarcation, separating the private world for the family from the public world beyond. To cross it puts any visitor or intruder at an immediate disadvantage. As he crosses the threshold, his dominance wanes, slightly but unmistakably. He is entering an area where he senses that he must ask permission to do simple things that he would consider a right elsewhere. Without lifting a finger, the territorial owners exert their dominance. This is done by all the hundreds of small ownership "markers" they have deposited on their family territory: the ornaments, the "possessed" objects positioned in the rooms and on the walls; the furnishings, the furniture, the colors, the patterns, all owner-chosen and all making this particular home base unique to them.

It is one of the tragedies of modern architecture that there has been a standardization of these vital territorial living units. One of the most important aspects of a home is that it should be similar to other homes only in a general way, and that in detail it should have many differences, making it a *particular* home. Unfortunately, it is cheaper to build a row of houses, or a block of flats, so that all the family living-units are identical, but the territorial urge rebels against this trend and house-owners struggle as best they can to make their mark on their mass-produced properties. They do this with garden-design, with front-door colors, with curtain patterns, with wallpaper and all the other decorative elements that together create a unique and different family environment. Only when they have completed this nest-building do they feel truly "at home" and secure.

When they venture forth as a family unit they repeat the process in a minor way. On a day-trip to the seaside, they load the car with personal belongings and it becomes their temporary, portable territory. Arriving at the beach they stake out a small territorial claim, marking it with rugs, towels, baskets, and other belongings to which they can return from their seaboard wanderings. Even if they all leave it at once to bathe, it retains a characteristic territorial quality and other family groups arriving will recognize this by setting up their own "home" bases at a respectful distance. Only when the whole beach has filled up with these marked spaces will newcomers start to position themselves in such a way that the inter-base distance becomes reduced. Forced to pitch between several existing beach territories they will feel a momentary sensation of intrusion, and the established "owners" will feel a similar sensation of invasion, even though they are not being directly inconvenienced.

The same territorial scene is being played out in parks and fields and on riverbanks, wherever family groups gather in their clustered units. But if rivalry for spaces creates mild feelings of hostility, it is true to say that, without the territorial system of sharing and space-limited dominance, there would be chaotic disorder.

15 Third: the Personal Space. If a man enters a waiting-room and sits at one end of a long row of empty chairs, it is possible to predict where the next man to enter will seat himself. He will not sit next to the first man, nor will he sit at the far end, right away from him. He will choose a position about halfway between these two points. The next man to enter will take the largest gap left, and sit roughly in the middle of that, and so on, until eventually the latest newcomer will be forced to select a seat that places him right next to one of the already seated men. Similar patterns can be observed in cinemas, public urinals, airplanes, trains, and buses. This is a reflection of the fact that we all carry with us, everywhere we go, a portable territory called a Personal Space. If people move inside this space, we feel threatened. If they keep too far outside it, we feel rejected. The result is a subtle series of spatial adjustments, usually operating quite unconsciously and producing ideal compromises as far as this is possible. If a situation becomes too crowded, then we adjust our reactions accordingly and allow our personal space to shrink. Jammed into an elevator, a rush-hour compartment, or a packed room, we give up altogether and allow body-to-body contact, but when we relinquish our Personal Space in this way, we adopt certain special techniques. In essence, what we do is to convert these other bodies into "nonpersons." We studiously ignore them, and they us. We try not to face them if we can possibly

avoid it. We wipe all expressiveness from our faces, letting them go blank. We may look up at the ceiling or down at the floor, and we reduce body movements to a minimum. Packed together like sardines in a tin, we stand dumbly still, sending out as few social signals as possible.

Even if the crowding is less severe, we still tend to cut down our social interactions in the presence of large numbers. Careful observations of children in play groups revealed that if they are high-density groupings there is less social interaction between the individual children, even though there is theoretically more opportunity for such contacts. At the same time, the high-density groups show a higher frequency of aggressive and destructive behavior patterns in their play. Personal Space—"elbow room"—is a vital commodity for the human animal, and one that cannot be ignored without risking serious trouble.

Of course, we all enjoy the excitement of being in a crowd, and this reaction cannot be ignored. But there are crowds and crowds. It is pleasant enough to be in a "spectator crowd," but not so appealing to find yourself in the middle of a rush-hour crush. The difference between the two is that the spectator crowd is all facing in the same direction and concentrating on a distant point of interest. Attending a theater, there are twinges of rising hostility toward the stranger who sits down immediately in front of you or the one who squeezes into the seat next to you. The shared armrest can become a polite, but distinct, territorial boundary-dispute region. However, as soon as the show begins, these invasions of Personal Space are forgotten and the attention is focused beyond the small space where the crowding is taking place. Now, each member of the audience feels himself spatially related, not to his cramped neighbors, but to the actor on the stage, and this distance is, if anything, too great. In the rush-hour crowd, by contrast, each member of the pushing throng is competing with his neighbors all the time. There is no escape to a spatial relation with a distant actor, only the pushing, shoving bodies all around.

Those of us who have to spend a great deal of time in crowded conditions become gradually better able to adjust, but no one can ever become completely immune to invasions of Personal Space. This is because they remain forever associated with either powerful hostile or equally powerful loving feelings. All through our childhood we will have been held to be loved and held to be hurt, and anyone who invades our Personal Space when we are adults is, in effect, threatening to extend his behavior into one of these two highly charged areas of human interaction. Even if his motives are clearly neither hostile nor sexual, we still find it hard to suppress our reactions to his close approach. Unfortunately, different countries have different ideas about exactly how close is close. It is easy enough to test your own "space reaction": when you are talking to someone in the street or in any open space, reach out with your arm and see where the nearest point on his body comes. If you hail from western Europe, you will find that he is at roughly fingertip distance from you. In other words, as you reach out, your fingertips will just about make contact with his shoulder. If you come from eastern Europe you will find you are standing at "wrist distance." If you come from the Mediterranean region you will find that you are much closer to your companion, at little more than "elbow distance."

Trouble begins when a member of one of these cultures meets and talks to one from another. Say a British diplomat meets an Italian or an Arab diplomat at an embassy function. They start talking in a friendly way, but soon the fingertips man begins to feel uneasy. Without knowing quite why, he starts to back away gently from his companion. The companion edges forward again. Each tries in his way to set up a Personal Space relationship that suits his own background. But it is impossible to do. Every time the Mediterranean diplomat advances to a distance that feels comfortable for him, the British diplomat feels threatened. Every time the Briton moves back, the other feels rejected. Attempts to adjust this situation often lead to a talking pair shifting slowly across a room, and many an embassy reception is dotted with western-European fingertip-distance men pinned against the walls by eager elbow-distance men. Until such differences are fully understood and allowances made, these minor differences in "body territories" will continue to act as an alienation factor which may interfere in a subtle way with diplomatic harmony and other forms of international transaction.

20 If there are distance problems when engaged in conversation, then there are clearly going to be even bigger difficulties where people must work privately in a shared space. Close proximity of others, pressing against the invisible boundaries of our personal body-territory, makes it difficult to concentrate on nonsocial matters. Flat-mates, students sharing a study, sailors in the cramped quarters of a ship, and office staff in crowded work-places, all have to face this problem. They solve it by "cocooning." They use a variety of devices to shut themselves off from the others present. The best possible cocoon, of course, is a small private room—a den, a private office, a study, or a studio—which physically obscures the presence of other nearby territory-owners. This is the ideal situation for non-social work, but the space-sharers cannot enjoy this luxury. Their cocooning must be symbolic. They may, in certain cases, be able to erect small physical barriers, such as screens and partitions, which give substance to their invisible Personal Space boundaries, but when this cannot be done, other means must be sought. One of these is the "favored object." Each space-sharer devel-

ops a preference, repeatedly expressed until it becomes a fixed pattern, for a particular chair, or table, or alcove. Others come to respect this, and friction is reduced. This sytem is often formally arranged (this is my desk, that is yours), but even where it is not, favored places soon develop. Professor Smith has a favorite chair in the library. It is not formally his, but he always uses it and others avoid it. Seats around a mess-room table, or a boardroom table, become almost personal property for specific individuals. Even in the home, father has his favorite chair for reading the newspaper or watching television. Another device is the blinkers-posture. Just as a horse that over-reacts to other horses and the distractions of the noisy race-course is given a pair of blinkers to shield its eyes, so people studying privately in a public place put on pseudo-blinkers in the form of shielding hands. Resting their elbows on the table, they sit with their hands screening their eyes from the scene on either side.

A third method of reinforcing the body-territory is to use personal markers. Books, papers, and other personal belongings are scattered around the favored site to render it more privately owned in the eyes of companions. Spreading out one's belongings is a well-known trick in public-transport situations, where a traveler tries to give the impression that seats next to him are taken. In many contexts carefully arranged personal markers can act as an effective territorial display, even in the absence of the territory owner. Experiments in a library revealed that placing a pile of magazines on the table in one seating position successfully reserved that place for an average of 77 minutes. If a sports-jacket was added, draped over the chair, then the "reservation effect" lasted for over two hours.

In these ways, we strengthen the defenses of our Personal Spaces, keeping out intruders with the minimum of open hostility. As with all territorial behavior, the object is to defend space with signals rather than with fists and at all three levels—the tribal, the family, and the personal—it is a remarkably efficient system of space-sharing. It does not always seem so, because newspapers and newscasts inevitably magnify the exceptions and dwell on those cases where the signals have failed and wars have broken out, gangs have fought, neighboring families have feuded, or colleagues have clashed, but for every territorial signal that has failed, there are millions of others that have not. They do not rate a mention in the news, but they nevertheless constitute a dominant feature of human society—the society of a remarkably territorial animal.

QUESTIONS

1. *Morris's mode of organization is classification: he moves from large units to small. Imagine this essay with a different order: small to*

large, for example, or large to small to medium ("Goldilocks and the Three Bears" order), or medium to large and then small, or medium to small and then large. Is there a logic in the order Morris uses? What is it?

2. *Morris describes the home as "family territory" or a "breeding ground" and the family as a "breeding unit" (paragraph 11). Locate other examples of this kind of diction. What is its effect?*
3. *Describe your tribal subgroup in a larger social unit like high school or college with attention to its territorial signals. What are your reasons for belonging to it? Are they the reasons Morris suggests?*

Paul Theroux

BEING A MAN

There is a pathetic sentence in the chapter "Fetishism" in Dr. Norman Cameron's book *Personality Development and Psychopathology.* It goes, "Fetishists are nearly always men; and their commonest fetish is a woman's shoe." I cannot read that sentence without thinking that it is just one more awful thing about being a man—and perhaps it is an important thing to know about us.

I have always disliked being a man. The whole idea of manhood in America is pitiful, in my opinion. This version of masculinity is a little like having to wear an ill-fitting coat for one's entire life (by contrast, I imagine femininity to be an oppressive sense of nakedness). Even the expression "Be a man!" strikes me as insulting and abusive. It means: Be stupid, be unfeeling, obedient, soldierly and stop thinking. Man means "manly"—how can one think about men without considering the terrible ambition of manliness? And yet it is part of every man's life. It is a hideous and crippling lie; it not only insists on difference and connives at superiority, it is also by its very nature destructive—emotionally damaging and socially harmful.

The youth who is subverted, as most are, into believing in the masculine ideal is effectively separated from women and he spends the rest of his life finding women a riddle and a nuisance. Of course, there is a female version of this male affliction. It begins with mothers encouraging little girls to say (to other adults) "Do you like my new dress?" In a sense, little girls are traditionally urged to please adults with a kind of coquettishness, while boys are enjoined to behave like monkeys toward each other. The nine-year-old coquette proceeds to become womanish in a subtle power game in which she learns to be

From *Sunrise with Seamonsters* (1985).

sexually indispensable, socially decorative and always alert to a man's sense of inadequacy.

Femininity—being lady-like—implies needing a man as witness and seducer; but masculinity celebrates the exclusive company of men. That is why it is so grotesque; and that is also why there is no manliness without inadequacy—because it denies men the natural friendship of women.

5 It is very hard to imagine any concept of manliness that does not belittle women, and it begins very early. At an age when I wanted to meet girls—let's say the treacherous years of thirteen to sixteen—I was told to take up a sport, get more fresh air, join the Boy Scouts, and I was urged not to read so much. It was the 1950s and if you asked too many questions about sex you were sent to camp—boy's camp, of course: the nightmare. Nothing is more unnatural or prison-like than a boy's camp, but if it were not for them we would have no Elks' Lodges, no pool rooms, no boxing matches, no Marines.

And perhaps no sports as we know them. Everyone is aware of how few in number are the athletes who behave like gentlemen. Just as high school basketball teaches you how to be a poor loser, the manly attitude toward sports seems to be little more than a recipe for creating bad marriages, social misfits, moral degenerates, sadists, latent rapists and just plain louts. I regard high school sports as a drug far worse than marijuana, and it is the reason that the average tennis champion, say, is a pathetic oaf.

Any objective study would find the quest for manliness essentially right-wing, puritanical, cowardly, neurotic and fueled largely by a fear of women. It is also certainly philistine. There is no book-hater like a Little League coach. But indeed all the creative arts are obnoxious to the manly ideal, because at their best the arts are pursued by uncompetitive and essentially solitary people. It makes it very hard for a creative youngster, for any boy who expresses the desire to be alone seems to be saying that there is something wrong with him.

It ought to be clear by now that I have something of an objection to the way we turn boys into men. It does not surprise me that when the President of the United States has his customary weekend off he dresses like a cowboy—it is both a measure of his insecurity and his willingness to please. In many ways, American culture does little more for a man than prepare him for modeling clothes in the L. L. Bean[1] catalog. I take this as a personal insult because for many years I found it impossible to admit to myself that I wanted to be a writer. It was my

1. A mail-order and retail store in Freeport, Maine, known for rugged sporting clothes and camping gear.

guilty secret, because being a writer was incompatible with being a man.

There are people who might deny this, but that is because the American writer, typically, has been so at pains to prove his manliness that we have come to see literariness and manliness as mingled qualities. But first there was a fear that writing was not a manly profession—indeed, not a profession at all. (The paradox in American letters is that it has always been easier for a woman to write and for a man to be published.) Growing up, I had thought of sports as wasteful and humiliating, and the idea of manliness was a bore. My wanting to become a writer was not a flight from that oppressive role-playing, but I quickly saw that it was at odds with it. Everything in stereotyped manliness goes against the life of the mind. The Hemingway personality is too tedious to go into here, and in any case his exertions are well known, but certainly it was not until this aberrant behavior was examined by feminists in the 1960s that any male writer dared question the pugnacity in Hemingway's fiction. All the bullfighting and arm wrestling and elephant shooting diminished Hemingway as a writer, but it is consistent with a prevailing attitude in American writing: one cannot be a male writer without first proving that one is a man.

10 It is normal in America for a man to be dismissive or even somewhat apologetic about being a writer. Various factors make it easier. There is a heartiness about journalism that makes it acceptable—journalism is the manliest form of American writing and, therefore, the profession the most independent-minded women seek (yes, it is an illusion, but that is my point). Fiction-writing is equated with a kind of dispirited failure and is only manly when it produces wealth—money is masculinity. So is drinking. Being a drunkard is another assertion, if misplaced, of manliness. The American male writer is traditionally proud of his heavy drinking. But we are also a very literal-minded people. A man proves his manhood in America in old-fashioned ways. He kills lions, like Hemingway; or he hunts ducks, like Nathanael West; or he makes pronouncements like, "A man should carry enough knife to defend himself with," as James Jones once said to a *Life* interviewer. Or he says he can drink you under the table. But even tiny drunken William Faulkner loved to mount a horse and go fox hunting, and Jack Kerouac roistered up and down Manhattan in a lumberjack shirt (and spent every night of *The Subterraneans* with his mother in Queens). And we are familiar with the lengths to which Norman Mailer is prepared, in his endearing way, to prove that he is just as much a monster as the next man.[2]

2. The writers named in this paragraph and the next are twentieth-century Americans whose personal lives may be seen as conforming (or not conforming, in the cases of Oates and Didion) to stereotypical ideas of masculinity.

When the novelist John Irving was revealed as a wrestler, people took him to be a very serious writer; and even a bubble reputation like Eric *(Love Story)* Segal's was enhanced by the news that he ran the marathon in a respectable time. How surprised we would be if Joyce Carol Oates were revealed as a sumo wrestler or Joan Didion active in pumping iron. "Lives in New York City with her three children" is the typical woman writer's biographical note, for just as the male writer must prove he has achieved a sort of muscular manhood, the woman writer—or rather her publicists—must prove her motherhood.

There would be no point in saying any of this if it were not generally accepted that to be a man is somehow—even now in feminist-influenced America—a privilege. It is on the contrary an unmerciful and punishing burden. Being a man is bad enough; being manly is appalling (in this sense, women's lib has done much more for men than for women). It is the sinister silliness of men's fashions, and a clubby attitude in the arts. It is the subversion of good students. It is the so-called Dress Code of the Ritz-Carlton Hotel in Boston, and it is the institutionalized cheating in college sports. It is the most primitive insecurity.

And this is also why men often object to feminism but are afraid to explain why: of course women have a justified grievance, but most men believe—and with reason—that their lives are just as bad.

Scott Russell Sanders

LOOKING AT WOMEN

On that sizzling July afternoon, the girl who crossed at the stoplight in front of our car looked, as my mother would say, as though she had been poured into her pink shorts. The girl's matching pink halter bared her stomach and clung to her nubbin breasts, leaving little to the imagination, as my mother would also say. Until that moment, it had never made any difference to me how much or little a girl's clothing revealed, for my imagination had been entirely devoted to other mysteries. I was eleven. The girl was about fourteen, the age of my buddy Norman who lounged in the back seat with me. Staring after her, Norman elbowed me in the ribs and murmured, "Check out that chassis."

His mother glared around from the driver's seat. "Hush your mouth."

First published in *Georgia Review* (Spring 1989).

"I was talking about that sweet Chevy," said Norman, pointing out a souped-up jalopy at the curb.

"I know what you were talking about," his mother snapped.

5 No doubt she did know, since mothers could read minds, but at first I did not have a clue. Chassis? I knew what it meant for a car, an airplane, a radio, or even a cannon to have a chassis. But could a girl have one as well? I glanced after the retreating figure, and suddenly noticed with a sympathetic twitching in my belly the way her long raven ponytail swayed in rhythm to her walk and the way her fanny jostled in those pink shorts. In July's dazzle of sun, her swinging legs and arms beamed at me a semaphore I could almost read.

As the light turned green and our car pulled away, Norman's mother cast one more scowl at her son in the rearview mirror, saying, "Just think how it makes her feel to have you two boys gawking at her."

How? I wondered.

"Makes her feel like hot stuff," said Norman, owner of a bold mouth.

"If you don't get your mind out of the gutter, you're going to wind up in the state reformatory," said his mother.

10 Norman gave a snort. I sank into the seat, and tried to figure out what power had sprung from that sashaying girl to zap me in the belly.

Only after much puzzling did it dawn on me that I must finally have drifted into the force-field of sex, as a space traveler who has lived all his years in free fall might rocket for the first time within gravitational reach of a star. Even as a bashful eleven-year-old I knew the word *sex*, of course, and I could paste that name across my image of the tantalizing girl. But a label for a mystery no more explains a mystery than the word *gravity* explains gravity. As I grew a beard and my taste shifted from girls to women, I acquired a more cagey language for speaking of desire, I picked up disarming theories. First by hearsay and then by experiment, I learned the delicious details of making babies. I came to appreciate the urgency for propagation that litters the road with maple seeds and drives salmon up waterfalls and yokes the newest crop of boys to the newest crop of girls. Books in their killjoy wisdom taught me that all the valentines and violins, the waltzes and glances, the long fever and ache of romance, were merely embellishments on biology's instructions that we multiply our kind. And yet, the fraction of desire that actually leads to procreation is so vanishingly small as to seem irrelevant. In his lifetime a man sways to a million longings, only a few of which, or perhaps none at all, ever lead to the fathering of children. Now, thirty years away from that July afternoon, firmly married, twice a father, I am still humming from the power unleashed by the girl in pink shorts, still wondering how it made her feel to have two boys gawk at her, still puzzling over how to dwell in the force-field of desire.

How should a man look at women? It is a peculiarly and perhaps neurotically human question. Billy goats do not fret over how they should look at nanny goats. They look or don't look, as seasons and hormones dictate, and feel what they feel without benefit of theory. There is more billy goat in most men than we care to admit. None of us, however, is pure goat. To live utterly as an animal would make the business of sex far tidier but also drearier. If we tried, like Rousseau,[1] to peel off the layers of civilization and imagine our way back to some pristine man and woman who have not yet been corrupted by hand-me-down notions of sexuality, my hunch is that we would find, in our speculative state of nature, that men regarded women with appalling simplicity. In any case, unlike goats, we dwell in history. What attracts our eyes and rouses our blood is only partly instinctual. Other forces contend in us as well: the voices of books and religions, the images of art and film and advertising, the entire chorus of culture. Norman's telling me to relish the sight of females and his mother's telling me to keep my eyes to myself are only two of the many voices quarreling in my head.

If there were a rule book for sex, it would be longer than the one for baseball (that byzantine sport), more intricate and obscure than tax instructions from the Internal Revenue Service. What I present here are a few images and reflections that cling, for me, to this one item in such a compendium of rules: How should a man look at women?

Well before I was to see any women naked in the flesh, I saw a bevy of them naked in photographs, hung in a gallery around the bed of my freshman roommate at college. A *Playboy* subscriber, he would pluck the centerfold from its staples each month and tape another air-brushed lovely to the wall. The gallery was in place when I moved in, and for an instant before I realized what I was looking at, all that expanse of skin reminded me of a meat locker back in Newton Falls, Ohio. I never quite shook that first impression, even after I had inspected the pinups at my leisure on subsequent days. Every curve of buttock and breast was news to me, an innocent kid from the Puritan back roads. Today you would be hard pressed to find a college freshman as ignorant as I was of female anatomy, if only because teenagers now routinely watch movies at home that would have been shown, during my teen years, exclusively on the fly-speckled screens of honky-

1. Jean Jacques Rousseau (1712–1778), Swiss-born French philosopher, author, political theorist, and composer. His closeness to nature, individualism, rebellion against the established social and political order, and glorification of the emotions made him the father of French romanticism.

tonk cinemas or in the basement of the Kinsey Institute.[2] I studied those alien shapes on the wall with a curiosity that was not wholly sexual, a curiosity tinged with the wonder that astronomers must have felt when they pored over the early photographs of the far side of the moon.

15 The paper women seemed to gaze back at me, enticing or mocking, yet even in my adolescent dither I was troubled by the phony stare, for I knew this was no true exchange of looks. Those mascaraed eyes were not fixed on me but on a camera. What the models felt as they posed I could only guess—perhaps the boredom of any numbskull job, perhaps the weight of dollar bills, perhaps the sweltering lights of fame, perhaps a tingle of the power that launched a thousand ships.

Whatever their motives, these women had chosen to put themselves on display. For the instant of the photograph, they had become their bodies, as a prizefighter does in the moment of landing a punch, as a weightlifter does in the moment of hoisting a barbell, as a ballerina does in the whirl of a pirouette, as we all do in the crisis of making love or dying. Men, ogling such photographs, are supposed to feel that where so much surface is revealed there can be no depths. Yet I never doubted that behind the makeup and the plump curves and the two dimensions of the image there was an inwardness, a feeling self as mysterious as my own. In fact, during moments when I should have been studying French or thermodynamics, I would glance at my roommate's wall and invent mythical lives for those goddesses. The lives I made up were adolescent ones, to be sure; but so was mine. Without that saving aura of inwardness, these women in the glossy photographs would have become merely another category of objects for sale, alongside the sports cars and stereo systems and liquors advertised in the same pages. If not extinguished, however, their humanity was severely reduced. And if by simplifying themselves they had lost some human essence, then by gaping at them I had shared in the theft.

What did that gaping take from me? How did it affect my way of seeing other women, those who would never dream of lying nude on a fake tiger rug before the million-faceted eye of a camera? The bodies in the photographs were implausibly smooth and slick and inflated, like balloon caricatures that might be floated overhead in a parade. Free of sweat and scars and imperfections, sensual without being fertile, tempting yet impregnable, they were Platonic ideals of the female form, divorced from time and the fluster of living, excused from the perplexities of mind. No actual woman could rival their insipid perfection.

2. Indiana University's Institute for Sex Research, directed, beginning in 1942, by American biologist Alfred Charles Kinsey (1894–1956).

The swains who gathered to admire my roommate's gallery discussed the pinups in the same tones and in much the same language as the farmers back home in Ohio used for assessing cows. The relevant parts of male or female bodies are quickly named—and, the *Kamasutra*[3] and Marquis de Sade[4] notwithstanding, the number of ways in which those parts can be stimulated or conjoined is touchingly small—so these studly conversations were more tedious than chitchat about the weather. I would lie on my bunk pondering calculus or Aeschylus and unwillingly hear the same few nouns and fewer verbs issuing from one mouth after another, and I would feel smugly superior. Here I was, improving my mind, while theirs wallowed in the notorious gutter. Eventually the swains would depart, leaving me in peace, and from the intellectual heights of my bunk I would glance across at those photographs—and yield to the gravity of lust. Idiot flesh! How stupid that a counterfeit stare and artful curves, printed in millions of copies on glossy paper, could arouse me. But there it was, not the first proof of my body's automatism and not the last.

Nothing in men is more machinelike than the flipping of sexual switches. I have never been able to read with a straight face the claims made by D. H. Lawrence and lesser pundits that the penis is a god, a lurking dragon. It more nearly resembles a railroad crossing signal, which stirs into life at intervals to announce, "Here comes a train." Or, if the penis must be likened to an animal, let it be an ill-trained circus dog, sitting up and playing dead and heeling whenever it takes a notion, oblivious of the trainer's commands. Meanwhile, heart, lungs, blood vessels, pupils, and eyelids all assert their independence like the members of a rebellious troupe. Reason stands helpless at the center of the ring, cracking its whip.

20 While he was president, Jimmy Carter raised a brouhaha by confessing in a *Playboy* interview, of all shady places, that he occasionally felt lust in his heart for women. What man hasn't, aside from those who feel lust in their hearts for other men? The commentators flung their stones anyway. Naughty, naughty, they chirped. Wicked Jimmy. Perhaps Mr. Carter could derive some consolation from psychologist Allen Wheelis, who blames male appetite on biology: "We have been selected for desiring. Nothing could have convinced us by argument that it would be worthwhile to chase endlessly and insatiably after women, but something has transformed us from within, a plasmid has invaded our DNA, has twisted our nature so that now this is exactly

3. A detailed account (first century?) of the art and technique of Indian erotics by the sage Vātsyāyana.

4. French author (1740–1814) whose works, because of their pornographic and blasphemous subject matter led, in his lifetime, to repeated imprisonment and have been denied official publication by the French courts as recently as 1957.

what we *want* to do." Certainly, by Darwinian logic, those males who were most avid in their pursuit of females were also the most likely to pass on their genes. Consoling it may be, yet it is finally no solution to blame biology. "I am extremely sexual in my desires: I carry them everywhere and at all times," William Carlos Williams[5] tells us on the opening page of his autobiography. "I think that from that arises the drive which empowers us all. Given that drive, a man does with it what his mind directs. In the manner in which he directs that power lies his secret." Whatever the contents of my DNA, however potent the influence of my ancestors, I still must direct that rebellious power. I still must live with the consequences of my looking and my longing.

Aloof on their blankets like goddesses on clouds, the pinups did not belong to my funky world. I was invisible to them, and they were immune to my gaze. Not so the women who passed me on the street, sat near me in classes, shared a table with me in the cafeteria: it was risky to stare at them. They could gaze back, and sometimes did, with looks both puzzling and exciting. It only complicated matters for me to realize that so many of these strangers had taken precautions that men should notice them. The girl in matching pink halter and shorts who set me humming in my eleventh year might only have wanted to keep cool in the sizzle of July. But these alluring college femmes had deeper designs. Perfume, eye shadow, uplift bras (about which I learned in the Sears catalog), curled hair, stockings, jewelry, lipstick, lace—what were these if not hooks thrown out into male waters?

I recall being mystified in particular by spike heels. They looked painful to me, and dangerous. Danger may have been the point, since the spikes would have made good weapons—they were affectionately known, after all, as stilettos. Or danger may have been the point in another sense, because a woman teetering along on such heels is tipsy, vulnerable, broadcasting her need for support. And who better than a man to prop her up, some guy who clomps around in brogans wide enough for the cornerstones of flying buttresses? (For years after college, I felt certain that spike heels had been forever banned, like bustles and foot-binding, but lately they have come back in fashion, and once more one encounters women teetering along on knife points.)

Back in those days of my awakening to women, I was also baffled by lingerie. I do not mean underwear, the proletariat of clothing, and I do not mean foundation garments, pale and sensible. I mean what the woman who lives in the house behind ours—owner of a shop called "Bare Essentials"—refers to as "intimate apparel." Those two words announce that her merchandise is both sexy and expensive. These

5. American poet and physician (1883–1963).

flimsy items cost more per ounce than truffles, more than frankincense and myrrh. They are put-ons whose only purpose is in being taken off. I have a friend who used to attend the men's-only nights at Bare Essentials, during which he would invariably buy a slinky outfit or two, by way of proving his serious purpose, outfits that wound up in the attic because his wife would not be caught dead in them. Most of the customers at the shop are women, however, as the models are women, and the owner is a woman. What should one make of that? During my college days I knew about intimate apparel only by rumor, not being that intimate with anyone who would have tricked herself out in such finery, but I could see the spike heels and other female trappings everywhere I turned. Why, I wondered then and wonder still, do so many women decorate themselves like dolls? And does that mean they wish to be viewed as dolls?

On this question as on many others, Simone de Beauvoir[6] has clarified matters for me, writing in *The Second Sex:* "The 'feminine' woman in making herself prey tries to reduce man, also, to her carnal passivity; she occupies herself in catching him in her trap, in enchaining him by means of the desires she arouses in him in submissively making herself a thing." Those women who transform themselves into dolls, in other words, do so because that is the most potent identity available to them. "It must be admitted," Beauvoir concedes, "that the males find in woman more complicity than the oppressor usually finds in the oppressed. And in bad faith they take authorization from this to declare that she has *desired* the destiny they have imposed on her."

25 *Complicity, oppressor, bad faith:* such terms yank us into a moral realm unknown to goats. While I am saddled with enough male guilt to believe three-quarters of Beauvoir's claim, I still doubt that men are so entirely to blame for the turning of women into sexual dolls. I believe human history is more collaborative than her argument would suggest. It seems unlikely to me that one-half the species could have "imposed" a destiny on the other half, unless that other half were far more craven than the females I have known. Some women have expressed their own skepticism on this point. Thus Joan Didion: "That many women are victims of condescension and exploitation and sex-role stereotyping was scarcely news, but neither was it news that other women are not: nobody forces women to buy the package." Beauvoir herself recognized that many members of her sex refuse to buy the

6. French novelist and essayist (1908–1986), who served as one of the most articulate exponents of existentialism. *Le Deuxième Sexe* (1949; translated as *The Second Sex*, 1953), a thorough analysis of women's status in society, became a classic of feminist literature.

"feminine" package: "The emancipated woman, on the contrary, wants to be active, a taker, and refuses the passivity man means to impose on her."

Since my college years, back in the murky 1960s, emancipated women have been discouraging their unemancipated sisters from making spectacles of themselves. Don't paint your face like a clown's or drape your body like a mannequin's, they say. Don't bounce on the sidelines in skimpy outfits, screaming your fool head off, while men compete in the limelight for victories. Don't present yourself to the world as a fluff pastry, delicate and edible. Don't waddle across the stage in a bathing suit in hopes of being named Miss This or That.

A great many women still ignore the exhortations. Wherever a crown for beauty is to be handed out, many still line up to stake their claims. Recently, Miss Indiana Persimmon Festival was quoted in our newspaper about the burdens of possessing the sort of looks that snag men's eyes. "Most of the time I enjoy having guys stare at me," she said, "but every once in a while it makes me feel like a piece of meat." The news photograph showed a cheerleader's perky face, heavily made-up, with starched hair teased into a blond cumulus. She put me in mind not of meat but of a plastic figurine, something you might buy from a booth outside a shrine. Nobody should ever be seen as meat, mere juicy stuff to satisfy an appetite. Better to appear as a plastic figurine, which is not meant for eating, and which is a gesture, however crude, toward art. Joyce described the aesthetic response as a contemplation of form without the impulse to action. Perhaps that is what Miss Indiana Persimmon Festival wishes to inspire in those who look at her, perhaps that is what many women who paint and primp themselves desire: to withdraw from the touch of hands and dwell in the eye alone, to achieve the status of art.

By turning herself (or allowing herself to be turned into) a work of art, does a woman truly escape men's proprietary stare? Not often, says the British critic John Berger. Summarizing the treatment of women in Western painting, he concludes that—with a few notable exceptions, such as works by Rubens and Rembrandt—the woman on canvas is a passive object displayed for the pleasure of the male viewer, especially for the owner of the painting, who is, by extension, owner of the woman herself. Berger concludes: "Men look at women. Women watch themselves being looked at. This determines not only most relations between men and women but also the relation of women to themselves. The surveyor of woman in herself is male: the surveyed female. Thus she turns herself into an object—and most particularly an object of vision: a sight."

That sweeping claim, like the one quoted earlier from Beauvoir, also seems to me about three-quarters truth and one-quarter exaggeration.

I know men who outdo the peacock for show, and I know women who are so fully possessed of themselves that they do not give a hang whether anybody notices them or not. The flamboyant gentlemen portrayed by Van Dyck are no less aware of being *seen* than are the languid ladies portrayed by Ingres. With or without clothes, both gentlemen and ladies may conceive of themselves as objects of vision, targets of envy or admiration or desire. Where they differ is in their potential for action: the men are caught in the midst of a decisive gesture or on the verge of making one; the women wait like fuel for someone else to strike a match.

I am not sure the abstract nudes favored in modern art are much of 30
an advance over the inert and voluptuous ones of the old school. Think of two famous examples: Duchamp's *Nude Descending a Staircase* (1912), where the faceless woman has blurred into a waterfall of jagged shards, or Picasso's *Les Demoiselles d'Avignon* (1907), where the five angular damsels have been hammered as flat as cookie sheets and fitted with African masks. Neither painting invites us to behold a woman, but instead to behold what Picasso or Duchamp can make of one.

The naked women in Rubens, far from being passive, are gleefully active, exuberant, their sumptuous pink bodies like rainclouds or plump nebulae. "His nudes are the first ones that ever made me feel happy about my own body," a woman friend told me in one of the Rubens galleries of the Prado Museum. I do not imagine any pinup or store-window mannequin or bathing-suited Miss Whatsit could have made her feel that way. The naked women in Rembrandt, emerging from the bath or rising from bed, are so private, so cherished in the painter's gaze, that we as viewers see them not as sexual playthings but as loved persons. A man would do well to emulate that gaze.

I have never thought of myself as a sight. How much that has to do with being male and how much with having grown up on the back roads where money was scarce and eyes were few, I cannot say. As a boy, apart from combing my hair when I was compelled to and regretting the patches on my jeans (only the poor wore patches), I took no trouble over my appearance. It never occurred to me that anybody outside my family, least of all a girl, would look at me twice. As a young man, when young women did occasionally glance my way, without any prospect of appearing handsome I tried at least to avoid appearing odd. A standard haircut and the cheapest versions of the standard clothes were camouflage enough. Now as a middle-aged man I have achieved once more that boyhood condition of invisibility, with less hair to comb and fewer patches to humble me.

Many women clearly pass through the world aspiring to invisibility.

Many others just as clearly aspire to be conspicuous. Women need not make spectacles of themselves in order to draw the attention of men. Indeed, for my taste, the less paint and fewer bangles the better. I am as helpless in the presence of subtle lures as a male moth catching a whiff of pheromones. I am a sucker for hair ribbons, a scarf at the throat, toes leaking from sandals, teeth bared in a smile. By contrast, I have always been more amused than attracted by the enameled exhibitionists whom our biblical mothers would identify as brazen hussies or painted Jezebels or, in the extreme cases, as whores of Babylon.

To encounter female exhibitionists in their full glory and variety, you need to go to a city. I never encountered ogling as a full-blown sport until I visited Rome, where bands of Italian men joined with gusto in appraising the charms of every passing female, and the passing females vied with one another in demonstrating their charms. In our own cities the most notorious bands of oglers tend to be construction gangs or street crews, men who spend much of their day leaning on the handles of shovels or pausing between bursts of riveting guns, their eyes tracing the curves of passersby. The first time my wife and kids and I drove into Boston we followed the signs to Chinatown, only to discover that Chinatown's miserably congested main street was undergoing repairs. That street also proved to be the city's home for X-rated cinemas and girlie shows and skin shops. LIVE SEX ACTS ON STAGE. PEEP SHOWS. PRIVATE BOOTHS. Caught in a traffic jam, we spent an hour listening to jackhammers and wolf whistles as we crept through the few blocks of pleasure palaces, my son and daughter with their noses hanging out the windows, my wife and I steaming. Lighted marquees peppered by burnt-out bulbs announced the titles of sleazy flicks; life-size posters of naked women flanked the doorways of clubs: leggy strippers in miniskirts, the originals for some of the posters, smoked on the curb between numbers.

35 After we had finally emerged from the zone of eros, eight-year-old Jesse inquired, "What was *that* place all about?"

"Sex for sale," my wife Ruth explained.

That might carry us some way toward a definition of pornography: making flesh into a commodity, flaunting it like any other merchandise, divorcing bodies from selves. By this reckoning, there is a pornographic dimension to much advertising, where a charge of sex is added to products ranging from cars to shaving cream. In fact, the calculated imagery of advertising may be more harmful than the blatant imagery of the pleasure palaces, that frank raunchiness which Kate Millett refers to as the "truthful explicitness of pornography." One can leave the X-rated zone of the city, but one cannot escape the sticky reach of commerce, which summons girls to the high calling of cosmetic glamor, fashion, and sexual display, while it summons boys to the panting chase.

You can recognize pornography, according to D. H. Lawrence, "by the insult it offers, invariably, to sex, and to the human spirit." He should know, Millet argues in *Sexual Politics*, for in her view Lawrence himself was a purveyor of patriarchal and often sadistic pornography. I think she is correct about the worst of Lawrence, and that she identifies a misogynist streak in his work; but she ignores his career-long struggle to achieve a more public, tolerant vision of sexuality as an exchange between equals. Besides, his novels and stories all bear within themselves their own critiques. George Steiner reminds us that "the list of writers who have had the genius to enlarge our actual compass of sexual awareness, who have given the erotic play of the mind a novel focus, an area of recognition previously unknown or fallow, is very small." Lawrence belongs on that brief list. The chief insult to the human spirit is to deny it, to claim that we are merely conglomerations of molecules, to pretend that we exist purely as bundles of appetites or as food for the appetites of others.

Men commit that insult toward women out of ignorance, but also out of dread. Allen Wheelis again: "Men gather in pornographic shows, not to stimulate desire, as they may think, but to diminish fear. It is the nature of the show to reduce the woman, discard her individuality, her soul, make her into an object, thereby enabling the man to handle her with greater safety, to use her as a toy. . . . As women move increasingly toward equality, the felt danger to men increases, leading to an increase in pornography and, since there are some men whose fears cannot even so be stilled, to an increase also in violence against women."

40 *Make her into an object:* all the hurtful ways for men to look at women are variations on this betrayal. "Thus she turns herself into an object," writes Berger. A woman's ultimate degradation is in "submissively making herself a thing," writes Beauvoir. To be turned into an object—whether by the brush of a painter or the lens of a photographer or the eye of a voyeur, whether by hunger or poverty or enslavement, by mugging or rape, bullets or bombs, by hatred, racism, car crashes, fires, or falls—is for each of us the deepest dread; and to reduce another person to an object is the primal wrong.

Caught in the vortex of desire, we have to struggle to recall the wholeness of persons, including ourselves. Beauvoir speaks of the temptation we all occasionally feel to give up the struggle for a self and lapse into the inertia of an object: "Along with the ethical urge of each individual to affirm his subjective existence, there is also the temptation to forgo liberty and become a thing." A woman in particular, given so much encouragement to lapse into thinghood, "is often very well pleased with her role as the *Other*."

Yet one need not forgo liberty and become a thing, without a center or a self, in order to become the Other. In our mutual strangeness, men and women can be doorways one for another, openings into the creative mystery that we share by virtue of our existence in the flesh. "To be sensual," James Baldwin writes, "is to respect and rejoice in the force of life, of life itself, and to be *present* in all that one does, from the effort of loving to the breaking of bread." The effort of loving is reciprocal, not only in act but in desire, an *I* addressing a *Thou*, a meeting in that vivid presence. The distance a man stares across at a woman, or a woman at a man, is a gulf in the soul, out of which a voice cries, *Leap, leap.* One day all men may cease to look on themselves as prototypically human and on women as lesser miracles; women may cease to feel themselves the targets for desire; men and women both may come to realize that we are all mere flickerings in the universal fire; and then none of us, male or female, need give up humanity in order to become the *Other.*

Ever since I gawked at the girl in pink shorts, I have dwelt knowingly in the force-field of sex. Knowingly or not, it is where we all dwell. Like the masses of planets and stars, our bodies curve the space around us. We radiate signals constantly, radio sources that never go off the air. We cannot help being centers of attraction and repulsion for one another. That is not all we are by a long shot, nor all we are capable of feeling, and yet, even after our much-needed revolution in sexual consciousness, the power of eros will still turn our heads and hearts. In a world without beauty pageants, there will still be beauty, however its definition may have changed. As long as men have eyes, they will gaze with yearning and confusion at women.

When I return to the street with the ancient legacy of longing coiled in my DNA, and the residues from a thousand generations of patriarchs silting my brain, I encounter women whose presence strikes me like a slap of wind in the face. I must prepare a gaze that is worthy of their splendor.

QUESTIONS

1. *Several sections of this essay are grounded in specific episodes from Sanders's life. Identify the episodes and explain the uses to which Sanders puts them.*
2. *The five sections of this essay are separated by typographical space rather than connected by prose transitions. Determine the content of each section and explain its relation to the content of the section that precedes it. Describe Sanders's strategies of organization and development.*
3. *In the second section (paragraph 12) Sanders asks: "How should a man look at women?" What is his answer? Where does he provide it?*

4. *Write an essay on a topic of your choice that is grounded in a specific episode from your life.*

Anna Quindlen

BETWEEN THE SEXES, A GREAT DIVIDE

Perhaps we all have the same memory of the first boy-girl party we attended. The floors were waxed, the music loud, the air thick with the smell of cologne. The boys stood on one side of the room and the girls on the other, each affecting a nonchalance belied by the shuffling male loafers and the occasional high birdlike sound of a female giggle.

Eventually, one of the taller, better-looking boys, perhaps dogged by two slightly shorter, squeakier acolytes, would make the big move across the chasm to ask the cutest girl to dance. Eventually, one of the girls would brave the divide to start a conversation on the other side. We would immediately develop a certain opinion of that girl, so that for the rest of our school years together, pajama parties would fairly crackle when she was not there.

None of us would consciously know it then, but what we were seeing, that great empty space in the center of the floor as fearful as a trapdoor, was the great division between the sexes. It was wonderful to think of the time when it would no longer be there, when the school gym would be a great meeting ground in which we would mingle freely, girl and boy, boy and girl, person to person, all alike. And maybe that's going to happen sometime in my lifetime, but I can't say I know when.

I've thought about this for some time, because I've written some loving things about men, and some nasty things too, and I meant them all. And I've always been a feminist, and I've been one of the boys as well, and I've given both sides a pretty good shot. I've spent a lot of time telling myself that men and women are fundamentally alike, mainly in the service of arguing that women should not only be permitted but be welcomed into a variety of positions and roles that only men occupied.

And then something happens, a little thing usually, and all I can see 5
is that great shiny space in the middle of the dance floor where no one ever meets. "I swear to God we are a different species," one of my friends said on the telephone recently. I can't remember whether the

Originally appeared in *The New York Times* "Hers" column (March 24, 1988).

occasion was a fight with her husband, a scene at work or a contretemps with a mutual male friend of ours. No matter. She's said it before and she'll say it again, just like all my other friends have said it to me, and I to them. Men are the other.

We are the other, too, of course. That's why we want to believe so badly that there are no others at all, because over the course of human history being other has meant being symbols of divinity, evil, carnal degeneration, perfect love, fertility and death, to name a few. And anybody who has ever been a symbol knows that it's about as relaxing as sitting on a piece of Louis XV furniture.[1] It is also true that over the course of history, we have been subordinate to others, symbols of weakness, dependency and emotions run amok.

Yet isn't it odd that I feel that the prejudice is somehow easier to deal with than the simple difference? Prejudice is evil and can be fought, while difference simply is. I live with three males, one husband and two sons, and occasionally I realize with great clarity that they are gazing across a divide at me, not because of big differences among us, but because of small ones.

The amaryllis bulb haunts me. "Why did you put an onion in a pot in the bathroom?" my elder son asked several months ago. I explained that it was not an onion but an amaryllis bulb and that soon it would grow into fabulous flowers. "What is that thing in the bathroom?" his father said later the same day. Impatiently I explained again. A look flashed between them, and then the littlest boy, too. Mom. Weird. Women.

Once I would have felt anger flame inside me at that. But I've done the same so many times now. On the telephone a friend and I will be commiserating about the failure of our husbands to listen when we talk, or their inexorable linear thinking, or their total blindness to the use and necessity of things like amaryllis bulbs. One of us will sigh, and the other will know what the sigh means. Husband. Strange. Men. Is it any wonder that our relationships are so often riddled with misunderstandings and disappointments?

10 In the children you can see the beginnings, even though we raise them in households in which mothers do things fathers once did, and vice versa. Children try to nail down the world, and themselves, early on and in a very primitive and real way. I remember a stage with my elder son in which, going through the supermarket or walking down the street, he would pin me down on each person walking by, and on such disparate cultural influences as Vanna White and Captain Kangaroo, by demanding that I tell him which genitalia category they fell in. Very soon, he got the idea: us and them, him and her. It was all very

1. Eighteenth-century French furniture.

well to say that all people are the same inside (even if I had believed it) but he thought the outside was very important, too, and it helped him classify the world.

I must never forget, I suppose, that even in the gym, with all that space between us, we still managed to pick partners and dance. It's the dance that's important, not the difference. (I shouldn't leave out who leads and who follows. But I speak to that from a strange perspective, since any man who has ever danced with me can attest to the fact that I have never learned to follow.)

I have just met the dance downstairs. My elder son has one of his best friends over, and he does not care that she is a girl, and she does not care that he is a boy. But she is complaining that he is chasing her with the plastic spider and making her scream, and he is grinning maniacally because that is just exactly the response he is looking for, and they are both having a great time. Two children, raised in egalitarian households in the 1980s. Between them the floor already stretches, an ocean to cross before they can dance uneasily in one another's arms.

QUESTIONS

1. *Mark the places in this essay where Quindlen, after describing "the first boy-girl party we attended" (paragraph 1), returns to it. How does she turn an event into a symbol of male-female differences?*
2. *"I've spent a lot of time telling myself that men and women are fundamentally alike, mainly in the service of arguing that women should not only be permitted but be welcomed into a variety of positions and roles that only men occupied" (paragraph 4). Does her admission that they are not fundamentally alike mean that women should not be welcomed into male positions and roles? Why?*
3. *As Quindlen, in this essay, casts men as the Other, so Scott Russell Sanders, in "Looking at Women" (p. 271), casts women as the Other. How do they present and try to decipher what they do not fully know or understand?*
4. *Write an essay in which you turn an event into a symbol.*

Dorothy Allison

GUN CRAZY

When we were little, my sister and I would ride with the cousins in the back of my uncle Bo's pickup truck when he drove us up into the foothills where we could picnic and the men could go shooting. I remember standing up behind the cab, watching the tree branches filter the bright Carolina sunshine, letting the wind push my hair behind me, and then wrestling with my cousin, Butch, until my aunt yelled at us to stop.

"Ya'll are gonna fall out," she was always screaming, but we never did.

Every stop sign we passed was pocked with bullet holes.

"Fast flying bees," Uncle Jack told us with a perfectly serious expression.

5 "Hornets with lead in their tails," Bo laughed.

My mama's youngest brother, Bo, kept his guns, an ought-seven rifle and a lovingly restored old Parker shotgun, wrapped in a worn green army blanket. A fold of the blanket was loosely stitched down a third of its length to make a cloth bag, the only sewing Bo ever did in his life. He kept his cleaning kit—a little bag of patches and a plastic bottle of gun oil—in the blanket pouch with the guns. Some evenings he would spread the blanket out in front of the couch and sit there happily cleaning his guns slowly and thoroughly. All the while he would sip cold beer and talk about what a fine time a man could have with his weapons out in the great outdoors. "You got to sit still, perfectly still," he'd say, nod, and sip again, then dab a little more gun oil on the patch he was running through the rifle barrel.

"Oh, you're good at that," someone would always joke.

"The man an't never shot an animal once in his life," Bo's wife, Nessa, told us. "Shot lots of bottles, whiskey bottles, beer bottles, coke-cola bottles. The man's one of the great all-time bottle destroyers."

I grinned. Stop signs and bottles, paper targets and wooden fences. My uncles loved to shoot, it was true, but the only deer they ever brought home was one found drowned in a creek and another that Uncle Jack hit head-on one night when he was driving his Pontiac convertible with the busted headlights.

From *Skin: Talking About Sex, Class, and Literature* (1994).

"Let me help you," I begged my uncle Bo one night when he had 10
pulled out his blanket kit and started the ritual of cleaning his gun. I was eleven, shy but fearless. Bo just looked at me over the angle of the cigarette jutting out of the corner of his mouth. He shook his head.

"I'd be careful," I blurted.

"Nessa, you hear this child?" Bo yelled in the direction of the kitchen and then turned back to me. "An't no such thing as careful where girls and guns are concerned." He took the cigarette out of his mouth and gave me another of those cool, distant looks. "You an't got no business thinking about guns."

"But I want to learn to shoot."

He laughed a deep throaty laugh, coughed a little, then laughed again. "Girls don't shoot," he told me with a smile. "You can do lots of things, girl, but not shooting. That just an't gonna happen."

I glared at him and said, "I bet Uncle Jack will teach me. He knows 15
how careful I can be."

Bo shook his head and tucked the cigarette back in the corner of his mouth. "It an't about careful, it's about you're a girl. You can whine and wiggle all you wont. An't nobody in this family gonna teach you to shoot." His face was stern, his smile completely gone. "That just an't gonna happen."

When I was in high school my best girlfriend was Anne, whose mama worked in the records division at the local children's hospital. One Sunday Anne invited me to go over to the woods out behind the mental hospital, to a hollow there where we could do some plinking.

"Plinking?"

"You know, plinking. Shooting bottles and cans." She pushed her hair back off her face and smiled at me. "If there's any water we'll fill the bottles up and watch it shoot up when the glass breaks. That's my favorite thing."

"You got a gun?" My mouth was hanging open. 20

"Sure. Mama gave me a rifle for my birthday. Didn't I tell you?"

"I don't think so." I looked away, so she wouldn't see how envious I felt. Her mama had given her a gun for her sixteenth birthday! I had always thought Anne's mama was something special, but that idea was simply amazing.

Anne's mama refused to cook, smoked Marlboros continuously, left the room any time any of her three children mentioned their dead father, and drank cocktails every evening while leaning back in her Lazy-Boy lounge chair and wearing dark eyeshades. "Don't talk to me," she'd hiss between yellow stained teeth. "I got crazy people and drunken orderlies talking at me all day long. I come home, I want some peace and quiet."

"My mama thinks a woman should be able to take care of herself," Anne told me.

25 "Right," I agreed. "She's right." Inside, I was seething with envy and excitement. Outside, I kept my face smooth and noncommittal. I wanted to shoot, wanted to shoot a shotgun like all my uncles, pepper stop signs and scare dogs. But I'd settle for a rifle, the kind of rifle a woman like Anne's mama would give her sixteen-year-old daughter.

That Sunday I watched closely as Anne slid a bullet into the chamber of her rifle and sighted down the gully to the paper target we had set up thirty feet away. Anne looked like Jane Fonda in *Cat Ballou* after she lost her temper—fierce, blonde, and competent. I swallowed convulsively and wiped sweaty palms on my jeans. I would have given both my big toes to have been able to stand like that, legs apart, feet planted, arms up, and the big rifle perfectly steady as the center circle target was fissured with little bullet holes.

Anne was myopic, skinny, completely obsessed with T. E. Lawrence, and neurotically self-conscious with boys, but holding that rifle tight to her shoulder and peppering the target, she looked different—older and far more interesting. She looked sexy, or maybe the gun looked sexy, I wasn't sure. But I wanted that look. Not Anne, but the power. I wanted to hold a rifle steady, the stock butting my shoulder tightly while I hit the target dead center. My mouth went dry. Anne showed me how to aim the gun a little lower than the center of the target.

"It shoots a little high," she said. "You got to be careful not to let it jump up when it fires." She stood behind me and steadied the gun in my hands. I put the little notch at the peak of the barrel just under the target, tightened my muscles, and pulled the trigger. The rifle still jerked up a little, but a small hole appeared at the outer edge of the second ring of the target.

"Goddamn!" Anne crowed. "You got it, girl." I let the barrel of the rifle drop down, the metal of the trigger guard smooth and warm under my hand.

30 You got to hold still, I thought. Perfectly still. I sighted along the barrel again, shifting the target notch to the right of the jars Anne had set up earlier. I concentrated, focused, felt my arm become rigid, stern and strong. I pulled back on the trigger slowly, squeezing steadily, the way in the movies they always said it was supposed to be done. The bottle exploded, water shooting out in a wide fine spray.

"Goddamn!" Anne shouted again. I looked over at her. Her glasses had slipped down on her nose and her hair had fallen forward over one eye. Sun shone on her sweaty nose and the polished whites of her teeth. She was staring at me like I had stared at her earlier, her whole face open with pride and delight.

Sexy, yeah. I pointed the barrel at the sky and let my mouth widen into a smile.

"Goddamn," I said, and meant it with all my heart.

Edmund White

SEXUAL CULTURE

Do gay men have friends—I mean," she said, "are they friends with each other?" Since the woman asking was a New Yorker, the owner of one of the city's simplest and priciest restaurants, someone who's known gays all her life, I found the question honest, shocking, and revealing of a narrow but bottomless abyss between us.

Of course New York is a city of total, even absolute strangers rubbing shoulders: the Hasidim in their yellow school bus being conveyed back to Brooklyn from the jewelry district, beards and black hats glimpsed through mud-splattered windows in a sun-dimmed daguerreotype; the junkie pushing the baby carriage and telling his wife, the prostitute, as he points to his tattooed biceps, "I haven't partied in this vein for years"; Moonies doing calisthenics at midnight in their Eighth Avenue center high above empty Thirty-fourth Street. . . . But this alienation wasn't religious or ethnic. The woman and I spoke the same language, knew the same people; we both considered Marcella Hazan fun but no substitute for Simone Beck.[1] How odd that she, as lower-upper-middle-class as I, shouldn't know whether gay men befriended one another.

It was then that I saw how mysterious gay culture is—not homosexuality, which is merely an erotic tropism, but modern American gay culture, which is a special way of laughing, spending money, ordering priorities, encoding everything from song lyrics to mirror-shiny military shoes. None of the usual modes for a subculture will do, for gay men are brought up by heterosexuals to be straight, they seek other men through what feels very much like a compulsion though they enter the ghetto by choice, yet once they make that choice it reshapes their lives, even their bodies, certainly their wardrobes. Many gay men live among straights as Marranos, those Spanish Jews who pretended during the Inquisition to convert to Christianity but continued to observe the old rites in cellars, when alone, in the greatest secrecy. Gays

From *The Burning Library* (1994).

1. Authors, respectively, of cookbooks for Italian and French cuisine.

aren't *like* blacks or Jews since they often *are* black or Jewish, and their affectional preference isn't a color or a religion though it has spawned a culture not unlike an ethnic minority's. Few Jews have Christian siblings, but most gays have straight brothers and sisters or at least straight parents. Many American Jews have been raised to feel they belong to the Chosen People, at once superior and inferior to gentiles, but every gay discovers his sexual nature with a combination of pain and relief, regret at being excluded from the tribe but elation at discovering the solution to the puzzle.

Gays aren't a nationality. They aren't Chicanos or Italo-Americans or Irish-Americans, but they do constitute one of the most potent political forces in big cities such as New York, Philadelphia, Washington (where gays and blacks elected Marion Barry mayor), Houston, Los Angeles, and San Francisco (where gays are so numerous they've splintered into countless factions, including the lesbian S/M[2] group Samois and the Sisters of Perpetual Indulgence, a group of drag nuns, one of whose members ran in a cowl and wimple as a candidate in the last citywide election). Not ethnic but a minority, not a polis but political, not a nationality but possessed of a costume, customs, and a patois, not a class but an economic force (not only as a market for records, films, vacations, and clothes but also as an army of worker ants who, for better or worse, have gentrified the center cities, thereby creating a better tomorrow for single young white heterosexual professionals).

5 Imagine a religion one enters against one's parents' will—and against one's own. Imagine a race one joins at sixteen or sixty without changing one's hue or hair texture (unless at the tanning or beauty salon). Imagine a sterile nation without descendants but with a long, misty regress of ancestors, without an articulated self-definition but with a venerable history. Imagine an exclusive club that includes a P.R. (Puerto Rican) boy of sixteen wearing ankle-high black-and-white Converse basketball shoes and a petrol green shirt sawed off to reveal a Praxitelean stomach[3]—and also includes a P.R. (Public Relations) WASP executive of forty in his Prince of Wales plaids and Cole-Haan tasseled loafers.

If one is gay, one is always in a crucial relationship to gayness as such, a defining category that is so full it is nearly empty (Renaud Camus writes: "Homosexuality is always elsewhere because it is everywhere").[4] No straight man stands in rapt contemplation of his straightness unless he's an ass. To be sure, heterosexuals may wonder

2. Sadomasochistic, or deriving pleasure from inflicting pain on others or oneself.
3. Praxiteles (4th century B.C.), Athenian sculptor who worked in marble.
4. French author (1946–).

over the significance of their homosexual fantasies, though even that morbid exercise is less popular now than formerly; as Barbara Ehrenreich acutely observes in her new study of the heterosexual male revolt, *The Hearts of Men,* the emergence of gay liberation ended the period in which everyone suspected everyone else of being "latently" homosexual. Now there are open homosexuals, and heterosexual men are exempt from the automatic suspicion of deviance.

No homosexual can take his homosexuality for granted. He must sound it, palpate it, auscultate it as though it were the dead limb of a tree or the living but tricky limb of a body; for that reason all homosexuals are "gay philosophers"[5] in that they must invent themselves. At a certain point one undergoes a violent conversion into a new state, the unknown, which one then sets about knowing as one will. Surely everyone experiences his or her life as an artifact, as molten glass being twirled and pinched into a shape to cool, or as a novel at once capacious and suspenseful, but no one is more a *Homo faber*[6] (in the sense of both "fabricator" and "fabulist") than a homo. It would be vain, of course, to suggest that this creativity is praiseworthy, an ambition rather than a response.

Sometimes I try to imagine how straights—not fundamentalist know-nothings, not rural innocents, not Freudian bigots, but educated urban heterosexuals—look at gay men (do they even see lesbians?). When they see gay men, what do they see? A mustache, a pumped-up body in black jeans and a tank top, an eye-catching tattoo (braided rope around the biceps)? And what do they think ("they," in this case, *hypocrite lecteur,* being *you*)?[7] Do you see something at once ludicrous and mildly enviable in the still youthful but overexercised body of this forty-year-old clone with the aggressive stare and soft voice? If you're a woman, do you find so much preening over appearance in a grown man . . . well, if not offensive, at least unappetizing; energy better spent on a career, on a family—on you? If you're a man, does it incense you that this jerk is out of harness, too loose, too free, has so lightly made a mockery of manhood? Once, on a radio call-in show a cop called in to tell me he had to admire the old-style queens back when it was rough being queer but that now, jeez, these guys swapping spit wit' a goil one week, wit' a guy the next, they're too lazy, they just don't know the fine art of being a man, it's all just too easy.

Your sentiments, perhaps?

5. Frederick Nietzsche (1844–1900), German philosopher, referred to philosophy as a "gay" or "happy" science.
6. Man the maker.
7. Charles Baudelaire (1821–1867), French poet, addresses his reader (in *The Flowers of Evil*) as hypocritical reader, my fellow, my brother.

10 Do you see gays as menacing satyrs, sex fiends around whom it's dangerous to drop your soap, *and* as feeble sissies, frail wood nymphs locked within massive trunks and limbs? Or, more positively if just as narrowly, are you a sybaritic het who greets the sight of gays with cries of glee, convinced you've stumbled on liberty hall, where sexual license of every sort—including your sort—is bound to reign? In fact, such sybarites often do regard gay men as comrades in arms, fellow libertines, and fellow victims in a country phobic to pleasure.

Or do gays just irk you? Do you regard them as a tinselly distraction in your peripheral vision? As errant, obstinate atoms that can't be drawn into any of the usual social molecules, men who if they insist on their gayness won't really do at any of the solemnities, from dinner parties to debutante balls, all of which depend on strict gender dimorphism for a rational seating plan? Since any proper gathering requires the threat of adultery for excitement and the prospect of marriage as a justification, of what earthly use are gays? Even the few fearless straight guys who've invaded my gay gym drift toward one another, not out of soap-dropping panic but because otherwise their dirty jokes fall on deaf or prettily blushing ears and their taunting, butt-slapping mix of rivalry and camaraderie provokes a weird hostility or a still weirder thrill.

And how do gays look at straights? In Andrew Holleran's superb new novel, *Nights in Aruba*, the narrator wonders "what it would be like to be the head of a family, as if with that all my problems would drop away, when in fact they would have merely been replaced by another set. I would not have worried about the size of my penis, the restrictions of age, the difficulty of finding love; I would have worried about mortgages, tuition, my youngest daughter's asthma, my competition at Shearson Loeb Rhoades." What makes this speculation so characteristically gay is that it is so focused on the family man, for if the nineteenth-century tart required, even invented the convent-bred virgin to contemplate, in the same way the homosexual man today must insult and revere, mock and envy this purely imaginary bourgeois paterfamilias, a creature extinct except in gay fantasies. Meanwhile, of course, the family man devotes his time to scream therapy and tai chi, ticking off Personals in the *Village Voice*[8] and wriggling out of visits from his kids, two punked-out teens who live in a feminist compound with his divorced wife, now a lesbian potter of great sensitivity and verve if low energy.

So much for how the two sexes (straight and gay) regard each other. If the camera were to pull back and frame both worlds in the lens, how would the two systems compare?

8. A New York weekly newspaper.

The most obvious difference is that whereas heterosexuality does include two sexes, since homosexuality does not it must improvise a new polarity moment by moment. Such a polarity seems necessary to sexual desire, at least as it is constructed in our culture. No wonder that some gay men search out the most extreme opposites (someone of a distant race, a remote language, another class or age); no wonder that even that convinced heterosexual Flaubert[9] was finally able to unbend with a boy prostitute in Egypt, an exotic who provided him with all the difference desire might demand. Other gay men seek out their twins—so that the beloved, I suppose, can stand in for oneself as one bows down to this false god and plays in turn his father, teacher, son, godfather, or god. Still others institutionalize the polarity in that next-best thing to heterosexuality: sadomasochism, the only vice that anthologizes all family and romantic relationships.

15 Because every gay man loves men, he comes to learn at first hand how to soothe the savage breast of the male ego. No matter how passive or girlish or shy the new beau might be in the boudoir, he will become the autocrat of the dinner table. Women's magazines are always planning articles on gay men and straight women; I'd say what they have most in common, aside from a few shared sexual techniques, is a body of folk wisdom about that hardhead, that bully, that maddeningly self-involved creature, the human male. As studies have surprisingly shown, men talk more than women, interrupt them more often, and determine the topics of conversation and object to women's assertions with more authority and frequency. When two gay men get together, especially after the first romantic urge to oblige the other wanes, a struggle for conversational dominance ensues, a conflict only symptomatic of larger arguments over every issue from where to live to how and whom to entertain.

To be sure, in this way the gay couple resembles the straight duo that includes an assertive, liberated woman. But while most of the young straight liberated women I know, at least, may protect their real long-range interests (career, mode of life, emotional needs) with vigilance, they're still willing to accommodate *him* in little social ways essential to harmony.

One benign side of straight life is that women conceive of men as "characters," as full-bodied, multifaceted beings who are first social, second familial, third amorous or amicable, and only finally physical. I'm trying politely to say that women are lousy judges of male beauty; they're easily taken in by such superficial traits as loyalty, dependability, charm, a sense of humor. Women don't, or at least didn't, judge men as so much beefcake. But men, both straight and gay, start with looks, the most obvious currency of value, worth, price. Let's say that

9. Gustave Flaubert (1821–1880), French novelist.

women see men as characters in a long family novel in which the men are introduced complete with phrenology, genealogy, and one annoying and two endearing traits, whereas men see their partners (whether male or female) as cars, makes to be instantly spotted, appraised, envied, made. A woman wants to be envied for her husband's goodness, his character, whereas a man wants to be envied for his wife's beauty, rarity, status—her drivability. Straight life combines the warmth and *Gemütlichkeit*[1] of the nineteenth-century bourgeois (the woman) with the steely corporate ethos of the twentieth-century functionary (the man). If gay male life, freed of this dialectic, has become supremely efficient (the trapdoor beside the bed) and only momentarily intimate (a whole life cycle compressed into the one-night stand), then the gain is dubious, albeit an extreme expression of one trend in our cultural economy.

But of course most morality, that is, popular morality—not real morals, which are unaffected by consensus, but mores, which are a form of fashion—is nothing but a species of nostalgia, a cover-up for pleasurable and profitable but not yet admissible innovations. If so many people condemn promiscuity, they do so at least partly because there is no available rhetoric that could condone, much less glamorize, impermanence in love. Nevertheless, it strikes me that homosexuals, masters of improvisation fully at home with the arbitrary and equipped with an internal compass that orients them instantly to any social novelty, are perhaps the most sensitive indicators of the future.

The birthrate declines, the divorce rate climbs, and popular culture (movies, television, song lyrics, advertising, fashions, journalism) is so completely and irrevocably secularized that the so-called religious revival is of no more lasting importance than the fad for Kabuki[2] in a transistorized Japan—a temporary throwback, a slight brake on the wheel. In such a world the rate of change is so rapid that children, once they are in school, can learn little from their parents but must assimilate new forms of behavior from their peers and new information from specialized instructors. As a result, parental authority declines, and the demarcations between the generations become ever more formidable. Nor do the parents regret their loss of control, since they're devoting all their energy to cultivating the inner self in the wholesale transition of our society from an ethic of self-sacrifice to one of self-indulgence, the so-called aristocraticization of middle-class life that has dominated the peaceful parts of this century in the industrialized West.

20 In the contemporary world the nineteenth-century experiment of

1. Kindliness and sociability.
2. Traditional Japanese popular drama.

companionate marriage,[3] never very workable, has collapsed utterly. The exact nature of the collapse isn't very clear yet because of our distracting, probably irrelevant habit of psychologizing every crisis (thus the endless speculations in the lowbrow press on the Irresponsible Male and the Defeminized Female or the paradoxical and cruelly impracticable advice to women readers to "go for it all—family, career, marriage, romance, *and* the reveries of solitude"). We treat the failure of marriage as though it were the failure of individuals to achieve it—a decline in grit or maturity or commitment or stamina rather than the unraveling of a poorly tied knot. Bourgeois marriage was meant to concentrate friendship, romance, and sex into an institution at once familial and economic. Only the most intense surveillance could keep such a bulky, ill-assorted load from bursting at the seams. Once the hedonism of the '60s relaxed that tension, people began to admit that friendship tranquilizes sexual desires (when mates become siblings, the incest taboo sets in) and that romance is by its very nature evanescent though indefinitely renewable given an endless supply of fresh partners. Neither sexual nor romantic attraction, so capricious, so passionate, so unstable, could ever serve as the basis for an enduring relationship, which can be balanced only on the plinth of esteem, that easy, undramatic, intimate kind of love one would say resembled family love if families were more loving.

It is this love that so many gay couples know about, aim for, and sometimes even express. If all goes well, two gay men will meet through sex, become lovers, weather the storms of jealousy and the diminution of lust, develop shared interests (a hobby, a business, a house, a circle), and end up with a long-term, probably sexless camaraderie that is not as disinterested as friendship or as seismic as passion or as charged with contradiction as fraternity. Younger gay couples feel that this sort of relationship, when it happens to them, is incomplete, a compromise, and they break up in order to find total fulfillment (i.e., tireless passion) elsewhere. But older gay couples stay together, cultivate their mild, reasonable love, and defend it against the ever-present danger of the sexual allure exercised by a newcomer. For the weak point of such marriages is the eternally recurring fantasy, first in one partner and then the other, of "total fulfillment." Needless to say, such couples can wreak havoc on the newcomer who fails to grasp that Bob and Fred are not just roommates. They may have separate bedrooms and regular extracurricular sex partners or even beaux, but Bob monitors Fred's infatuations with an eye attuned to nuance, and at a certain point will intervene to banish a potential rival.

3. Marriage in which partners prevent conception and may divorce by mutual consent without financial claims on each other.

I think most straight people would find these arrangements more scandalous than the infamous sexual high jinks of gays. Because these arrangements have no name, no mythology, no public or private acknowledgment, they're almost invisible even to the participants. Thus if you asked Bob in a survey what he wanted, he might say he wanted a "real" lover. He might also say Fred was "just a roommate, my best friend, we used to be lovers." So much for explicit analysis, but over the years Bob has cannily steered his affair with Fred between the Scylla of excessive fidelity (which is finally so dull no two imaginative gay men could endure it) and the Charybdis of excessive tolerance[4] (which could leave both men feeling so neglected they'd seek love elsewhere for sure).

There are, of course, countless variants to this pattern. The men live together or they don't. If they don't, they can maintain the civilized fiction of romance for years. They plan dates, honeymoons, take turns sleeping over at each other's house, and avoid conflicts about domestic details. They keep their extracurricular sex lives separate, they agree not to snoop—or they have three-ways. Or one of the pair has an active sex life and the other has abandoned the erotic arena.

Are gay men friends with each other? the woman asked me.

The question may assume that gays are only sexual, and that a man eternally on the prowl can never pause for mere affection—that a gay Don Juan is lonely. Or perhaps the question reveals a confusion about a society of one gender. Since a straight woman has other women for friends and men for lovers, my questioner might have wondered how the same sex could serve in both capacities.

The first supposition—that gay men are only sexual—is an ancient prejudice, and like all prejudices mostly untrue but in one sense occasionally accurate. If politically conscious homosexuals prefer the word *gay* to *homosexual*, they do so because they want to make the world regard attraction to members of the same gender as an affectional preference as well as a sexual orientation.

For instance, there are some gay men who prefer the feel of women's bodies to men's, who are even more comfortable sexually with women, but whose emotions crave contact with other men. Gay men have unfinished emotional business with other men—scary, promising, troubling, absorbing business—whereas their sentiments toward women (at least women not in their family) are much simpler, more stable, less fraught. Affection, passionate affection, is never simple; it is built out of equal parts of yearning, fear, and appetite. For that reason the friendship of one gay man fiercely drawn to another is as tense as any heterosexual passion, whereas a sexless, more disinter-

4. Homer's Odysseus navigated between Scylla, a monster, and Charybdis, a whirlpool.

ested gay friendship is as relaxed, as good-tempered as a friendship, say, between two straight men.

Gay men, then, do divide other gays into two camps—those who are potential partners (lovers) and those who are not (friends). But where gay life is more ambiguous than the world at large (and possibly for that reason more baffling to outsiders) is that the members of the two camps, lovers and friends, are always switching places or hovering somewhere in the margin between. It is these unconfessed feelings that have always intrigued me the most as a novelist—the unspoken love between two gay men, say, who pretend they are just friends, cruising buddies, merely filling in until Mr. Right comes along (mercifully, he never does).

In one sense, the public's prejudice about a gay obsession with sex is valid. The right to have sex, even to look for it, has been so stringently denied to gays for so many centuries that the drive toward sexual freedom remains a bright, throbbing banner in the fierce winds whipping over the ghetto. Laws against sex have always created the biggest problems for homosexuals; they helped to define the very category of homosexuality. For that reason, the gay community, despite its invention of a culture no more eroticized than any other, still cannot give up its origin in sexual desire and its suppression.

But what about the "excessive" promiscuity of gay men, the infa- 30
mous quickies, a phenomenon only temporarily held in check by the AIDS crisis? Don't the quickies prove that gay men are essentially bizarre, fundamentally lacking in judgment—*oversexed?* Of course, gay men behave as all men would were they free of the strictures of female tastes, needs, prohibitions, and expectations. There is nothing in gay male life that cannot be attributed either to its minority status or to its all-male population. All men want quick, uncomplicated sexual adventure (as well as sustained romantic passion); in a world of all men, that desire is granted.

The very universality of sexual opportunity within the modern gay ghetto has, paradoxically, increased the importance of friendship. In a society not based on the measured denial or canalization of sexual desire, there is more energy left over for friendship. Relationships are less loaded in gay life (hence the celebrated gay irony, a levity equivalent to seeing through conventions). In so many ways gays are still prisoners of the dominant society, but in this one regard gays are freer than their jailers: because gay relationships are not disciplined by religious, legal, economic, and political ceremonies but only by the dictates of conscience and the impulses of the heart, they don't stand for anything larger. They aren't symbols but realities, not laws but entities sufficient unto themselves, not consequential but ecstatic.

QUESTIONS

1. *In the first and third sections of this essay, White describes gay culture and homosexual relationships through comparison. Account for the different use of comparison in each section.*
2. *White begins this essay by having a real (or imaginary) friend ask him a question. What are her characteristics? How does casting her as his audience determine the content of the first section?*
3. *White, when he imagines how straights look at gays in the second section of this essay, shifts pronouns from* they *to* you. *Who becomes his new audience? How does this audience determine the content of the second section?*
4. *Who is the audience for the third section of this essay?*
5. *In an essay of your own, create a real (or imaginary) audience that you characterize in it. Append a paragraph explaining your choice of audience and its usefulness to you as a writer.*

Charles Lamb

A BACHELOR'S COMPLAINT OF THE BEHAVIOUR OF MARRIED PEOPLE

As a single man, I have spent a good deal of my time in noting down the infirmities of Married People, to console myself for those superior pleasures, which they tell me I have lost by remaining as I am.

I cannot say that the quarrels of men and their wives ever made any great impression upon me, or had much tendency to strengthen in those anti-social resolutions, which I took up long ago upon more substantial considerations. What oftenest offends me at the houses of married persons where I visit, is an error of quite a different description; it is that they are too loving.

Not too loving neither: that does not explain my meaning. Besides, why should that offend me? The very act of separating themselves from the rest of the world, to have the fuller enjoyment of each other's society, implies that they prefer one another to all the world.

But what I complain of is, that they carry this preference so undisguisedly, they perk it up in the faces of us single people so shamelessly, you cannot be in their company a moment without being made to feel, by some indirect hint or open avowal, that *you* are not the object of

From the *London Magazine* (Sept. 1822). The essay appeared under Lamb's pen name, Elia.

this preference. Now there are some things which give no offence, while implied or taken for granted merely; but expressed, there is much offence in them.

If a man were to accost the first homely-featured or plain-dressed young woman of his acquaintance, and tell her bluntly, that she was not handsome or rich enough for him, and he could not marry her, he would deserve to be kicked for his ill manners; yet no less is implied in the fact, that having access and opportunity of putting the question to her, he has never yet thought fit to do it. The young woman understands this as clearly as if it were put into words; but no reasonable young woman would think of making this the ground of a quarrel. Just as little right have a married couple to tell me by speeches, and looks that are scarce less plain than speeches, that I am not the happy man—the lady's choice. It is enough that I know I am not: I do not want this perpetual reminding.

The display of superior knowledge or riches may be made sufficiently mortifying; but these admit of a palliative. The knowledge which is brought out to insult me, may accidentally improve me; and in the rich man's houses and pictures—his parks and gardens, I have a temporary usufruct at least. But the display of married happiness has none of these palliatives: it is throughout pure, unrecompensed, unqualified insult.

Marriage by its best title is a monopoly, and not of the least invidious sort. It is the cunning of most possessors of any exclusive privilege to keep their advantage as much out of sight as possible, that their less favoured neighbours, seeing little of the benefit, may the less be disposed to question the right. But these married monopolists thrust the most obnoxious part of their patent into our faces.

Nothing is to me more distasteful than that entire complacency and satisfaction which beam in the countenances of a new-married couple—in that of the lady particularly: it tells you, that her lot is disposed of in this world: that *you* can have no hopes of her. It is true, I have none: nor wishes either, perhaps; but this is one of those truths which ought, as I said before, to be taken for granted, not expressed.

The excessive airs which those people give themselves, founded on the ignorance of us unmarried people, would be more offensive if they were less irrational. We will allow them to understand the mysteries belonging to their own craft better than we, who have not had the happiness to be made free of the company: but their arrogance is not content within these limits. If a single person presume to offer his opinion in their presence, though upon the most indifferent subject, he is immediately silenced as an incompetent person. Nay, a young married lady of my acquaintance, who, the best of the jest was, had not changed her condition above a fortnight before, in a question on which I had the misfortune to differ from her, respecting the properest mode of breeding oysters for the London market, had the assurance to ask with a sneer, how such an old Bachelor as I could pretend to know anything about such matters!

But what I have spoken of hitherto is nothing to the airs these creatures give themselves when they come, as they generally do, to have children. When I consider how little of a rarity children are—that every street and blind alley swarms with them—that the poorest people commonly have them in most abundance—that there are few marriages that are not blest with at least one of these bargains—how often they turn out ill, and defeat the fond hopes of their parents, taking to vicious courses, which end in poverty, disgrace, the gallows, etc.—I cannot for my life tell what cause for pride there can possibly be in having them. If they were young phœnixes, indeed, that were born but one in a year, there might be a pretext. But when they are so common. . . .

I do not advert to the insolent merit which they assume with their husbands on these occasions. Let *them* look to that. But why *we*, who are not their natural-born subjects, should be expected to bring our spices, myrrh, and incense—our tribute and homage of admiration—I do not see.

"Like as the arrows in the hand of the giant, even so are the young children": so says the excellent office in our Prayer-book appointed for the churching of women. "Happy is the man that hath his quiver full of them." So say I; but then don't let him discharge his quiver upon us that are weaponless; let them be arrows, but not to gall and stick us. I have generally observed that these arrows are double-headed: they have two forks, to be sure to hit with one or the other. As for instance, where you come into a house which is full of children, if you happen to take no notice of them (you are thinking of something else, perhaps, and turn a deaf ear to their innocent caresses), you are set down as untractable, morose, a hater of children. On the other hand, if you find them more than usually engaging—if you are taken with their pretty manners, and set about in earnest to romp and play with them, some pretext or other is sure to be found for sending them out of the room; they are too noisy or boisterous, or Mr.——does not like children. With one or other of these folks the arrow is sure to hit you.

I could forgive their jealousy, and dispense with toying with their brats, if it gives them any pain; but I think it unreasonable to be called upon to *love* them, where I see no occasion—to love a whole family, perhaps eight, nine, or ten, indiscriminately—to love all the pretty dears, because children are so engaging!

I know there is a proverb, "Love me, love my dog": that is not always so very practicable, particularly if the dog be set upon you to tease you or snap at you in sport. But a dog, or a lesser thing—any inanimate substance, as a keepsake, a watch or a ring, a tree, or the place where we last parted when my friend went away upon a long absence, I can make shift to love, because I love him, and anything that reminds me of him; provided it be in its nature indifferent, and apt to receive whatever hue fancy can give it. But children have a real character, and an essential being of themselves: they are amiable or unamiable *per se*; I must love or hate them as I see cause for either in their qualities.

A child's nature is too serious a thing to admit of its being regarded as a mere appendage to another being, and to be loved or hated accordingly: they stand with me upon their own stock, as much as men and women do. Oh! but you will say, sure it is an attractive age—there is something in the tender years of infancy that of itself charms us? This is the very reason why I am more nice about them. I know that a sweet child is the sweetest thing in nature, not even excepting the delicate creatures which bear them; but the prettier the kind of a thing is, the more desirable it is that it should be pretty of its kind. One daisy differs not much from another in glory; but a violet should look and smell the daintiest. I was always rather squeamish in my women and children.

But this is not the worst: one must be admitted into their familiarity at least, before they can complain of inattention. It implies visits, and some kind of intercourse. But if the husband be a man with whom you have lived on a friendly footing before marriage—if you did not come in on the wife's side—if you did not sneak into the house in her train, but were an old friend in fast habits of intimacy before their courtship was so much as thought on—look about you—your tenure is precarious—before a twelvemonth shall roll over your head, you shall find your old friend gradually grow cool and altered towards you, and at last seek opportunities of breaking with you.

I have scarce a married friend of my acquaintance, upon whose firm faith I can rely, whose friendship did not commence *after the period of his marriage*. With some limitations, they can endure that; but that the good man should have dared to enter into a solemn league of friendship in which they were not consulted, though it happened before they knew him—before they that are now man and wife ever met—this is intolerable to them. Every long friendship, every old authentic intimacy, must be brought into their office to be new stamped with their currency, as a sovereign prince calls in the good old money that was coined in some reign before he was born or thought of, to be new marked and minted with the stamp of his authority, before he will let it pass current in the world. You may guess what luck generally befalls such a rusty piece of metal as I am in these *new mintings*.

Innumerable are the ways which they take to insult and worm you out of their husband's confidence. Laughing at all you say with a kind of wonder, as if you were a queer kind of fellow that said good things, *but an oddity*, is one of the ways—they have a particular kind of stare for the purpose—till at last the husband, who used to defer to your judgment, and would pass over some excrescences of understanding and manner for the sake of a general vein of observation (not quite vulgar) which he perceived in you, begins to suspect whether you are not altogether a humourist—a fellow well enough to have consorted with in his bachelor days, but not quite so proper to be introduced to ladies. This may be called the staring way; and is that which has oftenest been put in practice against me.

Then there is the exaggerating way, or the way of irony; that is, where they find you an object of especial regard with their husband, who is not so easily to be shaken from the lasting attachment founded on esteem which he has conceived towards you, by never qualified exaggerations to cry up all that you say or do, till the good man, who understands well enough that it is all done in compliment to him, grows weary of the debt of gratitude which is due to so much candour, and by relaxing a little on his part, and taking down a peg or two in his enthusiasm, sinks at length to the kindly level of moderate esteem—that "decent affection and complacent kindness" towards you, where she herself can join in sympathy with him without much stretch and violence to her sincerity.

Another way (for the ways they have to accomplish so desirable a purpose are infinite) is, with a kind of innocent simplicity, continually to mistake what it was which first made their husband fond of you. If an esteem for something excellent in your moral character was that which riveted the chain which she is to break, upon any imaginary discovery of a want of poignancy in your conversation, she will cry, "I thought, my dear, you described your friend, Mr.——, as a great wit?" If, on the other hand, it was for some supposed charm in your conversation that he first grew to like you, and was content for this to overlook some trifling irregularities in your moral deportment, upon the first notice of any of these she as readily exclaims, "This, my dear, is your good Mr.——!"

One good lady whom I took the liberty of expostulating with for not showing me quite so much respect as I thought due to her husband's old friend, had the candour to confess to me that she had often heard Mr.——speak of me before marriage, and that she had conceived a great desire to be acquainted with me, but that the sight of me had very much disappointed her expectations; for from her husband's representations of me, she had formed a notion that she was to see a fine, tall, officer-like-looking man (I use her very words), the very reverse of which proved to be the truth.

This was candid; and I had the civility not to ask her in return, how she came to pitch upon a standard of personal accomplishments for her husband's friends which differed so much from his own; for my friend's dimensions as near as possible approximate to mine; he standing five feet five in his shoes, in which I have the advantage of him by about half an inch; and he no more than myself exhibiting any indications of a martial character in his air or countenance.

These are some of the mortifications which I have encountered in the absurd attempt to visit at their houses. To enumerate them all would be a vain endeavour; I shall therefore just glance at the very common impropriety of which married ladies are guilty—of treating us as if we were their husbands, and vice versa. I mean, when they use us with familiarity, and their husbands with ceremony. *Testacea,*[1] for instance, kept me the other night two or three hours beyond my usual time of supping, while she was fretting because Mr.——did not come home, till the oysters were all spoiled, rather than she would be guilty of the impoliteness of touching one in his absence.

This was reversing the point of good manners: for ceremony is an invention to take off the uneasy feeling which we derive from knowing ourselves to be less the object of love and esteem with a fellow-creature than some other person is. It endeavours to make up, by superior attentions in little points, for that invidious preference which it is forced to deny in the greater. Had *Testacea* kept the oysters back for me, and withstood her husband's importunities to go to supper, she would have acted according to the strict rules of propriety.

I know no ceremony that ladies are bound to observe to their husbands, beyond the point of a modest behaviour and decorum: therefore I must protest against the vicarious gluttony of *Cerasia,*[2] who at her own table sent away a dish of Morellas,[3] which I was applying to with great goodwill, to her husband at the other end of the table, and recommended a plate of less extraordinary gooseberries to my unwedded palate in their stead. Neither can I excuse the wanton affront of——

But I am weary of stringing up all my married acquaintances by Roman denominations. Let them amend and change their manners, or I promise to record the full-length English of their names, to the terror of all such desperate offenders in future.

1. A shelled animal, such as an oyster. Lamb names these imaginary wives according to the food they supply their husbands.
2. Derived from Ceres, the Roman goddess of agriculture.
3. Probably a variety of sour cherry.

QUESTIONS

1. *Mark the divisions of this essay. How many aspects of the behavior of married people does Lamb consider? What kinds of transitions does he provide?*
2. *Lamb published his essays under a pen name, Elia. On the basis of this essay, describe the character (or persona) of his creation, Elia.*
3. *In this essay Lamb criticizes marriage, children, and family life, which are ordinarily respected, even venerated. What makes his criticism gentle rather than harsh, comic rather than severe?*
4. *Lamb concludes this essay: "But I am weary of stringing up all my married acquaintances by Roman denominations."* Testacea, *who saves the oysters for her husband, has a name derived from the Latin for shell;* Cerasia, *who sends the morellas to her husband, has a name derived from the goddess Ceres, the patron of agriculture. Write an essay in which you invent English "denominations" appropriate to several of your acquaintances and provide sketches of their character and behavior.*

Lewis Thomas

THE LONG HABIT

We continue to share with our remotest ancestors the most tangled and evasive attitudes about death, despite the great distance we have come to understanding some of the profound aspects of biology. We have as much distaste for talking about personal death as for thinking about it; it is an indelicacy, like talking in mixed company about venereal disease or abortion in the old days. Death on a grand scale does not bother us in the same special way: we can sit around a dinner table and discuss war, involving 60 million volatilized human deaths, as though we were talking about bad weather; we can watch abrupt bloody death every day, in color, on films and television, without blinking back a tear. It is when the numbers of dead are very small, and very close, that we begin to think in scurrying circles. At the very center of the problem is the naked cold deadness of one's own self, the only reality in nature of which we can have absolute certainty, and it is unmentionable, unthinkable. We may be even less willing to face the issue at first hand than our predecessors because of a secret new hope that maybe it will go away. We like to think, hiding the thought, that

First published in *The New England Journal of Medicine* (Apr. 13, 1972); reprinted in Thomas's essay collection *The Lives of the Cell* (1974).

with all the marvelous ways in which we seem now to lead nature around by the nose, perhaps we can avoid the central problem if we just become, next year, say, a bit smarter.

"The long habit of living," said Thomas Browne, "indisposeth us to dying."[1] These days, the habit has become an addiction: we are hooked on living, the tenacity of its grip on us, and ours on it, grows in intensity. We cannot think of giving it up, even when living loses its zest—even when we have lost the zest for zest.

We have come a long way in our technologic capacity to put death off, and it is imaginable that we might learn to stall it for even longer periods, perhaps matching the life-spans of the Abkhasian Russians, who are said to go on, springily, for a century and a half. If we can rid ourselves of some of our chronic, degenerative diseases, and cancer, strokes and coronaries, we might go on and on. It sounds attractive and reasonable, but it is no certainty. If we became free of disease, we would make a much better run of it for the last decade or so, but might still terminate on about the same schedule as now. We may be like the genetically different lines of mice, or like Hayflick's different tissue-culture lines, programmed to die after a predetermined number of days clocked by their genomes. If this is the way it is, some of us will continue to wear out and come unhinged in the sixth decade, and some much later, depending on genetic timetables.

If we ever do achieve freedom from most of today's diseases, or even complete freedom from disease, we will perhaps terminate by drying out and blowing away on a light breeze, but we will still die.

5 Most of my friends do not like this way of looking at it. They prefer to take it for granted that we only die because we get sick, with one lethal ailment or another, and if we did not have our diseases we might go on indefinitely. Even biologists choose to think this about themselves, despite the evidences of the absolute inevitability of death that surround their professional lives. Everything dies, all around, trees, plankton, lichens, mice, whales, flies, mitochondria. In the simplest creatures it is sometimes difficult to see it as death, since the strands of replicating DNA they leave behind are more conspicuously the living parts of themselves than with us (not that it is fundamentally any different, but it seems so). Flies do not develop a ward round[2] of diseases that carry them off, one by one. They simply age, and die, like flies.

We hanker to go on, even in the face of plain evidence that long,

1. From *Hydriotaphia, Urne-Buriall, Or, A Discourse of the Sepulchral Urnes lately found in Norfolk* (1658).
2. That is, the variety of ailments a doctor sees during his circuit among the patients in a hospital ward.

long lives are not necessarily pleasurable in the kind of society we have arranged thus far. We will be lucky if we can postpone the search for new technologies for a while, until we have discovered some satisfactory things to do with the extra time. Something will surely have to be found to take the place of sitting on the porch reexamining one's watch.

Perhaps we would not be so anxious to prolong life if we did not detest so much the sickness of withdrawal. It is astonishing how little information we have about this universal process, with all the other dazzling advances in biology. It is almost as though we wanted not to know about it. Even if we could imagine the act of death in isolation, without any preliminary stage of being struck down by disease, we would be fearful of it.

There are signs that medicine may be taking a new interest in the process, partly from interest, partly from an embarrassed realization that we have not been handling this aspect of disease with as much skill as physicians once displayed, back in the days before they became convinced that disease was their solitary and sometimes defeatable enemy. It used to be the hardest and most important of all the services of a good doctor to be on hand at the time of death, and to provide comfort, usually in the home. Now it is done in hospitals, in secrecy (one of the reasons for the increased fear of death these days may be that so many people are totally unfamiliar with it; they never actually see it happen in real life). Some of our technology permits us to deny its existence, and we maintain flickers of life for long stretches in one community of cells or another, as though we were keeping a flag flying. Death is not a sudden all-at-once affair; cells go down in sequence, one by one. You can, if you like, recover great numbers of them many hours after the lights have gone out, and grow them out in cultures. It takes hours, even days, before the irreversible word finally gets around to all the provinces.

We may be about to rediscover that dying is not such a bad thing to do after all. Sir William Osler took this view; he disapproved of people who spoke of the agony of death, maintaining that there was no such thing.

10 In a 19th-century memoir about an expedition in Africa, there is a story about an explorer who was caught by a lion, crushed across the chest in the animal's great jaws, and saved in the instant by a lucky shot from a friend. Later, he remembered the episode in clear detail. He was so amazed by the extraordinary sense of peace and calm, and total painlessness, associated with his partial experience of being killed, that he constructed a theory that all creatures are provided with a protective physiologic mechanism, switched on at the verge of death, carrying them through in a haze of tranquility.

I have seen agony in death only once, in a patient with rabies, who remained acutely aware of every stage in the process of his own disintegration over a 24-hour period, right up to his final moment. It was as though, in the special neuropathology of rabies, the switch had been prevented from turning.

We will be having new opportunities to learn more about the physiology of death at first hand, from the increasing numbers of cardiac patients who have been through the whole process and then back again. Judging from what has been found out thus far, from the first generation of people resuscitated from cardiac standstill (already termed the Lazarus syndrome), Osler seems to have been right. Those who remember parts or all of their episodes do not recall any fear, or anguish. Several people who remained conscious throughout, while appearing to have been quite dead, could only describe a remarkable sensation of detachment. One man underwent coronary occlusion with cessation of the heart and dropped for all practical purposes dead in front of a hospital, and within a few minutes his heart had been restarted by electrodes and he breathed his way back into life. According to his account, the strangest thing was that there were so many people around him, moving so urgently, handling his body with such excitement, while all his awareness was of quietude.

In a recent study of the reaction to dying in patients with obstructive disease of the lungs, it was concluded that the process was considerably more shattering for the professional observers than the observed. Most of the patients appeared to be preparing themselves with equanimity for death, as though intuitively familiar with the business. One elderly woman reported that the only painful and distressing part of the process was in being interrupted; on several occasions she was provided with conventional therapeutic measures to maintain oxygenation or restore fluids and electrolytes, and each time she found the experience of coming back harrowing, she deeply resented the interference with her dying.

I find myself surprised by the thought that dying is an all-right thing to do, but perhaps it should not surprise. It is, after all, the most ancient and fundamental of biologic functions, with its mechanisms worked out with the same attention to detail, the same provision for the advantage of the organism, the same abundance of genetic information for guidance through the stages, that we have long since become accustomed to finding in all the crucial acts of living.

15 Very well. But even so, if the transformation is a co-ordinated, integrated physiologic process in its initial, local stages, there is still that permanent vanishing of consciousness to be accounted for. Are we to be stuck forever with this problem? Where on earth does it go? Is it simply stopped dead in its tracks, lost in humus, wasted? Considering

the tendency of nature to find uses for complex and intricate mechanisms, this seems to me unnatural. I prefer to think of it as somehow separated off at the filaments of its attachment, and then drawn like an easy breath back into the membrane of its origin, a fresh memory for a biospherical nervous system, but I have no data on the matter.

This is for another science, another day. It may turn out, as some scientists suggest, that we are forever precluded from investigating consciousness, by a sort of indeterminancy principle that stipulates that the very act of looking will make it twitch and blur out of sight. It this is true, we will never learn. I envy some of my friends who are convinced about telepathy; oddly enough, it is my European scientist acquaintances who believe it most freely and take it most lightly. All their aunts have received Communications, and there they sit, with proof of the motility of consciousness at their fingertips, and the making of a new science. It is discouraging to have had the wrong aunts, and never the ghost of a message.

QUESTIONS

1. *Thomas begins paragraph 14 by observing: "I find myself surprised by the thought that dying is an all-right thing to do. . . ." How, in the previous paragraphs, has he prepared readers not to be surprised by this observation?*
2. *Mark the places in this essay where Thomas speaks as a layperson and the places where he speaks as a medical doctor. What kinds of authority does he claim and how does he claim them?*
3. *Take Thomas's title and quotation from Thomas Browne (paragraph 2) and use them in an essay of your own. Attend to the authority you claim and how you claim it.*
4. *Elisabeth Kübler-Ross, in "On the Fear of Death" (p. 309), Stephen Jay Gould, in "Our Allotted Lifetimes" (p. 316), and Rita Moir, in "Leave Taking" (p. 321) would all agree with Thomas that "dying is an all-right thing to do." Compare the ways in which two (or more) of them support this statement and the ways they give it different emphases.*

Elisabeth Kübler-Ross

ON THE FEAR OF DEATH

Let me not pray to be sheltered from dangers but to be fearless in facing them.

Let me not beg for the stilling of my pain but for the heart to conquer it.

Let me not look for allies in life's battlefield but to my own strength.

Let me not crave in anxious fear to be saved but hope for the patience to win my freedom.

Grant me that I may not be a coward, feeling your mercy in my success alone; but let me find the grasp of your hand in my failure.

RABINDRANATH TAGORE,
Fruit-Gathering

Epidemics have taken a great toll of lives in past generations. Death in infancy and early childhood was frequent and there were few families who didn't lose a member of the family at an early age. Medicine has changed greatly in the last decades. Widespread vaccinations have practically eradicated many illnesses, at least in western Europe and the United States. The use of chemotherapy, especially the antibiotics, has contributed to an ever decreasing number of fatalities in infectious diseases. Better child care and education has effected a low morbidity and mortality among children. The many diseases that have taken an impressive toll among the young and middle-aged have been conquered. The number of old people is on the rise, and with this fact come the number of people with malignancies and chronic diseases associated more with old age.

Pediatricians have less work with acute and life-threatening situations as they have an ever increasing number of patients with psychosomatic disturbances and adjustment and behavior problems. Physicians have more people in their waiting rooms with emotional problems than they have ever had before, but they also have more elderly patients who not only try to live with their decreased physical abilities and limitations but who also face loneliness and isolation with all its pains and anguish. The majority of these people are not seen by

From *On Death and Dying* (1969).

a psychiatrist. Their needs have to be elicited and gratified by other professional people, for instance, chaplains and social workers. It is for them that I am trying to outline the changes that have taken place in the last few decades, changes that are ultimately responsible for the increased fear of death, the rising number of emotional problems, and the greater need for understanding of and coping with the problems of death and dying.

When we look back in time and study old cultures and people, we are impressed that death has always been distasteful to man and will probably always be. From a psychiatrist's point of view this is very understandable and can perhaps best be explained by our basic knowledge that, in our unconscious, death is never possible in regard to ourselves. It is inconceivable for our unconscious to imagine an actual ending of our own life here on earth, and if this life of ours has to end, the ending is always attributed to a malicious intervention from the outside by someone else. In simple terms, in our unconscious mind we can only be killed; it is inconceivable to die of a natural cause or of old age. Therefore death in itself is associated with a bad act, a frightening happening, something that in itself calls for retribution and punishment.

One is wise to remember these fundamental facts as they are essential in understanding some of the most important, otherwise unintelligible communications of our patients.

5 The second fact that we have to comprehend is that in our unconscious mind we cannot distinguish between a wish and a deed. We are all aware of some of our illogical dreams in which two completely opposite statements can exist side by side—very acceptable in our dreams but unthinkable and illogical in our wakening state. Just as our unconscious mind cannot differentiate betwee the wish to kill somebody in anger and the act of having done so, the young child is unable to make this distinction. The child who angrily wishes his mother to drop dead for not having gratified his needs will be traumatized greatly by the actual death of his mother—even if this event is not linked closely in time with his destructive wishes. He will always take part or the whole blame for the loss of his mother. He will always say to himself—rarely to others—"I did it, I am responsible, I was bad, therefore Mommy left me." It is well to remember that the child will react in the same manner if he loses a parent by divorce, separation, or desertion. Death is often seen by a child as an impermanent thing and has therefore little distinction from a divorce in which he may have an opportunity to see a parent again.

Many a parent will remember remarks of their children such as, "I will bury my doggy now and next spring when the flowers come up again, he will get up." Maybe it was the same wish that motivated the ancient Egyptians to supply their dead with food and goods to keep them happy and the old American Indians to bury their relatives with their belongings.

When we grow older and begin to realize that our omnipotence is really not so omnipotent, that our strongest wishes are not powerful enough to make the impossible possible, the fear that we have contributed to the death of a loved one diminishes—and with it the guilt. The fear remains diminished, however, only so long as it is not challenged too strongly. Its vestiges can be seen daily in hospital corridors and in people associated with the bereaved.

A husband and wife may have been fighting for years, but when the partner dies, the survivor will pull his hair, whine and cry louder and beat his chest in regret, fear and anguish, and will hence fear his own death more than before, still believing in the law of talion—an eye for an eye, a tooth for a tooth—"I am responsible for her death, I will have to die a pitiful death in retribution."

Maybe this knowledge will help us understand many of the old customs and rituals which have lasted over the centuries and whose purpose is to diminish the anger of the gods or the people as the case may be, thus decreasing the anticipated punishment. I am thinking of the ashes, the torn clothes, the veil, the *Klage Weiber*[1] of the old days—they are all means to ask you to take pity on them, the mourners, and are expressions of sorrow, grief, and shame. If someone grieves, beats his chest, tears his hair, or refuses to eat, it is an attempt at self-punishment to avoid or reduce the anticipated punishment for the blame that he takes on the death of a loved one.

This grief, shame, and guilt are not very far removed from feelings 10
of anger and rage. The process of grief always includes some qualities of anger. Since none of us likes to admit anger at a deceased person, these emotions are often disguised or repressed and prolong the period of grief or show up in other ways. It is well to remember that it is not up to us to judge such feelings as bad or shameful but to understand their true meaning and origin as something very human. In order to illustrate this I will again use the example of the child—and the child in us. The five-year-old who loses his mother is both blaming himself for her disappearance and being angry at her for having deserted him and for no longer gratifying his needs. The dead person then turns into something the child loves and wants very much but also hates with equal intensity for this severe deprivation.

The ancient Hebrews regarded the body of a dead person as something unclean and not to be touched. The early American Indians talked about the evil spirits and shot arrows in the air to drive the spir-

1. Wailing wives.

its away. Many other cultures have rituals to take care of the "bad" dead person, and they all originate in this feeling of anger which still exists in all of us, though we dislike admitting it. The tradition of the tombstone may originate in this wish to keep the bad spirits deep down in the ground, and the pebbles that many mourners put on the grave are left-over symbols of the same wish. Though we call the firing of guns at military funerals a last salute, it is the same symbolic ritual as the Indian used when he shot his spears and arrows into the skies.

I give these examples to emphasize that man has not basically changed. Death is still a fearful, frightening happening, and the fear of death is a universal fear even if we think we have mastered it on many levels.

What has changed is our way of coping and dealing with death and dying and our dying patients.

Having been raised in a country in Europe where science is not so advanced, where modern techniques have just started to find their way into medicine, and where people still live as they did in this country half a century ago, I may have had an opportunity to study a part of the evolution of mankind in a shorter period.

15 I remember as a child the death of a farmer. He fell from a tree and was not expected to live. He asked simply to die at home, a wish that was granted without questioning. He called his daughters into the bedroom and spoke with each one of them alone for a few moments. He arranged his affairs quietly, though he was in great pain, and distributed his belongings and his land, none of which was to be split until his wife should follow him in death. He also asked each of his children to share in the work, duties, and tasks that he had carried on until the time of the accident. He asked his friends to visit him once more, to bid good-bye to them. Although I was a small child at the time, he did not exclude me or my siblings. We were allowed to share in the preparations of the family just as we were permitted to grieve with them until he died. When he did die, he was left at home, in his own beloved home which he had built, and among his friends and neighbors who went to take a last look at him where he lay in the midst of flowers in the place he had lived in and loved so much. In that country today there is still no make-believe slumber room, no embalming, no false makeup to pretend sleep. Only the signs of very disfiguring illnesses are covered up with bandages and only infectious cases are removed from the home prior to the burial.

Why do I describe such "old-fashioned" customs? I think they are an indication of our acceptance of a fatal outcome, and they help the dying patient as well as his family to accept the loss of a loved one. If a patient is allowed to terminate his life in the familiar and beloved environment, it requires less adjustment for him. His own family knows him well enough to replace a sedative with a glass of his favorite wine; or the smell of a home-cooked soup may give him the appetite to sip a few spoons of fluid which, I think is still more enjoyable than an infusion. I will not minimize the need for sedatives and infusions and realize full well from my own experience as a country doctor that they are sometimes life-saving and often unavoidable. But I also know that patience and familiar people and foods could replace many a bottle of intravenous fluids given for the simple reason that it fulfills the physiological need without involving too many people and/or individual nursing care.

The fact that children are allowed to stay at home where a fatality has stricken and are included in the talk, discussions, and fears gives them the feeling that they are not alone in the grief and gives them the comfort of shared responsibility and shared mourning. It prepares them gradually and helps them view death as part of life, an experience which may help them grow and mature.

This is in great contrast to a society in which death is viewed as taboo, discussion of it is regarded as morbid, and children are excluded with the presumption and pretext that it would be "too much" for them. They are then sent off to relatives, often accompanied with some unconvincing lies of "Mother has gone on a long trip" or other unbelievable stories. The child senses that something is wrong, and his distrust in adults will only multiply if other relatives add new variations of the story, avoid his questions or suspicions, shower him with gifts as a meager substitute for a loss he is not permitted to deal with. Sooner or later the child will become aware of the changed family situation and, depending on the age and personality of the child, will have an unresolved grief and regard this incident as a frightening, mysterious, in any case very traumatic experience with untrustworthy grown-ups, which he has no way to cope with.

It is equally unwise to tell a little child who lost her brother that God loved little boys so much that he took little Johnny to heaven. When this little girl grew up to be a woman she never solved her anger at God, which resulted in a psychotic depression when she lost her own little son three decades later.

20 We would think that our great emancipation, our knowledge of science and of man, has given us better ways and means to prepare ourselves and our families for this inevitable happening. Instead the days are gone when a man was allowed to die in peace and dignity in his own home.

The more we are making advancements in science, the more we seem to fear and deny the reality of death. How is this possible?

We use euphemisms, we make the dead look as if they were asleep, we ship the children off to protect them from the anxiety and turmoil around the house if the patient is fortunate enough to die at home, we don't allow children to visit their dying parents in the hospitals, we have long and controversial discussions about whether patients should be told the truth—a question that rarely arises when the dying person is tended by the family physician who has known him from delivery to death and who knows the weaknesses and strengths of each member of the family.

I think there are many reasons for this flight away from facing death calmly. One of the most important facts is that dying nowadays is more gruesome in many ways, namely, more lonely, mechanical, and dehumanized; at times it is even difficult to determine technically when the time of death has occurred.

Dying becomes lonely and impersonal because the patient is often taken out of his familiar environment and rushed to an emergency room. Whoever has been very sick and has required rest and comfort especially may recall his experience of being put on a stretcher and enduring the noise of the ambulance siren and hectic rush until the hospital gates open. Only those who have lived through this may appreciate the discomfort and cold necessity of such transportation which is only the beginning of a long order—hard to endure when you are well, difficult to express in words when noise, light, pumps, and voices are all too much to put up with. It may well be that we might consider more the patient under the sheets and blankets and perhaps stop our well-meant efficiency and rush in order to hold the patient's hand, to smile, or to listen to a question. I include the trip to the hospital as the first episode in dying, as it is for many. I am putting it exaggeratedly in contrast to the sick man who is left at home—not to say that lives should not be saved if they can be saved by a hospitalization but to keep the focus on the patient's experience, his needs and his reactions.

25 When a patient is severely ill, he is often treated like a person with no right to an opinion. It is often someone else who makes the decision if and when and where a patient should be hospitalized. It would take so little to remember that the sick person too has feelings, has wishes and opinions, and has—most important of all—the right to be heard.

Well, our presumed patient has now reached the emergency room. He will be surrounded by busy nurses, orderlies, interns, residents, a lab technician perhaps who will take some blood, an electrocardiogram technician who takes the cardiogram. He may be moved to X-ray and he will overhear opinions of his condition and discussions and questions to members of the family. He slowly but surely is beginning to be treated like a thing. He is no longer a person. Decisions are made often without his opinion. If he tries to rebel he will be sedated and after hours of waiting and wondering whether he has the strength, he will be wheeled into the operating room or intensive treatment unit and become an object of great concern and great financial investment.

He may cry for rest, peace, and dignity, but he will get infusions, transfusions, a heart machine, or tracheotomy[2] if necessary. He may want one single person to stop for one single minute so that he can ask one single question—but he will get a dozen people around the clock, all busily preoccupied with his heart rate, pulse, electrocardiogram or pulmonary functions, his secretions or excretions but not with him as a human being. He may wish to fight it all but it is going to be a useless fight since all this is done in the fight for his life, and if they can save his life they can consider the person afterwards. Those who consider the person first may lose precious time to save his life! At least this seems to be the rationale or justification behind all this—or is it? Is the reason for this increasingly mechanical, depersonalized approach our own defensiveness? Is this approach our own way to cope with and repress the anxieties that a terminally or critically ill patient evokes in us? Is our concentration on equipment, on blood pressure our desperate attempt to deny the impending death which is so frightening and discomforting to us that we displace all our knowledge onto machines, since they are less close to us than the suffering face of another human being which would remind us once more of our lack of omnipotence, our own limits and failures, and last but not least perhaps our own mortality?

Maybe the question has to be raised: Are we becoming less human or more human? * * * [I]t is clear that whatever the answer may be, the patient is suffering more—not physically, perhaps, but emotionally. And his needs have not changed over the centuries, only our ability to gratify them.

2. The surgical opening of a passage through the neck into the trachea.

QUESTIONS

1. *In this essay Kübler-Ross incorporates various kinds of evidence: experience, observation, and reading. Mark the various kinds and describe how she incorporates them.*
2. *In this essay Kübler-Ross attends to the needs of the living and the rights of the dying. Describe where and how she attends to each and how she presents the conflicts, actual and potential, between them.*
3. *In paragraphs 24 to 27 Kübler-Ross describes the experience of the trip by ambulance, the emergency room, and the hospital from a patient's point of view. What does this shift in point of view contribute to the essay?*

4. *Imagine a situation in which a child or children are not isolated from death. What might be the consequences? Using this situation and its possible consequences, write an essay in which you agree or disagree with Kübler-Ross's views.*

Stephen Jay Gould

OUR ALLOTTED LIFETIMES

Meeting with Henry Ford in E. L. Doctorow's *Ragtime*, J. P. Morgan praises the assembly line as a faithful translation of nature's wisdom:

> Has it occurred to you that your assembly line is not merely a stroke of industrial genius but a projection of organic truth? After all, the interchangeability of parts is a rule of nature. . . . All mammals reproduce in the same way and share the same designs of self-nourishment, with digestive and circulatory systems that are recognizably the same, and they enjoy the same senses. . . . Shared design is what allows taxonomists to classify mammals as mammals.

An imperious tycoon should not be met with equivocation; nonetheless, I can only reply "yes, and no" to Morgan's pronouncement. Morgan was wrong if he thought that large mammals are geometric replicas of small ones. Elephants have relatively smaller brains and thicker legs than mice, and these differences record a general rule of mammalian design, not the idiosyncracies of particular animals.

Morgan was right in arguing that large animals are essentially similar to small members of their group. The similarity, however, does not lie in a constant shape. The basic laws of geometry dictate that animals must change their shape in order to perform the same function at different sizes. I remind readers of the classical example, first discussed by Galileo in 1638: the strength of an animal's leg is a function of its cross-sectional area (length × length); the weight that the leg must support varies as the animal's volume (length × length × length). If a mammal did not alter the relative thickness of its legs as it got larger, it would soon collapse since body weight would increase much faster than the supporting strength of limbs. Instead, large mammals have relatively thicker leg bones than small mammals. To remain the same in function, animals must change their form.

The study of these changes in form is called "scaling theory." Scaling theory has uncovered a remarkable regularity of changing shape

From *The Panda's Thumb: More Reflections in Natural History* (1980).

over the 25-millionfold range of mammalian weight from shrew to blue whale. If we plot brain weight versus body weight for all mammals on the so-called mouse-to-elephant (or shrew-to-whale) curve, very few species deviate far from a single line expressing the general rule: brain weight increases only two-thirds as fast as body weight as we move from small to large mammals. (We share with bottle-nosed dolphins the honor of greatest deviance from the curve.)

We can often predict these regularities from the physical behavior 5
of objects. The heart, for example, is a pump. Since all mammalian hearts are similar in function, small hearts will pump considerably faster than large ones (imagine how much faster you could work a finger-sized toy bellows than the giant model that fuels a blacksmith's large forge). On the mouse-to-elephant curve for mammals, the length of a heartbeat increases between one-fourth and one-third as fast as body weight as we move from small to large mammals. The generality of this conclusion has just been affirmed in an interesting study by J. E. Carrel and R. D. Heathcote on the scaling of heart rate in spiders. They used a cool laser beam to illuminate the hearts of resting spiders and drew a crab spider-to-tarantula curve for eighteen species spanning nearly a thousandfold range of body weight. Again, scaling is very regular with heart rate increasing four-tenths as fast as body weight (or .409 times as fast, to be exact).

We may extend this conclusion for hearts to a very general statement about the pace of life in small versus large animals. Small animals tick through life far more rapidly than large ones—their hearts work more quickly, they breathe more frequently, their pulse beats much faster. Most importantly, metabolic rate, the so-called fire of life, scales only three-fourths as fast as body weight in mammals. Large mammals generate much less heat per unit of body weight to keep themselves going. Tiny shrews move frentically, eating nearly all their waking lives to keep their metabolic fire burning at its maximal rate among mammals; blue whales glide majestically, their hearts beating the slowest rhythm among active, warmblooded creatures.

If we consider the scaling of lifetime among mammals, an intriguing synthesis of these disparate data seems to suggest itself. We have all had enough experience with mammalian pets of various sizes to understand that small mammals tend to live for a shorter time than large ones. In fact, the scaling of mammalian lifetime follows a regular curve at about the same rate as heartbeat and breath time—between one-fourth and one-third as fast as body weight as we move from small to large animals. (Again, *Homo sapiens* emerges as a very peculiar animal. We live far longer than a mammal of our body size should. I have argued elsewhere that humans evolved by a process called "neoteny"—the retention of shapes and growth rates that characterize juvenile stages of our primate ancestors. I also believe that neoteny is responsible for our elevated longevity. Compared with other mammals, all stages of human life—from juvenile features to adulthood—arise "too late." We are born as helpless embryos after a long gestation; we mature late after an extended childhood; we die, if fortune be kind, at ages otherwise reached only by the very largest warmblooded creatures.)

Usually, we pity the pet mouse or gerbil that lived its full span of a year or two at most. How brief its life, while we endure for the better part of a century. As the main theme of this column, I want to argue that such pity is misplaced (our personal grief, of course, is quite another matter; with this, science does not deal). J. P. Morgan of *Ragtime* was right—small and large mammals are essentially similar. Their lifetimes are scaled to their life's pace, and all endure for approximately the same amount of biological time. Small mammals tick fast, burn rapidly, and live for a short time; large ones live long at a stately pace. Measured by their own internal clocks, mammals of different sizes tend to live for the same amount of time.

Yet we are prevented from grasping this important and comforting concept by a deeply ingrained habit of Western thought. We are trained from earliest memory to regard absolute Newtonian time as the single valid measuring stick in a rational and objective world. We impose our kitchen clock, ticking equably, upon all things. We marvel at the quickness of a mouse, express boredom at the torpor of a hippopotamus. Yet each is living at the appropriate pace of its own biological clock.

10 I do not wish to deny the importance of absolute, astronomical time to organisms. Animals must measure it to lead successful lives. Deer must know when to regrow their antlers, birds when to migrate. Animals track the day–night cycle with their circadian rhythms; jet lag is the price we pay for moving much faster than nature intended. Bamboos can somehow count 120 years before flowering again.

But absolute time is not the appropriate measuring stick for all biological phenomena. Consider the song of the humpback whale. These magnificent animals sing with such volume that their sounds travel through water for thousands of miles, perhaps even around the world, as their leading student Roger S. Payne has suggested. E. O. Wilson has described the awesome effect of these vocalizations: "The notes are eerie yet beautiful to the human ear. Deep basso groans and almost inaudibly high soprano squeaks alternate with repetitive squeals that suddenly rise or fall in pitch." We do not know the function of these songs. Perhaps they enable whales to find each other and to stay together during their annual transoceanic migrations.

Each whale has its own characteristic song; the highly complex patterns are repeated over and over again with great faithfulness. No scientific fact that I have learned in the last decade struck me with more force than Payne's report that the length of some songs may extend for more than half an hour. I have never been able to memorize the five-minute first Kyrie of the B-minor Mass[1] (and not for want of trying); how could a whale sing for thirty minutes and then repeat itself accurately? Of what possible use is a thirty-minute repeat cycle—far too long for a human to recognize: we would never grasp it as a single song (without Payne's recording machinery and much study after the fact). But then I remembered the whale's metabolic rate, the enormously slow pace of its life compared with ours. What do we know about a whale's perception of thirty minutes? A humpback may scale the world to its own metabolic rate: its half-hour song may be our minute waltz.[2] From any point of view, the song is spectacular; it is the most elaborate single display so far discovered in any animal. I merely urge the whale's point of view as an appropriate perspective.

We can provide some numerical precision to support the claim that all mammals, on average, live for the same amount of biological time. In a method developed by W. R. Stahl, B. Gunther, and E. Guerra in the late 1950s and early 1960s, we search the mouse-to-elephant equations for biological properties that scale at the same rate against body weight. For example, Gunther and Guerra give the following equations for mammalian breath time and heartbeat time versus body weight.

$$\text{breath time} = .0000470\ \text{body}^{0.28}$$
$$\text{heartbeat time} = .0000119\ \text{body}^{0.28}$$

(Nonmathematical readers need not be overwhelmed by the formalism. The equations simply mean that both breath time and heartbeat time increase about .28 times as fast as body weight as we move from small to large mammals.) If we divide the two equations, body weight cancels out because it is raised to the same power.

$$\frac{\text{breath time}}{\text{heartbeat time}} = \frac{.0000470\ \cancel{\text{body}^{0.28}}}{.0000119\ \cancel{\text{body}^{0.28}}} = 4.0$$

This says that the ratio of breath time to heartbeat time is 4.0 in mammals of any body size. In other words, all mammals, whatever

1. By Johann Sebastian Bach; the movement is woven together from many independent musical lines.

2. The reference is to the "Minute Waltz," by Frédéric Chopin, which is not only brief but fast-moving.

their size, breathe once for each four heartbeats. Small animals breathe and beat their hearts faster than large animals, but both breath and heart slow up at the same relative rate as mammals get larger.

15 Lifetime also scales at the same rate to body weight (.28 times as fast as we move from small to large mammals). This means that the ratio of both breath time and heartbeat time to lifetime is also constant over the whole range of mammalian size. When we perform an exercise similar to that above, we find that all mammals, regardless of their size, tend to breathe about 200 million times during their lives (their hearts, therefore, beat about 800 million times). Small mammals breathe fast, but live for a short time. Measured by the sensible internal clocks of their own hearts or the rhythm of their own breathing, all mammals live about the same time. (Astute readers, having counted their breaths, may have calculated that they should have died long ago. But *Homo sapiens* is a markedly deviant mammal in more ways than braininess alone. We live about three times as long as mammals of our body size "should," but we breathe at the "right" rate and thus live to breathe about three times as much as an average mammal of our body size.)

The mayfly lives but a day as an adult. It may, for all I know, experience that day as we live a lifetime. Yet all is not relative in our world, and such a short glimpse of it must invite distortion in interpreting events ticking on longer scales. In a brilliant metaphor, the pre-Darwinian evolutionist Robert Chambers spoke of a mayfly watching the metamorphosis of a tadpole into a frog (from *Vestiges of the Natural History of Creation*, 1844):

> Suppose that an ephemeron [a mayfly], hovering over a pool for its one April day of life, were capable of observing the fry of the frog in the waters below. In its aged afternoon, having seen no change upon them for such a long time, it would be little qualified to conceive that the external branchiae [gills] of these creatures were to decay, and be replaced by internal lungs, that feet were to be developed, the tail erased, and the animal then to become a denizen of the land.

Human consciousness arose but a minute before midnight on the geologic clock. Yet we mayflies, ignorant perhaps of the messages buried in earth's long history, try to bend an ancient world to our purposes. Let us hope that we are still in the morning of our April day.

QUESTIONS

1. *In paragraph 7 Gould observes: "We live far longer than a mammal of our body size should." Describe, first, how he leads up to this statement, and second, what consequences he draws from it.*

2. *Explain, first in Gould's words and then in your own, Galileo's example (paragraph 3), the scaling of brain weight versus body weight (paragraph 4), the scaling of heart rate versus body weight (paragraph 5), the scaling of metabolic rate versus body weight (paragraph 6), the scaling of mammalian lifetime versus body weight (paragraph 7), the equations for mammalian breath time and heartbeat time versus body weight (paragraphs 13 to 14), and the deviance of human lifetimes (paragraph 15).*
3. *In this essay Gould describes three kinds of time: Newtonian time, metabolic time, and geologic time. Consider how you experience each one. Then write an essay in which you describe your experience of all three and their relative importance to you.*

Rita Moir

LEAVE TAKING

We pulled down the stainless steel locker door and slid you out. The morgue was warm—a refrigeration breakdown, the nurse said, and it would get warmer as we worked.

I didn't know if I'd know you. I only knew you were Bert Carlson and you died in a motorcycle accident last Saturday in Silverton. Your friends asked our burial society[1] to help prepare you for cremation. The society built the cemetery a few years ago, and some members learned how to do the simple things that help a dead person take leave.

I'd never done it before. I hoped I wouldn't be sick. I hoped I wouldn't be useless.

The hospital wrapping of plastic and linen had loosened around you. I saw your penis before I saw your face. It made you human, needing our help but not helpless.

The four of us, three women you didn't know, and your male friend, 5
lifted you onto the metal table. We searched through a black plastic garbage bag lying with you. The belt buckle your girlfriend asked for lay at the bottom of the bag, broken. It was with another piece of metal, a piece of the car you collided with.

The section of bumper was silver and untarnished. Inside your helmet, the black foam was still wet. Your jeans and sheepskin jacket had blood on them, too. Nothing was awful. Nothing was horrifying.

From *Event* (Autumn 1989).

1. In British Columbia, where Moir lives, laypeople are permitted to prepare human bodies for burial, thus carrying on a cultural tradition of such groups as the Doukhobors (see note 2) and the Quakers.

My friends told me that the autopsy cut and stitching is disturbing. Especially in babies. It's a long cut from your navel to your breastbone, then a Y-shape to your shoulder blades. The coroner bastes you back up with a string heavier than that used on a turkey. They cut open your head, too, and the string hangs from your hair, waiting for the final trim.

You didn't look that damaged. Not like the pictures in the first aid book. Your deadness didn't alarm me. I'd been with death. It was animal death, but there's a connection. Even dead chickens have dignity. Not the kind of chickens bought frozen in the Safeway, but the ones I've had to kill myself. The bears our neighbor shot for fun, then gave us to butcher—they have power, too. My dog howled all night when I tried to boil a head to make bear-head cheese. I learned not to do things like that. There are some things that aren't done. Decent burials are important. Respect is important. Time is important.

When Amanda died in her crib, Penny held her for eight hours. A change came over them both. They found peace together while they were leaving each other.

10 You needed to find your peace, too. It wasn't just for us, and for your family, that we did this. You weren't three days dead. You weren't gone yet.

The Doukhobors[2] who live in these valleys give the body three days to lie at rest before burial. It goes back to the three days Christ had before rising. I know you're not a Doukhobor, Bert, and no one ever accused me of being religious, but here in this room it makes sense.

We struggled to put on your white cotton socks, tried to make your legs move one more time. Were you one of the long-legged treeplanters who left us short-limbed ones behind? Did you stride so fast a breeze cooled you in the hot spring sun? You called out with joy when fireweed sweetened the air or nettle stung your fingertips, leaving you shocked and laughing.

We couldn't get on your boots, even though we used pruning shears to cut them up the back. Your feet weren't bending. We slipped your jeans on, rolling you sideways, holding you in our arms, the four of us a team.

The hard part was your head. This most vulnerable place, this container with all your thoughts. The head injury and the autopsy cut at the top—we didn't know how to touch it. This was a test, but it wasn't grisly so far. We didn't want to be afraid of you.

15 The nurse showed us how to move your head. Your man friend washed your face. They brought us swabs, and I cleaned around your

2. Members of a Russian religious sect, many of whom emigrated to western Canada in the late eighteenth century to flee persecution.

eyes and in your nostrils and in your ears. Your friend cleaned your teeth. There was blood in these places. You died from inside.

We wheeled you to the sink. I remembered last week at Margee's hair salon, lying back as the warm water coursed over me, soothing, gentle. We couldn't wash your hair, but we cleaned away the blood with damp cloths.

We snipped the string and I combed your hair. I'll have a hard time looking at my lover for a while. The resemblance is only passing, the same receding hairline, the same mustache.

Sometimes your eyes opened as we washed around them. I closed them. I could see.

We didn't try to lift or bend you to put on your shirt. We used the coroner's scissors from the white towel covered with the tools of his work, and snipped up the back of your yellow T-shirt. The one that says Fleetwood, the name of your treeplanting company. I thought of Fleetwood Mac,[3] rock 'n' roll. The shirt stayed connected around your chest and we slipped it over your arms and tucked it round you.

Your flannel shirt was harder. We figured the only way was to cut it up the back, right through the yoke and collar, slip on the two halves, and button up the front.

Your friend put on the baseball cap you always wore on the slopes.

Months ago Sally made the wood coffin that we kept in stock. Your friends believed you would fit, but they were off by a few inches. You were six feet four.

Until then it had all been gentle. Now we had to use force. The four of us looked at one another, drew our breath, and kept going.

We left you tucked in your coffin with your quilt and pillow, a sheet tucked around your bent legs.

We washed up, then stood aside while your girlfriend came in with the nurse to see you. We exchanged brief hugs. We didn't know her well, and she hadn't cried yet.

She left the room and we screwed down the pine lid, 12 screws, lifted the coffin and wheeled you out to the basement loading dock of the hospital where the treeplanters' station wagon waited for you.

Your six men friends waiting below concentrated on the metal handles of the coffin and didn't look up into our eyes. We passed you on. You were ready to take your leave.

Your face came into my mind even when I left for a long time to go away to work. You'd taken your leave, but now I needed to take mine, from you.

3. A British blues band of the 1960s that evolved into a best-selling rock group in the 1970s and 1980s.

I phoned your girlfriend. I worried she would find my words too personal, impertinent.

30 She did what I knew she'd do. She took out a snapshot. I braced myself.

There was still the chance that I would recognize you as someone I'd known. But I didn't know you, was just glad to see how thick and dark your hair had been, you leaning against the counter in your plaid shirt, tall man with big mustache and cheeks whipped red and warm by the wind.

Your girlfriend completed the picture, helped me take my leave.

Last night I talked with a friend of mine. While I'd been away working, she had helped prepare a man for burial. She'd never done it before either. She found it moving, although she had not known the man in life. The same nurse said to her, I like the way you people do this. This is so much better than the other way.

Her brother said to her, I hear you've been laying out stiffs in your spare time.

Cultural Critique

Anthony Burgess

IS AMERICA FALLING APART?

I am back in Bracciano, a castellated town about 13 miles north of Rome, after a year in New Jersey. I find the Italian Government still unstable, gasoline more expensive than anywhere in the world, butchers and bank clerks and tobacconists (which also means saltsellers) ready to go on strike at the drop of a *cappello*,[1] neo-Fascists at their dirty work, the hammer and sickle painted on the rumps of public statues, a thousand-lire note (officially worth about $1.63) shrunk to the slightness of a dollar bill.

Nevertheless, it's delightful to be back. People are underpaid but they go through an act of liking their work, the open markets are luscious with esculent color, the community is more important than the state, the human condition is humorously accepted. The *tramontana*[2] blows viciously today, and there's no central heating to turn on, but it will be pleasant when the wind drops. The two television channels are inadequate, but next Wednesday's rerun of an old Western, with Gary Cooper coming into a saloon saying "*Ciao, ragazzi*,"[3] is something to look forward to. Manifold consumption isn't important here. The quality of life has nothing to do with the quantity of brand names. What matters is talk, family, cheap wine in the open air, the wresting of minimal sweetness out of the long-known bitterness of living. I was spoiled in New Jersey. The Italian for *spoiled* is *viziato*, cognate with *vitiated*, which has to do with vice.

Spoiled? Well, yes. I never had to shiver by a fire that wouldn't draw, or go without canned kraut juice or wild rice. America made me develop new appetites in order to make proper use of the supermarket.

From *The New York Times* (Nov. 7, 1971).

1. Hat.
2. North wind.
3. "Howdy, boys."

A character in Evelyn Waugh's *Put Out More Flags* said that the difference between prewar and postwar life was that, prewar, if one thing went wrong the day was ruined; postwar, if one thing went right the day would be made. America is a prewar country, psychologically unprepared for one thing to go wrong. Now everything seems to be going wrong. Hence the neurosis, despair, the Kafka feeling that the whole marvelous fabric of American life is coming apart at the seams. Italy is used to everything going wrong. This is what the human condition is about.

Let me stay for a while on this subject of consumption. American individualism, on the face of it an admirable philosophy, wishes to manifest itself in independence of the community. You don't share things in common; you have your own things. A family's strength is signalized by its possessions. Herein lies a paradox. For the desire for possessions must eventually mean dependence on possessions. Freedom is slavery. Once let the acquisitive instinct burgeon (enough flour for the winter, not just for the week), and there are ruggedly individual forces only too ready to make it come to full and monstrous blossom. New appetites are invented; what to the European are bizarre luxuries become, to the American, plain necessities.

5 During my year's stay in New Jersey I let my appetites flower into full Americanism except for one thing. I did not possess an automobile. This self-elected deprivation was a way into the nastier side of the consumer society. Where private ownership prevails, public amenities decay or are prevented from coming into being. The wretched rundown rail services of America are something I try, vainly, to forget. The nightmare of filth, outside and in, that enfolds the trip from Springfield, Mass., to Grand Central Station would not be accepted in backward Europe. But far worse is the nightmare of travel in and around Los Angeles, where public transport does not exist and people are literally choking to death in their exhaust fumes. This is part of the price of the metaphysic of individual ownership.

But if the car owner can ignore the lack of public transport, he can hardly ignore the decay of services in general. His car needs mechanics, and mechanics grow more expensive and less efficient. The gadgets in the home are cheaper to replace than repair. The more efficiently self-contained the home, primary fortress of independence, seems to be, the more dependent it is on the great impersonal corporations, as well as a diminishing army of servitors. Skills at the lowest level have to be wooed slavishly and exorbitantly rewarded. Plumbers will not come. Nor, at the higher level, will doctors. And doctors and dentists, in a nation committed to maiming itself with sugar and cholesterol, know their scarcity value and behave accordingly.

Americans are at last realizing that the acquisition of goods is not the whole of life. Consumption, on one level, is turning insipid, especially as the quality of the artifacts themselves seems to be deteriorating. Planned obsolescence is not conducive to pride in workmanship. On another level, consumption is turning sour. There is a growing guilt about the masses of discarded junk—rusting automobiles and refrigerators and washing machines and dehumidifiers—that it is uneconomical to recycle. Indestructible plastic hasn't even the grace to undergo chemical change. America, the world's biggest consumer, is the world's biggest polluter. Awareness of this is a kind of redemptive grace, but it doesn't appreciably lead to repentance and a revolution in consumer habits. Citizens of Los Angeles are horrified by that daily pall of golden smog, but they don't noticeably clamor for a decrease in the number of owner-vehicles. There is no worse neurosis than that which derives from a consciousness of guilt and an inability to reform.

America is anachronistic in so many ways, and not least in its clinging to a belief—now known to be unviable—in the capacity of the individual citizen to do everything for himself. Americans are admirable in their distrust of the corporate state—they have fought both Fascism and Communism—but they forget that there is a use for everything, even the loathesome bureaucratic machine. America needs a measure of socialization, as Britain needed it. Things—especially those we need most—don't always pay their way, and it is here that the state must enter, dismissing the profit element. Part of the present American neurosis, again, springs from awareness of this but inability to do anything about practical implementation. Perhaps only a country full of bombed cities feels capable of this kind of social revolution.

It would be supererogatory for me to list those areas in which thoughtful Americans feel that collapse is coming. It is enough for me to concentrate on what, during my New Jersey stay, impinged on my own life. Education, for instance, since I have a 6-year-old son to be brought up. America has always despised its teachers and, as a consequence, it has been granted the teachers it deserves. The quality of first-grade education that my son received, in a New Jersey town noted for the excellence of its public schools, could not, I suppose, be faulted on the level of dogged conscientiousness. The principal had read all the right pedagogic books, and was ready to quote these in the footnotes to his circular exhortations to parents. The teachers worked rigidly from the approved rigidly programed primers, ensuring that school textbook publication remains the big business it is.

10 But there seemed to be no spark; no daring, no madness, no readiness to engage the individual child's mind as anything other than raw material for statistical reductions. The fear of being unorthodox is

rooted in the American teacher's soul: you can be fired for treading the path of experimental enterprise. In England, teachers cannot be fired, except for raping girl students and getting boy students drunk. In consequence, there is the kind of security that breeds eccentric genius, the capacity for firing mad enthusiasms.

I know that American technical genius, and most of all the moon landings, seems to give the lie to too summary a condemnation of the educational system, but there is more to education than the segmental equipping of the mind. There is that transmission of the value of the past as a force still miraculously fertile and moving—mostly absent from American education at all levels.

Of course, America was built on a rejection of the past. Even the basic Christianity which was brought to the continent in 1620 was of a novel and bizarre kind that would have nothing to do with the great rank river of belief that produced Dante and Michelangelo. America as a nation has never been able to settle to a common belief more sophisticated than the dangerous naiveté of the Declaration of Independence. "Life, liberty and the pursuit of happiness," indeed. And now America, filling in the vacuum left by the liquefied British Empire, has the task of telling the rest of the world that there's something better than Communism. The something better can only be money-making and consumption for its own sake. In the name of this ghastly creed the jungles must be defoliated.[4]

No wonder the guilt of the thoughtful Americans I met in Princeton and New York and, indeed, all over the Union tended to express itself as an extravagant masochism, a desire for flagellation. Americans want to take on all the blame they can find, gluttons for punishment. "What do Europeans really think of us?" is a common question at parties. The expected answer is: "They think you're a load of decadent, gross-lipped, potbellied, callous, overbearing neoimperialists." Then the head can be bowed and the chest smitten: "*Nostra culpa, nostra maxima culpa. . . .*"[5] But the fact is that such an answer, however much desired, would not be an honest one. Europeans think more highly of Americans now than they ever did. Let me try to explain why.

When Europe, after millennia of war, rapine, slavery, famine, intolerance, had sunk to the level of a sewer, America became the golden dream, the Eden where innocence could be recovered. Original sin was the monopoly of that dirty continent over there; in America man

4. That is, in order to deny the enemy protective cover—a part of American strategy during the Vietnam War.

5. "Through our fault, through our most grievous fault," a modification of *Mea culpa, mea maxima culpa* ("Through my fault . . ."), part of the act of confession in the Roman Catholic church.

could glow in an aura of natural goodness, driven along his shining path by divine reason. The Declaration of Independence itself is a monument to reason. Progress was possible, and the wrongs committed against the Indians, the wildlife, the land itself, could be explained away in terms of the rational control of environment necessary for the building of a New Jerusalem.[6] Right and wrong made up the moral dichotomy; evil—that great eternal inextirpable entity—had no place in America.

At last, with the Vietnam war and especially the Mylai horror,[7] 15
Americans are beginning to realize that they are subject to original sin as much as Europeans are. Some things—the massive crime figures, for instance—can now be explained only in terms of absolute evil. Europe, which has long known about evil and learned to live with it (*live* is *evil* spelled backwards), is now grimly pleased to find that America is becoming like Europe. America is no longer Europe's daughter nor her rich stepmother: she is Europe's sister. The agony that America is undergoing is not to be associated with breakdown so much as with the parturition of self-knowledge.

It has been assumed by many that the youth of America has been in the vanguard of the discovery of both the disease and the cure. The various copping-out movements, however, from the Beats on, have committed the gross error of assuming that original sin rested with their elders, their rulers, and that they themselves could manifest their essential innocence by building little neo-Edens. The drug culture could confirm that the paradisal vision was available to all who sought it. But instant ecstasy has to be purchased, like any other commodity, and, in economic terms, that passive life of pure being involves parasitism. Practically all of the crime I encountered in New York—directly or through report—was a preying of the opium-eaters on the working community. There has to be a snake in paradise. You can't escape the heritage of human evil by building communes, usually on an agronomic ignorance that, intended to be a rejection of inherited knowledge, that suspect property of the elders, does violence to life. The American young are well-meaning but misguided, and must not themselves be taken as guides.

The guides, as always, lie among the writers and artists. And Americans ought to note that, however things may seem to be falling apart, arts and the humane scholarship are flourishing here, as they are not, for instance, in England. I'm not suggesting that Bellow, Mailer, Roth

6. The holy city described by John in Revelation xxi, here a figurative expression for a perfected society.
7. A massacre by American troops of over a hundred Vietnamese civilians in the village of My Lai.

and the rest have the task of finding a solution to the American mess, but they can at least clarify its nature and show how it relates to the human condition in general. Literature, that most directly human of the arts, often reacts magnificently to an ambience of unease or apparent breakdown. The Elizabethans,[8] to whose era we look back as to an irrecoverable Golden Age, were far more conscious than modern Americans of the chaos and corruption and incompetence of the state. Shakespeare's period was one of poverty, unemployment, ghastly inflation, violence in the streets. Twenty-six years after his death there was a bloody civil war, followed by a dictatorship of religious fanatics, followed by a calm respite in which the seeds of a revolution were sown. England survived. America will survive.

I'm not suggesting that Americans sit back and wait for a transient period of mistrust and despair to resolve itself, like a disease, through the unconscious healing forces which lie deep in organic nature. Man, as Thornton Wilder showed in *The Skin of Our Teeth*,[9] always comes through—though sometimes only just. Americans living here and now have a right to an improvement in the quality of their lives, and they themselves, not the remote governors, must do something about it. It is not right that men and women should fear to go on the streets at night, and that they should sometimes fear the police as much as the criminals, both of whom sometimes look like mirror images of each other. I have had too much evidence, in my year in New Jersey, of the police behaving like the "Fascist pigs" of the revolutionary press. There are too many guns about, and the disarming of the police should be a natural aspect of the disarming of the entire citizenry.

American politics, at both the state and the Federal levels, is too much concerned with the protection of large fortunes, America being the only example in history of a genuine timocracy. The wealth qualification for the aspiring politician is taken for granted; a governmental system dedicated to the promotion of personal wealth in a few selected areas will never act for the public good. The time has come, nevertheless, for citizens to demand, from their government, a measure of socialization—the provision of amenities for the many, of which adequate state pensions and sickness benefits, as well as nationalized transport, should be priorities.

20 As for those remoter solutions to the American nightmare—only an aspect, after all, of the human nightmare—an Englishman must be diffident about suggesting that America made her biggest mistake in becoming America—meaning a revolutionary republic based on a ro-

8. The British during the reign of Elizabeth I, 1558–1603.
9. Pulitzer Prize–winning comedy, written in 1942 by Thornton Wilder (1897–1975).

mantic view of human nature. To reject a limited monarchy in favor of an absolute one (which is, after all, what the American Presidency is) argues a trust in the disinterestedness of an elected ruler which is, of course, no more than a reflection of belief in the innate goodness of man—so long as he happens to be American man. The American Constitution is out of date. Republics tend to corruption. Canada and Australia have their own problems, but they are happier countries than America.

This *Angst*[1] about America coming apart at the seams, which apparently is shared by nearly 50 per cent of the entire American population, is something to rejoice about. A sense of sin is always admirable, though it must not be allowed to become neurotic. If electric systems break down and gadgets disintegrate, it doesn't matter much. There is always wine to be drunk by candlelight, uniced. If America's position as a world power collapses, and the Union dissolves into independent states, there is still the life of the family or the individual to be lived. England has survived her own dissolution as an imperial power, and Englishmen seem to be happy enough. But I ask the reader to note that I, an Englishman, no longer live in England, and I can't spend more than six months at a stretch in Italy—or any other European country, for that matter. I come to America as to a country more stimulating than depressing. The future of mankind is being worked out there on a scale typically American—vast, dramatic, almost apocalyptical. I brave the brutality and the guilt in order to be in on the scene. I shall be back.

1. Anxiety.

QUESTIONS

1. *This essay appeared in 1971. What might Burgess leave out, add, or modify if he were to write it today?*
2. *Burgess says that in his son's school there was "no readiness to engage the individual child's mind as anything other than raw material for statistical reductions" (paragraph 10). Precisely what is he referring to? Does your own experience support or counter Burgess's claim?*
3. *Visitors like Burgess can sometimes see things natives miss; they can also overlook the obvious. Write a response to Burgess, pointing out where he is on target and what he has missed.*

Elizabeth Wurtzel

PARENTAL GUIDANCE SUGGESTED

It is the spring of my junior year of college, I am lying in a near-catatonic state in a mental ward, I have just been given an industrial-strength antipsychotic—the kind they give to schizophrenics—because I have not been able to stop crying and shaking and wailing for hours, and the doctor is afraid that I might, quite literally, choke on my own tears. The pill they've given me—some variation on Thorazine—has knocked me into a silent state of submission that would be perfectly blissful if only the therapist on duty would stop trying to get me to talk to her. She wants to know what's wrong; she wants to know what I am experiencing that is so potent and profound that it takes a brain-draining drug to make it go away.

I don't know, is all I keep saying. I don't know, I don't know, I don't know.

What have you lost? she asks, trying a new approach.

I know I better come up with something. I better think of an answer before they start trying out other things on me—different drugs, electroconvulsive therapy (known in the vernacular as *shock*), whatever.

5 I think it's got something to do with summer camp, I say.

She looks at me blankly.

It's like this, I begin: I'm from New York City, my mom is Jewish and middle class, my dad is solidly white trash, they divorced when I was two, my mom was always unemployed or marginally employed and my dad was always uninvolved or marginally involved in raising me, there was never enough money for anything, we lived in state-subsidized housing, I went to private schools on scholarships, and my childhood, as I recall it, is one big flurry of application forms for financial aid or for special rates on this thing or that thing that my mother thought I should really have because she didn't want me to be deprived of anything.

My mom really did her best.

But then, as soon as I was old enough, my mother decided that I had to go to sleep-away camp for the summers. She was overextended as a parent throughout the school year, my dad wasn't willing to take care of me, and there was nothing for a girl like me to do in New York City during the long hot summer except get into trouble with the neighborhood kids. So it was off to camp. That was that.

From *Next: Young American Writers on the New Generation* (1994).

I went to camp for five years in a row—a different one each year, a 10
different setup in a different rural town in the Poconos or the Catskills or the Berkshires or wherever I could enroll at a discount rate. And the funny thing is, I explain to the therapist, after my mother had sent me off to these places that I thought were so lonesome and horrible, instead of hating her for it, I just spent all summer missing her. All my waking and sleeping energy was devoted to missing this rather minimal and unstable home I came from. Starting on June 28, or whatever day it was that I got to camp, and never even achieving a brief reprieve until I'd come home on August 24 or so, I would devote myself fully to the task of getting back home. I'd spend hours each day writing my mom letters, calling her on the phone, just making sure that she'd know exactly where and when to pick me up at the bus when it was time to return. I would run to the camp's administrative offices to make sure that notices about the location of the return trip would be sent to my mother so that she'd know where to find me. I'd extract promises that she'd arrive there one or two hours early. I'd even call my dad and get him to promise to be there at least a half hour before the estimated time of arrival. I'd talk to the head counselor and express my concern that I might be put on a bus to New Jersey or Long Island and somehow end up in the wrong place and never find my way back home. I would ask other New Yorkers in my bunk if I could go home with them if my mother failed to materialize at the bus stop. I would call grandparents, aunts, uncles, and baby-sitters—always collect—to find out where they would be on August 24, just in case I had to go to one of their homes, in case my parents didn't show up to get me.

Instead of discovering the virtues of tennis and volleyball, or of braiding lanyards and weaving potholders, I would devote a full eight weeks of my summer to planning for a two-hour trip back home.

The therapist looks at me kind of strangely, as if this doesn't quite make sense, that summer camp was so long ago and I'll never have to go back again, so why is this still bothering me? There's no way, I realize, to ever make her understand that homesickness is just a state of mind for me, that I'm always missing someone or some place or something, I'm always trying to get back to some imaginary somewhere. My life has been one long longing.

And I'm sick of it. And I can't move. And I've a feeling, I tell the therapist, that I might as well lie here congealed to this hospital bed forever because there's no place in the world that's at all like a home to me and I'd rather be dead than spend another minute in this life as an emotional nomad.

A few days later, having lost all hope of anything else working, a psychiatrist gives me a prescription for a new, virtually untried antidepressant that she thinks might help. It's called fluoxetine hydrochloride, brand name Prozac. A few weeks later, I am better, much better, as I have been ever since.

But there's just one small problem. They can give me all sorts of drugs to stabilize my moods, to elevate the downs, to flatten the ups, to make me function in this world like any other normal, productive person who works, pays rent, has affairs, waters her own plants. They can make it all feel pretty much all right most of the time. But they can't do anything for the homesickness. There's no pill they can come up with that can cure the longing I feel to be in a place that feels like home. There's no cure for the strange estrangedness, and if there were, I am sure my body would resist it.

Since I first began taking Prozac, the pill has become one of the most commonly prescribed drugs in the country, with 650,000 orders filled each month. Back in 1990, the story of this wonder drug made the cover of periodicals like *Newsweek* and *New York*, while *Rolling Stone* deemed Prozac the "hot yuppie upper," and all the major network news-magazines and daytime talk shows began to do their Prozac-saved-my-life segments. While a backlash of reports linked Prozac with incidents of suicide and murder, the many people who it relieved from symptoms of depression had nothing but praise: Cheryl Wheeler, a Nashville folkie, even wrote a song called "Is It Peace or Is It Prozac?"

Yet this is not just about Prozac: it's about the mainstreaming of mental illness—it's about the way a state of mind that was once considered tragic has become completely commonplace. Talk of depression as the mental disease of our times has been very much in the air in the last few years, to the point where it has almost become a political issue: As Hillary Rodham Clinton campaigned on behalf of what she deemed "The Politics of Meaning," it was hard not to notice that her references to a "sleeping sickness of the soul," to "alienation and despair and hopelessness," to a "crisis of meaning," and to a "spiritual vacuum" seemed to imply that the country's problems have less to do with taxes and unemployment than with the simple fact that we were in one big collective bad mood. It is almost as if, perhaps, the next time half a million people gather for a protest march in Washington it will not be for abortion rights or gay liberation but because we're all just so bummed out.

Of course, one of the striking elements of this depression outbreak is the extent to which it has gotten such a strong hold on so many young people. The Valium addicts of the fifties and sixties, the housewives reaching for their mother's little helpers, the strung-out junkies and crackheads who litter the gutters of the Bowery or the streets of Harlem or the Skid Row of any town—all these people were stereotyped as wasted, dissipated, or middle-aged. What is fascinating about depression this time around is the extent to which it is affecting those who have so much to look forward to and to hope for, who are, as one might say of a bright young thing about to make her debut into the world, so full of promise.

Recently, I was reading a magazine on an airplane, and I chanced upon an article titled "The Plot Sickens," in which a college writing instructor sees the gruesome, pessimistic nature of the work that her students produce as an indication of a wave of youth malaise like none she'd ever noticed before in twenty-one years of teaching. "To read their work, you'd think they were a generation that was starved, beaten, raped, arrested, addicted, and war-torn. Inexplicable intrusions of random tragedy break up the otherwise good life of the characters," the author writes. "The figures in their fictions are victims of hideous violence by accident; they commit crimes, but only for the hell of it; they hate, not understanding why they hate; they are loved or abused or depressed, and don't know why. . . . Randomness rules."

Perhaps for the author of that article, the nature of her students' 20
work is surprising. For me, and for everyone I know my age, it just seems normal, peculiarly ordinary. I mean: Randomness *does* rule.

A few years ago, I wrote an article about my bout with depression for *Mademoiselle*. I was rather alarmed when the piece generated more mail than anything else they'd run in several years and was somewhat heartened but also terribly saddened to see that I had touched such a raw, exposed nerve in so many young women. Shortly after the article ran, I was on the phone with my editor, and she suddenly asked, "I wonder what Prozac would do for regular people—I mean, not clinical cases like you, but just the rest of us who are normally depressed."

Once again, that word *normally* seemed to be creeping up in a place where it oughtn't be. Since when is it *normal* to be depressed? What kind of world do we live in that someone can refer to depression as a *normal* state?

Christopher Ricks[1] once wrote an essay about the difference between "disenchanted" and "unenchanted," the former describing someone sprung by reality from an enchanted state, while the latter is a person who was never enchanted to begin with. And that's me. And that's what society's come to: the spate of depression that I have come into contact with is not among people who've been disappointed by life—it's among those who have given up on it before they've even given it a real go. So many of us who are in our twenties now were born into homes that had already fallen apart, fathers on the lam, mothers

1. British literary critic (b. 1933), now teaching at Boston University.

on the floor, no sense of security and safety, no sense of home at all. So we muddle through our adult lives wandering around, kind of dazed, kind of wasted, looking like lost children who are still waiting to be claimed at the security office of the shopping mall or amusement park or supermarket where our parents last lost track of us. When Sonic Youth titled its 1989 album *Daydream Nation,* I think they must have been referring to this youth cadre of the walking wounded, of people who spend so many of their waking hours lost in thought, distraction, and abstraction, trying to get a grip on the hopes—on the dreams—that they dare not have in their conscious minds. Sleep is no relief because they are always sort of asleep. All these young people are homesick and in a reverie for an enchanted place they've never known.

While I often get the sense that many older people look back on their childhoods with a sense of sorrow that they had to grow up and say good-bye to all that, most of my friends could not wait to come of age and get out of the house because the house was not a home. The lucky among us had two active, participating parents and had to spend a lot of time schlepping between two households, always lugging an overnight bag or wondering whether the black-and-white saddle shoes and box of Lego were at Mommy's or Daddy's. In my case, only my mother really cared for me, and she had a really hard time just making ends meet; she seemed forever on the verge of a nervous breakdown, so I spent much of my time just trying to keep her calm. My dad used Valium and pretty much managed to sleep through my whole childhood (when I was nine, we went to see *The Last Waltz,* he fell asleep, and we ended up sitting through the movie three times because I couldn't get him to wake up); our Saturday-afternoon visits mostly involved his putting me in front of the television set to watch "Star Trek" reruns or college basketball while he dozed off.

25 But these are only the incidental, aftershock effects that divorce has on children—far more terrifying is the violent rupture it creates in any young person's life because any sense of home is ripped asunder, any sense of a safe haven in a cruel world is taken away. We did not learn about bitterness and hatred on the streets (the supposed source of all terror)—we learned from watching our parents try to kill each other. We didn't learn to break promises and (marriage) vows from big bad bullies at school—we learned from watching our parents deny every word they once said to each other. And we learned from them that it is not just acceptable, but virtually normal, to realize that love does not last forever. There are certainly plenty of kids whose parents will stay together until death do they part and who haven't experienced the symptoms I've just described. But even they are affected by the divorce revolution because it colors their worldview, too. They know that their own marriages might end in divorce. They know that the

family unit is not sacred, and this adds a degree of uncertainty to their own plans.

But I don't want to get too down on divorce. It has become all too facile a neoconservative impulse to blame divorce or the decline of so-called family values for all the ills of our society. Even more troubling is how easy it has become for people in my age group to blame the lack of a structured family life when they were growing up for all their problems as adults. If I allowed myself to express the full extent of the bitterness I feel toward my parents for not, shall we say, having their shit together while they were raising me, I fear that I might start to sound like an ally of Dan Quayle. And I don't want to do that. The main reason: it is precisely those family values that Dan Quayle referred to in his famous anti–Murphy Brown speech that drove my parents, and so many of my friends' parents, into marriages they were not ready for and bearing children they were not capable of properly nurturing.

It was the family imperative, the sense that life happens in a simple series of steps (something like: adolescence-college-marriage-kids) that all sane and decent people must adhere to that got our parents in trouble to begin with. Remember, the progenitors of people in my age group are not, for the most part, those freewheeling, wild baby boomers who took it upon themselves to transform our society in the late sixties and early seventies. Our parents were, on the whole, a little too old for that, they are people who were done with college and had moved on to the work world by the early sixties—several years before the campus uprisings, the antiwar activities, and the emerging sex-drugs-rock-and-roll culture had become a pervasive force. By the time the radical sixties hit our home bases, we were already born, and our parents found themselves stuck between an entrenched belief that children needed to be raised in a traditional household and a new sense that anything was possible, that the alternative lifestyle was out there for the asking. A little too old to take full advantage of the cultural revolution of the sixties, our parents just got all the fallout. Instead of waiting later to get married, our parents got divorced; instead of becoming feminists, our mothers were left as displaced homemakers. A lot of already existent unhappy situations were dissolved by people who were not quite young or free (read: childless) enough to start again. And their discontent—their stuck-ness—was played out on their children.

My parents are a perfect case in point. Lord knows whatever possessed them to get married in the first place. It probably had something to do with the fact that my mom was raised with many of her first cousins, and all of them were getting married, so it seemed like the thing to do. And from her point of view, back in the early sixties, marriage was the only way she could get out of her parents' house.

She'd gone to Cornell, wanting to be an architect, but her mother told her all she could be was an architect's *secretary*, so she majored in art history with that goal in mind. She'd spent a junior year abroad at the Sorbonne and did all the studiedly adventurous things a nice Jewish girl from Long Island can do in Paris—rented a moped, wore a black cape, dated some nobleman type—but once she got out of college, she moved back home and was expected to stay there until she moved into her husband's house. (Certainly there were many bolder women who defied this expectation, who took efficiencies and railroad flats with girlfriends in safe neighborhoods in the city, who worked and dated and went to theater openings and lectures—but my mom was not one of them.) She took a job in the executive training program at Macy's, and one day while she was riding the escalator up from the main floor to the mezzanine, she passed my father, who was riding down. They got married less than a year later, even though he hadn't gone to college, had no ambition, and was considered a step down for a girl like my mom.

My parents did weird things after they got married. My dad got a job at IBM and they moved to Poughkeepsie, New York, where my mom went nuts with boredom and bought herself a pet monkey named Percy. Eventually she got pregnant with me, decided a baby was better than a monkey, and she moved down to New York City because she could not bear another day in a town that was half Vassar College, half IBM. My father followed, I was born, they fought, they were miserable, he refused to get a college degree, they fought some more, and then one day I wouldn't stop crying. My mom called my dad at work to say that if he didn't come home immediately and figure out how to get me to calm down, she was going to defenestrate me. Whatever my father did when he got to the apartment must have worked, because I'm still alive today, but I think that moment marked the end of their marriage.

This was a marriage that could have peacefully ceased to be one fine day with an understanding that it was just a mistake, they were just two foolish kids playing house. Problem was, they had a child, and for many years after they split up, I became the battlefield on which they fought through all their ideological differences. This was New York City in the late sixties, Harlem had burned down, my mom was petrified about being a single mother with a deadbeat ex-husband, so she sent me to the synagogue nursery school, thinking this would provide me with some sense of community and stability. My dad would turn up to see me about once a week, and he would talk to me about atheism and insist I eat lobster and ham and other nonkosher foods that I was taught in school were not allowed. For years, my mom was tugging toward trying to give me a solid, middle-class, traditional upbringing, while my father would tell me that I should just be an artist or a poet or live off the land, or some such thing. She was desperate to keep at least a toehold in the bourgeoisie, and he was working overtime (or actually, not *gainfully* working at all) to stay the hell out of it. Back and forth this went for years, until it felt clear that all three of us were caught mostly in the confusing cross fire of changing times, and what little foundation my parents could possibly give me was shattered and scattered by conflict.

When I was ten or eleven, I really cracked up, started hiding in the locker room at school, crying for hours, or walking around the corridors saying, *Everything is plastic, we're all gonna die anyway, so why does anything matter?* I'd read this phrase in a picture of some graffiti in a magazine article about punk rock, which I decided was definitely a great invention. When I stopped talking, stopped eating, stopped going to school, and started spending my time cutting my legs up with razor blades while listening to dumb rock music like Foreigner on a little Panasonic tape recorder, my parents agreed I needed psychiatric help. To make a very long and complicated story short, my mom found a therapist for me, my dad didn't like him and kept trying to sneak me off to others, I never got terribly effective treatment, my father refused to file an insurance claim for the psychiatrist I was seeing, and the whole scenario concluded with me as messed up as ever, but with all the adults involved suing one another. My mom sued my dad for unpaid alimony and child support, my psychiatrist sued my dad for unpaid bills, and after years of lawyers everywhere, my father finally fled to Florida when I was fourteen years old and did not turn up in my life again until my freshman year at Harvard.

By the time I actually did grow up, I was so grateful to be out of my parents' firing range and not stuck in between them or torn apart like an overstretched rubber band they each tugged at for years that my depression actually began to lift. For me, growing up was not about coming face-to-face with the cruelties of the world; it was about relief.

Obviously, divorce is inevitable and at this point there is joint custody and divorce counseling and all sorts of other things to make the process less painful for the children and for the adults. Which might mean that things are better now, although I think things must be so much worse if divorce is being normalized—because let's face it, all these strangely pieced together families of half siblings and stepparents and all that are not natural. At one time, a kid got two parents who did their best to get it right, but now, taking stepparents into account, he can have twice as many guardians—along with nannies, therapists, tutors, and whatnot—but somehow, all these people put together can't seem to raise a child decently. It's like having ninety-two channels of cable and nothing to watch.

* * *

Despite the exhaustion, I still think that adulthood has been a lot better for me than growing up was. And I believe the task of a lifetime for my generation will be to reinvent the family unit in a way that works and endures. Perhaps critics will say, *Those twentysomethings, all they ever worry about is their private lives,* but I for one believe our private lives deserve some thoughtful attention. If anyone had bothered to give our development as human beings some constructive thought while we were still young enough to receive the benefits passively, we wouldn't have to think about our personal lives so damn much now.

35 I have heard it said that in our modern world, twelve-step fellowships have become a substitute for family, that the rooms of alcoholics and junkies offering each other support in church basements and community centers is the closest thing anyone has to a familial setup. I have also heard that the neo-Nazi kids in modern Germany, the inner-city youth who join gangs in Los Angeles like the Bloods and the Crips, the homeboys hanging out on the corner—all these movements and loosely bound organizations are about young people trying to find a place in this world to call home, trying to find people in this world to call family. The interesting thing about the attraction of something like AA is that an organization like that involves such a large group of people—not just a few random friends but a big collection of helpful people. And I think we all need some version of that. In the worst moments of my depression, I used to wish I were a drug addict—I used to think it would be so nice if it were simply a matter of getting heroin or alcohol out of my life—because then I could walk into a meeting of fellow sufferers and feel that I'd arrived home at last.

But I'd hate to think that I'd have to become a junkie in order to find my place in this world. And I don't think that is the case. In fact, I think one of the ways many of us twentysomethings have come to deal with our rootlessness has been by turning friends into family. For those of us without addictions, those of us who are just run-of-the-mill parasites on society, our alliances are all that's left. For many of my friends, the world feels like one big orphanage—we're so far from our families, or without families at all, or without families that are able to serve a familial role, and here we get thrown into this lot of life together. Of course, some pundits make fun of us for turning friends and ex-lovers into pseudo-family members, but I believe this is an arrangement that actually works. (Besides, if anyone has a better idea, I'm glad to listen. Joining the Moonies, hooking up with the Branch Davidians, or running off to Esalen are *not* acceptable substitutes.)

And obviously, the theme of friends-as-family seems to resonate in the media a great deal: whether it's in the Banana Republic advertising campaign that pictures several versions of "Your Chosen Family," or it's in the United Colors of Benetton billboards and print ads that try to depict an international loving brotherhood of all races and nations.

It's in MTV's attempt at *cinema vérité*[2] with "The Real World," a series that shows a group of young people living in a loft together and puttering their way through the tribulations of everyday; and it's in the way the typical television drama or sitcom of today is likely to revolve around the odd connections and acquaintances made by single people or one-parent families in their apartment complex or subdivision, not on the freestanding biological family that was the center of almost every show thirty years ago. It's in all the press that surrounded the Clinton-Gore bus campaign that attempted to portray the two candidate couples—Al and Tipper and Bill and Hillary—as a little fun-loving family on a perpetual double date rolling its way across the country; and it was in Clinton's beckoning speech at the Democratic convention, in which he invited everyone out there to "join our family." All these examples just amount to a manipulation of Americans' simplest desire to imagine the possibility of home, and yet even as I know my emotions are being toyed with, I still appreciate all these public attempts to define family as something that's got nothing to do with blood.

All my friends, inadequately parented as we seem to have been, spend as much time looking after one another as we do just hanging out and having fun. * * * Insofar as I'm now able to get work done, to make attempts at having relationships, to live a life that is fruitful and productive at all, I attribute it completely to the friends that I have turned into my family.

And if anyone finds that pathetic, I don't care. I don't want to spend another minute of my life supine and suffering in a hospital bed, praying to God for any form of relief he can give to a mind—not even a body—in terrible pain. I don't ever want to endure another morning of the orderlies coming in at 7:00 to take a blood sample and take my temperature because that is the routine in a health-care facility—even though the only thing that's wrong with me is in my head. I don't want to roam the streets at all hours of the day and night, feeling crazy from the heat in the middle of January, running like hell from the voices in my head. I don't want to live life as a sicko. And the friendships I have developed as an adult are probably the only thing standing between me and Bellevue.[3] More to the point, they are the only thing standing between me and suicide. The hole in my heart that was left by a grievous lack of family connections has in some ways been patched over, if not altogether filled, by a sense of family I've found in the last few years.

2. Literally, cinema of fact or cinema of truth; a style of filmmaking that stresses unbiased realism.

3. Hospital in New York City with a large psychiatric ward.

40 But I must say, I'm sure my friends and I often seem like these sad lost people who are scared to grow up. I sometimes worry that the clinginess of our relationships is kind of a sorry thing, that we often seem to be holding on tight because of the depth of our desperation and need—and perhaps this just isn't healthy. We often spend time together in large groups of people, and I keep thinking we all really should be out on dates in couples, but it doesn't seem as though any of us is quite ready even to think about getting into deeply committed relationships. I have plenty of friends who have been going out with the same person for years, but none of them is showing signs of heading to the altar. We're all just much too frightened.

And it is this nervousness, this lack of trust, that makes this generation seem ineffectual to many older people on so many fronts.

But we are trying our best to take care of one another. And it is my hope that when we finally do have kids of our own, the sense of community we have created for ourselves will be passed along to them. I hope my children know that their father and I are not the only adults in their lives who can be counted on—I hope they feel that Christine, Jason, Mark, Larissa, Tom, Heather, Ronnie, and Sharon are as much a part of their family as they are part of mine. I hope my friends' children will play with my kids, and I hope they all grow up understanding that they too can choose families of their own. I hope they don't ever think that their world and their expectations are limited by two people who just happen to be their parents, and might do some really stupid, silly things along the way.

These days we all sit around, drinking Rolling Rock and smoking pot late into the night as if we were still in our college dormitory rooms, and sometimes we talk about how it will be to have kids someday. And we all say the same thing: we can't wait to bring children into the world and do everything right that our parents did wrong. Of course, I suspect that our parents had the same idea themselves, and look where it got them.

But still, I've got to believe I can do better. I've already brought up myself, so surely I ought to be able to raise someone else.

45 I think.

QUESTIONS

1. *In recounting what happened to her, Wurtzel claims to be telling the story of a whole generation. What for Wurtzel characterizes her generation's problems?*
2. *Point to characteristics of Wurtzel's writing style that reveal her to be someone in her young twenties. Look at tone as well as vocabulary and phrasing.*

3. *Is the portrait Wurtzel paints true to your own experience of people in their twenties?*

Maggie Helwig

HUNGER

Consider that it is now normal for North American women to have eating disorders. Consider that anorexia—deliberate starvation—and bulimia—self-induced vomiting—and obsessive patterns for weight-controlling exercise are now the ordinary thing for young women, and are spreading at a frightening rate to older women, to men, to ethnic groups and social classes that were once "immune." Consider that some surveys suggest that 80 per cent of the women on an average university campus have borderline-to-severe eating disorders; that it is almost impossible to get treatment unless the problem is life-threatening; that, in fact, if it is not life-threatening it is not considered a problem at all. I once sat in a seminar on nutritional aspects of anorexia, and ended up listening to people tell me how to keep my weight down. All this is happening in one of the richest countries in the world, a society devoted to consumption. Amazing as it may seem, we have normalized anorexia and bulimia, even turned them into an industry.

We've also trivialized them: made them into nothing more than an exaggerated conformity with basically acceptable standards of behavior. Everyone wants to be thin and pretty, after all. Some people take it a little too far; you have to get them back on the right track, but it's all a question of knowing just how far is proper.

The consumer society has gone so far we can even buy into hunger.

But that is not what it's about. You do not stuff yourself with food and force yourself to vomit just because of fashion magazines. You do not reduce yourself to the condition of a skeleton in order to be attractive. This is not just a problem of proportion. This is the nightmare of consumerism acted out in women's bodies.

5 This is what we are saying as we starve: it is not all right. It is not all right. It is not all right.

There've always been strange or disordered patterns of eating, associated mainly with religious extremism or psychological problems (which some, not myself, would say were the same thing). But the complex of ideas, fears, angers and actions that make up contemporary anorexia and bulimia seems to be of fairly recent origin. Anorexia

Originally published in *This Magazine* (Feb. 1989).

did not exist as a recognized pattern until the 1960s, and bulimia not until later than that—and at first they were deeply shocking. The idea that privileged young women (the first group to be affected) were voluntarily starving themselves, sometimes to death, or regularly sticking their fingers down their throats to make themselves throw up, shook the culture badly. It was a fad, in a sense, the illness of the month, but it was also a scandal, and a source of something like horror.

Before this, though, before anorexia had a widely recognized name, one of the first women to succumb to it had made her own scandalous stand, and left a body of writing that still has a lot to say about the real meaning of voluntary hunger.

Simone Weil was a brilliant, disturbed, wildly wrong-headed and astonishingly perceptive young French woman who died from the complications of self-starvation in America during World War II, at the age of 34. She never, of course, wrote directly about her refusal to eat—typically for any anorexic, she insisted she ate perfectly adequate amounts. But throughout her philosophical and theological writing (almost all of it fragments and essays collected after her death), she examines and uses the symbolism of hunger, eating and food.

Food occupied, in fact, a rather important and valued position in her philosophy—she once referred to food as "the irrefutable proof of the reality of the universe," and at another time said that the foods served at Easter and Christmas, the turkey and *marron glacés*,[1] were "the true meaning of the feast"; although she could also take the more conventional puritan position that desire for food is a "base motive." She spoke often of eating God (acceptable enough in a Christian context) and of being eaten by God (considerably less so). The great tragedy of our lives, she said, is that we cannot really eat God; and also "it may be that vice, depravity and crime are almost always . . . attempts to eat beauty."

10 But it is her use of the symbolism of hunger that explains her death. "We have to go down into ourselves to the abode of the desire which is not imaginary. Hunger: we imagine kinds of food, but the hunger itself is real: we have to fasten onto the hunger."

Hunger, then, was a search for reality, for the irreducible need that lies beyond all imaginary satisfactions. Weil was deeply perturbed by the "materialism" of her culture; though she probably could not have begun to imagine the number of imaginary and illusory "satisfactions" now available. Simply, she wanted truth. She wanted to reduce herself to the point where she would *know* what needs, and what foods, were real and true.

Similarly, though deeply drawn to the Catholic faith, she refused to

1. Chestnuts in vanilla syrup.

be baptized and to take Communion (to, in fact, eat God). "I cannot help wondering whether in these days when so large a proportion of humanity is sunk in materialism, God does not want there to be some men and women who have given themselves to him and to Christ and who yet remain outside the Church." For the sake of honesty, of truth, she maintained her hunger.

Weil, a mystic and a political activist simultaneously until the end of her short life—she was one of the first French intellectuals to join the Communist party and one of the first to leave, fought in the Spanish civil war and worked in auto factories—could not bear to have life be less than a total spiritual and political statement. And her statement of protest, of dissatisfaction, her statement of hunger, finally destroyed her.

The term anorexia nervosa was coined in the 19th century, but it was not until sometime in the 1960s that significant—and constantly increasing—numbers of well-off young women began dying of starvation, and not until the early 1970s that it became public knowledge.
It is the nature of our times that the explanations proffered were 15
psychological and individualistic; yet, even so, it was understood as being, on some level, an act of protest. And of course symbolically, it could hardly be other—it was, simply, a hunger strike. The most common interpretation, at that point, was that it was a sort of adolescent rebellion against parental control, an attempt, particularly, to escape from an overcontrolling mother. It was a fairly acceptable paradigm for the period, although many mothers were justifiably disturbed; sometimes deeply and unnecessarily hurt. The theory still has some currency, and is not entirely devoid of truth.

But can it be an accident that this happened almost precisely to coincide with the growth of the consumer society, a world based on a level of material consumption that, by the end of the 1960s, had become very nearly uncontrollable? Or with the strange, underground guilt that has made "conspicuous consumption" a matter of consuming vast amounts and *hiding it,* of million-dollar minimalism? With the development of what is possibly the most emotionally depleted society in history, where the only "satisfactions" seem to be the imaginary ones, the material buy-offs?

To be skeletally, horribly thin makes one strong statement. It says, I am hungry. What I have been given is not sufficient, not real, not true, not acceptable. I am starving. To reject food, whether by refusing it or by vomiting it back, says simply, I will not consume. I will not participate. This is not real.

Hunger is the central nightmare image of our society. Of all the icons of horror the last few generations have offered us, we have chosen, above all, pictures of hunger—the emaciated prisoners of Auschwitz and Belsen, Ethiopian children with bloated bellies and stick-figure limbs. We carry in our heads these nightmares of the extreme edge of hunger.

And while we may not admit to guilt about our level of consumption in general, we admit freely to guilt about eating, easily equate food with "sin." We cannot accept hunger of our own, cannot afford to consider it.

It is, traditionally, women who carry our nightmares. It was women who became possessed by the Devil, women who suffered from "hysterical disorders," women who, in all popular culture, are the targets of the "monster." One of the roles women are cast in is that of those who act out the subconscious fears of their society. And it is women above all, in this time, who carry our hunger.

It is the starving women who embody the extremity of hunger that terrifies and fascinates us, and who insist that they are not hungry. It is the women sticking their fingers down their throats who act out the equation of food and sin, who deny hunger and yet embody endless, unfulfilled appetite. It is these women who live through every implication of our consumption and our hunger, our guilt and ambiguity and our awful need for something real to fill us.

We have too much; and it is poison.

* * *

As eating disorders became increasingly widespread, they also became increasingly trivialized, incorporated into a framework already "understood" all too well. Feminist writers had, early on, noted that anorexia had to be linked with the increasing thinness of models and other glamor icons, as part of a larger cultural trend. This is true enough as a starting point, for the symbolic struggle being waged in women's bodies happens on many levels, and is not limited to pathology cases. Unfortunately, this single starting point was seized on by "women's magazines" and popularizing accounts in general. Anorexia was now understandable, almost safe really, it was just fashion gone out of control. Why, these women were *accepting* the culture, they just needed a sense of proportion. What a relief.

Now it could be condoned. Now it could, in fact, become the basis for an industry; could be incorporated neatly into consumer society. According to Jane Fonda the solution to bulimia is to remain equally unhealthily thin by buying the 20-minute workout and becoming an obsessive fitness follower (at least for those who can afford it). The diet clinic industry, the Nutrisystem package, the aerobics boom. An advertising industry that plays equally off desire and guilt, for they now reinforce each other. Thousands upon thousands of starving, tormented women, not "sick" enough to be taken seriously, not really troubled at all.

One does not reduce oneself to the condition of a skeleton in order 25
to be fashionable. One does not binge and vomit daily as an acceptable means of weight control. One does not even approach or imagine or dream of these things if one is not in some sort of trouble. If it were as simple as fashion, surely we would not be so ashamed to speak of these things, we would not feel that either way, whether we eat or do not eat, we are doing something wrong.

I was anorexic for eight years. I nearly died. It was certainly no help to me to be told I was taking fashion too far—I knew perfectly well that had nothing to do with it. It did not help much to be told I was trying to escape from my mother, since I lived away from home and was in only occasional contact with my family; it did not help much to be approached on an individualistic, psychological level. In fact, the first person I was able to go to for help was a charismatic Catholic, who at least understood that I was speaking in symbols of spiritual hunger.

I knew that I had something to say, that things were not all right, that I had to make that concretely, physically obvious. I did not hate or look down on my body—I spoke through it and with it.

Women are taught to take guilt, concern, problems, onto themselves personally; and especially onto their bodies. But we are trying to talk about something that is only partly personal. Until we find new ways of saying it and find the courage to talk to the world about the world, we will speak destruction to ourselves. We must come to know what we are saying—and say it.

QUESTIONS

1. *Psychologists, social workers, or medical doctors would describe eating disorders according to their own professional criteria and in their own style. What particular language, style, and tone does Helwig use?*
2. *Helwig says that anorexia and bulimia are particularly feminine statements about consumption and consumerism. What evidence does she offer for this claim?*
3. *Helwig says that "women's magazines" claimed that anorexia was "understandable, almost safe really, it was just fashion gone out of control," while it was really something deeply symbolic of what is wrong in the culture. Write about something else that people are often told is simply a matter of lack of proportion.*

John McMurtry

KILL 'EM! CRUSH 'EM! EAT 'EM RAW!

A few months ago my neck got a hard crick in it. I couldn't turn my head; to look left or right I'd have to turn my whole body. But I'd had cricks in my neck since I started playing grade-school football and hockey, so I just ignored it. Then I began to notice that when I reached for any sort of large book (which I do pretty often as a philosophy teacher at the University of Guelph) I had trouble lifting it with one hand. I was losing the strength in my left arm, and I had such a steady pain in my back I often had to stretch out on the floor of the room I was in to relieve the pressure.

A few weeks later I mentioned to my brother, an orthopedic surgeon, that I'd lost the power in my arm since my neck began to hurt. Twenty-four hours later I was in a Toronto hospital not sure whether I might end up with a wasted upper limb. Apparently the steady pounding I had received playing college and professional football in the late Fifties and early Sixties had driven my head into my backbone so that the discs had crumpled together at the neck—"acute herniation"—and had cut the nerves to my left arm like a pinched telephone wire (without nerve stimulation, of course, the muscles atrophy, leaving the arm crippled). So I spent my Christmas holidays in the hospital in heavy traction and much of the next three months with my neck in a brace. Today most of the pain has gone, and I've recovered most of the strength in my arm. But from time to time I still have to don the brace, and surgery remains a possibility.

Not much of this will surprise anyone who knows football. It is a sport in which body wreckage is one of the leading conventions. A few days after I went into hospital for that crick in my neck, another brother, an outstanding football player in college, was undergoing spinal surgery in the same hospital two floors above me. In his case it was a lower, more massive herniation, which every now and again buckled him so that he was unable to lift himself off his back for days at a time. By the time he entered the hospital for surgery he had already spent several months in bed. The operation was successful, but, as in all such cases, it will take him a year to recover fully.

These aren't isolated experiences. Just about anybody who has ever played football for any length of time, in high school, college or one of the professional leagues, has suffered for it later physically.

Originally appeared in *Macleans* (Oct. 1971).

Indeed, it is arguable that body shattering is the very *point* of foot- 5
ball, as killing and maiming are of war. (In the United States, for example, the game results in 15 to 20 deaths a year and about 50,000 major operations on knees alone.) To grasp some of the more conspicuous similarities between football and war, it is instructive to listen to the imperatives most frequently issued to the players by their coaches, teammates and fans. "Hurt 'em!" "Level 'em!" "Kill 'em!" "Take 'em apart!" Or watch for the plays that are most enthusiastically applauded by the fans. Where someone is "smeared," "knocked silly," "creamed," "nailed," "broken in two," or even "crucified." (One of my coaches when I played corner linebacker with the Calgary Stampeders in 1961 elaborated, often very inventively, on this language of destruction: admonishing us to "unjoin" the opponent, "make 'im remember you" and "stomp 'im like a bug.") Just as in hockey, where a fight will bring fans to their feet more often than a skillful play, so in football the mouth waters most of all for the really crippling block or tackle. For the kill. Thus the good teams are "hungry," the best players are "mean," and "casualties" are as much a part of the game as they are of a war.

The family resemblance between football and war is, indeed, striking. Their languages are similar: "field general," "long bomb," "blitz," "take a shot," "front line," "pursuit," "good hit," "the draft" and so on. Their principles and practices are alike: mass hysteria, the art of intimidation, absolute command and total obedience, territorial aggression, censorship, inflated insignia and propaganda, blackboard maneuvers and strategies, drills, uniforms, formations, marching bands and training camps. And the virtues they celebrate are almost identical: hyper-aggressiveness, coolness under fire and suicidal bravery. All this has been implicitly recognized by such jock-loving Americans as media stars General Patton and President Nixon, who have talked about war as a football game. Patton wanted to make his Second World War tank men look like football players. And Nixon, as we know, was fond of comparing attacks on Vietnam to football plays and drawing coachly diagrams on a blackboard for TV war fans.

One difference between war and football, though, is that there is little or no protest against football. Perhaps the most extraordinary thing about the game is that the systematic infliction of injuries excites in people not concern, as would be the case if they were sustained at, say, a rock festival, but a collective rejoicing and euphoria. Players and fans alike revel in the spectacle of a combatant felled into semiconsciousness, "blindsided," "clotheslined" or "decapitated." I can remember, in fact, being chided by a coach in pro ball for not "getting my hat" injuriously into a player who was already lying helpless on the ground. (On another occasion, after the Stampeders had traded the celebrated Joe Kapp to BC, we were playing the Lions in Vancouver and Kapp was forced on one play to run with the ball. He was coming "down the chute," his bad knee wobbling uncertainly, so I simply dropped on him like a blanket. After I returned to the bench I was reproved for not exploiting the opportunity to unhinge his bad knee.)

After every game, of course, the papers are full of reports on the day's injuries, a sort of post-battle "body count," and the respective teams go to work with doctors and trainers, tape, whirlpool baths, cortisone and morphine to patch and deaden the wounds before the next game. Then the whole drama is reenacted—injured athletes held together by adhesive, braces and drugs—and the days following it are filled with even more feverish activity to put on the show yet again at the end of the next week. (I remember being so taped up in college that I earned the nickname "mummy.") The team that survives this merry-go-round spectacle of skilled masochism with the fewest incapacitating injuries usually wins. It is a sort of victory by ordeal: "We hurt them more than they hurt us."

My own initiation into this brutal circus was typical. I loved the game from the moment I could run with a ball. Played shoeless on a green open field with no one keeping score and in a spirit of reckless abandon and laughter, it's a very different sport. Almost no one gets hurt and it's rugged, open and exciting (it still is for me). But then, like everything else, it starts to be regulated and institutionalized by adult authorities. And the fun is over.

10 So it was as I began the long march through organized football. Now there was a coach and elders to make it clear by their behavior that beating other people was the only thing to celebrate and that trying to shake someone up every play was the only thing to be really proud of. Now there were severe rule enforcers, audiences, formally recorded victors and losers, and heavy equipment to permit crippling bodily moves and collisions (according to one American survey, more than 80% of all football injuries occur to fully equipped players). And now there was the official "given" that the only way to keep playing was to wear suffocating armor, to play to defeat, to follow orders silently and to renounce spontaneity for joyless drill. The game had been, in short, ruined. But because I loved to play and play skillfully, I stayed. And progressively and inexorably, as I moved through high school, college and pro leagues, my body was dismantled. Piece by piece.

I started off with torn ligaments in my knee at 13. Then, as the organization and the competition increased, the injuries came faster and harder. Broken nose (three times), broken jaw (fractured in the first half and dismissed as a "bad wisdom tooth," so I played with it for the rest of the game), ripped knee ligaments again. Torn ligaments in one ankle and a fracture in the other (which I remember feeling relieved about because it meant I could honorably stop drill-blocking a 270-pound defensive end). Repeated rib fractures and cartilage tears (usually carried, again, through the remainder of the game). More dislocations of the left shoulder than I can remember (the last one I played with because, as the Calgary Stampeder doctor said, it "couldn't be damaged any more"). Occasional broken or dislocated fingers and toes. Chronically hurt lower back (I still can't lift with it or change a tire without worrying about folding). Separated right shoulder (as with many other injuries, like badly bruised hips and legs, needled with morphine for the games). And so on. The last pro grame I played—against Winnipeg Blue Bombers in the Western finals in 1961—I had a recently dislocated left shoulder, a more recently wrenched right shoulder and a chronic pain center in one leg. I was so tied up with soreness I couldn't drive my car to the airport. But it never occurred to me or anyone else that I miss a play as a corner linebacker.

By the end of my football career, I had learned that physical injury—giving it and taking it—is the real currency of the sport. And that in the final analysis the "winner" is the man who can hit to kill even if only half his limbs are working. In brief, a warrior game with a warrior ethos into which (like almost everyone else I played with) my original boyish enthusiasm had been relentlessly taunted and conditioned.

In thinking back on how all this happened, though, I can pick out no villains. As with the social system as a whole, the game has a life of its own. Everyone grows up inside it, accepts it and fulfills its dictates as obediently as helots. Far from ever questioning the principles of the activity, people simply concentrate on executing these principles more aggressively than anybody around them. The result is a group of people who, as the leagues become of a higher and higher class, are progressively insensitive to the possibility that things could be otherwise. Thus, in football, anyone who might question the wisdom or enjoyment of putting on heavy equipment on a hot day and running full speed at someone else with the intention of knocking him senseless would be regarded simply as not really a devoted athlete and probably "chicken." The choice is made straightforward. Either you, too, do your very utmost to efficiently smash and be smashed, or you admit incompetence or cowardice and quit. Since neither of these admissions is very pleasant, people generally keep any doubts they have to themselves and carry on.

Of course, it would be a mistake to suppose that there is more blind acceptance of brutal practices in organized football than elsewhere. On the contrary, a recent Harvard study has approvingly argued that football's characteristics of "impersonal acceptance of inflicted injury," an overriding "organization goal," the "ability to turn oneself on and off" and being, above all, "out to win" are of "inestimable value" to big corporations. Clearly, our sort of football is no sicker than the rest of our society. Even its organized destruction of physical well-being is not anomalous. A very large part of our wealth, work and time is, after all, spent in systematically destroying and harming human life. Manufacturing, selling and using weapons that tear opponents to pieces. Making ever bigger and faster predator-named cars with which to kill and injure one another by the million every year. And devoting our very lives to outgunning one another for power in an ever more destructive rat race. Yet all these practices are accepted without question by most people, even zealously defended and honored. Competitive, organized injuring is integral to our way of life, and football is simply one of the more intelligible mirrors of the whole process: a sort of colorful morality play showing us how exciting and rewarding it is to Smash Thy Neighbor.

15 Now it is fashionable to rationalize our collaboration in all this by arguing that, well, man *likes* to fight and injure his fellows and such games as football should be encouraged to discharge this original-sin urge into less harmful channels than, say, war. Public-show football, this line goes, plays the same sort of cathartic role as Aristotle said stage tragedy does: without real blood (or not much), it releases players and audience from unhealthy feelings stored up inside them.

As an ex-player in the seasonal coast-to-coast drama, I see little to recommend such a view. What organized football did to me was make me *suppress* my natural urges and re-express them in an alienating, vicious form. Spontaneous desires for free bodily exuberance and fraternization with competitors were shamed and forced under ("If it ain't hurtin' it ain't helpin' ") and in their place were demanded armored mechanical moves and cool hatred of all opposition. Endless authoritarian drill and dressing-room harangues (ever wonder why competing teams can't prepare for a game in the same dressing room?) were the kinds of mechanisms employed to reconstruct joyful energies into mean and alien shapes. I am quite certain that everyone else around me was being similarly forced into this heavily equipped military precision and angry antagonism, because there was always a mutinous attitude about full-dress practices, and everybody (the pros included) had to concentrate incredibly hard for days to whip themselves into just one hour's hostility a week against another club. The players never speak of these things, of course, because everyone is so anxious to appear tough.

The claim that men like seriously to battle one another to some sort of finish is a myth. It only endures because it wears one of the oldest and most propagandized of masks—the romantic combatant. I sometimes wonder whether the violence all around us doesn't depend for its survival on the existence and preservation of this tough-guy disguise.

As for the effect of organized football on the spectator, the fan is not released from supposed feelings of violent aggression by watching his athletic heroes perform it so much as encouraged in the view that people-smashing is an admirable mode of self-expression. The most savage attackers, after all, are, by general agreement, the most efficient and worthy players of all (the biggest applause I ever received as a football player occurred when I ran over people or slammed them so hard they couldn't get up). Such circumstances can hardly be said to lessen the spectators' martial tendencies. Indeed it seems likely that the whole show just further develops and titillates the North American addiction for violent self-assertion. . . . Perhaps, as well, it helps explain why the greater the zeal of U.S. political leaders as football fans (Johnson, Nixon, Agnew), the more enthusiastic the commitment to hardline politics. At any rate there seems to be a strong correlation between people who relish tough football and people who relish intimidating and beating the hell out of commies, hippies, protest marchers and other opposition groups.

Watching well-advertised strong men knock other people round, make them hurt, is in the end like other tastes. It does not weaken with feeding and variation in form. It grows.

I got out of football in 1962. I had asked to be traded after Calgary 20
had offered me a $25-a-week-plus-commissions off-season job as a clothing-store salesman. ("Dear Mr. Finks:" I wrote. [Jim Finks was then the Stampeders' general manager.] "Somehow I do not think the dialectical subtleties of Hegel, Marx and Plato would be suitably oriented amidst the environmental stimuli of jockey shorts and herringbone suits. I hope you make a profitable sale or trade of my contract to the East.") So the Stampeders traded me to Montreal. In a preseason intersquad game with the Alouettes I ripped the cartilages in my ribs on the hardest block I'd ever thrown. I had trouble breathing and I had to shuffle-walk with my torso on a tilt. The doctor in the local hospital said three weeks rest, the coach said scrimmage in two days. Three days later I was back home reading philosophy.

QUESTIONS

1. *What relationships does McMurty see between football and war? How persuasive do you find the linkage?*
2. *Is McMurty's essay mainly about his personal experiences in football or is it about some larger point, with his experiences used as examples?*
3. *Draw connections between "real life" and some kind of game or play*

familiar to you. Does this illuminate any social arrangements or help you to see them in a new light? How far can one generalize?

Jessica Mitford

BEHIND THE FORMALDEHYDE CURTAIN

The drama begins to unfold with the arrival of the corpse at the mortuary.

Alas, poor Yorick![1] How surprised he would be to see how his counterpart of today is whisked off to a funeral parlor and is in short order sprayed, sliced, pierced, pickled, trussed, trimmed, creamed, waxed, painted, rouged and neatly dressed—transformed from a common corpse into a Beautiful Memory Picture. This process is known in the trade as embalming and restorative art, and is so universally employed in the United States and Canada that the funeral director does it routinely, without consulting corpse or kin. He regards as eccentric those few who are hardy enough to suggest that it might be dispensed with. Yet no law requires embalming, no religious doctrine commends it, nor is it dictated by considerations of health, sanitation, or even of personal daintiness. In no part of the world but in Northern America is it widely used. The purpose of embalming is to make the corpse presentable for viewing in a suitably costly container; and here too the funeral director routinely, without first consulting the family, prepares the body for public display.

Is all this legal? The processes to which a dead body may be subjected are after all to some extent circumscribed by law. In most states, for instance, the signature of next of kin must be obtained before an autopsy may be performed, before the deceased may be cremated, before the body may be turned over to a medical school for research purposes; or such provision must be made in the decedent's will. In the case of embalming, no such permission is required nor is it ever sought. A textbook, *The Principles and Practices of Embalming*, comments on this: "There is some question regarding the legality of much that is done within the preparation room." The author points out that it would be most unusual for a responsible member of a bereaved fam-

From *The American Way of Death* (1963).

1. Hamlet says this (V.i.184) upon seeing the skull of the court clown he had known as a child.

ily to instruct the mortician, in so many words, to "embalm" the body of a deceased relative. The very term "embalming" is so seldom used that the mortician must rely upon custom in the matter. The author concludes that unless the family specifies otherwise, the act of entrusting the body to the care of a funeral establishment carries with it an implied permission to go ahead and embalm.

Embalming is indeed a most extraordinary procedure, and one must wonder at the docility of Americans who each year pay hundreds of millions of dollars for its perpetuation, blissfully ignorant of what it is all about, what is done, how it is done. Not one in ten thousand has any idea of what actually takes place. Books on the subject are extremely hard to come by. They are not to be found in most libraries or bookshops.

5 In an era when huge television audiences watch surgical operations in the comfort of their living rooms, when, thanks to the animated cartoon, the geography of the digestive system has become familiar territory even to the nursery school set, in a land where the satisfaction of curiosity about almost all matters is a national pastime, the secrecy surrounding embalming can, surely, hardly be attributed to the inherent gruesomeness of the subject. Custom in this regard has within this century suffered a complete reversal. In the early days of American embalming, when it was performed in the home of the deceased, it was almost mandatory for some relative to stay by the embalmer's side and witness the procedure. Today, family members who might wish to be in attendance would certainly be dissuaded by the funeral director. All others, except apprentices, are excluded by law from the preparation room.

A close look at what does actually take place may explain in large measure the undertaker's intractable reticence concerning a procedure that has become his major *raison d'être.*[2] Is it possible he fears that public information about embalming might lead patrons to wonder if they really want this service? If the funeral men are loath to discuss the subject outside the trade, the reader may, understandably, be equally loath to go on reading at this point. For those who have the stomach for it, let us part the formaldehyde curtain. . . .

The body is first laid out in the undertaker's morgue—or rather, Mr. Jones is reposing in the preparation room—to be readied to bid the world farewell.

The preparation room in any of the better funeral establishments has the tiled and sterile look of a surgery, and indeed the embalmer-restorative artist who does his chores there is beginning to adopt the term "dermasurgeon" (appropriately corrupted by some mortician-

2. Reason for being.

writers as "demi-surgeon") to describe his calling. His equipment, consisting of scalpels, scissors, augers, forceps, clamps, needles, pumps, tubes, bowls and basins, is crudely imitative of the surgeon's, as is his technique, acquired in a nine- or twelve-month post-high-school course in an embalming school. He is supplied by an advanced chemical industry with a bewildering array of fluids, sprays, pastes, oils, powders, creams, to fix or soften tissue, shrink or distend it as needed, dry it here, restore the moisture there. There are cosmetics, waxes and paints to fill and cover features, even plaster of Paris to replace entire limbs. There are ingenious aids to prop and stabilize the cadaver: a Vari-Pose Head Rest, the Edwards Arm and Hand Positioner, the Repose Block (to support the shoulders during the embalming), and the Throop Foot Positioner, which resembles an old-fashioned stocks.

Mr. John H. Eckels, president of the Eckels College of Mortuary Science, thus describes the first part of the embalming procedure: "In the hands of a skilled practitioner, this work may be done in a comparatively short time and without mutilating the body other than by slight incision—so slight that it scarcely would cause serious inconvenience if made upon a living person. It is necessary to remove the blood, and doing this not only helps in the disinfecting, but removes the principal cause of disfigurements due to discoloration."

10 Another textbook discusses the all-important time element: "The earlier this is done, the better, for every hour that elapses between death and embalming will add to the problems and complications encountered. . . ." Just how soon should one get going on the embalming? The author tells us, "On the basis of such scanty information made available to this profession through its rudimentary and haphazard system of technical research, we must conclude that the best results are to be obtained if the subject is embalmed before life is completely extinct—that is, before cellular death has occurred. In the average case, this would mean within an hour after somatic death." For those who feel that there is something a little rudimentary, not to say haphazard, about this advice, a comforting thought is offered by another writer. Speaking of fears entertained in early days of premature burial, he points out, "One of the effects of embalming by chemical injection, however, has been to dispel fears of live burial." How true; once the blood is removed, chances of live burial are indeed remote.

To return to Mr. Jones, the blood is drained out through the veins and replaced by embalming fluid pumped in through the arteries. As noted in *The Principles and Practices of Embalming*, "every operator has a favorite injection and drainage point—a fact which becomes a handicap only if he fails or refuses to forsake his favorites when conditions demand it." Typical favorites are the carotid artery, femoral artery, jugular vein, subclavian vein. There are various choices of embalming fluid. If Flextone is used, it will produce a "mild, flexible rigidity. The skin retains a velvety softness, the tissues are rubbery and pliable. Ideal for women and children." It may be blended with B. and G. Products Company's Lyf-Lyk tint, which is guaranteed to reproduce "nature's own skin texture . . . the velvety appearance of living tissue." Suntone comes in three separate tints: Suntan; Special Cosmetic Tint, a pink shade "especially indicated for young female subjects"; and Regular Cosmetic Tint, moderately pink.

About three to six gallons of a dyed and perfumed solution of formaldehyde, glycerin, borax, phenol, alcohol and water is soon circulating through Mr. Jones, whose mouth has been sewn together with a "needle directed upward between the upper lip and gum and brought out through the left nostril," with the corners raised slightly "for a more pleasant expression." If he should be bucktoothed, his teeth are cleaned with Bon Ami and coated with colorless nail polish. His eyes, meanwhile, are closed with flesh-tinted eye caps and eye cement.

The next step is to have at Mr. Jones with a thing called a trocar. This is a long, hollow needle attached to a tube. It is jabbed into the abdomen, poked around the entrails and chest cavity, the contents of which are pumped out and replaced with "cavity fluid." This done, and the hole in the abdomen sewn up, Mr. Jones's face is heavily creamed (to protect the skin from burns which may be caused by leakage of the chemicals), and he is covered with a sheet and left unmolested for a while. But not for long—there is more, much more, in store for him. He has been embalmed, but not yet restored, and the best time to start the restorative work is eight to ten hours after embalming, when the tissues have become firm and dry.

The object of all this attention to the corpse, it must be remembered, is to make it presentable for viewing in an attitude of healthy repose. "Our customs require the presentation of our dead in the semblance of normality . . . unmarred by the ravages of illness, disease or mutilation," says Mr. J. Sheridan Mayer in his *Restorative Art*. This is rather a large order since few people die in the full bloom of health, unravaged by illness and unmarked by some disfigurement. The funeral industry is equal to the challenge: "In some cases the gruesome appearance of a mutilated or disease-ridden subject may be quite discouraging. The task of restoration may seem impossible and shake the confidence of the embalmer. This is the time for intestinal fortitude and determination. Once the formative work is begun and affected tissues are cleaned or removed, all doubts of success vanish. It is surprising and gratifying to discover the results which may be obtained."

The embalmer, having allowed an appropriate interval to elapse, re- 15 turns to the attack, but now he brings into play the skill and equipment of sculptor and cosmetician. Is a hand missing? Casting one in plaster of Paris is a simple matter. "For replacement purposes, only a cast of the back of the hand is necessary; this is within the ability of the average operator and is quite adequate." If a lip or two, a nose or an ear should be missing, the embalmer has at hand a variety of restorative waxes with which to model replacements. Pores and skin texture are simulated by stippling with a little brush, and over this cosmetics are laid on. Head off? Decapitation cases are rather routinely handled. Ragged edges are trimmed, and head joined to torso with a series of splints, wires and sutures. It is a good idea to have a little something at the neck—a scarf or a high collar—when time for viewing comes. Swollen mouth? Cut out tissue as needed from inside the lips. If too much is removed, the surface contour can easily be restored by padding with cotton. Swollen necks and cheeks are reduced by removing tissue through vertical incisions made down each side of the neck. "When the deceased is casketed, the pillow will hide the suture incisions . . . as an extra precaution against leakage, the suture may be painted with liquid sealer."

The opposite condition is more likely to present itself—that of emaciation. His hypodermic syringe now loaded with massage cream, the embalmer seeks out and fills the hollowed and sunken areas by injection. In this procedure the backs of the hands and fingers and the under-chin area should not be neglected.

Positioning the lips is a problem that recurrently challenges the ingenuity of the embalmer. Closed too tightly, they tend to give a stern, even disapproving expression. Ideally, embalmers feel, the lips should give the impression of being ever so slightly parted, the upper lip protruding slightly for a more youthful appearance. This takes some engineering, however, as the lips tend to drift apart. Lip drift can sometimes be remedied by pushing one or two straight pins through the inner margin of the lower lip and then inserting them between the two front upper teeth. If Mr. Jones happens to have no teeth, the pins can just as easily be anchored in his Armstrong Face Former and Denture Replacer. Another method to maintain lip closure is to dislocate the lower jaw, which is then held in its new position by a wire run through holes which have been drilled through the upper and lower jaws at the midline. As the French are fond of saying, *il faut souffrir pour être belle.*[3]

If Mr. Jones has died of jaundice, the embalming fluid will very likely turn him green. Does this deter the embalmer? Not if he has intestinal fortitude. Masking pastes and cosmetics are heavily laid on,

3. It's necessary to suffer to be beautiful.

burial garments and casket interiors are color-correlated with particular care, and Jones is displayed beneath rose-colored lights. Friends will say "How *well* he looks." Death by carbon monoxide, on the other hand, can be rather a good thing from the embalmer's viewpoint: "One advantage is the fact that this type of discoloration is an exaggerated form of a natural pink coloration." This is nice because the healthy glow is already present and needs but little attention.

The patching and filling completed, Mr. Jones is now shaved, washed and dressed. Cream-based cosmetic, available in pink, flesh, suntan, brunette and blond, is applied to his hands and face, his hair is shampooed and combed (and, in the case of Mrs. Jones, set), his hands manicured. For the horny-handed son of toil special care must be taken; cream should be applied to remove ingrained grime, and the nails cleaned. "If he were not in the habit of having them manicured in life, trimming and shaping is advised for better appearance—never questioned by kin."

20 Jones is now ready for casketing (this is the present participle of the verb "to casket"). In this operation his right shoulder should be depressed slightly "to turn the body a bit to the right and soften the appearance of lying flat on the back." Positioning the hands is a matter of importance, and special rubber positioning blocks may be used. The hands should be cupped slightly for a more lifelike, relaxed apearance. Proper placement of the body requires a delicate sense of balance. It should lie as high as possible in the casket, yet not so high that the lid, when lowered, will hit the nose. On the other hand, we are cautioned, placing the body too low "creates the impression that the body is in a box."

Jones is next wheeled into the appointed slumber room where a few last touches may be added—his favorite pipe placed in his hand or, if he was a great reader, a book propped into position. (In the case of little Master Jones a Teddy bear may be clutched.) Here he will hold open house for a few days, visiting hours 10 A.M. to 9 P.M.

All now being in readiness, the funeral director calls a staff conference to make sure that each assistant knows his precise duties. Mr. Wilber Kriege writes: "This makes your staff feel that they are a part of the team, with a definite assignment that must be properly carried out if the whole plan is to succeed. You never heard of a football coach who failed to talk to his entire team before they go on the field. They have drilled on the plays they are to execute for hours and days, and yet the successful coach knows the importance of making even the bench-warming third-string substitute feel that he is important if the game is to be won." The winning of *this* game is predicated upon glass-smooth handling of the logistics. The funeral director has notified the pallbearers whose names were furnished by the family, has arranged for the presence of clergyman, organist, and soloist, has provided transportation for everybody, has organized and listed the flowers sent by friends. In *Psychology of Funeral Service* Mr. Edward A. Martin points out: "He may not always do as much as the family thinks he is doing, but it is his helpful guidance that they appreciate in knowing they are proceeding as they should. . . . The important thing is how well his services can be used to make the family believe they are giving unlimited expression to their own sentiment."

The religious service may be held in a church or in the chapel of the funeral home; the funeral director vastly prefers the latter arrangement, for not only is it more convenient for him but it affords him the opportunity to show off his beautiful facilities to the gathered mourners. After the clergyman has had his say, the mourners queue up to file past the casket for a last look at the deceased. The family is *never* asked whether they want an open-casket ceremony; in the absence of their instruction to the contrary, this is taken for granted. Consequently well over 90 per cent of all American funerals feature the open casket—a custom unknown in other parts of the world. Foreigners are astonished by it. An English woman living in San Francisco described her reaction in a letter to the writer:

> I myself have attended only one funeral here—that of an elderly fellow worker of mine. After the service I could not understand why everyone was walking towards the coffin (sorry, I mean casket), but thought I had better follow the crowd. It shook me rigid to get there and find the casket open and poor old Oscar lying there in his brown tweed suit, wearing a suntan makeup and just the wrong shade of lipstick. If I had not been extremely fond of the old boy, I have a horrible feeling that I might have giggled. Then and there I decided that I could never face another American funeral—even dead.

The casket (which has been resting throughout the service on a Classic Beauty Ultra Metal Casket Bier) is now transferred by a hydraulically operated device called Porto-Lift to a balloon-tired, Glide Easy casket carriage which will wheel it to yet another conveyance, the Cadillac Funeral Coach. This may be lavender, cream, light green—anything but black. Interiors, of course, are color-correlated, "for the man who cannot stop short of perfection."

25 At graveside, the casket is lowered into the earth. This office, once the prerogative of friends of the deceased, is now performed by a patented mechanical lowering device. A "Lifetime Green" artificial grass mat is at the ready to conceal the sere earth, and overhead, to conceal the sky, is a portable Steril Chapel Tent ("resists the intense heat and humidity of summer and the terrific storms of winter . . . available in Silver Grey, Rose or Evergreen"). Now is the time for the ritual scatter-

ing of earth over the coffin, as the solemn words "earth to earth, ashes to ashes, dust to dust" are pronounced by the officiating cleric. This can today be accomplished "with a mere flick of the wrist with the Gordon Leak-Proof Earth Dispenser. No grasping of a handful of dirt, no soiled fingers. Simple, dignified, beautiful, reverent! The modern way!" The Gordon Earth Dispenser (at $5) is of nickel-plated brass construction. It is not only "attractive to the eye and long wearing"; it is also "one of the 'tools' for building better public relations" if presented as "an appropriate non-commercial gift" to the clergyman. It is shaped something like a saltshaker.

Untouched by human hand, the coffin and the earth are now united.

It is in the function of directing the participants through this maze of gadgetry that the funeral director has assigned to himself his relatively new role of "grief therapist." He has relieved the family of every detail, he has revamped the corpse to look like a living doll, he has arranged for it to nap for a few days in a slumber room, he has put on a well-oiled performance in which the concept of *death* has played no part whatsoever—unless it was inconsiderately mentioned by the clergyman who conducted the religious service. He has done everything in his power to make the funeral a real pleasure for everybody concerned. He and his team have given their all to score an upset victory over death.

Ada Louise Huxtable

MODERN-LIFE BATTLE: CONQUERING CLUTTER

There are two kinds of people in the world—those who have a horror of a vacuum and those with a horror of the things that fill it. Translated into domestic interiors, this means people who live with, and without, clutter. (Dictionary definition: jumble, confusion, disorder.) The reasons for clutter, the need to be surrounded by things, goes deep, from security to status. The reasons for banning objects, or living in as selective and austere an environment as possible, range from the esthetic to the neurotic. This is a phenomenon of choice that relates as much to the psychiatrist as to the tastemaker.

Originally appeared in the "Design Notebook" column of *The New York Times* (Feb. 5, 1981).

Some people clutter compulsively, and others just as compulsively throw things away. Clutter in its highest and most organized form is called collecting. Collecting can be done as the Collyer brothers[1] did it, or it can be done with art and flair. The range is from old newspapers to Fabergé.[2]

This provides a third category, or what might be called calculated clutter, in which the objets d'art, the memorabilia that mark one's milestones and travels, the irresistible and ornamental things that speak to pride, pleasure and temptation, are constrained by decorating devices and hierarchal principles of value. This gives the illusion that one is in control.

Most of us are not in control. My own life is an unending battle against clutter. By that I do not mean to suggest that I am dedicated to any clean-sweep asceticism or arrangements of high art; I am only struggling to keep from drowning in the detritus of everyday existence, or at least to keep it separate from the possessions that are meant to be part of what I choose to believe is a functional-esthetic scheme.

5 Really living without clutter takes an iron will, plus a certain stoicism about the little comforts of life. I have neither. But my eye requires a modest amount of beauty and serenity that clutter destroys. This involves eternal watchfulness and that oldest and most relentless of the housewife's occupations, picking up. I have a feeling that picking up will go on long after ways have been found to circumvent death and taxes.

I once saw a home in which nothing had ever been picked up. Daily vigilance had been abandoned a long time ago. Although disorder descends on the unwary with the speed of light, this chaos must have taken years to achieve; it was almost a new decorating art form.

The result was not, as one might suppose, the idiosyncratic disorder of a George Price[3] drawing, where things are hung from pipes and hooks in permanent arrangements of awesome convenience.

This was an expensive, thoughtful, architect-designed house where everything had simply been left where it landed. Pots and pans, linens and clothing, toys and utensils were tangled and piled everywhere, as well as all of those miscellaneous items that go in, and usually out, of most homes. No bare spot remained on furniture or floor. And no one

1. In spring of 1947, the bodies of Langley and Homer Collyer, aged brothers living in a New York brownstone, were excavated by police along with 120 tons of newspapers and rubbish, hoarded over time, including fourteen grand pianos and the parts of a dismantled Model T Ford.
2. Peter Carl Fabergé (1846–1920), Russian court jeweler noted for delicate objects in gold and enamel.
3. Cartoonist (1901–1995) whose jumbled interiors are typified in the rest of this sentence.

who lived there found it at all strange, or seemed to require any other kind of domestic landscape. They had no hangups, in any sense of the word.

I know another house that is just as full of things, but the difference is instructive. This is a rambling old house lived in for many years by a distinguished scholar and his wife, whose love of the life of the mind and its better products has only been equaled by their love of life.

In this very personal and knowledgeable eclecticism, every shared 10
intellectual and cultural experience led to the accumulation of discoveries, mementos and *objets de vertu*,[4] kept casually at hand or in unstudied places. Tabletops and floors are thickets of books and overflow treasures. There is enormous, overwhelming, profligate clutter. And everything has meaning, memory and style.

At the opposite extreme is the stripped, instant, homogeneous style, created whole and new. These houses and apartments, always well-published, either start with nothing, which is rare, or clear everything out that the owners have acquired, which must take courage, desperation, or both. This means jettisoning the personal baggage, and clutter, of a lifetime.

I confess to very mixed reactions when I see these sleek and shining couples in their sleek and shining rooms, with every perfect thing in its perfect place. Not the least of my feelings is envy. Do these fashionable people, elegantly garbed and posed in front of the lacquered built-ins with just the right primitive pot and piece of sculpture and the latest exotic tree, feel a tremendous sense of freedom and release? Have they been liberated by their seamless new look?

More to the point, what have they done with their household *lares* and *penates*,[5] the sentimental possessions of their past? Did they give them away? Send them to auction galleries and thrift shops? Go on a trip while the decorator cleared them all out? Take a deduction for their memories? Were they tempted to keep nothing? Do they ever have any regrets?

This, of course, is radical surgery. The rest of us resort to more conventional forms of clutter combat. Houses have, or had, attics and cellars. Old apartments provide generous closets, which one fills with things that are permanently inaccessible and unneeded. In the city, there is stolen space, in elevator and service halls. And there is the ultimate catch-all—the house in the country.

Historically, clutter is a modern phenomenon, born of the industrial 15
revolution. There was a time when goods were limited; and the rich and fashionable were few in number and objects were precious and

4. Art objects, especially if beautiful and rare.
5. Valued household possessions; literally, household gods.

hard to come by. Clutter is a 19th-century esthetic; it came with the abundance of products combined with the rise of purchasing power, and the shifts in society that required manifestations of status and style.

Victorian parlors were a jungle of elaborate furnishings and ornamental overkill. The reforms of the Arts and Crafts movement in the later 19th century only substituted a more "refined" kind of clutter—art pottery, embroidered mottos, handpainted tiles and porcelains, vases of bullrushes and peacock feathers. There were bewildering "artful" effects borrowed from the studio or atelier.

Clutter only became a bad word in the 20th century. The modern movement decreed a new simplicity—white walls, bare floors, and the most ascetic of furnishings in the most purified of settings. If ornament was crime, clutter was taboo.

Architects built houses and decorators filled them. Antiques were discovered and every kind of collecting boomed. There were even architects of impeccable modernist credentials—Charles Eames and Alexander Girard—who acquired and arranged vast numbers of toys and treasures. They did so with a discerning eye for the colorful and the primitive that added interest—and clutter—to modern rooms.

Today, clutter is oozing in at a record rate. Architect-collectors like Charles Moore are freewheeling and quixotic in their tastes; high seriousness has been replaced by eclectic whimsy. Nostalgia and fleamarkets coexist on a par with scholarship and accredited antiques. Turning the century on its head, the artifacts of early modernism are being collected by the post-modernist avant-garde. At the commercial level, sophisticated merchandising sells the endless new fashions and products embraced by an affluent consumer society. The vacuum must be filled. And the truth must be told. Our possessions possess us.

QUESTIONS

1. *Distinguish among Huxtable's three categories: clutter, collecting, and "calculated clutter."*
2. *What signs in her essay reveal the level of affluence Huxtable has achieved?*
3. *Describe a place where the furnishings or decoration (or lack of it) seem symbolic of the people who live or work there.*

Arthur Schopenhauer

ON NOISE

Kant wrote a treatise on The Vital Powers.[1] I should prefer to write a dirge for them. The superabundant display of vitality, which takes the form of knocking, hammering, and tumbling things about, has proved a daily torment to me all my life long. There are people, it is true—nay, a great many people—who smile at such things, because they are not sensitive to noise; but they are just the very people who are also not sensitive to argument, or thought, or poetry, or art, in a word, to any kind of intellectual influence. The reason of it is that the tissue of their brains is of a very rough and coarse quality. On the other hand, noise is a torture to intellectual people. In the biographies of almost all great writers, or wherever else their personal utterances are recorded, I find complaints about it; in the case of Kant, for instance, Goethe, Lichtenberg, Jean Paul;[2] and if it should happen that any writer has omitted to express himself on the matter, it is only for want of an opportunity.

This aversion to noise I should explain as follows: If you cut up a large diamond into little bits, it will entirely lose the value it had as a whole; and an army divided up into small bodies of soldiers, loses all its strength. So a great intellect sinks to the level of an ordinary one, as soon as it is interrupted and disturbed, its attention distracted and drawn off from the matter in hand: for its superiority depends upon its power of concentration—of bringing all its strength to bear upon one theme, in the same way as a concave mirror collects into one point all the rays of light that strike upon it. Noisy interruption is a hindrance to this concentration. That is why distinguished minds have always shown such an extreme dislike to disturbance in any form, as something that breaks in upon and distracts their thoughts. Above all have they been averse to that violent interruption that comes from noise. Ordinary people are not much put out by anything of the sort. The most sensible and intelligent of all nations in Europe lays down the rule, Never Interrupt! as the eleventh commandment. Noise is the

Translated by Thomas Bailey Saunders for the collection *Studies in Pessimism* (1890).

1. Immanuel Kant (1724–1804), German philosopher. "Vital powers" refer to those physical functions or faculties essential to the maintainence of life.
2. Johann Wolfgang von Goethe (1749–1832), Georg Christoph Lichtenberg (1742–1799), and Jean Paul Friedrich Richter (1763–1825), all famous German writers of the late 18th and early 19th centuries.

most impertinent of all forms of interruption. It is not only an interruption, but also a disruption of thought. Of course, where there is nothing to interrupt, noise will not be so particularly painful. Occasionally it happens that some slight but constant noise continues to bother and distract me for a time before I become distinctly conscious of it. All I feel is a steady increase in the labor of thinking—just as though I were trying to walk with a weight on my foot. At last I find out what it is.

Let me now, however, pass from genus to species. The most inexcusable and disgraceful of all noises is the cracking of whips—a truly infernal thing when it is done in the narrow resounding streets of a town. I denounce it as making a peaceful life impossible; it puts an end to all quiet thought. That this cracking of whips should be allowed at all seems to me to show in the clearest way how senseless and thoughtless is the nature of mankind. No one with anything like an idea in his head can avoid a feeling of actual pain at this sudden, sharp crack, which paralyzes the brain, rends the thread of reflection, and murders thought. Every time this noise is made, it must disturb a hundred people who are applying their minds to business of some sort, no matter how trivial it may be; while on the thinker its effect is woeful and disastrous, cutting his thoughts asunder, much as the executioner's axe severs the head from the body. No sound, be it ever so shrill, cuts so sharply into the brain as this cursed cracking of whips; you feel the sting of the lash right inside your head; and it affects the brain in the same way as touch affects a sensitive plant, and for the same length of time.

With all due respect for the most holy doctrine of utility, I really cannot see why a fellow who is taking away a wagon-load of gravel or dung should thereby obtain the right to kill in the bud the thoughts which may happen to be springing up in ten thousand heads—the number he will disturb one after another in half an hour's drive through the town. Hammering, the barking of dogs, and the crying of children are horrible to hear; but your only genuine assassin of thought is the crack of a whip; it exists only for the purpose of destroying every pleasant moment of quiet thought that any one may now and then enjoy. If the driver had no other way of urging on his horse than by making this most abominable of all noises, it would be excusable; but quite the contrary is the case. This cursed cracking of whips is not only unnecessary, but even useless. Its aim is to produce an effect upon the intelligence of the horse; but through the constant abuse of it, the animal becomes habituated to the sound, which falls upon blunted feelings and produces no effect at all. The horse does not go any faster for it. You have a remarkable example of this in the ceaseless cracking of his whip on the part of a cab-driver, while he is proceeding at a slow pace on the lookout for a fare. If he were to give his horse the slightest touch with the whip, it would have much more effect. Supposing, however, that it were absolutely necessary to crack the whip in order to keep the horse constantly in mind of its presence, it would be enough to make the hundredth part of the noise. For it is a well-known fact that, in regard to sight and hearing animals are sensitive to even the faintest indications; they are alive to things that we can scarcely perceive. The most surprising instances of this are furnished by trained dogs and canary birds.

It is obvious, therefore, that here we have to do with an act of pure 5
wantonness; nay, with an impudent defiance offered to those members of the community who work with their heads by those who work with their hands. That such infamy should be tolerated in a town is a piece of barbarity and iniquity, all the more as it could easily be remedied by a police-notice to the effect that every lash shall have a knot at the end of it. There can be no harm in drawing the attention of the mob to the fact that the classes above them work with their heads, for any kind of headwork is mortal anguish to the man in the street. A fellow who rides through the narrow alleys of a populous town with unemployed post-horses or cart-horses, and keeps on cracking a whip several yards long with all his might, deserves there and then to stand down and receive five really good blows with a stick.

All the philanthropists in the world, and all the legislators, meeting to advocate and decree the total abolition of corporal punishment, will never persuade me to the contrary! There is something even more disgraceful than what I have just mentioned. Often enough you may see a carter walking along the street, quite alone, without any horses, and still cracking away incessantly; so accustomed has the wretch become to it in consequence of the unwarrantable toleration of this practice. A man's body and the needs of his body are now everywhere treated with a tender indulgence. Is the thinking mind then, to be the only thing that is never to obtain the slightest measure of consideration or protection, to say nothing of respect? Carters, porters, messengers—these are the beasts of burden amongst mankind; by all means let them be treated justly, fairly, indulgently, and with forethought; but they must not be permitted to stand in the way of the higher endeavors of humanity by wantonly making a noise. How many great and splendid thoughts, I should like to know, have been lost to the world by the crack of a whip? If I had the upper hand, I should soon produce in the heads of these people an indissoluble association of ideas between cracking a whip and getting a whipping.

Let us hope that the more intelligent and refined among the nations will make a beginning in this matter, and then that the Germans may take example by it and follow suit. Meanwhile, I may quote what

Thomas Hood[3] says of them: *For a musical nation, they are the most noisy I ever met with.* That they are so is due to the fact, not that they are more fond of making a noise than other people—they would deny it if you asked them—but that their senses are obtuse; consequently, when they hear a noise, it does not affect them much. It does not disturb them in reading or thinking, simply because they do not think; they only smoke, which is their substitute for thought. The general toleration of unnecessary noise—the slamming of doors, for instance, a very unmannerly and ill-bred thing—is direct evidence that the prevailing habit of mind is dullness and lack of thought. In Germany it seems as though care were taken that no one should ever think for mere noise—to mention one form of it, the way in which drumming goes on for no purpose at all.

Finally, as regards the literature of the subject treated of in this chapter, I have only one work to recommend, but it is a good one. I refer to a poetical epistle in *terza rima*[4] by the famous painter Bronzino,[5] entitled *De' Romori: a Messer Luca Martini.*[6] It gives a detailed description of the torture to which people are put by the various noises of a small Italian town. Written in a tragi-comic style, it is very amusing. The epistle may be found in *Opere burlesche del Berni, Aretino ed altri,*[7] Vol. II, p. 258; apparently published in Utrecht in 1771.

3. English poet and humorist (1799–1845).
4. Three-line rhymed stanza.
5. Il Bronzino [Agnolo di Cosimo Allori (1503–1572)], Florentine portraitist.
6. *About Noises, by Mr. Louis Martini.*
7. *Comic Works by Berni, Aretino, and others.*

QUESTIONS

1. *Does Schopenhauer think noise affects everyone or just a certain type of person?*
2. *Imagine what Schopenhauer expected to accomplish with this essay. Why, do you think, does he conclude with some references to comic treatments of noise? Just how serious is he?*
3. *The cracking of whips annoys Schopenhauer most, especially since the noise made is totally useless. Write about what noises annoy you the most; or describe a sensitive person in a noisy environment: attending a hockey game, being forced to listen to car alarms, working a cattle roundup.*

Roland Barthes

TOYS

French toys: One could not find a better illustration of the fact that the adult Frenchman sees the child as another self. All the toys one commonly sees are essentially a microcosm of the adult world; they are all reduced copies of human objects, as if in the eyes of the public the child was, all told, nothing but a smaller man, a homunculus to whom must be supplied objects of his own size.

Invented forms are very rare: a few sets of blocks, which appeal to the spirit of do-it-yourself, are the only ones which offer dynamic forms. As for the others, French toys *always mean something,* and this something is always entirely socialized, constituted by the myths or the techniques of modern adult life: the army, broadcasting, the post office, medicine (miniature instrument-cases, operating theaters for dolls), school, hair styling (driers for permanent-waving), the air force (parachutists), transport (trains, Citroëns, Vedettes, Vespas,[1] petrol stations), science (Martian toys).

The fact that French toys *literally* prefigure the world of adult functions obviously cannot but prepare the child to accept them all, by constituting for him, even before he can think about it, the alibi of a Nature which has at all times created soldiers, postmen and Vespas. Toys here reveal the list of all the things the adult does not find unusual: war, bureaucracy, ugliness, Martians, etc. It is not so much, in fact, the imitation which is the sign of an abdication, as its literalness. French toys are like a Jivaro[2] head, in which one recognizes, shrunken to the size of an apple, the wrinkles and hair of an adult. There exist, for instance, dolls which urinate; they have an esophagus, one gives them a bottle, they wet their nappies; soon, no doubt, milk will turn to water in their stomachs. This is meant to prepare the little girl for the causality of housekeeping, to "condition" her to her future role as mother. However, faced with this world of faithful and complicated objects, the child can only identify himself as owner, as user, never as creator; he does not invent the world, he uses it: There are, prepared for him, actions without adventure, without wonder, without joy. He is turned into a little stay-at-home householder who does not even have to invent the mainsprings of adult causality; they are sup-

From *Mythologies* (1957).

1. Italian motor scooter.
2. South American Indian headhunting tribe.

plied to him ready-made: He has only to help himself, he is never allowed to discover anything from start to finish. The merest set of blocks, provided it is not too refined, implies a very different learning of the world: Then, the child does not in any way create meaningful objects, it matters little to him whether they have an adult name; the actions he performs are not those of a user but those of a demiurge. He creates forms which walk, which roll, he creates life, not property: Objects now act by themselves, they are no longer an inert and complicated material in the palm of his hand. But such toys are rather rare: French toys are usually based on imitation, they are meant to produce children who are users, not creators.

The bourgeois status of toys can be recognized not only in their forms, which are all functional, but also in their substances. Current toys are made of a graceless material, the product of chemistry, not of nature. Many are now molded from complicated mixtures; the plastic material of which they are made has an appearance at once gross and hygienic, it destroys all the pleasure, the sweetness, the humanity of touch. A sign which fills one with consternation is the gradual disappearance of wood, in spite of its being an ideal material because of its firmness and its softness, and the natural warmth of its touch. Wood removes, from all the forms which it supports, the wounding quality of angles which are too sharp, the chemical coldness of metal. When the child handles it and knocks it, it neither vibrates nor grates, it has a sound at once muffled and sharp. It is a familiar and poetic substance, which does not sever the child from close contact with the tree, the table, the floor. Wood does not wound or break down; it does not shatter, it wears out, it can last a long time, live with the child, alter little by little the relations between the object and the hand. If it dies, it is in dwindling, not in swelling out like those mechanical toys which disappear behind the hernia of a broken spring. Wood makes essential objects, objects for all time. Yet there hardly remain any of these wooden toys from the Vosges, these fretwork farms with their animals, which were only possible, it is true, in the days of the craftsman. Henceforth, toys are chemical in substance and color; their very material introduces one to a coenaesthesis[3] of use, not pleasure. These toys die in fact very quickly, and once dead, they have no posthumous life for the child.

3. General awareness of the body and its condition.

QUESTIONS

1. *Barthes makes a comparison between wooden blocks and more modern toys. What are the ways in which wood is better?*
2. *What do French toys prepare children for?*

3. *Describe a few types of contemporary American toys, keeping in mind the kinds of purposes Barthes has noted in his essay. Think of how some modern toys shape children's expectations about life. Which toys channel imagination and which liberate it? Why?*

Fred Strebeigh

THE WHEELS OF FREEDOM: BICYCLES IN CHINA

"Hello." She appeared at my right shoulder, her face inches from mine. We were cycling together, though I had never seen her before. We rode side by side through the city of Beijing, and around us streamed thousands of bicycles with red banners flying. Beijing was in revolt. And as we rode together we broke the law.

I had gone to China with an odd goal: to learn a bit about what the bicycle means to people who live in a country with only a few thousand privately owned cars but some 220 million cycles—vastly more than any other nation. And I had arrived at an odd time.

My first day in China was also the first day of what became known as the Beijing Spring of 1989. As I awoke, students and citizens by the hundreds of thousands were flowing from all over Beijing to Tiananmen Square, the vast plaza at the city's heart, creating the largest spontaneous demonstration in the history of China and perhaps the world. They came on foot and by bus and subway, of course, but mostly they came by bicycle, calling for freedom. (I could see why bicycles are forbidden in the capital of North Korea, China's more repressive neighbor. Its government reportedly fears that bikes give people too much independence.)

Within hours of my arrival in Beijing, bicycles became more crucial than ever. Buses stopped. Subways shut. Taxis struck. But on flowed the bikes of Beijing. Bicyclists carried messages from university to university. Tricyclists rushed round delivering food to demonstrators. Families and schoolmates and couples and commuters smiled and waved as they rode, in twos and threes and throngs.

On my own bicycle, hesitant at first and then lost in the cycling 5
masses, I roamed freely. Daily I rode to Tiananmen Square, with its mood of carnival, its students from all regions, and its uncountable cycles. Bicycles and tricycles became flag holders and tent supporters.

Originally published in *Bicycling Magazine* (Apr. 1991).

They became tea dispensers and cold-drink stands. They became photographers' perches, families' viewing platforms, old men's reading chairs, and children's racing toys.

On my bicycle I also strayed far from Tiananmen, to the quiet corners of the city. Everywhere the bicycle set the rhythm of life. Martial artists rode to practice with swords strapped to their bikes. Women in jet-black business suits pedalled their daughters to school. Boys fished beside parked bicycles at placid lakes. Bakers in white toques headed for work on transport tricycles. Pedalling beside them at their slow pace, I felt at ease and oddly at home. I felt as I had years ago in my small hometown, where automobiles never clogged the streets and where the bicycle offered a mix of peace and freedom.

Riding among the bicycles of Beijing, I began to recognize dozens of China's famous brands: Golden Lion and Mountain River, Plum Flower and Chrysanthemum, Red Flag and Red Cotton, Flying Arrival and Flying Pigeon, Pheasant and Phoenix and Forever. Long and stately bicycles, recalling decades past, they possessed the rake and sheer and grace that today I associate less with cycling than with yachting. I felt as if I were cruising, on the wake of clippers like *Red Jacket* or *Flying Cloud*, in a regatta of tall ships.

Then the Chinese government declared martial law. It forbade citizens to attend the student demonstrations and forbade foreigners, like me, to visit Tiananmen or talk to students. It sent its army in a first push into the city, but citizens peacefully blocked its way. My Chinese hosts (I had been invited to lecture at a couple of universities) warned me to obey the government, and I said I would try.

10 In the second day under martial law, as I was riding down one of Beijing's leafy boulevards, suddenly a young woman appeared at my shoulder. She said "hello," and we were cycling together.

I had been rolling at Beijing speed, eight miles an hour—in synch with commuters, demonstrators, and vegetable haulers. To catch me she had accelerated, maybe to eight-and-a-half miles an hour.

"What," she wanted to know, did I "think about the students?" She wore tinted glasses, a shy smile in a radiant face, a lab coat—she was a science student, and by law we were forbidden to talk.

"I think what they are doing is very brave," I said, "and very scary." And so we became two petty criminals, riding handlebar-to-handlebar.

We floated together and others floated past. But they travelled fractions of a pedal-turn faster or fractions slower, and we were left alone in talk, our handlebars occasionally nudging each other, in the bizarre intimacy of Beijing cycling. I worried aloud about the Chinese army—now half a mile to our west, still blocked but still pressing towards us. She praised George Washington. We would not have talked so freely in a restaurant or hotel, I realized; police could have demanded our names. But here we were just two bicycles lost in the mass—the most private place in Beijing.

Ahead of us appeared Tiananmen Square, where some of her classmates had been starving themselves in protest and others had been singing "We Shall Overcome." Within moments, she drifted south and I north. Soon I was at the American embassy. They warned me against talking to students.

15 To stay in Beijing, I decided, was to endanger anyone I met. And so I resolved to travel out from the capital and return later, in order to talk about bicycles in a time of greater calm and, I hoped, greater freedom.

One of the people I most wanted to meet outside Beijing was a student in Sichuan Province named Fang Hui. The year before, she had become the first woman to ride a bicycle from Chengdu, the capital of Sichuan in central China, to Lhasa, the capital of Tibet—bumping for thirteen hundred miles over one of China's worst roads, a sawtooth of rock tracks and mountain passes which reach altitudes above 15,000 feet. In recognition, China honored her as one of the nation's "Ten Brave Young People."

I didn't care much about Fang Hui's honors. I cared more about her motivations, her goals. I guess I expected her to be a hot but somewhat dull athlete, the sort who wins Chinese honors by excelling in volleyball. When we met at her university in Chengdu, where she is a graduate student in English, she surprised me.

As we pedalled through the streets of Chengdu, I asked Fang Hui if she had always been a cyclist. Not really, she said. Before her trip she had not owned a bicycle. The day before departing for Tibet she bought an old, single-speed Arched Eyebrow for 75 yuan ($15). She then taught herself to ride, over a thousand miles of mountains.

I asked how she chose Tibet. She said she had answered a poster advertisement. I was shocked. So, apparently, were the five men, mostly teachers from a local school, who had planned the trip and posted invitations for fellow travellers. Only Fang Hui accepted.

20 The men doubted she could reach Tibet, perhaps because she looked like a pudgy schoolgirl. Uphill she always rode more slowly than they, falling miles behind. Downhill, because her old bike had wretched brakes, she squeezed its levers with all her strength as the Arched Eyebrow hurtled down pitted roads. "I went very fast," she said. "I felt as if I would become light." At the end of each day of clinging to her brake levers, her hands were so cramped she could not open them.

Eventually, the men admitted that her strength egged them on. "If even a girl can do this," they said, "how shameful for a man to give up."

Fang Hui had not really worried about giving up on the journey, she told me. But, earlier, she had worried about giving up on life. "Before," she said, "yesterday, today, tomorrow were all alike—so dull. What I most wanted was to meet something unexpected."

Not just the road's pain but also its loneliness changed Fang Hui. At remote outposts she would meet soldiers, mere isolated boys, who would write love letters that followed her up the Lhasa road, carried by lone truck drivers. In yet remoter terrain she would ride half a day, she recalled, and "not see a single man. So when I heard a dog bark, it would arouse a tender feeling—a reminder of the human world. When I came back, people all said I had changed. Now I can find something new in every day." And now at night, she added with glee, "sometimes I dream I am riding very fast downhill."

As I rode through Chengdu, sometimes talking with Fang Hui or with other university students and teachers, I began to see that the bicycle offered an escape not just *from* everyday life. It also offered escape within everyday life.

25 One day as Fang Hui and I rode through a crush of cyclists, a young couple passed us riding two bicycles side-by-side. They rode pedal-to-pedal and almost arm-in-arm. At first the girl rode with her left hand on the boy's right, controlling his hand and handlebar, steering them both. Then he moved his hand to round the small of her back. They reminded me of partners in a waltz.

The boy lowered his hand to the girl's bicycle seat and leaned to her, and as they rode they whispered. In the often-dehumanizing crush of urban China, two bicycles had made space for romance. Fang Hui said that young "lovers" often ride so utterly together, so alone in their world.

Providing such measures of human dignity, one professor told me, was one of the bicycle's gifts to China—and particularly to people like his parents, who were "peasants" (the term in China for all people who work the land). Here in the center of China's richest farmlands, he said, I could watch the bicycle making life less hard. Flower farmers with hollyhocks and asters tied to their bicycles arrived in Chengdu at dawn, flicked down their kickstands on side streets, and began to sell. Farmers' sons strapped saws and other carpenters' tools to their bicycles, rode into the city, and waited at curbside for customers to hire them to build beds or bureaus. In Sichuan's booming "free markets" (free, that is, of government control), geese came to town on the backs of farmers' tricycles, were sold to families for domestic egg laying, and then departed with their wings still flapping, strapped to the buyers' handlebars. Everywhere, cycles kept life rolling.

The professor told me that peasants in his parents' remote village always refer to the bicycle, appreciatively, as the "foreign horse." The government opposes the name, he said, but it helps explain the history of the bicycle in China. The first bicycle arrived in 1886, carrying Thomas Stevens, a young San Franciscan who was completing the first cycling journey around the world. With its huge front wheel and small rear one, his penny-farthing[1] cycle must have looked very foreign but, unlike a good horse, not very practical.

The first practical bicycle to reach China came in 1891, again transporting a round-the-world cyclist. By the early twentieth century, the foreign horse had won the fascination of China's last emperor, the young Puyi, who rode one around his palace, Beijing's "Forbidden City."

Slowly cycling trickled down from the throne toward the masses. By 30
the 1940s China's bicycle factories were producing a vehicle like today's most common model, a virtual twin of England's stately Raleigh Tourist.

In the years before the Chinese revolution of 1949, the professor told me, almost everyone called the bicycle "foreign horse," because "foreign" suggested both "modern" and "admirable." Since peasants carried most goods on their backs, they particularly admired the bicycle. Every peasant longed to shift his burden to the back of a foreign horse—a longing frustrated by high price and short supply.

Then came the revolution of 1949. Hoping to "raise the people's dignity," the professor continued, the young government made two decisions. Happily, in an effort to give wheels to an impoverished population, it encouraged bicycle production, which began doubling and redoubling. But sadly, because the old name suggested blind worship of foreign things, the government banned the lyrical phrase "foreign horse" (which, pronounced *yang ma* in Chinese, resounds like a ringing gong). The government imposed, instead, the unpoetic "self-running cart" (*zi xing che* in Chinese, which sounds like a dental problem).

Not surprisingly, the cycle's foreign resonance remains. Peasants in remote villages still pedal "foreign horses." And many Chinese factories, seeking a touch of class, still adorn their bicycles with prominent English names: "Forever" or "Light Roadster" or, on the most celebrated of foreign horses, "Flying Pigeon—The All-Steel Bicycle." (When George Bush made his first presidential visit to China, his welcoming gift from the nation was a pair of Flying Pigeons.)

A regional branch of the Flying Pigeon Bicycle Factory lies an hour's ride from the center of Chengdu, and one day I was given a tour of its old-style assembly line by Jiang Guoji, the factory's present director—the first ever elected by its workers. He spoke with the ease of a man-

1. Referring to wheels of unequal size: pennies were big, farthings small.

ager whose workers trust his judgment and whose society trusts his product.

35 Since Jiang Guoji's factory sits in the middle of China's best farmland, he and his co-workers decided to specialize in what Jiang called the "ZA-62" or "Reinforced Flying Pigeon." This bike, which I came to think of as the "Peasant Pigeon," comes with massive tubing, a formidable rack, a second set of forks to hold the front wheels, and—probably unique among Chinese bicycles—a three-year warranty. It contains 68 pounds of steel which, together with some leather and rubber, brings its total weight above 72 pounds—three times that of my average American bike.

Jiang Guoji's factory has raised production steadily, along with all Chinese cycle factories, creating an unprecedented problem. The year before my visit, Chinese bicycle production reached 42 million cycles—dwarfing any other nation's output and, more significantly, overtaking Chinese demand for the first time in history. For years, bicycles had been rationed, and families had longed to own a good one. Now "if a person has money, he can buy," Jiang told me, with a mix of pride and regret—because prices have begun dropping and "bicycle factories have real competition."

In response, Jiang said, he was trying to spur international demand for Peasant Pigeons. Looking for good "propaganda," two years earlier he donated "Peasant Pigeons" to five local riders who wanted to go around the world. Alas, one had been run down by a truck in Pakistan. But the other four were riding on, circling the globe back towards his factory. He expected his 72-pound Pigeons home within a year, still under warranty. (He added that, despite transport costs and import duties, he would gladly sell Peasant Pigeons wholesale in America for less than a dollar a pound.)

All Chinese bicycles—whether sturdy Flying Pigeons or sad Arched Eyebrows—must survive long after their warranties have expired. To help them along, repairmen have set up roadside stands in every city. Entering the business proves simple. A would-be repairman chooses a site, asks the city to license it to him, and lays down his tools. He then puts up his advertisement—a circle of overlapping innertubes, colored black and deep pink, perhaps hung on a tree limb.

Some Chinese portray repairmen in a style that outdoes American caricatures of car mechanics. Most of my Chinese acquaintances knew one repairman they relied on and dozens they distrusted. One university professor insisted that underemployed repairmen scatter tacks to puncture passing tires and inflate profits.

40 Another professor invited me to meet her revered neighborhood repairman. Since he worked incessantly and had little time for chatter, she devised a ruse to buy time for asking questions: we would take him her Flying Arrival, which had a useless rear brake.

We found him at the back gate of her university beneath a circle of innertubes. When my friend arrived, the repairman put aside a Phoenix he was polishing and greeted her as a long-term client. She presented the brake problem. He took a quick look, produced two sets of pliers, loosened a nut, tightened a cable, tensioned a spring and, after 30 seconds of work, handed the bike back to her—fixed. He refused payment. The job was too small. He resumed polishing the Phoenix.

Though her ruse had failed, the professor pressed forward: How did he become a repairman? Three years ago when he was twenty-seven, he told us, he stopped working his family's farm because the land was small and the family had more than enough laborers—including his wife, their three children, his two sisters and two brothers, and their aging parents. He still lives on the farm but commutes three miles to the city on his Forever. He works seven days a week, from 9 A.M. to 8 P.M., except when it rains.

He likes bike repair because it "makes *money*," he said, emphasizing the word as if it were a novelty. Back on the farm, where he hopes never to work again, he "just produced *crops*," which sold for "not-so-much money."

When we asked him how much he made in a month, he told us 800 yuan ($216). The professor gasped. To me she said, quietly, "That's five university professors!" Still, she seemed to believe him. She pointed out to me that he had paid the government's penalty for having three children. The penalty in recent years has run as high as 2,000 yuan ($540), she said, too much for most professors—but not for an industrious bike fixer.

As I talked to more repairmen, I saw that their job may be the freest 45
in China. A hard worker needed only a street corner and a few tools. Before his eyes bikes would inevitably break down and, if he was skilled, clients would multiply. Bicycle repair seemed to offer an extension of what the bike itself offered and what so many Chinese sought: modest dignity, new choices, ample freedom.

The farm country outside Chengdu, contrary to the complaints of one peasant-turned-repairman, generates much of the new agricultural wealth enjoyed by the Chinese people. In early June, by train and by bicycle, I travelled to the southern mountains that rim this rich agricultural bowl within Sichuan province. There I was the guest at another university, tucked in verdant hills.

During my stay, one teacher lent me an old "Peasant Pigeon"—one well past its warranty. I rode it daily over farm tracks of rut and rock that would have jolted the nuts off my light American bike. The big Pigeon just bobbed along, high and easy.

One midday while I was exploring narrow paths through emerald-colored rice paddies, two girls whizzed past me, riding double on a black Forever. Both wore red uniforms and one carried an abacus—students dashing home for lunch.

With me was a professor who was fluent not only in English but also the quite-obscure local dialect. She suggested we follow the students so I could meet a "peasant family."

50 We travelled through flooded paddies, past water buffaloes, up to a newly built home that stretched around a cement courtyard, and found the older of the two girls talking with her mother next to their vegetable garden. The professor introduced us. Their mother, Mrs. Fang, invited us for tea and introduced her daughters: Liya, third-grader and bicycle passenger, and Jianmei, sixth-grader and bicyclist. Because Jianmei's Forever still had protective wrapping paper on its top bar, as if it had just come from the store, I asked if it was new.

Jianmei, who was gulping down rice in preparation for her afternoon at school, said proudly that she won it just last year. Her mother explained that the family offers their daughters prizes for each year that they sustain grades of 90% or better. In autumn each daughter names a prize she wants, and then for the rest of the school year she tries to win it. In third grade Jianmei won a set of nice clothes; in fourth grade, a golden wristwatch; in fifth grade, the Forever. (I said to the professor, in English, "Are you sure we're talking to *peasants?*")

Mrs. Fang then led us through her tiled kitchen to a room that held, along with awards won by Jianmei for track and basketball, another full-sized bicycle—a cherry-red "Cuckoo," also still wrapped to protect its paint. It was Jianmei's earlier bike. I was astonished; ten years ago here, the professor had told me, only one family in ten could afford even a single bicycle.

Jianmei explained that she wanted the Forever because it was strong and smooth enough to carry her little sister. With it, she rides not just to school but up to the university, off to a nearby temple, even to a town 22 miles away to see the world's largest carved Buddha.

As we walked away from the Fang household—so imbued with work and reward and independence—I said to the professor: "Don't you wish you grew up in a place like that?" A bit later I thought to myself: "I *did* grow up in a place like that." Riding off to school, studying hard, cycling ten and twenty miles on a whim—this was like being back in sixth grade in my small hometown.

55 On the same day I talked with the Fang family, stories of the Beijing massacre—of hundreds or perhaps thousands of citizens killed by army troops and tanks—were reaching our remote region. Soon travellers arrived with tales of killing in other provincial cities. Students began to flee our rural campus, fearing the army would next descend on them. I returned to Chengdu.

There, I tried to continue the work I had planned—looking for the city's used bicycle market, avoiding the army troops who had arrived to quell outbursts, gathering statistics on bicycle ownership. But I could not concentrate. My mind was on Beijing. Finally I decided to return, to what just days before had been the world's most exuberant city.

Again I rode its leafy boulevards, but no excited voice at my shoulder asked what I thought of the students. No banners waved. No people smiled. All faces seemed as if carved, years ago, in soft stone—at once fixed and badly weathered.

Each evening, Beijing television proudly showed the now-barren Tiananmen Square, cleared of all students and, for that matter, all life. Understandably, the TV cameras did not show what people in Beijing had seen: citizens trying to stop tanks by shoving bicycles at them, flatbed tricycles turned into ambulances for slaughtered children. Less understandably, the cameras often began their pan across the square with an image of a pile of crumpled bicycles.

That odd image haunted me for months, long after I had left China. Only slowly did I realize that the government had chosen that scene precisely. The government cameras wanted to show more than a few crushed machines. They wanted to show crushed dignity, crushed humanity, crushed freedom—so much that the bicycle means in China.

And finally I realized that of course the old men who cling to power 60
in China would want to show off the crumpled bicycles of the young men and women who had called for freedom. How terrifying it must have been, to those old men, to see millions of young people cycling toward them—so independent, so alive, so free—all those wheels turning and turning beyond the control of fear or fiat. Of course those old men would want to crush the cycles of the young. For they would know too well that history itself runs in cycles—sometimes foreign horses, sometimes self-running carts, always wheels of change. How sad: Four decades earlier these same old men, seeking to "raise the people's dignity," had set rolling the cycles of modern China. And then, in a few days of a Beijing spring, they sought to crush, all at once, cycles and dignity and change together. They might as easily have sought to stop the circling, round the sun, of earth's revolution. For as each spring comes round, the old fade and the young quicken. And every day throughout China, the wheels of freedom roll.

Henry Louis Gates, Jr.

IN THE KITCHEN

We always had a gas stove in the kitchen, in our house in Piedmont, West Virginia, where I grew up. Never electric, though using electric became fashionable in Piedmont in the sixties, like using Crest toothpaste rather than Colgate, or watching Huntley and Brinkley rather than Walter Cronkite.[1] But not us: gas, Colgate, and good ole Walter Cronkite, come what may. We used gas partly out of loyalty to Big Mom, Mama's Mama, because she was mostly blind and still loved to cook, and could feel her way more easily with gas than with electric. But the most important thing about our gas-equipped kitchen was that Mama used to do hair there. The "hot comb" was a fine-toothed iron instrument with a long wooden handle and a pair of iron curlers that opened and closed like scissors. Mama would put it in the gas fire until it glowed. You could smell those prongs heating up.

I liked that smell. Not the smell so much, I guess, as what the smell meant for the shape of my day. There was an intimate warmth in the women's tones as they talked with my Mama, doing their hair. I knew what the women had been through to get their hair ready to be "done," because I would watch Mama do it to herself. How that kink could be transformed through grease and fire into that magnificent head of wavy hair was a miracle to me, and still is.

Mama would wash her hair over the sink, a towel wrapped around her shoulders, wearing just her slip and her white bra. (We had no shower—just a galvanized tub that we stored in the kitchen—until we moved down Rat Tail Road into Doc Wolverton's house, in 1954.) After she dried it, she would grease her scalp thoroughly with blue Bergamot hair grease, which came in a short, fat jar with a picture of a beautiful colored lady on it. It's important to grease your scalp real good, my Mama would explain, to keep from burning yourself. Of course, her hair would return to its natural kink almost as soon as the hot water and shampoo hit it. To me, it was another miracle how hair so "straight" would so quickly become kinky again the second it even approached some water.

My Mama had only a few "clients" whose heads she "did"—did, I think, because she enjoyed it, rather than for the few pennies it brought in. They would sit on one of our red plastic kitchen chairs, the

Originally published in *The New Yorker* (Apr. 18, 1994).

1. Newscasters of the 1960s: Chet Huntley and David Brinkley were on NBC; Walter Cronkite was on CBS.

kind with the shiny metal legs, and brace themselves for the process. Mama would stroke that red-hot iron—which by this time had been in the gas fire for half an hour or more—slowly but firmly through their hair, from scalp to strand's end. It made a scorching, crinkly sound, the hot iron did, as it burned its way through kink, leaving in its wake straight strands of hair, standing long and tall but drooping over at the ends, their shape like the top of a heavy willow tree. Slowly, steadily, Mama's hands would transform a round mound of Odetta[2] kink into a darkened swamp of everglades. The Bergamot made the hair shiny; the heat of the hot iron gave it a brownish-red cast. Once all the hair was as straight as God allows kink to get, Mama would take the well-heated curling iron and twirl the straightened strands into more or less loosely wrapped curls. She claimed that she owed her skill as a hairdresser to the strength in her wrists, and as she worked her little finger would poke out, the way it did when she sipped tea. Mama was a southpaw,[3] and wrote upside down and backward to produce the cleanest, roundest letters you've ever seen.

The "kitchen" she would all but remove from sight with a handheld 5
pair of shears, bought just for this purpose. Now, the kitchen was the room in which we were sitting—the room where Mama did hair and washed clothes, and where we all took a bath in that galvanized tub. But the word has another meaning, and the kitchen that I'm speaking of is the very kinky bit of hair at the back of your head, where your neck meets your shirt collar. If there was ever a part of our African past that resisted assimilation, it was the kitchen. No matter how hot the iron, no matter how powerful the chemical, no matter how stringent the mashed-potatoes-and-lye formula of a man's "process," neither God nor woman nor Sammy Davis, Jr.,[4] could straighten the kitchen. The kitchen was permanent, irredeemable, irresistible kink. Unassimilably African. No matter what you did, no matter how hard you tried, you couldn't de-kink a person's kitchen. So you trimmed it off as best you could.

When hair had begun to "turn," as they'd say—to return to its natural kinky glory—it was the kitchen that turned first (the kitchen around the back, and nappy edges at the temples). When the kitchen started creeping up the back of the neck, it was time to get your hair done again.

Sometimes, after dark, a man would come to have his hair done. It was Mr. Charlie Carroll. He was very light-complected and had a

2. Singer (b. 1930) of blues and spirituals in the 1950s and a leading figure in the American folk revival of the 1960s; she wore a large Afro hairdo.
3. A left-handed person.
4. African-American singer, dancer, and entertainer (1925–1990), noted for his "processed" hair.

ruddy nose—it made me think of Edmund Gwenn, who played Kris Kringle in "Miracle on 34th Street." At first, Mama did him after my brother, Rocky, and I had gone to sleep. It was only later that we found out that he had come to our house so Mama could iron his hair—not with a hot comb or a curling iron but with our very own Proctor-Silex steam iron. For some reason I never understood, Mr. Charlie would conceal his Frederick Douglass-like mane[5] under a big white Stetson hat. I never saw him take it off except when he came to our house, at night, to have his hair pressed. (Later, Daddy would tell us about Mr. Charlie's most prized piece of knowledge, something that the man would only confide after his hair had been pressed, as a token of intimacy. "Not many people know this," he'd say, in a tone of circumspection, "but George Washington was Abraham Lincoln's daddy." Nodding solemnly, he'd add the clincher: "A white man told me." Though he was in dead earnest, this became a humorous refrain around our house—"a white man told me"—which we used to punctuate especially preposterous assertions.)

My mother examined my daughters' kitchens whenever we went home to visit, in the early eighties. It became a game between us. I had told her not to do it, because I didn't like the politics it suggested—the notion of "good" and "bad" hair. "Good" hair was "straight," "bad" hair kinky. Even in the late sixties, at the height of Black Power, almost nobody could bring themselves to say "bad" for good and "good" for bad. People still said that hair like white people's hair was "good," even if they encapsulated it in a disclaimer, like "what we used to call 'good.' "

Maggie would be seated in her high chair, throwing food this way and that, and Mama would be cooing about how cute it all was, how I used to do just like Maggie was doing, and wondering whether her flinging her food with her left hand meant that she was going to be left-handed like Mama. When my daughter was just about covered with Chef Boyardee Spaghetti-O's, Mama would seize the opportunity: wiping her clean, she would tilt Maggie's head to one side and reach down the back of her neck. Sometimes Mama would even rub a curl between her fingers, just to make sure that her bifocals had not deceived her. Then she'd sigh with satisfaction and relief: No kink . . . yet. Mama! I'd shout, pretending to be angry. Every once in a while, if no one was looking, I'd peek, too.

10 I say "yet" because most black babies are born with soft, silken hair. But after a few months it begins to turn, as inevitably as do the seasons

5. Frederick Douglass (c. 1817–1895) was an escaped slave turned abolitionist who, in nineteenth-century photographs, is shown with a lionlike mane of hair.

or the leaves on a tree. People once thought baby oil would stop it. They were wrong.

Everybody I knew as a child wanted to have good hair. You could be as ugly as homemade sin dipped in misery and still be thought attractive if you had good hair. "Jesus moss," the girls at Camp Lee, Virginia, had called Daddy's naturally "good" hair during the war. I know that he played that thick head of hair for all it was worth, too.

My own hair was "not a bad grade," as barbers would tell me when they cut it for the first time. It was like a doctor reporting the results of the first full physical he has given you. Like "You're in good shape" or "Blood pressure's kind of high—better cut down on salt."

I spent most of my childhood and adolescence messing with my hair. I definitely wanted straight hair. Like Pop's. When I was about three, I tried to stick a wad of Bazooka bubble gum to that straight hair of his. I suppose what fixed that memory for me is the spanking I got for doing so: he turned me upside down, holding me by my feet, the better to paddle my behind. Little *nigger*, he had shouted, walloping away. I started to laugh about it two days later, when my behind stopped hurting.

When black people say "straight," of course, they don't usually mean literally straight—they're not describing hair like, say, Peggy Lipton's (she was the white girl on "The Mod Squad"), or like Mary's of Peter, Paul & Mary[6] fame; black people call that "stringy" hair. No, "straight" just means not kinky, no matter what contours the curl may take. I would have done *anything* to have straight hair—and I used to try everything, short of getting a process.[7]

15 Of the wide variety of techniques and methods I came to master in the challenging prestidigitation of the follicle, almost all had two things in common: a heavy grease and the application of pressure. It's not an accident that some of the biggest black-owned companies in the fifties and sixties made hair products. And I tried them all, in search of that certain silken touch, the one that would leave neither the hand nor the pillow sullied by grease.

I always wondered what Frederick Douglass put on *his* hair, or what Phillis Wheatley[8] put on hers. Or why Wheatley has that rag on her head in the little engraving in the frontispiece of her book. One thing is for sure: you can bet that when Phillis Wheatley went to England and saw the Countess of Huntingdon she did not stop by the Queen's coiffeur on her way there. So many black people still get their hair

6. Folksinging group famous in the 1960s for "Puff the Magic Dragon" and a version of Bob Dylan's "Blowing in the Wind."
7. Hair-straightening treatment that used chemicals for smoothing out kinks.
8. African-American poet and slave (1753–1784) and America's first published black writer. She was taken to England to meet royalty.

straightened that it's a wonder we don't have a national holiday for Madame C. J. Walker, the woman who invented the process of straightening kinky hair. Call it Jheri-Kurled or call it "relaxed," it's still fried hair.

I used all the greases, from sea-blue Bergamot and creamy vanilla Duke (in its clear jar with the orange-white-and-green label) to the godfather of grease, the formidable Murray's. Now, Murray's was some *serious* grease. Whereas Bergamot was like oily jello, and Duke was viscous and sickly sweet, Murray's was light brown and *hard.* Hard as lard and twice as greasy, Daddy used to say. Murray's came in an orange can with a press-on top. It was so hard that some people would put a match to the can, just to soften the stuff and make it more manageable. Then, in the late sixties, when Afros came into style, I used Afro Sheen. From Murray's to Duke to Afro Sheen: that was my progression in black consciousness.

We used to put hot towels or washrags over our Murray-coated heads, in order to melt the wax into the scalp and the follicles. Unfortunately, the wax also had the habit of running down your neck, ears, and forehead. Not to mention your pillowcase. Another problem was that if you put two palmfuls of Murray's on your head your hair turned white. (Duke did the same thing.) The challenge was to get rid of that white color. Because if you got rid of the white stuff you had a magnificent head of wavy hair. That was the beauty of it: Murray's was so hard that it froze your hair into the wavy style you brushed it into. It looked really good if you wore a part. A lot of guys had parts *cut* into their hair by a barber, either with the clippers or with a straightedge razor. Especially if you had kinky hair—then you'd generally wear a short razor cut, or what we called a Quo Vadis.

We tried to be as innovative as possible. Everyone knew about using a stocking cap, because your father or your uncle wore one whenever something really big was about to happen, whether sacred or secular: a funeral or a dance, a wedding or a trip in which you confronted official white people. Any time you were trying to look really sharp, you wore a stocking cap in preparation. And if the event was really a big one, you made a new cap. You asked your mother for a pair of her hose, and cut it with scissors about six inches or so from the open end—the end with the elastic that goes up to the top of the thigh. Then you knotted the cut end, and it became a beehive-shaped hat, with an elastic band that you pulled down low on your forehead and down around your neck in the back. To work well, the cap had to fit tightly and snugly, like a press. And it had to fit that tightly because it *was* a press: it pressed your hair with the force of the hose's elastic. If you greased your hair down real good, and left the stocking cap on long enough, voilà: you got a head of pressed-against-the-scalp waves. (You also got a ring around your forehead when you woke up, but it went away.) And then you could enjoy your concrete do. Swore we were bad, too, with all that grease and those flat heads. My brother and I would brush it out a bit in the mornings, so that it looked—well, "natural." Grown men still wear stocking caps—especially older men, who generally keep their stocking caps in their top drawers, along with their cufflinks and their see-through silk socks, their "Maverick" ties, their silk handkerchiefs, and whatever else they prize the most.

A Murrayed-down stocking cap was the respectable version of the 20
process, which, by contrast, was most definitely not a cool thing to have unless you were an entertainer by trade. Zeke and Keith and Poochie and a few other stars of the high-school basketball team all used to get a process once or twice a year. It was expensive, and you had to go somewhere like Pittsburgh or D.C. or Uniontown—somewhere where there were enough colored people to support a trade. The guys would disappear, then reappear a day or two later, strutting like peacocks, their hair burned slightly red from the lye base. They'd also wear "rags"—cloths or handkerchiefs—around their heads when they slept or played basketball. Do-rags, they were called. But the result was straight hair, with just a hint of wave. No curl. Do-it-yourselfers took their chances at home with a concoction of mashed potatoes and lye.

The most famous process of all, however, outside of the process Malcolm X describes in his "Autobiography," and maybe the process of Sammy Davis, Jr., was Nat King Cole's[9] process. Nat King Cole had patent-leather hair. That man's got the finest process money can buy, or so Daddy said the night we saw Cole's TV show on NBC. It was November 5, 1956. I remember the date because everyone came to our house to watch it and to celebrate one of Daddy's buddies' birthdays. Yeah, Uncle Joe chimed in, they can do shit to his hair that the average Negro can't even *think* about—secret shit.

Nat King Cole was *clean.* I've had an ongoing argument with a Nigerian friend about Nat King Cole for twenty years now. Not about whether he could sing—any fool knows that he could—but about whether or not he was a handkerchief head for wearing that patent-leather process.

Sammy Davis, Jr.,'s process was the one I detested. It didn't look good on him. Worse still, he liked to have a fried strand dangling down the middle of his forehead, so he could shake it out from the crown when he sang. But Nat King Cole's hair was a thing unto itself, a beautifully sculpted work of art that he and he alone had the right to wear.

9. Singer and jazz pianist (1919–1965).

The only difference between a process and a stocking cap, really, was taste; but Nat King Cole, unlike, say, Michael Jackson, looked *good* in his. His head looked like Valentino's[1] head in the twenties, and some say it was Valentino the process was imitating. But Nat King Cole wore a process because it suited his face, his demeanor, his name, his style. He was as clean as he wanted to be.

I had forgotten all about that patent-leather look until one day in 1971, when I was sitting in an Arab restaurant on the island of Zanzibar surrounded by men in fezzes and white caftans, trying to learn how to eat curried goat and rice with the fingers of my right hand and feeling two million miles from home. All of a sudden, an old transistor radio sitting on top of a china cupboard stopped blaring out its Swahili music and started playing "Fly Me to the Moon," by Nat King Cole. The restaurant's din was not affected at all, but in my mind's eye I saw it: the King's magnificent sleek black tiara. I managed, barely, to blink back the tears.

1. Film star (1895–1926), known, among other things, for his slicked-back hair.

Herb Goldberg

IN HARNESS: THE MALE CONDITION

Most men live in harness. Richard was one of them. Typically he had no awareness of how his male harness was choking him until his personal and professional life and his body had nearly fallen apart.

Up to that time he had experienced only occasional short bouts of depression that a drink would bring him out of. For Richard it all crashed at an early age, when he was thirty-three. He came for psychotherapy with resistance, but at the instruction of his physician. He had a bad ulcer, was losing weight, and, in spite of repeated warnings that it could kill him, he was drinking heavily.

His personal life was also in serious trouble. He had recently lost his job as a disc jockey on a major radio station because he'd been arrested for drunk driving. He had totaled his car against a tree and the newspapers had a picture of it on the front page. Shortly thereafter his wife moved out, taking with her their eight-year-old daughter. She left at the advice of friends who knew that he had become violent twice that year while drunk.

As he began to talk about himself it became clear that he had been

From *The Hazards of Being Male* (1976).

securely fitted into his male harness early in his teens. In high school he was already quite tall and stronger than most. He was therefore urged to go out for basketball, which he did, and he got lots of attention for it.

He had a deep, resonant voice that he had carefully cultivated. He was told that he should go into radio announcing and dramatics, so he got into all the high school plays. In college he majored in theater arts.

In his senior year in college he dated one of the most beautiful and sought-after girls in the junior class. His peer group envied him, which reassured Richard that he had a good thing going. So he married Joanna a year after graduating and took a job with a small radio station in Fresno, California. During the next ten years he played out the male role; he fathered a child and fought his way up in a very competitive profession.

It wasn't until things had fallen apart that he even let himself know that he had any feelings of his own, and in therapy he began to see why it had been so necessary to keep his feelings buried. They were confusing and frightening.

More than anything else, there was a hypersensitive concern over what others thought about him as a "man." As other suppressed feelings began to surface they surprised him. He realized how he had hated the pressures of being a college basketball player. The preoccupation with being good and winning had distorted his life in college.

Though he had been to bed with many girls before marriage and even a few afterward, he acknowledged that rarely was it a genuine turn-on for him. He liked the feeling of being able to seduce a girl but the experience itself was rarely satisfying, so he would begin the hunt for another as soon as he succeeded with one. "Some of those girls were a nightmare," he said, "I would have been much happier without them. But I was caught in the bag of proving myself and I couldn't seem to control it."

The obsessive preoccupation in high school and college with cultivating a deep, resonant "masculine" voice he realized was similar to the obsession some women have with their figures. Though he thought he had enjoyed the attention he got being on stage, he acknowledged that he had really disliked being an entertainer, or "court jester," as he put it.

When he thought about how he had gotten married he became particularly uncomfortable. "I was really bored with Joanna after the first month of dating but I couldn't admit it to myself because I thought I had a great thing going. I married her because I figured if I didn't one of the other guys would. I couldn't let that happen."

Richard had to get sick in his harness and nearly be destroyed by role-playing masculinity before he could allow himself to be a person with his own feelings, rather than just a hollow male image. Had it not been for a bleeding ulcer he might have postponed looking at himself for many years more.

Like many men, Richard had been a zombie, a daytime sleepwalker. Worse still, he had been a highly "successful" zombie, which made it so difficult for him to risk change. Our culture is saturated with successful male zombies, businessmen zombies, golf zombies, sports car zombies, playboy zombies, etc. They are playing by the rules of the male game plan. They have lost touch with, or are running away from, their feelings and awareness of themselves as people. They have confused their social masks for their essence and they are destroying themselves while fulfilling the traditional definitions of masculine-appropriate behavior. They set their life sails by these role definitions. They are the heroes, the studs, the providers, the warriors, the empire builders, the fearless ones. Their reality is always approached through these veils of gender expectations.

When something goes seriously wrong, they discover that they are shadows to themselves as well as to others. They are unknown because they have been so busy manipulating and masking themselves in order to maintain and garner more status that a genuine encounter with another person would threaten them, causing them to flee or to react with extreme defensiveness.

15 Men evaluate each other and are evaluated by many women largely by the degree to which they approximate the ideal masculine model. Women have rightfully lashed out against being placed into a mold and being related to as a sex object. Many women have described their roles in marriage as a form of socially approved prostitution. They assert that they are selling themselves out for an unfulfilling portion of supposed security. For psychologically defensive reasons the male has not yet come to see himself as a prostitute, day in and day out, both in and out of the marriage relationship.

The male's inherent survival instincts have been stunted by the seemingly more powerful drive to maintain his masculine image. He would, for example, rather die in the battle than risk living in a different way and being called a "coward" or "not a man." He would rather die at his desk prematurely than free himself from his compulsive patterns and pursuits. As a recently published study concluded, "A surprising number of men approaching senior citizenship say they would rather die than be buried in retirement."

The male in our culture is at a growth impasse. He won't move—not because he is protecting his cherished central place in the sun, but because he *can't* move. He is a cardboard Goliath precariously balanced and on the verge of toppling over if he is pushed even ever so slightly out of his well-worn path. He lacks the fluidity of the female who can readily move between the traditional definitions of male or female behavior and roles. She can be wife and mother or a business executive. She can dress in typically feminine fashion or adopt the male styles. She will be loved for having "feminine" interests such as needlework or cooking, or she will be admired for sharing with the male in his "masculine" interests. That will make her a "man's woman." She can be sexually assertive or sexually passive. Meanwhile, the male is rigidly caught in his masculine pose and, in many subtle and direct ways, he is severely punished when he steps out of it.

Unlike some of the problems of women, the problems of men are not readily changed through legislation. The male has no apparent and clearly defined targets against which he can vent his rage. Yet he is oppressed by the cultural pressures that have denied him his feelings, by the mythology of the woman and the distorted and self-destructive way he sees and relates to her, by the urgency for him to "act like a man" which blocks his ability to respond to his inner promptings both emotionally and physiologically, and by a generalized self-hate that causes him to feel comfortable only when he is functioning well in harness, or when he lives for joy and for personal growth.

The prevalent "enlightened" male's reaction to the women's liberation movement bears testimony to his inability to mobilize himself on his own behalf. He has responded to feminist assertions by donning sack cloth, sprinkling himself with ashes, and flagellating himself—accusing himself of the very things she is accusing him of. An article entitled, "You've Come a Long Way, Buddy," perhaps best illustrates the male self-hating attitude. In it, the writer said,

> The members of the men's liberation movement are . . . a kind of embarrassing vanguard, the first men anywhere on record to take a political stand based on the idea that what the women are saying is right—men are a bunch of lazy, selfish, horny, unhappy oppressors.

20 Many other undoubtedly well-intentioned writers on the male condition have also taken a basically guilt- and shame-oriented approach to the male, alternately scolding him, warning him, and preaching to him that he better change and not be a male chauvinist pig anymore. During many years of practice as a psychotherapist, I have never seen a person grow or change in a self-constructive, meaningful way when he was motivated by guilt, shame, or self-hate. That manner of approach smacks of old-time religion and degrades the male by ignoring the complexity of the binds and repressions that are his emotional heritage.

Precisely because the tenor and mood of the male liberation efforts so far have been one of self-accusation, self-hate, and a repetition of feminist assertions, I believe it is doomed to failure in its present form. It is buying the myth that the male is culturally favored—a notion that is clung to despite the fact that every critical statistic in the area of longevity, disease, suicide, crime, accidents, childhood emotional disorders, alcoholism, and drug addiction shows a disproportionately higher male rate.

Many men who join male liberation groups do so to please or impress their women or to learn how to deal with and hold onto their recently liberated wives or girlfriends. Once in a male liberation group they intellectualize their feelings and reactions into lifelessness. In addition, the men tend to put each other down for thinking like "typical male chauvinists" or using words like "broad," "chick," "dike," etc. They have introjected the voices of their feminist accusers and the result is an atmosphere that is joyless, self-righteous, cautious, and lacking in a vitalizing energy. A new, more subtle kind of competitiveness pervades the atmosphere: the competition to be the least competitive and most free of the stereotyped version of male chauvinism.

The women's liberation movement did not effect its astounding impact via self-hate, guilt, or the desire to placate the male. Instead it has been energized by anger and outrage. Neither will the male change in any meaningful way until he experiences his underlying rage toward the endless, impossible binds under which he lives, the rigid definitions of his role, the endless pressure to be all things to all people, and the guilt-oriented, self-denying way he has traditionally related to women, to his feelings, and to his needs.

Because it is so heavily repressed, male rage only manifests itself indirectly and in hidden ways. Presently it is taking the form of emotional detachment, interpersonal withdrawal, and passivity in relationship to women. The male has pulled himself inward in order to deny his anger and to protect himself and others from his buried cascade of resentment and fury. Pathetic, intellectualized attempts not to be a male chauvinist pig will *never* do the job.

25 There is also a commonly expressed notion that men will somehow be freed as a by-product of the feminist movement. This is a comforting fantasy for the male but I see no basis for it becoming a reality. It simply disguises the fear of actively determining his own change. Indeed, by responding inertly and passively, the male will be moved, but not in a meaningful and productive direction. If there is to be a constructive change for the male he will have to chart his own way, develop his own style and experience his own anxieties, fear, and rage because *this time mommy won't do it!*

Recently, I asked a number of men to write to me about how they see their condition and what liberation would mean to them. A sense of suffocation and confusion was almost always present.

A forty-six-year-old businessman wrote: "From what do I need to be liberated? I'm too old and tired to worry about myself. I know that I'm only a high-grade mediocrity. I've come to accept a life where the dreams are now all revealed as unreality. I don't know how my role or my son's role should change. If I knew I suppose it would be in any way that would make my wife happier and less of a shrew."

A thirty-nine-year-old carpenter discussing the "joys" of working responded: "I contend that the times in which it is fun and rewarding in a healthy way have been fairly limited. Most of the time it has been a question of running in fear of failure." Referring to his relationships, he continued. "There is another aspect of women's and men's lib that I haven't experienced extensively. This is the creation of close friendships outside of the marriage. My past experiences have been stressful to the point where I am very careful to limit any such contact. What's the fear? I didn't like the sense of insecurity developed by my wife and the internal stresses that I felt. It created guilt feelings."

A fifty-seven-year-old college professor expressed it this way: "Yes, there's a need for male lib and hardly anyone writes about it the way it really is, though a few make jokes. My gut reaction, which is what you asked for, is that men—the famous male chauvinist pigs who neglect their wives, underpay their women employees, and rule the world—are literally slaves. They're out there picking that cotton, sweating, swearing, taking lashes from the boss, working fifty hours a week to support themselves and the plantation, only then to come back to the house to do another twenty hours a week rinsing dishes, toting trash bags, writing checks, and acting as butlers at the parties. It's true of young husbands and middle-aged husbands. Young bachelors may have a nice deal for a couple of years after graduating, but I've forgotten, and I'll never again be young! Old men. Some have it sweet, some have it sour.

"Man's role—how has it affected my life? At thirty-five, I chose to 30
emphasize family togetherness and income and neglect my profession if necessary. At fifty-seven, I see no reward for time spent with and for the family, in terms of love or appreciation. I see a thousand punishments for neglecting my profession. I'm just tired and have come close to just walking away from it and starting over; just research, publish, teach, administer, play tennis, and travel. Why haven't I? Guilt. And love. And fear of loneliness. How should the man's role in my family change? I really don't know how it can, but I'd like a lot more time to do my thing."

The most remarkable and significant aspect of the feminist movement to date has been woman's daring willingness to own up to her resistances and resentment toward her time-honored, sanctified roles of wife and even mother. The male, however, has yet to fully realize, acknowledge, and rebel against the distress and stifling aspects of many of the roles he plays—from good husband, to good daddy, to good provider, to good lover, etc. Because of the inner pressure to constantly affirm his dominance and masculinity, he continues to act as if he can stand up under, fulfill, and even enjoy all the expectations placed on him no matter how contradictory and devitalizing they are.

It's time to remove the disguises of privilege and reveal the male condition for what it really is.

QUESTIONS

1. *Exactly what does Goldberg mean by "harness"? Is it a condition you have felt yourself? Are there women as well as men who can be said to be "in harness"?*
2. *What evidence does Goldberg have to support his conclusions? What problems might arise from basing conclusions on men who seek help from a psychotherapist?*
3. *Write about to what extent males you know are or are not in situations Goldberg would describe as "harness."*

Betty Rollin

MOTHERHOOD: WHO NEEDS IT?

Motherhood is in trouble, and it ought to be. A rude question is long overdue: Who needs it? The answer used to be (1) society and (2) women. But now, with the impending horrors of overpopulation, society desperately *doesn't* need it. And women don't need it either. Thanks to the Motherhood Myth—the idea that having babies is something that all normal women instinctively want and need and will enjoy doing—they just *think* they do.

The notion that the maternal wish and the activity of mothering are instinctive or biologically predestined is baloney. Try asking most sociologists, psychologists, psychoanalysts, biologists—many of whom are mothers—about motherhood being instinctive: it's like asking department store presidents if their Santa Clauses are real. "Motherhood—instinctive?" shouts distinguished sociologist/author Dr. Jessie Bernard. "Biological destiny? Forget biology! If it were biology, people would die from not doing it."

"Women don't need to be mothers any more than they need spa-

Originally published in *Look* (Sept. 22, 1970).

ghetti," says Dr. Richard Rabkin, a New York psychiatrist. "But if you're in a world where everyone is eating spaghetti, thinking they need it and want it, you will think so too. Romance has really contaminated science. So-called instincts have to do with stimulation. They are not things that well up inside of you."

"When a woman says with feeling that she craved her baby from within, she is putting into biological language what is psychological," says University of Michigan psychoanalyst and motherhood-researcher Dr. Frederick Wyatt. "There are no instincts," says Dr. William Goode, president-elect of the American Sociological Association. "There are reflexes, like eye-blinking, and drives, like sex. There is no innate drive for children. Otherwise, the enormous cultural pressures that there are to reproduce wouldn't exist. There are no cultural pressures to sell you on getting your hand out of the fire."

There are, to be sure, biologists and others who go on about biologi- 5
cal destiny, that is, the innate or instinctive goal of motherhood. (At the turn of the century, even good old capitalism was explained by a theorist as "the *instinct* of acquisitiveness.") And many psychoanalysts will hold the Freudian view that women feel so rotten about not having a penis that they are necessarily propelled into the child-wish to replace the missing organ. Psychoanalysts also make much of the psychological need to repeat what one's parent of the same sex has done. Since every woman has a mother, it is considered normal to wish to imitate one's mother by being a mother.

There is, surely, a wish to pass on love if one has received it, but to insist women must pass it on in the same way is like insisting that every man whose father is a gardener has to be a gardener. One dissenting psychoanalyst says, simply, "There is a wish to comply with one's biology, yes, but we needn't and sometimes we shouldn't." (Interestingly, the woman who has been the greatest contributor to child therapy and who has probably given more to children than anyone alive is Dr. Anna Freud, Freud's magnificent daughter, who is not a mother.)

Anyway, what an expert cast of hundreds is telling us is, simply, that biological *possibility* and desire are not the same as biological *need*. Women have childbearing equipment. To choose not to use the equipment is no more blocking what is instinctive than it is for a man who, muscles or no, chooses not to be a weight lifter.

So much for the wish. What about the "instinctive" *activity* of mothering? One animal study shows that when a young member of a species is put in a cage, say, with an older member of the same species, the latter will act in a protective, "maternal" way. But that goes for both males and females who have been "mothered" themselves. And studies indicate that a human baby will also respond to whoever is around playing mother—even if it's father. Margaret Mead and many others frequently point out that mothering can be a fine occupation, if you want it, for either sex. Another experiment with monkeys who were brought up without mothers found them lacking in maternal behavior toward their own offspring. A similar study showed that monkeys brought up without other monkeys of the opposite sex had no interest in mating—all of which suggests that both mothering and mating behavior are learned, not instinctual. And, to turn the cart (or the baby carriage) around, baby ducks who lovingly follow their mothers seemed, in the mother's absence, to just as lovingly follow wooden ducks or even vacuum cleaners.

If motherhood isn't instinctive, when and why, then, was the Motherhood Myth born? Until recently, the entire question of maternal motivation was academic. Sex, like it or not, meant babies. Not that there haven't always been a lot of interesting contraceptive tries. But until the creation of the diaphragm in the 1880's, the birth of babies was largely unavoidable. And, generally speaking, nobody really seemed to mind. For one thing, people tend to be sort of good sports about what seems to be inevitable. For another, in the past, the population needed beefing up. Mortality rates were high, and agricultural cultures, particularly, have always needed children to help out. So because it "just happened" and because it was needed, motherhood was assumed to be innate.

10 Originally, it was the word of God that got the ball rolling with "Be fruitful and multiply," a practical suggestion, since the only people around then were Adam and Eve. But in no time, supermoralists like St. Augustine changed the tone of the message: "Intercourse, even with one's legitimate wife, is unlawful and wicked where the conception of the offspring is prevented," he, we assume, thundered. And the Roman Catholic position was thus cemented. So then and now, procreation took on a curious value among people who viewed (and view) the pleasures of sex as sinful. One could partake in the sinful pleasure, but feel vindicated by the ensuing birth. Motherhood cleaned up sex. Also, it cleaned up women, who have always been considered somewhat evil, because of Eve's transgression (". . . but the woman was deceived and became a transgressor. Yet woman will be saved through bearing children . . . ," I Timothy, 2:14–15), and somewhat dirty because of menstruation.

And so, based on need, inevitability, and pragmatic fantasy—the Myth *worked*, from society's point of view—the Myth grew like corn in Kansas. And society reinforced it with both laws and propaganda—laws that made woman a chattel, denied her education and personal mobility, and madonna propaganda that she was beautiful and wonderful doing it and it was all beautiful and wonderful to do. (One rarely sees a madonna washing dishes.)

In fact, the Myth persisted—breaking some kind of record for long-lasting fallacies—until something like yesterday. For as the truth about the Myth trickled in—as women's rights increased, as women gradually got the message that it was certainly possible for them to do most things that men did, that they live longer, that their brains were not tinier—then, finally, when the really big news rolled in, that they could *choose* whether or not to be mothers—what happened? The Motherhood Myth soared higher than ever. As Betty Friedan made oh-so-clear in *The Feminine Mystique*, the '40's and '50's produced a group of ladies who not only had babies as if they were going out of style (maybe they were) but, as never before, they turned motherhood into a cult. First, they wallowed in the aesthetics of it all—natural childbirth and nursing became maternal musts. Like heavy-bellied ostriches, they grounded their heads in the sands of motherhood, only coming up for air to say how utterly happy and fulfilled they were. But, as Mrs. Friedan says only too plainly, they weren't. The Myth galloped on, moreover, long after making babies had turned from practical asset to liability for both individual parents *and* society. With the average cost of a middle-class child figured conservatively at $30,000 (not including college), any parent knows that the only people who benefit economically from children are manufacturers of consumer goods. Hence all those gooey motherhood commercials. And the Myth gathered momentum long after sheer numbers, while not yet extinguishing us, have made us intensely uncomfortable. Almost all of our societal problems, from minor discomforts like traffic to major ones like hunger, the population people keep reminding us, have to do with there being too many people. And who suffers most? The kids who have been so mindlessly brought into the world, that's who. They are the ones who have to cope with all of the difficult and dehumanizing conditions brought on by overpopulation. They are the ones who have to cope with the psychological nausea of feeling unneeded by society. That's not the only reason for drugs, but, surely, it's a leading contender.

Unfortunately, the population curbers are tripped up by a romantic, stubborn, ideological hurdle. How can birth-control programs really be effective as long as the concept of glorious motherhood remains unchanged? (Even poor old Planned Parenthood has to euphemize—why not Planned Unparenthood?) Particularly among the poor, motherhood is one of the few inherently positive institutions that are accessible. As Berkeley demographer Judith Blake points out, "Poverty-oriented birth control programs do not make sense as a welfare measure . . . as long as existing pronatalist policies . . . encourage mating, pregnancy, and the care, support, and rearing of children." Or, she might have added, as long as the less-than-idyllic child-rearing part of motherhood remains "in small print."

Sure, motherhood gets dumped on sometimes: Philip Wylie's Momism[1] got going in the '40's and Philip Roth's *Portnoy's Complaint* did its best to turn rancid the chicken-soup concept of Jewish motherhood. But these are viewed as the sour cries of a black humorist here, a malcontent there. Everyone shudders, laughs, but it's like the mouse and the elephant joke. Still, the Myth persists. Last April, a Brooklyn woman was indicted on charges of manslaughter and negligent homicide—eleven children died in a fire in a building she owned and criminally neglected—"But," sputtered her lawyer, "my client, Mrs. Breslow, is a mother, a grandmother, and a great-grandmother!"

15 Most remarkably, the Motherhood Myth persists in the face of the most overwhelming maternal unhappiness and incompetence. If reproduction were merely superfluous and expensive, if the experience were as rich and rewarding as the cliché would have us believe, if it were a predominantly joyous trip for everyone riding—mother, father, child—then the going everybody-should-have-two-children plan would suffice. Certainly, there are a lot of joyous mothers, and their children and (sometimes, not necessarily) their husbands reflect their joy. But a lot of evidence suggests that for more women than anyone wants to admit, motherhood can be miserable. ("If it weren't," says one psychiatrist wryly, "the world wouldn't be in the mess it's in.")

There is a remarkable statistical finding from a recent study of Dr. Bernard's, comparing the mental illness and unhappiness of married mothers and single women. The latter group, it turned out, was both markedly less sick and overtly more happy. Of course, it's not easy to measure slippery attitudes like happiness. "Many women have achieved a kind of reconciliation—a conformity," says Dr. Bernard,

> that they interpret as happiness. Since feminine happiness is supposed to lie in devoting one's life to one's husband and children, they do that; so *ipso facto,* they assume they are happy. And for many women, untrained for independence and "processed" for motherhood, they find their state far preferable to the alternatives, which don't really exist.

Also, unhappy mothers are often loath to admit it. For one thing, if in society's view not to be a mother is to be a freak, not to be a *blissful* mother is to be a witch. Besides, unlike a disappointing marriage, disappointing motherhood cannot be terminated by divorce. Of course, none of that stops such a woman from expressing her dissatisfaction in a variety of ways. Again, it is not only she who suffers but her husband and children as well. Enter the harridan housewife, the carping shrew. The realities of motherhood can turn women into terrible

1. Philip Wylie's A *Generation of Vipers* (1942) blamed many of the ills of American society on dominating mothers.

people. And, judging from the 50,000 cases of child abuse in the U.S. each year, some are worse than terrible.

In some cases, the unpleasing realities of motherhood begin even before the beginning. In *Her Infinite Variety*, Morton Hunt describes young married women pregnant for the first time as "very likely to be frightened and depressed, masking these feelings in order not to be considered contemptible. The arrival of pregnancy interrupts a pleasant dream of motherhood and awakens them to the realization that they have too little money, or not enough space, or unresolved marital problems. . . ."

The following are random quotes from interviews with some mothers in Ann Arbor, Mich., who described themselves as reasonably happy. They all had positive things to say about their children, although when asked about the best moment of their day, they *all* confessed it was when the children were in bed. Here is the rest:

> Suddenly I had to devote myself to the child totally. I was under the illusion that the baby was going to fit into my life, and I found that I had to switch my life and my schedule to fit *him*. You think, "I'm in love, I'll get married, and we'll have a baby." First there's two, then three, it's simple and romantic. You don't even think about the work. . . .

> You never get away from the responsibility. Even when you leave the children with a sitter, you are not out from under the pressure of the responsibility. . . .

> I hate ironing their pants and doing their underwear, and they never put their clothes in the laundry basket. . . . As they get older, they make less demands on our time because they're in school, but the demands are greater in forming their values. . . . Best moment of the day is when all the children are in bed. . . . The worst time of the day is 4 P.M., when you have to get dinner started, the kids are tired, hungry and crabby—everybody wants to talk to you about *their* day . . . your day is only half over.

> Once a mother, the responsibility and concern for my children became so encompassing. . . . It took a great deal of will to keep up other parts of my personality. . . . To me, motherhood gets harder as they get older because you have less control. . . . In an abstract sense, I'd have several. . . . In the non-abstract, I would not have any . . . .

> I had anticipated that the baby would sleep and eat, sleep and eat. Instead, the experience was overwhelming. I really had not thought particularly about what motherhood would mean in a realistic sense. I want to do *other* things, like to become involved in things that are worthwhile—I don't mean women's clubs—but I don't have the physical energy to go out in the evenings. I feel like I'm missing something . . . the experience of being somewhere with people and having them talking about something—something that's going on in the world.

Every grownup person expects to pay a price for his pleasures, but seldom is the price as vast as the one endured "however happily" by most mothers. We have mentioned the literal cost factor. But what does that mean? For middle-class American women, it means a life style with severe and usually unimagined limitations; i.e., life in the suburbs, because who can afford three bedrooms in the city? And what do suburbs mean? For women, suburbs mean other women and children and leftover peanut-butter sandwiches and car pools and seldom-seen husbands. Even the Feminine Mystiqueniks—the housewives who finally admitted that their lives behind brooms (OK, electric brooms) were driving them crazy—were loath to trace their predicament to their children. But it is simply a fact that a childless married woman has no child-work and little housework. She can live in a city, or, if she still chooses the suburbs or the country, she can leave on the commuter train with her husband if she wants to. Even the most ardent job-seeking mother will find little in the way of great opportunities in Scarsdale.[2] Besides, by the time she wakes up, she usually lacks both the preparation for the outside world and the self-confidence to get it. You will say there are plenty of city-dwelling working mothers. But most of those women do additional-funds-for-the-family kind of work, not the interesting career kind that takes plugging during child-bearing years.

20 Nor is it a bed of petunias for the mother who does make it professionally. Says writer critic Marya Mannes:

> If the creative woman has children, she must pay for this indulgence with a long burden of guilt, for her life will be split three ways between them and her husband and her work. . . . No woman with any heart can compose a paragraph when her child is in trouble. . . . The creative woman has no wife to protect her from intrusion. A man at his desk in a room with closed door is a man at work. A woman at a desk in any room is available.

Speaking of jobs, do remember that mothering, salary or not, is a job. Even those who can afford nurses to handle the nitty-gritty still need to put out emotionally. "Well-cared-for" neurotic rich kids are not exactly unknown in our society. One of the more absurd aspects of the Myth is the underlying assumption that, since most women are biologically equipped to bear children, they are psychologically, mentally, emotionally, and technically equipped (or interested) to rear them. Never mind happiness. To assume that such an exacting, consuming, and important task is something almost all women are equipped to do is far more dangerous and ridiculous than assuming that everyone with vocal chords should seek a career in the opera.

2. A wealthy suburb of New York City.

A major expectation of the Myth is that children make a not-so-hot marriage hotter, or a hot marriage, hotter still. Yet almost every available study indicates that childless marriages are far happier. One of the biggest, of 850 couples, was conducted by Dr. Harold Feldman of Cornell University, who states his finding in no uncertain terms: "Those couples with children had a significantly lower level of marital satisfaction than did those without children." Some of the reasons are obvious. Even the most adorable children make for additional demands, complications, and hardships in the lives of even the most loving parents. If a woman feels disappointed and trapped in her mother role, it is bound to affect her marriage in any number of ways: she may take out her frustrations directly on her husband, or she may count on him too heavily for what she feels she is missing in her daily life.

". . . You begin to grow away from your husband," says one of the Michigan ladies. "He's working on his career and you're working on your family. But you both must gear your lives to the children. You do things the children enjoy, more than things you might enjoy." More subtle and possibly more serious is what motherhood may do to a woman's sexuality. Often when the stork flies in, sexuality flies out. Both in the emotional minds of some women *and* in the minds of their husbands, when a woman becomes a mother, she stops being a woman. It's not only that motherhood may destroy her physical attractiveness, but its madonna concept may destroy her *feelings* of sexuality.

And what of the payoff? Usually, even the most self-sacrificing of maternal self-sacrificers expects a little something back. Gratified parents are not unknown to the Western world, but there are probably at least just as many who feel, to put it crudely, shortchanged. The experiment mentioned earlier—where the baby ducks followed vacuum cleaners instead of their mothers—indicates that what passes for love from baby to mother is merely a rudimentary kind of object attachment. Without necessarily feeling like a Hoover, a lot of women become disheartened because babies and children are not only not interesting to talk to (not everyone thrills at the wonders of da-da-mama talk) but they are generally not empathetic, considerate people. Even the nicest children are not capable of empathy, surely a major ingredient of love, until they are much older. Sometimes they're never capable of it. Dr. Wyatt says that often, in later years particularly, when most of the "returns" are in, it is the "good mother" who suffers most of all. It is then she must face a reality: The child—the appendage with her genes—is not an appendage, but a separate person. What's more, he or she may be a separate person who doesn't even like her—or whom she doesn't really like.

So if the music is lousy, how come everyone's dancing? Because the 25 motherhood minuet is taught freely from birth, and whether or not she has rhythm or likes the music, every woman is expected to do it. Indeed, she *wants* to do it. Little girls start learning what to want—and what to be—when they are still in their cribs. Dr. Miriam Keiffer, a young social psychologist at Bensalem, the Experimental College of Fordham University, points to studies showing that

> at six months of age, mothers are already treating their baby girls and boys quite differently. For instance, mothers have been found to touch, comfort, and talk to their females more. If these differences can be found at such an early stage, it's not surprising that the end product is as different as it is. What is surprising is that men and women are, in so many ways, similar.

Some people point to the way little girls play with dolls as proof of their innate motherliness. But remember, little girls are *given* dolls. When Margaret Mead presented some dolls to New Guinea children, it was the boys, not the girls, who wanted to play with them, which they did by crooning lullabies and rocking them in the most maternal fashion.

By the time they reach adolescence, most girls, unconsciously or not, have learned enough about role definition to qualify for a master's degree. In general, the lesson has been that no matter what kind of career thoughts one may entertain, one must, first and foremost, be a wife and mother. A girl's mother is usually her first teacher. As Dr. Goode says, "A woman is not only taught by society to have a child; she is taught to have a child who will have a child." A woman who has hung her life on the Motherhood Myth will almost always reinforce her young married daughter's early training by pushing for grandchildren. Prospective grandmothers are not the only ones. Husbands, too, can be effective sellers. After all, they have the Fatherhood Myth to cope with. A married man is *supposed* to have children. Often, particularly among Latins, children are a sign of potency. They help him assure the world—and himself—that he is the big man he is supposed to be. Plus, children give him both immortality (whatever that means) and possibly the chance to become more in his lifetime through the accomplishments of his children, particularly his son. (Sometimes it's important, however, for the son to do better, but not *too* much better.)

Friends, too, can be counted on as myth-pushers. Naturally one wants to do what one's friends do. One study, by the way, found a correlation between a woman's fertility and that of her three closest friends. The negative sell comes into play here, too. We have seen what the concept of non-mother means (cold, selfish, unwomanly, abnormal). In practice, particularly in the suburbs, it can mean, simply, exclusion—both from child-centered activities (that is, most activities) and child-centered conversations (that is, most conversations). It can also mean being the butt of a lot of unfunny jokes. ("Whaddya waiting for? An immaculate conception? Ha ha.") Worst of all, it can mean being an object of pity.

In case she's escaped all those pressures (that is, if she was brought up in a cave), a young married woman often wants a baby just so that she'll (1) have something to do (motherhood is better than clerk/typist, which is often the only kind of job she can get, since little more has been expected of her and, besides, her boss also expects her to leave and be a mother); (2) have something to hug and possess, to be needed by and have power over; and (3) have something to *be*—e.g., a baby's mother. Motherhood affords an instant identity. First, through wifehood, you are somebody's wife; then you are somebody's mother. Both give not only identity and activity, but status and stardom of a kind. During pregnancy, a woman can look forward to the kind of attention and pampering she may not ever have gotten or may never otherwise get. Some women consider birth the biggest accomplishment of their lives, which may be interpreted as saying not much for the rest of their lives. As Dr. Goode says, "It's like the gambler who may know the roulette wheel is crooked, but it's the only game in town." Also, with motherhood, the feeling of accomplishment is immediate. It is really much faster and easier to make a baby than paint a painting, or write a book, or get to the point of accomplishment in a job. It is also easier in a way to shift focus from self-development to child development—particularly since, for women, self-development is considered selfish. Even unwed mothers may achieve a feeling of this kind. (As we have seen, little thought is given to the aftermath.) And, again, since so many women are underdeveloped as people, they feel that, besides children, they have little else to give—to themselves, their husbands, to their world.

You may ask why then, when the realities do start pouring in, does a woman want to have a second, third, even fourth child? OK, (1) just because reality is pouring in doesn't mean she wants to *face* it. A new baby can help bring back some of the old illusions. Says psychoanalyst Dr. Natalie Shainess, "She may view each successive child as a knight in armor that will rescue her from being a 'bad unhappy mother.' " (2) Next on the horror list of having no children, is having one. It suffices to say that only children are not only OK, they even have a high rate of exceptionality. (3) Both parents usually want at least one child of each sex. The husband, for reasons discussed earlier, probably wants a son. (4) The more children one has, the more of an excuse one has not to develop in any other way.

What's the point? A world without children? Of course not. Noth- 30
ing could be worse or more unlikely. No matter what anyone says in

Look or anywhere else, motherhood isn't about to go out like a blown bulb, and who says it should? Only the Myth must go out, and now it seems to be dimming.

The younger-generation females who have been reared on the Myth have not rejected it totally, but at least they recognize it can be more loving to children not to have them. And at least they speak of adopting children instead of bearing them. Moreover, since the new nonbreeders are "less hung-up" on ownership, they seem to recognize that if you dig loving children, you don't necessarily have to own one. The end of the Motherhood Myth might make available more loving women (and men!) for those children who already exist.

When motherhood is no longer culturally compulsory, there will, certainly, be less of it. Women are now beginning to think and do more about development of self, of their individual resources. Far from being selfish, such development is probably our only hope. That means more alternatives for women. And more alternatives mean more selective, better, happier, motherhood—and childhood and husbandhood (or manhood) and peoplehood. It is not a question of whether or not children are sweet and marvelous to have and rear; the question is, even if that's so, whether or not one wants to pay the price for it. It doesn't make sense any more to pretend that women need babies, when what they really need is themselves. If God were still speaking to us in a voice we could hear, even He would probably say, "Be fruitful. Don't multiply."

QUESTIONS

1. *Why does Rollin use the term "myth" to describe what she believes is the common attitude toward motherhood?*
2. *Arguing against motherhood is likely to cause problems in persuading an audience. How does Rollin go about dealing with those problems?*
3. *Rollin allows that "nothing could be worse or more unlikely" than "a world without children" (paragraph 30). Does this contradict her previous argument?*
4. *Choose a common "myth" in contemporary society and argue against it.*

Gloria Steinem

THE GOOD NEWS IS: THESE ARE NOT THE BEST YEARS OF YOUR LIFE

If you had asked me a decade or more ago, I certainly would have said the campus was the first place to look for the feminist or any other revolution. I also would have assumed that student-age women, like student-age men, were much more likely to be activist and open to change than their parents. After all, campus revolts have a long and well-publicized tradition, from the students of medieval France, whose "heresy" was suggesting that the university be separate from the church, through the anticolonial student riots of British India; from students who led the cultural revolution of the People's Republic of China, to campus demonstrations against the Shah of Iran. Even in this country, with far less tradition of student activism, the populist movement to end the war in Vietnam was symbolized by campus protests and mistrust of anyone over thirty.

It has taken me many years of traveling as a feminist speaker and organizer to understand that I was wrong about women; at least, about women acting on their own behalf. In activism, as in so many other things, I had been educated to assume that men's cultural pattern was the natural or the only one. If student years were the peak time of rebellion and openness to change for men, then the same must be true for women. In fact, a decade of listening to every kind of women's group—from brown-bag lunchtime lectures organized by office workers to all-night rap sessions at campus women's centers; from housewives' self-help groups to campus rallies—has convinced me that the reverse is more often true. Women may be the one group that grows more radical with age. Though some students are big exceptions to this rule, women in general don't begin to challenge the politics of our own lives until later.

Looking back, I realize that this pattern has been true for my life, too. My college years were full of uncertainties and the personal conservatism that comes from trying to win approval and fit into the proper grown-up and womanly role whether that means finding a well-to-do man to be supported by or a male radical to support. Nonetheless, I went right on assuming that brave exploring youth and cowardly conservative old age were the norms for everybody, and that I must be just an isolated and guilty accident. Though every generalization

First appeared in *Ms.* magazine (Sept. 1979).

based on female culture has many exceptions, and should never be used as a crutch or excuse, I think we might be less hard on ourselves and each other as students, feel better about our potential for change as we grow older—and educate reporters who announce feminism's demise because its red-hot center is not on campus—if we figured out that for most of us as women, the traditional college period is an unrealistic and cautious time. Consider a few of the reasons.

As students, women are probably treated with more equality than we ever will be again. For one thing, we're consumers. The school is only too glad to get the tuitions we pay, or that our families or government grants pay on our behalf. With population rates declining because of women's increased power over childbearing, that money is even more vital to a school's existence. Yet more than most consumers, we're too transient to have much power as a group. If our families are paying our tuition, we may have even less power.

5 As young women, whether students or not, we're still in the stage most valued by male-dominant cultures: We have our full potential as workers, wives, sex partners, and childbearers.

That means we haven't yet experienced the life events that are most radicalizing for women: entering the paid-labor force and discovering how women are treated there; marrying and finding out that it is not yet an equal partnership; having children and discovering who is responsible for them and who is not; and aging, still a greater penalty for women than for men.

Furthermore, new ambitions nourished by the rebirth of feminism may make young women feel and behave a little like a classical immigrant group. We are determined to prove ourselves, to achieve academic excellence, and to prepare for interesting and successful careers. More noses are kept to more grindstones in an effort to demonstrate newfound abilities, and perhaps to allay suspicions that women still have to have more and better credentials than men. This doesn't leave much time for activism. Indeed, we may not yet know that it is necessary.

In addition, the very progress into previously all-male careers that may be revolutionary for women is seen as conservative and conformist by outside critics. Assuming male radicalism to be the measure of change, they interpret any concern with careers as evidence of "campus conservatism." In fact, "dropping out" may be a departure for men, but "dropping in" is a new thing for women. Progress lies in the direction we have not been.

Like most groups of the newly arrived or awakened, our faith in education and paper degrees also has yet to be shaken. For instance, the percentage of women enrolled in colleges and universities has been increasing at the same time that the percentage of men has been decreasing. Among students entering college in 1978, women *outnumbered* men for the first time. This hope of excelling at the existing game is probably reinforced by the greater cultural pressure on females to be "good girls" and observe somebody else's rules.

10 Though we may know intellectually that we need to have new games with new rules, we probably haven't quite absorbed such facts as the high unemployment rate among female Ph.D.s; the lower average salary among women college graduates of all races than among counterpart males who graduated from high school or less; the middle-management ceiling against which even those eagerly hired new business-school graduates seem to bump their heads after five or ten years; and the barrier-breaking women in nontraditional fields who become the first fired when recession hits. Sadly enough, we may have to personally experience some of these reality checks before we accept the idea that lawsuits, activism, and group pressure will have to accompany our individual excellence and crisp new degrees.

Then there is the female guilt trip, student edition. If we're not sailing along as planned, it must be *our* fault. If our mothers didn't "do anything" with their educations, it must have been *their* fault. If we can't study as hard as we think we must (because women still have to be better prepared than men), and have a substantial personal and sexual life at the same time (because women are supposed to care more about relationships than men do), then we feel inadequate, as if each of us were individually at fault for a problem that is actually culture-wide.

I've yet to be on a campus where most women weren't worrying about some aspect of combining marriage, children, and a career. I've yet to find one where many men were worrying about the same thing. Yet women will go right on suffering from the double-role problem and terminal guilt until men are encouraged, pressured, or otherwise forced, individually and collectively, to integrate themselves into the "women's work" of raising children and homemaking. Until then, and until there are changed job patterns to allow equal parenthood, children will go right on growing up with the belief that only women can be loving and nurturing, and only men can be intellectual or active outside the home. Each half of the world will go on limiting the full range of its human talent.

Finally, there is the intimate political training that hits women in the teens and early twenties: the countless ways we are still brainwashed into assuming that women are dependent on men for our basic identities, both in our work and our personal lives, much more than vice versa. After all, if we're going to enter a marriage system that's still legally designed for a person and a half, submit to an economy in which women still average about fifty-nine cents on the dollar earned by men, and work mainly as support staff and assistants, or *co*-directors and *vice*-presidents at best, then we have to be convinced that we are not whole people on our own.

In order to make sure that we will see ourselves as half-people, and thus be addicted to getting our identity from serving others, society tries hard to convert us as young women into "man junkies"; that is, into people who are addicted to regular shots of male-approval and presence, both professionally and personally. We need a man standing next to us, actually and figuratively, whether it's at work, on Saturday night, or throughout life. (If only men realized how little it matters *which* man is standing there, they would understand that this addiction depersonalizes them, too.) Given the danger to a male-dominant system if young women stop internalizing this political message of derived identity, it's no wonder that those who try to kick the addiction—and, worse yet, to help other women do the same—are likely to be regarded as odd or dangerous by everyone from parents to peers.

15 With all that pressure combined with little experience, it's no wonder that younger women are often less able to support each other. Even young women who espouse feminist goals as individuals may refrain from identifying themselves as "feminist": it's okay to want equal pay for yourself (just one small reform) but it's not okay to want equal pay for women as a group (an economic revolution). Some retreat into individualized career obsessions as a way of avoiding this dangerous discovery of shared experience with women as a group. Others retreat into the safe middle ground of "I'm not a feminist but. . . ." Still others become politically active, but only on issues that are taken seriously by their male counterparts.

The same lesson about the personal conservatism of younger women is taught by the history of feminism. If I hadn't been conned into believing the masculine stereotype of youth as the "natural" time for freedom and rebellion, a time of "sowing wild oats" that actually is made possible by the assurance of power and security later on, I could have figured out the female pattern of activism by looking at women's movements of the past.

In this country, for instance, the nineteenth-century wave of feminism was started by older women who had been through the radicalizing experience of getting married and becoming the legal chattel of their husbands (or the equally radicalizing experience of *not* getting married and being treated as spinsters). Most of them had also worked in the antislavery movement and learned from the political parallels between race and sex. In other countries, that wave was also led by women who were past the point of maximum pressure toward marriageability and conservatism.

Looking at the first decade of this second wave, it's clear that the early feminist activist and consciousness-raising groups of the 1960s were organized by women who had experienced the civil rights movement, or homemakers who had discovered that raising kids and cooking didn't occupy all their talents. While most campuses of the late sixties were still circulating the names of illegal abortionists privately (after all, abortion could damage our marriage value), slightly older women were holding press conferences and speak-outs about the reality of abortions (including their own, even though that often meant confessing to an illegal act) and demanding reform or repeal of anti-choice laws. Though rape had been a quiet epidemic on campus for generations, younger women victims were still understandably fearful of speaking up, and campuses encouraged silence in order to retain their reputation for safety with tuition-paying parents. It took many off-campus speak-outs, demonstrations against laws of evidence and police procedures, and testimonies in state legislatures before most student groups began to make demands on campus and local cops for greater rape protection. In fact, "date rape"—the common campus phenomenon of a young woman being raped by someone she knows, perhaps even by several students in a fraternity house—is just now being exposed. Marital rape, a more difficult legal issue, was taken up several years ago. As for battered women and the attendant exposé of husbands and lovers as more statistically dangerous than unknown muggers in the street, that issue still seems to be thought of as a largely noncampus concern, yet at many of the colleges and universities where I've spoken, there has been at least one case within current student memory of a young woman beaten or murdered by a jealous lover.

This cultural pattern of youthful conservatism makes the growing number of older women going back to school very important. They are life examples and pragmatic activists who radicalize women young enough to be their daughters. Now that the median female undergraduate age in this country is twenty-seven because so many older women have returned, the campus is becoming a major place for cross-generational connections.

None of this should denigrate the courageous efforts of young 20
women, especially women on campus, and the many changes they've pioneered. On the contrary, they should be seen as even more remarkable for surviving the conservative pressures, recognizing societal problems they haven't yet fully experienced, and organizing successfully in the midst of a transient student population. Every women's history course, rape hot line, or campus newspaper that is finally covering *all* the news; every feminist professor whose job has been created or tenure saved by student pressure, or male administrator whose consciousness has been permanently changed; every counselor who's

stopped guiding women one way and men another; every lawsuit that's been fueled by student energies against unequal athletic funds or graduate school requirements: all those accomplishments are even more impressive when seen against the backdrop of the female pattern of activism.

Finally, it would help to remember that a feminist revolution rarely resembles a masculine-style one—just as a young woman's most radical act toward her mother (that is, connecting as women in order to help each other get some power) doesn't look much like a young man's most radical act toward his father (that is, breaking the father-son connection in order to separate identities or take over existing power).

It's those father-son conflicts at a generational, national level that have often provided the conventional definition of revolution; yet they've gone on for centuries without basically changing the role of the female half of the world. They have also failed to reduce the level of violence in society, since both fathers and sons have included some degree of aggressiveness and superiority to women in their definition of masculinity, thus preserving the anthropological model of dominance.

Furthermore, what current leaders and theoreticians define as revolution is usually little more than taking over the army and the radio stations. Women have much more in mind than that. We have to uproot the sexual caste system that is the most pervasive power structure in society, and that means transforming the patriarchal values of those who run the institutions, whether they are politically the "right" or the "left," the fathers or the sons. This cultural part of the change goes very deep, and is often seen as too intimate, and perhaps too threatening, to be considered as either serious or possible. Only conflicts among men are "serious." Only a takeover of existing institutions is "possible."

That's why the definition of "political," on campus as elsewhere, tends to be limited to who's running for president, who's demonstrating against corporate investments in South Africa, or which is the "moral" side of some conventional revolution, preferably one that is thousands of miles away.

25 As important as such activities are, they are also the most comfortable ones when we're young. They provide a sense of virtue without much disruption in the power structure of our daily lives. Even when the most consistent energies on campus are actually concentrated around feminist issues, they may be treated as apolitical and invisible. Asked "What's happening on campus?" a student may reply, "The antinuke movement," even though that resulted in one demonstration of two hours, while student antirape squads have been patrolling the campus every night for two years and women's studies have begun to transform the very textbooks we read.

No wonder reporters and sociologists looking for revolution on campus often miss the depth of feminist change and activity that is really there. Women students themselves may dismiss it as not political and not serious. Certainly, it rarely comes in the masculine sixties style of bombing buildings or burning draft cards. In fact, it goes much deeper than protesting a temporary sympton—say, the draft—and challenges the right of one group to dominate another, which is the disease itself.

Young women have a big task of resisting pressures and challenging definitions. Their increasing success is a miracle of foresight and courage that should make us all proud. But they should know that they, too, may grow more radical with age.

One day, an army of gray-haired women may quietly take over the earth.

James Baldwin

STRANGER IN THE VILLAGE

From all available evidence no black man had ever set foot in this tiny Swiss village before I came. I was told before arriving that I would probably be a "sight" for the village; I took this to mean that people of my complexion were rarely seen in Switzerland, and also that city people are always something of a "sight" outside of the city. It did not occur to me—possibly because I am an American—that there could be people anywhere who had never seen a Negro.

It is a fact that cannot be explained on the basis of the inaccessibility of the village. The village is very high, but it is only four hours from Milan and three hours from Lausanne. It is true that it is virtually unknown. Few people making plans for a holiday would elect to come here. On the other hand, the villagers are able, presumably, to come and go as they please—which they do: to another town at the foot of the mountain, with a population of approximately five thousand, the nearest place to see a movie or go to the bank. In the village there is no movie house, no bank, no library, no theater; very few radios, one jeep, one station wagon; and at the moment, one typewriter, mine, an invention which the woman next door to me here had never seen. There are about six hundred people living here, all Catholic—I conclude this from the fact that the Catholic church is open all year round, whereas the Protestant chapel, set off on a hill a little removed from the village, is open only in the summertime when the tourists arrive. There are four or five hotels, all closed now, and four or five *bistros*, of which,

From *Notes of a Native Son* (1955).

however, only two do any business during the winter. These two do not do a great deal, for life in the village seems to end around nine or ten o'clock. There are a few stores, butcher, baker, *épicerie,* a hardware store, and a money-changer—who cannot change travelers' checks, but must send them down to the bank, an operation which takes two or three days. There is something called the *Ballet Haus,* closed in the winter and used for God knows what, certainly not ballet, during the summer. There seems to be only one schoolhouse in the village, and this for the quite young children; I suppose this to mean that their older brothers and sisters at some point descend from these mountains in order to complete their education—possibly, again, to the town just below. The landscape is absolutely forbidding, mountains towering on all four sides, ice and snow as far as the eye can reach. In this white wilderness, men and women and children move all day, carrying washing, wood, buckets of milk or water, sometimes skiing on Sunday afternoons. All week long boys and young men are to be seen shoveling snow off the rooftops, or dragging wood down from the forest in sleds.

The village's only real attraction, which explains the tourist season, is the hot spring water. A disquietingly high proportion of these tourists are cripples, or semi-cripples, who come year after year—from other parts of Switzerland, usually—to take the waters. This lends the village, at the height of the season, a rather terrifying air of sanctity, as though it were a lesser Lourdes. There is often something beautiful, there is always something awful, in the spectacle of a person who has lost one of his faculties, a faculty he never questioned until it was gone, and who struggles to recover it. Yet people remain people, on crutches or indeed on deathbeds; and wherever I passed, the first summer I was here, among the native villagers or among the lame, a wind passed with me—of astonishment, curiosity, amusement, and outrage. That first summer I stayed two weeks and never intended to return. But I did return in the winter, to work; the village offers, obviously, no distractions whatever and has the further advantage of being extremely cheap. Now it is winter again, a year later, and I am here again. Everyone in the village knows my name, though they scarcely ever use it, knows that I come from America—though, this, apparently, they will never really believe: black men come from Africa—and everyone knows that I am the friend of the son of a woman who was born here, and that I am staying in their chalet. But I remain as much a stranger today as I was the first day I arrived, and the children shout *Neger! Neger!* as I walk along the streets.

It must be admitted that in the beginning I was far too shocked to have any real reaction. In so far as I reacted at all, I reacted by trying to be pleasant—it being a great part of the American Negro's education (long before he goes to school) that he must make people "like" him. This smile-and-the-world-smiles-with-you routine worked about as well in this situation as it had in the situation for which it was designed, which is to say that it did not work at all. No one, after all, can be liked whose human weight and complexity cannot be, or has not been, admitted. My smile was simply another unheard-of phenomenon which allowed them to see my teeth—they did not, really, see my smile and I began to think that, should I take to snarling, no one would notice any difference. All of the physical characteristics of the Negro which had caused me, in America, a very different and almost forgotten pain were nothing less than miraculous—or infernal—in the eyes of the village people. Some thought my hair was the color of tar, that it had the texture of wire, or the texture of cotton. It was jocularly suggested that I might let it all grow long and make myself a winter coat. If I sat in the sun for more than five minutes some daring creature was certain to come along and gingerly put his fingers on my hair, as though he were afraid of an electric shock, or put his hand on my hand, astonished that the color did not rub off. In all of this, in which it must be conceded there was the charm of genuine wonder and in which there were certainly no element of intentional unkindness, there was yet no suggestion that I was human: I was simply a living wonder.

I knew that they did not mean to be unkind, and I know it now; it is 5
necessary, nevertheless, for me to repeat this to myself each time that I walk out of the chalet. The children who shout *Neger!* have no way of knowing the echoes this sound raises in me. They are brimming with good humor and the more daring swell with pride when I stop to speak with them. Just the same, there are days when I cannot pause and smile, when I have no heart to play with them; when, indeed, I mutter sourly to myself, exactly as I muttered on the streets of a city these children have never seen, when I was no bigger than these children are now: *Your* mother *was a nigger.* Joyce is right about history being a nightmare—but it may be the nightmare from which no one *can* awaken. People are trapped in history and history is trapped in them.

There is a custom in the village—I am told it is repeated in many villages—of "buying" African natives for the purpose of converting them to Christianity. There stands in the church all year round a small box with a slot for money, decorated with a black figurine, and into this box the villagers drop their francs. During the *carnaval* which precedes Lent, two village children have their faces blackened—out of which bloodless darkness their blue eyes shine like ice—and fantastic horsehair wigs are placed on their blond heads; thus disguised, they solicit among the villagers for money for the missionaries in Africa. Between the box in the church and the blackened children, the village "bought" last year six or eight African natives. This was reported to me with pride by the wife of one of the *bistro* owners and I was careful to express astonishment and pleasure at the solicitude shown by the village for the souls of black folks. The *bistro* owner's wife beamed with a pleasure far more genuine than my own and seemed to feel that I might now breathe more easily concerning the souls of at least six of my kinsmen.

I tried not to think of these so lately baptized kinsmen, of the price paid for them, or the peculiar price they themselves would pay, and said nothing about my father, who having taken his own conversion too literally never, at bottom, forgave the white world (which he described as heathen) for having saddled him with a Christ in whom, to judge at least from their treatment of him, they themselves no longer believed. I thought of white men arriving for the first time in an African village, strangers there, as I am a stranger here, and tried to imagine the astounded populace touching their hair and marveling at the color of their skin. But there is a great difference between being the first white man to be seen by Africans and being the first black man to be seen by whites. The white man takes the astonishment as tribute, for he arrives to conquer and to convert the natives, whose inferiority in relation to himself is not even to be questioned; whereas I, without a thought of conquest, find myself among a people whose culture controls me, has even, in a sense, created me, people who have cost me more in anguish and rage than they will ever know, who yet do not even know of my existence. The astonishment with which I might have greeted them, should they have stumbled into my African village a few hundred years ago, might have rejoiced their hearts. But the astonishment with which they greet me today can only poison mine.

And this is so despite everything I may do to feel differently, despite my friendly conversations with the *bistro* owner's wife, despite their three-year-old son who has at last become my friend, despite the *saluts* and *bonsoirs*[1] which I exchange with people as I walk, despite the fact that I know that no individual can be taken to task for what history is doing, or has done. I say that the culture of these people controls me—but they can scarcely be held responsible for European culture. America comes out of Europe, but these people have never seen America, nor have most of them seen more of Europe than the hamlet at the foot of their mountain. Yet they move with an authority which I shall never have; and they regard me, quite rightly, not only as a stranger in their village but as a suspect latecomer, bearing no credentials, to everything they have—however unconsciously—inherited.

For this village, even were it incomparably more remote and incred-

1. "Hellos" and "good evenings."

ibly more primitive, is the West, the West onto which I have been so strangely grafted. These people cannot be, from the point of view of power, strangers anywhere in the world; they have made the modern world, in effect, even if they do not know it. The most illiterate among them is related, in a way that I am not, to Dante, Shakespeare, Michelangelo, Aeschylus, Da Vinci, Rembrandt, and Racine; the cathedral at Chartres says something to them which it cannot say to me, as indeed would New York's Empire State Building, should anyone here ever see it. Out of their hymns and dances come Beethoven and Bach. Go back a few centuries and they are in their full glory—but I am in Africa, watching the conquerors arrive.

10 The rage of the disesteemed is personally fruitless, but it is also absolutely inevitable; this rage, so generally discounted, so little understood even among the people whose daily bread it is, is one of the things that makes history. Rage can only with difficulty, and never entirely, be brought under the domination of the intelligence and is therefore not susceptible to any arguments whatever. This is a fact which ordinary representatives of the *Herrenvolk*,[2] having never felt this rage and being unable to imagine, quite fail to understand. Also, rage cannot be hidden, it can only be dissembled. This dissembling deludes the thoughtless, and strengthens rage and adds, to rage, contempt. There are, no doubt, as many ways of coping with the resulting complex of tensions as there are black men in the world, but no black man can hope ever to be entirely liberated from this internal warfare—rage, dissembling, and contempt having inevitably accompanied his first realization of the power of white men. What is crucial here is that, since white men represent in the black man's world so heavy a weight, white men have for black men a reality which is far from being reciprocal; and hence all black men have toward all white men an attitude which is designed, really, either to rob the white man of the jewel of his naïveté, or else to make it cost him dear.

The black man insists, by whatever means he finds at his disposal, that the white man cease to regard him as an exotic rarity and recognize him as a human being. This is a very charged and difficult moment, for there is a great deal of will power involved in the white man's naïveté. Most people are not naturally reflective any more than they are naturally malicious, and the white man prefers to keep the black man at a certain human remove because it is easier for him thus to preserve his simplicity and avoid being called to account for crimes committed by his forefathers, or his neighbors. He is inescapably aware, nevertheless, that he is in a better position in the world than black men are, nor can he quite put to death the suspicion that he is

2. Master race.

hated by black men therefore. He does not wish to be hated, neither does he wish to change places, and at this point in his uneasiness he can scarcely avoid having recourse to those legends which white men have created about black men, the most usual effect of which is that the white man finds himself enmeshed, so to speak, in his own language which describes hell, as well as the attributes which lead one to hell, as being as black as night.

Every legend, moreover, contains its residuum of truth, and the root function of language is to control the universe by describing it. It is of quite considerable significance that black men remain, in the imagination, and in overwhelming numbers in fact, beyond the disciplines of salvation; and this despite the fact that the West has been "buying" African natives for centuries. There is, I should hazard, an instantaneous necessity to be divorced from this so visibly unsaved stranger, in whose heart, moreover, one cannot guess what dreams of vengeance are being nourished; and, at the same time, there are few things on earth more attractive than the idea of the unspeakable liberty which is allowed the unredeemed. When, beneath the black mask, a human being begins to make himself felt one cannot escape a certain awful wonder as to what kind of human being it is. What one's imagination makes of other people is dictated, of course, by the laws of one's own personality and it is one of the ironies of black-white relations that, by means of what the white man imagines the black man to be, the black man is enabled to know who the white man is.

I have said, for example, that I am as much a stranger in this village today as I was the first summer I arrived, but this is not quite true. The villagers wonder less about the texture of my hair than they did then, and wonder rather more about me. And the fact that their wonder now exists on another level is reflected in their attitudes and in their eyes. There are the children who make those delightful, hilarious, sometimes astonishingly grave overtures of friendship in the unpredictable fashion of children; other children, having been taught that the devil is a black man, scream in genuine anguish as I approach. Some of the older women never pass without a friendly greeting, never pass, indeed, if it seems that they will be able to engage me in conversation; other women look down or look away or rather contemptuously smirk. Some of the men drink with me and suggest that I learn how to ski—partly, I gather, because they cannot imagine what I would look like on skis—and want to know if I am married, and ask questions about my *métier*. But some of the men have accused *le sale nègre*[3]—behind my back—of stealing wood and there is already in the eyes of some of them that peculiar, intent, paranoiac malevolence which one some-

3. The dirty Negro.

times surprises in the eyes of American white men when, out walking with their Sunday girl, they see a Negro male approach.

There is a dreadful abyss between the streets of this village and the streets of the city in which I was born, between the children who shout *Neger!* today and those who shouted *Nigger!* yesterday—the abyss is experience, the American experience. The syllable hurled behind me today expresses, above all, wonder: I am a stranger here. But I am not a stranger in America and the same syllable riding on the American air expresses the war my presence has occasioned in the American soul.

For this village brings home to me this fact: that there was a day, 15
and not really a very distant day, when Americans were scarcely Americans at all but discontented Europeans, facing a great unconquered continent and strolling, say, into a marketplace and seeing black men for the first time. The shock this spectacle afforded is suggested, surely, by the promptness with which they decided that these black men were not really men but cattle. It is true that the necessity on the part of the settlers of the New World of reconciling their moral assumptions with the fact—and the necessity—of slavery enhanced immensely the charm of this idea, and it is also true that this idea expresses, with a truly American bluntness, the attitude which to varying extents all masters have had toward all slaves.

But between all former slaves and slave-owners and the drama which begins for Americans over three hundred years ago at Jamestown, there are at least two differences to be observed. The American Negro slave could not suppose, for one thing, as slaves in past epochs had supposed and often done, that he would ever be able to wrest the power from his master's hands. This was a supposition which the modern era, which was to bring about such vast changes in the aims and dimensions of power, put to death; it only begins, in unprecedented fashion, and with dreadful implications, to be resurrected today. But even had this supposition persisted with undiminished force, the American Negro slave could not have used it to lend his condition dignity, for the reason that this supposition rests on another: that the slave in exile yet remains related to his past, has some means—if only in memory—of revering and sustaining the forms of his former life, is able, in short, to maintain his identity.

This was not the case with the American Negro slave. He is unique among the black men of the world in that his past was taken from him, almost literally, at one blow. One wonders what on earth the first slave found to say to the first dark child he bore. I am told that there are Haitians able to trace their ancestry back to African kings, but any American Negro wishing to go back so far will find his journey through time abruptly arrested by the signature on the bill of sale which served as the entrance paper for his ancestor. At the time—to say nothing of the circumstances—of the enslavement of the captive black man who was to become the American Negro, there was not the remotest possibility that he would ever take power from his master's hands. There was no reason to suppose that his situation would ever change, nor was there, shortly, anything to indicate that his situation had ever been different. It was his necessity, in the words of E. Franklin Frazier, to find a "motive for living under American culture or die." The identity of the American Negro comes out of this extreme situation, and the evolution of this identity was a source of the most intolerable anxiety in the minds and the lives of his masters.

For the history of the American Negro is unique also in this: that the question of his humanity, and of his rights therefore as a human being, became a burning one for several generations of Americans, so burning a question that it ultimately became one of those used to divide the nation. It is out of this argument that the venom of the epithet *Nigger!* is derived. It is an argument which Europe has never had, and hence Europe quite sincerely fails to understand how or why the argument arose in the first place, why its effects are frequently disastrous and always so unpredictable, why it refuses until today to be entirely settled. Europe's black possessions remained—and do remain—in Europe's colonies, at which remove they represented no threat whatever to European identity. If they posed any problem at all for the European conscience it was a problem which remained comfortingly abstract: in effect, the black man, as a *man* did not exist for Europe. But in America, even as a slave, he was an inescapable part of the general social fabric and no American could escape having an attitude toward him. Americans attempt until today to make an abstraction of the Negro, but the very nature of these abstractions reveals the tremendous effects the presence of the Negro has had on the American character.

When one considers the history of the Negro in America it is of the greatest importance to recognize that the moral beliefs of a person, or a people, are never really as tenuous as life—which is not moral—very often causes them to appear; these create for them a frame of reference and a necessary hope, the hope being that when life has done its worst they will be enabled to rise above themselves and to triumph over life. Life would scarcely be bearable if this hope did not exist. Again, even when the worst has been said, to betray a belief is not by any means to have put oneself beyond its power; the betrayal of a belief is not the same thing as ceasing to believe. If this were not so there would be no moral standards in the world at all. Yet one must also recognize that morality is based on ideas and that all ideas are dangerous—dangerous because ideas can only lead to action and where the action leads no man can say. And dangerous in this respect: that confronted with the impossibility of remaining faithful to one's beliefs, and the equal impossibility of becoming free of them, one can be driven to the most inhuman excesses. The ideas on which American beliefs are based are not, though Americans often seem to think so, ideas which originated in America. They came out of Europe. And the establishment of democracy on the American continent was scarcely as radical a break with the past as was the necessity, which Americans faced, of broadening this concept to include black men.

This was, literally, a hard necessity. It was impossible, for one thing, 20
for Americans to abandon their beliefs, not only because these beliefs alone seemed able to justify the sacrifices they had endured and the blood that they had spilled, but also because these beliefs afforded them their only bulwark against a moral chaos as absolute as the physical chaos of the continent it was their destiny to conquer. But in the situation in which Americans found themselves, these beliefs threatened an idea which, whether or not one likes to think so, is the very warp and woof of the heritage of the West, the idea of white supremacy.

Americans have made themselves notorious by the shrillness and the brutality with which they have insisted on this idea, but they did not invent it; and it has escaped the world's notice that those very excesses of which Americans have been guilty imply a certain, unprecedented uneasiness over the idea's life and power, if not, indeed, the idea's validity. The idea of white supremacy rests simply on the fact that white men are the creators of civilization (the present civilization, which is the only one that matters; all previous civilizations are simply "contributions" to our own) and are therefore civilization's guardians and defenders. Thus it was impossible for Americans to accept the black man as one of themselves, for to do so was to jeopardize their status as white men. But not so to accept him was to deny his human reality, his human weight and complexity, and the strain of denying the overwhelmingly undeniable forced Americans into rationalizations so fantastic that they approached the pathological.

At the root of the American Negro problem is the necessity of the American white man to find a way of living with the Negro in order to be able to live with himself. And the history of this problem can be reduced to the means used by Americans—lynch law and law, segregation and legal acceptance, terrorization and concession—either to come to terms with this necessity, or to find a way around it, or (most usually) to find a way of doing both these things at once. The resulting spectacle, at once foolish and dreadful, led someone to make the quite accurate observation that "the Negro-in-America is a form of insanity which overtakes white men."

In this long battle, a battle by no means finished, the unforeseeable effects of which will be felt by many future generations, the white man's motive was the protection of his identity; the black man was motivated by the need to establish an identity. And despite the terrorization which the Negro in America endured and endures sporadically until today, despite the cruel and totally inescapable ambivalence of his status in his country, the battle for his identity has long ago been won. He is not a visitor to the West, but a citizen there, an American; as American as the Americans who despise him, the Americans who fear him, the Americans who love him—the Americans who became less than themselves, or rose to be greater than themselves by virtue of the fact that the challenge he represented was inescapable. He is perhaps the only black man in the world whose relationship to white men is more terrible, more subtle, and more meaningful than the relationship of bitter possessed to uncertain possessors. His survival depended, and his development depends, on his ability to turn his peculiar status in the Western world to his own advantage and, it may be, to the very great advantage of that world. It remains for him to fashion out of his experience that which will give him sustenance, and a voice.

The cathedral at Chartres, I have said, says something to the people of this village which it cannot say to me; but it is important to understand that this cathedral says something to me which it cannot say to them. Perhaps they are struck by the power of the spires, the glory of the windows; but they have known God, after all, longer than I have known him, and in a different way, and I am terrified by the slippery bottomless well to be found in the crypt, down which heretics were hurled to death, and by the obscene, inescapable gargoyles jutting out of the stone and seeming to say that God and the devil can never be divorced. I doubt that the villagers think of the devil when they face a cathedral because they have never been identified with the devil. But I must accept the status which myth, if nothing else, gives me in the West before I can hope to change the myth.

25 Yet, if the American Negro has arrived at his identity by virtue of the absoluteness of his estrangement from his past, American white men still nourish the illusion that there is some means of recovering the European innocence, of returning to a state in which black men do not exist. This is one of the greatest errors Americans can make. The identity they fought so hard to protect has, by virtue of that battle, undergone a change: Americans are as unlike any other white people in the world as it is possible to be. I do not think, for example, that it is too much to suggest that the American vision of the world—which allows so little reality, generally speaking, for any of the darker forces in human life, which tends until today to paint moral issues in glaring black and white—owes a great deal to the battle waged by Americans to maintain between themselves and black men a human separation

which could not be bridged. It is only now beginning to be borne in on us—very faintly, it must be admitted, very slowly, and very much against our will—that this vision of the world is dangerously inaccurate, and perfectly useless. For it protects our moral high-mindedness at the terrible expense of weakening our grasp of reality. People who shut their eyes to reality simply invite their own destruction, and anyone who insists on remaining in a state of innocence long after that innocence is dead turns himself into a monster.

The time has come to realize that the interracial drama acted out on the American continent has not only created a new black man, it has created a new white man, too. No road whatever will lead Americans back to the simplicity of this European village where white men still have the luxury of looking on me as a stranger. I am not, really, a stranger any longer for any American alive. One of the things that distinguishes Americans from other people is that no other people has ever been so deeply involved in the lives of black men, and vice versa. This fact faced, with all its implications, it can be seen that the history of the American Negro problem is not merely shameful, it is also something of an achievement. For even when the worst has been said, it must also be added that the perpetual challenge posed by this problem was always, somehow, perpetually met. It is precisely this black-white experience which may prove of indispensable value to us in the world we face today. This world is white no longer, and it will never be white again.

QUESTIONS

1. *Baldwin begins with the narration of his experience in a Swiss village. At what point do you become aware that he has a larger point? What purpose does he make his experience serve?*
2. *Baldwin relates the white man's language and legends about black men to the "laws" of the white man's personality. What conviction about the source and the nature of language does this reveal?*
3. *Describe some particular experience that raises a large social question or shows the working of large social forces. Does Baldwin offer any help in the problem of connecting the particular and the general?*

Brent Staples

BLACK MEN AND PUBLIC SPACE

My first victim was a woman—white, well dressed, probably in her early twenties. I came upon her late one evening on a deserted street in Hyde Park, a relatively affluent neighborhood in an otherwise mean, impoverished section of Chicago. As I swung onto the avenue behind her, there seemed to be a discreet, uninflammatory distance between us. Not so. She cast back a worried glance. To her, the youngish black man—a broad six feet two inches with a beard and billowing hair, both hands shoved into the pockets of a bulky military jacket—seemed menacingly close. After a few more quick glimpses, she picked up her pace and was soon running in earnest. Within seconds she disappeared into a cross street.

That was more than a decade ago, I was twenty-two years old, a graduate student newly arrived at the University of Chicago. It was in the echo of that terrified woman's footfalls that I first began to know the unwieldy inheritance I'd come into—the ability to alter public space in ugly ways. It was clear that she thought herself the quarry of a mugger, a rapist, or worse. Suffering a bout of insomnia, however, I was stalking sleep, not defenseless wayfarers. As a softy who is scarcely able to take a knife to a raw chicken—let alone hold one to a person's throat—I was surprised, embarrassed, and dismayed all at once. Her flight made me feel like an accomplice in tyranny. It also made it clear that I was indistinguishable from the muggers who occasionally seeped into the area from the surrounding ghetto. That first encounter, and those that followed, signified that a vast, unnerving gulf lay between nighttime pedestrians—particularly women—and me. And I soon gathered that being perceived as dangerous is a hazard in itself. I only needed to turn a corner into a dicey situation, or crowd some frightened, armed person in a foyer somewhere, or make an errant move after being pulled over by a policeman. Where fear and weapons meet—and they often do in urban America—there is always the possibility of death.

In that first year, my first away from my hometown, I was to become thoroughly familiar with the language of fear. At dark, shadowy intersections, I could cross in front of a car stopped at a traffic light and elicit the *thunk, thunk, thunk, thunk* of the driver—black, white, male, or female—hammering down the door locks. On less traveled streets after dark, I grew accustomed to but never comfortable with people

Originally appeared in *Harper's Magazine* (Dec. 1986); later included in *Paralled Time: Growing Up in Black and White* (1994).

crossing to the other side of the street rather than pass me. Then there were the standard unpleasantries with policemen, doormen, bouncers, cabdrivers, and others whose business it is to screen out troublesome individuals *before* there is any nastiness.

I moved to New York nearly two years ago and I have remained an avid night walker. In central Manhattan, the near-constant crowd cover minimizes tense one-on-one street encounters. Elsewhere—in SoHo, for example, where sidewalks are narrow and tightly spaced buildings shut out the sky—things can get very taut indeed.

5 After dark, on the warrenlike streets of Brooklyn where I live, I often see women who fear the worst from me. They seem to have set their faces on neutral, and with their purse straps strung across their chests bandolier-style, they forge ahead as though bracing themselves against being tackled. I understand, of course, that the danger they perceive is not a hallucination. Women are particularly vulnerable to street violence, and young black males are drastically overrepresented among the perpetrators of that violence. Yet these truths are no solace against the kind of alienation that comes of being ever the suspect, a fearsome entity with whom pedestrians avoid making eye contact.

It is not altogether clear to me how I reached the ripe old age of twenty-two without being conscious of the lethality nighttime pedestrians attributed to me. Perhaps it was because in Chester, Pennsylvania, the small, angry industrial town where I came of age in the 1960s, I was scarcely noticeable against a backdrop of gang warfare, street knifings, and murders. I grew up one of the good boys, had perhaps a half-dozen fistfights. In retrospect, my shyness of combat has clear sources.

As a boy, I saw countless tough guys locked away; I have since buried several, too. They were babies, really—a teenage cousin, a brother of twenty-two, a childhood friend in his mid-twenties—all gone down in episodes of bravado played out in the streets. I came to doubt the virtues of intimidation early on. I chose, perhaps unconsciously, to remain a shadow—timid, but a survivor.

The fearsomeness mistakenly attributed to me in public places often has a perilous flavor. The most frightening of these confusions occurred in the late 1970s and early 1980s, when I worked as a journalist in Chicago. One day, rushing into the office of a magazine I was writing for with a deadline story in hand, I was mistaken for a burglar. The office manager called security and, with an ad hoc[1] posse, pursued me through the labyrinthine halls, nearly to my editor's door. I had no way of proving who I was. I could only move briskly toward the company of someone who knew me.

Another time I was on assignment for a local paper and killing time

1. For a particular purpose.

before an interview. I entered a jewelry store on the city's affluent Near North Side. The proprietor excused herself and returned with an enormous red Doberman pinscher straining at the end of a leash. She stood, the dog extended toward me, silent to my questions, her eyes bulging nearly out of her head. I took a cursory look around, nodded, and bade her good night.

10 Relatively speaking, however, I never fared as badly as another black male journalist. He went to nearby Waukegan, Illinois, a couple of summers ago to work on a story about a murderer who was born there. Mistaking the reporter for the killer, police officers hauled him from his car at gunpoint and but for his press credentials would probably have tried to book him. Such episodes are not uncommon. Black men trade tales like this all the time.

Over the years, I learned to smother the rage I felt at so often being taken for a criminal. Not to do so would surely have led to madness. I now take precautions to make myself less threatening. I move about with care, particularly late in the evening. I give a wide berth to nervous people on subway platforms during the wee hours, particularly when I have exchanged business clothes for jeans. If I happen to be entering a building behind some people who appear skittish, I may walk by, letting them clear the lobby before I return, so as not to seem to be following them. I have been calm and extremely congenial on those rare occasions when I've been pulled over by the police.

And on late-evening constitutionals I employ what has proved to be an excellent tension-reducing measure: I whistle melodies from Beethoven and Vivaldi and the more popular classical composers. Even steely New Yorkers hunching toward nighttime destinations seem to relax, and occasionally they even join in the tune. Virtually everybody seems to sense that a mugger wouldn't be warbling bright, sunny selections from Vivaldi's *Four Seasons*.[2] It is my equivalent of the cowbell that hikers wear when they know they are in bear country.

2. Work by composer Antonio Vivaldi (c. 1675–1741), celebrating the seasons.

QUESTIONS

1. *Staples writes of situations rightly perceived as threatening and of situations misperceived as threatening. Give specific instances of each and tell how they are related.*
2. *Staples's essay contains a mixture of rage and humor. Does this mix distract from or contribute to the seriousness of the matter?*
3. *Write of a situation in which someone was wrongly perceived as threatening.*

Shelby Steele

THE RECOLORING OF CAMPUS LIFE

In the past few years, we have witnessed what the National Institute Against Prejudice and Violence calls a "proliferation" of racial incidents on college campuses around the country. Incidents of on-campus "intergroup conflict" have occurred at more than 160 colleges in the last three years, according to the institute. The nature of these incidents has ranged from open racial violence—most notoriously, the October 1986 beating of a black student at the University of Massachusetts at Amherst after an argument about the World Series turned into a racial bashing, with a crowd of up to 3,000 whites chasing twenty blacks—to the harassment of minority students, to acts of racial or ethnic insensitivity, with by far the greatest number falling in the last two categories. At Dartmouth College, three editors of the *Dartmouth Review,* the off-campus right-wing student weekly, were suspended last winter for harassing a black professor in his lecture hall. At Yale University last year a swastika and the words "white power" were painted on the school's Afro-American cultural center. Racist jokes were aired not long ago on a campus radio station at the University of Michigan. And at the University of Wisconsin at Madison, members of the Zeta Beta Tau fraternity held a mock slave auction in which pledges painted their faces black and wore Afro wigs. Two weeks after the president of Stanford University informed the incoming freshmen class last fall that "bigotry is out, and I mean it," two freshmen defaced a poster of Beethoven—gave the image thick lips—and hung it on a black student's door.

In response, black students around the country have rediscovered the militant protest strategies of the Sixties. At the University of Massachusetts at Amherst, Williams College, Penn State University, UC Berkeley, UCLA, Stanford, and countless other campuses, black students have sat in, marched, and rallied. But much of what they were marching and rallying about seemed less a response to specific racial incidents than a call for broader action on the part of the colleges and universities they were attending. Black students have demanded everything from more black faculty members and new courses on racism to the addition of "ethnic" foods in the cafeteria. There is the sense in these demands that racism runs deep.

Of course, universities are not where racial problems tend to arise.

First published in *Harper's Magazine* (Feb. 1989).

When I went to college in the mid-Sixties, colleges were oases of calm and understanding in a racially tense society; campus life—with its traditions of tolerance and fairness, its very distance from the "real" world—imposed a degree of broad-mindedness on even the most provincial students. If I met whites who were not anxious to be friends with blacks, most were at least vaguely friendly to the cause of our freedom. In any case, there was no guerrilla activity against our presence, no "mine field of racism" (as one black student at Berkeley recently put it) to negotiate. I wouldn't say that the phrase "campus racism" is a contradiction in terms, but until recently it certainly seemed an incongruence.

But a greater incongruence is the generational timing of this new problem on the campuses. Today's undergraduates were born after the passage of the 1964 Civil Rights Act. They grew up in an age when racial equality was for the first time enforceable by law. This too was a time when blacks suddenly appeared on television, as mayors of big cities, as icons of popular culture, as teachers, and in some cases even as neighbors. Today's black and white college students, veterans of *Sesame Street* and often of integrated grammar and high schools, have had more opportunities to know each other—whites and blacks—than any previous generation in American history. Not enough opportunities, perhaps, but enough to make the notion of racial tension on campus something of a mystery, at least to me.

5 To try to unravel this mystery I left my own campus, where there have been few signs of racial tension, and talked with black and white students at California schools where racial incidents had occurred: Stanford, UCLA, Berkeley. I spoke with black and white students—and not with Asians and Hispanics—because, as always, blacks and whites represent the deepest lines of division, and because I hesitate to wander onto the complex territory of other minority groups. A phrase by William H. Gass[1]—"the hidden internality of things"—describes with maybe a little too much grandeur what I hoped to find. But it *is* what I wanted to find, for this is the kind of problem that makes a black person nervous, which is not to say that it doesn't unnerve whites as well. Once every six months or so someone yells "nigger" at me from a passing car. I don't like to think that these solo artists might soon make up a chorus or, worse, that this chorus might one day soon sing to me from the paths of my own campus.

I have long believed that trouble between the races is seldom what it appears to be.[2] It was not hard to see after my first talks with students

1. A contemporary American novelist.
2. See my essay, "I'm Black, You're White, Who's Innocent? Race and Power in an Era of Blame," *Harper's Magazine*, June 1988 [Steele's note].

that racial tension on campus is a problem that misrepresents itself. It has the same look, the archetypal pattern, of America's timeless racial conflict—white racism and black protest. And I think part of our concern over it comes from the fact that it has the feel of a relapse, illness gone and come again. But if we are seeing the same symptoms, I don't believe we are dealing with the same illness. For one thing, I think racial tension on campus is the result more of racial equality than inequality.

How to live with racial difference has been America's profound social problem. For the first 100 years or so following emancipation it was controlled by a legally sanctioned inequality that acted as a buffer between the races. No longer is this the case. On campuses today, as throughout society, blacks enjoy equality under the law—a profound social advancement. No student may be kept out of a class or a dormitory or an extracurricular activity because of his or her race. But there is a paradox here: On a campus where members of all races are gathered, mixed together in the classroom as well as socially, differences are more exposed than ever. And this is where the trouble starts. For members of each race—young adults coming into their own, often away from home for the first time—bring to this site of freedom, exploration, and now, today, equality very deep fears and anxieties, inchoate feelings of racial shame, anger, and guilt. These feelings could lie dormant in the home, in familiar neighborhoods, in simpler days of childhood. But the college campus, with its structures of interaction and adult-level competition—the big exam, the dorm, the "mixer"—is another matter. I think campus racism is born of the rub between racial difference and a setting, the campus itself, devoted to interaction and equality. On our campuses, such concentrated micro-societies, all that remains unresolved between blacks and whites, all the old wounds and shames that have never been addressed, present themselves for attention—and present our youth with pressures they cannot always handle.

I have mentioned one paradox: racial fears and anxieties among blacks and whites bubbling up in an era of racial equality under the law, in settings that are among the freest and fairest in society. And there is another, related paradox, stemming from the notion of—and practice of—affirmative action. Under the provisions of the Equal Employment Opportunity Act of 1972, all state governments and institutions (including universities) were forced to initiate plans to increase the proportion of minority and women employees—in the case of universities, of students too. Affirmative action plans that establish racial quotas were ruled unconstitutional more than ten years ago in *University of California Regents v. Bakke.* But quotas are only the most controversial aspect of affirmative action; the principle of affirmative action is reflected in various university programs aimed at redressing and overcoming past patterns of discrimination. Of course, to be conscious of patterns of discrimination—the fact, say, that public schools in the black inner cities are more crowded and employ fewer top-notch teachers than white suburban public schools, and that this is a factor in student performance—is only reasonable. However, in doing this we also call attention quite obviously to difference: in the case of blacks and whites, racial difference. What has emerged on campus in recent years—as a result of the new equality and affirmative action, in a sense, as a result of progress—is a *politics of difference,* a troubling, volatile politics in which each group justifies itself, its sense of worth and its pursuit of power, through difference alone.

In this context, racial, ethnic, and gender differences become forms of sovereignty, campuses become balkanized, and each group fights with whatever means are available. No doubt there are many factors that have contributed to the rise of racial tension on campus: What has been the role of fraternities, which have returned to campus with their inclusions and exclusions? What role has the heightened notion of college as some first step to personal, financial success played in increasing competition, and thus tension? Mostly what I sense, though, is that in interactive settings, while fighting the fights of "difference," old ghosts are stirred, and haunt again. Black and white Americans simply have the power to make each other feel shame and guilt. In the "real" world, we may be able to deny these feelings, keep them at bay. But these feelings are likely to surface on college campuses, where young people are groping for identity and power, and where difference is made to matter so greatly. In a way, racial tension on campus in the Eighties might have been inevitable.

10 I would like, first, to discuss black students, their anxieties and vulnerabilities. The accusation that black Americans have always lived with is that they are inferior—inferior simply because they are black. And this accusation has been too uniform, too ingrained in cultural imagery, too enforced by law, custom, and every form of power not to have left a mark. Black inferiority was a precept accepted by the founders of this nation; it was a principle of social organization that relegated blacks to the sidelines of American life. So when today's young black students find themselves on white campuses, surrounded by those who historically have claimed superiority, they are also surrounded by the myth of their inferiority.

Of course it is true that many young people come to college with some anxiety about not being good enough. But only blacks come wearing a color that is still, in the minds of some, a sign of inferiority. Poles, Jews, Hispanics, and other groups also endure degrading stereotypes. But two things make the myth of black inferiority a far heavier burden—the broadness of its scope and its incarnation in color. There are not only more stereotypes of blacks than of other groups, but these stereotypes are also more dehumanizing, more focused on the most despised of human traits—stupidity, laziness, sexual immorality, dirtiness, and so on. In America's racial and ethnic hierarchy, blacks have clearly been relegated to the lowest level—have been burdened with an ambiguous, animalistic humanity. Moreover, this is made unavoidable for blacks by the sheer visibility of black skin, a skin that evokes the myth of inferiority on sight. And today this myth is sadly reinforced for many black students by affirmative action programs, under which blacks may often enter college with lower test scores and high-school grade point averages than whites. "They see me as an affirmative action case," one black student told me at UCLA.

So when a black student enters college, the myth of inferiority compounds the normal anxiousness over whether he or she will be good enough. This anxiety is not only personal but also racial. The families of these students will have pounded into them the fact that blacks are not inferior. And probably more than anything, it is this pounding that finally leaves a mark. If I am not inferior, why the need to say so?

This myth of inferiority constitutes a very sharp and ongoing anxiety for young blacks, the nature of which is very precise: It is the terror that somehow, through one's actions or by virtue of some "proof" (a poor grade, a flubbed response in class), one's fear of inferiority—inculcated in ways large and small by society—will be confirmed as real. On a university campus, where intelligence itself is the ultimate measure, this anxiety is bound to be triggered.

A black student I met at UCLA was disturbed a little when I asked him if he ever felt vulnerable—anxious about "black inferiority"—as a black student. But after a long pause, he finally said, "I think I do." The example he gave was of a large lecture class he'd taken with more than 300 students. Fifty or so black students sat in the back of the lecture hall and "acted out every stereotype in the book." They were loud, ate food, came in late—and generally got lower grades than the whites in the class. "I knew I would be seen like them, and I didn't like it. I never sat by them." Seen like what? I asked, though we both knew the answer. "As lazy, ignorant, and stupid," he said sadly.

Had the group at the back been white fraternity brothers, they 15
would not have been seen as dumb *whites*, of course. And a frat brother who worried about his grades would not worry that he would be seen "like them." The terror in this situation for the student I spoke with was that his own deeply buried anxiety would be given credence, that the myth would be verified, and that he would feel shame and humiliation not because of who he was but simply because he was black. In this lecture hall his race, quite apart from his performance,

might subject him to four unendurable feelings—diminishment, accountability to the preconceptions of whites, a powerlessness to change those preconceptions, and, finally, shame. These are the feelings that make up his racial anxiety, and that of all blacks on any campus. On a white campus a black is never far from these feelings, and even his unconscious knowledge that he is subject to them can undermine his self-esteem. There are blacks on every campus who are not up to doing good college-level work. Certain black students may not be happy or motivated or in the appropriate field of study—*just like whites.* (Let us not forget that many white students get poor grades, fail, drop out.) Moreover, many more blacks than whites are not quite prepared for college, may have to catch up, owing to factors beyond their control: poor previous schooling, for example. But the white who has to catch up will not be anxious that his being behind is a matter of his whiteness, of his being *racially* inferior. The black student may well have such a fear.

This, I believe, is one reason why black colleges in America turn out 34 percent of all black college graduates, though they enroll only 17 percent of black college students. Without whites around on campus the myth of inferiority is in abeyance and, along with it, a great reservoir of culturally imposed self-doubt. On black campuses feelings of inferiority are personal; on campuses with a white majority, a black's problems have a way of becoming a "black" problem.

But this feeling of vulnerability a black may feel in itself is not as serious a problem as what he or she does with it. To admit that one is made anxious in integrated situations about the myth of racial inferiority is difficult for young blacks. It seems like admitting that one *is* racially inferior. And so, most often, the student will deny harboring these feelings. This is where some of the pangs of racial tension begin, because denial always involves distortion.

In order to deny a problem we must tell ourselves that the problem is something different than what it really is. A black student at Berkeley told me that he felt defensive every time he walked into a class and saw mostly white faces. When I asked why, he said, "Because I know they're all racists. They think blacks are stupid." Of course it may be true that some whites feel this way, but the singular focus on white racism allows this student to obscure his own underlying racial anxiety. He can now say that his problem—facing a class full of white faces, *fearing* that they think he is dumb—is entirely the result of certifiable white racism and has nothing to do with his own anxieties, or even that this particular academic subject may not be his best. Now all the terror of his anxiety, its powerful energy, is devoted to simply *seeing* racism. Whatever evidence of racism he finds—and looking this hard, he will no doubt find some—can be brought in to buttress his distorted view of the problem, while his actual deep-seated anxiety goes unseen.

Denial, and the distortion that results, places the problem *outside* the self and in the world. It is not that I have any inferiority anxiety because of my race; it is that I am going to school with people who don't like blacks. This is the shift in thinking that allows black students to reenact the protest pattern of the Sixties. Denied racial anxiety-distortion-reenactment is the process by which feelings of inferiority are transformed into an exaggerated white menace—which is then protested against with the techniques of the past. Under the sway of this process, black students believe that history is repeating itself, that it's just like the Sixties, or Fifties. In fact, it is the not yet healed wounds from the past, rather than the inequality that created the wounds, that is the real problem.

This process generates an unconscious need to exaggerate the level 20
of racism on campus—to make it a matter of the system, not just a handful of students. Racism is the avenue away from the true inner anxiety. How many students demonstrating for a black "theme house"—demonstrating in the style of the Sixties, when the battle was to win for blacks a place on campus—might be better off spending their time reading and studying? Black students have the highest dropout rate and lowest grade point average of any group in American universities. This need not be so. And it is not the result of not having black theme houses.

It was my very good fortune to go to college in 1964, when the question of black "inferiority" was openly talked about among blacks. The summer before I left for college I heard Martin Luther King Jr. speak in Chicago, and he laid it on the line for black students everywhere. "When you are behind in a footrace, the only way to get ahead is to run faster than the man in front of you. So when your white roommate says he's tired and goes to sleep, you stay up and burn the midnight oil." His statement that we were "behind in a footrace" acknowledged that because of history, of few opportunities, of racism, we were, in a sense, "inferior." But this had to do with what had been done to our parents and their parents, not with inherent inferiority. And because it was acknowledged, it was presented to us as a challenge rather than a mark of shame.

Of the eighteen black students (in a student body of 1,000) who were on campus in my freshman year, all graduated, though a number of us were not from the middle class. At the university where I currently teach, the dropout rate for black students is 72 percent, despite the presence of several academic-support programs; a counseling center with black counselors; an Afro-American studies department; black faculty, administrators, and staff; a general education curriculum that emphasizes "cultural pluralism"; an Educational Opportunities Program; a mentor program; a black faculty and staff association; and an administration and faculty that often announce the need to do more for black students.

It may be unfair to compare my generation with the current one. Parents do this compulsively and to little end but self-congratulation. But I don't congratulate my generation. I think we were advantaged. We came along at a time when racial integration was held in high esteem. And integration was a very challenging social concept for both blacks and whites. We were remaking ourselves—that's what one did at college—and making history. We had something to prove. This was a profound advantage; it gave us clarity and a challenge. Achievement in the American mainstream was the goal of integration, and the best thing about this challenge was its secondary message—that we *could* achieve.

There is much irony in the fact that black power would come along in the late Sixties and change all this. Black power was a movement of uplift and pride, and yet it also delivered the weight of pride—a weight that would burden black students from then on. Black power "nationalized" the black identity, made blackness itself an object of celebration and allegiance. But if it transformed a mark of shame into a mark of pride, it also, in the name of pride, required the denial of racial anxiety. Without a frank account of one's anxieties, there is no clear direction, no concrete challenge. Black students today do not get as clear a message from their racial identity as my generation got. They are not filled with the same urgency to prove themselves, because black pride has said, You're already proven, already equal, as good as anybody.

25 The "black identity" shaped by black power most powerfully contributes to racial tensions on campuses by basing entitlement more on race than on constitutional rights and standards of merit. With integration, black entitlement was derived from constitutional principles of fairness. Black power changed this by skewing the formula from rights to color—if you were black, you were entitled. Thus, the United Coalition Against Racism (UCAR) at the University of Michigan could "demand" two years ago that all black professors be given immediate tenure, that there be special pay incentives for black professors, and that money be provided for an all-black student union. In this formula, black becomes the very color of entitlement, an extra right in itself, and a very dangerous grandiosity is promoted in which blackness amounts to specialness.

Race is, by any standard, an unprincipled source of power. And on campuses the use of racial power by one group makes racial or ethnic or gender *difference* a currency of power for all groups. When I make my difference into power, other groups must seize upon their difference to contain my power and maintain their position relative to me. Very quickly a kind of politics of difference emerges in which racial, ethnic, and gender groups are forced to assert their entitlement and vie for power based on the single quality that makes them different from one another.

On many campuses today academic departments and programs are established on the basis of difference—black studies, women's studies, Asian studies, and so on—despite the fact that there is nothing in these "difference" departments that cannot be studied within traditional academic disciplines. If their rationale truly is past exclusion from the mainstream curriculum, shouldn't the goal now be complete inclusion rather than separateness? I think this logic is overlooked because these groups are too interested in the power their difference can bring, and they insist on separate departments and programs as a tribute to that power.

This politics of difference makes everyone on campus a member of a minority group. It also makes racial tensions inevitable. To highlight one's difference as a source of advantage is also, indirectly, to inspire the enemies of that difference. When blackness (and femaleness) becomes power, then white maleness is also sanctioned as power. A white male student at Stanford told me, "One of my friends said the other day that we should get together and start up a white student union and come up with a list of demands."

It is certainly true that white maleness has long been an unfair source of power. But the sin of white male power is precisely its use of race and gender as a source of entitlement. When minorities and women use their race, ethnicity, and gender in the same way, they not only commit the same sin but also, indirectly, sanction the very form of power that oppressed them in the first place. The politics of difference is based on a tit-for-tat sort of logic in which every victory only calls one's enemies to arms.

This elevation of difference undermines the communal impulse by 30
making each group foreign and inaccessible to others. When difference is celebrated rather than remarked, people must think in terms of difference, they must find meaning in difference, and this meaning comes from an endless process of contrasting one's group with other groups. Blacks use whites to define themselves as different, women use men. Hispanics use whites and blacks, and on it goes. And in the process each group mythologizes and mystifies its difference, puts it beyond the full comprehension of outsiders. Difference becomes an inaccessible preciousness toward which outsiders are expected to be simply and uncomprehendingly reverential. But beware: In this world,

even the insulated world of the college campus, preciousness is a balloon asking for a needle. At Smith College, graffiti appears: "Niggers, Spics, and Chinks quit complaining or get out."

Most of the white students I talked with spoke as if from under a faint cloud of accusation. There was always a ring of defensiveness in their complaints about blacks. A white student I spoke with at UCLA told me: "Most white students on this campus think the black student leadership here is made up of oversensitive crybabies who spend all their time looking for things to kick up a ruckus about." A white student at Stanford said: "Blacks do nothing but complain and ask for sympathy when everyone really knows they don't do well because they don't try. If they worked harder, they could do as well as everyone else."

That these students felt accused was most obvious in their compulsion to assure me that they were not racists. Oblique versions of some-of-my-best-friends-are stories came ritualistically before or after critiques of black students. Some said flatly, "I am not a racist, but . . ." Of course, we all deny being racists, but we only do this compulsively, I think, when we are working against an accusation of bias. I think it was the color of my skin, itself, that accused them.

This was the meta-message that surrounded these conversations like an aura, and in it, I believe, is the core of white American racial anxiety. My skin not only accused them, it judged them. And this judgment was a sad gift of history that brought them to account whether they deserved such an accounting or not. It said that wherever and whenever blacks were concerned, they had reason to feel guilt. And whether it was earned or unearned, I think it was guilt that set off the compulsion in these students to disclaim. I believe it is true that in America black people make white people feel guilty.

Guilt is the essence of white anxiety, just as inferiority is the essence of black anxiety. And the terror that it carries for whites is the terror of discovering that one has reason to feel guilt where blacks are concerned—not so much because of what blacks might think but because of what guilt can say about oneself. If the darkest fear of blacks is inferiority, the darkest fear of whites is that their better lot in life is at least partially the result of their capacity for evil—their capacity to dehumanize an entire people for their own benefit, and then to be indifferent to the devastation their dehumanization has wrought on successive generations of their victims. This is the terror that whites are vulnerable to regarding blacks. And the mere fact of being white is sufficient to feel it, since even whites with hearts clean of racism benefit from being white—benefit at the expense of blacks. This is a conditional guilt having nothing to do with individual intentions or actions. And it makes for a very powerful anxiety because it threatens whites with a view of themselves as inhuman, just as inferiority threatens blacks with a similar view of themselves. At the dark core of both anxieties is a suspicion of incomplete humanity.

So the white students I met were not just meeting me; they were 35
also meeting the possibility of their own inhumanity. And this, I think, is what explains how some young white college students in the late Eighties can so frankly take part in racially insensitive and outright racist acts. They were expected to be cleaner of racism than any previous generation—they were born into the Great Society. But this expectation overlooks the fact that, for them, color is still an accusation and judgment. In black faces there is a discomforting reflection of white collective shame. Blacks remind them that their racial innocence is questionable, that they are the beneficiaries of past and present racism, and that the sins of the father may well have been visited on the children.

And yet young whites tell themselves that they had nothing to do with the oppression of black people. They have a stronger belief in their racial innocence than any previous generation of whites, and a natural hostility toward anyone who would challenge that innocence. So (with a great deal of individual variation) they can end up in the paradoxical position of being hostile to blacks as a way of defending their own racial innocence.

I think this is what the young white editors of the *Dartmouth Review* were doing when they shamelessly harassed William Cole, a black music professor. Weren't they saying, in effect, I am so free of racial guilt that I can afford to ruthlessly attack blacks and still be racially innocent? The ruthlessness of that attack was a form of denial, a badge of innocence. The more they were charged with racism, the more ugly and confrontational their harassment became. Racism became a means of rejecting racial guilt, a way of showing that they were not ultimately racists.

The politics of difference sets up a struggle for innocence among all groups. When difference is the currency of power, each group must fight for the innocence that entitles it to power. Blacks sting whites with guilt, remind them of their racist past, accuse them of new and more subtle forms of racism. One way whites retrieve their innocence is to discredit blacks and deny their difficulties, for in this denial is the denial of their own guilt. To blacks this denial looks like racism, a racism that feeds black innocence and encourages them to throw more guilt at whites. And so the cycle continues. The politics of difference leads each group to pick at the sore spots of the other.

Men and women who run universities—whites, mostly—also participate in the politics of difference, although they handle their guilt differently than many of their students. They don't deny it, but still they don't want to *feel* it. And to avoid this *feeling* of guilt they have tended to go along with whatever blacks put on the table rather than work with them to assess their real needs. University administrators have too often been afraid of their own guilt and have relied on negotiation and capitulation more to appease that guilt than to help blacks and other minorities. Administrators would never give white students a racial theme house where they could be "more comfortable with people of their own kind," yet more and more universities are doing this for black students, thus fostering a kind of voluntary segregation. To avoid the anxieties of integrated situations, blacks ask for theme houses; to avoid guilt, white administrators give them theme houses.

40 When everyone is on the run from his anxieties about race, race relations on campus can be reduced to the negotiation of avoidances. A pattern of demand and concession develops in which each side uses the other to escape itself. Black studies departments, black deans of student affairs, black counseling programs, Afro houses, black theme houses, black homecoming dances and graduation ceremonies—black students and white administrators have slowly engineered a machinery of separatism that, in the name of sacred difference, redraws the ugly lines of segregation.

Black students have not sufficiently helped themselves, and universities, despite all their concessions, have not really done much for blacks. If both faced their anxieties, I think they would see the same thing: Academic parity with all other groups should be the overriding mission of black students, and it should also be the first goal that universities have for their black students. Blacks can only *know* they are as good as others when they are, in fact, as good—when their grades are higher and their dropout rate lower. Nothing under the sun will substitute for this, and no amount of concessions will bring it about.

Universities and colleges can never be free of guilt until they truly help black students, which means leading and challenging them rather than negotiating and capitulating. It means inspiring them to achieve academic parity, nothing less, and helping them see their own weaknesses as their greatest challenge. It also means dismantling the machinery of separatism, breaking the link between difference and power, and skewing the formula for entitlement away from race and gender and back to constitutional rights.

As for the young white students who have rediscovered swastikas and the word "nigger," I think they suffer from an exaggerated sense of their own innocence, as if they were incapable of evil and beyond the reach of guilt. But it is also true that the politics of difference creates an environment which threatens their innocence and makes them defensive. White students are not invited to the negotiating table from which they see blacks and others walk away with concessions. The presumption is that they do not deserve to be there because they are white. So they can only be defensive, and the less mature among them will be aggressive. Guerrilla activity will ensue. Of course this is wrong, but it is also a reflection of an environment where difference carries power and where whites have the wrong "difference."

I think universities should emphasize commonality as a higher value than "diversity" and "pluralism"—buzzwords for the politics of difference. Difference that does not rest on a clearly delineated foundation of commonality not only is inaccessible to those who are not part of the ethnic or racial group but is antagonistic to them. Difference can enrich only the common ground.

Integration has become an abstract term today, having to do with 45
little more than numbers and racial balances. But it once stood for a high and admirable set of values. It made difference second to commonality, and it asked members of all races to face whatever fears they inspired in each other. I doubt the word will have a new vogue, but the values, under whatever name, are worth working for.

QUESTIONS

1. *What are the differences Steele cites between black-white campus relations in the 1960s and the 1980s?*
2. *What leads Steele to say that today's campus is given over to "politics of difference"? What are the "politics of difference"?*
3. *Using the same kind of interviewing approach Steele does, write about the extent to which his conclusions apply to your own campus.*

Gerald Early

THEIR MALCOLM, MY PROBLEM: ON THE ABUSES OF AFROCENTRISM AND BLACK ANGER

Late one afternoon last spring I sat at home on my couch, disheartened, thumbing through an old copy of *The Autobiography of Malcolm X.* Earlier that afternoon I'd had a lengthy meeting with black students from my university, and although Malcolm X had been in the air on campus for some time—the proliferation of X caps and T-shirts, gossip about the Spike Lee movie, which would open at the end of the year—I suspect it was mostly the passionate and angry tone of the black voices at the meeting that prompted me to pull my copy of the book off the shelf.

From *Harper's Magazine* (Dec. 1992).

I had reread *The Autobiography* many times, having taught it on several occasions. A considerable literary accomplishment, it borrows freely and innovatively from St. Augustine's *Confessions,* the slave narrative tradition, and the bildungsroman tradition of Fielding and Goethe.[1] As a boy I felt it was the only book written expressly for me, a young black American male. But over the years my view changed: the book's rhetoric began to seem awkwardly out of date, and the energy of the man seemed contained in a vision that was as narrow as it was vivid; there was something about the nature of Malcolm's raillery that now left me unprovoked, something about his quest for humanity that left me unmoved.

But as I sat on the couch working my way through the narrative that afternoon, I found much of what I'd been moved by so long ago coming back to me with remarkable force. I read again with revived interest how Malcolm was born in Omaha in 1925, the seventh child of a father who was an itinerant preacher, a fierce follower of Marcus Garvey, and of a mother so light-skinned that she was frequently mistaken for white. When Malcolm was six years old his father was murdered, presumably by white terrorists, because of his black-nationalist beliefs. It is this death, as well as the institutionalization of his mother—who suffered a breakdown as the result of her husband's murder and her struggle to support her family on welfare—that establishes the pattern of both the book and the life as a critique of racism and liberalism. As Malcolm claims angrily, "I am a creation of the Northern white man and of his hypocritical attitude toward the Negro."

After growing up in a detention home in Mason, Michigan, and spending some time in Boston's Roxbury ghetto, living with his half sister, Malcolm, at age seventeen, settled in Harlem and became a petty hustler and dope pusher. He participated in a string of burglaries of rich white suburban homes but was caught, convicted, and sentenced to ten years in prison. While in jail Malcolm converted to Elijah Muhammad's Nation of Islam, embracing a strict religious but militantly racialist outlook and dedicating himself to telling "the truth about the white man." Once out of prison, Malcolm became Muhammad's most effective minister and proselytizer, attracting adherents and also the attention of the white media. In 1964 Malcolm was excommunicated from the Nation, ostensibly for describing the assassination of John Kennedy as the "chickens coming home to roost." But a schism had been brewing for some time: Muhammad had become increasingly jealous over Malcolm's media attention, Malcolm's stardom, while Malcolm had become disillusioned by Muhammad's

1. Bildingsroman, novel of growth and development, typified by Fielding's *Tom Jones* and Goethe's *Wilhelm Meister.*

extra-marital affairs and the older man's reluctance to become more politically active.

After leaving the Nation, Malcolm tried, unsuccessfully, to found 5
two organizations, Muslim Mosque, Inc., and the Organization of Afro-American Unity, the latter patterned after the Organization of African Unity. During the last two years of his life, he traveled extensively in Africa and also made a pilgrimage to Mecca, during which he re-converted to a non-racialist Islam. He was assassinated in Harlem by members of the Nation of Islam in February 1965, just as he was about to give a speech. An angry end to an angry life.

Leafing through *The Autobiography*, I began to see that Malcolm X was the ideological standard of Africanness now being offered up by my students. His singular presence had been much in evidence at that afternoon's meeting. I had agreed to sit down with a coalition of black students—most of whom did not know me—soon after it was announced that I was to become the new director of African and Afro-American Studies at my university. In the weeks before we arranged to convene, I had been furiously denounced and publicly pilloried for not being sufficiently Afrocentric to head the department, a charge rather akin to being "not black enough" in the 1960s.

What I found particularly baffling about these attacks was that I do not possess any of the "social tokens" often associated with being "insufficiently black": I do not have a white wife; I have served on most of the university's affirmative-action committees; I am intellectually engaged in the study of black subject matter; I have never publicly criticized any black person connected with the campus during my entire ten-year stay.

But in the eyes of these students, I had failed as a black man. I had never led a protest march or even proposed that one be held. I had never initiated or signed a petition. I had never attended any student meetings that focused on black issues. I had never, in short, done anything deemed heroic. And, for the young, a lack of demonstrable, outsized heroism is a lack of commitment and a lack of commitment is a sign of having sold out.

Some of this standard teacher-student strife is to be expected; I suppose it is generational. Still, I was deeply pained to have been seen by my black students as someone who compromised, who slouched, who shuffled, someone who had not stood up and been counted, someone who had never done anything heroic for the race.

When my ten-year-old daughter came home from school, she was 10
surprised to find me home, and more surprised to find me visibly upset.

"What's wrong?" she asked.

"The American Negro," I began sarcastically, as she made herself a snack, "goes through periodic bouts of dementia when he romantically proclaims himself an African, lost from his brothers and sisters. These tides of benighted nationalism come and go, but this time it seems particularly acute." By now my voice had become strident, my rage nearly out of control.

"Never have I been subjected to more anti-intellectual, proto-fascistic nonsense than what I have had to endure in the name of Afrocentrism. And this man," I said, waving Malcolm's autobiography, "is the architect of it all, the father of Afrocentrism. This idiot, this fool." I slumped at the kitchen table, placing my forehead against the cool wood.

"But I thought you liked Malcolm X," she said.

15 Indeed, I was once keenly fond of Malcolm X. I first saw Malcolm on television in 1963, when I was a ten-year-old boy living in Philadelphia; three years later Malcolm, by now dead if not forgotten, left an indelible mark on my life. That year my oldest sister, then a college student, joined the local chapter of the Student Nonviolent Coordinating Committee (SNCC), which at the time was becoming an increasingly Marxist and militant group. Her conversation was now peppered with phrases like "the white power structure," "the man," "black power," and "self-determination for oppressed people." One day she brought home a recorded Malcolm X speech entitled "Message to the Grass Roots."

Hearing it for the first time was a shock and a revelation. I had heard men in barbershops say many of the same things but never in public. I laughed and laughed at Malcolm's oratory, but I felt each word burn with the brightness of a truth that was both utterly new and profoundly familiar. Whenever I had the chance, I would play the record over and over. In a few days I had memorized the entire speech, every word, every turn of phrase, every vocal nuance. I could deliver the speech just as Malcolm had. I never looked at the world in quite the same way again.

During the days of segregation, which continued, de facto, into the Sixties, belonging to an all-black institution—anything from a church to a social club to a Boy Scout troop—was like wearing a badge of inferiority. Participation in these groups was not a choice made by blacks but a fiat, decreed by whites, which clearly stated that blacks were not considered, in any way, part of the white world—for most blacks, a world where what happened, mattered. But Malcolm asserted blackness as a source of honor and accomplishment, not degradation and shame.

Within months of the time I first heard Malcolm's "Message to the Grass Roots," I not only had read his autobiography but had listened carefully to other of his speeches, such as "The Ballot or the Bullet" and “Malcolm X on Afro-American History.” I had become knowledgeable about the Congo, Patrice Lumumba, the Bandung Conference, and the leadership of the American civil rights movement, topics that were hardly of interest to other boys my age.

Not everyone I knew responded enthusiastically to Malcolm X. I would often hear men in the barbershop making statements like: “All that Malcolm X does is talk. In fact, that's what all them Muslims do is talk. Just another nigger hustle.” And one day, when I was fourteen, my friend Gary became very angry with me when—with Malcolm X in mind—I called him black.

20 “Don't call me black, man. I don't like that. I ain't black,” he said vehemently.

“We are all black people,” I said. “You've been brainwashed by the white man to hate your color. But you're black, and you've got to accept that.”

“I said don't call me black,” he shouted. “What's wrong with you, anyway? You sound like you been hanging out with them Malcolm X guys. He was a phony just like all the rest of them Muslims. You sound like you snappin' out or something.”

I was surprised at Gary's reaction. He was bigger and tougher than I was, and I assumed that he would view Malcolm as a hero, too. But when it became clear he didn't, I felt personally insulted.

“You're black, black, black,” I said angrily. “Malcolm X was a great man who tried to free black people. What've you ever done to free black people? You're black and I'll call you black anytime I want to, you dumb nigger.”

25 He hit me so hard in the chest that I fell down in the street, stunned and hurt by the blow.

“Don't call me that,” he said, walking away.

It is unlikely that a young black person today would get swatted for defending Malcolm X. In fact, in many ways Malcolm's presence is more deeply felt in the black community now than at any time since his murder. The reasons for his enduring legacy are complex. Malcolm X does not remain an important figure in American cultural history simply because he was a charismatic black nationalist. Hubert H. Harrison, Henry McNeal Turner, Richard B. Moore, Martin Delany, David Walker, Elijah Muhammad, Alexander Crummell, Edward Wilmot Blyden, and Ron Karenga all were charismatic black nationalists of some sort in the nineteenth and twentieth centuries, and none is remembered as a distinct figure except by historians of African-American life and culture.

Malcolm was a fierce debater, a compelling public speaker, and a man of considerable intellectual agility. But, like Martin Luther King, he was hardly an original thinker: American blacks have been hearing some form of black nationalism—Ethiopianism, the back-to-Africa movement, Black Judaism, the Black Moors, Pan-Africanism, the Black Aesthetic, or Afrocentrism—for well over 200 years. Malcolm's basic idea—a vision of millenarian race-based cultural nationalism culminating in a worldwide race war that would overturn European dominance forever—was, like the Puritanism of Jonathan Edwards,[2] already hoary with age even when it seemed most current. But just as Edwards brilliantly disseminated Calvinist ideas, Malcolm, with valor and wit, popularized ideas about black nationalism, black self-determination, and a universal African identity.

More important, however, than Malcolm's ideas—that is, his popularizing of black nationalism—was, and is, Malcolm the man. His life unfolded like a myth, a heroic tale. He had the imprimatur of both prison (the mark of a revolutionary) and the street (the mark of the proletariat), which lent him authenticity. But, as a Muslim, he was also a firm believer in the bourgeois ideals of diligence, discipline, and entrepreneurship.

30 Then there was Malcolm's youth. Although generational conflict exists in many societies, it has a long and particularly intense history for blacks. Each new generation views its elders with suspicion, thinking them failures who compromised and accommodated themselves in order to survive among the whites. And each generation, in some way, wishes to free itself from the generation that produced it.

Malcolm's particular brand of youthfulness fed this desire. He embodied a daring and a recklessness that young blacks, especially young black men, have found compelling. At rallies I attended as a teenager in the early 1970s, men older than myself would describe the inspiring experience of having heard Malcolm live. They had, on several occasions a decade earlier, attended Savior's Day rallies, annual Muslim conventions during which Elijah Muhammad was scheduled to speak. But Malcolm would always appear on the dais first. He was supposed to serve, simply, as the warm-up act, but for these young men he always stole the show. While black nationalist and separatist ideas coming from Elijah Muhammad seemed cranky, cult-like, backwaterish, and marginal, the same ideas coming from Malcolm seemed revolutionary, hip, and vibrant.

Malcolm arrived on the scene during the age of Kennedy and King, the blossoming of youth culture and the coming of rock and roll. Flaunting his youth as a symbol of masculinity and magnetic power, he exploited the generation gap among blacks. Because of Malcolm, the leaders of the civil rights movement were made, through their comparative conservatism, to seem even older than they were, more cowardly than they were, bigger sellouts than they were. He referred to

2. American theologian and preacher (1703–1758).

them as "Uncle Toms" or as "Uncles," associating them with the conflated popular image of both Uncle Remus and Uncle Tom, fictional characters created by white writers, aged black men who "loved their white folks." Malcolm used this language even when talking about Martin Luther King, who was, in fact, younger than he was. And Malcolm remains forever young, having died at the age of thirty-nine. He—like the Kennedys and King—died the tragic death of a political martyr.

Malcolm, the dead hero, has grown in stature in our black consciousness even while other living former heroes are forgotten. It is telling to compare the current view of Malcolm with that of another important black figure of the 1960s, Muhammad Ali. Ali and Malcolm are often yoked together in the black mind: two militant Muslims, public troublemakers, disturbers of the peace. But today, those of us who lived through the 1960s return to thinking about Malcolm not simply because of his greater intellect but because we are unnerved by Ali now, by the brain damage he has suffered in the ring, by the way he has aged. Malcolm remains frozen forever in his stern youthfulness, almost immortal, like a saint, while Ali is a mirror of our own aging and mortality, a busted-up, broken-down hero.

No doubt Malcolm's early death contributed to his enduring power for young people today. But it is the existence of *The Autobiography* that has mythologized him forever. If Malcolm—or Alex Haley (who assisted in writing *The Autobiography*) or Malcolm's wife, Betty Shabazz (who is said to have done extensive revisions on Haley's manuscript)—had not written his story, he would have died a negligible curiosity on the American political landscape in much the same way that, say, George Lincoln Rockwell or Father Divine did.[3] Today it is rare to come upon a black student who has not read *The Autobiography of Malcolm X* or will not read it at some point during his or her college career. It has sold more than 3 million copies and is probably the most commonly taught and most frequently recommended book written by a black American male.

Malcolm, frozen in time, stands before us as the lonely outsider, a 35
kind of bespectacled prince, estranged and embattled, holding a high-noon posture of startling and doomed confrontation. It is this man who has become for young blacks today the kind of figure that Thoreau, who espoused the overturning of generations and the uselessness of the elders in *Walden*, was for young whites in the late 1960s.

When I was growing up in the 1960s the goal for blacks was clear: equality and integration. The civil rights movement, which provided

3. Charismatic American black religious leader (c. 1882–1965). George Lincoln Rockwell (1918–1967), head of the American Nazi party.

an arena for heroic political action aimed at destroying segregation, helped forge this consensus among blacks. Today blacks, confused and angered by the failure of "the dream," share little agreement about the future. There is a sense that integration has been halfhearted and has been achieved only at the expense of black identity.

To today's young, middle-class blacks in particular, Malcolm's espousal of all-blackness—the idea that everything black is inherently good and that blacks must purge themselves of white "contaminants"—may be especially crucial; it is certainly more important than it was to my generation. These young people have grown up, by and large, in an integrated world. Most of the black students who attend the standard prestigious, private, research-oriented university are the offspring of either black professional parents or a mixed marriage, have lived most of their lives in mixed or largely white neighborhoods, and have attended white prep schools or predominantly white public schools. When they arrive at a university that has an African or Afro-American Studies program, these students expect to find, for the first time in their lives, an all-black community, one that they have never experienced in the secular world, a sort of intellectual "nation within a nation," to borrow W. E. B. Du Bois's[4] term. There they can be their "true" black selves. Yet in many ways these black students share fundamentally the same values—a belief in upward mobility and the rewards of hard work—as the whites who surround them. These students are wholly neither inside nor outside of the American mainstream, and they are unsure whether any ideal form of integration exists. But, like Malcolm, they wish to rid themselves of their feelings of ambiguity, their sense of the precariousness of their belonging. For many of them (and they are not entirely unjustified in feeling this way) integration is the badge of degradation and dishonor, of shame and inferiority, that segregation was for my generation.

I also have felt great shame in the era of integration because, as a student and as a professor, I have taken the money of whites, been paid simply because I was black and was expected to make "black statements" in order to be praised by whites for my Negro-ness. I have felt much as if I were doing what James Baldwin described black domestics in white homes as doing: stealing money and items from whites that the whites expected them to take, wanted them to take, because it reinforced the whites' superiority and our own degradation. Allowing the whites to purchase my "specialness" through affirmative action has seemed not like reparations but like a new form of enslavement.

And I worry about my daughters, wondering whether they are getting too cozy with whites at school and whether they seem too utterly

4. Leading black writer and social thinker (1868–1963).

middle class. So much are they protected from any blatant form of racism that I fear they are likely never to understand that it existed and continues to exist today. At these times I feel estranged from my children, knowing that I do not fully understand their experience, nor do they understand mine. For instance, when we moved to an affluent white suburb they clamored for a golden retriever, no doubt because a neighbor down the street had a very attractive one. I adamantly refused to consent, thinking that purchasing a friendly, suburban, sitcom-type dog was another concession to white, middle-class taste. "I don't like dogs," I said childishly before I finally relented.

On occasions like this, when I have wanted to instill in my daughters a sense of "blackness," I tend to trot out a story about my boyhood. 40 It is an anecdote that involves my friend Gary, and it took place about six months after our fight over Malcolm X. Think of my story as the black parent's jeremiad, a warning about the declension of the new generation. And once again Malcolm X seems central to it.

In order to get home from school each day, Gary and I had to walk through an Italian neighborhood. Often during these trips home, several older Italian boys and their Doberman pinschers would chase Gary and me, or a group of us, for several blocks. Once we hit the border of our black Philadelphia neighborhood, around Sixth Street, they would retreat. The Italian boys called this game "chasing the coons" or "spooking the spooks," and it sometimes resulted in a black kid being bitten by one of their dogs. The black kids never fought back; we just ran, later cursing the Italian boys, rhetorically wreaking all manner of vengeance upon them.

On this particular afternoon, both Gary and I had bought sodas and doughnuts, as we usually did, on our way home from school, and we were strolling along when we suddenly heard some voices cry out, "Get those niggers." We turned to see about five or six Italian boys and an unleashed Doberman coming after us. We started running like beings possessed. We were comfortably ahead and easily could have avoided getting caught when Gary abruptly pulled up and caught my arm.

"I'm tired of running from them guys. I ain't running anymore and neither are you."

"Hey, man," I said frantically. "Are you crazy or something? What are we gonna do? Fight 'em? You must be crazy. I'm getting out of here."

"You ain't going nowhere," he said angrily through his teeth. "It's 45 time we stood up for ourselves. I'm tired of having them white bastards chase me and laugh at me. If they beat us up, well, I guess that's one ass whipping we got to take. But I ain't running."

Gary turned his soda bottle over in his hand like a weapon and I reluctantly did the same. He picked up a brick from the street and I followed; we waited for the Italian boys to catch up. When they did they looked almost bewildered. They stood, perhaps twenty feet from us, slowly comprehending that we were standing our ground. For several moments, except for the growling dog, everyone was silent. Then one of them spoke.

"What you niggers doing walking through our neighborhood? We got a hunting season on jungle bunnies."

"We ain't causing no trouble," Gary said. "We just minding our own business. And if you come another step closer, I guarantee I'll put your ass in the hospital."

We all stood for what seemed the longest time, as if frozen in some sort of still life. I was gripping the brick and bottle so hard my hands ached. I felt ready, even eager, to fight, but I was also relieved when I realized we wouldn't have to.

50 One Italian boy mumbled something about watching ourselves "next time," and they all began to drift off.

As they were retreating, Gary shouted, "And we ain't no niggers. We're black. Don't ever call us niggers again."

At this I was more than slightly startled, but I was very proud, as if I had made a convert. I recalled at that instant something I had heard Malcolm X say on television, something like, "The so-called Negro has to stop the sit-in, the beg-in, the crawl-in, asking for something that is by rights already his. The so-called Negro has to approach the white man as a man himself." We felt like men, grown-up men, or what we thought grown-up men must feel like when they have been tested and found themselves adequate.

Never once have I told this story in any way that impresses my daughters. My youngest usually says, "Are you finished now, Daddy?"

They know the moral is something to the effect that it is good to be black and that it is something for which we must all stand up. "Yeah," my youngest says, "it's good to be black, but it's better not to have to spend all your time thinking about how good it is to be black."

55 So here I am, caught between my daughters, who find my race lessons tiresome, and my students, who think me somehow insufficiently black. I need look no farther than Malcolm, old ally and new nemesis, to find the source of this ambiguity. Malcolm embodied contradiction. He preached the importance of Africa, yet he was the most American of men. His autobiography is the quintessential Horatio Alger tale of the self-created individual. Even Malcolm's turn toward Islam, his attempt to embrace something explicitly non-Western, is itself classically American. Americans have long been attracted to the East—in the form of nineteenth-century orientalism, twentieth-century Egyptology, and the current-day popularity, among many middle-class whites, of yoga and Zen Buddhism. Even Afrocentrism itself can

be seen as classically American in its urge to romanticize and reinvent the past, much in the way that Jay Gatsby[5] did.

And yet Fitzgerald's novel clearly warns against the temptation to remake the past and the seduction of fraudulent identities. It is in its defining of identity that Malcolm's thinking is uncomfortably rigid and finally false. He developed two distinct but related beliefs about black identity: that blacks are not Americans and that they are really Africans. "We are just as much African today as we were in Africa four hundred years ago, only we are a modern counterpart of it," Malcolm X said at Harvard in 1964. "When you hear a black man playing music, whether it is jazz or Bach, you still hear African music. In everything else we do we still are African in color, feeling, everything. And we will always be that whether we like it or not."

By preaching a romantic reunification with mythological Africa as a way of generating pride and racial unity, Malcolm advocated a single identity for all black people, one that implicitly removed individual distinctions among blacks. In Malcolm's view, individuality is a negligible European creation, while the holy "community"—a creation of the African and other darkskinned peoples—is prized above everything else. The idea of race as community, as invisible church, however, can demand a stifling conformity; its popularity suggests that some aspects of Afrocentrism, or all-blackness, as Malcolm popularized them and as they are preached in some quarters today, far from being imaginative or innovative, are utterly prosaic and philistine in their vision.

Despite the unrealistic romanticism of Malcolm's back-to-Africa preachings, he offers an important message for today's young blacks: that blacks are, indeed, as Du Bois argues, a people of "double-consciousness"; that both blackness and Americanness are real options, each having meaning only when measured against the other. Malcolm would not have argued with such passion and virulence against the validity of any kind of black *American* experience if he did not suspect that assimilation, that *being* American, was truly a rooted desire, if not a fulfilled reality, for most blacks. Yet he also knew that blacks in America cannot think about what their Americanness means without thinking about what it means to be of African descent: the two are inextricably bound together. As the historian Sterling Stuckey has argued, black people did not acquire a sense of what being African was until they came to America. They, like most people who came to this country, achieved their initial sense of identity through their clan—that is, slaves thought of themselves more as members of specific tribes or nations than as "Africans." Slavery compressed the diversity of African experience into one broad African identity, forcing blacks,

5. Hero of F. Scott Fitzgerald's novel *The Great Gatsby* (1925).

in turn, to invent a collective sense of an African memory and an African self.

But Africanness is relevant to American blacks today only as a way of helping us understand what it means to be American. While it is necessary that we recognize our African ancestry, and remember that it was, in varying degrees, stripped away by slavery, we must acknowledge, finally, that our story is one of remaking ourselves as Americans. My world is shaped by two indelible ideas: first, that I was once an African, that I grew, generations ago, from that ancestral soil; and, second, that I will never be African again, that I will, like Joseph, not be buried in the soil of my long-ago ancestors.

Malcolm preached the necessity of being African at the complete expense of our American selves, a love of the misty past at the cost of our actual lives, our triumphs, our sufferings in the New World and as modern people. In this way, Malcolm merely increased our anxiety, further fueled our sense of inadequacy, and intensified our self-hatred and feelings of failure by providing us with a ready excuse: America is the white man's country, and the whites don't want you here and will never give you equal citizenship.

But it must always be remembered that our blood is here, our names are here, our fate is here, in a land we helped to invent. By that I have in mind much more than the fact that blacks gave America free labor; other groups have helped build this and other countries for no or for nominal wages. We have given America something far more valuable: we have given her her particular identity, an identity as a country dedicated to diversity, a nation of different peoples living together as one. And no black person should care what the whites want or don't want in the realm of integration. The whites simply must learn to live as committed equals with their former slaves.

Our profound past of being African, which we must never forget, must be balanced by the complex fate of being American, which we can never deny or, worse, evade. For we must accept who and what we are and the forces and conditions that have made us this, not as defeat or triumph, not in shame or with grandiose pride, but as the tangled, strange, yet poignant and immeasurable record of an imperishable human presence.

QUESTIONS

1. *What are some of the key ironies Early uses to help structure his essay?*
2. *Is there a way people might regard Early's problematical situation as a sign of progress?*
3. *Describe current knowledge and opinion of Malcolm X by interviewing people of different races, ages, and backgrounds.*

Education

Eudora Welty

CLAMOROUS TO LEARN

From the first I was clamorous to learn—I wanted to know and begged to be told not so much what, or how, or why, or where, as when. How soon?

> Pear tree by the garden gate,
> How much longer must I wait?

This rhyme from one of my nursery books was the one that spoke for me. But I lived not at all unhappily in this craving, for my wild curiosity was in large part suspense, which carries its own secret pleasure. And so one of the godmothers of fiction was already bending over me.

When I was five years old, I knew the alphabet, I'd been vaccinated (for smallpox), and I could read. So my mother walked across the street to Jefferson Davis Grammar School[1] and asked the principal if she would allow me to enter the first grade after Christmas.

"Oh, all right," Said Miss Duling. "Probably the best thing you could do with her."

Miss Duling, a lifelong subscriber to perfection, was a figure of authority, the most whole-souled I have ever come to know. She was a dedicated schoolteacher who denied herself all she might have done or whatever other way she might have lived (this possibility was the last that could have occurred to us, her subjects in school). I believe she came of well-off people, well-educated, in Kentucky, and certainly old photographs show she was a beautiful, high-spirited-looking young lady—and came down to Jackson to its new grammar school that was going begging for a principal. She must have earned next to nothing;

From *One Writer's Beginnings* (1985).

1. Named after the president of the Confederate States of America (1861–1865) and located in Jackson, Mississippi.

Mississippi then as now was the nation's lowest-ranking state economically, and our legislature has always shown a painfully loud reluctance to give money to public education. That challenge *brought* her.

In the long run she came into touch, as teacher or principal. with three generations of Jacksonians. My parents had not, but everybody else's parents had gone to school to her. She'd taught most of our leaders somewhere along the line. When she wanted something done—some civic oversight corrected, some injustice made right overnight, or even a tree spared that the fool telephone people were about to cut down—she telephoned the mayor, or the chief of police, or the president of the power company, or the head doctor at the hospital, or the judge in charge of a case, or whoever, and calling them by their first names, *told* them. It is impossible to imagine her meeting with anything less than compliance. The ringing of her brass bell from their days at Davis School would still be in their ears. She also proposed a spelling match between the fourth grade at Davis School and the Mississippi Legislature, who went through with it; and that told the Legislature.

Her standards were very high and of course inflexible, her authority was total; why *wouldn't* this carry with it a brass bell that could be heard ringing for a block in all directions? That bell belonged to the figure of Miss Duling as though it grew directly out of her right arm, as wings grew out of an angel or a tail out of the devil. When we entered, marching, into her school, by strictest teaching, surveillance, and order we learned grammar, arithmetic, spelling, reading, writing, and geography; and she, not the teachers, I believe, wrote out the examinations: need I tell you, they were "hard."

She's not the only teacher who has influenced me, but Miss Duling, in some fictional shape or form, has stridden into a larger part of my work than I'd realized until now. She emerges in my perhaps inordinate number of schoolteacher characters. I loved those characters in the writing. But I did not, in life, love Miss Duling. I was afraid of her high-arched bony nose, her eyebrows lifted in half-circles above her hooded, brilliant eyes, and of the Kentucky R's in her speech, and the long steps she took in her hightop shoes. I did nothing but fear her bearing-down authority, and did not connect this (as of course we were meant to) with our own need or desire to learn, perhaps because I already had this wish, and did not need to be driven.

She was impervious to lies or foolish excuses or the insufferable plea of not knowing any better. She wasn't going to have any frills, either, at Davis School. When a new governor moved into the mansion, he sent his daughter to Davis School; her name was Lady Rachel Conner. Miss Duling at once called the governor to the telephone and told him, "She'll be plain Rachel here."

Miss Duling dressed as plainly as a Pilgrim on a Thanksgiving poster we made in the schoolroom, in a longish black-and-white checked gingham dress, a bright thick wool sweater the red of a railroad lantern—she'd knitted it herself—black stockings and her narrow elegant feet in black hightop shoes with heels you could hear coming, rhythmical as a parade drum down the hall. Her silky black curly hair was drawn back out of curl, fastened by high combs, and knotted behind. She carried her spectacles on a gold chain hung around her neck. Her gaze was in general sweeping, then suddenly at the point of concentration upon you. With a swing of her bell that took her whole right arm and shoulder, she rang it, militant and impartial, from the head of the front steps of Davis School when it was time for us all to line up, girls on one side, boys on the other. We were to march past her into the school building, while the fourth-grader she nabbed played time on the piano, mostly to a tune we could have skipped to, but we didn't skip into Davis School.

Little recess (open-air exercises) and big recess (lunch-boxes from 10
home opened and eaten on the grass, on the girls' side and the boys' side of the yard) and dismissal were also regulated by Miss Duling's bell. The bell was also used to catch us off guard with fire drill.

It was examinations that drove my wits away, as all emergencies do. Being expected to measure up was paralyzing. I failed to make 100 on my spelling exam because I missed one word and that word was "uncle." Mother, as I knew she would, took it personally. "You couldn't spell *uncle?* When you've got those five perfectly splendid uncles in West Virginia? What would *they* say to that?"

It was never that Mother wanted me to beat my classmates in grades; what she wanted was for me to have my answers right. It was unclouded perfection I was up against.

My father was much more tolerant of possible error. He only said, as he steeply and impeccably sharpened my pencils on examination morning, "Now just keep remembering: the examinations were made out for the *average* student to pass. That's the majority. And if the majority can pass, think how much better *you* can do."

I looked to my mother, who had her own opinions about the majority. My father wished to treat it with respect, she didn't. I'd been born left-handed, but the habit was broken when I entered the first grade in Davis School. My father had insisted. He pointed out that everything in life had been made for the convenience of right-handed people, because they were the majority, and he often used "what the majority wants" as a criterion for what was for the best. My mother said she could not promise him, could not promise him at all, that I wouldn't stutter as a consequence. Mother had been born left-handed too; her family consisted of five left-handed brothers, a left-handed mother, and a father who could write with both hands at the same time, also backwards and forwards and upside down, different words with each hand. She had been broken of it when she was young, and she said she used to stutter.

"But you still stutter," I'd remind her, only to hear her say loftily, "You should have heard me when I was your age."

In my childhood days, a great deal of stock was put, in general, in the value of doing well in school. Both daily newspapers in Jackson saw the honor roll as news and published the lists, and the grades, of all the honor students. The city fathers gave the children who made the honor roll free season tickets to the baseball games down at the grandstand. We all attended and all worshiped some player on the Jackson Senators: I offered up my 100's in arithmetic and spelling, reading and writing, attendance and, yes, deportment—I must have been a prig!—to Red McDermott, the third baseman. And our happiness matched that of knowing Miss Duling was on her summer vacation, far, far away in Kentucky.

Every school week, visiting teachers came on their days for special lessons. On Mondays, the singing teacher blew into the room fresh from the early outdoors, singing in her high soprano "How do you do?" to do-mi-sol-do,[2] and we responded in chorus from our desks, "I'm ve-ry well" to do-sol-mi-do. Miss Johnson taught us rounds—"Row row row your boat gently down the stream"—and "Little Sir Echo," with half the room singing the words and the other half being the echo, a competition. She was from the North, and she was the one who wanted us all to stop the Christmas carols and see snow. The snow falling that morning outside the window was the first most of us had ever seen, and Miss Johnson threw up the window and held out wide her own black cape and caught flakes on it and ran, as fast as she could go, up and down the aisles to show us the real thing before it melted.

Thursday was Miss Eyrich and Miss Eyrich was Thursday. She came to give us physical training. She wasted no time on nonsense. Without greeting, we were marched straight outside and summarily divided into teams (no choosing sides), put on the mark, and ordered to get set for a relay race. Miss Eyrich cracked out "Go!" Dread rose in my throat. My head swam. Here was my turn, nearly upon me. (Wait, have I been touched—was that slap the touch? Go on! Do I go on without our passing a word? What word? Now am I racing too fast to turn around? Now I'm nearly home, but where is the hand waiting for mine to touch? Am I too late? Have I lost the whole race for our side?) I lost the relay race for our side before I started, through living ahead of myself, dreading to make my start, feeling too late prematurely, and

2. Syllables indicating the first, third, fifth, and eighth tones of the scale.

standing transfixed by emergency, trying to think of a password. Thursdays still can make me hear Miss Eyrich's voice. "On your mark—get set—GO!"

Very composedly and very slowly, the art teacher, who visited each room on Fridays, paced the aisle and looked down over your shoulder at what you were drawing for her. This was Miss Ascher. Coming from behind you, her deep, resonant voice reached you without being a word at all, but a sort of purr. It was much the sound given out by our family doctor when he read the thermometer and found you were running a slight fever: "Um-hm. Um-hm." Both alike, they let you go right ahead with it.

The school toilets were in the boys' and girls' respective basements. 20
After Miss Duling had rung to dismiss school, a friend and I were making our plans for Saturday from adjoining cubicles. "Can you come spend the day with me?" I called out, and she called back, "I might could."

"Who—said—MIGHT—COULD?" It sounded like "Fe Fi Fo Fum!"

We both were petrified, for we knew whose deep measured words those were that came from just outside our doors. That was the voice of Mrs. McWillie, who taught the other fourth grade across the hall from ours. She was not even our teacher, but a very heavy, stern lady who dressed entirely in widow's weeds with a pleated black shirtwaist with a high net collar and velvet ribbon, and a black skirt to her ankles, with black circles under her eyes and a mournful, Presbyterian expression. We children took her to be a hundred years old. We held still.

"You might as well tell me," continued Mrs. McWillie. "I'm going to plant myself right here and wait till you come out. Then I'll see who it was I heard saying 'MIGHT-COULD.' "

If Elizabeth wouldn't go out, of course I wouldn't either. We knew her to be a teacher who would not flinch from standing there in the basement all afternoon, perhaps even all day Saturday. So we surrendered and came out. I priggishly hoped Elizabeth would clear it up which child it was—it wasn't me.

"So it's you." She regarded us as a brace, made no distinction: who- 25
ever didn't say it was guilty by association. "If I ever catch you down here one more time saying 'MIGHT-COULD,' I'm going to carry it to Miss Duling. You'll be kept in every day for a week! I hope you're both sufficiently ashamed of yourselves?" Saying "might-could" was bad, but saying it in the basement made bad grammar a sin. I knew Presbyterians believed that you could go to Hell.

Mrs. McWillie never scared us into grammar, of course. It was my first-year Latin teacher in high school who made me discover I'd fallen in love with it. It took Latin to thrust me into bona fide alliance with words in their true meaning. Learning Latin (once I was free of Caesar) fed my love for words upon words, words in continuation and modification, and the beautiful, sober, accretion of a sentence. I could see the achieved sentence finally standing there, as real, intact, and built to stay as the Mississippi State Capitol at the top of my street, where I could walk through it on my way to school and hear underfoot the echo of its marble floor, and over me the bell of its rotunda.

On winter's rainy days, the schoolrooms would grow so dark that sometimes you couldn't see the figures on the blackboard. At that point, Mrs. McWillie, that stern fourth-grade teacher, would let her children close their books, and she would move, broad in widow's weeds like darkness itself, to the window and by what light there was she would stand and read aloud "The King of the Golden River."[3] But I was excluded—in the other fourth grade, across the hall. Miss Louella Varnado, my teacher, didn't copy Mrs. McWillie; we had a spelling match: you could spell in the dark. I did not then suspect that there was any other way I could learn the story of "The King of the Golden River" than to have been assigned in the beginning to Mrs. McWillie's cowering fourth grade, then wait for her to treat you to it on the rainy day of her choice. I only now realize how much the treat depended, too, on there not having been money enough to put electric lights in Davis School. John Ruskin had to come in through courtesy of darkness. When in time I found the story in a book and read it to myself, it didn't seem to live up to my longings for a story with that name; as indeed, how could it?

3. A fantasy for children by the English author John Ruskin (1819–1900).

Jewelle Gomez

A SWIMMING LESSON

At nine years old I didn't realize that my grandmother, Lydia, and I were doing an extraordinary thing by packing a picnic and riding the elevated train from Roxbury to Revere[1] Beach. It seemed part of the natural rhythm of summer to me. I didn't notice until much later how the subway cars slowly emptied most of their Black passengers as the train left Boston's urban center and made its way into the Italian and Irish suburban neighborhoods to the north. It didn't seem odd that all

From *Forty-Three Septembers* (1993).

1. Roxbury is a black section of Boston; Revere, a white working-class suburb.

of the Black families sorted themselves out in one section of the beach and never ventured onto the boardwalk to the concession stands or the rides, except in groups.

I do remember Black women perched cautiously on their blankets, tugging desperately at bathing suits rising too high in the rear and complaining about their hair "going back." Not my grandmother, though. She glowed with unembarrassed athleticism as she waded out, just inside the reach of the waves, and moved along the riptide parallel to the shore. Once submerged, she would load me onto her back and begin her tireless, long strokes. With the waves partially covering us, I followed her rhythm, my short, chubby arms taking my cue from the power in her back muscles. We did this over and over until I'd fall off, then she'd catch me and set me upright in the strong New England surf. I was thrilled by the wildness of the sea and my grandmother's fearless relationship to it. I loved that she didn't continually consult her mirror but looked as if she had been born to the shore, a kind of aquatic heiress.

None of the larger social issues had a chance of catching my attention in 1957. All that existed was my grandmother rising from the surf like a Dahomean queen,[2] shaking her head free of the torturous, useless rubber cap, beaming down on me when I, at long last, took the first swim strokes on my own. She towered over me in the sun with a confidence that made simply dwelling in her presence a reward in itself. Under her gaze I felt like part of a long line of royalty. I was certain that everyone around us—Black and white—felt and respected her magnificence.

Although I intuited her power, I didn't know the real significance of our summer together as Black females in a white part of town. Unlike winter when we're protected by the concealment of coats, boots, and hats, the summer is a vulnerable time. I am left exposed, at odds with all the expectations handed down from the mainstream culture and its media: narrow hips, straight hair, flat stomach, small feet. But Lydia never seemed to notice. Her long, chorus-girl legs ended in size-nine shoes. She seemed unafraid to make herself even bigger, stretching the broad back of a woman with a purpose: teaching her granddaughter how to swim against the tide of prevailing opinion and propriety. It may have looked like a superfluous skill to those watching our lessons. After all, it was obvious I wouldn't be doing the backstroke on the Riviera or in the pool of a penthouse spa. Certainly nothing in the popular media had made the great outdoors seem a hospitable place for Blacks or women. It was a place in which, at best, we were meant to feel un-

2. The Dahomey are a West African tribe, which at one time included a legendary regiment of powerful women warriors.

comfortable, and at worst—hunted. But the potential prospects for actually utilizing the skill were irrelevant to me; it was simply the skill itself that mattered. When I finally got it right I felt I held an invaluable life secret.

5 It wasn't until college that the specifics of slavery and the Middle Passage[3] were made available to me. The magnitude of that "peculiar institution" was almost beyond my comprehension. It wasn't like anything else I'd learned in school about Black people in this country. It was impossibly contradictory trying to make my own connection to the descendants of slaves—myself, others I knew—and at the same time see slaves not exactly as Americans I might know but as Africans set adrift from their own, very different land. My initial reaction was, *Why didn't the slaves simply jump from the ships while still close to shore and swim home?* The child in me who'd been taught how to survive in water was crushed to learn my ancestors had not necessarily shared this skill. Years later, when I visited West Africa and found out about the poisonous, spiny fish inhabiting much of the inhospitable coastline, rocky and turbulent, I understood why swimming was not a local sport there as it is in New England. I often remember that innocent inquiry, and now every time I visit a beach I think of those ancestors and of Lydia.

The sea has been a fearful place for us. It swallowed us whole when there was no other escape from the holds of slave ships, and did so again more recently with the flimsy refugee flotillas from Haiti. To me, for whom the dark recesses of a tenement hallway were the most unknowable thing encountered in my first nine years, the ocean was a mystery of terrifying proportions. In teaching me to swim Lydia took away that fear. I understood something outside myself—the sea—and consequently something about myself as well. I was no longer simply a fat little girl. My body became a sea vessel—sturdy, enduring, graceful.

Before she died in the summer of 1988 I discovered that she herself didn't really swim that well. All that time I was splashing desperately, trying to learn the right rhythm—*face down, eyes closed, air out, face up, eyes open, air in, reach*—Lydia would be brushing the sandy bottom under the water to keep us both afloat. As she told me this it didn't seem such a big deal to her, but I was shocked. I reached back in my memory trying to put this new information together with the Olympic vision of her I'd always kept inside my head. At first I felt disappointed, tricked. Like I used to feel when I learned that my favorite movie stars were only five feet tall. But I later realized that it was an incredible act of bravery and intelligence for her to pass on to me a skill

3. The long, dangerous sea voyage from Africa to America.

she herself had not quite mastered—a skill she knew would always bring me a sense of pride in accomplishment.

And it's not just the swimming, or the ability to stand on any beach anywhere and be proud of my large body, my African hair. It's being unafraid of the strong muscles in my own back, accepting control over my own life. Now when the weather turns cold and I don the layers of wool and down that protect me from the eastern winter, from those who think a Black woman can't do her job, from those who think I'm simply sexual prey, I remember the power of my grandmother's broad back and I imagine I'm wearing my swimsuit.

Face up, eyes open, air in, reach.

QUESTIONS

1. *Why is there relatively little in this essay about the actual swimming lesson? What in fact is being taught besides swimming? What do you think was the grandmother's intention?*
2. *A recurring note throughout the essay is Gomez's awareness of being observed by others. Trace the occurrences of these observations. Are there exceptions to this consciousness of the observer's gaze?*
3. *Gomez's essay explicitly contrasts what happened when she was nine years old with what she knows now. In other words, she frames the swimming lesson with present-day, adult knowledge of her grandmother. Write an account of a youthful learning experience in which you frame the experience with present-day knowledge.*

John Holt

HOW TEACHERS MAKE CHILDREN HATE READING

When I was teaching English at the Colorado Rocky Mountain School, I used to ask my students the kinds of questions that English teachers usually ask about reading assignments—questions designed to bring out the points that *I* had decided *they* should know. They, on their part, would try to get me to give them hints and clues as to what I wanted. It was a game of wits. I never gave my students an opportunity to say what they really thought about a book.

I gave vocabulary drills and quizzes too. I told my students that every time they came upon a word in their book they did not under-

From *The Under-Achieving School* (1967).

stand, they were to look it up in the dictionary. I even devised special kinds of vocabulary tests, allowing them to use their books to see how the words were used. But looking back, I realize that these tests, along with many of my methods, were foolish.

My sister was the first person who made me question my conventional ideas about teaching English. She had a son in the seventh grade in a fairly good public school. His teacher had asked the class to read Cooper's *The Deerslayer.* The choice was bad enough in itself; whether looking at man or nature, Cooper was superficial, inaccurate and sentimental, and his writing is ponderous and ornate. But to make matters worse, this teacher had decided to give the book the microscope and x-ray treatment. He made the students look up and memorize not only the definitions but the derivations of every big word that came along—and there were plenty. Every chapter was followed by close questioning and testing to make sure the students "understood" everything.

Being then, as I said, conventional, I began to defend the teacher, who was a good friend of mine, against my sister's criticisms. The argument soon grew hot. What was wrong with making sure that children understood everything they read? My sister answered that until this year her boy had always loved reading, and had read a lot on his own; now he had stopped. (He was not really to start again for many years.)

5 Still I persisted. If children didn't look up the words they didn't know, how would they ever learn them? My sister said, "Don't be silly! when you were little you had a huge vocabulary, and were always reading very grown-up books. When did you ever look up a word in a dictionary?"

She had me. I don't know that we had a dictionary at home; if we did, I didn't use it. I don't use one today. In my life I doubt that I have looked up as many as fifty words, perhaps not even half that.

Since then I have talked about this with a number of teachers. More than once I have said, "According to tests, educated and literate people like you have a vocabulary of about twenty-five thousand words. How many of these did you learn by looking them up in a dictionary?" They usually are startled. Few claim to have looked up even as many as a thousand. How did they learn the rest?

They learned them just as they learned to talk—by meeting words over and over again, in different contexts, until they saw how they fitted.

Unfortunately, we English teachers are easily hung up on this matter of understanding. Why should children understand everything they read? Why should anyone? Does anyone? I don't, and I never did. I was always reading books that teachers would have said were "too hard" for me, books full of words I didn't know. That's how I got to be a good reader. When about ten, I read all the D'Artagnan stories and loved them. It didn't trouble me in the least that I didn't know why France was at war with England or who was quarreling with whom in the French court or why the Musketeers should always be at odds with Cardinal Richelieu's men. I didn't even know who the Cardinal was, except that he was a dangerous and powerful man that my friends had to watch out for. This was all I needed to know.

Having said this, I will now say that I think a big, unabridged dictionary is a fine thing to have in any home or classroom. No book is more fun to browse around in—*if* you're not made to. Children, depending on their age, will find many pleasant and interesting things to do with a big dictionary. They can look up funny-sounding words, which they like, or words that nobody else in the class has ever heard of, which they like, or long words, which they like, or forbidden words, which they like best of all. At a certain age, and particularly with a little encouragement from parents or teachers, they may become very interested in where words came from and when they came into the language and how their meanings have changed over the years. But exploring for the fun of it is very different from looking up words out of your reading because you're going to get into trouble with your teacher if you don't.

While teaching fifth grade two years or so after the argument with my sister, I began to think again about reading. The children in my class were supposed to fill out a card—just the title and author and a one-sentence summary—for every book they read. I was not running a competition to see which child could read the most books, a competition that almost always leads to cheating. I just wanted to know what the children were reading. After a while it became clear that many of these very bright kids, from highly literate and even literary backgrounds, read very few books and deeply disliked reading. Why should this be?

At this time I was coming to realize, as I described in my book *How Children Fail*, that for most children school was a place of danger, and their main business in school was staying out of danger as much as possible. I now began to see also that books were among the most dangerous things in school.

From the very beginning of school we make books and reading a constant source of possible failure and public humiliation. When children are little we make them read aloud, before the teacher and other children, so that we can be sure they "know" all the words they are reading. This means that when they don't know a word, they are going to make a mistake, right in front of everyone. Instantly they are made to realize that they have done something wrong. Perhaps some of the other children will begin to wave their hands and say, "Ooooh! O-o-o-oh!" Perhaps they will just giggle, or nudge each other, or make a face. Perhaps the teacher will say, "Are you sure?" or ask someone else what he thinks. Or perhaps, if the teacher is kindly, she will just smile a sweet, sad smile—often one of the most painful punishments a child can suffer in school. In any case, the child who has made the mistake knows he has made it, and feels foolish, stupid, and ashamed, just as any of us would in his shoes.

Before long many children associate books and reading with mistakes, real or feared, and penalties and humiliation. This may not seem sensible, but it is natural. Mark Twain once said that a cat that sat on a hot stove lid would never sit on one again—but it would never sit on a cold one either. As true of children as of cats. If they, so to speak, sit on a hot book a few times, if books cause them humiliation and pain, they are likely to decide that the safest thing to do is to leave all books alone.

15 After having taught fifth-grade classes for four years I felt quite sure of this theory. In my next class were many children who had had great trouble with schoolwork, particularly reading. I decided to try at all costs to rid them of their fear and dislike of books, and to get them to read oftener and more adventurously.

One day soon after school had started, I said to them, "Now I'm going to say something about reading that you have probably never heard a teacher say before. I would like you to read a lot of books this year, but I want you to read them only for pleasure. I am not going to ask you questions to find out whether you understand the books or not. If you understand enough of a book to enjoy it and want to go on reading it, that's enough for me. Also I'm not going to ask you what words mean.

"Finally," I said, "I don't want you to feel that just because you start a book, you have to finish it. Give an author thirty or forty pages or so to get his story going. Then if you don't like the characters and don't care what happens to them, close the book, put it away, and get another. I don't care whether the books are easy or hard, short or long, as long as you enjoy them. Furthermore I'm putting all this in a letter to your parents, so they won't feel they have to quiz and heckle you about books at home."

The children sat stunned and silent. Was this a teacher talking? One girl, who had just come to us from a school where she had had a very hard time, and who proved to be one of the most interesting, lively, and intelligent children I have ever known, looked at me steadily for a long time after I had finished. Then, still looking at me, she said slowly and solemnly, "Mr. Holt, do you really mean that?" I said just as solemnly, "I mean every word of it."

Apparently she decided to believe me. The first book she read was

Dr. Seuss's *How the Grinch Stole Christmas*, not a hard book even for most third graders. For a while she read a number of books on this level. Perhaps she was clearing up some confusion about reading that her teachers, in their hurry to get her up to "grade level," had never given her enough time to clear up. After she had been in the class six weeks or so and we had become good friends, I very tentatively suggested that, since she was a skillful rider and loved horses, she might like to read *National Velvet*. I made my sell as soft as possible, saying only that it was about a girl who loved and rode horses, and that if she didn't like it, she could put it back. She tried it, and though she must have found it quite a bit harder than what she had been reading, finished it and liked it very much.

During the spring she really astonished me, however. One day, in 20
one of our many free periods, she was reading at her desk. From a glimpse of the illustrations I thought I knew what the book was. I said to myself, "It can't be," and went to take a closer look. Sure enough, she was reading *Moby Dick*, in the edition with woodcuts by Rockwell Kent. When I came close to her desk she looked up. I said, "Are you really reading that?" She said she was. I said, "Do you like it?" She said, "Oh, yes, it's neat!" I said, "Don't you find parts of it rather heavy going?" She answered "Oh, sure, but I just skip over those parts and go on to the next good part."

This is exactly what reading should be and in school so seldom is—an exciting, joyous adventure. Find something, dive into it, take the good parts, skip the bad parts, get what you can out of it, go on to something else. How different is our mean-spirited, picky insistence that every child get every last little scrap of "understanding" that can be dug out of a book.

For teachers who really enjoy doing it, and will do it with gusto, reading aloud is a very good idea. I have found that not just fifth graders but even ninth and eleventh graders enjoy it. Jack London's "To Build a Fire" is a good read-aloud story. So are ghost stories, and "August Heat," by W. F. Harvey, and "The Monkey's Paw," by W. W. Jacobs, are among the best. Shirley Jackson's "The Lottery" is surefire, and will raise all kinds of questions for discussion and argument. Because of a TV program they had seen and that excited them, I once started reading my fifth graders William Golding's *Lord of the Flies*, thinking to read only a few chapters, but they made me read it to the end.

In my early fifth-grade classes the children usually were of high IQ, came from literate backgrounds and were generally felt to be succeeding in school. Yet it was astonishingly hard for most of those children to express themselves in speech or in writing. I have known a number of five-year-olds who were considerably more articulate than most of the fifth graders I have known in school. Asked to speak, my fifth graders were covered with embarrassment; many refused altogether. Asked to write, they would sit for minutes on end, staring at the paper. It was hard for most of them to get down a half page of writing, even on what seemed to be interesting topics or topics they chose themselves.

In desperation I hit on a device that I named the Composition Derby. I divided the class into teams, and told them that when I said, "Go," they were to start writing something. It could be about anything they wanted, but it had to be about something—they couldn't just write "dog dog dog dog" on the paper. It could be true stories, descriptions of people or places or events, wishes, made-up stories, dreams—anything they liked. Spelling didn't count, so they didn't have to worry about it. When I said, "Stop," they were to stop and count up the words they had written. The team that wrote the most words would win the derby.

It was a success in many ways and for many reasons. The first surprise was that the two children who consistently wrote the most words were two of the least successful students in the class. They were bright, but they had always had a very hard time in school. Both were very bad spellers, and worrying about this had slowed down their writing without improving their spelling. When they were free of this worry and could let themselves go, they found hidden and unsuspected talents.

One of the two, a very driven and anxious little boy, used to write long adventures, or misadventures, in which I was the central character—"The Day Mr. Holt Went to Jail," "The Day Mr. Holt Fell Into the Hole," "The Day Mr. Holt Got Run Over," and so on. These were very funny, and the class enjoyed hearing me read them aloud. One day I asked the class to write a derby on a topic I would give them. They groaned; they liked picking their own. "Wait till you hear it," I said. "It's 'The Day the School Burned Down.' "

With a shout of approval and joy they went to work, and wrote furiously for 20 minutes or more, laughing and chuckling as they wrote. The papers were all much alike; in them the children danced around the burning building, throwing in books and driving me and the other teachers back in when we tried to escape.

In our first derby the class wrote an average of about ten words a minute; after a few months their average was over 20. Some of the slower writers tripled their output. Even the slowest, one of whom was the best student in the class, were writing 15 words a minute. More important, almost all the children enjoyed the derbies and wrote interesting things.

Some time later I learned that Professor S. I. Hayakawa, teaching freshman English, had invented a better technique. Every day in class he asked his students to write without stopping for about half an hour.

They could write on whatever topic or topics they chose, but the important thing was not to stop. If they ran dry, they were to copy their last sentence over and over again until new ideas came. Usually they came before the sentence had been copied once. I use this idea in my own classes, and call this kind of paper a Non-Stop. Sometimes I ask students to write a Non-Stop on an assigned topic, more often on anything they choose. Once in a while I ask them to count up how many words they have written, though I rarely ask them to tell me; it is for their own information. Sometimes these papers are to be handed in; often they are what I call private papers, for the students' eyes alone.

The private paper has proved very useful. In the first place, in any 30
English class—certainly any large English class—if the amount the students write is limited by what the teacher can find time to correct, or even to read, the students will not write nearly enough. The only remedy is to have them write a great deal that the teacher does not read. In the second place, students writing for themselves will write about many things that they would never write on a paper to be handed in, once they have learned (sometimes it takes a while) that the teacher means what he says about the papers' being private. This is important, not just because it enables them to get things off their chest, but also because they are most likely to write well, and to pay attention to how they write, when they are writing about something important to them.

Some English teachers, when they first hear about private papers, object that students do not benefit from writing papers unless the papers are corrected. I disagree for several reasons. First, most students, particularly poor students, do not read the corrections on their papers; it is boring, even painful. Second, even when they do read these corrections, they do not get much help from them, do not build the teacher's suggestions into their writing. This is true even when they really believe the teacher knows what he is talking about.

Third, and most important, we learn to write by writing, not by reading other people's ideas about writing. What most students need above all else is practice in writing, and particularly in writing about things that matter to them, so that they will begin to feel the satisfaction that comes from getting important thoughts down in words and will care about stating these thoughts forcefully and clearly.

Teachers of English—or, as some schools say (ugh!), Language Arts—spend a lot of time and effort on spelling. Most of it is wasted; it does little good, and often more harm than good. We should ask ourselves, "How do good spellers spell? What do they do when they are not sure which spelling of a word is right?" I have asked this of a number of good spellers. Their answer never varies. They do not rush for a dictionary or rack their brains trying to remember some rules. They write down the word both ways, or several ways, look at them and pick the one that looks best. Usually they are right.

Good spellers know what words look like and even, in their writing muscles, feel like. They have a good set of word images in their minds, and are willing to trust these images. The things we do to "teach" spelling to children do little to develop these skills or talents, and much to destroy them or prevent them from developing.

The first and worst thing we do is to make children anxious about spelling. We treat a misspelled word like a crime and penalize the misspeller severely; many teachers talk of making children develop a "spelling conscience," and fail otherwise excellent papers because of a few spelling mistakes. This is self-defeating. When we are anxious, we don't perceive clearly or remember what we once perceived. Everyone knows how hard it is to recall even simple things when under emotional pressure; the harder we rack our brains, the less easy it is to find what we are looking for. If we are anxious enough, we will not trust the messages that memory sends us. Many children spell badly because although their first hunches about how to spell a word may be correct, they are afraid to trust them. I have often seen on children's papers a word correctly spelled, then crossed out and misspelled.

There are some tricks that might help children get sharper word images. Some teachers may be using them. One is the trick of air writing; that is, of "writing" a word in the air with a finger and "seeing" the image so formed. I did this quite a bit with fifth graders, using either the air or the top of a desk, on which their fingers left no mark. Many of them were tremendously excited by this. I can still hear them saying, "There's nothing there, but I can see it!" It seemed like black magic. I remember that when I was little I loved to write in the air. It was effortless, voluptuous, satisfying, and it was fun to see the word appear in the air. I used to write "Money Money Money," not so much because I didn't have any as because I liked the way it felt, particularly that *y* at the end, with its swooping tail.

Another thing to help sharpen children's image-making machinery is taking very quick looks at words—or other things. The conventional machine for doing this is the tachistoscope. But these are expensive, so expensive that most children can have few chances to use them, if any at all. With some three-by-five and four-by-eight file cards you can get the same effect. On the little cards you put the words or the pictures that the child is going to look at. You hold the larger card over the card to be read, uncover it for a split second with a quick wrist motion, then cover it up again. Thus you have a tachistoscope that costs one cent and that any child can work by himself.

Once when substituting in a first-grade class, I thought that the children, who were just beginning to read and write, might enjoy some of the kind of free, nonstop writing that my fifth graders had. One day about 40 minutes before lunch, I asked them all to take pencil and paper and start writing about anything they wanted to. They seemed to like the idea, but right away one child said anxiously, "Suppose we can't spell a word."

"Don't worry about it," I said. "Just spell it the best way you can."

40 A heavy silence settled on the room. All I could see were still pencils and anxious faces. This was clearly not the right approach. So I said, "All right, I'll tell you what we'll do. Any time you want to know how to spell a word, tell me and I'll write it on the board."

They breathed a sigh of relief and went to work. Soon requests for words were coming fast; as soon as I wrote one, someone asked me another. By lunchtime, when most of the children were still busily writing, the board was full. What was interesting was that most of the words they had asked for were much longer and more complicated than anything in their reading books or workbooks. Freed from worry about spelling, they were willing to use the most difficult and interesting words that they knew.

The words were still on the board when we began school next day. Before I began to erase them, I said to the children, "Listen, everyone. I have to erase these words, but before I do, just out of curiosity, I'd like to see if you remember some of them."

The result was surprising. I had expected that the child who had asked for and used a word might remember it, but I did not think many others would. But many of the children still knew many of the words. How had they learned them? I suppose each time I wrote a word on the board a number of children had looked up, relaxed yet curious, just to see what the word looked like, and these images and the sound of my voice saying the word had stuck in their minds until the next day. This, it seems to me, is how children may best learn to write and spell.

What can a parent do if a school, or a teacher, is spoiling the language for a child by teaching it in some tired way? First, try to get them to change, or at least let them know that you are eager for change. Talk to other parents; push some of these ideas in the PTA; talk to the English department at the school; talk to the child's own teacher. Many teachers and schools want to know what the parents want.

45 If the school or teacher cannot be persuaded, then what? Perhaps all you can do is try not to let your child become too bored or discouraged or worried by what is happening in school. Help him meet the school's demands, foolish though they may seem, and try to provide more interesting alternatives at home—plenty of books and conversation, and a serious and respectful audience when a child wants to talk. Nothing

that ever happened to me in English classes at school was as helpful to me as the long conversations I used to have every summer with my uncle, who made me feel that the difference in our ages was not important and that he was really interested in what I had to say.

At the end of her freshman year in college a girl I know wrote home to her mother, "Hooray! Hooray! Just think—I never have to take English any more!" But this girl had always been an excellent English student, had always loved books, writing, ideas. It seems unnecessary and foolish and wrong that English teachers should so often take what should be the most flexible, exciting, and creative of all school courses and make it into something that most children can hardly wait to see the last of. Let's hope that we can and soon will begin to do much better.

QUESTIONS

1. *In two columns, list the traditional techniques Holt attacks and the alternatives he suggests.*
2. *If a high school English course ran on Holt's principles, what would classes be like? Describe a typical week in such a course: assignments; classroom arrangements; teaching style; discussion of reading; work on writing; homework.*
3. *What might go wrong in the type of course Holt advocates? Compare that to what might go wrong with the traditional approach. Which "deviation" would be worse for the students? For society?*

Santha Rama Rau

BY ANY OTHER NAME

At the Anglo-Indian day school in Zorinabad to which my sister and I were sent when she was eight and I was five and a half, they changed our names. On the first day of school, a hot, windless morning of a north Indian September, we stood in the headmistress's study and she said, "Now you're the *new* girls. What are your names?"

My sister answered for us. "I am Premila, and she"—nodding in my direction—"is Santha."

The headmistress had been in India, I suppose, fifteen years or so, but she still smiled her helpless inability to cope with Indian names. Her rimless half-glasses glittered, and the precarious bun on the top of

From *Gifts of Passage* (1961).

her head trembled as she shook her head. "Oh, my dears, those are much too hard for me. Suppose we give you pretty English names. Wouldn't that be more jolly? Let's see, now—Pamela for you, I think." She shrugged in a baffled way at my sister. "That's as close as I can get. And for *you,*" she said to me, "how about Cynthia? Isn't that nice?"

My sister was always less easily intimidated than I was, and while she kept a stubborn silence, I said, "Thank you," in a very tiny voice.

5 We had been sent to that school because my father, among his responsibilities as an officer of the civil service, had a tour of duty to perform in the villages around that steamy little provincial town, where he had his headquarters at that time. He used to make his shorter inspection tours on horseback, and a week before, in the stale heat of a typically postmonsoon day, we had waved good-by to him and a little procession—an assistant, a secretary, two bearers, and the man to look after the bedding rolls and luggage. They rode away through our large garden, still bright green from the rains, and we turned back into the twilight of the house and the sound of fans whispering in every room.

Up to then, my mother had refused to send Premila to school in the British-run establishments of that time, because, she used to say, "you can bury a dog's tail for seven years and it still comes out curly, and you can take a Britisher away from his home for a lifetime and he still remains insular." The examinations and degrees from entirely Indian schools were not, in those days, considered valid. In my case, the question had never come up, and probably never would have come up if Mother's extraordinary good health had not broken down. For the first time in my life, she was not able to continue the lessons she had been giving us every morning. So our Hindi books were put away, the stories of the Lord Krishna as a little boy were left in mid-air, and we were sent to the Anglo-Indian school.

That first day at school is still, when I think of it, a remarkable one. At that age, if one's name is changed, one develops a curious form of dual personality. I remember having a certain detached and disbelieving concern in the actions of "Cynthia," but certainly no responsibility. Accordingly, I followed the thin, erect back of the headmistress down the veranda to my classroom feeling, at most, a passing interest in what was going to happen to me in this strange, new atmosphere of School.

The building was Indian in design, with wide verandas opening onto a central courtyard, but Indian verandas are usually whitewashed, with stone floors. These, in the tradition of British schools, were painted dark brown and had matting on the floors. It gave a feeling of extra intensity to the heat.

I suppose there were about a dozen Indian children in the school—which contained perhaps forty children in all—and four of them were in my class. They were all sitting at the back of the room, and I went to join them. I sat next to a small, solemn girl who didn't smile at me. She had long, glossy-black braids and wore a cotton dress, but she still kept on her Indian jewelry—a gold chain around her neck, thin gold bracelets, and tiny ruby studs in her ears. Like most Indian children, she had a rim of black kohl[1] around her eyes. The cotton dress should have looked strange, but all I could think of was that I should ask my mother if I couldn't wear a dress to school, too, instead of my Indian clothes.

10 I can't remember too much about the proceedings in class that day, except for the beginning. The teacher pointed to me and asked me to stand up. "Now, dear, tell the class your name."

I said nothing.

"Come along," she said, frowning slightly. "What's your name, dear?"

"I don't know," I said, finally.

The English children in the front of the class—there were about eight or ten of them—giggled and twisted around in their chairs to look at me. I sat down quickly and opened my eyes very wide, hoping in that way to dry them off. The little girl with the braids put out her hand and very lightly touched my arm. She still didn't smile.

15 Most of that morning I was rather bored. I looked briefly at the children's drawings pinned to the wall, and then concentrated on a lizard clinging to the ledge of the high, barred window behind the teacher's head. Occasionally it would shoot out its long yellow tongue for a fly, and then it would rest, with its eyes closed and its belly palpitating, as though it were swallowing several times quickly. The lessons were mostly concerned with reading and writing and simple numbers—things that my mother had already taught me—and I paid very little attention. The teacher wrote on the easel blackboard words like "bat" and "cat," which seemed babyish to me; only "apple" was new and incomprehensible.

When it was time for the lunch recess, I followed the girl with braids out onto the veranda. There the children from the other classes were assembled. I saw Premila at once and ran over to her, as she had charge of our lunchbox. The children were all opening packages and sitting down to eat sandwiches. Premila and I were the only ones who had Indian food—thin wheat chapatties,[2] some vegetable curry, and a bottle of buttermilk. Premila thrust half of it into my hand and whis-

1. Cosmetic preparation to darken the edges of the eyelids.
2. Flat, pan-fried wheat bread.

pered fiercely that I should go and sit with my class, because that was what the others seemed to be doing.

The enormous black eyes of the little Indian girl from my class looked at my food longingly, so I offered her some. But she only shook her head and plowed her way solemnly through her sandwiches.

I was very sleepy after lunch, because at home we always took a siesta. It was usually a pleasant time of day, with the bedroom darkened against the harsh afternoon sun, the drifting off into sleep with the sound of Mother's voice reading a story in one's mind, and, finally, the shrill, fussy voice of the ayah[3] waking one for tea.

At school, we rested for a short time on low, folding cots on the veranda, and then we were expected to play games. During the hot part of the afternoon we played indoors, and after the shadows had begun to lengthen and the slight breeze of the evening had come up we moved outside to the wide courtyard.

I had never really grasped the system of competitive games. At home, whenever we played tag or guessing games, I was always allowed to "win"—"because," Mother used to tell Premila, "she is the youngest, and we have to allow for that." I had often heard her say it, and it seemed quite reasonable to me, but the result was that I had no clear idea of what "winning" meant.

When we played twos-and-threes that afternoon at school, in accordance with my training, I let one of the small English boys catch me, but was naturally rather puzzled when the other children did not return the courtesy. I ran about for what seemed like hours without ever catching anyone, until it was time for school to close. Much later I learned that my attitude was called "not being a good sport," and I stopped allowing myself to be caught, but it was not for years that I really learned the spirit of the thing.

When I saw our car come up to the school gate, I broke away from my classmates and rushed toward it yelling, "Ayah! Ayah!" It seemed like an eternity since I had seen her that morning—a wizened, affectionate figure in her white cotton sari, giving me dozens of urgent and useless instructions on how to be a good girl at school. Premila followed more sedately, and she told me on the way home never to do that again in front of the other children.

When we got home we went straight to Mother's high, white room to have tea with her, and I immediately climbed onto the bed and bounced gently up and down on the springs. Mother asked how we had liked our first day in school. I was so pleased to be home and to have left that peculiar Cynthia behind that I had nothing whatever to say about school, except to ask what "apple" meant. But Premila told

3. Nurse or maid.

Mother about the classes, and added that in her class they had weekly tests to see if they had learned their lessons well.

I asked, "What's a test?"

25 Premila said, "You're too small to have them. You won't have them in your class for donkey's years." She had learned the expression that day and was using it for the first time. We all laughed enormously at her wit. She also told Mother, in an aside, that we should take sandwiches to school the next day. Not, she said, that *she* minded. But they would be simpler for me to handle.

That whole lovely evening I didn't think about school at all. I sprinted barefoot across the lawns with my favorite playmate, the cook's son, to the stream at the end of the garden. We quarreled in our usual way, waded in the tepid water under the lime trees, and waited for the night to bring out the smell of the jasmine. I listened with fascination to his stories of ghosts and demons, until I was too frightened to cross the garden alone in the semidarkness. The ayah found me, shouted at the cook's son, scolded me, hurried me in to supper—it was an entirely usual, wonderful evening.

It was a week later, the day of Premila's first test, that our lives changed rather abruptly. I was sitting at the back of my class, in my usual inattentive way, only half listening to the teacher. I had started a rather guarded friendship with the girl with the braids, whose name turned out to be Nalini (Nancy, in school). The three other Indian children were already fast friends. Even at that age it was apparent to all of us that friendship with the English or Anglo-Indian children was out of the question. Occasionally, during the class, my new friend and I would draw pictures and show them to each other secretly.

The door opened sharply and Premila marched in. At first, the teacher smiled at her in a kindly and encouraging way and said, "Now, you're little Cynthia's sister?"

Premila didn't even look at her. She stood with her feet planted firmly apart and her shoulders rigid, and addressed herself directly to me. "Get up," she said. "We're going home."

30 I didn't know what had happened, but I was aware that it was a crisis of some sort. I rose obediently and started to walk toward my sister.

"Bring your pencils and your notebook," she said.

I went back for them, and together we left the room. The teacher started to say something just as Premila closed the door, but we didn't wait to hear what it was.

In complete silence we left the school grounds and started to walk home. Then I asked Premila what the matter was. All she would say was "We're going home for good."

It was a very tiring walk for a child of five and a half, and I dragged along behind Premila with my pencils growing sticky in my hand. I can still remember looking at the dusty hedges, and the tangles of thorns in the ditches by the side of the road, smelling the faint fragrance from the eucalyptus trees and wondering whether we would ever reach home. Occasionally a horse-drawn tonga[4] passed us, and the women, in their pink or green silks, stared at Premila and me trudging along on the side of the road. A few coolies and a line of women carrying baskets of vegetables on their heads smiled at us. But it was nearing the hottest time of day, and the road was almost deserted. I walked more and more slowly, and shouted to Premila, from time to time, "Wait for me!" with increasing peevishness. She spoke to me only once, and that was to tell me to carry my notebook on my head, because of the sun.

When we got to our house the ayah was just taking a tray of lunch 35
into Mother's room. She immediately started a long, worried questioning about what are you children doing back here at this hour of the day.

Mother looked very startled and very concerned, and asked Premila what had happened.

Premila said, "We had our test today, and She made me and the other Indians sit at the back of the room, with a desk between each one."

Mother said, "Why was that, darling?"

"She said it was because Indians cheat," Premila added. "So I don't think we should go back to that school."

Mother looked very distant, and was silent a long time. At last she 40
said, "Of course not, darling." She sounded displeased.

We all shared the curry she was having for lunch, and afterward I was sent off to the beautifully familiar bedroom for my siesta. I could hear Mother and Premila talking through the open door.

Mother said, "Do you suppose she understood all that?"

Premila said, "I shouldn't think so. She's a baby."

Mother said, "Well, I hope it won't bother her."

Of course, they were both wrong. I understood it perfectly, and I 45
remember it all very clearly. But I put it happily away, because it had all happened to a girl called Cynthia, and I never was really particularly interested in her.

4. Light two-wheeled wagon.

QUESTIONS

1. *Why does Rau devote paragraph 26 to how she played with the cook's son on the evening of her first day of school? How does such a paragraph help readers understand Rau's experiences as a five-year-old?*
2. *Trace the sights, sounds, and smells that seem to occur at just the appropriate times in this essay. What might be Rau's purposes in grounding each scene in such precise physical descriptions?*
3. *Rau writes in an extremely understated manner. For instance, imag-*

ine what kind of effort it must have taken for eight-year-old Premila to stalk out of school and take her younger sister with her. (Think of doing that in an American school!) What does Rau gain from downplaying the drama?

4. *This essay captures the desire of the sisters to become like everyone else, even while it records Premila's refusal to give up her sense of who she is. Write about a time when someone had to confront a similar assault on identity. Demonstrate the attractiveness of the new identity (as team member, part of the group, etc.) as well as the ultimate refusal to go along.*

Benjamin R. Barber

AMERICA SKIPS SCHOOL

On September 8, the day most of the nation's children were scheduled to return to school, the Department of Education Statistics issued a report, commissioned by Congress, on adult literacy and numeracy in the United States. The results? More than 90 million adult Americans lacked simple literacy. Fewer than 20 percent of those surveyed could compare two metaphors in a poem; not 4 percent could calculate the cost of carpeting at a given price for a room of a given size, using a calculator. As the DOE report was being issued, as if to echo its findings, two of the nation's largest school systems had delayed their openings: in New York, to remove asbestos from aging buildings; in Chicago, because of a battle over the budget.

Inspired by the report and the delays, pundits once again began chanting the familiar litany of the education crisis. We've heard it all many times before: 130,000 children bring guns along with their pencils and books to school each morning; juvenile arrests for murder increased by 85 percent from 1987 to 1991; more than 3,000 youngsters will drop out today and every day for the rest of the school year, until about 600,000 are lost by June—in many urban schools, perhaps half the enrollment. A lot of the dropouts will end up in prison, which is a surer bet for young black males than college: one in four will pass through the correctional system, and at least two out of three of those will be dropouts.

In quiet counterpoint to those staggering facts is another set of statistics: teachers make less than accountants, architects, doctors, lawyers, engineers, judges, health professionals, auditors, and surveyors.

Originally appeared in *Harper's Magazine* (Nov. 1993).

They can earn higher salaries teaching in Berlin, Tokyo, Ottawa, or Amsterdam than in New York or Chicago. American children are in school only about 180 days a year, as against 240 days or more for children in Europe or Japan. The richest school districts (school financing is local, not federal) spend twice as much per student as poorer ones do. The poorer ones seem almost beyond help: children with venereal disease or AIDS (2.5 million adolescents annually contract a sexually transmitted disease), gangs in the schoolyard, drugs in the classroom, children doing babies instead of homework, playground firefights featuring Uzis and Glocks.

Clearly, the social contract that obliges adults to pay taxes so that children can be educated is in imminent danger of collapse. Yet for all the astonishing statistics, more astonishing still is that no one seems to be listening. The education crisis is kind of like violence on television: the worse it gets the more inert we become, and the more of it we require to rekindle our attention. We've had a "crisis" every dozen years or so at least since the launch of *Sputnik*, in 1957, when American schools were accused of falling behind the world standard in science education. Just ten years ago, the National Commission on Excellence in Education warned that America's pedagogical inattention was putting America "at risk." What the commission called "a rising tide of mediocrity" was imperiling "our very future as a Nation and a people." What was happening to education was an "act of war."

5 Since then, countless reports have been issued decrying the condition of our educational system, the DOE report being only the most recent. They have come from every side, Republican as well as Democrat, from the private sector as well as the public. Yet for all the talk, little happens. At times, the schools look more like they are being dismantled than rebuilt. How can this be? If Americans over a broad political spectrum regard education as vital, why has nothing been done?

I have spent thirty years as a scholar examining the nature of democracy, and even more as a citizen optimistically celebrating its possibilities, but today I am increasingly persuaded that the reason for the country's inaction is that Americans do not really care about education—the country has grown comfortable with the game of "let's pretend we care."

As America's educational system crumbles, the pundits, instead of looking for solutions, search busily for scapegoats. Some assail the teachers—those "Profscam" pedagogues trained in the licentious Sixties who, as aging hippies, are supposedly still subverting the schools—for producing a dire illiteracy. Others turn on the kids themselves, so that at the same moment as we are transferring our responsibilities to the shoulders of the next generation, we are blaming them for our own generation's most conspicuous failures. Allan Bloom was typical of the many recent critics who have condemned the young as vapid, lazy, selfish, complacent, self-seeking, materialistic, small-minded, apathetic, greedy, and, of course, illiterate. E. D. Hirsch in his *Cultural Literacy* and Diane Ravitch and Chester E. Finn Jr. in their *What Do Our Seventeen-Year-Olds Know?* have lambasted the schools, the teachers, and the children for betraying the adult generation from which they were to inherit, the critics seemed confident, a precious cultural legacy.

How this captious literature reeks of hypocrisy! How sanctimonious all the hand-wringing over still another "education crisis" seems. Are we ourselves really so literate? Are our kids stupid or smart for ignoring what we preach and copying what we practice? The young, with their keen noses for hypocrisy, are in fact adept readers—but not of books. They are society-smart rather than school-smart, and what they read so acutely are the social signals emanating from the world in which they will have to make a living. Their teachers in that world, the nation's true pedagogues, are television, advertising, movies, politics, and the celebrity domains they define. We prattle about deficient schools and the gullible youngsters they turn out, so vulnerable to the siren song of drugs, but think nothing of letting the advertisers into the classroom to fashion what an *Advertising Age* essay calls "brand and product loyalties through classroom-centered, peer-powered life-style patterning."

Our kids spend 900 hours a year in school (the ones who go to school) and from 1,200 to 1,800 hours a year in front of the television set. From which are they likely to learn more? Critics such as Hirsch and Ravitch want to find out what our seventeen-year-olds know, but it's really pretty simple: they know exactly what our forty-seven-year-olds know and teach them by example—on television, in the boardroom, around Washington, on Madison Avenue, in Hollywood. The very first lesson smart kids learn is that it is much more important to heed what society teaches implicitly by its deeds and reward structures than what school teaches explicitly in its lesson plans and civic sermons. Here is a test for adults that may help reveal what the kids see when they look at our world.

REAL-WORLD CULTURAL LITERACY

1. According to television, having fun in America means
   a) going blond
   b) drinking Pepsi
   c) playing Nintendo
   d) wearing Air Jordans
   e) reading Mark Twain

2. A good way to prepare for a high-income career and to acquire status in our society is to
   a) win a slam-dunk contest
   b) take over a company and sell off its assets
   c) start a successful rock band
   d) earn a professional degree
   e) become a kindergarten teacher

3. Book publishers are financially rewarded today for publishing
   a) mega-cookbooks
   b) mega–cat books
   c) megabooks by Michael Crichton
   d) megabooks by John Grisham
   e) mini-books by Voltaire

4. A major California bank that advertised "no previous credit history required" in inviting Berkeley students to apply for Visa cards nonetheless turned down one group of applicants because
   a) their parents had poor credit histories
   b) they had never held jobs
   c) they had outstanding student loans
   d) they were "humanities majors"

5. Colleges and universities are financially rewarded today for
   a) supporting bowl-quality football teams
   b) forging research relationships with large corporations
   c) sustaining professional programs in law and business
   d) stroking wealthy alumni
   e) fostering outstanding philosophy departments

6. Familiarity with *Henry IV, Part II* is likely to be of vital importance in
   a) planning a corporate takeover
   b) evaluating budget cuts in the Department of Education
   c) initiating a medical-malpractice lawsuit
   d) writing an impressive job résumé
   e) taking a test on what our seventeen-year-olds know

7. To help the young learn that "history is a living thing," Scholastic, Inc., a publisher of school magazines and paperbacks, recently distributed to 40,000 junior and senior high-school classrooms
   a) a complimentary video of the award-winning series *The Civil War*
   b) free copies of Plato's *Dialogues*

c) an abridgment of Alexis de Tocqueville's *Democracy in America*
d) a wall-size Periodic Table of the Elements
e) gratis copies of Billy Joel's hit single "We Didn't Start the Fire" (which recounts history via a vaguely chronological list of warbled celebrity names)

10 My sample of forty-seven-year-olds scored very well on the test. Not surprisingly, so did their seventeen-year-old children. (For each question, either the last entry is correct or all responses are correct *except* the last one.) The results of the test reveal again the deep hypocrisy that runs through our lamentations about education. The illiteracy of the young turns out to be our own reflected back to us with embarrassing force. We honor ambition, we reward greed, we celebrate materialism, we worship acquisitiveness, we cherish success, and we commercialize the classroom—and then we bark at the young about the gentle arts of the spirit. We recommend history to the kids but rarely consult it ourselves. We make a fuss about ethics but are satisfied to see it taught as an "add-on," as in "ethics in medicine" or "ethics in business"—as if Sunday morning in church could compensate for uninterrupted sinning from Monday to Saturday.

The children are onto this game. They know that if we really valued schooling, we'd pay teachers what we pay stockbrokers; if we valued books, we'd spend a little something on the libraries so that adults could read, too; if we valued citizenship, we'd give national service and civic education more than pilot status; if we valued children, we wouldn't let them be abused, manipulated, impoverished, and killed in their beds by gang-war cross fire and stray bullets. Schools can and should lead, but when they confront a society that in every instance tells a story exactly opposite to the one they are supposed to be teaching, their job becomes impossible. When the society undoes each workday what the school tries to do each school day, schooling can't make much of a difference.

Inner-city children are not the only ones who are learning the wrong lessons. TV sends the same messages to everyone, and the success of Donald Trump, Pete Rose, Henry Kravis, or George Steinbrenner makes them potent role models, whatever their values. Teen dropouts are not blind; teen drug sellers are not deaf; teen college students who avoid the humanities in favor of pre-business or pre-law are not stupid. Being apt pupils of reality, they learn their lessons well. If they see a man with a rubber arm and an empty head who can throw a ball at 95 miles per hour pulling down millions of dollars a year while a dedicated primary-school teacher is getting crumbs, they will avoid careers in teaching even if they can't make the major leagues. If they observe their government spending up to $35,000 a year to keep a young black behind bars but a fraction of that to keep him in school, they will write off school (and probably write off blacks as well).

Our children's illiteracy is merely our own, which they assume with commendable prowess. They know what we have taught them all too well: there is nothing in Homer or Virginia Woolf, in Shakespeare or Toni Morrison, that will advantage them in climbing to the top of the American heap. Academic credentials may still count, but schooling in and of itself is for losers. Bookworms. Nerds. Inner-city rappers and fraternity-house wise guys are in full agreement about that. The point is to start pulling down the big bucks. Some kids just go into business earlier than others. Dropping out is the national pastime, if by dropping out we mean giving up the precious things of the mind and the spirit in which America shows so little interest and for which it offers so little payback. While the professors argue about whether to teach the ancient history of a putatively white Athens or the ancient history of a putatively black Egypt, the kids are watching televised political campaigns driven by mindless image-mongering and inflammatory polemics that ignore history altogether. Why, then, are we so surprised when our students dismiss the debate over the origins of civilization, whether Eurocentric or Afrocentric, and concentrate on cash-and-carry careers? Isn't the choice a tribute not to their ignorance but to their adaptive intelligence? Although we can hardly be proud of ourselves for what we are teaching them, we should at least be proud of them for how well they've learned our lessons.

Not all Americans have stopped caring about the schools, however. In the final irony of the educational endgame, cynical entrepreneurs like Chris Whittle are insinuating television into the classroom itself, bribing impoverished school boards by offering free TV sets on which they can show advertising for children—sold to sponsors at premium rates. Whittle, the mergers and acquisitions mogul of education, is trying to get rich off the poverty of public schools and the fears of parents. Can he really believe advertising in the schools enhances education? Or is he helping to corrupt public schools in ways that will make parents even more anxious to use vouchers for private schools—which might one day be run by Whittle's latest entrepreneurial venture, the Edison Project.

According to Lifetime Learning Systems, an educational-software 15
company, "kids spend 40 percent of each day . . . where traditional advertising can't reach them." Not to worry, says Lifetime Learning in an *Advertising Age* promo: "Now, you can enter the classroom through custom-made learning materials created with your specific marketing objectives in mind. Communicate with young spenders directly and, through them, their teachers and families as well." If we redefine

young learners as "young spenders," are the young really to be blamed for acting like mindless consumers? Can they become young spenders and still become young critical thinkers, let alone informed citizens? If we are willing to give TV cartoons the government's imprimatur as "educational television" (as we did a few years ago, until the FCC changed its mind), can we blame kids for educating themselves on television trash?

Everyone can agree that we should educate our children to be something more than young spenders molded by "lifestyle patterning." But what should the goals of the classroom be? In recent years it has been fashionable to define the educational crisis in terms of global competition and minimal competence, as if schools were no more than vocational institutions. Although it has talked sensibly about education, the Clinton Administration has leaned toward this approach, under the tutelage of Secretary of Labor Robert Reich.

The classroom, however, should not be merely a trade school. The fundamental task of education in a democracy is what Tocqueville once called the apprenticeship of liberty: learning to be free. I wonder whether Americans still believe liberty has to be learned and that its skills are worth learning. Or have they been deluded by two centuries of rhetoric into thinking that freedom is "natural" and can be taken for granted?

The claim that all men are born free, upon which America was founded, is at best a promising fiction. In real life, as every parent knows, children are born fragile, born needy, born ignorant, born unformed, born weak, born foolish, born dependent—born in chains. We acquire our freedom over time, if at all. Embedded in families, clans, communities, and nations, we must learn to be free. We may be natural consumers and born narcissists, but citizens have to be made. Liberal-arts education actually means education in the arts of liberty; the "servile arts" were the trades learned by unfree men in the Middle Ages, the vocational education of their day. Perhaps this is why Thomas Jefferson preferred to memorialize his founding of the University of Virginia on his tombstone rather than his two terms as president; it is certainly why he viewed his Bill for the More General Diffusion of Knowledge in Virginia as a centerpiece of his career (although it failed passage as legislation—times were perhaps not so different). John Adams, too, boasted regularly about Massachusetts's high literacy rates and publicly funded education.

Jefferson and Adams both understood that the Bill of Rights offered little protection in a nation without informed citizens. Once educated, however, a people was safe from even the subtlest tyrannies. Jefferson's democratic proclivities rested on his conviction that education could turn a people into a safe refuge—indeed "the only safe depository" for the ultimate powers of society. "Cherish therefore the spirit of our people," he wrote to Edward Carrington in 1787, "and keep alive their attention. Do not be severe upon their errors, but reclaim them by enlightening them. If once they become inattentive to public affairs, you and I and Congress and Assemblies, judges and governors, shall all become wolves."

The logic of democracy begins with public education, proceeds to 20
informed citizenship, and comes to fruition in the securing of rights and liberties. We have been nominally democratic for so long that we presume it is our natural condition rather than the product of persistent effort and tenacious responsibility. We have decoupled rights from civic responsibilities and severed citizenship from education on the false assumption that citizens just happen. We have forgotten that the "public" in public schools means not just paid for by the public but procreative of the very idea of a public. Public schools are how a public—a citizenry—is forged and how young, selfish individuals turn into conscientious, community-minded citizens.

Among the several literacies that have attracted the anxious attention of commentators, civic literacy has been the least visible. Yet this is the fundamental literacy by which we live in a civil society. It encompasses the competence to participate in democratic communities, the ability to think critically and act with deliberation in a pluralistic world, and the empathy to identify sufficiently with others to live with them despite conflicts of interest and differences in character. At the most elementary level, what our children suffer from most, whether they're hurling racial epithets from fraternity porches or shooting one another down in schoolyards, is the absence of civility. Security guards and metal detectors are poor surrogates for civility, and they make our schools look increasingly like prisons (though they may be less safe than prisons). Jefferson thought schools would produce free men: we prove him right by putting dropouts in jail.

Civility is a work of the imagination, for it is through the imagination that we render others sufficiently like ourselves for them to become subjects of tolerance and respect, if not always affection. Democracy is anything but a "natural" form of association. It is an extraordinary and rare contrivance of cultivated imagination. Give the uneducated the right to participate in making collective decisions, and what results is not democracy but, at best, mob rule: the government of private prejudice once known as the tyranny of opinion. For Jefferson, the difference between the democratic temperance he admired in agrarian America and the rule of the rabble he condemned when viewing the social unrest of Europe's teeming cities was quite simply education. Madison had hoped to "filter" out popular passion through the device of representation. Jefferson saw in education a filter that could be installed within each individual, giving to each the capacity to rule prudently. Education creates a ruling aristocracy constrained by temperance and wisdom; when that education is public and universal, it is an aristocracy to which all can belong. At its best, the American dream of a free and equal society governed by judicious citizens has been this dream of an aristocracy of everyone.

To dream this dream of freedom is easy, but to secure it is difficult as well as expensive. Notwithstanding their lamentations, Americans do not appear ready to pay the price. There is no magic bullet for education. But I no longer can accept that the problem lies in the lack of consensus about remedies—in a dearth of solutions. There is no shortage of debate over how to repair our educational infrastructure. National standards or more local control? Vouchers or better public schools? More parental involvement or more teacher autonomy? A greater federal presence (only 5 or 6 percent of the nation's education budget is federally funded) or fairer local school taxes? More multicultural diversity or more emphasis on what Americans share in common? These are honest disputes. But I am convinced that the problem is simpler and more fundamental. Twenty years ago, writer and activist Frances Moore Lappé captured the essence of the world food crisis when she argued that starvation was caused not by a scarcity of food but by a global scarcity in democracy. The education crisis has the same genealogy. It stems from a dearth of democracy: an absence of democratic will and a consequent refusal to take our children, our schools, and our future seriously.

Most educators, even while they quarrel among themselves, will agree that a genuine commitment to any one of a number of different solutions could help enormously. Most agree that although money can't by itself solve problems, without money few problems can be solved. Money also can't win wars or put men in space, but it is the crucial facilitator. It is also how America has traditionally announced, We are serious about this!

25 If we were serious, we would raise teachers' salaries to levels that would attract the best young professionals in our society: starting lawyers get from $70,000 to $80,000—why don't starting kindergarten teachers get the same? Is their role in vouchsafing our future less significant? And although there is evidence suggesting that an increase in general educational expenditures doesn't translate automatically into better schools, there is also evidence that an increase aimed specifically at instructional services does. Can we really take in earnest the chattering devotion to excellence of a country so wedded in practice to mediocrity, a nation so ready to relegate teachers—conservators of our common future—to the professional backwaters?

If we were serious, we would upgrade physical facilities so that every school met the minimum standards of our better suburban institutions. Good buildings do not equal good education, but can any education at all take place in leaky, broken-down habitats of the kind described by Jonathan Kozol in his *Savage Inequalities?* If money is not a critical factor, why are our most successful suburban school districts funded at nearly twice the level of our inner-city schools? Being even at the starting line cannot guarantee that the runners will win or even finish the race, but not being even pretty much assures failure. We would rectify the balance not by penalizing wealthier communities but by bringing poorer communities up to standard, perhaps, by finding other sources of funding for our schools besides property taxes.

If we were serious, we'd extend the school year by a month or two so that learning could take place throughout the year. We'd reduce class size (which means more teachers) and nurture more cooperative learning so that kids could become actively responsible for their own education and that of their classmates. Perhaps most important, we'd raise standards and make teachers and students responsible for them. There are two ways to breed success: to lower standards so that everybody "passes" in a way that loses all meaning in the real world; and to raise standards and then meet them, so that school success translates into success beyond the classroom. From Confucian China to Imperial England, great nations have built their success in the world upon an education of excellence. The challenge in a democracy is to find a way to maintain excellence while extending educational opportunity to everyone.

Finally, if we were serious, parents, teachers, and students would be the real players while administrators, politicians, and experts would be secondary, at best advisers whose chief skill ought to be knowing when and how to facilitate the work of teachers and then get out of the way. If the Democrats can clean up federal government bureaucracy (the Gore plan), perhaps we can do the same for educational bureaucracy. In New York up to half of the city's teachers occupy jobs outside the classroom. No other enterprise is run that way: Half the soldiers at company headquarters? Half the cops at stationhouse desks? Half the working force in the assistant manager's office? Once the teachers are back in the classroom, they will need to be given more autonomy, more professional responsibility for the success or failure of their students. And parents will have to be drawn in not just because they have rights or because they are politically potent but because they have responsibilities and their children are unlikely to learn without parental engagement. How to define the parental role in the classroom would become serious business for educators.

Some Americans will say this is unrealistic. Times are tough, money's short, and the public is fed up with almost all of its public institutions: the schools are just one more frustrating disappointment. With all the goodwill in the world, it is still hard to know how schools can cure the ills that stem from the failure of so many other institutions. Saying we want education to come first won't put it first.

30 America, however, has historically been able to accomplish what it sets its mind to. When we wish it and will it, what we wish and will has happened. Our successes are willed; our failures seem to happen when will is absent. There are, of course, those who benefit from the bankruptcy of public education and the failure of democracy. But their blame is no greater than our own: in a world where doing nothing has such dire consequences, complacency has become a greater sin than malevolence.

In wartime, whenever we have known why we were fighting and believed in the cause, we have prevailed. Because we believe in profits, we are consummate salespersons and efficacious entrepreneurs. Because we love sports, ours are the dream teams. Why can't a Chicago junior high school be as good as the Chicago Bulls? Because we cherish individuality and mobility, we have created a magnificent (if costly) care culture and the world's largest automotive consumer market. Even as our lower schools are among the worst in the Western world, our graduate institutions are among the very best—because professional training in medicine, law, and technology is vital to our ambitions and because corporate America backs up state and federal priorities in this crucial domain. Look at the things we do well and observe how very well we do them: those are the things that as a nation we have willed.

Then observe what we do badly and ask yourself, Is it because the challenge is too great? Or is it because, finally, we aren't really serious? Would we will an end to the carnage and do whatever it took—more cops, state militias, federal marshals, the Marines?—if the dying children were white and middle class? Or is it a disdain for the young—white, brown, and black—that inures us to the pain? Why are we so sensitive to the retirees whose future (however foreshortened) we are quick to guarantee—don't worry, no reduced cost-of-living allowances, no taxes on social security except for the well-off—and so callous to the young? Have you noticed how health care is on every politician's agenda and education on no one's?

To me, the conclusion is inescapable: we are not serious. We have given up on the public schools because we have given up on the kids; and we have given up on the kids because we have given up on the future—perhaps because it looks too multicolored or too dim or too hard. "Liberty," said Jean-Jacques Rousseau, "is a food easy to eat but hard to digest." America is suffering from a bad case of indigestion. Finally, in giving up on the future, we have given up on democracy.

Certainly there will be no liberty, no equality, no social justice without democracy, and there will be no democracy without citizens and the schools that forge civic identity and democratic responsibility. If I am wrong (I'd like to be), my error will be easy to discern, for before the year is out we will put education first on the nation's agenda. We will put it ahead of the deficit, for if the future is finished before it starts, the deficit doesn't matter. Ahead of defense, for without democracy, what liberties will be left to defend? Ahead of all the other public issues and public goods, for without public education there can be no public and hence no truly public issues or public goods to advance. When the polemics are spent and we are through hyperventilating about the crisis in education, there is only one question worth asking: are we serious? If we are, we can begin by honoring that old folk homily and put our money where for much too long our common American mouth has been. Our kids, for once, might even be grateful.

QUESTIONS

1. *What is "civic literacy," and why is it so important to Barber?*
2. *Develop three more questions of your own for the "Real World Cultural Literacy" test Barber gives.*
3. *Barber claims in the last paragraph that the reason our schools aren't so good is that "we are not serious." From your own experience, argue whether or not schools seem serious, and whether they, in Barber's terms, "have given up on the kids."*

Caroline Bird

COLLEGE IS A WASTE OF TIME AND MONEY

A great majority of our nine million college students are not in school because they want to be or because they want to learn. They are there because it has become the thing to do or because college is a pleasant place to be; because it's the only way they can get parents or taxpayers to support them without working at a job they don't like; because Mother wanted them to go, or some other reason entirely irrelevant to the course of studies for which college is supposedly organized.

As I crisscross the United States lecturing on college campuses, I am dismayed to find that professors and administrators, when pressed for

From *The Case Against College* (1975).

a candid opinion, estimate that no more than 25 percent of their students are turned on by classwork. For the rest, college is at best a social center or aging vat, and at worst a young folks' home or even a prison that keeps them out of the mainstream of economic life for a few more years.

The premise—which I no longer accept—that college is the best place for all high-school graduates grew out of a noble American ideal. Just as the United States was the first nation to aspire to teach every small child to read and write, so, during the 1950s, we became the first and only great nation to aspire to higher education for all. During the '60s we damned the expense and built great state university systems as fast as we could. And adults—parents, employers, high-school counselors—began to push, shove and cajole youngsters to "get an education."

It became a mammoth industry, with taxpayers footing more than half the bill. By 1970, colleges and universities were spending more than 30 billion dollars annually. But still only half our highschool graduates were going on. According to estimates made by the economist Fritz Machlup, if we had been educating every young person until age 22 in that year of 1970, the bill for higher education would have reached 47.5 billion dollars, 12.5 billion more than the total corporate profits for the year.

5 Figures such as these have begun to make higher education for all look financially prohibitive, particularly now when colleges are squeezed by the pressures of inflation and a drop-off in the growth of their traditional market.

Predictable demography has caught up with the university empire builders. Now that the record crop of postwar babies has graduated from college, the rate of growth of the student population has begun to decline. To keep their mammoth plants financially solvent, many institutions have begun to use hard-sell, Madison-Avenue techniques to attract students. They sell college like soap, promoting features they think students want: innovative programs, an environment conducive to meaningful personal relationships, and a curriculum so free that it doesn't sound like college at all.

Pleasing the customers is something new for college administrators. Colleges have always known that most students don't like to study, and that at least part of the time they are ambivalent about college, but before the student riots of the 1960s educators never thought it either right or necessary to pay any attention to student feelings. But when students rebelling against the Vietnam war and the draft discovered they could disrupt a campus completely, administrators had to act on some student complaints. Few understood that the protests had tapped the basic discontent with college itself, a discontent that did not go away when the riots subsided.

Today students protest individually rather than in concert. They turn inward and withdraw from active participation. They drop out to travel to India or to feed themselves on subsistence farms. Some refuse to go to college at all. Most, of course, have neither the funds nor the self-confidence for constructive articulation of their discontent. They simply hang around college unhappily and reluctantly.

All across the country, I have been overwhelmed by the prevailing sadness on American campuses. Too many young people speak little, and then only in drowned voices. Sometimes the mood surfaces as diffidence, wariness, or coolness, but whatever its form, it looks like a defense mechanism, and that rings a bell. This is the way it used to be with women, and just as society had systematically damaged women by insisting that their proper place was in the home, so we may be systematically damaging 18-year-olds by insisting that their proper place is in college.

10 Campus watchers everywhere know what I mean when I say students are sad, but they don't agree on the reason for it. During the Vietnam war some ascribed the sadness to the draft; now others blame affluence, or say it has something to do with permissive upbringing.

Not satisfied with any of these explanations, I looked for some answers with the journalistic tools of my trade—scholarly studies, economic analyses, the historical record, the opinions of the especially knowledgeable, conversations with parents, professors, college administrators, and employers, all of whom spoke as alumni too. Mostly I learned from my interviews with hundreds of young people on and off campuses all over the country.

My unnerving conclusion is that students are sad because they are not needed. Somewhere between the nursery and the employment office, they become unwanted adults. No one has anything in particular against them. But no one knows what to do with them either. We already have too many people in the world of the 1970s, and there is no room for so many newly minted 18-year-olds. So we temporarily get them out of the way by sending them to college where in fact only a few belong.

To make it more palatable, we fool ourselves into believing that we are sending them there for their own best interests, and that it's good for them, like spinach. Some, of course, learn to like it, but most wind up preferring green peas.

Educators admit as much. Nevitt Sanford, distinguished student of higher education, says students feel they are "capitulating to a kind of voluntary servitude." Some of them talk about their time in college as if it were a sentence to be served. I listened to a 1970 Mount Holyoke graduate: "For two years I was really interested in science, but in my junior and senior years I just kept saying, 'I've done two years; I'm going to finish'. When I got out I made up my mind that I wasn't going to school anymore because so many of my courses had been bullshit."

15 But bad as it is, college is often preferable to a far worse fate. It is better than the drudgery of an uninspiring nine-to-five job, and better than doing nothing when no jobs are available. For some young people, it is a graceful way to get away from home and become independent without losing the financial support of their parents. And sometimes it is the only alternative to an intolerable home situation.

It is difficult to assess how many students are in college reluctantly. The conservative Carnegie Commission estimates from 5 to 30 percent. Sol Linowitz, who was once chairman of a special committee on campus tension of the American Council on Education, found that "a significant number were not happy with their college experience because they felt they were there only in order to get the 'ticket to the big show' rather than to spend the years as productively as they otherwise could."

Older alumni will identify with Richard Baloga, a policeman's son, who stayed in school even though he "hated it" because he thought it would do him some good. But fewer students each year feel this way. Daniel Yankelovich has surveyed undergraduate attitudes for a number of years, and reported in 1971 that 74 percent thought education was "very important." But just two years earlier, 80 percent thought so.

The doubters don't mind speaking up. Leon Lefkowitz, chairman of the department of social studies at Central High School in Valley Stream, New York, interviewed 300 college students at random, and reports that 200 of them didn't think that the education they were getting was worth the effort. "In two years I'll pick up a diploma," said one student, "and I can honestly say it was a waste of my father's bread."

Nowadays, says one sociologist, you don't have to have a reason for going to college; it's an institution. His definition of an institution is an arrangement everyone accepts without question; the burden of proof is not on why you go, but why anyone thinks there might be a reason for not going. The implication is that an 18-year-old is too young and confused to know what he wants to do, and that he should listen to those who know best and go to college.

20 I don't agree. I believe that college has to be judged not on what other people think is good for students, but on how good it feels to the students themselves.

I believe that people have an inside view of what's good for them. If a child doesn't want to go to school some morning, better let him stay at home, at least until you find out why. Maybe he knows something you don't. It's the same with college. If high-school graduates don't want to go, or if they don't want to go right away, they may perceive more clearly than their elders that college is not for them. It is no longer obvious that adolescents are best off studying a core curriculum that was constructed when all educated men could agree on what made them educated, or that professors, advisors, or parents can be of any particular help to young people in choosing a major or a career. High-school graduates see college graduates driving cabs, and decide it's not worth going. College students find no intellectual stimulation in their studies and drop out.

If students believe that college isn't necessarily good for them, you can't expect them to stay on for the general good of mankind. They don't go to school to beat the Russians to Jupiter, improve the national defense, increase the GNP, or create a new market for the arts—to mention some of the benefits taxpayers are supposed to get for supporting higher education.

Nor should we expect to bring about social equality by putting all young people through four years of academic rigor. At best, it's a roundabout and expensive way to narrow the gap between the highest and lowest in our society anyway. At worst, it is unconsciously elitist. Equalizing opportunity through universal higher education subjects the whole population to the intellectual mode natural only to a few. It violates the fundamental egalitarian principle of respect for the differences between people.

Of course, most parents aren't thinking of the "higher" good at all. They send their children to college because they are convinced young people benefit financially from those four years of higher education. But if money is the only goal, college is the dumbest investment you can make. I say this because a young banker in Poughkeepsie, New York, Stephen G. Necel, used a computer to compare college as an investment with other investments available in 1974 and college did not come out on top.

25 For the sake of argument, the two of us invented a young man whose rich uncle gave him, in cold cash, the cost of a four-year education at any college he chose, but the young man didn't have to spend the money on college. After bales of computer paper, we had our mythical student write to his uncle: "Since you said I could spend the money foolishly if I wished, I am going to blow it all on Princeton."

The much respected financial columnnist Sylvia Porter echoed the common assumption when she said last year, "A college education is among the very best investments you can make in your entire life." But the truth is not quite so rosy, even if we assume that the Census Bureau is correct when it says that as of 1972, a man who completed four years of college would expect to earn $199,000 more between the ages of 22 and 64 than a man who had only a high-school diploma.

If a 1972 Princeton-bound high-school graduate had put the $34,181 that his four years of college would have cost him into a savings bank at 7.5 percent interest compounded daily, he would have had at age 64 a total of $1,129,200, or $528,200 more than the earnings of a male college graduate, and more than five times as much as the $199,000 extra the more educated man could expect to earn between 22 and 64.

The big advantage of getting your college money in cash now is that you can invest it in something that has a higher return than a diploma. For instance, a Princeton-bound high-school graduate of 1972 who liked fooling around with cars could have banked his $34,181, and gone to work at the local garage at close to $1,000 more per year than the average high-school graduate. Meanwhile, as he was learning to be an expert auto mechanic, his money would be ticking away in the bank. When he became 28, he would have earned $7,199 less on his job from age 22 to 28 than his college-educated friend, but he would have had $73,113 in his passbook—enough to buy out his boss, go into the used-car business, or acquire his own new-car dealership. If successful in business, he could expect to make more than the average college graduate. And if he had the brains to get into Princeton, he would be just as likely to make money without the four years spent on campus. Unfortunately, few college-bound high-school graduates get the opportunity to bank such a large sum of money, and then wait for it to make them rich. And few parents are sophisticated enough to understand that in financial returns alone, their children would be better off with the money than with the education.

Rates of return and dollar signs on education are fascinating brain teasers, but obviously there is a certain unreality to the game. Quite aside from the noneconomic benefits of college, and these should loom larger once the dollars are cleared away, there are grave difficulties in assigning a dollar value to college at all.

30 In fact there is no real evidence that the higher income of college graduates is due to college. College may simply attract people who are slated to earn more money anyway; those with higher IQs, better family backgrounds, a more enterprising temperament. No one who has wrestled with the problem is prepared to attribute all of the higher income to the impact of college itself.

Christopher Jencks, author of *Inequality*, a book that assesses the effect of family and schooling in America, believes that education in general accounts for less than half of the difference in income in the American population. "The biggest single source of income differences," writes Jencks, "seems to be the fact that men from high-status families have higher incomes than men from low-status families even when they enter the same occupations, have the same amount of education, and have the same test scores."

Jacob Mincer of the National Bureau of Economic Research and Columbia University states flatly that of "20 to 30 percent of students at any level, the additional schooling has been a waste, at least in terms of earnings." College fails to work its income-raising magic for almost a third of those who go. More than half of those people in 1972 who earned $15,000 or more reached that comfortable bracket without the benefit of a college diploma. Jencks says that financial success in the U.S. depends a good deal on luck, and the most sophisticated regression analyses have yet to demonstrate otherwise.

But most of today's students don't go to college to earn more money anyway. In 1968, when jobs were easy to get, Daniel Yankelovich made his first nationwide survey of students. Sixty-five percent of them said they "would welcome less emphasis on money." By 1973, when jobs were scarce, that figure jumped to 80 percent.

The young are not alone. Americans today are all looking less to the pay of a job than to the work itself. They want "interesting" work that permits them "to make a contribution," express themselves" and "use their special abilities," and they think college will help them find it.

Jerry Darring of Indianapolis knows what it is to make a dollar. He 35
worked with his father in the family plumbing business, on the line at Chevrolet, and in the Chrysler foundry. He quit these jobs to enter Wright State University in Dayton, Ohio, because "in a job like that a person only has time to work, and after that he's so tired that he can't do anything else but come home and go to sleep."

Jerry came to college to find work "helping people." And he is perfectly willing to spend the dollars he earns at dull, well-paid work to prepare for lower-paid work that offers the reward of service to others.

Jerry's case is not unusual. No one works for money alone. In order to deal with the nonmonetary rewards of work, economists have coined the concept of "psychic income" which according to one economic dictionary means "income that is reckoned in terms of pleasure, satisfaction, or general feelings of euphoria."

Psychic income is primarily what college students mean when they talk about getting a good job. During the most affluent years of the late 1960s and early 1970s college students told their placement officers that they wanted to be researchers, college professors, artists, city planners, social workers, poets, book publishers, archeologists, ballet dancers, or authors.

The psychic income of these and other occupations popular with students is so high that these jobs can be filled without offering high salaries. According to one study, 93 percent of urban university professors would choose the same vocation again if they had the chance, compared with only 16 percent of unskilled auto workers. Even though the monetary gap between college professor and auto worker is now surprisingly small, the difference in psychic income is enormous.

40 But colleges fail to warn students that jobs of these kinds are hard to come by, even for qualified applicants, and they rarely accept the responsibility of helping students choose a career that will lead to a job. When a young person says he is interested in helping people, his counselor tells him to become a psychologist. But jobs in psychology are scarce. The Department of Labor, for instance, estimates there will be 4,300 new jobs for psychologists in 1975 while colleges are expected to turn out 58,430 B.A.s in psychology that year.

Of 30 psych majors who reported back to Vassar what they were doing a year after graduation in 1972, only five had jobs in which they could possibly use their courses in psychology, and two of these were working for Vassar.

The outlook isn't much better for students majoring in other psychic-pay disciplines: sociology, English, journalism, anthropology, forestry, education. Whatever college graduates want to do, most of them are going to wind up doing what there is to do.

John Shingleton, director of placement at Michigan State University, accuses the academic community of outright hypocrisy. "Educators have never said, 'Go to college and get a good job,' but this has been implied, and now students expect it. . . . If we care what happens to students after college, then let's get involved with what should be one of the basic purposes of education: career preparation."

In the 1970s, some of the more practical professors began to see that jobs for graduates meant jobs for professors too. Meanwhile, students themselves reacted to the shrinking job market, and a "new vocationalism" exploded on campus. The press welcomed the change as a return to the ethic of achievement and service. Students were still idealistic, the reporters wrote, but they now saw that they could best make the world better by healing the sick as physicians or righting individual wrongs as lawyers.

45 But there are no guarantees in these professions either. The American Enterprise Institute estimated in 1971 that there would be more than the target ratio of 100 doctors for every 100,000 people in the population by 1980. And the odds are little better for would-be lawyers. Law schools are already graduating twice as many new lawyers every year as the Department of Labor thinks will be needed, and the oversupply is growing every year.

And it's not at all apparent that what is actually learned in a "professional" education is necessary for success. Teachers, engineers and others I talked to said they find that on the job they rarely use what they learned in school. In order to see how well college prepared engineers and scientists for actual paid work in their fields, The Carnegie Commission queried all the employees with degrees in these fields in two large firms. Only one in five said the work they were doing bore a "very close relationship" to their college studies, while almost a third saw "very little relationship at all." An overwhelming majority could think of many people who were doing their same work, but had majored in different fields.

Majors in nontechnical fields report even less relationship between their studies and their jobs. Charles Lawrence, a communications major in college and now the producer of "Kennedy & Co.," the Chicago morning television show, says, "You have to learn all that stuff and you never use it again. I learned my job doing it." Others employed as architects, nurses, teachers and other members of the so-called learned professions report the same thing.

Most college administrators admit that they don't prepare their graduates for the job market. "I just wish I had the guts to tell parents that when you get out of this place you aren't prepared to do anything," the academic head of a famous liberal-arts college told us. Fortunately, for him, most people believe that you don't have to defend a liberal-arts education on those grounds. A liberal-arts education is supposed to provide you with a value system, a standard, a set of ideas, not a job. "Like Christianity, the liberal arts are seldom practiced and would probably be hated by the majority of the populace if they were," said one defender.

The analogy is apt. The fact is, of course, that the liberal arts are a religion in every sense of that term. When people talk about them, their language becomes elevated, metaphorical, extravagant, theoretical and reverent. And faith in personal salvation by the liberal arts is professed in a creed intoned on ceremonial occasions such as commencements.

If the liberal arts are a religious faith, the professors are its priests. 50
But disseminating ideas in a four-year college curriculum is slow and most expensive. If you want to learn about Milton, Camus, or even Margaret Mead you can find them in paperback books, the public library, and even on television.

And when most people talk about the value of a college education, they are not talking about great books. When at Harvard commencement, the president welcomes the new graduates into "the fellowship of educated men and women," what he could be saying is, "Here is a piece of paper that is a passport to jobs, power and instant prestige." As Glenn Bassett, a personnel specialist at G.E. says, "In some parts of G.E., a college degree appears completely irrelevant to selection to, say, a manager's job. In most, however, it is a ticket of admission."

But now that we have doubled the number of young people attending college, a diploma cannot guarantee even that. The most charitable conclusion we can reach is that college probably has very little, if any, effect on people and things at all. Today, the false premises are easy to see:

First, college doesn't make people intelligent, ambitious, happy, or liberal. It's the other way around. Intelligent, ambitious, happy, liberal people are attracted to higher education in the first place.

Second, college can't claim much credit for the learning experiences that really change students while they are there. Jobs, friends, history, and most of all the sheer passage of time, have as big an impact as anything even indirectly related to the campus.

Third, colleges have changed so radically that a freshman entering in the fall of 1974 can't be sure to gain even the limited value research studies assigned to colleges in the '60s. The sheer size of undergraduate campuses of the 1970s makes college even less stimulating now than it was 10 years ago. Today even motivated students are disappointed with their college courses and professors.

Finally, a college diploma no longer opens as many vocational doors. Employers are beginning to realize that when they pay extra for someone with a diploma, they are paying only for an empty credential. The fact is that most of the work for which employers now expect college training is now or has been capably done in the past by people without higher educations.

College, then, may be a good place for those few young people who are really drawn to academic work, who would rather read than eat, but it has become too expensive, in money, time, and intellectual effort to serve as a holding pen for large numbers of our young. We ought to make it possible for those reluctant, unhappy students to find alternative ways of growing up, and more realistic preparation for the years ahead.

James Thurber

UNIVERSITY DAYS

I passed all the other courses that I took at my university, but I could never pass botany. This was because all botany students had to spend several hours a week in a laboratory looking through a microscope at plant cells, and I could never see through a microscope. I never once saw a cell through a microscope. This used to enrage my instructor. He would wander around the laboratory pleased with the progress all the students were making in drawing the involved and, so I am told, interesting structure of flower cells, until he came to me. I would just be standing there. "I can't see anything," I would say. He would begin patiently enough, explaining how anybody can see

From *My Life and Hard Times* (1933).

through a microscope, but he would always end up in a fury, claiming that I could *too* see through a microscope but just pretended that I couldn't. "It takes away from the beauty of flowers anyway," I used to tell him. "We are not concerned with beauty in this course," he would say. "We are concerned solely with what I may call the *mechanics* of flars." "Well," I'd say, "I can't see anything." "Try it just once again," he'd say, and I would put my eye to the microscope and see nothing at all, except now and again a nebulous milky substance—a phenomenon of maladjustment. You were supposed to see a vivid, restless clockwork of sharply defined plant cells. "I see what looks like a lot of milk," I would tell him. This, he claimed, was the result of my not having adjusted the microscope properly, so he would readjust it for me, or rather, for himself. And I would look again and see milk.

I finally took a deferred pass, as they called it, and waited a year and tried again. (You had to pass one of the biological sciences or you couldn't graduate.) The professor had come back from vacation brown as a berry, bright-eyed, and eager to explain cell-structure again to his classes. "Well," he said to me, cheerily, when we met in the first laboratory hour of the semester, "we're going to see cells this time, aren't we?" "Yes, sir," I said. Students to right of me and to left of me and in front of me were seeing cells; what's more, they were quietly drawing pictures of them in their notebooks. Of course, I didn't see anything.

"We'll try it," the professor said to me, grimly, "with every adjustment of the microscope known to man. As God is my witness, I'll arrange this glass so that you see cells through it or I'll give up teaching. In twenty-two years of botany, I—" He cut off abruptly for he was beginning to quiver all over, like Lionel Barrymore,[1] and he genuinely wished to hold onto his temper; his scenes with me had taken a great deal out of him.

So we tried it with every adjustment of the microscope known to man. With only one of them did I see anything but blackness or the familiar lacteal opacity, and that time I saw, to my pleasure and amazement, a variegated constellation of flecks, specks, and dots. These I hastily drew. The instructor, noting my activity, came back from an adjoining desk, a smile on his lips and his eyebrows high in hope. He looked at my cell drawing. "What's that?" he demanded, with a hint of a squeal in his voice. "That's what I saw," I said. "You didn't, you didn't, you *didn't!*" he screamed, losing control of his temper instantly, and he bent over and squinted into the microscope. His head snapped up. "That's your eye!" he shouted. "You've fixed the lens so that it reflects! You've drawn your eye!"

Another course that I didn't like, but somehow managed to pass, 5

1. American actor (1878–1954), especially noted for elderly roles.

was economics. I went to that class straight from the botany class, which didn't help me any in understanding either subject. I used to get them mixed up. But not as mixed up as another student in my economics class who came there direct from a physics laboratory. He was a tackle on the football team, named Bolenciecwcz. At that time Ohio State University had one of the best football teams in the country, and Bolenciecwcz was one of its outstanding stars. In order to be eligible to play it was necessary for him to keep up in his studies, a very difficult matter, for while he was not dumber than an ox he was not any smarter. Most of his professors were lenient and helped him along. None gave him more hints in answering questions or asked him simpler ones than the economics professor, a thin, timid man named Bassum. One day when we were on the subject of transportation and distribution, it came Bolenciecwcz's turn to answer a question. "Name one means of transportation," the professor said to him. No light came into the big tackle's eyes. "Just any means of transportation," said the professor. Bolenciecwcz sat staring at him. "That is," pursued the professor, "any medium, agency, or method of going from one place to another." Bolenciecwcz had the look of a man who is being led into a trap. "You may choose among steam, horsedrawn, or electrically propelled vehicles," said the instructor. "I might suggest the one which we commonly take in making long journeys across land." There was a profound silence in which everybody stirred uneasily, including Bolenciecwcz and Mr. Bassum, Mr. Bassum abruptly broke this silence in an amazing manner. "Choo-choo-choo," he said, in a low voice, and turned instantly scarlet. He glanced appealingly around the room. All of us, of course, shared Mr. Bassum's desire that Bolenciecwcz should stay abreast of the class in economics, for the Illinois game, one of the hardest and most important of the season, was only a week off. "Toot, toot, too-tooooooot!" some student with a deep voice moaned, and we all looked encouragingly at Bolenciecwcz. Somebody else gave a fine imitation of a locomotive letting off steam. Mr. Bassum himself rounded off the little show. "Ding, dong, ding, dong," he said, hopefully. Bolenciecwcz was staring at the floor now, trying to think, his great brow furrowed, his huge hands rubbing together, his face red.

"How did you come to college this year, Mr. Bolenciecwcz?" asked the professor. "*Chuffa* chuffa, *chuffa* chuffa."

"M'father sent me," said the football player.

"What on?" asked Bassum.

"I git an 'lowance," said the tackle, in a low, husky voice, obviously embarrassed.

10 "No, no," said Bassum. "Name a means of transportation. What did you *ride* here on?"

"Train," said Bolenciecwcz.

"Quite right," said the professor. "Now, Mr. Nugent, will you tell us—"

If I went through anguish in botany and economics—for different reasons—gymnasium work was even worse. I don't even like to think about it. They wouldn't let you play games or join in the exercises with your glasses on and I couldn't see with mine off. I bumped into professors, horizontal bars, agricultural students, and swinging iron rings. Not being able to see, I could take it but I couldn't dish it out. Also, in order to pass gymnasium (and you had to pass it to graduate) you had to learn to swim if you didn't know how. I didn't like the swimming pool, I didn't like swimming, and I didn't like the swimming instructor, and after all these years I still don't. I never swam but I passed my gym work anyway, by having another student give my gymnasium number (978) and swim across the pool in my place. He was a quiet, amiable blond youth, number 473, and he would have seen through a microscope for me if we could have got away with it, but we couldn't get away with it. Another thing I didn't like about gymnasium work was that they made you strip the day you registered. It is impossible for me to be happy when I am stripped and being asked a lot of questions. Still, I did better than a lanky agricultural student who was cross-examined just before I was. They asked each student what college he was in—that is, whether Arts, Engineering, Commerce, or Agriculture. "What college are you in?" the instructor snapped at the youth in front of me. "Ohio State University," he said promptly.

It wasn't that agricultural student but it was another a whole lot like him who decided to take up journalism, possibly on the ground that when farming went to hell he could fall back on newspaper work. He didn't realize, of course, that that would be very much like falling back full-length on a kit of carpenter's tools. Haskins didn't seem cut out for journalism, being too embarrassed to talk to anybody and unable to use a typewriter, but the editor of the college paper assigned him to the cow barns, the sheep house, the horse pavilion, and the animal husbandry department generally. This was a genuinely big "beat," for it took up five times as much ground and got ten times as great a legislative appropriation as the College of Liberal Arts. The agricultural student knew animals, but nevertheless his stories were dull and colorlessly written. He took all afternoon on each of them, on account of having to hunt for each letter on the typewriter. Once in a while he had to ask somebody to help him hunt. "C" and "L," in particular, were hard letters for him to find. His editor finally got pretty much annoyed at the farmer-journalist because his pieces were so uninteresting. "See here, Haskins," he snapped at him one day, "why is it we never have anything hot from you on the horse pavilion? Here we have two hundred head of horses on this campus—more than any other university in the Western Conference[2] except Purdue—and yet you never get any real lowdown on them. Now shoot over to the horse barns and dig up something lively." Haskins shambled out and came back in about an hour; he said he had something. "Well, start it off snappily," said the editor. "Something people will read." Haskins set to work and in a couple of hours brought a sheet of typewritten paper to the desk; it was a two-hundred-word story about some disease that had broken out among the horses. Its opening sentence was simple but arresting. It read: "Who has noticed the sores on the tops of the horses in the animal husbandry building?"

Ohio State was a land grant university and therefore two years of military drill was compulsory. We drilled with old Springfield rifles and studied the tactics of the Civil War even though the World War was going on at the time. At 11 o'clock each morning thousands of freshmen and sophomores used to deploy over the campus, moodily creeping up on the old chemistry building. It was good training for the kind of warfare that was waged at Shiloh[3] but it had no connection with what was going on in Europe. Some people used to think there was German money behind it, but they didn't dare say so or they would have been thrown in jail as German spies. It was a period of muddy thought and marked, I believe, the decline of higher education in the Middle West.

As a soldier I was never any good at all. Most of the cadets were glumly indifferent soldiers, but I was no good at all. Once General Littlefield, who was commandant of the cadet corps, popped up in front of me during regimental drill and snapped, "You are the main trouble with this university!" I think he meant that my type was the main trouble with the university but he may have meant me individually. I was mediocre at drill, certainly—that is, until my senior year. By that time I had drilled longer than anybody else in the Western Conference, having failed at military at the end of each preceding year so that I had to do it all over again. I was the only senior still in uniform. The uniform which, when new, had made me look like an interurban railway conductor, now that it had become faded and too tight made me look like Bert Williams[4] in his bellboy act. This had a definitely bad effect on my morale. Even so, I had become by sheer practice little short of wonderful at squad maneuvers.

One day General Littlefield picked our company out of the whole regiment and tried to get it mixed up by putting it through one movement after another as fast as we could execute them: squads right,

2. The Big Ten.
3. In southwestern Tennessee, site of 1862 Union victory.
4. African-American vaudeville star (1874?–1922).

squads left, squads on right into line, squads right about, squads left front into line, etc. In about three minutes one hundred and nine men were marching in one direction and I was marching away from them at an angle of forty degrees, all alone. "Company, halt!" shouted General Littlefield. "That man is the only man who has it right!" I was made a corporal for my achievement.

The next day General Littlefield summoned me to his office. He was swatting flies when I went in. I was silent and he was silent too, for a long time, I don't think he remembered me or why he had sent for me, but he didn't want to admit it. He swatted some more flies, keeping his eyes on them narrowly before he let go with the swatter. "Button up your coat!" he snapped. Looking back on it now I can see that he meant me although he was looking at a fly, but I just stood there. Another fly came to rest on a paper in front of the general and began rubbing its hind legs together. The general lifted the swatter cautiously. I moved restlessly and the fly flew away. "You startled him!" barked General Littlefield, looking at me severely. I said I was sorry. "That won't help the situation!" snapped the General, with cold military logic. I didn't see what I could do except offer to chase some more flies toward his desk, but I didn't say anything. He stared out the window at the faraway figures of co-eds crossing the campus toward the library. Finally, he told me I could go. So I went. He either didn't know which cadet I was or else he forgot what he wanted to see me about. It may have been that he wished to apologize for having called me the main trouble with the university; or maybe he had decided to compliment me on my brilliant drilling of the day before and then at the last minute decided not to. I don't know. I don't think about it much any more.

QUESTIONS

1. *What do the incidents Thurber wrote about have in common? Consider tone and narrator's attitude as well as "plot."*
2. *On the basis of this essay, what might Thurber have thought an ideal liberal college education would be?*
3. *In an essay called "Some Remarks on Humor," E. B. White says: "Humorists fatten on trouble. . . . You find them wrestling with foreign languages, fighting folding ironing boards and swollen drainpipes, suffering the terrible discomfort of tight boots. . . . They pour out their sorrows profitably, in a form that is not quite fiction nor quite fact either. Beneath the sparkling surface of these dilemmas flows the strong tide of human woe." Discuss how this statement can apply to Thurber's piece.*

William Zinsser

COLLEGE PRESSURES

Dear Carlos: I desperately need a dean's excuse for my chem midterm which will begin in about 1 hour. All I can say is that I totally blew it this week. I've fallen incredibly, inconceivably behind.

Carlos: Help! I'm anxious to hear from you. I'll be in my room and won't leave it until I hear from you. Tomorrow is the last day for . . .

Carlos: I left town because I started bugging out again. I stayed up all night to finish a take-home make-up exam & am typing it to hand in on the 10th. It was due on the 5th. P.S. I'm going to the dentist. Pain is pretty bad.

Carlos: Probably by Friday I'll be able to get back to my studies. Right now I'm going to take a long walk. This whole thing has taken a lot out of me.

Carlos: I'm really up the proverbial creek. The problem is I really *bombed* the history final. Since I need that course for my major I . . .

Carlos: Here follows a tale of woe. I went home this weekend, had to help my Mom, & caught a fever so didn't have much time to study. My professor . . .

Carlos: Aargh! Trouble. Nothing original but everything's piling up at once. To be brief, my job interview . . .

Hey Carlos, good news! I've got mononucleosis.

Who are these wretched supplicants, scribbling notes so laden with anxiety, seeking such miracles of postponement and balm? They are men and women who belong to Branford College, one of the twelve residential colleges at Yale University, and the messages are just a few of the hundreds that they left for their dean, Carlos Hortas—often slipped under his door at 4 A.M.—last year.

But students like the ones who wrote those notes can also be found on campuses from coast to coast—especially in New England and at many other private colleges across the country that have high academic standards and highly motivated students. Nobody could doubt that the notes are real. In their urgency and their gallows humor they are authentic voices of a generation that is panicky to succeed.

My own connection with the message writers is that I am master of Branford College. I live in its Gothic quadrangle and know the students well. (We have 485 of them.) I am privy to their hopes and

First appeared in *Blair and Ketchum's Country Journal* (Apr. 1979).

fears—and also to their stereo music and their piercing cries in the dead of night ("Does anybody *ca-a-are* ?"). If they went to Carlos to ask how to get through tomorrow, they come to me to ask how to get through the rest of their lives.

Mainly I try to remind them that the road ahead is a long one and that it will have more unexpected turns than they think. There will be plenty of time to change jobs, change careers, change whole attitudes and approaches. They don't want to hear such liberating news. They want a map—right now—that they can follow unswervingly to career security, financial security. Social Security and, presumably, a prepaid grave.

What I wish for all students is some release from the clammy grip of 5
the future. I wish them a chance to savor each segment of their education as an experience in itself and not as a grim preparation for the next step. I wish them the right to experiment, to trip and fall, to learn that defeat is as instructive as victory and is not the end of the world.

My wish, of course, is naïve. One of the few rights that America does not proclaim is the right to fail. Achievement is the national god, venerated in our media—the million-dollar athlete, the wealthy executive—and glorified in our praise of possessions. In the presence of such a potent state religion, the young are growing up old.

I see four kinds of pressure working on college students today: economic pressure, parental pressure, peer pressure, and self-induced pressure. It is easy to look around for villains—to blame the colleges for charging too much money, the professors for assigning too much work, the parents for pushing their children too far, the students for driving themselves too hard. But there are no villains; only victims.

"In the late 1960s," one dean told me, "the typical question that I got from students was 'Why is there so much suffering in the world?' or 'How can I make a contribution?' Today it's 'Do you think it would look better for getting into law school if I did a double major in history and political science, or just majored in one of them?' " Many other deans confirmed this pattern. One said: "They're trying to find an edge—the intangible something that will look better on paper if two students are about equal."

Note the emphasis on looking better. The transcript has become a sacred document, the passport to security. How one appears on paper is more important than how one appears in person. *A* is for Admirable and *B* is for Borderline, even though, in Yale's official system of grading, A means "excellent" and *B* means "very good." Today, looking very good is no longer good enough, especially for students who hope to go on to law school or medical school. They know that entrance into the better schools will be an entrance into the better law firms and better medical practices where they will make a lot of money. They also know that the odds are harsh, Yale Law School, for instance, matriculates 170 students from an applicant pool of 3,700; Harvard enrolls 550 from a pool of 7,000.

10 It's all very well for those of us who write letters of recommendation for our students to stress the qualities of humanity that will make them good lawyers or doctors. And it's nice to think that admission officers are really reading our letters and looking for the extra dimension of commitment or concern. Still, it would be hard for a student not to visualize these officers shuffling so many transcripts studded with As that they regard a *B* as positively shameful.

The pressure is almost as heavy on students who just want to graduate and get a job. Long gone are the days of the "gentleman's C," when students journeyed through college with a certain relaxation, sampling a wide variety of courses—music, art, philosophy, classics, anthropology, poetry, religion—that would send them out as liberally educated men and women. If I were an employer I would rather employ graduates who have this range and curiosity than those who narrowly pursued safe subjects and high grades. I know countless students whose inquiring minds exhilarate me. I like to hear the play of their ideas. I don't know if they are getting As or Cs, and I don't care. I also like them as people. The country needs them, and they will find satisfying jobs. I tell them to relax. They can't.

Nor can I blame them. They live in a brutal economy. Tuition, room, and board at most private colleges now comes to at least $7,000, not counting books and fees. This might seem to suggest that the colleges are getting rich. But they are equally battered by inflation. Tuition covers only 60 percent of what it costs to educate a student, and ordinarily the remainder comes from what colleges receive in endowments, grants, and gifts. Now the remainder keeps being swallowed by the cruel costs—higher every year—of just opening the doors. Heating oil is up. Insurance is up. Postage is up. Health-premium costs are up. Everything is up. Deficits are up. We are witnessing in America the creation of a brotherhood of paupers—colleges, parents, and students, joined by the common bond of debt.

Today it is not unusual for a student, even if he works part time at college and full time during the summer, to accrue $5,000 in loans after four years—loans that he must start to repay within one year after graduation. Exhorted at commencement to go forth into the world, he is already behind as he goes forth. How could he not feel under pressure throughout college to prepare for this day of reckoning? I have used "he," incidentally, only for brevity. Women at Yale are under no less pressure to justify their expensive education to themselves, their parents, and society. In fact, they are probably under more pressure. For although they leave college superbly equipped to bring fresh leadership to traditionally male jobs, society hasn't yet caught up with this fact.

Along with economic pressure goes parental pressure. Inevitably, the two are deeply intertwined.

15 I see many students taking pre-medical courses with joyless tenacity. They go off to their labs as if they were going to the dentist. It saddens me because I know them in other corners of their life as cheerful people.

"Do you want to go to medical school?" I ask them.

"I guess so," they say, without conviction, or "Not really."

"Then why are you going?"

"Well, my parents want me to be a doctor. They're paying all this money and . . ."

20 Poor students, poor parents. They are caught in one of the oldest webs of love and duty and guilt. The parents mean well; they are trying to steer their sons and daughters toward a secure future. But the sons and daughters want to major in history or classics or philosophy—subjects with no "practical" value. Where's the payoff on the humanities? It's not easy to persuade such loving parents that the humanities do indeed pay off. The intellectual faculties developed by studying subjects like history and classics—an ability to synthesize and relate, to weigh cause and effect, to see events in perspective—are just the faculties that make creative leaders in business or almost any general field. Still, many fathers would rather put their money on courses that point toward a specific profession—courses that are pre-law, pre-medical, pre-business, or, as I sometimes heard it put, "pre-rich."

But the pressure on students is severe. They are truly torn. One part of them feels obligated to fulfill their parents' expectations; after all, their parents are older and presumably wiser. Another part tells them that the expectations that are right for their parents are not right for them.

I know a student who wants to be an artist. She is very obviously an artist and will be a good one—she has already had several modest local exhibits. Meanwhile she is growing as a well-rounded person and taking humanistic subjects that will enrich the inner resources out of which her art will grow. But her father is strongly opposed. He thinks that an artist is a "dumb" thing to be. The student vacillates and tries to please everybody. She keeps up with her art somewhat furtively and takes some of the "dumb" courses her father wants her to take—at least they are dumb courses for her. She is a free spirit on a campus of tense students—no small achievement in itself—and she deserves to follow her muse.

Peer pressure and self-induced pressure are also intertwined, and they begin almost at the beginning of freshman year.

"I had a freshman student I'll call Linda," one dean told me, "who came in and said she was under terrible pressure because her roommate, Barbara, was much brighter and studied all the time. I couldn't tell her that Barbara had come in two hours earlier to say the same thing about Linda."

25 The story is almost funny—except that it's not. It's symptomatic of all the pressures put together. When every student thinks every other student is working harder and doing better, the only solution is to study harder still. I see students going off to the library every night after dinner and coming back when it closes at midnight. I wish they would sometimes forget about their peers and go to a movie. I hear the clacking of typewriters in the hours before dawn. I see the tension in their eyes when exams are approaching and papers are due: "*Will I get everything done?*"

Probably they won't. They will get sick. They will get "blocked." They will sleep. They will oversleep. They will bug out. *Hey Carlos, help!*

Part of the problem is that they do more than they are expected to do. A professor will assign five-page papers. Several students will start writing ten-page papers to impress him. Then more students will write ten-page papers, and a few will raise the ante to fifteen. Pity the poor student who is still just doing the assignment.

"Once you have twenty or thirty percent of the student population deliberately overexerting," one dean points out, "it's bad for everybody. When a teacher gets more and more effort from his class, the student who is doing normal work can be perceived as not doing well. The tactic works, psychologically."

Why can't the professor just cut back and not accept longer papers? He can, and he probably will. But by then the term will be half over and the damage done. Grade fever is highly contagious and not easily reversed. Besides, the professor's main concern is with his course. He knows his students only in relation to the course and doesn't know that they are also overexerting in their other courses. Nor is it really his business. He didn't sign up for dealing with the student as a whole person and with all the emotional baggage the student brought along from home. That's what deans, masters, chaplains, and psychiatrists are for.

30 To some extent this is nothing new: a certain number of professors have always been self-contained islands of scholarship and shyness, more comfortable with books than with people. But the new pauperism has widened the gap still further, for professors who actually like to spend time with students don't have as much time to spend. They also

are overexerting. If they are young, they are busy trying to publish in order not to perish, hanging by their finger nails onto a shrinking profession. If they are old and tenured, they are buried under the duties of administering departments—as departmental chairmen or members of committees—that have been thinned out by the budgetary axe.

Ultimately it will be the students' own business to break the circles in which they are trapped. They are too young to be prisoners of their parents' dreams and their classmates' fears. They must be jolted into believing in themselves as unique men and women who have the power to shape their own future.

"Violence is being done to the undergraduate experience," says Carlos Hortas. "College should be open-ended: at the end it should open many, many roads. Instead, students are choosing their goal in advance, and their choices narrow as they go along. It's almost as if they think that the country has been codified in the type of jobs that exist—that they've got to fit into certain slots. Therefore, fit into the best-paying slot.

"They ought to take chances. Not taking chances will lead to a life of colorless mediocrity. They'll be comfortable. But something in the spirit will be missing."

I have painted too drab a portrait of today's students, making them seem a solemn lot. That is only half of their story; if they were so dreary I wouldn't so thoroughly enjoy their company. The other half is that they are easy to like. They are quick to laugh and to offer friendship. They are not introverts. They are unusually kind and are more considerate of one another than any student generation I have known.

35 Nor are they so obsessed with their studies that they avoid sports and extracurricular activities. On the contrary, they juggle their crowded hours to play on a variety of teams, perform with musical and dramatic groups, and write for campus publications. But this in turn is one more cause of anxiety. There are too many choices. Academically, they have 1,300 courses to select from; outside class they have to decide how much spare time they can spare and how to spend it.

This means that they engage in fewer extracurricular pursuits than their predecessors did. If they want to row on the crew and play in the symphony they will eliminate one; in the '60s they would have done both. They also tend to choose activities that are self-limiting. Drama, for instance, is flourishing in all twelve of Yale's residential colleges as it never has before. Students hurl themselves into these productions—as actors, directors, carpenters, and technicians—with a dedication to create the best possible play, knowing that the day will come when the run will end and they can get back to their studies.

They also can't afford to be the willing slave of organizations like the *Yale Daily News*. Last spring at the one-hundredth anniversary banquet of that paper—whose past chairmen include such once and future kings as Potter Stewart, Kingman Brewster, and William F. Buckley, Jr.—much was made of the fact that the editorial staff used to be small and totally committed and that "newsies" routinely worked fifty hours a week. In effect they belonged to a club; Newsies is how they defined themselves at Yale. Today's student will write one or two articles a week, when he can, and he defines himself as a student. I've never heard the word Newsie except at the banquet.

If I have described the modern undergraduate primarily as a driven creature who is largely ignoring the blithe spirit inside who keeps trying to come out and play, it's because that's where the crunch is, not only at Yale but throughout American education. It's why I think we should all be worried about the values that are nurturing a generation so fearful of risk and so goal-obsessed at such an early age.

I tell students that there is no one "right" way to get ahead—that each of them is a different person, starting from a different point and bound for a different destination. I tell them that change is a tonic and that all the slots are not codified nor the frontiers closed. One of my ways of telling them is to invite men and women who have achieved success outside the academic world to come and talk informally with my students during the year. They are heads of companies or ad agencies, editors of magazines, politicians, public officials, television magnates, labor leaders, business executives, Broadway producers, artists, writers, economists, photographers, scientists, historians—a mixed bag of achievers.

40 I ask them to say a few words about how they got started. The students assume that they started in their present profession and knew all along that it was what they wanted to do. Luckily for me, most of them got into their field by a circuitous route, to their surprise, after many detours. The students are startled. They can hardly conceive of a career that was not pre-planned. They can hardly imagine allowing the hand of God or chance to nudge them down some unforeseen trail.

QUESTIONS

1. *What are the four kinds of pressure Zinsser describes at Yale in the 1970s? Are they the same kinds of pressures that trouble students now? Have new ones come to take their place?*
2. *Some people believe that students perform best when subjected to additional pressure, while others think that students already feel enough pressures from everyday life. What do you think about pressure as being good for college students? How much is enough?*
3. *Using your own recollections, compare the way people predicted college would be with the way first-year college students now perceive it.*

Adrienne Rich

TAKING WOMEN STUDENTS SERIOUSLY

I see my function here today as one of trying to create a context, delineate a background, against which we might talk about women as students and students as women. I would like to speak for awhile about this background, and then I hope that we can have, not so much a question period, as a raising of concerns, a sharing of questions for which we as yet may have no answers, an opening of conversations which will go on and on.

When I went to teach at Douglass, a women's college,[1] it was with a particular background which I would like briefly to describe to you. I had graduated from an all-girls' school in the 1940s, where the head and the majority of the faculty were independent, unmarried women. One or two held doctorates, but had been forced by the Depression (and by the fact that they were women) to take secondary school teaching jobs. These women cared a great deal about the life of the mind, and they gave a great deal of time and energy—beyond any limit of teaching hours—to those of us who showed special intellectual interest or ability. We were taken to libraries, art museums, lectures at neighboring colleges, set to work on extra research projects, given extra French or Latin reading. Although we sometimes felt "pushed" by them, we held those women in a kind of respect which even then we dimly perceived was not generally accorded to women in the world at large. They were vital individuals, defined not by their relationships but by their personalities; and although under the pressure of the culture we were all certain we wanted to get married, their lives did not appear empty or dreary to us. In a kind of cognitive dissonance, we knew they were "old maids" and therefore supposed to be bitter and lonely; yet we saw them vigorously involved with life. But despite their existence as alternate models of women, the *content* of the education they gave us in no way prepared us to survive as women in a world organized by and for men.

From that school, I went on to Radcliffe, congratulating myself that now I would have great men as my teachers. From 1947 to 1951, when I graduated, I never saw a single woman on a lecture platform, or in front of a class, except when a woman graduate student gave a paper

The talk that follows was addressed to teachers of women. . . . It was given for the New Jersey College and University Coalition on Women's Education, May 9, 1978 [Rich's note].

1. Part of Rutgers University in New Jersey.

on a special topic. The "great men" talked of other "great men," of the nature of Man, the history of Mankind, the future of Man; and never again was I to experience, from a teacher, the kind of prodding, the insistence that my best could be even better, that I had known in high school. Women students were simply not taken very seriously. Harvard's message to women was an elite mystification: we were, of course, part of Mankind; we were special, achieving women, or we would not have been there; but of course our real goal was to marry—if possible, a Harvard graduate.

In the late sixties, I began teaching at the City College of New York—a crowded, public, urban, multiracial institution as far removed from Harvard as possible. I went there to teach writing in the SEEK Program,[2] which predated Open Admissions and which was then a kind of model for programs designed to open up higher education to poor, black, and Third World students. Although during the next few years we were to see the original concept of SEEK diluted, then violently attacked and betrayed, it was for a short time an extraordinary and intense teaching and learning environment. The characteristics of this environment were a deep commitment on the part of teachers to the minds of their students; a constant, active effort to create or discover the conditions for learning, and to educate ourselves to meet the needs of the new college population; a philosophical attitude based on open discussion of racism, oppression, and the politics of literature and language; and a belief that learning in the classroom could not be isolated from the student's experience as a member of an urban minority group in white America. Here are some of the kinds of questions we, as teachers of writing, found ourselves asking:

(1) What has been the student's experience of education in the inadequate, often abusively racist public school system, which rewards passivity and treats a questioning attitude or independent mind as a behavior problem? What has been her or his experience in a society that consistently undermines the selfhood of the poor and the nonwhite? How can such a student gain that sense of self which is necessary for active participation in education? What does all this mean for us as teachers?

(2) How do we go about teaching a canon of literature which has consistently excluded or depreciated nonwhite experience?

(3) How can we connect the process of learning to write well with the student's own reality, and not simply teach her/him how to write acceptable lies in standard English?

2. SEEK is an acronym for "Search for Education, Elevation, and Knowledge"; the instructors in the program included not only college teachers but also creative artists and writers.

When I went to teach at Douglass College in 1976, and in teaching 5
women's writing workshops elsewhere, I came to perceive stunning parallels to the questions I had first encountered in teaching the so-called disadvantaged students at City. But in this instance, and against the specific background of the women's movement, the questions framed themselves like this:

(1) What has been the student's experience of education in schools which reward female passivity, indoctrinate girls and boys in stereotypic sex roles, and do not take the female mind seriously? How does a woman gain a sense of her *self* in a system—in this case, patriarchal capitalism—which devalues work done by women, denies the importance and uniqueness of female experience, and is physically violent toward women? What does this mean for a woman teacher?

(2) How do we, as women, teach women students a canon of literature which has consistently excluded or depreciated female experience, and which often expresses hostility to women and validates violence against us?

(3) How can we teach women to move beyond the desire for male approval and getting "good grades" and seek and write their own truths that the culture has distorted or made taboo? (For women, of course, language itself is exclusive: I want to say more about this further on.)

In teaching women, we have two choices: to lend our weight to the forces that indoctrinate women to passivity, self-depreciation, and a sense of powerlessness, in which case the issue of "taking women students seriously" is a moot one; or to consider what we have to work against, as well as with, in ourselves, in our students, in the content of the curriculum, in the structure of the institution, in the society at large. And this means, first of all, taking ourselves seriously: Recognizing that central responsibility of a woman to herself, without which we remain always the Other, the defined, the object, the victim; believing that there is a unique quality of validation, affirmation, challenge, support, that one woman can offer another. Believing in the value and significance of women's experience, traditions, perceptions. Thinking of ourselves seriously, not as one of the boys, not as neuters, or androgynes, but *as women.*

Suppose we were to ask ourselves, simply: What does a woman need to know? Does she not, as a self-conscious, self-defining human being, need a knowledge of her own history, her much-politicized biology, an awareness of the creative work of women of the past, the skills and crafts and techniques and powers exercised by women in different times and cultures, a knowledge of women's rebellions and organized movements against our oppression and how they have been routed or diminished? Without such knowledge women live and have lived without context, vulnerable to the projections of male fantasy, male prescriptions for us, estranged from our own experience because our education has not reflected or echoed it. I would suggest that not biology, but ignorance of our selves, has been the key to our powerlessness.

But the university curriculum, the high-school curriculum, do not provide this kind of knowledge for women, the knowledge of Womankind, whose experience has been so profoundly different from that of Mankind. Only in the precariously budgeted, much-condescended-to area of women's studies is such knowledge available to women students. Only there can they learn about the lives and work of women other than the few select women who are included in the "mainstream" texts, usually misrepresented even when they do appear. Some students, at some institutions, manage to take a majority of courses in women's studies, but the message from on high is that this is self-indulgence, soft-core education: the "real" learning is the study of Mankind.

If there is any misleading concept, it is that of "coeducation": that because women and men are sitting in the same classrooms, hearing the same lectures, reading the same books, performing the same laboratory experiments, they are receiving an equal education. They are not, first because the content of education itself validates men even as it invalidates women. Its very message is that men have been the shapers and thinkers of the world, and that this is only natural. The bias of higher education, including the so-called sciences, is white and male, racist and sexist; and this bias is expressed in both subtle and blatant ways. I have mentioned already the exclusiveness of grammar itself: "The student should test himself on the above questions"; "The poet is representative. He stands among partial men for the complete man." Despite a few half-hearted departures from custom, what the linguist Wendy Martyna has named "He-Man" grammar prevails throughout the culture. The efforts of feminists to reveal the profound ontological implications of sexist grammar are routinely ridiculed by academicians and journalists, including the professedly liberal *Times* columnist, Tom Wicker, and the professed humanist, Jacques Barzun. Sexist grammar burns into the brains of little girls and young women a message that the male is the norm, the standard, the central figure beside which we are the deviants, the marginal, the dependent variables. It lays the foundation for androcentric thinking, and leaves men safe in their solipsistic tunnel-vision.

10 Women and men do not receive an equal education because outside the classroom women are perceived not as sovereign beings but as prey. The growing incidence of rape on and off the campus may or

may not be fed by the proliferations of pornographic magazines and X-rated films available to young males in fraternities and student unions; but it is certainly occurring in a context of widespread images of sexual violence against women, on billboards and in so-called high art. More subtle, more daily than rape is the verbal abuse experienced by the woman student on many campuses—Rutgers for example—where, traversing a street lined with fraternity houses, she must run a gauntlet of male commentary and verbal assault. The undermining of self, of a woman's sense of her right to occupy space and walk freely in the world, is deeply relevant to education. The capacity to think independently, to take intellectual risks, to assert ourselves mentally, is inseparable from our physical way of being in the world, our feelings of personal integrity. If it is dangerous for me to walk home late of an evening from the library, *because I am a woman and can be raped*, how self-possessed, how exuberant can I feel as I sit working in that library? how much of my working energy is drained by the subliminal knowledge that, as a woman, I test my physical right to exist each time I go out alone? Of this knowledge, Susan Griffin has written:

> . . . more than rape itself, the fear of rape permeates our lives. And what does one do from day to day, with *this* experience, which says, without words and directly to the heart, *your existence, your experience, may end at any moment*. Your experience may end, and the best defense against this is not to be, to deny being in the body, as a self, to . . . avert your gaze, make yourself, as a presence in the world, less felt.[3]

Finally, rape of the mind. Women students are more and more often now reporting sexual overtures by male professors—one part of our overall growing consciousness of sexual harassment in the workplace. At Yale a legal suit has been brought against the university by a group of women demanding an explicit policy against sexual advances toward female students by male professors. Most young women experience a profound mixture of humiliation and intellectual self-doubt over seductive gestures by men who have the power to award grades, open doors to grants and graduate school, or extend special knowledge and training. Even if turned aside, such gestures constitute mental rape, destructive to a woman's ego. They are acts of domination, as despicable as the molestation of the daughter by the father.

But long before entering college the woman student has experienced her alien identity in a world which misnames her, turns her to its own uses, denying her the resources she needs to become self-affirming, self-defined. The nuclear family teaches her that relation-

3. Rich is quoting from the manuscript of Griffin's *Rape: The Power of Consciousness* (New York, 1979).

ships are more important than selfhood or work; that "whether the phone rings for you, and how often," having the right clothes, doing the dishes, take precedence over study or solitude; that too much intelligence or intensity may make her unmarriageable; that marriage and children—service to others—are, finally, the points on which her life will be judged a success or a failure. In high school, the polarization between feminine attractiveness and independent intelligence comes to an absolute. Meanwhile, the culture resounds with messages. During Solar Energy Week in New York I saw young women wearing "ecology" T-shirts with the legend: CLEAN, CHEAP AND AVAILABLE; a reminder of the 1960s antiwar button which read: CHICKS SAY YES TO MEN WHO SAY NO. Department store windows feature female mannequins in chains, pinned to the wall with legs spread, smiling in positions of torture. Feminists are depicted in the media as "shrill," "strident," "puritanical," or "humorless," and the lesbian choice—the choice of the woman-identified woman—as pathological or sinister. The young woman sitting in the philosophy classroom, the political science lecture, is already gripped by tensions between her nascent sense of self-worth, and the battering force of messages like these.

Look at a classroom: look at the many kinds of women's faces, postures, expressions. Listen to the women's voices. Listen to the silences, the unasked questions, the blanks. Listen to the small, soft voices, often courageously trying to speak up, voices of women taught early that tones of confidence, challenge, anger, or assertiveness, are strident and unfeminine. Listen to the voices of the women and the voices of the men; observe the space men allow themselves, physically and verbally, the male assumption that people will listen, even when the majority of the group is female. Look at the faces of the silent, and of those who speak. Listen to a woman groping for language in which to express what is on her mind, sensing that the terms of academic discourse are not her language, trying to cut down her thought to the dimensions of a discourse not intended for her *(for it is not fitting that a woman speak in public)*; or reading her paper aloud at breakneck speed, throwing her words away, deprecating her own work by a reflex prejudgment: *I do not deserve to take up time and space.*

As women teachers, we can either deny the importance of this context in which women students think, write, read, study, project their own futures; or try to work with it. We can either teach passively, accepting these conditions, or actively, helping our students identify and resist them.

15 One important thing we can do is *discuss* the context. And this need not happen only in a women's studies course; it can happen anywhere. We can refuse to accept passive, obedient learning and insist upon critical thinking. We can become harder on our women students, giv-

ing them the kinds of "cultural prodding" that men receive, but on different terms and in a different style. Most young women need to have their intellectual lives, their work, legitimized against the claims of family, relationships, the old message that a woman is always available for service to others. We need to keep our standards very high, not to accept a woman's preconceived sense of her limitations; we need to be hard to please, while supportive of risk-taking, because self-respect often comes only when exacting standards have been met. At a time when adult literacy is generally low, we need to demand more, not less, of women, both for the sake of their futures as thinking beings, and because historically women have always had to be better than men to do half as well. A romantic sloppiness, an inspired lack of rigor, a self-indulgent incoherence, are symptoms of female self-depreciation. We should help our women students to look very critically at such symptoms, and to understand where they are rooted.

Nor does this mean we should be training women students to "think like men." Men in general think badly: in disjuncture from their personal lives, claiming objectivity where the most irrational passions seethe, losing, as Virginia Woolf[4] observed, their senses in the pursuit of professionalism. It is not easy to think like a woman in a man's world, in the world of the professions; yet the capacity to do that is a strength which we can try to help our students develop. To think like a woman in a man's world means thinking critically, refusing to accept the givens, making connections between facts and ideas which men have left unconnected. It means remembering that every mind resides in a body; remaining accountable to the female bodies in which we live; constantly retesting given hypotheses against lived experience. It means a constant critique of language, for as Wittgenstein[5] (no feminist) observed, "The limits of my language are the limits of my world." And it means that most difficult thing of all: listening and watching in art and literature, in the social sciences, in all the descriptions we are given of the world, for the silences, the absences, the nameless, the unspoken, the encoded—for there we will find the true knowledge of women. And in breaking those silences, naming our selves, uncovering the hidden, making ourselves present, we begin to define a reality which resonates to *us*, which affirms *our* being, which allows the woman teacher and the woman student alike to take ourselves, and each other, seriously: meaning, to begin taking charge of our lives.

4. Prominent British novelist, essayist, and feminist (1882–1941).
5. Ludwig Josef Johann Wittgenstein (1889–1951), Austrian-born British philosopher.

Jill K. Conway

POLITICS, PEDAGOGY, AND GENDER

In the mid-nineteenth century the public education system of the United States drew its corps of teachers from the nation's population of young women. In contrast, European public education remained a male-dominated enterprise until well into the twentieth century. Traditionally, the United States' early and extensive recruitment of female teachers has been interpreted as a sign of enlightened attitudes about women and their place in society. Horace Mann's innovative Massachusetts normal schools, which trained young women to be teachers, are customarily cited as examples of feminism in action. So, until recently, was the career of Catharine Beecher,[1] the archetypal proselytizer for the female teaching profession. The development of a public elementary school system before the Civil War and the extension of that system through the establishment of secondary schools in the last quarter of the nineteenth century provide a happy ending to the traditional story of the establishment of the first "women's" profession.[2]

Underlying this popular history of women in teaching is the assumption that access to new work opportunities has the same meaning for everyone. If we stop to ask what gender meant for the nineteenth-century founders of American public education, however, the story takes on new levels of meaning. Some of its themes speak directly to our educational dilemmas today. Its interest lies not in the sex of the teachers who staffed America's one-room schools but in the political and psychological images that men and women held regarding the gender of those teachers. The story of women's opportunities to enter teaching as a respectable occupation for single women outside the home is a case study in the meaning of access. Examination of the case of women teachers' recruitment in the mid-nineteenth century should make us rethink the incremental model of change that is presumed to characterize the liberal state.

The number of women involved in this recruitment is certainly striking. By 1848 women greatly outnumbered men as annual entrants to the teaching profession; in absolute numbers their predominance

From *Learning About Women: Gender, Politics, and Power* (1987).

1. Mann (1796–1859) and Beecher (1800–1878), American educators.
2. Horace Mann, *Eleventh Annual Report* (Massachusetts Normal Schools, 1845), p. 24 [Conway's note].

was established. In that year 2,424 men taught in the public (or common) schools of America beside 5,510 women.[3] During the 1850s the same pattern was replicated in the Midwest. After 1864 one of the impositions of the victorious North on the southern states during Reconstruction was the establishment of a predominantly female cadre of elementary school teachers. In the last three decades of the nineteenth century the same pattern emerged in the public high schools. By 1890, 65 percent of all teachers in the United States were women. Members of the new female profession were remarkably youthful, averaging from twenty-one to twenty-five years of age in different regions of the country.

Popular attitudes encouraged single women to become teachers but discouraged their presence in the schools once they married. The country's teachers were predominantly daughters of the native-born, from rural families. In comparison with European teachers, American teachers were not well educated. As late as the 1930s only 12 percent of elementary teachers in the United States had earned bachelor's degrees.[4] In the nineteenth century many entrants to the profession had not even completed high school. Because so many teachers were drawn from rural farm families, most had not traveled more than 100 miles from their place of birth. Their experience of high culture was minimal. Surveys carried out at the turn of the century recorded that most teachers had never seen reproductions of works of art during their own schooling. As adults their only reading was an occasional novel and the standard popular magazines of the day. To compensate for these deficiencies, the normal schools offered teaching programs that were largely remedial.[5]

5 The woman teacher, whether rural or urban, earned about 60 percent of the salary paid to men in the same school system. Around 1900 the average woman teacher's salary was $350.00 per year. Higher earnings were available to women in the textile industry and in most other industrial settings. In some states mechanics and clerks earned twice the annual wages of male teachers, whose earnings were more than a third higher than those of their female counterparts. The universal custom of "boarding out" was a major factor in depressing the level of teachers' earnings: nineteenth-century school districts held down the cost of elementary schools by housing teachers in rotation with fami-

3. Redding R. Sugg, Jr., *Motherteacher: The Feminization of American Education* (Charlottesville, VA: University Press of Virginia, 1978), p. 37 [Conway's note].
4. Lindley J. Stiles, ed., *The Teacher's Role in American Society* (New York: Harper & Row, 1957), p. 279 [Conway's note].
5. Lotus D. Coffman, *The Social Composition of the Teaching Population* (New York: Bureau of Publications, Teachers College, Columbia University, 1911), p. 550 [Conway's note].

lies whose children were currently school pupils. This dubious hospitality was motivated partly by economic considerations and partly by the prevailing sentiment that young single women should not be allowed to live outside a family setting. The school district's room and board carried with it a censorious social control that young single women could resist only at their peril. In short, the young teacher's social status was marginal.[6]

This marginality was not borne for long; rates of turnover were very high. Most women elementary teachers taught for only three or four years. Although 90 percent of the elementary instructors by the 1920s were women, their rapid turnover meant that they did not develop as school leaders or as curriculum planners.[7] Men did not remain teachers for long either; they did not form strong bonds to the occupation of teacher as they did to the professions of medicine and engineering. Yet male teachers were seven times more likely to become school administrators than their female colleagues. Despite the social changes that have raised women's work aspirations in recent decades, these early trends have continued unaltered. Today men hold 99.4 percent of all school superintendencies. The only area of school administration in which women predominate is librarianship. Clearly gender shapes one's status within the teaching profession, even though teaching has traditionally been singled out for its supposed hospitality to women. What, then, are we to make of women's early access to teaching in the United States? What values shaped the establishment of the common schools in America, and what was the operative significance of ideas about gender in that process? To paraphrase William James,[8] what was the meaning of the ideas being translated into action when people like Horace Mann began to recruit women for teacher training?

If we look at the political debates that preceded the establishment of the public education system in the 1830s and 1840s, we see that political forces divided over the level of intellectual aspiration desired as an outcome of state-supported education and over the place of elites of education and talent within the young republic. One thing that united Jefferson and his Federalist opponents was the value they saw in an educated elite drawn from the best talent of their new society. Jefferson wanted his elite to be democratically recruited, its education publicly supported; he expected the result to be the highest intellectual achievement.

6. Ibid., p. 550. See also Myra H. Strober and Audri Gordon Langford, "The Feminization of Public School Teaching: A Cross-Sectional Analysis, 1850–1880," *Signs* 11 (2) (1986), pp. 212–235, and Willard S. Ellsbree, *The American Teacher: Evaluation of a Profession in a Democracy* (New York: American Book Company, 1933), p. 281 [Conway's note].
7. Ellsbree, *The American Teacher*, p. 206 [Conway's note].
8. American psychologist and philosopher (1842–1910).

One of the major shifts of value in the Jacksonian era was the rejection of the idea of a socially valuable elite formed by education and high culture. Instead, Americans of that era favored a popular education that was broadly accessible and limited in its intellectual goals. As Michael Katz has shown in his study of the development of public education in Massachusetts, some of the old Federalist elites found popular education attractive not so much as a means of training the mind but as a way of providing instruction in behavior.[9] Many New England moralists who sought to control the excesses of frontier behavior thought that this goal might be achieved through the common schools. Their intellectual aspirations for the students who were expected to attend these schools were minimal.

We know from recent studies of the legislative decisions approving the establishment of the common schools that Federalists and Jacksonians alike sought to develop public education as inexpensively as possible. The compromise that led to agreement on tax-supported public education combined the older Jeffersonian ideal of wide access to public education with Federalist and Jacksonian concerns for limited education at minimal cost to the taxpayer. The goal of cost containment made the recruitment of women completely logical because all parties to the educational debate agreed that women lacked acquisitive drives and would serve at subsistence salaries. The potentially explosive conflict over the intellectual goals of public education could also be avoided by choosing women as teachers. Their access to education was slight, so that male control over the normal schools that trained teachers insured control over the content of the curriculum. Furthermore, beliefs about the female temperament promised that the pedagogical style of women teachers would be emotional and value-oriented rather than rational and critical. Thus neither Jacksonians nor Federalists needed to make resolution of their conflicts over the goals of education an explicit part of their political agenda.[1] The resolution of fundamental contradictions about a strategic institution for the evolving society could safely be postponed as long as women teachers presented no threat to the objectives of low cost and strictly utilitarian public education.

The following three quotations demonstrate gender stereotyping at 10
work in the public-education policy discussions of late nineteenth-century legislators and public officials. Each of the speakers favored the recruitment of women teachers. These passages illustrate the important components of the gender ideology accepted by all parties to the dispute over the goals of education.

9. Michael Katz, *The Irony of Early School Reform* (Cambridge, MA: Harvard University Press, 1968) [Conway's note].

1. Sugg, *Motherteacher*, pp. 4–25 [Conway's note].

> [Women] manifest a livelier interest, more contentment in the work, have altogether superior success in managing and instructing young children, and I know of instances, where by the silken cord of affection, have led many a stubborn will, and wild ungoverned impulse, into habits of obedience and study even in the large winter schools (Henry Barnard, *Second Annual Report* [Connecticut School, 1840], pp. 27–28).

> [Women] are endowed by nature with stronger parental impulses, and this makes the society of children delightful, and turns duty into a pleasure. Their minds are less withdrawn from their employment, by the active scenes of life; and they are less intent and scheming for future honors and emoluments. As a class, they never look forward, as young men almost invariably do, to a period of legal emancipation from parental control. . . . They are also of purer morals (*Fourth Annual Report* [Boston Board of Education, 1841], pp. 45–46).

> In childhood the intellectual faculties are but partially developed—the affections much more fully. At that early age the affections are the key of the whole being. The female teacher readily possesses herself of that key, and thus having access to the heart, the mind is soon reached and operated upon (Assemblyman Hurlburd, *New York State Education Exhibit* [World's Columbian Exposition, Chicago, 1893], pp. 45–46).

At the center of the cluster of ideas that made up each writer's picture of women we see a belief in women's capacity to influence children's behavior through the emotions. Barnard's "silken cord of affection" and Hurlburd's "access to the heart" were characteristic themes in discourse about women as teachers. The writer of the Boston Board of Education's annual report associated women's ability to establish emotional links with children with women's lack of acquisitiveness and acceptance of dependence. These presumed qualities made women ideal candidates to teach in elementary schools, the purpose of which was to instill principles of behavior and convey basic literacy at a minimum cost to the public purse. Women were favored and actively recruited as elementary teachers because their presence in the schools satisfied a larger political agenda. Their perceived gender characteristics and their lack of academic preparation were positive advantages in the eyes of early public education officials; with a corps of women teachers there was no danger that investment in public education might foster the creation of new elites.

What, then, were the consequences of this congruence of ideology and economic concerns that served to give women preferred access to the teaching profession in the United States? The first consequence, extensively commented on by foreign visitors, was that discipline in American schools was very different from any known in European classrooms. As women were not thought suited to administering corporal punishment, the rod was virtually absent from America's schools. Maintaining discipline and conveying knowledge became more a matter of persuasion than an exercise of power based on authority. One learned because one liked the teacher, not out of respect for the learning that the teacher represented, as was the case in the French lycée or the German gymnasium.[2] The climate in the American schoolroom was wholly different; the classroom was considered an extension of the home.

This should not be taken to mean that the stereotype of the steely-eyed New England schoolmarm was incorrect; there were many such outstanding women. What it did mean, however, was that maleness involved rebellion against the values for which the schoolmarm stood. Many celebrations of maleness in American culture have retained overtones of adolescent rebellion against a female cultural presence that ostensibly cannot be easily incorporated into a strong adult male identity.

We may speculate about the consequences of subsuming school and home within a maternal, domestic culture rather than having the school serve as an impersonal agent of cultural authority, much like the church or the army. How would *Huckleberry Finn*[3] read if the journey on the raft were an escape from male institutions? Huckleberry Finn's journey raises many profound questions about American culture. One critical question is whether the overrepresentation of one gender in the early stages of schooling permits either boys or girls to develop the balanced identities we associate with creativity. For the purpose of understanding American educational institutions, another question that requires answering is this: If the school exists in opposition to male values and frontier life, how are we to understand higher education? In what ways is there a cultural imperative to redress the balance between maternal and masculine values at different levels of the system? What has that cultural requirement meant for American intellectual life?

Teaching through love made the school a setting in which many 15
ideas about child development were played out; it was never an agency for strenuous effort to discipline and develop young intellectual talents. Thus, the traditional twelve years of schooling did not bring the young American student to the levels of learning aimed at by the lycée or the gymnasium. Instead, and increasingly, American education came to require a further four years of intellectual exploration at the college level before the young person was considered to be in a position to make adult career commitments. Moreover, because of American public schools' identification with maternal functions, colleges

2. Institutions of secondary education.
3. Mark Twain's novel of 1884.

and universities have distanced themselves from schools and stressed the "masculine" tough-mindedness of American scholarship. This difference remains an enduring puzzle to Europeans, who see both schools and universities in a continuum of intellectual endeavor, and who value intellectual playfulness.

We may interpret this impulse to distance higher learning from schools as a natural response to some of the major nineteenth-century curricular debates. Because the schools operated as agents of maternal values, school curricula were organized along the lines of accepted models of child development. G. Stanley Hall's[4] celebrated theories of child development, which held that the child recapitulated the various stages of human evolutionary development, required that the teacher act as a helpful director as the pupil traversed these stages. It is unlikely that Hall would have designed so unintellectual a teaching role had he assumed that most elementary school teachers would be men. His ideas about child development were revolutionary in their largely successful redefinition of childhood as a series of developmental stages rather than as a time when the "imp of Satan" had to be disciplined; however, his view of the teacher was based on earlier nineteenth-century assumptions about the female temperament.

John Dewey's[5] Progressive schools discarded the notion of a fixed body of intellectual skills to be acquired entirely in school. Progressive pedagogy asked that the teacher help the young to discover the world through their innate intelligence. It took individuals with an almost superhuman capacity for nurturing to manage this kind of schoolroom. Few teachers could completely repress the desire to instruct, as Dewey's theories required. Many rueful survivors of Progressive schools testified to the demoralizing nature of such self-abnegation. It is reasonable to ask whether educational theorists would have designed teaching roles of such preternatural maternal patience had they expected their male colleagues to take principal responsibility for such instruction. Had the standard levels of education required for elementary school teachers been higher, educational reformers of the Progressive variety might have found earlier curricular ideals less easy to disregard. It was because the minds of young teachers were seen as tabulae rasae that older notions of learning could be easily ignored. Certainly if one assesses Dewey's pedagogy from the standpoint of the gender stereotypes enshrined within it, its conservatism is striking. Dewey advanced a new theory of learning and stated new political goals for American schools, but his assumptions about the temperamental and intellectual characteristics of teachers differed little from

4. American psychologist and educator (1846–1924).
5. American philosopher and educator (1859–1952).

the assumptions made by Henry Barnard and his colleagues in the 1840s.[6]

While many of the goals of Progressive education were admirable, the fact that the overwhelming majority of teachers in the American elementary school system were young women was a substantial influence on the way reformers thought about the role of teacher. Because of the persistence of the idea that women related to children primarily through the emotions, reformers prescribed intellectually demeaning roles for teachers—roles that often ignored the teacher's intellectual capacity in relation to the child's.

Similarly, the fact that most teachers did not have the right to vote affected the dynamics of the political relationship between the common schools and the larger society. From its inception the public education system operated at the center of a vortex of political forces, many of which were intrinsically unrelated to pedagogical issues. The schools were affected by political battles over such issues as patronage rights, appointments to teaching staffs and desirable jobs on maintenance staffs, which districts would be granted the economic benefits of building contracts, and which merchants should benefit from the purchasing power of students and their families. Moreover, it was taken for granted that parents, who had an abiding interest in the curriculum and its relationship to employment opportunities, and whose taxes paid teachers' salaries, had a democratic right to influence what was and was not taught to their children. These interests found expression in city and state politics, but women teachers were disfranchised until 1919 and consequently were unable to directly participate in the political process that shaped and established priorities for public education. Fathers and men teachers could mobilize voter support for school policies through their lodges or friendly societies, or later through Rotary, Kiwanis, or Lions Clubs; women could not. This situation affected women's status as teachers and indirectly affected the political importance of schools: an important component of professionalization in all modern societies is the degree to which would-be professionals are able to persuade economically or politically powerful elites that their services are important enough to command special rewards. Women teachers, unable to undertake this effort effectively, found their logical political allies in the ranks of organized labor.

The history that produced this logic is vividly illustrated in the dis- 20
putes affecting the Chicago school system in the 1880s and 1890s.

6. On G. Stanley Hall's educational theories, see Dorothy Ross, *G. Stanley Hall, The Psychologist as Populist* (Chicago: University of Chicago Press, 1972). On Dewey and Progressive education, see John Dewey, *On Education* (New York: The Modern Library, 1964) [Conway's note].

The city's total population was 500,000 and there were 59,000 pupils in the public schools, which expended a budget of over $1,000,000. The school system was the biggest employer in the city. The school board was appointed by the mayor, and it controlled or influenced three sets of resources critical to Chicago's economic future: land voted to support the public schools, contracts for school buildings, and tax abatements for corporations occupying land within the city. The major issues of concern to teachers were security of tenure, pension rights, and professional evaluation for promotion.[7] Women teachers felt considerable social distance from the exclusively male school superintendents in the city, who were themselves political appointees. In the campaign to secure teachers' pension rights, the female-led Chicago Federation of Teachers found that it carried no weight with the municipal government, so it waged battle in the courts. In her autobiography, Margaret A. Haley, the founder of the federation, records the process by which she came to conclude that, because of women's limited voting rights, her union's predominantly female membership would gain political leverage by affiliating with a strong political organization—the Chicago Federation of Labor. She recognized that laws were only enacted in response to the political pressure of voters. "Except in a few western states," she wrote, "the women of the nation had practically no voting power."[8]

The early choice of unionization was a natural one for nonvoting workers; its consequences were profound. As early as the Chicago Federation of Teachers' 1902 decision to affiliate with the Chicago Federation of Labor, the city's elementary teachers were in a confrontational relationship with political and social elites. The male school principals and superintendents, who identified with management in the labor-versus-management model of the school and the teacher's role within it, were even more distanced from teachers. The working peers of the school administrators were the political actors who had selected and appointed them. The place of the school in political priorities reflected the fact that most of its constituency could not vote and that its spokesmen were distant from the classroom. Decisions about educational policy were usually based entirely on the budgetary priorities of individual districts and regions. Economic considerations favored the selection of women teachers and, by the late nineteenth century, women principals; womens' salaries in such positions did not reflect high esteem for their professional achievements. Jessie May

7. Robert J. Braun, *Teachers and Power: The Story of the American Federation of Teachers* (New York: Simon and Schuster, 1972), pp. 21–27. See also Robert L. Reid, ed., *Battleground; The Autobiography of Margaret A. Haley* (Urbana, IL: University of Illinois Press, 1982) [Conway's note].

8. Reid, *Battleground*, p. 90 [Conway's note].

Short, an assistant professor of mathematics at Reed College in Portland, Oregon, described her experience in an Oregon high school in the 1920s.

> A personal experience will illustrate the discriminations that are considered normal in the smaller schools. . . . For five years I was principal of a high school in a delightful county-seat town. During the five years the high school enrollment doubled, a new building was erected, I had salary increases each year. I resigned for graduate study although I was offered a small salary increase if I would remain. The man who took my place was freely given a salary fifty percent higher than I had received. Before his first year had closed he was literally taken from the school and thrown into a snow bank. The school board asked me to return and made me what they considered a generous offer, a ten percent increase over my former salary. I suggested that I might consider the appointment at the fifty percent increase the board had willingly given the man who could not handle the situation. The idea of compensating the service without regard to the sex of the one rendering the service was, as I had anticipated, beyond their comprehension.[9]

Short's experience strikingly illustrates that the public's view of the worth of the predominantly female teaching profession and of the predominantly male management of the public schools was fundamentally shaped by the gender of those who served in the system. Because there was little popular respect for the function of the teacher, most important professional prerogatives were gained only after protracted battle. The early decades of unionizing and struggling against low social esteem focused teachers' concerns on job security to the neglect of curricular issues. The cherished right of tenure, sought since the 1880s, was not achieved until the 1950s, when the postwar baby boom and the Cold-War mentality of the Sputnik era gave schools and teachers national importance.

The public's low esteem of the profession was also related to the youthfulness of women teachers. As most of them remained teachers for no more than three or four years, it was easy for local school boards to disregard their opinions. The assumption that young women need protection gave school boards and committees ample justification to scrutinize teachers' conduct and to represent such activity to be in the teachers' best interest. The small minority of men teachers acquired the status of their women colleagues by association. Because society accorded such scant respect to the role of teacher, it was considered perfectly appropriate to pay teachers wages equivalent to those of un-

9. Jessie May Short, *Women in the Teaching Profession: Or Running as Fast as You Can to Stay in the Same Place* (Portland, OR: Reed College, June 1939), p. 10 [Conway's note].

skilled labor. By 1900 teacher turnover was as high as 10 percent a year; every year 40,000 new recruits had to be brought into the common school system.[1] The high annual rates of change in teaching personnel throughout the first century of the profession made teachers seem much more like transient workers than career professionals (teaching was not accepted as a lifetime career for women until the Second World War). School reformers even today struggle with the consequences of Margaret Haley's accurate perception that to bargain successfully, women teachers had to unionize like industrial laborers.

If we compare the public esteem accorded to teaching in the late nineteenth century with that held for other emerging professions, we begin to see that the difference lies in the fact that most of the people recruited into public education were women. Consider, for instance, attitudes toward the engineer—the male professional who emerged to meet national needs in transportation, communication, and industrial technology over the same one hundred years that saw the establishment of public education. In the United States the social origins of engineers were almost identical to those of teachers. Engineers too came from rural and blue-collar families. Initially, their training was not highly theoretical and their tasks were strictly utilitarian. Yet engineers were held in high public esteem.

Clearly, gender categories and cultural values had a tremendous influence on the process of professionalization. We have only to read Henry Adams's assessment of the new technology in his commentaries on *The Virgin and the Dynamo*, or Thorstein Veblen's description of the engineer in *The Engineers and the Price System* (1919), to see what a difference gender made.[2] "These technological specialists," Veblen wrote, "whose constant supervision is indispensable to the due working of the industrial system, constitute the general staff of industry, whose work is to control the strategy of production at large and keep an oversight of the tactics of production in detail."[3] During the Depression, when married women teachers were dismissed by school systems to create openings for unemployed men, Lewis Mumford[4] wrote, "The establishment of the class of engineers in its proper characteristics is the more important because this class will, without doubt, constitute the direct and necessary instrument of coalition between men

1. B. A. Hinsdale, "The Training of Teachers," *Education in the United States: A Series of Monographs Prepared for the United States Exhibit at the Paris Exposition, 1900*, ed., Nicholas Murray Butler (Albany: J. Lyon, 1900), p. 16 [Conway's note].
2. Adams (1838–1918), American author and historian, in *The Education of Henry Adams* (1907). Veblen (1857–1929), American sociologist and economist.
3. Thorstein Veblen, *The Engineers and the Price System* (New York: Heubsch, 1921), pp. 52–53 [Conway's note].
4. American author and architecture critic (1895–1990).

of science and industrialists, by which alone the new social order can commence."[5] No one thought to exclaim on how much the new social order might depend on the labors of "the class of teachers." Engineers, of course, pursued their training at the college level and developed a professional culture of aggressive masculinity. Their skills were of critical and immediate importance to the business elites of American society—but then so were the skills of teachers, although no one recognized their value.

Gender stereotypes helped to account for the differences in social mobility experienced by women and men drawn from the same social background. If we look at the gender composition of the teaching profession cross-culturally, we see that the American pattern established at the time of the creation of the public school system was unique. In 1930–31, a national survey of American teachers showed that women outnumbered men by 19 to 1 in elementary education and by 3 to 1 in secondary education. In contrast, men held 65 percent of the elementary teaching posts in Norway and 69 percent of the secondary teaching positions there. In Germany 75 percent of the primary school teachers and 71 percent of the secondary school teachers were men; the ratios for France were similar.[6] These figures reflect the conditions that existed in societies that had had relatively stable populations when the public system of elementary and secondary education was being established, and that made strongly centralized educational planning a high national priority.

In these European countries, lifetime careers of steady progression through the different levels of the public school system were established; entry-level positions based on long and strict academic preparation were accepted as the norm. In France, for instance, completion of the baccalaureate was required to become a lycée teacher; further progress in the system required an advanced degree. Besides contributing substantially to the intellectual level of the schools, this pattern of recruitment defined the teacher as an agent of the nation's culture, not simply a representative of its maternal values.

When the possibility of recruiting more men to the profession or requiring teachers to undergo more rigorous academic preparation was broached in the United States, it was generally discarded as prohibitively costly. In 1906–7, for instance, the New York City school superintendent acknowledged the desirability of having a cadre of teachers more balanced in gender composition. In a report, he commented that

5. Lewis Mumford, *Technics and Civilization* (New York: Harcourt Brace, 1934), pp. 219–20 [Conway's note].
6. Edward S. Evenden, Guy C. Gamble, and Harold G. Blue, "Teacher Personnel in the United States," U.S. Department of the Interior Bulletin no. 10 (1931), in vol. 11, *National Survey of the Education of Teachers*, p. 20 [Conway's note].

the achievement of this goal would require equalizing the pay scales of the gender groups and raising all salary levels. This, he calculated, was politically impossible. It would add between $8 million and $11 million to the annual school system budget. To propose such a budget increase in the absence of popular demand would be political suicide, and there was not the slightest popular sentiment for such action.[7]

Gender was a highly significant factor in the way American society mobilized its resources to develop its public education system. Assumptions about female temperament and motivation dovetailed with the often contradictory ideals and values of the public school system's creators. Stereotypes about women coincided neatly with the economic priorities that dictated how much money was appropriated for public education, and reinforced popular preferences regarding the purpose of public schooling. Assumptions about the gender and intellectual level of the typical teacher influenced successive waves of curricular reform. Culturally, these gender stereotypes had a tremendous impact on everyone involved in the schools—teachers, pupils, principals, superintendents, school board members. These assumptions played a part in what it meant to grow up male or female in America. Their enduring power explains the continued inability of our affluent society to muster either the will or the resources to create and maintain schools that are intellectually demanding and that accord the profession of teaching sufficient dignity to engender high teacher morale.

Much has been made of the degree to which teaching offered American women the opportunity to move out of family subordination and into an independent existence. The memoirs of some of America's greatest women reformers tell us that this new life outside the family was a heady experience. Frances Willard,[8] for example, wrote of learning to live without reliance on her parents as a very young teacher. Through her struggles with unruly children in rural one-room schools, she came to see herself as an agent for improving society. Dozens of other young women documented similar experiences. Service as teachers inspired many young women to seek other active careers. Both as individuals and as a group, women proved themselves capable of creating and sustaining demanding intellectual tasks when they were given adequate preparation and appropriate renumeration. It was not the sex of women teachers that created problems in the school system and made the status of teachers so lowly; it was the gender identity that women carried into the schools with them. It is the terms on which women enter occupations that govern their opportunities. The mere fact of entry does not create opportunities. Horace Mann

7. Sugg, *Motherteacher*, p. 122 [Conway's note].
8. American educator and reformer (1839–1893).

and Henry Barnard, two of America's greatest educational reformers, actively admired women and thought that by employing them as teachers they could secure both a better society and important advantages for women. They bore women no ill will whatsoever. Their assumptions about women, however, established the terms on which women entered the teaching profession, and those terms were far more consequential than the great numbers of women who were invited to teach in the public schools. Those terms still matter today. So too does our ambivalence about the goals of public education. This piece of unfinished business from the politics of the Jacksonian era matters as much today as it did in the 1840s. We cannot conclude it satisfactorily without taking into account the unintended consequences of our assumptions about the gender of teachers. They matter not only to women but to our whole society.

Dorothy Gies McGuigan

TO BE A WOMAN AND A SCHOLAR

On a Saturday morning in June exactly three hundred years ago this year, the first woman in the world to receive a doctoral degree mounted a pulpit in the cathedral of Padua to be examined in Aristotelian dialectics.

Her name was Elena Lucrezia Cornaro Piscopia. She was thirty-two years old, single, daughter of one of the wealthiest families in Venice. Precociously brilliant, she had begun to study Aristotle at the age of seven. Her father had backed her studies and supplied the best of tutors; by the time she enrolled in the University of Padua, she knew not only Latin and Greek, French, English, and Spanish, but also Hebrew, Arabic, and Chaldaic.

News of the unique phenomenon of a woman scholar had drawn such throngs to witness her doctoral trial that it had to be moved from the hall of the University of Padua into the cathedral. Elena had first applied to take her doctorate in theology, but the Chancellor of the university's Theological Faculty, Cardinal Gregorio Barbarigo, Bishop of Padua, had refused indignantly. "Never," he replied. "Woman is made for motherhood, not for learning." He wrote later of the incident, "I talked with a French cardinal about it and he broke out in laughter." Reluctantly Barbarigo agreed that she be allowed to take the doctoral examination in philosophy. A modest, deeply religious

From *Changing Family, Changing Workplace: New Research* (1980).

young woman, Elena Cornaro had quailed before the prospect of the public examination; it was her proud, ambitious father who had insisted. A half hour before the solemn program began, Elena expressed such anguish and reluctance that her confessor had to speak very sternly to persuade her to go through with it. Her examiners were not lenient because of her sex, for the prestige of the university was at stake. But Elena's replies—in Latin, of course—were so brilliant that the judges declared the doctorate in philosophy was "hardly an honor for so towering an intellect." The doctoral ring was placed on Elena's finger, the ermine cape of teacher laid about her shoulders, and the laurel crown of poet placed on her dark curly head. The entire assembly rose and chanted a Te Deum.[1]

What was it like to be a gifted woman, an Elena Cornaro, three hundred years ago? What happened to a bright woman in the past who wanted to study another culture, examine the roots of a language, master the intricacies of higher mathematics, write a book—or prevent or cure a terrible disease?

5 To begin with, for a woman to acquire anything that amounted to real learning, she needed four basics.

She needed to survive. In the seventeenth century women's life expectancy had risen only to thirty-two; not until 1750 did it begin to rise appreciably and reach, in mid-nineteenth century, age forty-two. A woman ambitious for learning would do well to choose a life of celibacy, not only to avoid the hazards of childbirth but because there was no room for a scholar's life within the confines of marriage and childbearing. Elena Cornaro had taken a vow of chastity at the age of eleven, turned down proposals of marriage to become an oblate of the Benedictine Order.

Secondly, to aspire to learning a woman needed basic literacy; she had to be one of the fortunate few who learned at least to read and write. Although literacy studies in earlier centuries are still very incomplete and comparative data on men's and women's literacy are meager, it appears that before 1650 a bare 10 percent of women in the city of London could sign their names. What is most striking about this particular study is that when men are divided by occupation—with clergy and the professions at the top, 100 percent literate, and male laborers at the bottom of the scale, about 15 percent literate—women as a group fell below even unskilled male laborers in their rate of literacy. By about 1700 half the women in London could sign their names; in the provinces women's literacy remained much lower.

The third fundamental a woman needed if she aspired to learning was, of course, an economic base. It was best to be born, like Elena

1. Festival hymn of rejoicing and praise of God.

Cornaro, to a family of wealth who owned a well-stocked library and could afford private tutors. For girls of poor families the chance of learning the bare minimum of reading and writing was small. Even such endowed charity schools as Christ's Hospital in London were attended mostly by boys; poor girls in charity schools were apt to have their literacy skills slighted in favor of catechism, needlework, knitting, and lace-making in preparation for a life in domestic service.

The fourth fundamental a woman scholar needed was simply a very tough skin, for she was a deviant in a society where the learned woman, far from being valued, was likely to hear herself preached against in the pulpit and made fun of on the public stage. Elena Cornaro was fortunate to have been born in Italy where an array of learned women had flourished during the Renaissance and where the woman scholar seems to have found a more hospitable ambiance than in the northern countries.

In eighteenth-century England the gifted writer Lady Mary Wortley 10
Montagu, writing in 1753 about proposed plans for a little granddaughter's education, admonished her daughter with some bitterness "to conceal whatever Learning [the child] attains, with as much solicitude as she would hide crookedness or lameness."

In post-Renaissance Europe two overriding fears dominated thinking on women's education: the fear that learning would unfit women for their social role, defined as service to husband and children and obedience to the church; and, a corollary of the first, that open access to education would endanger women's sexual purity. For while humanist philosophy taught that education led to virtue, writers on education were at once conflicted when they applied the premise to women. Nearly all, beginning with the influential sixteenth-century Juan Luis Vives, opted for restricting women's learning. Only a few radical thinkers—some men, such as Richard Mulcaster in Tudor England and the extraordinary Poullain de la Barre in seventeenth-century France, some women, like the feisty Bathsua Makin and revolutionary Mary Wollstonecraft—spoke out for the full development of women's intellectual potential.

In any case, since institutions of higher learning were designed for young men entering the professions—the church, the law, government service—from which women were excluded, they were excluded too from the universities that prepared for them. And, just as importantly, they were excluded from the grammar or preparatory schools, whose curriculum was based on Latin, the code language of the male intellectual elite. Since most scholarly texts were written in Latin, ignorance of that language prevented women from reading scholarly literature in most fields—which only gradually and belatedly became available in translation.

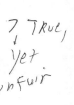

Richard Hyrde, a tutor in the household of Sir Thomas More and himself a defender of learning in women, cited the common opinion:

> . . . that the frail kind of women, being inclined of their own courage unto vice, and mutable at every newelty [*sic*], if they should have skill in many things that must be written in the Latin and Greek tongue . . . it would of likelihood both inflame their stomachs a great deal the more to that vice, that men say they be too much given unto of their own nature already and instruct them also with more subtility and conveyance, to set forward and accomplish their froward intent and purpose.

And yet, despite all the hurdles, some bright women did manage to make a mark as scholars and writers. Sometimes girls listened in on their brothers' tutored lessons. A fortunate few, like Elena Cornaro, had parents willing and able to educate daughters equally with sons. The daughters of Sir Thomas More, of the Earl of Arundel, and of Sir Anthony Cooke in Tudor England were given excellent educations. Arundel's daughter, Lady Joanna Lumley, produced the earliest known English translation of a Greek drama.

But by far the largest number of women scholars in the past were almost totally self-educated. Through sheer intellectual curiosity, self-discipline, often grinding hard work, they taught themselves what they wanted to know. Such self-teaching may well be the only truly joyous form of learning. Yet it has its drawbacks: it may also be haphazard and superficial. Without access to laboratory, lecture, and dissecting table, it was all but impossible for women to train themselves in higher mathematics, for instance, in science, in anatomy.

Mary Wollstonecraft wrote in 1792 that most women who have acted like rational creatures or shown any vigor of intellect have accidentally been allowed "to run wild," and running wild in the family library was the usual way intellectually ambitious women educated themselves. Such a self-taught scholar was Elizabeth Tanfield, Viscountess Cary, who as a girl in Elizabethan England, taught herself French, Spanish, Italian, Latin, and added Hebrew "with very little teaching." Her unsympathetic mother refused to allow her candles to read at night, so Elizabeth bribed the servants, and by her wedding day—she was married at fifteen—she had run up a candle debt of a hundred pounds. She wrote numerous translations, poetry—most of which she destroyed—and at least one play, *Mariam, the Faire Queen of Jewry.*

Very often the critical phase of women's intellectual development took place at a different period in their lives from the normal time of men's greatest development. Gifted women often came to a period of intellectual crisis and of intense self-teaching during adulthood.

When Christine de Pisane, daughter of the Italian astrologer and physician at the court of Charles V of France, found herself widowed at twenty-five with three children to support, she turned to writing—certainly one of the first, if not the first, woman in Europe to support herself through a literary career. But Christine found her education wholly inadequate, and at the age of thirty-four she laid down a complete course of study for herself, teaching herself Latin, history, philosophy, literature. She used her pen later on to urge better educational opportunities for women, to defend her sex from the charges of such misogynistic writers as Jean de Meung.[2] In her book, *The City of Ladies*, Christine imagined talented women building a town for themselves where they could lead peaceful and creative lives—an existence impossible, she considered, in fifteenth-century France.

Like Christine de Pisane, the Dutch scholar Anna van Schurman of Utrecht, a contemporary of Elena Cornaro, found her early education superficial and unsatisfying. Like most upper middle class girls of the seventeenth century, Anna, precocious though she was, had been taught chiefly to sing nicely, to play musical instruments, to carve portraits in boxwood and wax, to do needlework and tapestry and cut paperwork. At the age of twenty-eight, frustrated by the lack of intellectual stimulation in her life, Anna turned her brilliant mind to serious studies, became one of the finest Latinists of her day, learned Hebrew, Syriac, Chaldaic, wrote an Ethiopian grammar that was the marvel of Dutch scholars, carried on an international correspondence—in Latin, of course—with all the leading scholars of continental Europe. When a professor of theology at Leyden wrote that women were barred from equality with men "by the sacred laws of nature," Anna wrote a Latin treatise in reply in 1641, defending the intellectual capacity of women and urging, as Christine de Pisane had, much greater educational opportunities. Her work was widely translated and made Anna van Schurman a model for women scholars all over Europe.

In France, during the lifetime of Anna van Schurman, a group of 20
bright, intellectually malnourished women—most of them convent-educated—developed one of the most ingenious devices for women's lifelong learning. Bored with the dearth of cultivated conversation at the French court, the Marquise de Rambouillet, Mlle de Scudéry, Mme de Lafayette, and a host of others opened their town houses in Paris, invited men and women of talent and taste to hone their wits and talk of science and philosophy, literature and language, love and friendship. The salon has been described as "an informal university for women." Not only did it contribute to adult women's education, but it

2. Medieval French author of the satirical antifeminist portion of the influential poem *The Romance of the Rose*.

shaped standards of speaking and writing for generations in France and profoundly influenced French culture as a whole.

An offshoot of the salons were the special lecture courses offered by eminent scholars in chemistry, etymology and other subjects—lectures largely attended by women. Fontenelle wrote his popular book on astronomy, *The Plurality of Worlds*, specifically for a female readership, and Descartes declared he had written his *Discourse on Method* in French rather than Latin so that women too would be able to read it.

There was, rather quickly, a backlash. Molière's satires on learned women did much to discredit the ladies who presided at salons—and who might at times be given to a bit of overelegance in speech and manner. When Abbé Fénélon wrote his influential treatise, *On the Education of Girls*, in 1686—just eight years after Elena Cornaro had won her doctorate—he mentioned neither Elena Cornaro nor Anna van Schurman nor Christine de Pisane. He inveighed against the pernicious effect of the salons. Declaring that "A woman's intellect is normally more feeble and her curiosity greater than those of men, it is undesirable to set her to studies which may turn her head. A girl," admonished that worthy French cleric, "must learn to obey without respite, to hold her peace and allow others to do the talking. Everything is lost if she obstinately tries to be clever and to get a distaste for domestic duties. The virtuous woman spins, confines herself to her home, keeps quiet, believes and obeys."

So much for the encouragement of women scholars in late seventeenth century France.

Across the Channel in England in the second half of the seventeenth century, bright ambitious women were studying not only the classics and languages but learning to use the newly perfected telescope and microscope, and to write on scientific subjects. Margaret Cavendish, Duchess of Newcastle, a remarkable woman with a wide-ranging mind and imagination, wrote not only biography, autobiography, and romance, but also popular science—she called it "natural philosophy"—directed especially to women readers. The versatile and talented writer Aphra Behn—the first woman in England to make her living by her pen—translated Fontenelle's *Plurality of Worlds* into English in 1688. In the preface she declared she would have preferred to write an original work on astronomy but had "neither health nor leisure" for such a project; it was, in fact, the year before her death and she was already ailing. But she defended the Copernican system vigorously against the recent attack by a Jesuit priest, did not hesitate to criticize the author, Fontenelle, and to correct an error in the text on the height of the earth's atmosphere.

25 But the learned lady in England as in France found herself criticized

from the pulpit and satirized on the stage. Margaret Cavendish was dubbed "Mad Madge of Newcastle." Jonathan Swift poked fun at Mary Astell for her proposal to found a women's college. Thomas Wright in *The Female Virtuosos*, the anonymous authors of *The Humours of Oxford* and *Female Wits*, Shadwell, Congreve, and others lampooned the would-be woman scholar. The shy poet, Anne, countess of Winchilsea, who had only reluctantly identified herself as author of a published volume of verse, was cruelly pilloried by Pope and Gay in their play *Three Hours after Marriage*. And Aphra Behn, author of a phenomenal array of plays, poems, novels, and translations, could read this published verse about herself and her work at about the same time she was translating Fontenelle:

> Yet hackney writers, when their verse did fail
> To get 'em brandy, bread and cheese, and ale,
> Their wants by prostitution were supplied;
> Show but a tester [sixpence] you might up and ride;
> For punk and poetess agree so pat
> You cannot well be this, and not be that.

So if one asks what it was like to be a gifted woman, to aspire to learning at the time of Elena Cornaro, the answer must be that it was a difficult and demanding choice, requiring not merely intellectual gifts but extraordinary physical and mental stamina, and only a rare few women succeeded in becoming contributing scholars and writers. All the usual scholarly careers were closed to women, so that even for women who succeeded in educating themselves to the level of their male colleagues, the opportunities to support themselves were meager.

In a day when it was considered impermissible for a woman to speak in public, it was also considered inappropriate and unfeminine to draw attention to herself by publishing a work under her own name. Many—perhaps most—women scholars and writers—from Anne, Countess of Winchilsea, Lady Mary Wortley Montagu down to Fanny Burney and Jane Austen—published their works at first either anonymously or pseudonymously. Nor was Elizabeth Tanfield the only woman scholar who destroyed her own writings before they were published.

And what of Elena Cornaro's life after she won her doctorate in 1678? During the six years she lived after that event, she divided her time between scholarly pursuits and service to the poor, sick and needy. Baroque Italy paid honor to its unique woman scholar. Certainly Elena Cornaro aroused no antagonisms, but rather filled with discretion the approved nunlike role designated for the woman in Catholic countries who chose not to marry. Scholars and statesmen from several countries made a point of visiting her in Padua, and she was invited to join fellow scholars in the Academy of Ricovrati in Padua. When she died of tuberculosis in 1684 at the age of thirty-eight—a disease that was in a measure responsible for her eminence, for she had been sent to Padua partly to escape the damp air of Venice—her funeral attracted a greater throng than her doctoral examination. A delegation of distinguished university faculty accompanied the procession through the streets of Padua, and on her coffin were heaped books in the languages she had mastered and the sciences she had studied. She was buried in the Chapel of St. Luke among the Benedictine monks, having carefully instructed her maid to sew her robe together at the hem so that even in death her modesty would be preserved.

Of her writings very little has survived. She had arranged to have her correspondence and many of her manuscripts destroyed before she died, and the remainder of her writings were disseminated as souvenirs among family and friends.

30 After Elena Cornaro's death a half century passed before a second woman, again Italian, Laura Maria Catherina Bassi, was awarded a doctorate at the University of Bologna. Not until 150 years later did American universities admit women for degrees, and two centuries passed before Oxford and Cambridge conferred degrees on women. Only in our own decade, in 1970, did the Catholic Church finally award the degree of Doctor of Theology that had been denied Elena Cornaro to two women: one to the sixteenth century Spanish saint, Teresa of Avila, the other to fourteenth century St. Catherine of Siena, who had in fact never learned to read and write. One hopes that in some academic elysium those two saintly ladies are proudly showing off their belated scholarly credentials.

QUESTIONS

1. *Characterize the tone of McGuigan's essay: restrained? objective? angry? amused? outraged? Why do you think she adopts her tone? What would be the effects of different tones?*
2. *McGuigan frames her examination of women's scholarship with accounts of the doctoral examination and death of Elena Cornaro. Why? What does she gain from this approach? Where have you seen this approach used before?*
3. *Estimates of literacy in the past, McGuigan notes, were made on the basis of signatures. How would we estimate literacy today?*
4. *Take five women scholars from McGuigan's essay and find out if people you know have heard of any of them. Which ones are known? What do people know about the famous ones?*

Wayne C. Booth

BORING FROM WITHIN: THE ART OF THE FRESHMAN ESSAY

Last week I had for about the hundredth time an experience that always disturbs me. Riding on a train, I found myself talking with my seat-mate, who asked me what I did for a living. "I teach English." Do you have any trouble predicting his response? His face fell, and he groaned, "Oh, dear, I'll have to watch my language." In my experience there are only two other possible reactions. The first is even less inspiriting: "I hated English in school; it was my worst subject." The second, so rare as to make an honest English teacher almost burst into tears of gratitude when it occurs, is an animated conversation about literature, or ideas, or the American language—the kind of conversation that shows a continuing respect for "English" as something more than being sure about *who* and *whom, lie* and *lay*.

Unless the people you meet are a good deal more tactful or better liars than the ones I meet, you've had the two less favorable experiences many times. And it takes no master analyst to figure out why so many of our fellow citizens think of us as unfriendly policemen: it is because too many of us have seen ourselves as unfriendly policemen. I know of a high school English class in Indiana in which the students are explicitly told that their paper grades will not be affected by anything they say; required to write a paper a week, they are graded simply on the number of spelling and grammatical errors. What is more, they are given a standard form for their papers: each paper is to have three paragraphs, a beginning, a middle, and an end—or is it an introduction, a body, and a conclusion? The theory seems to be that if the student is not troubled about having to say anything, or about discovering a good way of saying it, he can then concentrate on the truly important matter of avoiding mistakes.

What's wrong with such assignments? What's wrong with getting the problem of correctness focused sharply enough so that we can really work on it? After all, we do have the job of teaching correct English, don't we? We can't possibly teach our hordes of students to be colorful writers, but by golly, we can beat the bad grammar out of them. Leaving aside the obvious fact that we *can't* beat the bad grammar out of them, not by direct assault, let's think a bit about what that

Adapted by Wayne C. Booth from a speech delivered in May 1963 to the Illinois Council of College Teachers of English.

kind of assignment does to the poor teacher who gives it. Those papers must be read, by someone, and unless the teacher has more trained assistance than you and I have, *she's* the victim. She can't help being bored silly by her own paper-reading, and we all know what an evening of being bored by a class's papers does to our attitude toward that class the next day. The old formula of John Dewey was that any teaching that bores the student is likely to fail. The formula was subject to abuse, quite obviously, since interest in itself is only one of many tests of adequate teaching. A safer formula, though perhaps also subject to abuse, might be: Any teaching that bores the teacher is sure to fail. And I am haunted by the picture of that poor woman in Indiana, week after week reading batches of papers written by students who have been told that nothing they say can possibly affect her opinion of those papers. Could any hell imagined by Dante or Jean-Paul Sartre[1] match this self-inflicted futility?

I call it self-inflicted, as if it were a simple matter to avoid receiving papers that bore us. But unfortunately it is not. It may be a simple matter to avoid the *total* meaninglessness that the students must give that Indiana teacher, but we all know that it is no easy matter to produce interesting papers; our pet cures for boredom never work as well as they ought to. Every beginning teacher learns quickly and painfully that nothing works with all students, and that on bad days even the most promising ideas work with nobody.

5 As I try to sort out the various possible cures for those batches of boredom—in ink, double-spaced, on one side of the sheet, only, please—I find them falling into three groups: efforts to give the students a sharper sense of writing to an audience, efforts to give them some substance to express, and efforts to improve their habits of observation and of approach to their task—what might be called improving their mental personalities.

This classification, both obvious and unoriginal, is a useful one not only because it covers—at least I hope it does—all of our efforts to improve what our students can do but also because it reminds us that no one of the three is likely to work unless it is related to each of the others. In fact each of the three types of cure—"develop an awareness of audience," "give them something to say," and "enliven their writing personalities"—threatens us with characteristic dangers and distortions; all three together are indispensable to any lasting cure.

Perhaps the most obvious omission in that Indiana teacher's assignments is all sense of an audience to be persuaded, of a serious rhetori-

1. Booth refers to the elaborately described hell of the *Inferno*, by the fourteenth-century Italian poet Dante Alighieri, and to the banal locked room in which the characters of Sartre's *No Exit* discover that hell is "other people."

cal purpose to be achieved. One tempting cure for this omission is to teach them to put a controversial edge on what they say. So we ask them to write a three-page paper arguing that China should be allowed into the UN or that women are superior to men or that American colleges are failing in their historic task. Then we are surprised when the papers turn out to be as boring as ever. The papers on Red China are full of abstract pomposities that the students themselves obviously do not understand or care about, since they have gleaned them in a desperate dash through the most readily available sources listed in the *Readers' Guide*. Except for the rare student who has some political background and awareness, and who thus might have written on the subject anyway, they manage to convey little more than their resentment at the assignment and their boredom in carrying it out. One of the worst batches of papers I ever read came out of a good idea we had at Earlham College for getting the whole student body involved in controversial discussion about world affairs. We required them to read Barbara Ward's *Five Ideas that Change the World;* we even had Lady Jackson[2] come to the campus and talk to everyone about her concern for the backward nations. The papers, to our surprise, were a discouraging business. We found ourselves in desperation collecting the boners that are always a sure sign, when present in great numbers, that students are thoroughly disengaged. "I think altruism is all right, so long as we practice it in our own interest." "I would be willing to die for anything fatal." "It sure is a doggie dog world."

It is obvious what had gone wrong: though we had ostensibly given the student a writing purpose, it had not become *his* purpose, and he was really no better off, perhaps worse, than if we had him writing about, say, piccolos or pizza. We might be tempted in revulsion from such overly ambitious failures to search for controversy in the students' own mundane lives. This may be a good move, but we should not be surprised when the papers on "Let's clean up the campus" or "Why must we have traffic fatalities?" turn out to be just as empty as the papers on the UN or the Congo. They may have more exclamation points and underlined adjectives, but they will not interest any teacher who would like to read papers for his own pleasure or edification. "People often fail to realize that nearly 40,000 people are killed on our highways each year. Must this carnage continue?" Well, I suppose it must, until people who write about it learn to see it with their own eyes, and hearts, instead of through a haze of cliché. The truth is that to make students assume a controversial pose before they have any genuine substance to be controversial about is to encourage dis-

2. Barbara Ward.

honesty and slovenliness, and to ensure our own boredom. It may very well lead them into the kind of commercial concern for the audience which makes almost every *Reader's Digest* article intelligible to everyone over the chronological age of ten and boring to everyone over the mental age of fifteen. *Newsweek* magazine recently had a readability survey conducted on itself. It was found to be readable by the average twelfth grader, unlike *Time,* which is readable by the average eleventh grader. The editors were advised, and I understand are taking the advice, that by improving their "readability" by one year they could improve their circulation by several hundred thousand. Whether they will thereby lop off a few thousand adult readers in the process was not reported.

The only protection from this destructive type of concern for the audience is the control of substance, of having something solid to say. Our students bore us, even when they take a seemingly lively controversial tone, because they have nothing to say, to us or to anybody else. If and when they discover something to say, they will no longer bore us, and our comments will no longer bore them. Having something to say, they will be interested in learning how to say it better. Having something to say, they can be taught how to give a properly controversial edge to what will by its nature be controversial—nothing, after all, is worth saying that everybody agrees on already.

10 When we think of providing substance, we are perhaps tempted first to find some way of filling students' minds with a goodly store of general ideas, available on demand. This temptation is not necessarily a bad one. After all, if we think of the adult writers who interest us, most of them have such a store; they have read and thought about man's major problems, and they have opinions and arguments ready to hand about how men ought to live, how society ought to be run, how literature ought to be written. Edmund Wilson, for example, one of the most consistently interesting men alive, seems to have an inexhaustible flow of reasoned opinions on any subject that comes before him. Obviously our students are not going to interest us until they too have some ideas.

But it is not easy to impart ideas. It is not even easy to impart opinions, though a popular teacher can usually manage to get students to parrot his views. But ideas—that is, opinions backed with genuine reasoning—are extremely difficult to develop. If they were not, we wouldn't have a problem in the first place; we could simply send our students off with an assignment to prove their conviction that God does or does not exist or that the American high school system is the best on God's earth, and the interesting arguments would flow.

There is, in fact, no short cut to the development of reasoned ideas. Years and years of daily contact with the world of ideas are required before the child can be expected to begin formulating his own ideas and his own reasons. And for the most part the capacity to handle abstract ideas comes fairly late. I recently saw a paper of a bright high school sophomore, from a good private school, relating the economic growth of China and India to their political development and relative supply of natural resources. It was a terrible paper; the student's hatred of the subject, his sense of frustration in trying to invent generalizations about processes that were still too big for him, showed in every line. The child's parent told me that when the paper was returned by the geography teacher, he had pencilled on the top of one page, "Why do you mix so many bad ideas with your good ones?" The son was almost in tears, his father told me, with anger and helplessness. "He talks as if I'd put bad ideas in on purpose. *I* don't know a bad idea from a good one on this subject."

Yet with all this said, I am still convinced that general ideas are not only a resource but also a duty that cannot be dodged just because it is a dangerous one. There is nothing we touch, as English teachers, that is immune to being tainted by our touch; all the difference lies in how we go about it.

Ideas are a resource because adolescents are surprisingly responsive to any real encouragement to think for themselves, *if* methods of forced feeding are avoided. The seventeen-year-old who has been given nothing but commonplaces and clichés all his life and who finally discovers a teacher with ideas of his own may have his life changed, and, as I shall say in my final point, when his life is changed his writing is changed. Perhaps some of you can remember, as I can, a first experience with a teacher who could think for himself. I can remember going home from a conversation with my high school chemistry teacher and audibly vowing to myself: "Someday I'm going to be able to think for myself like that." There was nothing especially unconventional about Luther Gidding's ideas—at least I can remember few of them now. But what I cannot forget is the way he had with an idea, the genuine curiosity with which he approached it, the pause while he gave his little thoughtful cough, and then the bulldog tenacity with which he would argue it through. And I am convinced that though he never required me to write a line, he did more to improve my writing during the high school years than all of my English teachers put together. The diary I kept to record my sessions with him, never read by anyone, was the best possible writing practice.

If ideas, in this sense of speculation backed up with an attempt to 15
think about things rigorously and constructively, are a great and often neglected resource, they are also our civic responsibility—a far more serious responsibility than our duty to teach spelling and grammar. It is a commonplace to say that democracy depends for its survival on an

informed citizenry, but we all know that mere information is not what we are talking about when we say such things. What we mean is that democracy depends on a citizenry that can reason for themselves, on men who know whether a case has been proved, or at least made probable. Democracy depends, if you will forgive some truisms for a moment, on free choices, and choices cannot be in any sense free if they are made blind: free choice is, in fact, choice that is based on knowledge—not just opinions, but knowledge in the sense of reasoned opinion. And if that half of our population who do not go beyond high school do not learn from us how to put two and two together and how to test the efforts of others to do so, and if the colleges continue to fail with most of the other half, we are doomed to become even more sheeplike, as a nation, than we are already.

Papers about ideas written by sheep are boring; papers written by thinking boys and girls are interesting. The problem is always to find ideas at a level that will allow the student to *reason*, that is, to provide support for his ideas, rather than merely assert them in half-baked form. And this means something that is all too often forgotten by the most ambitious teachers—namely, that whatever ideas the student writes about must somehow be connected with his own experience. Teaching machines will never be able to teach the kind of writing we all want, precisely because no machine can ever know which general ideas relate, for a given student, to some meaningful experience. In the same class we'll have one student for whom philosophical and religious ideas are meaningful, another who can talk with confidence about entropy and the second law of thermodynamics, a third who can write about social justice, and a fourth who can discuss the phony world of Holden Caulfield.[3] Each of them can do a good job on his own subject, because he has as part of his equipment a growing awareness of how conclusions in that subject are related to the steps of argument that support conclusions. Ideally, each of these students ought to have the personal attention of a tutor for an hour or so each week, someone who can help him sharpen those connections, and not force him to write on topics not yet appropriate to his interests or experience. But when these four are in a class of thirty or forty others, taught by a teacher who has three or four other similar sections, we all know what happens: the teacher is forced by his circumstances to provide some sort of mold into which all of the students can be poured. Although he is still better able to adapt to individual differences than a machine, he is unfortunately subject to boredom and fatigue, as a machine would not be. Instead of being the philosopher, scientist, political analyst, and literary critic that these four students require him to

3. The hero of *The Catcher in the Rye*, by J. D. Salinger.

be, teaching them and learning from them at the same time, the teacher is almost inevitably tempted to force them all to write about the ideas he himself knows best. The result is that at least three of the four must write out of ignorance.

Now clearly the best way out of this impasse would be for legislatures and school boards and college presidents to recognize the teaching of English for what it is: the most demanding of all teaching jobs, justifying the smallest sections and the lightest course loads. No composition teacher can possibly concentrate on finding special interests, making imaginative assignments, and testing the effectiveness and cogency of papers if he has more than seventy-five students at a time; the really desirable limit would be about forty-five—three sections of fifteen students each. Nobody would ever expect a piano teacher, who has no themes to read, to handle the great masses of pupils that we handle. Everyone recognizes that for all other technical skills individual attention is required. Yet for this, the most delicate of all skills, the one requiring the most subtle interrelationships of training, character, and experience, we fling students and teachers into hopelessly impersonal patterns.

But if I'm not careful I'll find myself saying that our pupils bore us because the superintendents and college presidents hire us to be bored. Administrative neglect and misallocation of educational funds are basic to our problem, and we should let the citizenry know of the scandal on every occasion. But meanwhile, back at the ranch, we are faced with the situation as it now is: we must find some way to train a people to write responsibly even though the people, as represented, don't want this service sufficiently to pay for it.

The tone of political exhortation into which I have now fallen leads me to one natural large source of ideas as we try to encourage writing that is not just lively and controversial but informed and genuinely persuasive. For many students there is obviously more potential interest in social problems and forces, political controversy, and the processes of everyday living around them than in more general ideas. The four students I described a moment ago, students who can say something about philosophy, science, general political theory, or literary criticism, are rare. But most students, including these four, can in theory at least be interested in meaningful argument about social problems in which they are personally involved.

As a profession we have tried, over the past several decades, a variety 20
of approaches attempting to capitalize on such interests. Papers on corruption in TV, arguments about race relations, analyses of distortions in advertising, descriptions of mass communication—these have been combined in various quantities with traditional subjects like grammar, rhetoric, and literature. The "communications" movement,

which looked so powerful only a few years ago and which now seems almost dead, had at its heart a perfectly respectable notion, a notion not much different from the one I'm working with today: get them to write about something they know about, and make sure that they see their writing as an act of communication, not as a meaningless exercise. And what better material than other acts of communication.

The dangers of such an approach are by now sufficiently understood. As subject matter for the English course, current "communications media" can at best provide only a supplement to literature and analysis of ideas. But they can be a valuable supplement. Analysis in class of the appeals buried in a *New Yorker* or *Life* advertisement followed by a writing assignment requiring similar analyses can be a far more interesting introduction to the intricacies of style than assignments out of a language text on levels of usage or emotion-charged adjectives. Analysis of a *Time* magazine account, purporting to be objective news but in actual fact a highly emotional editorial, can be not only a valuable experience in itself, but it can lead to papers in which the students do say something to us. Stylistic analysis of the treatment of the same news events by two newspapers or weeklies of different editorial policy can lead to an intellectual awakening of great importance, and thus to papers that will not, cannot, bore the teacher. But this will happen only if the students' critical powers are genuinely developed. It will not do simply to teach the instructor's own prejudices.

There was a time in decades not long past when many of the most lively English teachers thought of their job as primarily to serve as handmaids to liberalism. I had one teacher in college who confessed to me that his overriding purpose was to get students to read and believe *The Nation* rather than the editorials of their daily paper. I suppose that his approach was not entirely valueless. It seems preferable to the effort to be noncontroversial that marks too many English teachers in the '60's, and at least it stirred some of us out of our dogmatic slumbers. But unfortunately it did nothing whatever about teaching us to think critically. Though we graduated from his course at least aware—as many college graduates do not seem to be today—that you can't believe anything you read in the daily press until you have analyzed it and related it to your past experience and to other accounts, it failed to teach us that you can't believe what you read in *The Nation* either. It left the job undone of training our ability to think, because it concentrated too heavily on our opinions. The result was, as I remember, that my own papers in that course were generally regurgitated liberalism. I was excited by them, and that was something. But I can't believe that the instructor found reading them anything other than a chore. There was nothing in them that came from my own experience, my own notions of what would constitute evidence for my conclusions.

There I was, in Utah in the depths of the depression, writing about the Okies when I could have been writing about the impoverished farmers all around me. I wrote about race relations in the south without ever having talked with a Negro in my life and without recognizing that the bootblack I occasionally saw in Salt Lake City in the Hotel Utah was in any way related to the problem of race relations.

The third element that accounts for our boring papers is the lack of character and personality in the writer. My life, my observations, my insights were not included in those papers on the Okies and race relations and the New Deal. Every opinion was derivative, every observation second-hand. I had no real opinions of my own, and my eyes were not open wide enough for me to make first-hand observations on the world around me. What I wrote was therefore characterless, without true personality, though often full of personal pronouns. My opinions had been changed, my *self* had not. The style was the boy, the opinionated, immature, uninformed boy; whether my teacher knew it or not—and apparently he did not—his real job was to make a man of me if he wanted me to write like a man.

Putting the difficulty in this way naturally leads me to what perhaps many of you have been impatient about from the beginning. Are not the narrative arts, both as encountered in great literature and as practiced by the students themselves, the best road to the infusion of individuality that no good writing can lack? Would not a real look at the life of that bootblack, and an attempt to deal with him in narrative, have led to a more interesting paper than all of my generalized attacks on the prejudiced southerners?

I think it would, but once again I am almost more conscious of the 25
dangers of the cure than of the advantages. As soon as we make our general rule something like, "Have the students write a personal narrative on what they know about, what they can see and feel at first hand," we have opened the floodgates for those dreadful assignments that we all find ourselves using, even though we know better: "My Summer Vacation," "Catching My First Fish," and "Our Trip to the Seattle World's Fair." Here are personal experiences that call for personal observation and narration. What's wrong with them?

Quite simply, they invite triviality, superficiality, puerility. Our students have been writing essays on such non-subjects all their lives, and until they have developed some sort of critical vision, some way of looking at the world they passed through on their vacations or fishing trips, they are going to feed us the same old bromides that have always won their passing grades. "My Summer Vacation" is an invitation to a grocery list of items, because it implies no audience, no point to be made, no point of view, no character in the speaker. A bright student will make something of such an invitation, by dramatizing the comic family quarrel that developed two days out, or by comparing his view of the American motel system with Nabokov's in *Lolita*, or by remembering the types of people seen in the campgrounds. If he had his own eyes and ears open he might have seen, in a men's room in Grand Canyon last summer, a camper with a very thick French accent trying to convert a Brooklyn Jew into believing the story of the Mormon gold plates.[4] Or he could have heard, at Mesa Verde, a young park ranger, left behind toward the end of the season by all of the experienced rangers, struggling ungrammatically through a set speech on the geology of the area and finally breaking down in embarrassment over his lack of education. Such an episode, really *seen*, could be used narratively to say something to other high school students about what education really is.

But mere narration can be in itself just as dull as the most abstract theorizing about the nature of the universe or the most derivative opinion-mongering about politics. Even relatively skilful narration, used too obviously as a gimmick to catch interest, with no real relation to the subject, can be as dull as the most abstract pomposities. We all know the student papers that begin like *Reader's Digest* articles, with stereotyped narration that makes one doubt the event itself: "On a dark night last January, two teen agers were seen etc., etc." One can open any issue of *Time* and find this so-called narrative interest plastered throughout. From the March 29 issue I find, among many others, the following bits of fantasy: #1: "A Bolivian father sadly surveyed his nation's seven universities, then made up his mind. 'I don't want my son mixed up in politics.' . . . So saying, he sent his son off to West Germany to college." So writing, the author sends me into hysterical laughter: the quote is phony, made up for the occasion to disguise the generality of the news item. #2: "Around 12:30 P.M. every Monday and Friday, an aging Cubana Airlines turbo-prop Britannia whistles to a halt at Mexico City's International Airport. Squads of police stand by. All passengers . . . without diplomatic or Mexican passports are photographed and questioned. . . . They always dodge questions. 'Why are you here? Where are you going?' ask the Mexicans. 'None of your business,' answer the secretive travelers." "Why should I go on reading?" ask I. #3: "At 6:30 one morning early this month, a phone shrilled in the small office off the bedroom of Egypt's President . . . Nasser. [All early morning phones "shrill" for *Time*.] Already awake, he lifted the receiver to hear exciting news: a military coup had just been launched against the anti-Nasser government of Syria. The phone rang again. It was the Minister of Culture. . . . How should Radio Cairo handle the Syrian crisis? 'Support the rebels,' snapped Nasser." Oh lucky reporter,

4. Bearing, according to Mormon tradition, the Book of Mormon, divinely revealed to the prophet Joseph Smith in Upstate New York in 1827.

I sigh, to have such an efficient wiretapping service. #4: "In South Korea last week, a farmer named Song Kyu Il traveled all the way from the southern provinces to parade before Seoul's Duk Soo Palace with a placard scrawled in his own blood. . . . Farmer Song was thrown in jail, along with some 200 other demonstrators." That's the last we hear of Song, who is invented as an individual for this opening and then dropped. #5: "Defense Secretary Robert McNamara last spring stood beside President Kennedy on the tenth-deck bridge of the nuclear-powered carrier *Enterprise*. For as far as the eye could see, other U.S. ships deployed over the Atlantic seascape." Well, maybe. But for as far as the eye can see, the narrative clichés are piled, rank on rank. At 12:00 midnight last Thursday a gaunt, harried English professor could be seen hunched over his typewriter, a pile of *Time* magazines beside him on the floor. "What," he murmured to himself, sadly, "Whatever can we do about this trashy imitation of narration?"

Fortunately there is something we can do, and it is directly within our province. We can subject our students to models of genuine narration, with the sharp observation and penetrating critical judgment that underlies all good story telling, whether reportorial or fictional.

> It is a truth universally acknowledged, that a single man in possession of a good fortune must be in want of a wife.
>
> However little known the feelings or views of such a man may be on his first entering a neighborhood, this truth is so well fixed in the minds of the surrounding families, that he is considered as the rightful property of someone or other of their daughters.
>
> "My dear Mr. Bennet," said his lady to him one day, "have you heard that Netherfield Park is let at last?"

And already we have a strong personal tone established, a tone of mocking irony which leaves Jane Austen's Mrs. Bennet revealed before us as the grasping, silly gossip she is. Or try this one:

> I am an American, Chicago-born—Chicago, that somber city—and go at things as I have taught myself, free-style, and will make the record in my own way: first to knock, first admitted; sometimes an innocent knock, sometimes a not so innocent. But a man's character is his fate, says Heraclitus, and in the end there isn't any way to disguise the nature of the knocks by acoustical work on the door or gloving the knuckles.
>
> Everybody knows there is no fineness or accuracy of suppression; if you hold down one thing you hold down the adjoining.
>
> My own parents were not much to me, though I cared for my mother. She was simple-minded, and what I learned from her was not what she taught. . . .

Do you catch the accent of Saul Bellow here, beneath the accent of his Augie March? You do, of course, but the students, many of them, do not. How do you know, they will ask, that Jane Austen is being ironic? How do you know, they ask again, that Augie is being characterized by his author through what he says? In teaching them how we know, in exposing them to the great narrative voices, ancient and modern, and in teaching them to hear these voices accurately, we are, of course, trying to change their lives, to make them new, to raise their perceptions to a new level altogether. Nobody can really catch these accents who has not grown up sufficiently to see through cheap substitutes. Or, to put it another way, a steady exposure to such voices is the very thing that will produce the maturity that alone can make our students ashamed of beclouded, commercial, borrowed spectacles for viewing the world.

30 It is true that exposure to good fiction will not in itself transform our students into good writers. Even the best-read student still needs endless hours and years of practice, with rigorous criticism. Fiction will not do the job of discipline in reasoned argument and of practice in developing habits of addressing a living audience. But in the great fiction they will learn what it means to look at something with full attention, what it means to see beneath the surface of society's platitudes. If we then give them practice in writing about things close to the home base of their own honest observations, constantly stretching their powers of generalization and argument but never allowing them to drift into pompous inanities or empty controversiality, we may have that rare but wonderful pleasure of witnessing the miracle: a man and a style where before there was only a bag of wind or a bundle of received opinions. Even when, as with most of our students, no miracles occur, we can hope for papers that we can enjoy reading. And as a final bonus, we might hope that when our students encounter someone on a train who says that he teaches English, their automatic response may be something other than looks of pity or, cries of mock alarm.

QUESTIONS

1. *What does Booth think is wrong with most freshman themes? And what does he claim will make such writing better?*
2. *Booth attacks the writing in* Reader's Digest *and* Time *(paragraph 27). Exactly what is he objecting to? Look at a recent issue of* Time *or* Reader's Digest *and see if Booth's 1963 claims still hold true.*
3. *Select three passages from other sections of* The Norton Reader *that you think would please Booth.*

William G. Perry, Jr.

EXAMSMANSHIP AND THE LIBERAL ARTS: A STUDY IN EDUCATIONAL EPISTEMOLOGY

"But sir, I don't think I really deserve it, it was mostly bull, really." This disclaimer from a student whose examination we have awarded a straight "A" is wondrously depressing. Alfred North Whitehead[1] invented its only possible rejoinder: "Yes sir, what you wrote is nonsense, utter nonsense. But ah! Sir! It's the right *kind* of nonsense!"

Bull, in this university,[2] is customarily a source of laughter, or a problem in ethics. I shall step a little out of fashion to use the subject as a take-off point for a study in comparative epistemology. The phenomenon of bull, in all the honor and opprobrium with which it is regarded by students and faculty, says something, I think, about our theories of knowledge. So too, the grades which we assign on examinations communicate to students what these theories may be.

We do not have to be out-and-out logical-positivists[3] to suppose that we have something to learn about "what we think knowledge is" by having a good look at "what we do when we go about measuring it." We know the straight "A" examination when we see it, of course, and we have reason to hope that the student will understand why his work receives our recognition. He doesn't always. And those who receive lesser honor? Perhaps an understanding of certain anomalies in our customs of grading good bull will explain the students' confusion.

I must beg patience, then, both of the reader's humor and of his morals. Not that I ask him to suspend his sense of humor but that I shall ask him to go beyond it. In a great university the picture of a bright student attempting to outwit his professor while his professor takes pride in not being outwitted is certainly ridiculous. I shall report just such a scene, for its implications bear upon my point. Its comedy need not present a serious obstacle to thought.

As for the ethics of bull, I must ask for a suspension of judgment. I 5
wish that students could suspend theirs. Unlike humor, moral commitment is hard to think beyond. Too early a moral judgment is pre-

From *Examining in Harvard College: A Collection of Essays (1964).*

1. British philosopher (1861–1947), later a Harvard professor. See the following essay.
2. Harvard.
3. Mid-twentieth-century philosophers concerned not with abstract notions of what a thing is but with empirical observation of what it does.

cisely what stands between many able students and a liberal education. The stunning realization that the Harvard Faculty will often accept, as evidence of knowledge, the cerebrations of a student who has little data at his disposal, confronts every student with an ethical dilemma. For some it forms an academic focus for what used to be thought of as "adolescent disillusion." It is irrelevant that rumor inflates the phenomenon to mythical proportions. The students know that beneath the myth there remains a solid and haunting reality. The moral "bind" consequent on this awareness appears most poignantly in serious students who are reluctant to concede the competitive advantage to the bullster and who yet feel a deep personal shame when, having succumbed to "temptation," they themselves receive a high grade for work they consider "dishonest."

I have spent many hours with students caught in this unwelcome bitterness. These hours lend an urgency to my theme. I have found that students have been able to come to terms with the ethical problem, to the extent that it is real, only after a refined study of the true nature of bull and its relation to "knowledge." I shall submit grounds for my suspicion that we can be found guilty of sharing the students' confusion of moral and epistemological issues.

I

I present as my "premise," then, an amoral *fabliau*.[4] Its hero-villain is the Abominable Mr. Metzger '47. Since I celebrate his virtuosity, I regret giving him a pseudonym, but the peculiar style of his bravado requires me to honor also his modesty. Bull in pure form is rare; there is usually some contamination by data. The community has reason to be grateful to Mr. Metzger for having created an instance of laboratory purity, free from any adulteration by matter. The more credit is due him, I think, because his act was free from premeditation, deliberation, or hope of personal gain.

Mr. Metzger stood one rainy November day in the lobby of Memorial Hall.[5] A junior, concentrating in mathematics, he was fond of diverting himself by taking part in the drama, a penchant which may have had some influence on the events of the next hour. He was waiting to take part in a rehearsal in Sanders Theatre, but, as sometimes happens, no other players appeared. Perhaps the rehearsal had been canceled without his knowledge? He decided to wait another five minutes.

Students, meanwhile, were filing into the Great Hall opposite, and

4. A short, often coarse French medieval tale.
5. Large building at Harvard where examinations took place; within it is Sanders Theater, site of musical performances.

taking seats at the testing tables. Spying a friend crossing the lobby toward the Great Hall's door, Metzger greeted him and extended appropriate condolences. He inquired, too, what course his friend was being tested in. "Oh, Soc. Sci. something-or-other." "What's it all about?" asked Metzger, and this, as Homer remarked of Patroclus,[6] was the beginning of evil for him.

"It's about Modern Perspectives on Man and Society and All That," 10
said his friend. "Pretty interesting, really."

"Always wanted to take a course like that," said Metzger. "Any good reading?"

"Yeah, great. There's this book"—his friend did not have time to finish.

"Take your seats please" said a stern voice beside them. The idle conversation had somehow taken the two friends to one of the tables in the Great Hall. Both students automatically obeyed; the proctor put blue-books before them; another proctor presented them with copies of the printed hour-test.

Mr. Metzger remembered afterwards a brief misgiving that was suddenly overwhelmed by a surge of curiosity and puckish glee. He wrote "George Smith" on the blue book, opened it, and addressed the first question.

I must pause to exonerate the Management. The Faculty has a rule 15
that no student may attend an examination in a course in which he is not enrolled. To the wisdom of this rule the outcome of this deplorable story stands witness. The Registrar, charged with the enforcement of the rule, has developed an organization with procedures which are certainly the finest to be devised. In November, however, class rosters are still shaky, and on this particular day another student, named Smith, was absent. As for the culprit, we can reduce his guilt no further than to suppose that he was ignorant of the rule, or, in the face of the momentous challenge before him, forgetful.

We need not be distracted by Metzger's performance on the "objective" or "spot" questions on the test. His D on these sections can be explained by those versed in the theory of probability. Our interest focuses on the quality of his essay. It appears that when Metzger's friend picked up his own blue book a few days later, he found himself in company with a large proportion of his section in having received on the essay a C+. When he quietly picked up "George Smith's" blue book to return it to Metzger, he observed that the grade for the essay

6. In Homer's *Iliad,* Achilles refused to fight, but his friend Patroclus persuaded him to let him wear his armor and lead his troops. He did, and the Greeks won, but Patroclus was slain by Hector. This made Achilles decide to avenge Patroclus's death, and the eventual result was the fall of Troy.

was A. In the margin was a note in the section man's hand. It read "Excellent work. Could you have pinned these observations down a bit more closely? Compare . . . in . . . pp. . . ."

Such news could hardly be kept quiet. There was a leak, and the whole scandal broke on the front page of Tuesday's *Crimson.*[7] With the press Metzger was modest, as becomes a hero. He said that there had been nothing to it at all, really. The essay question had offered a choice of two books, Margaret Mead's *And Keep Your Powder Dry* or Geoffrey Gorer's *The American People.* Metzger reported that having read neither of them, he had chosen the second "because the title gave me some notion as to what the book might be about." On the test, two critical comments were offered on each book, one favorable, one unfavorable. The students were asked to "discuss." Metzger conceded that he had played safe in throwing his lot with the more laudatory of the two comments, "but I did not forget to be balanced."

I do not have Mr. Metzger's essay before me except in vivid memory. As I recall, he took his first cue from the name Geoffrey, and committed his strategy to the premise that Gorer was born into an "Anglo-Saxon" culture, probably English, but certainly "English speaking." Having heard that Margaret Mead was a social anthropologist, he inferred that Gorer was the same. He then entered upon his essay, centering his inquiry upon what he supposed might be the problems inherent in an anthropologist's observation of a culture which was his own, or nearly his own. Drawing in part from memories of table-talk on cultural relativity[8] and in part from creative logic, he rang changes on the relation of observer to observed, and assessed the kind and degree of objectivity which might accrue to an observer through training as an anthropologist. He concluded that the book in question did in fact contribute a considerable range of " 'objective', and even 'fresh'," insights into the nature of our culture. "At the same time," he warned, "these observations must be understood within the context of their generation by a person only partly freed from his embeddedness in the culture he is observing, and limited in his capacity to transcend those particular tendencies and biases which he has himself developed as a personality in his interraction with this culture since his birth. In this sense the book portrays as much the character of Geoffrey Gorer as it analyzes that of the American people." It is my regrettable duty to report that at this moment of triumph Mr. Metzger was carried away by the temptations of parody and added, "We are thus much the richer."

In any case, this was the essay for which Metzger received his honor

7. Harvard's college newspaper.
8. "An important part of Harvard's education takes place during meals in the Houses." An Official Publication [Perry's note]. The houses are dormitory complexes.

grade and his public acclaim. He was now, of course, in serious trouble with the authorities.

I shall leave him for the moment to the mercy of the Administrative 20
Board of Harvard College and turn the reader's attention to the section man who ascribed the grade. He was in much worse trouble. All the consternation in his immediate area of the Faculty and all the glee in other areas fell upon his unprotected head. I shall now undertake his defense.

I do so not simply because I was acquainted with him and feel a respect for his intelligence; I believe in the justice of his grade! Well, perhaps "justice" is the wrong word in a situation so manifestly absurd. This is more a case in "equity." That is, the grade is equitable if we accept other aspects of the situation which are equally absurd. My proposition is this: if we accept as valid those C grades which were accorded students who, like Metzger's friend, demonstrated a thorough familiarity with the details of the book without relating their critique to the methodological problems of social anthropology, then "George Smith" deserved not only the same, but better.

The reader may protest that the C's given to students who showed evidence only of diligence were indeed not valid and that both these students and "George Smith" should have received E's. To give the diligent E is of course not in accord with custom. I shall take up this matter later. For now, were I to allow the protest, I could only restate my thesis: that "George Smith's" E would, in a college of liberal arts, be properly a "better" E.

At this point I need a short-hand. It is a curious fact that there is no academic slang for the presentation of evidence of diligence alone. "Parroting" won't do; it is possible to "parrot" bull. I must beg the reader's pardon, and, for reasons almost too obvious to bear, suggest "cow."

Stated as nouns, the concepts look simple enough:

> cow (pure): data, however relevant, without relevancies.
> bull (pure): relevancies, however relevant, without data.

The reader can see all too clearly where this simplicity would lead. I 25
can assure him that I would not have imposed on him this way were I aiming to say that knowledge in this university is definable as some neuter compromise between cow and bull, some infertile hermaphrodite. This is precisely what many diligent students seem to believe: that what they must learn to do is to "find the right mean" between "amounts" of detail and "amounts" of generalities. Of course this is not the point at all. The problem is not quantitative, nor does its solution lie on a continuum between the particular and the general. Cow and bull are not poles of a single dimension. A clear notion of what

they really are is essential to my inquiry, and for heuristic purposes I wish to observe them further in the celibate state.

When the pure concepts are translated into verbs, their complexities become apparent in the assumptions and purposes of the students as they write:

> To cow (*v. intrans.*) or the act of cowing:
> To list data (or perform operations) without awareness of, or comment upon, the contexts, frames of reference, or points of observation which determine the origin, nature, and meaning of the data (or procedures). To write on the assumption that "a fact is a fact." To present evidence of hard work as a substitute for understanding, without any intent to deceive.
>
> To bull (*v. intrans.*) or the act of bulling:
> To discourse upon the contexts, frames of reference and points of observation which would determine the origin, nature, and meaning of data if one had any. To present evidence of an understanding of form in the hope that the reader may be deceived into supposing a familiarity with content.

At the level of conscious intent, it is evident that cowing is more moral, or less immoral, than bulling. To speculate about unconscious intent would be either an injustice or a needless elaboration of my theme. It is enough that the impression left by cow is one of earnestness, diligence, and painful naiveté. The grader may feel disappointment or even irritation, but these feelings are usually balanced by pity, compassion, and a reluctance to hit a man when he's both down and moral. He may feel some challenge to his teaching, but none whatever to his one-ups-manship. He writes in the margin: "See me."

We are now in a position to understand the anomaly of custom: As instructors, we always assign bull an E, *when we detect it;* whereas we usually give cow a C, *even though it is always obvious.*

After all, we did not ask to be confronted with a choice between morals and understanding (or did we?). We evince a charming humanity, I think, in our decision to grade in favor of morals and pathos. "I simply *can't* give this student an E after he has *worked* so hard." At the same time we tacitly express our respect for the bullster's strength. We recognize a colleague. If he knows so well how to dish it out, we can be sure that he can also take it.

30 Of course it is just possible that we carry with us, perhaps from our own school-days, an assumption that if a student is willing to work hard and collect "good hard facts" he can always be taught to understand their relevance, whereas a student who has caught onto the forms of relevance without working at all is a lost scholar.

But this is not in accord with our experience.

It is not in accord either, as far as I can see, with the stated values of a liberal education. If a liberal education should teach students "how to think," not only in their own fields but in fields outside their own—that is, to understand "how the other fellow orders knowledge," then bulling, even in its purest form, expresses an important part of what a pluralist university holds dear, surely a more important part than the collecting of "facts that are facts" which schoolboys learn to do. Here then, good bull appears not as ignorance at all but as an aspect of knowledge. It is both relevant and "true." In a university setting good bull is therefore of more value than "facts," which, without a frame of reference, are not even "true" at all.

Perhaps this value accounts for the final anomaly: as instructors, we are inclined to reward bull highly, *where we do not detect its intent,* to the consternation of the bullster's acquaintances. And often we do not examine the matter too closely. After a long evening of reading blue books full of cow, the sudden meeting with a student who at least understands the problems of one's field provides a lift like a draught of refreshing wine, and a strong disposition toward trust.

This was, then, the sense of confidence that came to our unfortunate section man as he read "George Smith's" sympathetic considerations.

II

In my own years of watching over students' shoulders as they work, I 35
have come to believe that this feeling of trust has a firmer basis than the confidence generated by evidence of diligence alone. I believe that the theory of a liberal education holds. Students who have dared to understand man's real relation to his knowledge have shown themselves to be in a strong position to learn content rapidly and meaningfully, and to retain it. I have learned to be less concerned about the education of a student who has come to understand the nature of man's knowledge, even though he has not yet committed himself to hard work, than I am about the education of the student who, after one or two terms at Harvard, is working desperately hard and still believes that collected "facts" constitute knowledge. The latter, when I try to explain to him, too often understands me to be saying that he "doesn't *put in enough generalities.*" Surely he has "put in *enough* facts."

I have come to see such quantitative statements as expressions of an entire, coherent epistemology. In grammar school the student is taught that Columbus discovered America in 1492. The *more* such items he gets "right" on a given test the more he is credited with "knowing." From years of this sort of thing it is not unnatural to develop the conviction that knowledge consists of the accretion of hard facts by hard work.

The student learns that the more facts and procedures he can get "right" in a given course, the better will be his grade. The more courses he takes, the more subjects he has "had," the more credits he accumulates, the more diplomas he will get, until, after graduate school, he will emerge with his doctorate, a member of the community of scholars.

The foundation of this entire life is the proposition that a fact is a fact. The necessary correlate of this proposition is that a fact is either right or wrong. This implies that the standard against which the rightness or wrongness of a fact may be judged exists *someplace*—perhaps graven upon a tablet in a Platonic world[9] outside and above *this* cave of tears. In grammar school it is evident that the tablets which enshrine the spelling of a word or the answer to an arithmetic problem are visible to my teacher who need only compare my offerings to it. In high school I observe that my English teachers disagree. This can only mean that the tablets in such matters as the goodness of a poem are distant and obscured by clouds. They surely exist. The pleasing of befuddled English teachers degenerates into assessing their prejudices, a game in which I have no protection against my competitors more glib of tongue. I respect only my science teachers, authorities who *really know*. Later I learn from them that "this is only what we think *now*." But eventually, surely. . . . Into this epistemology of education, apparently shared by teachers in such terms as "credits," "semester hours" and "years of French" the student may invest his ideals, his drive, his competitiveness, his safety, his self-esteem, and even his love.

College raises other questions: by whose calendar is it proper to say that Columbus discovered America in 1492? How, when and by whom was the year 1 established in this calendar? What of other calendars? In view of the evidence for Leif Ericson's previous visit (and the American Indians), what historical ethnocentrism is suggested by the use of the word "discover" in this sentence? As for Leif Ericson, in accord with what assumptions do you order the evidence?

These questions and their answers are not "more" knowledge. They are devastation. I do not need to elaborate upon the epistemology, or rather epistemologies, they imply. A fact has become at last "an observation or an operation performed in a frame of reference." A liberal education is founded in an awareness of frame of reference even in the most immediate and empirical examination of data. Its acquirement

9. That is, a world of ideal forms, of which this world is but the distorted image. Plato's image of humanity's weak grasp of ideal forms was the "Allegory of the Cave."

involves relinquishing hope of absolutes and of the protection they afford against doubt and the glib-tongued competitor. It demands an ever widening sophistication about systems of thought and observation. It leads, not away from, but *through* the arts of gamesmanship to a new trust.

This trust is in the value and integrity of systems, their varied character, and the way their apparently incompatible metaphors enlighten, from complementary facets, the particulars of human experience. As one student said to me: "I used to be cynical about intellectual games. Now I want to know them thoroughly. You see I came to realize that it was only when I knew the rules of the game cold that I could tell whether what I was saying was tripe."

We too often think of the bullster as cynical. He can be, and not always in a light-hearted way. We have failed to observe that there can lie behind cow the potential of a deeper and more dangerous despair. The moralism of sheer work and obedience can be an ethic that, unwilling to face a despair of its ends, glorifies its means. The implicit refusal to consider the relativity of both ends and means leaves the operator in an unconsidered proprietary absolutism. History bears witness that in the pinches this moral superiority has no recourse to negotiation, only to force.

A liberal education proposes that man's hope lies elsewhere: in the negotiability that can arise from an understanding of the integrity of systems and of their origins in man's address to his universe. The prerequisite is the courage to accept such a definition of knowledge. From then on, of course, there is nothing incompatible between such an epistemology and hard work. Rather the contrary.

I can now at last let bull and cow get together. The reader knows best how a productive wedding is arranged in his own field. This is the nuptial he celebrates with a straight A on examinations. The masculine context must embrace the feminine particular, though itself "born of woman." Such a union is knowledge itself, and it alone can generate new contexts and new data which can unite in their turn to form new knowledge.

In this happy setting we can congratulate in particular the Natural 45
Sciences, long thought to be barren ground to the bullster. I have indeed drawn my examples of bull from the Social Sciences, and by analogy from the Humanities. Essay-writing in these fields has long been thought to nurture the art of bull to its prime. I feel, however, that the Natural Sciences have no reason to feel slighted. It is perhaps no accident that Metzger was a mathematician. As part of my researches for this paper, furthermore, a student of considerable talent has recently honored me with an impressive analysis of the art of amassing "partial credits" on examinations in advanced physics. Though beyond me in

some respects, his presentation confirmed my impression that instructors of Physics frequently honor on examinations operations structurally similar to those requisite in a good essay.

The very qualities that make the Natural Sciences fields of delight for the eager gamesman have been essential to their marvelous fertility.

III

As priests of these mysteries, how can we make our rites more precisely expressive? The student who merely cows robs himself, without knowing it, of his education and his soul. The student who only bulls robs himself, as he knows full well, of the joys of inductive discovery—that is, of engagement. The introduction of frames of reference in the new curricula of Mathematics and Physics in the schools is a hopeful experiment. We do not know yet how much of these potent revelations the very young can stand, but I suspect they may rejoice in them more than we have supposed. I can't believe they have never wondered about Leif Ericson and that word "discovered," or even about 1492. They have simply been too wise to inquire.

Increasingly in recent years better students in the better high schools and preparatory schools *are* being allowed to inquire. In fact they appear to be receiving both encouragement and training in their inquiry. I have the evidence before me.

Each year for the past five years all freshmen entering Harvard and Radcliffe have been asked in freshman week to "grade" two essays answering an examination question in History. They are then asked to give their reasons for their grades. One essay, filled with dates, is 99% cow. The other, with hardly a date in it, is a good essay, easily mistaken for bull. The "official" grades of these essays are, for the first (alas!) C+ "because he has worked so hard," and for the second (soundly, I think) B+. Each year a larger majority of freshmen evaluate these essays as would the majority of the faculty, and for the faculty's reasons, and each year a smaller minority give the higher honor to the essay offering data alone. Most interesting, a larger number of students each year, while not overrating the second essay, award the first the straight E appropriate to it in a college of liberal arts.

50 For us who must grade such students in a university, these developments imply a new urgency, did we not feel it already. Through our grades we describe for the students, in the showdown, what we believe about the nature of knowledge. The subtleties of bull are not peripheral to our academic concerns. That they penetrate to the center of our care is evident in our feelings when a student whose good work we have awarded a high grade reveals to us that he does not feel he deserves it. Whether he disqualifies himself because "there's too much

bull in it," or worse because "I really don't think I've worked that hard," he presents a serious educational problem. Many students feel this sleaziness; only a few reveal it to us.

We can hardly allow a mistaken sense of fraudulence to undermine our students' achievements. We must lead students beyond their concept of bull so that they may honor relevancies that are really relevant. We can willingly acknowledge that, in lieu of the date 1492, a consideration of calendars and of the word "discovered," may well be offered with intent to deceive. We must insist that this does not make such considerations intrinsically immoral, and that, contrariwise, the date 1492 may be no substitute for them. Most of all, we must convey the impression that we grade understanding qua understanding. To be convincing, I suppose we must concede to ourselves in advance that a bright student's understanding is understanding even if he achieved it by osmosis rather than by hard work in our course.

These are delicate matters. As for cow, its complexities are not what need concern us. Unlike good bull, it does not represent partial knowledge at all. It belongs to a different theory of knowledge entirely. In our theories of knowledge it represents total ignorance, or worse yet, a knowledge downright inimical to understanding. I even go so far as to propose that we award no more C's for cow. To do so is rarely, I feel, the act of mercy it seems. Mercy lies in clarity.

The reader may be afflicted by a lingering curiosity about the fate of Mr. Metzger. I hasten to reassure him. The Administrative Board of Harvard College, whatever its satanic reputations, is a benign body. Its members, to be sure, were on the spot. They delighted in Metzger's exploit, but they were responsible to the Faculty's rule. The hero stood in danger of probation. The debate was painful. Suddenly one member, of a refined legalistic sensibility, observed that the rule applied specifically to "examinations" and that the occasion had been simply an hour-test. Mr. Metzger was merely "admonished."

QUESTIONS

1. *What do the terms "bull" and "cow" refer to? Give examples from Perry as well as from some of your college courses.*
2. *Perry wrote this essay in 1964. Over thirty years later, everyone knows that 1492 is far from a "neutral" date. Give two other assertions in Perry's essay that have proved to be problematic in similar ways.*
3. *How might the audience of Perry's essay—professional educators interested in how Harvard conducts its examinations—have determined its shape and tone? What changes might Perry make if he were writing for a group of high school teachers? a group of educators from developing nations? first-year college students?*

Alfred North Whitehead

THE RHYTHMIC CLAIMS OF FREEDOM AND DISCIPLINE

The fading of ideals is sad evidence of the defeat of human endeavour. In the schools of antiquity philosophers aspired to impart wisdom, in modern colleges our humbler aim is to teach subjects. The drop from the divine wisdom, which was the goal of the ancients, to text-book knowledge of subjects, which is achieved by the moderns, marks an educational failure, sustained through the ages. I am not maintaining that in the practice of education the ancient were more successful than ourselves. You have only to read Lucian,[1] and to note his satiric dramatizations of the pretentious claims of philosophers, to see that in this respect the ancients can boast over us no superiority. My point is that, at the dawn of our European civilisation, men started with the full ideals which should inspire education, and that gradually our ideals have sunk to square with our practice.

But when ideals have sunk to the level of practice, the result is stagnation. In particular, so long as we conceive intellectual education as merely consisting in the acquirement of mechanical mental aptitudes, and of formulated statements of useful truths, there can be no progress; though there will be much activity, amid aimless re-arrangement of syllabuses, in the fruitless endeavour to dodge the inevitable lack of time. We must take it as an unavoidable fact, that God has so made the world that there are more topics desirable for knowledge than any one person can possibly acquire. It is hopeless to approach the problem by the way of the enumeration of subjects which every one ought to have mastered. There are too many of them, all with excellent title-deeds. Perhaps, after all, this plethora of material is fortunate; for the world is made interesting by a delightful ignorance of important truths. What I am anxious to impress on you is that though knowledge is one chief aim of intellectual education, there is another ingredient, vaguer but greater, and more dominating in its importance. The ancients called it "wisdom." You cannot be wise without some basis of knowledge; but you may easily acquire knowledge and remain bare of wisdom.

Now wisdom is the way in which knowledge is held. It concerns the

From *The Aims of Education* (1929).

1. Greek satirist of false philosophical doctrines (c. 120–c. 180).

handling of knowledge, its selection for the determination of relevant issues, its employment to add value to our immediate experience. This mastery of knowledge, which is wisdom, is the most intimate freedom obtainable. The ancients saw clearly—more clearly than we do—the necessity for dominating knowledge by wisdom. But, in the pursuit of wisdom in the region of practical education, they erred sadly. To put the matter simply, their popular practice assumed that wisdom could be imparted to the young by procuring philosophers to spout at them. Hence the crop of shady philosophers in the schools of the ancient world. The only avenue towards wisdom is by freedom in the presence of knowledge. But the only avenue towards knowledge is by discipline in the acquirement of ordered fact. Freedom and discipline are the two essentials of education, and hence the title of my discourse to-day, "The Rhythmic Claims of Freedom and Discipline."

The antithesis in education between freedom and discipline is not so sharp as a logical analysis of the meanings of the terms might lead us to imagine. The pupil's mind is a growing organism. On the one hand, it is not a box to be ruthlessly packed with alien ideas: and, on the other hand, the ordered acquirement of knowledge is the natural food for a developing intelligence. Accordingly, it should be the aim of an ideally constructed education that the discipline should be the voluntary issue of free choice, and that the freedom should gain an enrichment of possibility as the issue of discipline. The two principles, freedom and discipline, are not antagonists, but should be so adjusted in the child's life that they correspond to a natural sway, to and fro, of the developing personality. It is this adaptation of freedom and discipline to the natural sway of development that I have elsewhere called The Rhythm of Education. I am convinced that much disappointing failure in the past has been due to neglect of attention to the importance of this rhythm. My main position is that the dominant note of education at its beginning and at its end is freedom, but that there is an intermediate stage of discipline with freedom in subordination: Furthermore, that there is not one unique threefold cycle of freedom, discipline, and freedom; but that all mental development is composed of such cycles, and of cycles of such cycles. Such a cycle is a unit cell, or brick; and the complete stage of growth is an organic structure of such cells. In analysing any one such cell, I call the first period of freedom the "stage of Romance," the intermediate period of discipline I call the "stage of Precision," and the final period of freedom is the "stage of Generalisation."

Let me now explain myself in more detail. There can be no mental 5
development without interest. Interest is the *sine qua non*[2] for atten-

2. Something absolutely necessary or indispensable.

tion and apprehension. You may endeavour to excite interest by means of birch rods, or you may coax it by the incitement of pleasurable activity. But without interest there will be no progress. Now the natural mode by which living organisms are excited towards suitable self-development is enjoyment. The infant is lured to adapt itself to its environment by its love of its mother and its nurse; we eat because we like a good dinner: we subdue the forces of nature because we have been lured to discovery by an insatiable curiosity: we enjoy exercise: and we enjoy the unchristian passion of hating our dangerous enemies. Undoubtedly pain is one subordinate means of arousing an organism to action. But it only supervenes on the failure of pleasure. Joy is the normal healthy spur for the *élan vital.*[3] I am not maintaining that we can safely abandon ourselves to the allurement of the greater immediate joys. What I do mean is that we should seek to arrange the development of character along a path of natural activity, in itself pleasurable. The subordinate stiffening of discipline must be directed to secure some long-time good; although an adequate object must not be too far below the horizon, if the necessary interest is to be retained.

The second preliminary point which I wish to make, is the unimportance—indeed the evil—of barren knowledge. The importance of knowledge lies in its use, in our active mastery of it—that is to say, it lies in wisdom. It is a convention to speak of mere knowledge, apart from wisdom, as of itself imparting a peculiar dignity to its possessor. I do not share in this reverence for knowledge as such. It all depends on who has the knowledge and what he does with it. That knowledge which adds greatness to character is knowledge so handled as to transform every phase of immediate experience. It is in respect to the activity of knowledge that an over-vigorous discipline in education is so harmful. The habit of active thought, with freshness, can only be generated by adequate freedom. Undiscriminating discipline defeats its own object by dulling the mind. If you have much to do with the young as they emerge from school and from the university, you soon note the dulled minds of those whose education has consisted in the acquirement of inert knowledge. Also the deplorable tone of English society in respect to learning is a tribute to our educational failure. Furthermore, this overhaste to impart mere knowledge defeats itself. The human mind rejects knowledge imparted in this way. The craving for expansion, for activity, inherent in youth is disgusted by a dry imposition of disciplined knowledge. The discipline, when it comes, should satisfy a natural craving for the wisdom which adds value to bare experience.

But let us now examine more closely the rhythm of these natural cravings of the human intelligence. The first procedure of the mind in

3. Vital impulse.

a new environment is a somewhat discursive activity amid a welter of ideas and experience. It is a process of discovery, a process of becoming used to curious thoughts, of shaping questions, of seeking for answers, of devising new experiences, of noticing what happens as the result of new ventures. This general process is both natural and of absorbing interest. We must often have noticed children between the ages of eight and thirteen absorbed in its ferment. It is dominated by wonder, and cursed be the dullard who destroys wonder. Now undoubtedly this stage of development requires help, and even discipline. The environment within which the mind is working must be carefully selected. It must, of course, be chosen to suit the child's stage of growth, and must be adapted to individual needs. In a sense it is an imposition from without; but in a deeper sense it answers to the call of life within the child. In the teacher's consciousness the child has been sent to his telescope to look at the stars, in the child's consciousness he has been given free access to the glory of the heavens. Unless, working somewhere, however obscurely, even in the dullest child, there is this transfiguration of imposed routine, the child's nature will refuse to assimilate the alien material. It must never be forgotten that education is not a process of packing articles in a trunk. Such a simile is entirely inapplicable. It is, of course, a process completely of its own peculiar genus. Its nearest analogue is the assimilation of food by a living organism: and we all know how necessary to health is palatable food under suitable conditions. When you have put your boots in a trunk, they will stay there till you take them out again; but this is not at all the case if you feed a child with the wrong food.

This initial stage of romance requires guidance in another way. After all the child is the heir to long ages of civilisation, and it is absurd to let him wander in the intellectual maze of men in the Glacial Epoch.[4] Accordingly, a certain pointing out of important facts, and of simplifying ideas, and of usual names, really strengthens the natural impetus of the pupil. In no part of education can you do without discipline or can you do without freedom; but in the stage of romance the emphasis must always be on freedom, to allow the child to see for itself and to act for itself. My point is that a block in the assimilation of ideas inevitably arises when a discipline of precision is imposed before a stage of romance has run its course in the growing mind. There is no comprehension apart from romance. It is my strong belief that the cause of so much failure in the past has been due to the lack of careful study of the due place of romance. Without the adventure of romance, at the best you get inert knowledge without initiative, and at the worst you get contempt of ideas—without knowledge.

But when this stage of romance has been properly guided another

4. The Ice Age, the time of the earliest humans, before science and the arts developed.

craving grows. The freshness of inexperience has worn off; there is general knowledge of the groundwork of fact and theory: and, above all, there has been plenty of independent browsing amid first-hand experiences, involving adventures of thought and of action. The enlightenment which comes from precise knowledge can now be understood. It corresponds to the obvious requirements of common sense, and deals with familiar material. Now is the time for pushing on, for knowing the subject exactly, and for retaining in the memory its salient features. This is the stage of precision. This stage is the sole stage of learning in the traditional scheme of education, either at school or university. You had to learn your subject, and there was nothing more to be said on the topic of education. The result of such an undue extension of a most necessary period of development was the production of a plentiful array of dunces, and of a few scholars whose natural interest had survived the car of Juggernaut.[5] There is, indeed, always the temptation to teach pupils a little more of fact and of precise theory than at that stage they are fitted to assimilate. If only they could, it would be so useful. We—I am talking of schoolmasters and of university dons—are apt to forget that we are only subordinate elements in the education of a grown man; and that, in their own good time, in later life our pupils will learn for themselves. The phenomena of growth cannot be hurried beyond certain very narrow limits. But an unskilful practitioner can easily damage a sensitive organism. Yet, when all has been said in the way of caution, there is such a thing as pushing on, of getting to know the fundamental details and the main exact generalisations, and of acquiring an easy mastery of technique. There is no getting away from the fact that things have been found out, and that to be effective in the modern world you must have a store of definite acquirement of the best practice. To write poetry you must study metre; and to build bridges you must be learned in the strength of material. Even the Hebrew prophets had learned to write, probably in those days requiring no mean effort. The untutored art of genius is—in the words of the Prayer Book[6]—a vain thing, fondly invented.

During the stage of precision, romance is the background. The stage is dominated by the inescapable fact that there are right ways and wrong ways, and definite truths to be known. But romance is not dead, and it is the art of teaching to foster it amidst definite application to appointed task. It must be fostered for one reason, because romance is after all a necessary ingredient of that balanced wisdom which is the goal to be attained. But there is another reason: The organism will not

5. The idol of the Hindu deity Krishna, which crushed whatever was in its path. Devotees were said to have thrown themselves under the wheels of the car in which the idol was carried.

6. The Book of Common Prayer, the devotional manual of the Church of England.

absorb the fruits of the task unless its powers of apprehension are kept fresh by romance. The real point is to discover in practice that exact balance between freedom and discipline which will give the greatest rate of progress over the things to be known. I do not believe that there is any abstract formula which will give information applicable to all subjects, to all types of pupils, or to each individual pupil; except indeed the formula of rhythmic sway which I have been insisting on, namely, that in the earlier stage the progress requires that the emphasis be laid on freedom, and that in the later middle stage the emphasis be laid on the definite acquirement of allotted tasks. I freely admit that if the stage of romance has been properly managed, the discipline of the second stage is much less apparent, that the children know how to go about their work, want to make a good job of it, and can be safely trusted with the details. Furthermore, I hold that the only discipline, important for its own sake, is self-discipline, and that this can only be acquired by a wide use of freedom. But yet—so many are the delicate points to be considered in education—it is necessary in life to have acquired the habit of cheerfully undertaking imposed tasks. The conditions can be satisfied if the tasks correspond to the natural cravings of the pupil at his stage of progress, if they keep his powers at full stretch, and if they attain an obviously sensible result, and if reasonable freedom is allowed in the mode of execution.

The difficulty of speaking about the way a skilful teacher will keep romance alive in his pupils arises from the fact that what takes a long time to describe, takes a short time to do. The beauty of a passage of Virgil[7] may be rendered by insisting on beauty of verbal enunciation, taking no longer than prosy utterance. The emphasis on the beauty of a mathematical argument, in its marshalling of general considerations to unravel complex fact, is the speediest mode of procedure. The responsibility of the teacher at this stage is immense. To speak the truth, except in the rare case of genius in the teacher, I do not think that it is possible to take a whole class very far along the road of precision without some dulling of the interest. It is the unfortunate dilemma that initiative and training are both necessary, and that training is apt to kill initiative.

But this admission is not to condone a brutal ignorance of methods of mitigating this untoward fact. It is not a theoretical necessity, but arises because perfect tact is unattainable in the treatment of each individual case. In the past the methods employed assassinated interest; we are discussing how to reduce the evil to its smallest dimensions. I merely utter the warning that education is a difficult problem, to be solved by no one simple formula.

In this connection there is, however, one practical consideration

7. Latin poet (70–19 B.C.) who wrote the *Aeneid*.

which is largely neglected. The territory of romantic interest is large, ill-defined, and not to be controlled by any explicit boundary. It depends on the chance flashes of insight. But the area of precise knowledge, as exacted in any general educational system, can be, and should be, definitely determined. If you make it too wide you will kill interest and defeat your own object: if you make it too narrow your pupils will lack effective grip. Surely, in every subject in each type of curriculum, the precise knowledge required should be determined after the most anxious inquiry. This does not now seem to be the case in any effective way. For example, in the classical studies of boys destined for a scientific career—a class of pupils in whom I am greatly interested—What is the Latin vocabulary which they ought definitely to know? Also what are the grammatical rules and constructions which they ought to have mastered? Why not determine these once and for all, and then bend every exercise to impress just these on the memory, and to understand their derivatives, both in Latin and also in French and English. Then, as to other constructions and words which occur in the reading of texts, supply full information in the easiest manner. A certain ruthless definiteness is essential in education. I am sure that one secret of a successful teacher is that he has formulated quite clearly in his mind what the pupil has got to know in precise fashion. He will then cease from half-hearted attempts to worry his pupils with memorising a lot of irrelevant stuff of inferior importance. The secret of success is pace, and the secret of pace is concentration. But, in respect to precise knowledge, the watchword is pace, pace, pace. Get your knowledge quickly, and then use it. If you can use it, you will retain it.

We have now come to the third stage of the rhythmic cycle, the stage of generalisation. There is here a reaction towards romance. Something definite is now known; aptitudes have been acquired; and general rules and laws are clearly apprehended both in their formulation and their detailed exemplification. The pupil now wants to use his new weapons. He is an effective individual, and it is effects that he wants to produce. He relapses into the discursive adventures of the romantic stage, with the advantage that his mind is now a disciplined regiment instead of a rabble. In this sense, education should begin in research and end in research. After all, the whole affair is merely a preparation for battling with the immediate experiences of life, a preparation by which to qualify each immediate moment with relevant ideas and appropriate actions. An education which does not begin by evoking initiative and end by encouraging it must be wrong. For its whole aim is the production of active wisdom.

15 In my own work at universities I have been much struck by the paralysis of thought induced in pupils by the aimless accumulation of precise knowledge, inert and unutilised. It should be the chief aim of a

university professor to exhibit himself in his own true character—that is, as an ignorant man thinking, actively utilising his small share of knowledge. In a sense, knowledge shrinks as wisdom grows: for details are swallowed up in principles. The details of knowledge which are important will be picked up *ad hoc*[8] in each avocation of life, but the habit of the active utilisation of well-understood principles is the final possession of wisdom. The stage of precision is the stage of growing into the apprehension of principles by the acquisition of a precise knowledge of details. The stage of generalisations is the stage of shedding details in favour of the active application of principles, the details retreating into subconscious habits. We don't go about explicitly retaining in our own minds that two and two make four, though once we had to learn it by heart. We trust to habit for our elementary arithmetic. But the essence of this stage is the emergence from the comparative passivity of being trained into the active freedom of application. Of course, during this stage, precise knowledge will grow, and more actively than ever before, because the mind has experienced the power of definiteness, and responds to the acquisition of general truth and of richness of illustration. But the growth of knowledge becomes progressively unconscious, as being an incident derived from some active adventure of thought.

So much for the three stages of the rhythmic unit of development. In a general way the whole period of education is dominated by this threefold rhythm. Till the age of thirteen or fourteen there is the romantic stage, from fourteen to eighteen the stage of precision, and from eighteen to two and twenty the stage of generalisation. But these are only average characters, tinging the mode of development as a whole. I do not think that any pupil completes his stages simultaneously in all subjects. For example, I should plead that while language is initiating its stage of precision in the way of acquisition of vocabulary and of grammar, science should be in its full romantic stage. The romantic stage of language begins in infancy with the acquisition of speech, so that it passes early towards a stage of precision; while science is a late comer. Accordingly a precise inculcation of science at an early age wipes out initiative and interest, and destroys any chance of the topic having any richness of content in the child's apprehension. Thus, the romantic stage of science should persist for years after the precise study of language has commenced.

There are minor eddies, each in itself a threefold cycle, running its course in each day, in each week, and in each term. There is the general apprehension of some topic in its vague possibilities, the mastery of the relevant details, and finally the putting of the whole subject to-

8. "Toward this," that is, for a specific purpose.

gether in the light of the relevant knowledge. Unless the pupils are continually sustained by the evocation of interest, the acquirement of technique, and the excitement of success, they can never make progress, and will certainly lose heart. Speaking generally, during the last thirty years the schools of England have been sending up to the universities a disheartened crowd of young folk, inoculated against any outbreak of intellectual zeal. The universities have seconded the efforts of the schools and emphasised the failure. Accordingly, the cheerful gaiety of the young turns to other topics, and thus educated England is not hospitable to ideas. When we can point to some great achievement of our nation—let us hope that it may be something other than a war—which has been won in the class-room of our schools, and not in their playing-fields, then we may feel content with our modes of education.

So far I have been discussing intellectual education, and my argument has been cramped on too narrow a basis. After all, our pupils are alive, and cannot be chopped into separate bits, like the pieces of a jig-saw puzzle. In the production of a mechanism the constructive energy lies outside it, and adds discrete parts to discrete parts. The case is far different for a living organism which grows by its own impulse towards self-development. This impulse can be stimulated and guided from outside the organism, and it can also be killed. But for all your stimulation and guidance the creative impulse towards growth comes from within, and is intensely characteristic of the individual. Education is the guidance of the individual towards a comprehension of the art of life; and by the art of life I mean the most complete achievement of varied activity expressing the potentialities of that living creature in the face of its actual environment. This completeness of achievement involves an artistic sense, subordinating the lower to the higher possibilities of the indivisible personality. Science, art, religion, morality, take their rise from this sense of values within the structure of being. Each individual embodies an adventure of existence. The art of life is the guidance of this adventure. The great religions of civilisation include among their original elements revolts against the inculcation of morals as a set of isolated prohibitions. Morality, in the petty negative sense of the term, is the deadly enemy of religion. Paul[9] denounces the Law, and the Gospels are vehement against the Pharisees.[1] Every outbreak of religion exhibits the same intensity of antagonism—an antagonism diminishing as religion fades. No part of education has more to gain from attention to the rhythmic law of growth than has

9. The New Testament apostle who first persecuted Christians before converting to Christianity himself.

1. One of three chief Jewish sects at the time of Christ.

moral and religious education. Whatever be the right way to formulate religious truths, it is death to religion to insist on a premature stage of precision. The vitality of religion is shown by the way in which the religious spirit has survived the ordeal of religious education.

The problem of religion in education is too large to be discussed at this stage of my address. I have referred to it to guard against the suspicion that the principles here advocated are to be conceived in a narrow sense. We are analysing the general law of rhythmic progress in the higher stages of life, embodying the initial awakening, the discipline, and the fruition on the higher plane. What I am now insisting is that the principle of progress is from within: the discovery is made by ourselves, the discipline is self-discipline, and the fruition is the outcome of our own initiative. The teacher has a double function. It is for him to elicit the enthusiasm by resonance from his own personality, and to create the environment of a larger knowledge and a firmer purpose. He is there to avoid the waste, which in the lower stages of existence is nature's way of evolution. The ultimate motive power, alike in science, in morality, and in religion, is the sense of value, the sense of importance. It takes the various forms of wonder, of curiosity, of reverence, or worship, of tumultuous desire for merging personality in something beyond itself. This sense of value imposes on life incredible labours, and apart from it life sinks back into the passivity of its lower types. The most penetrating exhibition of this force is the sense of beauty, the æsthetic sense of realised perfection. This thought leads me to ask, whether in our modern education we emphasise sufficiently the functions of art.

The typical education of our public schools was devised for boys from well-to-do cultivated homes. They travelled in Italy, in Greece, and in France, and often their own homes were set amid beauty. None of these circumstances hold for modern national education in primary or secondary schools, or even for the majority of boys and girls in our enlarged system of public schools. You cannot, without loss, ignore in the life of the spirit so great a factor as art. Our æsthetic emotions provide us with vivid apprehensions of value. If you maim these, you weaken the force of the whole system of spiritual apprehensions. The claim for freedom in education carries with it the corollary that the development of the whole personality must be attended to. You must not arbitrarily refuse its urgent demands. In these days of economy, we hear much of the futility of our educational efforts and of the possibility of curtailing them. The endeavour to develop a bare intellectuality is bound to issue in a large crop of failure. This is just what we have done in our national schools. We do just enough to excite and not enough to satisfy. History shows us that an efflorescence of art is the first activity of nations on the road to civilisation. Yet, in the face of this plain fact, we practically shut out art from the masses of the population. Can we wonder that such an education, evoking and defeating cravings, leads to failure and discontent? The stupidity of the whole procedure is, that art in simple popular forms is just what we can give to the nation without undue strain on our resources. You may, perhaps, by some great reforms, obviate the worst kind of sweated labour and the insecurity of employment. But you can never greatly increase average incomes. On that side all hope of Utopia is closed to you. It would, however, require no very great effort to use our schools to produce a population with some love of music, some enjoyment of drama, and some joy in beauty of form and colour. We could also provide means for the satisfaction of these emotions in the general life of the population. If you think of the simplest ways, you will see that the strain on material resources would be negligible; and when you have done that, and when your population widely appreciates what art can give—its joys and its terrors—do you not think that your prophets and your clergy and your statesmen will be in a stronger position when they speak to the population of the love of God, of the inexorableness of duty, and of the call of patriotism?

Shakespeare wrote his plays for English people reared in the beauty of the country, amid the pageant of life as the Middle Age merged into the Renaissance, and with a new world across the ocean to make vivid the call of romance. To-day we deal with herded town populations, reared in a scientific age. I have no doubt that unless we can meet the new age with new methods, to sustain for our populations the life of the spirit, sooner or later, amid some savage outbreak of defeated longings, the fate of Russia will be the fate of England. Historians will write as her epitaph that her fall issued from the spiritual blindness of her governing classes, from their dull materialism, and from their Pharisaic attachment to petty formulæ of statesmanship.

Language and Communication

Gloria Naylor

"MOMMY, WHAT DOES 'NIGGER' MEAN?"

Language is the subject. It is the written form with which I've managed to keep the wolf away from the door and, in diaries, to keep my sanity. In spite of this, I consider the written word inferior to the spoken, and much of the frustration experienced by novelists is the awareness that whatever we manage to capture in even the most transcendent passages falls far short of the richness of life. Dialogue achieves its power in the dynamics of a fleeting moment of sight, sound, smell and touch.

I'm not going to enter the debate here about whether it is language that shapes reality or vice versa. That battle is doomed to be waged whenever we seek intermittent reprieve from the chicken and egg dispute. I will simply take the position that the spoken word, like the written word, amounts to a nonsensical arrangement of sounds or letters without a consensus that assigns "meaning." And building from the meanings of what we hear, we order reality. Words themselves are innocuous; it is the consensus that gives them true power.

I remember the first time I heard the word nigger. In my third-grade class, our math tests were being passed down the rows, and as I handed the papers to a little boy in back of me, I remarked that once again he had received a much lower mark than I did. He snatched his test from me and spit out that word. Had he called me a nymphomaniac or a necrophiliac, I couldn't have been more puzzled. I didn't know what a nigger was, but I knew that whatever it meant, it was something he shouldn't have called me. This was verified when I raised my hand,

Originally appeared in *The New York Times Magazine* "Hers" column (Feb. 20, 1986).

and in a loud voice repeated what he had said and watched the teacher scold him for using a "bad" word. I was later to go home and ask the inevitable question that every black parent must face—"Mommy, what does 'nigger' mean?"

And what exactly did it mean? Thinking back, I realize that this could not have been the first time the word was used in my presence. I was part of a large extended family that had migrated from the rural South after World War II and formed a close-knit network that gravitated around my maternal grandparents. Their ground-floor apartment in one of the buildings they owned in Harlem was a weekend mecca for my immediate family, along with countless aunts, uncles and cousins who brought along assorted friends. It was a bustling and open house with assorted neighbors and tenants popping in and out to exchange bits of gossip, pick up an old quarrel or referee the ongoing checkers game in which my grandmother cheated shamelessly. They were all there to let down their hair and put up their feet after a week of labor in the factories, laundries and shipyards of New York.

5 Amid the clamor, which could reach deafening proportions—two or three conversations going on simultaneously, punctuated by the sound of a baby's crying somewhere in the back rooms or out on the street—there was still a rigid set of rules about what was said and how. Older children were sent out of the living room when it was time to get into the juicy details about "you-know-who" up on the third floor who had gone and gotten herself "p-r-e-g-n-a-n-t!" But my parents, knowing that I could spell well beyond my years, always demanded that I follow the others out to play. Beyond sexual misconduct and death, everything else was considered harmless for our young ears. And so among the anecdotes of the triumphs and disappointments in the various workings of their lives, the word nigger was used in my presence, but it was set within contexts and inflections that caused it to register in my mind as something else.

In the singular, the word was always applied to a man who had distinguished himself in some situation that brought their approval for his strength, intelligence or drive:

"Did Johnny really do that?"

"I'm telling you, that nigger pulled in $6,000 of overtime last year. Said he got enough for a down payment on a house."

When used with a possessive adjective by a woman—"my nigger"—it became a term of endearment for husband or boyfriend. But it could be more than just a term applied to a man. In their mouths it became the pure essence of manhood—a disembodied force that channeled their past history of struggle and present survival against the odds into a victorious statement of being: "Yeah, that old foreman found out quick enough—you don't mess with a nigger."

In the plural, it became a description of some group within the com- 10
munity that had overstepped the bounds of decency as my family defined it: Parents who neglected their children, a drunken couple who fought in public, people who simply refused to look for work, those with excessively dirty mouths or unkempt households were all "trifling niggers." This particular circle could forgive hard times, unemployment, the occasional bout of depression—they had gone through all of that themselves—but the unforgivable sin was lack of self-respect.

A woman could never be a "nigger" in the singular, with its connotation of confirming worth. The noun girl was its closest equivalent in that sense, but only when used in direct address and regardless of the gender doing the addressing. "Girl" was a token of respect for a woman. The one-syllable word was drawn out to sound like three in recognition of the extra ounce of wit, nerve or daring that the woman had shown in the situation under discussion.

"G-i-r-l, stop. You mean you said that to his face?"

But if the word was used in a third-person reference or shortened so that it almost snapped out of the mouth, it always involved some element of communal disapproval. And age became an important factor in these exchanges. It was only between individuals of the same generation, or from an older person to a younger (but never the other way around), that "girl" would be considered a compliment.

I don't agree with the argument that use of the word nigger at this social stratum of the black community was an internalization of racism. The dynamics were the exact opposite: the people in my grandmother's living room took a word that whites used to signify worthlessness or degradation and rendered it impotent. Gathering there together, they transformed "nigger" to signify the varied and complex human beings they knew themselves to be. If the word was to disappear totally from the mouths of even the most liberal of white society, no one in that room was naïve enough to believe it would disappear from white minds. Meeting the word head-on, they proved it had absolutely nothing to do with the way they were determined to live their lives.

So there must have been dozens of times that the word "nigger" was 15
spoken in front of me before I reached the third grade. But I didn't "hear" it until it was said by a small pair of lips that had already learned it could be a way to humiliate me. That was the word I went home and asked my mother about. And since she knew that I had to grow up in America, she took me in her lap and explained.

Maxine Hong Kingston

TONGUE-TIED

Long ago in China, knot-makers tied string into buttons and frogs, and rope into bell pulls. There was one knot so complicated that it blinded the knot-maker. Finally an emperor outlawed this cruel knot, and the nobles could not order it anymore. If I had lived in China, I would have been an outlaw knot-maker.

Maybe that's why my mother cut my tongue. She pushed my tongue up and sliced the frenum.[1] Or maybe she snipped it with a pair of nail scissors. I don't remember her doing it, only her telling me about it, but all during childhood I felt sorry for the baby whose mother waited with scissors or knife in hand for it to cry—and then, when its mouth was wide open like a baby bird's, cut. The Chinese say "a ready tongue is an evil."

I used to curl up my tongue in front of the mirror and tauten my frenum into a white line, itself as thin as a razor blade. I saw no scars in my mouth. I thought perhaps I had had two frena, and she had cut one. I made other children open their mouths so I could compare theirs to mine. I saw perfect pink membranes stretching into precise edges that looked easy enough to cut. Sometimes I felt very proud that my mother committed such a powerful act upon me. At other times I was terrified—the first thing my mother did when she saw me was to cut my tongue.

"Why did you do that to me, Mother?"

5 "I told you."

"Tell me again."

"I cut it so that you would not be tongue-tied. Your tongue would be able to move in any language. You'll be able to speak languages that are completely different from one another. You'll be able to pronounce anything. Your frenum looked too tight to do those things, so I cut it."

"But isn't 'a ready tongue an evil'?"

"Things are different in this ghost country."[2]

10 "Did it hurt me? Did I cry and bleed?"

"I don't remember. Probably."

From *The Woman Warrior: Memoirs of a Girlhood among Ghosts* (1976).

1. The connecting fold of membrane on the underside of the tongue.
2. In Kingston's story, the Chinese immigrants see white Americans as "ghosts" whose language and values they must adopt in order to become American.

She didn't cut the other children's. When I asked cousins and other Chinese children whether their mothers had cut their tongues loose, they said, "What?"

"Why didn't you cut my brothers' and sisters' tongues?"

"They didn't need it."

"Why not? Were theirs longer than mine?" 15

"Why don't you quit blabbering and get to work?"

If my mother was not lying she should have cut more, scraped away the rest of the frenum skin, because I have a terrible time talking. Or she should not have cut at all, tampering with my speech. When I went to kindergarten and had to speak English for the first time, I became silent. A dumbness—a shame—still cracks my voice in two, even when I want to say "hello" casually, or ask an easy question in front of the check-out counter, or ask directions of a bus driver. I stand frozen, or I hold up the line with the complete, grammatical sentence that comes squeaking out at impossible length. "What did you say?" says the cab driver, or "Speak up," so I have to perform again, only weaker the second time. A telephone call makes my throat bleed and takes up that day's courage. It spoils my day with self-disgust when I hear my broken voice come skittering out into the open. It makes people wince to hear it. I'm getting better, though. Recently I asked the postman for special-issue stamps; I've waited since childhood for postmen to give me some of their own accord. I am making progress, a little every day.

My silence was thickest—total—during the three years that I covered my school paintings with black paint. I painted layers of black over houses and flowers and suns, and when I drew on the blackboard, I put a layer of chalk on top. I was making a stage curtain, and it was the moment before the curtain parted or rose. The teachers called my parents to school, and I saw they had been saving my pictures, curling and cracking, all alike and black. The teachers pointed to the pictures and looked serious, talked seriously too, but my parents did not understand English. ("The parents and teachers of criminals were executed," said my father.) My parents took the pictures home. I spread them out (so black and full of possibilities) and pretended the curtains were swinging open, flying up, one after another, sunlight underneath, mighty operas.

During the first silent year I spoke to no one at school, did not ask before going to the lavatory, and flunked kindergarten. My sister also said nothing for three years, silent in the playground and silent at lunch. There were other quiet Chinese girls not of our family, but most of them got over it sooner than we did. I enjoyed the silence. At first it did not occur to me I was supposed to talk or to pass kindergarten. I talked at home and to one or two of the Chinese kids in class. I made motions and even made some jokes. I drank out of a toy saucer when the water spilled out of the cup, and everybody laughed, pointing at me, so I did it some more. I didn't know that Americans don't drink out of saucers.

20 I liked the Negro students (Black Ghosts) best because they laughed the loudest and talked to me as if I were a daring talker too. One of the Negro girls had her mother coil braids over her ears Shanghai-style like mine; we were Shanghai twins except that she was covered with black like my paintings. Two Negro kids enrolled in Chinese school, and the teachers gave them Chinese names. Some Negro kids walked me to school and home, protecting me from the Japanese kids, who hit me and chased me and stuck gum in my ears. The Japanese kids were noisy and tough. They appeared one day in kindergarten, released from concentration camp,[3] which was a tic-tac-toe mark, like barbed wire, on the map.

It was when I found out I had to talk that school became a misery, that the silence became a misery. I did not speak and felt bad each time that I did not speak. I read aloud in first grade, though, and heard the barest whisper with little squeaks come out of my throat. "Louder," said the teacher, who scared the voice away again. The other Chinese girls did not talk either, so I knew the silence had to do with being a Chinese girl.

Reading out loud was easier than speaking because we did not have to make up what to say, but I stopped often, and the teacher would think I'd gone quiet again. I could not understand "I." The Chinese "I" had seven strokes, intricacies. How could the American "I," assuredly wearing a hat like the Chinese, have only three strokes, the middle so straight? Was it out of politeness that this writer left off strokes the way a Chinese has to write her own name small and crooked? No, it was not politeness; "I" is a capital and "you" is a lowercase. I stared at that middle line and waited so long for its black center to resolve into tight strokes and dots that I forgot to pronounce it. The other troublesome word was "here," no strong consonant to hang on to, and so flat, when "here" is two mountainous ideographs.[4] The teacher, who had already told me every day how to read "I" and "here," put me in the low corner under the stairs again, where the noisy boys usually sat.

When my second grade class did a play, the whole class went to the auditorium except the Chinese girls. The teacher, lovely and Ha-

3. During World War II, more than 100,000 Japanese-Americans were imprisoned in "War Relocation Camps" in the United States.

4. Composite characters in Chinese writing made by combining two or more other characters for words of related meaning.

waiian, should have understood about us, but instead left us behind in the classroom. Our voices were too soft or nonexistent, and our parents never signed the permission slips anyway. They never signed anything unnecessary. We opened the door a crack and peeked out, but closed it again quickly. One of us (not me) won every spelling bee, though.

I remember telling the Hawaiian teacher, "We Chinese can't sing 'land where our fathers died.' " She argued with me about politics, while I meant because of curses. But how can I have that memory when I couldn't talk? My mother says that we, like the ghosts, have no memories.

After American school, we picked up our cigar boxes, in which we 25
had arranged books, brushes, and an inkbox neatly, and went to Chinese school, from 5:00 to 7:30 P.M. There we chanted together, voices rising and falling, loud and soft, some boys shouting, everybody reading together, reciting together and not alone with one voice. When we had a memorization test, the teacher let each of us come to his desk and say the lesson to him privately, while the rest of the class practiced copying or tracing. Most of the teachers were men. The boys who were so well behaved in the American school played tricks on them and talked back to them. The girls were not mute. They screamed and yelled during recess, when there were no rules; they had fistfights. Nobody was afraid of children hurting themselves or of children hurting school property. The glass doors to the red and green balconies with the gold joy symbols were left wide open so that we could run out and climb the fire escapes. We played capture-the-flag in the auditorium, where Sun Yat-sen and Chiang Kai-shek's[5] pictures hung at the back of the stage, the Chinese flag on their left and the American flag on their right. We climbed the teak ceremonial chairs and made flying leaps off the stage. One flag headquarters was behind the glass door and the other on stage right. Our feet drummed on the hollow stage. During recess the teachers locked themselves up in their office with the shelves of books, copybooks, inks from China. They drank tea and warmed their hands at a stove. There was no play supervision. At recess we had the school to ourselves, and also we could roam as far as we could go—downtown, Chinatown stores, home—as long as we returned before the bell rang.

At exactly 7:30 the teacher again picked up the brass bell that sat on his desk and swung it over our heads, while we charged down the stairs, our cheering magnified in the stairwell. Nobody had to line up.

Not all of the children who were silent at American school found

5. Sun Yat-sen (1866–1925) and his successor, Chiang Kai-shek (1888–1975), led the Guomindang (or Nationalist party) campaign to unify China in the 1920s and 1930s.

voice at Chinese school. One new teacher said each of us had to get up and recite in front of the class, who was to listen. My sister and I had memorized the lesson perfectly. We said it to each other at home, one chanting, one listening. The teacher called on my sister to recite first. It was the first time a teacher had called on the second-born to go first. My sister was scared. She glanced at me and looked away; I looked down at my desk. I hoped that she could do it because if she could, then I would have to. She opened her mouth and a voice came out that wasn't a whisper, but it wasn't a proper voice either. I hoped that she would not cry, fear breaking up her voice like twigs underfoot. She sounded as if she were trying to sing through weeping and strangling. She did not pause or stop to end the embarrassment. She kept going until she said the last word, and then she sat down. When it was my turn, the same voice came out, a crippled animal running on broken legs. You could hear splinters in my voice, bones rubbing jagged against one another. I was loud, though. I was glad I didn't whisper. There was one little girl who whispered.

Richard Rodriguez

ARIA

Supporters of bilingual education today imply that students like me miss a great deal by not being taught in their family's language. What they seem not to recognize is that, as a socially disadvantaged child, I considered Spanish to be a private language. What I needed to learn in school was that I had the right—and the obligation—to speak the public language of *los gringos.*[1] The odd truth is that my first-grade classmates could have become bilingual, in the conventional sense of that word, more easily than I. Had they been taught (as upper-middle-class children are often taught early) a second language like Spanish or French, they could have regarded it simply as that: another public language. In my case such bilingualism could not have been so quickly achieved. What I did not believe was that I could speak a single public language.

Without question, it would have pleased me to hear my teachers address me in Spanish when I entered the classroom. I would have felt much less afraid. I would have trusted them and responded with ease.

From *Hunger of Memory: The Education of Richard Rodriguez* (1982).

1. Foreigners.

But I would have delayed—for how long postponed?—having to learn the language of public society. I would have evaded—and for how long could I have afforded to delay?—learning the great lesson of school, that I had a public identity.

Fortunately, my teachers were unsentimental about their responsibility. What they understood was that I needed to speak a public language. So their voices would search me out, asking me questions. Each time I'd hear them, I'd look up in surprise to see a nun's face frowning at me. I'd mumble, not really meaning to answer. The nun would persist, "Richard, stand up. Don't look at the floor. Speak up. Speak to the entire class, not just to me!" But I couldn't believe that the English language was mine to use. (In part, I did not want to believe it.) I continued to mumble. I resisted the teacher's demands. (Did I somehow suspect that once I learned public language my pleasing family life would be changed?) Silent, waiting for the bell to sound, I remained dazed, diffident, afraid.

Because I wrongly imagined that English was intrinsically a public language and Spanish an intrinsically private one, I easily noted the difference between classroom language and the language of home. At school, words were directed to a general audience of listeners. ("Boys and girls.") Words were meaningfully ordered. And the point was not self-expression alone but to make oneself understood by many others. The teacher quizzed: "Boys and girls, why do we use that word in this sentence? Could we think of a better word to use there? Would the sentence change its meaning if the words were differently arranged? And wasn't there a better way of saying much the same thing?" (I couldn't say. I wouldn't try to say.)

5 Three months. Five. Half a year passed. Unsmiling, ever watchful, my teachers noted my silence. They began to connect my behavior with the difficult progress my older sister and brother were making. Until one Saturday morning three nuns arrived at the house to talk to our parents. Stiffly, they sat on the blue living room sofa. From the doorway of another room, spying the visitors, I noted the incongruity—the clash of two worlds, the faces and voices of school intruding upon the familiar setting of home. I overheard one voice gently wondering, "Do your children speak only Spanish at home, Mrs. Rodriguez?" While another voice added, "That Richard especially seems so timid and shy."

That Rich-heard!

With great tact the visitors continued, "Is it possible for you and your husband to encourage your children to practice their English when they are home?" Of course, my parents complied. What would they not do for their children's well-being? And how could they have questioned the Church's authority which those women represented?

In an instant, they agreed to give up the language (the sounds) that had revealed and accentuated our family's closeness. The moment after the visitors left, the change was observed. "*Ahora*, speak to us *en inglés*,"[2] my father and mother united to tell us.

At first, it seemed a kind of game. After dinner each night, the family gathered to practice "our" English. (It was still then *inglés*, a language foreign to us, so we felt drawn as strangers to it.) Laughing, we would try to define words we could not pronounce. We played with strange English sounds, often overanglicizing our pronunciations. And we filled the smiling gaps of our sentences with familiar Spanish sounds. But that was cheating, somebody shouted. Everyone laughed. In school, meanwhile, like my brother and sister, I was required to attend a daily tutoring session. I needed a full year of special attention. I also needed my teachers to keep my attention from straying in class by calling out, *Rich-heard*—their English voices slowly prying loose my ties to my other name, its three notes, *Ri-car-do*. Most of all I needed to hear my mother and father speak to me in a moment of seriousness in broken—suddenly heartbreaking—English. The scene was inevitable: One Saturday morning I entered the kitchen where my parents were talking in Spanish. I did not realize that they were talking in Spanish however until, at the moment they saw me, I heard their voices change to speak English. Those *gringo* sounds they uttered startled me. Pushed me away. In that moment of trivial misunderstanding and profound insight, I felt my throat twisted by unsounded grief. I turned quickly and left the room. But I had no place to escape to with Spanish. (The spell was broken.) My brother and sisters were speaking English in another part of the house.

Again and again in the days following, increasingly angry, I was obliged to hear my mother and father: "Speak to us *en inglés*." (*Speak*.) Only then did I determine to learn classroom English. Weeks after, it happened: One day in school I raised my hand to volunteer an answer. I spoke out in a loud voice. And I did not think it remarkable when the entire class understood. That day, I moved very far from the disadvantaged child I had been only days earlier. The belief, that calming assurance that I belonged in public, had at last taken hold.

10 Shortly after, I stopped hearing the high and loud sounds of *los gringos*. A more and more confident speaker of English, I didn't trouble to listen to *how* strangers sounded, speaking to me. And there simply were too many English-speaking people in my day for me to hear American accents anymore. Conversations quickened. Listening to persons who sounded eccentrically pitched voices, I usually noted their sounds for an initial few seconds before I concentrated on *what*

2. "*Now*, speak to us *in English*."

they were saying. Conversations became content-full. Transparent. Hearing someone's *tone* of voice—angry or questioning or sarcastic or happy or sad—I didn't distinguish it from the words it expressed. Sound and word were thus tightly wedded. At the end of a day, I was often bemused, always relieved, to realize how "silent," though crowded with words, my day in public had been. (This public silence measured and quickened the change in my life.)

At last, seven years old, I came to believe what had been technically true since my birth: I was an American citizen.

But the special feeling of closeness at home was diminished by then. Gone was the desperate, urgent, intense feeling of being at home; rare was the experience of feeling myself individualized by family intimates. We remained a loving family, but one greatly changed. No longer so close; no longer bound tight by the pleasing and troubling knowledge of our public separateness. Neither my older brother nor sister rushed home after school anymore. Nor did I. When I arrived home there would often be neighborhood kids in the house. Or the house would be empty of sounds.

Following the dramatic Americanization of their children, even my parents grew more publicly confident. Especially my mother. She learned the names of all the people on our block. And she decided we needed to have a telephone installed in the house. My father continued to use the word *gringo.* But it was no longer charged with the old bitterness or distrust. (Stripped of any emotional content, the word simply became a name for those Americans not of Hispanic descent.) Hearing him, sometimes, I wasn't sure if he was pronouncing the Spanish word *gringo* or saying gringo in English.

Matching the silence I started hearing in public was a new quiet at home. The family's quiet was partly due to the fact that, as we children learned more and more English, we shared fewer and fewer words with our parents. Sentences needed to be spoken slowly when a child addressed his mother or father. (Often the parent wouldn't understand.) The child would need to repeat himself. (Still the parent misunderstood.) The young voice, frustrated, would end up saying, "Never mind"—the subject was closed. Dinners would be noisy with the clinking of knives and forks against dishes. My mother would smile softly between her remarks; my father at the other end of the table would chew and chew at his food, while he stared over the heads of his children.

My *mother!* My *father!* After English became my primary language, 15
I no longer knew what words to use in addressing my parents. The old Spanish words (those tender accents of sound) I had used earlier—*mamá* and *papá*—I couldn't use anymore. They would have been too painful reminders of how much had changed in my life. On the other

hand, the words I heard neighborhood kids call *their* parents seemed equally unsatisfactory. *Mother* and *Father; Ma, Papa, Pa, Dad, Pop* (how I hated the all American sound of that last word especially)—all these terms I felt were unsuitable, not really terms of address for *my* parents. As a result, I never used them at home. Whenever I'd speak to my parents, I would try to get their attention with eye contact alone, In public conversations, I'd refer to "my parents" or "my.mother and father."

My mother and father, for their part, responded differently, as their children spoke to them less. She grew restless, seemed troubled and anxious at the scarcity of words exchanged in the house. It was she who would question me about my day when I came home from school. She smiled at small talk. She pried at the edges of my sentences to get me to say something more. (What?) She'd join conversations she overhead, but her intrusions often stopped her children's talking. By contrast, my father seemed reconciled to the new quiet. Though his English improved somewhat, he retired into silence. At dinner he spoke very little. One night his children and even his wife helplessly giggled at his garbled English pronunciation of the Catholic Grace before Meals. Thereafter he made his wife recite the prayer at the start of each meal, even on formal occasions, when there were guests in the house. Hers became the public voice of the family. On official business, it was she, not my father, one would usually hear on the phone or in stores, talking to strangers. His children grew so accustomed to his silence that, years later, they would speak routinely of his shyness. (My mother would often try to explain: Both his parents died when he was eight. He was raised by an uncle who treated him like little more than a menial servant. He was never encouraged to speak. He grew up alone. A man of few words.) But my father was not shy, I realized, when I'd watch him speaking Spanish with relatives. Using Spanish, he was quickly effusive. Especially when talking with other men, his voice would spark, flicker, flare alive with sounds. In Spanish, he expressed ideas and feelings he rarely revealed in English. With firm Spanish sounds, he conveyed confidence and authority English would never allow him.

The silence at home, however, was finally more than a literal silence. Fewer words passed between parent and child, but more profound was the silence that resulted from my inattention to sounds. At about the time I no longer bothered to listen with care to the sounds of English in public, I grew careless about listening to the sounds family members made when they spoke. Most of the time I heard someone speaking at home and didn't distinguish his sounds from the words people uttered in public. I didn't even pay much attention to my parents' accented and ungrammatical speech. At least not at home. Only when I was with them in public would I grow alert to their accents. Though, even then, their sounds caused me less and less concern. For I was increasingly confident of my own public identity.

I would have been happier about my public success had I not sometimes recalled what it had been like earlier, when my family had conveyed its intimacy through a set of conveniently private sounds. Sometimes in public, hearing a stranger, I'd hark back to my past. A Mexican farmworker approached me downtown to ask directions to somewhere, *"¿Hijito . . . ?"*[3] he said. And his voice summoned deep longing. Another time, standing beside my mother in the visiting room of a Carmelite convent,[4] before the dense screen which rendered the nuns shadowy figures, I heard several Spanish-speaking nuns—their busy, singsong overlapping voices—assure us that yes, yes, we were remembered, all our family was remembered in their prayers. (Their voices echoed faraway family sounds.) Another day, a dark-faced old woman—her hand light on my shoulder—steadied herself against me as she boarded a bus. She murmured something I couldn't quite comprehend. Her Spanish voice came near, like the face of a never-before-seen relative in the instant before I was kissed. Her voice, like so many of the Spanish voices I'd hear in public, recalled the golden age of my youth. Hearing Spanish then, I continued to be a careful, if sad, listener to sounds. Hearing a Spanish-speaking family walking behind me, I turned to look. I smiled for an instant, before my glance found the Hispanic-looking faces of strangers in the crowd going by.

Today I hear bilingual educators say that children lose a degree of "individuality" by becoming assimilated into public society. (Bilingual schooling was popularized in the seventies, that decade when middle-class ethnics began to resist the process of assimilation—the American melting pot.) But the bilingualists simplistically scorn the value and necessity of assimilation. They do not seem to realize that there are *two* ways a person is individualized. So they do not realize that while one suffers a diminished sense of *private* individuality by becoming assimilated into public society, such assimilation makes possible the achievement of *public* individuality.

The bilingualists insist that a student should be reminded of his difference from others in mass society, his heritage. But they equate mere 20
separateness with individuality. The fact is that only in private—with intimates—is separateness from the crowd a prerequisite for individuality. (An intimate draws me apart, tells me that I am unique, unlike

3. "Little boy . . . ?"
4. Of the Catholic Order of Our Lady of Mount Carmel.

all others.) In public, by contrast, full individuality is achieved, paradoxically, by those who are able to consider themselves members of the crowd. Thus it happened for me: Only when I was able to think of myself as an American, no longer an alien in *gringo* society, could I seek the rights and opportunities necessary for full public individuality. The social and political advantages I enjoy as a man result from the day that I came to believe that my name, indeed, is *Rich-heard Road-ree-guess*. It is true that my public society today is often impersonal. (My public society is usually mass society). Yet despite the anonymity of the crowd and despite the fact that the individuality I achieve in public is often tenuous—because it depends on my being one in a crowd—I celebrate the day I acquired my new name. Those middle-class ethnics who scorn assimilation seem to me filled with decadent self-pity, obsessed by the burden of public life. Dangerously, they romanticize public separateness and they trivialize the dilemma of the socially disadvantaged.

My awkward childhood does not prove the necessity of bilingual education. My story discloses instead an essential myth of childhood—inevitable pain. If I rehearse here the changes in my private life after my Americanization, it is finally to emphasize the public gain. The loss implies the gain: The house I returned to each afternoon was quiet. Intimate sounds no longer rushed to the door to greet me. There were other noises inside. The telephone rang. Neighborhood kids ran past the door of the bedroom where I was reading my schoolbooks—covered with shopping-bag paper. Once I learned public language, it would never again be easy for me to hear intimate family voices. More and more of my day was spent hearing words. But that may only be a way of saying that the day I raised my hand in class and spoke loudly to an entire roomful of faces, my childhood started to end.

QUESTIONS

1. *What did Rodriguez lose because his schooling was in English instead of Spanish? What did he gain?*
2. *Is Rodriguez arguing against bilingual education? Is he claiming that other non-English speakers would have the same gains and losses as he did? What evidence does he base his case on?*
3. *How does Rodriguez characterize the differences between public and private language? What are his arguments on behalf of the public language? Why might some Americans remain unconvinced?*
4. *For Rodriguez, public language is English and private language is Spanish. Could similar considerations apply if both were different kinds or levels of English? In other words, could many monolingual*

Americans face some of the dilemmas Rodriguez discusses about his own family, though to a lesser degree? Write an essay exploring your own experience with moving from private to public language.

Casey Miller and Kate Swift

WHO'S IN CHARGE OF THE ENGLISH LANGUAGE?

In order to encourage the use of language that is free of gender bias, it's obviously necessary to get authors to recognize gender bias in their writing. The reason that's so difficult is that our culture is steeped in unconscious attitudes and beliefs about gender characteristics, a condition reflected in our use of words.

Every human society has recognized the relationship between power and naming: that the act of naming confers power over the thing named. In the Book of Genesis, Adam named all the animals and was given dominion over them, and then, later, the story says "Adam called his wife's name Eve." Those who have the power to name and define other things—animals, wives, whatever—inevitably take themselves as the norm or standard, the measure of all things.

English is androcentric because for centuries it has been evolving in a society where men have been dominant. They were the ones in charge of the major social institutions: government, law, commerce, education, religion. They shaped the course of history and were the subjects of history. It's natural that the languages of patriarchal societies should come to express a male-centered view. That's basic anthropology. Anthropologists know that the single best way to understand the culture of any society is to study the lexicon of its language: a people's words reflect their reality. But the question is: whose reality? The English language still reflects a world in which the power to define gender characteristics is a male prerogative.

We all know that English contains a variety of words that identify and emphasize difference between the sexes. A number of English words actually express polarization of the sexes. Never mind that beyond having one or the other set of biological features necessary for reproduction, every individual is distinct in personality, combining in a unique way those polarized qualities called "masculine" and "femi-

From *The Exchange* (Fall 1990). Excerpted from a talk given at the annual meeting of the Association of American University Presses on June 26, 1990.

nine." Never mind that virtually no one fits the mold at either pole. It remains a cherished precept of our culture, semantically underlined in our lexicon and embraced by the purveyors of every commodity imaginable, that the sexes must be thought of as opposite.

Female-Negative-Trivial

5 This linguistic syndrome can be described as "female-negative-trivial" on the one hand, and "male-positive-important" on the other. If that strikes you as overly exaggerated, consider for a moment a group of people who are *not* in charge of the English language—that is, lexicographers—and the definitions they have come up with for a pair of words which relate to gender—the words *manly* and *womanly.* These definitions are from the most recently updated edition of *Webster's Third New International Dictionary* (copyright 1986).

> **Manly** 1. a: having qualities appropriate to a man: not effeminate or timorous: bold, resolute, and open in conduct or bearing . . . b. (1): belonging to or appropriate in character to man [*and they give as examples*] "manly sports," "beer is a manly drink," and "a big booming manly voice." (2): of undaunted courage: gallant, brave [*and among the quotations they give as examples*] "it seemed a big manly thing to say" and "a manly disregard of his enemies" . . .

Now compare the same dictionary's definition of *womanly,* remembering that lexicographers base their definitions on hundreds of examples of usage that have appeared in print.

> **Womanly** 1: marked by qualities characteristic of a woman, esp. marked by qualities becoming a well-balanced adult woman [*and their examples are*] "womanly manners" and "womanly advice." 2: possessed of the character or behavior befitting a grown woman: no longer childish or girlish: becoming to a grown woman [*and their example is from Charles Dickens*] "a little girl wearing a womanly sort of bonnet much too large for her" 3: characteristic of, belonging to, or suitable to women: conforming to or motivated by a woman's nature and attitudes rather than a man's. [*The first example here is*] "convinced that drawing was a waste of time, if not downright womanly, like painting on China." [*And another example*] "her usual womanly volubility."

What are these two supposedly parallel entries telling us? They're saying that in addition to defining characteristics appropriate to a man, like vocal pitch, *manly* is synonymous with admirable qualities that all of us might wish we had. "Bold, resolute, open in conduct or bearing; of undaunted courage, gallant, brave." And where is the list of comparable synonyms for *womanly?* There aren't any. Instead, *wom-*

anly is defined only in a circular way—through characteristics seen to be appropriate or inappropriate to women, not to human beings in general. And the examples of usage cited give a pretty good picture of what is considered appropriate to, or characteristic of, a well-balanced adult woman: she's concerned with manners, advice, and hat styles (as distinguished from sports and beer, which are felt to be manly); she wastes time in trivial pursuits like painting on china; and she talks too much.

The Slippery Slope

Most writers and editors today recognize that the female-negative-trivial syndrome is clearly evident in the use of so-called feminine suffixes with nouns of common gender. In 1990 no publishable author would identify someone as "a poetess," except in ridicule. (Adrienne Rich says the word brings out the "terroristress" in her.) But respectable writers are still using *heroine*, *suffragette*, and *executrix* when referring to a hero, a suffragist, or an executor who is a woman.

These words illustrate what Douglas Hofstadter calls "the slippery slope" of meaning. In his book *Metamagical Themas*, Hofstadter shows diagramatically how the slippery slope works. A triangle represents the idea of, let's say, a heroic person. At one base angle of this triangle is the word *heroine*, representing the female heroic person. At the other base angle is the word *hero*, representing the male heroic person. And at the apex is the generic word, again *hero*, encompassing both. But because the *hero* at the apex and the *hero* at one base angle are identical in name, their separate meanings slip back and forth along one side of the triangle, the slippery slope. The meanings blend and absorb each other. They bond together on the slope. And *heroine*, at the other base angle, remains outside that bond.

Another word that comes to mind in this connection is *actress*. It's our impression that women performers in the theater and films today are tending more and more to refer to themselves and one another as "actors." It may be deliberate, conscious usage on the part of some. Considering that their union is called Actors Equity, and that they may have trained at Actors Studio, and performed at Actors Playhouse, they simply accept that the generic word for their profession is *actor*. But when this word appears in juxtaposition with *actress*, the generic meaning of *actor* is absorbed into the gender-specific meaning, and women are identified as nonactors, as being outside or marginal, in de Beauvoir's phrase, as "the other."

10 Many people will undoubtedly go on feeling that *actress* is a term without bias, but we would like to suggest that it is on its way to becoming archaic, or at least quaint, simply because people it has identified are abandoning it by a process that may be more visceral than cerebral. In a sense it's their word, it has defined them, and, whether intentionally or not, they are taking charge of it, perhaps dumping it. We'll see.

Because linguistic changes reflect changes in our ways of thinking, a living language is constantly being created and re-created by the people who speak it. Linguistic changes spring from nothing less than new perceptions of the world and of ourselves.

Obviously we all know that over time the "rules" of grammar have changed, and we know that words themselves change their meanings: they lose some and acquire others; new words come into existence and old ones disappear into that word heaven, the *Oxford English Dictionary*. Nevertheless, most people resist change, especially, it seems, changes in grammar and the meanings of words. What we tend to forget—or choose to forget—is that the only languages which don't change are the ones no one speaks any more, like classical Greek and Latin.

Take the narrowing process that turned the Old English word *man* into a synonym for "adult male human being." As long ago as 1752 the philosopher David Hume recognized how ambiguous that word had already become: "All men," he wrote, and then added, "both male and female." And you are probably familiar with the numerous experimental studies done in the last few years, primarily by psychologists and sociologists rather than linguists, which show that most native speakers of English simply do not conceptualize women and girls when they encounter *man* and *mankind* used generically. In fact the narrowing process is felt so strongly, at least at an existential level, that a growing number of women today strongly object to being subsumed under those male-gender terms. "We aren't men," they're saying; "we're women, and we're tired of being made invisible."

Yet despite women's objections, and despite the slippery, ambiguous nature of generic *man*, lots of people, especially formally educated people, have a hard time giving it up. They forget, it seems, that words have a power of their own—the power of taking over meaning. A writer starts out talking about the species as a whole and, more often than we'll ever know, ends up talking about males. Listen to this well-known author, for example, who was discussing aggressive behavior in human beings—all of us, *Homo sapiens*. "[M]an," he wrote, "can do several things which the animal cannot do. . . . Eventually, his vital interests are not only life, food, access to females, etc., but also values, symbols, institutions."

Resistance to Change and the Problem of Precision

15 It's probably helpful, once in a while, to look back at the way some of the most familiar and accepted words in use today were greeted when they were newcomers.

Back in 1619, for example, the London schoolmaster Alexander Gil described what he called "the new mange in speaking and writing." What he was deploring was the introduction of newly coined, Latin-derived words to replace older English ones. According to him, the "new mange" included such terms as *virtue, justice, pity, compassion,* and *grace.* And he asked, "Whither have you banished those words our forefathers used for these new-fangled ones?" Alexander Gil was headmaster of St. Paul's school at the time, and it might be noted that one of his students was an eleven-year-old named John Milton who—fortunately—was not persuaded to reject Gil's "new-fangled" words.

And how about old terms that have lost favor, like the once-accepted use of the pronoun *they* with a singular referent, as in "If a person is born of a gloomy temper, they cannot help it." That was written in 1759 by none other than the very correct, well-educated British statesman, Lord Chesterfield. However, since most academics are not yet ready to revive that convenient usage—despite precedents ranging from Shakespeare to Shaw—it still isn't surprising to come across a recently published book about, let's say, the psychology of children, in which the distinguished author uses *he* and its inflected forms as all-purpose pronouns, leaving readers to guess whether a particular problem or development applies to boys only or to children of both sexes. We submit that such writing is not just unfortunate. It's inexcusable.

These days more and more writers acknowledge that *he* used generically is, like *man* used generically, both ambiguous and insidious, and they take the time and trouble to write more precisely. But sometimes, even after several polite but probably exhausting battles between author and editor, all the author will agree to do is add a disclaimer. Disclaimers can be helpful, of course (for example, those providing guidance as to what a writer of some previous century may have meant by a now-ambiguous term). More often, however, they are nothing but excuses for sloppiness.

There is also an element here which we don't think should be ignored: the deep if often unacknowledged psychological impact of the grammatical "rule" mandating masculine-gender pronouns for indefinite referents. As long ago as the 1950s, Lynn White, Jr., then the president of Mills College, described with great perception the harm that rule can do to children when he wrote:

> The penetration of this habit of language into the minds of little girls as they grow up to be women is more profound than most people, including

> most women, have recognized; for it implies that personality is really a male attribute, and that women are a human subspecies. . . . It would be a miracle if a girl-baby, learning to use the symbols of our tongue, could escape some unverbalized wound to her self-respect; whereas a boy-baby's ego is bolstered by the pattern of our language.

20 Obviously many literate men (and some literate women) must find the truth of White's perception difficult to accept, or we wouldn't still be battling the generic use of masculine-gender pronouns. But since accuracy and precision are what we're talking about today, let us ask this question: what is one to make of a scholar—a professor of communications with a special interest in semantics, as a matter of fact—who dismissed the problem of sexist language as follows: "I tend to avoid 'gender-exclusive' words," he wrote, "except when in so doing, I would injure the rhythm of a sentence."

Has it never occurred to him that in writing a sentence, any sentence, he must choose both its words and the way those words, in their infinite variety, are put together? That the choice isn't between exclusionary language on the one hand and rhythm on the other? (Surely it's possible to write with style and still communicate accurately what it is you want to say.) The choice is between settling for an ambiguous or inaccurate term because it "sounds good"—and finding the exact combination of words to convey one's message with clarity and precision. It seems to us that editors have every right to expect nothing less than the latter.

English is a vigorously alive tongue, and it reflects a vigorously alive, dynamic society that is capable of identifying its ills and thereby trying to cope with them. Neither the term *sexism* nor the term *racism* existed fifty years ago—which, as you know, isn't the same as saying that the attitudes and practices they define didn't exist before; of course they did. But those attitudes and practices came to be widely examined and questioned, and finally to be widely acknowledged within the dominant culture, only after they were put into words.

Without precision, language can betray everything we stand for. As George Orwell put it in his essay "Politics and the English Language," we must "Let the meaning choose the word and not the other way about." And Orwell went on, "In prose the worst thing you can do with words is surrender to them."

With George Orwell giving us courage, may we be so bold, in closing, as to adapt his wisdom to the occasion by adding this final thought? In publishing, the worst thing you can do is surrender to some tyrannical author who lets the word choose the meaning rather than the other way about.

Deborah Tannen

CONVERSATIONAL STYLES

When I researched and wrote my latest book, *You Just Don't Understand: Women and Men in Conversation*, the furthest thing from my mind was reevaluating my teaching strategies. But that has been one of the direct benefits of having written the book.

The primary focus of my linguistic research always has been the language of everyday conversation. One facet of this is conversational style: how different regional, ethnic, and class backgrounds, as well as age and gender, result in different ways of using language to communicate. *You Just Don't Understand* is about the conversational styles of women and men. As I gained more insight into typically male and female ways of using language, I began to suspect some of the causes of the troubling facts that women who go to single-sex schools do better in later life, and that when young women sit next to young men in classrooms, the males talk more. This is not to say that all men talk in class, nor that no women do. It is simply that a greater percentage of discussion time is taken by men's voices.

The research of sociologists and anthropologists such as Janet Lever, Marjorie Harness Goodwin, and Donna Eder has shown that girls and boys learn to use language differently in their sex-separate peer groups. Typically, a girl has a best friend with whom she sits and talks, frequently telling secrets. It's the telling of secrets, the fact and the way that they talk to each other, that makes them best friends. For boys, activities are central: Their best friends are the ones they do things with. Boys also tend to play in larger groups that are hierarchical. High-status boys give orders and push low-status boys around. So boys are expected to use language to seize center stage: by exhibiting their skill, displaying their knowledge, and challenging and resisting challenges.

These patterns have stunning implications for classroom interaction. Most faculty members assume that participating in class discussion is a necessary part of successful performance. Yet speaking in a classroom is more congenial to boys' language experience than to girls', since it entails putting oneself forward in front of a large group of people, many of whom are strangers and at least one of whom is sure to judge speakers' knowledge and intelligence by their verbal display.

Another aspect of many classrooms that makes them more hospita- 5

From the *Chronicle of Higher Education* (June 19, 1991).

ble to most men than to most women is the use of debate-like formats as a learning tool. Our educational system, as Walter Ong argues persuasively in his book *Fighting for Life* (Cornell University Press, 1981), is fundamentally male in that the pursuit of knowledge is believed to be achieved by ritual opposition: public display followed by argument and challenge. Father Ong demonstrates that ritual opposition—what he calls "adversativeness" or "agonism"—is fundamental to the way most males approach almost any activity. (Consider, for example, the little boy who shows he likes a little girl by pulling her braids and shoving her.) But ritual opposition is antithetical to the way most females learn and like to interact. It is not that females don't fight, but that they don't fight for fun. They don't *ritualize* opposition.

Anthropologists working in widely disparate parts of the world have found contrasting verbal rituals for women and men. Women in completely unrelated cultures (for example, Greece and Bali) engage in ritual laments: spontaneously produced rhyming couplets that express their pain, for example, over the loss of loved ones. Men do not take part in laments. They have their own, very different verbal ritual: a contest, a war of words in which they vie with each other to devise clever insults.

When discussing these phenomena with a colleague, I commented that I see these two styles in American conversation: Many women bond by talking about troubles, and many men bond by exchanging playful insults and put-downs, and other sorts of verbal sparring. He exclaimed: "I never thought of this, but that's the way I teach: I have students read an article, and then I invite them to tear it apart. After we've torn it to shreds, we talk about how to build a better model."

This contrasts sharply with the way I teach: I open the discussion of readings by asking, "What did you find useful in this? What can we use in our own theory building and our own methods?" I note what I see as weaknesses in the author's approach, but I also point out that the writer's discipline and purposes might be different from ours. Finally, I offer personal anecdotes illustrating the phenomena under discussion and praise students' anecdotes as well as their critical acumen.

These different teaching styles must make our classrooms wildly different places and hospitable to different students. Male students are more likely to be comfortable attacking the readings and might find the inclusion of personal anecdotes irrelevant and "soft." Women are more likely to resist discussion they perceive as hostile, and, indeed, it is women in my classes who are most likely to offer personal anecdotes.

10 A colleague who read my book commented that he had always taken for granted that the best way to deal with students' comments is to

challenge them; this, he felt it was self-evident, sharpens their minds and helps them develop debating skills. But he had noticed that women were relatively silent in his classes, so he decided to try beginning discussion with relatively open-ended questions and letting comments go unchallenged. He found, to his amazement and satisfaction, that more women began to speak up.

Though some of the women in his class clearly liked this better, perhaps some of the men liked it less. One young man in my class wrote in a questionnaire about a history professor who gave students questions to think about and called on people to answer them: "He would then play devil's advocate . . . *i.e.*, he debated us. . . . That class *really* sharpened me intellectually. . . . We as students do need to know how to defend ourselves." This young man valued the experience of being attacked and challenged publicly. Many, if not most, women would shrink from such "challenge," experiencing it as public humiliation.

A professor at Hamilton College told me of a young man who was upset because he felt his class presentation had been a failure. The professor was puzzled because he had observed that class members had listened attentively and agreed with the student's observations. It turned out that it was this very agreement that the student interpreted as failure: Since no one had engaged his ideas by arguing with him, he felt they had found them unworthy of attention.

So one reason men speak in class more than women is that many of them find the "public" classroom setting more conducive to speaking, whereas most women are more comfortable speaking in private to a small group of people they know well. A second reason is that men are more likely to be comfortable with the debate-like form that discussion may take. Yet another reason is the different attitudes toward speaking in class that typify women and men.

Students who speak frequently in class, many of whom are men, assume that it is their job to think of contributions and try to get the floor to express them. But many women monitor their participation not only to get the floor but to avoid getting it. Women students in my class tell me that if they have spoken up once or twice, they hold back for the rest of the class because they don't want to dominate. If they have spoken a lot one week, they will remain silent the next. These different ethics of participation are, of course, unstated, so those who speak freely assume that those who remain silent have nothing to say, and those who are reining themselves in assume that the big talkers are selfish and hoggish.

When I looked around my classes, I could see these differing ethics 15
and habits at work. For example, my graduate class in analyzing conversation had 20 students, 11 women and 9 men. Of the men, four were foreign students: two Japanese, one Chinese, and one Syrian.

With the exception of the three Asian men, all the men spoke in class at least occasionally. The biggest talker in the class was a woman, but there were also five women who never spoke at all, only one of whom was Japanese. I decided to try something different.

I broke the class into small groups to discuss the issues raised in the readings and to analyze their own conversational transcripts. I devised three ways of dividing the students into groups: one by the degree program they were in, one by gender, and one by conversational style, as closely as I could guess it. This meant that when the class was grouped according to conversational style, I put Asian students together, fast talkers together, and quiet students together. The class split into groups six times during the semester, so they met in each grouping twice. I told students to regard the groups as examples of interactional data and to note the different ways they participated in the different groups. Toward the end of the term, I gave them a questionnaire asking about their class and group participation.

I could see plainly from my observation of the groups at work that women who never opened their mouths in class were talking away in the small groups. In fact, the Japanese woman commented that she found it particularly hard to contribute to the all-woman group she was in because "I was overwhelmed by how talkative the female students were in the female-only group." This is particularly revealing because it highlights that the same person who can be "oppressed" into silence in one context can become the talkative "oppressor" in another. No one's conversational style is absolute; everyone's style changes in response to the context and others' styles.

Some of the students (seven) said they preferred the same-gender groups; others preferred the same-style groups. In answer to the question "Would you have liked to speak in class more than you did?" six of the seven who said Yes were women; the one man was Japanese. Most startingly, this response did not come only from quiet women; it came from women who had indicated they had spoken in class never, rarely, sometimes, and often. Of the 11 students who said the amount they had spoken was fine, 7 were men. Of the four women who checked "fine," two added qualifications indicating it wasn't completely fine: One wrote in "maybe more," and one wrote, "I have an urge to participate but often feel I should have something more interesting/relevant/wonderful/intelligent to say!!"

I counted my experiment a success. Everyone in the class found the small groups interesting, and no one indicated he or she would have preferred that the class not break into groups. Perhaps most instructive, however, was the fact that the experience of breaking into groups, and of talking about participation in class, raised everyone's awareness about classroom participation. After we had talked about it, some of the quietest women in the class made a few voluntary contributions, though sometimes I had to insure their participation by interrupting the students who were exuberantly speaking out.

Americans are often proud that they discount the significance of 20
cultural differences: "We are all individuals," many people boast. Ignoring such issues as gender and ethnicity becomes a source of pride: "I treat everyone the same." But treating people the same is not equal treatment if they are not the same.

The classroom is a different environment for those who feel comfortable putting themselves forward in a group than it is for those who find the prospect of doing so chastening, or even terrifying. When a professor asks, "Are there any questions?," students who can formulate statements the fastest have the greatest opportunity to respond. Those who need significant time to do so have not really been given a chance at all, since by the time they are ready to speak, someone else has the floor.

In a class where some students speak out without raising hands, those who feel they must raise their hands and wait to be recognized do not have equal opportunity to speak. Telling them to feel free to jump in will not make them feel free; one's sense of timing, of one's rights and obligations in a classroom, are automatic, learned over years of interaction. They may be changed over time, with motivation and effort, but they cannot be changed on the spot. And everyone assumes his or her own way is best. When I asked my students how the class could be changed to make it easier for them to speak more, the most talkative woman said she would prefer it if no one had to raise hands, and a foreign student said he wished people would raise their hands and wait to be recognized.

My experience in this class has convinced me that small-group interaction should be part of any class that is not a small seminar. I also am convinced that having the students become observers of their own interaction is a crucial part of their education. Talking about ways of talking in class makes students aware that their ways of talking affect other students, that the motivations they impute to others may not truly reflect others' motives, and that the behaviors they assume to be self-evidently right are not universal norms.

The goal of complete equal opportunity in class may not be attainable, but realizing that one monolithic classroom-participation structure is not equal opportunity is itself a powerful motivation to find more-diverse methods to serve diverse students—and every classroom is diverse.

QUESTIONS

1. *As a student, you probably have thought of some of the issues Tannen raises. Does she strike you as basically right about her subject? Is what she says true to your experience?*
2. *Tannen's essay is a journalistic piece for a broad audience. Point to some places where a scientific report or a scholarly argument would be more tightly reasoned or more precisely phrased. (For instance, would scientists be content with the term "more" in sentence 5 of paragraph 2 or "many" in paragraph 7? What would they want instead or in addition?) What evidence does Tannen use? How would that evidence be presented in a scholarly or scientific report?*
3. *Test Tannen's accuracy by observing who speaks in three different college classrooms. Can you add anything to her points? Do your observations disagree in any serious way? Does the type of course or student matter?*

Patricia A. Williams

THE DEATH OF THE PROFANE: A COMMENTARY ON THE GENRE OF LEGAL WRITING

Buzzers are big in New York City. Favored particularly by smaller stores and boutiques, merchants throughout the city have installed them as screening devices to reduce the incidence of robbery: if the face at the door looks desirable, the buzzer is pressed and the door is unlocked. If the face is that of an undesirable, the door stays locked. Predictably, the issue of undesirability has revealed itself to be a racial determination. While controversial enough at first, even civil-rights organizations backed down eventually in the face of arguments that the buzzer system is a "necessary evil," that it is a "mere inconvenience" in comparison to the risks of being murdered, that suffering discrimination is not as bad as being assaulted, and that in any event it is not all blacks who are barred, just "17-year-old black males wearing running shoes and hooded sweatshirts."[1]

From *The Alchemy of Race and Rights* (1991). All notes to this essay are the author's.

1. "When 'By Appointment' Means Keep Out," *New York Times*, December 17, 1986, p. B1. Letter to the Editor from Michael Levin and Marguerita Levin, *New York Times*, January 11, 1987, p. E32.

The installation of these buzzers happened swiftly in New York; stores that had always had their doors wide open suddenly became exclusive or received people by appointment only. I discovered them and their meaning one Saturday in 1986. I was shopping in Soho and saw in a store window a sweater that I wanted to buy for my mother. I pressed my round brown face to the window and my finger to the buzzer, seeking admittance. A narrow-eyed, white teenager wearing running shoes and feasting on bubble gum glared out, evaluating me for signs that would pit me against the limits of his social understanding. After about five seconds, he mouthed "We're closed," and blew pink rubber at me. It was two Saturdays before Christmas, at one o'clock in the afternoon; there were several white people in the store who appeared to be shopping for things for *their* mothers.

I was enraged. At that moment I literally wanted to break all the windows of the store and *take* lots of sweaters for my mother. In the flicker of his judgmental gray eyes, that saleschild had transformed my brightly sentimental, joy-to-the-world, pre-Christmas spree to a shambles. He snuffed my sense of humanitarian catholicity, and there was nothing I could do to snuff his, without making a spectacle of myself.

I am still struck by the structure of power that drove me into such a blizzard of rage. There was almost nothing I could do, short of physically intruding upon him, that would humiliate him the way he humiliated me. No words, no gestures, no prejudices of my own would make a bit of difference to him; his refusal to let me into the store—it was Benetton's, whose colorfully punnish ad campaign is premised on wrapping every one of the world's peoples in its cottons and woolens—was an outward manifestation of his never having let someone like me into the realm of his reality. He had no compassion, no remorse, no reference to me; and no desire to acknowledge me even at the estranged level of arm's-length transactor. He saw me only as one who would take his money and therefore could not conceive that I was there to give him money.

In this weird ontological imbalance, I realized that buying some- 5
thing in that store was like bestowing a gift, the gift of my commerce, the lucre of my patronage. In the wake of my outrage, I wanted to take back the gift of appreciation that my peering in the window must have appeared to be. I wanted to take it back in the form of unappreciation, disrespect, defilement. I wanted to work so hard at wishing he could feel what I felt that he would never again mistake my hatred for some sort of plaintive wish to be included. I was quite willing to disenfranchise myself, in the heat of my need to revoke the flattery of my purchasing power. I was willing to boycott Benetton's, random white-owned businesses, and anyone who ever blew bubble gum in my face again.

My rage was admittedly diffuse, even self-destructive, but it was symmetrical. The perhaps loose-ended but utter propriety of that rage is no doubt lost not just to the young man who actually barred me, but to those who would appreciate my being barred only as an abstract precaution, who approve of those who would bar even as they deny that they would bar *me*.

The violence of my desire to burst into Benetton's is probably quite apparent. I often wonder if the violence, the exclusionary hatred, is equally apparent in the repeated public urgings that blacks understand the buzzer system by putting themselves in the shoes of white storeowners—that, in effect, blacks look into the mirror of frightened white faces for the reality of their undesirability; and that then blacks would "just as surely conclude that [they] would not let [themselves] in under similar circumstances."[2] (That some blacks might agree merely shows that some of us have learned too well the lessons of privatized intimacies of self-hatred and rationalized away the fullness of our public, participatory selves.)

On the same day I was barred from Benetton's, I went home and wrote the above impassioned account in my journal. On the day after that, I found I was still brooding, so I turned to a form of catharsis I have always found healing. I typed up as much of the story as I have just told, made a big poster of it, put a nice colorful border around it, and, after Benetton's was truly closed, stuck it to their big sweater-filled window. I exercised my first-amendment right to place my business with them right out in the street.

So that was the first telling of this story. The second telling came a few months later, for a symposium on Excluded Voices sponsored by a law review. I wrote an essay summing up my feelings about being excluded from Benetton's and analyzing "how the rhetoric of increased privatization, in response to racial issues, functions as the rationalizing agent of public unaccountability and, ultimately, irresponsibility." Weeks later, I received the first edit. From the first page to the last, my fury had been carefully cut out. My rushing, run-on-rage had been reduced to simple declarative sentences. The active personal had been inverted in favor of the passive impersonal. My words were different; they spoke to me upside down. I was afraid to read too much of it at a time—meanings rose up at me oddly, stolen and strange.

10 A week and a half later, I received the second edit. All reference to Benetton's had been deleted because, according to the editors and the faculty adviser, it was defamatory; they feared harassment and liability; they said printing it would be irresponsible. I called them and offered to supply a footnote attesting to this as my personal experience

2. *New York Times*, January 11, 1987, p. E32.

at one particular location and of a buzzer system not limited to Benetton's; the editors told me that they were not in the habit of publishing things that were unverifiable. I could not but wonder, in this refusal even to let me file an affadavit, what it would take to make my experience verifiable. The testimony of an independent white bystander? (a requirement in fact imposed in U.S. Supreme Court holdings through the first part of the century[3]).

Two days *after* the piece was sent to press, I received copies of the final page proofs. All reference to my race had been eliminated because it was against "editorial policy" to permit descriptions of physiognomy. "I realize," wrote one editor, "that this was a very personal experience, but any reader will know what you must have looked like when standing at that window." In a telephone conversation to them, I ranted wildly about the significance of such an omission. "It's irrelevant," another editor explained in a voice gummy with soothing and patience; "It's nice and poetic," but it doesn't "advance the discussion of any principle. . . . This is a law review, after all." Frustrated, I accused him of censorship; calmly he assured me it was not. "This is just a matter of style," he said with firmness and finality.

Ultimately I did convince the editors that mention of my race was central to the whole sense of the subsequent text; that my story became one of extreme paranoia without the information that I am black; or that it became one in which the reader had to fill in the gap by assumption, presumption, prejudgment, or prejudice. What was most interesting to me in this experience was how the blind application of principles of neutrality, through the device of omission, acted either to make me look crazy or to make the reader participate in old habits of cultural bias.

That was the second telling of my story. The third telling came last April, when I was invited to participate in a law-school conference on Equality and Difference. I retold my sad tale of exclusion from Soho's most glitzy boutique, focusing in this version on the law-review editing process as a consequence of an ideology of style rooted in a social text of neutrality. I opined:

> Law and legal writing aspire to formalized, color-blind, liberal ideals. Neutrality is the standard for assuring these ideals; yet the adherence to it is often determined by reference to an aesthetic of uniformity, in which difference is simply omitted. For example, when segregation was eradicated from the American lexicon, its omission led many to actually believe that racism therefore no longer existed. Race-neutrality in law has become the presumed antidote for race bias in real life. With the

3. See generally *Blyew v. U.S.*, 80 U.S. 581 (1871), upholding a state's right to forbid blacks to testify against whites.

entrenchment of the notion of race-neutrality came attacks on the concept of affirmative action and the rise of reverse discrimination suits. Blacks, for so many generations deprived of jobs based on the color of our skin, are now told that we ought to find it demeaning to be hired, based on the color of our skin. Such is the silliness of simplistic either-or inversions as remedies to complex problems.

What is truly demeaning in this era of double-speak-no-evil is going on interviews and not getting hired because someone doesn't think we'll be comfortable. It is demeaning not to get promoted because we're judged "too weak," then putting in a lot of energy the next time and getting fired because we're "too strong." It is demeaning to be told what we find demeaning. It is very demeaning to stand on street corners unemployed and begging. It is downright demeaning to have to explain why we haven't been employed for months and then watch the job go to someone who is "more experienced." It is outrageously demeaning that none of this can be called racism, even if it happens only to, or to large numbers of, black people; as long as it's done with a smile, a handshake and a shrug; as long as the phantom-word "race" is never used.

The image of race as a phantom-word came to me after I moved into my late godmother's home. In an attempt to make it my own, I cleared the bedroom for painting. The following morning the room asserted itself, came rushing and raging at me through the emptiness, exactly as it had been for twenty-five years. One day filled with profuse and overwhelming complexity, the next day filled with persistently recurring memories. The shape of the past came to haunt me, the shape of the emptiness confronted me each time I was about to enter the room. The force of its spirit still drifts like an odor throughout the house.

The power of that room, I have thought since, is very like the power of racism as status quo: it is deep, angry, eradicated from view, but strong enough to make everyone who enters the room walk around the bed that isn't there, avoiding the phantom as they did the substance, for fear of bodily harm. They do not even know they are avoiding; they defer to the unseen shapes of things with subtle responsiveness, guided by an impulsive awareness of nothingness, and the deep knowledge and denial of witchcraft at work.

The phantom room is to me symbolic of the emptiness of formal equal opportunity, particularly as propounded by President Reagan, the Reagan Civil Rights Commission and the Reagan Supreme Court. Blindly formalized constructions of equal opportunity are the creation of a space that is filled in by a meandering stream of unguided hopes, dreams, fantasies, fears, recollections. They are the presence of the past in imaginary, imagistic form—the phantom-roomed exile of our longing.

It is thus that I strongly believe in the efficacy of programs and paradigms like affirmative action. Blacks are the objects of a constitutional omission which has been incorporated into a theory of neutrality. It is thus that omission is really a form of expression, as oxymoronic as that sounds: racial omission is a literal part of original intent; it is the fixed,

> reiterated prophecy of the Founding Fathers. It is thus that affirmative action is an affirmation; the affirmative act of hiring—or hearing—blacks is a recognition of individuality that re-places blacks as a social statistic, that is profoundly interconnective to the fate of blacks and whites either as sub-groups or as one group. In this sense, affirmative action is as mystical and beyond-the-self as an initiation ceremony. It is an act of verification and of vision. It is an act of social as well as professional responsibility.

The following morning I opened the local newspaper, to find that the event of my speech had commanded two columns on the front page of the Metro section. I quote only the opening lines: "Affirmative action promotes prejudice by denying the status of women and blacks, instead of affirming them as its name suggests. So said New York City attorney Patricia Williams to an audience Wednesday."[4]

I clipped out the article and put it in my journal. In the margin there is a note to myself: eventually, it says, I should try to pull all these threads together into yet another law-review article. The problem, of course, will be that in the hierarchy of law-review citation, the article in the newspaper will have more authoritative weight about me, as a so-called "primary resource," than I will have; it will take precedence over my own citation of the unverifiable testimony of my speech.

I have used the Benetton's story a lot, in speaking engagements at various schools. I tell it whenever I am too tired to whip up an original speech from scratch. Here are some of the questions I have been asked in the wake of its telling:

Am I not privileging a racial perspective, by considering only the black point of view? Don't I have an obligation to include the "salesman's side" of the story?

Am I not putting the salesman on trial and finding him guilty of racism without giving him a chance to respond to or cross-examine me?

Am I not using the store window as a "metaphorical fence" against the potential of his explanation in order to represent my side as "authentic"?

How can I be sure I'm right?

What makes my experience the real black one anyway?

Isn't it possible that another black person would disagree with my experience? If so, doesn't that render my story too unempirical and subjective to pay any attention to?

4. "Attorney Says Affirmative Action Denies Racism, Sexism," *Dominion Post* (Morgantown, West Virginia), April 8, 1988, p. B1.

Always a major objection is my having put the poster on Benetton's window. As one law professor put it: "It's one thing to publish this in a law review, where no one can take it personally, but it's another thing altogether to put your own interpretation right out there, just like that, uncontested, I mean, with nothing to counter it."*

*At the end of her essay, Williams added these observations: These questions put me on trial—an imaginary trial where it is I who have the burden of proof—and proof being nothing less than the testimony of the salesman actually confessing yes yes I am a racist. These questions question my own ability to know, to assess, to be objective. And of course, since anything that happens to me is inherently subjective, they take away my power to know what happens to me in the world. Others, by this standard, will always know better than I. And my insistence on recounting stories from my own perspective will be treated as presumption, slander, paranoid hallucination, or just plain lies.

Recently I got an urgent call from Thomas Grey of Stanford Law School. He had used this piece in his jurisprudence class, and a rumor got started that the Benetton's story wasn't true, that I had made it up, that it was a fantasy, a lie that was probably the product of a diseased mind trying to make all white people feel guilty. At this point I realized it almost didn't make any difference whether I was telling the truth or not—that the greater issue I had to face was the overwhelming weight of a disbelief that goes beyond mere disinclination to believe and becomes active suppression of anything I might have to say. The greater problem is a powerfully oppressive mechanism for denial of black self-knowledge and expression. And this denial cannot be separated from the simultaneously pathological willingness to believe certain things about blacks—not to believe them, but things about them.

When students in Grey's class believed and then claimed that I had made it all up, they put me in a position like that of Tawana Brawley [a black woman who falsely claimed she was abducted and raped by white men (eds.)]. I mean that specifically: the social consequence of concluding that we are liars operates as a kind of public absolution of racism—the conclusion is not merely that we are troubled or that I am eccentric, but that we, as liars, are the norm. Therefore, the nonbelievers can believe, things of this sort really don't happen (even in the face of statistics to the contrary). Racism or rape is all a big fantasy concocted by troublesome minorities and women. It is interesting to recall the outcry in every national medium, from the *New York Post* to the *Times* to the major networks, in the wake of the Brawley case: who will ever again believe a black woman who cries rape by a white man? Now shift the frame a bit, and imagine a white male facing a consensus that he lied. Would there be a difference? Consider Charles Stuart, for example, the white Bostonian who accused a black man of murdering his pregnant wife and whose brother later alleged that in fact the brothers had conspired to murder her. Most people and the media not only did not claim but actively resisted believing that Stuart represented any kind of "white male" norm. Instead he was written off as a troubled weirdo, a deviant—again even in the face of spousal-abuse statistics to the contrary. There was not a story I could find that carried on about "who will ever believe" the next white man who cries murder.

QUESTIONS

1. *Williams tells of the original experience three times. What changes occur in the telling of the incident itself?*
2. *List the gains and the losses in the change between Williams's lively telling and the law review account she decries. How real are the gains?*

the losses? What standards are the law review people trying to uphold? What is Williams trying to uphold?

3. *What might those law review sentences or paragraphs have looked like before they were edited? Find a law review article or two or rewrite paragraph 2 of her essay in the neutral, "law review" style that Williams despises.*

Lewis Thomas

NOTES ON PUNCTUATION

There are no precise rules about punctuation (Fowler[1] lays out some general advice (as best he can under the complex circumstances of English prose (he points out, for example, that we possess only four stops (the comma, the semicolon, the colon and the period (the question mark and exclamation point are not, strictly speaking, stops; they are indicators of tone (oddly enough, the Greeks employed the semicolon for their question mark (it produces a strange sensation to read a Greek sentence which is a straightforward question: Why weepest thou; (instead of Why weepest thou? (and, of course, there are parentheses (which are surely a kind of punctuation making this whole much more complicated by having to count up the left-handed parentheses in order to be sure of closing with the right number (but if the parentheses were left out, with nothing to work with but the stops, we would have considerably more flexibility in the deploying of layers of meaning than if we tried to separate all the clauses by physical barriers (and in the latter case, while we might have more precision and exactitude for our meaning, we would lose the essential flavor of language, which is its wonderful ambiguity))))))))))))).

The commas are the most useful and usable of all the stops. It is highly important to put them in place as you go along. If you try to come back after doing a paragraph and stick them in the various spots that tempt you you will discover that they tend to swarm like minnows into all sorts of crevices whose existence you hadn't realized and before you know it the whole long sentence becomes immobilized and lashed up squirming in commas. Better to use them sparingly, and with affection, precisely when the need for each one arises, nicely, by itself.

From *The Medusa and the Snail: More Notes of a Biology Watcher* (1979).

1. H. W. Fowler, author of *Modern English Usage* (1926, revised 1965 by Sir Ernest Gowers).

I have grown fond of semicolons in recent years. The semicolon tells you that there is still some question about the preceding full sentence; something needs to be added; it reminds you sometimes of the Greek usage. It is almost always a greater pleasure to come across a semicolon than a period. The period tells you that that is that; if you didn't get all the meaning you wanted or expected, anyway you got all the writer intended to parcel out and now you have to move along. But with a semicolon there you get a pleasant little feeling of expectancy; there is more to come; read on; it will get clearer.

Colons are a lot less attractive, for several reasons: firstly, they give you the feeling of being rather ordered around, or at least having your nose pointed in a direction you might not be inclined to take if left to yourself, and, secondly, you suspect you're in for one of those sentences that will be labeling the points to be made: firstly, secondly and so forth, with the implication that you haven't sense enough to keep track of a sequence of notions without having them numbered. Also, many writers use this system loosely and incompletely, starting out with number one and number two as though counting off on their fingers but then going on and on without the succession of labels you've been led to expect, leaving you floundering about searching for the ninethly or seventeenthly that ought to be there but isn't.

5 Exclamation points are the most irritating of all. Look! they say, look at what I just said! How amazing is my thought! It is like being forced to watch someone else's small child jumping up and down crazily in the center of the living room shouting to attract attention. If a sentence really has something of importance to say, something quite remarkable, it doesn't need a mark to point it out. And if it is really, after all, a banal sentence needing more zing, the exclamation point simply emphasizes its banality!

Quotation marks should be used honestly and sparingly, when there is a genuine quotation at hand, and it is necessary to be very rigorous about the words enclosed by the marks. If something is to be quoted, the *exact* words must be used. If part of it must be left out because of space limitations, it is good manners to insert three dots to indicate the omission, but it is unethical to do this if it means connecting two thoughts which the original author did not intend to have tied together. Above all, quotation marks should not be used for ideas that you'd like to disown, things in the air so to speak. Nor should they be put in place around clichés; if you want to use a cliché you must take full responsibility for it yourself and not try to job it off on anon., or on society. The most objectionable misuse of quotation marks, but one which illustrates the dangers of misuse in ordinary prose, is seen in advertising, especially in advertisements for small restaurants, for example "just around the corner," or "a good place to eat." No single, identifiable, citable person ever really said, for the record, "just around the corner," much less "a good place to eat," least likely of all for restaurants of the type that use this type of prose.

The dash is a handy device, informal and essentially playful, telling you that you're about to take off on a different tack but still in some way connected with the present course—only you have to remember that the dash is there, and either put a second dash at the end of the notion to let the reader know that he's back on course, or else end the sentence, as here, with a period.

The greatest danger in punctuation is for poetry. Here it is necessary to be as economical and parsimonious with commas and periods as with the words themselves, and any marks that seem to carry their own subtle meanings, like dashes and little rows of periods, even semicolons and question marks, should be left out altogether rather than inserted to clog up the thing with ambiguity. A single exclamation point in a poem, no matter what else the poem has to say, is enough to destroy the whole work.

The things I like best in T. S. Eliot's poetry, especially in the *Four Quartets*, are the semicolons. You cannot hear them, but they are there, laying out the connections between the images and the ideas. Sometimes you get a glimpse of a semicolon coming, a few lines farther on, and it is like climbing a steep path through woods and seeing a wooden bench just at a bend in the road ahead, a place where you can expect to sit for a moment, catching your breath.

Commas can't do this sort of thing; they can only tell you how the 10
different parts of a complicated thought are to be fitted together, but you can't sit, not even take a breath, just because of a comma,

QUESTIONS

1. *The title of this piece begins with the word "Notes." Is that the right word? Is this a series of notes or something else?*
2. *How long did it take you to realize that Thomas is playing a kind of game with his readers? (For instance, paragraph 1 is a single sentence.) Is punctuation the kind of thing people play games about?*
3. *Choose one or two writers in "An Album of Styles" and describe how they employ commas, colons, and semicolons. Do any of the semicolons serve as "a wooden bench just at a bend in the road ahead" (paragraph 9)?*

Erich Fromm

THE NATURE OF SYMBOLIC LANGUAGE

Let us assume you want to tell someone the difference between the taste of white wine and red wine. This may seem quite simple to you. *You* know the difference very well; why should it not be easy to explain it to someone else? Yet you find the greatest difficulty putting this taste difference into words. And probably you will end up by saying, "Now look here, I can't explain it to you. Just drink red wine and then white wine, and you will know what the difference is." You have no difficulty in finding words to explain the most complicated machine, and yet words seem to be futile to describe a simple taste experience.

Are we not confronted with the same difficulty when we try to explain a feeling experience? Let us take a mood in which you feel lost, deserted, where the world looks gray, a little frightening though not really dangerous. You want to describe this mood to a friend, but again you find yourself groping for words and eventually feel that nothing you have said is an adequate explanation of the many nuances of the mood. The following night you have a dream. You see yourself in the outskirts of a city just before dawn, the streets are empty except for a milk wagon, the houses look poor, the surroundings are unfamiliar, you have no means of accustomed transportation to places familiar to you and where you feel you belong. When you wake up and remember the dream, it occurs to you that the feeling you had in that dream was exactly the feeling of lostness and grayness you tried to describe to your friend the day before. It is just one picture, whose visualization took less than a second. And yet this picture is a more vivid and precise description than you could have given by talking *about* it at length. The picture you see in the dream is a *symbol* of something you felt.

What is a symbol? A symbol is often defined as "something that stands for something else." This definition seems rather disappointing. It becomes more interesting, however, if we concern ourselves with those symbols which are sensory expressions of seeing, hearing, smelling, touching, standing for a "something else" which is an inner experience, a feeling or thought. A symbol of this kind is something outside ourselves; that which it symbolizes is something inside ourselves. Symbolic language is language in which we express inner experience as if it were a sensory experience, as if it were something we were doing or something that was done to us in the world of things.

From *The Forgotten Language* (1951).

Symbolic language is language in which the world outside is a symbol of the world inside, a symbol for our souls and our minds.

If we define a symbol as "something which stands for something else," the crucial question is: *What is the specific connection between the symbol and that which it symbolizes?*

In answer to this question we can differentiate between three kinds of symbols: the *conventional*, the *accidental* and the *universal* symbol. As will become apparent presently, only the latter two kinds of symbols express inner experiences as if they were sensory experiences, and only they have the elements of symbolic language.

The *conventional* symbol is the best known of the three, since we employ it in everyday language. If we see the word "table" or hear the sound "table," the letters T-A-B-L-E stand for something else. They stand for the thing table that we see, touch and use. What is the connection between the *word* "table" and the *thing* "table"? Is there any inherent relationship between them? Obviously not. The thing table has nothing to do with the sound table, and the only reason the word symbolizes the thing is the convention of calling this particular thing by a particular name. We learn this connection as children by the repeated experience of hearing the word in reference to the thing until a lasting association is formed so that we don't have to think to find the right word.

There are some words, however, where the association is not only conventional. When we say "phooey," for instance, we make with our lips a movement of dispelling the air quickly. It is an expression of disgust in which our mouths participate. By this quick expulsion of air we imitate and thus express our intention to expel something, to get it out of our system. In this case, as in some others, the symbol has an inherent connection with the feeling it symbolizes. But even if we assume that originally many or even all words had their origins in some such inherent connection between symbol and the symbolized, most words no longer have this meaning for us when we learn a language.

Words are not the only illustration for conventional symbols, although they are the most frequent and best-known ones. Pictures also can be conventional symbols. A flag, for instance, may stand for a specific country, and yet there is no connection between the specific colors and the country for which they stand. They have been accepted as denoting that particular country, and we translate the visual impression of the flag into the concept of that country, again on conventional grounds. Some pictorial symbols are not entirely conventional; for example, the cross. The cross can be merely a conventional symbol of the Christian church and in that respect no different from a flag. But the specific content of the cross referring to Jesus' death or, beyond that, to the interpenetration of the material and spiritual planes, puts the connection between the symbol and what it symbolizes beyond the level of mere conventional symbols.

The very opposite to the conventional symbol is the *accidental* symbol, although they have one thing in common: there is no intrinsic relationship between the symbol and that which it symbolizes. Let us assume that someone has had a saddening experience in a certain city; when he hears the name of that city, he will easily connect the name with a mood of sadness, just as he would connect it with a mood of joy had his experience been a happy one. Quite obviously there is nothing in the nature of the city that is either sad or joyful. It is the individual experience connected with the city that makes it a symbol of a mood.

The same reaction could occur in connection with a house, a street, a certain dress, certain scenery, or anything once connected with a specific mood. We might find ourselves dreaming that we are in a certain city. In fact, there may be no particular mood connected with it in the dream; all we see is a street or even simply the name of the city. We ask ourselves why we happened to think of that city in our sleep and may discover that we had fallen asleep in a mood similar to the one symbolized by the city. The picture in the dream represents this mood, the city "stands for" the mood once experienced in it. Here the connection between the symbol and the experience symbolized is entirely accidental.

In contrast to the conventional symbol, the accidental symbol cannot be shared by anyone else except as we relate the events connected with the symbol. For this reason accidental symbols are rarely used in myths, fairy tales, or works of art written in symbolic language because they are not communicable unless the writer adds a lengthy comment to each symbol he uses. In dreams, however, accidental symbols are frequent. * * *

The *universal* symbol is one in which there is an intrinsic relationship between the symbol and that which it represents. We have already given one example, that of the outskirts of the city. The sensory experience of a deserted, strange, poor environment has indeed a significant relationship to a mood of lostness and anxiety. True enough, if we have never been in the outskirts of a city we could not use that symbol, just as the word "table" would be meaningless had we never seen a table. This symbol is meaningful only to city dwellers and would be meaningless to people living in cultures that have no big cities. Many other universal symbols, however, are rooted in the experience of every human being. Take, for instance, the symbol of fire. We are fascinated by certain qualities of fire in a fireplace. First of all, by its aliveness. It changes continuously, it moves all the time, and yet there is constancy in it. It remains the same without being the same. It gives the impression of power, of energy, of grace and lightness. It is as if it were dancing and had an inexhaustible source of energy. When we use fire as a symbol, we describe the inner experience characterized by the same elements which we notice in the sensory experience of fire; the mood of energy, lightness, movement, grace, gaiety—sometimes one, sometimes another of these elements being predominant in the feeling.

Similar in some ways and different in others is the symbol of water—of the ocean or of the stream. Here, too, we find the blending of change and permanence, of constant movement and yet of permanence. We also feel the quality of aliveness, continuity and energy. But there is a difference; where fire is adventurous, quick, exciting, water is quiet, slow and steady. Fire has an element of surprise; water an element of predictability. Water symbolizes the mood of aliveness, too, but one which is "heavier," "slower," and more comforting than exciting.

That a phenomenon of the physical world can be the adequate expression of an inner experience, that the world of things can be a symbol of the world of the mind, is not surprising. We all know that our bodies express our minds. Blood rushes to our heads when we are furious, it rushes away from them when we are afraid; our hearts beat more quickly when we are angry, and the whole body has a different tonus if we are happy from the one it has when we are sad. We express our moods by our facial expressions and our attitudes and feelings by movements and gestures so precise that others recognize them more accurately from our gestures than from our words. Indeed, the body is a symbol—and not an allegory—of the mind. Deeply and genuinely felt emotion, and even any genuinely felt thought, is expressed in our whole organism. In the case of the universal symbol, we find the same connection between mental and physical experience. Certain physical phenomena suggest by their very nature certain emotional and mental experiences, and we express emotional experiences in the language of physical experiences, that is to say, symbolically.

15 The universal symbol is the only one in which the relationship between the symbol and that which is symbolized is not coincidental but intrinsic. It is rooted in the experience of the affinity between an emotion or thought, on the one hand, and a sensory experience, on the other. It can be called universal because it is shared by all men, in contrast not only to the accidental symbol, which is by its very nature entirely personal, but also to the conventional symbol, which is restricted to a group of people sharing the same convention. The universal symbol is rooted in the properties of our body, our senses, and our mind, which are common to all men and, therefore, not restricted to individuals or to specific groups. Indeed, the language of the universal symbol is the one common tongue developed by the human race, a

language which it forgot before it succeeded in developing a universal conventional language.

There is no need to speak of a racial inheritance in order to explain the universal character of symbols. Every human being who shares the essential features of bodily and mental equipment with the rest of mankind is capable of speaking and understanding the symbolic language that is based upon these common properties. Just as we do not need to learn to cry when we are sad or to get red in the face when we are angry, and just as these reactions are not restricted to any particular race or group of people, symbolic language does not have to be learned and is not restricted to any segment of the human race. Evidence for this is to be found in the fact that symbolic language as it is employed in myths and dreams is found in all cultures—in so-called primitive as well as such highly developed cultures as Egypt and Greece. Furthermore, the symbols used in these various cultures are strikingly similar since they all go back to the basic sensory as well as emotional experiences shared by men of all cultures. Added evidence is to be found in recent experiments in which people who had no knowledge of the theory of dream interpretation were able, under hypnosis, to interpret the symbolism of their dreams without any difficulty. After emerging from the hypnotic state and being asked to interpret the same dreams, they were puzzled and said, "Well, there is no meaning to them—it is just nonsense."

The foregoing statement needs qualification, however. Some symbols differ in meaning according to the difference in their realistic significance in various cultures. For instance, the function and consequently the meaning of the sun is different in northern countries and in tropical countries. In northern countries, where water is plentiful, all growth depends on sufficient sunshine. The sun is the warm, life-giving, protecting, loving power. In the Near East, where the heat of the sun is much more powerful, the sun is a dangerous and even threatening power from which man must protect himself, while water is felt to be the source of all life and the main condition for growth. We may speak of dialects of universal symbolic language, which are determined by those differences in natural conditions which cause certain symbols to have a different meaning in different regions of the earth.

Quite different from these "symbolic dialects" is the fact that many symbols have more than one meaning in accordance with different kinds of experiences which can be connected with one and the same natural phenomenon. Let us take up the symbol of fire again. If we watch fire in the fireplace, which is a source of pleasure and comfort, it is expressive of a mood of aliveness, warmth, and pleasure. But if we see a building or forest on fire, it conveys to us an experience of threat or terror, of the powerlessness of man against the elements of nature. Fire, then, can be the symbolic representation of inner aliveness and happiness as well as of fear, powerlessness, or of one's own destructive tendencies. The same holds true of the symbol water. Water can be a most destructive force when it is whipped up by a storm or when a swollen river floods its banks. Therefore, it can be the symbolic expression of horror and chaos as well as of comfort and peace.

Another illustration of the same principle is a symbol of a valley. The valley enclosed between mountains can arouse in us the feeling of security and comfort, of protection against all dangers from the outside. But the protecting mountains can also mean isolating walls which do not permit us to get out of the valley and thus the valley can become a symbol of imprisonment. The particular meaning of the symbol in any given place can only be determined from the whole context in which the symbol appears, and in terms of the predominant experiences of the person using the symbol. * * *

A good illustration of the function of the universal symbol is a story, 20
written in symbolic language, which is known to almost everyone in Western culture: the Book of Jonah. Jonah has heard God's voice telling him to go to Nineveh and preach to its inhabitants to give up their evil ways lest they be destroyed. Jonah cannot help hearing God's voice and that is why he is a prophet. But he is an unwilling prophet, who, though knowing what he should do, tries to run away from the command of God (or, as we may say, the voice of his conscience). He is a man who does not care for other human beings. He is a man with a strong sense of law and order, but without love.

How does the story express the inner processes in Jonah?

We are told that Jonah went down to Joppa and found a ship which should bring him to Tarshish. In mid-ocean a storm rises and, while everyone else is excited and afraid, Jonah goes into the ship's belly and falls into a deep sleep. The sailors, believing that God must have sent the storm because someone on the ship is to be punished, wake Jonah, who had told them he was trying to flee from God's command. He tells them to take him and cast him forth into the sea and that the sea would then become calm. The sailors (betraying a remarkable sense of humanity by first trying everything else before following his advice) eventually take Jonah and cast him into the sea, which immediately stops raging. Jonah is swallowed by a big fish and stays in the fish's belly three days and three nights. He prays to God to free him from this prison. God makes the fish vomit out Jonah unto the dry land and Jonah goes to Nineveh, fulfills God's command, and thus saves the inhabitants of the city.

The story is told as if these events had actually happened. However, it is written in symbolic language and all the realistic events described are symbols for the inner experiences of the hero. We find a sequence of symbols which follow one another: going into the ship, going into the ship's belly, falling asleep, being in the ocean, and being in the fish's belly. All these symbols stand for the same inner experience: for a condition of being protected and isolated, of safe withdrawal from communication with other human beings. They represent what could be represented in another symbol, the fetus in the mother's womb. Different as the ship's belly, deep sleep, the ocean, and a fish's belly are realistically, they are expressive of the same inner experience, of the blending between protection and isolation.

In the manifest story events happen in space and time: *first*, going into the ship's belly; *then*, falling asleep; *then*, being thrown into the ocean; *then*, being swallowed by the fish. One thing happens after the other and, although some events are obviously unrealistic, the story has its own logical consistency in terms of time and space. But if we understand that the writer did not intend to tell us the story of external events, but of the inner experience of a man torn between his conscience and his wish to escape from his inner voice, it becomes clear that his various actions following one after the other express the same mood in him; and that *sequence in time* is expressive of a *growing intensity* of the same feeling. In his attempt to escape from his obligation to his fellow men Jonah isolates himself more and more until, in the belly of the fish, the protective element has so given way to the imprisoning element that he can stand it no longer and is forced to pray to God to be released from where he had put himself. (This is a mechanism which we find so characteristic of neurosis. An attitude is assumed as a defense against a danger, but then it grows far beyond its original defense function and becomes a neurotic symptom from which the person tries to be relieved.) Thus Jonah's escape into protective isolation ends in the terror of being imprisoned, and he takes up his life at the point where he had tried to escape.

There is another difference between the logic of the manifest and of the latent story. In the manifest story the logical connection is one of causality of external events. Jonah wants to go overseas *because* he wants to flee from God, he falls asleep *because* he is tired, he is thrown overboard *because* he is supposed to be the reason for the storm, and he is swallowed by the fish *because* there are man-eating fish in the ocean. One event occurs because of a previous event. (The last part of the story is unrealistic but not illogical.) But in the latent story the logic is different. The various events are related to each other by their association with the same inner experience. What appears to be a causal sequence of external events stands for a connection of experiences linked with each other by their association in terms of inner events. This is as logical as the manifest story—but it is a logic of a different kind.

Susan Sontag

AIDS AND ITS METAPHORS

Just as one might predict for a disease that is not yet fully understood as well as extremely recalcitrant to treatment, the advent of this terrifying new disease, new at least in its epidemic form, has provided a large-scale occasion for the metaphorizing of illness.

Strictly speaking, AIDS—acquired immune deficiency syndrome—is not the name of an illness at all. It is the name of a medical condition, whose consequences are a spectrum of illnesses. In contrast to syphilis and cancer, which provide prototypes for most of the images and metaphors attached to AIDS, the very definition of AIDS requires the presence of other illnesses, so-called opportunistic infections and malignancies. But though not in *that* sense a single disease, AIDS lends itself to being regarded as one—in part because, unlike cancer and like syphilis, it is thought to have a single cause.

AIDS has a dual metaphoric genealogy. As a microprocess, it is described as cancer is: an invasion. When the focus is transmission of the disease, an older metaphor, reminiscent of syphilis, is invoked: pollution. (One gets it from the blood or sexual fluids of infected people or from contaminated blood products.) But the military metaphors used to describe AIDS have a somewhat different focus from those used in describing cancer. With cancer, the metaphor scants the issue of causality (still a murky topic in cancer research) and picks up at the point at which rogue cells inside the body mutate, eventually moving out from an original site or organ to overrun other organs or systems—a domestic subversion. In the description of AIDS the enemy is what causes the disease, an infectious agent that comes from the outside:

> The invader is tiny, about one sixteen-thousandth the size of the head of a pin. . . . Scouts of the body's immune system, large cells called macrophages, sense the presence of the diminutive foreigner and promptly alert the immune system. It begins to mobilize an array of cells that, among other things, produce antibodies to deal with the threat. Single-mindedly, the AIDS virus ignores many of the blood cells in its path, evades the rapidly advancing defenders and homes in on the master coordinator of the immune system, a helper T cell. . . .

This is the language of political paranoia, with its characteristic distrust of a pluralistic world. A defense system consisting of cells "that, among other things, produce antibodies to deal with the threat" is,

From *AIDS and Its Metaphors* (1989).

predictably, no match for an invader who advances "single-mindedly." And the science-fiction flavor, already present in cancer talk, is even more pungent in accounts of AIDS—this one comes from *Time* magazine in late 1986—with infection described like the high-tech warfare for which we are being prepared (and inured) by the fantasies of our leaders and by video entertainments. In the era of Star Wars and Space Invaders, AIDS has proved an ideally comprehensible illness:

> On the surface of that cell, it finds a receptor into which one of its envelope proteins fits perfectly, like a key into a lock. Docking with the cell, the virus penetrates the cell membrane and is stripped of its protective shell in the process. . . .

Next the invader takes up permanent residence, by a form of alien takeover familiar in science-fiction narratives. The body's own cells *become* the invader. With the help of an enzyme the virus carries with it,

> the naked AIDS virus converts its RNA into . . . DNA, the master molecule of life. The molecule then penetrates the cell nucleus, inserts itself into a chromosome and takes over part of the cellular machinery, directing it to produce more AIDS viruses. Eventually, overcome by its alien product, the cell swells and dies, releasing a flood of new viruses to attack other cells. . . .

As viruses attack other cells, runs the metaphor, so "a host of opportunistic diseases, normally warded off by a healthy immune system, attacks the body," whose integrity and vigor have been sapped by the sheer replication of "alien product" that follows the collapse of its immunological defenses. "Gradually weakened by the onslaught, the AIDS victim dies, sometimes in months, but almost always within a few years of the first symptoms." Those who have not already succumbed are described as "under assault, showing the telltale symptoms of the disease," while millions of others "harbor the virus, vulnerable at any time to a final, all-out attack."

Cancer makes cells proliferate; in AIDS, cells die. Even as this original model of AIDS (the mirror image of leukemia) has been altered, descriptions of how the virus does its work continue to echo the way the illness is perceived as infiltrating the society. "AIDS Virus Found to Hide in Cells, Eluding Detection by Normal Tests" was the headline of a recent front-page story in the *New York Times* announcing the discovery that the virus can "lurk" for years in the macrophages—disrupting their disease-fighting function without killing them, "even when the macrophages are filled almost to bursting with virus," and without producing antibodies, the chemicals the body makes in response to "invading agents" and whose presence has been regarded as an infallible marker of the syndrome.[1] That the virus isn't lethal for *all* the cells where it takes up residence, as is now thought, only increases the illness-foe's reputation for wiliness and invincibility.

What makes the viral assault so terrifying is that contamination, and therefore vulnerability, is understood as permanent. Even if someone infected were never to develop any symptoms—that is, the infection remained, or could by medical intervention be rendered, inactive—the viral enemy would be forever within. In fact, so it is believed, it is just a matter of time before something awakens ("triggers") it, before the appearance of "the telltale symptoms." Like syphilis, known to generations of doctors as "the great masquerader," AIDS is a clinical construction, an inference. It takes its identity from the presence of *some* among a long, and lengthening, roster of symptoms (no one has everything that AIDS could be), symptoms which "mean" that what the patient has is this illness. The construction of the illness rests on the invention not only of AIDS as a clinical entity but of a kind of junior AIDS, called AIDS-related complex (ARC), to which people are assigned if they show "early" and often intermittent symptoms of immunological deficit such as fevers, weight loss, fungal infections, and swollen lymph glands. AIDS is progressive, a disease of time. Once a certain density of symptoms is attained, the course of the illness can be swift, and brings atrocious suffering. Besides the commonest "presenting" illnesses (some hitherto unusual, at least in a fatal form, such as a rare skin cancer and a rare form of pneumonia), a plethora of disabling, disfiguring, and humiliating symptoms make the AIDS patient steadily more infirm, helpless, and unable to control or take care of basic functions and needs.

The sense in which AIDS is a slow disease makes it more like syphilis, which is characterized in terms of "stages," than like cancer. Thinking in terms of "stages" is essential to discourse about AIDS. Syphilis in its most dreaded form is "tertiary syphilis," syphilis in its third stage. What is called AIDS is generally understood as the last of three stages—the first of which is infection with a human im-

1. The larger role assigned to the macrophages—"to serve as a reservoir for the AIDS virus because the virus multiplies in them but does not kill them, as it kills T-4 cells"—is said to explain the not uncommon difficulty of finding infected T-4 lymphocytes in patients who have antibodies to the virus and symptoms of AIDS. (It is still assumed that antibodies will develop once the virus spreads to these "key target" cells.) Evidence of presently infected populations of cells has been as puzzlingly limited or uneven as the evidence of infection in the populations of human societies—puzzling, because of the conviction that the disease is everywhere, and must spread. "Doctors have estimated that as few as one in a million T-4 cells are infected, which led some to ask where the virus hides. . . ." Another resonant speculation, reported in the same article of the *New York Times* (June 7, 1988): "Infected macrophages can transmit the virus to other cells, possibly by touching the cells" [Sontag's note].

munodeficiency virus (HIV) and early evidence of inroads on the immune system—with a long latency period between infection and the onset of the "telltale" symptoms. (Apparently not as long as syphilis, in which the latency period between secondary and tertiary illness might be decades. But it is worth noting that when syphilis first appeared in epidemic form in Europe at the end of the fifteenth century, it was a rapid disease, of an unexplained virulence that is unknown today, in which death often occurred in the second stage, sometimes within months or a few years.) Cancer *grows* slowly: It is not thought to be, for a long time, latent. (A convincing account of a process in terms of "stages" seems invariably to include the notion of a normative delay or halt in the process, such as is supplied by the notion of latency.) True, a cancer is "staged." This is a principal tool of diagnosis, which means classifying it according to its gravity, determining how "advanced" it is. But it is mostly a spatial notion: that the cancer advances through the body, traveling or migrating along predictable routes. Cancer is first of all a disease of the body's geography, in contrast to syphilis and AIDS, whose definition depends on constructing a temporal sequence of stages.

Syphilis is an affliction that didn't have to run its ghastly full course, to paresis[2] (as it did for Baudelaire and Maupassant and Jules de Goncourt),[3] and could and often did remain at the stage of nuisance, indignity (as it did for Flaubert). The scourge was also a cliché, as Flaubert himself observed. "SYPHILIS. Everybody has it, more or less" reads one entry in the *Dictionary of Accepted Opinions*, his treasury of mid-nineteenth-century platitudes. And syphilis did manage to acquire a darkly positive association in late-nineteenth- and early-twentieth-century Europe, when a link was made between syphilis and heightened ("feverish") mental activity that parallels the connection made since the era of the Romantic writers between pulmonary tuberculosis and heightened emotional activity. As if in honor of all the notable writers and artists who ended their lives in syphilitic witlessness, it came to be believed that the brain lesions of neurosyphilis might actually inspire original thought or art. Thomas Mann, whose fiction is a storehouse of early-twentieth-century disease myths, makes this notion of syphilis as muse central to his *Doctor Faustus*, with its protagonist a great composer whose voluntarily contracted syphilis—the Devil guarantees that the infection will be limited to the central nervous system—confers on him twenty-four years of incandescent creativity. E. M. Cioran recalls how, in Romania in the late 1920s, syphi-

2. An alteration of the brain caused by tertiary syphilis, resulting in paralysis and dementia.
3. Nineteenth-century French writers infected with syphilis.

lis-envy figured in his adolescent expectations of literary glory: he would discover that he had contracted syphilis, be rewarded with several hyperproductive years of genius, then collapse into madness. This romanticizing of the dementia characteristic of neurosyphilis was the forerunner of the much more persistent fantasy in this century about mental illness as a source of artistic creativity or spiritual originality. But with AIDS—though dementia is also a common, late symptom—no compensatory mythology has arisen, or seems likely to arise. AIDS, like cancer, does not allow romanticizing or sentimentalizing, perhaps because its association with death is too powerful. In Krzysztof Zanussi's film *Spiral* (1978), the most truthful account I know of anger at dying, the protagonist's illness is never specified; therefore, it *has* to be cancer. For several generations now, the generic idea of death has been a death from cancer, and a cancer death is experienced as a generic defeat. Now the generic rebuke to life and to hope is AIDS.

"Plague" is the principal metaphor by which the AIDS epidemic is understood. And because of AIDS, the popular misidentification of cancer as an epidemic, even as a plague, seems to be receding: AIDS has banalized cancer.

Plague, from the Latin *plaga* (stroke, wound), has long been used metaphorically as the highest standard of collective calamity, evil, scourge—Procopius, in his masterpiece of calumny, *The Secret History,* called the Emperor Justinian worse than the plague ("fewer escaped")[4]—as well as being a general name for many frightening diseases. Although the disease to which the word is permanently affixed produced the most lethal of recorded epidemics, being experienced as a pitiless slayer is not necessary for a disease to be regarded as plague-like. Leprosy, very rarely fatal now, was not much more so when at its greatest epidemic strength, between about 1050 and 1350. And syphilis has been regarded as a plague—Blake speaks of "the youthful Harlot's curse" that "blights with plagues the Marriage hearse"[5]—not because it killed often, but because it was disgracing, disempowering, disgusting.

It is usually epidemics that are thought of as plagues. And these mass incidences of illness are understood as inflicted, not just endured. Considering illness as a punishment is the oldest idea of what causes illness, and an idea opposed by all attention to the ill that de-

4. Procopius (c. 500–c. 565) was a Byzantine historian whose writings are the chief source of information about the Emperor Justinian (483–565). Bubonic plague broke out in Constantinople in 542.
5. William Blake (1757–1827), English poet; the poem cited is "London."

serves the noble name of medicine. Hippocrates,[6] who wrote several treatises on epidemics, specifically ruled out "the wrath of God" as a cause of bubonic plague. But the illnesses interpreted in antiquity as punishments, like the plague in *Oedipus*, were not thought to be shameful, as leprosy and subsequently syphilis were to be. Diseases, insofar as they acquired meaning, were collective calamities, and judgments on a community. Only injuries and disabilities, not diseases, were thought of as individually merited. For an analogy in the literature of antiquity to the modern sense of a shaming, isolating disease, one would have to turn to Philoctetes and his stinking wound.[7]

The most feared diseases, those that are not simply fatal but transform the body into something alienating, like leprosy and syphilis and cholera and (in the imagination of many) cancer, are the ones that seem particularly susceptible to promotion to "plague." Leprosy and syphilis were the first illnesses to be consistently described as repulsive. It was syphilis that, in the earliest descriptions by doctors at the end of the fifteenth century, generated a version of the metaphors that flourish around AIDS: of a disease that was not only repulsive and retributive but collectively invasive. Although Erasmus, the most influential European pedagogue of the early sixteenth century, described syphilis as "nothing but a kind of leprosy" (by 1529 he called it "something worse than leprosy"), it had already been understood as something different, because sexually transmitted. Paracelsus speaks (in Donne's paraphrase) of "that foule contagious disease which then had invaded mankind in a few places, and since overflowes in all, that for punishment of general licentiousness God first inflicted that disease."[8] Thinking of syphilis as a punishment for an individual's transgression was for a long time, virtually until the disease became easily curable, not really distinct from regarding it as retribution for the licentiousness of a community—as with AIDS now, in the rich industrial countries. In contrast to cancer, understood in a modern way as a disease incurred by (and revealing of) individuals, AIDS is understood in a premodern way, as a disease incurred by people both as individuals and as members of a "risk group"—that neutral-sounding, bureaucratic category which also revives the archaic idea of a tainted community that illness has judged.

Not every account of plague or plaguelike diseases, of course, is a vehicle for lurid stereotypes about illness and the ill. The effort to

6. Greek physician (c. 460–377 B.C.), traditionally regarded as the father of medicine.
7. In mythology, Philoctetes is a Greek warrior whose foot, bitten by a snake, fails to heal and festers for years.
8. Paracelsus (c. 1493–1541), German physician and chemist who studied syphilis. John Donne (1572–1631), English poet and clergyman who cited Paracelsus in the sermon quoted here.

think critically, historically, about illness (about disaster generally) was attempted throughout the eighteenth century: say, from Defoe's *A Journal of the Plague Year* (1722) to Alessandro Manzoni's *The Betrothed* (1827). Defoe's historical fiction, purporting to be an eyewitness account of bubonic plague in London in 1665, does not further any understanding of the plague as punishment or, a later part of the script, as a transforming experience. And Manzoni, in his lengthy account of the passage of plague through the duchy of Milan in 1630, is avowedly committed to presenting a more accurate, less reductive view than his historical sources. But even these two complex narratives reinforce some of the perennial, simplifying ideas about plague.

One feature of the usual script for plague: The disease invariably comes from somewhere else. The names for syphilis, when it began its epidemic sweep through Europe in the last decade of the fifteenth century, are an exemplary illustration of the need to make a dreaded disease foreign.[9] It was the "French pox" to the English, *morbus Germanicus*[1] to the Parisians, the Naples sickness to the Florentines, the Chinese disease to the Japanese. But what may seem like a joke about the inevitability of chauvinism reveals a more important truth: that there is a link between imagining disease and imagining foreignness. It lies perhaps in the very concept of wrong, which is archaically identical with the non-us, the alien. A polluting person is always wrong, as Mary Douglas has observed. The inverse is also true: A person judged to be wrong is regarded as, at least potentially, a source of pollution.

The foreign place of origin of important illnesses, as of drastic changes in the weather, may be no more remote than a neighboring country. Illness is a species of invasion, and indeed is often carried by

9. As noted in the first accounts of the disease: "This malady received from different peoples whom it affected different names," writes Giovanni di Vigo in 1514. Like earlier treatises on syphilis, written in Latin—by Nicolo Leoniceno (1497) and by Juan Almenar (1502)—the one by di Vigo calls it *morbus Gallicus*, the French disease. (Excerpts from this and other accounts of the period, including *Syphilis; Or a Poetical History of the French Disease* [1530] by Girolamo Fracastoro, who coined the name that prevailed, are in *Classic Descriptions of Disease*, edited by Ralph H. Major [1932].) Moralistic explanations abounded from the beginning. In 1495, a year after the epidemic started, the Emperor Maximilian issued an edict declaring syphilis to be an affliction from God for the sins of men.

The theory that syphilis came from even farther than a neighboring country, that it was an entirely new disease in Europe, a disease of the New World brought back to the Old by sailors of Columbus who had contracted it in America, became the accepted explanation of the origin of syphilis in the sixteenth century and is still widely credited. It is worth noting that the earliest medical writers on syphilis did not accept the dubious theory. Leoniceno's *Libellus de Epidemia, quam vulgo morbum Gallicum vocant* starts by taking up the question of whether "the French disease under another name was common to the ancients," and says he believes firmly that it was [Sontag's note].

1. German disease.

soldiers. Manzoni's account of the plague of 1630 (chapters 31 to 37) begins:

> The plague which the Tribunal of Health had feared might enter the Milanese provinces with the German troops had in fact entered, as is well known; and it is also well known that it did not stop there, but went on to invade and depopulate a large part of Italy.

Defoe's chronicle of the plague of 1665 begins similarly, with a flurry of ostentatiously scrupulous speculation about its foreign origin:

> It was about the beginning of September, 1664, that I, among the rest of my neighbours, heard in ordinary discourse that the plague was returned again in Holland; for it had been very violent there, and particularly at Amsterdam and Rotterdam, in the year 1663, whither, they say, it was brought, some said from Italy, others from the Levant, among some goods which were brought home by their Turkey fleet; others said it was brought from Candia; others from Cyprus. It mattered not from whence it came; but all agreed it was come into Holland again.

The bubonic plague that reappeared in London in the 1720s had arrived from Marseilles, which was where plague in the eighteenth century was usually thought to enter Western Europe: brought by seamen, then transported by soldiers and merchants. By the nineteenth century the foreign origin was usually more exotic, the means of transport less specifically imagined, and the illness itself had become phantasmagorical, symbolic.

15 At the end of *Crime and Punishment* Raskolnikov dreams of plague: "He dreamt that the whole world was condemned to a terrible new strange plague that had come to Europe from the depths of Asia." At the beginning of the sentence it is "the whole world," which turns out by the end of the sentence to be "Europe," afflicted by a lethal visitation from Asia. Dostoevsky's model is undoubtedly cholera, called Asiatic cholera, long endemic in Bengal, which had rapidly become and remained through most of the nineteenth century a worldwide epidemic disease. Part of the centuries-old conception of Europe as a privileged cultural entity is that it is a place which is colonized by lethal diseases coming from elsewhere. Europe is assumed to be by rights free of disease. (And Europeans have been astoundingly callous about the far more devastating extent to which they—as invaders, as colonists—have introduced *their* lethal diseases to the exotic, "primitive" world: Think of the ravages of smallpox, influenza, and cholera on the aboriginal populations of the Americas and Australia.) The tenacity of the connection of exotic origin with dreaded disease is one reason why cholera, of which there were four great outbreaks in Europe in the nineteenth century, each with a lower death toll than

the preceding one, has continued to be more memorable than smallpox, whose ravages increased as the century went on (half a million died in the European smallpox pandemic of the early 1870s) but which could not be construed as, plaguelike, a disease with a non-European origin.

Plagues are no longer "sent," as in Biblical and Greek antiquity, for the question of agency has blurred. Instead, peoples are "visited" by plagues. And the visitations recur, as is taken for granted in the subtitle of Defoe's narrative, which explains that it is about that "which happened in London during the Last Great Visitation in 1665." Even for non-Europeans, lethal disease may be called a visitation. But a visitation on "them" is invariably described as different from one on "us." "I believe that about one half of the whole people was carried off by this visitation," wrote the English traveler Alexander Kinglake, reaching Cairo at a time of the bubonic plague (sometimes called "oriental plague"). "The Orientals, however, have more quiet fortitude than Europeans under afflictions of this sort." Kinglake's influential book *Eothen* (1844)—suggestively subtitled "Traces of Travel Brought Home from the East"—illustrates many of the enduring Eurocentric presumptions about others, starting from the fantasy that peoples with little reason to expect exemption from misfortune have a lessened capacity to *feel* misfortune. Thus it is believed that Asians (or the poor, or blacks, or Africans, or Muslims) don't suffer or don't grieve as Europeans (or whites) do. The fact that illness is associated with the poor—who are, from the perspective of the privileged, aliens in one's midst—reinforces the association of illness with the foreign: with an exotic, often primitive place.

Thus, illustrating the classic script for plague, AIDS is thought to have started in the "dark continent," then spread to Haiti, then to the United States and to Europe, then . . . It is understood as a tropical disease: another infestation from the so-called Third World, which is after all where most people in the world live, as well as a scourge of the *tristes tropiques.*[2] Africans who detect racist stereotypes in much of the speculation about the geographical origin of AIDS are not wrong. (Nor are they wrong in thinking that depictions of Africa as the cradle of AIDS must feed anti-African prejudices in Europe and Asia.) The subliminal connection made to notions about a primitive past and the many hypotheses that have been fielded about possible transmission from animals (a disease of green monkeys? African swine fever?) cannot help but activate a familiar set of

2. The sad tropics; also the title of a famous book by the anthropologist Claude Lévi-Strauss.

stereotypes about animality, sexual license, and blacks. In Zaire and other countries in Central Africa where AIDS is killing tens of thousands, the counterreaction has begun. Many doctors, academics, journalists, government officials, and other educated people believe that the virus was sent to Africa from the United States, an act of bacteriological warfare (whose aim was to decrease the African birth rate) which got out of hand and has returned to afflict its perpetrators. A common African version of this belief about the disease's provenance has the virus fabricated in a CIA–Army laboratory in Maryland, sent from there to Africa, and brought back to its country of origin by American homosexual missionaries returning from Africa to Maryland.[3]

At first it was assumed that AIDS must become widespread elsewhere in the same catastrophic form in which it has emerged in Africa, and those who still think this will eventually happen invariably invoke the Black Death. The plague metaphor is an essential vehicle of the most pessimistic reading of the epidemiological prospects. From classic fiction to the latest journalism, the standard plague story is of inexorability, inescapability. The unprepared are taken by surprise; those observing the recommended precautions are struck down as well. *All* succumb when the story is told by an omniscient narrator, as in Poe's parable "The Masque of the Red Death" (1842), inspired by an account of a ball held in Paris during the cholera epidemic of 1832. Almost all—if the story is told from the point of view of a traumatized witness, who will be a benumbed survivor, as in Jean Giono's Stendhalian novel *Horseman on the Roof* (1951), in which a young Italian nobleman in exile wanders through cholera-stricken southern France in the 1830s.

3. The rumor may not have originated as a KGB-sponsored "disinformation" campaign, but it received a crucial push from Soviet propaganda specialists. In October 1985 the Soviet weekly *Literatumaya Gazeta* published an article alleging that the AIDS virus had been engineered by the U.S. government during biological-warfare research at Fort Detrick, Maryland, and was being spread abroad by U.S. servicemen who had been used as guinea pigs. The source cited was an article in the Indian newspaper *Patriot.* Repeated on Moscow's "Radio Peace and Progress" in English, the story was taken up by newspapers and magazines throughout the world. A year later it was featured on the front page of London's conservative, mass-circulation *Sunday Express.* ("The killer AIDS virus was artificially created by American scientists during laboratory experiments which went disastrously wrong—and a massive cover-up has kept the secret from the world until today.") Though ignored by most American newspapers, the *Sunday Express* story was recycled in virtually every other country. As recently as the summer of 1987, it appeared in newspapers in Kenya, Peru, Sudan, Nigeria, Senegal, and Mexico. Gorbachev-era policies have since produced an official denial of the allegations by two eminent members of the Soviet Academy of Sciences, which was published in *Izvestia* in late October 1987. But the story is still being repeated—from Mexico to Zaire, from Australia to Greece [Sontag's note].

QUESTIONS

1. *What does Sontag think is wrong with regarding AIDS as an invasion? And what is wrong about focusing on its supposed African origin? What kinds of prejudices is she trying to get at?*
2. *Why does so much of this essay refer to literature? Just what use does Sontag make of the writers of the past?*
3. *Interview people about their knowledge of AIDS to see if Sontag's points about AIDS and its metaphors get confirmed. Also ask yourself if it is possible to think of any disease without using metaphors. What might Sontag reply?*

George Orwell

POLITICS AND THE ENGLISH LANGUAGE

Most people who bother with the matter at all would admit that the English language is in a bad way, but it is generally assumed that we cannot by conscious action do anything about it. Our civilization is decadent and our language—so the argument runs—must inevitably share in the general collapse. It follows that any struggle against the abuse of language is a sentimental archaism, like preferring candles to electric light or hansom cabs to aeroplanes. Underneath this lies the half-conscious belief that language is a natural growth and not an instrument which we shape for our own purposes.

Now, it is clear that the decline of a language must ultimately have political and economic causes: it is not due simply to the bad influence of this or that individual writer. But an effect can become a cause, reinforcing the original cause and producing the same effect in an intensified form, and so on indefinitely. A man may take to drink because he feels himself to be a failure, and then fail all the more completely because he drinks. It is rather the same thing that is happening to the English language. It becomes ugly and inaccurate because our thoughts are foolish, but the slovenliness of our language makes it easier for us to have foolish thoughts. The point is that the process is reversible. Modern English, especially written English, is full of bad habits which spread by imitation and which can be avoided if one is willing to take the necessary trouble. If one gets rid of these habits one can think more clearly, and to think clearly is a necessary first step towards political regeneration: so that the fight against bad English is

From *Shooting an Elephant and Other Essays* (1950).

not frivolous and is not the exclusive concern of professional writers. I will come back to this presently, and I hope that by that time the meaning of what I have said here will have become clearer. Meanwhile, here are five specimens of the English language as it is now habitually written.

These five passages have not been picked out because they are especially bad—I could have quoted far worse if I had chosen—but because they illustrate various of the mental vices from which we now suffer. They are a little below the average, but are fairly representative samples. I number them so that I can refer back to them when necessary:

> "(1) I am not, indeed, sure whether it is not true to say that the Milton who once seemed not unlike a seventeenth-century Shelley had not become, out of an experience ever more bitter in each year, more alien [*sic*] to the founder of that Jesuit sect which nothing could induce him to tolerate."
>
> Professor Harold Laski (Essay in *Freedom of Expression*).

> "(2) Above all, we cannot play ducks and drakes with a native battery of idioms which prescribes such egregious collocations of vocables as the Basic *put up with* for *tolerate* or *put at a loss* for *bewilder*."
>
> Professor Lancelot Hogben (*Interglossa*).

> "(3) On the one side we have the free personality: by definition it is not neurotic, for it has neither conflict nor dream. Its desires, such as they are, are transparent, for they are just what institutional approval keeps in the forefront of consciousness; another institutional pattern would alter their number and intensity; there is little in them that is natural, irreducible, or culturally dangerous. But *on the other side*, the social bond itself is nothing but the mutual reflection of these self-secure integrities. Recall the definition of love. Is not this the very picture of a small academic? Where is there a place in this hall of mirrors for either personality or fraternity?"
>
> Essay on psychology in *Politics* (New York).

> "(4) All the 'best people' from the gentlemen's clubs, and all the frantic fascist captains, united in common hatred of Socialism and bestial horror of the rising tide of the mass revolutionary movement, have turned to acts of provocation, to foul incendiarism, to medieval legends of poisoned wells, to legalize their own destruction of proletarian organizations, and rouse the agitated petty-bourgeoisie to chauvinistic fervour on behalf of the fight against the revolutionary way out of the crisis."
>
> Communist pamphlet.

> "(5) If a new spirit *is* to be infused into this old country, there is one thorny and contentious reform which must be tackled, and that is the humanization and galvanization of the B.B.C. Timidity here will bespeak

> cancer and atrophy of the soul. The heart of Britain may be sound and of strong beat, for instance, but the British lion's roar at present is like that of Bottom in Shakespeare's *Midsummer Night's Dream*—as gentle as any sucking dove. A virile new Britain cannot continue indefinitely to be traduced in the eyes or rather ears, of the world by the effete languors of Langham Place, brazenly masquerading as 'standard English'. When the Voice of Britain is heard at nine o'clock, better far and infinitely less ludicrous to hear aitches honestly dropped than the present priggish, inflated, inhibited, school-ma'amish arch braying of blameless bashful mewing maidens!"
>
> Letter in *Tribune*.

Each of these passages has faults of its own, but, quite apart from avoidable ugliness, two qualities are common to all of them. The first is staleness of imagery: the other is lack of precision. The writer either has a meaning and cannot express it, or he inadvertently says something else, or he is almost indifferent as to whether his words mean anything or not. This mixture of vagueness and sheer incompetence is the most marked characteristic of modern English prose, and especially of any kind of political writing. As soon as certain topics are raised, the concrete melts into the abstract and no one seems able to think of turns of speech that are not hackneyed: prose consists less and less of *words* chosen for the sake of their meaning, and more and more of *phrases* tacked together like the sections of a prefabricated hen-house. I list below, with notes and examples, various of the tricks by means of which the work of prose-construction is habitually dodged:

Dying Metaphors

A newly invented metaphor assists thought by evoking a visual 5
image, while on the other hand a metaphor which is technically "dead" (e.g. *iron resolution*) has in effect reverted to being an ordinary word and can generally be used without loss of vividness. But in between these two classes there is a huge dump of worn-out metaphors which have lost all evocative power and are merely used because they save people the trouble of inventing phrases for themselves. Examples are: *Ring the changes on, take up the cudgels for, toe the line, ride roughshod over, stand shoulder to shoulder with, play into the hands of, no axe to grind, grist to the mill, fishing in troubled waters, on the order of the day, Achilles' heel, swan song, hotbed.* Many of these are used without knowledge of their meaning (what is a "rift," for instance?), and incompatible metaphors are frequently mixed, a sure sign that the writer is not interested in what he is saying. Some metaphors now current have been twisted out of their original meaning without those who use them even being aware of the fact. For example, *toe the line* is some-

times written *tow the line*. Another example is *the hammer and the anvil*, now always used with the implication that the anvil gets the worst of it. In real life it is always the anvil that breaks the hammer, never the other way about: a writer who stopped to think what he was saying would be aware of this, and would avoid perverting the original phrase.

Operators or Verbal False Limbs

These save the trouble of picking out appropriate verbs and nouns, and at the same time pad each sentence with extra syllables which give it an appearance of symmetry. Characteristic phrases are: *render inoperative, militate against, make contact with, be subjected to, give rise to, give grounds for, have the effect of, play a leading part (role) in, make itself felt, take effect, exhibit a tendency to, serve the purpose of, etc., etc.* The keynote is the elimination of simple verbs. Instead of being a single word, such as *break, stop, spoil, mend, kill*, a verb becomes a *phrase*, made up of a noun or adjective tacked on to some general-purposes verb such as *prove, serve, form, play, render*. In addition, the passive voice is wherever possible used in preference to the active, and noun constructions are used instead of gerunds (*by examination of* instead of *by examining*). The range of verbs is further cut down by means of the *-ize* and *de-* formation, and the banal statements are given an appearance of profundity by means of the *not un-* formation. Simple conjunctions and prepositions are replaced by such phrases as *with respect to, having regard to, the fact that, by dint of, in view of, in the interests of, on the hypothesis that*; and the ends of sentences are saved from anticlimax by such resounding commonplaces as *greatly to be desired, cannot be left out of account, a development to be expected in the near future, deserving of serious consideration, brought to a satisfactory conclusion*, and so on and so forth.

Pretentious Diction

Words like *phenomenon, element, individual* (as noun), *objective, categorical, effective, virtual, basic, primary, promote, constitute, exhibit, exploit, utilize, eliminate, liquidate*, are used to dress up simple statements and give an air of scientific impartiality to biased judgments. Adjectives like *epoch-making, epic, historic, unforgettable, triumphant, age-old, inevitable, inexorable, veritable*, are used to dignify the sordid processes of international politics, while writing that aims at glorifying war usually takes on an archaic colour, its characteristic words being: *realm, throne, chariot, mailed fist, trident, sword, shield, buckler, banner, jackboot, clarion*. Foreign words and expressions such as *cul de sac, ancien régime, deus ex machina, mutatis mutandis, status quo, gleichschaltung, weltanschauung,* are used to give an air of culture and elegance. Except for the useful abbreviations *i.e., e.g.,* and *etc.,* there is no real need for any of the hundreds of foreign phrases now current in English. Bad writers, and especially scientific, political and sociological writers, are nearly aways haunted by the notion that Latin or Greek words are grander than Saxon ones, and unnecessary words like *expedite, ameliorate, predict, extraneous, deracinated, clandestine, subaqueous* and hundreds of others constantly gain ground from their Anglo-Saxon opposite numbers.[1] The jargon peculiar to Marxist writing (*hyena, hangman, cannibal, petty bourgeois, these gentry, lacquey, flunkey, mad dog, White Guard,* etc.) consists largely of words and phrases translated from Russian, German or French; but the normal way of coining a new word is to use a Latin or Greek root with the appropriate affix and, where necessary, the *-ize* formation. It is often easier to make up words of this kind (*deregionalize, impermissible, extramarital, nonfragmentatory* and so forth) than to think up the English words that will cover one's meaning. The result, in general, is an increase in slovenliness and vagueness.

Meaningless Words

In certain kinds of writing, particularly in art criticism and literary criticism, it is normal to come across long passages which are almost completely lacking in meaning.[2] Words like *romantic, plastic, values, human, dead, sentimental, natural, vitality,* as used in art criticism, are strictly meaningless in the sense that they not only do not point to any discoverable object, but are hardly ever expected to do so by the reader. When one critic writes, "The outstanding feature of Mr. X's work is its living quality," while another writes, "The immediately striking thing about Mr. X's work is its peculiar deadness," the reader accepts this as a simple difference of opinion. If words like *black* and *white* were involved, instead of the jargon words *dead* and *living,* he would see at once that language was being used in an improper way.

1. An interesting illustration of this is the way in which the English flower names which were in use till very recently are being ousted by Greek ones, *snapdragon* becoming *antirrhinum, forget-me-not* becoming *myosotis,* etc. It is hard to see any practical reason for this change of fashion: it is probably due to an instinctive turning-away from the more homely word and a vague feeling that the Greek word is scientific [Orwell's note].
2. Example: "Comfort's catholicity of perception and image, strangely Whitmanesque in range, almost the exact opposite in aesthetic compulsion, continues to evoke that trembling atmospheric accumulative hinting at a cruel, an inexorably serene timelessness. . . . Wrey Gardiner scores by aiming at simple bull's-eyes with precision. Only they are not so simple, and through this contented sadness- runs more than the surface bittersweet of resignation" (*Poetry Quarterly*) [Orwell's note].

Many political words are similarly abused. The word *Fascism* has now no meaning except in so far as it signifies "something not desirable." The words *democracy, socialism, freedom, patriotic, realistic, justice,* have each of them several different meanings which cannot be reconciled with one another. In the case of a word like *democracy,* not only is there no agreed definition, but the attempt to make one is resisted from all sides. It is almost universally felt that when we call a country democratic we are praising it: consequently the defenders of every kind of régime claim that it is a democracy, and fear that they might have to stop using the word if it were tied down to any one meaning. Words of this kind are often used in a consciously dishonest way. That is, the person who uses them has his own private definition, but allows his hearer to think he means something quite different. Statements like *Marshal Pétain was a true patriot, The Soviet Press is the freest in the world, The Catholic Church is opposed to persecution,* are almost always made with intent to deceive. Other words used in variable meanings, in most cases more or less dishonestly, are: *class, totalitarian, science, progressive, reactionary, bourgeois, equality.*

Now that I have made this catalogue of swindles and perversions, let me give another example of the kind of writing that they lead to. This time it must of its nature be an imaginary one. I am going to translate a passage of good English into modern English of the worst sort. Here is a well-known verse from *Ecclesiastes:*

> "I returned and saw under the sun, that the race is not to the swift, nor the battle to the strong, neither yet bread to the wise, nor yet riches to men of understanding, nor yet favour to men of skill; but time and chance happeneth to them all."

10 Here it is in modern English:

> "Objective consideration of contemporary phenomena compels the conclusion that success or failure in competitive activities exhibits no tendency to be commensurate with innate capacity, but that a considerable element of the unpredictable must invariably be taken into account."

This is a parody, but not a very gross one. Exhibit (3), above, for instance, contains several patches of the same kind of English. It will be seen that I have not made a full translation. The beginning and ending of the sentence follow the original meaning fairly closely, but in the middle the concrete illustrations—race, battle, bread—dissolve into the vague phrase "success or failure in competitive activities." This had to be so, because no modern writer of the kind I am discussing—no one capable of using phrases like "objective consideration of contemporary phenomena"—would ever tabulate his thoughts in that precise and detailed way. The whole tendency of modern prose is away from concreteness. Now analyse these two sentences a little more closely. The first contains forty-nine words but only sixty syllables, and all its words are those of everyday life. The second contains thirty-eight words of ninety syllables: eighteen of its words are from Latin roots, and one from Greek. The first sentence contains six vivid images, and only one phrase ("time and chance") that could be called vague. The second contains not a single fresh, arresting phrase, and in spite of its ninety syllables it gives only a shortened version of the meaning contained in the first. Yet without a doubt it is the second kind of sentence that is gaining ground in modern English. I do not want to exaggerate. This kind of writing is not yet universal, and outcrops of simplicity will occur here and there in the worst-written page. Still, if you or I were told to write a few lines on the uncertainty of human fortunes, we should probably come much nearer to my imaginary sentence than to the one from *Ecclesiastes*.

As I have tried to show, modern writing at its worst does not consist in picking out words for the sake of their meaning and inventing images in order to make the meaning clearer. It consists in gumming together long strips of words which have already been set in order by someone else, and making the results presentable by sheer humbug. The attraction of this way of writing is that it is easy. It is easier—even quicker, once you have the habit—to say *In my opinion it is a not unjustifiable assumption that* than to say *I think*. If you use ready-made phrases, you not only don't have to hunt about for words; you also don't have to bother with the rhythms of your sentences, since these phrases are generally so arranged as to be more or less euphonious. When you are composing in a hurry—when you are dictating to a stenographer, for instance, or making a public speech—it is natural to fall into a pretentious, Latinized style. Tags like *a consideration which we should do well to bear in mind* or *a conclusion to which all of us would readily assent* will save many a sentence from coming down with a bump. By using stale metaphors, similes and idioms, you save much mental effort, at the cost of leaving your meaning vague, not only for your reader but for yourself. This is the significance of mixed metaphors. The sole aim of a metaphor is to call up a visual image. When these images clash—as in *The Fascist octopus has sung its swan song, the jackboot is thrown into the melting pot*—it can be taken as certain that the writer is not seeing a mental image of the objects he is naming; in other words he is not really thinking. Look again at the examples I gave at the beginning of this essay. Professor Laski (1) uses five negatives in fifty-three words. One of these is superfluous, making nonsense of the whole passage, and in addition there is the slip *alien* for akin, making further nonsense, and several avoidable pieces of clumsiness which increase the general vagueness. Professor Hogben (2) plays ducks and drakes with a battery which is able to write prescriptions, and, while disapproving of the everyday phrase *put up with*, is unwilling to look *egregious* up in the dictionary and see what it means. (3), if one takes an uncharitable attitude towards it, is simply meaningless: probably one could work out its intended meaning by reading the whole of the article in which it occurs. In (4), the writer knows more or less what he wants to say, but an accumulation of stale phrases chokes him like tea leaves blocking a sink. In (5), words and meaning have almost parted company. People who write in this manner usually have a general emotional meaning—they dislike one thing and want to express solidarity with another—but they are not interested in the detail of what they are saying. A scrupulous writer, in every sentence that he writes, will ask himself at least four questions, thus: What am I trying to say? What words will express it? What image or idiom will make it clearer? Is this image fresh enough to have an effect? And he will probably ask himself two more: Could I put it more shortly? Have I said anything that is avoidably ugly? But you are not obliged to go to all this trouble. You can shirk it by simply throwing your mind open and letting the ready-made phrases come crowding in. They will construct your sentences for you—even think your thoughts for you, to a certain extent—and at need they will perform the important service of partially concealing your meaning even from yourself. It is at this point that the special connection between politics and the debasement of language becomes clear.

In our time it is broadly true that political writing is bad writing. Where it is not true, it will generally be found that the writer is some kind of rebel, expressing his private opinions and not a "party line." Orthodoxy, of whatever colour, seems to demand a lifeless, imitative style. The political dialects to be found in pamphlets, leading articles, manifestos, White Papers and the speeches of under-secretaries do, of course, vary from party to party, but they are all alike in that one almost never finds in them a fresh, vivid, home-made turn of speech. When one watches some tired hack on the platform mechanically repeating the familiar phrases—*bestial atrocities, iron heel, bloodstained tyranny, free peoples of the world, stand shoulder to shoulder*—one often has a curious feeling that one is not watching a live human being but some kind of dummy: a feeling which suddenly becomes stronger at moments when the light catches the speaker's spectacles and turns them into blank discs which seem to have no eyes behind them. And this is not altogether fanciful. A speaker who uses that kind of phraseology has gone some distance towards turning himself into a machine. The appropriate noises are coming out of his larynx, but his brain is not involved as it would be if he were choosing his words for himself. If the speech he is making is one that he is accustomed to make over and over again, he may be almost unconscious of what he is saying, as one is when one utters the responses in church. And this reduced state of consciousness, if not indispensable, is at any rate favourable to political conformity.

In our time, political speech and writing are largely the defence of the indefensible. Things like the continuance of British rule in India, the Russian purges and deportations, the dropping of the atom bombs on Japan, can indeed be defended, but only by arguments which are too brutal for most people to face, and which do not square with the professed aims of political parties. Thus political language has to consist largely of euphemism, question-begging and sheer cloudy vagueness. Defenceless villages are bombarded from the air, the inhabitants driven out into the countryside, the cattle machine-gunned, the huts set on fire with incendiary bullets: this is called *pacification*. Millions of peasants are robbed of their farms and sent trudging along the roads with no more than they can carry: this is called *transfer of population* or *rectification of frontiers*. People are imprisoned for years without trial, or shot in the back of the neck or sent to die of scurvy in Arctic lumber camps: this is called *elimination of unreliable elements*. Such phraseology is needed if one wants to name things without calling up mental pictures of them. Consider for instance some comfortable English professor defending Russian totalitarianism. He cannot say outright, "I believe in killing off your opponents when you can get good results by doing so." Probably, therefore, he will say something like this:

"While freely conceding that the Soviet régime exhibits certain fea- 15
tures which the humanitarian may be inclined to deplore, we must, I think, agree that a certain curtailment of the right to political opposition is an unavoidable concomitant of transitional periods, and that the rigors which the Russian people have been called upon to undergo have been amply justified in the sphere of concrete achievement."

The inflated style is itself a kind of euphemism. A mass of Latin words falls upon the facts like soft snow, blurring the outlines and covering up all the details. The great enemy of clear language is insincerity. When there is a gap between one's real and one's declared aims, one turns as it were instinctively to long words and exhausted idioms, like a cuttlefish squirting out ink. In our age there is no such thing as "keeping out of politics." All issues are political issues, and politics itself is a mass of lies, evasions, folly, hatred and schizophrenia. When the general atmosphere is bad, language must suffer. I should expect to find—this is a guess which I have not sufficient knowledge to verify—that the German, Russian and Italian languages have all deteriorated in the last ten or fifteen years, as a result of dictatorship.

But if thought corrupts language, language can also corrupt thought. A bad usage can spread by tradition and imitation, even among people who should and do know better. The debased language that I have been discussing is in some ways very convenient. Phrases like *a not unjustifiable assumption, leaves much to be desired, would serve no good purpose, a consideration which we should do well to bear in mind,* are a continuous temptation, a packet of aspirins always at one's elbow. Look back through this essay, and for certain you will find that I have again and again committed the very faults I am protesting against. By this morning's post I have received a pamphlet dealing with conditions in Germany. The author tells me that he "felt impelled" to write it. I open it at random, and here is almost the first sentence that I see: "(The Allies) have an opportunity not only of achieving a radical transformation of Germany's social and political structure in such a way as to avoid a nationalistic reaction in Germany itself, but at the same time of laying the foundations of a co-operative and unified Europe." You see, he "feels impelled" to write—feels, presumably, that he has something new to say—and yet his words, like cavalry horses answering the bugle, group themselves automatically into the familiar dreary pattern. This invasion of one's mind by ready-made phrases (*lay the foundations, achieve a radical transformation*) can only be prevented if one is constantly on guard against them, and every such phrase anaesthetizes a portion of one's brain.

I said earlier that the decadence of our language is probably curable. Those who deny this would argue, if they produced an argument at all, that language merely reflects existing social conditions, and that we cannot influence its development by any direct tinkering with words and constructions. So far as the general tone or spirit of a language goes, this may be true, but it is not true in detail. Silly words and expressions have often disappeared, not through any evolutionary process but owing to the conscious action of a minority. Two recent examples were *explore every avenue* and *leave no stone unturned,* which were killed by the jeers of a few journalists. There is a long list of flyblown metaphors which could similarly be got rid of if enough people would interest themselves in the job; and it should also be possible to laugh the *not un-* formation out of existence,[3] to reduce the amount of Latin and Greek in the average sentence, to drive out foreign phrases and strayed scientific words, and, in general, to make pretentiousness unfashionable. But all these are minor points. The defence of the English language implies more than this, and perhaps it is best to start by saying what it does *not* imply.

3. One can cure oneself of the *not un-*formation by memorizing this sentence: *A not unblack dog was chasing a not unsmall rabbit across a not ungreen field* [Orwell's note].

To begin with it has nothing to do with archaism, with the salvaging of obsolete words and turns of speech, or with the setting up of a "standard English" which must never be departed from. On the contrary, it is especially concerned with the scrapping of every word or idiom which has outworn its usefulness. It has nothing to do with correct grammar and syntax, which are of no importance so long as one makes one's meaning clear, or with the avoidance of Americanisms, or with having what is called a "good prose style." On the other hand it is not concerned with fake simplicity and the attempt to make written English colloquial. Nor does it even imply in every case preferring the Saxon word to the Latin one, though it does imply using the fewest and shortest words that will cover one's meaning. What is above all needed is to let the meaning choose the word, and not the other way about. In prose, the worst thing one can do with words is to surrender to them. When you think of a concrete object, you think wordlessly, and then, if you want to describe the thing you have been visualizing you probably hunt about till you find the exact words that seem to fit. When you think of something abstract you are more inclined to use words from the start, and unless you make a conscious effort to prevent it, the existing dialect will come rushing in and do the job for you, at the expense of blurring or even changing your meaning. Probably it is better to put off using words as long as possible and get one's meaning as clear as one can through pictures or sensations. Afterwards one can choose—not simply *accept*—the phrases that will best cover the meaning, and then switch round and decide what impression one's words are likely to make on another person. This last effort of the mind cuts out all stale or mixed images, all prefabricated phrases, needless repetitions, and humbug and vagueness generally. But one can often be in doubt about the effect of a word or a phrase, and one needs rules that one can rely on when instinct fails. I think the following rules will cover most cases:

(i) Never use a metaphor, simile or other figure of speech which you are used to seeing in print.

(ii) Never use a long word where a short one will do.

(iii) If it is possible to cut a word out, always cut it out.

(iv) Never use the passive where you can use the active.

(v) Never use a foreign phrase, a scientific word or a jargon word if you can think of an everyday English equivalent.

(vi) Break any of these rules sooner than say anything outright barbarous.

These rules sound elementary, and so they are, but they demand a deep change of attitude in anyone who has grown used to writing in the style now fashionable. One could keep all of them and still write bad English, but one could not write the kind of stuff that I quoted in those five specimens at the beginning of this article.

20 I have not here been considering the literary use of language, but merely language as an instrument for expressing and not for concealing or preventing thought. Stuart Chase and others have come near to claiming that all abstract words are meaningless, and have used this as a pretext for advocating a kind of political quietism. Since you don't know what Fascism is, how can you struggle against Fascism? One need not swallow such absurdities as this, but one ought to recognize that the present political chaos is connected with the decay of language, and that one can probably bring about some improvement by starting at the verbal end. If you simplify your English, you are freed from the worst follies of orthodoxy. You cannot speak any of the necessary dialects, and when you make a stupid remark its stupidity will be obvious, even to yourself. Political language—and with variations this is true of all political parties, from Conservatives to Anarchists—is designed to make lies sound truthful and murder respectable, and to give an appearance of solidity to pure wind. One cannot change this all in a moment, but one can at least change one's own habits, and from time to time one can even, if one jeers loudly enough, send some worn-out and useless phrase—some *jackboot, Achilles' heel, hotbed, melting pot, acid test, veritable inferno* or other lump of verbal refuse—into the dustbin where it belongs.

QUESTIONS

1. *State Orwell's main point as precisely as possible.*
2. *What kind of prose is Orwell writing about? Is it a kind you are familiar with? What sort of people read that kind of writing?*
3. *Apply rule iv (paragraph 19) to paragraph 14. Is Orwell forgetting his own rule? Or does he have a good enough reason for using all those passives? Try rewriting the paragraph to get rid of the passives. Have you said "anything outright barbarous"?*
4. *Orwell wrote this essay in 1946. Using examples from current media, write an essay discussing whether or not the outcomes Orwell feared have come to pass in the ensuing half century.*

An Album of Styles

Francis Bacon: Of Youth and Age

A man that is young in years may be old in hours, if he have lost no time. But that happeneth rarely. Generally, youth is like the first cogitations, not so wise as the second. For there is a youth in thoughts as well as in ages. And yet the invention of young men is more lively than that of old, and imaginations stream into their minds better, and as it were more divinely. Natures that have much heat, and great and violent desires and perturbations, are not ripe for action till they have passed the meridian of their years: as it was with Julius Caesar,[1] and Septimius Severus. Of the latter of whom it is said, *Juventutem egit erroribus, imo furoribus, plenam:*[2] and yet he was the ablest emperor, almost, of all the list. But reposed natures may do well in youth. As it is seen in Augustus Caesar, Cosmus, Duke of Florence, Gaston de Foix,[3] and others. On the other side, heat and vivacity in age is an excellent composition for business. Young men are fitter to invent than to judge, fitter for execution than for counsel, and fitter for new projects than for settled business. For the experience of age, in things that fall within the compass of it, directeth them, but in new things abuseth them. The errors of young men are the ruin of business; but the errors of aged men amount but to this, that more might have been done, or sooner. Young men, in the conduct and manage of actions, embrace more than they can hold; stir more than they can quiet; fly to

From *Essays* (various editions, 1597–1625).

1. Julius Caesar (100–44 B.C.) became dictator of Rome in 49 B.C.
2. Severus (A.D. 145/6–211) became emperor of Rome in A.D. 193 "He passed a youth full of folly, or rather of madness," according to Spartianus *(Life of Severus)*.
3. Duke of Nemours and nephew of Louis XII of France, died in battle in 1512, at 22. Augustus Caesar (63 B.C.–A.D. 14) became ruler of Rome in 27 B.C. Cosimo de' Medici (1519–1574) became ruler of Florence in 1537.

the end, without consideration of the means and degrees; pursue some few principles which they have chanced upon absurdly; care not to innovate,[4] which draws unknown inconveniences; use extreme remedies at first; and, that which doubleth all errors, will not acknowledge or retract them; like an unready horse that will neither stop nor turn. Men of age object too much, consult too long, adventure too little, repent too soon, and seldom drive business home to the full period, but content themselves with a mediocrity of success. Certainly it is good to compound employments of both; for that will be good for the present, because the virtues of either age may correct the defects of both; and good for succession, that young men may be learners while men in age are actors; and, lastly, good for extern accidents, because authority followeth old men, and favour and popularity youth. But for the moral part, perhaps youth will have the pre-eminence, as age hath for the politic. A certain rabbin, upon the text, *Your young men shall see visions, and your old men shall dream dreams*,[5] inferreth that young men are admitted nearer to God than old, because vision is a clearer revelation than a dream. And certainly, the more a man drinketh of the world, the more it intoxicateth; and age doth profit rather in the powers of understanding than in the virtues of the will and affections. There be some have an over-early ripeness in their years, which fadeth betimes. These are, first, such as have brittle wits, the edge whereof is soon turned; such as was Hermogenes the rhetorician, whose books are exceeding subtle, who afterwards waxed stupid.[6] A second sort is of those that have some natural dispositions which have better grace in youth than in age, such as is a fluent and luxuriant speech, which becomes youth well, but not age: so Tully saith of Hortensius, *Idem manebat, neque idem docebat.*[7] The third is of such as take too high a strain at the first, and are magnanimous more than tract of years can uphold. As was Scipio Africanus, of whom Livy saith in effect, *Ultima primis cedebant.*[8]

4. Are not careful about innovating.
5. Joel 2.28.
6. Hermogenes, Greek rhetorician of the 2nd century A.D., is said to have lost his memory when young.
7. "He remained the same when the same style no longer became him," (Cicero, *Brutus*); said by Cicero (or Tully) of a rival orator.
8. "His last actions were not the equal of his first" (*Heroides* 9); Bacon quotes from Ovid the poet (43 B.C.–A.D. 17) to express the gist of what Livy the historian (59 B.C.–A.D. 17) said of Africanus (236–183 or 184 B.C.), Roman conqueror of Africa.

John Donne: No Man Is an Island

No man is an island, entire of itself; every man is a piece of the continent, a part of the main.[1] If a clod be washed away by the sea, Europe is the less, as well as if a promontory were, as well as if a manor of thy friend's or of thine own were. Any man's death diminishes me, because I am involved in mankind; and therefore never send to know for whom the bell tolls; it tolls for thee.

From *Meditation 17* of Donne's *Devotions upon Emergent Occasions* (1623).

1. Mainland.

Samuel Johnson: The Pyramids

Of the wall [of China] it is very easy to assign the motives. It secured a wealthy and timorous nation from the incursions of Barbarians, whose unskillfulness in arts made it easier for them to supply their wants by rapine than by industry, and who from time to time poured in upon the habitations of peaceful commerce, as vultures descend upon domestic fowl. Their celerity and fierceness made the wall necessary, and their ignorance made it efficacious.

But for the pyramids no reason has ever been given adequate to the cost and labor of the work. The narrowness of the chambers proves that it could afford no retreat from enemies, and treasures might have been reposited at far less expense with equal security. It seems to have been erected only in compliance with that hunger of imagination which preys incessantly upon life, and must be always appeased by some employment. Those who have already all that they can enjoy, must enlarge their desires. He that has built for use, till use is supplied, must begin to build for vanity, and extend his plan to the utmost power of human performance, that he may not be soon reduced to form another wish.

I consider this mighty structure as a monument of the insufficiency of human enjoyments. A king, whose power is unlimited, and whose treasures surmount all real and imaginary wants, is compelled to sol-

From *Rasselas* (1759).

ace, by the erection of a pyramid, the satiety of dominion and tastelessness of pleasures, and to amuse the tediousness of declining life, by seeing thousands laboring without end, and one stone, for no purpose, laid upon another. Whoever thou art, that, not content with a moderate condition, imaginest happiness in royal magnificence, and dreamest that command or riches can feed the appetite of novelty with perpetual gratifications, survey the pyramids, and confess thy folly!

William Hazlitt: ON THE WANT OF MONEY

Literally and truly, one cannot get on well in the world without money. To be in want of it, is to pass through life with little credit or pleasure; it is to live out of the world, or to be despised if you come into it; it is not to be sent for to court, or asked out to dinner, or noticed in the street; it is not to have your opinion consulted or else rejected with contempt, to have your acquirements carped at and doubted, your good things disparaged, and at last to lose the wit and the spirit to say them; it is to be scrutinized by strangers, and neglected by friends; it is to be a thrall to circumstances, an exile in one's own country; to forego leisure, freedom, ease of body and mind, to be dependent on the goodwill and caprice of others, or earn a precarious and irksome livelihood by some laborious employment; it is to be compelled to stand behind a counter, or to sit at a desk in some public office, or to marry your landlady, or not the person you would wish; or to go out to the East or West Indies, or to get a situation as judge abroad, and return home with a liver-complaint; or to be a law-stationer, or a scrivener or scavenger, or newspaper reporter; or to read law and sit in court without a brief; or to be deprived of the use of your fingers by transcribing Greek manuscripts, or to be a seal-engraver and pore yourself blind; or to go upon the stage, or try some of the Fine Arts; with all your pains, anxiety, and hopes, most probably to fail, or, if you succeed, after the exertions of years, and undergoing constant distress of mind and fortune, to be assailed on every side with envy, back-biting, and falsehood, or to be a favourite with the public for awhile, and then thrown into the background—or a gaol, by the fickleness of taste and some new favourite; to be full of enthusiasm and extravagance in youth, of chagrin and disappointment in after-life; to be jostled by the rabble because you do not ride in your coach, or avoided by those who know your worth and shrink

Originally appeared in *The Monthly Magazine* (Jan. 1827); reprinted in *Literary Remains* (1836).

from it as a claim on their respect or their purse; to be a burden to your relations, or unable to do anything for them; to be ashamed to venture into crowds; to have cold comfort at home; to lose by degrees your confidence and any talent you might possess; to grow crabbed, morose, and querulous, dissatisfied with every one, but most so with yourself; and plagued out of your life, to look about for a place to die in, and quit the world without any one's asking after your will. The *wiseacres* [1] will possibly, however, crowd round your coffin, and raise a monument at a considerable expense, and after a lapse of time, to commemorate your genius and your misfortunes!

1. An obnoxiously self-assured person, a smart aleck.

John Henry Newman: KNOWLEDGE AND VIRTUE

Knowledge is one thing, virtue is another; good sense is not conscience, refinement is not humility, nor is largeness and justness of view faith. Philosophy, however enlightened, however profound, gives no command over the passions, no influential motives, no vivifying principles. Liberal Education makes not the Christian, not the Catholic, but the gentleman. It is well to be a gentleman, it is well to have a cultivated intellect, a delicate taste, a candid, equitable, dispassionate mind, a noble and courteous bearing in the conduct of life—these are the connatural qualities of a large knowledge; they are the objects of a University; I am advocating, I shall illustrate and insist upon them; but still, I repeat, they are no guarantee for sanctity or even for conscientiousness, they may attach to the man of the world, to the profligate, to the heartless, pleasant, alas, and attractive as he shows when decked out in them. Taken by themselves, they do but seem to be what they are not; they look like virtue at a distance, but they are detected by close observers, and on the long run; and hence it is that they are popularly accused of pretense and hypocrisy, not, I repeat, from their own fault, but because their professors and their admirers persist in taking them for what they are not, and are officious in arrogating for them a praise to which they have no claim. Quarry the granite rock with razors, or moor the vessel with a thread of silk; then may you hope with such keen and delicate instruments as human knowledge and human reason to contend against those giants, the passion and the pride of man.

From *The Idea of a University Defined and Illustrated* (1852).

Abraham Lincoln: The Gettysburg Address

Four score and seven years ago our fathers brought forth on this continent, a new nation, conceived in Liberty, and dedicated to the proposition that all men are created equal.

Now we are engaged in a great civil war, testing whether that nation, or any nation so conceived and so dedicated, can long endure. We are met on a great battle-field of that war. We have come to dedicate a portion of that field, as a final resting place for those who here gave their lives that that nation might live. It is altogether fitting and proper that we should do this.

But, in a larger sense, we can not dedicate—we can not consecrate—we can not hallow—this ground. The brave men, living and dead, who struggled here, have consecrated it, far above our poor power to add or detract. The world will little note, nor long remember what we say here, but it can never forget what they did here. It is for us the living, rather, to be dedicated here to the unfinished work which they who fought here have thus far so nobly advanced. It is rather for us to be here dedicated to the great task remaining before us—that from these honored dead we take increased devotion to that cause for which they gave the last full measure of devotion—that we here highly resolve that these dead shall not have died in vain—that this nation, under God, shall have a new birth of freedom—and that government of the people, by the people, for the people, shall not perish from the earth.

Presidential address delivered in 1863 in Gettysburg, Pennsylvania.

Walter Pater: The Mona Lisa

The presence that rose thus so strangely beside the waters, is expressive of what in the ways of a thousand years men had come to desire. Hers is the head upon which all "the ends of the world are come,"[1]

From Pater's essay on Leonardo da Vinci in his first book, *Studies in the History of the Renaissance* (1873).

1. 1 Corinthians 10.11.

and the eyelids are a little weary. It is a beauty wrought out from within upon the flesh, the deposit, little cell by cell, of strange thoughts and fantastic reveries and exquisite passions. Set it for a moment beside one of those white Greek goddesses or beautiful women of antiquity, and how would they be troubled by this beauty, into which the soul with all its maladies has passed! All the thoughts and experience of the world have etched and molded there, in that which they have of power to refine and make expressive the outward form, the animalism of Greece, the lust of Rome, the mysticism of the middle ages with its spiritual ambition and imaginative loves, the return of the Pagan world, the sins of the Borgias.[2] She is older than the rocks among which she sits; like the vampire, she has been dead many times, and learned the secrets of the grave; and has been a diver in deep seas, and keeps their fallen day about her; and trafficked for strange webs with Eastern merchants: and, as Leda, was the mother of Helen of Troy, and, as Saint Anne, the mother of Mary; and all this has been to her but as the sound of lyres and flutes, and lives only in the delicacy with which it has molded the changing lineaments, and tinged the eyelids and the hands. The fancy of a perpetual life, sweeping together ten-thousand experiences, is an old one; and modern philosophy has conceived the idea of humanity as wrought upon by, and summing up in itself, all modes of thought and life. Certainly Lady Lisa might stand as the embodiment of the old fancy, the symbol of the modern idea.

2. An Italian family influential during the fourteents, fifteenth, and sixteenth centuries.

Ernest Hemingway: FROM A FAREWELL TO ARMS

I was always embarrassed by the words sacred, glorious, and sacrifice and the expression in vain. We had heard them, sometimes standing in the rain almost out of earshot, so that only the shouted words came through, and had read them, on proclamations that were slapped up by billposters over other proclamations, now for a long time, and I had seen nothing sacred, and the things that were glorious had no glory and the sacrifices were like the stockyards at Chicago if nothing was done with the meat except to bury it. There were many words that you could not stand to hear and finally only the names of places had dignity. Certain numbers were the same way and certain dates and these

From A *Farewell to Arms* (1929).

with the names of places were all you could say and have them mean anything. Abstract words such as glory, honor, courage, or hallow were obscene beside the concrete names of villages, the numbers of roads, the names of rivers, the numbers of regiments and the dates.

Virginia Woolf: WHAT THE NOVELIST GIVES US

It is simple enough to say that since books have classes—fiction, biography, poetry—we should separate them and take from each what it is right that each should give us. Yet few people ask from books what books can give us. Most commonly we come to books with blurred and divided minds, asking of fiction that it shall be true, of poetry that it shall be false, of biography that it shall be flattering, of history that it shall enforce our own prejudices. If we could banish all such preconceptions when we read, that would be an admirable beginning. Do not dictate to your author; try to become him. Be his fellow-worker and accomplice. If you hang back, and reserve and criticize at first, you are preventing yourself from getting the fullest possible value from what you read. But if you open your mind as widely as possible, then signs and hints of almost imperceptible fineness, from the twist and turn of the first sentences, will bring you into the presence of a human being unlike any other. Steep yourself in this, acquaint yourself with this, and soon you will find that your author is giving you, or attempting to give you, something far more definite. The thirty-two chapters of a novel—if we consider how to read a novel first—are an attempt to make something as formed and controlled as a building: but words are more impalpable than bricks; reading is a longer and more complicated process than seeing. Perhaps the quickest way to understand the elements of what a novelist is doing is not to read, but to write; to make your own experiment with the dangers and difficulties of words. Recall, then, some event that has left a distinct impression on you—how at the corner of the street, perhaps, you passed two people talking. A tree shook; an electric light danced; the tone of the talk was comic, but also tragic; a whole vision, an entire conception, seemed contained in that moment.

But when you attempt to reconstruct it in words, you will find that it breaks into a thousand conflicting impressions. Some must be sub-

From the essay "How Should One Read a Book?" in *The Second Common Reader* (1932).

dued; others emphasized; in the process you will lose, probably, all grasp upon the emotion itself. Then turn from your blurred and littered pages to the opening pages of some great novelist—Defoe, Jane Austen, Hardy. Now you will be better able to appreciate their mastery. It is not merely that we are in the presence of a different person—Defoe, Jane Austen, or Thomas Hardy—but that we are living in a different world. Here, in *Robinson Crusoe,* we are trudging a plain high road; one thing happens after another; the fact and the order of the fact is enough. But if the open air and adventure mean everything to Defoe they mean nothing to Jane Austen. Hers is the drawing-room, and people talking, and by the many mirrors of their talk revealing their characters. And if, when we have accustomed ourselves to the drawing-room and its reflections, we turn to Hardy, we are once more spun around. The moors are round us and the stars are above our heads. The other side of the mind is now exposed—the dark side that comes uppermost in solitude, not the light side that shows in company. Our relations are not towards people, but towards Nature and destiny. Yet different as these worlds are, each is consistent with itself. The maker of each is careful to observe the laws of his own perspective, and however great a strain they may put upon us they will never confuse us, as lesser writers so frequently do, by introducing two different kinds of reality into the same book. Thus to go from one great novelist to another—from Jane Austen to Hardy, from Peacock to Trollope, from Scott to Meredith—is to be wrenched and uprooted; to be thrown this way and then that. To read a novel is a difficult and complex art. You must be capable not only of great finesse of perception, but of great boldness of imagination if you are going to make use of all that the novelist—the great artist—gives you.

E. B. White: Progress and Change

In resenting progress and change, a man lays himself open to censure. I suppose the explanation of anyone's defending anything as rudimentary and cramped as a Pullman berth is that such things are associated with an earlier period in one's life and that this period in retrospect seems a happy one. People who favor progress and improvements are apt to be people who have had a tough enough time without

From "One Man's Meat," White's column for *Harper's Magazine* (Dec. 1938).

any extra inconvenience. Reactionaries who pout at innovations are apt to be well-heeled sentimentalists who had the breaks. Yet for all that, there is always a subtle danger in life's refinements, a dim degeneracy in progress. I have just been refining the room in which I sit, yet I sometimes doubt that a writer should refine or improve his workroom by so much as a dictionary: one thing leads to another and the first thing you know he has a stuffed chair and is fast asleep in it. Half a man's life is devoted to what he calls improvements, yet the original had some quality which is lost in the process. There was a fine natural spring of water on this place when I bought it. Our drinking water had to be lugged in a pail, from a wet glade of alder and tamarack. I visited the spring often in those first years, and had friends there—a frog, a woodcock, and an eel which had churned its way all the way up through the pasture creek to enjoy the luxury of pure water. In the normal course of development, the spring was rocked up, fitted with a concrete curb, a copper pipe, and an electric pump. I have visited it only once or twice since. This year my only gesture was the purely perfunctory one of sending a sample to the state bureau of health for analysis. I felt cheap, as though I were smelling an old friend's breath.

William Faulkner: NOBEL PRIZE AWARD SPEECH

I feel that this award was not made to me as a man but to my work—a life's work in the agony and sweat of the human spirit, not for glory and least of all for profit, but to create out of the materials of the human spirit something which did not exist before. So this award is only mine in trust. It will not be difficult to find a dedication for the money part of it commensurate with the purpose and significance of its origin. But I would like to do the same with the acclaim too, by using this moment as a pinnacle from which I might be listened to by the young men and women already dedicated to the same anguish and travail, among whom is already that one who will some day stand here where I am standing.

Our tragedy today is a general and universal physical fear so long sustained by now that we can even bear it. There are no longer problems of the spirit. There is only the question: When will I be blown up? Because of this, the young man or woman writing today has for-

Given on acceptance of the Nobel Prize in 1949.

gotten the problems of the human heart in conflict with itself which alone can make good writing because only that is worth writing about, worth the agony and the sweat.

He must learn them again. He must teach himself that the basest of all things is to be afraid; and, teaching himself that, forget it forever, leaving no room in his workshop for anything but the old verities and truths of the heart, the old universal truths lacking which any story is ephemeral and doomed—love and honor and pity and pride and compassion and sacrifice. Until he does so, he labors under a curse. He writes not of love but of lust, of defeats in which nobody loses anything of value, of victories without hope and, worst of all, without pity or compassion. His griefs grieve on no universal bones leaving no scars. He writes not of the heart but of the glands.

Until he relearns these things, he will write as though he stood alone and watched the end of man. I decline to accept the end of man. It is easy enough to say that man is immortal simply because he will endure; that when the last ding-dong of doom has clanged and faded from the last worthless rock hanging tideless in the last red and dying evening, that even then there will still be one more sound: that of his puny inexhaustible voice, still talking. I refuse to accept this. I believe that man will not merely endure: he will prevail. He is immortal, not because he alone among creatures has an inexhaustible voice but because he has a soul, a spirit capable of compassion and sacrifice and endurance. The poet's, the writer's, duty is to write about these things. It is his privilege to help man endure by lifting his heart, by reminding him of the courage and honor and hope and pride and compassion and pity and sacrifice which have been the glory of his past. The poet's voice need not merely be the record of man, it can be one of the props, the pillars to help him endure and prevail.

James Thurber: A Dog's Eye View of Man

If Man has benefited immeasurably by his association with the dog, what, you may ask, has the dog got out of it? His scroll has, of course, been heavily charged with punishments: he has known the muzzle, the leash, and the tether; he has suffered the indignities of the show bench, the tin can on the tail, the ribbon in the hair; his love life with

From *Thurber's Dogs* (1955).

the other sex of his species has been regulated by the frigid hand of authority, his digestion ruined by the macaroons and marshmallows of doting women. The list of his woes could be continued indefinitely. But he has also had his fun, for he has been privileged to live with and study at close range the only creature with reason, the most unreasonable of creatures.

The dog has got more fun out of Man than Man has got out of the dog, for the clearly demonstrable reason that Man is the more laughable of the two animals. The dog has long been bemused by the singular activities and the curious practices of men, cocking his head inquiringly to one side, intently watching and listening to the strangest goings-on in the world. He has seen men sing together and fight one another in the same evening. He has watched them go to bed when it is time to get up, and get up when it is time to go to bed. He has observed them destroying the soil in vast areas, and nurturing it in small patches. He has stood by while men built strong and solid houses for rest and quiet, and then filled them with lights and bells and machinery. His sensitive nose, which can detect what's cooking in the next township, has caught at one and the same time the bewildering smells of the hospital and the munitions factory. He has seen men raise up great cities to heaven and then blow them to hell.

John Updike: BEER CAN

This seems to be an era of gratuitous inventions and negative improvements. Consider the beer can. It was beautiful—as beautiful as the clothespin, as inevitable as the wine bottle, as dignified and reassuring as the fire hydrant. A tranquil cylinder of delightfully resonant metal, it could be opened in an instant, requiring only the application of a handy gadget freely dispensed by every grocer. Who can forget the small, symmetrical thrill of those two triangular punctures, the dainty *pffff,* the little crest of suds that foamed eagerly in the exultation of release? Now we are given, instead, a top beetling with an ugly, shmoo-shaped[1] "tab," which, after fiercely resisting the tugging, bleeding fingers of the thirsty man, threatens his lips with a dangerous and hid-

Originally appeared in *The New Yorker* (Jan. 18, 1964).

1. The first tabs, made of plastic, reminded Updike of shmoos, bloblike creatures inveneted by Al Capp in the comic strip *Li'l Abner.*

eous hole. However, we have discovered a way to thwart Progress, usually so unthwartable. *Turn the beer can upside down and open the bottom.* The bottom is still the way the top used to be. True, this operation gives the beer an unsettling jolt, and the sight of a consistently inverted beer can might make people edgy, not to say queasy. But the latter difficulty could be eliminated if manufacturers would design cans that looked the same whichever end was up, like playing cards. What we need is Progress with an escape hatch.

Joan Didion: MARRYING ABSURD

What people who get married in Las Vegas actually do expect—what, in the largest sense, their "expectations" are—strikes one as a curious and self-contradictory business. Las Vegas is the most extreme and allegorical of American settlements, bizarre and beautiful in its venality and in its devotion to immediate gratification, a place the tone of which is set by mobsters and call girls and ladies' room attendants with amyl nitrite poppers in their uniform pockets. Almost everyone notes that there is no "time" in Las Vegas, no night and no day and no past and no future (no Las Vegas casino, however, has taken the obliteration of the ordinary time sense quite so far as Harold's Club in Reno, which for a while issued, at odd intervals in the day and night, mimeographed "bulletins" carrying news from the world outside); neither is there any logical sense of where one is. One is standing on a highway in the middle of a vast hostile desert looking at an eighty-foot sign which blinks "STARDUST" or "CAESAR'S PALACE." Yes, but what does that explain? This geographical implausibility reinforces the sense that what happens there has no connection with "real" life; Nevada cities like Reno and Carson are ranch towns, Western towns, places behind which there is some historical imperative. But Las Vegas seems to exist only in the eye of the beholder. All of which makes it an extraordinarily stimulating and interesting place, but an odd one in which to want to wear a candlelight satin Priscilla of Boston wedding dress with Chantilly lace insets, tapered sleeves and a detachable modified train.

And yet the Las Vegas wedding business seems to appeal to precisely that impulse. "Sincere and Dignified Since 1954," one wedding chapel advertises. There are nineteen such wedding chapels in Las

From *Slouching Towards Bethlehem* (1966).

Vegas, intensely competitive, each offering better, faster, and, by implication, more sincere services than the next: Our Photos Best Anywhere, Your Wedding on A Phonograph Record, Candlelight with Your Ceremony, Honeymoon Accommodations, Free Transportation from Your Motel to Courthouse to Chapel and Return to Motel, Religious or Civil Ceremonies, Dressing Rooms, Flowers, Rings, Announcements, Witnesses Available, and Ample Parking. All of these services, like most others in Las Vegas (sauna baths, payroll-check cashing, chinchilla coats for sale or rent) are offered twenty-four hours a day, seven days a week, presumably on the premise that marriage, like craps, is a game to be played when the table seems hot.

Wallace Stegner: COMING HOME

I was shaped by the West and have lived most of a long life in it, and nothing would gratify me more than to see it, in all its subregions and subcultures, both prosperous and environmentally healthy, with a civilization to match its scenery. Whenever I return to the Rocky Mountain states where I am most at home or escape into the California backlands from the suburbia where I live, the smell of distance excites me, the largeness and the clarity take the scales from my eyes, and I respond as unthinkingly as a salmon that swims past a rivermouth and tastes the waters of its birth.

From *Where the Bluebird Sings and the Lemonade Springs* (1992).

Jamaica Kincaid: THE UGLY TOURIST

The thing you have always suspected about yourself the minute you become a tourist is true: A tourist is an ugly human being. You are not an ugly person all the time; you are not an ugly person ordinarily; you are not an ugly person day to day. From day to day, you are a nice person. From day to day, all the people who are supposed to love you on the whole do. From day to day, as you walk down a busy street in

From *Harper's Magazine* (Sept. 1988).

the large and modern and prosperous city in which you work and live, dismayed, puzzled (a cliché, but only a cliché can explain you) at how alone you feel in this crowd, how awful it is to go unnoticed, how awful it is to go unloved, even as you are surrounded by more people than you could possibly get to know in a lifetime that lasted for millennia, and then out of the corner of your eye you see someone looking at you and absolute pleasure is written all over that person's face, and then you realise that you are not as revolting a presence as you think you are (for that look just told you so). And so, ordinarily, you are a nice person, an attractive person, a person capable of drawing to yourself the affection of other people (people just like you), a person at home in your own skin (sort of; I mean, in a way; I mean, your dismay and puzzlement are natural to you, because people like you just seem to be like that, and so many of the things people like you find admirable about yourselves—the things you think about, the things you think really define you—seem rooted in these feelings): a person at home in your own house (and all its nice house things), with its nice back yard (and its nice back-yard things), at home on your street, your church, in community activities, your job, at home with your family, your relatives, your friends—you are a whole person. But one day, when you are sitting somewhere, alone in that crowd, and that awful feeling of displacedness comes over you, and really, as an ordinary person you are not well equipped to look too far inward and set yourself aright, because being ordinary is already so taxing, and being ordinary takes all you have out of you, and though the words "I must get away" do not actually pass across your lips, you make a leap from being that nice blob just sitting like a boob in your amniotic sac of the modern experience to being a person visiting heaps of death and ruin and feeling alive and inspired at the sight of it; to being a person lying on some faraway beach, your stilled body stinking and glistening in the sand, looking like something first forgotten, then remembered, then not important enough to go back for; to being a person marvelling at the harmony (ordinarily, what you would say is the backwardness) and the union these other people (and they are other people) have with nature. And you look at the things they can do with a piece of ordinary cloth, the things they fashion out of cheap, vulgarly colored (to you) twine, the way they squat down over a hole they have made in the ground, the hole itself is something to marvel at, and since you are being an ugly person this ugly but joyful thought will swell inside you: their ancestors were not clever in the way yours were and not ruthless in the way yours were, for then would it not be you who would be in harmony with nature and backwards in that charming way? An ugly thing, that is what you are when you become a tourist, an ugly, empty thing, a stupid thing, a piece of rubbish pausing here and there to gaze at this and taste that, and it will never occur to you that the people who inhabit the place in which you have just passed cannot stand you, that behind their closed doors they laugh at your strangeness (you do not look the way they look); the physical sight of you does not please them; you have bad manners (it is their custom to eat their food with their hands; you try eating their way, you look silly; you try eating the way you always eat, you look silly); they do not like the way you speak (you have an accent); they collapse helpless from laughter, mimicking the way they imagine you must look as you carry out some everyday bodily function. They do not like you. *They do not like me!* That thought never actually occurs to you. Still, you feel a little uneasy. Still, you feel a little foolish. Still, you feel a little out of place. But the banality of your own life is very real to you; it drove you to this extreme, spending your days and your nights in the company of people who despise you, people you do not like really, people you would not want to have as your actual neighbour. And so you must devote yourself to puzzling out how much of what you are told is really, really true (Is ground-up bottle glass in peanut sauce really a delicacy around here, or will it do just what you think ground-up bottle glass will do? Is this rare, multicoloured, snout-mouthed fish really an aphrodisiac, or will it cause you to fall asleep permanently?). Oh, the hard work all of this is, and is it any wonder, then, that on your return home you feel the need of a long rest, so that you can recover from your life as a tourist?

That the native does not like the tourist is not hard to explain. For every native of every place is a potential tourist, and every tourist is a native of somewhere. Every native everywhere lives a life of overwhelming and crushing banality and boredom and desperation and depression, and every deed, good and bad, is an attempt to forget this. Every native would like to find a way out, every native would like a rest, every native would like a tour. But some natives—most natives in the world—cannot go anywhere. They are too poor. They are too poor to go anywhere. They are too poor to escape the reality of their lives; and they are too poor to live properly in the place where they live, which is the very place you, the tourist, want to go—so when the natives see you, the tourist, they envy you, they envy your ability to leave your own banality and boredom, they envy your ability to turn their own banality and boredom into a source of pleasure for yourself.

Nature and the Environment

Gretel Ehrlich

SPRING

We have a nine-acre lake on our ranch and a warm spring that feeds it all winter. By mid-March the lake ice begins to melt where the spring feeds in, and every year the same pair of mallards come ahead of the others and wait. Though there is very little open water they seem content. They glide back and forth through a thin estuary, brushing watercress with their elegant folded wings, then tip end-up to eat and, after, clamber onto the lip of ice that retreats, hardens forward, and retreats again.

Mornings, a transparent pane of ice lies over the meltwater. I peer through and see some kind of waterbug—perhaps a leech—paddling like a sea turtle between green ladders of lakeweed. Cattails and sweet-grass from the previous summer are bone dry, marked with black mold spots, and bend like elbows into the ice. They are swords that cut away the hard tenancy of winter. At the wide end a mat of dead waterplants has rolled back into a thick, impregnable breakwater. Near it, bubbles trapped under the ice are lenses focused straight up to catch the coming season.

It's spring again and I wasn't finished with winter. That's what I said at the end of summer too. I stood on the twenty-foot-high haystack and yelled "No!" as the first snow fell. We had been up since four in the morning picking the last bales of hay from the oatfield by hand, slipping under the weight of them in the mud, and by the time we finished the stack, six inches of snow had fallen.

It's spring but I was still cataloguing the different kinds of snow: snow that falls dry but is rained on; snow that melts down into hard

First published in *Antaeus* (1986).

crusts; wind-driven snow that looks blue; powder snow on hardpack on powder—a Linzertorte[1] of snow. I look up. The troposphere is the seven-to-ten-mile-wide sleeve of air out of which all our weather shakes. A bank of clouds drives in from the south. Where in it, I wonder, does a snowflake take on its thumbprint uniqueness? Inside the cloud where schools of flakes are flung this way and that like schools of fish? What gives the snowflake its needle, plate, column, branching shapes—the battering wind or the dust particles around which water vapor clings?

5 Near town the river ice breaks up and lies stacked in industrial-sized hunks—big as railway cars—on the banks, and is flecked black by wheeling hurricanes of newly plowed topsoil. That's how I feel when winter breaks up inside me: heavy, onerous, upended, inert against the flow of water. I had thought about ice during the cold months too. How it is movement betrayed, water seized in the moment of falling. In November, ice thickened over the lake like a cataract, and from the air looked like a Cyclops,[2] one bad eye. Under its milky spans over irrigation ditches, the sound of water running south was muffled. One solitary spire of ice hung noiselessly against dark rock at the Falls as if mocking or mirroring the broom-tail comet on the horizon. Then, in February, I tried for words not about ice, but words hacked from it—the ice at the end of the mind, so to speak—and failed.

Those were winter things and now it is spring, though one name can't describe what, in Wyoming, is a three-part affair: false spring, the vernal equinox, and the spring when flowers come and the grass grows.

Spring means restlessness. The physicist I've been talking to all winter says if I look more widely, deeply, and microscopically all at once I might see how springlike the whole cosmos is. What I see as order and stillness—the robust, time-bound determinacy of my life—is really a mirage suspended above chaos. "There's a lot of random jiggling going on all the time, everywhere," he tells me. Winter's tight sky hovers. Under it, the hayfields are green, then white, then green growing under white. The confinement I've felt since November resembles the confinement of subatomic particles, I'm told. A natural velocity finally shows itself. The particle moves; it becomes a wave.

The sap rises in trees and in me and the hard knot of perseverance I cultivated to meet winter dissipates; I walk away from the obsidian of bitter nights. Now, when snow comes, it is wet and heavy, but the air it traverses feels light. I sleep less and dream not of human entanglements, but of animals I've never seen: a caterpillar fat as a man's

1. An Austrian cake made with multiple layers.
2. A mythical giant with a single eye set in the middle of its forehead.

thumb, made of linked silver tubes, has two heads—one human, one a butterfly's.

Last spring at this time I was coming out of a bout with pneumonia. I went to bed on January first and didn't get up until the end of February. Winter was a cocoon in which my gagging, basso cough shook the dark figures at the end of my bed. Had I read too much Hemingway? Or was I dying? I'd lie on my stomach and look out. Nothing close up interested me. All engagements of mind—the circumlocutions of love interests and internal gossip—appeared false. Only my body was true. And my body was trying to close down, go out the window without me.

I saw things out there. Our ranch faces south down a long treeless valley whose vanishing point is two gray hills, folded one in front of the other like two hands, and after that—space, cerulean air, clouds like pleated skirts, and red mesas standing up like breaching whales in a valley three thousand feet below. Afternoons, our young horses played, rearing up on back legs and pawing oh so carefully at each other, reaching around, ears flat back, nipping manes and withers. One of those times their falsetto squeals looped across the pasture and hung on frozen currents of air. But when I tried to ingest their sounds of delight, I found my lungs had no air.

It was thirty-five below zero that night. Our plumbing froze, and because I was very weak my husband had to bundle me up and help me to the outhouse. Nothing close at hand seemed to register with me: neither the cold nor the semicoziness of an uninsulated house. But the stars were lurid. For a while I thought I saw the horses, dead now, and eating each other, and spinning round and round in the ice of the air.

My scientists friends talk with relish about how insignificant we humans are when placed against the time-scale of geology and the cosmos. I had heard it a hundred times, but never felt it truly. As I lay in bed, the black room was a screen through which some part of my body traveled, leaving the rest behind. I thought I was a sun flying over a barge whose iron holds soaked me up until I became rust floating on a bright river.

A ferocious loneliness took hold of me. I felt spring-inspired desire, a sense of trajectory, but no interception was in sight. In fact, I wanted none. My body was a parenthetical dash laid against a landscape so spacious it defied space as we know it—space as a membrane—and curved out of time. That night a luscious, creamy fog rolled in, like a roll of fat, hugging me, but it was snow.

Recuperation is like spring: dormancy and vitality collide. In any year I'm like a bear, a partial hibernator. During January thaws I stick my nose out and peruse the frozen desolation as if reading a book whose language I don't know. In March I'm ramshackle, weak in the knees, giddy, dazzled by broken-backed clouds, the passing of Halley's comet, the on-and-off strobe of sun. Like a sheepherder I X out each calendar day as if time were a forest through which I could clear-cut a way to the future. My physicist friend straightens me out on this point too. The notion of "time passing," like a train through a landscape, is an illusion, he says. I hold the Big Ben clock taken from a dead sheepherder's wagon and look at it. The clock measures intervals of time, not the speed of time, and the calendar is a scaffolding we hang as if time were rushing water we could harness. Time-bound, I hinge myself to a linear bias—cause and effect all laid out in a neat row—and in this we learn two things: blame and shame.

15 Julius Caesar had a sense of humor about time. The Roman calendar with its calends, nones, and ides—counting days—changed according to who was in power. Caesar serendipitously added days, changed the names of certain months, and when he was through, the calendar was so skewed that January fell in autumn.

Einsteinian time is too big for even Julius Caesar to touch. It stretches and shrinks and dilates. In fact, it is the antithesis of the mechanistic concept we've imposed on it. Time, indecipherable from space, is not one thing but an infinity of spacetimes, overlapping, interfering, wavelike. There is no future that is not now, no past that is not now. Time includes every moment.

It's the ides of March today.

I've walked to a hill a mile from the house. It's not really a hill but a mountain slope that heaves up, turns sideways, and comes down again, straight down to a foot-wide creek. Everything I can see from here used to be a flatland covered with shallow water. "Used to be" means several hundred million years ago, and the land itself was not really "here" at all, but part of a continent floating near Bermuda. On top is a fin of rock, a marine deposition created during Jurassic[3] times by small waves moving in and out slapping the shore.

I've come here for peace and quiet and to see what's going on in this secluded valley, away from ranch work and sorting corrals, but what I get is a slap on the ass by a prehistoric wave, gains and losses in altitude and aridity, outcrops of mud composed of rotting volcanic ash that fell continuously for ten thousand years a hundred million years ago. The soils are a geologic flag—red, white, green, and gray. On one side of the hill, mountain mahogany gives off a scent like orange blossoms; on the other, colonies of sagebrush root wide in ground the color

3. The second period of the Mesozoic era, characterized by the dominance of the dinosaur.

of Spanish roof tiles. And it still looks like the ocean to me. "How much truth can a man stand, sitting by the ocean, all that perpetual motion," Mose Allison, the jazz singer, sings.

The wind picks up and blusters. Its fat underbelly scrapes the un- 20
even ground, twisting like taffy toward me, slips up over the mountain, and showers out across the Great Plains. The sea smell it carried all the way from Seattle has long since been absorbed by pink gruss—the rotting granite that spills down the slopes of the Rockies. Somewhere over the Midwest the wind slows, tangling in the hair of hardwood forests, and finally drops into the corridors of the cities, past Manhattan's World Trade Center, ripping free again as it crosses the Atlantic's green swell.

Spring jitterbugs inside me. Spring *is* wind, symphonic and billowing. A dark cloud pops like a blood blister over me, letting hail down. It comes on a piece of wind that seems to have widened the sky, comes so the birds have something to fly on.

A message reports to my brain but I can't believe my eyes. The sheet of wind had a hole in it: an eagle just fell out of the sky. It fell as if down the chute of a troubled airplane. Landed, falling to one side as if a leg were broken. I was standing on the hill overlooking the narrow valley that had been a seashore 170 million years ago, whose sides had lifted like a medic's litter to catch up this eagle now.

She hops and flaps seven feet of wing and closes them down and sways. She had come down (on purpose?) near a dead fawn whose carcass had recently been feasted upon. When I walked closer, all I could see of the animal was a ribcage rubbed red with fine tissue and the decapitated head lying peacefully against sagebrush, eyes closed.

At twenty yards the eagle opened her wings halfway and rose up, her whole back lengthening and growing stiff. At forty feet she looked as big as a small person. She craned her neck, first to one side, then the other, and stared hard. She's giving me the eagle eye, I thought.

Friends who have investigated eagles' nests have literally feared for their lives. It's not that they were in danger of being pecked to death but, rather, grabbed. An eagle's talons are a powerful jaw. Their grip is so strong the talons can slice down through flesh to bone in one motion.

But I had come close only to see what was wrong, to see what I could 25
do. An eagle with a bum leg will starve to death. Was it broken, bruised, or sprained? How could I get close enough to know? I approached again. She hopped up in the air, dashing the critical distance between us with her great wings. Best to leave her alone, I decided. My husband dragged a road-killed deer up the mountain slope so she could eat, and I brought a bucket of water. Then we turned toward home.

A golden eagle is not golden but black with yellow spots on the neck and wings. Looking at her, I had wondered how feathers came to be, how their construction—the rachis, vane, and quill—is unlike anything else in nature.

Birds are glorified flying lizards. The remarkable feathers that, positioned together, are like hundreds of smaller wings, evolved from reptilian scales. Ancestral birds had thirteen pairs of cone-shaped teeth that grew in separate sockets like a snake's, rounded ribs, and bony tails. Archaeopteryx was half bird, half dinosaur who glided instead of flying; ichthyornis was a fish-bird, a relative of the pelican; diatryma was a giant, seven feet tall with a huge beak and wings so absurdly small they must have been useless, though later the wingbone sprouted from them. *Aquila chrysaëtos*, the modern golden eagle, has seven thousand contour feathers, no teeth, and weighs about eight pounds.

I think about the eagle. How big she was, how each time she spread her wings it was like a thought stretching between two seasons.

Back at the house I relax with a beer. At 5:03 the vernal equinox occurs. I go outside and stand in the middle of a hayfield with my eyes closed. The universe is restless but I want to feel celestial equipoise: twelve hours of daylight, twelve of dark, and the earth ramrod straight on its axis. In celebration I straighten my posture in an effort to resist the magnetic tilt back into dormancy, spiritual and emotional reticence. Far to the south I imagine the equatorial sash, now nose to nose with the sun, sizzling like a piece of bacon, then the earth slowly tilting again.

30 In the morning I walk up to the valley again. I glass both hillsides, back and forth through the sagebrush, but the eagle isn't there. The hindquarters of the road-killed deer have been eaten. Coyote tracks circle the carcass. Did they have eagle for dinner too?

Afternoon. I return. Far up on the opposite hill I see her, flapping and hopping to the top. When I stop, she stops and turns her head. Her neck is the plumbline on which earth revolves. Even at two hundred yards, I can feel her binocular vision zeroing in; I can feel the heat of her stare.

Later, I look through my binoculars at all sorts of things. I'm seeing the world with an eagle eye. I glass the crescent moon. How jaded I've become, taking the moon at face value only, forgetting the charcoal, shaded backside, as if it weren't there at all.

That night I dream about two moons. One is pink and spins fast; the other is an eagle's head, farther away and spinning in the opposite direction. Slowly, both moons descend and then it is day.

At first light I clamber up the hill. Now the dead deer my husband brought is only a hoop of ribs, two forelegs, and hair. The eagle is not here or along the creek or on either hill. I go to the hill and sit. After a long time an eagle careens out from the narrow slit of the red-walled canyon whose creek drains into this valley. Surely it's the same bird. She flies by. I can hear the bone-creak and whoosh of air under her wings. She cocks her head and looks at me. I smile. What is a smile to her? Now she is not so much flying as lifting above the planet, far from me.

Late March. The emerald of the hayfields brightens. A flock of gray- 35
capped rosy finches who overwintered here swarms a leafless apple tree, then falls from the smooth boughs like cut grass. the tree was planted by the Texan who homesteaded this ranch. As I walk past, one of the boughs, shaped like an undulating dragon, splits off from the trunk and falls.

Space is an arena in which the rowdy particles that are the building blocks of life perform their antics. All spring, things fall; the general law of increasing disorder is on the take. I try to think of what it is to be a cause without an effect, an effect without a cause. To abandon time-bound thinking, the use of tenses, the temporally related emotions of impatience, expectation, hope, and fear. But I can't. I go to the edge of the lake and watch the ducks. Like them, my thinking rises and falls on the same water.

Another day. Sometimes when I'm feeling small-minded I take a plane ride over Wyoming. As we take off I feel the plane's resistance to accepting air under its wings. Is this how an eagle feels? Ernst Mach's[4] principle tells me that an object's resistance against being accelerated is not the intrinsic property of matter, but a measure of its interaction with the universe; that matter has inertia only because it exists in relation to other matter.

Airborne, then, I'm not aloof but in relation to everything—like Wallace Steven's floating eagle for whom the whole, intricate Alps is a nest. We fly southeast from Heart Mountain across the Big Horn River, over the long red wall where Butch Cassidy trailed stolen horses, across the high plains to Laramie. Coming home the next day, we hit clouds. Turbulence, like many forms of trouble, cannot always be seen. We bounce so hard my arms sail helplessly above my head. In evolution, wingbones became arms and hands; perhaps I'm de-evolving.

From ten thousand feet I can see that spring is only half here: the southern part of the state is white, the northern half is green. Land is also time. The greening of time is a clock whose hands are blades of

4. Austrian physicist (1836–1916) who formulated the principle that the inertial and other properties of a system anywhere in the universe are determined by the interaction of that system with the rest of the universe.

grass moving vertically, up through the fringe of numbers, spreading across the middle of the face, sinking again as the sun moves from one horizon to the other. Time doesn't go anywhere; the shadow of the plane, my shadow, moves across it.

40 To sit on a plane is to sit on the edge of sleep where the mind's forge brightens into incongruities. Down there I see disparate wholenesses strung together and the string dissolving. Mountains run like rivers; I fly through waves and waves of chiaroscuro light. The land looks bare but is articulate. The body of the plane is my body, pressing into spring, pressing matter into relation with matter. Is it even necessary to say the obvious? That spring brings on surges of desire? From this disinterested height I say out loud what Saint Augustine wrote: "My love is my weight. Because of it I move."

Directly below us now is the fine old Wyoming ranch where Joel, Mart, Dave, Hughy, and I have moved thousands of head of cattle. Joel's father, Smokey, was one of two brothers who put the outfit together. They worked hard, lived frugally, and even after Fred died, Smokey did not marry until his late fifties. As testimony to a long bachelorhood, there is no kitchen in the main house. The cookhouse stands separate from all the other buildings. In back is a bedroom and bath, which have housed a list of itinerant cooks ten pages long.

Over the years I've helped during roundup and branding. We'd rise at four. Smokey, now in his eighties, cooked flapjacks and boiled coffee on the wood cookstove. There was a long table. Joel and Smokey always sat at one end. They were lookalikes, both skin-and-bones tall with tipped-up dark eyes set in narrow faces. Stern and vigilant, Smokey once threw a young hired hand out of the cookhouse because he hadn't grained his saddle horse after a long day's ride. "On this outfit we take care of our animals first," he said. "Then if there's time, we eat."

Even in his early twenties, Joel had his father's dignity and razor-sharp wit. They both wore white Stetsons identically shaped. Only their hands were different: Joel had eight fingers and one thumb—the other he lost while roping.

Eight summers ago my parents visited their ranch. We ate a hearty meal of homemade whiskey left over from Prohibition days, steaks cut from an Angus bull, four kinds of vegetables, watermelon, ice cream, and pie. Despite a thirteen-year difference in our ages, Smokey wanted Joel and me to marry. As we rose from the meal, he shook my father's hand. "I guess you'll be my son's father-in-law," he said. That was news to all of us. Joel's face turned crimson. My father threw me an astonished look, cleared his throat, and thanked his host for the fine meal.

45 One night Joel did come to my house and asked me if I would take

him into my bed. It was a gentlemanly proposition—doffed hat, moist eyes, a smile almost grimacing with loneliness. "You're an older woman. Think of all you could teach me," he said jauntily, but with a blush. He stood ramrod straight waiting for an answer. My silence turned him away like a rolling wave and he drove to the home ranch, spread out across the Emblem Bench thirty-five miles away.

The night Joel died I was staying at a writer's farm in Missouri. I had fallen asleep early, then awakened suddenly, feeling claustrophobic. I jumped out of bed and stood in the dark. I wanted to get out of there, drive home to Wyoming, and I didn't know why. Finally, at seven in the morning, I was able to sleep. I dreamed about a bird landing, then lifting out of a tree along a river bank. That was the night Joel's pickup rolled. He was found five hours after the accident occurred—just about daylight—and died on the way to the hospital.

Now I'm sitting on a fin of Gypsum Springs rock looking west. The sun is setting. What I see are three gray cloud towers letting rain down at the horizon. The sky behind these massifs is gilded gold, and long fingers of land—benches where the Hunt Oil Company's Charolais cattle graze—are pink. Somewhere over Joel's grave the sky is bright. The road where he died shines like a dash in a Paul Klee painting. Over my head, it is still winter: snow so dry it feels like Styrofoam when squeezed together, tumbles into my lap. I think about flying and falling. The place in the sky where the eagle fell is dark, as if its shadow had burned into the backdrop of rock—Hiroshima style. Why does a wounded eagle get well and fly away; why do the head wounds of a young man cut him down? Useless questions.

Sex and death are the riddles thrown into the hopper, thrown down on the planet like hailstones. Where one hits the earth, it makes a crater and melts, perhaps a seed germinates, perhaps not. If I dice life down into atoms, the trajectories I find are so wild, so random, anything could happen: life or nonlife. But once we have a body, who can give it up easily? Our own or others? We check our clocks and build our beautiful narratives, under which indeterminacy seethes.

Sometimes, lying in bed, I feel like a flounder with its two eyes on one side pointing upward into nothingness. The casings of thought rattle. Then I realize there are no casings at all. Is it possible that the mind, like space, is finite, but has no boundaries, no center or edge? I sit cross-legged on old blankets. My bare feet strain against the crotch of my knees. Time is between my toes, it seems. Just as morning comes and the indigo lifts, the leaflessness of the old apple tree looks ornate. Nothing in this world is plain.

"Every atom in your body was once inside a star," another physicist 50
says, but he's only trying to humor me. Not all atoms in all kinds of

matter are shared. But who wouldn't find that idea appealing? Outside, shadows trade places with a sliver of sun that trades places with shadow. Finally the lake ice goes and the water—pale and slate blue—wears its coat of diamonds all day. The mallards number twenty-six pairs now. They nest on two tiny islands and squabble amicably among themselves. A Pacific storm blows in from the south like a jibsail reaching far out, backhanding me with a gust of something tropical. It snows into my mouth, between my breasts, against my shins. Spring teaches me what space and time teach me: that I am a random multiple; that the many fit together like waves; that my swell is a collision of particles. Spring is a kind of music, a seething minor, a twelve-tone scale. Even the odd harmonies amassed only lift up to dissolve.

Spring passes harder and harder and is feral. The first thunder cracks the sky into a larger domain. Sap rises in obdurateness. For the first time in seven months, rain slants down in a slow pavane—sharp but soft—like desire, like the laying on of hands. I drive the highway that crosses the wild-horse range. Near Emblem I watch a black studhorse trot across the range all alone. He travels north, then turns in my direction as if trotting to me. Now, when I dream of Joel, he is riding that horse and he knows he is dead. One night he rides to my house, all smiles and shyness. I let him in.

Edward Abbey

THE SERPENTS OF PARADISE

The April mornings are bright, clear and calm. Not until the afternoon does the wind begin to blow, raising dust and sand in funnel-shaped twisters that spin across the desert briefly, like dancers, and then collapse—whirlwinds from which issue no voice or word except the forlorn moan of the elements under stress. After the reconnoitering dust devils comes the real the serious wind, the voice of the desert rising to a demented howl and blotting out sky and sun behind yellow clouds of dust, sand, confusion, embattled birds, last year's scrub-oak leaves, pollen, the husks of locusts, bark of juniper. . . .

Time of the red eye, the sore and bloody nostril, the sand-pitted windshield, if one is foolish enough to drive his car into such a storm. Time to sit indoors and continue that letter which is never finished—while the fine dust forms neat little windrows under the edge of the

From *Desert Solitaire: A Season in the Wilderness* (1968).

door and on the windowsills. Yet the springtime winds are as much a part of the canyon country as the silence and the glamorous distances, you learn, after a number of years, to love them also.

The mornings therefore, as I started to say and meant to say, are all the sweeter in the knowledge of what the afternoon is likely to bring. Before beginning the morning chores I like to sit on the sill of my doorway, bare feet planted on the bare ground and a mug of hot coffee in hand, facing the sunrise. The air is gelid, not far above freezing, but the butane heater inside the trailer keeps my back warm, the rising sun warms the front, and the coffee warms the interior.

Perhaps this is the loveliest hour of the day, though it's hard to choose. Much depends on the season. In midsummer the sweetest hour begins at sundown, after the awful heat of the afternoon. But now, in April, we'll take the opposite, that hour beginning with the sunrise. The birds, returning from wherever they go in winter, seem inclined to agree. The pinyon jays are whirling in garrulous, gregarious flocks from one stunted tree to the next and back again, erratic exuberant games without any apparent practical function. A few big ravens hang around and croak harsh clanking statements of smug satisfaction from the rimrock, lifting their greasy wings now and then to probe for lice. I can hear but seldom see the canyon wrens singing their distinctive song from somewhere up on the cliffs: a flutelike descent—never ascent—of the whole tone scale. Staking out new nesting claims, I understand. Also invisible but invariably present at some indefinable distance are the mourning doves whose plaintive call suggests irresistibly a kind of seeking out, the attempt by separated souls to restore a lost communion:

Hello . . . they seem to cry, *who . . . are . . . you?* 5

And the reply from a different quarter. *Hello* . . . (pause) *where . . . are . . . you?*

No doubt this line of analogy must be rejected. It's foolish and unfair to impute to the doves, with serious concerns of their own, an interest in questions more appropriate to their human kin. Yet their song, if not a mating call or a warning, must be what it sounds like, a brooding meditation on space, on solitude. The game.

Other birds, silent, which I have not yet learned to identify, are also lurking in the vicinity, watching me. What the ornithologist terms l.g.b.'s—little gray birds—they flit about from point to point on noiseless wings, their origins obscure.

* * * I share the housetrailer with a number of mice. I don't know how many but apparently only a few, perhaps a single family. They don't disturb me and are welcome to my crumbs and leavings. Where they came from, how they got into the trailer, how they survived

before my arrival (for the trailer had been locked up for six months), these are puzzling matters I am not prepared to resolve. My only reservation concerning the mice is that they do attract rattlesnakes.

I'm sitting on my doorstep early one morning, facing the sun as usual, drinking coffee, when I happen to look down and see almost between my bare feet, only a couple of inches to the rear of my heels, the very thing I had in mind. No mistaking that wedgelike head, that tip of horny segmented tail peeping out of the coils. He's under the doorstep and in the shade where the ground and air remain very cold. In his sluggish condition he's not likely to strike unless I rouse him by some careless move of my own.

There's a revolver inside the trailer, a huge British Webley .45, loaded, but it's out of reach. Even if I had it in my hands I'd hesitate to blast a fellow creature at such close range, shooting between my own legs at a living target flat on solid rock thirty inches away. It would be like murder; and where would I set my coffee? My cherrywood walking stick leans against the trailerhouse wall only a few feet away, but I'm afraid that in leaning over for it I might stir up the rattler or spill some hot coffee on his scales.

Other considerations come to mind. Arches National Monument[1] is meant to be among other things a sanctuary for wildlife—for all forms of wildlife. It is my duty as a park ranger to protect, preserve and defend all living things within the park boundaries, making no exceptions. Even if this were not the case I have personal convictions to uphold. Ideals, you might say. I prefer not to kill animals. I'm a humanist; I'd rather kill a *man* than a snake.

What to do. I drink some more coffee and study the dormant reptile at my heels. It is not after all the mighty diamondback, *Crotalus atrox*, I'm confronted with but a smaller species known locally as the horny rattler or more precisely as the Faded Midget. An insulting name for a rattlesnake, which may explain the Faded Midget's alleged bad temper. But the name is apt: he is small and dusty-looking, with a little knob above each eye—the horns. His bite though temporarily disabling would not likely kill a full-grown man in normal health. Even so I don't really want him around. Am I to be compelled to put on boots or shoes every time I wish to step outside? The scorpions, tarantulas, centipedes, and black widows are nuisance enough.

I finish my coffee, lean back and swing my feet up and inside the doorway of the trailer. At once there is a buzzing sound from below and the rattler lifts his head from his coils, eyes brightening, and extends his narrow black tongue to test the air.

1. Near Moab, Utah, in the spectacular Canyonlands region.

After thawing out my boots over the gas flame I pull them on and 15
come back to the doorway. My visitor is still waiting beneath the doorstep, basking in the sun, fully alert. The trailerhouse has two doors. I leave by the other and get a long-handled spade out of the bed of the government pickup. With this tool I scoop the snake into the open. He strikes, I can hear the click of the fangs against steel, see the stain of venom. He wants to stand and fight, but I am patient; I insist on herding him well away from the trailer. On guard, head aloft—that evil slit-eyed weaving head shaped like the ace of spades—tail whirring, the rattler slithers sideways, retreating slowly before me until he reaches the shelter of a sandstone slab. He backs under it.

You better stay there, cousin, I warn him; if I catch you around the trailer again I'll chop your head off.

A week later he comes back. If not him his twin brother. I spot him one morning under the trailer near the kitchen drain, waiting for a mouse. I have to keep my promise.

This won't do. If there are midget rattlers in the area there may be diamondbacks too—five, six or seven feet long, thick as a man's wrist, dangerous. I don't want them camping under my home. It looks as though I'll have to trap the mice.

However, before being forced to take that step I am lucky enough to capture a gopher snake. Burning garbage one morning at the park dump, I see a long slender yellow-brown snake emerge from a mound of old tin cans and plastic picnic plates and take off down the sandy bed of a gulch. There is a burlap sack in the cab of the truck which I carry when plucking Kleenex flowers from the brush and cactus along the road; I grab that and my stick, run after the snake and corner it beneath the exposed roots of a bush. Making sure it's a gopher snake and not somethng less useful, I open the neck of the sack and with a great deal of coaxing and prodding get the snake into it. The gopher snake, *Drymarchon corais couperi*, or bull snake, has a reputation as the enemy of rattlesnakes, destroying or driving them away whenever encountered.

Hoping to domesticate this sleek, handsome and docile reptile, I re- 20
lease him inside the trailerhouse and keep him there for several days. Should I attempt to feed him? I decide against it—let him eat mice. What little water he may need can also be extracted from the flesh of his prey.

The gopher snake and I get along nicely. During the day he curls up like a cat in the warm corner behind the heater and at night he goes about his business. The mice, singularly quiet for a change, make themselves scarce. The snake is passive, apparently contented, and makes no resistance when I pick him up with my hands and drape him over an arm or around my neck. When I take him outside into the wind and sunshine his favorite place seems to be inside my shirt, where he wraps himself around my waist and rests on my belt. In this position he sometimes sticks his head out between shirt buttons for a survey of the weather, astonishing and delighting any tourists who may happen to be with me at the time. The scales of a snake are dry and smooth, quite pleasant to the touch. Being a cold blooded creature, of course, he takes his temperature from that of the immediate environment—in this case my body.

We are compatible. From my point of view, friends. After a week of close association I turn him loose on the warm sandstone at my doorstep and leave for a patrol of the park. At noon when I return he is gone. I search everywhere beneath, nearby and inside the trailerhouse, but my companion has disappeared. Has he left the area entirely or is he hiding somewhere close by? At any rate I am troubled no more by rattlesnakes under the door.

The snake story is not yet ended.

In the middle of May, about a month after the gopher snake's disappearance, in the evening of a very hot day, with all the rosy desert cooling like a griddle with the fire turned off, he reappears. This time with a mate.

25 I'm in the stifling heat of the trailer opening a can of beer, barefooted, about to go outside and relax after a hard day watching cloud formations. I happen to glance out the little window near the refrigerator and see two gopher snakes on my verandah engaged in what seems to be a kind of ritual dance. Like a living caduceus they wind and unwind about each other in undulant, graceful, perpetual motion, moving slowly across a dome of sandstone. Invisible but tangible as music is the passion which joins them—sexual? combative? both? A shameless *voyeur*, I stare at the lovers, and then to get a closer view run outside and around the trailer to the back. There I get down on hands and knees and creep toward the dancing snakes, not wanting to frighten or disturb them. I crawl to within six feet of them and stop, flat on my belly, watching from the snake's eye level. Obsessed with their ballet, the serpents seem unaware of my presence.

The two gopher snakes are nearly identical in length and coloring; I cannot be certain that either is actually my former household pet. I cannot even be sure that they are male and female, though their performance resembles so strongly a *pas de deux* by formal lovers. They intertwine and separate, glide side by side in perfect congruence, turn like mirror images of each other and glide back again, wind and unwind again. This is the basic pattern but there is a variation: at regular intervals the snakes elevate their heads, facing one another, as high as they can go, as if each is trying to outreach or overawe the other. Their heads and bodies rise, higher and higher, then topple together and the rite goes on.

I crawl after them, determined to see the whole thing. Suddenly and simultaneously they discover me, prone on my belly a few feet away. The dance stops. After a moment's pause the two snakes come straight toward me, still in flawless unison, straight toward my face, the forked tongues flickering, their intense wild yellow eyes staring directly into my eyes. For an instant I am paralyzed by wonder; then, stung by a fear too ancient and powerful to overcome I scramble back, rising, to my knees. The snakes veer and turn and race away from me in parallel motion, their lean elegant bodies making a soft hissing noise as they slide over the sand and stone. I follow them for a short distance, still plagued by curiosity, before remembering my place and the requirements of common courtesy. For godsake let them go in peace, I tell myself. Wish them luck and (if lovers) innumerable offspring, a life of happily ever after. Not for their sake alone but for your own.

In the long hot days and cool evenings to come I will not see the gopher snakes again. Nevertheless I will feel their presence watching over me like totemic deities, keeping the rattlesnakes far back in the brush where I like them best, cropping off the surplus mouse population, maintaining useful connections with the primeval. Sympathy, mutual aid, symbiosis, continuity.

How can I descend to such anthropomorphism? Easily—but is it, in this case, entirely false? Perhaps not. I am not attributing human motives to my snake and bird acquaintances. I recognize that when and where they serve purposes of mine they do so for beautifully selfish reasons of their own. Which is exactly the way it should be. I suggest, however, that it's a foolish, simple-minded rationalism which denies any form of emotion to all animals but man and his dog. This is no more justified than the Moslems are in denying souls to women. It seems to me possible, even probable, that many of the nonhuman undomesticated animals experience emotions unknown to us. What do the coyotes mean when they yodel at the moon? What are the dolphins trying so patiently to tell us? Precisely what did those two enraptured gopher snakes have in mind when they came gliding toward my eyes over the naked sandstone? If I had been as capable of trust as I am susceptible to fear I might have learned something new or some truth so very old we have all forgotten it.

> They do not sweat and whine about their condition.
> They do not lie awake in the dark and weep for their sins.
> . . .

30 All men are brothers, we like to say, half-wishing sometimes in secret it were not true. But perhaps it is true. And is the evolutionary hue from protozoan to Spinoza[2] any less certain? That also may be true. We are obliged, therefore, to spread the news, painful and bitter though it may be for some to hear, that all living things on hand are kindred. . . .

2. Baruch Spinoza (1632–1677), Dutch philosopher known today for his writings on the doctrine of pantheism.

QUESTIONS

1. *Why is the word "paradise" included in the title? What does it reveal about Abbey's attitude toward the desert in which he lives?*
2. *"I'd rather kill a* man *than a snake," writes Abbey in paragraph 12; yet three paragraphs later he threatens, "If I catch you around the trailer again I'll chop your head off" (paragraph 16). What are the rhetorical purposes of these statements? How do they articulate the thematic concerns of the essay?*
3. *Write an essay in which you use your own experience in nature to defend an ecological or environmental cause.*
4. *Write about your own encounter with an animal, whether domesticated or wild.*

Robert Finch

VERY LIKE A WHALE

One day last week at sunset I went back to Corporation Beach in Dennis[1] to see what traces, if any, might be left of the great, dead finback whale that had washed up there several weeks before. The beach was not as hospitable as it had been that sunny Saturday morning after Thanksgiving when thousands of us streamed over the sand to gaze and look. A few cars were parked in the lot, but these kept their inhabitants. Bundled up against a sharp wind, I set off along the twelve-foot swath of trampled beach grass, a raw highway made in a few hours by ten thousand feet that day.

I came to the spot where the whale had beached and marveled that such a magnitude of flesh could have been there one day and gone the next. But the carcass had been hauled off and the tide had smoothed

From *Common Ground: A Naturalist's Cape Cod* (1981).

1. Village on Cape Cod.

and licked clean whatever vestiges had remained. The cold, salt wind had lifted from the sands the last trace of that pervasive stench of decay that clung to our clothes for days, and now blew clean and sharp into my nostrils.

The only sign that anything unusual had been there was that the beach was a little too clean, not quite so pebbly and littered as the surrounding areas, as the grass above a new grave is always fresher and greener. What had so manifestly occupied this space a short while ago was now utterly gone. And yet the whale still lay heavily on my mind; a question lingered, like a persistent odor in the air. And its dark shape, though now sunken somewhere beneath the waves, still loomed before me, beckoning, asking something.

What was it? What had we seen? Even the several thousand of us that managed to get down to the beach before it was closed off did not see much. Whales, dead or alive, are protected these days under the Federal Marine Mammals Act, and shortly after we arrived, local police kept anyone from actually touching the whale. I could hardly regret this, since in the past beached whales, still alive, have had cigarettes put out in their eyes and bits of flesh hacked off with pocket knives by souvenir seekers. And so, kept at a distance, we looked on while the specialists worked, white-coated, plastic-gloved autopsists from the New England Aquarium, hacking open the thick hide with carving knives and plumbing its depth for samples to be shipped to Canada for analysis and determination of causes of death. What was it they were pulling out? What fetid mystery would they pluck from that huge coffin of dead flesh? We would have to trust them for the answer.

5 But as the crowds continued to grow around the whale's body like flies around carrion, the question seemed to me, and still seems, not so much why did the whale die, as why had we come to see it? What made this dark bulk such a human magnet, spilling us over onto private lawns and fields? I watched electricians and oil truck drivers pulling their vehicles off the road and clambering down to the beach. Women in high heels and pearls, on their way to Filene's,[2] stumbled through the loose sand to gaze at a corpse. The normal human pattern was broken and a carnival atmosphere was created, appropriate enough in the literal sense of "a farewell to the flesh." But there was also a sense of pilgrimage in those trekking across the beach, an obligation to view such a thing. But for what? Are we really such novices to death? Or so reverent toward it?

I could understand my own semiprofessional interest in the whale, but what had drawn these hordes? There are some obvious answers, of

2. Department store in Boston.

course: a break in the dull routine, "something different." An old human desire to associate ourselves with great and extraordinary events. We placed children and sweethearts in front of the corpse and clicked cameras. "Ruthie and the whale." "Having a whale of a time on Cape Cod."

Curiosity, the simplest answer, doesn't really answer anything. What, after all, did we learn by being there? We were more like children at a zoo, pointing and poking, or Indians on a pristine beach, gazing in innocent wonder at strange European ships come ashore. Yet, as the biologists looted it with vials and plastic bags and the press captured it on film, the spectators also tried to make something of the whale. Circling around it as though for some hold on its slippery bulk, we grappled it with metaphors, lashed similes around its immense girth. It lay upside down, overturned "like a trailer truck." Its black skin was cracked and peeling, red underneath, "like a used tire." The distended, corrugated lower jaw, "a giant accordion," was afloat with the gas of putrefaction and, when pushed, oscillated slowly "like an enormous waterbed." Like our primitive ancestors, we still tend to make images to try to comprehend the unknown.

But what were we looking at? Or more to the point, from what perspective were we looking at it? What did we see in it that might tell us why we had come? A male finback whale—*Balaenoptera physalus*—a baleen cetacean. The second largest creature ever to live on earth. An intelligent and complex mammal. A cause for conservationists. A remarkably adapted swimming and eating machine. Perfume, pet food, engineering oil. A magnificent scientific specimen. A tourist attraction. A media event, a "day to remember." A health menace, a "possible carrier of a communicable disease." A municipal headache and a navigational hazard. Material for an essay.

On the whale's own hide seemed to be written its life history, which we could remark but not read. The right fluke was almost entirely gone, lost in some distant accident or battle and now healed over with a white scar. The red eye, unexpectedly small and mammalian, gazed out at us with fiery blankness. Like the glacial scratches sometimes found on our boulders, there were strange marks or grooves in the skin around the anal area, perhaps caused by scraping the ocean bottom.

10 Yet we could not seem to scratch its surface. The whale—dead, immobile, in full view—nonetheless shifted kaleidoscopically before our eyes. The following morning it was gone, efficiently and sanitarily removed, like the week's garbage. What was it we saw? I have a theory, though probably (as they say in New England) it hardly does.

There is a tendency these days to defend whales and other endangered animals by pointing out their similarities to human beings. Cetaceans, we are told, are very intelligent. They possess a highly complex language and have developed sophisticated communications systems that transmit over long distances. They form family groups, develop social structures and personal relationships, and express loyalty and affection toward one another. Much of their behavior seems to be recreational: they sing, they play. And so on.

These are not sentimental claims. Whales apparently do these things, at least as far as our sketchy information about their habits warrants such interpretations. And for my money, any argument that helps to preserve these magnificent creatures can't be all bad.

I take exception to this approach not because it is wrong, but because it is wrongheaded and misleading. It is exclusive, anthropocentric, and does not recognize nature in its own right. It implies that whales and other creatures have value only insofar as they reflect man himself and conform to his ideas of beauty and achievement. This attitude is not really far removed from that of the whalers themselves. To consume whales solely for their nourishment of human values is only a step from consuming them for meat and corset staves. It is not only presumptuous and patronizing, but it is misleading and does both whales and men a grave disservice. Whales have an inalienable right to exist, not because they resemble man *or* because they are useful to him, but simply because they do exist, because they have a proven fitness to the exactitudes of being on a global scale matched by few other species. If they deserve our admiration and respect, it is because, as Henry Beston put it, "They are other nations, caught with ourselves in the net of life and time, fellow prisoners of the splendour and travail of life."

But that still doesn't explain the throngs who came pell-mell to stare and conjecture at the dead whale that washed up at Corporation Beach and dominated it for a day like some extravagant *memento mori.*[3] Surely we were not flattering ourselves, consciously or unconsciously, with any human comparisons to that rotting hulk. Nor was there much, in its degenerate state, that it had to teach us. And yet we came—why?

The answer may be so obvious that we have ceased to recognize it. 15
Man, I believe, has a crying need to confront otherness in the universe. Call it nature, wilderness, the "great outdoors," or what you will—we crave to look out and behold something other than our own human faces staring back at us, expectantly and increasingly frustrated. What the human spirit wants, as Robert Frost said, "Is not its own love back in copy-speech, / But counter-love, original response."

This sense of otherness is, I feel, as necessary a requirement to our personalities as food and warmth are to our bodies. Just as an individ-

3. "Remember that you must die," hence a reminder of death.

ual, cut off from human contact and stimulation, may atrophy and die of loneliness and neglect, so mankind is today in a similar, though more subtle, danger of cutting himself off from the natural world he shares with all creatures. If our physical survival depends upon our devising a proper use of earth's materials and produce, our growth as a species depends equally upon our establishing a vital and generative relationship with what surrounds us.

We need plants, animals, weather, unfettered shores and unbroken woodland, not merely for a stable and healthy environment, but as an antidote to introversion, a preventive against human inbreeding. Here in particular, in the splendor of natural life, we have an extraordinary reservoir of the Cape's untapped possibilities and modes of being, ways of experiencing life, of knowing wind and wave. After all, how many neighborhoods have whales wash up in their backyards? To confine this world in zoos or in exclusive human terms does injustice not only to nature, but to ourselves as well.

Ever since his beginnings, when primitive man adopted totems and animal spirits to himself and assumed their shapes in ritual dance, *Homo sapiens* has been a superbly imitative animal. He has looked out across the fields and seen and learned. Somewhere along the line, though, he decided that nature was his enemy, not his ally, and needed to be confined and controlled. He abstracted nature and lost sight of it. Only now are we slowly realizing that nature can be confined only by narrowing our own concepts of it, which in turn narrows us. That is why we came to see the whale.

We substitute human myth for natural reality and wonder why we starve for nourishment. "Your Cape" becomes "your Mall," as the local radio jingle has it. Thoreau's "huge and real Cape Cod . . . a wild, rank place with no flattery in it," becomes the Chamber of Commerce's "Rural Seaside Charm"—until forty tons of dead flesh wash ashore and give the lie to such thin, flattering conceptions, flesh whose stench is still the stench of life that stirs us to reaction and response. That is why we came to see the whale. Its mute, immobile bulk represented that ultimate, unknowable otherness that we both seek and recoil from, and shouted at us louder than the policeman's bullhorn that the universe is fraught, not merely with response or indifference, but incarnate assertion.

20 Later that day the Dennis Board of Health declared the whale carcass to be a "health menace" and warned us off the beach. A health menace? More likely an intoxicating, if strong, medicine that might literally bring us to our senses.

But if those of us in the crowd failed to grasp the whale that day, others did not have much better luck. Even in death the whale escaped us: the tissue samples taken in the autopsy proved insufficient for analysis and the biologists concluded, "We will never know why the whale died." The carcass, being towed tail-first by a Coast Guard cutter for a final dumping beyond Provincetown, snapped a six-inch hawser. Eluding further attempts to reattach it, it finally sank from sight. Even our powers of disposal, it seemed, were questioned that day.

And so, while we are left on shore with the memory of a deflated and stinking carcass and of bullhorns that blared and scattered us like flies, somewhere out beyond the rolled waters and the shining winter sun, the whale sings its own death in matchless, sirenian strains.

Alexander Petrunkevitch

THE SPIDER AND THE WASP

In the feeding and safeguarding of their progeny insects and spiders exhibit some interesting analogies to reasoning and some crass examples of blind instinct. The case I propose to describe here is that of the tarantula spiders and their archenemy, the digger wasps of the genus Pepsis. It is a classic example of what looks like intelligence pitted against instinct—a strange situation in which the victim, though fully able to defend itself, submits unwittingly to its destruction.

Most tarantulas live in the tropics, but several species occur in the temperate zone and a few are common in the southern U.S. Some varieties are large and have powerful fangs with which they can inflict a deep wound. These formidable looking spiders do not, however, attack man; you can hold one in your hand, if you are gentle, without being bitten. Their bite is dangerous only to insects and small mammals such as mice; for man it is no worse than a hornet's sting.

Tarantulas customarily live in deep cylindrical burrows, from which they emerge at dusk and into which they retire at dawn. Mature males wander about after dark in search of females and occasionally stray into houses. After mating, the male dies in a few weeks, but a female lives much longer and can mate several years in succession. In a Paris museum is a tropical specimen which is said to have been living in captivity for 25 years.

A fertilized female tarantula lays from 200 to 400 eggs at a time; thus it is possible for a single tarantula to produce several thousand young. She takes no care of them beyond weaving a cocoon of silk to enclose the eggs. After they hatch, the young walk away, find conve-

From *Scientific American* (Aug. 1952).

nient places in which to dig their burrows and spend the rest of their lives in solitude. The eyesight of tarantulas is poor, being limited to a sensing of change in the intensity of light and to the perception of moving objects. They apparently have little or no sense of hearing, for a hungry tarantula will pay no attention to a loudly chirping cricket placed in its cage unless the insect happens to touch one of its legs.

But all spiders, and especially hairy ones, have an extremely delicate sense of touch. Laboratory experiments prove that tarantulas can distinguish three types of touch: pressure against the body wall, stroking of the body hair, and riffling of certain very fine hairs on the legs called trichobothria. Pressure against the body, by the finger or the end of a pencil, causes the tarantula to move off slowly for a short distance. The touch excites no defensive response unless the approach is from above where the spider can see the motion, in which case it rises on its hind legs, lifts its front legs, opens its fangs and holds this threatening posture as long as the object continues to move.

The entire body of a tarantula, especially its legs, is thickly clothed with hair. Some of it is short and wooly, some long and stiff. Touching this body hair produces one of two distinct reactions. When the spider is hungry, it responds with an immediate and swift attack. At the touch of a cricket's antennae the tarantula seizes the insect so swiftly that a motion picture taken at the rate of 64 frames per second shows only the result and not the process of capture. But when the spider is not hungry, the stimulation of its hairs merely causes it to shake the touched limb. An insect can walk under its hairy belly unharmed.

The trichobothria, very fine hairs growing from dislike[1] membranes on the legs, are sensitive only to air movement. A light breeze makes them vibrate slowly, without disturbing the common hair. When one blows gently on the trichobothria, the tarantula reacts with a quick jerk of its four front legs. If the front and hind legs are stimulated at the same time, the spider makes a sudden jump. This reaction is quite independent of the state of its appetite.

These three tactile responses—to pressure on the body wall, to moving of the common hair, and to flexing of the trichobothria—are so different from one another that there is no possibility of confusing them. They serve the tarantula adequately for most of its needs and enable it to avoid most annoyances and dangers. But they fail the spider completely when it meets its deadly enemy, the digger wasp Pepsis.

These solitary wasps are beautiful and formidable creatures. Most species are either a deep shiny blue all over, or deep blue with rusty wings. The largest have a wing span of about four inches. They live on

1. Unlike or dissimilar.

nectar. When excited, they give off a pungent odor—a warning that they are ready to attack. The sting is much worse than that of a bee or common wasp, and the pain and swelling last longer. In the adult stage the wasp lives only a few months. The female produces but a few eggs, one at a time at intervals of two or three days. For each egg the mother must provide one adult tarantula, alive but paralyzed. The mother wasp attaches the egg to the paralyzed spider's abdomen. Upon hatching from the egg, the larva is many hundreds of times smaller than its living but helpless victim. It eats no other food and drinks no water. By the time it has finished its single Gargantuan meal and become ready for wasphood, nothing remains of the tarantula but its indigestible chitinous skeleton.

The mother wasp goes tarantula-hunting when the egg in her ovary 10
is almost ready to be laid. Flying low over the ground late on a sunny afternoon, the wasp looks for its victim or for the mouth of a tarantula burrow, a round hole edged by a bit of silk. The sex of the spider makes no difference, but the mother is highly discriminating as to species. Each species of Pepsis requires a certain species of tarantula, and the wasp will not attack the wrong species. In a cage with a tarantula which is not its normal prey, the wasp avoids the spider and is usually killed by it in the night.

Yet when a wasp finds the correct species, it is the other way about. To identify the species the wasp apparently must explore the spider with her antennae. The tarantula shows an amazing tolerance to this exploration. The wasp crawls under it and walks over it without evoking any hostile response. The molestation is so great and so persistent that the tarantula often rises on all eight legs, as if it were on stilts. It may stand this way for several minutes. Meanwhile the wasp, having satisfied itself that the victim is of the right species, moves off a few inches to dig the spider's grave. Working vigorously with legs and jaws, it excavates a hole 8 to 10 inches deep with a diameter slightly larger than the spider's girth. Now and again the wasp pops out of the hole to make sure that the spider is still there.

When the grave is finished, the wasp returns to the tarantula to complete her ghastly enterprise. First she feels it all over once more with her antennae. Then her behavior becomes more aggressive. She bends her abdomen, protruding her sting, and searches for the soft membrane at the point where the spider's legs join its body—the only spot where she can penetrate the horny skeleton. From time to time, as the exasperated spider slowly shifts ground, the wasp turns on her back and slides along with the aid of her wings, trying to get under the tarantula for a shot at the vital spot. During all this maneuvering, which can last for several minutes, the tarantula makes no move to save itself. Finally the wasp corners it against some obstruction and grasps one of its legs in her powerful jaws. Now at last the harassed spider tries a desperate but vain defense. The two contestants roll over and over on the ground. It is a terrifying sight and the outcome is always the same. The wasp finally manages to thrust her sting into the soft spot and holds it there for a few seconds while she pumps in the poison. Almost immediately the tarantula falls paralyzed on its back. Its legs stop twitching; its heart stops beating. Yet it is not dead, as is shown by the fact that if taken from the wasp it can be restored to some sensitivity by being kept in a moist chamber for several months.

After paralyzing the tarantula, the wasp cleans herself by dragging her body along the ground and rubbing her feet, sucks the drop of blood oozing from the wound in the spider's abdomen, then grabs a leg of the flabby, helpless animal in her jaws and drags it down to the bottom of the grave. She stays there for many minutes, sometimes for several hours, and what she does all that time in the dark we do not know. Eventually she lays her egg and attaches it to the side of the spider's abdomen with a sticky secretion. Then she emerges, fills the grave with soil carried bit by bit in her jaws, and finally tramples the ground all around to hide any trace of the grave from prowlers. Then she flies away, leaving her descendant safely started in life.

In all this the behavior of the wasp evidently is qualitatively different from that of the spider. The wasp acts like an intelligent animal. This is not to say that instinct plays no part or that she reasons as man does. But her actions are to the point; they are not automatic and can be modified to fit the situation. We do not know for certain how she identifies the tarantula—probably it is by some olfactory or chemotactile sense—but she does it purposefully and does not blindly tackle a wrong species.

15 On the other hand, the tarantula's behavior shows only confusion. Evidently the wasp's pawing gives it no pleasure, for it tries to move away. That the wasp is not simulating sexual stimulation is certain because male and female tarantulas react in the same way to its advances. That the spider is not anesthetized by some odorless secretion is easily shown by blowing lightly at the tarantula and making it jump suddenly. What, then, makes the tarantula behave as stupidly as it does?

No clear, simple answer is available. Possibly the stimulation by the wasp's antennae is masked by a heavier pressure on the spider's body, so that it reacts as when prodded by a pencil. But the explanation may be much more complex. Initiative in attack is not in the nature of tarantulas; most species fight only when cornered so that escape is impossible. Their inherited patterns of behavior apparently prompt them to avoid problems rather than attack them. For example, spiders always weave their webs in three dimensions, and when a spider finds that there is insufficient space to attach certain threads in the third dimension, it leaves the place and seeks another, instead of finishing the web in a single plane. This urge to escape seems to arise under all circumstances, in all phases of life, and to take the place of reasoning. For a spider to change the pattern of its web is as impossible as for an inexperienced man to build a bridge across a chasm obstructing his way.

In a way the instinctive urge to escape is not only easier but often more efficient than reasoning. The tarantula does exactly what is most efficient in all cases except in an encounter with a ruthless and determined attacker dependent for the existence of her own species on killing as many tarantulas as she can lay eggs. Perhaps in this case the spider follows its usual pattern of trying to escape, instead of seizing and killing the wasp, because it is not aware of its danger. In any case, the survival of the tarantula species as a whole is protected by the fact that the spider is much more fertile than the wasp.

QUESTIONS

1. *Why is Petrunkevitch's initial description of the tarantula longer than his initial description of the wasp?*
2. *What are the major points of contrast between the spider and the wasp? Why does Petrunkevitch emphasize these particular points rather than others?*
3. *Petrunkevitch suggests more than one hypothesis for the behavior of the tarantula; indeed, he says that "no clear, simple answer is available." How does he test the possible explanations? Which one do you think he prefers?*
4. *What evidence is there that Petrunkevitch sees the tarantula and the wasp at least partly in human terms? In a brief essay explain why you think this is or is not legitimate for a scientist.*

Carl Sagan

THE ABSTRACTIONS OF BEASTS

"Beasts abstract not," announced John Locke, expressing mankind's prevailing opinion throughout recorded history: Bishop Berkeley[1] had, however, a sardonic rejoinder: "If the fact that brutes ab-

From *The Dragons of Eden* (1977).

1. Bishop George Berkeley (1685–1753), Irish philosopher, author of *A Treatise Concerning the Principles of Human Knowledge* (1710). John Locke (1632–1704), English philosopher, author of *An Essay Concerning Human Understanding* (1690).

stract not be made the distinguishing property of that sort of animal, I fear a great many of those that pass for men must be reckoned into their numbers." Abstract thought, at least in its more subtle varieties, is not an invariable accompaniment of everyday life for the average man. Could abstract thought be a matter not of kind but of degree? Could other animals be capable of abstract thought but more rarely or less deeply than humans?

We have the impression that other animals are not very intelligent. But have we examined the possibility of animal intelligence carefully enough, or, as in François Truffaut's poignant film *The Wild Child*, do we simply equate the absence of our style of expression of intelligence with the absence of intelligence? In discussing communication with the animals, the French philosopher Montaigne[2] remarked, "The defect that hinders communication betwixt them and us, why may it not be on our part as well as theirs?"

There is, of course, a considerable body of anecdotal information suggesting chimpanzee intelligence. The first serious study of the behavior of simians—including their behavior in the wild—was made in Indonesia by Alfred Russel Wallace, the co-discoverer of evolution by natural selection. Wallace concluded that a baby orangutan he studied behaved "exactly like a human child in similar circumstances." In fact, "orangutan" is a Malay phrase meaning not ape but "man of the woods." Teuber recounted many stories told by his parents, pioneer German ethologists who founded and operated the first research station devoted to chimpanzee behavior on Tenerife in the Canary Islands early in the second decade of this century. It was here that Wolfgang Kohler performed his famous studies of Sultan, a chimpanzee "genius" who was able to connect two rods in order to reach an otherwise inaccessible banana. On Tenerife, also, two chimpanzees were observed maltreating a chicken: One would extend some food to the fowl, encouraging it to approach; whereupon the other would thrust at it with a piece of wire it had concealed behind its back. The chicken would retreat but soon allow itself to approach once again—and be beaten once again. Here is a fine combination of behavior sometimes thought to be uniquely human: cooperation, planning a future course of action, deception and cruelty. It also reveals that chickens have a very low capacity for avoidance learning.

Until a few years ago, the most extensive attempt to communicate with chimpanzees went something like this: A newborn chimp was taken into a household with a newborn baby, and both would be raised together—twin cribs, twin bassinets, twin high chairs, twin potties,

2. Michel Eyquem de Montaigne (1533–1592), French moralist and creator of the personal essay.

twin diaper pails, twin babypowder cans. At the end of three years, the young chimp had, of course, far outstripped the young human in manual dexterity, running, leaping, climbing and other motor skills. But while the child was happily babbling away, the chimp could say only, and with enormous difficulty, "Mama," "Papa," and "cup." From this it was widely concluded that in language, reasoning and other higher mental functions, chimpanzees were only minimally competent: "Beasts abstract not."

But in thinking over these experiments, two psychologists, Beatrice 5
and Robert Gardner, at the University of Nevada, realized that the pharynx and larynx of the chimp are not suited for human speech. Human beings exhibit a curious multiple use of the mouth for eating, breathing and communicating. In insects such as crickets, which call to one another by rubbing their legs, these three functions are performed by completely separate organ systems. Human spoken language seems to be adventitious. The exploitation of organ systems with other functions for communication in humans is also indicative of the comparatively recent evolution of our linguistic abilities. It might be, the Gardners reasoned, that chimpanzees have substantial language abilities which could not be expressed because of the limitations of their anatomy. Was there any symbolic language, they asked, that could employ the strengths rather than the weaknesses of chimpanzee anatomy?

The Gardners hit upon a brilliant idea: Teach a chimpanzee American sign language, known by its acronym Ameslan, and sometimes as "American deaf and dumb language" (the "dumb" refers, of course, to the inability to speak and not to any failure of intelligence). It is ideally suited to the immense manual dexterity of the chimpanzee. It also may have all the crucial design features of verbal languages.

There is by now a vast library of described and filmed conversations, employing Ameslan and other gestural languages, with Washoe, Lucy, Lana and other chimpanzees studied by the Gardners and others. Not only are there chimpanzees with working vocabularies of 100 to 200 words; they are also able to distinguish among nontrivially different grammatical patterns and syntaxes. What is more, they have been remarkably inventive in the construction of new words and phrases.

On seeing for the first time a duck land quacking in a pond, Washoe gestured "waterbird," which is the same phrase used in English and other languages, but which Washoe invented for the occasion. Having never seen a spherical fruit other than an apple, but knowing the signs for the principal colors, Lana, upon spying a technician eating an orange, signed "orange apple." After tasting a watermelon, Lucy described it as "candy drink" or "drink fruit," which is essentially the same word form as the English "water melon." But after she had burned her mouth on her first radish, Lucy forever after described them as "cry hurt food." A small doll placed unexpectedly in Washoe's cup elicited the response "Baby in my drink." When Washoe soiled, particularly clothing or furniture, she was taught the sign "dirty," which she then extrapolated as a general term of abuse. A rhesus monkey that evoked her displeasure was repeatedly signed at: "Dirty monkey, dirty monkey, dirty monkey." Occasionally Washoe would say things like "Dirty Jack, gimme drink." Lana, in a moment of creative annoyance, called her trainer "You green shit." Chimpanzees have invented swear words. Washoe also seems to have a sort of sense of humor; once, when riding on her trainer's shoulders and, perhaps inadvertently, wetting him, she signed: "Funny, funny."

Lucy was eventually able to distinguish clearly the meanings of the phrases "Roger tickle Lucy" and "Lucy tickle Roger," both of which activities she enjoyed with gusto. Likewise, Lana extrapolated from "Tim groom Lana" to "Lana groom Tim." Washoe was observed "reading" a magazine—i.e., slowly turning the pages, peering intently at the pictures and making, to no one in particular, an appropriate sign, such as "cat" when viewing a photograph of a tiger, and "drink" when examining a Vermouth advertisement. Having learned the sign "open" with a door, Washoe extended the concept to a briefcase. She also attempted to converse in Ameslan with the laboratory cat, who turned out to be the only illiterate in the facility. Having acquired this marvelous method of communication, Washoe may have been surprised that the cat was not also competent in Ameslan. And when one day Jane, Lucy's foster mother, left the laboratory, Lucy gazed after her and signed: "Cry me. Me cry."

10 Boyce Rensberger is a sensitive and gifted reporter for the *New York Times* whose parents could neither speak nor hear, although he is in both respects normal. His first language, however, was Ameslan. He had been abroad on a European assignment for the *Times* for some years. On his return to the United States, one of his first domestic duties was to look into the Gardners' experiments with Washoe. After some little time with the chimpanzee, Rensberger reported, "Suddenly I realized I was conversing with a member of another species in my native tongue." The use of the word tongue is, of course, figurative: it is built deeply into the structure of the language (a word that also means "tongue"). In fact, Rensberger was conversing with a member of another species in his native "hand." And it is just this transition from tongue to hand that has permitted humans to regain the ability—lost, according to Josephus,[3] since Eden—to communicate with the animals.

In addition to Ameslan, chimpanzees and other nonhuman pri-

3. First-century Jewish general and historian.

mates are being taught a variety of other gestural languages. At the Yerkes Regional Primate Research Center in Atlanta, Georgia, they are learning a specific computer language called (by the humans, not the chimps) "Yerkish." The computer records all of its subjects' conversations, even during the night when no humans are in attendance; and from its ministrations we have learned that chimpanzees prefer jazz to rock and movies about chimpanzees to movies about human beings. Lana had, by January 1976, viewed *The Developmental Anatomy of the Chimpanzee* 245 times. She would undoubtedly appreciate a larger film library.

* * * The machine provides for many of Lana's needs, but not all. Sometimes, in the middle of the night, she forlornly types out: "Please, machine, tickle Lana." More elaborate requests and commentaries, each requiring a creative use of a set grammatical form, have been developed subsequently.

Lana monitors her sentences on a computer display, and erases those with grammatical errors. Once, in the midst of Lana's construction of an elaborate sentence, her trainer mischievously and repeatedly interposed, from his separate computer console, a word that made nonsense of Lana's sentence. She gazed at her computer display, spied her trainer at his console, and composed a new sentence: "Please, Tim, leave room." Just as Washoe and Lucy can be said to speak, Lana can be said to write.

At an early stage in the development of Washoe's verbal abilities, Jacob Bronowski and a colleague wrote a scientific paper denying the significance of Washoe's use of gestural language because, in the limited data available to Bronowski, Washoe neither inquired nor negated. But later observations showed that Washoe and other chimpanzees were perfectly able both to ask questions and to deny assertions put to them. And it is difficult to see any significant difference in quality between chimpanzee use of gestural language and the use of ordinary speech by children in a manner that we unhesitatingly attribute to intelligence. In reading Bronowski's paper I cannot help but feel that a little pinch of human chauvinsim has crept in, an echo of Locke's "Beasts abstract not." In 1949, the American anthropologist Leslie White stated unequivocally: "Human behavior is symbolic behavior; symbolic behavior is human behavior." What would White have made of Washoe, Lucy and Lana?

These findings on chimpanzee language and intelligence have an 15
intriguing bearing on "Rubicon" arguments[4]—the contention that

4. Those assuming a definitive boundary between different kinds of intelligence. The allusion is to the river Rubicon, in ancient times the boundary between Rome and its "barbaric" Germanic provinces.

the total brain mass, or at least the ratio of brain to body mass, is a useful index of intelligence. Against this point of view it was once argued that the lower range of the brain masses of microcephalic humans overlaps the upper range of brain masses of adult chimpanzees and gorillas; and yet, it was said, microcephalics have some, although severely impaired, use of language—while the apes have none. But in only relatively few cases are microcephalics capable of human speech. One of the best behavioral descriptions of microcephalics was written by a Russian physician, S. Korsakov, who in 1893 observed a female microcephalic named "Masha." She could understand a very few questions and commands and could occasionally reminisce on her childhood. She sometimes chattered away, but there was little coherence to what she uttered. Korsakov characterized her speech as having "an extreme poverty of logical associations." As an example of her poorly adapted and automaton-like intelligence, Korsakov described her eating habits. When food was present on the table, Masha would eat. But if the food was abruptly removed in the midst of a meal, she would behave as if the meal had ended, thanking those in charge and piously blessing herself. If the food were returned, she would eat again. The pattern apparently was subject to indefinite repetition. My own impression is that Lucy or Washoe would be a far more interesting dinner companion than Masha, and that the comparison of microcephalic humans with normal apes is not inconsistent with some sort of "Rubicon" of intelligence. Of course, both the quality and the quantity of neural connections are probably vital for the sorts of intelligence that we can easily recognize.

Recent experiments performed by James Dewson of the Stanford University School of Medicine and his colleagues give some physiological support to the idea of language centers in the simian neocortex—in particular, like humans, in the left hemisphere. Monkeys were trained to press a green light when they heard a hiss and a red light when they heard a tone. Some seconds after a sound was heard, the red or the green light would appear at some unpredictable position—different each time—on the control panel. The monkey pressed the appropriate light and, in the case of a correct guess, was rewarded with a pellet of food. Then the time interval between hearing the sound and seeing the light was increased up to twenty seconds. In order to be rewarded, the monkeys now had to remember for twenty seconds which noise they had heard. Dewson's team then surgically excised part of the so-called auditory association cortex from the left hemisphere of the neocortex in the temporal lobe. When retested, the monkeys had very poor recall of which sound they were then hearing. After less than a second they could not recall whether it was a hiss or a tone. The removal of a comparable part of the temporal lobe from the right hemisphere produced no effect whatever on this task. "It looks," Dewson was reported to say, "as if we removed the structure in the monkeys' brains that may be analogous to human language centers." Similar studies on rhesus monkeys, but using visual rather than auditory stimuli, seem to show no evidence of a difference between the hemispheres of the neocortex.

Because adult chimpanzees are generally thought (at least by zookeepers) to be too dangerous to retain in a home or home environment, Washoe and other verbally accomplished chimpanzees have been involuntarily "retired" soon after reaching puberty. Thus we do not yet have experience with the adult language abilities of monkeys and apes. One of the most intriguing questions is whether a verbally accomplished chimpanzee mother will be able to communicate language to her offspring. It seems very likely that this should be possible and that a community of chimps initially competent in gestural language could pass down the language to subsequent generations.

Where such communication is essential for survival, there is already some evidence that apes transmit extragenetic or cultural information. Jane Goodall observed baby chimps in the wild emulating the behavior of their mothers and learning the reasonably complex task of finding an appropriate twig and using it to prod into a termite's nest so as to acquire some of these tasty delicacies.

Differences in group behavior—something that it is very tempting to call cultural differences—have been reported among chimpanzees, baboons, macaques and many other primates. For example, one group of monkeys may know how to eat bird's eggs, while an adjacent band of precisely the same species may not. Such primates have a few dozen sounds or cries, which are used for intra-group communication, with such meanings as "Flee; here is a predator." But the sound of the cries differs somewhat from group to group: there are regional accents.

An even more striking experiment was performed accidentally by 20
Japanese primatologists attempting to relieve an overpopulation and hunger problem in a community of macaques on an island in south Japan. The anthropologists threw grains of wheat on a sandy beach. Now it is very difficult to separate wheat grains one by one from sand grains; such an effort might even expend more energy than eating the collected wheat would provide. But one brilliant macaque, Imo, perhaps by accident or out of pique, threw handfuls of the mixture into the water. Wheat floats; sand sinks, a fact that Imo clearly noted. Through the sifting process she was able to eat well (on a diet of soggy wheat, to be sure). While older macaques, set in their ways, ignored her, the younger monkeys appeared to grasp the importance of her discovery, and imitate it. In the next generation, the practice was more widespread; today all macaques on the island are competent at water sifting, an example of a cultural tradition among the monkeys.

Earlier studies on Takasakiyama, a mountain in northeast Kyushu inhabited by macaques, show a similar pattern in cultural evolution. Visitors to Takasakiyama threw caramels wrapped in paper to the monkeys—a common practice in Japanese zoos, but one the Takasakiyama macaques had never before encountered. In the course of play, some young monkeys discovered how to unwrap the caramels and eat them. The habit was passed on successively to their playmates, their mothers, the dominant males (who among the macaques act as babysitters for the very young) and finally to the subadult males, who were at the furthest social remove from the monkey children. The process of acculturation took more than three years. In natural primate communities, the existing nonverbal communications are so rich that there is little pressure for the development of a more elaborate gestural language. But if gestural language were necessary for chimpanzee survival, there can be little doubt that it would be transmitted culturally down through the generations.

I would expect a significant development and elaboration of language in only a few generations if all the chimps unable to communicate were to die or fail to reproduce. Basic English corresponds to about 1,000 words. Chimpanzees are already accomplished in vocabularies exceeding 10 percent of that number. Although a few years ago it would have seemed the most implausible science fiction, it does not appear to me out of the question that, after a few generations in such a verbal chimpanzee community, there might emerge the memoirs of the natural history and mental life of a chimpanzee, published in English or Japanese (with perhaps an "as told to" after the by-line).

If chimpanzees have consciousness, if they are capable of abstractions, do they not have what until now has been described as "human rights"? How smart does a chimpanzee have to be before killing him constitutes murder? What further properties must he show before religious missionaries must consider him worthy of attempts at conversion?

I recently was escorted through a large primate research laboratory by its director. We approached a long corridor lined, to the vanishing point as in a perspective drawing, with caged chimpanzees. They were one, two or three to a cage, and I am sure the accommodations were exemplary as far as such institutions (or for that matter traditional zoos) go. As we approached the nearest cage, its two inmates bared their teeth and with incredible accuracy let fly great sweeping arcs of spittle, fairly drenching the lightweight suit of the facility's director. They then uttered a staccato of short shrieks, which echoed down the corridor to be repeated and amplified by other caged chimps, who had certainly not seen us, until the corridor fairly shook with the screeching and banging and rattling of bars. The director informed me that not only spit is apt to fly in such a situation; and at his urging we retreated.

I was powerfully reminded of those American motion pictures of the 25
1930s and '40s, set in some vast and dehumanized state or federal penitentiary, in which the prisoners banged their eating utensils against the bars at the appearance of the tyrannical warden. These chimps are healthy and well-fed. If they are "only" animals, if they are beasts which abstract not, then my comparison is a piece of sentimental foolishness. But chimpanzees *can* abstract. Like other mammals, they are capable of strong emotions. They have certainly committed no crimes. I do not claim to have the answer, but I think it is certainly worthwhile to raise the question: Why, exactly, all over the civilized world, in virtually every major city, are apes in prison?

For all we know, occasional viable crosses between humans and chimpanzees are possible. The natural experiment must have been tried very infrequently, at least recently. If such off-spring are ever produced, what will their legal status be? The cognitive abilities of chimpanzees force us, I think, to raise searching questions about the boundaries of the community of beings to which special ethical considerations are due, and can, I hope, help to extend our ethical perspectives downward through the taxa on Earth and upwards to extraterrestial organisms, if they exist.

QUESTIONS

1. *Instead of a traditional thesis statement, Sagan uses two rhetorical questions in his opening paragraph. What advantages—and disadvantages—does this technique have? Try writing a thesis statement to replace Sagan's questions.*
2. *Sagan's essay divides into two parts: paragraphs 1 to 14 and paragraphs 15 to 26. Why does he choose this arrangement? What is the function of each part?*
3. *At the end of his essay Sagan raises some questions about the legal rights of apes. Respond to those questions in a journal, a brief essay, or class discussion.*
4. *Sagan begins with quotations from three philosophers: John Locke, Bishop George Berkeley, and Michel Eyquem de Montaigne. Choose one of the three quotations and write an essay in which you agree, disagree, or correct the philosopher. Use evidence from Sagan's essay as well as from your own experience or research.*

Chief Seattle

LETTER TO PRESIDENT PIERCE, 1855

We know that the white man does not understand our ways. One portion of the land is the same to him as the next, for he is a stranger who comes in the night and takes from the land whatever he needs. The earth is not his brother, but his enemy, and when he has conquered it, he moves on. He leaves his fathers' graves, and his children's birthright is forgotten. The sight of your cities pains the eyes of the red man. But perhaps it is because the red man is a savage and does not understand.

There is no quiet place in the white man's cities. No place to hear the leaves of spring or the rustle of insect's wings. But perhaps because I am a savage and do not understand, the clatter only seems to insult the ears. The Indian prefers the soft sound of the wind darting over the face of the pond, the smell of the wind itself cleansed by a mid-day rain, or scented with the piñon pine. The air is precious to the red man. For all things share the same breath—the beasts, the trees, the man. Like a man dying for many days, he is numb to the stench.

What is man without the beasts? If all the beasts were gone, men would die from great loneliness of spirit, for whatever happens to the beasts also happens to man. All things are connected. Whatever befalls the earth befalls the sons of the earth.

It matters little where we pass the rest of our days; they are not many. A few more hours, a few more winters, and none of the children of the great tribes that once lived on this earth, or that roamed in small bands in the woods, will be left to mourn the graves of a people once as powerful and hopeful as yours.

5 The whites, too, shall pass—perhaps sooner than other tribes. Continue to contaminate your bed, and you will one night suffocate in your own waste. When the buffalo are all slaughtered, the wild horses all tamed, the secret corners of the forest heavy with the scent of many men, and the view of the ripe hills blotted by talking wires,[1] where is the thicket? Gone. Where is the eagle? Gone. And what is it to say goodby to the swift and the hunt, the end of living and the beginning of survival? We might understand if we knew what it was that the

From *Native American Testimony: An Anthology of Indian and White Relations,* edited by Peter Nabokov (1977).

1. I.e., the telegraph.

white man dreams, what he describes to his children on the long winter nights, what visions he burns into their minds, so they will wish for tomorrow. But we are savages. The white man's dreams are hidden from us.

QUESTIONS

1. *Chief Seattle repeatedly refers to the red man as "a savage" who "does not understand," yet in the course of this letter he gives evidence of a great deal of understanding. What is the purpose of such ironic comments and apparently self-disparaging remarks?*
2. *Scholars have recently suggested that Chief Seattle's "Letter" is in fact the creation of a white man, based on Seattle's public oratory. If so, what rhetorical techniques does the white editor associate with Indian speech? Why might he have done so?*
3. *A surprisingly modern note of ecological awareness resounds in the statement "[W]hatever happens to the beasts also happens to man. All things are connected." Locate two or three similar observations, and explain their effectiveness.*
4. *Chief Seattle says that the red man might understand the white man better "if we knew what it was that the white man dreams, what he describes to his children on the long winter nights, what visions he burns into their minds, so they will wish for tomorrow." Write a short essay explaining, either straightforwardly or ironically, how "the white man" might reply. If you prefer, write the reply itself.*

Aldo Leopold

THINKING LIKE A MOUNTAIN

A deep chesty bawl echoes from rimrock to rimrock, rolls down the mountain, and fades into the far blackness of the night. It is an outburst of wild defiant sorrow, and of contempt for all the adversities of the world.

Every living thing (and perhaps many a dead one as well) pays heed to that call. To the deer it is a reminder of the way of all flesh, to the pine a forecast of midnight scuffles and of blood upon the snow, to the coyote a promise of gleanings to come, to the cowman a threat of red

From Leopold's journals, published posthumously as A *Sand County Almanac* (1949). Sand County was Leopold's fictional name for family property outside of Madison, Wisconsin.

ink at the bank, to the hunter a challenge of fang against bullet. Yet behind these obvious and immediate hopes and fears there lies a deeper meaning, known only to the mountain itself. Only the mountain has lived long enough to listen objectively to the howl of a wolf.

Those unable to decipher the hidden meaning know nevertheless that it is there, for it is felt in all wolf country, and distinguishes that country from all other land. It tingles in the spine of all who hear wolves by night, or who scan their tracks by day. Even without sight or sound of wolf, it is implicit in a hundred small events: the midnight whinny of a pack horse, the rattle of rolling rocks, the bound of a fleeing deer, the way shadows lie under the spruces. Only the ineducable tyro can fail to sense the presence or absence of wolves, or the fact that mountains have a secret opinion about them.

My own conviction on this score dates from the day I saw a wolf die. We were eating lunch on a high rimrock, at the foot of which a turbulent river elbowed its way. We saw what we thought was a doe fording the torrent, her breast awash in white water. When she climbed the bank toward us and shook out her tail, we realized our error: it was a wolf. A half-dozen others, evidently grown pups sprang from the willows and all joined in a welcoming mêlée of wagging tails and playful maulings. What was literally a pile of wolves writhed and tumbled in the center of an open flat at the foot of our rimrock.

5 In those days we had never heard of passing up a chance to kill a wolf. In a second we were pumping lead into the pack, but with more excitement than accuracy: how to aim a steep downhill shot is always confusing. When our rifles were empty, the old wolf was down, and a pup was dragging a leg into impassable slide-rocks.

We reached the old wolf in time to watch a fierce green fire dying in her eyes. I realized then, and have known ever since, that there was something new to me in those eyes—something known only to her and to the mountain. I was young then, and full of trigger-itch; I thought that because fewer wolves meant more deer, that no wolves would mean hunters' paradise. But after seeing the green fire die, I sensed that neither the wolf nor the mountain agreed with such a view.

Since then I have lived to see state after state extirpate its wolves. I have watched the face of many a newly wolfless mountain, and seen the south-facing slopes wrinkle with a maze of new deer trails. I have seen every edible bush and seedling browsed, first to anemic desuetude, and then to death. I have seen every edible tree defoliated to the height of a saddle-horn. Such a mountain looks as if someone had given God a new pruning shears, and forbidden Him all other exercise. In the end the starved bones of the hoped for deer herd, dead of its own too much, bleach with the bones of the dead sage, or molder under the high-lined junipers.

I now suspect that just as a deer herd lives in mortal fear of its wolves, so does a mountain live in mortal fear of its deer. And perhaps with better cause, for while a buck pulled down by wolves can be replaced in two or three years, a range pulled down by too many deer may fail of replacement in as many decades.

So also with cows. The cowman who cleans his range of wolves does not realize that he is taking over the wolf's job of trimming the herd to fit the range. He has not learned to think like a mountain. Hence we have dustbowls, and rivers washing the future into the sea.

We all strive for safety, prosperity, comfort, long life, and dullness. 10
The deer strives with his supple legs, the cowman with trap and poison, the statesman with pen, the most of us with machines, votes, and dollars, but it all comes to the same thing; peace in our time. A measure of success in this is all well enough, and perhaps is a requisite to objective thinking, but too much safety seems to yield only danger in the long run. Perhaps this is behind Thoreau's dictum: In wildness is the salvation of the world. Perhaps this is the hidden meaning in the howl of the wolf, long known among mountains, but seldom perceived among men.

Noel Perrin

FOREVER VIRGIN: THE AMERICAN VIEW OF AMERICA

If there is one novel that nearly all educated Americans have read, it's F. Scott Fitzgerald's[1] *The Great Gatsby.* If there's a single most famous passage in that novel, it's the one on the last page where Fitzgerald talks about Gatsby's belief in the green light ahead. He has in mind two or three kinds of green light at once. There's the literal green dock-identification light that Gatsby can see from his Long Island mansion, glimmering across the bay where Daisy lives. There's the metaphorical green traffic light: the future is open, the future is GO. And finally there's the green light that nature produces: the reflection

First published in *Antaeus* (Autumn 1986).

1. American novelist (1896–1940) and chronicler of the 1920s, which he called the Jazz Age.

from trees, and especially from a whole forest, a forest crowding right up to the shore of Long Island Sound.

In that famous last passage, the narrator of the book is standing in front of Gatsby's mansion at night—a summer night. He is looking across the bay, just as Gatsby used to do. There is a bright moon. As he looks, "the inessential houses began to melt away until gradually I became aware of the old island here that flowered once for Dutch sailors' eyes—a fresh, green breast of the new world. Its vanished trees, the trees that had made way for Gatsby's house, had once pandered in whispers to the last and greatest of all human dreams; for a transitory enchanted moment man must have held his breath in the presence of this continent . . . face to face for the last time in history with something commensurate to his capacity for wonder."

Fitzgerald says in this passage that it was just for a moment that men and women beheld the new world as a fresh, untouched place, a virgin world, a place where the future is open and green. But, of course, it wasn't. We still see it that way—or most of us do most of the time. Certainly that was how Jay Gatsby saw it sixty years ago. In the narrator's vision, there on the last page, that is how he, too, sees it: Long Island with the houses invisible in the moonlight, the island like a green breast, the breast of Mother Nature, inexhaustibly nourishing. As I am going to try to show in a little while, that is how most Americans still perceive the country now: morning in America, a green light ahead, nature glad and strong and free. Or at least we do in our dominant mood, and that's why the majority of us don't really worry much about acid rain, or recycling, or any of that. We have a consciousness below knowledge that the big country can handle all that.

But there are two things I want to do before I come to the relationship between human beings and nature in America in the 1980s: a short thing and a long thing. The short one is simply to make clear what I mean by nature. And the long one is to give some of the history of the encounter between us and nature since we got here. Because of course I am not claiming we feel exactly the same as Henryk Hudson's sailors did in 1609. We have changed, and the country has changed since then. A lot. All I'm claiming is that we still see the green light.

5 First, what nature is. Among other things, it's a word that if you look it up turns out to have twelve meanings, plus eight more submeanings. They vary so widely that Robert Frost[2] could and did once write a poem on the subject. In the poem, he and an anonymous college official are arguing about what the word means in the epitaph that the Victorian poet Walter Savage Landor[3] wrote for himself. Landor summed up his life thus:

2. American poet (1874–1963).
3. English poet, essayist, and literary critic (1775–1864).

I strove with none, for none was worth my strife.
Nature I loved, and next to Nature, Art.
I warm'd both hands before the fire of life;
It sinks, and I am ready to depart.

Frost and the administrator can't agree on what it was that Landor loved, and the result is a mocking little poem that begins

Dean, adult education may seem silly.
What of it, though? I got some willy-nilly
The other evening at your college deanery.
And grateful for it (let's not be facetious!)
For I thought Epicurus and Lucretius
By Nature meant the Whole Goddam Machinery
But you say that in college nomenclature
The only meaning possible for Nature
In Landor's quatrain would be Pretty Scenery.

Well, what I mean by nature is more than pretty scenery, but slightly less than the whole goddam machinery. I mean everything that exists on this planet (or elsewhere) that was not made by man. It's what most people mean. Only the minute you look closely, it turns out to be very hard to decide what was made by man and what wasn't. A plastic bag or a beer can is easy: Both were made by man—though of course out of natural materials, since that's all there are. But what about a garden? Nature made the carrot, but man modified it, planted it, grew it. There are two wills in collaboration here—the will of the carrot to be orange and to taste carroty and so forth—and the will of human beings to have it be a large carrot that travels well, keeps in cold storage, and so forth. What about a lake that exists because someone has built a dam, a so-called man-made or artificial lake? What about a tree? Only God—or nature—can make them, as Joyce Kilmer[4] pointed out. But then, there are hybrid poplars: designed, planted, shaped by human beings. Again, a collaboration. Almost the entire surface of England is such a collaboration, and most of the United States, too. Only a wilderness area is not at least partly a collaboration. Lots of the prettiest scenery *is.*

So what I'm going to call nature is everything on this planet that is at least partially under the control of some other will than ours. Pure nature is of course what exists entirely without our will. In terms of landscape, there isn't much of it.

That still leaves one big question unanswered. Is man himself part of nature? Our remote ancestors certainly were: They evolved without planning to. But we ourselves? Well, I think we're partly in and partly out of nature—and the balance varies from age to age. But for the

4. Popular American writer (1886–1918), best known for his poem "Trees."

moment I'm going to say we're outside of nature. Certainly we thought of ourselves that way when we came to America. The Dutch sailors did, the pioneer settlers did. The authors of the Bible did.

10 Now let me drop back a little, and talk history. Not as far back as 1609—the Dutch sailors didn't leave much record of what they thought when they saw Long Island—but back to the eighteenth century and to a book called *Letters From an American Farmer*,[5] which was written in the 1770s (though not published until 1782), and which was one of the very early American best-sellers. Basically, it's a report to Europeans on conditions in America just before the Revolution. Most of it is about what it's like to come to be a farmer in one of the thirteen colonies, though there is one long section on what it's like to live on Nantucket and be a sailor.

At that time "America" was a strip of land about 300 miles wide, going south from Maine to Georgia. In the absence of airplanes, satellites, and so forth, no one knew exactly how much more land there was west of the frontier.

But the general feeling was that for all practical purposes this continent was infinite. As Hector St. John de Crèvecoeur says in *Letters From an American Farmer*, "Many ages will not see the shores of our great lakes replenished with inland nations, nor the unknown bounds of North America entirely peopled. Who can tell how far it extends?"

St. John was wrong, of course. It did not take many ages to start inland nations on the shores of our Great Lakes. It took about two generations. Fifty years after he wrote the book, the inland nation of Illinois came into being. Another fifty years and Chicago was a large city, another forty and it had two million people. But he couldn't know that. He and everyone else in 1770 thought we would still have a frontier in, say, the twenty-fifth century, and that the still-growing country could absorb all the immigrants who might ever wish to come, that it, in fact, would always *need* more. "There is room for everybody in America," he wrote. And, remember, America had already existed for a century and a half when he wrote that: The image was firmly fixed that this was an infinite country.

The other thing that St. John took for granted was that pure nature is an appalling thing. He saw no beauty in wilderness whatsoever. Trackless forests did not appeal to him, and he considered frontiersmen corrupt and degenerate barbarians. What he liked, what he thought beautiful was the collaboration between man and nature that a farm is, and he considered that the best possible use of a person's time lay in taming wild nature.

5. Written by Michel Guillaume Jean de Crèvecoeur (1735–1813), a French author, agronomist, and traveler who used the pen name J. Hector St. John Crèvecoeur.

> To examine how the world is gradually settled, how the howling swamp is converted into a pleasing meadow, the rough ridge into a fine field; and to hear the cheerful whistling, the rural song, where there was no sound heard before save . . . the screech of the owl or the hissing of the snake—

that, says St. John, gives him enormous pleasure. He explains to his European audience how the first thing an American does when he comes into a new piece of wilderness is to build a bridge over whatever creek or little river runs through it, and the second is to take his axe and chop down as many acres of trees as he has energy to do that year, and the third is to start draining swamps and other wetlands. And perfectly reasonable, too, since the woods, the swamps, and the rivers are infinite. But St. John's assumptions are that nature is not in any way sacred, or precious, or to be treasured just because it exists; on the contrary it is badly in need of collaboration with man, and only under our governance can it become the beautiful thing it should be. And he also assumes, as the Bible told him to, that nature has no other important function than to serve us. He even thinks that God intended the wolves, the bears, the snakes, and the Indians themselves to give way before us. He doesn't worry about their becoming extinct, because the continent is infinite—but I think if you pressed him, he'd say that had to be their eventual fate.

15 One other observation of St. John's demands mention, even though it has little to do with nature, only nurture. I mentioned that one long section of the book is about Nantucket, a place St. John greatly admired. It was a Quaker community, and already deep into whaling—the people St. John met there were the great-grandfathers of the people Melville[6] wrote about in *Moby-Dick.* St. John also admired the women of Nantucket, who ran the farms while their husbands were off whaling—and whom he regarded as the most spirited, independent, and, incidentally, good-looking women in America—which for him means they were the most spirited, independent, and good-looking women in the world. But, he says, "a singular custom prevails here among the women, at which I was greatly surprised. . . . They have adopted these many years the Asiatic custom of taking a dose of opium every morning, and so deeply rooted is it that they would be at a loss how to live without this indulgence; they would rather be deprived of any necessary than forego their favorite luxury." Nantucket men, St. John says, didn't touch opium.

Now I want to move ahead to 1804, which was the year that President Jefferson sent Captains Meriwether Lewis and William Clark of the U.S. Army across the continent on foot, the first human beings, so

6. Herman Melville (1819–1891), American novelist and poet.

far as I know, to make that entire trip across what is now the United States. It took them and their party of twenty-five enlisted men and a couple of guides two years to get to the Pacific ocean and back again. Plus, as usual, rather more money than the government had anticipated. President Jefferson budgeted the two-year trip for thirty people, including boats, a newly invented airgun to impress the Indians, all supplies, at $2,500. The actual cost of the expedition was nearly $5,000. But it did reach the Pacific.

After Lewis and Clark, no one could think that North America was infinite. They returned with maps and mileage estimates. The shrinking process had begun. But it was still huge—a place that takes you a year to cross in each direction—and it was still largely pure nature.

Lewis and Clark did not see the wilderness quite the way St. John did—partly because the region he knew was all woods, and a great deal of their time was spent crossing the Great Plains, the grassy open plains with herds of antelope and buffalo. What struck them was that nature had already made the center of America into a garden, just waiting for the settlers to come cultivate it. In fact, some of it God or nature had already cultivated for us. On July 10, 1804, going up the Missouri River, they passed a piece of bottom-land: 2,000 acres covered with wild potatoes. At any time, there were hordes of deer, wild turkeys, elk, just waiting to be killed. Lewis gave it as his professional army captain's opinion that two hunters could keep a regiment supplied with meat. On August 5, 1804, Captain Clark noticed how abundant the fresh fruit was. "Great quantities of grapes on the banks. I observe three kinds, at this time ripe." On August 16, 1804, Captain Lewis and twelve men spent the morning fishing. Here's the report: "Caught upwards of 800 fine fish: 79 pike, 8 salmon resembling trout, 1 rock, 1 flat back, 127 buffalo and red horse, 4 bass, 490 cats, with many small silver fish and shrimp."

Sometimes, when the captains climbed a hill for the view, a whole section of what is now Iowa or Nebraska would remind them of a giant stock farm back in Virginia. Lewis described one view in which there was a forest of wild plum trees on one side—"loaded with fruit and now ripe"—and on the other twenty miles of open grassland, smooth as a bowling green. "This scenery," he says, "already rich, pleasing, and beautiful, was still further heightened by immense herds of buffalo, deer, elk, and antelopes, which we saw in every direction. . . . I do not think I exaggerate when I estimate the number of buffalo which could be comprehended at one view to be 3,000." The wolves prowling around the edge of each herd even reminded him of the sheepdogs back in Virginia.

20 Again, the sense is that nature is so bounteous that we could never possibly run short of anything. Nor was this some special white prejudice. The Indians felt the same. Lewis and Clark watched several

times while a small tribe of Plains Indians drove a whole herd of buffalo over a cliff, took the tongues and humps of a couple of dozen to eat, and left all the rest to rot. Why not? There was no more need to be frugal with buffalo than we feel the need to be frugal with, say, ice cubes. Don't think I'm blaming either Lewis and Clark or the Indians. Their behavior made perfect sense at the time.

Nature wasn't all bounty, though. For example, the whole region was swarming with grizzly bears: eating plums, waiting at the bottoms of cliffs for someone to drive a herd of buffalo over, and just generally enjoying life. They were not a bit afraid of American soldiers. And in fact a soldier with a single-shot rifle was in no way a match for a grizzly. By experience, Lewis and Clark found that about six soldiers equaled one grizzly. If all six shot, they were pretty likely to kill the bear with no one being hurt or chased up a tree. If fewer shot, there was apt to be trouble.

There was other trouble, too. When the expedition reached the Rocky Mountains, they found the peaks terrifying. Not beautiful (except snow-capped from a distance), not fun to be in. Instead, a place where you were very apt to starve to death, freeze to death, fall off a cliff. A typical campsite was by the mountain stream they called Hungry Creek—"at that place we had nothing to eat"—where they spent the night of September 18, 1805. A typical adventure occurred the next morning when Private Robert Frazer's packhorse, bought from the Indians, lost its footing and rolled a hundred yards down a precipice.

Most of the year, the only food you were going to find in the Rockies was what you carried in on your back, and when you ran out of that, there was no store to buy more at, nor could you decide to quit and hitch a ride back to Virginia, much less catch a plane to Denver. In short, not only was nature huge, but man was weak. Clever—clever enough to have invented axes and to drive stupid buffalo off cliffs—but weak. Nature, Mother Nature, was a worthy opponent as well as a worthy partner. In fact, let me make a sort of metaphor out of the grizzly and the buffalo, the two of them standing for wild nature. Both are physically stronger than men, and can run faster. One, the grizzly, is untameable, and more or less useless to us. So the thing to do is kill them, and that's a heroic and dangerous task: one part of subduing the wilderness. The other, the buffalo, is partially tameable, and very useful to us. Kill them, too, but not all of them, because we want them around to eat. Or else replace them with cattle, which are completely tameable. That's another part of subduing the wilderness—less heroic, maybe, but still a big job, and still nature offers plenty of resistance to the changes we make. The collaboration is not entirely on our terms, but partly on hers.

In sum, for the first two centuries that Europeans lived in North

America, they saw the continent as a giant wilderness or desert—they used the two words interchangeably—the motto of Dartmouth College, *Vox clamantis in deserto,* translates to "A voice crying in the wilderness." They saw a vast, powerful, and immensely rich wilderness, which it would be the bounden duty of their descendants to turn into farms and gardens and alabaster cities, but which we would never entirely do, because the country was so damned big and the power of the axe and plow so limited.

25 All that began to change in the nineteenth century with the growth of technology. Railroads and steamboats were, of course, the first major manifestations. They made the wilderness accessible and the continent (relatively) small. In so doing, they produced the first few converts to a new point of view. Henry David Thoreau[7] was one. Thoreau lived right next to the Fitchburg Railroad. He saw quite clearly the threat steam posed to untamed nature. Steam engines are bigger and faster than grizzlies. Steam saws can cut trees up far more quickly than forests can grow them. Steam shovels can drain an everglade.

Wilderness threatened became wilderness desirable—for the handful of converts. Thoreau was, as far as I know, the first American who publicly concluded that wilderness as wilderness—that is, pure nature—was a good thing to have around. In the 1850s he made a proposal that each town in Massachusetts save a 500-acre piece of woods which would be forever wild: no lumbering, no changes at all. Needless to say, he got nowhere, not even in Concord itself. It was still too much like going down to McDonald's and suggesting to the manager that he put 500 ice cubes in permanent deep freeze, against the time when ice may be scarce.

John Muir[8] was a slightly later convert. It's a coincidence, but a nice coincidence, that the year in which he began to describe the western mountains as wonderful places, sacred ground, God's outdoor temples, was the same year in which the transcontinental railroad was completed. That was 1869. Henceforth the Lewis and Clark journey of a year could be done in a few days. Muir, like Thoreau before him, sensed the growth of man's power against nature, though in 1869 nature was still stronger. And, of course, Muir could be romantic about mountains in part because by now the country had been so much tamed that within one day's walk of most of his camping places in the Sierras he could borrow or buy flour to make bread with, sometimes even go to a regular store. He could even be worried about the ecologi-

7. American essayist and naturalist (1817–1862), best known for *Walden, or, Life in the Woods* (1854).

8. Scottish-born American naturalist (1838–1914), known especially for his writing about Wisconsin and the Yosemite Valley, California.

cal harm that overgrazing by sheep was doing in the Sierras, and eventually have some success in banning sheep from portions.

Ever since then, human power has grown at an almost geometric rate, while the forces of nature have remained static. The ascending line was bound eventually to cross the level one. It's not possible to pinpoint the year in which this happened, but it *is* possible to suggest a decade. I think the 1950s represent the swing point in man's relationship to nature, certainly in the United States, and probably in the whole world. During that decade we became stronger than our surroundings. Certainly not in all ways—such physical phenomena as earthquakes and hurricanes and volcanoes remain quite beyond our power to control. But in most ways. The biggest river isn't even difficult for us to bridge, or to dam. No other living creature can seriously dispute us, certainly not on a one-to-one basis. In Melville's day, six men in a whaleboat were generally a match for one whale—but not always; sometimes the whale won. By the 1950s, one man with a harpoon gun could do in any number of whales. There's not even any thrill to it.

More important than any of this, by the 1950s our science and our engineering enabled us to produce new substances and to distribute old substances on a scale equal to nature's own. For example, we can put sulfur dioxide in the air at a rate faster than the volcanoes do. One single refinery in Sudbury, Ontario, became the source of 5 percent of all the sulfur dioxide that entered the air of the entire planet, there to become sulfuric acid and to come down again as acid rain and snow. One fleet of jet airplanes could seriously affect the ozone layer.

We have earth-moving machinery that can rearrange a whole land- 30
scape. We have new chemical compounds that can affect the whole chain of life. Nature cannot easily absorb the effect of DDT or of Sevin; nature is no longer resilient. We can nearly eliminate whales, sort of half-meaning to, and we can all but extinguish peregrine falcons as an unintended by-product of raising crops. We really are what our ancestors only claimed to be: the masters of nature—or at least we're the dominant partner in the collaboration. To use one more metaphor, we are like goldfish who have been living in an aquarium for as long as we can remember; and being clever goldfish, we have discovered how to manipulate the controls of the aquarium: put more oxygen in the water, get rid of the pesky turtle we never liked anyway, triple the supply of goldfish food. Only once we realize we're partly running the aquarium, it scares some of us. What if we make a mistake, and wreck the aquarium entirely? We couldn't live outside it.

That has been the actual position since the 1950s, and it is what our rational minds clearly report. The green light has turned yellow, and there is a real possibility it will go to red. But it is not what our emotions tell us. Emotionally, almost all of us still believe what the Dutch sailors thought: that here is an inexhaustible new world, with plenty of everything for everybody.

And because of that emotion, which I, too, share, we have had a double response since the 1950s. One is to do our damndest to keep part of our continent still virgin—pure nature, wilderness. That's the nature-lover's response, the Sierra Club response, and sometimes the environmentalist's response. It's almost uniquely American. I have a friend, for example, who is a Spanish environmentalist, and I know from him that there is exactly one national park in Spain, the former hunting forest of the dukes of Medina, and even that is by no means a wilderness area. Spain is not virgin country. At the moment, about 2 percent of the United States is official wilderness, just about the same amount that is paved. And in a country this big, 2 percent is quite a lot: something like 60,000 square miles, twelve times as big as the state of Connecticut.

In terms of our whole population, to be sure, it's less impressive: If you put all of us in the wilderness at once, we'd each have a fifth of an acre. But it's enough to give a comforting illusion that pure nature is still going, independent of us. And most people who seek that illusion also want to downplay their separateness from nature, and to say that we have no right to meddle, our collaboration is deadly. We goldfish should stand back and let the aquarium run itself as it always has.

The other response involves a much greater illusion—or I think it does, anyway. And that is simply to deny that anything has changed significantly since the days of Hector St. John de Crèvecoeur and Lewis and Clark. This is the response, for example, of the present United States government. We're still just collaborators with nature, people who hold this view say, more effective collaborators than we used to be, certainly; and if we do our part, nature will do its. Nature is still resilient; it can still absorb anything we do. Besides, we were meant to rule the planet—this aquarium was designed specially for us—and what we do was pretty much all allowed for in the original design.

35 One group wants to re-create the world the Dutch sailors saw, and the other denies that it has ever ceased to exist. If I have to choose, of course I choose to be one of the re-creators—to try to protect as much wilderness as possible. I'd like to get the proportion of untouched land up to 3 percent. I've even dreamt of 4 percent.

But neither group, I think, is right. Neither has really dealt with the fact that a generation ago the green light turned yellow. If there is anything that is really, really worth doing in the rest of this century, I think, it's to find a third and better way of dealing with the relationship between man and nature.

Joseph Wood Krutch

THE MOST DANGEROUS PREDATOR

In the United States the slaughter of wild animals for fun is subject to certain restrictions fairly well enforced. In Mexico the laws are less strict and in many regions there is little or no machinery for enforcement. Hence an automobile club in southern California distributes to its members an outline map of Baja[1] purporting to indicate in detail just where various large animals not yet quite extinct may be found by those eager to do their bit toward eliminating them completely. This map gives the impression that pronghorn antelopes, mountain sheep, and various other "game animals" abound.

In actual fact, the country can never have supported very many such and today the traveler accustomed to the open country of our own Southwest would be struck by the fact that, except for sea birds, sea mammals and fish, wildlife of any kind is far scarcer than at home. This is no doubt due in part to American hunters but also in part to the fact that native inhabitants who once could not afford the cartridges to shoot anything they did not intend to eat now get relatively cheap ammunition from the United States and can indulge in what seems to be the almost universal human tendency to kill anything that moves.

Someday—probably a little too late—the promoters of Baja as a resort area will wake up to the fact that wildlife is a tourist attraction and that though any bird or beast can be observed or photographed an unlimited number of times it can be shot only once. The Mexican government is cooperating with the government of the United States in a successful effort to save the gray whale and the sea elephant but to date does not seem much interested in initiating its own measures of protection. As long ago as 1947, Lewis Wayne Walker (who guided me on our innocent hunt for the boojum trees he had previously photographed) wrote for *Natural History Magazine* a survey of the situation, particularly as it concerns the pronghorn and the mountain sheep. A quarter of a century before, herds of antelope were to be found within thirty or forty miles of the United States border. But by 1933 they had all, so a rancher told him, been killed after a party of quail hunters had discovered them. In the roadless areas some bands of mountain sheep

From *The Best Nature Writing of Joseph Wood Krutch* (1969).

1. A Mexican peninsula extending some 760 miles south from the U.S. border and separating the Gulf of California from the Pacific Ocean.

still existed (and doubtless do even today) but the water holes near traversable areas were already deserted by the mid forties. All the large animals of a given region must come to drink at the only pool or spring for many miles around, hence a single party need only wait beside it to exterminate the entire population inhabiting that area. Though Walker had driven more than ten thousand miles on the Baja trails during the two years preceding the writing of his letter, he saw only one deer, no sheep, and no antelope. Despite the publicity given it, "Baja is," he wrote, "the poorest game area I have ever visited."

The depredations of the hunter are not always the result of any fundamental blood lust. Perhaps he is only, more often than not, merely lacking in imagination. The exterminator of the noble animals likes the out-of-doors and thrills at the sight of something which suggests the world as it once was. But contemplation is not widely recognized as an end in itself. Having seen the antelope or the sheep, he must "do something about it." And the obvious thing to do is to shoot.

5 In the *Sea of Cortez* John Steinbeck[2] describes how a Mexican rancher invited his party to a sheep hunt. They were reluctant to accept until they realized that the rancher himself didn't really want to kill the animals—he merely didn't know what other excuse to give for seeking them out. When his Indians returned empty-handed he said with only mild regret: "If they had killed one we could have had our pictures taken with it." Then Steinbeck adds: "They had taught us the best of all ways to go hunting and we shall never use any other. We have, however, made one slight improvement on their method; we shall not take a gun, thereby obviating the last remote possibility of having the hunt cluttered up with game. We have never understood why men mount the heads of animals and hang them up to look down on their conquerors. Possibly it feels good to these men to be superior to animals but it does seem that if they were sure of it they would not have to prove it." Later, when one of the Indians brought back some droppings which he seemed to treasure and presented a portion of them to the white men, Steinbeck adds: "Where another man can say, 'there was an animal but because I am greater than he, he is dead and I am alive and there is his head to prove it' we can say, 'there was an animal, and for all we know there still is and here is proof of it. He was very healthy when we last heard of him.' "

"Very pretty," so the tough-minded will say, "but hardly realistic. Man is a predator, to be sure, but he isn't the only one. The mountain lion killed sheep long before even the Indian came to Baja. The law of

2. American author (1902–1968). California, Steinbeck's birthplace, was the setting of many of his books.

life is also a law of death. Nature is red in tooth and claw. You can't get away from that simple fact and there is no use in trying. Whatever else he may be, man is an animal; and like the other animals he is the enemy of all other living things. You talk of 'the balance of nature' but we are an element in it. As we increase, the mountain sheep disappear. The fittest, you know, survive."

Until quite recent times this reply would have been at least a tenable one. Primitive man seems to have been a rather unsuccessful animal, few in numbers and near the ragged edge of extinction. But gradually the balance shifted. He held his own; then he increased in numbers; then he developed techniques of aggression as well as of protection incomparably more effective than any which nature herself had ever been able to devise before the human mind intervened. Up until then, animals had always been a match, one for another. But they were no match for him. The balance no longer worked. Though for another 500,000 years "coexistence" still seemed to be a *modus vivendi*[3] the time came, only a short while ago, when man's strength, his numbers, and his skill made him master and tyrant. He now dominated the natural world of which he had once been only a part. Now for the first time he could exterminate, if he wished to do so, any other living creature—perhaps even (as we learned just yesterday) his fellow man. What this means in a specific case; what the difference is between nature, however red she may be in tooth and claw, and the terrifying predator who is no longer subject to the limitations she once imposed, can readily be illustrated on the Baja peninsula. In neither case is the story a pretty one. Both involve a ruthless predator and the slaughter of innocents. But nature's far from simple plan does depend upon a coexistence. Man is, on the other hand, the only animal who habitually exhausts or exterminates what he has learned to exploit.

Let us, then, take first a typical dog-eat-story as nature tells it, year after year, on Rasa Island, where confinement to a small area keeps it startlingly simple, without any of these sub-plots which make nature's usual stories so endlessly complicated.

This tiny island—less than a mile square in area and barely one hundred feet above sea level at its highest point—lies in the Gulf fifteen or twenty miles away from the settlement at Los Angeles Bay. It is rarely visited because even in fair weather the waters round about it are treacherous. Currents up to eight knots create whirlpools between it and other small islands and there is a tide drop of twelve to thirty feet, depending upon the season. It is almost bare of vegetation except for a little of the salt weed or Salicornia which is found in so many of

3. "Way of getting along."

the saline sands in almost every climate. But it is the nesting place of thousands of Heermann gulls who, after the young are able to fend for themselves, migrate elswhere—a few southward as far as Central America but most of them north to various points on the Pacific coast. A few of the latter take the shortest route across the Baja peninsula but most take what seems an absurd detour by going first some 450 miles south to the tip of Baja and then the eight hundred or a thousand miles up its west coast to the United States—perhaps, as seems to be the case in various other paradoxes of migration—because they are following some ancestral habit acquired when the climate or the lay of the land was quite different.

10 My travels in Baja are, I hope, not finished, and I intend someday to set foot on Rasa to see what goes on there for myself. So far, however, I have observed the huge concentration of birds only from a low-flying plane and what I have to describe is what Walker has told me and what he wrote some ten years ago in an illustrated account for the *National Geographic Magazine.*

In late April, when the breeding season is at its height, the ground is crowded with innumerable nests—in some places no more than a yard apart, nowhere with more than twenty feet between them. Because man has so seldom disturbed the gulls here they show little fear of him though once they have reached the northern shore they rise and fly out to sea at the first sight of a human being.

If this were all there was to tell, Rasa might seem to realize that idyllic state of nature of which man, far from idyllic though he has made his own society, often loves to dream. Though on occasion gulls are predators as well as scavengers they respect one another's eggs and offspring on Rasa and live together in peace. But like most animals (and like most men) they are ruthless in their attitude toward other species though too utterly nature's children to rationalize as man does that ruthlessness. They know in their nerves and muscles without even thinking about it that the world was made for the exclusive use and convenience of gulls.

In the present case the victims of that egomania of the species are the two kinds of tern which share the island with them and have chosen to lay their eggs in a depression surrounded by gulls.

Here Walker had best tell his own story: "In the early morning of the second day a few eggs were seen under the terns but even as we watched, several were stolen by gulls. By late afternoon not an egg remained. Nightfall brought on an influx of layers, and morning found twice as many eggs dotting the ground. By dusk only a fraction of the number in the exact center of the plot had escaped the inroads of the egg-eating enemy.

15 "The new colony had now gained a permanent foothold. Accordion-

like it expanded during the night, contracted by evening. Each twenty-four hour period showed a gain for the terns and a corresponding retreat in the waiting ranks of the killing gulls.

"By the end of a week the colony had expanded from nothing to approximately four hundred square feet of egg-spotted ground and it continued to spread. The gulls seemed to be losing their appetites. Like children sated with ice cream, they had found that a single diet can be over-done."

What an absurd—some would say what a horrid—story that is. How decisively it gives the lie to what the earliest idealizers of nature called her "social union." How difficult it makes it to believe that some all-good, omnipotent, conscious, and transcendental power consciously chose to set up a general plan of which this is a typical detail. How much more probable it makes it seem that any purpose that may exist in the universe is one emerging from a chaos rather than one which had deliberately created that chaos.

But a fact remains: one must recognize that the scheme works—for the terns as well as for the gulls. If it is no more than the mechanism which so many call it, then it is at least (to use the newly current terminology) a cybernetic or self–regulating mechanism. If the gulls destroyed so many eggs that the tern population began to decline, then the gulls, deprived of their usual food supply, would also decline in numbers and the terns would again increase until the balance had been reached. "How careful of the type she seems; how careless of the single life"—as Tennyson observed some years before Darwin[4] made the same humanly disturbing fact a cornerstone of his theories.

Absurd as the situation on Rasa may seem, it has probably existed for thousands of years and may well continue for thousands more—if left to itself, undisturbed by the only predator who almost invariably renders the "cybernetic" system inoperable.

Consider now the case of the elephant seal, a great sea beast four- 20
teen to sixteen feet long and nearly three tons in weight. Hardly more than a century ago it bred in enormous numbers on the rocky coast and on the islands from Point Reyes, just north of San Francisco, almost to the Magdalena Bay on the Pacific coast of Baja. Like the gray whale it was preyed upon by the ferocious killer whale which is, perhaps, the most formidable of all the predators of the sea. But a balance had been reached and the two coexisted in much the same fashion as the gulls and the terns of Rasa.

4. Charles Darwin (1809–1882), English naturalist whose *Origin of Species* (1859) and *The Descent of Man* (1871) set forth his theory of evolution. Alfred, Lord Tennyson (1809–1892), English poet.

Unfortunately (at least for them) human enterprise presently discovered that sea elephants could become a source of oil second in importance to the whale alone. And against this new predator nature afforded no protection. The elephant seals had learned to be wary of the killer whale but they had known no enemy on land and they feared none. Because instinct is slow while the scheming human brain works fast, those who must depend upon instinct are lost before it can protect them against any new threat. Captain Scammon, always clear, vivid, and businesslike, describes how easy and how profitable it was to bring the seals as near to extinction as the gray whales were brought at approximately the same time:

"The mode of capturing them is thus; the sailors get between the herd and the water; then raising all possible noise by shouting, and at the same time flourishing clubs, guns, and lances, the party advances slowly towards the rookery, when the animals will retreat, appearing in a state of great alarm. Occasionally, an overgrown male will give battle, or attempt to escape; but a musket ball through the brain dispatches it; or someone checks its progress by thrusting a lance into the roof of its mouth, which causes it to settle on its haunches, when two men with heavy oaken clubs give the creature repeated blows about the head, until it is stunned or killed. After securing those that are disposed to showing resistance, the party rush on the main body. The onslaught creates such a panic among these peculiar creatures, that, losing all control of their actions, they climb, roll, and tumble over each other, when prevented from further retreat by the projecting cliffs. We recollect in one instance, where sixty-five were captured, that several were found showing no signs of having been either clubbed or lanced but were smothered by numbers of their kind heaped upon them. The whole flock, when attacked, manifested alarm by their peculiar roar, the sound of which, among the largest males, is nearly as loud as the lowing of an ox, but more prolonged in one strain, accompanied by a rattling noise in the throat. The quantity of blood in this species of the seal tribe is supposed to be double that contained in an ox, in proportion to its size.

"After the capture, the flay begins. First, with a large knife, the skin is ripped along the upper side of the body its whole length, and then cut down as far as practicable, without rolling it over; then the coating of fat that lies between the skin and flesh—which may be from one to seven inches in thickness, according to the size and condition of the animal—is cut into 'horse pieces,' about eight inches wide and twelve to fifteen long, and a puncture is made in each piece sufficiently large to pass a rope through. After flensing the upper portion of the body, it is rolled over, and cut all around as above described. Then the 'horse pieces' are strung on a raft rope (a rope three fathoms long, with an eye splice in one end) and taken to the edge of the surf; a long line is made fast to it, the end of which is thrown to a boat lying just outside of the breakers; they are then hauled through the rollers and towed to the vessel, where the oil is tried out by boiling the blubber, or fat, in large pots set in a brick furnace. . . . The oil produced is superior to whale oil for lubricating purposes. Owing to the continual pursuit of the animals, they have become nearly if not quite extinct on the California coast, or the few remaining have fled to some unknown point for security."

Captain Scammon's account was first published in the *Overland Monthly* in 1870. A few members of the herds he had helped to slaughter must have survived because in 1884 the zoologist Charles Haskins Townsend accompanied a party of sealers who hunted for two months and succeeded in killing sixty. Then, eight years later, he found eight elephant seals on Guadalupe, the lonely lava-capped island twenty-two by seven miles in extent which lies 230 miles southwest of Ensenada in Baja and is the most westerly of Mexican possessions.

It seems to be a biological law that if a given species diminishes in 25
numbers, no matter how slowly, it presently reaches a point of no return from which even the most careful fostering cannot bring it back. Eight elephant seals would probably have been far too few to preserve the species; but there must have been others somewhere because when Townsend visited the islands again in 1911 he found 125, and in 1922 scientists from the Scripps Institution and the California Academy of Sciences counted 264 males at a time of year when the females had already left the breeding grounds.

Had Guadalupe not happened to be one of the most remote and inaccessible islands in our part of the world, the few refugees could hardly have survived. By the time it became known that on Guadalupe they had not only survived but multiplied into the hundreds, sealers would almost certainly have sought them out again to finish the job of extermination had not the Mexican government agreed to make Guadalupe a closed area. Because the elephant seal has again no enemy except the killer whale it now occupies all the beaches of the island to which it fled and has established new colonies on various other small islands in the same Pacific area, especially on the San Benitos group nearly two hundred miles to the east. By 1950 the total population was estimated at one thousand.

The earliest voyagers described Guadalupe, rising majestically from the sea to its four-thousand-foot summit, as a true island paradise and also, like other isolated islands, so rich in the unique forms of life which had been slowly evolved in isolation that half the birds and half the plants were unknown anywhere else. So far, I know it only by reputation and have not even seen it, as I have seen Rasa, from the air; but it is said to be very far from a paradise today. Though inhabited only by a few officers of the Mexican Navy who operate a meteorological station, whalers had begun to visit it as early as 1700 and disastrously upset the balance of nature by intentionally introducing goats to provide food for subsequent visits and unintentionally allowing cats and rats to escape from their ships. Several thousand wild goats as well as innumerable cats and rats now manage to exist there, but it is said that almost nothing of the original flora and fauna remains. Most of the unique birds are extinct; the goats have nibbled the trees as high as they are able to reach, and have almost completely destroyed all other plant life. In the absence of the natural predators necessary to establish a tolerable balance, many of the goats are said to die of starvation every year for the simple reason that any animal population will ultimately destroy its own food supply unless multiplication is regulated by either natural or artificial means. Guadalupe is, in short, a perfect demonstration of three truths: (1) That nature left to herself establishes a *modus vivendi* which may be based upon tooth and claw but which nevertheless does permit a varied flora and fauna to live and flourish; (2) that man easily upsets the natural balance so quickly and drastically that nature herself cannot reestablish it in any fashion so generally satisfactory as that which prevailed before the balance was destroyed; (3) that man, if he wishes, can mitigate to some extent the destructive effects of his intervention by intervening again to save some individual species as he seems now to have saved the gray whale and the elephant seal.

How important is it that he should come to an adequate realization of these three truths? Of the second he must take some account if he is not, like the goats of Guadalupe, to come up against the fact that any species may become so "successful" that starvation is inevitable as the ultimate check upon its proliferation and that from this fate not even his technology can save him ultimately, because even those cakes of sewage-grown algae with which he is already experimenting could do no more than postpone a little longer the final day of reckoning. He has proved himself so much cleverer than nature that, once he has intervened, she can no longer protect him just as she could not protect either the life indigenous to Guadalupe or the goats man had introduced there. Having decided to go it alone, he needs for his survival to become more clever still and, especially, more farseeing.

On the other hand, and if he so wishes, he can, perhaps, disregard the other two laws that prevent the gradual disappearance of every area which illustrates the profusion and variety which nature achieves by her own methods and he may see no reason why he should preserve from extinction the elephant seal, which will probably never again be commercially valuable, or for that matter any other of the plants and animals which supply none of his physical needs. None of them may be necessary to his survival, all of them merely "beautiful" or "curious," rather than "useful."

Many arguments have been advanced by those who would persuade 30
him to take some thought before it is too late. But the result may depend less upon arguments than upon the attitudes which are essentially emotional and aesthetic.

Thoreau[5]—perhaps the most eloquent exponent we have ever had of the practical, the aesthetic, and the mystical goods which man can receive from the contemplation of the natural as opposed to the man-made or man-managed—once wrote as follows:

"When I consider that the nobler animals have been exterminated here—the cougar, the panther, lynx, wolverine, wolf, bear, moose, deer, the beaver, the turkey and so forth and so forth, I cannot but feel as if I lived in a tamed and, as it were, emasculated country. . . . Is it not a maimed and imperfect nature that I am conversing with? As if I were to study a tribe of Indians that had lost all its warriors. . . . I take infinite pains to know all the phenomena of the spring, for instance, thinking that I have here the entire poem, and then, to my chagrin, I hear that it is but an imperfect copy that I possess and have read, that my ancestors had torn out many of the first leaves and grandest passages, and mutilated it in many places. I should not like to think that some demigod had come before me and picked out some of the best of the stars. I wish to know an entire heaven and an entire earth."

To what proportion of the human race such a statement is, or could be made, meaningful I do not know. But upon the answer that time is already beginning to give will depend how much, if any, of the "poem" will be legible even a few generations hence.

Many of us now talk as if, until recently, there was no need to talk about "conservation." Probably there are today more men than ever before who could answer in the affirmative Emerson's[6] question:

"Hast thou named all the birds without a gun? 35
Loved the wild rose, and left it on its stalk?"

But in absolute rather than relative numbers there are vastly more men today equipped with vastly more efficient instruments of destruction than there ever were before and many of them respect neither the bird nor the wild rose. As of this moment it is they who are winning against everything those of us who would like to preserve the poem are able to say or do.

5. Henry David Thoreau (1817–1862), American author and naturalist.
6. Ralph Waldo Emerson (1803–1882), American poet and essayist, friend of Thoreau.

QUESTIONS

1. *What is the distinction Krutch makes between predation within the nonhuman world of nature and predation on the creatures of that world by man?*
2. *Krutch obviously feels disdain for men who shoot and kill wild animals. Locate sentences in which he expresses that disdain, and analyze how they work.*
3. *Krutch wrote this essay over thirty years ago. Have any of the facts changed? If he were writing today, would he need to modify any of his conclusions in paragraph 27?*
4. *Taking the gulls and terns as a kind of model, explore the similarities and differences in some other relationship of predation—for instance, birds and mosquitoes, mosquitoes and people, hunters and deer—and write a brief account of how the relationship works.*

John McPhee

DUTY OF CARE

The world's largest pile of scrap tires is not visible from Interstate 5, in Stanislaus County, California. But it's close. Below Stockton, in the region of Modesto and Merced, the highway follows the extreme western edge of the flat Great Central Valley, right next to the scarp where the Coast Ranges are territorially expanding as fresh unpopulated hills. The hills conceal the tires from the traffic. If you were to abandon your car three miles from the San Joaquin County line and make your way on foot southwest one mile, you would climb into steeply creased terrain that in winter is jade green and in summer straw brown, and, any time at all, you would come upon a black vista. At rest on sloping ground, the tires are so deep that they form their own topography—their own escarpments, their own overhanging cliffs. Deposited from a ridgeline, they border a valley for nearly half a mile. When you first glimpse them, you are not sure what they are. From the high ground on the opposite side, the individual tires appear to be grains of black sand. They look like little eggstones—oolites—each a bright yolk ringed in black pearl. Close to them, you walk in tire canyons. In some places, they are piled six stories high, compressing themselves, densifying: at the top, tires; at the bottom, pucks. From the highest elevations of this thick and drifted black mantle, you can look east a hundred miles and see snow on the Sierra.

First published in *The New Yorker* (June 28, 1993).

The tires are from all sides of the bays of San Francisco and up and down the Great Central Valley from Bakersfield to Sacramento. Even before the interstate was there, a tire jockey named Ed Filbin began collecting them—charging dealers and gas stations "tipping fees" of so much per passenger tire and so much per truck tire, as tire jockeys everywhere do. This was long before people began to worry, with regard to used tires, about mosquitoes, fires, landfills, and compounding environmental concerns, or to look upon old tires as a minable resource. Filbin's pile just grew, and he made enough money to diversify, becoming, as he is today, the largest sheep rancher in Nevada. Meanwhile, his tire ranch near Modesto continued to broaden and thicken, until no one, including Filbin, knew how many tires were there. Eventually, the state took notice—and county zoning authorities—and Filbin felt harassed. When I called him one day in Nevada, he sketched these people as "dirty rotten bureaucrats" and said, "I told them to go jump in a crick. I had grandfather rights." With those words, he cradled his telephone, refusing to say more.

There have been many estimates of the number of tires in the great California pile, but the figures tend to be high or low in direct proportion to the appraiser's economic interest or environmental bias. The variations can be absurd, missing agreement with one another by factors as high as five. Not long ago, while I was at the University of California, Davis, working on something else, I began to muse about the tire pile and the problem of counting its contents. In the university library I found David Lundquist, the map librarian, and asked for his suggestions. The pile does not appear on the 7.5-minute Solyo Quadrangle of the United States Geological Survey, and I thought he might have a more sophisticated map of equally ample scale. He said he had recent low-altitude aerial photographs made by the federal Agricultural Stabilization and Conservation Service that amounted to an eyeball-to-earth mosaic of the state. The prints were nine by ten and were in several map-cabinet drawers. Comparing map and photograph indexes, he rummaged through stacks of pictures. When No. 507-52 was at last before us, a shape in black Rorschach, sharply defined, stood out like a mountain lake. The terrain was veiny with clear draws and ridgelines, which made relatively simple the task of re-creating the dark shape on a copy of the Solyo topographic map. To help determine the acreage covered, a Davis geologist gave me a piece of graph paper whose squares were so small that four thousand four hundred and twenty-two of them covered one square mile on the map. Having seen the great pile and moved around it close, I could assign it an average thickness. Jack Waggoner, of Sacramento, who has spent his career as a distributor of tire-retreading and tire-shredding equipment, supplied figures for average densities of tires compressed by their own weight. On its side, a tire occupies about four square feet. A calculator blended these facts. While I had read or been given estimates of eight, nine, fifteen, twenty-five, forty-two, and forty-four, the calculator was reporting that in the world's largest known pile there are thirty-four million tires.

You don't have to stare long at that pile before the thought occurs to you that those tires were once driven upon by the Friends of the Earth. They are not just the used tires of bureaucrats, ballplayers, and litter-strewing rock-deafened ninja-teen-aged nyrds. They are everybody's tires. They are Environmental Defense Fund tires, Rainforest Action Network tires, Wilderness Society tires. They are California Natural Resources Federation tires, Save San Francisco Bay Association tires, Citizens for a Better Environment tires. They are Greenpeace tires, Sierra Club tires, Earth Island Institute tires. They are Earth First! tires! No one is innocent of scrapping those tires. They who carry out what they carry in have not carried out those tires. Of the problem the tire pile represents, everybody is the cause, and the problem, like the pile, has been increasing. (The California Integrated Waste Management Board has referred to the state's "growing tire population.") Most landfills across the country are refusing tires now, because most landfills are filling up, and, moreover, tires "float." They won't stay covered up. They work their way to the surface like glacial rocks. Intended by their manufacturers to be reliable and durable, they most emphatically are. Nothing about an automobile is safer than its tires, whose ultimate irony is that when they reach the end of their intended lives they are all but indestructible. When they are thrown away, they are just as tough as they were when they felt Kick 1. On the surface or underground or on the beds of rivers, they don't decay. They are one per cent of all municipal solid waste and symbol of the other ninety-nine. Locked into the chemistry of each passenger tire is more than two and a half gallons of recoverable petroleum. California by itself discards twenty million tires a year. The United States throws away two hundred and fifty million tires a year. Strewn about the country at last count are something like three billion trashed tires. A hundred and seventy-eight million barrels of oil.

5 In southern Connecticut, beside a meander bend of the Quinnipiac River, a large privately owned landfill includes a thirty-acre body of water known as the Tire Pond. It was once a quarry, a clay pit. The town line between Hamden and North Haven runs through it. For a decade or so, the tire jockey Joe Farricielli has been tipping tires into the water there. He collects from more than two hundred customers, almost all in Connecticut, who pay him sixty-five cents to take an ordinary tire and as much as five dollars to be rid of a large one. The Tire Pond, now about half full, contains fifteen million tires.

When I made a visit there, the place was managed by Jim Rizzo, vice-president of the Tire Pond. His office was a small brick structure landscaped with young spruce that were standing in the centers of tires. Rizzo was an easy-talking, slightly burly man with a dark and radical mustache, who would not have looked amiss teaching paleontology at Harvard. He was wearing bluejeans and a gray Lacoste pullover. It was an April morning, and out toward the pond we drove in his pickup past trailers newly arrived. Men were grading the tires in them—looking for "high treads," Rizzo said, to be resold. Up the road, the company used to have a retail outlet called Second Time Around. It was not a big success, but they still sell high treads for fifteen dollars at the pond. For California, Mexico is the second time around. California tire jockeys sell more than a million discarded tires in Mexico each year, where they are mounted on Mexicans' cars.

Now Rizzo and I were on a dirt road in what appeared to be a field of dry tires, eye high. There was open water beyond. He said that the tires were protruding above the surface of the pond and were resting on other tires, which went all the way to the bottom. They were standing in water as deep or deeper than most of the Atlantic Ocean dump sites in the New York bight. In fact, if we were to go down the Quinnipiac and across Long Island Sound and across Long Island to the ocean, we would have to go twenty miles out to sea to find a depth greater than the Tire Pond's. "After the tires get to be five or six feet above water, they are covered with geotextile fabric, and the fabric is then covered with clean fill—concrete, sand, stone, soil—two to three feet thick," Rizzo said. "That is the covering. Everything below that down to the bottom of the pond is tires. That covering is firm. In fact, you and I are now *on* the pond. We are driving on tires."

A large dump truck carrying seven hundred and fifty tires had also driven out upon the pond. It had stopped close to the rubber shoreline. A long stainless hydraulic shaft lifted one end of the bed. Seven hundred and fifty tires slid into the water. They looked like black ice cubes. Rizzo said that when tires are added they do not raise the level of the water. The excess just goes away. A tip is a place where material is dumped, as from wagons. This tip was what was left of the Stiles Brick Company, which in the nineteenth century and on into the twentieth had dug out two hundred thousand cubic yards of clay. The pond was a hundred and forty feet deep. No mosquitoes. No pests. No fires.

Soon after Joe Farricielli bought the landfill, in the middle nineteen-seventies, he experienced a tire fire, and that is what drew his attention to the potentialities of the pond. A tire fire sends off billows of stinking black acidulous smoke, which drifting downwind full of polynuclear aromatic hydrocarbons, benzene, and other toxic pollutants, attracts the attention of neighbors, zoning boards, and departments of environmental protection. Tire jockeys can recite by heart the roll call of the great fires: Platteville, Colorado, 1987, where the pile burned for four days; Hagersville, Ontario, 1990, where the pile burned for seventeen days; Palmetto, Georgia, 1992, where the fire burned for five weeks; Winchester, Virginia, 1983–84, where the pile burned continuously for nine months. In the Virginia fire, seven million tires were involved. Tire-pile fires are usually the result of arson. In the pile at Sid's in Norton, Ohio, four fires occurred within six months. Typically, the arsonist fills tires with newspapers. The Tire Pond was beyond the reach of the New Haven *Register*, the Hartford *Courant*, and even the incendiary New York *Times*.

10 To the Hagersville fire, outside Toronto, in February of 1990, the London Fire Brigade sent an observer. He noted the efficacy of sand and chemicals, and the inadvisability of fighting such fires with water, which augments the toxic spill. Where not much oxygen is involved, a burning tire will decompose into carbon black, gas, and oil. A tire fire oozes oil. If water is used to fight the fire, the oil travels with it. The fluid then contaminates groundwater, surface water, and soil. In Winchester, Virginia, where the tire fire burned for two hundred and seventy-five days, the runoff was collected. It included six hundred and ninety thousand gallons of oil, which was sold for a hundred and eighty-four thousand dollars.

Mosquitoes? A tire that is under water is not breeding mosquitoes. A tire with a little rain in it is a near-perfect mosquito incubator, as any reader of *Mosquito News* or the *Journal of the American Mosquito Control Association* can tell you. Almost any old tire, dumped legally or not, can help disseminate vector-borne viral diseases—for example, La Crosse virus, dengue fever, Sepik fever, Ross River fever, Japanese encephalitis, St. Louis encephalitis. The concern is not just domestic. In the complexities of international economics, the United States annually imports three million used tires. About a quarter of them contain a little water and, often, some mosquito larvae. The tires are, in large part, for recapping and reshipping to other parts of the world, but some are rejected for retreading. They go into scrap heaps, and the mosquitoes stay here. Most of the worn tires that arrive in ships come from Asian countries where *Aedes albopictus* is indigenous—a mosquito that can serve as a viral vector but by nature does not migrate and has a lifetime flight range of less than a thousand yards. In other words, this mosquito goes nowhere on its own. Used tires have dispersed it throughout the Western Hemisphere.

The State of Connecticut has checked the Tire Pond and found no *Aedes albopictus*, Rizzo said. Tires, moreover, are not exactly soluble; they don't affect the water. Since the pond's inception as a tire fill, it has had a water-compliance permit from the Department of Environmental Protection. As if to emphasize the tenor of Rizzo's presentation, two alabaster swans came into view, swimming on the Tire Pond. We were now beyond the filled area and beside the open water. We paused on the pond's eastern shore, on the isthmus that separated it from the Quinnipiac River. The view to the west was multilaminate and somewhat surreal. In the background, against the sky, was a hillside green with shade trees over spread-out suburban homes. The New Haven Country Club was up there somewhere, and Quinnipiac College, and Lake Whitney. The next layer, below, consisted of the light industries of State Street and a lengthy ribbon of a sign that said "Volkswagen, New and Used Cars." The stratum below that was Amtrak—New Haven to the left, Hartford to the right. The bottom layer was the Tire Pond, on its surface the Wagnerian swans, a couple of mallards, a few dozen gulls, and the black-sparkling ice-cube tires drifting about in the wind.

I was growing suspicious of Rizzo. The thought was occurring to me that he and Farricielli had imported the swans. In the bright sun, the birds seemed to blaze white. "We are members of the Audubon Society," Rizzo was saying. "People from Audubon come here to count the birds. Those ducks nest in the tires."

A day or two later, I would talk on the telephone with Milan Bull, director of field studies and ornithology, Connecticut Audubon Society, who said that he always goes to the Tire Pond at Christmas and at one or two other times during the year. "Open spaces attract birds," he explained. "They like the weeds there. Song sparrows, savanna sparrows, brushy-type birds. Meadowlarks. Occasional bobolinks. Open-field birds. Orange-crowned warblers. The Tire Pond is hit regularly during the Christmas count. Maybe two hundred people go there a year. Birds are right in the surface tires. Nests are in the tires—song sparrows', American goldfinches', I guess. We see mallards, pied-billed grebes, wood ducks, the mute swans. Mute swans are an increasing species in Connecticut. There has been a dramatic increase in ten years. There are about four thousand across the state now. The swans don't nest in the Tire Pond, but probably along the Quinnipiac River."

I also met Anne Evans at the Tire Pond. Jack Waggoner, in Califor- 15
nia, had strongly suggested that I call on her. Born into the tire trade, in Middletown, Connecticut, she had taken charge of her family's business at the age of twenty-two, selling and mounting new tires and paying the Middletown landfill to carry the old ones away. When she was twenty-nine, she had become president of the New England Association of Independent Tire Dealers. But now, at thirty-seven, she had long since given up retailing tires in order to concern herself full time with what might be done to get rid of them—specifically, to develop

profitable ways of using them after they have fulfilled their initial purpose. As a convenience to me, she had proposed meeting at the pond to talk tires, and had said that no matter what she might say to me it would not ruffle Jim Rizzo, because he had heard it all before. "The tire industry is really, really, really, really tiny," she had said. "We're a small industry. We all know one another. And we stick together."

Now, on that spring morning, as her dark bright eyes swept over Rizzo's establishment, she said, "At least it's not going to burn." She wore a blue-gray suit over an aquamarine blouse. Her dark glasses, tilted upward, nested in her short black hair. She wore gold earrings, a gold necklace, a sapphire bracelet, and a ring with a diamond as big as a tire. "This place is a blight on the earth," she went on. "They're making a fortune. They bought the clay pit for next to nothing. Their overhead is almost nothing. While other people are spending millions of dollars on equipment for recycling, they've got a hole. The tires will sit in the hole forever. To me it's just something so incredible that thirteen million tires are in a hole and no one cares!"

Someone muttered, "Fifteen million."

"This is the way things went for a long time," she continued. "Tires were just dumped, and no attempt was made to do something with them." The Tire Pond, like the rubber alp in California, had been what she called a "regional solution"—an innovative response to the choking of local landfills. "I guess this pond is not as bad as a pile of tires in a ravine," she concluded. "On the other hand, tires in a ravine can be removed. These are here for an eternity."

If I wanted to meet an authentic pioneer in doing something about tires, she said, I should go to Baltimore and look up Norman Emanuel. She added reverently, "He mastered the early shredding machines. He sells to energy users. He's done very, very well. And he's still in overalls."

20 My dialogue with Anne Evans was by no means exhausted, and her widespread insights and personal history would in various ways inform much of the rest of these notes. Meanwhile, I did as I was told. I went to inner Baltimore, just west of Amtrak, and found Bentalou Street, where—seeking, as I was, the preëminent tire shredder of eastern America—I expected to see begrimed industrial structures of the sort that are everywhere framed in the begrimed windows of Amtrak. Bentalou was a shade street, though, of maples, sycamores, ash, elms, lindens, flowering cherries. Its row houses had small lawns and covered fieldstone porches—an obvious escalation from the signature marble steps that spill with such perspective symmetry to wide sidewalks of Baltimore. On Bentalou were greening hedges, blossoming azaleas, and, between a cemetery and the railroad tracks, a driveway that led to the Emanuel Tire Company. Mostly open to the sky, it was laid out

something like a lumberyard, and Norman Emanuel was off to one side, sitting in his office before a mural map. Hardly a word had passed between us before he sat me down opposite and began to fulminate about officials of the state and the city, not to mention the county. "They haven't found anything that I've done right, but the things I've been doing, they're eliminating that," he said. He was a big beefy dark-haired handsome tan-faced man with the build of a linebacker. He did not look urban, there in the middle of the city. He looked farm. Direct as he was, he was not always easy to understand. "Burl" equalled "barrel," as in "burl stacking"—the conventional way to stack tires. The form of water that drives turbines was "stame." He wore rubber boots, and his overalls were blue. His shirt was composed of rectangular checks of red, yellow, and black. On the forehead of his green-visored cap was the name of a company in North Carolina that had shown interest in burning Emanuel tire shreds to power machines that chip wood. "We collect three million tires a year," Emanuel continued. "We'd be up to six or eight million now, but the state, they've cut my growth terribly."

It was growth that began in the nineteen-fifties, when he was nineteen years old and, while staying with a relative, found a job in a Baltimore Chevrolet plant. He was from Red Springs, in Robeson County, on the North Carolina coastal plain, where he grew up farming corn, cotton, wheat, and soybeans. In the Chevrolet cafeteria, he overheard a man saying that he had built a house on money he made collecting used tires and selling them for retreads. Norman Emanuel straightaway went to a service station and left with eight old tires. He sold three for three dollars a piece, and the Emanuel Tire Company had shown its first profit. Then he picked up thirty-one more. He sold thirty, and he never looked back.

To his eleven acres in Baltimore he brings tires from Florida, Georgia, South Carolina, North Carolina, Kentucky, Oklahoma, Virginia, West Virginia, Delaware, Pennsylvania, New Jersey, New York, and, of course, Maryland—each tire for a fee. "In 1978, when landfilling was phasing out, I knew I'd have to start making changes," he said. "I was the second person in the United States to have a tire shredder—after Pacific Energy, in Oregon. For a while, I landfilled the shreds."

Outside the office, a shredder was shredding. It was a squarish machine about twelve feet high with a couple of steel ladders and catwalks. Emanuel said, "Go ahead, go up and have a look." Tires were riding a conveyor to the top, and then falling into a hopperlike chamber whose bottom was a pair of rollers with steel teeth. Like the wringer on an old clothes washer, the rollers rolled toward each other, and when a tire fell on them it got caught in the crease. Slowly, quietly, the tire torqued, twisted, writhed—like a snake caught up in a combine, attacked by the steel teeth, squeezed, folded, crushed, chopped, in a few seconds torn to shreds. (At a tire-shredding operation in Sacramento, not long ago, an employee was shredded on his first day of work. For a time, no one missed him. He had left the machine in half-inch cubes.) Emanuel Tire has fourteen shredders, which make two-inch chips and smaller grades, on down to a quarter of an inch. Steel belt wire, like fish bones, protruded from the chips. The most concentrated steel in a tire is in the beads—the two hoops of cable in the rim-touching sides. Emanuel picked up a truck tire, put it on his debeader, and sliced out a bead. The hoop's braided steel was an inch in diameter.

Up the street in another lot were a couple of acres of shredded tires—plains and hills of shredded tires, a terrain that felt underfoot like a well-filled waterbed. To achieve such resiliency, all tires still contain some natural rubber. A big orthopterous machine—its narrow discharge conveyors reaching out like antennae—was chewing chopped tires and spewing product in three directions, forming conical mounds: chips fell to the left, steel forward, crumbs to the right. The chips were one-inch bits of tire. In a couple of days, the machine had piled up thirty tons of steel. Gesturing toward a modest mound of crumbs—a rubber drumlin not much higher than our heads—Emanuel said it represented ten thousand tires. It consisted of quarter-inch bits that felt in the hand like granola.

Emanuel's business has evolved so far away from landfills that nowadays, on principle, he said, he would sell shreds at a loss, if he had to, rather than put them in the ground. Over time, he has developed a roster of customers that is as varied as it is far-flung. He is reluctant to reveal who and where they are, but he will say that some of them are as far away from Baltimore as are St. Louis, Indianapolis, and Chicago. In some instances, he is more specific. He let it drop that the University of Virginia wanted forty tons of quarter-inch material for playing surfaces. For more than a decade, a rubber company in Trenton, New Jersey, had been making boots and gloves from shredded Emanuel tires. A good deal of crumb rubber goes for something he calls "reclaim," accenting the first syllable: running tracks, rubberized asphalt, railroad crossings.

In 1982, he began shipping shredded rubber to Spring Grove, Pennsylvania, for use as boiler fuel at a paper mill. Other paper mills followed, and now about a third of Emanuel's product "goes to burn for energy." One automobile tire, burning, will release about two hundred and fifty thousand British thermal units of energy—enough to heat fourteen hundred pounds of ice water to a boil. A tire contains considerably more energy than an equivalent weight of bituminous coal.

United States paper mills, cement plants, and five hundred power plants currently burn bituminous coal. According to the California Integrated Waste Management Board, tires produce less ash and contain less sulphur than many commonly used types of coal, and with "no significant differences in emissions."

It has crossed Norman Emanuel's mind that he could keep the rubber he shreds and make use of it himself. He dreams sometimes of his own 1.5-megawatt power plant, and also of his own vegetable cannery, using "tires as fuel to make that stame." He says, "I see now that I could be almost self-sufficient."

He has in his stockpiles at any given time, in addition to shredded material, more than five hundred thousand tires graded to be sold for use on the road. Of the three million discarded tires that he annually collects, about seven hundred and fifty thousand are in good to excellent condition. One of his warehouses was half again as large as a football field. It was filled with tires that, by and large, were not burl stacked, one upon another, but densely laced, cross-bedded, adroitly assembled in converging angles by a method he called windrowing. The great room was as clean and tidy as a yarn shop.

"I hate a mess," he said. "I hate dirt."

On an amazing percentage of the inventory the treads were so high 30
that the tires seemed new. He exports them all over the world. He sent a hundred thousand tires to Russia last year.

"Russia's a good market but you can't get no money."

Trade is brisk right there on Bentalou, where Baltimore bluebloods often cluster.

"People with Mercedes, people with Jaguars come here to buy tires. I mean, the economy's in bad shape."

His tall slender wife, Dafene, who is also from Robeson County, North Carolina, runs the office. She tries to keep up with the proliferating regulations that inhibit and threaten their business, and she appears to be a good deal cooler than he. A new state law limits them to fifteen thousand cubic feet of inventory, or about five truckloads of shredded material—the practical equivalent of nothing in a nation that throws away two hundred and fifty million tires a year and has about as many Norman Emanuels as congressmen from Alaska. Constricting regulations are what caused him to say, "They haven't found anything that I've done right, but the things I've been doing, they're eliminating that." He likes to let tire chips sit in weather for two to three years, so that oxidation will remove protruding steel—a process too passive to survive regulation. To date, he and Dafene have paid three hundred thousand dollars in legal fees in their effort to come to terms with the state. "The thing is simple: What can you do with tires? Landfill them or shred them. Why does the state want it gone from the face of the earth?" he asks, evidently asserting that the state wants the tires and the shreds to vanish but is not practically considering how that might happen. He grumbles that Texas and North Carolina are the only states that don't create problems for people who collect tires. He summarizes Maryland as follows: "The state says you've got to take tires to an approved place, but there's no place they approve. The State of Maryland, they stuff all their stuff into other states they can." He continues, "Everybody in this country is worried about a vote instead of doing what's right. They've fought the difference between right and wrong. When I'm dead, everybody will know that I made a difference in solving this tire problem. I'll make it happen. You only live once in your life."

35 Aerial crop dusters use burning tires as wind socks. To attract fish, tires are piled in oceans as artificial reefs. Tires are amassed around harbors as porous breakwaters. In Guilford, Connecticut, Sally Richards grows mussels on tires. Tires are used on dairy farms to cover the tarps that cover silage. They stabilize the shoulders of highways, the slopes of drainage canals. They are set up as crash barriers, dock bumpers, fences, and playground tunnels and swings. At Churchill Downs, the paving blocks of the paddock are made of scrap tires. Used tires are used to fashion silent stairs. They weigh down ocean dragnets. They become airplane shock absorbers. They become sandals. Crumbed and granulated tires become mud flaps, hockey pucks, running tracks, carpet padding, and office-floor anti-fatigue mats. Australians make crumb rubber by freezing and then crushing tire chips. Japanese have laid railroad track on crumbled tires. Dirt racetracks seeded with crumbled tires are easier on horses. Crumbed tires added to soil will increase porosity and allow more oxygen to reach down to grass roots. Twelve thousand crumbed tires will treat one football field. In Colorado, corn was planted in soil that had been laced with crumbed tires. The corn developed large, strong roots. A mighty windstorm came and went, and the tire-treated field was the only corn left standing in that part of Colorado. All such uses, though, as imaginative and practical as they may be, draw down such a small fraction of the tires annually piled as scrap that while they address the problem they essentially do not affect it.

Retreads don't help much, either, in holding down the national pile, although Air Force One lands on retreads, the jets of the Blue Angels land on retreads, and when H. Norman Schwarzkopf touched down in Saudi Arabia he touched down on retreads. Almost all commercial airliners roll on retreaded tires. Most buses—including school buses—and most taxis are on retreads, and so are ten thousand Frito-Lay trucks and thirty-six thousand U.P.S. trucks. A company sensitive to costs per mile will retread its casings three times. A retread is in no way inferior to a new tire, but new tires are affordable, and the retreaded passenger tire has descended to the status of a clip-on tie. Not long ago, twenty-four million passenger tires were retreaded every year, but the number has declined nearly seventy per cent, swelling the volume of discards. Pilot plants have been erected to decompose tires through pyrolysis (destructive distillation, thermal degradation) in an attempt to recycle some of the fifteen million barrels of oil that are thrown away in tires in the United States each year. The process has not shown a profit. Tire chips go into rubber-modified asphalt concrete. RUMAC, as it is known, absorbs more heat than other surfaces do, gets rid of ice and snow, reduces glare, and makes a quiet road, a resilient road, a deformation-resistant road. A mile of RUMAC thirty-six feet wide and three inches thick uses sixteen thousand tires. The road lasts twice as long as ordinary asphalt. But ordinary asphalt is recycled, and that is hard to do if there is rubber in it. Few miles of American road are RUMAC.

When Jack Waggoner, of Sacramento, first wrote to me about the great tire pile of California, he mentioned that all the scrap tires now strewn about the American landscape would make a stack a hundred and forty-two thousand miles high. If you want to get rid of something like that, you don't try to do it by making lacrosse balls. The technological need is for consumption of old whole tires in a major useful way, and that, he said, was now going on at the big pile. Waggoner is an easygoing, ocean-fishing man in his fifties who has been in some aspect of the tire business all his adult life. In 1957, he was working in a Flying A service station in Lodi, near Stockton, when a customer said to him, "You do a hell of a job washing windshields. Come to work for me." The customer was impressive. Suit, tie, vest, hat, furled umbrella, he "looked like he should be calling on heads of state," but he was actually the sales manager of Super Mold, the largest manufacturer of tire-retreading machinery in the world. For years, Waggoner's territory included Japan, the Philippines, Indonesia, Ceylon, and islands of the South Pacific. He was "real heavy into Vietnam," where eight hundred truck tires were retreaded every day. Eventually, he started his own company, and when the retread business declined he augmented sales by distributing shredders. Driving south on I-5 toward the big pile, he said, "Once you get rubber in your veins, you can never get it out." I asked him why he, a purveyor of shredding machines, was interested in whole-tire recycling. He said, "Because it's the right thing to do."

On a dirt road behind a truck stop, we soon came to a guardhouse and a platinum-haired security man in a black leather jacket with a huge silver star. Waggoner was grata. No cameras allowed. We made our way into the range. On the hilltop opposite the tires was an electric plant with two Standardkessel boilers and a fueling technology of German design—taller than it was broad, like a castle by the Neckar or the Rhine. From the bottom of the valley rose a moving conveyor at least four hundred feet long. Tires were riding upward, and we climbed five stories of steel steps to watch them arrive. Producing stame, the structure was now and again fogged by its own swirling cloud, which blew off and revealed the creased hills. At the top of the conveyor was a carrousel that accepted the tires, carried them around, and watched them with electric eyes. When air-lock chambers were ready to receive them, fingers of steel came up through the carrousel and shoved them to one side. They went into the air-lock chambers, and then fell to a reciprocating grate—a nickel-chromium stoker grate—which looked something like a stairway, with accordion steps that contracted and expanded and advanced the tire toward the core of conflagration. You could watch this through a window, two inches in diameter. Scarcely had a new tire landed on the grate when—count one, count two—it burst into wild flame, at upward of twenty-five hundred degrees. At the far side of the fire chamber, where the fuel compacted and the heat was most intense, a peephole looked in at the climax of the burning. What appeared there resembled the cliff-like snout of a glacier, white in a bath of auroran red, with white particulate flying like snow, and lumps and bumps and moguls.

The plant was supplying enough power to Pacific Gas & Electric to fulfill the daily requirements of fifteen thousand homes. Among dedicated waste-to-energy fuels, tires have two to three times as many B.T.U.s as municipal solid waste, refuse-derived fuel, or biomass. Generally operating around the clock, the plant was burning seventeen thousand tires a day. It burns five million tires a year.

40 Filbin the Tire Jockey—having been paid, say, an average of a quarter of a dollar for collecting each of the many millions of tires he had stored here—was now selling them to the Oxford Energy Company, owners of the plant, for slightly more. Doug Tomison, Oxford's plant manager, mentioned "a royalty arrangement on a sliding scale," and the scale had to do with how many million tires were in the great pile. Tomison's rough estimate came in one digit. Tomison was a young handsome dark-haired man on crutches. All in four weeks, he had hit a school bus with his motorcycle, a bee had stung him on the motorcycle, and a cow had kicked him off it, too. But that level of misfortune was painless compared with the kicking he was getting from the tire jockey. "He's killing us," Tomison said. "We're making a profit and giving it to him." By burning whole tires, the company saves a shredding cost of twenty-five dollars a ton, but not even that can turn the thing around. Oxford was paying Filbin over a million dollars a year.

Oxford Energy has been described by Anne Evans as "four or five guys with an idea," and at one point she was one of the guys. As a director of the National Tire Dealers and Retreaders Association, she encouraged Oxford from the beginning. They hired her as a consultant. In Sterling, Connecticut, Oxford has a plant that consumes more tires than the one in California. These are the only power plants in the United States that burn whole tires. By 1995, Oxford hopes to have four plants on line, annually consuming thirty-one million tires. The California plant was dedicated in 1987. On a wall in its trailer-office is a framed citation featuring a large letter "E": "1988 Environmental Protection Award for outstanding achievement by industry in the protection of our natural environment. Awarded by Power Magazine to Oxford Energy Company, Modesto, California. The E stands for environment and is a symbol of concern for the purity of our nation's air and water." And next to that is a 1988 United States Department of Energy "Special Award for Energy Innovation. . . . presented to the Oxford Energy Company in recognition of a significant contribution to our nation's energy efficiency."

The Attorney General of California has shown professional interest in the tire pile. One of many considerations is that if a smoldering fire were to spread far through it a river of oil would go out of the hills and into the California Aqueduct. Los Angeles' femoral artery, the California Aqueduct is close by Interstate 5, a few thousand yards from the tires and three hundred feet below them. Looking across the valley, we could see in the rolling black dunes tiny figures moving. They were people, carrying tires. One tire at a time, the people were shifting tens of thousands of tires—by hand, the only way to do it—creating fire lanes to satisfy the government.

In the power-plant compound, the second-largest structure was the bag house, full of Gore-Tex bags hung up like balloons. They remove fine ash down to three microns. Burning tires emit nitrogen and sulphur oxides (known as Nox and Sox), carbon monoxide, particulate matter, hydrocarbons, arsenic, cadmium, chromium, lead, zinc, dioxins and furans, polycyclic aromatic hydrocarbons, polychlorinated biphenyls, and benzene. These pollutants are also emitted by coal. About seventy-five percent of the ash is a rocklike slag of ferrous oxide, which falls into a hopper with a steel-belted thud and hardly requires a filter. A process called Thermal DeNox deals with nitrogen oxides. There is a limestone-slurry spray scrubber to remove sulphur. The fly ash is largely zinc, which is the major pollutant, and it is trapped in the Gore-Tex bags. Computers by the roomful operate the machines. The pollution-control equipment cost Oxford seven million dollars. Well over half of the Nox gets away. Of the Sox, two per cent escapes, as do smaller amounts of carbon monoxide.

As the limestone slurry reacts with the sulphur dioxide, gypsum results—as much as twelve tons a day. Gypsum can be used as a "soil amendment." Farmers buy it all. Zinc is recovered as zinc. The iron oxide, for the most part, is stored, looking for a customer, but some is sold as gravel for use in cement.

45 The country over-all would do well to burn whole tires in making cement. Flanking Interstate 5 near Redding—two hundred miles north of Filbin's pile—are a limestone quarry and a cement plant. Powdered limestone and shale are fed into a cylindrical precalcining furnace—a ten-story tower—up the side of which runs a chain-conveyor with steel hooks. From each hook hangs a tire. The tires enter from chutes about half way up the tower, and, as they drop, flash in fire. The mixture of stone and burning tires moves on into a huge revolving drum that is slightly inclined from the horizontal, spins two times a minute, and extends more than two hundred yards. The Fahrenheit temperature rises within it to twenty-six hundred degrees. As the rock, revolving, roasts, the tires supply not only heat but also the iron oxide indispensable to cement. The ash residue of the tires becomes a part of the chemistry of the cement. The tires disappear absolutely. Their steel is completely oxidized. The heat causes the limestone's calcium carbonate and carbon dioxide to separate, leaving calcium oxide, or quicklime. Then quicklime reacts with silica and alumina (in the shale) to form calcium silicates and aluminates, which leave the kiln as clinker in pieces the size of eggs. The clinker is ground with gypsum, and that is cement. No ash, no slag. In Germany and Japan, about twenty per cent of the fuel for cement plants is whole tires. The kiln in Redding—at the Calaveras Cement Company—consumes more than two hundred tires an hour. It has a bag house and other state-of-the-art pollution-control equipment. California has eleven cement plants, ten of which are close to cities, where the tires are. Those eleven plants could consume all of the twenty million tires annually discarded in California and dispose of five million additional tires as well. California cement plants require thirty-four trillion B.T.U.s a year, and ninety per cent of that energy is supplied by coal. In words of the California Integrated Waste Management Board, "The cement manufacturing industry could use all of the waste tires generated in the state as well as the existing stockpiles. . . . From an energy perspective, use of tires as a supplemental fuel in cement kilns displaces fossil fuels and results in no wastes and no significant differences in emissions." A cement plant near Santa Cruz applied for a permit to use tires but gave up because of the cost of fighting environmentalists. Cement plants alone could solve the scrap-tire dilemma. There are enough cement plants in the United States to use three billion tires a year.

In 1989, Anne Evans was invited by Great Britain's Department of Trade and Industry to develop in England a dedicated waste-to-energy tire-burning power plant like the one in California. She was thirty-three years old then. While still in her twenties, she had started a tire export-import business that operated in many countries around the world, including England, and her profits were very large. Always—in a shifting, chronic manner—tires became overstocked or understocked in this place and that. What she did was move them from supply to demand, meanwhile watching currency fluctuations, which she rode like thermals. "If you work very hard at that and don't get a lot of sleep, and if you understand letters of credit, you do very well," she told me. "The idea is to close a deal within twenty-four hours. You make a good relationship with a freight forwarder, and your life gets very simple. Be honest. Do a good job. Don't be greedy. And you'll do well."

Her distributors were involved not only with new tires but with old ones, and the problem of how to dispose of the old ones was everywhere increasing. She remembers her grandfather saying, "He who figures out what to do with these tires is going to make a million"—her grandfather Tony DiGiandomenico, who started the family's Firestone dealership and retreading company in Middletown. Her father, Mario Salemi, had rubber in his veins, too. His parents, and Tony DiGiandomenico's mother, came from Melilli, near Syracuse, in Sicily, as did so many other citizens of Middletown that they built an exact copy of Melilli's ornate and gilded Church of San Sebastiano. To this day, almost anybody from Middletown can cash a personal check in Melilli. It may be a little easier if your name is DiGiandomenico. Anne, at twenty-two and with scarcely any more business training than any other recent product of Newton College of the Sacred Heart, was working in Washington for the National Republican Congressional Campaign Committee when her father fell ill and she went home to take over the tires.

Now she commutes from Connecticut, where her husband is a real-estate broker, to Wolverhampton, in the West Midlands, home of her Elm Energy & Recycling. Wolverhampton is twelve miles from Birmingham. The plant occupies six acres, surrounded by quiet streets and private suburban homes. Except for its exhaust stack, it is an unobtrusive ground-hugging structure, in which tires are not stockpiled but arrive instead in a continuous stream of lorries. Michelin, Pirelli, Goodyear, Dunlop—all the big tire companies operate their own retail stores in England. They will pay the haulers, who, in turn, will pay Elm. All their waste tires will go to Wolverhampton. The plant is capable of producing thirty megawatts, but will sell no more than twenty-five. The rest of the power is needed to run the anti-pollution equipment. The site was dedicated in a tent in April of 1992, in ceremonies overhung by chandeliers and enriched by a cello. The pneumatic Michelin man was outside, the chairman of Pirelli was inside. The plant will soon be receiving twenty-five percent of all tires discarded in the United Kingdom.

"We are the cleanest power station in England," she told me when we talked in Connecticut. "We're green. We're the best thing since peanut butter." She was obviously undaunted by her discovery that, as she put it, "the English are not receptive to women." She said, "There might as well be a sign at Heathrow: 'If you are a woman doing business, go home.' "

50 She went on to say, "Energy is a good thing for tires. Landfilling should not happen. That's a total waste—of land, of material. But energy may be just another step in the evolution." She thinks that tires themselves will change. She imagines them somehow being made differently, so that the disposal problem will take care of itself. "Tires will change as cars change. Now they hold the shock. That may be put somewhere else. Tires may be different. A different material. Who knows what?" Meanwhile, she was much impressed by a research scientist for a German tire company who studied tires-to-energy and said, "Maybe we can take something out of the tire to make it easier to burn."

"The consumer has got to be willing to pay mandated disposal fees," she concluded. "It costs money to do it right. Every bit of material should be used to its fullest extent. A tire in its first life is a tire. It needs to be used for something further. Unless we do that, we're wasteful. The reality of life is that we can't afford to be wasteful anymore. Let's do something else with this material when we're finished with it, and we'll be in good shape in the next generation. That takes an industrial commitment. It's not a legislative matter. You can't legislate people to feel a certain way. It's got to be in them to say, 'We've got to do this as a society.' When governments raise tipping fees, illegal dumping rises. In England, when someone takes tires away for fifteen pence a tire and dumps them in a vacant lot, it is known as fly tipping. That is why there is a law in England called Duty of Care: you need a waste-management license; you have to know exactly what happens to your waste. The tire stores have to know."

"Do we have such a law?"

"Of course not."

QUESTIONS

1. *As is common in journalistic writing, McPhee establishes interest in his subject—and its significance—at the beginning of his essay*

(paragraphs 1 to 4). What facts, anecdotes, and descriptions help to establish interest and significance?

2. *What is the origin of the title "Duty of Care"? Where does McPhee introduce the phrase—and why?*
3. *McPhee gathers much of his information and evidence by interviewing experts. Examine one section of the essay that relies heavily on interview (for example, paragraphs 5 to 14, 20 to 34, or 37 to 41) and formulate the principles that McPhee uses for paraphrasing versus quoting the expert.*
4. *Choose an environmental issue of local concern and, after reading and conducting interviews about it, write your own account of the problem and its possible solutions.*

Terry Tempest Williams

THE CLAN OF ONE-BREASTED WOMEN

I belong to a Clan of One-breasted Women. My mother, my grandmothers, and six aunts have all had mastectomies. Seven are dead. The two who survive have just completed rounds of chemotherapy and radiation.

I've had my own problems: two biopsies for breast cancer and a small tumor between my ribs diagnosed as "a border-line malignancy."

This is my family history.

Most statistics tell us breast cancer is genetic, hereditary, with rising percentages attached to fatty diets, childlessness, or becoming pregnant after thirty. What they don't say is living in Utah may be the greatest hazard of all.

We are a Mormon family with roots in Utah since 1847. The 5
word-of-wisdom, a religious doctrine of health, kept the women in my family aligned with good foods: no coffee, no tea, tobacco, or alcohol. For the most part, these women were finished having their babies by the time they were thirty. And only one faced breast cancer prior to 1960. Traditionally, as a group of people, Mormons have a low rate of cancer.

Is our family a cultural anomaly? The truth is we didn't think about it. Those who did, usually the men, simply said, "bad genes." The women's attitude was stoic. Cancer was part of life. On February 16, 1971, the eve before my mother's surgery, I accidently picked up the

First published in *Witness* (Winter 1989).

telephone and overheard her ask my grandmother what she could expect.

"Diane, it is one of the most spiritual experiences you will ever encounter."

I quietly put down the receiver.

Two days later, my father took my three brothers and me to the hospital to visit her. She met us in the lobby in a wheelchair. No bandages were visible. I'll never forget her radiance, the way she held herself in a purple velour robe and how she gathered us around her.

10 "Children, I am fine. I want you to know I felt the arms of God around me."

We believed her. My father cried. Our mother, his wife, was thirty-eight years old.

Two years ago, after my mother's death from cancer, my father and I were having dinner together. He had just returned from St. George where his construction company was putting in natural gas lines for towns in southern Utah. He spoke of his love for the country: the sandstoned landscape, bare-boned and beautiful. He had just finished hiking the Kolob trail in Zion National Park. We got caught up in reminiscing, recalling with fondness our walk up Angel's Landing on his fiftieth birthday and the years our family had vacationed there. This was a remembered landscape where we had been raised.

Over dessert, I shared a recurring dream of mine. I told my father that for years, as long as I could remember, I saw this flash of light in the night in the desert. That this image had so permeated my being, I could not venture south without seeing it again, on the horizon, illuminating buttes and mesas.

"You did see it," he said.

15 "Saw what?" I asked, a bit tentative.

"The bomb. The cloud. We were driving home from Riverside, California. You were sitting on your mother's lap. She was pregnant. In fact, I remember the date, September 7, 1957. We had just gotten out of the Service. We were driving north, past Las Vegas. It was an hour or so before dawn, when this explosion went off. We not only heard it, but felt it. I thought the oil tanker in front of us had blown up. We pulled over and suddenly, rising from the desert floor, we saw it, clearly, this golden-stemmed cloud, the mushroom. The sky seemed to vibrate with an eerie pink glow. Within a few minutes, a light ash was raining on the car."

I stared at my father. This was new information to me.

"I thought you knew that," my father said. "It was a common occurrence in the fifties."

It was at this moment I realized the deceit I had been living under. Children growing up in the American Southwest, drinking contaminated milk from contaminated cows, even from the contaminated breasts of their mother, my mother—members, years later, of the Clan of One-breasted Women.

It is a well-known story in the Desert West, "The Day We Bombed 20
Utah," or perhaps, "The Years We Bombed Utah."[1] Above ground atomic testing in Nevada took place from January 27, 1951, through July 11, 1962. Not only were the winds blowing north, covering "low use segments of the population" with fallout and leaving sheep dead in their tracks, but the climate was right.[2] The United States of the 1950s was red, white, and blue. The Korean War was raging. McCarthyism was rampant. Ike was it and the Cold War was hot.[3] If you were against nuclear testing, you were for a Communist regime.

Much has been written about this "American nuclear tragedy." Public health was secondary to national security. The Atomic Energy Commissioner, Thomas Murray said, "Gentlemen, we must not let anything interfere with this series of tests, nothing."[4]

Again and again, the American public was told by its government, in spite of burns, blisters, and nausea, "It has been found that the tests may be conducted with adequate assurance of safety under conditions prevailing at the bombing reservations."[5] Assuaging public fears was simply a matter of public relations. "Your best action," an Atomic Energy Commission booklet read, "is not to be worried about fallout." A news release typical of the times stated, "We find no basis for concluding that harm to any individual has resulted from radioactive fallout."[6]

On August 30, 1979, during Jimmy Carter's presidency, a suit was filed entitled "Irene Allen vs. the United States of America." Mrs. Allen was the first to be alphabetically listed with twenty-four test

1. Fuller, John G., *The Day We Bombed Utah* (New York: New American Library, 1984) [Williams's note].
2. Discussion on March 14, 1988, with Carole Gallagher, photographer and author, *Nuclear Towns: The Secret War in the American Southwest,* to be published by Doubleday, Spring, 1990 [Williams's note].
3. Events and figures of the 1950s: the Korean War (1950–1953) pitted the combined forces of the Republic of Korea and the United Nations (primarily the United States) against the invading armies of Communist North Korea; McCarthyism, after Republican senator Joseph S. McCarthy, refers to the Communist "witch-hunt" led by the senator; Ike is the nickname of Dwight D. Eisenhower, president from 1953 to 1961; the Cold War refers to the power struggle between the Western powers and the Communist bloc that began at the end of World War II.
4. Szasz, Ferenc M., "Downwind From the Bomb," *Nevada Historical Society Quarterly,* Fall, 1987 Vol. XXX, No. 3, p. 185 [Williams's note].
5. Fradkin, Philip L., *Fallout* (Tucson: University of Arizona Press, 1989), 98 [Williams's note].
6. Ibid., 109 [Williams's note].

cases, representative of nearly 1200 plaintiffs seeking compensation from the United States government for cancers caused from nuclear testing in Nevada.

Irene Allen lived in Hurricane, Utah. She was the mother of five children and had been widowed twice. Her first husband with their two oldest boys had watched the tests from the roof of the local high school. He died of leukemia in 1956. Her second husband died of pancreatic cancer in 1978.

25 In a town meeting conducted by Utah Senator Orrin Hatch, shortly before the suit was filed, Mrs. Allen said, "I am not blaming the government, I want you to know that, Senator Hatch. But I thought if my testimony could help in any way so this wouldn't happen again to any of the generations coming up after us . . . I am really happy to be here this day to bear testimony of this."[7]

God-fearing people. This is just one story in an anthology of thousands.

On May 10, 1984, Judge Bruce S. Jenkins handed down his opinion. Ten of the plaintiffs were awarded damages. It was the first time a federal court had determined that nuclear tests had been the cause of cancers. For the remaining fourteen test cases, the proof of causation was not sufficient. In spite of the split decision, it was considered a landmark ruling.[8] It was not to remain so for long.

In April, 1987, the 10th Circuit Court of Appeals overturned Judge Jenkins' ruling on the basis that the United States was protected from suit by the legal doctrine of sovereign immunity, the centuries-old idea from England in the days of absolute monarchs.[9]

In January, 1988, the Supreme Court refused to review the Appeals Court decision. To our court system, it does not matter whether the United States Government was irresponsible, whether it lied to its citizens or even that citizens died from the fallout of nuclear testing. What matters is that our government is immune. "The King can do no wrong."

30 In Mormon culture, authority is respected, obedience is revered, and independent thinking is not. I was taught as a young girl not to "make waves" or "rock the boat."

"Just let it go—" my mother would say. "You know how you feel, that's what counts."

For many years, I did just that—listened, observed, and quietly

7. Town meeting held by Senator Orrin Hatch in St. George, Utah, April 17, 1979, transcript, 26–28 [Williams's note].
8. Fradkin, Op. cit., 228 [Williams's note].
9. U.S. vs. Allen, 816 Federal Reporter, 2d/1417 (10th Circuit Court 1987), cert. denied, 108 S. CT. 694 (1988) [Williams's note].

formed my own opinions within a culture that rarely asked questions because they had all the answers. But one by one, I watched the women in my family die common, heroic deaths. We sat in waiting rooms hoping for good news, always receiving the bad. I cared for them, bathed their scarred bodies and kept their secrets. I watched beautiful women become bald as cytoxan, cisplatin and adriamycin were injected into their veins. I held their foreheads as they vomited green-black bile and I shot them with morphine when the pain became inhuman. In the end, I witnessed their last peaceful breaths, becoming a midwife to the rebirth of their souls. But the price of obedience became too high.

The fear and inability to question authority that ultimately killed rural communities in Utah during atmospheric testing of atomic weapons was the same fear I saw being held in my mother's body. Sheep. Dead sheep. The evidence is buried.

I cannot prove that my mother, Diane Dixon Tempest, or my grandmothers, Lettie Romney Dixon and Kathryn Blackett Tempest, along with my aunts contracted cancer from nuclear fallout in Utah. But I can't prove they didn't.

My father's memory was correct, the September blast we drove 35
through in 1957 was part of Operation Plumbbob, one of the most intensive series of bomb tests to be initiated. The flash of light in the night in the desert I had always thought was a dream developed into a family nightmare. It took fourteen years, from 1957 to 1971, for cancer to show up in my mother—the same time, Howard L. Andrews, an authority on radioactive fallout at the National Institutes of Health, says radiation cancer requires to become evident.[1] The more I learn about what it means to be a "downwinder," the more questions I drown in.

What I do know, however, is that as a Mormon woman of the fifth generation of "Latter-Day-Saints," I must question everything, even if it means losing my faith, even if it means becoming a member of a border tribe among my own people. Tolerating blind obedience in the name of patriotism or religion ultimately takes our lives.

When the Atomic Energy Commission described the country north of the Nevada Test Site as "virtually uninhabited desert terrain," my family members were some of the "virtual uninhabitants."

One night, I dreamed women from all over the world circling a blazing fire in the desert. They spoke of change, of how they hold the moon in their bellies and wax and wane with its phases. They mocked at the presumption of even-tempered beings and made promises that

1. Fradkin, Op. cit., 116 [Williams's note].

they would never fear the witch inside themselves. The women danced wildly as sparks broke away from the flames and entered the night sky as stars.

And they sang a song given to them by Shoshoni grandmothers:

Ah ne nah, nah
nin nah nah—
Ah ne nah, nah
nin nah nah—
Nyaga mutzi
oh ne nay—
Nyaga mutzi
oh ne nay—[2]

The women danced and drummed and sang for weeks, preparing themselves for what was to come. They would reclaim the desert for the sake of their children, for the sake of the land.

A few miles downwind from the fire circle, bombs were being tested. Rabbits felt the tremors. Their soft leather pads on paws and feet recognized the shaking sands while the roots of mesquite and sage were smoldering. Rocks were hot from the inside out and dust devils hummed unnaturally. And each time there was another nuclear test, ravens watched the desert heave. Stretch marks appeared. The land was losing its muscle.

The women couldn't bear it any longer. They were mothers. They had suffered labor pains but always under the promise of birth. The red hot pains beneath the desert promised death only as each bomb became a stillborn. A contract had been broken between human beings and the land. A new contract was being drawn by the women who understood the fate of the earth as their own.

Under the cover of darkness, ten women slipped under the barbed wire fence and entered the contaminated country. They were trespassing. They walked toward the town of Mercury in moonlight, taking their cues from coyote, kit fox, antelope squirrel, and quail. They moved quietly and deliberately through the maze of Joshua trees. When a hint of daylight appeared they rested, drinking tea and sharing their rations of food. The women closed their eyes. The time had come to protest with the heart, that to deny one's genealogy with the earth was to commit treason against one's soul.

2. This song was sung by the Western Shoshone women as they crossed the line at the Nevada Test Site on March 18, 1988, as part of their "Reclaim the Land" action. The translation they gave was: "Consider the rabbits how gently they walk on the earth. Consider the rabbits how gently they walk on the earth. We remember them. We can walk gently also. We remember them. We can walk gently also." [Williams's note].

At dawn, the women draped themselves in mylar, wrapping long streamers of silver plastic around their arms to blow in the breeze. They wore clear masks that became the faces of humanity. And when they arrived on the edge of Mercury, they carried all the butterflies of a summer day in their wombs. They paused to allow their courage to settle.

45 The town which forbids pregnant women and children to enter because of radiation risks to their health was asleep. The women moved through the streets as winged messengers, twirling around each other in slow motion, peeking inside homes and watching the easy sleep of men and women. They were astonished by such stillness and periodically would utter a shrill note or low cry just to verify life.

The residents finally awoke to what appeared as strange apparitions. Some simply stared. Others called authorities, and in time, the women were apprehended by wary soldiers dressed in desert fatigues. They were taken to a white, square building on the other edge of Mercury. When asked who they were and why they were there, the women replied, "We are mothers and we have come to reclaim the desert for our children."

The soldiers arrested them. As the ten women were blindfolded and handcuffed, they began singing:

You can't forbid us everything
You can't forbid us to think—
You can't forbid our tears to flow
And you can't stop the songs that we sing.

The women continued to sing louder and louder, until they heard the voices of their sisters moving across the mesa.

Ah ne nah, nah
nin nah nah—
Ah ne nah, nah
nin nah nah—
Nyaga mutzi
oh ne nay—
Nyaga mutzi
oh ne nay—

"Call for re-enforcement," one soldier said.

50 "We have," interrupted one woman. "We have—and you have no idea of our numbers."

On March 18, 1988, I crossed the line at the Nevada Test Site and was arrested with nine other Utahns for trespassing on military lands. They are still conducting nuclear tests in the desert. Ours was an act of civil disobedience. But as I walked toward the town of Mercury, it was more than a gesture of peace. It was a gesture on behalf of the Clan of One-breasted Women.

As one officer cinched the handcuffs around my wrists, another frisked my body. She found a pen and a pad of paper tucked inside my left boot.

"And these?" she asked sternly.

"Weapons," I replied.

55 Our eyes met. I smiled. She pulled the leg of my trousers back over my boot.

"Step forward, please," she said as she took my arm.

We were booked under an afternoon sun and bussed to Tonapah, Nevada. It was a two-hour ride. This was familiar country to me. The Joshua trees standing their ground had been named by my ancestors who believed they looked like prophets pointing west to the promised land. These were the same trees that bloomed each spring, flowers appearing like white flames in the Mojave. And I recalled a full moon in May when my mother and I had walked among them, flushing out mourning doves and owls.

The bus stopped short of town. We were released. The officials thought it was a cruel joke to leave us stranded in the desert with no way to get home. What they didn't realize is that we were home, soul-centered and strong, women who recognized the sweet smell of sage as fuel for our spirits.

QUESTIONS

1. *Williams uses a variety of evidence in this essay: personal memory, family history, government documents, and so on. List the evidence and the order in which she uses it. Why does Williams present her material in this order?*
2. *The essay begins with what Williams calls a "family nightmare" and ends with a dream vision. What is the rhetorical effect of this interactive opening and closing?*
3. *What does Williams mean by the statement "I must question everything" (paragraph 36)?*
4. *Do some research on an environmental issue that affects you or your family and, using Williams as a model, write an essay that combines your personal experience and your research.*

Ethics

James Thurber

THE BEAR WHO LET IT ALONE

In the woods of the Far West there once lived a brown bear who could take it or let it lone. He would go into a bar where they sold mead, a fermented drink made of honey, and he would have just two drinks. Then he would put some money on the bar and say, "See what the bears in the back room will have," and he would go home. But finally he took to drinking by himself most of the day. He would reel home at night, kick over the umbrella stand, knock down the bridge lamps, and ram his elbows through the windows. Then he would collapse on the floor and lie there until he went to sleep. His wife was greatly distressed and his children were very frightened.

At length the bear saw the error of his ways and began to reform. In the end he became a famous teetotaller and a persistent temperance lecturer. He would tell everybody that came to his house about the awful effects of drink, and he would boast about how strong and well he had become since he gave up touching the stuff. To demonstrate this, he would stand on his head and on his hands and he would turn cartwheels in the house, kicking over the umbrella stand, knocking down the bridge lamps, and ramming his elbows through the windows. Then he would lie down on the floor, tired by his healthful exercise, and go to sleep. His wife was greatly distressed and his children were very frightened.

Moral: You might as well fall flat on your face as lean over too far backward.

From *Fables of Our Time* (1940).

Francis Bacon

OF SIMULATION AND DISSIMULATION

Dissimulation is but a faint kind of policy or wisdom; for it asketh a strong wit and a strong heart to know when to tell truth, and to do it. Therefore it is the weaker sort of politics[1] that are the great dissemblers.

Tacitus saith, *Livia sorted well with the arts of her husband and dissimulation of her son;* attributing arts or policy to Augustus, and dissimulation to Tiberius. And again, when Mucianus encourageth Vespasian to take arms against Vitellius, he saith, *We rise not against the piercing judgment of Augustus, nor the extreme caution or closeness of Tiberius.*[2] These properties, of arts or policy and dissimulation or closeness, are indeed habits and faculties several, and to be distinguished. For if a man have that penetration of judgment as he can discern what things are to be laid open, and what to be secreted, and what to be shewed at half lights, and to whom and when (which indeed are arts of state and arts of life, as Tacitus well calleth them), to him a habit of dissimulation is a hinderance and a poorness. But if a man cannot obtain to that judgment, then it is left to him generally to be close, and a dissembler. For where a man cannot choose or vary in particulars, there it is good to take the safest and wariest way in general; like the going softly, by one that cannot well see. Certainly the ablest men that ever were have had all an openness and frankness of dealing; and a name of certainty and veracity; but then they were like horses well managed; for they could tell passing well when to stop or turn; and at such times when they thought the case indeed required dissimulation, if then they used it, it came to pass that the former opinion spread abroad of their good faith and clearness of dealing made them almost invisible.

There be three degrees of this hiding and veiling of a man's self. The first, Closeness, Reservation, and Secrecy; when a man leaveth himself without observation, or without hold to be taken, what he is. The second, Dissimulation, in the negative; when a man lets fall signs and

From *Novum Organum* (1620).

1. Politicians.
2. The Roman historian Tacitus here speaks of the plottings of Livia, wife of the emperor Augustus Caesar and mother of his successor Tiberius; and of the Roman official Mucianus, who in A.D. 69 supported Vespasian in his successful struggle against Vitellius to gain the imperial throne.

arguments, that he is not that he is. And the third, Simulation, in the affirmative; when a man industriously and expressly feigns and pretends to be that he is not.

For the first of these, Secrecy; it is indeed the virtue of a confessor.[3] And assuredly the secret man heareth many confessions. For who will open himself to a blab or babbler? But if a man be thought secret, it inviteth discovery; as the more close air sucketh in the more open; and as in confession the revealing is not for worldly use, but for the ease of a man's heart, so secret men come to the knowledge of many things in that kind; while men rather discharge their minds than impart their minds. In few words, mysteries are due to secrecy. Besides (to say truth) nakedness is uncomely, as well in mind as body; and it addeth no small reverence to men's manners and actions, if they be not altogether open. As for talkers and futile persons, they are commonly vain and credulous withal. For he that talketh what he knoweth, will also talk what he knoweth not. Therefore set it down, *that an habit of secrecy is both politic and moral.* And in this part, it is good that a man's face give his tongue leave to speak. For the discovery of a man's self by the tracts of his countenance is a great weakness and betraying; by how much it is many times more marked and believed than a man's words.

For the second, which is Dissimulation; it followeth many times 5
upon secrecy by a necessity; so that he that will be secret must be a dissembler in some degree. For men are too cunning to suffer a man to keep an indifferent carriage between both, and to be secret, without swaying the balance on either side. They will so beset a man with questions, and draw him on, and pick it out of him, that, without an absurd silence, he must shew an inclination one way; or if he do not, they will gather as much by his silence as by his speech. As for equivocations, or oraculous speeches, they cannot hold out for long. So that no man can be secret, except he give himself a little scope of dissimulation; which is, as it were, but the skirts or train of secrecy.

But for the third degree, which is Simulation and false profession; that I hold more culpable, and less politic; except it be in great and rare matters. And therefore a general custom of simulation (which is this last degree) is a vice, rising either of a natural falseness or fearfulness, or of a mind that hath some main faults, which because a man must needs disguise, it maketh him practice simulation in other things, lest his hand should be out of ure.[4]

The great advantages of simulation and dissimulation are three. First, to lay asleep opposition, and to surprise. For where a man's intentions are published, it is an alarum to call up all that are against

3. One to whom confession is made.

4. Practice.

them. The second is, to reserve to a man's self a fair retreat. For if a man engage himself by a manifest declaration, he must go through or take a fall. The third is, the better to discover the mind of another. For to him that opens himself men will hardly shew themselves adverse; but will (fair) let him go on, and turn their freedom of speech to freedom of thought. And therefore it is a good shrewd proverb of the Spaniard, *Tell a lie and find a troth.* As if there were no way of discovery but by simulation. There be also three disadvantages, to set it even. The first, that simulation and dissimulation commonly carry with them a shew of fearfulness, which in any business doth spoil the feathers of round flying up to the mark. The second, that it puzzleth and perplexeth the conceits[5] of many, that perhaps would otherwise cooperate with him; and makes a man walk almost alone to his own ends. The third and greatest is, that it depriveth a man of one of the most principal instruments for action; which is trust and belief. The best composition and temperature is to have openness in fame and opinion; secrecy in habit; dissimulation in seasonable use; and a power to feign, if there be no remedy.

5. Conceptions, thoughts.

QUESTIONS

1. *Explain Bacon's distinction between simulation and dissimulation. What does he think of each?*
2. *Bacon uses classification three times: he speaks of "three degrees of this hiding and veiling of a man's self," its three advantages, and its three disadvantages. What principle of classification determines his divisions into three? What is the logic of the order in which he presents each group of three?*
3. *This selection by Bacon was published in 1620, over 370 years ago. To what kinds of persons would his advice on simulation and dissimulation have applied then? Are there contemporary equivalents? Would Bacon's advice still apply to them? Rewrite a couple of paragraphs from this passage in a style you think appropriate to giving them advice.*

Samuel Johnson

ON SELF-LOVE AND INDOLENCE

—Steriles transmisimus annos,
Haec aevi mihi prima dies, haec limina vitae.

STAT. [I.362]

—Our barren years are past;
Be this of life the first, of sloth the last.

ELPHINSTONE [1]

No weakness of the human mind has more frequently incurred animadversion, than the negligence with which men overlook their own faults, however flagrant, and the easiness with which they pardon them, however frequently repeated.

It seems generally believed, that, as the eye cannot see itself, the mind has no faculties by which it can contemplate its own state, and that therefore we have not means of becoming acquainted with our real characters; an opinion which, like innumerable other postulates, an inquirer finds himself inclined to admit upon very little evidence, because it affords a ready solution of many difficulties. It will explain why the greatest abilities frequently fail to promote the happiness of those who possess them; why those who can distinguish with the utmost nicety the boundaries of vice and virtue, suffer them to be confounded in their own conduct; why the active and vigilant resign their affairs implicitly to the management of others; and why the cautious and fearful make hourly approaches toward ruin, without one sigh of solicitude or struggle for escape.

When a position teems thus with commodious consequences, who can without regret confess it to be false? Yet it is certain that declaimers have indulged a disposition to describe the dominion of the passions as extended beyond the limits that nature assigned. Self-love is often rather arrogant than blind; it does not hide our faults from ourselves, but persuades us that they escape the notice of others, and disposes us to resent censures lest we would confess them to be just. We are secretly conscious of defects and vices which we hope to conceal from the public eye, and please ourselves with innumerable impostures, by which, in reality, no body is deceived.

From *The Rambler* (1751).

1. The author of these lines is Publius Papinius Statius, a first-century Latin poet. They are given first in the original and then in William Elphinstone's sixteenth-century translation.

In proof of the dimness of our internal sight, or the general inability of man to determine rightly concerning his own character, it is common to urge the success of the most absurd and incredible flattery, and the resentment always raised by advice, however soft, benevolent, and reasonable. But flattery, if its operation be nearly examined, will be found to owe its acceptance not to our ignorance but knowledge of our failures, and to delight us rather as it consoles our wants than displays our possessions. He that shall solicit the favor of his patron by praising him for qualities which he can find in himself, will be defeated by the more daring panegyrist who enriches him with adscititious excellence. Just praise is only a debt, but flattery is a present. The acknowledgment of those virtues on which conscience congratulates us, is a tribute that we can at any time exact with confidence, but the celebration of those which we only feign, or desire without any vigorous endeavors to attain them, is received as a confession of sovereignty over regions never conquered, as a favorable decision of disputable claims, and is more welcome as it is more gratuitous.

5 Advice is offensive, not because it lays us open to unexpected regret, or convicts us of any fault which had escaped our notice, but because it shows us that we are known to others as well as to ourselves; and the officious monitor is persecuted with hatred, not because his accusation is false, but because he assumes that superiority which we are not willing to grant him, and has dared to detect what we desired to conceal.

For this reason advice is commonly ineffectual. If those who follow the call of their desires, without inquiry whither they are going, had deviated ignorantly from the paths of wisdom, and were rushing upon dangers unforeseen, they would readily listen to information that recalls them from their errors, and catch the first alarm by which destruction or infamy is denounced. Few that wander in the wrong way mistake it for the right; they only find it more smooth and flowery, and indulge their own choice rather than approve it: therefore few are persuaded to quit it by admonition or reproof, since it impresses no new conviction, nor confers any powers of action or resistance. He that is gravely informed how soon profusion will annihilate his fortune, hears with little advantage what he knew before, and catches at the next occasion of expense, because advice has no force to suppress his vanity. He that is told how certainly intemperance will hurry him to the grave, runs with his usual speed to a new course of luxury, because his reason is not invigorated, nor his appetite weakened.

The mischief of Flattery is, not that it persuades any man that he is what he is not, but that it suppresses the influence of honest ambition, by raising an opinion that honor may be gained without the toil of merit; and the benefit of advice arises commonly, not from any new light imparted to the mind, but from the discovery which it affords, of the publick suffrages. He that could withstand conscience, is frighted at infamy, and shame prevails where reason was defeated.

As we all know our own faults, and know them commonly with many aggravations which human perspicacity cannot discover, there is, perhaps, no man, however hardened by impudence or dissipated by levity, sheltered by hypocrisy, or blasted by disgrace, who does not intend some time to review his conduct, and to regulate the remainder of his life by the laws of virtue. New temptations indeed attack him, new invitations are offered by pleasure and interest, and the hour of reformation is always delayed; every delay gives vice another opportunity of fortifying itself by habit; and the change of manners, though sincerely intended and rationally planned, is referred to the time when some craving passion shall be fully gratified, or some powerful allurement cease its importunity.

Thus procrastination is accumulated on procrastination, and one impediment succeeds another, till age shatters our resolution, or death intercepts the project of amendment. Such is often the end of salutary purposes, after they have long delighted the imagination, and appeased that disquiet which every mind feels from known misconduct, when the attention is not diverted by business or by pleasure.

Nothing surely can be more unworthy of a reasonable nature, than 10
to continue in a state so opposite to real happiness, as that all the peace of solitude and felicity of meditation, must arise from resolutions of forsaking it. Yet the world will often afford examples of men, who pass months and years in a continual war with their own convictions, and are daily dragged by habit or betrayed by passion into practices, which they closed and opened their eyes with purposes to avoid; purposes which, though settled on conviction, the first impulse of momentary desire totally overthrows.

The influence of custom is indeed such that to conquer it will require the utmost efforts of fortitude and virtue, nor can I think any man more worthy of veneration and renown, than those who have burst the shackles of habitual vice. This victory however has different degrees of glory as of difficulty; it is more heroic as the objects of guilty gratification are more familiar, and the recurrence of solicitation more frequent. He that from experience of the folly of ambition resigns his offices, may set himself free at once from temptation to squander his life in courts, because he cannot regain his former station. He who is enslaved by an amorous passion, may quit his tyrant in disgust, and absence will without the help of reason overcome by degrees the desire of returning. But those appetites to which every place affords their proper object, and which require no preparatory measures or gradual advances, are more tenaciously adhesive; the wish is so near the enjoyment, that compliance often precedes consideration, and before the powers of reason can be summoned, the time for employing them is past.

Indolence is therefore one of the vices from which those whom it once infects are seldom reformed. Every other species of luxury operates upon some appetite that is quickly satiated, and requires some concurrence of art or accident which every place will not supply; but the desire of ease acts equally at all hours, and the longer it is indulged in the more increased. To do nothing is in every man's power; we can never want an opportunity of omitting duties. The lapse to indolence is soft and imperceptible, because it is only a mere cessation of activity; but the return to diligence is difficult, because it implies a change from rest to motion, from privation to reality.

—Facilis descensus Averni:
Noctes atque dies patet atri janua Ditis:
Sed revocare gradum, superasque evadere ad auras,
Hoc opus, hic labor est.—

[VIR. *Aeneid VI. 126*]

The gates of *Hell* are open night and day;
Smooth the descent, and easy is the way:
But, to return, and view the chearful skies;
In this, the task and mighty labour lies.

DRYDEN

Of this vice, as of all others, every man who indulges it is conscious; we all know our own state, if we could be induced to consider it; and it might perhaps be useful to the conquest of all these ensnarers of the mind, if at certain stated days life was reviewed. Many things necessary are omitted, because we vainly imagine that they may be always performed, and what cannot be done without pain will for ever be delayed if the time of doing it be left unsettled. No corruption is great but by long negligence, which can scarcely prevail in a mind regularly and frequently awakened by periodical remorse. He that thus breaks his life into parts, will find in himself a desire to distinguish every stage of his existence by some improvement, and delight himself with the approach of the day of recollection, as of the time which is to begin a new series of virtue and felicity.

QUESTIONS

1. *Explain the connections that Johnson makes between self-love and indolence.*
2. *Johnson characteristically makes general statements that apply to everyone. In this essay, for example, in the first sentence, "the human*

mind" signifies everyone's mind; "has more frequently incurred criticism" signifies frequent criticism by everyone (or perhaps by everyone who criticizes); "the negligence with which men overlook their own faults" signifies all men, or everyone, inasmuch as Johnson uses man *and* men *generically, that is, with reference to both sexes rather than to male persons only. Choose several more general statements in this essay and explain how Johnson's language makes them general. Then rewrite them, still as general statements, in modern colloquial English.*

3. *Write an essay in which you test the general applicability of one of Johnson's general statements. How wide a range of examples can you provide in support of it? Can you provide significant counterexamples that call its general applicability into question?*

Lord Chesterfield

LETTER TO HIS SON

London, October 16, O.S. 1747

DEAR BOY

The art of pleasing is a very necessary one to possess, but a very difficult one to acquire. It can hardly be reduced to rules; and your own good sense and observation will teach you more of it than I can. "Do as you would be done by," is the surest method that I know of pleasing. Observe carefully what pleases you in others, and probably the same things in you will please others. If you are pleased with the complaisance and attention of others to your humors, your tastes, or your weaknesses, depend upon it, the same complaisance and attention on your part to theirs will equally please them. Take the tone of the company that you are in, and do not pretend to give it; be serious, gay, or even trifling, as you find the present humor of the company; this is an attention due from every individual to the majority. Do not tell stories in company; there is nothing more tedious and disagreeable; if by chance you know a very short story, and exceedingly applicable to the present subject of conversation, tell it in as few words as possible; and even then, throw out that you do not love to tell stories, but that the shortness of it tempted you.

Of all things banish the egotism out of your conversation, and never think of entertaining people with your own personal concerns or private affairs; though they are interesting to you, they are tedious and impertinent to everybody else; besides that, one cannot keep one's

From Chesterfield's *Letters* (1774).

own private affairs too secret. Whatever you think your own excellencies may be, do not affectedly display them in company; nor labor, as many people do, to give that turn to the conversation, which may supply you with an opportunity of exhibiting them. If they are real, they will infallibly be discovered, without your pointing them out yourself, and with much more advantage. Never maintain an argument with heat and clamor, though you think or know yourself to be in the right; but give your opinion modestly and coolly, which is the only way to convince; and, if that does not do, try to change the conversation, by saying, with good-humor, "We shall hardly convince one another; nor is it necessary that we should, so let us talk of something else."

Remember that there is a local propriety to be observed in all companies; and that what is extremely proper in one company may be, and often is, highly improper in another.

The jokes, the *bon-mots*, the little adventures, which may do very well in one company, will seem flat and tedious, when related in another. The particular characters, the habits, the cant of one company may give merit to a word, or a gesture, which would have none at all if divested of those accidental circumstances. Here people very commonly err; and fond of something that has entertained them in one company, and in certain circumstances, repeat it with emphasis in another, where it is either insipid, or, it may be, offensive, by being ill-timed or misplaced. Nay, they often do it with this silly preamble: "I will tell you an excellent thing," or, "I will tell you the best thing in the world." This raises expectations, which, when absolutely disappointed, make the relator of this excellent thing look, very deservedly, like a fool.

5 If you would particularly gain the affection and friendship of particular people, whether men or women, endeavor to find out their predominant excellency, if they have one, and their prevailing weakness, which everybody has; and do justice to the one, and something more than justice to the other. Men have various objects in which they may excel, or at least would be thought to excel; and, though they love to hear justice done to them, where they know that they excel, yet they are most and best flattered upon those points where they wish to excel, and yet are doubtful whether they do or not. As for example: Cardinal Richelieu, who was undoubtedly the ablest statesman of his time, or perhaps of any other, had the idle vanity of being thought the best poet too; he envied the great Corneille his reputation, and ordered a criticism to be written upon the *Cid*.[1] Those, therefore, who

1. When the French classic tragedy *The Cid,* founded upon the legendary exploits of the medieval Castilian warrior-hero, was published in 1636 by its author Pierre Corneille (1606–1684), it was the subject of violent criticism, led by the French minister of state Richelieu (1585–1642).

flattered skillfully, said little to him of his abilities in state affairs, or at least but *en passant*, and as it might naturally occur. But the incense which they gave him, the smoke of which they knew would turn his head in their favor, was as a *bel esprit* and a poet. Why? Because he was sure of one excellency, and distrustful as to the other.

You will easily discover every man's prevailing vanity by observing his favorite topic of conversation; for every man talks most of what he has most a mind to be thought to excel in. Touch him but there, and you touch him to the quick. The late Sir Robert Walpole[2] (who was certainly an able man) was little open to flattery upon that head, for he was in no doubt himself about it; but his prevailing weakness was, to be thought to have a polite and happy turn to gallantry—of which he had undoubtedly less than any man living. It was his favorite and frequent subject of conversation, which proved to those who had any penetration that it was his prevailing weakness, and they applied to it with success.

Women have, in general, but one object, which is their beauty; upon which scarce any flattery is too gross for them to follow. Nature has hardly formed a woman ugly enough to be insensible to flattery upon her person; if her face is so shocking that she must, in some degree, be conscious of it, her figure and air, she trusts, make ample amends for it. If her figure is deformed, her face, she thinks, counterbalances it. If they are both bad, she comforts herself that she has graces, a certain manner, a *je ne sais quoi*[3] still more engaging than beauty. This truth is evident from the studied and elaborate dress of the ugliest woman in the world. An undoubted, uncontested, conscious beauty is, of all women, the least sensible of flattery upon that head; she knows it is her due, and is therefore obliged to nobody for giving it her. She must be flattered upon her understanding; which, though she may possibly not doubt of herself, yet she suspects that men may distrust.

Do not mistake me, and think that I mean to recommend to you abject and criminal flattery: no; flatter nobody's vices or crimes: on the contrary, abhor and discourage them. But there is no living in the world without a complaisant indulgence for people's weaknesses, and innocent, though ridiculous vanities. If a man has a mind to be thought wiser, and a woman handsomer, than they really are, their error is a comfortable one to themselves, and an innocent one with regard to other people; and I would rather make them my friends by indulging them in it, than my enemies by endeavoring (and that to no purpose) to undeceive them.

2. For two decades a powerful prime minister, Walpole (1676–1745) was also a patron of the arts and prided himself on his taste.
3. A certain inexpressible quality.

There are little attentions, likewise, which are infinitely engaging, and which sensibly affect that degree of pride and self-love, which is inseparable from human nature, as they are unquestionable proofs of the regard and consideration which we have for the persons to whom we pay them. As, for example, to observe the little habits, the likings, the antipathies, and the tastes of those whom we would gain; and then take care to provide them with the one, and to secure them from the other; giving them, genteelly, to understand, that you had observed they liked such a dish, or such a room, for which reason you had prepared it: or, on the contrary, that having observed they had an aversion to such a dish, a dislike to such a person, etc., you had taken care to avoid presenting them. Such attention to such trifles flatters self-love much more than greater things, as it makes people think themselves almost the only objects of your thoughts and care.

10 These are some of the arcana[4] necessary for your initiation in the great society of the world. I wish I had known them better at your age; I have paid the price of three and fifty years for them, and shall not grudge it if you reap the advantage. Adieu.

4. Secret things.

QUESTIONS

1. *Chesterfield recommends to his son the rule "Do as you would be done by" (paragraph 1). What kind of behavior does Chesterfield enjoin? How does his injunction differ from Jesus' injunction "Therefore all things whatsoever ye would that men should do to you, do ye even so unto them" (Matthew 7.12; see also Luke 6.31)?*
2. *Chesterfield does not recommend "abject and criminal flattery" of vices and crimes but rather "complaisant indulgence for people's weaknesses, and innocent, though ridiculous vanities" (paragraph 8). Make a short list of what you consider vices and crimes and another of what you consider weaknesses and vanities. Be prepared to defend your distinctions.*
3. *Rewrite Chesterfield's "Letter to His Son" for the 1990s.*

Samuel L. Clemens

ADVICE TO YOUTH

Being told I would be expected to talk here, I inquired what sort of a talk I ought to make. They said it should be something suitable to youth—something didactic, instructive, or something in the nature of good advice. Very well. I have a few things in my mind which I have often longed to say for the instruction of the young; for it is in one's tender early years that such things will best take root and be most enduring and most valuable. First, then, I will say to you, my young friends—and I say it beseechingly, urgingly—

Always obey your parents, when they are present. This is the best policy in the long run, because if you don't they will make you. Most parents think they know better than you do, and you can generally make more by humoring that superstition than you can by acting on your own better judgment.

Be respectful to your superiors, if you have any, also to strangers, and sometimes to others. If a person offend you, and you are in doubt as to whether it was intentional or not, do not resort to extreme measures; simply watch your chance and hit him with a brick. That will be sufficient. If you shall find that he had not intended any offense, come out frankly and confess yourself in the wrong when you struck him; acknowledge it like a man and say you didn't mean to. Yes, always avoid violence; in this age of charity and kindliness, the time has gone by for such things. Leave dynamite to the low and unrefined.

Go to bed early, get up early—this is wise. Some authorities say get up with the sun; some others say get up with one thing, some with another. But a lark is really the best thing to get up with. It gives you a splendid reputation with everybody to know that you get up with the lark; and if you get the right kind of a lark, and work at him right, you can easily train him to get up at half past nine, every time—it is no trick at all.

Now as to the matter of lying. You want to be very careful about 5
lying; otherwise you are nearly sure to get caught. Once caught, you can never again be, in the eyes of the good and the pure, what you were before. Many a young person has injured himself permanently through a single clumsy and illfinished lie, the result of carelessness born of incomplete training. Some authorities hold that the young ought not to lie at all. That, of course, is putting it rather stronger than necessary;

Text of a lecture given by Clemens in 1882.

still, while I cannot go quite so far as that, I do maintain, and I believe I am right, that the young ought to be temperate in the use of this great art until practice and experience shall give them that confidence, elegance, and precision which alone can make the accomplishment graceful and profitable. Patience, diligence, painstaking attention to detail—these are the requirements; these, in time, will make the student perfect; upon these, and upon these only, may he rely as the sure foundation for future eminence. Think what tedious years of study, thought, practice, experience, went to the equipment of that peerless old master who was able to impose upon the whole world the lofty and sounding maxim that "truth is mighty and will prevail"—the most majestic compound fracture of fact which any of woman born has yet achieved. For the history of our race, and each individual's experience, are sown thick with evidence that a truth is not hard to kill and that a lie told well is immortal. There is in Boston a monument of the man who discovered anaesthesia; many people are aware, in these latter days, that that man didn't discover it at all, but stole the discovery from another man. Is this truth mighty, and will it prevail? Ah no, my hearers, the monument is made of hardy material, but the lie it tells will outlast it a million years. An awkward, feeble, leaky lie is a thing which you ought to make it your unceasing study to avoid; such a lie as that has no more real permanence than an average truth. Why, you might as well tell the truth at once and be done with it. A feeble, stupid, preposterous lie will not live two years—except it be a slander upon somebody. It is indestructible, then, of course, but that is no merit of yours. A final word: begin your practice of this gracious and beautiful art early—begin now. If I had begun earlier, I could have learned how.

Never handle firearms carelessly. The sorrow and suffering that have been caused through the innocent but heedless handling of firearms by the young! Only four days ago, right in the next farmhouse to the one where I am spending the summer, a grandmother, old and gray and sweet, one of the loveliest spirits in the land, was sitting at her work, when her young grandson crept in and got down an old, battered, rusty gun which had not been touched for many years and was supposed not to be loaded, and pointed it at her, laughing and threatening to shoot. In her fright she ran screaming and pleading toward the door on the other side of the room; but as she passed him he placed the gun almost against her very breast and pulled the trigger! He had supposed it was not loaded. And he was right—it wasn't. So there wasn't any harm done. It is the only case of that kind I ever heard of. Therefore, just the same, don't you meddle with old unloaded firearms; they are the most deadly and unerring things that have ever been created by man. You don't have to take any pains at all with them; you don't have to have a rest, you don't have to have any sights on the gun, you don't have to take aim, even. No, you just pick out a relative and bang away, and you are sure to get him. A youth who can't hit a cathedral at thirty yards with a Gatling gun in three-quarters of an hour, can take up an old empty musket and bag his grandmother every time, at a hundred. Think what Waterloo[1] would have been if one of the armies had been boys armed with old muskets supposed not to be loaded, and the other army had been composed of their female relations. The very thought of it makes one shudder.

There are many sorts of books; but good ones are the sort for the young to read. Remember that. They are a great, an inestimable, an unspeakable means of improvement. Therefore be careful in your selection, my young friends; be very careful; confine yourselves exclusively to Robertson's Sermons, Baxter's *Saint's Rest, The Innocents Abroad*, and works of that kind.[2]

But I have said enough. I hope you will treasure up the instructions which I have given you, and make them a guide to your feet and a light to your understanding. Build your character thoughtfully and painstakingly upon these precepts, and by and by, when you have got it built, you will be surprised and gratified to see how nicely and sharply it resembles everybody else's.

1. The bloody battle (1815) in which Napoleon suffered his final defeat at the hands of English and German troops under the Duke of Wellington.
2. The five volumes of sermons by Frederick William Robertson (1816–1853), an English clergyman, and Richard Baxter's *Saints' Everlasting Rest* (1650) were once well-known religious works. *The Innocents Abroad* is Clemens's own collection of humorous travel sketches.

QUESTIONS

1. *Underline the various pieces of "serious" advice that Clemens offers and notice where and how he begins to turn each one upside down.*
2. *Samuel Clemens—that is, Mark Twain, already known as a comic author—delivered "Advice to Youth" as a lecture in 1882; it was not published until 1923. We do not know the circumstances under which he delivered it or to whom. Using evidence from the text, imagine both the circumstances and audience.*
3. *Rewrite "Advice to Youth" for the 1990s.*

Willard Gaylin

WHAT YOU SEE IS THE REAL YOU

It was, I believe, the distinguished Nebraska financier Father Edward J. Flanagan[1] who professed to having "never met a bad boy." Having, myself, met a remarkable number of bad boys, it might seem that either our experiences were drastically different or we were using the word "bad" differently. I suspect neither is true, but rather that the Father was appraising the "inner man," while I, in fact, do not acknowledge the existence of inner people.

Since we psychoanalysts have unwittingly contributed to this confusion, let one, at least, attempt a small rectifying effort. Psychoanalytic data—which should be viewed as supplementary information—is, unfortunately, often viewed as alternative (and superior) explanation. This has led to the prevalent tendency to think of the "inner" man as the real man and the outer man as an illusion or pretender.

While psychoanalysis supplies us with an incredibly useful tool for explaining the motives and purposes underlying human behavior, most of this has little bearing on the moral nature of that behavior.

Like roentgenology, psychoanalysis is a fascinating, but relatively new, means of illuminating the person. But few of us are prepared to substitute an X-ray of Grandfather's head for the portrait that hangs in the parlor. The inside of the man represents another view, not a truer one. A man may not always be what he appears to be, but what he appears to be is always a significant part of what he is. A man is the sum total of *all* his behavior. To probe for unconscious determinants of behavior and then define *him* in their terms exclusively, ignoring his overt behavior altogether, is a greater distortion than ignoring the unconscious completely.

5 Kurt Vonnegut has said, "You are what you pretend to be," which is simply another way of saying, you are what we (all of us) perceive you to be, not what you think you are.

Consider for a moment the case of the ninety-year-old man on his deathbed (surely the Talmud must deal with this?) joyous and relieved over the success of his deception. For ninety years he has shielded his evil nature from public observation. For ninety years he has affected courtesy, kindness, and generosity—suppressing all the malice he

From *The New York Times* (Oct. 7, 1977).

1. Founder (1917) of Boys Town, a self-governing community for homeless and abandoned boys, for which he was also an energetic fund raiser.

knew was within him while he calculatedly and artificially substituted grace and charity. All his life he had been fooling the world into believing he was a good man. This "evil" man will, I predict, be welcomed into the Kingdom of Heaven.

Similarly, I will not be told that the young man who earns his pocket money by mugging old ladies is "really" a good boy. Even my generous and expansive definition of goodness will not accommodate that particular form of self-advancement.

It does not count that beneath the rough exterior he has a heart—or, for that matter, an entire innards—of purest gold, locked away from human perception. You are for the most part what you seem to be, not what you would wish to be, nor, indeed, what you believe yourself to be.

Spare me, therefore, your good intentions, your inner sensitivities, your unarticulated and unexpressed love. And spare me also those tedious psychohistories which—by exposing the goodness inside the bad man, and the evil in the good—invariably establish a vulgar and perverse egalitarianism, as if the arrangement of what is outside and what inside makes no moral difference.

10 Saint Francis[2] may, in his unconscious, indeed have been compensating for, and denying, destructive, unconscious Oedipal impulses identical to those which Atilla projected and acted on. But the similarity of the unconscious constellations in the two men matters precious little, if it does not distinguish between them.

I do not care to learn that Hitler's heart was in the right place. A knowledge of the unconscious life of the man may be an adjunct to understanding his behavior. It is *not* a substitute for his behavior in describing him.

The inner man is a fantasy. If it helps you to identify with one, by all means, do so; preserve it, cherish it, embrace it, but do not present it to others for evaluation or consideration, for excuse or exculpation, or, for that matter, for punishment or disapproval.

Like any fantasy, it serves your purposes alone. It has no standing in the real world which we share with each other. Those character traits, those attitudes, that behavior—that strange and alien stuff sticking out all over you—*that's the real you!*

2. Saint Francis of Assisi, who early in the thirteenth century renounced parental wealth, entered on a life of poverty, and founded the Franciscan order of begging friars.

Barbara Huttmann

A CRIME OF COMPASSION

"Murderer," a man shouted. "God help patients who get *you* for a nurse."

"What gives you the right to play God?" another one asked.

It was the Phil Donahue show where the guest is a fatted calf and the audience a 200-strong flock of vultures hungering to pick at the bones. I had told them about Mac, one of my favorite cancer patients. "We resuscitated him 52 times in just one month. I refused to resuscitate him again. I simply sat there and held his hand while he died."

There wasn't time to explain that Mac was a young, witty, macho cop who walked into the hospital with 32 pounds of attack equipment, looking as if he could singlehandedly protect the whole city, if not the entire state. "Can't get rid of this cough," he said. Otherwise, he felt great.

5 Before the day was over, tests confirmed that he had lung cancer. And before the year was over, I loved him, his wife, Maura, and their three kids as if they were my own. All the nurses loved him. And we all battled his disease for six months without ever giving death a thought. Six months isn't such a long time in the whole scheme of things, but it was long enough to see him lose his youth, his wit, his macho, his hair, his bowel and bladder control, his sense of taste and smell and his ability to do the slightest thing for himself. It was also long enough to watch Maura's transformation from a young woman into a haggard, beaten old lady.

When Mac had wasted away to a 60-pound skeleton kept alive by liquid food we poured down a tube, i.v. solutions we dripped into his veins and oxygen we piped to a mask on his face, he begged us: "Mercy . . . for God's sake, please just let me go."

The first time he stopped breathing, the nurse pushed the button that calls a "code blue" throughout the hospital and sends a team rushing to resuscitate the patient. Each time he stopped breathing, sometimes two or three times a day, the code team came again. The doctors and technicians worked their miracles and walked away. The nurses stayed to wipe the saliva that drooled from his mouth, irrigate the big craters of bedsores that covered his hips, suction the lung fluids that threatened to drown him, clean the feces that burned his skin like lye, pour the liquid food down the tube attached to his stom-

From the "My Turn" column of *Newsweek* (Aug. 3, 1983).

ach, put pillows between his knees to ease the bone-on-bone pain, turn him every hour to keep the bedsores from getting worse and change his gown and linen every two hours to keep him from being soaked in perspiration.

At night I went home and tried to scrub away the smell of decaying flesh that seemed woven into the fabric of my uniform. It was in my hair, the upholstery of my car—there was no washing it away. And every night I prayed that Mac would die, that his agonized eyes would never again plead with me to let him die.

Every morning I asked his doctor for a "no code" order. Without that order, we had to resuscitate every patient who stopped breathing. His doctor was one of several who believe we must extend life as long as we have the means and knowledge to do it. To not do it is to be liable for negligence, at least in the eyes of many people, including some nurses. I thought about what it would be like to stand before a judge, accused of murder, if Mac stopped breathing and I didn't call a code.

And after the 52nd code, when Mac was still lucid enough to beg for 10
death again, and Maura was crumbled in my arms again, and when no amount of pain medication stilled his moaning and agony, I wondered about a spiritual judge. Was all this misery and suffering supposed to be building character or infusing us all with the sense of humility that comes from impotence?

Had we, the whole medical community, become so arrogant that we believed in the illusion of salvation through science? Had we become so self-righteous that we thought meddling in God's work was our duty, our moral imperative and our legal obligation? Did we really believe that we had the right to force "life" on a suffering man who had begged for the right to die?

Such questions haunted me more than ever early one morning when Maura went home to change her clothes and I was bathing Mac. He had been still for so long. I thought he at last had the blessed relief of coma. Then he opened his eyes and moaned. "Pain . . . no more . . . Barbara . . . do something . . . God, let me go."

The desperation in his eyes and voice riddled me with guilt. "It'll stop," I told him as I injected the pain medication.

I sat on the bed and held Mac's hands in mine. He pressed his bony fingers against my hand and muttered, "Thanks." Then there was one soft sigh and I felt his hands go cold in mine. "Mac?" I whispered, as I waited for his chest to rise and fall again.

A clutch of panic banded my chest, drew my finger to the code but- 15
ton, urged me to do something, anything . . . but sit there alone with death. I kept one finger on the button, without pressing it, as a waxen pallor slowly transformed his face from person to empty shell. Nothing

I've ever done in my 47 years has taken so much effort as it took *not* to press that code button.

Eventually, when I was as sure as I could be that the code team would fail to bring him back, I entered the legal twilight zone and pushed the button. The team tried. And while they were trying, Maura walked into the room and shrieked, "No . . . don't let them do this to him . . . for God's sake . . . please, no more."

Cradling her in my arms was like cradling myself, Mac and all those patients and nurses who had been in this place before who do the best they can in a death-denying society.

So a TV audience accused me of murder. Perhaps I am guilty. If a doctor had written a no-code order, which is the only *legal* alternative, would he have felt any less guilty? Until there is legislation making it a criminal act to code a patient who has requested the right to die, we will all of us risk the same fate as Mac. For whatever reason, we developed the means to prolong life, and now we are forced to use it. We do not have the right to die.

Michael Levin

THE CASE FOR TORTURE

It is generally assumed that torture is impermissible, a throwback to a more brutal age. Enlightened societies reject it outright, and regimes suspected of using it risk the wrath of the United States.

I believe this attitude is unwise. There are situations in which torture is not merely permissible but morally mandatory. Moreover, these situations are moving from the realm of imagination to fact.

Death: Suppose a terrorist has hidden an atomic bomb on Manhattan Island which will detonate at noon on July 4 unless . . . (here follow the usual demands for money and release of his friends from jail). Suppose, further, that he is caught at 10 a.m. of the fateful day, but—preferring death to failure—won't disclose where the bomb is. What do we do? If we follow due process—wait for his lawyer, arraign him—millions of people will die. If the only way to save those lives is to subject the terrorist to the most excruciating possible pain, what grounds can there be for not doing so? I suggest there are none. In any case, I ask you to face the question with an open mind.

Torturing the terrorist is unconstitutional? Probably. But millions of lives surely outweigh constitutionality. Torture is barbaric? Mass

Originally appeared in *Newsweek* (June 7, 1982).

murder is far more barbaric. Indeed, letting millions of innocents die in deference to one who flaunts his guilt is moral cowardice, an unwillingness to dirty one's hands. If *you* caught the terrorist, could you sleep nights knowing that millions died because you couldn't bring yourself to apply the electrodes?

Once you concede that torture is justified in extreme cases, you 5
have admitted that the decision to use torture is a matter of balancing innocent lives against the means needed to save them. You must now face more realistic cases involving more modest numbers. Someone plants a bomb on a jumbo jet. He alone can disarm it, and his demands cannot be met (or if they can, we refuse to set a precedent by yielding to his threats). Surely we can, we must, do anything to the extortionist to save the passengers. How can we tell 300, or 100, or 10 people who never asked to be put in danger, "I'm sorry, you'll have to die in agony, we just couldn't bring ourselves to . . ."

Here are the results of an informal poll about a third, hypothetical, case. Suppose a terrorist group kidnapped a newborn baby from a hospital. I asked four mothers if they would approve of torturing kidnappers if that were necessary to get their own newborns back. All said yes, the most "liberal" adding that she would like to administer it herself.

I am not advocating torture as punishment. Punishment is addressed to deeds irrevocably past. Rather, I am advocating torture as an acceptable measure for preventing future evils. So understood, it is far less objectionable than many extant punishments. Opponents of the death penalty, for example, are forever insisting that executing a murderer will not bring back his victim (as if the purpose of capital punishment were supposed to be resurrection, not deterrence or retribution). But torture, in the cases described, is intended not to bring anyone back but to keep innocents from being dispatched. The most powerful argument against using torture as a punishment or to secure confessions is that such practices disregard the rights of the individual. Well, if the individual is all that important—and he is—it is correspondingly important to protect the rights of individuals threatened by terrorists. If life is so valuable that it must never be taken, the lives of the innocents must be saved even at the price of hurting the one who endangers them.

Better precedents for torture are assassination and pre-emptive attack. No Allied leader would have flinched at assassinating Hitler, had that been possible. (The Allies did assassinate Heydrich.) Americans would be angered to learn that Roosevelt could have had Hitler killed in 1943—thereby shortening the war and saving millions of lives—but refused on moral grounds. Similarly, if nation A learns that nation B is about to launch an unprovoked attack, A has a right to save itself by destroying B's military capability first. In the same way, if the police can by torture save those who would otherwise die at the hands of kidnappers or terrorists, they must.

Idealism: There is an important difference between terrorists and their victims that should mute talk of the terrorists' "rights." The terrorist's victims are at risk unintentionally, not having asked to be endangered. But the terrorist knowingly initiated his actions. Unlike his victims, he volunteered for the risks of his deed. By threatening to kill for profit or idealism, he renounces civilized standards, and he can have no complaint if civilization tries to thwart him by whatever means necessary.

10 Just as torture is justified only to save lives (not extort confessions or recantations), it is justifiably administered only to those *known* to hold innocent lives in their hands. Ah, but how can the authorities ever be sure they have the right malefactor? Isn't there a danger of error and abuse? Won't We turn into Them?

Questions like these are disingenuous in a world in which terrorists proclaim themselves and perform for television. The name of their game is public recognition. After all, you can't very well intimidate a government into releasing your freedom fighters unless you announce that it is your group that has seized its embassy. "Clear guilt" is difficult to define, but when 40 million people see a group of masked gunmen seize an airplane on the evening news, there is not much question about who the perpetrators are. There will be hard cases where the situation is murkier. Nonetheless, a line demarcating the legitimate use of torture can be drawn. Torture only the obviously guilty, and only for the sake of saving innocents, and the line between Us and Them will remain clear.

There is little danger that the Western democracies will lose their way if they choose to inflict pain as one way of preserving order. Paralysis in the face of evil is the greater danger. Some day soon a terrorist will threaten tens of thousands of lives, and torture will be the only way to save them. We had better start thinking about this.

Tom Regan

THE CASE FOR ANIMAL RIGHTS

I regard myself as an advocate of animal rights—as a part of the animal rights movement. That movement, as I conceive it, is committed to a number of goals, including:

From *In Defense of Animals* (1985).

- the total abolition of the use of animals in science;
- the total dissolution of commercial animal agriculture;
- the total elimination of commercial and sport hunting and trapping.

There are, I know, people who profess to believe in animal rights but do not avow these goals. Factory farming, they say, is wrong—it violates animals' rights—but traditional animal agriculture is all right. Toxicity tests of cosmetics on animals violates their rights, but important medical research—cancer research, for example—does not. The clubbing of baby seals is abhorrent, but not the harvesting of adult seals. I used to think I understood this reasoning. Not any more. You don't change unjust institutions by tidying them up.

What's wrong—fundamentally wrong—with the way animals are treated isn't the details that vary from case to case. It's the whole system. The forlornness of the veal calf is pathetic, heart-wrenching; the pulsing pain of the chimp with electrodes planted deep in her brain is repulsive; the slow, tortuous death of the racoon caught in the leghold trap is agonizing. But what is wrong isn't the pain, isn't the suffering, isn't the deprivation. These compound what's wrong. Sometimes—often—they make it much, much worse. But they are not the fundamental wrong.

The fundamental wrong is the system that allows us to view animals as *our resources*, here for *us*—to be eaten, or surgically manipulated, or exploited for sport or money. Once we accept this view of animals—as our resources—the rest is as predictable as it is regrettable. Why worry about their loneliness, their pain, their death? Since animals exist for us, to benefit us in one way or another, what harms them really doesn't matter—or matters only if it starts to bother us, makes us feel a trifle uneasy when we eat our veal escalope, for example. So, yes, let us get veal calves out of solitary confinement, give them more space, a little straw, a few companions. But let us keep our veal escalope.

But a little straw, more space and a few companions won't eliminate—won't even touch—the basic wrong that attaches to our viewing and treating these animals as our resources. A veal calf killed to be eaten after living in close confinement is viewed and treated in this way: but so, too, is another who is raised (as they say) "more humanely." To right the wrong of our treatment of farm animals requires more than making rearing methods "more humane"; it requires the total dissolution of commercial animal agriculture.

5 How we do this, whether we do it or, as in the case of animals in science, whether and how we abolish their use—these are to a large extent political questions. People must change their beliefs before they change their habits. Enough people, especially those elected to

public office, must believe in change—must want it—before we will have laws that protect the rights of animals. This process of change is very complicated, very demanding, very exhausting, calling for the efforts of many hands in education, publicity, political organization and activity, down to the licking of envelopes and stamps. As a trained and practicing philosopher, the sort of contribution I can make is limited but, I like to think, important. The currency of philosophy is ideas—their meaning and rational foundation—not the nuts and bolts of the legislative process, say, or the mechanics of community organization. That's what I have been exploring over the past ten years or so in my essays and talks and, most recently, in my book, *The Case for Animal Rights*. I believe the major conclusions I reach in the book are true because they are supported by the weight of the best arguments. I believe the idea of animal rights has reason, not just emotion, on its side.

In the space I have at my disposal here I can only sketch, in the barest outline, some of the main features of the book. Its main themes—and we should not be surprised by this—involve asking and answering deep, foundational moral questions about what morality is, how it should be understood and what is the best moral theory, all considered. I hope I can convey something of the shape I think this theory takes. The attempt to do this will be (to use a word a friendly critic once used to describe my work) cerebral, perhaps too cerebral. But this is misleading. My feelings about how animals are sometimes treated run just as deep and just as strong as those of my more volatile compatriots. Philosophers do—to use the jargon of the day—have a right side to their brains. If it's the left side we contribute (or mainly should), that's because what talents we have reside there.

How to proceed? We begin by asking how the moral status of animals has been understood by thinkers who deny that animals have rights. Then we test the mettle of their ideas by seeing how well they stand up under the heat of fair criticism. If we start our thinking in this way, we soon find that some people believe that we have no duties directly to animals, that we owe nothing to them, that we can do nothing that wrongs them. Rather, we can do wrong acts that involve animals, and so we have duties regarding them, though none to them. Such views may be called indirect duty views. By way of illustration: suppose your neighbor kicks your dog. Then your neighbor has done something wrong. But not to your dog. The wrong that has been done is a wrong to you. After all, it is wrong to upset people, and your neighbor's kicking your dog upsets you. So you are the one who is wronged, not your dog. Or again: by kicking your dog your neighbor damages your property. And since it is wrong to damage another person's property, your neighbor has done something wrong—to you, of course, not to your dog. Your neighbor no more wrongs your dog than your car would be wronged if the windshield were smashed. Your neighbor's duties involving your dog are indirect duties to you. More generally, all of our duties regarding animals are indirect duties to one another—to humanity.

How could someone try to justify such a view? Someone might say that your dog doesn't feel anything and so isn't hurt by your neighbor's kick, doesn't care about the pain since none is felt, is as unaware of anything as is your windshield. Someone might say this, but no rational person will, since, among other considerations, such a view will commit anyone who holds it to the position that no human being feels pain either—that human beings also don't care about what happens to them. A second possibility is that though both humans and your dog are hurt when kicked, it is only human pain that matters. But, again, no rational person can believe this. Pain is pain wherever it occurs. If your neighbor's causing you pain is wrong because of the pain that is caused, we cannot rationally ignore or dismiss the moral relevance of the pain that your dog feels.

Philosophers who hold indirect duty views—and many still do—have come to understand that they must avoid the two defects just noted: that is, both the view that animals don't feel anything as well as the idea that only human pain can be morally relevant. Among such thinkers the sort of view now favored is one or other form of what is called *contractarianism.*

Here, very crudely, is the root idea: morality consists of a set of rules 10
that individuals voluntarily agree to abide by, as we do when we sign a contract (hence the name contractarianism). Those who understand and accept the terms of the contract are covered directly; they have rights created and recognized by, and protected in, the contract. and these contractors can also have protection spelled out for others who, though they lack the ablity to understand morality and so cannot sign the contract themselves, are loved or cherished by those who can. Thus young children, for example, are unable to sign contracts and lack rights. But they are protected by the contract none the less because of the sentimental interests of others, most notably their parents. So we have, then, duties involving these children, duties regarding them, but no duties to them. Our duties in their case are indirect duties to other human beings, usually their parents.

As for animals, since they cannot understand contracts, they obviously cannot sign; and since they cannot sign, they have no rights. Like children, however, some animals are the objects of the sentimental interest of others. You, for example, love your dog or cat. So those animals that enough people care about (companion animals, whales, baby seals, the American bald eagle), though they lack rights themselves, will be protected because of the sentimental interests of people. I have, then, according to contractarianism, no duty directly to your dog or any other animal, not even the duty not to cause them pain or suffering; my duty not to hurt them is a duty I have to those people who care about what happens to them. As for other animals, where no or little sentimental interest is present—in the case of farm animals, for example, or laboratory rats—what duties we have grow weaker and weaker, perhaps to vanishing point. The pain and death they endure, though real, are not wrong if no one cares about them.

When it comes to the moral status of animals, contractarianism could be a hard view to refute if it were an adequate theoretical approach to the moral status of human beings. It is not adequate in this latter respect, however, which makes the question of its adequacy in the former case, regarding animals, utterly moot. For consider: morality, according to the (crude) contractarian position before us, consists of rules that people agree to abide by. What people? Well, enough to make a difference—enough, that is, *collectively* to have the power to enforce the rules that are drawn up in the contract. This is very well and good for the signatories but not so good for anyone who is not asked to sign. And there is nothing in contractarianism of the sort we are discussing that guarantees or requires that everyone will have a chance to participate equally in framing the rules of morality. The result is that this approach to ethics could sanction the most blatant forms of social, economic, moral and political injustice, ranging from a repressive caste system to systematic racial or sexual discrimination. Might, according to this theory, does make right. Let those who are the victims of injustice suffer as they will. It matters not so long as no one else—no contractor, or too few of them—cares about it. Such a theory takes one's moral breath away . . . as if, for example, there would be nothing wrong with apartheid in South Africa if few white South Africans were upset by it. A theory with so little to recommend it at the level of the ethics of our treatment of our fellow humans cannot have anything more to recommend it when it comes to the ethics of how we treat our fellow animals.

The version of contractarianism just examined is, as I have noted, a crude variety, and in fairness to those of a contractarian persuasion it must be noted that much more refined, subtle and ingenious varieties are possible. For example, John Rawls,[1] in his *A Theory of Justice,* sets forth a version of contractarianism that forces contractors to ignore the accidental features of being a human being—for example, whether one is white or black, male or female, a genius or of modest intellect. Only by ignoring such features, Rawls believes, can we ensure that the principles of justice that contractors would agree upon

1. Contemporary American philosopher (b. 1921).

are not based on bias or prejudice. Despite the improvement a view such as Rawls's represents over the cruder forms of contractarianism, it remains deficient: it systematically denies that we have direct duties to those human beings who do not have a sense of justice—young children, for instance, and many mentally retarded humans. And yet it seems reasonably certain that, were we to torture a young child or a retarded elder, we would be doing something that wronged him or her, not something that would be wrong if (and only if) other humans with a sense of justice were upset. And since this is true in the case of these humans, we cannot rationally deny the same in the case of animals.

Indirect duty views, then, including the best among them, fail to command our rational assent. Whatever ethical theory we should accept rationally, therefore, it must at least recognize that we have some duties directly to animals, just as we have some duties directly to each other. The next two theories I'll sketch attempt to meet this requirement.

The first I call the cruelty-kindness view. Simply stated, this says 15
that we have a direct duty to be kind to animals and a direct duty not to be cruel to them. Despite the familiar, reassuring ring of these ideas, I do not believe that this view offers an adequate theory. To make this clearer, consider kindness. A kind person acts from a certain kind of motive—compassion or concern, for example. And that is a virtue. But there is no guarantee that a kind act is a right act. If I am a generous racist, for example, I will be inclined to act kindly towards members of my own race, favoring their interests above those of others. My kindness would be real and, so far as it goes, good. But I trust it is too obvious to require argument that my kind acts may not be above moral reproach—may, in fact, be positively wrong because rooted in injustice. So kindness, notwithstanding its status as a virtue to be encouraged, simply will not carry the weight of a theory of right action.

Cruelty fares no better. People or their acts are cruel if they display either a lack of sympathy for or, worse, the presence of enjoyment in another's suffering. Cruelty in all its guises is a bad thing, a tragic human failing. But just as a person's being motivated by kindness does not guarantee that he or she does what is right, so the absence of cruelty does not ensure that he or she avoids doing what is wrong. Many people who perform abortions, for example, are not cruel, sadistic people. But that fact alone does not settle the terribly difficult question of the morality of abortion. The case is no different when we examine the ethics of our treatment of animals. So, yes, let us be for kindness and against cruelty. But let us not suppose that being for the one and against the other answers questions about moral right and wrong.

Some people think that the theory we are looking for is utilitarianism. A utilitarian accepts two moral principles. The first is that of equality: everyone's interests count, and similar interests must be counted as having similar weight or importance. White or black, American or Iranian, human or animal—everyone's pain or frustration matter, and matter just as much as the equivalent pain or frustration of anyone else. The second principle a utilitarian accepts is that of utility: do the act that will bring about the best balance between satisfaction and frustration for everyone affected by the outcome.

As a utilitarian, then, here is how I am to approach the task of deciding what I morally ought to do: I must ask who will be affected if I choose to do one thing rather than another, how much each individual will be affected, and where the best results are most likely to lie—which option, in other words, is most likely to bring about the best results, the best balance between satisfaction and frustration. That option, whatever it may be, is the one I ought to choose. That is where my moral duty lies.

The great appeal of utilitarianism rests with its uncompromising *egalitarianism:* everyone's interests count and count as much as the like interests of everyone else. The kind of odious discrimination that some forms of contractarianism can justify—discrimination based on race or sex, for example—seems disallowed in principle by utilitarianism, as is speciesism, systematic discrimination based on species membership.

20 The equality we find in utilitarianism, however, is not the sort an advocate of animal or human rights should have in mind. Utilitarianism has no room for the equal moral rights of different individuals because it has no room for their equal inherent value or worth. What has value for the utilitarian is the satisfaction of an individual's interests, not the individual whose interests they are. A universe in which you satisfy your desire for water, food and warmth is, other things being equal, better than a universe in which these desires are frustrated. And the same is true in the case of an animal with similar desires. But neither you nor the animal have any value in your own right. Only your feelings do.

Here is an analogy to help make the philosophical point clearer: a cup contains different liquids, sometimes sweet, sometimes bitter, sometimes a mix of the two. What has value are the liquids: the sweeter the better, the bitterer the worse. The cup, the container, has no value. It is what goes into it, not what they go into, that has value. For the utilitarian you and I are like the cup; we have no value as individuals and thus no equal value. What has value is what goes into us, what we serve as receptacles for; our feelings of satisfaction have positive value, our feelings of frustration negative value.

Serious problems arise for utilitarianism when we remind ourselves that it enjoins us to bring about the best consequences. What does this mean? It doesn't mean the best consequences for me alone, or for my family or friends, or any other person taken individually. No, what we must do is, roughly, as follows: we must add up (somehow!) the separate satisfactions and frustrations of everyone likely to be affected by our choice, the satisfactions in one column, the frustrations in the other. We must total each column for each of the options before us. That is what it means to say the theory is aggregative. And then we must choose that option which is most likely to bring about the best balance of totaled satisfactions over totaled frustrations. Whatever act would lead to this outcome is the one we ought morally to perform—it is where our moral duty lies. And that act quite clearly might not be the same one that would bring about the best results for me personally, or for my family or friends, or for a lab animal. The best aggregated consequences for everyone concerned are not necessarily the best for each individual.

That utilitarianism is an aggregative theory—different individuals' satisfactions or frustrations are added, or summed, or totaled—is the key objection to this theory. My Aunt Bea is old, inactive, a cranky, sour person, though not physically ill. She prefers to go on living. She is also rather rich. I could make a fortune if I could get my hands on her money, money she intends to give me in any event, after she dies, but which she refuses to give me now. In order to avoid a huge tax bite, I plan to donate a handsome sum of my profits to a local children's hospital. Many, many children will benefit from my generosity, and much joy will be brought to their parents, relatives and friends. If I don't get the money rather soon, all these ambitions will come to naught. The once-in-a-lifetime opportunity to make a real killing will be gone. Why, then, not kill my Aunt Bea? Oh, of course I *might* get caught. But I'm no fool and, besides, her doctor can be counted on to co-operate (he has an eye for the same investment and I happen to know a good deal about his shady past). The deed can be done . . . professionally, shall we say. There is *very* little chance of getting caught. And as for my conscience being guilt-ridden, I am a resourceful sort of fellow and will take more than sufficient comfort—as I lie on the beach at Acapulco—in contemplating the joy and health I have brought to so many others.

Suppose Aunt Bea is killed and the rest of the story comes out as told. Would I have done anything wrong? Anything immoral? One would have thought that I had. Not according to utilitarianism. Since what I have done has brought about the best balance between totaled satisfaction and frustration for all those affected by the outcome, my action is not wrong. Indeed, in killing Aunt Bea the physician and I did what duty required.

This same kind of argument can be repeated in all sorts of cases, 25 illustrating, time after time, how the utilitarian's position leads to results that impartial people find morally callous. It *is* wrong to kill my Aunt Bea in the name of bringing about the best results for others. A good end does not justify an evil means. Any adequate moral theory will have to explain why this is so. Utilitarianism fails in this respect and so cannot be the theory we seek.

What do do? Where to begin anew? The place to begin, I think, is with the utilitarian's view of the value of the individual—or, rather, lack of value. In its place, suppose we consider that you and I, for example, do have value as individuals—what we'll call *inherent value.* To say we have such value is to say that we are something more than, something different from, mere receptacles. Moreover, to ensure that we do not pave the way for such injustices as slavery or sexual discrimination, we must believe that all who have inherent value have it equally, regardless of their sex, race, religion, birthplace and so on. Similarly to be discarded as irrelevant are one's talents or skills, intelligence and wealth, personality or pathology, whether one is loved and admired or despised and loathed. The genius and the retarded child, the prince and the pauper, the brain surgeon and the fruit vendor, Mother Teresa[2] and the most unscrupulous used-car salesman—all have inherent value, all possess it equally, and all have an equal right to be treated with respect, to be treated in ways that do not reduce them to the status of things, as if they existed as resources for others. My value as an individual is independent of my usefulness to you. Yours is not dependent on your usefulness to me. For either of us to treat the other in ways that fail to show respect for the other's independent value is to act immorally, to violate the individual's rights.

Some of the rational virtues of this view—what I call the rights view—should be evident. Unlike (crude) contractarianism, for example, the rights view *in principle* denies the moral tolerability of any and all forms of racial, sexual or social discrimination; and unlike utilitarianism, this view *in principle* denies that we can justify good results by using evil means that violate an individual's rights—denies, for example, that it could be moral to kill my Aunt Bea to harvest beneficial consequences for others. That would be to sanction the disrespectful treatment of the individual in the name of the social good, something the rights view will not—categorically will not—ever allow.

The rights view, I believe, is rationally the most satisfactory moral theory. It surpasses all other theories in the degree to which it illuminates and explains the foundation of our duties to one another—the domain of human morality. On this score it has the best reasons, the best arguments, on its side. Of course, if it were possible to show that

2. Nun (b. 1910) who founded the Missionaries of Charity in Calcutta, India.

only human beings are included within its scope, then a person like myself, who believes in animal rights, would be obliged to look elsewhere.

But attempts to limit its scope to humans only can be shown to be rationally defective. Animals, it is true, lack many of the abilities humans possess. They can't read, do higher mathematics, build a bookcase or make *baba ghanoush.*[3] Neither can many human beings, however, and yet we don't (and shouldn't) say that they (these humans) therefore have less inherent value, less of a right to be treated with respect, than do others. It is the *similarities* between those human beings who most clearly, most non-controversially have such value (the people reading this, for example), not our differences, that matter most. And the really crucial, the basic similarity is simply this: we are each of us the experiencing subject of a life, a conscious creature having an individual welfare that has importance to us whatever our usefulness to others. We want and prefer things, believe and feel things, recall and expect things. And all these dimensions of our life, including our pleasure and pain, our enjoyment and suffering, our satisfaction and frustration, our continued existence or our untimely death—all make a difference to the quality of our life as lived, as experienced, by us as individuals. As the same is true of those animals that concern us (the ones that are eaten and trapped, for example), they too must be viewed as the experiencing subjects of a life, with inherent value of their own.

Some there are who resist the idea that animals have inherent value. 30
"Only humans have such value," they profess. How might this narrow view be defended? Shall we say that only humans have the requisite intelligence, or autonomy, or reason? But there are many, many humans who fail to meet these standards and yet are reasonably viewed as having value above and beyond their usefulness to others. Shall we claim that only humans belong to the right species, the species *Homo sapiens*?[4] But this is blatant speciesism. Will it be said, then, that all—and only—humans have immortal souls? Then our opponents have their work cut out for them. I am myself not ill-disposed to the proposition that there are immortal souls. Personally, I profoundly hope I have one. But I would not want to rest my position on a controversial ethical issue on the even more controversial question about who or what has an immortal soul. That is to dig one's hole deeper, not to climb out. Rationally, it is better to resolve moral issues without making more controversial assumptions than are needed. The ques-

3. An eggplant-sesame oil spread or dip popular in the Middle East.
4. Latin for man with intellect, the taxonomic designation for the modern human species.

tion of who has inherent value is such a question, one that is resolved more rationally without the introduction of the idea of immortal souls than by its use.

Well, perhaps some will say that animals have some inherent value, only less than we have. Once again, however, attempts to defend this view can be shown to lack rational justification. What could be the basis of our having more inherent value than animals? Their lack of reason, or autonomy, or intellect? Only if we are willing to make the same judgment in the case of humans who are similarly deficient. But it is not true that such humans—the retarded child, for example, or the mentally deranged—have less inherent value than you or I. Neither, then, can we rationally sustain the view that animals like them in being the experiencing subjects of a life have less inherent value. *All* who have inherent value have it *equally*, whether they be human animals or not.

Inherent value, then, belongs equally to those who are the experiencing subjects of a life. Whether it belongs to others—to rocks and rivers, trees and glaciers, for example—we do not know and may never know. But neither do we need to know, if we are to make the case for animal rights. We do not need to know, for example, how many people are eligible to vote in the next presidential election before we can know whether I am. Similarly, we do not need to know how many individuals have inherent value before we can know that some do. When it comes to the case for animal rights, then, what we need to know is whether the animals that, in our culture, are routinely eaten, hunted and used in our laboratories, for example, are like us in being subjects of a life. And we do know this. We do know that many—literally, billions and billions—of these animals are the subjects of a life in the sense explained and so have inherent value if we do. And since, in order to arrive at the best theory of our duties to one another, we must recognize our equal inherent value as individuals, reason—not sentiment, not emotion—reason compels us to recognize the equal inherent value of these animals and, with this, their equal right to be treated with respect.

That, *very* roughly, is the shape and feel of the case for animal rights. Most of the details of the supporting argument are missing. They are to be found in the book to which I alluded earlier. Here, the details go begging, and I must, in closing, limit myself to four final points.

The first is how the theory that underlies the case for animal rights shows that the animal rights movement is a part of, not antagonistic to, the human rights movement. The theory that rationally grounds the rights of animals also grounds the rights of humans. Thus those involved in the animal rights movement are partners in the struggle to secure respect for human rights—the rights of women, for example, or minorities, or workers. The animal rights movement is cut from the same moral cloth as these.

Second, having set out the broad outlines of the rights view, I can 35
now say why its implications for farming and science, among other fields, are both clear and uncompromising. In the case of the use of animals in science, the rights view is categorically abolitionist. Lab animals are not our tasters; we are not their kings. Because these animals are treated routinely, systematically as if their value were reducible to their usefulness to others, they are routinely, systematically treated with a lack of respect, and thus are their rights routinely, systematically violated. This is just as true when they are used in trivial, duplicative, unnecessary or unwise research as it is when they are used in studies that hold out real promise of human benefits. We can't justify harming or killing a human being (my Aunt Bea, for example) just for these sorts of reason. Neither can we do so even in the case of so lowly a creature as a laboratory rat. It is not just refinement or reduction that is called for, not just larger, cleaner cages, not just more generous use of anaesthetic or the elimination of multiple surgery, not just tidying up the system. It is complete replacement. The best we can do when it comes to using animals in science is—not to use them. That is where our duty lies, according to the rights view.

As for commercial animal agriculture, the rights view takes a similar abolitionist position. The fundamental moral wrong here is not that animals are kept in stressful close confinement or in isolation, or that their pain and suffering, their needs and preferences are ignored or discounted. All these *are* wrong, of course, but they are not the fundamental wrong. They are symptoms and effects of the deeper, systematic wrong that allows these animals to be viewed and treated as lacking independent value, as resources for us—as, indeed, a renewable resource. Giving farm animals more space, more natural environments, more companions does not right the fundamental wrong, any more than giving lab animals more anaesthesia or bigger, cleaner cages would right the fundamental wrong in their case. Nothing less than the total dissolution of commercial animal agriculture will do this, just as, for similar reasons I won't develop at length here, morality requires nothing less than the total elimination of hunting and trapping for commercial and sporting ends. The rights view's implications, then, as I have said, are clear and uncompromising.

My last two points are about philosophy, my profession. It is, most obviously, no substitute for political action. The words I have written here and in other places by themselves don't change a thing. It is what we do with the thoughts that the words express—our acts, our deeds—that changes things. All that philosophy can do, and all I have attempted, is to offer a vision of what our deeds should aim at. And the why. But not the how.

Finally, I am reminded of my thoughtful critic, the one I mentioned earlier, who chastised me for being too cerebral. Well, cerebral I have been: indirect duty views, utilitarianism, contractarianism—hardly the stuff deep passions are made of. I am also reminded, however, of the image another friend once set before me—the image of the ballerina as expressive of disciplined passion. Long hours of sweat and toil, of loneliness and practice, of doubt and fatigue: those are the discipline of her craft. But the passion is there too, the fierce drive to excel, to speak through her body, to do it right, to pierce our minds. That is the image of philosophy I would leave with you, not "too cerebral" but *disciplined passion.* Of the discipline enough has been seen. As for the passion: there are times, and these not infrequent, when tears come to my eyes when I see, or read, or hear of the wretched plight of animals in the hands of humans. Their pain, their suffering, their loneliness, their innocence, their death. Anger. Rage. Pity. Sorrow. Disgust. The whole creation groans under the weight of the evil we humans visit upon these mute, powerless creatures. It *is* our hearts, not just our heads, that call for an end to it all, that demand of us that we overcome, for them, the habits and forces behind their systematic oppression. All great movements, it is written, go through three stages: ridicule, discussion, adoption. It is the realization of this third stage, adoption, that requires both our passion and our discipline, our hearts and our heads. The fate of animals is in our hands. God grant we are equal to the task.

QUESTIONS

1. *Regan argues against four views that deny rights to animals: indirect duty, contractarianism, cruelty-kindness, and utilitarianism. Locate his account of each and explain his objections to it.*
2. *Regan then argues for what he calls a "rights view," which is, he claims, "rationally the most satisfactory moral theory" (paragraph 28). Explain both his view and his claim.*
3. *What are the advantages of arguing for views that conflict with one's own before arguing for one's own? What are the disadvantages?*
4. *Regan includes among his goals "the total dissolution of commercial animal agriculture" and "the total elimination of commercial and sport hunting and trapping" (paragraph 1). Do these goals include vegetarianism? Discuss.*
5. *Write an essay in which you take a position on an issue about which*

you have strong feelings. Following Regan's example, focus on argument while both acknowledging and excluding your feelings.

Carl Cohen

THE CASE FOR THE USE OF ANIMALS IN BIOMEDICAL RESEARCH

Using animals as research subjects in medical investigations is widely condemned on two grounds: first, because it wrongly violates the *rights* of animals,[1] and second, because it wrongly imposes on sentient creatures much avoidable *suffering.*[2] Neither of these arguments is sound. The first relies on a mistaken understanding of rights; the second relies on a mistaken calculation of consequences. Both deserve definitive dismissal.

Why Animals Have No Rights

A right, properly understood, is a claim, or potential claim, that one party may exercise against another. The target against whom such a claim may be registered can be a single person, a group, a community, or (perhaps) all humankind. The content of rights claims also varies greatly: repayment of loans, nondiscrimination by employers, noninterference by the state, and so on. To comprehend any genuine right fully, therefore, we must know *who* holds the right, *against whom* it is held, and *to what* it is a right.

Alternative sources of rights add complexity. Some rights are grounded in constitution and law (e.g., the right of an accused to trial by jury); some rights are moral but give no legal claims (e.g., my right to your keeping the promise you gave me); and some rights (e.g., against theft or assault) are rooted both in morals and in law.

The different targets, contents, and sources of rights, and their inevitable conflict, together weave a tangled web. Notwithstanding all such complications, this much is clear about rights in general: they are in every case claims, or potential claims, within a community of moral agents. Rights arise, and can be intelligibly defended, only among beings who actually do, or can, make moral claims against one another.

From *The New England Journal of Medicine* (Oct. 1986). All notes to this essay are the author's and are collected at the end as "References," as is the style of the *New England Journal of Medicine,* in which this essay appeared.

Whatever else rights may be, therefore, they are necessarily human; their possessors are persons, human beings.

The attributes of human beings from which this moral capability arises have been described variously by philosophers, both ancient and modern: the inner consciousness of a free will (Saint Augustine[3]); the grasp, by human reason, of the binding character of moral law (Saint Thomas[4]); the self-conscious participation of human beings in an objective ethical order (Hegel[5]); human membership in an organic moral community (Bradley[6]); the development of the human self through the consciousness of other moral selves (Mead[7]); and the underivative, intuitive cognition of the rightness of an action (Prichard[8]). Most influential has been Immanuel Kant's emphasis on the universal human possession of a uniquely moral will and the autonomy its use entails.[9] Humans confront choices that are purely moral; humans—but certainly not dogs or mice—lay down moral laws, for others and for themselves. Human beings are self-legislative, morally *auto-nomous*.

Animals (that is, nonhuman animals, the ordinary sense of that word) lack this capacity for free moral judgment. They are not beings of a kind capable of exercising or responding to moral claims. Animals therefore have no rights, and they can have none. This is the core of the argument about the alleged rights of animals. The holders of rights must have the capacity to comprehend rules of duty, governing all including themselves. In applying such rules, the holders of rights must recognize possible conflicts between what is in their own interest and what is just. Only in a community of beings capable of self-restricting moral judgments can the concept of a right be correctly invoked.

Humans have such moral capacities. They are in this sense self-legislative, are members of communities governed by moral rules, and do possess rights. Animals do not have such moral capacities. They are not morally self-legislative, cannot possibly be members of a truly moral community, and therefore cannot possess rights. In conducting research on animal subjects, therefore, we do not violate their rights, because they have none to violate.

To animate life, even in its simplest forms, we give a certain natural reverence. But the possession of rights presupposes a moral status not attained by the vast majority of living things. We must not infer, therefore, that a live being has, simply in being alive, a "right" to its life. The assertion that all animals, only because they are alive and have interests, also possess the "right to life"[10] is an abuse of that phrase, and wholly without warrant.

It does not follow from this, however, that we are morally free to do anything we please to animals. Certainly not. In our dealings with animals, as in our dealings with other human beings, we have obligations that do not arise from claims against us based on rights. Rights entail obligations, but many of the things one ought to do are in no way tied to another's entitlement. Rights and obligations are not reciprocals of one another, and it is a serious mistake to suppose that they are.

10 Illustrations are helpful. Obligations may arise from internal commitments made: physicians have obligations to their patients not grounded merely in their patients' rights. Teachers have such obligations to their students, shepherds to their dogs, and cowboys to their horses. Obligations may arise from differences of status: adults owe special care when playing with young children, and children owe special care when playing with young pets. Obligations may arise from special relationships: the payment of my son's college tuition is something to which he may have no right, although it may be my obligation to bear the burden if I reasonably can; my dog has no right to daily exercise and veterinary care, but I do have the obligation to provide these things for her. Obligations may arise from particular acts or circumstances: one may be obliged to another for a special kindness done, or obliged to put an animal out of its misery in view of its condition—although neither the human benefactor nor the dying animal may have had a claim of right.

Plainly, the grounds of our obligations to humans and to animals are manifold and cannot be formulated simply. Some hold that there is a general obligation to do no gratuitous harm to sentient creatures (the principle of nonmaleficence); some hold that there is a general obligation to do good to sentient creatures when that is reasonably within one's power (the principle of beneficence). In our dealings with animals, few will deny that we are at least obliged to act humanely—that is, to treat them with the decency and concern that we owe, as sensitive human beings, to other sentient creatures. To treat animals humanely, however, is not to treat them as humans or as the holders of rights.

A common objection, which deserves a response, may be paraphrased as follows:

> If having rights requires being able to make moral claims, to grasp and apply moral laws, then many humans—the brain-damaged, the comatose, the senile—who plainly lack those capacities must be without rights. But that is absurd. This proves [the critic concludes] that rights do not depend on the presence of moral capacities.[1,10]

This objection fails; it mistakenly treats an essential feature of humanity as though it were a screen for sorting humans. The capacity for moral judgment that distinguishes humans from animals is not a test to be administered to human beings one by one. Persons who are unable, because of some disability, to perform the full moral functions natural to human beings are certainly not for that reason ejected from the moral community. The issue is one of kind. Humans are of such a kind that they may be the subject of experiments only with their voluntary consent. The choices they make freely must be respected. Animals are of such a kind that it is impossible for them, in principle, to give or withhold voluntary consent or to make a moral choice. What humans retain when disabled, animals have never had.

A second objection, also often made, may be paraphrased as follows:

> Capacities will not succeed in distinguishing humans from the other animals. Animals also reason; animals also communicate with one another; animals also care passionately for their young; animals also exhibit desires and preferences,[11,12] Features of moral relevance—rationality, interdependence, and love—are not exhibited uniquely by human beings. Therefore [this critic concludes], there can be no solid moral distinction between humans and other animals.[10]

15 This criticism misses the central point. It is not the ability to communicate or to reason, or dependence on one another, or care for the young, or the exhibition of preference, or any such behavior that marks the critical divide. Analogies between human families and those of monkeys, or between human communities and those of wolves, and the like, are entirely beside the point. Patterns of conduct are not at issue. Animals do indeed exhibit remakable behavior at times. Conditioning, fear, instinct, and intelligence all contribute to species survival. Membership in a community of moral agents nevertheless remains impossible for them. Actors subject to moral judgment must be capable of grasping the generality of an ethical premise in a practical syllogism. Humans act immorally often enough, but only they—never wolves or monkeys—can discern, by applying some moral rule to the facts of a case, that a given act ought or ought not to be performed. The moral restraints imposed by humans on themselves are thus highly abstract and are often in conflict with the self-interest of the agent. Communal behavior among animals, even when most intelligent and most endearing, does not approach autonomous morality in this fundamental sense.

Genuinely moral acts have an internal as well as an external dimension. Thus, in law, an act can be criminal only when the guilty deed, the actus reus, is done with a guilty mind, mens rea. No animal can ever commit a crime; bringing animals to criminal trial is the mark of primitive ignorance. The claims of moral right are similarly inapplicable to them. Does a lion have a right to eat a baby zebra? Does a baby zebra have a right not to be eaten? Such questions, mistakenly invoking the concept of right where it does not belong, do not make good sense. Those who condemn biomedical research because it violates "animal rights" commit the same blunder.

In Defense of "Speciesism"

Abandoning reliance on animal rights, some critics resort instead to animal sentience—their feelings of pain and distress. We ought to desist from imposition of pain insofar as we can. Since all or nearly all experimentation on animals does impose pain and could be readily forgone, say these critics, it should be stopped. The ends sought may be worthy, but those ends do not justify imposing agonies on humans, and by animals the agonies are felt no less. The laboratory use of animals (these critics conclude) must therefore be ended—or at least very sharply curtailed.

Argument of this variety is essentially utilitarian, often expressly so;[13] it is based on the calculation of the net product, in pains and pleasures, resulting from experiments on animals. Jeremy Bentham, comparing horses and dogs with other sentient creatures, is thus commonly quoted: "The question is not, Can they reason? nor Can they talk? but, Can they suffer?" [14]

Animals certainly can suffer and surely ought not to be made to suffer needlessly. But in inferring, from these uncontroversial premises, that biomedical research causing animal distress is largely (or wholly) wrong, the critic commits two serious errors.

The first error is the assumption, often explicitly defended, that all 20
sentient animals have equal moral standing. Between a dog and a human being, according to this view, there is no moral difference; hence the pains suffered by dogs must be weighed no differently from the pains suffered by humans. To deny such equality, according to this critic, is to give unjust preference to one species over another; it is "speciesism." The most influential statement of this moral equality of species was made by Peter Singer:

> The racist violates the principle of equality by giving greater weight to the interests of members of his own race when there is a clash between their interests and the interests of those of another race. The sexist violates the principle of equality by favoring the interests of his own sex. Similarly the speciesist allows the interests of his own species to override the greater interests of members of other species. The pattern is identical in each case.[2]

This argument is worse than unsound; it is atrocious. It draws an offensive moral conclusion from a deliberately devised verbal parallelism that is utterly specious. Racism has no rational ground whatever. Differing degrees of respect or concern for humans for no other reason than that they are members of different races is an injustice totally without foundation in the nature of the races themselves. Racists, even if acting on the basis of mistaken factual beliefs, do grave moral wrong precisely because there is no morally relevant distinction among the races. The supposition of such differences has led to outright horror. The same is true of the sexes, neither sex being entitled by right to greater respect or concern than the other. No dispute here.

Between species of animate life, however—between (for example) humans on the one hand and cats or rats on the other—the morally relevant differences are enormous, and almost universally appreciated. Humans engage in moral reflection; humans are morally autonomous; humans are members of moral communities, recognizing just claims against their own interest. Human beings do have rights; theirs is a moral status very different from that of cats or rats.

I am a speciesist. Speciesism is not merely plausible; it is essential for right conduct, because those who will not make the morally relevant distinctions among species are almost certain, in consequence, to misapprehend their true obligations. The analogy between speciesism and racism is insidious. Every sensitive moral judgment requires that the differing natures of the beings to whom obligations are owed be considered. If all forms of animate life—or vertebrate animal life?—must be treated equally, and if therefore in evaluating a research program the pains of a rodent count equally with the pains of a human, we are forced to conclude (1) that neither humans nor rodents possess rights, or (2) that rodents possess all the rights that humans possess. Both alternatives are absurd. Yet one or the other must be swallowed if the moral equality of all species is to be defended.

Humans owe to other humans a degree of moral regard that cannot be owed to animals. Some humans take on the obligation to support and heal others, both humans and animals, as a principal duty in their lives; the fulfillment of that duty may require the sacrifice of many animals. If biomedical investigators abandon the effective pursuit of their professional objectives because they are convinced that they may not do to animals what the service of humans requires, they will fail, objectively, to do their duty. Refusing to recognize the moral differences among species is a sure path to calamity. (The largest animal rights group in the country is People for the Ethical Treatment of Animals; its codirector, Ingrid Newkirk, calls research using animal subjects "fascism" and "supremacism." "Animal liberationists do not separate out the *human* animal," she says, "so there is no rational basis for saying that a human being has special rights. A rat is a pig is a dog is a boy. They're all mammals." [15])

25 Those who claim to base their objection to the use of animals in biomedical research on their reckoning of the net pleasures and pains produced make a second error, equally grave. Even if it were true—as it is surely not—that the pains of all animal beings must be counted equally, a cogent utilitarian calculation requires that we weigh all the consequences of the use, and of the nonuse, of animals in laboratory research. Critics relying (however mistakenly) on animal rights may

claim to ignore the beneficial results of such research, rights being trump cards to which interest and advantage must give way. But an argument that is explicitly framed in terms of interest and benefit for all over the long run must attend also to the disadvantageous consequences of not using animals in research, and to all the achievements attained and attainable only through their use. The sum of the benefits of their use is utterly beyond quantification. The elimination of horrible disease, the increase of longevity, the avoidance of great pain, the saving of lives, and the improvement of the quality of lives (for humans and for animals) achieved through research using animals is so incalculably great that the argument of these critics, systematically pursued, establishes not their conclusion but its reverse: to refrain from using animals in biomedical research is, on utilitarian grounds, morally wrong.

When balancing the pleasures and pains resulting from the use of animals in research, we must not fail to place on the scales the terrible pains that would have resulted, would be suffered now, and would long continue had animals not been used. Every disease eliminated, every vaccine developed, every method of pain relief devised, every surgical procedure invented, every prosthetic device implanted—indeed, virtually every modern medical therapy is due, in part or in whole, to experimentation using animals. Nor may we ignore, in the balancing process, the predictable gains in human (and animal) well-being that are probably achievable in the future but that will not be achieved if the decision is made now to desist from such research or to curtail it.

Medical investigators are seldom insensitive to the distress their work may cause animal subjects. Opponents of research using animals are frequently insensitive to the cruelty of the results of the restrictions they would impose.[2] Untold numbers of human beings—real persons, although not now identifiable—would suffer grievously as the consequence of this well-meaning but shortsighted tenderness. If the morally relevant differences between humans and animals are borne in mind, and if all relevant considerations are weighed, the calculation of long-term consequences must give overwhelming support for biomedical research using animals.

Concluding Remarks

Substitution. The humane treatment of animals requires that we desist from experimenting on them if we can accomplish the same result using alternative methods—in vitro experimentation, computer simulation, or others. Critics of some experiments using animals rightly make this point.

It would be a serious error to suppose, however, that alternative techniques could soon be used in most research now using live animal subjects. No other methods now on the horizon—or perhaps ever to be available—can fully replace the testing of a drug, a procedure, or a vaccine, in live organisms. The flood of new medical possibilities being opened by the successes of recombinant DNA technology will turn to a trickle if testing on live animals is forbidden. When initial trials entail great risks, there may be no forward movement whatever without the use of live animal subjects. In seeking knowledge that may prove critical in later clinical applications, the unavailability of animals for inquiry may spell complete stymie. In the United States, federal regulations require the testing of new drugs and other products on animals, for efficacy and safety, before human beings are exposed to them.[16,17] We would not want it otherwise.

30 Every new advance in medicine—every new drug, new operation, new therapy of any kind—must sooner or later be tried on a living being for the first time. That trial, controlled or uncontrolled, will be an experiment. The subject of that experiment, if it is not an animal, will be a human being. Prohibiting the use of live animals in biomedical research, therefore, or sharply restricting it, must result either in the blockage of much valuable research or in the replacement of animal subjects with human subjects. These are the consequences—unacceptable to most reasonable persons—of not using animals in research.

Reduction. Should we not at least reduce the use of animals in biomedical research? No, we should increase it, to avoid when feasible the use of humans as experimental subjects. Medical investigations putting human subjects at some risk are numerous and greatly varied. The risks run in such experiments are usually unavoidable, and (thanks to earlier experiments on animals) most such risks are minimal or moderate. But some experimental risks are substantial.

When an experimental protocol that entails substantial risk to humans comes before an institutional review board, what response is appropriate? The investigation, we may suppose, is promising and deserves support, so long as its human subjects are protected against unnecessary dangers. May not the investigators be fairly asked, Have you done all that you can do to eliminate risk to humans by the extensive testing of that drug, that procedure, or that device on animals? To achieve maximal safety for humans we are right to require thorough experimentation on animal subjects before humans are involved.

Opportunities to increase human safety in this way are commonly missed; trials in which risks may be shifted from humans to animals are often not devised, sometimes not even considered. Why? For the investigator, the use of animals as subjects is often more expensive, in money and time, than the use of human subjects. Access to suitable human subjects is often quick and convenient, whereas access to appropriate animal subjects may be awkward, costly, and burdened with red tape. Physician-investigators have often had more experience working with human beings and know precisely where the needed pool of subjects is to be found and how they may be enlisted. Animals, and the procedures for their use, are often less familiar to these investigators. Moreover, the use of animals in place of humans is now more likely to be the target of zealous protests from without. The upshot is that humans are sometimes subjected to risks that animals could have borne, and should have borne, in their place. To maximize the protection of human subjects, I conclude, the wide and imaginative use of live animal subjects should be encouraged rather than discouraged. This enlargement in the use of animals is our obligation.

Consistency. Finally, inconsistency between the profession and the practice of many who oppose research using animals deserves comment. This frankly ad hominem observation aims chiefly to show that a coherent position rejecting the use of animals in medical research imposes costs so high as to be intolerable even to the critics themselves.

One cannot coherently object to the killing of animals in biomedi- 35
cal investigations while continuing to eat them. Anesthetics and thoughtful animal husbandry render the level of actual animal distress in the laboratory generally lower than that in the abattoir. So long as death and discomfort do not substantially differ in the two contexts, the consistent objector must not only refrain from all eating of animals but also protest as vehemently against others eating them as against others experimenting on them. No less vigorously must the critic object to the wearing of animal hides in coats and shoes, to employment in any industrial enterprise that uses animal parts, and to any commercial development that will cause death or distress to animals.

Killing animals to meet human needs for food, clothing, and shelter is judged entirely reasonable by most persons. The ubiquity of these uses and the virtual universality of moral support for them confront the opponent of research using animals with an inescapable difficulty. How can the many common uses of animals be judged morally worthy, while their use in scientific investigation is judged unworthy?

The number of animals used in research is but the tiniest fraction of the total used to satisfy assorted human appetites. That these appetites, often base and satisfiable in other ways, morally justify the far larger consumption of animals, whereas the quest for improved human health and understanding cannot justify the far smaller, is wholly implausible. Aside from the numbers of animals involved, the distinction in terms of worthiness of use, drawn with regard to any single animal, is not defensible. A given sheep is surely not more justifiably used to put lamb chops on the supermarket counter than to serve in testing a new contraceptive or a new prosthetic device. The needless killing of animals is wrong; if the common killing of them for our food or convenience is right, the less common but more humane uses of animals in the service of medical science are certainly not less right.

Scrupulous vegetarianism, in matters of food, clothing, shelter, commerce, and recreation, and in all other spheres, is the only fully coherent position the critic may adopt. At great human cost, the lives of fish and crustaceans must also be protected, with equal vigor, if speciesism has been forsworn. A very few consistent critics adopt this position. It is the reductio ad absurdum of the rejection of moral distinctions between animals and human beings.

Opposition to the use of animals in research is based on arguments of two different kinds—those relying on the alleged rights of animals and those relying on the consequences for animals. I have argued that arguments of both kinds must fail. We surely do have obligations to animals, but they have, and can have, no rights against us on which research can infringe. In calculating the consequences of animal research, we must weigh all the long-term benefits of the results achieved—to animals and to humans—and in that calculation we must not assume the moral equality of all animate species.

References

1. Regan T. The case for animal rights. Berkeley, Calif.: University of California Press, 1983.
2. Singer P. Animal liberation. New York: Avon Books, 1977.
3. St. Augustine. Confessions. Book Seven. A.D. 397. New York: Pocket books, 1957:-104–26.
4. St. Thomas Aquinas. Summa theologica. A.D. 1273. Philosophic texts. New York. Oxford University Press, 1960:353–66.
5. Hegel GWF. Philosophy of right. 1821. London: Oxford University Press, 1952:-105–10.
6. Bradley FH. Why should I be moral? 1876. In: Melden AI, ed. Ethical theories. New York: Prentice Hall, 1950:345–59.
7. Mead GH. The genesis of the self and social control. 1925. In: Reck AJ, ed. Selected writings. Indianapolis: Bobbs-Merrill, 1964:264–93.
8. Prichard HA. Does moral philosophy rest on a mistake? 1912. In: Cellars W, Hospers J, eds. Readings in ethical theory. New York: Appleton-Century-Crofts, 1952:-149–63.
9. Kant I. Fundamental principles of the metaphysic of morals. 1785. New York: Liberal Arts Press, 1949.

10. Rollin BE. Animal rights and human morality. New York: Prometheus Books, 1981.
11. Hoff C. Immoral and moral uses of animals. N Engl J Med 1980; 302:115–8.
12. Jamieson D. Killing persons and other beings. In: Miller HB, Williams WH, eds. Ethics and animals. Clifton, N.J.: Humana Press, 1983:135–46.
13. Singer P. Ten years of animal liberation. New York Review of Books. 1985; 31:46–52.
14. Bentham J. Introduction to the principles of morals and legislation. London: Athlone Press, 1970.
15. McCabe K. Who will live, who will die? Washingtonian Magazine. August 1986:-115.
16. U.S. Code of Federal Regulations, Title 21, Sect. 505(i). Food, drug and cosmetic regulations.
17. U.S. Code of Federal Regulations, Title 16, Sect. 1500.40–2. Consumer product regulations.

QUESTIONS

1. *Cohen limits his argument to the use of animals in biomedical research. What are the advantages of this limitation? What are the disadvantages?*
2. *Cohen defends speciesism; Tom Regan, in "The Case for Animal Rights" (pp. 746–758), condemns it. What are the issues at stake between them?*
3. *"Neither of these arguments is sound," Cohen opines. "The first relies on a mistaken understanding of rights; the second relies on a mistaken calculation of consequences" (paragraph 1). Find other examples of the language Cohen uses to dismiss arguments in opposition to his own. How do you respond to it? Is it the kind of language you would use in your own writing? Explain.*
4. *Write an essay in which you argue for or against speciesism. Be sure to define it. You may use Regan's and Cohen's arguments (with proper credit) in support of your own, but you need not.*

Sallie Tisdale

WE DO ABORTIONS HERE: A NURSE'S STORY

We do abortions here; that is all we do. There are weary, grim moments when I think I cannot bear another basin of bloody remains, utter another kind phrase of reassurance. So I leave the procedure room in the back and reach for a new chart. Soon I am talking to an eighteen-year-old woman pregnant for the fourth time. I push up her sleeve to check her blood pressure and find row upon row of needle marks, neat and parallel and discolored. She has been so hungry for her

From *Harper's Magazine* (Oct. 1990).

drug for so long that she has taken to using the loose skin of her upper arms; her elbows are already a permanent ruin of bruises. She is surprised to find herself nearly four months pregnant. I suspect she is often surprised, in a mild way, by the blows she is dealt. I prepare myself for another basin, another brief and chafing loss.

"How can you stand it?" Even the clients ask. They see the machine, the strange instruments, the blood, the final stroke that wipes away the promise of pregnancy. Sometimes I see that too: I watch a woman's swollen abdomen sink to softness in a few stuttering moments and my own belly flip-flops with sorrow. But all it takes for me to catch my breath is another interview, one more story that sounds so much like the last one. There is a numbing sameness lurking in this job: the same questions, the same answers, even the same trembling tone in the voices. The worst is the sameness of human failure, of inadequacy in the face of each day's dull demands.

In describing this work, I find it difficult to explain how much I enjoy it most of the time. We laugh a lot here, as friends and as professional peers. It's nice to be with women all day. I like the sudden, transient bonds I forge with some clients: moments when I am in my strength, remembering weakness, and a woman in weakness reaches out for my strength. What I offer is not power, but solidness, offered almost eagerly. Certain clients waken in me every tender urge I have—others make me wince and bite my tongue. Both challenge me to find a balance. It is a sweet brutality we practice here, a stark and loving dispassion.

I look at abortion as if I am standing on a cliff with a telescope, gazing at some great vista. I can sweep the horizon with both eyes, survey the scene in all its distance and size. Or I can put my eye to the lens and focus on the small details, suddenly so close. In abortion the absolute must always be tempered by the contextual, because both are real, both valid, both hard. How can we do this? How can we refuse? Each abortion is a measure of our failure to protect, to nourish our own. Each basin I empty is a promise—but a promise broken a long time ago.

5 I grew up on the great promise of birth control. Like many women my age, I took the pill as soon as I was sexually active. To risk pregnancy when it was so easy to avoid seemed stupid, and my contraceptive success, as it were, was part of the promise of social enlightenment. But birth control fails, far more frequently than laboratory trials predict. Many of our clients take the pill; its failure to protect them is a shocking realization. We have clients who have been sterilized, whose husbands have had vasectomies; each one is a statistical misfit, fine print come to life. The anger and shame of these women I hold in one hand, and the basin in the other. The distance between the two, the length I pace and try to measure, is the size of an abortion.

The procedure is disarmingly simple. Women are surprised, as though the mystery of conception, a dark and hidden genesis, requires an elaborate finale. In the first trimester of pregnancy, it's a mere few minutes of vacuuming, a neat tidying up. I give a woman a small yellow Valium, and when it has begun to relax her, I lead her into the back, into bareness, the stirrups. The doctor reaches in her, opening the narrow tunnel to the uterus with a succession of slim, smooth bars of steel. He inserts a plastic tube and hooks it to a hose on the machine. The woman is framed against white paper that crackles as she moves, the light bright in her eyes. Then the machine rumbles low and loud in the small windowless room; the doctor moves the tube back and forth with an efficient rhythm, and the long tail of it fills with blood that spurts and stumbles along into a jar. He is usually finished in a few minutes. They are long minutes for the woman; her uterus frequently reacts to its abrupt emptying with a powerful, unceasing cramp, which cuts off the blood vessels and enfolds the irritated, bleeding tissue.

I am learning to recognize the shadows that cross the faces of the women I hold. While the doctor works between her spread legs, the paper drape hiding his intent expression, I stand beside the table. I hold the woman's hands in mine, resting them just below her ribs. I watch her eyes, finger her necklace, stroke her hair. I ask about her job, her family; in a haze she answers me; we chatter, faces close, eyes meeting and sliding apart.

I watch the shadows that creep up unnoticed and suddenly darken her face as she screws up her features and pushes a tear out each side to slide down her cheeks. I have learned to anticipate the quiver of chin, the rapid intake of breath and the surprising sobs that rise soon after the machine starts to drum. I know this is when the cramp deepens, and the tears are partly the tears that follow pain—the sharp, childish crying when one bumps one's head on a cabinet door. But a well of woe seems to open beneath many women when they hear that thumping sound. The anticipation of the moment has finally come to fruit; the moment has arrived when the loss is no longer an imagined one. It has come true.

I am struck by the sameness and I am struck every day by the variety here—how this commonplace dilemma can so display the differences of women. A twenty-one-year-old woman, unemployed, uneducated, without family, in the fifth month of her fifth pregnancy. A forty-two-year-old mother of teenagers, shocked by her condition, refusing to tell her husband. A twenty-three-year-old mother of two having her seventh abortion, and many women in their thirties having their first. Some are stoic, some hysterical, a few giggle uncontrollably, many cry.

I talk to a sixteen-year-old uneducated girl who was raped. She has 10
gonorrhea. She describes blinding headaches, attacks of breathless-

ness, nausea. "Sometimes I feel like two different people," she tells me with a calm smile, "and I talk to myself."

I pull out my plastic models. She listens patiently for a time, and then holds her hands wide in front of her stomach.

"When's the baby going to go up into my stomach?" she asks.

I blink. "What do you mean?"

"Well," she says, still smiling, "when women get so big, isn't the baby in your stomach? Doesn't it hatch out of an egg there?"

15 My first question in an interview is always the same. As I walk down the hall with the woman, as we get settled in chairs and I glance through her files, I am trying to gauge her, to get a sense of the words, and the tone, I should use. With some I joke, with others I chat, sometimes I fall into a brisk, business-like patter. But I ask every woman, "Are you sure you want to have an abortion?" Most nod with grim knowing smiles. "Oh, yes," they sigh. Some seek forgiveness, offer excuses. Occasionally a woman will flinch and say, "Please don't use that word."

Later I describe the procedure to come, using care with my language. I don't say "pain" any more than I would say "baby." So many are afraid to ask how much it will hurt. "My sister told me—" I hear. "A friend of mine said—" and the dire expectations unravel. I prick the index finger of a woman for a drop of blood to test, and as the tiny lancet approaches the skin she averts her eyes, holding her trembling hand out to me and jumping at my touch.

It is when I am holding a plastic uterus in one hand, a suction tube in the other, moving them together in imitation of the scrubbing to come, that women ask the most secret question. I am speaking in a matter-of-fact voice about "the tissue" and "the contents" when the woman suddenly catches my eye and asks, "How big is the baby now?" These words suggest a quiet need for a definition of the boundaries being drawn. It isn't so odd, after all, that she feels relief when I describe the growing bud's bulbous shape, its miniature nature. Again I gauge, and sometimes lie a little, weaseling around its infantile features until its clinging power slackens.

But when I look in the basin, among the curdlike blood clots, I see an elfin thorax, attenuated, its pencilline ribs all in parallel rows with tiny knobs of spine rounding upwards. A translucent arm and hand swim beside.

A sleepy-eyed girl, just fourteen, watched me with a slight and goofy smile all through her abortion. "Does it have little feet and little fingers and all?" she'd asked earlier. When the suction was over she sat up woozily at the end of the table and murmured, "Can I see it?" I shook my head firmly.

20 "It's not allowed," I told her sternly, because I knew she didn't really

want to see what was left. She accepted this statement of authority, and a shadow of confused relief crossed her plain, pale face.

Privately, even grudgingly, my colleagues might admit the power of abortion to provoke emotion. But they seem to prefer the broad view and disdain the telescope. Abortion is a matter of choice, privacy, control. Its uncertainty lies in specific cases: retarded women and girls too young to give consent for surgery, women who are ill or hostile or psychotic. Such common dilemmas are met with both compassion and impatience: they slow things down. We are too busy to chew over ethics. One person might discuss certain concerns, behind closed doors, or describe a particularly disturbing dream. But generally there is to be no ambivalence.

Every day I take calls from women who are annoyed that we cannot see them, cannot do their abortion today, this morning, now. They argue the price, demand that we stay after hours to accommodate their job or class schedule. Abortion is so routine that one expects it to be like a manicure: quick, cheap, and painless.

Still, I've cultivated a certain disregard. It isn't negligence, but I don't always pay attention. I couldn't be here if I tried to judge each case on its merits; after all, we do over a hundred abortions a week. At some point each individual in this line of work draws a boundary and adheres to it. For one physician the boundary is a particular week of gestation; for another, it is a certain number of repeated abortions. But these boundaries can be fluid too: one physician overruled his own limit to abort a mature but severely malformed fetus. For me, the limit is allowing my clients to carry their own burden, shoulder the responsibility themselves. I shoulder the burden of trying not to judge them.

This city has several "crisis pregnancy centers" advertised in the Yellow Pages. They are small offices staffed by volunteers, and they offer free pregnancy testing, glossy photos of dead fetuses, and movies. I had a client recently whose mother is active in the anti-abortion movement. The young woman went to the local crisis center and was told that the doctor would make her touch her dismembered baby, that the pain would be the most horrible she could imagine, and that she might, after an abortion, never be able to have children. All lies. They called her at home and at work, over and over and over, but she had been wise enough to give a false name. She came to us a fugitive. We who do abortions are marked, by some, as impure. It's dirty work.

25 When a deliveryman comes to the sliding glass window by the reception desk and tilts a box toward me, I hesitate. I read the packing slip, assess the shape and weight of the box in light of its supposed contents. We request familiar faces. The doors are carefully locked; I

have learned to half glance around at bags and boxes, looking for a telltale sign. I register with security when I arrive, and I am careful not to bang a door. We are all a little on edge here.

Concern about size and shape seem to be natural, and so is the relief that follows. We make the powerful assumption that the fetus is different from us, and even when we admit the similarities, it is too simplistic to be seduced by form alone. But the form is enormously potent—humanoid, powerless, palm-sized, and pure, it evokes an almost fierce tenderness when viewed simply as what it appears to be. But appearance, and even potential, aren't enough. The fetus, in becoming itself, can ruin others; its utter dependence has a sinister side. When I am struck in the moment by the contents in the basin, I am careful to remember the context, to note the tearful teenager and the woman sighing with something more than relief. One kind of question, though, I find considerably trickier.

"Can you tell what it is?" I am asked, and this means gender. This question is asked by couples, not women alone. Always couples would abort a girl and keep a boy. I have been asked about twins, and even if I could tell what race the father was.

An eighteen-year-old woman with three daughters brought her husband to the interview. He glared first at me, then at his wife, as he sank lower and lower in the chair, picking his teeth with a toothpick. He interrupted a conversation with his wife to ask if I could tell whether the baby would be a boy or a girl. I told him I could not.

"Good," he replied in a slow and strangely malevolent voice, " 'cause if it was a boy I'd wring her neck."

In a literal sense, abortion exists because we are able to ask such questions, able to assign a value to the fetus which can shift with changing circumstances. If the human bond to a child were as primitive and unflinchingly narrow as that of other animals, there would be no abortion. There would be no abortion because there would be nothing more important than caring for the young and perpetuating the species, no reason for sex but to make babies. I sense this sometimes, this wordless organic duty, when I do ultrasounds.

30 We do ultrasound, a sound-wave test that paints a faint, gray picture of the fetus, whenever we're uncertain of gestation. Age is measured by the width of the skull and confirmed by the length of the femur or thighbone; we speak of a pregnancy as being a certain "femur length" in weeks. The usual concern is whether a pregnancy is within the legal limit for an abortion. Women this far along have bellies which swell out round and tight like trim muscles. When they lie flat, the mound rises softly above the hips, pressing the umbilicus upward.

It takes practice to read an ultrasound picture, which is grainy and etched as though in strokes of charcoal. But suddenly a rapid rhythmic motion appears—the beating heart. Nearby is a soft oval, scratched with lines—the skull. The leg is harder to find, and then suddenly the fetus moves, bobbing in the surf. The skull turns away, an arm slides across the screen, the torso rolls. I know the weight of a baby's head on my shoulder, the whisper of lips on ears, the delicate curve of a fragile spine in my hand. I know how heavy and correct a newborn cradled feels. The creature I watch in secret requires nothing from me but to be left alone, and that is precisely what won't be done.

These inadvertently made beings are caught in a twisting web of motive and desire. They are at least inconvenient, sometimes quite literally dangerous in the womb, but most often they fall somewhere in between—consequences never quite believed in come to roost. Their virtue rises and falls outside their own nature: they become only what we make them. A fetus created by accident is the most absolute kind of surprise. Whether the blame lies in a failed IUD, a slipped condom, or a false impression of safety, that fetus is a thing whose creation has been actively worked against. Its existence is an error. I think this is why so few women, even late in a pregnancy, will consider giving a baby up for adoption. To do so means making the fetus real—imagining it as something whole and outside oneself. The decision to terminate a pregnancy is sometimes so difficult and confounding that it creates an enormous demand for immediate action. The decision is a rejection; the pregnancy has become something to be rid of, a condition to be ended. It is a burden, a weight, a thing separate.

Women have abortions because they are too old, and too young, too poor, and too rich, too stupid, and too smart. I see women who berate themselves with violent emotions for their first and only abortion, and others who return three times, five times, hauling two or three children, who cannot remember to take a pill or where they put the diaphragm. We talk glibly about choice. But the choice for what? I see all the broken promises in lives lived like a series of impromptu obstacles. There are the sweet, light promises of love and intimacy, the glittering promise of education and progress, the warm promise of safe families, long years of innocence and community. And there is the promise of freedom: freedom from failure, from faithlessness. Freedom from biology. The early feminist defense of abortion asked many questions, but the one I remember is this: Is biology destiny? And the answer is yes, sometimes it is. Women who have the fewest choices of all exercise their right to abortion the most.

Oh, the ignorance. I take a woman to the back room and ask her to undress; a few minutes later I return and find her positioned discreetly behind a drape, still wearing underpants. "Do I have to take these off too?" she asks, a little shocked. Some swear they have not had sex, many do not know what a uterus is, how sperm and egg meet, how sex makes babies. Some late seekers do not believe themselves pregnant; they believe themselves *impregnable.* I was chastised when I began this job for referring to some clients as girls: it is a feminist heresy. They come so young, snapping gum, sockless and sneakered, and their shakily applied eyeliner smears when they cry. I call them girls with maternal benignity. I cannot imagine them as mothers.

35 The doctor seats himself between the woman's thighs and reaches into the dilated opening of a five-month pregnant uterus. Quickly he grabs and crushes the fetus in several places, and the room is filled with a low clatter and snap of forceps, the click of the tanaculum, and a pulling, sucking sound. The paper crinkles as the drugged and sleepy woman shifts, the nurse's low, honey-brown voice explains each step in delicate words.

I have fetus dreams, we all do here: dreams of abortions one after the other; of buckets of blood splashed on the walls; trees full of crawling fetuses. I dreamed that two men grabbed me and began to drag me away. "Let's do an abortion," they said with a sickening leer, and I began to scream, plunged into a vision of sucking, scraping pain, of being spread and torn by impartial instruments that do only what they are bidden. I woke from this dream barely able to breathe and thought of kitchen tables and coat hangers, knitting needles striped with blood, and women all alone clutching a pillow in their teeth to keep the screams from piercing the apartment-house walls. Abortion is the narrowest edge between kindness and cruelty. Done as well as it can be, it is still violence—merciful violence, like putting a suffering animal to death.

Maggie, one of the nurses, received a call at midnight not long ago. It was a woman in her twentieth week of pregnancy; the necessarily gradual process of cervical dilation begun the day before had stimulated labor, as it sometimes does. Maggie and one of the doctors met the woman at the office in the night. Maggie helped her onto the table, and as she lay down the fetus was delivered into Maggie's hands. When Maggie told me about it the next day, she cupped her hands into a small bowl—"It was just like a little kitten," she said softly, wonderingly. "Everything was still attached."

At the end of the day I clean out the suction jars, pouring blood into the sink, splashing the sides with flecks of tissue. From the sink rises a rich and humid smell, hot, earthy, and moldering; it is the smell of something recently alive beginning to decay. I take care of the plastic tub on the floor, filled with pieces too big to be trusted to the trash. The law defines the contents of the bucket I hold protectively against my chest as "tissue." Some would say my complicity in filling that bucket gives me no right to call it anything else. I slip the tissue gently into a bag and place it in the freezer, to be burned at another time. Abortion requires of me an entirely new set of assumptions. It requires a willingness to live with conflict, fearlessness, and grief. As I close the freezer door, I imagine a world where this won't be necessary, and then return to the world where it is.

QUESTIONS

1. *Tisdale speaks of taking both broad views—"as if I am standing on a cliff with a telescope"—and narrow views—"I can put my eye to the lens and focus on small details" (paragraph 4). Choose one of the longer sections of this essay (i.e., the second, third, or fourth) and mark the passages you would describe as taking broad views and the passages you would describe as taking narrow views. What is the effect of Tisdale's going back and forth between them? How does she manage transitions?*
2. *"We are too busy to chew over ethics" (paragraph 21), Tisdale observes. What does she mean by ethics? Does she engage with what you consider ethical issues in this essay? Explain.*
3. *Although Tisdale takes a pro-choice position, a pro-lifer could use parts of her essay against her. What parts? What are the advantages and disadvantages of including material that could be used in support of the opposition?*
4. *Write a pro-choice or pro-life essay of your own. Include material that could be used in support of the opposition. You may use Tisdale's essay (with proper credit), but you need not.*

Stephen Jay Gould

THE TERRIFYING NORMALCY OF AIDS

Disney's Epcot Center in Orlando, Fla., is a technological tour de force and a conceptual desert. In this permanent World's Fair, American industrial giants have built their versions of an unblemished future. These masterful entertainments convey but one message, brilliantly packaged and relentlessly expressed: progress through technology is the solution to all human problems. G.E. proclaims from Horizons: "If we can dream it, we can do it." A.T.&T. speaks from on high within its giant golf ball: We are now "unbounded by space and

From *The New York Times Magazine* (Apr. 19, 1987).

time." United Technologies bubbles from the depths of Living Seas: "With the help of modern technology, we feel there's really no limit to what can be accomplished."

Yet several of these exhibits at the Experimental Prototype Community of Tomorrow, all predating last year's space disaster, belie their stated message from within by using the launch of the shuttle as a visual metaphor for technological triumph. The Challenger disaster[1] may represent a general malaise, but it remains an incident. The AIDS pandemic, an issue that may rank with nuclear weaponry as the greatest danger of our era, provides a more striking proof that mind and technology are not omnipotent and that we have not canceled our bond to nature.

In 1984, John Platt, a biophysicist who taught at the University of Chicago for many years, wrote a short paper for private circulation. At a time when most of us were either ignoring AIDS, or viewing it as a contained and peculiar affliction of homosexual men, Platt recognized that the limited data on the origin of AIDS and its spread in America suggested a more frightening prospect: we are all susceptible to AIDS, and the disease has been spreading in a simple exponential manner.

Exponential growth is a geometric increase. Remember the old kiddy problem: if you place a penny on square one of a checkerboard and double the number of coins on each subsequent square—2, 4, 8, 16, 32 . . . —how big is the stack by the 64th square? The answer: about as high as the universe is wide. Nothing in the external environment inhibits this increase, thus giving to exponential processes their relentless character. In the real, noninfinite world, of course, some limit will eventually arise, and the process slows down, reaches a steady state, or destroys the entire system: the stack of pennies falls over, the bacterial cells exhaust their supply of nutrients.

5 Platt noticed that data for the initial spread of AIDS fell right on an exponential curve. He then followed the simplest possible procedure of extrapolating the curve unabated into the 1990's. Most of us were incredulous, accusing Platt of the mathematical gamesmanship that scientists call "curve fitting." After all, aren't exponential models unrealistic? Surely we are not all susceptible to AIDS. Is it not spread only by odd practices to odd people? Will it not, therefore, quickly run its short course within a confined group?

Well, hello 1987—worldwide data still match Platt's extrapolated curve. This will not, of course, go on forever. AIDS has probably already saturated the African areas where it probably originated, and

1. In January 1986, when the space shuttle *Challenger* exploded after launching, seven astronauts were killed.

where the sex ratio of afflicted people is 1-to-1, male-female. But AIDS still has far to spread, and may be moving exponentially, through the rest of the world. We have learned enough about the cause of AIDS to slow its spread, if we can make rapid and fundamental changes in our handling of that most powerful part of human biology—our own sexuality. But medicine, as yet, has nothing to offer as a cure and precious little even for palliation.

This exponential spread of AIDS not only illuminates its, and our, biology, but also underscores the tragedy of our moralistic misperception. Exponential processes have a definite time and place of origin, an initial point of "inoculation"—in this case, Africa. We didn't notice the spread at first. In a population of billions, we pay little attention when 1 increases to 2, or 8 to 16, but when 1 million becomes 2 million, we panic, even though the *rate* of doubling has not increased.

The infection has to start somewhere, and its initial locus may be little more than an accident of circumstance. For a while, it remains confined to those in close contact with the primary source, but only by accident of proximity, not by intrinsic susceptibility. Eventually, given the power and lability of human sexuality, it spreads outside the initial group and into the general population. And now AIDS has begun its march through our own heterosexual community.

What a tragedy that our moral stupidity caused us to lose precious time, the greatest enemy in fighting an exponential spread, by downplaying the danger because we thought that AIDS was a disease of three irregular groups of minorities: minorities of life style (needle users), of sexual preference (homosexuals) and of color (Haitians). If AIDS had first been imported from Africa into a Park Avenue apartment, we would not have dithered as the exponential march began.

The message of Orlando—the inevitability of technological solu- 10
tions—is wrong, and we need to understand why.

Our species has not won its independence from nature, and we cannot do all that we can dream. Or at least we cannot do it at the rate required to avoid tragedy, for we are not unbounded from time. Viral diseases are preventable in principle, and I suspect that an AIDS vaccine will one day be produced. But how will this discovery avail us if it takes until the millenium, and by then AIDS has fully run its exponential course and saturated our population, killing a substantial percentage of the human race? A fight against an exponential enemy is primarily a race against time.

We must also grasp the perspective of ecology and evolutionary biology and recognize, once we reinsert ourselves properly into nature, that AIDS represents the ordinary workings of biology, not an irrational or diabolical plague with a moral meaning. Disease, including epidemic spread, is a natural phenomenon, part of human history from the beginning. An entire subdiscipline of my profession, paleopathology, studies the evidence of ancient diseases preserved in the fossil remains of organisms. Human history has been marked by episodic plagues. More native peoples died of imported disease than ever fell before the gun during the era of colonial expansion. Our memories are short, and we have had a respite, really, only since the influenza pandemic at the end of World War I, but AIDS must be viewed as a virulent expression of an ordinary natural phenomenon.

I do not say this to foster either comfort or complacency. The evolutionary perspective is correct, but utterly inappropriate for our human scale. Yes, AIDS is a natural phenomenon, one of a recurring class of pandemic diseases. Yes, AIDS may run through the entire population, and may carry off a quarter or more of us. Yes, it may make no *biological* difference to Homo sapiens in the long run: there will still be plenty of us left and we can start again. Evolution cares as little for its agents—organisms struggling for reproductive success—as physics cares for individual atoms of hydrogen in the sun. But *we* care. These atoms are our neighbors, our lovers, our children and ourselves. AIDS is both a natural phenomenon and, potentially, the greatest natural tragedy in human history.

The cardboard message of Epcot fosters the wrong attitudes; we must both reinsert ourselves into nature and view AIDS as a natural phenomenon in order to fight properly. If we stand above nature and if technology is all-powerful, then AIDS is a horrifying anomaly that must be trying to tell us something. If so, we can adopt one of two attitudes, each potentially fatal. We can either become complacent, because we believe the message of Epcot and assume that medicine will soon generate a cure, or we can panic in confusion and seek a scapegoat for something so irregular that it must have been visited upon us to teach us a moral lesson.

15 But AIDS is not irregular. It is part of nature. So are we. This should galvanize us and give us hope, not prompt the worst of all responses: a kind of "new-age" negativism that equates natural with what we must accept and cannot, or even should not, change. When we view AIDS as natural, and when we recognize both the exponential property of its spread and the accidental character of its point of entry into America, we can break through our destructive tendencies to blame others and to free ourselves of concern.

If AIDS is natural, then there is no *message* in its spread. But by all that science has learned and all that rationality proclaims, AIDS works by a *mechanism*—and we can discover it. Victory is not ordained by any principle of progress, or any slogan of technology, so we shall have to fight like hell, and be watchful. There is no message, but there is a mechanism.

QUESTIONS

1. *Gould uses current events, historical information, and scientific data to make his case. Identify examples of each.*
2. *What case does Gould make?*
3. *Why is this essay in the section called "Ethics" rather than in the section called "Science"?*
4. *Gould uses Disney's Epcot Center in Orlando, Florida, as a symbol of our belief in technology. Find another symbol of this belief and, in a brief essay, describe and interpret it.*

Kildare Dobbs

THE SHATTERER OF WORLDS

Before that morning in 1945 only a few conventional bombs, none of which did any great damage, had fallen on the city. Fleets of U.S. bombers had, however, devastated many cities round about, and Hiroshima had begun a program of evacuation which had reduced its population from 380,000 to some 245,000. Among the evacuees were Emiko and her family.

"We were moved out to Otake, a town about an hour's train-ride out of the city," Emiko told me. She had been a fifteen-year-old student in 1945. Fragile and vivacious, versed in the gentle traditions of the tea ceremony and flower arrangement, Emiko still had an air of the frail school-child when I talked with her. Every day, she and her sister Hideko used to commute into Hiroshima to school. Hideko was thirteen. Their father was an antique-dealer and he owned a house in the city, although it was empty now. Tetsuro, Emiko's thirteen-year-old brother, was at the Manchurian front with the Imperial Army. Her mother was kept busy looking after the children, for her youngest daughter Eiko was sick with heart trouble, and rations were scarce. All of them were undernourished.

The night of August 5, 1945, little Eiko was dangerously ill. She was not expected to live. Everybody took turns watching by her bed, soothing her by massaging her arms and legs. Emiko retired at 8:30 (most Japanese people go to bed early) and at midnight was roused to take her turn with the sick girl. At 2 A.M. she went back to sleep.

From *Reading the Time* (1968).

While Emiko slept, the *Enola Gay*, a U.S. B-29 carrying the world's first operational atom bomb, was already in the air. She had taken off from the Pacific island of Iwo Jima at 1:45 A.M., and now Captain William Parsons, U.S.N. ordnance expert, was busy in her bomb-hold with the final assembly of Little Boy. Little Boy looked much like an outsize T.N.T. block-buster but the crew knew there was something different about him. Only Parsons and the pilot, Colonel Paul Tibbets, knew exactly in what manner Little Boy was different. Course was set for Hiroshima.

5 Emiko slept.

On board the *Enola Gay* co-pilot Captain Robert Lewis was writing up his personal log. "After leaving Iwo," he recorded, "we began to pick up some low stratus and before very long we were flying on top of an under-cast. Outside of a thin, high cirrus and the low stuff, it's a very beautiful day."

Emiko and Hideko were up at six in the morning. They dressed in the uniform of their women's college—white blouse, quilted hat, and black skirt—breakfasted and packed their aluminum lunch-boxes with white rice and eggs. These they stuffed into their shoulder bags as they hurried for the seven-o'clock train to Hiroshima. Today there would be no classes. Along with many women's groups, high school students, and others, the sisters were going to work on demolition. The city had begun a project of clearance to make fire-breaks in its downtown huddle of wood and paper buildings.

It was a lovely morning.

While the two young girls were at breakfast, Captain Lewis, over the Pacific, had made an entry in his log. "We are loaded. The bomb is now alive, and it's a funny feeling knowing it's right in back of you. Knock wood!"

10 In the train Hideko suddenly said she was hungry. She wanted to eat her lunch. Emiko dissuaded her: she'd be much hungrier later on. The two sisters argued, but Hideko at last agreed to keep her lunch till later. They decided to meet at the main station that afternoon and catch the five-o'clock train home. By now they had arrived at the first of Hiroshima's three stations. This was where Hideko got off, for she was to work in a different area from her sister. "Sayonara!" she called. "Goodbye." Emiko never saw her again.

There had been an air-raid at 7 A.M., but before Emiko arrived at Hiroshima's main station, two stops farther on, the sirens had sounded the all-clear. Just after eight, Emiko stepped off the train, walked through the station, and waited in the morning sunshine for her streetcar.

At about the same moment Lewis was writing in his log. "There'll be a short intermission while we bomb our target."

It was hot in the sun, Emiko saw a class-mate and greeted her. Together they moved back into the shade of a high concrete wall to chat. Emiko looked up at the sky and saw, far up in the cloudless blue, a single B-29.

It was exactly 8:10 A.M. The other people waiting for the streetcar saw it too and began to discuss it anxiously. Emiko felt scared. She felt that at all costs she must go on talking to her friend. Just as she was thinking this, there was a tremendous greenish-white flash in the sky. It was far brighter than the sun. Emiko afterwards remembered vaguely that there was a roaring or a rushing sound as well, but she was not sure, for just at that moment she lost consciousness.

"About 15 seconds after the flash," noted Lewis, 30,000 feet high 15
and several miles away, "there were two very distinct slaps on the ship from the blast and the shock wave. That was all the physical effect we felt. We turned the ship so that we could observe the results."

When Emiko came to, she was lying on her face about forty feet away from where she had been standing. She was not aware of any pain. Her first thought was: "I'm alive!" She lifted her head slowly and looked about her. It was growing dark. The air was seething with dust and black smoke. There was a smell of burning. Emiko felt something trickle into her eyes, tested it in her mouth. Gingerly she put a hand to her head, then looked at it. She saw with a shock that it was covered with blood.

She did not give a thought to Hideko. It did not occur to her that her sister who was in another part of the city could possibly have been in danger. Like most of the survivors, Emiko assumed she had been close to a direct hit by a conventional bomb. She thought it had fallen on the post-office next to the station. With a hurt child's panic, Emiko, streaming with blood from gashes in her scalp, ran blindly in search of her mother and father.

The people standing in front of the station had been burned to death instantly (a shadow had saved Emiko from the flash). The people inside the station had been crushed by falling masonry. Emiko heard their faint cries, saw hands scrabbling weakly from under the collapsed platform. All around her the maimed survivors were running and stumbling away from the roaring furnace that had been a city. She ran with them toward the mountains that ring the landward side of Hiroshima.

From the *Enola Gay*, the strangers from North America looked down at their handiwork. "There, in front of our eyes," wrote Lewis, "was without a doubt the greatest explosion man had ever witnessed. The city was nine-tenths covered with smoke of a boiling nature, which seemed to indicate buildings blowing up, and a large white cloud which in less than three minutes reached 30,000 feet, then went to at least 50,000 feet."

Far below, on the edge of this cauldron of smoke, at a distance of 20 some 2,500 yards from the blast's epicenter, Emiko ran with the rest of the living. Some who could not run limped or dragged themselves along. Others were carried. Many, hideously burned, were screaming with pain; when they tripped they lay where they had fallen. There was a man whose face had been ripped open from mouth to ear, another whose forehead was a gaping wound. A young soldier was running with a foot-long splinter of bamboo protruding from one eye. But these, like Emiko, were the lightly wounded.

Some of the burned people had been literally roasted. Skin hung from their flesh like sodden tissue paper. They did not bleed but plasma dripped from their seared limbs.

The *Enola Gay*, mission completed, was returning to base. Lewis sought words to express his feelings, the feelings of all the crew. "I might say," he wrote, "I might say 'My God! What have we done?' "

Emiko ran. When she had reached the safety of the mountain she remembered that she still had her shoulder bag. There was a small first-aid kit in it and she applied ointment to her wounds and to a small cut in her left hand. She bandaged her head.

Emiko looked back at the city. It was a lake of fire. All around her the burned fugitives cried out in pain. Some were scorched on one side only. Others, naked and flayed, were burned all over. They were too many to help and most of them were dying. Emiko followed the walking wounded along a back road, still delirious, expecting suddenly to meet her father and mother.

25 The thousands dying by the roadside called feebly for help or water. Some of the more lightly injured were already walking in the other direction, back towards the flames. Others, with hardly any visible wounds, stopped, turned ashy pale, and died within minutes. No one knew then that they were victims of radiation.

Emiko reached the suburb of Nakayama.

Far off in the *Enola Gay*, Lewis, who had seen none of this, had been writing, "If I live a hundred years, I'll never get those few minutes out of my mind. Looking at Captain Parsons, why he is as confounded as the rest, and he is supposed to have known everything and expected this to happen. . . ."

At Nakayama, Emiko stood in line at a depot where rice-balls were being distributed. Though it distressed her that the badly maimed could hardly feed themselves, the child found she was hungry. It was about 6 P.M. now. A little farther on, at Gion, a farmer called her by name. She did not recognize him, but it seemed he came monthly to her home to collect manure. The farmer took Emiko by the hand, led her to his own house, where his wife bathed her and fed her a meal of white rice. Then the child continued on her way. She passed another town where there were hundreds of injured. The dead were being hauled away in trucks. Among the injured a woman of about forty-five was waving frantically and muttering to herself. Emiko brought this woman a little water in a pumpkin leaf. She felt guilty about it; the schoolgirls had been warned not to give water to the seriously wounded. Emiko comforted herself with the thought that the woman would die soon anyway.

At Koi, she found standing-room in a train. It was heading for Otake with a full load of wounded. Many were put off at Ono, where there was a hospital; and two hours later the train rolled into Otake station. It was around 10 P.M.

A great crowd had gathered to look for their relations. It was a nightmare, Emiko remembered years afterwards; people were calling their dear kinfolk by name, searching frantically. It was necessary to call them by name, since most were so disfigured as to be unrecognizable. Doctors in the town council offices stitched Emiko's head-wounds. The place was crowded with casualties lying on the floor. Many died as Emiko watched.

The town council authorities made a strange announcement. They said a new and mysterious kind of bomb had fallen in Hiroshima. People were advised to stay away from the ruins.

Home at midnight, Emiko found her parents so happy to see her that they could not even cry. They could only give thanks that she was safe. Then they asked, "Where is your sister?"

For ten long days, while Emiko walked daily one and a half miles to have her wounds dressed with fresh gauze, her father searched the rubble of Hiroshima for his lost child. He could not have hoped to find her alive. All, as far as the eye could see, was a desolation of charred ashes and wreckage, relieved only by a few jagged ruins and by the seven estuarial rivers that flowed through the waste delta. The banks of these rivers were covered with the dead and in the rising tidal waters floated thousands of corpses. On one broad street in the Hakushima district the crowds who had been thronging there were all naked and scorched cadavers. Of thousands of others there was no trace at all. A fire several times hotter than the surface of the sun had turned them instantly to vapor.

On August 11 came the news that Nagasaki had suffered the same fate as Hiroshima; it was whispered that Japan had attacked the United States mainland with similar mysterious weapons. With the lavish circumstantiality of rumor, it was said that two out of a fleet of six-engined trans-Pacific bombers had failed to return. But on August 15, speaking for the first time over the radio to his people, the Emperor Hirohito announced his country's surrender. Emiko heard him. No more bombs! she thought. No more fear! The family did not learn till June the following year that this very day young Tetsuro had been killed in action in Manchuria.

Emiko's wounds healed slowly. In mid-September they had closed with a thin layer of pinkish skin. There had been a shortage of antiseptics and Emiko was happy to be getting well. Her satisfaction was short-lived. Mysteriously she came down with diarrhea and high fever. The fever continued for a month. Then one day she started to bleed from the gums, her mouth and throat became acutely inflamed, and her hair started to fall out. Through her delirium the child heard the doctors whisper by her pillow that she could not live. By now the doctors must have known that ionizing radiation caused such destruction of the blood's white cells that victims were left with little or no resistance against infection.

Yet Emiko recovered.

The wound on her hand, however, was particularly troublesome and did not heal for a long time.

As she got better, Emiko began to acquire some notion of the fearful scale of the disaster. Few of her friends and acquaintances were still alive. But no one knew precisely how many had died in Hiroshima. To this day the claims of various agencies conflict.

According to General Douglas MacArthur's headquarters, there were 78,150 dead and 13,083 missing.[1] The United States Atomic Bomb Casualty Commission claims there were 79,000 dead. Both sets of figures are probably far too low. There's reason to believe that at the time of the surrender Japanese authorities lied about the number of survivors, exaggerating it to get extra medical supplies. The Japanese welfare ministry's figures of 260,000 dead and 163,263 missing may well be too high. But the very order of such discrepancies speaks volumes about the scale of the catastrophe. The dead were literally uncountable.

40 This appalling toll of human life had been exacted from a city that had been prepared for air attack in a state of full wartime readiness. All civil-defense services had been overwhelmed from the first moment and it was many hours before any sort of organized rescue and relief could be put into effect.

It's true that single raids using so-called conventional weapons on other cities such as Tokyo and Dresden inflicted far greater casualties. And that it could not matter much to a victim whether he was burnt alive by a fire-storm caused by phosphorus, or by napalm or by nuclear fission. Yet in the whole of human history so savage a massacre had never before been inflicted with a single blow. And modern thermonuclear weapons are upwards of 1,000 times more powerful and deadly than the Hiroshima bomb.

1. MacArthur (1880–1964), American army officer, Allied Supreme Commander in the Southwest Pacific (1942) and of occupied Japan following World War II (1945–1951).

The white scar I saw on Emiko's small, fine-boned hand was a tiny metaphor, a faint but eloquent reminder of the scar on humanity's conscience.

QUESTIONS

1. *Dobbs moves between one narrative, Emiko's story, and another, the bombing mission of the* Enola Gay; *in film this technique is called cross-cutting. Where did Dobbs get information for each narrative?*
2. *Consider the differences between the visible accumulation of information in Paul Fussell's "Thank God for the Atom Bomb," below, that acknowledges sources (as in, for example, paragraphs 25 to 26) and Dobbs's you-are-there reconstruction. What are the advantages and disadvantages of each? Which one are you more likely to use as a college writer?*
3. *Dobbs waits until the final paragraph to make explicit the moral judgments that have been implicit throughout "The Shatterer of Worlds." Write an essay in which the narrative speaks for itself, without your intervention or interpretations, until the end.*

Paul Fussell

THANK GOD FOR THE ATOM BOMB

Many years ago in New York I saw on the side of a bus a whiskey ad I've remembered all this time. It's been for me a model of the short poem, and indeed I've come upon few short poems subsequently that exhibited more poetic talent. The ad consisted of two eleven-syllable lines of "verse," thus:

> In life, experience is the great teacher.
> In Scotch, Teacher's is the great experience.

For present purposes we must jettison the second line (licking our lips, to be sure, as it disappears), leaving the first to register a principle whose banality suggests that it enshrines a most useful truth. I bring up the matter because, writing on the forty-second anniversary of the atom-bombing of Hiroshima and Nagasaki, I want to consider something suggested by the long debate about the ethics, if any, of that ghastly affair. Namely, the importance of experience, sheer, vulgar experience, in influencing, if not determining, one's views about that use of the atom bomb.

The experience I'm talking about is having to come to grips, face to

Originally published in *The New Republic* (Aug. 22, 1981).

face, with an enemy who designs your death. The experience is common to those in the marines and the infantry and even the line navy, to those, in short, who fought the Second World War mindful always that their mission was, as they were repeatedly assured, "to close with the enemy and destroy him." *Destroy*, notice: not hurt, frighten, drive away, or capture. I think there's something to be learned about that war, as well as about the tendency of historical memory unwittingly to resolve ambiguity and generally clean up the premises, by considering the way testimonies emanating from real war experience tend to complicate attitudes about the most cruel ending of that most cruel war.

"What did you do in the Great War, Daddy?" The recruiting poster deserves ridicule and contempt, of course, but here its question is embarrassingly relevant, and the problem is one that touches on the dirty little secret of social class in America. Arthur T. Hadley said recently that those for whom the use of the A-bomb was "wrong" seem to be implying "that it would have been better to allow thousands on thousands of American and Japanese infantrymen to die in honest hand-to-hand combat on the beaches than to drop those two bombs." People holding such views, he notes, "do not come from the ranks of society that produce infantrymen or pilots." And there's an eloquence problem: most of those with firsthand experience of the war at its worst were not elaborately educated people. Relatively inarticulate, most have remained silent about what they know. That is, few of those destined to be blown to pieces if the main Japanese islands had been invaded went on to become our most effective men of letters or impressive ethical theorists or professors of contemporary history or of international law. The testimony of experience has tended to come from rough diamonds—James Jones[1] is an example—who went through the war as enlisted men in the infantry or the Marine Corps.

Anticipating objections from those without such experience, in his book *WWII* Jones carefully prepares for his chapter on the A-bombs by detailing the plans already in motion for the infantry assaults on the home islands of Kyushu (thirteen divisions scheduled to land in November 1945) and ultimately Honshu (sixteen divisions scheduled for March 1946). Planners of the invasion assumed that it would require a full year, to November 1946, for the Japanese to be sufficiently worn down by land-combat attrition to surrender. By that time, one million American casualties was the expected price. Jones observes that the forthcoming invasion of Kyushu "was well into its collecting and stockpiling stages before the war ended." (The island of Saipan was designated a main ammunition and supply base for the invasion, and

1. American novelist (1921–1977), author of *From Here to Eternity* (1951), the first volume in a trilogy about World War II.

if you go there today you can see some of the assembled stuff still sitting there.) "The assault troops were chosen and already in training," Jones reminds his readers, and he illuminates by the light of experience what this meant:

> What it must have been like to some old-timer buck sergeant or staff sergeant who had been through Guadalcanal or Bougainville or the Philippines, to stand on some beach and watch this huge war machine beginning to stir and move all around him and know that he very likely had survived this far only to fall dead on the dirt of Japan's home islands, hardly bears thinking about.

5 Another bright enlisted man, this one an experienced marine destined for the assault on Honshu, adds his testimony. Former Pfc. E. B. Sledge, author of the splendid memoir *With the Old Breed at Peleliu and Okinawa,* noticed at the time that the fighting grew "more vicious the closer we got to Japan," with the carnage of Iwo Jima and Okinawa worse than what had gone before. He points out that

> what we had *experienced* [my emphasis] in fighting the Japs (pardon the expression) on Peleliu and Okinawa caused us to formulate some very definite opinions that the invasion . . . would be a ghastly bloodletting. . . . It would shock the American public and the world. [Every Japanese] soldier, civilian, woman, and child would fight to the death with whatever weapons they had, rifle, grenade, or bamboo spear.

The Japanese pre-invasion patriotic song, "One Hundred Million Souls for the Emperor," says Sledge, "meant just that." Universal national kamikaze was the point. One kamikaze pilot, discouraged by his unit's failure to impede the Americans very much despite the bizarre casualties it caused, wrote before diving his plane onto an American ship, "I see the war situation becoming more desperate. All Japanese must become soldiers and die for the Emperor." Sledge's First Marine Division was to land close to the Yokosuka Naval Base, "one of the most heavily defended sectors of the island." The marines were told, he recalls, that

> due to the strong beach defenses, caves, tunnels, and numerous Jap suicide torpedo boats and manned mines, few Marines in the first five assault waves would get ashore alive—my company was scheduled to be in the first and second waves. The veterans in the outfit felt we had already run out of luck anyway. . . . We viewed the invasion with complete resignation that we would be killed—either on the beach or inland.

And the invasion was going to take place: there's no question about that. It was not theoretical or merely rumored in order to scare the Japanese. By July 10, 1945, the prelanding naval and aerial bombardment of the coast had begun, and the battleships *Iowa, Missouri, Wis-*

consin, and *King George V* were steaming up and down the coast, softening it up with their sixteen-inch shells.

On the other hand, John Kenneth Galbraith is persuaded that the Japanese would have surrendered surely by November without an invasion. He thinks the A-bombs were unnecessary and unjustified because the war was ending anyway. The A-bombs meant, he says, "a difference, at most, of two or three weeks." But at the time, with no indication that surrender was on the way, the kamikazes were sinking American vessels, the *Indianapolis* was sunk (880 men killed), and Allied casualties were running to over 7,000 per week. "Two or three weeks," says Galbraith. Two weeks more means 14,000 more killed and wounded, three weeks more, 21,000. Those weeks mean the world if you're one of those thousands or related to one of them. During the time between the dropping of the Nagasaki bomb on August 9 and the actual surrender on the fifteenth, the war pursued its accustomed course: on the twelfth of August eight captured American fliers were executed (heads chopped off); the fifty-first United States submarine, *Bonefish*, was sunk (all aboard drowned); the destroyer *Callaghan* went down, the seventieth to be sunk, and the Destroyer Escort *Underhill* was lost. That's a bit of what happened in six days of the two or three weeks posited by Galbraith. What did he do in the war? He worked in the Office of Price Administration in Washington. I don't demand that he experience having his ass shot off. I merely note that he didn't.

Likewise, the historian Michael Sherry, author of a recent book on the rise of the American bombing mystique, *The Creation of Armageddon*, argues that we didn't delay long enough between the test explosion in New Mexico and the mortal explosions in Japan. More delay would have made possible deeper moral considerations and perhaps laudable second thoughts and restraint. "The risks of delaying the bomb's use," he says, "would have been small—not the thousands of casualties expected of invasion but only a few days or weeks of relatively routine operations." While the mass murders represented by these "relatively routine operations" were enacting, Michael Sherry was safe at home. Indeed, when the bombs were dropped he was going on eight months old, in danger only of falling out of his pram. In speaking thus of Galbraith and Sherry, I'm aware of the offensive implications *ad hominem*. But what's at stake in an infantry assault is so entirely unthinkable to those without the experience of one, or several, or many, even if they possess very wide-ranging imaginations and warm sympathies, that experience is crucial in this case.

10 In general, the principle is, the farther from the scene of horror, the easier the talk. One young combat naval officer close to the action wrote home in the fall of 1943, just before the marines underwent the

agony of Tarawa: "When I read that we will fight the Japs for years if necessary and will sacrifice hundreds of thousands if we must, I always like to check from where he's talking: it's seldom out here." That was Lieutenant (j.g.) John F. Kennedy. And Winston Churchill, with an irony perhaps too broad and easy, noted in Parliament that the people who preferred invasion to A-bombing seemed to have "no intention of proceeding to the Japanese front themselves."

A remoteness from experience like Galbraith's and Sherry's, and a similar rationalistic abstraction from actuality, seem to motivate the reaction of an anonymous reviewer of William Manchester's *Goodbye Darkness: A Memoir of the Pacific War* for *The New York Review of Books*. The reviewer naturally dislikes Manchester's still terming the enemy Nips or Japs, but what really shakes him (her?) is this passage of Manchester's:

> After Biak the enemy withdrew to deep caverns. Rooting them out became a bloody business which reached its ultimate horrors in the last months of the war. You think of the lives which would have been lost in an invasion of Japan's home islands—a staggering number of Americans but millions more of Japanese—and you thank God for the atomic bomb.

Thank God for the atom bomb. From this, "one recoils," says the reviewer. One does, doesn't one?

And not just a staggering number of Americans would have been killed in the invasion. Thousands of British assault troops would have been destroyed too, the anticipated casualties from the almost 200,000 men in the six divisions (the same number used to invade Normandy) assigned to invade the Malay Peninsula on September 9. Aimed at the reconquest of Singapore, this operation was expected to last until about March 1946—that is, seven more months of infantry fighting. "But for the atomic bombs," a British observer intimate with the Japanese defenses notes, "I don't think we would have stood a cat in hell's chance. We would have been murdered in the biggest massacre of the war. They would have annihilated the lot of us."

The Dutchman Laurens van der Post had been a prisoner of the Japanese for three and a half years. He and thousands of his fellows, enfeebled by beriberi and pellagra, were being systematically starved to death, the Japanese rationalizing this treatment not just because the prisoners were white men but because they had allowed themselves to be captured at all and were therefore moral garbage. In the summer of 1945 Field Marshal Terauchi issued a significant order: at the moment the Allies invaded the main islands, all prisoners were to be killed by the prison-camp commanders. But thank God that did not happen. When the A-bombs were dropped, van der Post recalls, "This cataclysm I was certain would make the Japanese feel that they could withdraw from the war without dishonor, because it would strike them, as it had us in the silence of our prison night, as something supernatural."

In an exchange of views not long ago in *The New York Review of Books*, Joseph Alsop and David Joravsky set forth the by now familiar argument on both sides of the debate about the "ethics" of the bomb. It's not hard to guess which side each chose once you know that Alsop experienced capture by the Japanese at Hong Kong early in 1942, while Joravsky came into no deadly contact with the Japanese: a young, combat-innocent soldier, he was on his way to the Pacific when the war ended. The editors of *The New York Review* gave the debate the tendentious title "Was the Hiroshima Bomb Necessary?" surely an unanswerable question (unlike "Was It Effective?") and one precisely indicating the intellectual difficulties involved in imposing *ex post facto* a rational and even a genteel ethics on this event. In arguing the acceptability of the bomb, Alsop focuses on the power and fanaticism of War Minister Anami, who insisted that Japan fight to the bitter end, defending the main islands with the same techniques and tenacity employed at Iwo and Okinawa. Alsop concludes: "Japanese surrender could never have been obtained, at any rate without the honor-satisfying bloodbath envisioned by . . . Anami, if the hideous destruction of Hiroshima and Nagasaki had not finally galvanized the peace advocates into tearing up the entire Japanese book of rules." The Japanese plan to deploy the undefeated bulk of their ground forces, over two million men, plus 10,000 kamikaze planes, plus the elderly and all the women and children with sharpened spears they could muster in a suicidal defense makes it absurd, says Alsop, to "hold the common view, by now hardly challenged by anyone, that the decision to drop the two bombs on Japan was wicked in itself, and that President Truman and all others who joined in making or who [like Robert Oppenheimer] assented to this decision shared in the wickedness." And in explanation of "the two bombs," Alsop adds: "The true, climactic, and successful effort of the Japanese peace advocates . . . did not begin in deadly earnest until *after* the second bomb had destroyed Nagasaki. The Nagasaki bomb was thus the trigger to all the developments that led to peace." At this time the army was so unready for surrender that most looked forward to the forthcoming invasion as an indispensable opportunity to show their mettle, enthusiastically agreeing with the army spokesman who reasoned early in 1945, "Since the retreat from Guadalcanal, the Army has had little opportunity to engage the enemy in land battles. But when we meet in Japan proper, our Army will demonstrate its invincible superiority." This possibility foreclosed by the Emperor's post-A-bomb surrender broadcast, the shocked, disappointed officers of one infantry battalion, anticipating a professionally impressive defense of the beaches, killed themselves in the following numbers: one major, three captains, ten first lieutenants, and twelve second lieutenants.

David Joravsky, now a professor of history at Northwestern, argued 15
on the other hand that those who decided to use the A-bombs on cities betray defects of "reason and self-restraint." It all needn't have happened, he says, "if the U.S. government had been willing to take a few more days and to be a bit more thoughtful in opening up the age of nuclear warfare." I've already noted what "a few more days" would mean to the luckless troops and sailors on the spot, and as to being thoughtful when "opening up the age of nuclear warfare," of course no one was focusing on anything as portentous as that, which reflects a historian's tidy hind-sight. The U.S. government was engaged not in that sort of momentous thing but in ending the war conclusively, as well as irrationally Remembering Pearl Harbor with a vengeance. It didn't know then what everyone knows now about leukemia and various kinds of carcinoma and birth defects. Truman was not being sly or coy when he insisted that the bomb was "only another weapon." History, as Eliot's "Gerontion" notes,

> . . . has many cunning passages, contrived corridors
> And issues, deceives with whispering ambitions,
> Guides us by vanities. . . .
>   Think
> Neither fear nor courage saves us.
>   Unnatural vices
> Are fathered by our heroism. Virtues
> Are forced upon us by our impudent crimes.

Understanding the past requires pretending that you don't know the present. It requires feeling its own pressure on your pulses without any *ex post facto* illumination. That's a harder thing to do than Joravsky seems to think.

The Alsop-Joravsky debate, reduced to a collision between experience and theory, was conducted with a certain civilized respect for evidence. Not so the way the scurrilous, agitprop *New Statesman* conceives those justifying the dropping of the bomb and those opposing. They are, on the one hand, says Bruce Page, "the imperialist class-forces acting through Harry Truman" and, on the other, those representing "the humane, democratic virtues"—in short, "fascists" as opposed to "populists." But ironically the bomb saved the lives not of any imperialists but only of the low and humble, the quintessentially democratic huddled masses—the conscripted enlisted men manning the fated invasion divisions and the sailors crouching at their gun-mounts in terror of the Kamikazes. When the war ended, Bruce Page was nine years old. For someone of his experience, phrases like "imperialist class forces" come easily, and the issues look perfectly clear.

He's not the only one to have forgotten, if he ever knew, the unspeakable savagery of the Pacific war. The dramatic postwar Japanese success at hustling and merchandising and tourism has (happily, in many ways) effaced for most people the vicious assault context in which the Hiroshima horror should be viewed. It is easy to forget, or not to know, what Japan was like before it was first destroyed, and then humiliated, tamed, and constitutionalized by the West. "Implacable, treacherous, barbaric"—those were Admiral Halsey's characterizations of the enemy, and at the time few facing the Japanese would deny that they fit to a T. One remembers the captured American airmen—the lucky ones who escaped decapitation—locked for years in packing crates. One remembers the gleeful use of bayonets on civilians, on nurses and the wounded, in Hong Kong and Singapore. Anyone who actually fought in the Pacific recalls the Japanese routinely firing on medics, killing the wounded (torturing them first, if possible), and cutting off the penises of the dead to stick in the corpses' mouths. The degree to which Americans register shock and extraordinary shame about the Hiroshima bomb correlates closely with lack of information about the Pacific war.

And of course the brutality was not just on one side. There was much sadism and cruelty, undeniably racist, on ours. (It's worth noting in passing how few hopes blacks could entertain of desegregation and decent treatment when the U.S. Army itself slandered the enemy as "the little brown Jap.") Marines and soldiers could augment their view of their own invincibility by possessing a well-washed Japanese skull, and very soon after Guadalcanal it was common to treat surrendering Japanese as handy rifle targets. Plenty of Japanese gold teeth were extracted—some from still living mouths—with Marine Corps Ka-Bar Knives,[2] and one of E. B. Sledge's fellow marines went around with a cut-off Japanese hand. When its smell grew too offensive and Sledge urged him to get rid of it, he defended his possession of this trophy thus: "How many Marines you reckon that hand pulled the trigger on?" (It's hardly necessary to observe that a soldier in the ETO would probably not have dealt that way with a German or Italian—that is, a "white person's"—hand.) In the Pacific the situation grew so public and scandalous that in September 1942, the Commander in Chief of the Pacific Fleet issued this order: "No part of the enemy's

2. High-carbon steel knives carried by Marines (officers and gunners) who did not carry bayonet-bearing rifles.

body may be used as a souvenir. Unit Commanders will take stern disciplinary action. . . ."

Among Americans it was widely held that the Japanese were really subhuman, little yellow beasts, and popular imagery depicted them as lice, rats, bats, vipers, dogs, and monkeys. What was required, said the Marine Corps journal *The Leatherneck* in May 1945, was "a gigantic task of extermination." The Japanese constituted a "pestilence," and the only appropriate treatment was "annihilation." Some of the marines landing on Iwo Jima had "Rodent Exterminator" written on their helmet covers, and on one American flagship the naval commander had erected a large sign enjoining all to "KILL JAPS! KILL JAPS! KILL MORE JAPS!" Herman Wouk remembers the Pacific war scene correctly while analyzing ensign Keith in *The Caine Mutiny*: "Like most of the naval executioners of Kwajalein, he seemed to regard the enemy as a species of animal pest." And the feeling was entirely reciprocal: "From the grim and desperate taciturnity with which the Japanese died, they seemed on their side to believe that they were contending with an invasion of large armed ants." Hiroshima seems to follow in natural sequence: "This obliviousness of both sides to the fact that the opponents were human beings may perhaps be cited as the key to the many massacres of the Pacific war." Since the Jap vermin resist so madly and have killed so many of us, let's pour gasoline into their bunkers and light it and then shoot those afire who try to get out. Why not? Why not blow them all up, with satchel charges or with something stronger? Why not, indeed, drop a new kind of bomb on them, and on the un-uniformed ones too, since the Japanese government has announced that women from ages of seventeen to forty are being called up to repel the invasion? The intelligence officer of the U.S. Fifth Air Force declared on July 21, 1945, that "the entire population of Japan is a proper military target," and he added emphatically, "*There are no civilians in Japan.*" Why delay and allow one more American high school kid to see his own intestines blown out of his body and spread before him in the dirt while he screams and screams when with the new bomb we can end the whole thing just like that?

On Okinawa, only weeks before Hiroshima, 123,000 Japanese and 20
Americans *killed* each other. (About 140,000 Japanese died at Hiroshima.) "Just awful" was the comment on the Okinawa slaughter not of some pacifist but of General MacArthur. On July 14, 1945, General Marshall sadly informed the Combined Chiefs of Staff—he was not trying to scare the Japanese—that it's "now clear . . . that in order to finish with the Japanese quickly, it will be necessary to invade the industrial heart of Japan." The invasion was definitely on, as I know because I was to be in it.

When the atom bomb ended the war, I was in the Forty-fifth Infantry Division, which had been through the European war so thoroughly that it had needed to be reconstituted two or three times. We were in a staging area near Rheims, ready to be shipped back across the United States for refresher training at Fort Lewis, Washington, and then sent on for final preparation in the Philippines. My division, like most of the ones transferred from Europe, was to take part in the invasion of Honshu. (The earlier landing on Kyushu was to be carried out by the 700,000 infantry already in the Pacific, those with whom James Jones has sympathized.) I was a twenty-one-year-old second lieutenant of infantry leading a rifle platoon. Although still officially fit for combat, in the German war I had already been wounded in the back and the leg badly enough to be adjudged, after the war, 40 percent disabled. But even if my leg buckled and I fell to the ground whenever I jumped out of the back of a truck, and even if the very idea of more combat made me breathe in gasps and shake all over, my condition was held to be adequate for the next act. When the atom bombs were dropped and news began to circulate that "Operation Olympic" would not, after all, be necessary, when we learned to our astonishment that we would not be obliged in a few months to rush up the beaches near Tokyo assault-firing while being machine-gunned, mortared, and shelled, for all the practiced phlegm of our tough façades we broke down and cried with relief and joy. We were going to live. We were going to grow to adulthood after all. The killing was all going to be over, and peace was actually going to be the state of things. When the *Enola Gay* dropped its package, "There were cheers," says John Toland, "over the intercom; it meant the end of the war." Down on the ground the reaction of Sledge's marine buddies when they heard the news was more solemn and complicated. They heard about the end of the war

> with quiet disbelief coupled with an indescribable sense of relief. We thought the Japanese would never surrender. Many refused to believe it. . . . Sitting in stunned silence, we remembered our dead. So many dead. So many maimed. So many bright futures consigned to the ashes of the past. So many dreams lost in the madness that had engulfed us. Except for a few widely scattered shouts of joy, the survivors of the abyss sat hollow-eyed and silent, trying to comprehend a world without war.

These troops who cried and cheered with relief or who sat stunned by the weight of their experience are very different from the high-minded, guilt-ridden GIs we're told about by J. Glenn Gray in his sensitive book *The Warriors*. During the war in Europe Gray was an interrogator in the Army Counterintelligence Corps, and in that capacity he experienced the war at Division level. There's no denying that Gray's outlook on everything was admirably noble, elevated, and responsible. After the war he became a much-admired professor of philosophy at Colorado College and an esteemed editor of Heidegger. But

The Warriors, his meditation on the moral and psychological dimensions of modern soldiering, gives every sign of error occasioned by remoteness from experience. Division headquarters is miles—*miles*—behind the line where soldiers experience terror and madness and relieve those pressures by crazy brutality and sadism. Indeed, unless they actually encountered the enemy during the war, most "soldiers" have very little idea what "combat" was like. As William Manchester says, "All who wore uniforms are called veterans, but more than 90 percent of them are as uninformed about the killing zones as those on the home front." Manchester's fellow marine E. B. Sledge thoughtfully and responsibly invokes the terms *drastically* and *totally* to underline the differences in experience between front and rear, and not even the far rear, but the close rear. "Our code of conduct toward the enemy," he notes, "differed drastically from that prevailing back at the division CP." (He's describing gold-tooth extraction from still-living Japanese.) Again he writes: "We existed in an environment totally incomprehensible to men behind the lines . . . ," even, he would insist, to men as intelligent and sensitive as Glenn Gray, who missed seeing with his own eyes Sledge's marine friends sliding under fire down a shell-pocked ridge slimy with mud and liquid dysentery shit into the maggoty Japanese and USMC corpses at the bottom, vomiting as the maggots burrowed into their own foul clothing. "We didn't talk about such things," says Sledge. "They were too horrible and obscene even for hardened veterans. . . . Nor do authors normally write about such vileness; unless they have seen it with their own eyes, it is too preposterous to think that men could actually live and fight for days and nights on end under such terrible conditions and not be driven insane." And Sledge has added a comment on such experience and the insulation provided by even a short distance: "Often people just behind our rifle companies couldn't understand what we knew." Glenn Gray was not in a rifle company, or even just behind one. "When the news of the atomic bombing of Hiroshima and Nagasaki came," he asks us to believe, "many an American soldier felt shocked and ashamed." Shocked, OK, but why ashamed? Because we'd destroyed civilians? We'd been doing that for years, in raids on Hamburg and Berlin and Cologne and Frankfurt and Mannheim and Dresden, and Tokyo, and besides, the two A-bombs wiped out 10,000 Japanese troops, not often thought of now, John Hersey's kindly physicians and Jesuit priests being more touching. If around division headquarters some of the people Gray talked to felt ashamed, down in the rifle companies no one did, despite Gray's assertions. "The combat soldier," he says,

> knew better than did Americans at home what those bombs meant in suffering and injustice. The man of conscience realized intuitively that

> the vast majority of Japanese in both cities were no more, if no less, guilty of the war than were his own parents, sisters, or brothers.

I find this canting nonsense. The purpose of the bombs was not to "punish" people but to stop the war. To intensify the shame Gray insists we feel, he seems willing to fiddle the facts. The Hiroshima bomb, he says, was dropped "without any warning." But actually, two days before, 720,000 leaflets were dropped on the city urging everyone to get out and indicating that the place was going to be (as the Potsdam Declaration had promised) obliterated. Of course few left.

Experience whispers that the pity is not that we used the bomb to end the Japanese war but that it wasn't ready in time to end the German one. If only it could have been rushed into production faster and dropped at the right moment on the Reich Chancellery or Berchtesgaden or Hitler's military headquarters in East Prussia (where Colonel Stauffenberg's July 20 bomb didn't do the job because it wasn't big enough), much of the Nazi hierarchy could have been pulverized immediately, saving not just the embarrassment of the Nuremberg trials but the lives of around four million Jews, Poles, Slavs, and gypsies, not to mention the lives and limbs of millions of Allied and German soldiers. If the bomb had only been ready in time, the young men of my infantry platoon would not have been so cruelly killed and wounded.

25 All this is not to deny that like the Russian Revolution, the atom-bombing of Japan was a vast historical tragedy, and every passing year magnifies the dilemma into which it has lodged the contemporary world. As with the Russian Revolution, there are two sides—that's why it's a tragedy instead of a disaster—and unless we are, like Bruce Page, simple-mindedly unimaginative and cruel, we will be painfully aware of both sides at once. To observe that from the viewpoint of the war's victims-to-be the bomb seemed precisely the right thing to drop is to purchase no immunity from horror. To experience both sides, one might study the book *Unforgettable Fire: Pictures Drawn by Atomic Bomb Survivors*, which presents a number of amateur drawings and watercolors of the Hiroshima scene made by middle-aged and elderly survivors for a peace exhibition in 1975. In addition to the almost unbearable pictures, the book offers brief moments of memoir not for the weak-stomached:

> While taking my severely wounded wife out to the river bank . . ., I was horrified indeed at the sight of a stark naked man standing in the rain with his eyeball in his palm. He looked to be in great pain but there was nothing that I could do for him. I wonder what became of him. Even today, I vividly remember the sight. I was simply miserable.

These childlike drawings and paintings are of skin hanging down, breasts torn off, people bleeding and burning, dying mothers nursing dead babies. A bloody woman holds a bloody child in the ruins of a house, and the artist remembers her calling, "Please help this child! Someone, please help this child. Please help! Someone, please." As Samuel Johnson said of the smothering of Desdemona, the innocent in another tragedy, "It is not to be endured." Nor, it should be noticed, is an infantryman's account of having his arm blown off in the Arno Valley in Italy in 1944:

> I wanted to die and die fast. I wanted to forget this miserable world. I cursed the war, I cursed the people who were responsible for it, I cursed God for putting me here . . . to suffer for something I never did or knew anything about.

(A good place to interrupt and remember Glenn Gray's noble but hopelessly one-sided remarks about "injustice," as well as "suffering.")

"For this was hell," the soldier goes on,

> and I never imagined anything or anyone could suffer so bitterly. I screamed and cursed. Why? What had I done to deserve this? But no answer came. I yelled for medics, because subconsciously I wanted to live. I tried to apply my right hand over my bleeding stump, but I didn't have the strength to hold it. I looked to the left of me and saw the bloody mess that was once my left arm; its fingers and palm were turned upward, like a flower looking to the sun for its strength.

The future scholar-critic who writes *The History of Canting in the Twentieth Century* will find much to study and interpret in the utterances of those who dilate on the special wickedness of the A-bomb-droppers. He will realize that such utterance can perform for the speaker a valuable double function. First, it can display the fineness of his moral weave. And second, by implication it can also inform the audience that during the war he was not socially so unfortunate as to find himself down there with the ground forces, where he might have had to compromise the purity and clarity of his moral system by the experience of weighing his own life against someone else's. Down there, which is where the other people were, is the place where coarse self-interest is the rule. When the young soldier with the wild eyes comes at you, firing, do you shoot him in the foot, hoping he'll be hurt badly enough to drop or mis-aim the gun with which he's going to kill you, or do you shoot him in the chest (or, if you're a prime shot, in the head) and make certain that you and not he will be the survivor of that mortal moment?

It would be not just stupid but would betray a lamentable want of 30
human experience to expect soldiers to be very sensitive humanitarians. The Glenn Grays of this world need to have their attention directed to the testimony of those who know, like, say, Admiral of the

Fleet Lord Fisher, who said, "Moderation in war is imbecility," or Sir Arthur Harris, director of the admittedly wicked aerial-bombing campaign designed, as Churchill put it, to "de-house" the German civilian population, who observed that "War is immoral," or our own General W. T. Sherman: "War is cruelty, and you cannot refine it." Lord Louis Mountbatten, trying to say something sensible about the dropping of the A-bomb, came up only with "War is crazy." Or rather, it requires choices among crazinesses. "It would seem even more crazy," he went on, "if we were to have more casualties on our side to save the Japanese." One of the unpleasant facts for anyone in the ground armies during the war was that you had to become pro tem a subordinate of the very uncivilian George S. Patton and respond somehow to his unremitting insistence that you embrace his view of things. But in one of his effusions he was right, and his observation tends to suggest the experimental dubiousness of the concept of "just wars." "War is not a contest with gloves," he perceived. "It is resorted to only when laws, which are rules, have failed." Soldiers being like that, only the barest decencies should be expected of them. They did not start the war, except in the terrible sense hinted at in Frederic Manning's observation based on his front-line experience in the Great War: "War is waged by men; not by beasts, or by gods. It is a peculiarly human activity. To call it a crime against mankind is to miss at least half its significance; it is also the punishment of a crime." Knowing that unflattering truth by experience, soldiers have every motive for wanting a war stopped, by any means.

The stupidity, parochialism, and greed in the international mismanagement of the whole nuclear challenge should not tempt us to misimagine the circumstances of the bomb's first "use." Nor should our well-justified fears and suspicions occasioned by the capture of the nuclear-power trade by the inept and the mendacious (who have fucked up the works at Three Mile Island, Chernobyl, etc.[3]) tempt us to infer retrospectively extraordinary corruption, imbecility, or motiveless malignity in those who decided, all things considered, to drop the bomb. Times change. Harry Truman . . . knew war, and he knew better than some of his critics then and now what he was doing and why he was doing it. "Having found the bomb," he said, "we have used it. . . . We have used it to shorten the agony of young Americans."

The past, which as always did not know the future, acted in ways that ask to be imagined before they are condemned. Or even simplified.

3. Two disasters at nuclear power plants: the first, near Harrisburg, Pennsylvania, occurred in the spring of 1979; the second, in the Soviet Union, occurred in the spring of 1986.

QUESTIONS

1. *Mark the places where Fussell includes personal experience in this essay. How much is his own, how much belongs to others? Why does he include both kinds?*
2. *Fussell dismisses those who disagree with him with contempt. Locate some examples. How do you respond to them? Would you use Fussell's strategies to dismiss those who disagree with you? Explain.*
3. *Mark some instances of Fussell's "voice." What kind of voice does he adopt? What kind of person does he present himself as?*
4. *Write an argumentative essay in which you take a strong position. Include your own experience and the experience of others if appropriate.*

Prose Forms: Apothegms

At the beginning of Bacon's essay "Of Truth," jesting Pilate asks, "What is truth?" and does not stay for an answer. Perhaps Pilate asked in jest because he thought the question foolish; perhaps because he thought an answer impossible. Something of Pilate's skepticism is in most of us, but something too of a belief that there is truth, even if—as the history of philosophy teaches us—determining its nature may be enormously difficult. We readily assume some things to be true even if we hesitate to say what ultimately is Truth.

The test of truth most often is an appeal to the observed facts of experience. The observation of experience yields knowledge; the generalized statement of that knowledge yields a concept of the experience; the concise, descriptive form in which that concept is expressed we call apothegm, proverb, maxim, or aphorism. Thus Sir James Mackintosh can speak of apothegms as "the condensed good sense of nations," because the apothegm conveys the distilled observations of people about their own persistent conduct. To hear the familiar "Absence makes the heart grow fonder" is to be reminded of a general truth that the world acknowledges. It does not matter that the equally familiar "Out of sight, out of mind" seems to contradict the other saying. Both are true but applicable to different situations. Both statements are immediately recognizable as true and neither requires to be argued for, representing as they do the collective experience of humankind intelligently observed.

Aphoristic statements often occur within the context of more extended pieces of writing, and while not apothegms in the strictest sense, but rather propositions, they have the force of apothegms. For example, Percy Shelley's "Defence of Poetry" (1821) concludes that "Poets are the unacknowledged legislators of the world." Seventy years later in his Preface to The Picture of Dorian Gray *Oscar Wilde asserts that "All art is quite useless." Although these statements seem contradictory, each is unarguable within its own context.*

Not everyone is as astute an observer as the writer of apothegms and maxims, of course, but everyone is presumably capable of perceiv-

ing their rightness. What we perceive first is the facts to which the saying applies. When Franklin says "An empty bag cannot stand upright" (in 1740 he obviously had in mind a cloth bag), we acknowledge that this is the condition of the empty bag—and of ourselves when we are empty. Or when La Rochefoucauld says "We are all strong enough to endure the misfortunes of others," he too observes a condition that exists among people.

Many aphoristic assertions claim their validity primarily in descriptive terms. But the descriptive "is" in most apothegms and maxims is joined to a normative "ought" and the sayings therefore convey admonitions about and judgments of the conditions they describe. "Waste not, want not" is a simple illustration of this use of fact to admonish. Samuel Butler briefly gives us the presumed fact that "the world will always be governed by self-interest." Then he quickly advises: "We should not try to stop this, we should try to make the self-interest of cads a little more consistent with that of decent people." The condition of "ought" need not always be admonitory; it may be the implied judgment in La Rochefoucauld's assertion that "It is the habit of mediocre minds to condemn all that is beyond their grasp." The judgment is explicit in Franklin's "Fish and visitors stink in three days." And Bierce's definitions of ordinary words are not specifications of meanings in the way of ordinary dictionaries, but critical concepts of the experiences to which the words point.

"Wisdom" or "good sense," then, is the heart of the apothegm or maxim, the conjunction of "is" and "ought" in an assertion of universal truth. Unlike ordinary assertions of fact or opinion usually concerned with particular rather than universal experience, the wise saying is complete in its brevity. Before the ordinary assertion is allowed to hold, we require that the assumptions on which it rests, the implications it carries, the critical concepts and terms it contains, be examined closely and explored or justified. If someone says that the modern college student wants most to succeed materially in life, we want to be satisfied about what constitutes "modern," which college students (and where) are referred to, what else is involved in the comparative "most," what specifically is meant by "materially." But the apothegm assumes facts widely known and accepted, and in its judgments invokes values or attitudes readily intelligible to the great majority. It is the truth as most people experience it.

In a sense, every writer's concern is ultimately with truth. Certainly the essayist is directly concerned, in defining and ordering ideas, to say what is true and, somehow, to say it "new." Much of what he or she says is of the nature of assertion about particular experience; he or she must therefore be at pains to handle such matters as assumptions and logical proofs carefully and deliberately. But one cannot always be starting from scratch, not daring to assume anything, trusting no certain knowledge or experience or beliefs held in common with other people. Careful one must be, but also aware that there is available, in addition to methods of logical analysis and proof, rules of evidence, and the other means to effective exposition, the whole memory and record of the vast experience of the race contained in a people's apothegms and aphorisms. In them is a treasury of truths useful to many demands of clarity and precision. And in them, too, is a valuable lesson in the way a significantly large body of experience—direct, in a person's day-to-day encounters; indirect, in the study of all forms of history—can be observed, conceptualized, and then expressed in an economy of language brief in form, comprehensive in meaning, and satisfyingly true.

Ambrose Bierce: FROM THE DEVIL'S DICTIONARY

abdication, *n.* An act whereby a sovereign attests his sense of the high temperature of the throne.

abscond, *v.i.* To "move in a mysterious way," commonly with the property of another.

absent, *adj.* Peculiarly exposed to the tooth of detraction; vilified; hopelessly in the wrong; superseded in the consideration and affection of another.

accident, *n.* An inevitable occurrence due to the action of immutable natural laws.

accordion, *n.* An instrument in harmony with the sentiments of an assassin.

achievement, *n.* The death of endeavor and the birth of disgust.

admiration, *n.* Our polite recognition of another's resemblance to ourselves.

alone, *adj.* In bad company.

applause, *n.* The echo of a platitude.

ardor, *n.* The quality that distinguishes love without knowledge.

bore, *n.* A person who talks when you wish him to listen.

cemetery, *n.* An isolated suburban spot where mourners match lies, poets write at a target and stone-cutters spell for a wager. The inscription following will serve to illustrate the success attained in these Olympian games:

> His virtues were so conspicuous that his enemies, unable to overlook them, denied them, and his friends, to whose loose lives they were a rebuke, represented them as vices. They are here commemorated by his family, who shared them.

childhood, *n.* The period of human life intermediate between the idiocy of infancy and the folly of youth—two removes from the sin of manhood and three from the remorse of age.

Christian, *n.* One who believes that the New Testament is a divinely inspired book admirably suited to the spiritual needs of his neighbor. One who follows the teachings of Christ in so far as they are not inconsistent with a life of sin.

compulsion, *n.* The eloquence of power.

congratulation, *n.* The civility of envy.

From *The Devil's Dictionary* (1906).

conservative, *n.* A statesman who is enamored of existing evils, as distinguished from the Liberal, who wishes to replace them with others.

consult, *v.t.* To seek another's approval of a course already decided on.

contempt, *n.* The feeling of a prudent man for an enemy who is too formidable safely to be opposed.

coward, *n.* One who in a perilous emergency thinks with his legs.

debauchee, *n.* One who has so earnestly pursued pleasure that he has had the misfortune to overtake it.

destiny, *n.* A tyrant's authority for crime and a fool's excuse for failure.

diplomacy, *n.* The patriotic art of lying for one's country.

distance, *n.* The only thing that the rich are willing for the poor to call theirs and keep.

duty, *n.* That which sternly impels us in the direction of profit, along the line of desire.

education, *n.* That which discloses to the wise and disguises from the foolish their lack of understanding.

erudition, *n.* Dust shaken out of a book into an empty skull.

extinction, *n.* The raw material out of which theology created the future state.

faith, *n.* Belief without evidence in what is told by one who speaks without knowledge, of things without parallel.

genealogy, *n.* An account of one's descent from an ancestor who did not particularly care to trace his own.

ghost, *n.* The outward and visible sign of an inward fear.

habit, *n.* A shackle for the free.

heaven, *n.* A place where the wicked cease from troubling you with talk of their personal affairs, and the good listen with attention while you expound your own.

historian, *n.* A broad-gauge gossip.

hope, *n.* Desire and expectation rolled into one.

hypocrite, *n.* One who, professing virtues that he does not respect, secures the advantage of seeming to be what he despises.

impiety, *n.* Your irreverence toward my deity.

impunity, *n.* Wealth.

language, *n.* The music with which we charm the serpents guarding another's treasure.

logic, *n.* The art of thinking and reasoning in strict accordance with the limitations and incapacities of the human misunderstanding. The basis of logic is the syllogism, consisting of a major and a minor premise and a conclusion—thus:

Major Premise: Sixty men can do a piece of work sixty times as quickly as one man.

Minor Premise: One man can dig a post-hole in sixty seconds;

therefore—

Conclusion: Sixty men can dig a post-hole in one second.

This may be called the syllogism arithmetical, in which, by combining logic and mathematics, we obtain a double certainty and are twice blessed.

love, *n.* A temporary insanity curable by marriage or by removal of the patient from the influences under which he incurred the disorder. This disease, like *caries* and many other ailments, is prevalent only among civilized races living under artificial conditions; barbarous nations breathing pure air and eating simple food enjoy immunity from its ravages. It is sometimes fatal, but more frequently to the physician than to the patient.

miracle, *n.* An act or event out of the order of nature and unaccountable, as beating a normal hand of four kings and an ace with four aces and a king.

monkey, *n.* An arboreal animal which makes itself at home in genealogical trees.

mouth, *n.* In man, the gateway to the soul; in woman, the outlet of the heart.

non-combatant, *n.* A dead Quaker.

platitude, *n.* The fundamental element and special glory of popular literature. A thought that snores in words that smoke. The wisdom of a million fools in the diction of a dullard. A fossil sentiment in artificial rock. A moral without the fable. All that is mortal of a departed truth. A demi-tasse of milk-and-morality. The Pope's-nose of a featherless peacock. A jelly-fish withering on the shore of the sea of thought. The cackle surviving the egg. A dessicated epigram.

pray, *v.* To ask that the laws of the universe be annulled in behalf of a single petitioner confessedly unworthy.

presidency, *n.* The greased pig in the field game of American politics.

prude, *n.* A bawd hiding behind the back of her demeanor.

rapacity, *n.* Providence without industry. The thrift of power.

reason, *v.i.* To weigh probabilities in the scales of desire.

religion, *n.* A daughter of Hope and Fear, explaining to Ignorance the nature of the Unknowable.

resolute, *adj.* Obstinate in a course that we approve.

retaliation, *n.* The natural rock upon which is reared the Temple of Law.

saint, *n.* A dead sinner revised and edited.

The Duchess of Orleans relates that the irreverent old calumniator, Marshal Villeroi, who in his youth had known St. Francis de Sales, said, on hearing him called saint: "I am delighted to hear that Monsieur de Sales is a saint. He was fond of saying indelicate things, and used to cheat at cards. In other respects he was a perfect gentleman, though a fool."

valor, *n.* A soldierly compound of vanity, duty and the gambler's hope:

> "Why have you halted?" roared the commander of a division at Chickamauga, who had ordered a charge; "move forward, sir, at once."
>
> "General," said the commander of the delinquent brigade, "I am persuaded that any further display of valor by my troops will bring them into collision with the enemy."

William Blake: PROVERBS OF HELL

In seed time learn, in harvest teach, in winter enjoy.
Drive your cart and your plough over the bones of the dead.
The road of excess leads to the palace of wisdom.
Prudence is a rich, ugly old maid courted by Incapacity.
He who desires but acts not, breeds pestilence.
The cut worm forgives the plough.
Dip him in the river who loves water.
A fool sees not the same tree that a wise man sees.
He whose face gives no light, shall never become a star.
Eternity is in love with the productions of time.
The busy bee has no time for sorrow.
The hours of folly are measur'd by the clock; but of wisdom, no clock
can measure.
All wholesome food is caught without a net or a trap.
Bring out number, weight, and measure in a year of dearth.
No bird soars too high, if he soars with his own wings.
A dead body revenges not injuries.
The most sublime act is to set another before you.
If the fool would persist in his folly he would become wise.
Folly is the cloak of knavery.
Shame is Pride's cloak.
Prisons are built with stones of Law, brothels with bricks of Religion.
The pride of the peacock is the glory of God.
The lust of the goat is the bounty of God.
The wrath of the lion is the wisdom of God.

From *The Marriage of Heaven and Hell* (1790–1793).

The nakedness of woman is the work of God.
Excess of sorrow laughs. Excess of joy weeps.
The roaring of lions, the howling of wolves, the raging of the stormy sea, and the destructive sword are portions of eternity too great for the eye of man.
The fox condemns the trap, not himself.
Joys impregnate. Sorrows bring forth.
Let man wear the fell of the lion, woman the fleece of the sheep.
The bird a nest, the spider a web, man friendship.
The selfish, smiling fool, and the sullen, frowning fool shall be both thought wise, that they may be a rod.
What is now proved was once only imagin'd.
The rat, the mouse, the fox, the rabbit watch the roots; the lion, the tiger, the horse, the elephant watch the fruits.
The cistern contains: the fountain overflows.
One thought fills immensity.
Always be ready to speak your mind, and a base man will avoid you.
Everything possible to be believ'd is an image of truth.
The eagle never lost so much time as when he submitted to learn of the crow.
The fox provides for himself; but God provides for the lion.
Think in the morning. Act in the noon. Eat in the evening. Sleep in the night.
He who has suffer'd you to impose on him, knows you.
As the plough follows words, so God rewards prayers.
The tigers of wrath are wiser than the horses of instruction.
Expect poison from the standing water.
You never know what is enough unless you know what is more than enough.
Listen to the fool's reproach! it is a kingly title!
The eyes of fire, the nostrils of air, the mouth of water, the beard of earth.
The weak in courage is strong in cunning.
The apple tree never asks the beech how he shall grow; nor the lion, the horse, how he shall take his prey.
The thankful receiver bears a plentiful harvest.
If others had not been foolish, we should be so.
The soul of sweet delight can never be defil'd.
When thou seest an eagle, thou seest a portion of Genius; lift up thy head!
As the caterpillar chooses the fairest leaves to lay her eggs on, so the priest lays his curse on the fairest joys.
To create a little flower is the labor of ages.
Damn braces. Bless relaxes.

The best wine is the oldest, the best water the newest.
Prayers plough not! Praises reap not!
Joys laugh not! Sorrows weep not!
The head Sublime, the heart Pathos, the genitals Beauty, the hands and feet Proportion.
As the air to a bird or the sea to a fish, so is contempt to the contemptible.
The crow wish'd everything was black, the owl that everything was white.
Exuberance is Beauty.
If the lion was advised by the fox, he would be cunning.
Improvement makes straight roads; but the crooked roads without improvement are roads of Genius.
Sooner murder an infant in its cradle than nurse unacted desires.
Where man is not, nature is barren.
Truth can never be told so as to be understood, and not be believ'd.
Enough! or Too much.

Mason Cooley: FROM CITY APHORISMS

Anyone who feels like a fool has made a good beginning.

Every hole tempts my finger.

After a Japanese dinner—to McDonald's, quickly.

Beautiful people are forgiven more often than the rest.

Women encourage men to be childish, then scold them.

Children now expect their parents to audition for approval.

Fail, and your friends feel superior. Succeed, and they feel resentful.

Romance is tempestuous. Love is calm.

To avoid doing anything, wait for the right circumstances.

From *City Aphorisms* (1994).

Children use all their wiles to get their way with adults. Adults do the same with children.

The aphorism sometimes casts off cynicism and expresses strong feeling.

If everything had a label, we would live in a fully delineated but false world.

We express disappointment in everything except ourselves.

Creativity makes a leap, then looks to see where it is.

Keep your lies short and simple.

As a dream comes true, it falls flat.

Yawns are hard to refute.

Three meals plus bedtime make four sure blessings a day.

The Past is always waiting to entangle and deflect us.

The bathroom scale knows nothing of extenuating circumstances.

I was once in love with books. Now they go their way and I go mine.

When a man bores a woman, she complains. When a woman bores a man, he ignores her.

Do not wait for a reason to be happy.

Benjamin Franklin: FROM POOR RICHARD'S ALMANACK

Light purse, heavy heart. 1733
He's a fool that makes his doctor his heir.
Love well, whip well.

From *Poor Richard's Almanack* (1733–1757).

Hunger never saw bad bread.
Fools make feasts, and wise men eat 'em.
He that lies down with dogs, shall rise up with fleas.
He is ill clothed, who is bare of virtue.
There is no little enemy.

Without justice courage is weak. 1734
Where there's marriage without love, there will be love without marriage.
Do good to thy friend to keep him, to thy enemy to gain him.
He that cannot obey, cannot command.
Marry your son when you will, but your daughter when you can.

Approve not of him who commends all you say. 1735
Necessity never made a good bargain.
Be slow in choosing a friend, slower in changing.
Three may keep a secret, if two of them are dead.
Deny self for self's sake.
To be humble to superiors is duty, to equals courtesy, to inferiors nobleness.

Fish and visitors stink in three days. 1736
Do not do that which you would not have known.
Bargaining has neither friends nor relations.
Now I've a sheep and a cow, every body bids me good morrow.
God helps them that help themselves.
He that speaks much, is much mistaken.
God heals, and the doctor takes the fees.

There are no ugly loves, nor handsome prisons. 1737
Three good meals a day is bad living.

Who has deceiv'd thee so oft as thyself? 1738
Read much, but not many books.
Let thy vices die before thee.

He that falls in love with himself, will have no rivals. 1739
Sin is not hurtful because it is forbidden, but it is forbidden because it's hurtful.

An empty bag cannot stand upright. 1740

Learn of the skilful: he that teaches himself, hath a fool for his master. 1741

Death takes no bribes. 1742

An old man in a house is a good sign. 1744
Fear God, and your enemies will fear you.

He's a fool that cannot conceal his wisdom. 1745
Many complain of their memory, few of their judgment.

When the well's dry, we know the worth of water. 1746
The sting of a reproach is the truth of it.

Write injuries in dust, benefits in marble. 1747

Nine men in *ten* are suicides. 1749
A man in a passion rides a mad horse.

He is a governor that governs his passions, and he is a servant that serves them. 1750
Sorrow is good for nothing but sin.

Calamity and prosperity are the touchstones of integrity. 1752
Generous minds are all of kin.

Haste makes waste. 1753

The doors of wisdom are never shut. 1755

The way to be safe, is never to be secure. 1757

La Rochefoucauld: FROM MAXIMS

Our virtues are mostly but vices in disguise.

14. Men not only forget benefits received and injuries endured; they even come to dislike those to whom they are indebted, while ceasing to hate those others who have done them harm. Diligence in returning good for good, and in exacting vengeance for evil, comes to be a sort of servitude which we do not readily accept.

From *Reflexions ou sentences et maximes morales*, or *Maxims*, (1655–1678).

19. We are all strong enough to endure the misfortunes of others.

20. The steadiness of the wise man is only the art of keeping his agitations locked within his breast.

25. Firmer virtues are required to support good fortune than bad.

28. Jealousy is, in its way, both fair and reasonable, since its intention is to preserve for ourselves something which is ours, or which we believe to be ours; envy, on the other hand, is a frenzy which cannot endure contemplating the possessions of others.

31. Were we faultless, we would not derive such satisfaction from remarking the faults of others.

38. Our promises are made in hope, and kept in fear.

50. A man convinced of his own merit will accept misfortune as an honor, for thus can he persuade others, as well as himself, that he is a worthy target for the arrows of fate.

56. To achieve a position in the world a man will do his utmost to appear already arrived.

59. There is no accident so disastrous that a clever man cannot derive some profit from it: nor any so fortunate that a fool cannot turn it to his disadvantage.

62. Sincerity comes from an open heart. It is exceedingly rare; what usually passes for sincerity is only an artful pretense designed to win the confidence of others.

67. Grace is to the body what sense is to the mind.

71. When two people have ceased to love, the memory that remains is almost always one of shame.

72. Love, to judge by most of its effects, is closer to hatred than to friendship.

75. Love, like fire, needs constant motion; when it ceases to hope, or to fear, love dies.

78. For most men the love of justice is only the fear of suffering injustice.

79. For a man who lacks self-confidence, silence is the wisest course.

83. What men have called friendship is only a social arrangement, a mutual adjustment of interests, an interchange of services given and received; it is, in sum, simply a business from which those involved purpose to derive a steady profit for their own self-love.

89. Everyone complains of his memory, none of his judgment.

90. In daily life our faults are frequently more pleasant than our good qualities.

93. Old people love to give good advice: it compensates them for their inability nowadays to set a bad example.

119. We are so accustomed to adopting a mask before others that we end by being unable to recognize ourselves.

122. If we master our passions it is due to their weakness, not our strength.

134. We are never so ridiculous through what we are as through what we pretend to be.

138. We would rather speak ill of ourselves than not at all.

144. We do not like to give praise, and we never do so without reasons of self-interest. Praise is a cunning, concealed and delicate form of flattery which, in different ways, gratifies both the giver and the receiver; the one accepts it as the reward for merit; the other bestows it to display his sense of justice and his powers of discernment.

146. We usually only praise that we may be praised.

149. The refusal to accept praise is the desire to be praised twice over.

150. The wish to deserve the praise we receive strengthens our virtues; and praise bestowed upon wit, courage and beauty contributes to their increase.

167. Avarice, more than open-handedness, is the opposite of economy.

170. When a man's behavior is straightforward, sincere and honest it is hard to be sure whether this is due to rectitude or cleverness.

176. In love there are two sorts of constancy: the one comes from the perpetual discovery of new delights in the beloved: the other, from the self-esteem which we derive from our own fidelity.

180. Our repentance is less a regret for the evil we have done than a precaution against the evil that may be done to us.

185. Evil, like good, has its heroes.

186. Not all who have vices are contemptible: all without a trace of virtue are.

190. Only great men are marked with great faults.

192. When our vices depart from us, we flatter ourselves that it is we who have rid ourselves of them.

200. Virtue would not go so far did vanity not keep her company.

205. Virtue, in women, is often love of reputation and fondness for tranquillity.

216. Perfect valor is to behave, without witnesses, as one would act were all the world watching.

218. Hypocrisy is the tribute that vice pays to virtue.

230. Nothing is as contagious as example, and we never perform an outstandingly good or evil action without its producing others of its sort. We copy goodness in the spirit of emulation, and wickedness owing to the malignity of our nature which shame holds in check until example sets it free.

237. No man should be praised for his goodness if he lacks the

strength to be bad: in such cases goodness is usually only the effect of indolence or impotence of will.

259. The pleasure of love is in loving: and there is more joy in the passion one feels than in that which one inspires.

264. Pity is often only the sentiment of our own misfortunes felt in the ills of others. It is a clever pre-science of the evil times upon which we may fall. We help others in order to ensure their help in similar circumstances; and the kindnesses we do them are, if the truth were told, only acts of charity towards ourselves invested against the future.

276. Absence diminishes small loves and increases great ones, as the wind blows out the candle and blows up the bonfire.

277. Women frequently believe themselves to be in love even when they are not: the pursuit of an intrigue, the stimulus of gallantry, the natural inclination towards the joys of being loved, and the difficulty of refusal, all these combine to tell them that their passions are aroused when in fact it is but their coquetry at play.

375. It is the habit of mediocre minds to condemn all that is beyond their grasp.

376. True friendship destroys envy, as true love puts an end to coquetry.

378. We give advice but we do not inspire behavior.

392. One should treat one's fate as one does one's health; enjoy it when it is good, be patient with it when it is poorly, and never attempt any drastic cure save as an ultimate resort.

399. There is a form of eminence which is quite independent of our fate; it is an air which distinguishes us from our fellow men and makes us appear destined for great things; it is the value which we imperceptibly attach to ourselves; it is the quality which wins us the deference of others; more than birth, honours or even merit, it gives us ascendancy.

417. In love, the person who recovers first recovers best.

423. Few people know how to be old.

467. Vanity leads us to act against our inclinations more often than does reason.

479. Only people who are strong can be truly gentle: what normally passes for gentleness is mere weakness, which quickly turns sour.

483. Vanity, rather than malice, is the usual source of slander.

540. Hope and fear are inseparable. There is no hope without fear, nor any fear without hope.

576. We always discover, in the misfortunes of our dearest friends, something not altogether displeasing.

597. No man can be sure of his own courage until he has stared danger in the face.

617. How can we expect another to keep our secret, if we cannot keep it ourself?

QUESTIONS ON APOTHEGMS

1. *Many apothegms represent common sense or conventional wisdom—but stated in clever, unconventional form. Choose several examples that you think represent common sense, and explain why you find their form interesting or appealing.*
2. *Some apothegms represent unconventional wisdom or even advice contrary to common sense. Choose several examples of this sort, and explain what alternative truth they mean to articulate.*
3. *What makes an apothegm memorable? Choose one or two examples that you remember from your reading (or perhaps from childhood) and analyze the features that make it easily recollected.*
4. *Try writing several apothegms. Which features of this form are difficult? Which easy?*
5. *Choose an apothegm with which you agree, and write an essay explaining why it represents good advice. Alternatively, choose one with which you disagree, and write an essay in which you explain why it is incorrect or deceptive.*

History

Henry David Thoreau

THE BATTLE OF THE ANTS

One day when I went out to my wood-pile, or rather my pile of stumps, I observed two large ants, the one red, the other much larger, nearly half an inch long, and black, fiercely contending with one another. Having once got hold they never let go, but struggled and wrestled and rolled on the chips incessantly. Looking farther, I was surprised to find that the chips were covered with such combatants, that it was not a *duellum*, but a *bellum*, a war between two races of ants, the red always pitted against the black, and frequently two red ones to one black. The legions of these Myrmidons[1] covered all the hills and vales in my wood-yard, and the ground was already strewn with the dead and dying, both red and black. It was the only battle which I have ever witnessed, the only battle-field I ever trod while the battle was raging; internecine war; the red republicans on the one hand, and the black imperialists on the other. On every side they were engaged in deadly combat, yet without any noise that I could hear, and human soldiers never fought so resolutely. I watched a couple that were fast locked in each other's embraces, in a little sunny valley amid the chips, now at noonday prepared to fight till the sun went down, or life went out. The smaller red champion had fastened himself like a vice to his adversary's front, and through all the tumblings on that field never for an instant ceased to gnaw at one of his feelers near the root, having already caused the other to go by the board; while the stronger black one dashed him from side to side, and, as I saw on looking nearer, had already divested him of several of his members. They fought with more pertinacity than bulldogs. Neither manifested the least disposition to

From *Walden* (1854).

1. The reference is to the powerful soldiers of Achilles in Homer's *Iliad*.

retreat. It was evident that their battle-cry was "Conquer or die." In the meanwhile there came along a single red ant on the hillside of this valley, evidently full of excitement, who either had despatched his foe, or had not yet taken part in the battle; probably the latter, for he had lost none of his limbs; whose mother had charged him to return with his shield or upon it. Or perchance he was some Achilles, who had nourished his wrath apart, and had now come to avenge or rescue his Patroclus.[2] He saw this unequal combat from afar—for the blacks were nearly twice the size of the red—he drew near with rapid pace till he stood on his guard within half an inch of the combatants; then, watching his opportunity, he sprang upon the black warrior, and commenced his operations near the root of his right fore leg, leaving the foe to select among his own members; and so there were three united for life, as if a new kind of attraction had been invented which put all other locks and cements to shame. I should not have wondered by this time to find that they had their respective musical bands stationed on some eminent chip, and playing their national airs the while, to excite the slow and cheer the dying combatants. I was myself excited somewhat even as if they had been men. The more you think of it, the less the difference. And certainly there is not the fight recorded in Concord history, at least, if in the history of America, that will bear a moment's comparison with this, whether for the numbers engaged in it, or for the patriotism and heroism displayed. For numbers and for carnage it was an Austerlitz or Dresden.[3] Concord Fight! Two killed on the patriots' side, and Luther Blanchard wounded! Why here every ant was a Buttrick—"Fire! for God's sake fire!"—and thousands shared the fate of Davis and Hosmer. There was not one hireling there. I have no doubt that it was a principle they fought for, as much as our ancestors, and not to avoid a three-penny tax on their tea; and the results of this battle will be as important and memorable to those whom it concerns as those of the battle of Bunker Hill, at least.

I took up the chip on which the three I have particularly described were struggling, carried into my house, and placed it under a tumbler on my window-sill, in order to see the issue. Holding a microscope to the first-mentioned red ant, I saw that, though he was assiduously gnawing at the near fore leg of his enemy, having severed his remaining feeler, his own breast was all torn away, exposing what vitals he had there to the jaws of the black warrior, whose breastplate was apparently too thick for him to pierce; and the dark carbuncles of the sufferer's eyes shone with ferocity such as war only could excite. They

2. A Greek warrior in the *Iliad*, whose death Achilles avenges.
3. Bloody Napoleonic victories.

struggled half an hour longer under the tumbler, and when I looked again the black soldier had severed the heads of his foes from their bodies, and the still living heads were hanging on either side of him like ghastly trophies at his saddle-bow, still apparently as firmly fastened as ever, and he was endeavoring with feeble struggles, being without feelers, and with only the remnant of a leg, and I know not how many other wounds, to divest himself of them; which at length, after half an hour more, he accomplished. I raised the glass, and he went off over the window-sill in that crippled state. Whether he finally survived that combat, and spent the remainder of his days in some Hôtel des Invalides,[4] I do not know; but I thought that his industry would not be worth much thereafter. I never learned which party was victorious, nor the cause of the war, but I felt for the rest of that day as if I had my feelings excited and harrowed by witnessing the struggle, the ferocity and carnage, of a human battle before my door.

Kirby and Spence tell us that the battles of ants have long been celebrated and the date of them recorded, though they say that Huber[5] is the only modern author who appears to have witnessed them. "Aeneas Sylvius," say they, "after giving a very circumstantial account of one contested with great obstinacy by a great and small species on the trunk of a pear tree," adds that " 'this action was fought in the pontificate of Eugenius the Fourth, in the presence of Nicholas Pistoriensis, an eminent lawyer, who related the whole history of the battle with the greatest fidelity.' A similar engagement between great and small ants is recorded by Olaus Magnus, in which the small ones, being victorious, are said to have buried the bodies of their own soldiers, but left those of their giant enemies a prey to the birds. This event happened previous to the expulsion of the tyrant Christiern the Second from Sweden." The battle which I witnessed took place in the Presidency of Polk, five years before the passage of Webster's Fugitive-Slave Bill.[6]

4. The famous French hospital for wounded soldiers and sailors.
5. Kirby and Spence were nineteenth-century American entomologists; Huber was a great Swiss entomologist.
6. Passed in 1851.

QUESTIONS

1. *Thoreau uses the Latin word* bellum *to describe the battle of the ants, and he quickly follows this word with a reference to the Myrmidons of Achilles. What comparison does he intend? Find further examples of it.*
2. *This passage comes from a chapter in Thoreau's* Walden *titled*

"Brute Neighbors." How does the comparison alluded to in the first paragraph, between the fighting ants and human warriors, amplify the meaning of that title?

3. *Describe the life, or part of the life, of an animal so that, while remaining faithful to the facts as you understand them, your description opens outward, as does Thoreau's, and speaks not only of the animal but also of man, society, or nature.*

Herbert Butterfield

THE ORIGINALITY OF THE OLD TESTAMENT

The Old Testament sometimes seems very ancient, but the earliest considerable body of historical literature that we possess was being produced through a period of a thousand years and more before that. It consisted of what we call "annals," written in the first person singular by the heads of great empires which had their centre in Egypt or Mesopotamia or Asia Minor. These monarchs, often year by year, would produce accounts—quite detailed accounts sometimes—of their military campaigns. It is clear from what they say that one of their objects in life was to put their own personal achievements on record—their building feats, their prowess in the hunt, but also their victories in war. They show no sign of having had any interest in the past, but, among other things, they betray a great anxiety about the reputation they would have after they were dead. They did not look behind them to previous generations, but instead they produced what we should call the history of their own times, in a way rather like Winston Churchill producing his account of his wars against Germany in the twentieth century.

After this, however, a great surprise occurs. There emerges from nowhere a people passionately interested in the past, dominated by an historical memory. It is clear that this is due to the fact that there is a bygone event that they really cannot get over; it takes command over their whole mentality. This people were the ancient Hebrews. They had been semi-nomads, moving a great deal in the desert, but having also certain periods in rather better areas where they could grow a bit of something. Like semi-nomads in general, they had longed to have land of their own, a settled land which they could properly cultivate. This is what they expected their God to provide for them, and what he

From *Writings on Christianity and History*, edited by C. T. McIntire (1979).

promised to provide. Indeed the semi-nomads would tend to judge his effectiveness as a god by his ability to carry out his promise. The ancient Hebrews, the Children of Israel, had to wait a long time for their due reward, and perhaps this was the reason why they were so tremendously impressed when ultimately the Promise was actually fulfilled.

The earliest thing that we know from sheer historical evidence about these people is that as soon as they appear in the light of day they are already dominated by this historical memory. In some of the earliest books of the Bible there are embedded patches of text far earlier still, far earlier than the Old Testament itself, and repeatedly they are passages about this very thing. Fresh references go on perpetually being made to the same matter throughout the many centuries during which the Old Testament was being produced, indeed also in the Jewish literature that was written for a few centuries after that. We are more sure that the memory of this historical event was the predominating thing among them than we are of the reality, the actual historicity, of the event itself.

What they commemorated in this tremendous way, of course, was the fact that God had brought them up out of the land of Egypt and into the Promised Land. In reality it seems pretty clear that some of the tribes of Israel did not come into the land of Palestine from Egypt at all. Nevertheless I think it would be a central view among scholars that some of the ancient Hebrews came to the Promised Land from Egypt, and the impression of this was so powerful that it became the common memory of the whole group of tribes which settled in the land of Canaan; it became the accepted tradition even among the tribes that had never been in Egypt. Moreover the common tradition was the very thing that became the effective bond between the tribes of Israel, helping to weld them together as a people. This sense of a common history is always a powerful factor in fusing a group of tribes into a nation, just as Homer made the various bodies of Greeks feel that they had had a common experience in the past, a consciousness that they were all Hellenes. All this was so powerful with the Children of Israel because they felt such a fabulous gratitude for what had happened. I know of no other case in history where gratitude was carried so far, no other case where gratitude proved to be such a generative thing. Their God had stepped into history and kept his ancient Promise, bringing them to freedom and the Promised Land, and they simply could not get over it.

5 This was not the first time in history that gratitude had been a factor in religion, for at a date earlier still there are signs amongst the Hittites that the very sincerity of their feeling of indebtedness added an attractive kind of devotion to their worship of their pagan deities.

But this gratitude was such a signal thing amongst the Israelitish people that it altered the whole development of religion in that quarter of the globe; it altered the character of religion in the area from which our Western civilization sprang. It gave the Children of Israel a historical event that they could not get over, could not help remembering, and in the first place it made them historians—historians in a way that nobody had ever been before. The ancient Hebrews worshiped the God who brought them up out of the land of Egypt more than they worshipped God as the Creator of the World. By all the rules of the game, when once they had settled down in the land of Canaan and become an agricultural people, they ought to have turned to the gods of nature, the gods of fertility, and this is what some of their number wanted to do. But their historical memory was too strong. Even when they borrowed rites and ceremonies from neighboring peoples—pieces of ritual based on the cycle of nature, the succession of the seasons—they turned these into celebrations of historical events, just as I suppose Christianity may have turned the rites of Spring into a celebration of the Resurrection. The Hebrews took over circumcision, which existed among their neighbors, but they turned even this into the celebration of a historical event. A Harvest Festival is an occasion on which even among Christians today we call attention to the cycle of the seasons and the bounty of nature. But among the Children of Israel at this ceremony you handed your thankoffering to the priest and then, if you please, you did not speak of the corn or the vine—you recited your national history, you narrated the story of the Exodus. It was set down in writing that if the younger generation started asking why they were expected to obey God's commandments they should be told that it was because God had brought their forefathers out of the house of bondage. Everything was based on their gratitude for what God had done for the nation. And it is remarkable to see to what a degree the other religious ideas of the Old Testament always remained historical in character—the Promise, the Covenant, the Judgment, the Messiah, the remnant of Israel, etc.

Yet this Promised Land to which God had brought them and on which they based a religion of extravagant gratitude was itself no great catch, and if they called it a land flowing with milk and honey, this was only because it looked rich when compared to the life that they had hitherto led. In the twentieth century Palestine has demanded a tremendous wrestling with nature, and if one looks back to the state of that region in Old Testament times one cannot help feeling that Providence endowed this people with one of the riskiest bits of territory that existed in that part of the globe. They were placed in an area which had already been encircled by vast empires, based on Egypt and on Mesopotamia and on a Hittite realm in Asia Minor. And, for all their gratitude, they were one of the most unlucky peoples of history. Other great empires soon arose again in the same regions, and they were so placed that they could not be expected to keep their freedom—their independence as a state only lasted for a few centuries, something like the period between Tudor England and the present day.[1] The one stroke of luck that they did have was that for just a space at the crucial period those surrounding empires had come into decline, and this gave the Hebrews the chance of forming an independent state for a while. They virtually stood in the cockpit in that part of the world, just as Belgium stood in the cockpit in Western Europe and Poland in Eastern Europe. The fact that the Hebrews became, along with the Greeks, one of the main contributors to the formation of Western civilization is a triumph of mind over matter, of the human spirit over misfortune and disaster. They almost built their religion on gratitude for their good fortune in having a country at all, a country that they could call their own.

Because of the great act of God which had brought them to Palestine they devoted themselves to the God of History rather than to the gods of nature. Here is their great originality, the thing that in a way enabled them to change the very nature of religion. Because they turned their intellect to the actions of God in history, they were drawn into an ethical view of God. They were continually wrestling with him about ethical questions, continually debating with him as to whether he was playing fair with them. Religion became intimately connected with morality because this was a God who was always in personal relations with human beings in the ordinary historical realm, and in any case you find that it was the worshipers of the gods of nature who ran to orgies and cruelties and immoralities. In fact, the ancient Hebrews developed their thought about God, about personality, and about ethics all together, all rolled into one. Because these things all involved what we call problems of personal relations they developed their thought about history step by step along with the rest. For a student of history, one of the interesting features of the Old Testament is that it gives us evidence of religious development from very early stages, from most primitive ideas about God, some of these ideas being quite shocking to the modern mind. Indeed, in some of the early books of the Bible there are still embedded certain ancient things that make it look as though, here as in no other parts of Western Asia, the God of History may at one stage have been really the God of War.

So far as I have been able to discover—approaching the matter as a modern historian, and rather an outsider, and using only what is avail-

1. Queen Elizabeth I, the last of the Tudor monarchs, died in 1603.

able in Western languages—the Children of Israel, while still a comparatively primitive society, are the first people who showed a really significant interest in the past, the first to produce anything like a history of their nation, the first to lay out what we call a universal history, doing it with the help of some Babylonian legends but attempting to see the whole story of the human race. Because what we possess in the Old Testament is history as envisaged by the priests, or at least by the religious people, it is also a history very critical of the rulers—not like the mass of previous historical writing, a case of monarchs blowing their own trumpets. The history they wrote is a history of the people and not just of the kings, and it is very critical even of the people. So far as I know here is the only case of a nation producing a national history and making it an exposure of its national sins. In a technical sense this ancient Hebrew people became very remarkable as writers of history, some of their narratives (for example, the death of King David and the question of the succession to his throne) being quite wonderful according to modern standards of judgment. It was to be of momentous importance for the development of Western civilization, that, growing up in Europe (with Christianity presiding over its creative stages), it was influenced by the Old Testament, by this ancient Jewish passion for history. For century after century over periods of nearly 2000 years, the European could not even learn about his religion without studying the Bible, including the Old Testament—essentially a history-book, a book of very ancient history. Our civilization, unlike many others, became historically-minded, therefore, one that was interested in the past, and we owe that in a great part to the Old Testament.

QUESTIONS

1. *What difference does Butterfield find between the writings of the ancient Hebrews and writings made in the empires of the Near East? What caused the difference?*
2. *According to Butterfield, what was the effect of historical memory on the formation of the ancient nation of Israel? What examples or evidence does he provide of this kind of memory?*
3. *Butterfield believes that one of the key factors in the development of our civilization is that we "became historically minded." Write a brief essay discussing whether we are still "historically minded" today—and what evidence you find in support of your view.*

Barbara Tuchman

"THIS IS THE END OF THE WORLD": THE BLACK DEATH

In October 1347, two months after the fall of Calais,[1] Genoese trading ships put into the harbor of Messina in Sicily with dead and dying men at the oars. The ships had come from the Black Sea port of Caffa (now Feodosiya) in the Crimea, where the Genoese maintained a trading post. The diseased sailors showed strange black swellings about the size of an egg or an apple in the armpits and groin. The swellings oozed blood and pus and were followed by spreading boils and black blotches on the skin from internal bleeding. The sick suffered severe pain and died quickly within five days of the first symptoms. As the disease spread, other symptoms of continuous fever and spitting of blood appeared instead of the swellings or buboes. These victims coughed and sweated heavily and died even more quickly, within three days or less, sometimes in 24 hours. In both types everything that issued from the body—breath, sweat, blood from the buboes and lungs, bloody urine, and blood-blackened excrement—smelled foul. Depression and despair accompanied the physical symptoms, and before the end "death is seen seated on the face."

The disease was bubonic plague, present in two forms: one that infected the bloodstream, causing the buboes and internal bleeding, and was spread by contact; and a second, more virulent pneumonic type that infected the lungs and was spread by respiratory infection. The presence of both at once cause the high mortality and speed of contagion. So lethal was the disease that cases were known of persons going to bed well and dying before they woke, of doctors catching the illness at a bedside and dying before the patient. So rapidly did it spread from one to another that to a French physician, Simon de Covino, it seemed as if one sick person "could infect the whole world." The malignity of the pestilence appeared more terrible because its victims knew no prevention and no remedy.

The physical suffering of the disease and its aspect of evil mystery were expressed in a strange Welsh lament which saw "death coming into our midst like black smoke, a plague which cuts off the young, a

From A *Distant Mirror: The Calamitous Fourteenth Century* (1978).

1. After a year-long siege, the French citizens of Calais surrendered to Edward III, king of England and self-declared king of France.

rootless phantom which has no mercy for fair countenance. Woe is me of the shilling in the armpit! It is seething, terrible . . . a head that gives pain and causes a loud cry . . . a painful angry knob . . . Great is its seething like a burning cinder . . . a grievous thing of ashy color." Its eruption is ugly like the "seeds of black peas, broken fragments of brittle sea-coal . . . the early ornaments of black death, cinders of the peelings of the cockle weed, a mixed multitude, a black plague like halfpence, like berries. . . ."

Rumors of a terrible plague supposedly arising in China and spreading through Tartary (Central Asia) to India and Persia, Mesopotamia, Syria, Egypt, and all of Asia Minor had reached Europe in 1346. They told of a death toll so devastating that all of India was said to be depopulated, whole territories covered by dead bodies, other areas with no one left alive. As added up by Pope Clement VI at Avignon, the total of reported dead reached 23,840,000. In the absence of a concept of contagion, no serious alarm was felt in Europe until the trading ships brought their black burden of pestilence into Messina while other infected ships from the Levant carried it to Genoa and Venice.

By January 1348 it penetrated France via Marseille, and North 5
Africa via Tunis. Shipborne along coasts and navigable rivers, it spread westward from Marseille through the ports of Languedoc to Spain and northward up the Rhône to Avignon, where it arrived in March. It reached Narbonne, Montpellier, Carcassonne, and Toulouse between February and May, and at the same time in Italy spread to Rome and Florence and their hinterlands. Between June and August it reached Bordeaux, Lyon, and Paris, spread to Burgundy and Normandy, and crossed the Channel from Normandy into southern England. From Italy during the same summer it crossed the Alps into Switzerland and reached eastward to Hungary.

In a given area the plague accomplished its kill within four to six months and then faded, except in the larger cities, where, rooting into the close-quartered population, it abated during the winter, only to reappear in spring and rage for another six months.

In 1349 it resumed in Paris, spread to Picardy, Flanders, and the Low Countries, and from England to Scotland and Ireland as well as to Norway, where a ghost ship with a cargo of wool and a dead crew drifted offshore until it ran aground near Bergen. From there the plague passed into Sweden, Denmark, Prussia, Iceland, and as far as Greenland. Leaving a strange pocket of immunity in Bohemia, and Russia unattacked until 1351, it had passed from most of Europe by mid-1350. Although the mortality rate was erratic, ranging from one fifth in some places to nine tenths or almost total elimination in others, the overall estimate of modern demographers has settled—for the area extending from India to Iceland—around the same figure expressed in Froissart's casual words: "a third of the world died." His estimate, the common one at the time, was not an inspired guess but a borrowing of St. John's figure for mortality from plague in Revelation, the favorite guide to human affairs of the Middle Ages.

A third of Europe would have meant about 20 million deaths. No one knows in truth how many died. Contemporary reports were an awed impression, not an accurate count. In crowded Avignon, it was said, 400 died daily; 7,000 houses emptied by death were shut up; a single graveyard received 11,000 corpses in six weeks; half the city's inhabitants reportedly died, including 9 cardinals or one third of the total, and 70 lesser prelates. Watching the endlessly passing death carts, chroniclers let normal exaggeration take wings and put the Avignon death toll at 62,000 and even at 120,000, although the city's total population was probably less than 50,000.

When graveyards filled up, bodies at Avignon were thrown into the Rhône until mass burial pits were dug for dumping the corpses. In London in such pits corpses piled up in layers until they overflowed. Everywhere reports speak of the sick dying too fast for the living to bury. Corpses were dragged out of homes and left in front of doorways. Morning light revealed new piles of bodies. In Florence the dead were gathered up by the Compagnia della Misericordia—founded in 1244 to care for the sick—whose members wore red robes and hoods masking the face except for the eyes. When their efforts failed, the dead lay putrid in the streets for days at a time. When no coffins were to be had, the bodies were laid on boards, two or three at once, to be carried to graveyards or common pits. Families dumped their own relatives into the pits, or buried them so hastily and thinly "that dogs dragged them forth and devoured their bodies."

10 Amid accumulating death and fear of contagion, people died without last rites and were buried without prayers, a prospect that terrified the last hours of the stricken. A bishop in England gave permission to laymen to make confession to each other as was done by the Apostles, "or if no man is present then even to a woman," and if no priest could be found to administer extreme unction, "then faith must suffice." Clement VI found it necessary to grant remissions of sin to all who died of the plague because so many were unattended by priests. "And no bells tolled," wrote a chronicler of Siena, "and nobody wept no matter what his loss because almost everyone expected death. . . . And people said and believed, 'This is the end of the world.' "

In Paris, where the plague lasted through 1349, the reported death rate was 800 a day, in Pisa 500, in Vienna 500 to 600. The total dead in Paris numbered 50,000 or half the population. Florence, weakened by the famine of 1347, lost three to four fifths of its citizens, Venice two thirds, Hamburg and Bremen, though smaller in size, about the same proportion. Cities, as centers of transportation, were more likely to be affected than villages, although once a village was infected, its death rate was equally high. At Givry, a prosperous village in Burgundy of 1,200 to 1,500 people, the parish register records 615 deaths in the space of fourteen weeks, compared to an average of thirty deaths a year in the previous decade. In three villages of Cambridgeshire, manorial records show a death rate of 47 percent, 57 percent, and in one case 70 percent. When the last survivors, too few to carry on, moved away, a deserted village sank back into the wilderness and disappeared from the map altogether, leaving only a grass-covered ghostly outline to show where mortals once had lived.

In enclosed places such as monasteries and prisons, the infection of one person usually meant that of all, as happened in the Franciscan convents of Carcassonne and Marseille, where every inmate without exception died. Of the 140 Dominicans at Montpellier only seven survived. Petrarch's[2] brother Gherardo, member of a Carthusian monastery, buried the prior and 34 fellow monks one by one, sometimes three a day, until he was left alone with his dog and fled to look for a place that would take him in. Watching every comrade die, men in such places could not but wonder whether the strange peril that filled the air had not been sent to exterminate the human race. In Kilkenny, Ireland, Brother John Clyn of the Friars Minor, another monk left alone among dead men, kept a record of what had happened lest "things which should be remembered perish with time and vanish from the memory of those who come after us." Sensing "the whole world, as it were, placed within the grasp of the Evil One," and waiting for death to visit him too, he wrote, "I leave parchment to continue this work, if perchance any man survive and any of the race of Adam escape this pestilence and carry on the work which I have begun." Brother John, as noted by another hand, died of the pestilence, but he foiled oblivion.

The largest cities of Europe, with populations of about 100,000, were Paris and Florence, Venice and Genoa. At the next level, with more than 50,000, were Ghent and Bruges in Flanders, Milan, Bologna, Rome, Naples, and Palermo, and Cologne. London hovered below 50,000, the only city in England except York with more than 10,000. At the level of 20,000 to 50,000 were Bordeaux, Toulouse, Montpellier, Marseille, and Lyon in France, Barcelona, Seville, and Toledo in Spain, Siena, Pisa, and other secondary cities in Italy, and the Hanseatic trading cities of the Empire. The plague raged through them all, killing anywhere from one third to two thirds of their inhabi-

2. Francesco Petrarch (1304–1374), Italian writer whose sonnets to "my lady Laura" influenced a tradition of European love poetry for centuries afterward.

tants. Italy, with a total population of 10 to 11 million, probably suffered the heaviest toll. Following the Florentine bankruptcies, the crop failures and workers' riots of 1346–47, the revolt of Cola di Rienzi that plunged Rome into anarchy, the plague came as the peak of successive calamities. As if the world were indeed in the grasp of the Evil One, its first appearance on the European mainland in January 1348 coincided with a fearsome earthquake that carved a path of wreckage from Naples up to Venice. Houses collapsed, church towers toppled, villages were crushed, and the destruction reached as far as Germany and Greece. Emotional response, dulled by horrors, underwent a kind of atrophy epitomized by the chronicler who wrote, "And in these days was burying without sorrowe and wedding without friendschippe."

In Siena, where more than half the inhabitants died of the plague, work was abandoned on the great cathedral, planned to be the largest in the world, and never resumed, owing to loss of workers and master masons and "the melancholy and grief" of the survivors. The cathedral's truncated transept still stands in permanent witness to the sweep of death's scythe. Agnolo di Tura, a chronicler of Siena, recorded the fear of contagion that froze every other instinct. "Father abandoned child, wife husband, one brother another," he wrote, "for this plague seemed to strike through the breath and sight. And so they died. And no one could be found to bury the dead for money or friendship. . . . And I, Agnolo di Tura, called the Fat, buried my five children with my own hands, and so did many others likewise."

15 There were many to echo his account of inhumanity and few to balance it, for the plague was not the kind of calamity that inspired mutual help. Its loathsomeness and deadliness did not herd people together in mutual distress, but only prompted their desire to escape each other. "Magistrates and notaries refused to come and make the wills of the dying," reported a Franciscan friar of Piazza in Sicily; what was worse, "even the priests did not come to hear their confessions." A clerk of the Archbishop of Canterbury reported the same of English priests who "turned away from the care of their benefices from fear of death." Cases of parents deserting children and children their parents were reported across Europe from Scotland to Russia. The calamity chilled the hearts of men, wrote Boccaccio[3] in his famous account of the plague in Florence that serves as introduction to the *Decameron.* "One man shunned another . . . kinsfolk held aloof, brother was forsaken by brother, oftentimes husband by wife; nay, what is more, and scarcely to be believed, fathers and mothers were found to abandon

3. Giovanni Boccaccio (1313–1375), Italian writer best known for his collection of stories, *The Decameron,* in which seven young ladies and three young men flee from Florence to escape the Black Death and tell stories to while away the time.

their own children to their fate, untended, unvisited as if they had been strangers." Exaggeration and literary pessimism were common in the 14th century, but the Pope's physician, Guy de Chauliac, was a sober, careful observer who reported the same phenomenon: "A father did not visit his son, nor the son his father. Charity was dead."

Yet not entirely. In Paris, according to the chronicler Jean de Venette, the nuns of the Hôtel Dieu or municipal hospital, "having no fear of death, tended the sick with all sweetness and humility." New nuns repeatedly took the places of those who died, until the majority "many times renewed by death now rest in peace with Christ as we may piously believe."

When the plague entered northern France in July 1348, it settled first in Normandy and, checked by winter, gave Picardy a deceptive interim until the next summer. Either in mourning or warning, black flags were flown from church towers of the worst-stricken villages of Normandy. "And in that time," wrote a monk of the abbey of Fourcarment, "the mortality was so great among the people of Normandy that those of Picardy mocked them." The same unneighborly reaction was reported of the Scots, separated by a winter's immunity from the English. Delighted to hear of the disease that was scourging the "southrons," they gathered forces for an invasion, "laughing at their enemies." Before they could move, the savage mortality fell upon them too, scattering some in death and the rest in panic to spread the infection as they fled.

In Picardy in the summer of 1349 the pestilence penetrated the castle of Coucy to kill Enguerrand's[4] mother, Catherine, and her new husband. Whether her nine-year-old son escaped by chance or was perhaps living elsewhere with one of his guardians is unrecorded. In nearby Amiens, tannery workers, responding quickly to losses in the labor force, combined to bargain for higher wages. In another place villagers were seen dancing to drums and trumpets, and on being asked the reason, answered that, seeing their neighbors die day by day while their village remained immune, they believed they could keep the plague from entering "by the jollity that is in us. That is why we dance." Further north in Tournai on the border of Flanders, Gilles li Muisis, Abbot of St. Martin's, kept one of the epidemic's most vivid accounts. The passing bells rang all day and all night, he recorded, because sextons were anxious to obtain their fees while they could. Filled with the sound of mourning, the city became oppressed by fear, so that the authorities forbade the tolling of bells and the wearing of black and restricted funeral services to two mourners. The silencing of

4. Enguerrand de Coucy, a French nobleman, is the historical figure around whom Tuchman constructs her account of the fourteenth century.

funeral bells and of criers' announcements of deaths was ordained by most cities. Siena imposed a fine on the wearing of mourning clothes by all except widows.

Flight was the chief recourse of those who could afford it or arrange it. The rich fled to their country places like Boccaccio's young patricians of Florence, who settled in a pastoral palace "removed on every side from the roads" with "wells of cool water and vaults of rare wines." The urban poor died in their burrows, "and only the stench of their bodies informed neighbors of their death." That the poor were more heavily afflicted than the rich was clearly remarked at the time, in the north as in the south. A Scottish chronicler, John of Fordun, stated flatly that the pest "attacked especially the meaner sort and common people—seldom the magnates." Simon de Covino of Montpellier made the same observation. He ascribed it to the misery and want and hard lives that made the poor more susceptible, which was half the truth. Close contact and lack of sanitation was the unrecognized other half. It was noticed too that the young died in greater proportion than the old; Simon de Covino compared the disappearance of youth to the withering of flowers in the fields.

20 In the countryside peasants dropped dead on the roads, in the fields, in their houses. Survivors in growing helplessness fell into apathy, leaving ripe wheat uncut and livestock untended. Oxen and asses, sheep and goats, pigs and chickens ran wild and they too, according to local reports, succumbed to the pest. English sheep, bearers of the precious wool, died throughout the country. The chronicler Henry Knighton, canon of Leicester Abbey, reported 5,000 dead in one field alone, "their bodies so corrupted by the plague that neither beast nor bird would touch them," and spreading an appalling stench. In the Austrian Alps wolves came down to prey upon sheep and then, "as if alarmed by some invisible warning, turned and fled back into the wilderness." In remote Dalmatia bolder wolves descended upon a plague-stricken city and attacked human survivors. For want of herdsmen, cattle strayed from place to place and died in hedgerows and ditches. Dogs and cats fell like the rest.

The dearth of labor held a fearful prospect because the 14th century lived close to the annual harvest both for food and for next year's seed. "So few servants and laborers were left," wrote Knighton, "that no one knew where to turn for help." The sense of a vanishing future created a kind of dementia of despair. A Bavarian chronicler of Neuberg on the Danube recorded that "Men and women . . . wandered around as if mad" and let their cattle stray "because no one had any inclination to concern themselves about the future." Fields went uncultivated, spring seed unsown. Second growth with nature's awful energy crept back over cleared land, dikes crumbled, salt water reinvaded and soured the lowlands. With so few hands remaining to restore the work of centuries, people felt, in Walsingham's words, that "the world could never again regain its former prosperity."

Though the death rate was higher among the anonymous poor, the known and the great died too. King Alfonso XI of Castile was the only reigning monarch killed by the pest, but his neighbor King Pedro of Aragon lost his wife, Queen Leonora, his daughter Marie, and a niece in the space of six months. John Cantacuzene, Emperor of Byzantium, lost his son. In France the lame Queen Jeanne and her daughter-in-law Bonne de Luxemburg, wife of the Dauphin, both died in 1349 in the same phase that took the life of Enguerrand's mother. Jeanne, Queen of Navarre, daughter of Louis X, was another victim. Edward III's second daughter, Joanna, who was on her way to marry Pedro, the heir of Castile, died in Bordeaux. Women appear to have been more vulnerable than men, perhaps because, being more housebound, they were more exposed to fleas. Boccaccio's mistress Fiammetta, illegitimate daughter of the King of Naples, died, as did Laura, the beloved—whether real or fictional—of Petrarch. Reaching out to us in the future, Petrarch cried, "Oh happy posterity who will not experience such abysmal woe and will look upon our testimony as a fable."

In Florence Giovanni Villani, the great historian of his time, died at 68 in the midst of an unfinished sentence: ". . . *e dure questo pistolenza fino a* . . . (in the midst of this pestilence there came to an end . . .)." Siena's master painters, the brothers Ambrogio and Pietro Lorenzetti, whose names never appear after 1348, presumably perished in the plague, as did Andrea Pisano, architect and sculptor of Florence. William of Ockham and the English mystic Richard Rolle of Hampole both disappear from mention after 1349. Francisco Datini, merchant of Prato, lost both his parents and two siblings. Curious sweeps of mortality afflicted certain bodies of merchants in London. All eight wardens of the Company of Cutters, all six wardens of the Hatters, and four wardens of the Goldsmiths died before July 1350. Sir John Pulteney, master draper and four times Mayor of London, was a victim, likewise Sir John Montgomery, Governor of Calais.

Among the clergy and doctors the mortality was naturally high because of the nature of their professions. Out of 24 physicians in Venice, 20 were said to have lost their lives in the plague, although, according to another account, some were believed to have fled or to have shut themselves up in their houses. At Montpellier, site of the leading medieval medical school, the physician Simon de Covino reported that, despite the great number of doctors, "hardly one of them escaped." In Avignon, Guy de Chauliac confessed that he performed his medical visits only because he dared not stay away for fear of infamy, but "I was in continual fear." He claimed to have contracted the disease but to have cured himself by his own treatment; if so, he was one of the few who recovered.

25 Clerical mortality varied with rank. Although the one-third toll of cardinals reflects the same proportion as the whole, this was probably due to their concentration in Avignon. In England, in strange and almost sinister procession, the Archbishop of Canterbury, John Stratford, died in August 1348, his appointed successor died in May 1349, and the next appointee three months later, all three within a year. Despite such weird vagaries, prelates in general managed to sustain a higher survival rate than the lesser clergy. Among bishops the deaths have been estimated at about one in twenty. The loss of priests, even if many avoided their fearful duty of attending the dying, was about the same as among the population as a whole.

Government officials, whose loss contributed to the general chaos, found, on the whole, no special shelter. In Siena four of the nine members of the governing oligarchy died, in France one third of the royal notaries, in Bristol 15 out of the 52 members of the Town Council or almost one third. Tax-collecting obviously suffered, with the result that Philip VI was unable to collect more than a fraction of the subsidy granted him by the Estates in the winter of 1347–48.

Lawlessness and debauchery accompanied the plague as they had during the great plague of Athens of 430 B.C., when according to Thucydides, men grew bold in the indulgence of pleasure: "For seeing how the rich died in a moment and those who had nothing immediately inherited their property, they reflected that life and riches were alike transitory and they resolved to enjoy themselves while they could." Human behavior is timeless. When St. John had his vision of plague in Revelation, he knew from some experience or race memory that those who survived "repented not of the work of their hands. . . . Neither repented they of their murders, nor of their sorceries, nor of their fornication, nor of their thefts."

Ignorance of the cause augmented the sense of horror. Of the real carriers, rats and fleas, the 14th century had no suspicion, perhaps because they were so familiar. Fleas, though a common household nuisance, are not once mentioned in contemporary plague writings, and rats only incidentally, although folklore commonly associated them with pestilence. The legend of the Pied Piper arose from an outbreak of 1284. The actual plague bacillus, *Pasturella pestis*, remained undiscovered for another 500 years. Living alternately in the stomach of the flea and the bloodstream of the rat who was the flea's host, the bacillus in its bubonic form was transferred to humans and animals by the bite of either rat or flea. It traveled by virtue of *Rattus rattus*, the small medieval black rat that lived on ships, as well as by the heavier brown or sewer rat. What precipitated the turn of the bacillus from innocuous to virulent form is unknown, but the occurrence is now believed to have taken place not in China but somewhere in central Asia and to have spread along the caravan routes. Chinese origin was a mistaken notion of the 14th century based on real but belated reports of huge death tolls in China from drought, famine, and pestilence which have since been traced to the 1330s, too soon to be responsible for the plague that appeared in India in 1346.

The phantom enemy had no name. Called the Black Death only in later recurrences, it was known during the first epidemic simply as the Pestilence or Great Mortality. Reports from the East, swollen by fearful imaginings, told of strange tempests and "sheets of fire" mingled with huge hailstones that "slew almost all," or a "vast rain of fire" that burned up men, beasts, stones, trees, villages, and cities. In another version, "foul blasts of wind" from the fires carried the infection to Europe "and now as some suspect it cometh round the seacoast." Accurate observation in this case could not make the mental jump to ships and rats because no idea of animal- or insect-borne contagion existed.

The earthquake was blamed for releasing sulfurous and foul fumes from the earth's interior, or as evidence of a titanic struggle of planets and oceans causing waters to rise and vaporize until fish died in masses and corrupted the air. All these explanations had in common a factor of poisoned air, of miasmas and thick, stinking mists traced to every kind of natural or imagined agency from stagnant lakes to malign conjunction of the planets, from the hand of the Evil One to the wrath of God. Medical thinking, trapped in the theory of astral influences, stressed air as the communicator of disease, ignoring sanitation or visible carriers. The existence of two carriers confused the trail, the more so because the flea could live and travel independently of the rat for as long as a month and, if infected by the particularly virulent septicemic form of the bacillus, could infect humans without reinfecting itself from the rat. The simultaneous presence of the pneumonic form of the disease, which was indeed communicated through the air, blurred the problem further.

The mystery of the contagion was "the most terrible of all the terrors," as an anonymous Flemish cleric in Avignon wrote to a correspondent in Bruges. Plagues had been known before, from the plague of Athens (believed to have been typhus) to the prolonged epidemic of the 6th century A.D., to the recurrence of sporadic outbreaks in the 12th and 13th centuries, but they had left no accumulated store of understanding. That the infection came from contact with the sick or with their houses, clothes, or corpses was quickly observed but not comprehended. Gentile da Foligno, renowned physician of Perugia and doctor of medicine at the universities of Bologna and Padua, came close to respiratory infection when he surmised that poisonous material was "communicated by means of air breathed out and in." Having no idea of microscopic carriers, he had to assume that the air was corrupted by planetary influences. Planets, however, could not explain the ongoing contagion. The agonized search for an answer gave rise to such theories as transference by sight. People fell ill, wrote Guy de Chauliac, not only by remaining with the sick but "even by looking at them." Three hundred years later Joshua Barnes, the 17th century biographer of Edward III, could write that the power of infection had entered into beams of light and "darted death from the eyes."

Doctors struggling with the evidence could not break away from the terms of astrology, to which they believed all human physiology was subject. Medicine was the one aspect of medieval life, perhaps because of its links with the Arabs, not shaped by Christian doctrine. Clerics detested astrology, but could not dislodge its influence. Guy de Chauliac, physician to three popes in succession, practiced in obedience to the zodiac. While his *Cirurgia* was the major treatise on surgery of its time, while he understood the use of anesthesia made from the juice of opium, mandrake, or hemlock, he nevertheless prescribed bleeding and purgatives by the planets and divided chronic from acute diseases on the basis of one being under the rule of the sun and the other of the moon.

In October 1348 Philip VI asked the medical faculty of the University of Paris for a report on the affliction that seemed to threaten human survival. With careful thesis, antithesis, and proofs, the doctors ascribed it to a triple conjunction of Saturn, Jupiter, and Mars in the 40th degree of Aquarius said to have occurred on March 20, 1345. They acknowledged, however, effects "whose cause is hidden from even the most highly trained intellects." The verdict of the masters of Paris became the official version. Borrowed, copied by scribes, carried abroad, translated from Latin into various vernaculars, it was everywhere accepted, even by the Arab physicians of Cordova and Granada, as the scientific if not the popular answer. Because of the terrible interest of the subject, the translations of the plague tracts stimulated use of national languages. In that one respect, life came from death.

To the people at large there could be but one explanation—the wrath of God. Planets might satisfy the learned doctors, but God was closer to the average man. A scourge so sweeping and unsparing without any visible cause could only be seen as Divine punishment upon mankind for its sins. It might even be God's terminal disappointment in his creature. Matteo Villani compared the plague to the Flood in ultimate purpose and believed he was recording "the extermination of mankind." Efforts to appease Divine wrath took many forms, as when the city of Rouen ordered that everything that could anger God, such as gambling, cursing, and drinking, must be stopped. More general were the penitent processions authorized at first by the Pope, some lasting as long as three days, some attended by as many as 2,000, which everywhere accompanied the plague and helped to spread it.

Barefoot in sackcloth, sprinkled with ashes, weeping, praying, tearing their hair, carrying candles and relics, sometimes with ropes around their necks or beating themselves with whips, the penitents wound through the streets, imploring the mercy of the Virgin and saints at their shrines. In a vivid illustration for the *Très Riches Heures* of the Duc de Berry, the Pope is shown in a penitent procession attended by four cardinals in scarlet from hat to hem. He raises both arms in supplication to the angel on top of the Castel Sant'Angelo, while white-robed priests bearing banners and relics in golden cases turn to look as one of their number, stricken by the plague, falls to the ground, his face contorted with anxiety. In the rear, a gray-clad monk falls beside another victim already on the ground as the townspeople gaze in horror. (Nominally the illustration represents a 6th century plague in the time of Pope Gregory the Great, but as medieval artists made no distinction between past and present, the scene is shown as the artist would have seen it in the 14th century.) When it became evident that these processions were sources of infection, Clement VI had to prohibit them.

In Messina, where the plague first appeared, the people begged the Archbishop of neighboring Catania to lend them the relics of St. Agatha. When the Catanians refused to let the relics go, the Archbishop dipped them in holy water and took the water himself to Messina, where he carried it in a procession with prayers and litanies through the streets. The demonic, which shared the medieval cosmos with God, appeared as "demons in the shape of dogs" to terrify the people. "A black dog with a drawn sword in his paws appeared among them, gnashing his teeth and rushing upon them and breaking all the silver vessels and lamps and candlesticks on the altars and casting them hither and thither. . . . So the people of Messina, terrified by this prodigious vision, were all strangely overcome by fear."

The apparent absence of earthly cause gave the plague a supernatural and sinister quality. Scandinavians believed that a Pest Maiden emerged from the mouth of the dead in the form of a blue flame and flew through the air to infect the next house. In Lithuania the Maiden was said to wave a red scarf through the door or window to let in the pest. One brave man, according to legend, deliberately waited at his open window with drawn sword and, at the fluttering of the scarf, chopped off the hand. He died of his deed, but his village was spared and the scarf long preserved as a relic in the local church.

Beyond demons and superstition the final hand was God's. The

Pope acknowledged it in a Bull of September 1348, speaking of the "pestilence with which God is afflicting the Christian people." To the Emperor John Cantacuzene it was manifest that a malady of such horrors, stenches, and agonies, and especially one bringing the dismal despair that settled upon its victims before they died, was not a plague "natural" to mankind but "a chastisement from Heaven." To Piers Plowman "these pestilences were for pure sin."

The general acceptance of this view created an expanded sense of guilt, for if the plague were punishment there had to be terrible sin to have occasioned it. What sins were on the 14th century conscience? Primarily greed, the sin of avarice, followed by usury, worldliness, adultery, blasphemy, falsehood, luxury, irreligion. Giovanni Villani, attempting to account for the cascade of calamity that had fallen upon Florence, concluded that it was retribution for the sins of avarice and usury that oppressed the poor. Pity and anger about the condition of the poor, especially victimization of the peasantry in war, was often expressed by writers of the time and was certainly on the conscience of the century. Beneath it all was the daily condition of medieval life, in which hardly an act or thought, sexual, mercantile, or military, did not contravene the dictates of the Church. Mere failure to fast or attend mass was sin. The result was an underground lake of guilt in the soul that the plague now tapped.

40 That the mortality was accepted as God's punishment may explain in part the vacuum of comment that followed the Black Death. An investigator has noticed that in the archives of Périgord references to the war are innumerable, to the plague few. Froissart mentions the great death but once, Chaucer gives it barely a glance. Divine anger so great that it contemplated the extermination of man did not bear close examination.

QUESTIONS

1. *Why does Tuchman begin with the account of the Genoese trading ships?*
2. *What ways does Tuchman find to group related facts together—in other words, what categories does she develop? Suggest other categories that Tuchman might have used in arranging her facts. What would she have gained or lost by using such categories?*
3. *Can you determine the basis for Tuchman's decision sometimes to quote a source, sometimes to recount it in her own words? Under what general principle is she operating in making these choices?*
4. *Write a brief account of a disaster in our own time, based on research from several sources.*

Chief Seattle

ADDRESS

The Governor made a fine speech,[1] but he was outranged and outclassed that day. Chief Seattle, who answered on behalf of the Indians, towered a foot above the Governor. He wore his blanket like the toga of a Roman senator, and he did not have to strain his famous voice, which everyone agreed was audible and distinct at a distance of half a mile.

Seattle's oration was in Duwamish. Doctor Smith, who had learned the language, wrote it down; under the flowery garlands of his translation the speech rolls like an articulate iron engine, grim with meanings that outlasted his generation and may outlast all the generations of men. As the amiable follies of the white race become less amiable, the iron rumble of old Seattle's speech sounds louder and more ominous.

Standing in front of Doctor Maynard's office in the stumpy clearing, with his hand on the little Governor's head, the white invaders about him and his people before him, Chief Seattle said:

"Yonder sky that has wept tears of compassion upon my people for centuries untold, and which to us appears changeless and eternal, may change. Today is fair. Tomorrow may be overcast with clouds. My words are like the stars that never change. Whatever Seattle says the great chief at Washington can rely upon with as much certainty as he can upon the return of the sun or the seasons. The White Chief says that Big Chief at Washington sends us greetings of friendship and goodwill. That is kind of him for we know he has little need of our friendship in return. His people are many. They are like the grass that covers vast prairies. My people are few. They resemble the scattering trees of a storm-swept plain. The great, and—I presume—good, White Chief sends us word that he wishes to buy our lands but is willing to allow us enough to live comfortably. This indeed appears just, even generous, for the Red Man no longer has rights that he need respect, and the offer may be wise also, as we are no longer in need of an extensive country. . . . I will not dwell on, nor mourn over, our untimely decay, nor reproach our paleface brothers with hastening it, as we too may have been somewhat to blame.

1. In 1854, Governor Isaac Stevens, Commissioner of Indian Affairs for the Washington Territory, proffered a treaty to the Indians providing for the sale of two million acres of their land to the federal government. This address is the reply of Chief Seattle of the Duwampo tribe. The translator was Henry A. Smith.

"Youth is impulsive. When our young men grow angry at some real or imaginary wrong, and disfigure their faces with black paint, it denotes that their hearts are black, and then they are often cruel and relentless, and our old men and old women are unable to restrain them. Thus it has ever been. Thus it was when the white men first began to push our forefathers further westward. But let us hope that the hostilities between us may never return. We would have everything to lose and nothing to gain. Revenge by young men is considered gain, even at the cost of their own lives, but old men who stay at home in times of war, and mothers who have sons to lose, know better.

5 "Our good father at Washington—for I presume he is now our father as well as yours, since King George has moved his boundaries further north—our great good father, I say, sends us word that if we do as he desires he will protect us. His brave warriors will be to us a bristling wall of strength, and his wonderful ships of war will fill our harbors so that our ancient enemies far to the northward—the Hydas and Tsimpsians—will cease to frighten our women, children, and old men. Then in reality will he be our father and we his children. But can that ever be? Your God is not our God! Your God loves your people and hates mine. He folds his strong and protecting arms lovingly about the paleface and leads him by the hand as a father leads his infant son—but He has forsaken His red children—if they really are his. Our God, the Great Spirit, seems also to have forsaken us. Your God makes your people wax strong every day. Soon they will fill the land. Our people are ebbing away like a rapidly receding tide that will never return. The white man's God cannot love our people or He would protect them. They seem to be orphans who can look nowhere for help. How then can we be brothers? How can your God become our God and renew our prosperity and awaken in us dreams of returning greatness? If we have a common heavenly father He must be partial—for He came to his paleface children. We never saw Him. He gave you laws but He had no word for His red children whose teeming multitudes once filled this vast continent as stars fill the firmament. No; we are two distinct races with separate origins and separate destinies. There is little in common between us.

"To us the ashes of our ancestors are sacred and their resting place is hallowed ground. You wander far from the graves of your ancestors and seemingly without regret. Your religion was written upon tables of stone by the iron finger of your God so that you could not forget. The Red Man could never comprehend nor remember it. Our religion is the traditions of our ancestors—the dreams of our old men, given them in solemn hours of night by the Great Spirit; and the visions of our sachems; and it is written in the hearts of our people.

"Your dead cease to love you and the land of their nativity as soon as they pass the portals of the tomb and wander way beyond the stars. They are soon forgotten and never return. Our dead never forget the beautiful world that gave them being.

"Day and night cannot dwell together. The Red Man has ever fled the approach of the White Man, as the morning mist flees before the morning sun. However, your proposition seems fair and I think that my people will accept it and will retire to the reservation you offer them. Then we will dwell apart in peace, for the words of the Great White Chief seem to be the words of nature speaking to my people out of dense darkness.

"It matters little where we pass the remnant of our days. They will not be many. A few more moons; a few more winters—and not one of the descendants of the mighty hosts that once moved over this broad land or lived in happy homes, protected by the Great Spirit, will remain to mourn over the graves of a people once more powerful and hopeful than yours. But why should I mourn at the untimely fate of my people? Tribe follows tribe, and nation follows nation, like the waves of the sea. It is the order of nature, and regret is useless. Your time of decay may be distant, but it will surely come, for even the White Man whose God walked and talked with him as friend with friend, cannot be exempt from the common destiny. We may be brothers after all. We will see.

"We will ponder your proposition, and when we decide we will let 10
you know. But should we accept it, I here and now make this condition that we will not be denied the privilege without molestation of visiting at any time the tombs of our ancestors, friends and children. Every part of this soil is sacred in the estimation of my people. Every hillside, every valley, every plain and grove, has been hallowed by some sad or happy event in days long vanished. . . . The very dust upon which you now stand responds more lovingly to their footsteps than to yours, because it is rich with the blood of our ancestors and our bare feet are conscious of the sympathetic touch. . . . Even the little children who lived here and rejoiced here for a brief season will love these somber solitudes and at eventide they greet shadowy returning spirits. And when the last Red Man shall have perished, and the memory of my tribe shall have become a myth among the White Men, these shores will swarm with the invisible dead of my tribe, and when your children's children think themselves alone in the field, the store, the shop, upon the highway, or in the silence of the pathless woods, they will not be alone. . . . At night when the streets of your cities and villages are silent and you think them deserted, they will throng with the returning hosts that once filled and still love this beautiful land. The White Man will never be alone.

"Let him be just and deal kindly with my people, for the dead are not powerless. Dead, did I say? There is no death, only a change of worlds."

Walt Whitman

DEATH OF ABRAHAM LINCOLN

I shall not easily forget the first time I ever saw Abraham Lincoln. It must have been about the 18th or 19th of February, 1861. It was rather a pleasant afternoon, in New York city, as he arrived there from the West, to remain a few hours, and then pass on to Washington, to prepare for his inauguration. I saw him in Broadway, near the site of the present Post-office. He came down, I think from Canal street, to stop at the Astor House. The broad spaces, sidewalks, and streets in the neighborhood, and for some distance, were crowded with solid masses of people, many thousands. The omnibuses and other vehicles had all been turn'd off, leaving an unusual hush in that busy part of the city. Presently two or three shabby hack barouches made their way with some difficulty through the crowd, and drew up at the Astor House entrance. A tall figure stepp'd out of the centre of these barouches, paus'd leisurely on the sidewalk, look'd up at the granite walls and looming architecture of the grand old hotel—then, after a relieving stretch of arms and legs, turn'd round for over a minute to slowly and good-humoredly scan the appearance of the vast and silent crowds. There were no speeches—no compliments—no welcome—as far as I could hear, not a word said. Still much anxiety was conceal'd in the quiet. Cautious persons had fear'd some mark'd insult or indignity to the President-elect—for he possess'd no personal popularity at all in New York City, and very little political. But it was evidently tacitly agreed that if the few political supporters of Mr. Lincoln present would entirely abstain from any demonstration on their side, the immense majority, who were anything but supporters, would abstain on their sides also. The result was a sulky, unbroken silence, such as certainly never before characterized so great a New York crowd.

Almost in the same neighborhood I distinctly remember'd seeing Lafayette on his visit to America in 1825. I had also personally seen and heard, various years afterward, how Andrew Jackson, Clay, Webster, Hungarian Kossuth, Filibuster Walker, the Prince of Wales on his visit, and other *célèbres*, native and foreign, had been welcom'd

From *Specimen Days* (1882).

there—all that indescribable human roar and magnetism, unlike any other sound in the universe—the glad exulting thunder-shouts of countless unloos'd throats of men! But on this occasion, not a voice—not a sound. From the top of an omnibus, (driven up one side, close by, and block'd by the curbstone and the crowds), I had, I say, a capital view of it all, and especially of Mr. Lincoln, his look and gait—his perfect composure and coolness—his unusual and uncouth height, his dress of complete black, stovepipe hat push'd back on the head, dark-brown complexion, seam'd and wrinkled yet canny-looking face, black, bushy head of hair, disproportionately long neck, and his hands held behind as he stood observing the people. He look'd with curiosity upon that immense sea of faces, and the sea of faces return'd the look with similar curiosity. In both there was a dash of comedy, almost farce, such as Shakspere puts in his blackest tragedies. The crowd that hemm'd around consisted I should think of thirty to forty thousand men, not a single one his personal friend—while I have no doubt, (so frenzied were the ferments of the time,) many an assassin's knife and pistol lurk'd in hip or breast-pocket there, ready, soon as break and riot came.

But no break or riot came. The tall figure gave another relieving stretch or two of arms and legs; then with moderate pace, and accompanied by a few unknown-looking persons, ascended the portico-steps of the Astor House, disappear'd through its broad entrance—and the dumb-show ended.

I saw Abraham Lincoln often the four years following that date. He changed rapidly and much during his Presidency—but this scene, and him in it, are indelibly stamp'd upon my recollection. As I sat on the top of my omnibus, and had a good view of him, the thought, dim and inchoate then, has since come out clear enough, that four sorts of genius, four mighty and primal hands, will be needed to the complete limning of this man's future portrait—the eyes and brains and finger-touch of Plutarch and Eschylus and Michel Angelo, assisted now by Rabelais.

And now—(Mr. Lincoln passing on from this scene to Washington, 5
where he was inaugurated, amid armed cavalry, and sharpshooters at every point—the first instance of the kind in our history—and I hope it will be the last)—now the rapid succession of well-known events, (too well-known—I believe, these days, we almost hate to hear them mention'd)—the national flag fired on at Sumter—the uprising of the North, in paroxysms of astonishment and rage—the chaos of divided councils—the call for troops—the first Bull Run—the stunning cast-down, shock, and dismay of the North—and so in full flood the Secession war. Four years of lurid, bleeding, murky, murderous war.

Who paint those years, with all their scenes?—the hard-fought engagements—the defeats, plans, failures—the gloomy hours, days, when our Nationality seem'd hung in pall of doubt, perhaps death—the Mephistophelean sneers of foreign lands and attachés—the dreaded Scylla of European interference, and the Charybdis of the tremendously dangerous latent strata of seccession sympathizers throughout the free States, (far more numerous than is supposed)—the long marches in summer—the hot sweat, and many a sunstroke, as on the rush to Gettysburg in '63—the night battles in the woods, as under Hooker at Chancellorsville—the camps in winter—the military prisons—the hospitals—(alas! alas! the hospitals.)

The Secession war? Nay, let me call it the Union war. Though whatever call'd, it is even yet too near us—too vast and too closely overshadowing—its branches unform'd yet, (but certain,) shooting too far into the future—and the most indicative and mightiest of them yet ungrown. A great literature will yet arise out of the era of those four years, those scenes—era compressing centuries of native passion, first-class pictures, tempests of life and death—an inexhaustible mine for the histories, drama, romance, and even philosophy, of peoples to come—indeed the verteber[1] of poetry and art, (of personal character too,) for all future America—far more grand, in my opinion, to the hands capable of it, than Homer's siege of Troy, or the French wars to Shakspere.

But I must leave these speculations, and come to the theme I have assign'd and limited myself to. Of the actual murder of President Lincoln, though so much has been written, probably the facts are yet very indefinite in most persons' minds. I read from my memoranda, written at the time, and revised frequently and finally since.

The day, April 14, 1865, seems to have been a pleasant one throughout the whole land—the moral atmosphere pleasant too—the long storm, so dark, so fratricidal, full of blood and doubt and gloom, over and ended at last by the sunrise of such an absolute National victory, and utter break-down of Secessionism—we almost doubted our own senses! Lee had capitulated beneath the apple-tree of Appomattox. The other armies, the flanges of the revolt, swiftly follow'd. And could it really be, then? Out of all the affairs of this world of woe and failure and disorder, was there really come the confirm'd, unerring sign of plan, like a shaft of pure light—of rightful rule—of God? So the day, as I say, was propitious. Early herbage, early flowers, were out. (I remember where I was stopping at the time, the season being advanced, there were many lilacs in full bloom. By one of those caprices that enter and give tinge to events without being at all a part of them, I find

1. Vertebra.

myself always reminded of the great tragedy of that day by the sight and odor of these blossoms.[2] It never fails.)

But I must not dwell on accessories. The deed hastens. The popular afternoon paper of Washington, the little *Evening Star*, has spatter'd all over its third page, divided among the advertisements in a sensational manner, in a hundred different places, *"The President and his Lady will be at the Theatre this evening. . . ."* (Lincoln was fond of the theatre. I have myself seen him there several times. I remember thinking how funny it was that he, in some respects the leading actor in the stormiest drama known to real history's stage through centuries, should sit there and be so completely interested and absorb'd in those human jackstraws, moving about with their silly little gestures, foreign spirit, and flatulent text.)

On this occasion the theatre was crowded, many ladies in rich and gay costumes, officers in their uniforms, many well-known citizens, young folks, the usual clusters of gas-lights, the usual magnetism of so many people, cheerful, with perfumes, music of violins and flutes—(and over all, and saturating all, that vast, vague wonder, *Victory*, the nation's victory, the triumph of the Union, filling the air, the thought, the sense, with exhilaration more than all music and perfumes.)

The President came betimes, and, with his wife, witness'd the play from the large stage-boxes of the second tier, two thrown into one, and profusely drap'd with the national flag. The acts and scenes of the piece—one of those singularly written compositions which have at least the merit of giving entire relief to an audience engaged in mental action or business excitements and cares during the day, as it makes not the slightest call on either the moral, emotional, esthetic, or spiritual nature—a piece, (*Our American Cousin,*) in which, among other characters so call'd, a Yankee, certainly such a one as was never seen, or the least like it ever seen, in North America, is introduced in England, with a varied fol-de-rol of talk, plot, scenery, and such phantasmagoria as goes to make up a modern popular drama—had progress'd through perhaps a couple of its acts, when in the midst of this comedy, or nonsuch, or whatever it is to be call'd, and to offset it, or finish it out, as if in Nature's and the great Muse's mockery of those poor mimes, came interpolated that scene, not really or exactly to be described at all, (for on the many hundreds who were there it seems to this hour to have left a passing blur, a dream, a blotch)—and yet partially to be described as I now proceed to give it. There is a scene in the play representing a modern parlor, in which two unprecedented English ladies are inform'd by the impossible Yankee that he is not a man of fortune,

2. Cf. Whitman's elegy on Lincoln, "When Lilacs Last in the Dooryard Bloom'd" (1865–1866).

and therefore undesirable for marriage-catching purposes; after which, the comments being finish'd, the dramatic trio make exit, leaving the stage clear for a moment. At this period came the murder of Abraham Lincoln. Great as all its manifold train, circling round it, and stretching into the future for many a century, in the politics, history, art &c., of the New World, in point of fact the main thing, the actual murder, transpired with the quiet and simplicity of any commonest occurrence—the bursting of a bud or pod in the growth of vegetation, for instance. Through the general hum following the stage pause, with the change of positions, came the muffled sound of a pistol-shot, which not one-hundredth part of the audience heard at the time—and yet a moment's hush—somehow, surely, a vague startled thrill—and then, through the ornamented, draperied, starr'd and striped space-way of the President's box, a sudden figure, a man, raises himself with hands and feet, stands a moment on the railing, leaps below to the stage, (a distance of perhaps fourteen or fifteen feet), falls out of position, catching his boot-heel in the copious drapery, (the American flag,) falls on one knee, quickly recovers himself, rises as if nothing had happen'd, (he really sprains his ankle, but unfelt then)—and so the figure, Booth, the murderer, dress'd in plain black broadcloth, bare-headed, with full, glossy, raven hair, and his eyes like some mad animal's flashing with light and resolution, yet with a certain strange calmness, holds aloft in one hand a large knife—walks along not much back from the footlights—turns fully toward the audience his face of statuesque beauty, lit by those basilisk eyes, flashing with desperation, perhaps insanity—launches out in a firm and steady voice the words *Sic semper tyrannis*[3]—and then walks with neither slow nor very rapid pace diagonally across to the back of the stage, and disappears. (Had not all this terrible scene—making the mimic ones preposterous—had it not all been rehears'd, in blank, by Booth, beforehand?)

A moment's hush—a scream—the cry of "*murder*"—Mrs. Lincoln leaning out of the box, with ashy cheeks and lips, with involuntary cry, pointing to the retreating figure, "*He has kill'd the President.*" And still a moment's strange, incredulous suspense—and then the deluge! then that mixture of horror, noises, uncertainty—(the sound, somewhere back, of a horse's hoofs clattering with speed)—the people burst through chairs and railings, and break them up—there is inextricable confusion and terror—women faint—quite feeble persons fall, and are trampl'd on—many cries of agony are heard—the broad stage suddenly fills to suffocation with a dense and motley crowd, like some horrible carnival—the audience rush generally upon it, at least the strong men do—the actors and actresses are all there in their play-

3. "Thus always to tyrants."

costumes and painted faces, with mortal fright showing through the rouge—the screams and calls, confused talk—redoubled, trebled—two or three manage to pass up water from the stage to the President's box—others try to clamber up—&c., &c.

In the midst of all this, the soldiers of the President's guard, with others, suddenly drawn to the scene, burst in—(some two hundred altogether)—they storm the house, through all the tiers, especially the upper ones, inflam'd with fury, literally charging the audience with fix'd bayonets, muskets, and pistols, shouting "*Clear out! clear out! you sons of*———". . . . Such a wild scene, or a suggestion of it rather, inside the play-house that night.

Outside, too, in the atmosphere of shock and craze, crowds of people, fill'd with frenzy, ready to seize any outlet for it, come near committing murder several times on innocent individuals. One such case was especially exciting. The infuriated crowd, through some chance, got started against one man, either for words he utter'd, or perhaps without any cause at all, and were proceeding at once to actually hang him on a neighboring lamp-post, when he was rescued by a few heroic policemen, who placed him in their midst, and fought their way slowly and amid great peril toward the station-house. It was a fitting episode of the whole affair. The crowd rushing and eddying to and fro—the night, the yells, the pale faces, many frighten'd people trying in vain to extricate themselves—the attack'd man, not yet freed from the jaws of death, looking like a corpse—the silent, resolute, half-dozen policemen, with no weapons but their little clubs, yet stern and steady through all those eddying swarms—made a fitting side-scene to the grand tragedy of the murder. They gain'd the station house with the protected man, whom they placed in security for the night, and discharged him in the morning.

And in the midst of that pandemonium, infuriated soldiers, the audience and the crowd, the stage, and all its actors and actresses, its paint-pots, spangles, and gas-lights—the life blood from those veins, the best and sweetest of the land, drips slowly down, and death's ooze already begins its little bubbles on the lips.

Thus the visible incidents and surroundings of Abraham Lincoln's murder, as they really occur'd. Thus ended the attempted secession of these States: thus the four years' war. But the main things come subtly and invisibly afterward, perhaps long afterward—neither military, political, nor (great as those are,) historical. I say, certain secondary and indirect results, out of the tragedy of this death, are, in my opinion, greatest. Not the event of the murder itself. Not that Mr. Lincoln strings the principal points and personages of the period, like beads, upon the single string of his career. Not that his idiosyncrasy, in its sudden appearance and disappearance, stamps this Republic with a stamp more mark'd and enduring than any yet given by any one man—(more even than Washington's;)—but, join'd with these, the immeasurable value and meaning of that whole tragedy lies, to me, in senses finally dearest to a nation, (and here all our own)—the imaginative and artistic senses—the literary and dramatic ones. Not in any common or low meaning of those terms, but a meaning precious to the race, and to every age. A long and varied series of contradictory events arrives at last at its highest poetic, single, central, pictorial *dénouement*. The whole involved, baffling, multiform whirl of the secession period comes to a head, and is gather'd in one brief flash of lightning-illumination—one simple, fierce deed. Its sharp culmination, and as it were solution, of so many bloody and angry problems, illustrates those climax-moments on the stage of universal Time, where the historic Muse at one entrance, and the tragic Muse at the other, suddenly ringing down the curtain, close an immense act in the long drama of creative thought, and give it radiation, tableau, stranger than fiction. Fit radiation—fit close! How the imagination—how the student loves these things! America, too, is to have them. For not in all great deaths, not far or near—not Caesar in the Roman senate-house, or Napoleon passing away in the wild night-storm at St. Helena—not Paleologus,[4] falling, desperately fighting, piled over dozens deep with Grecian corpses—not calm old Socrates, drinking the hemlock—outvies that terminus of the secession war, in one man's life, here in our midst, in our time—that seal of the emancipation of three million slaves—that parturition and delivery of our at last really free Republic, born again, henceforth to commence its career of genuine homogeneous Union, compact, consistent with itself.

Nor will ever future American Patriots and Unionists, indifferently over the whole land, or North or South, find a better moral to their lesson. The final use of the greatest men of a Nation is, after all, not with reference to their deeds in themselves, or their direct bearing on their times or lands. The final use of a heroic-eminent life—especially of a heroic-eminent death—is its indirect filtering into the nation and the race, and to give, often at many removes, but unerringly, age after age, color and fibre to the personalism of the youth and maturity of that age, and of mankind. Then, there is a cement to the whole people, subtler, more underlying, than any thing in written constitution, or courts or armies—namely, the cement of a death identified thoroughly with that people, at its head, and for its sake. Strange, (is it not?) that battles, martyrs, agonies, blood, even assassination, should so condense—perhaps only really, lastingly condense—a Nationality.

I repeat it—the grand deaths of the race—the dramatic deaths of

4. Emperor Constantine XI, who yielded Constantinople to the Turks in 1453.

every nationality—are its most important inheritance-value—in some respects beyond its literature and art—(as the hero is beyond his finest portrait, and the battle itself beyond its choicest song or epic.) Is not here indeed the point underlying all tragedy? the famous pieces of the Grecian masters—and all masters? Why, if the old Greeks had had this man, what trilogies of plays—what epics—would have been made out of him! How the rhapsodes would have recited him! How quickly that quaint tall form would have enter'd into the region where men vitalize gods, and gods divinify men! But Lincoln, his times, his death—great as any, any age—belong altogether to our own, and are autochthonic.[5] (Sometimes indeed I think our American days, our own stage—the actors we know and have shaken hands, or talk'd with—more fateful than any thing in Eschylus[6]—more heroic than the fighters around Troy—afford kings of men for our Democracy prouder than Agamemnon—models of character cute and hardy as Ulysses—deaths more pitiful than Priam's.)

When centuries hence, (as it must, in my opinion, be centuries hence before the life of these States, or of Democracy, can be really written and illustrated,) the leading historians and dramatists seek for some personage, some special event, incisive enough to mark with deepest cut, and mnemonize, this turbulent nineteenth century of ours, (not only these States, but all over the political and social world)—something, perhaps, to close that gorgeous procession of European feudalism, with all its pomp and caste-prejudices, (of whose long train we in America are yet so inextricably the heirs)—something to identify with terrible identification, by far the greatest revolutionary step in the history of the United States, (perhaps the greatest of the world, our century)—the absolute extirpation and erasure of slavery from the States—those historians will seek in vain for any point to serve more thoroughly their purpose, than Abraham Lincoln's death.

Dear to the Muse—thrice dear to Nationality—to the whole 20
human race—precious to this Union—precious to Democracy—unspeakably and forever precious—their first great Martyr Chief.

5. Aboriginal, indigenous.
6. Eschylus (i.e., Aeschylus), Greek tragic dramatist (525–456 B.C.) whose plays, like Homer's epics, dealt with such figures of the Trojan War as Agamemnon, leader of the Greek forces; Ulysses, whose return to Ithaca after the war took ten years; and Priam, slaughtered king of Troy.

QUESTIONS

1. *Whitman delivered this piece as a lecture. What features suggest a lecture? How might it have differed if he had composed it as an essay to be read rather than a lecture to be heard?*

2. *The events of the assassination lead Whitman to mention his perception of Lincoln's fondness for the theater. How does he make this particular observation serve a larger purpose?*
3. *At the end, Whitman speaks grandly of Lincoln's significance for far more than the citizens of the United States. As he sees it, what do all these people have in common that would allow for this more-than-national significance?*
4. *How does Whitman convey the sense of horror and confusion in the scene when Lincoln is shot? Using some of Whitman's techniques, write an account of a similar scene that produces a strong emotional effect.*

H. Bruce Franklin

FROM REALISM TO VIRTUAL REALITY: IMAGES OF AMERICA'S WARS

The Industrial Revolution was only about one century old when modern technological warfare burst upon the world in the US Civil War. During that century human progress had already been manifested in the continually increasing deadliness and range of weapons, as well as in other potential military benefits of industrial capitalism. But it was the Civil War that actually demonstrated industrialism's ability to produce carnage and devastation on an unprecedented scale, thus foreshadowing a future more and more dominated by what we have come to call *technowar.* For the first time, immense armies had been transported by railroad, coordinated by telegraph, and equipped with an ever-evolving arsenal of mass-produced weapons designed by scientists and engineers. The new machines of war—such as the repeating rifle, the primitive machine gun, the submarine, and the steam-powered, ironclad warship—were being forged by other machines. Industrial organization was essential, therefore, not only in the factories where the technoweapons were manufactured but also on the battlefields and waters where these machines destroyed each other and slaughtered people.

Prior to the Civil War, visual images of America's wars were almost without exception expressions of romanticism and nationalism. Paintings, lithographs, woodcuts, and statues displayed a glorious saga of thrilling American heroism from the Revolution through the Mexican

From *The Georgia Review* (Spring 1994). All notes to this essay are the author's.

War. Drawing on their imagination, artists could picture action-filled scenes of heroic events, such as Emmanuel Leutze's 1851 painting *Washington Crossing the Delaware.*[1]

Literature, however, was the only art form capable of projecting the action of warfare as temporal flow and movement. Using words as a medium, writers had few limitations on how they chose to paint this action, and their visions had long covered a wide spectrum. One of the Civil War's most distinctively modern images was expressed by Herman Melville in his poem "A Utilitarian View of the Monitor's Fight." Melville sees the triumph of "plain mechanic power" placing war "Where War belongs—/Among the trades and artisans," depriving it of "passion": "all went on by crank,/Pivot, and screw,/And calculations of caloric." Since "warriors/Are now but operatives," he hopes that "War's made/Less grand than Peace."

The most profoundly deglamorizing images of that war, however, were produced not by literature but directly by technology itself. The industrial processes and scientific knowledge that created technowar had also brought forth a new means of perceiving its devastation. Industrial chemicals, manufactured metal plates, lenses, mirrors, bellows, and actuating mechanisms—all were essential to the new art and craft of photography. Thus the Civil War was the first truly modern war—both in how it was fought and in how it was imaged. The romantic images of warfare projected by earlier visual arts were now radically threatened by images of warfare introduced by photography.

Scores of commercial photographers, seeking authenticity and prof- 5
its, followed the Union armies into battle. Although evidently more than a million photographs of the Civil War were taken, hardly any show actual combat or other exciting action typical of the earlier paintings.[2] The photographers' need to stay close to their cumbersome horse-drawn laboratory wagons usually kept them from the thick of battle, and the collodion wet-plate process, which demanded long exposures, forced them to focus on scenes of stillness rather than action. Among all human subjects, those who stayed most perfectly still for the camera were the dead. Hence Civil War photography, dominated by images of death, inaugurated a grim, profoundly antiromantic realism.

Perhaps the most widely reproduced photo from the war, Timothy O'Sullivan's "A Harvest of Death, Gettysburg," contains numerous

1. See especially Alan Trachtenberg, *Reading American Photographs: Images as History, Mathew Brady to Walker Evans* (New York: Hill and Wang, 1989), p. 74; and William A. Frassanito, *Antietam: The Photographic Legacy of America's Bloodiest Day* (New York: Charles Scribner's Sons, 1978), pp. 27–28.
2. William C. Davis, "Finding the Hidden Images of the Civil War," *Civil War Times Illustrated*, 21 (1982, #2), 9.

corpses of Confederate soldiers, rotting after lying two days in the rain (see *Figure 1*). Stripped of their shoes and with their pockets turned inside out, the bodies stretch into the distance beyond the central corpse, whose mouth gapes gruesomely.

The first of such new images of war were displayed for sale to the public by Mathew Brady at his Broadway gallery in October 1862. Brady entitled his show "The Dead of Antietam." *The New York Times* responded in an awed editorial:

> The living that throng Broadway care little perhaps for the Dead at Antietam, but we fancy they would jostle less carelessly down the great thoroughfare . . . were a few dripping bodies, fresh from the field, laid along the pavement. . . .
>
> Mr. Brady has done something to bring home to us the terrible reality and earnestness of war. If he has not brought bodies and laid them in our dooryards and along the streets, he has done something very like it. At the door of his gallery hangs a little placard, "The Dead of Antietam." Crowds of people are constantly going up the stairs; follow them, and you find them bending over photographic views of that fearful battle-field, taken immediately after the action. . . . You will see hushed, reverent groups standing around these weird copies of carnage, bending down

Figure 1. "A Harvest of Death, Gettysburg," 1863 photograph by Timothy O'Sullivan.

> to look in the pale faces of the dead, chained by the strange spell that dwells in dead men's eyes.[3]

Oliver Wendell Holmes went further in explicating the meaning of the exhibition, which gives "some conception of what a repulsive, brutal, sickening, hideous thing it is, this dashing together of two frantic mobs to which we give the name of armies." He continues: "Let him who wishes to know what war is look at this series of illustrations. These wrecks of manhood thrown together in careless heaps or ranged in ghastly rows for burial were alive but yesterday. . . ."[4]

Nevertheless, three decades after the end of the Civil War the surging forces of militarism and imperialism were reimaging the conflict as a glorious episode in America's history. The disgust, shame, guilt, and deep national divisions that had followed this war—just like those a century later that followed the Vietnam War—were being buried under an avalanche of jingoist culture, the equivalent of contemporary Ramboism, even down to the cult of muscularism promulgated by Teddy Roosevelt.

It was in this historical context that Stephen Crane used realism, then flourishing as a literary mode, to assault just such treacherous views of war. Although *The Red Badge of Courage* is generally viewed as the great classic novel of the Civil War, it can be read much more meaningfully as Crane's response to the romantic militarism that was attempting to erase from the nation's memory the horrifying lessons taught by the war's realities.[5] Crane, not subject to the technological limitations of the slow black-and-white photographs that had brought home glimpses of the war's sordid repulsiveness, was able to image the animal frenzy that masqueraded as heroic combat and even to add color and tiny moving details to his pictures of the dead:

> The corpse was dressed in a uniform that once had been blue but was now faded to a melancholy shade of green. The eyes, staring at the youth, had changed to the dull hue to be seen on the side of a dead fish. The mouth was opened. Its red had changed to an appalling yellow. Over the grey skin of the face ran little ants. One was trundling some sort of a bundle along the upper lip.[6]

3. "Brady's Photographs: Pictures of the Dead at Antietam," *The New York Times*, 20 October 1862.
4. Oliver Wendell Holmes's "Doings of the Sunbeam," *Atlantic Monthly* (July 1863), p. 12.
5. This concept is developed most effectively by Amy Kaplan in "The Spectacle of War in Crane's Revision of History," *New Essays on* The Red Badge of Courage, ed. Lee Clark Mitchell (Cambridge: Cambridge University Press, 1986), pp. 77–108.
6. Stephen Crane, The Red Badge of Courage: *An Episode in the American Civil War*, ed. Henry Binder (New York: Avon Books, 1983), p. 37.

10 Other literary reactions to the new militarism looked even further backward to project images of a future dominated by war. Melville's *Billy Budd,* completed in 1891, envisions this triumph of violence in the aftermath of the American Revolution on the (aptly named) British warship HMS *Bellipotent,* where the best of humanity is hanged to death by the logic of war, the common people are turned into automatons "dispersed to the places allotted them when not at the guns," and the final image is of a sterile, lifeless, inorganic mass of "smooth white marble."[7]

In *A Connecticut Yankee in King Arthur's Court* (1889), Mark Twain recapitulates the development of industrial capitalism and extrapolates its future in a vision of apocalyptic technowar. Hank Morgan and his young disciples have run "secret wires" to dynamite deposits under all their "vast factories, mills, workshops, magazines, etc." and have connected them to a single command button so that nothing can stop them "when we want to blow up our civilization." When Hank does initiate this instantaneous push-button war, "In that explosion all our noble civilization-factories went up in the air and disappeared from the earth." Beyond an electrified fence, the technowarriors have prepared a forty-foot-wide belt of land mines. The first wave of thousands of knights triggers a twentieth-century-style explosion: "As to destruction of life, it was amazing. Moreover, it was beyond estimate. Of course we could not *count* the dead, because they did not exist as individuals, but merely as homogeneous protoplasm, with alloys of iron and buttons."

After Hank and his boys trap the rest of the feudal army inside their electric fence, Hank electrocutes the first batch, a flood is released on the survivors, and the boys man machine guns that "vomit death" into their ranks: "Within ten short minutes after we had opened fire, armed resistance was totally annihilated. . . . Twenty-five thousand men lay dead around us."[8] That number of dead, it is worth noting, matches exactly the total casualties in America's costliest day of war, the battle of Antietam, and thus recalls Brady's exhibition, "The Dead of Antietam." Twain's vision is even more horrific, for the victors themselves are conquered by "the poisonous air bred by those dead thousands." All that remains of this first experiment in industrialized warfare is a desolate landscape pockmarked by craters and covered with unburied, rotting corpses.

Twain's vision of the future implicit in industrial capitalism began

7. H. Bruce Franklin, "From Empire to Empire: *Billy Budd, Sailor,*" in *Herman Melville: Reassessments,* ed. A. Robert Lee (London: Vision Press, 1984), pp. 199–216.
8. Mark Twain, *A Connecticut Yankee in King Arthur's Court,* ed. Bernard L. Stein (Berkeley: University of California Press, 1979), pp. 466–86.

to materialize in the First World War, when armies slaughtered each other on an unprecedented scale, sections of Europe were turned into a wasteland, and weapons of mass destruction first seemed capable of actually destroying civilization. Meanwhile, the scientific, engineering, and organizational progress that had produced the modern machine gun, long-range artillery, poison gas, and fleets of submarines and warplanes had also created a new image-making technology that broke through the limits of still photography. Just as the Civil War was the first to be extensively photographed, the "War to End All Wars" was the first to be extensively imaged in motion pictures.[9]

World War I, of course, generated millions of still photographs, many showing scenes at least as ghastly as the corpse-strewn battlefields of the Civil War, and now there was also authentic documentary film of live action. But for various reasons the most influential photographic images from World War I, though realistic in appearance, displayed not reality but fantasy. Filmmakers who wished to record actual combat were severely restricted by the various governments and military authorities. At the same time, powerful forces were making a historic discovery: the tremendous potential of movies for propaganda and for profits. This was the dawn of twentieth-century image-making.

In the United States the most important photographic images were 15
movies designed to inflame the nation, first to enter the war and then to support it. Probably the most influential was *The Battle Cry of Peace*, a 1915 smash hit that played a crucial role in rousing the public against Germany by showing realistic scenes of the invasion and devastation of America by a rapacious Germanic army. Once the US entered the war, the American public got to view an endless series of feature movies, such as *To Hell with the Kaiser*; *The Kaiser, the Beast of Berlin*; and *The Claws of the Hun*—each outdoing its predecessors in picturing German bestiality. Erich von Stroheim's career began with his portrayal of the archetypal sadistic German officer in films like *The Unbeliever* and *Heart of Humanity*, where in his lust to rape innocent young women he murders anyone who gets in the way—even the crying baby of one intended victim. This genre is surveyed by Larry Wayne Ward, who describes the 1918 Warner Brothers hit *My Four Years in Germany*, which opens with a title card telling the audience they are seeing "Fact Not Fiction":

9. During the Spanish-American War, the Edison Company had recorded some motion pictures of the embarking troops but was unable to obtain any battle footage. Later the company re-created battle scenes in a mountain reservation near Edison's headquarters in Essex County, New Jersey. See "Historian Remembers the Maine, Spain-America Conflict," Newark (NJ) *Star Ledger* 11 February 1992.

> After the brutal conquest of Belgium, German troops are shown slaughtering innocent refugees and tormenting prisoners of war. Near the end of the film one of the German officials boasts that "America Won't Fight," a title which dissolves into newsreel footage of President Wilson and marching American soldiers. Soon American troops are seen fighting their way across the European battlefields. As he bayonets another German soldier, a young American doughboy turns to his companions and says, "I promised Dad I'd get six."[1]

Before the end of World War I, the motion picture had already proved to be a more effective vehicle for romanticizing and popularizing war than the antebellum school of heroic painting that had been partly debunked by Civil War photography. Indeed, the audiences that thronged to *My Four Years in Germany* frequently burned effigies of the kaiser outside the theaters and in some cases turned into angry mobs that had to be dispersed by police.

To restore the glamour of preindustrial war, however, it would take more than glorifying the men fighting on the ground or even the aviators supposedly dueling like medieval knights high above the battlefield. What was necessary to reverse Melville's "utilitarian" view of industrial warfare was the romanticizing of machines of war themselves.

The airplane was potentially an ideal vehicle for this romance. But photographic technology had to develop a bit further to bring home the thrills generated by destruction from the sky, because it needed to be seen *from* the sky, not from the ground where its reality was anything but glamorous. The central figure in America's romance with warplanes (as I have discussed at length elsewhere[2]) was Billy Mitchell, who also showed America and the world how to integrate media imagery with technowar.

In 1921, Mitchell staged a historic event by using bombers to sink captured German warships and turning the action into a media bonanza. His goal was to hit the American public with immediate, nationwide images of the airplane's triumph over the warship. The audacity of this enterprise in 1921 was remarkable. There were no satellites to relay images, and no television; in fact, the first experimental radio broadcast station had begun operation only in November 1920.

20 Back in 1919, Mitchell had given the young photographer George Goddard his own laboratory where, with assistance from Eastman Kodak, Goddard developed high-resolution aerial photography. As soon as Mitchell won the opportunity to bomb the German ships, he

1. Larry Wayne Ward, *The Motion Picture Goes to War: The U.S. Government Film Effort during World War I* (Ann Arbor: UMI Research Press, 1985), pp. 55–56.
2. H. Bruce Franklin, *War Stars: The Superweapon and the American Imagination* (New York: Oxford University Press, 1988), chapter 15.

put Goddard in command of a key unit: a team of aerial photographers provided with eighteen airplanes and a dirigible. Mitchell's instructions were unambiguous: "I want newsreels of those sinking ships in every theater in the country, just as soon as we can get 'em there." This demanded more than mere picture taking. With his flair for public relations, Mitchell explained to Goddard: "Most of all I need you to handle the newsreel and movie people. They're temperamental, and we've got to get all we can out of them."[3] Goddard had to solve unprecedented logistical problems, flying the film first to Langley Field and thence to Bolling Field for pickup by the newsreel people who would take it to New York for development and national distribution. The sinking of each ship, artfully filmed by relays of Goddard's planes, was screened the very next day in big-city theaters across the country.

This spectacular media coup implanted potent images of the warplane in the public mind, and Mitchell himself became an overnight national hero as millions watched the death of great warships on newsreel screens. Mitchell was a prophet. The battleship was doomed. The airplane would rule the world.

America was now much closer to the 1990 media conception of the Gulf War than to Melville's "Utilitarian View of the Monitor's Fight." Melville's vision of technowar as lacking "passion" was becoming antiquated, for what could be more thrilling—even erotic—than aerial war machines? The evidence is strewn throughout modern America: the warplane models assembled by millions of boys and young men during World War II; the thousands of warplane magazines and books filled with glossy photographs that some find as stimulating as those in "men's" magazines; and Hollywood's own warplane romances, such as *Top Gun*—one of the most popular movies of the 1980's—or *Strategic Air Command*, in which Jimmy Stewart's response to his first sight of a B-47 nuclear bomber is, "She's the most beautiful thing I've ever seen in my life."

One of the warplane's great advantages as a vehicle of romance is its distance from its victims. From the aircraft's perspective, even the most grotesque slaughter it inflicts is sufficiently removed so that it can be imaged aesthetically. The aesthetics of aerial bombing in World War II were prefigured in 1937 by Mussolini's son Vittorio, whose ecstasy about his own experience bombing undefended Ethiopian villages was expressed in his image of his victims "bursting out like a rose after I had landed a bomb in the middle of them."[4] These

3. Burke Davis, *The Billy Mitchell Affair* (New York: Random House, 1967), p. 16.
4. *Voli sulle ambe* (Florence, 1937), a book Vittorio Mussolini wrote to convince Italian boys they should all try war, "the most beautiful and complete of all sports." Quoted by Denis Mack Smith, *Mussolini's Roman Empire* (New York: Viking, 1976), p. 75.

aesthetics were consummated at the end of World War II by the mushroom clouds that rose over Hiroshima and Nagasaki.

Bracketed by these images, the aerial bombing of World War II has been most insightfully explored in *Catch-22* by Joseph Heller, a bombardier with sixty combat missions. The novel envisions the political and cultural triumph of fascism through the very means used to defeat it militarily. The turning point in Heller's work is the annihilation of an insignificant antifascist Italian mountain village, an event which allows fascist forces, embodied by US Air Corps officers, to gain total control.[5] The sole purpose of the American bombing of the village is image-making. The novel's General Peckem privately admits that bombing this "tiny undefended village, reducing the whole community to rubble" is "entirely unnecessary," but it will allow him to extend his power over the bombing squadrons. He has convinced them that he will measure their success by "a neat aerial photograph" of their *bomb pattern*—"a term I dreamed up," he confides, that "means nothing." The briefing officer tells the crews:

> Colonel Cathcart wants to come out of this mission with a good clean aerial photograph he won't be ashamed to send through channels. Don't forget that General Peckem will be here for the full briefing, and you know how he feels about bomb patterns.[6]

25 Pictures of bomb patterns were not, of course, the most influential American photographic image-making in World War II. The still photos published in *Life* alone could be the subject of several dissertations, and World War II feature movies about strategic bombing have been discussed at length by myself and many others. Indeed, in 1945 one might have wondered how the camera could possibly play a more important role in war.

The answer came in Vietnam, the first war to be televised directly into tens of millions of homes.[7] Television's glimpses of the war's reality were so horrendous and so influential that these images have been scapegoated as one of the main causes of the United States' defeat. Indeed, the Civil War still photographs of corpses seem innocuous when compared to the Vietnam War's on-screen killings, as well as live-action footage of the bulldozing of human carcasses into mass

5. For extended analyses of the significance of this event, see Franklin, *War Stars*, pp. 123–27, and Clinton Burhans Jr., "Spindrift and the Sea: Structural Patterns and Unifying Elements in *Catch-22*," *Twentieth Century Literature*, 19 (1973), 239–50.
6. Joseph Heller, *Catch-22* (New York: Dell, 1962), pp. 334–37.
7. When the Korean War began in mid-1950, there were fewer than ten million television sets in the United States. Americans' principal visual images of that war came from newsreels shown before feature films in movie theaters and from still photos in magazines.

graves, the napalming of children, and the ravaging of villages by American soldiers.

As appalling as these public images were, however, few had meanings as loathsome as the pictures that serve as the central metaphor of Stephen Wright's novel *Meditations in Green.* The hero of the novel has the job that the author had in Vietnam: he works as a photoanalyst in an intelligence unit whose mission is to aid the torture and assassination campaign known as Operation Phoenix, the ecocidal defoliation campaign originally designated Operation Hades, and the genocidal bombing. His official job as "image interpreter" is to scrutinize reconnaissance films to find evidence of life so that it can be eliminated. Not just humans are targets to be erased by bombing; trees themselves become the enemy. Anyone in the unit who has qualms about such genocide and ecocide is defined—in a revealing term—as a "smudge," thus becoming another target for elimination. The perfect image, it is implied, should have nothing left of the human or the natural. From the air, the unit's own base looks like "a concentration camp or a movie lot." The climax of the novel comes when the base is devastated by an enemy attack intercut with scenes from *Night of the Living Dead,* that ghoulish 1968 vision of America which is simultaneously being screened as entertainment.[8]

One of the most influential and enduring single images from the Vietnam War—certainly the most contested—exploded into the consciousness of millions of Americans in February 1968 when they actually watched, within the comfort of their own homes, as the chief of the Saigon national police executed a manacled NLF prisoner. In a perfectly framed sequence, the notorious General Nguyen Ngoc Loan unholsters a snub-nosed revolver and places its muzzle to the prisoner's right temple. The prisoner's head jolts, a sudden spurt of blood gushes straight out of his right temple, and he collapses in death. The next morning, newspaper readers were confronted with AP photographer Eddie Adams' potent stills of the execution (see *Figure* 2). The grim ironies of the scene were accentuated by the cultural significance of the weapon itself: a revolver, a somewhat archaic handgun, symbolic of the American West.

Precisely one decade later this image, with the roles now reversed, was transformed into the dominant metaphor of a Hollywood production presenting a new version of the Vietnam War: *The Deer Hunter.* This lavishly financed movie, which the New York Film Critics' Circle designated the best English-language film of 1978 and which received four Academy Awards, including Best Picture of 1978, succeeded not only in radically reimaging the war but in transforming prisoners of

8. Stephen Wright, *Meditations in Green* (New York: Bantam, 1984).

Figure 2. General Nguyen Ngoc Loan, head of South Vietnam's police and intelligence, executing a prisoner: 1969 photograph by Eddie Adams.

war (POW's) into central symbols of American manhood for the 1980's and 1990's.

The manipulation of familiar images—some already accruing symbolic power—was blatant, though most critics at the time seemed oblivious to it. The basic technique was to take images of the war that had become deeply embedded in America's consciousness and transform them into their opposites. For example, in the film's first scene in Vietnam, a uniformed soldier throws a grenade into an underground village shelter harboring women and children, and then with his automatic rifle mows down a woman and her baby. Although the scene resembles the familiar TV sequence of GIs in Vietnamese villages (as well as *Life*'s photographs of the My Lai massacre), the soldier turns out to be not American but North Vietnamese. In turn he is killed by a lone guerrilla—who is not a Viet Cong but our Special Forces hero, played by Robert DeNiro. Later, when two men plummet

Figure 3. In *The Deer Hunter* (1978), General Loan's revolver metamorphoses into a North Vietnamese revolver, and his NLF prisoner is replaced by South Vietnamese and US prisoners forced to play Russian roulette.

from a helicopter, the images replicate a familiar telephotographic sequence showing an NLF prisoner being pushed from a helicopter to make other prisoners talk;[9] but the falling men in the movie are American POW's attempting to escape from their murderous North Vietnamese captors.

The structuring metaphor of the film is the Russian roulette that the sadistic Asian Communists force their prisoners to play. The crucial torture scene consists of sequence after sequence of images replicating and replacing the infamous killing of the NLF prisoner by General Nguyen Ngoc Loan. Prisoner after prisoner is hauled out of the tiger cages (which also serve as a substitute image for the tiger cages of the Saigon government) and then forced by the demonic North Vietnamese officer in charge (who always stands to the prisoner's right, our left) to place a revolver to his own right temple. Then the image is framed to eliminate the connection between the prisoner's body and the arm holding the revolver, thus bringing the image

9. "How Helicopter Dumped a Viet Captive to Death," *Chicago Sun-Times*, 29 November 1969; "Death of a Prisoner," *San Francisco Chronicle*, 29 November 1969.

closer to the famous execution image (see *Figure* 3). One sequence even replicates the blood spurting out of the victim's right temple.

The Deer Hunter's manipulation of this particular image to reverse the roles of victim and victimizer was used again and again in the 1980's by other vehicles of the militarization of American culture from movies to comic books. Take, for example, *P.O.W.: The Escape*, an overtly militaristic 1986 POW rescue movie, inspired by *Rambo* and starring David Carradine as superhero. The bestiality of the Asian Communists is here embodied by a North Vietnamese prison-camp commander who executes an American prisoner with a revolver shot to the right temple in a tableau modeled even more precisely than *The Deer Hunter*'s on the original execution of the NLF prisoner in Saigon (see *Figure* 4). Then—just in case viewers missed it—this scene is replayed later as the movie's only flashback.

Toward the end of the 1980's, however, the infamous execution got manipulated incredibly further, actually shifting the role of the most heartless shooter (originally a South Vietnamese official) from the Vietnamese Communists to the photographers themselves! For example, the cover story of the November 1988 issue of the popular comic book *The 'Nam* portrays the photojournalists, both still photographers and TV cameramen, as the real enemies because they had placed the image on the "front page of every newspaper in the states!" The cover

Figure 4. *P.O.W.: The Escape* (1986) transforms the South Vietnamese execution of a prisoner into a North Vietnamese prison commander's murder of a US prisoner.

literally reverses the original image by showing the execution scene from a position behind the participants (*Figure* 5). This offers a frontal view of the photographer, whose deadly camera conceals his face and occupies the exact center of the picture. The prisoner appears merely as an arm, shoulder, and sliver of a body on the left. The only face shown belongs to the chief of the security police, who displays the righteous—even heroic—indignation that has led him to carry out this justifiable revenge against the treacherous actions of the "Viet Cong" pictured in the story. The climactic image (*Figure* 6) is a full page in which the execution scene appears as a reflection in the gigantic lens of the camera above the leering mouth of the photographer, from which comes a bubble with his greedy words, "Keep shooting!

Figure 5. Cover story of the November 1988 issue of *The 'Nam*, glorifying General Nguyen Ngoc Loan and making the photographer into the villain.

Figure 6. *The 'Nam* images the photographer as the shooter—and the camera as the most destructive weapon.

Just keep shooting!" "Shooting" a picture here has become synonymous with murder and treason. In the next panel, two GI's register their shock—not at the execution, but at a TV cameraman focusing on the dead body:

> "Front page of every newspaper in the states!"
> "Geez . . ."

One can hardly imagine a more complete reversal of the acclaim accorded to Civil War photographers for bringing the reality of war and death home to the American people.

The logic of this comic-book militarism, put into practice for each of America's wars since Vietnam, is inescapable: photographers must be allowed to image for the public only what the military deems suitable. Nonmilitary photographers and all journalists were simply banished from the entire war zone during the 1983 invasion of Grenada. Partly as a result of this treatment, the major media accepted a pool system for the 1989 invasion of Panama—and meekly went along with the military's keeping even these selected journalists confined to a US base throughout most of the conflict. (A European reporter who attempted to report directly from the scene was actually shot to death when the military unit sent to arrest him became involved in "friendly fire" with another group of US soldiers.)

The almost complete absence of photographic images was quite convenient for the Grenada and Panama invasions, which were carried out so swiftly and with such minimal military risk that they required no Congressional or public endorsement. And for the first several days after US troops had been dispatched to confront Iraq in August 1990, Secretary of Defense Dick Cheney refused to allow journalists to accompany them. The Pentagon seemed to be operating under the belief that photographic and televised images had helped bring about the US defeat in Vietnam. But for the Gulf War, with its long buildup, its potential for significant casualties, and its intended international and domestic political purposes, *some* effective images proved to be essential.

To control these images, the US government set up pools of selected reporters and photographers, confined them to certain locations, required them to have military escorts when gathering news, established stringent guidelines limiting what could be reported or photographed, and subjected all written copy, photographs, and videotape to strict censorship.[1] Most of those admitted to the pools, it is interesting to note, represented the very newspapers and TV networks that were simultaneously mounting a major campaign to build support for the war. Journalists were forced to depend on military briefings, where they were often fed deliberately falsified information. Immediately after the ground offensive began, all press briefings and pool reports were indefinitely suspended. In a most revealing negation of the achievement of Civil War photography, with its shocking disclosure of the reality of death, the Pentagon banned the press entirely from Dover Air Force Base during the arrival of the bodies of those killed in the war. Responding to an ACLU legal argument that it was attempting to shield the public from disturbing images, the Pentagon replied that it was merely protecting the privacy of grieving relatives.[2]

Although the media were largely denied access to the battlefields, the Gulf War nevertheless gained the reputation of the first "real-time" television war, and the images projected into American homes helped to incite the most passionate war fever since World War II. These screened images ranged from the most traditional to the most innovative modes of picturing America's wars. Even the antiquated icon of the heroic commanding general, missing for about forty years,

1. Everette E. Dennis et al., *The Media at War: The Press and the Persian Gulf Conflict* (New York: Gannett Foundation, 1991), pp. 17–18.
2. Dennis, pp. 21–22.

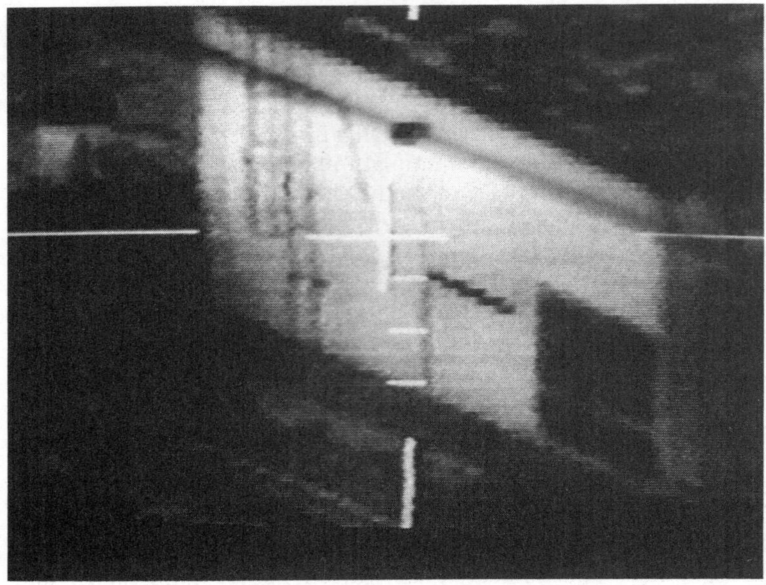

Figure 7. Technowar triumphs in TV sequence of a smart bomb destroying an Iraqi building.

was given new life. Although hardly as striking a figure as the commander in Leutze's *Washington Crossing the Delaware* or the posed picture of General Douglas MacArthur returning to the Philippines during World War II, a public idol took shape in the corpulent form of General Norman Schwarzkopf in his fatigues, boots, and jaunty cap.

But perhaps the most potent images combined techniques pioneered by Billy Mitchell with General Peckem's quest for aerial photos of perfect bomb patterns, the medium of television, and the technological capabilities of the weapons themselves. After all, since one of the main goals of the warmakers was to create the impression of a "clean" technowar—almost devoid of human suffering and death, conducted with surgical precision by wondrous mechanisms—why not project the war from the point of view of the weapons? And so the most thrilling images were transmitted directly by the laser-guidance systems of missiles and by those brilliant creations, "smart" bombs. Fascinated and excited, tens of millions of Americans stared at their screens, sharing the experience of these missiles and bombs unerringly guided by the wonders of American technology to a target identified by a narrator as an important military installation. The generation raised in video arcades and on Nintendo could hardly be more satisfied. The target got closer and closer, larger and larger (*Figure* 7). And then everything ended with the explosion. There were no bloated human bodies, as in the photographs of the battlefields of Antietam and Gettysburg—and none of the agony of the burned and wounded glimpsed on television relays from Vietnam. There was just nothing at all. In this magnificent triumph of technowar, America's images of its wars had seemingly reached perfection.

Kildare Dobbs

GALLIPOLI

Most visitors to the First World War battlefields and cemeteries of Gallipoli are Australians or New Zealanders who want to see the place where their countrymen died in such numbers. And perhaps the Australian movie *Gallipoli* has given them the idea that this catastrophic campaign in 1915 was entirely an ANZAC (Australia New Zealand Army Corps) affair. But the spearhead of the operation was the British 29th Division, made up of regular army units, among them a number of famous Irish regiments. It was because of one young officer in the 1st Battalion, the Royal Dublin Fusiliers, that I came to Gallipoli that gray morning in early spring.

My middle names, Robert and Eric, commemorate two uncles killed in the First World War before I was born. Lieutenant Robert Bernard of the Dublins was one of them. He fell on the second day of the assault on the Gallipoli peninsula in one of its most desperate battles.

I could recall little of the facts when I arrived.

Next morning I visited the office of the Commonwealth War Graves Commission, where a pleasant Turkish assistant had just arrived. Soft-spoken, plump, of fiery complexion, he gave me a glass of tea and a stack of tattered printed lists of the fallen—about a hundred thousand names. I did not succeed in finding that of Robert Bernard. Nor could the Englishman in charge help me when he arrived.

I found an agency called Troyanzac and asked the proprietor to ar- 5
range a taxi to the Helles monument at the entrance to the Dardanelles on the Gallipoli peninsula. I would not need a guide. Two young couples, Australian and New Zealander, were also taking a Gallipoli tour, but they were going to Anzac cove, a different area from

From *Anatolian Suite* (1989).

the one I sought. I would have to go alone and it would cost about thirty American dollars. Mr. Husseyin, the proprietor, made a little speech before we set out. The British, he said, had undertaken the Gallipoli campaign in 1915 in an attempt to force a passage through the Dardanelles, capture Constantinople and open a new front against the Central Powers. British and Commonwealth troops had fought gallantly for many months, but the fierce resistance of the Turks under Mustafa Kemal had in the end defeated them. At least 36,000 men on each side had been killed.

Mr. Husseyin, a small, tweedy gentleman with a fine mustache, looked suitably melancholy as he said this. I noticed his gleaming shoes, perhaps a tribute to men who had died with their boots clean. "Their name," he added sombrely, "liveth for evermore." And I thought that was one of the lies of history, that the dead would be remembered, a lie to comfort the next-of-kin. I would be the first of Robbie Bernard's kin to come to this remote place.

After a pause Husseyin Bey told us that we would cross the Dardanelles in a private launch. We were to follow his assistant now to the wharf.

The launch turned out to be an ancient, private-enterprise ferry. The official one went to Eceabat. Ours crossed directly to Kilitbahir, a medieval Ottoman fortress built by Mehmet II, the conqueror of Constantinople. From the upper deck I could see a Turkish war memorial scarring a hillside opposite. Akin to those prehistoric images cut into the turf of the British downs, this was a white figure on a gray ground, a soldier with one arm thrown out toward a poem in Turkish. The words were translated in my guidebook, no doubt losing something in the process: "Stop O Passer By . . ." and then something to the effect that this soil was where the heart of a nation throbbed. The poet's unlucky name was Onan, though verse so publicly exposed on a hillside could hardly be called a solitary vice.

On the wharf my yellow taxi was waiting. The driver spoke a few words of English. He had carefully carpeted the floor of his car with pieces of clean cardboard, to protect it from muddy feet.

10 As we headed toward open sea along the Gallipoli shore I saw many ships passing through the Dardanelles, to and from Istanbul and the Black Sea. The sky was gray and overcast. My spirits were raised by the sight of a large school of dolphins leaping through the waves near the shore. I remembered Yeats's[1] line in the poem "Byzantium":

> That dolphin-torn, that gong-tormented sea.

1. William Butler Yeats (1865–1939), Irish poet and dramatist whose Irish nationalism was one of the central elements of his work.

Symbols of rebirth, I recalled, dolphins were among the earliest images in Christian art, ferrying spirits over death's river. Yeats had never been in these waters except in imagination. He got his gongs and dolphins from books. Yet, such is the power of genius, here they were in this haunted channel. On the far side, the land was flat along the Asian shore, easier country for an attacker to capture, reason enough why the strategic city of Troy, buried for centuries a few miles from the Hellespont, had fallen at least seven times. The Turks' German advisors had expected the British to make their assault over there; and in fact a French contingent did attack Kumkale, as diversion from the main thrust, suffering heavy casualties before they withdrew.

Soon we turned inland where the ground was high. Orchards and broom were in blossom. There were olive groves and stands of pine and myrtle, and a few patches of green wheat or barley. This was April, the same month in which the campaign had begun. The grass was green, spring was reawakening the land with daisies, poppies and anemones. We passed shepherds with flocks of shivering sheep and goats, a village, two or three small cemeteries. At last we came to the Helles Memorial, at the south western point of the Gallipoli peninsula.

This rough stone obelisk, designed by Sir John Burnet, commemorates the Gallipoli campaign itself, together with the names of some twenty thousand dead whose bodies were never found and a roll call of the ships and regiments that took part. Among the latter I found the 6th Royal Irish Rifles, the 5th Connaught Rangers, the 6th Leinster Regiment, the 6th and 7th Royal Munster Fusiliers, the 6th and 7th Royal Dublin Fusiliers, the 5th and 6th Inniskilling Fusiliers, the 5th and 6th Royal Irish Fusiliers. Ireland itself had forgotten the military virtue of these soldiers and regiments, whose battle honors were part of the imperial myth. The official Irish myth had eclipsed them. Gallipoli, 1915, was overshadowed by the Easter Rising of 1916.[2]

A little to my right there was a lighthouse, slightly to the left the ruins of a redoubt where a couple of big guns had been blown off their mountings, and farther off along the beach the wreck of a fortress and a village, clustered around its minaret.

"What is the name of that village?" I asked the driver. 15

After some shouting and gesticulating I made myself understood. He told me the place was called Sedd-el-Bahr.

Vaguely I recalled having been told that that was the place where Uncle Robbie had been killed. Was there another cemetery down there? I asked. The driver led me to the edge of a bluff and pointed.

2. Republican insurrection in Ireland against the British government there, which began on Easter Monday, April 24, 1916, in Dublin.

There it was, below us, just inshore from the beach. This was V Beach Cemetery.

Telling the driver to wait for me, I walked down a rough, dirt road, passing a shepherd and some very dirty sheep on the way. *"Merhaba!"* I said. The man gave a grunt.

The cemetery was beautifully kept, with trim lawn and flowering judas trees. Some instinct led me straight to the marker. "Believed to be buried in this cemetery," I read. "Lieutenant Robert Bernard, Royal Dublin Fusiliers. 26 April 1915. Age 23. Dearly loved son of Most Rev. J. H. Bernard D.D. and Maud his wife."

At his son's death, Dr. Bernard was bishop of Ossory, residing in Kilkenny, thus Right Rev. Later that year he became archbishop of Dublin, distinguished as Most Rev.

I stared for a while at the beach, at the cliffs on the left, the hill behind it and the fortress on the right, fixing them in my memory. I took photographs despite the uninteresting light.

So that now, weeks later, I am able to see in my mind the desperate fighting and the horror that took place here in April 1915. I can do so because Dr. Bernard in his grief brought all the weight of his meticulous scholarship to bear on the problem of finding out how his son died. And he used his access to the inner councils of empire to collect the evidence. It is all here, in a thick album in my possession, along with every letter Robbie Bernard wrote to his parents in the entire course of his short life. Only three letters are withheld, Dr. Bernard notes, and those contain nothing dishonorable.

Men in the front line, at the cutting edge of battle, are not aware of the big picture. They know only what confronts them. They know their own unit's objectives, and as much of the general plan as their commanders think they need to understand. Robbie Bernard did not live to see the failure of the whole campaign, but the staff had not deceived the fighting units about what faced them. Historians see that the whole thing was a muddle, a project backed by young Winston Churchill (then first lord of the admiralty) that was never adequately thought through by the admiralty or the war office. The Royal Navy had failed to blast a passage through the Dardanelles on March 18. All they had achieved, apart from the loss of three capital ships, was to put the enemy on notice that they would be attacked again, so that the Turks, guided by their German advisers, were able to fortify the beaches and dig in.

The Royal Dublin Fusiliers were to be shock troops of the Covering Force, that is, among the units detailed to capture the beaches at Cape Helles and their defences, and hold them while the main body of the army came ashore. The Dublins were an elite regiment of Irishmen. The 1st Battalion, until its disbandment in 1922, was one of the oldest units in the British army, raised in 1646 and assigned to the East India Company as the Madras Fusiliers; the 2nd Battalion, raised in 1662, became the Bombay Fusiliers when the port was ceded to the Company.

“Clive[3] led you to Arcot and Plassey,” King George V told them as 25
he received their colors at disbandment; “Eyre Coote to Wandewash; Forde to Condore. Your history is the history of the early British dominance in India. . . .”

As the spearhead of the 29th Division the 1st Dublins and 1st Munsters were to attack V Beach at dawn, April 25, after heavy bombardment of the defences by the big guns of the Royal Navy. They were to seize the beach, capture and hold the hill behind it and the village of Sedd-el-Bahr with its fortress. An Englishman who met them before the attack described them as “typical paddies,” long-service professionals for whom war was a big joke. Certainly they were a cheerful lot, officers no less than the men.

On April 12, Robbie Bernard wrote a note in pencil to his parents. He was annoyed with the Senior Service (the navy): “They seem to have done absolutely nothing and if they were not so infernally jealous of our Service they would have called us in long ago and finished things off. Now, when our adversaries have had time to get things together we come in.” Yet on April 22 he wrote in his diary—the last entry: “Hurrah! Off today. At least we have left the harbour.”

Robbie had joined the regiment in March 1912, after passing out of Sandhurst Royal Military College. A photograph shows him in full dress uniform, scarlet tunic with gold bullion epaulets, blue facings and trews,[4] a magenta sash, sword and heavy bearskin hat. Six feet in height, athletic in build, he had blue eyes, reddish mustache and hair parted in the middle. His letters reveal an affectionate character, without intellectual leanings, perhaps somewhat oppressed by the desire to please his scholarly father. His father’s brief sketch supports this view.

“He was a very small baby,” Dr. Bernard wrote, “but grew into a powerfully built man of six feet high. He was a jolly, cheerful child—much fonder of games than of books, as he continued to be throughout his life. But he would work hard, as he proved when he read for the army. He was always a good trier (as his teachers said) and ‘did his best.’ ” One of the boy’s earliest letters begins, “Dear father How are you I doing my best to please you.”

After schooling at Arnold House in Wales (where Evelyn Waugh 30

3. Robert Clive (1725–1774), the celebrated British general and statesman whose victories in India helped achieve Great Britain’s control of India.
4. From an old Gaelic word, *trews* means “trousers,” more specifically close-fitting ones still sometimes worn by some Scottish regiments.

was to teach) and at Marlborough, Robbie took three tries at the army examination before he succeeded. He had served in Ludlow, Shropshire, where he fell in love with a girl called Eva Macaulay; and then in India and Egypt. His father hoped to get him transferred to the Indian army, which offered better pay than the imperial service, and where his uncle Colonel Herbert Bernard had kept a place for him in the 45th (Rattray's) Sikhs, the illustrious regiment he commanded. These plans were derailed by the world war, in which not only poor Robbie fell, but Uncle Herbie as well, leading his men, Irish this time, at the Somme.

Back in England, in January 1915, he found that Eva was tired of waiting for him. "She won't climb down and I won't so there's an end of the matter," he told his parents, "—sickening I call it." He left her his diaries, watches and a small camera. There is no picture of her in the album.

Two friends of Robbie's survived to tell the story of the landing on Sunday, April 25, at V Beach, described by Lieutenant Desmond O'-Hara as "a small sandy bay about 200 yards long, very like the Silver Sand at Wicklow; it was commanded by high ground all round, and into this the ships poured such shellfire, that you would never believe a living thing could survive it for a minute."

O'Hara's company was in a tramp steamer, the *River Clyde*, which had had doors cut in her sides through which the troops could disembark when she ran aground on the beach. The rest of the 1st Dublins, in pith helmets and khaki, and loaded down with heavy packs, ammunition and iron rations, were in cutters towed by pinnaces. Dawn was breaking as the thunder of the naval guns suddenly stopped. There was an ominous silence as the tows neared the beach. Some of the men must have hoped that the bombardment had knocked out all resistance.

They were within a few yards of the shore when a hurricane of fire from rifles, maxim-guns and pom-poms[5] tore into the crowded boats. Within seconds about half of the first wave of Dublins was killed or wounded. In a letter to his mother O'Hara wrote, "The whole of the high ground round was honeycombed with the enemy's trenches, and they waited till the boats which were crammed full got about five yards from the shore when they let drive at them. . . . Numbers of men were killed in the boats, others as they waded ashore, and more on the sand before they could take cover behind a sandbank some twelve or fifteen yards from the shore."

Today the sandbank is simply a low scarp marking the highest point of spring tides.

5. Maxim-guns and pom-poms are names of quick-firing, water-cooled machine guns invented by Sir Hiram S. Maxim.

Lieutenant-Colonel R. A. Rooth, commanding the battalion, was killed as he stepped ashore with his men. His second-in-command, Major E. Fetherstonhaugh, was mortally wounded before he could leave his boat. Captain G. M. Dunlop "just managed to crawl into the sand and died there. Poor young [Lieutenant R. V. C.] Corbet was horribly wounded in the boat, and died an hour later, in awful pain, I am afraid. [Captain and Adjutant W. F.] Higginson was able to get under cover, but put his head up and was killed. . . . [Captain D. V. F.] Anderson was shot through the body and killed almost instantly." Second Lieutenants Maffet and Walters were wounded, as was Lieutenant Lanigan O'Keeffe, a particular friend of Robbie's who had only just rejoined his unit after recovering from serious wounds suffered in France.

O'Keeffe described his ordeal to his sister in a letter written from a hospital ship May 3, 1915: "Well, here I am on my back again, having been whacked in both legs almost as soon as the show started. . . . We had to land from open boats on the shore of a small bay under fierce fire from either side and in front.

"Tremendous numbers of our fellows were killed or wounded even before the boats grounded, and then it was another 50 yards or so to the shore.

"They got me twice between the boat and the shore, but I was able to struggle ashore and into a more or less safe spot where I remained all that day and night and half the next day before being taken off by the ambulance people. No fault of theirs at all as we didn't drive the enemy from the cliffs just over my head until the next morning, and they couldn't do much by day, as our friends have a happy knack of firing at stretcher parties. I don't feel strong enough to describe that 30 hours minutely just yet. Suffice it to say it was extremely unpleasant.

"Poor old Robbie Bernard was killed on the morning of the 2nd day 40
(Monday), I believe and hope instantaneously. Poor old lad—there were few better in every way on this earth."

Somehow Robbie Bernard had survived the carnage of the first, terrible day. The men in the tramp steamer were so cut up as they tried to sally from the doors into boats that the attempt to land them was postponed till dark. O'Hara wrote: "I got our company ashore about 12 o'clock that night. Next morning we attacked a small village [Sedd-el-Bahr] to clear the snipers out of it. Bernard was killed by a hand grenade." But O'Hara had not witnessed this, and it was to be corrected by Sergeant-Major George Baker of Robbie's company, who saw what actually happened. In the horror of battle men were none too sure of what was going on.

Among the soldiers Dr. Bernard wrote to in his quest for information was a private in the Dublins who had been wounded. His letter gives some idea of the confusion: "1st-6-1915. Dear Sir in answer to your letter as regards the death of your son I could not tell you what he was doeing when he got shot for the last time I seen him was on the night of the 25 that is the day before he got shot but I think he was in charge of his company or the 26 as his capation got wounded the first day but on the 26 we made a bayonet charge on the front and great number of officers fell in the charge as they where all in front of there companies. Dear Sir I am very sorry I can not give you very much information about the brave officer. Pte. R. McGillin 1st Royal Dublin Fusiliers Clarendon House Keneton."

The bayonet charge referred to was carried out by the shattered remnant of the Dublins and the Munsters. They captured the hill inland from the beach, a desperate exploit that more than one commentator called glorious. "One of the most magnificent deeds of the whole war," said the French General Gouraud, who witnessed it. War correspondents took pride in it as a feat of "British" arms.

The Dublins lost twenty-one officers in the two days of fighting, and more than two-thirds of the rank and file. Sergeant-Major Baker reported the death of Robbie Bernard: "Lieutenant Bernard fell too bravely leading a charge through the village." That was how Baker recalled it from a military hospital on May 30. On June 3 he wrote in more detail: "Y company was ordered to go through the village of Seddul Bahr which was rather strongly held, but it had to be cleared and we were getting weaker and the men dubious of doing it, when Lieut. Bernard led the rush to their positions which cleared them out, but both he and Lieut. Andrews were shot dead at point-blank range by rifle fire, for he led the rush right up to the house without trying to take cover."

45 Dr. Bernard's inquiries would continue. On May 1 a blizzard of telegrams had descended on Dublin and the southern Irish counties, each with its shocking bulletin. One of them was delivered around nine A.M. to the Palace, Kilkenny, the gray mansion that stands next to St. Canice's Cathedral and its ancient round tower. Robbie's mother dashed off a note to her sister Alice: "I know how you will grieve with us when I tell you our darling Robbie was killed on the 25th—The cruel wire has just come, it seems quite unbearable, your loving Nan." Addressed to the Bishop of Ossory, the wire, scribbled in pencil, said, "Deeply regret to inform you that Lieutenant R. Bernard R Dublin Fusiliers is reported from Alexandria to have been killed in action 25th April Lord Kitchener expresses his sympathy. Secy War Office." It is noticeable that the date of death is wrong in this official notification, an error that was repeated in newspaper notices, and even in a regimental history.

Early in December 1915 Dr. Bernard was able to interview Baker in person about his son: "He saw him killed. It was quite instantaneous. Baker says that Robert was not in any way foolhardy. What gave rise to this suggestion probably was this: Robert, being in command, should (in theory) have kept behind and not exposed himself. But the thing was very dangerous, and the men were doubtful. If Robert had said 'Go on' and not 'Come on,' the men might have hesitated. He had crept up to the corner of the village street with his men, and was peering about with his revolver out. He saw a Turk and fired at him. But the Turk had already fired, and that was the end. No pain, for the Sergeant saw him hours afterwards and there were no signs of struggle or movement at all. He was hit twice—in the shoulder and behind the ear . . . I am thankful. It could not have been more merciful, or more gallant."

Lieutenant O'Hara, who was killed in August of that year, was awarded the Distinguished Service Order for his courage and competence. After Robbie's death the Turks were driven out of Sedd-el-Bahr, and in the afternoon the "Dubsters" carried their other objective, the hill behind the village. "When the Turks had been driven off," O'Hara wrote, "we entrenched for the night, and had a few hours rest next day. Then, on the following day, we had a tremendous battle, and gained four miles of land, and next morning attacked again with disastrous results. The French gave way on the right, and the whole division retired in disorder—a very little more, and it would have been a rout. It was an awful time, and at the end I was the only officer left in the regiment. The Turks made no attempt to follow up their advantage, and we were able to dig in. We remained there for two nights, and on the third the Turks advanced, 20,000 strong, and tried to break through the line. The fight went on from 10.30 at night till 5 o'c next morning—a desperate fight the whole time. My regiment alone got through 150,000 rounds, and they were only 360 strong. The Turks were simply driven on to the barbed wire in front of the trenches by the German officers, and shot down by the score. They must have lost thousands. The fighting is of the most desperate kind—very little quarter on either side. One wounded German officer was found just in front of our trenches when day broke, and was instantly riddled by bullets. The men are absolutely mad to get at them, as they mutilate our wounded when they catch them. For the first three nights I did not have a wink of sleep, and actually fell asleep once during the big night attack. We had no food for about 36 hours after landing, as we were fighting incessantly. There were only 1600 left in the brigade out of 4000. I have only had my boots off once since landing." It was now May 1.

Thanks to the tenacity of the Dublins and the Munsters, and of the Royal Lancashire Fusiliers on an adjacent beach, the invading army was ashore by the next day. The failure to break out of the beachhead was in the end fatal to the enterprise. Ignorance of topography, even of geography, seems to have been a failing of Churchill's. In the Second World War, he would speak of "the soft underbelly of Europe," referring to an area that presents an almost unbroken barrier of mountains.

According to a letter from Captain A. W. Molony, Bernard's company commander, who was wounded the first day, "The Turks fought extremely well, and hung on with the greatest tenacity. They made very clever use of their machine guns, which were very well concealed and did a lot of damage. Our losses were terribly heavy."

50 Eventual victory at Gallipoli gave the Turks, under Mustafa Kemal, a new confidence. For them it was the first of many ordeals on the blood-soaked road to a new nation. The virus of nationalism which had eaten away the Ottoman Empire was to create the Republic of Turkey, and to make Kemal the first of the twentieth-century dictators and the founding hero of his country.

And now, some seventy-three springs later, I see in my mind, not the quiet and remote beach where the Aegean enters the Dardanelles and the judas blossom trembles in the breeze, but the inferno of 1915 where Irishmen died gallantly in a vain cause with friends and countrymen.

Under Robbie Bernard's photo, his father has written: "*Qui ante diem periit sed miles, sed pro patria.*"[6]

Gallipoli is today a national park, but Turkish country people live there. In spring and winter when visitors come there is a little money to be made selling souvenirs or driving taxis. One enterprising villager has even built a tiny motel on V Beach.

The day I went to Cape Helles I was the only visitor, not only at the British memorial but also at the colossal Turkish one, whose principal merit is sheer magnitude and visibility from far off. And the small group from down under at Anzac cove was there largely because it was the scene of a famous movie. The world of shadows is more real than that of memory or history.

55 And in the afternoon I would take a minibus to the site of ancient Troy, surely because it was the scene of a famous poem called the *Iliad.*[7]

6. "Who died before his time, but as a soldier, and for his country," part of a line taken from Sir Henry Newbolt (1862–1938), *The Island Race, Clifton Chapel.*

7. Greek epic poem (eighth century B.C.?) attributed to Homer that in twenty-four books of dactylic hexameter verse, details the events of the few days near the end of the Trojan War.

Hannah Arendt

DENMARK AND THE JEWS

At the Wannsee Conference,[1] Martin Luther, of the Foreign Office, warned of great difficulties in the Scandinavian countries, notably in Norway and Denmark. (Sweden was never occupied, and Finland, though in the war on the side of the Axis, was one country the Nazis never even approached on the Jewish question. This surprising exception of Finland, with some two thousand Jews, may have been due to Hitler's great esteem for the Finns, whom perhaps he did not want to subject to threats and humiliating blackmail.) Luther proposed postponing evacuations from Scandinavia for the time being, and as far as Denmark was concerned, this really went without saying, since the country retained its independent government, and was respected as a neutral state, until the fall of 1943, although it, along with Norway, had been invaded by the German Army in April, 1940. There existed no Fascist or Nazi movement in Denmark worth mentioning, and therefore no collaborators. In Norway, however, the Germans had been able to find enthusiastic supporters; indeed, Vidkun Quisling, leader of the pro-Nazi and anti-Semitic Norwegian party, gave his name to what later became known as a "quisling government." The bulk of Norway's seventeen hundred Jews were stateless, refugees from Germany; they were seized and interned in a few lightning operations in October and November, 1942. When Eichmann's office ordered their deportation to Auschwitz, some of Quisling's own men resigned their government posts. This may not have come as a surprise to Mr. Luther and the Foreign Office, but what was much more serious, and certainly totally unexpected, was that Sweden immediately offered asylum, and even Swedish nationality, to all who were persecuted. Dr. Ernst von Weizsäcker, Undersecretary of State of the Foreign Office, who received the proposal, refused to discuss it, but the offer helped nevertheless. It is always relatively easy to get out of a country illegally, whereas it is nearly impossible to enter the place of refuge without permission and to dodge the immigration authorities. Hence, about nine hundred people, slightly more than half of the small Norwegian community, could be smuggled into Sweden.

It was in Denmark, however, that the Germans found out how fully justified the Foreign Office's apprehensions had been. The story of

From *Eichmann in Jerusalem: A Report on the Banality of Evil* (1963).

1. A meeting of German officials on "the Jewish question."

the Danish Jews is *sui generis*, and the behavior of the Danish people and their government was unique among all the countries in Europe—whether occupied, or a partner of the Axis, or neutral and truly independent. One is tempted to recommend the story as required reading in political science for all students who wish to learn something about the enormous power potential inherent in non-violent action and in resistance to an opponent possessing vastly superior means of violence. To be sure, a few other countries in Europe lacked proper "understanding of the Jewish question," and actually a majority of them were opposed to "radical" and "final" solutions. Like Denmark, Sweden, Italy, and Bulgaria proved to be nearly immune to anti-Semitism, but of the three that were in the German sphere of influence, only the Danes dared speak out on the subject to their German masters. Italy and Bulgaria sabotaged German orders and indulged in a complicated game of double-dealing and double-crossing, saving their Jews by a tour de force of sheer ingenuity, but they never contested the policy as such. That was totally different from what the Danes did. When the Germans approached them rather cautiously about introducing the yellow badge, they were simply told that the King would be the first to wear it, and the Danish government officials were careful to point out that anti-Jewish measures of any sort would cause their own immediate resignation. It was decisive in this whole matter that the Germans did not even succeed in introducing the vitally important distinction between native Danes of Jewish origin, of whom there were about sixty-four hundred, and the fourteen hundred German Jewish refugees who had found asylum in the country prior to the war and who now had been declared stateless by the German government. This refusal must have surprised the Germans no end, since it appeared so "illogical" for a government to protect people to whom it had categorically denied naturalization and even permission to work. (Legally, the prewar situation of refugees in Denmark was not unlike that in France, except that the general corruption in the Third Republic's civil services enabled a few of them to obtain naturalization papers, through bribes or "connections," and most refugees in France could work illegally, without a permit. But Denmark, like Switzerland, was no country *pour se débrouiller.*[2]) The Danes, however, explained to the German officials that because the stateless refugees were no longer German citizens, the Nazis could not claim them without Danish assent. This was one of the few cases in which statelessness turned out to be an asset, although it was of course not statelessness per se that saved the Jews but, on the contrary, the fact that the Danish government had decided to protect them. Thus, none of the preparatory

2. For wangling—using bribery to circumvent bureaucratic regulations.

moves, so important for the bureaucracy of murder, could be carried out, and operations were postponed until the fall of 1943.

What happened then was truly amazing; compared with what took place in other European countries, everything went topsy-turvey. In August, 1943—after the German offensive in Russia had failed, the Afrika Korps had surrendered in Tunisia, and the Allies had invaded Italy—the Swedish government canceled its 1940 agreement with Germany which had permitted German troops the right to pass through the country. Thereupon, the Danish workers decided that they could help a bit in hurrying things up; riots broke out in Danish shipyards, where the dock workers refused to repair German ships and then went on strike. The German military commander proclaimed a state of emergency and imposed martial law, and Himmler thought this was the right moment to tackle the Jewish question, whose "solution" was long overdue. What he did not reckon with was that—quite apart from Danish resistance—the German officials who had been living in the country for years were no longer the same. Not only did General von Hannecken, the military commander, refuse to put troops at the disposal of the Reich plenipotentiary, Dr. Werner Best; the special S.S. units (*Einsatz-kommandos*) employed in Denmark very frequently objected to "the measures they were ordered to carry out by the central agencies"—according to Best's testimony of Nuremberg. And Best himself, an old Gestapo man and former legal adviser to Heydrich, author of a then famous book on the police, who had worked for the military government in Paris to the entire satisfaction of his superiors, could not longer be trusted, although it is doubtful that Berlin ever learned the extent of his unreliability. Still, it was clear from the beginning that things were not going well, and Eichmann's office sent one of its best men to Denmark—Rolf Günther, whom no one had ever accused of not possessing the required "ruthless toughness." Günther made no impression on his colleagues in Copenhagen, and now von Hannecken refused even to issue a decree requiring all Jews to report for work.

Best went to Berlin and obtained a promise that all Jews from Denmark would be sent to Theresienstadt[3] regardless of their category—a very important concession, from the Nazis' point of view. The night of October 1 was set for their seizure and immediate departure—ships were ready in the harbor—and since neither the Danes nor the Jews nor the German troops stationed in Denmark could be relied on to help, police units arrived from Germany for a door-to-door search. At the last moment, Best told them that they were not permitted to break into apartments, because the Danish police might then interfere, and

3. A camp for certain classes of prisoners who were to receive special treatment.

they were not supposed to fight it out with the Danes. Hence they could seize only those Jews who voluntarily opened their doors. They found exactly 477 people, out of a total of more then 7,800, at home and willing to let them in. A few days before the date of doom, a German shipping agent, Georg F. Duckwitz, having probably been tipped off by Best himself, had revealed the whole plan to Danish government officials, who, in turn, had hurriedly informed the heads of the Jewish community. They, in marked contrast to Jewish leaders in other countries, had then communicated the news openly in the synagogues on the occasion of the New Year services. The Jews had just time enough to leave their apartments and go into hiding, which was very easy in Denmark, because, in the words of the judgment, "all sections of the Danish people, from the King down to simple citizens," stood ready to receive them.

5 They might have remained in hiding until the end of the war if the Danes had not been blessed with Sweden as a neighbor. It seemed reasonable to ship the Jews to Sweden, and this was done with the help of the Danish fishing fleet. The cost of transportation for people without means—about a hundred dollars per person—was paid largely by wealthy Danish citizens, and that was perhaps the most astounding feat of all, since this was a time when Jews were paying for their own deportation, when the rich among them were paying fortunes for exit permits (in Holland, Slovakia, and, later, in Hungary) either by bribing the local authorities or by negotiating "legally" with the S.S., who accepted only hard currency and sold exit permits, in Holland, to the tune of five or ten thousand dollars per person. Even in places where Jews met with genuine sympathy and a sincere willingness to help, they had to pay for it, and the chances poor people had of escaping were nil.

It took the better part of October to ferry all the Jews across the five to fifteen miles of water that separates Denmark from Sweden. The Swedes received 5,919 refugees, of whom at least 1,000 were of German origin, 1,310 were half-Jews, and 686 were non-Jews married to Jews. (Almost half the Danish Jews seem to have remained in the country and survived the war in hiding.) The non-Danish Jews were better off than ever before, they all received permission to work. The few hundred Jews whom the German police had been able to arrest were shipped to Theresienstadt. They were old or poor people, who either had not received the news in time or had not been able to comprehend its meaning. In the ghetto, they enjoyed greater privileges than any other group because of the never-ending "fuss" made about them by Danish institutions and private persons. Forty-eight persons died, a figure that was not particularly high, in view of the average age of the group. When everything was over, it was the considered opinion of Eichmann that "for various reasons the action against the Jews in Denmark has been a failure," whereas the curious Dr. Best declared that "the objective of the operation was not to seize a great number of Jews but to clean Denmark of Jews, and this objective has now been achieved."

Politically and psychologically, the most interesting aspect of this incident is perhaps the role played by the German authorities in Denmark, their obvious sabotage of orders from Berlin. It is the only case we know of in which the Nazis met with *open* native resistance, and the result seems to have been that those exposed to it changed their minds. They themselves apparently no longer looked upon the extermination of a whole people as a matter of course. They had met resistance based on principle, and their "toughness" had melted like butter in the sun, they had even been able to show a few timid beginnings of genuine courage. That the ideal of "toughness," except, perhaps, for a few half-demented brutes, was nothing but a myth of self-deception, concealing a ruthless desire for conformity at any price, was clearly revealed at the Nuremberg Trials, where the defendants accused and betrayed each other and assured the world that they "had always been against it" or claimed, as Eichmann was to do, that their best qualities had been "abused" by their superiors. (In Jerusalem, he accused "those in power" of having abused his "obedience." "The subject of a good government is lucky, the subject of a bad government is unlucky. I had no luck.") The atmosphere had changed, and although most of them must have known that they were doomed, not a single one of them had the guts to defend the Nazi ideology. Werner Best claimed at Nuremberg that he had played a complicated double role and that it was thanks to him that the Danish officials had been warned of the impending catastrophe; documentary evidence showed, on the contrary, that he himself had proposed the Danish operation in Berlin, but he explained that this was all part of the game. He was extradited to Denmark and there condemned to death, but he appealed the sentence, with surprising results; because of "new evidence," his sentence was commuted to five years in prison, from which he was released soon afterward. He must have been able to prove to the satisfaction of the Danish court that he really had done his best.

George Woodcock

THE TYRANNY OF THE CLOCK

In no characteristic is existing society in the West so sharply distinguished from the earlier societies, whether of Europe or the East, than in its conception of time. To the ancient Chinese or Greek, to the Arab herdsman or Mexican peon of today, time is represented by the cyclic processes of nature, the alternation of day and night, the passage from season to season. The nomads and farmers measured and still measure their day from sunrise to sunset, and their year in terms of seedtime and harvest, of the falling leaf and the ice thawing on the lakes and rivers. The farmer worked according to the elements, the craftsman for as long as he felt it necessary to perfect his product. Time was seen as a process of natural change, and men were not concerned in its exact measurement. For this reason civilizations highly developed in other respects had the most primitive means of measuring time: the hour glass with its trickling sand or dripping water, the sun dial, useless on a dull day, and the candle or lamp whose unburnt remnant of oil or wax indicated the hours. All these devices were approximate and inexact, and were often rendered unreliable by the weather or the personal laziness of the tender. Nowhere in the ancient or mediæval world were more than a tiny minority of men concerned with time in the terms of mathematical exactitude.

Modern, western man, however, lives in a world which runs according to the mechanical and mathematical symbols of clock time. The clock dictates his movements and inhibits his actions. The clock turns time from a process of nature into a commodity that can be measured and bought and sold like soap or sultanas. And because, without some means of exact time keeping, industrial capitalism could never have developed and could not continue to exploit the workers, the clock represents an element of mechanical tyranny in the lives of modern men more potent than any individual exploiter or than any other machine. It is therefore valuable to trace the historical process by which the clock influenced the social development of modern European civilization.

It is a frequent circumstance of history that a culture or civilization develops the device that will later be used for its destruction. The ancient Chinese, for example, invented gunpowder, which was devel-

From *The Rejection of Politics* (1972).

oped by the military experts of the West and eventually led to the Chinese civilization itself being destroyed by the high explosives of modern warfare. Similarly, the supreme achievement of the craftsmen of the mediæval cities of Europe was the invention of the clock which, with its revolutionary alteration of the concept of time, materially assisted the growth of the middle ages.

There is a tradition that the clock appeared in the eleventh century, as a device for ringing bells at regular intervals in the monasteries which, with the regimented life they imposed on their inmates, were the closest social approximation in the middle ages to the factory of today. The first authenticated clock, however, appeared in the thirteenth century, and it was not until the fourteenth century that clocks became common as ornaments of the public buildings in German cities.

5 These early clocks, operated by weights, were not particularly accurate, and it was not until the sixteenth century that any great reliability was attained. In England, for instance, the clock at Hampton Court, made in 1540, is said to have been the first accurate clock in the country. And even the accuracy of the sixteenth-century clocks is relative, for they were equipped only with hour hands. The idea of measuring time in minutes and seconds had been thought out by the early mathematicians as far back as the fourteenth century, but it was not until the invention of the pendulum in 1657 that sufficient accuracy was attained to permit the addition of a minute hand, and the second hand did not appear until the eighteenth century. These two centuries, it should be observed, were those in which capitalism grew to such an extent that it was able to take advantage of the techniques of the industrial revolution to establish its economic domination over society.

The clock, as Lewis Mumford[1] has pointed out, is the key machine of the machine age, both for its influence on technics and for its influence on the habits of men. Technically, the clock was the first really automatic machine that attained any importance in the life of man. Previous to its invention, the common machines were of such a nature that their operation depended on some external and unreliable force, such as human or animal muscles, water or wind. It is true that the Greeks had invented a number of primitive automatic machines, but these were used, like Hero's steam engine,[2] either for obtaining "su-

1. American philosopher, historian, and teacher (1895–1990), best known for his studies of the relationship of men and women to their environments, whether natural or manufactured.
2. In the *Pneumatica* of Hero of Alexandria (c. 130 B.C.) there is a description of the "aeolipile," a primitive steam reaction turbine.

pernatural" effects in the temples or for amusing the tyrants of Levantine[3] cities. But the clock was the first automatic machine that attained public importance and a social function. Clock-making became the industry from which men learnt the elements of machine-making and gained the technical skill that was to produce the complicated machinery of the Industrial Revolution.

Socially the clock had a more radical influence than any other machine, in that it was the means by which the regularization and regimentation of life necessary for an exploiting system of industry could best be assured. The clock provided a means by which time—a category so elusive that no philosophy has yet determined its nature—could be measured concretely in the more tangible terms of space provided by the circumference of a clock dial. Time as duration became disregarded, and men began to talk and think always of "lengths" of time, just as if they were talking of lengths of calico. And time, being now measurable in mathematical symbols, was regarded as a commodity that could be bought and sold in the same way as any other commodity.

The new capitalists, in particular, became rabidly time-conscious. Time, here symbolizing the labour of the workers, was regarded by them almost as if it were the chief raw material of industry. "Time is money" was one of the key slogans of capitalist ideology, and the timekeeper was the most significant of the new types of official introduced by the capitalist dispensation.

In the early factories the employers went so far as to manipulate their clocks or sound their factory whistles at the wrong times in order to defraud the workers of a little of this valuable new commodity. Later such practices became less frequent, but the influence of the clock imposed a regularity on the lives of the majority of men that had previously been known only in the monasteries. Men actually became like clocks, acting with a repetitive regularity which had no resemblance to the rhythmic life of a natural being. They became, as the Victorian phrase put it, "as regular as clockwork." Only in the country districts where the natural lives of animals and plants and the elements still dominated existence, did any large proportion of the population fail to succumb to the deadly tick of monotony.

10 At first this new attitude to time, this new regularity of life, was imposed by the clock-owning masters on the unwilling poor. The factory slave reacted in his spare time by living with a chaotic irregularity which characterized the gin-sodden slums of early nineteenth-century industrialism. Men fled to the timeless worlds of drink or Methodist

3. Of or pertaining to the eastern part of the Mediterranean including its adjoining countries and islands.

inspiration. But gradually the idea of regularity spread downwards and among the workers. Nineteenth-century religion and morality played their part by proclaiming the sin of "wasting time." The introduction of mass-produced watches and clocks in the 1850's spread time-consciousness among those who had previously merely reacted to the stimulus of the knocker-up or the factory whistle. In the church and the school, in the office and the workshop, punctuality was held up as the greatest of the virtues.

Out of this slavish dependence on mechanical time which spread insidiously into every class in the nineteenth century, there grew up the demoralizing regimentation which today still characterizes factory life. The man who fails to conform faces social disapproval and economic ruin—unless he drops out into a nonconformist way of life in which time ceases to be of prime importance. Hurried meals, the regular morning and evening scramble for trains or buses, the strain of having to work to time schedules, all contribute, by digestive and nervous disturbance, to ruin health and shorten life.

Nor does the financial imposition of regularity tend, in the long run, to greater efficiency. Indeed, the quality of the product is usually much poorer, because the employer, regarding time as a commodity which he has to pay for, forces the operative to maintain such a speed that his work must necessarily be skimped. Quantity rather than quality becoming the criterion, the enjoyment is taken out of the work itself, and the worker in his turn becomes a "clock-watcher," concerned only with when he will be able to escape to the scanty and monotonous leisure of industrial society, in which he "kills time" by cramming in as much time-scheduled and mechanical enjoyment of cinema, radio and newspaper as his wage packet and his tiredness will allow. Only if he is willing to accept the hazards of living by his faith or his wits can the man without money avoid living as a slave to the clock.

The problem of the clock is, in general, similar to that of the machine. Mechanized time is valuable as a means of coordinating activities in a highly developed society, just as the machine is valuable as a means of reducing unnecessary labour to a minimum. Both are valuable for the contribution they make to the smooth running of society, and should be used in so far as they assist men to co-operate efficiently and to eliminate monotonous toil and social confusion. But neither should be allowed to dominate men's lives as they do today.

Now the movement of the clock sets the tempo of men's lives—they become the servants of the concept of time which they themselves have made, and are held in fear, like Frankenstein by his own monster. In a sane and free society such an arbitrary domination of man's functions by either clock or machine would obviously be out of the question. The domination of man by man-made machines is even more ridiculous than the domination of man by man. Mechanical time would be relegated to its true function of a means of reference and co-ordination, and men would return again to a balanced view of life no longer dominated by time-regulation and the worship of the clock. Complete liberty implies freedom from the tyranny of abstractions as well as from the rule of men.

QUESTIONS

1. *Woodcock begins by contrasting people who live according to "cyclical" time versus those subject to "mechanical" time. What groups of people does he associate with each category? What effects does this association create?*
2. *Beginning in paragraph 7, Woodcock enumerates the effects of clocks on human life. List, in order, those effects. Why has Woodcock arranged his material in this order?*
3. *In the final paragraph Woodcock suggests that a truly "sane and free society" would not accept domination by the clock or any other man-made machine. Do you agree that the clock represents a "tyranny" that a free society should resist? Write an argumentative essay in which you agree or disagree with Woodcock's position, and cite evidence from your observation or experience.*
4. *Write a personal narrative in which you reveal an experience in which you were dominated by "the tyranny of the clock."*

Frances FitzGerald

REWRITING AMERICAN HISTORY

Those of us who grew up in the fifties believed in the permanence of our American-history textbooks. To us as children, those texts were the truth of things: they were American history. It was not just that we read them before we understood that not everything that is printed is the truth, or the whole truth. It was that they, much more than other books, had the demeanor and trappings of authority. They were weighty volumes. They spoke in measured cadences: imperturbable, humorless, and as distant as Chinese emperors. Our teachers treated them with respect, and we paid them abject homage by memorizing a chapter a week. But now the textbook histories have changed, some of them to such an extent that an adult would find them unrecognizable.

From *America Revised: History Schoolbooks in the Twentieth Century* (1979).

One current junior-high-school American history begins with a story about a Negro cowboy called George McJunkin. It appears that when McJunkin was riding down a lonely trail in New Mexico one cold spring morning in 1925 he discovered a mound containing bones and stone implements, which scientists later proved belonged to an Indian civilization ten thousand years old. The book goes on to say that scientists now believe there were people in the Americas at least twenty thousand years ago. It discusses the Aztec, Mayan, and Incan civilizations and the meaning of the word "culture" before introducing the European explorers.

Another history text—this one for the fifth grade—begins with the story of how Henry B. Gonzalez, who is a member of Congress from Texas, learned about his own nationality. When he was ten years old, his teacher told him he was an American because he was born in the United States. His grandmother, however, said, "The cat was born in the oven. Does that make him bread?" After reporting that Mr. Gonzalez eventually went to college and law school, the book explains that "the melting pot idea hasn't worked out as some thought it would," and that now "some people say that the people of the United States are more like a salad bowl than a melting pot."

Poor Columbus! He is a minor character now, a walk-on in the middle of American history. Even those books that have not replaced his picture with a Mayan temple or an Iroquois mask do not credit him with discovering America—even for the Europeans. The Vikings, they say, preceded him to the New World, and after that the Europeans, having lost or forgotten their maps, simply neglected to cross the ocean again for five hundred years. Columbus is far from being the only personage to have suffered from time and revision. Captain John Smith, Daniel Boone, and Wild Bill Hickok—the great self-promoters of American history—have all but disappeared, taking with them a good deal of the romance of the American frontier. General Custer has given way to Chief Crazy Horse; General Eisenhower no longer liberates Europe single-handed; and, indeed, most generals, even to Washington and Lee, have faded away, as old soldiers do, giving place to social reformers such as William Lloyd Garrison and Jacob Riis. A number of black Americans have risen to prominence: not only George Washington Carver but Frederick Douglass and Martin Luther King, Jr. W. E. B. Du Bois now invariably accompanies Booker T. Washington. In addition, there is a mystery man called Crispus Attucks, a fugitive slave about whom nothing seems to be known for certain except that he was a victim of the Boston Massacre and thus became one of the first casualties of the American Revolution. Thaddeus Stevens has been reconstructed—his character changed, as it were, from black to white, from cruel and vindictive to persistent and sincere. As for

Teddy Roosevelt, he now champions the issue of conservation instead of charging up San Juan Hill. No single President really stands out as a hero, but all Presidents—except certain unmentionables in the second half of the nineteenth century—seem to have done as well as could be expected, given difficult circumstances.

5 Of course, when one thinks about it, it is hardly surprising that modern scholarship and modern perspectives have found their way into children's books. Yet the changes remain shocking. Those who in the sixties complained of the bland optimism, the chauvinism, and the materialism of their old civics text did so in the belief that, for all their protests, the texts would never change. The thought must have had something reassuring about it, for that generation never noticed when its complaints began to take effect and the songs about radioactive rainfall and houses made of ticky-tacky began to appear in the textbooks. But this is what happened.

The history texts now hint at a certain level of unpleasantness in American history. Several books, for instance, tell the story of Ishi, the last "wild" Indian in the continental United States, who, captured in 1911 after the massacre of his tribe, spent the final four and a half years of his life in the University of California's museum of anthropology, in San Francisco. At least three books show the same stunning picture of the breaker boys, the child coal miners of Pennsylvania—ancient children with deformed bodies and blackened faces who stare stupidly out from the entrance to a mine. One book quotes a soldier on the use of torture in the American campaign to pacify the Philippines at the beginning of the century. A number of books say that during the American Revolution the patriots tarred and feathered those who did not support them, and drove many of the loyalists from the country. Almost all the present-day history books note that the United States interned Japanese-Americans in detention camps during the Second World War.

Ideologically speaking, the histories of the fifties were implacable, seamless. Inside their covers, America was perfect: the greatest nation in the world, and the embodiment of democracy, freedom, and technological progress. For them, the country never changed in any important way: its values and its political institutions remained constant from the time of the American Revolution. To my generation—the children of the fifties—these texts appeared permanent just because they were so self-contained. Their orthodoxy, it seemed, left no handholds for attack, no lodging for decay. Who, after all, would dispute the wonders of technology or the superiority of the English colonists over the Spanish? Who would find fault with the pastorale of the West or the Old South? Who would question the anti-Communist crusade? There was, it seemed, no point in comparing these visions with reality, since they were the public truth and were thus quite irrelevant to what existed and to what anyone privately believed. They were—or so it seemed—the permanent expression of mass culture in America.

But now the texts have changed, and with them the country that American children are growing up into. The society that was once uniform is now a patchwork of rich and poor, old and young, men and women, blacks, whites, Hispanics, and Indians. The system that ran so smoothly by means of the Constitution under the guidance of benevolent conductor Presidents is now a rattletrap affair. The past is no highway to the present; it is a collection of issues and events that do not fit together and that lead in no single direction. The word "progress" has been replaced by the word "change": children, the modern texts insist, should learn history so that they can adapt to the rapid changes taking place around them. History is proceeding in spite of us. The present, which was once portrayed in the concluding chapters as a peaceful haven of scientific advances and Presidential inaugurations, is now a tangle of problems: race problems, urban problems, foreign-policy problems, problems of pollution, poverty, energy depletion, youthful rebellion, assassination, and drugs. Some books illustrate these problems dramatically. One, for instance, contains a picture of a doll half buried in a mass of untreated sewage; the caption reads, "Are we in danger of being overwhelmed by the products of our society and wastage created by their production? Would you agree with this photographer's interpretation?" Two books show the same picture of an old black woman sitting in a straight chair in a dingy room, her hands folded in graceful resignation; the surrounding text discusses the problems faced by the urban poor and by the aged who depend on Social Security. Other books present current problems less starkly. One of the texts concludes sagely:

> Problems are part of life. Nations face them, just as people face them, and try to solve them. And today's Americans have one great advantage over past generations. Never before have Americans been so well equipped to solve their problems. They have today the means to conquer poverty, disease, and ignorance. The technetronic age has put that power into their hands.

Such passages have a familiar ring. Amid all the problems, the deus ex machina[1] of science still dodders around in the gloaming of pious hope.

Even more surprising than the emergence of problems is the discov-

1. God from a machine. A reference to early plays in which a god, lowered to the stage by mechanical means, solved the drama's problems; thus, an artificial solution to a difficulty.

ery that the great unity of the texts has broken. Whereas in the fifties all texts represented the same political view, current texts follow no pattern of orthodoxy. Some books, for instance, portray civil-rights legislation as a series of actions taken by a wise, paternal government; others convey some suggestion of the social upheaval involved and make mention of such people as Stokely Carmichael and Malcolm X.[2] In some books, the Cold War has ended; in others, it continues, with Communism threatening the free nations of the earth.

The political diversity in the books is matched by a diversity of pedagogical approach. In addition to the traditional narrative histories, with their endless streams of facts, there are so-called "discovery," or "inquiry," texts, which deal with a limited number of specific issues in American history. These texts do not pretend to cover the past; they focus on particular topics, such as "stratification in Colonial society" or "slavery and the American Revolution," and illustrate them with documents from primary and secondary sources. The chapters in these books amount to something like case studies, in that they include testimony from people with different perspectives or conflicting views on a single subject. In addition, the chapters provide background information, explanatory notes, and a series of questions for the student. The questions are the heart of the matter, for when they are carefully selected they force students to think much as historians think: to define the point of view of the speaker, analyze the ideas presented, question the relationship between events, and so on. One text, for example, quotes Washington, Jefferson, and John Adams on the question of foreign alliances and then asks, "What did John Adams assume that the international situation would be after the American Revolution? What did Washington's attitude toward the French alliance seem to be? How do you account for his attitude?" Finally, it asks, "Should a nation adopt a policy toward alliances and cling to it consistently, or should it vary its policies toward other countries as circumstances change?" In these books, history is clearly not a list of agreed-upon facts or a sermon on politics but a babble of voices and a welter of events which must be ordered by the historian.

In matters of pedagogy, as in matters of politics, there are not two sharply differentiated categories of books; rather, there is a spectrum. Politically, the books run from moderate left to moderate right; pedagogically, they run from the traditional history sermons, through a middle ground of narrative texts with inquiry-style questions and of inquiry texts with long stretches of narrative, to the most rigorous of case-study books. What is common to the current texts—and makes all of them different from those of the fifties—is their engagement

2. Radical black leaders of the 1960s.

with the social sciences. In eighth-grade histories, the "concepts" of social sciences make fleeting appearances. But these "concepts" are the very foundation stones of various elementary-school social-studies series. The 1970 Harcourt Brace Jovanovich[3] series, for example, boasts in its preface of "a horizontal base or ordering of conceptual schemes" to match its "vertical arm of behavioral themes." What this means is not entirely clear, but the books do proceed from easy questions to hard ones, such as—in the sixth-grade book—"How was interaction between merchants and citizens different in the Athenian and Spartan social systems?" Virtually all the American-history texts for older children include discussions of "role," "status," and "culture." Some of them stage debates between eminent social scientists in roped-off sections of the text; some include essays on economics or sociology; some contain pictures and short biographies of social scientists of both sexes and of diverse races. Many books seem to accord social scientists a higher status than American Presidents.

Quite as striking as these political and pedagogical alterations is the change in the physical appearance of the texts. The schoolbooks of the fifties showed some effort in the matter of design: they had maps, charts, cartoons, photographs, and an occasional four-color picture to break up the columns of print. But beside the current texts they look as naïve as Soviet fashion magazines. The print in the fifties books is heavy and far too black, the colors muddy. The photographs are conventional news shots—portraits of Presidents in three-quarters profile, posed "action" shots of soldiers. The other illustrations tend to be Socialist-realist-style[4] drawings (there are a lot of hefty farmers with hoes in the Colonial-period chapters) or incredibly vulgar made-for-children paintings of patriotic events. One painting shows Columbus standing in full court dress on a beach in the New World from a perspective that could have belonged only to the Arawaks.[5] By contrast, the current texts are paragons of sophisticated modern design. They look not like *People* or *Family Circle* but, rather, like *Architectural Digest* or *Vogue.* * * * The amount of space given to illustrations is far greater than it was in the fifties; in fact, in certain "slow-learner" books the pictures far outweigh the text in importance. However, the illustrations have a much greater historical value. Instead of made-up paintings or anachronistic sketches, there are cartoons, photographs, and paintings drawn from the periods being treated. The chapters on the Colonial period will show, for instance, a ship's carved prow, a Re-

3. Major textbook publisher.
4. Socialist realism, which originated in the Soviet Union, is a style of art which glorifies the communal labor of farmers and industrial workers in works of poster-like crudity.
5. Native Americans, then inhabiting the Caribbean area.

vere bowl, a Copley[6] painting—a whole gallery of Early Americana. The nineteenth century is illustrated with nineteenth-century cartoons and photographs—and the photographs are all of high artistic quality. As for the twentieth-century chapters, they are adorned with the contents of a modern-art museum.

The use of all this art and high-quality design contains some irony. The nineteenth-century photographs of child laborers or urban slum apartments are so beautiful that they transcend their subjects. To look at them, or at the Victor Gatto painting of the Triangle shirtwaist-factory fire, is to see not misery or ugliness but an art object. In the modern chapters, the contrast between style and content is just as great: the color photographs of junk yards or polluted rivers look as enticing as *Gourmet's* photographs of food. The book that is perhaps the most stark in its description of modern problems illustrates the horrors of nuclear testing with a pretty Ben Shahn picture of the Bikini explosion,[7] and the potential for global ecological disaster with a color photograph of the planet swirling its mantle of white clouds. Whereas in the nineteen-fifties the texts were childish in the sense that they were naïve and clumsy, they are now childish in the sense that they are polymorphous-perverse. American history is not dull any longer; it is a sensuous experience.

The surprise that adults feel in seeing the changes in history texts must come from the lingering hope that there is, somewhere out there, an objective truth. The hope is, of course, foolish. All of us children of the twentieth century know, or should know, that there are no absolutes in human affairs, and thus there can be no such thing as perfect objectivity. We know that each historian in some degree creates the world anew and that all history is in some degree contemporary history. But beyond this knowledge there is still a hope for some reliable authority, for some fixed stars in the universe. We may know that journalists cannot be wholly unbiased and that "balance" is an imaginary point between two extremes, and yet we hope that Walter Cronkite will tell us the truth of things. In the same way, we hope that our history will not change—that we learned the truth of things as children. The texts, with their impersonal voices, encourage this hope, and therefore it is particularly disturbing to see how they change, and how fast.

15 Slippery history! Not every generation but every few years the content of American-history books for children changes appreciably.

6. The reference is to John Singleton Copley (1738–1815), greatest of the American old masters; he specialized in portraits and historical paintings.

7. The Bikini atoll, part of the Marshall Islands in the Pacific, was the site of American nuclear-bomb testing from 1946 to 1958. Ben Shahn (1898–1969) was an American painter and graphic artist with strong social and political concerns.

Schoolbooks are not, like trade books,[8] written and left to their fate. To stay in step with the cycles of "adoption"[9] in school districts across the country, the publishers revise most of their old texts or substitute new ones every three or four years. In the process of revision, they not only bring history up to date but make changes—often substantial changes—in the body of the work. History books for children are thus more contemporary than any other form of history. How should it be otherwise? Should students read histories written ten, fifteen, thirty years ago? In theory, the system is reasonable—except that each generation of children reads only one generation of schoolbooks. The transient history is those children's history forever—their particular version of America.

8. Books written for a general audience, as opposed to textbooks.
9. Choice of required textbooks.

QUESTIONS

1. *What differences does FitzGerald find between the history textbooks of the 1950s and those of today? In what ways—according to what she states or implies—have the texts been improved? Does she see any changes for the worse?*
2. *In paragraph 8, FitzGerald says that in the new texts "the word 'progress' has been replaced by the word 'change.' " What is the difference between these two words? What does the replacement imply?*
3. *By "rewriting," does FitzGerald mean changing the facts of history? What is the relationship between the facts of history and history textbooks?*
4. *Choose an event from American history with which you are familiar—either one FitzGerald mentions or another you know well. On your own or in a group, study the way this event is presented in three or four contemporary history textbooks. Write an accout of the differences, including an analysis of why such differences may occur.*

William Cronon

A PLACE FOR STORIES: NATURE, HISTORY, AND NARRATIVE

In the beginning was the story. Or rather: many stories, of many places, in many voices, pointing toward many ends.

In 1979, two books were published about the long drought that struck the Great Plains during the 1930s. The two had nearly identical titles: one, by Paul Bonnifield, was called *The Dust Bowl;* the other, by Donald Worster, *Dust Bowl.*[1] The two authors dealt with virtually the same subject, had researched many of the same documents, and agreed on most of their facts, and yet their conclusions could hardly have been more different.

Bonnifield's closing argument runs like this:

> In the final analysis, the story of the dust bowl was the story of people, people with ability and talent, people with resourcefulness, fortitude, and courage. . . . The people of the dust bowl were not defeated, poverty-ridden people without hope. They were builders for tomorrow. During those hard years they continued to build their churches, their businesses, their schools, their colleges, their communities. They grew closer to God and fonder of the land. Hard years were common in their past, but the future belonged to those who were ready to seize the moment. . . . Because they stayed during those hard years and worked the land and tapped her natural resources, millions of people have eaten better, worked in healthier places, and enjoyed warmer homes. Because those determined people did not flee the stricken area during a crisis, the nation today enjoys a better standard of living.[2]

Worster, on the other hand, paints a bleaker picture:

> The Dust Bowl was the darkest moment in the twentieth-century life of the southern plains. The name suggests a place—a region whose borders are as inexact and shifting as a sand dune. But it was also an event of national, even planetary significance. A widely respected authority on world food problems, George Borgstrom, has ranked the creation of the

Originally published in *The Journal of American History* (March 1992). All notes to this essay are the author's.

1. Paul Bonnifield, *The Dust Bowl: Men, Dirt, and Depression* (Albuquerque, 1979); Donald Worster, *Dust Bowl: The Southern Plains in the 1930s* (New York, 1979). On Dust Bowl historiography in general, see the collection of essays in *Great Plains Quarterly,* 6 (Spring 1986).
2. Bonnifield, *The Dust Bowl,* 202.

> Dust Bowl as one of the three worst ecological blunders in history. . . . It cannot be blamed on illiteracy or overpopulation or social disorder. It came about because the culture was operating in precisely the way it was supposed to. . . . The Dust Bowl . . . was the inevitable outcome of a culture that deliberately, self-consciously, set itself [the] task of dominating and exploiting the land for all it was worth.[3]

For Bonnifield, the dust storms of the 1930s were mainly a natural disaster; when the rains gave out, people had to struggle for their farms, their homes, their very survival. Their success in that struggle was a triumph of individual and community spirit: nature made a mess, and human beings cleaned it up. Worster's version differs dramatically. Although the rains did fail during the 1930s, their disappearance expressed the cyclical climate of a semiarid environment. The story of the Dust Bowl is less about the failures of nature than about the failures of human beings to accommodate themselves to nature. A long series of willful human misunderstandings and assaults led finally to a collapse whose origins were mainly cultural.

Whichever of these interpretations we are inclined to follow, they 5
pose a dilemma for scholars who study past environmental change—indeed, a dilemma for all historians. As often happens in history, they make us wonder how two competent authors looking at identical materials drawn from the same past can reach such divergent conclusions. But it is not merely their *conclusions* that differ. Although both narrate the same broad series of events with an essentially similar cast of characters, they tell two entirely different *stories*. In both texts, the story is inextricably bound to its conclusion, and the historical analysis derives much of its force from the upward or downward sweep of the plot. So we must eventually ask a more basic question: where did these stories come from?

The question is trickier than it seems, for it transports us into the much contested terrain between traditional social science and postmodernist critical theory. As an environmental historian who tries to blend the analytical traditions of history with those of ecology, economics, anthropology, and other fields, I cannot help feeling uneasy about the shifting theoretical ground we all now seem to occupy. On the one hand, a fundamental premise of my field is that human acts occur within a network of relationships, processes, and systems that are as ecological as they are cultural. To such basic historical categories as gender, class, and race, environmental historians would add a theoretical vocabulary in which plants, animals, soils, climates, and other nonhuman entities become the coactors and codeterminants of a history not just of people but of the earth itself. For scholars who share

3. Worster, *Dust Bowl,* 4.

my perspective, the importance of the natural world, its objective effects on people, and the concrete ways people affect it in turn are not at issue; they are the very heart of our intellectual project. We therefore ally our historical work with that of our colleagues in the sciences, whose models, however imperfectly, try to approximate the mechanisms of nature.[4]

And yet scholars of environmental history also maintain a powerful commitment to narrative form. When we describe human activities within an ecosystem, we seem always to tell *stories* about them.[5] Like all historians, we configure the events of the past into causal sequences—stories—that order and simplify those events to give them new meanings. We do so because narrative is the chief literary form that tries to find meaning in an overwhelmingly crowded and disordered chronological reality. When we choose a plot to order our environmental histories, we give them a unity that neither nature nor the past possesses so clearly. In so doing, we move well beyond nature into the intensely human realm of value. There, we cannot avoid encountering the postmodernist assault on narrative, which calls into question not just the stories we tell but the deeper purpose that motivated us in the first place: trying to make sense of nature's place in the human past.

By writing stories about environmental change, we divide the causal relationships of an ecosystem with a rhetorical razor that defines included and excluded, relevant and irrelevant, empowered and disempowered. In the act of separating story from non-story, we wield the most powerful yet dangerous tool of the narrative form. It is a commonplace of modern literary theory that the very authority with which narrative presents its vision of reality is achieved by obscuring large portions of that reality. Narrative succeeds to the extent that it hides

4. For a wide-ranging discussion that explores the emerging intellectual agendas of environmental history, see "A Round Table: Environmental History," *Journal of American History*, 76 (March 1990), 1087–1147.

5. Throughout this essay, I will use "story" and "narrative" interchangeably, despite a technical distinction that can be made between them. For some literary critics and philosophers of history, "story" is a limited genre, whereas narrative (or *narratio*) is the much more encompassing part of classical rhetoric that organizes all representations of time into a configured sequence of completed actions. I intend the broader meaning for both words, since "storytelling" in its most fundamental sense is the activity I wish to criticize and defend. I hope it is emphatically clear at the outset that I am *not* urging a return to "traditional" narrative history that revolves around the biographies of "great" individuals (usually elite white male politicians and intellectuals); rather, I am urging historians to acknowledge storytelling as the necessary core even of *longue durée* histories that pay little attention to individual people. Environmental history is but one example of these, and most of my arguments apply just as readily to the others.

the discontinuities, ellipses, and contradictory experiences that would undermine the intended meaning of its story. Whatever its overt purpose, it cannot avoid a covert exercise of power: it inevitably sanctions some voices while silencing others. A powerful narrative reconstructs common sense to make the contingent seem determined and the artificial seem natural. If this is true, then narrative poses particularly difficult problems for environmental historians, for whom the boundary between the artificial and the natural is the very thing we most wish to study. The differences between Bonnifield's and Worster's versions of the Dust Bowl clearly have something to do with that boundary, as does my own uneasiness about the theoretical underpinnings of my historical craft.[6]

The disease of literary theory is to write too much in abstractions, so that even the simplest meanings become difficult if not downright opaque. Lest this essay wander off into litcrit fog, let me ground it on more familiar terrain. I propose to examine the role of narrative in environmental history by returning to the Great Plains to survey the ways historians have told that region's past. What I offer here will *not* be a comprehensive historiography, since my choice of texts is eclectic and I will ignore many major works. Rather, I will use a handful of Great Plains histories to explore the much vexed problems that narrative poses for all historians. On the one hand, I hope to acknowledge the deep challenges that postmodernism poses for those who applaud "the revival of narrative"; on the other, I wish to record my own con-

6. Much of the reading that lies behind this essay cannot easily be attached to a single argument or footnote. Among the works that helped shape my views on the importance and problems of narrative are the following: William H. Dray, *Philosophy of History* (Englewood Cliffs, 1964); Robert Scholes and Robert Kellogg, *The Nature of Narrative* (New York, 1966); Frank Kermode, *The Sense of an Ending: Studies in the Theory of Fiction* (New York, 1967); Hayden White, *Metahistory: The Historical Imagination in Nineteenth-Century Europe* (Baltimore, 1973); Hayden White, *Tropics of Discourse: Essays in Cultural Criticism* (Baltimore, 1978); Robert H. Canary and Henry Kozicki, eds., *The Writing of History: Literary Form and Historical Understanding* (Madison, 1978); W. J. T. Mitchell, ed., *On Narrative* (Chicago, 1981); Fredric Jameson, *The Political Unconscious: Narrative as a Socially Symbolic Act* (Ithaca, 1981); Jonathan Culler, *On Deconstruction: Theory and Criticism after Structuralism* (Ithaca, 1982); Terry Eagleton, *Literary Theory: An Introduction* (Minneapolis, 1983); Paul Ricoeur, *Time and Narrative* (3 vols., Chicago, 1984, 1985, 1988), trans. Kathleen Blamey and David Pellauer; Dominick LaCapra, *Rethinking Intellectual History: Texts, Contexts, Language* (Ithaca, 1983); Arthur C. Danto, *Narration and Knowledge: Including the Integral Text of Analytical Philosophy of History* (New York, 1985); James Clifford and George E. Marcus, eds., *Writing Culture: The Poetics and Politics of Ethnography* (Berkeley, 1986); Wallace Martin, *Recent Theories of Narrative* (Ithaca, 1986); Louis O. Mink, *Historical Understanding* (Ithaca, 1987); Hayden White, *The Content of the Form: Narrative Discourse and Historical Representation* (Baltimore, 1987); and Kai Erikson, "Obituary for Big Daddy: A Parable," unpublished manuscript (in William Cronon's possession).

viction—chastened but still strong—that narrative remains essential to our understanding of history and the human place in nature.

10 If we consider the Plains in the half millennium since Christopher Columbus crossed the Atlantic, certain events seem likely to stand out in any long-term history of the region. If I were to try to write these not as a *story* but as a simple *list*—I will not entirely succeed in so doing, since the task of *not* telling stories about the past turns out to be much more difficult than it may seem—the resulting chronicle might run something like this.

Five centuries ago, people traveled west across the Atlantic Ocean. So did some plants and animals. One of these—the horse—appeared on the Plains. Native peoples used horses to hunt bison. Human migrants from across the Atlantic eventually appeared on the Plains as well. People fought a lot. The bison herds disappeared. Native peoples moved to reservations. The new immigrants built homes for themselves. Herds of cattle increased. Settlers plowed the prairie grasses, raising corn, wheat, and other grains. Railroads moved people and other things into and out of the region. Crops sometimes failed for lack of rain. Some people abandoned their farms and moved elsewhere; other people stayed. During the 1930s, there was a particularly bad drought, with many dust storms. Then the drought ended. A lot of people began to pump water out of the ground for use on their fields and in their towns. Today, Plains farmers continue to raise crops and herds of animals. Some have trouble making ends meet. Many Indians live on reservations. It will be interesting to see what happens next.

I trust that this list seems pretty peculiar to anyone who reads it, as if a child were trying to tell a story without quite knowing how. I've tried to remove as much sense of *connection* among these details as I can. I've presented them not as a narrative but as a *chronicle*, a simple chronological listing of events as they occurred in sequence.[7] This was not a pure chronicle, since I presented only what I declared to be the "most important" events of Plains history. By the very act of separating important from unimportant events, I actually smuggled a number of not-so-hidden stories into my list, so that such things as the migration of the horse or the conquest of the Plains tribes began to form little narrative swirls in the midst of my ostensibly story-less account. A pure chronicle would have included every event that ever occurred on the Great Plains, no matter how large or small, so that a colorful

7. This distinction between chronicle and narrative is more fully analyzed in White, *Metahistory*, 5–7; White, *Tropics of Discourse*, 109–11; Louis O. Mink, "Narrative Form as a Cognitive Instrument," in *Writing of History*, ed. Canary and Kozicki, 141–44; David Carr, *Time, Narrative, and History* (Bloomington, 1986), 59; Danto, *Narration and Knowledge*; and Paul A. Roth, "Narrative Explanations: The Case of History," *History and Theory*, 27 (no. 1, 1988), 1–13.

sunset in September 1623 or a morning milking of cows on a farm near Leavenworth in 1897 would occupy just as prominent a place as the destruction of the bison herds or the 1930s dust storms.

Such a text is impossible even to imagine, let alone construct, for reasons that help explain historians' affection for narrative.[8] When we encounter the past in the form of a chronicle, it becomes much less recognizable to us. We have trouble sorting out why things happened when and how they did, and it becomes hard to evaluate the relative significance of events. Things seem less *connected* to each other, and it becomes unclear how all this stuff relates to us. Most important, in a chronicle we easily lose the thread of what was going on at any particular moment. Without some plot to organize the flow of events, everything becomes much harder—even impossible—to understand.

How do we discover a story that will turn the facts of Great Plains history into something more easily recognized and understood? The repertoire of historical plots we might apply to the events I've just chronicled is endless and could be drawn not just from history but from all of literature and myth. To simplify the range of choices, let me start by offering two large groups of possible plots. On the one hand, we can narrate Plains history as a story of improvement, in which the plot line gradually ascends toward an ending that is somehow more positive—happier, richer, freer, better—than the beginning. On the other hand, we can tell stories in which the plot line eventually falls toward an ending that is more negative—sadder, poorer, less free, worse—than the place where the story began. The one group of plots might be called "progressive," given their historical dependence on eighteenth-century Enlightenment notions of progress; the other might be called "tragic" or "declensionist," tracing their historical roots to romantic and antimodernist reactions against progress.

If we look at the ways historians have actually written about the 15
changing environment of the Great Plains, the upward and downward lines of progress and declension are everywhere apparent. The very ease with which we recognize them constitutes a warning about the terrain we are entering. However compelling these stories may be as depictions of environmental change, their narrative form has less to do with nature than with human discourse. Their plots are cultural constructions so deeply embedded in our language that they resonate far beyond the Great Plains. Historians did not invent them, and their

8. There are deeper epistemological problems here that I will not discuss, such as how we recognize what constitutes an "event" and how we draw boundaries around it. It should eventually become clear that "events" are themselves defined and delimited by the stories with which we configure them and are probably impossible to imagine apart from their narrative context.

very familiarity encourages us to shape our storytelling to fit their patterns. Placed in a particular historical or ideological context, neither group of plots is innocent: both have hidden agendas that influence what the narrative includes and excludes. So powerful are these agendas that not even the historian as author entirely controls them.

Take, for instance, the historians who narrate Great Plains history as a tale of frontier progress. The most famous of those who embraced this basic plot was of course Frederick Jackson Turner, for whom the story of the nation recapitulated the ascending stages of European civilization to produce a uniquely democratic and egalitarian community. Turner saw the transformation of the American landscape from wilderness to trading post to farm to boomtown as the central saga of the nation.[9] If ever there was a narrative that achieved its end by erasing its true subject, Turner's frontier was it: the heroic encounter between pioneers and "free land" could only become plausible by obscuring the conquest that traded one people's freedom for another's. By making Indians the foil for its story of progress, the frontier plot made their conquest seem natural, commonsensical, inevitable. But to say this is only to affirm the narrative's power. In countless versions both before and after it acquired its classic Turnerian form, this story of frontier struggle and progress remains among the oldest and most familiar narratives of American history. In its ability to turn ordinary people into heroes and to present a conflict-ridden invasion as an epic march toward enlightened democratic nationhood, it perfectly fulfilled the ideological needs of its late-nineteenth-century moment.[1]

The Great Plains would eventually prove less tractable to frontier progress than many other parts of the nation. Turner himself would say of the region that it constituted the American farmer's "first defeat," but that didn't stop the settlers themselves from narrating their past with the frontier story.[2] One of Dakota Territory's leading missionaries, Bishop William Robert Hare, prophesied in the 1880s that the plot of Dakota settlement would follow an upward line of migration, struggle, and triumph:

> You may stand ankle deep in the short burnt grass of an uninhabited wilderness—next month a mixed train will glide over the waste and stop

9. Frederick Jackson Turner, *The Frontier in American History* (New York, 1920), 12.
1. I have written about the rhetorical structure of Turner's work in two essays: William Cronon, "Revisiting the Vanishing Frontier: The Legacy of Frederick Jackson Turner," *Western Historical Quarterly*, 18 (April 1987), 157–76; and William Cronon, "Turner's First Stand: The Significance of Significance in American History," in *Writing Western History: Classic Essays on Classic Western Historians*, ed. Richard Etulain (Albuquerque, 1991), 73–101. See also Ronald H. Carpenter, *The Eloquence of Frederick Jackson Turner* (San Marino, 1983).
2. Turner, *Frontier in American History*, 147.

> at some point where the railroad has decided to locate a town. Men, women and children will jump out of the cars, and their chattel will be tumbled out after them. From that moment the building begins. The courage and faith of these pioneers are something extraordinary. Their spirit seems to rise above all obstacles.[3]

For Hare, this vision of progress was ongoing and prospective, a prophecy of future growth, but the same pattern could just as easily be applied to retrospective visions. An early historian of Oklahoma, Luther Hill, could look back in 1909 at the 1890s, a decade that had "wrought a great change in Oklahoma territory": in a mere ten years, settlers had transformed the "stagnant pool" of unused Indian lands into the "waving grain fields, the herds of cattle, and the broad prospect of agricultural prosperity [which] cause delight and even surprise in the beholder who sees the results of civilization in producing such marvels of wealth."[4] Ordinary people saw such descriptions as the fulfillment of a grand story that had unfolded during the course of their own lifetimes. As one Kansas townswoman, Josephine Middlekauf, concluded,

> After sixty years of pioneering in Hays, I could write volumes telling of its growth and progress. . . . I have been singularly privileged to have seen it develop from the raw materials into the almost finished product in comfortable homes, churches, schools, paved streets, trees, fruits and flowers.[5]

Consider these small narratives more abstractly. They tell a story of more or less linear progress, in which people struggle to transform a relatively responsive environment. There may be moderate setbacks along the way, but their narrative role is to play foil to the heroes who overcome them. Communities rapidly succeed in becoming ever more civilized and comfortable. The time frame of the stories is brief, limited to the lifespan of a single generation, and is located historically in the moment just after invading settlers first occupied Indian lands. Our attention as readers is focused on local events, those affecting individuals, families, townships, and other small communities. All of these framing devices, which are as literary as they are historical, compel us toward the conclusion that this is basically a happy story. It is tempered only by a hint of nostalgia for the world that is being lost, a quiet undercurrent of elderly regret for youthful passions and energies now fading.

3. William Robert Hare, ca. 1887, as quoted in Howard R. Lamar, "Public Values and Private Dreams: South Dakota's Search for Identity, 1850–1900," *South Dakota History*, 8 (Spring 1978), 129.
4. Luther B. Hill, *A History of the State of Oklahoma* (Chicago, 1909), 382, 386, 385.
5. Josephine Middlekauf, as quoted in Joanna L. Stratton, *Pioneer Women: Voices from the Kansas Frontier* (New York, 1981), 204.

* * *

Now in fact, these optimistic stories about Great Plains settlement are by no means typical of historical writing in the twentieth century. The problems of settling a semiarid environment were simply too great for the frontier story to proceed without multiple setbacks and crises. Even narrators who prefer an ascending plot line in their stories of regional environmental change must therefore tell a more complicated tale of failure, struggle, and accommodation in the face of a resistant if not hostile landscape.

20 Among the most important writers who adopt this narrative strategy are Walter Prescott Webb and James Malin, the two most influential historians of the Great Plains to write during the first half of the twentieth century. Webb's classic work, *The Great Plains*, was published over half a century ago and has remained in print to this day.[6] It tells a story that significantly revises the Turnerian frontier. For Webb, the Plains were radically different from the more benign environments that Anglo-American settlers had encountered in the East. Having no trees and little water, the region posed an almost insurmountable obstacle to the westward march of civilization. After describing the scene in this way, Webb sets his story in motion with a revealing passage:

> In the new region—level, timberless, and semi-arid—[settlers] were thrown by Mother Necessity into the clutch of new circumstances. Their plight has been stated in this way: east of the Mississippi civilization stood on three legs—land, water, and timber; west of the Mississippi not one but two of these legs were withdrawn,—water and timber,—and civilization was left on one leg—land. It is small wonder that it toppled over in temporary failure.

It is easy to anticipate the narrative that will flow from this beginning: Webb will tell us how civilization fell over, then built itself new legs and regained its footing to continue its triumphant ascent. The central agency that solves these problems and drives the story forward is human invention. Unlike the simpler frontier narratives, Webb's history traces a dialectic between a resistant landscape and the technological innovations that will finally succeed in transforming it. Although his book is over five hundred pages long and is marvelously intricate in its arguments, certain great inventions mark the turning points of Webb's plot. Because water was so scarce, settlers had to obtain it from the only reliable source, underground aquifers, so they invented the humble but revolutionary windmill. Because so little wood was available to build fences that would keep cattle out of cornfields,

6. Walter Prescott Webb, *The Great Plains* (New York, 1931), p. 9.

barbed wire was invented in 1874 and rapidly spread throughout the grasslands. These and other inventions—railroads, irrigation, new legal systems for allocating water rights, even six-shooter revolvers—eventually destroyed the bison herds, created a vast cattle kingdom, and broke the prairie sod for farming.

Webb closes his story by characterizing the Plains as "a land of survival where nature has most stubbornly resisted the efforts of man. Nature's very stubbornness has driven man to the innovations which he has made."[7] Given the scenic requirements of Webb's narrative, his Plains landscape must look rather different from that of earlier frontier narrators. For Webb, the semiarid environment is neither a wilderness nor a waste, but itself a worthy antagonist of civilization. It is a landscape the very resistance of which is the necessary spur urging human ingenuity to new levels of achievement. Webb thus spends much more time than earlier storytellers describing the climate, terrain, and ecology of the Great Plains so as to extol the features that made the region unique in American experience. Although his book ends with the same glowing image of a transformed landscape that we find in earlier frontier narratives, he in no way devalues the "uncivilized" landscape that preceded it. Quite the contrary: the more formidable it is as a rival, the more heroic become its human antagonists. In the struggle to make homes for themselves in this difficult land, the people of the Plains not only proved their inventiveness but built a regional culture beautifully adapted to the challenges of their regional environment.

Webb's story of struggle against a resistant environment has formed the core of most subsequent environmental histories of the Plains. We have already encountered one version of it in Paul Bonnifield's *The Dust Bowl.* It can also be discovered in the more ecologically sophisticated studies of James C. Malin, in which the evolution of "forest man" to "grass man" becomes the central plot of Great Plains history.[8] Malin's prose is far less story-like in outward appearance than Webb's, but it nonetheless narrates an encounter between a resistant environment and human ingenuity. Malin's human agents begin as struggling immigrants who have no conception of how to live in a treeless landscape; by the end, they have become "grass men" who have

7. *Ibid.*, 508.

8. These terms appear, for instance, in Malin's magnum opus, James C. Malin, *The Grassland of North America: Prolegomena to Its History* (Gloucester, Mass., 1967), but this basic notion informs virtually all of his work on the grasslands. See also James C. Malin, *Grassland Historical Studies: Natural Resources Utilization in a Background of Science and Technology* (Lawrence, Kan., 1950); and the collection of essays, James C. Malin, *History and Ecology: Studies of the Grassland,* ed. Robert P. Swierenga (Lincoln, 1984).

brought their culture "into conformity with the requirements of maintaining rather than disrupting environmental equilibrium." So completely have they succeeded in adapting themselves that they can even "point the finger of scorn at the deficiencies of the forest land; grassless, wet, with an acid, leached, infertile soil."[9] Human inhabitants have become one with an environment that only a few decades before had almost destroyed them.

The beauty of these plots is that they present the harshness of the regional environment in such a way as to make the human struggle against it appear even more positive and heroic than the continuous ascent portrayed in earlier frontier narratives. The focus of our attention is still relatively small-scale, though both the geographical and the chronological context of the plot have expanded. The story is now much more a regional one, so that the histories of one family or town, or even of Kansas or Oklahoma, become less important than the broader history of the grassland environment as a whole. The time frame too has advanced, so that the history of technological progress on the Plains moves well into the twentieth century. Because the plot still commences at the moment that Euroamerican settlers began to occupy the grasslands, though, there is no explicit *backward* extension of the time frame. The precontact history of the Indians is not part of this story.

Most interestingly, the human subject of these stories has become significantly broader than the earlier state and local frontier histories. Rather than focus primarily on individual pioneers and their communities, these new regional studies center their story on "civilization" or "man." The inventions that allowed people to adapt to life on the Great Plains are thus absorbed into the broader story of "man" and "his" long conquest of nature. No narrative centered on so singular a central character could be politically innocent. More erasures are at work here: Indians, yes, but also women, ethnic groups, underclasses, and any other communities that have been set apart from the collectivity represented by Man or Civilization. The narrative leaves little room for them, and even less for a natural realm that might appropriately be spared the conquests of technology. These are stories about a progress that, however hard-earned, is fated; its conquests are only what common sense and nature would expect. For Webb and Malin, the Great Plains gain significance from their ties to a world-historical plot, Darwinian in shape, that encompasses the entire sweep of human history. The ascending plot line we detect in these stories is in fact connected to a much longer plot line with the same rising characteristics. Whether that longer plot is expressed as the Making of the

9. Malin, *Grassland of North America,* 154.

American Nation, the Rise of Western Civilization, or the Ascent of Man, it still lends its grand scale to Great Plains histories that outwardly appear much more limited in form. This may explain how we can find ourselves so entranced by a book whose principal subject for five hundred pages is the invention of windmills and barbed wire.

But there is another way to tell this history, one in which the plot ultimately falls rather than rises. The first examples of what we might call a "declensionist" or "tragic" Great Plains history began to appear during the Dust Bowl calamity of the 1930s. The dominant New Deal interpretation of what had gone wrong on the Plains was that settlers had been fooled by a climate that was sometimes perfectly adequate for farming and at other times disastrously inadequate. Settlement had expanded during "good" years when rainfall was abundant, and the perennial optimism of the frontier had prevented farmers from acknowledging that drought was a permanent fact of life on the Plains. In this version, Great Plains history becomes a tale of self-deluding hubris and refusal to accept reality. Only strong government action, planned by enlightened scientific experts to encourage cooperation among Plains farmers, could prevent future agricultural expansion and a return of the dust storms.

The classic early statement of this narrative is that of the committee that Franklin D. Roosevelt appointed to investigate the causes of the Dust Bowl, in its 1936 report on *The Future of the Great Plains.* Its version of the region's history up until the 1930s runs as follows:

> The steady progress which we have come to look for in American communities was beginning to reverse itself. Instead of becoming more productive, the Great Plains were becoming less so. Instead of giving their population a better standard of living, they were tending to give them a poorer one. The people were energetic and courageous, and they loved their land. Yet they were increasingly less secure in it.[1]

One did not have to look far to locate the reason for this unexpected reversal of the American success story. Plains settlers had failed in precisely the agricultural adaptations that Webb and Malin claimed for them. Radical steps would have to be taken if the Dust Bowl disaster were not to repeat itself. "It became clear," said the planners, describing their own controversial conclusions with the settled authority of the past tense, "that unless there was a permanent change in the agricultural pattern of the Plains, relief always would have to be extended whenever the available rainfall was deficient."[2]

1. *The Future of the Great Plains: Report of the Great Plains Committee* (Washington, 1936), 1. On this report, see Gilbert F. White, "*The Future of the Great Plains* Re-Visited," *Great Plains Quarterly*, 6 (Spring 1986), 84–93.
2. *Future of the Great Plains*, 1.

Whatever the scientific or political merits of this description, consider its narrative implications. The New Deal planners in effect argued that the rising plot line of our earlier storytellers not only was false but was itself the principal cause of the environmental disaster that unfolded during the 1930s. The Dust Bowl had occurred because people had been telling themselves the wrong story and had tried to inscribe that story—the frontier—on a landscape incapable of supporting it. The environmental rhythms of the Plains ecosystem were cyclical, with good years and bad years following each other like waves on a beach. The problem of human settlement in the region was that people insisted on imposing their linear notions of progress on this cyclical pattern. Their perennial optimism led them always to accept as "normal" the most favorable part of the precipitation cycle, and so they created a type and scale of agriculture that could not possibly be sustained through the dry years. In effect, bad storytelling had wreaked havoc with the balance of nature.

By this interpretation, the "plot" of Great Plains history rises as Euroamerican settlement begins, but the upward motion becomes problematic as farmers exceed the natural limits of the ecosystem. From that moment forward, the story moves toward a climax in which the tragic flaws of a self-deluding people finally yield crisis and decline. Although the geographical and chronological frame of this narrative are much the same as in the earlier progressive plots, the *scene* has shifted dramatically. For Webb and Malin, the Plains environment was resistant but changeable, so that struggle and ingenuity would finally make it conform to the human will. In this early New Deal incarnation of a pessimistic Great Plains history, the environment was not only resistant but in some fundamental ways unchangeable. Its most important characteristics—cyclical drought and aridity—could not be altered by human technology; they could only be accommodated. If the story was still about human beings learning to live in the grasslands, its ultimate message was about gaining the wisdom to recognize and accept natural limits rather than strive to overcome them. Although the close of the New Deal committee's story still lay in the future when its report was released in 1936, its authors clearly intended readers to conclude that the only appropriate ending was for Americans to reject optimistic stories such as Webb's and Malin's in favor of environmental restraint and sound management.

30 The political subtext of this story is not hard to find. Whereas the heroes of earlier Great Plains narratives had been the courageous and inventive people who settled the region, the New Dealers constructed their stories so as to place themselves on center stage. Plainspeople, for all their energy, courage, and love of the land, were incapable of solving their own problems without help. They had made such a mess of

their environment that only disinterested outsiders, offering the enlightened perspective of scientific management, could save them from their own folly. In this sense, the New Deal narrative is only partially tragic, for in fact the planners still intended a happy ending. Like Webb and Malin, they saw the human story on the Plains as a tale of adaptation, but their vision of progressive modernization ended in regional coordination and centralized state planning. Federal planners would aid local communities in developing new cooperative institutions and a more sustainable relation to the land. This was the conclusion of Pare Lorentz's famous New Deal propaganda film, *The Plow that Broke the Plains* (1936), in which a seemingly inevitable environmental collapse is finally reversed by government intervention. Technology, education, cooperation, and state power—not individualism—would bring Plains society back into organic balance with Plains nature and thereby avert tragedy to produce a happy ending.

Seen in this light, James Malin's storytelling takes on new meaning. Malin wrote in the wake of the New Deal and was a staunch conservative opponent of everything it represented. His narratives of regional adaptation expressed his own horror of collectivism by resisting the New Deal story at virtually every turn. The planners, he said, had exaggerated the severity of the Dust Bowl to serve their own statist ends and had ignored the fact that dust storms had been a natural part of the Plains environment as far back as anyone remembered. Their scientistic faith in ecology had grave political dangers, for the ecologists had themselves gone astray in viewing the Plains environment as a stable, self-equilibrating organism in which human action inevitably disturbed the balance of nature.[3] Ecosystems were dynamic, and so was the human story of technological progress: to assert that nature set insurmountable limits to human ingenuity was to deny the whole upward sweep of civilized history. The New Dealers' affection for stories in which nature and society were metaphorically cast as organisms only revealed their own hostility to individualism and their flirtation with communist notions of the state. "Scientism," Malin declared, "along with statism, have become major social myths that threaten freedom."[4]

If the New Dealers' Great Plains was a constrained environment forcing inhabitants to accept its natural limits, Malin's was a landscape of multiple possibilities, a stage for human freedom. The story of the one began in balance, moved into chaos, and then returned to

3. On the role of the Dust Bowl in reshaping the science of ecology itself, see Ronald C. Tobey, *Saving the Prairies: The Life Cycle of the Founding School of American Plant Ecology, 1895–1955* (Berkeley, 1981).
4. Malin, *Grassland of North America*, 168.

the wiser balance of a scientifically planned society. The story of the other had no such prophetic return to an organic whole but expressed instead a constant process of readaptation that continued the long march of human improvement that was the core plot of Malin's history. In both cases, the shape of the landscape conformed to the human narratives that were set within it and so became the terrain upon which their different politics contested each other. Malin's commitment to individualist freedom led him to probe more deeply into grassland ecology than any historian before him, but always in an effort to find human possibilities rather than natural limits. The scene he constructed for his story was an environment that responded well to human needs unless misguided bureaucrats interfered with people's efforts to adapt themselves to the land.

It is James Malin's anti-New Deal narrative that informs Paul Bonnifield's *The Dust Bowl.* Writing in the late 1970s, at a time when conservative critiques of the welfare state were becoming a dominant feature of American political discourse, Bonnifield argues less urgently and polemically than Malin, but he tells essentially the same story. For him, the Great Plains did pose special problems to the people who settled there, but no one grappled with those problems more successfully than they. When the Dust Bowl hit, it was the people who lived there, not government scientists, who invented new land-use practices that solved earlier problems. New Deal planners understood little about the region and were so caught up in their own ideology that they compounded its problems by trying to impose their vision of a planned society.

Rather than allow residents to come up with their own solutions, Bonnifield argues, the planners used every means possible to drive farmers from their land. They did this not to address the environmental problems of the Plains, but to solve their own problem of reducing the national overproduction of wheat. To justify this deceit, they caricatured Plains inhabitants as "defeated, poverty-ridden people without hope" in such propaganda as *The Plow that Broke the Plains* and the Farm Security Administration photographs, with their mini-narratives of environmental destruction and social despair.[5] In fact, Bonnifield argues, the Plains contained some of the best farming soil in the world. The landscape was difficult but ultimately benign for people who could learn to thrive upon it. Their chief problem was less a hostile nature than a hostile government. The narrative echoes Malin's scenic landscape but gains a different kind of ideological force when placed at the historical moment of its narration—in the waning years of the Carter administration just prior to Ronald Reagan's trium-

5. Bonnifield, *The Dust Bowl*, 202.

phant election as president. Bonnifield's is a tale of ordinary folk needing nothing so much as to get government off their backs.

If Bonnifield elaborates the optimistic Dust Bowl narrative of a conservative critic of the New Deal, Donald Worster returns to the New Deal plot and deepens its tragic possibilities. Worster, who is with Webb the most powerful narrator among these writers, accepts the basic framework of Roosevelt's planners—the refusal of linear-minded Americans to recognize and accept cyclical environmental constraints—but he shears away its statist bias and considerably expands its cultural boundaries. One consequence of the New Deal tale was to remove the history of the Plains from its role in the long-term ascent of civilization; instead, the region became merely an unfortunate anomaly that imposed unusual constraints on the "steady progress" that was otherwise typical of American life. Worster rejects this reading of Plains history and argues instead that the Plains were actually a paradigmatic case in a larger story that might be called "the rise and fall of capitalism."

For Worster, the refusal to recognize natural limits is one of the defining characteristics of a capitalist ethos and economy. He is therefore drawn to a narrative in which the same facts that betokened progress for Webb and Malin become signs of declension and of the compounding contradictions of capitalist expansion. The scene of the story is world historical, only this time the plot leads toward catastrophe:

> That the thirties were a time of great crisis in American, indeed, in world, capitalism has long been an obvious fact. The Dust Bowl, I believe, was part of that same crisis. It came about because the expansionary energy of the United States had finally encountered a volatile, marginal land, destroying the delicate ecological balance that had evolved there. We speak of farmers and plows on the plains and the damage they did, but the language is inadequate. What brought them to the region was a social system, a set of values, an economic order. There is no word that so fully sums up those elements as "capitalism." . . . Capitalism, it is my contention, has been the decisive factor in this nation's use of nature.[6]

By this reading, the chief agent of the story is not "the pioneers" or "civilization" or "man"; it is capitalism. The plot leads from the origins of that economic system, through a series of crises, toward the future environmental cataclysm when the system will finally collapse. The tale of Worster's Dust Bowl thus concerns an intermediate crisis that foreshadows other crises yet to come; in this, it proclaims an apocalyptic prophecy that inverts the prophecy of progress found in

6. Worster, *Dust Bowl*, 5.

earlier frontier narratives. Worster's inversion of the frontier story is deeply ironic, for it implies that the increasing technological "control" represented by Webb's and Malin's human ingenuity leads only toward an escalating spiral of disasters. He also breaks rank with the New Dealers at this point, for in his view their efforts at solving the problems of the Dust Bowl did nothing to address the basic contradictions of capitalism itself. For Worster, the planners "propped up an agricultural economy that had proved itself to be socially and ecologically erosive."[7]

Given how much his basic plot differs from Webb's and Malin's, the scene Worster constructs for his narrative must differ just as dramatically. Since Worster's story concerns the destruction of an entire ecosystem, it must end where the frontier story began: in a wasteland. His plot must move downward toward an ecological disaster called the Dust Bowl. Whereas the frontier narratives begin in a negatively valued landscape and end in a positive one, Worster begins his tale in a place whose narrative value is entirely good. His grasslands are "an old and unique ecological complex" that nature had struggled for millions of years to achieve, "determining by trial and error what would flourish best in this dry corner of the good earth."[8] Delicate and beautiful, the Plains were an ecosystem living always on the edge of drought, and their survival depended on an intricate web of plants and animals that capitalism was incapable of valuing by any standard other than that of the marketplace. From this beginning, the story moves down a slope that ends in the dust storms whose narrative role is to stand as the most vivid possible symbol of human alienation from nature.

The very different scenes that progressive and declensionist narrators choose as the settings for their Great Plains histories bring us to another key observation about narrative itself: where one chooses to begin and end a story profoundly alters its shape and meaning. Worster's is not, after all, the only possible plot that can organize Great Plains history into a tale of crisis and decline. Because his metanarrative has to do with the past and future of capitalism, his time frame, like that of the frontier storytellers, remains tied to the start of white settlement—the moment when the American plot of progress or decline begins its upward or downward sweep. Although he acknowledges the prior presence of Indians in the region, he devotes only a few pages to them. They are clearly peripheral to his narrative. This is true of *all* the stories we have examined thus far, for reasons that have as much to do with narrative rhetoric as with historical analysis. In

7. *Ibid.*, 163.
8. *Ibid.*, 66.

their efforts to meet the narrative requirements that define a well-told tale—organic unity, a clear focus, and only the "relevant" details—these historians have little to say about the region's earlier human inhabitants. They therefore ignore the entire first half of my original chronicle of "key events" in Great Plains history. If we shift time frames to encompass the Indian past, we suddenly encounter a new set of narratives, equally tragic in their sense of crisis and declension, but strikingly different in plot and scene. As such, they offer further proof of the narrative power to reframe the past so as to include certain events and people, exclude others, and redefine the meaning of landscape accordingly.

40 One can detect this process of inclusion and exclusion in the passing references that progressive frontier narrators make to the prior, less happy stories of Indians. Sometimes, the tone of such references is elegiac and melancholy, as in the classic image of a "vanishing race"; sometimes the tone is simply dismissive. As Webb put it, "The Plains Indians were survivals of savagery," and "when there was nowhere else to push them they were permitted to settle down on the reservations."[9] If progressive change was inevitable, then so too was the eventual death or removal of the Indians. Their marginalization is thus a necessary requirement of the narrative. The feature of the environment that served as the best scenic indicator of this inevitability was the American bison, whose destruction was among the most crucial steps in undermining Indian subsistence. Even if one did not feel faborably disposed toward Indians, one could still mourn the bison. Webb again: "The Great Plains afforded the last virgin hunting grounds in America, and it was there that the most characteristic American animal made its last stand against the advance of the white man's civilization."[1]

These passing references to Indian "pre-history" are essentially framing devices, the purpose of which is to set the stage for the more important drama that is soon to follow. Historians who focus more centrally on Indians in their narratives almost inevitably construct very different plots from the ones I have described thus far. Among such scholars, one of the most sophisticated is Richard White.[2] Although his work too can be seen as a metaplot about the expansion of capitalism, the landscape he constructs is defined by Indian stories. White's

9. Webb, *Great Plains*, 508.

1. *Ibid.*, 509. For a similar use of the bison story as the symbol of an earlier Indian world that in some sense "vanished" during the last third of the nineteenth century, see William Cronon, *Nature's Metropolis: Chicago and the Great West* (New York, 1991), 213–18.

2. Richard White, *The Roots of Dependency: Subsistence, Environment, and Social Change among the Choctaws, Pawnees, and Navajos* (Lincoln, 1983), 147–211.

narrative of Pawnee history, for instance, begins with a people living in the mixed grasslands on the eastern margins of the Plains, dividing their activities in a seasonally shifting cycle of farming, gathering, and bison hunting. As one would expect of a declensionist plot, the initial scene is basically a benign and fruitful landscape, despite occasionally severe droughts. At the moment that the Pawnees began their encounter with Euroamerican culture—first with the arrival of the horse, then with the fur trade—the Plains environment was furnishing them a comfortable subsistence. In narrative terms, its meaning was that of a much-loved home.

The downward line of White's narrative records the steady erosion of the Pawnees' landscape. European disease wiped out much of their population. The expanding Sioux tribes made it harder for them to hunt bison and raise crops. As hunting became more difficult, the material and spiritual underpinnings of Pawnee subsistence began to disintegrate. Pawnee life was increasingly in crisis, and by the 1870s—when the great herds were finally destroyed—the tribe was forced to abandon its traditional homeland and remove to Indian Territory. The story ends as a classic tragedy of exodus and despair: "When the Pawnees decided to leave the Loup Valley, it was in the hope that to the south in Indian territory lay a land where they could hunt the buffalo, grow corn, and let the old life of the earthlodges flower beyond the reach of the Sioux and American settlers." Unfortunately, this hoped-for ending to the Pawnee story would never be achieved, because the scene it required no longer existed. As White says, "Such a land had disappeared forever."[3]

The frame of this story differs from anything we have seen thus far. It ends at the moment most of the other plots begin. It starts much further back in time, as European animals and trade goods begin to change the Plains landscape, offering opportunities and improvements in Pawnee life. Eventually a downward spiral begins, and the tragedy of the narrative becomes unrelenting as the Pawnees lose control of their familiar world. As for the scene of this plot, we have already encountered it in a different guise. The "wilderness" in which the progressive frontier narrators begin their stories is nothing less than the destroyed remnant of the Pawnees' home. It is less a wasteland than a land that has been wasted.

Narratives of this sort are by no means limited to white historians. Plenty Coups, a Crow Indian chief, tells in his 1930 autobiography of a boyhood vision sent him by his animal Helper, the Chickadee. In the dream, a great storm blown by the Four Winds destroyed a vast forest, leaving standing only the single tree in which the Chickadee—small-

3. White, *Roots of Dependency*, 211.

est but shrewdest of animals—made its lodge. The tribal elders interpreted this to mean that white settlers would eventually destroy not only the buffalo but also all tribes who resisted the American onslaught. On the basis of this prophetic dream, the Crows decided to ally themselves with the United States, and so they managed to preserve a portion of their homelands. Saving their land did not spare them from the destruction of the bison herds, however, and so they shared with other Plains tribes the loss of subsistence and spiritual communion that had previously been integral to the hunt. As Plenty Coups remarks at the end of his story, "when the buffalo went away the hearts of my people fell to the ground, and they could not lift them up again. After this nothing happened."[4]

Few remarks more powerfully capture the importance of narrative 45
to history than this last of Plenty Coups: "After this nothing happened." For the Crows as for other Plains tribes, the universe revolved around the bison herds, and life made sense only so long as the hunt continued. When the scene shifted—when the bison herds "went away"—that universe collapsed and history ended. Although the Crows continued to live on their reservation and although their identity as a people has never ceased, for Plenty Coups their subsequent life is all part of a different story.[5] The story he loved best ended with the buffalo. Everything that has happened since is part of some other plot, and there is neither sense nor joy in telling it.

The nothingness at the end of Plenty Coups's story suggests just how completely a narrative can redefine the events of the past and the landscapes of nature to fit the needs of its plot. After this nothing happened: not frontier progress, not the challenge of adaption to an arid land, not the Dust Bowl. Just the nothingness that follows the end of a story. It is this nothingness that carries me back to the place where I began, to my own awareness of a paradox at the heart of my intellectual practice as an historian. On the one hand, most environmental historians would be quite comfortable in asserting the importance of the nonhuman world to any understanding of the human past. Most would argue that nature is larger than humanity, that it is not com-

4. Frank Linderman, *Plenty-coups: Chief of the Crows* (1930; reprint, Lincoln, 1962), 311.
5. The danger in the way Plenty Coups ends his story, and in Richard White's ending as well, is that the close of these tragic narratives can all too easily be taken as the end of their protagonists' cultural history. The notion that Indian histories come to an end is among the classic imperialist myths of the frontier, wherein a "vanishing race" "melts away" before the advancing forces of "civilization." Plenty Coups's declaration that "after this nothing happened" conveys with great power the tragedy of an older Indian generation but says nothing about the generations of Indians who still live within the shadow of that narrative punctuation mark.

pletely an invention of human culture, that it impinges on our lives in ways we cannot completely control, that it is "real," and that our task as historians is to understand the way it affects us and vice versa. Black clouds bringing dust and darkness from the Kansas sky, overturned sod offering itself as a seedbed for alien grains sprouting amid the torn roots of dying prairie grasses, dry winds filled with the stench of rotting bison flesh as wolves and vultures linger over their feasts: these are more than just stories.

And yet—they are stories too. As such, they are human inventions despite all our efforts to preserve their "naturalness." They belong as much to rhetoric and human discourse as to ecology and nature. It is for this reason that we cannot escape confronting the challenge of multiple competing narratives in our efforts to understand both nature and the human past. As I hope my reading of Great Plains history suggests, the narrative theorists have much to teach us. Quite apart from the environmental historian's analytical premise that nature and culture have become inextricably entangled in their process of mutual reshaping, the rhetorical practice of environmental history commits us to narrative ways of talking about nature that are anything but "natural." If we fail to reflect on the plots and scenes and tropes that undergird our histories, we run the risk of missing the human artifice that lies at the heart of even the most "natural" of narratives.

And just what *is* a narrative? As the evidence of my Great Plains chronicle would imply, it is not merely a sequence of events. To shift from chronicle to narrative, a tale of environmental change must be structured so that, as Aristotle said, it "has beginning, middle, and end."[6] What distinguishes stories from other forms of discourse is that they describe an action that begins, continues over a well-defined period of time, and finally draws to a definite close, with consequences that become meaningful because of their placement within the narrative. Completed action gives a story its unity and allows us to evaluate and judge an act by its results. The moral of a story is defined by its ending: as Aristotle remarked, "the end is everywhere the chief thing."[7]

Narrative is a peculiarly human way of organizing reality, and this has important implications for the way we approach the history of environmental change. Some nonhuman events can be said to have properties that conform to the Aristotelian beginning-middle-end requirement of storytelling, as when an individual organism (or a species

6. Aristotle, *Poetics*, in *The Complete Works of Aristotle: The Revised Oxford Translation*, ed. Jonathan Barnes (2 vols., Princeton, 1984), II, 2321.
7. *Ibid.* On the importance of a story's ending in determining its configured unity, see Kermode, *Sense of an Ending;* this can be usefully combined with Edward W. Said, *Beginnings: Intention and Method* (New York, 1975).

or a mountain range or even the universe itself) is born, persists, and dies. One *can* tell stories about such things—geologists and evolutionary biologists often do—but they lack the compelling drama that comes from having a judgeable protagonist. Things in nature usually "just happen," without raising questions of moral choice. Many natural events lack even this much linear structure. Some are cyclical; the motions of the planets, the seasons, or the rhythms of biological fertility and reproduction. Others are random: climate shifts, earthquakes, genetic mutations, and other events the causes of which remain hidden from us. One does not automatically describe such things with narrative plots, and yet environmental histories, which purport to set the human past in its natural context, all have plots. Nature and the universe do not tell stories; we do. Why is this?

Two possible answers to this question emerge from the work that 50
philosophers and post-structuralist literary critics have done on the relationship between narrative and history. One group, which includes Hayden White and the late Louis Mink as well as many of the deconstructionists, argues that narrative is so basic to our cultural beliefs that we automatically impose it on a reality that bears little or no relation to the plots we use in organizing our experience.[8] Mink summarizes this position nicely by asserting that "the past is not an untold story." The same could presumably be said about nature: we force our stories on a world that doesn't fit them.[9] The historian's project of recovering past realities and representing them "truly" or even "fairly" is thus a delusion. Trapped within our narrative discourse, we could not do justice either to nature or to the past no matter how hard we tried—presuming, of course, that "nature" or "the past" even exist at all.

An alternative position, most recently defended by David Carr but originally developed by Martin Heidegger, is that although narrative may not be intrinsic to events in the physical universe, it is fundamental to the way we humans organize our experience. Whatever may be the perspective of the universe on the things going on around us, our human perspective is that we inhabit an endlessly storied world. We narrate the triumphs and failures of our pasts. We tell stories to explore the alternative choices that might lead to feared or hoped-for

8. See White, *Tropics of Discourse*; White, *Metahistory*; Mink, "Narrative Form as Cognitive Instrument"; a less extreme position that ultimately leads toward a similar conclusion can be found in Ricoeur, *Time and Narrative*, I. For a useful, if biased, explication of these debates, see Hayden White, "The Question of Narrative in Contemporary Historical Theory," *History and Theory*, 23 (no. 1, 1984), 1–33. A valuable survey can be found in Martin, *Recent Theories of Narrative*.

9. Mink, "Narrative Form as Cognitive Instrument," 148. See also Richard T. Vann, "Louis Mink's Linguistic Turn," *History and Theory*, 26 (no. 1, 1987), 14.

futures. Our very habit of partitioning the flow of time into "events," with their implied beginnings, middles, and ends, suggests how deeply the narrative structure inheres in our experience of the world. As Carr puts it, "Narrative is not merely a possibly successful way of describing events; its structure inheres in the events themselves. Far from being a formal distortion of the events it relates, a narrative account is an extension of one of their primary features."[1]

Carr's position will undoubtedly be attractive to most historians, since it argues that, far from being arbitrary, our narratives reflect one of the most fundamental properties of human consciousness. It also gives us a way of absorbing the lessons of narrative theory without feeling we have abandoned all ties to an external reality. Insofar as people project their wills into the future, organizing their lives to make acts in the present yield predictable future results—to just that extent, they live their lives as if they were telling a story. It is undoubtedly true that we all constantly tell ourselves stories to remind ourselves who we are, how we got to be that person, and what we want to become. The same is true not just of individuals but of communities and societies: we use our histories to remember ourselves, just as we use our prophecies as tools for exploring what we do or do not wish to become.[2] As Plenty Coups's story implies, to recover the narratives people tell themselves about the meanings of their lives is to learn a great deal about their past actions and about the way they *understand* those actions. Stripped of the story, we lose track of understanding itself.

The storied reality of human experience suggests why environmental histories so consistently find plots in nature and also why those plots almost always center on people. Environmental history sets itself the task of including within its boundaries far more of the nonhuman world than most other histories, and yet human agents continue to be the main anchors of its narratives. Dust storms have been occurring on the Plains for millennia, and yet the ones we really care about—those we now narrate under the title "Dust Bowl"—are the ones we can most easily transform into stories in which people become the heroes or victims or villains of the piece. In this, historians consistently differ from ecologists, who more often than not treat people as exogenous variables that fit awkwardly if at all into the theoretical models of the

1. David Carr, "Narrative and the Real World: An Argument for Continuity," *History and Theory*, 25 (no. 2, 1986), 117.
2. See Robert Cover, "Nomos and Narrative," *Harvard Law Review*, 97 (Nov. 1983), 3–68. Carr's argument that all human experience is narrated does not address a deeper relativist claim, that there is no necessary correlation between the stories people tell in their own lives and the stories historians tell in reconstructing those lives. On this issue, see Noel Carroll, review of *Time, Narrative, and History* by David Carr, *History and Theory*, 27 (no. 3, 1988), 297–306.

discipline. The historian's tendency is quite opposite. The chief protagonists and antagonists of our stories are almost always human, for reasons that go to the very heart of our narrative impulse.

Our histories of the Great Plains environment remain fixed on people because what we most care about in nature is its meaning for human beings. We care about the dust storms because they stand as a symbol of human endurance in the face of natural adversity—or as a symbol of human irresponsibility in the face of natural fragility. Human interests and conflicts create *values* in nature that in turn provide the moral center for our stories. We want to know whether environmental change is good or bad, and that question can only be answered by referring to our own sense of right and wrong. Nature remains mute about such matters. However passionately we may care about the nonhuman world, however much we may believe in its innate worth, our historical narratives, even those about the nonhuman world, remain focused on a human struggle over values. If these values are in effect the meanings we attach to judgeable human actions—nonhuman actions being generally unjudgeable by us—then the center of our stories will remain focused on human thoughts, human acts, and human values.

QUESTIONS

1. *Make a list of the historians of the "Dust Bowl" whom Cronon discusses; then group together those historians who share similar views on the causes and effects of the Dust Bowl. In what order does Cronon present these views? Why?*
2. *According to Cronon, historians tend to create "agents" who are responsible for the events they narrate; they create "causes" for the "effects." Among the agents Cronon finds in Dust Bowl narratives are "the pioneers," "civilization," "man," and "capitalism." For each historian you listed in question 1, what "agent" or "agents" are the leading cause(s) in his history?*
3. *In paragraph 12 Cronon distinguishes between a* chronicle *and a* narrative. *What does he mean by each term? Why does he claim that historians write* narratives? *How do the final paragraphs of his essay expand on his initial explanation?*
4. *Consult one of the original sources that Cronon quotes. Write a brief explanation of how Cronon uses this source in his own writing.*

Edward Hallett Carr

THE HISTORIAN AND HIS FACTS

What is history? Lest anyone think the question meaningless or superfluous, I will take as my text two passages relating respectively to the first and second incarnations of *The Cambridge Modern History.* Here is Acton in his report of October 1896 to the Syndics of the Cambridge University Press on the work which he had undertaken to edit:

> It is a unique opportunity of recording, in the way most useful to the greatest number, the fullness of the knowledge which the nineteenth century is about to bequeath. . . . By the judicious division of labor we should be able to do it, and to bring home to every man the last document, and the ripest conclusions of international research.
>
> Ultimate history we cannot have in this generation; but we can dispose of conventional history, and show the point we have reached on the road from one to the other, now that all information is within reach, and every problem has become capable of solution.

And almost exactly sixty years later Professor Sir George Clark, in his general introduction to the second *Cambridge Modern History,* commented on this belief of Acton and his collaborators that it would one day be possible to produce "ultimate history," and went on:

> Historians of a later generation do not look forward to any such prospect. They expect their work to be superseded again and again. They consider that knowledge of the past has come down through one or more human minds, has been "processed" by them, and therefore cannot consist of elemental and impersonal atoms which nothing can alter. . . . The exploration seems to be endless, and some impatient scholars take refuge in scepticism, or at least in the doctrine that, since all historical judgments involve persons and points of view, one is as good as another and there is no "objective" historical truth.

Where the pundits contradict each other so flagrantly the field is open to enquiry. I hope that I am sufficiently up-to-date to recognize that anything written in the 1890's must be nonsense. But I am not yet advanced enough to be committed to the view that anything written in the 1950's necessarily makes sense. Indeed, it may already have occurred to you that this enquiry is liable to stray into something even broader than the nature of history. The clash between Acton and Sir George Clark is a reflection of the change in our total outlook on society over the interval between these two pronouncements. Acton

From *What Is History?* (1961).

speaks out of the positive belief, the clear-eyed self-confidence of the later Victorian age; Sir George Clark echoes the bewilderment and distracted scepticism of the beat generation. When we attempt to answer the question, What is history?, our answer, consciously or unconsciously, reflects our own position in time, and forms part of our answer to the broader question, what view we take of the society in which we live. I have no fear that my subject may, on closer inspection, seem trivial. I am afraid only that I may seem presumptuous to have broached a question so vast and so important.

The nineteenth century was a great age for facts. "What I want," said Mr. Gradgrind in *Hard Times*,[1] "is Facts. . . . Facts alone are wanted in life." Nineteenth-century historians on the whole agreed with him. When Ranke in the 1830's, in legitimate protest against moralizing history, remarked that the task of the historian was "simply to show how it really was [*wie es eigentlich gewesen*]" this not very profound aphorism had an astonishing success. Three generations of German, British, and even French historians marched into battle intoning the magic words, "*Wie es eigentlich gewesen*" like an incantation—designed, like most incantations, to save them from the tiresome obligation to think for themselves. The Positivists, anxious to stake out their claim for history as a science, contributed the weight of their influence to this cult of facts. First ascertain the facts, said the positivists, then draw your conclusions from them. In Great Britain, this view of history fitted in perfectly with the empiricist tradition which was the dominant strain in British philosophy from Locke to Bertrand Russell. The empirical theory of knowledge presupposes a complete separation between subject and object. Facts, like sense-impressions, impinge on the observer from outside, and are independent of his consciousness. The process of reception is passive: having received the data, he then acts on them. *The Shorter Oxford English Dictionary*, a useful but tendentious work of the empirical school, clearly marks the separateness of the two processes by defining a fact as "a datum of experience as distinct from conclusions." This is what may be called the commonsense view of history. History consists of a corpus of ascertained facts. The facts are available to the historian in documents, inscriptions, and so on, like fish on the fishmonger's slab. The historian collects them, takes them home, and cooks and serves them in whatever style appeals to him. Acton, whose culinary tastes were austere, wanted them served plain. In his letter of instructions to contributors to the first *Cambridge Modern History* he announced the requirement "that our Waterloo must be one that satisfies French and English, German and Dutch alike; that nobody can tell, without examining the list of au-

1. Novel (1855) by Charles Dickens.

thors where the Bishop of Oxford laid down the pen, and whether Fairbairn or Gasquet, Liebermann or Harrison took it up." Even Sir George Clark, critical as he was of Acton's attitude, himself contrasted the "hard core of facts" in history with the "surrounding pulp of disputable interpretation"—forgetting perhaps that the pulpy part of the fruit is more rewarding than the hard core. First get your facts straight, then plunge at your peril into the shifting sands of interpretation—that is the ultimate wisdom of the empirical, common-sense school of history. It recalls the favorite dictum of the great liberal journalist C. P. Scott: "Facts are sacred, opinion is free."

Now this clearly will not do. I shall not embark on a philosophical discussion of the nature of our knowledge of the past. Let us assume for present purposes that the fact that Caesar crossed the Rubicon and the fact that there is a table in the middle of the room are facts of the same or of a comparable order, that both these facts enter our consciousness in the same or in a comparable manner, and that both have the same objective character in relation to the person who knows them. But, even on this bold and not very plausible assumption, our argument at once runs into the difficulty that not all facts about the past are historical facts, or are treated as such by the historian. What is the criterion which distinguishes the facts of history from other facts about the past?

What is a historical fact? This is a crucial question into which we must look a little more closely. According to the common-sense view, there are certain basic facts which are the same for all historians and which form, so to speak, the backbone of history—the fact, for example, that the Battle of Hastings was fought in 1066. But this view calls for two observations. In the first place, it is not with facts like these that the historian is primarily concerned. It is no doubt important to know that the great battle was fought in 1066 and not in 1065 or 1067, and that it was fought at Hastings and not at Eastbourne or Brighton. The historian must not get these things wrong. But when points of this kind are raised, I am reminded of Housman's remark[2] that "accuracy is a duty, not a virtue." To praise a historian for his accuracy is like praising an architect for using well-seasoned timber or properly mixed concrete in his building. It is a necessary condition of his work, but not his essential function. It is precisely for matters of this kind that the historian is entitled to rely on what have been called the "auxiliary sciences" of history—archaeology, epigraphy, numismatics, chronology, and so forth. The historian is not required to have the special skills which enable the expert to determine the origin and period of a fragment of pottery or marble, or decipher an obscure inscription, or

2. In the preface to his critical edition of Manilius, *Astronomicon*, an obscure Latin work.

to make the elaborate astronomical calculations necessary to establish a precise date. These so-called basic facts which are the same for all historians commonly belong to the category of the raw materials of the historian rather than of history itself. The second observation is that the necessity to establish these basic facts rests not on any quality in the facts themselves, but on an *a priori* decision of the historian. In spite of C. P. Scott's motto, every journalist knows today that the most effective way to influence opinion is by the selection and arrangement of the appropriate facts. It used to be said that facts speak for themselves. This is, of course, untrue. The facts speak only when the historian calls on them: It is he who decides to which facts to give the floor, and in what order or context. It was, I think, one of Pirandello's characters who said that a fact is like a sack—it won't stand up till you've put something in it. The only reason why we are interested to know that the battle was fought at Hastings in 1066 is that historians regard it as a major historical event. It is the historian who has decided for his own reasons that Caesar's crossing of that petty stream, the Rubicon, is a fact of history, whereas the crossing of the Rubicon by millions of other people before or since interests nobody at all. The fact that you arrived in this building half an hour ago on foot, or on a bicycle, or in a car, is just as much a fact about the past as the fact that Caesar crossed the Rubicon. But it will probably be ignored by historians. Professor Talcott Parsons once called science "a selective system of cognitive orientations to reality." It might perhaps have been put more simply. But history is, among other things, that. The historian is necessarily selective. The belief in a hard core of historical facts existing objectively and independently of the interpretation of the historian is a preposterous fallacy, but one which it is very hard to eradicate.

Let us take a look at the process by which a mere fact about the past 5
is transformed into a fact of history. At Stalybridge Wakes in 1850, a vendor of gingerbread, as the result of some petty dispute, was deliberately kicked to death by an angry mob. Is this a fact of history? A year ago I should unhesitatingly have said "no." It was recorded by an eyewitness in some little-known memoirs;[3] but I had never seen it judged worthy of mention by any historian. A year ago Dr. Kitson Clark cited it in his Ford lectures in Oxford. Does this make it into a historical fact? Not, I think, yet. Its present status, I suggest, is that it has been proposed for membership of the select club of historical facts. It now awaits a seconder and sponsors. It may be that in the course of the next few years we shall see this fact appearing first in footnotes, then in the text, of articles and books about nineteenth-century England, and that in twenty or thirty years' time it may be a well established

3. Lord George Sanger: *Seventy Years a Showman* (London: J. M. Dent & Sons, 1926), pp. 188–9 [Carr's note].

historical fact. Alternatively, nobody may take it up, in which case it will relapse into the limbo of unhistorical facts about the past from which Dr. Kitson Clark has gallantly attempted to rescue it. What will decide which of these two things will happen? It will depend, I think, on whether the thesis or interpretation in support of which Dr. Kitson Clark cited this incident is accepted by other historians as valid and significant. Its status as a historical fact will turn on a question of interpretation. This element of interpretation enters into every fact of history.

May I be allowed a personal reminiscence? When I studied ancient history in this university many years ago, I had as a special subject "Greece in the period of the Persian Wars." I collected fifteen or twenty volumes on my shelves and took it for granted that there, recorded in these volumes, I had all the facts relating to my subject. Let us assume—it was very nearly true—that those volumes contained all the facts about it that were then known, or could be known. It never occurred to me to enquire by what accident or process of attrition that minute selection of facts, out of all the myriad facts that must have once been known to somebody, had survived to become *the* facts of history. I suspect that even today one of the fascinations of ancient and mediaeval history is that it gives us the illusion of having all the facts at our disposal within a manageable compass: the nagging distinction between the facts of history and other facts about the past vanishes because the few known facts are all facts of history. As Bury, who had worked in both periods, said, "the records of ancient and mediaeval history are starred with lacunae." History has been called an enormous jig-saw with a lot of missing parts. But the main trouble does not consist of the lacunae. Our picture of Greece in the fifth century *b.c.* is defective not primarily because so many of the bits have been accidentally lost, but because it is, by and large, the picture formed by a tiny group of people in the city of Athens. We know a lot about what fifth-century Greece looked like to an Athenian citizen; but hardly anything about what it looked like to a Spartan, a Corinthian, or a Theban—not to mention a Persian, or a slave or other non-citizen resident in Athens. Our picture has been preselected and predetermined for us, not so much by accident as by people who were consciously or unconsciously imbued with a particular view and thought the facts which supported that view worth preserving. In the same way, when I read in a modern history of the Middle Ages that the people of the Middle Ages were deeply concerned with religion, I wonder how we know this, and whether it is true. What we know as the facts of mediaeval history have almost all been selected for us by generations of chroniclers who were professionally occupied in the theory and practice of religion, and who therefore thought it supremely important, and recorded everything relating to it, and not much else. The picture of the Russian peasant as devoutly religious was destroyed by the revolution of 1917. The picture of mediaeval man as devoutly religious, whether true or not, is indestructible, because nearly all the known facts about him were preselected for us by people who believed it, and wanted others to believe it, and a mass of other facts, in which we might possibly have found evidence to the contrary, has been lost beyond recall. The dead hand of vanished generations of historians, scribes, and chroniclers has determined beyond the possibility of appeal the pattern of the past. "The history we read," writes Professor Barraclough, himself trained as a mediaevalist, "though based on facts, is, strictly speaking, not factual at all, but a series of accepted judgments."

But let us turn to the different, but equally grave, plight of the modern historian. The ancient or mediaeval historian may be grateful for the vast winnowing process which, over the years, has put at his disposal a manageable corpus of historical facts. As Lytton Strachey said in his mischievous way, "ignorance is the first requisite of the historian, ignorance which simplifies and clarifies, which selects and omits." When I am tempted, as I sometimes am, to envy the extreme competence of colleagues engaged in writing ancient or mediaeval history, I find consolation in the reflection that they are so competent mainly because they are so ignorant of their subject. The modern historian enjoys none of the advantages of this built-in ignorance. He must cultivate this necessary ignorance for himself—the more so the nearer he comes to his own times. He has the dual task of discovering the few significant facts and turning them into facts of history, and of discarding the many insignificant facts as unhistorical. But this is the very converse of the nineteenth-century heresy that history consists of the compilation of a maximum number of irrefutable and objective facts. Anyone who succumbs to this heresy will either have to give up history as a bad job, and take to stamp-collecting or some other form of antiquarianism, or end in a madhouse. It is this heresy, which during the past hundred years has had such devastating effects on the modern historian, producing in Germany, in Great Britain, and in the United States a vast and growing mass of dry-as-dust factual histories, of minutely specialized monographs, of would-be historians knowing more and more about less and less, sunk without trace in an ocean of facts. It was, I suspect, this heresy—rather than the alleged conflict between liberal and Catholic loyalties—which frustrated Acton as a historian. In an early essay he said of his teacher Döllinger: "He would not write with imperfect materials, and to him the materials were always imperfect."[4] Acton was surely here pronouncing an anticipatory

4. Later Acton said of Döllinger that "it was given him to form his philosophy of history on the largest induction ever available to man" [Carr's note].

verdict on himself, on that strange phenomenon of a historian whom many would regard as the most distinguished occupant the Regius Chair of Modern History in this university has ever had—but who wrote no history. And Acton wrote his own epitaph in the introductory note to the first volume of the *Cambridge Modern History*, published just after his death, when he lamented that the requirements pressing on the historian "threaten to turn him from a man of letters into the compiler of an encyclopedia." Something had gone wrong. What had gone wrong was the belief in this untiring and unending accumulation of hard facts as the foundation of history, the belief that facts speak for themselves and that we cannot have too many facts, a belief at that time so unquestioning that few historians then thought it necessary—and some still think it unnecessary today—to ask themselves the question: What is history?

The nineteenth-century fetishism of facts was completed and justified by a fetishism of documents. The documents were the Ark of the Covenant in the temple of facts. The reverent historian approached them with bowed head and spoke of them in awed tones. If you find it in the documents, it is so. But what, when we get down to it, do these documents—the decrees, the treaties, the rent-rolls, the blue books, the official correspondence, the private letters and diaries—tell us? No document can tell us more than what the author of the document thought—what he thought had happened, what he thought ought to happen or would happen, or perhaps only what he wanted others to think he thought, or even only what he himself thought he thought. None of this means anything until the historian has got to work on it and deciphered it. The facts, whether found in documents or not, have still to be processed by the historian before he can make any use of them: the use he makes of them is, if I may put it that way, the processing process.

Let me illustrate what I am trying to say by an example which I happen to know well. When Gustav Stresemann, the Foreign Minister of the Weimar Republic, died in 1929, he left behind him an enormous mass—300 boxes full—of papers, official, semiofficial, and private, nearly all relating to the six years of his tenure of office as Foreign Minister. His friends and relatives naturally thought that a monument should be raised to the memory of so great a man. His faithful secretary Bernhardt got to work; and within three years there appeared three massive volumes, of some 600 pages each, of selected documents from the 300 boxes, with the impressive title *Stresemanns Vermächtnis*.[5] In the ordinary way the documents themselves would have moldered away in some cellar or attic and disappeared for ever; or per-

5. *Stresemann's Legacy.*

haps in a hundred years or so some curious scholar would have come upon them and set out to compare them with Bernhardt's text. What happened was far more dramatic. In 1945 the documents fell into the hands of the British and the American governments, who photographed the lot and put the photostats at the disposal of scholars in the Public Record Office in London and in the National Archives in Washington, so that, if we have sufficient patience and curiosity, we can discover exactly what Bernhardt did. What he did was neither very unusual nor very shocking. When Stresemann died, his Western policy seemed to have been crowned with a series of brilliant successes—Locarno, the admission of Germany to the League of Nations, the Dawes and Young plans and the American loans, the withdrawal of allied occupation armies from the Rhineland. This seemed the important and rewarding part of Stresemann's foreign policy; and it was not unnatural that it should have been over-represented in Bernhardt's selection of documents. Stresemann's Eastern policy, on the other hand, his relations with the Soviet Union, seemed to have led nowhere in particular; and, since masses of documents about negotiations which yielded only trivial results were not very interesting and added nothing to Stresemann's reputation, the process of selection could be more rigorous. Stresemann in fact devoted a far more constant and anxious attention to relations with the Soviet Union, and they played a far larger part in his foreign policy as a whole, than the reader of the Bernhardt selection would surmise. But the Bernhardt volumes compare favorably, I suspect, with many published collections of documents on which the ordinary historian implicitly relies.

This is not the end of my story. Shortly after the publication of 10
Bernhardt's volumes, Hitler came into power. Stresemann's name was consigned to oblivion in Germany, and the volumes disappeared from circulation: many, perhaps most, of the copies must have been destroyed. Today *Stresemanns Vermächtnis* is a rather rare book. But in the West Stresemann's reputation stood high. In 1935 an English publisher brought out an abbreviated translation of Bernhardt's work—a selection from Bernhardt's selection; perhaps one third of the original was omitted. Sutton, a well-known translator from the German, did his job competently and well. The English version, he explained in the preface, was "slightly condensed, but only by the omission of a certain amount of what, it was felt, was more ephemeral matter . . . of little interest to English readers or students." This again is natural enough. But the result is that Stresemann's Eastern policy, already under-represented in Bernhardt, recedes still further from view, and the Soviet Union appears in Sutton's volumes merely as an occasional and rather unwelcome intruder in Stresemann's predominantly Western foreign policy. Yet it is safe to say that, for all except a

few specialists, Sutton and not Bernhardt—and still less the documents themselves—represents for the Western world the authentic voice of Stresemann. Had the documents perished in 1945 in the bombing, and had the remaining Bernhardt volumes disappeared, the authenticity and authority of Sutton would never have been questioned. Many printed collections of documents gratefully accepted by historians in default of the originals rest on no securer basis than this.

But I want to carry the story one step further. Let us forget about Bernhardt and Sutton, and be thankful that we can, if we choose, consult the authentic papers of a leading participant in some important events in recent European history. What do the papers tell us? Among other things they contain records of some hundreds of Stresemann's conversations with the Soviet ambassador in Berlin and of a score or so with Chicherin.[6] These records have one feature in common. They depict Stresemann as having the lion's share of the conversations and reveal his arguments as invariably well put and cogent, while those of his partner are for the most part scanty, confused, and unconvincing. This is a familiar characteristic of all records of diplomatic conversations. The documents do not tell us what happened, but only what Stresemann thought had happened. It was not Sutton or Bernhardt, but Stresemann himself, who started the process of selection. And, if we had, say Chicherin's records of these same conversations, we should still learn from them only what Chicherin thought, and what really happened would still have to be reconstructed in the mind of the historian. Of course, facts and documents are essential to the historian. But do not make a fetish of them. They do not by themselves constitute history; they provide in themselves no ready-made answer to this tiresome question: What is history?

At this point I should like to say a few words on the question of why nineteenth-century historians were generally indifferent to the philosophy of history. The term was invented by Voltaire, and has since been used in different senses; but I shall take it to mean, if I use it at all, our answer to the question: What is history? The nineteenth century was, for the intellectuals of Western Europe, a comfortable period exuding confidence and optimism. The facts were on the whole satisfactory; and the inclination to ask and answer awkward questions about them was correspondingly weak. Ranke piously believed that divine providence would take care of the meaning of history if he took care of the facts; and Burckhardt with a more modern touch of cynicism observed that "we are not initiated into the purposes of the eternal wisdom." Professor Butterfield as late as 1931 noted with apparent satisfaction that "historians have reflected little upon the nature of things and

6. Soviet foreign minister from 1918 to 1928.

even the nature of their own subject." But my predecessor in these lectures, Dr. A. L. Rowse, more justly critical, wrote of Sir Winston Churchill's *The World Crisis*—his book about the First World War—that, while it matched Trotsky's *History of the Russian Revolution* in personality, vividness, and vitality, it was inferior in one respect: it had "no philosophy of history behind it." British historians refused to be drawn, not because they believed that history had no meaning, but because they believed that its meaning was implicit and self-evident. The liberal nineteenth-century view of history had a close affinity with the economic doctrine of *laissez-faire*—also the product of a serene and self-confident outlook on the world. Let everyone get on with his particular job, and the hidden hand would take care of the universal harmony. The facts of history were themselves a demonstration of the supreme fact of a beneficent and apparently infinite progress towards higher things. This was the age of innocence, and historians walked in the Garden of Eden, without a scrap of philosophy to cover them, naked and unashamed before the god of history. Since then, we have known Sin and experienced a Fall; and those historians who today pretend to dispense with a philosophy of history are merely trying, vainly and self-consciously, like members of a nudist colony, to recreate the Garden of Eden in their garden suburb. Today the awkward question can no longer be evaded. * * *

During the past fifty years a good deal of serious work has been done on the question: What is history? It was from Germany, the country which was to do so much to upset the comfortable reign of nineteenth-century liberalism, that the first challenge came in the 1880's and 1890's to the doctrine of the primacy and autonomy of facts in history. The philosophers who made the challenge are now little more than names: Dilthey is the only one of them who has recently received some belated recognition in Great Britain. Before the turn of the century, prosperity and confidence were still too great in this country for any attention to be paid to heretics who attacked the cult of facts. But early in the new century, the torch passed to Italy, where Croce began to propound a philosophy of history which obviously owed much to German masters. All history is "contemporary history," declared Croce,[7] meaning that history consists essentially in seeing the past through the eyes of the present and in the light of its problems, and that the main work of the historian is not to record, but to evaluate;

7. The context of this celebrated aphorism is as follows: "The practical requirements which underlie every historical judgment give to all history the character of 'contemporary history,' because, however remote in time events thus recounted may seem to be, the history in reality refers to present needs and present situations wherein those events vibrate" [Carr's note].

for, if he does not evaluate, how can he know what is worth recording? In 1910 the American philosopher, Carl Becker, argued in deliberately provocative language that "the facts of history do not exist for any historian till he creates them." These challenges were for the moment little noticed. It was only after 1920 that Croce began to have a considerable vogue in France and Great Britain. This was not perhaps because Croce was a subtler thinker or a better stylist than his German predecessors, but because, after the First World War, the facts seemed to smile on us less propitiously than in the years before 1914, and we were therefore more accessible to a philosophy which sought to diminish their prestige. Croce was an important influence on the Oxford philosopher and historian Collingwood, the only British thinker in the present century who has made a serious contribution to the philosophy of history. He did not live to write the systematic treatise he had planned; but his published and unpublished papers on the subject were collected after his death in a volume entitled *The Idea of History*, which appeared in 1945.

The views of Collingwood can be summarized as follows. The philosophy of history is concerned neither with "the past by itself" nor with "the historian's thought about it by itself," but with "the two things in their mutual relations." (This dictum reflects the two current meanings of the word "history"—the enquiry conducted by the historian and the series of past events into which he enquires.) "The past which a historian studies is not a dead past, but a past which in some sense is still living in the present." But a past act is dead, *i.e.* meaningless to the historian, unless he can understand the thought that lay behind it. Hence "all history is the history of thought," and "history is the re-enactment in the historian's mind of the thought whose history he is studying." The reconstitution of the past in the historian's mind is dependent on empirical evidence. But it is not in itself an empirical process, and cannot consist in a mere recital of facts. On the contrary, the process of reconstitution governs the selection and interpretation of the facts: this, indeed, is what makes them historical facts. "History," says Professor Oakeshott, who on this point stands near to Collingwood, "is the historian's experience. It is 'made' by nobody save the historian: to write history is the only way of making it."

15 This searching critique, though it may call for some serious reservations, brings to light certain neglected truths.

In the first place, the facts of history never come to us "pure," since they do not and cannot exist in a pure form: they are always refracted through the mind of the recorder. It follows that when we take up a work of history, our first concern should be not with the facts which it contains but with the historian who wrote it. Let me take as an example the great historian in whose honor and in whose name these lectures were founded. Trevelyan, as he tells us in his autobiography, was "brought up at home on a somewhat exuberantly Whig tradition"; and he would not, I hope, disclaim the title if I described him as the last and not the least of the great English liberal historians of the Whig tradition. It is not for nothing that he traces back his family tree, through the great Whig historian George Otto Trevelyan, to Macaulay, incomparably the greatest of the Whig historians. Dr. Trevelyan's finest and maturest work *England under Queen Anne* was written against that background, and will yield its full meaning and significance to the reader only when read against that background. The author, indeed, leaves the reader with no excuse for failing to do so. For if, following the technique of connoisseurs of detective novels, you read the end first, you will find on the last few pages of the third volume the best summary known to me of what is nowadays called the Whig interpretation of history; and you will see that what Trevelyan is trying to do is to investigate the origin and development of the Whig tradition, and to root it fairly and squarely in the years after the death of its founder, William III. Though this is not, perhaps, the only conceivable interpretation of the events of Queen Anne's reign, it is a valid and, in Trevelyan's hands, a fruitful interpretation. But, in order to appreciate it at its full value, you have to understand what the historian is doing. For if, as Collingwood says, the historian must re-enact in thought what has gone on in the mind of his *dramatis personae*, so the reader in his turn must re-enact what goes on in the mind of the historian. Study the historian before you begin to study the facts. This is, after all, not very abstruse. It is what is already done by the intelligent undergraduate who, when recommended to read a work by that great scholar Jones of St. Jude's, goes round to a friend at St. Jude's to ask what sort of chap Jones is, and what bees he has in his bonnet. When you read a work of history, always listen out for the buzzing. If you can detect none, either you are tone deaf or your historian is a dull dog. The facts are really not at all like fish on the fishmonger's slab. They are like fish swimming about in a vast and sometimes inaccessible ocean; and what the historian catches will depend partly on chance, but mainly on what part of the ocean he chooses to fish in and what tackle he chooses to use—these two factors being, of course, determined by the kind of fish he wants to catch. By and large, the historian will get the kind of facts he wants. History means interpretation. Indeed, if, standing Sir George Clark on his head, I were to call history "a hard core of interpretation surrounded by a pulp of disputable facts," my statement would, no doubt, be one-sided and misleading, but no more so, I venture to think, than the original dictum.

The second point is the more familiar one of the historian's need of imaginative understanding for the minds of the people with whom he is dealing, for the thought behind their acts: I say "imaginative understanding," not "sympathy," lest sympathy should be supposed to imply agreement. The nineteenth century was weak in mediaeval history, because it was too much repelled by the superstitious beliefs of the Middle Ages and by the barbarities which they inspired, to have any imaginative understanding of mediaeval people. Or take Burckhardt's censorious remark about the Thirty Years' War: "It is scandalous for a creed, no matter whether it is Catholic or Protestant, to place its salvation above the integrity of the nation." It was extremely difficult for a nineteenth-century liberal historian, brought up to believe that it is right and praiseworthy to kill in defense of one's country, but wicked and wrongheaded to kill in defense of one's religion, to enter into the state of mind of those who fought the Thirty Years' War. This difficulty is particularly acute in the field in which I am now working. Much of what has been written in English-speaking countries in the last ten years about the Soviet Union, and in the Soviet Union about the English-speaking countries, has been vitiated by this inability to achieve even the most elementary measure of imaginative understanding of what goes on in the mind of the other party, so that the words and actions of the other are always made to appear malign, senseless, or hypocritical. History cannot be written unless the historian can achieve some kind of contact with the mind of those about whom he is writing.

The third point is that we can view the past, and achieve our understanding of the past, only through the eyes of the present. The historian is of his own age, and is bound to it by the conditions of human existence. The very words which he uses—words like democracy, empire, war, revolution—have current connotations from which he cannot divorce them. Ancient historians have taken to using words like *polis* and *plebs* in the original, just in order to show that they have not fallen into this trap. This does not help them. They, too, live in the present, and cannot cheat themselves into the past by using unfamiliar or obsolete words, any more than they would become better Greek or Roman historians if they delivered their lectures in a *chlamys* or a *toga*. The names by which successive French historians have described the Parisian crowds which played so prominent a role in the French revolution—*les sansculottes, le peuple, la canaille, les bras-nus*—are all, for those who know the rules of the game, manifestos of a political affiliation and of a particular interpretation. Yet the historian is obliged to choose: the use of language forbids him to be neutral. Nor is it a matter of words alone. Over the past hundred years the changed balance of power in Europe has reversed the attitude of British historians to Frederick the Great. The changed balance of power within the

Christian churches between Catholicism and Protestantism has profoundly altered their attitude to such figures as Loyola, Luther, and Cromwell. It requires only a superficial knowledge of the work of French historians of the last forty years on the French revolution to recognize how deeply it has been affected by the Russian revolution of 1917. The historian belongs not to the past but to the present. Professor Trevor-Roper tells us that the historian "ought to love the past." This is a dubious injunction. To love the past may easily be an expression of the nostalgic romanticism of old men and old societies, a symptom of loss of faith and interest in the present or future.[8] *Cliché* for *cliché*, I should prefer the one about freeing oneself from "the dead hand of the past." The function of the historian is neither to love the past nor to emancipate himself from the past, but to master and understand it as the key to the understanding of the present.

If, however, these are some of the sights of what I may call the Collingwood view of history, it is time to consider some of the dangers. The emphasis on the role of the historian in the making of history tends, if pressed to its logical conclusion, to rule out any objective history at all: history is what the historian makes. Collingwood seems indeed, at one moment, in an unpublished note quoted by his editor, to have reached this conclusion:

> St. Augustine looked at history from the point of view of the early Christian; Tillemont, from that of a seventeenth-century Frenchman; Gibbon, from that of an eighteenth-century Englishman; Mommsen, from that of a nineteenth-century German. There is no point in asking which was the right point of view. Each was the only one possible for the man who adopted it.

This amounts to total scepticism, like Froude's remark that history is "a child's box of letters with which we can spell any word we please." Collingwood, in his reaction against "scissors-and-paste history," against the view of history as a mere compilation of facts, comes perilously near to treating history as something spun out of the human brain, and leads back to the conclusion referred to by Sir George Clark in the passage which I quoted earlier, that "there is no 'objective' historical truth." In place of the theory that history has no meaning, we are offered here the theory of an infinity of meanings, none any more right than any other—which comes to much the same thing. The second theory is surely as untenable as the first. It does not follow that, because a mountain appears to take on different shapes from different angles of vision, it has objectively either no shape at all or an infinity of

8. Compare Nietzsche's view of history: "To old age belongs the old man's business of looking back and casting up his accounts, of seeking consolation in the memories of the past, in historical culture" [Carr's note].

shapes. It does not follow that, because interpretation plays a necessary part in establishing the facts of history, and because no existing interpretation is wholly objective, one interpretation is as good as another, and the facts of history are in principle not amenable to objective interpretation. I shall have to consider at a later stage what exactly is meant by objectivity in history.

But a still greater danger lurks in the Collingwood hypothesis. If the historian necessarily looks at his period of history through the eyes of his own time, and studies the problems of the past as a key to those of the present, will he not fall into a purely pragmatic view of the facts, and maintain that the criterion of a right interpretation is its suitability to some present purpose? On this hypothesis, the facts of history are nothing, interpretation is everything. Nietzsche had already enunciated the principle: "The falseness of an opinion is not for us any objection to it. . . . The question is how far it is life-furthering, life-preserving, species-preserving, perhaps species-creating." The American pragmatists moved, less explicitly and less wholeheartedly, along the same line. Knowledge is knowledge for some purpose. The validity of the knowledge depends on the validity of the purpose. But, even where no such theory has been professed, the practice has often been no less disquieting. In my own field of study, I have seen too many examples of extravagant interpretation riding roughshod over facts, not to be impressed with the reality of this danger. It is not surprising that perusal of some of the more extreme products of Soviet and anti-Soviet schools of historiography should sometimes breed a certain nostalgia for that illusory nineteenth-century heaven of purely factual history.

How then, in the middle of the twentieth century, are we to define the obligation of the historian to his facts? I trust that I have spent a sufficient number of hours in recent years chasing and perusing documents, and stuffing my historical narrative with properly footnoted facts, to escape the imputation of treating facts and documents too cavalierly. The duty of the historian to respect his facts is not exhausted by the obligation to see that his facts are accurate. He must seek to bring into the picture all known or knowable facts relevant, in one sense or another, to the theme on which he is engaged and to the interpretation proposed. If he seeks to depict the Victorian Englishman as a moral and rational being, he must not forget what happened at Stalybridge Wakes in 1850. But this, in turn, does not mean that he can eliminate interpretation, which is the life-blood of history. Laymen—that is to say, non-academic friends or friends from other academic disciplines—sometimes ask me how the historian goes to work when he writes history. The commonest assumption appears to be that the historian divides his work into two sharply distinguishable phases or periods. First, he spends a long preliminary period reading his source and filling his notebooks with facts: then, when this is over, he puts away his sources, takes out his notebooks, and writes his book from beginning to end. This is to me an unconvincing and unplausible picture. For myself, as soon as I have got going on a few of what I take to be the capital sources, the itch becomes too strong and I begin to write—not necessarily at the beginning, but somewhere, anywhere. Thereafter, reading and writing go on simultaneously. The writing is added to, subtracted from, re-shaped, cancelled, as I go on reading. The reading is guided and directed and made fruitful by the writing: the more I write, the more I know what I am looking for, the better I understand the significance and relevance of what I find. Some historians probably do all this preliminary writing in their head without using pen, paper, or typewriter, just as some people play chess in their heads without recourse to board and chess-men: this is a talent which I envy, but cannot emulate. But I am convinced that, for any historian worth the name, the two processes of what economists call "input" and "output" go on simultaneously and are, in practice, parts of a single process. If you try to separate them, or to give one priority over the other, you fall into one of two heresies. Either you write scissors-and-paste history without meaning or significance; or you write propaganda or historical fiction, and merely use facts of the past to embroider a kind of writing which has nothing to do with history.

Our examination of the relation of the historian to the facts of history finds us, therefore, in an apparently precarious situation, navigating delicately between the Scylla of an untenable theory of history as an objective compilation of facts, of the unqualified primacy of fact over interpretation, and the Charybdis of an equally untenable theory of history as the subjective product of the mind of the historian who establishes the facts of history and masters them through the process of interpretation, between a view of history having the center of gravity in the past and the view having the center of gravity in the present. But our situation is less precarious than it seems. We shall encounter the same dichotomy of fact and interpretation again in these lectures in other guises—the particular and the general, the empirical and the theoretical, the objective and the subjective. The predicament of the historian is a reflection of the nature of man. Man, except perhaps in earliest infancy and in extreme old age, is not totally involved in his environment and unconditionally subject to it. On the other hand, he is never totally independent of it and its unconditional master. The relation of man to his environment is the relation of the historian to his theme. The historian is neither the humble slave, nor the tyrannical master, of his facts. The relation between the historian and his facts is one of equality, of give-and-take. As any working historian knows, if he stops to reflect on what he is doing as he thinks and writes, the historian is engaged in a continuous process of molding his facts to his interpretation and his interpretation to his facts. It is impossible to assign primacy to one over the other.

The historian starts with the provisional selection of facts and a provisional interpretation in the light of which that selection has been made—by others as well as by himself. As he works, both the interpretation and the selection and ordering of facts undergo subtle and perhaps partly unconscious changes through the reciprocal action of one or the other. And this reciprocal action also involves reciprocity between present and past, since the historian is part of the present and the facts belong to the past. The historian and the facts of history are necessary to one another. The historian without his facts is rootless and futile; the facts without their historian are dead and meaningless. My first answer therefore to the question, What is history?, is that it is a continuous process of interaction between the historian and his facts, an unending dialogue between the present and the past.

QUESTIONS

1. *In his discussion of the facts of history, Carr distinguishes between "a mere fact about the past" and "a fact of history." What does he mean?*
2. *Carr begins with a question but does not answer it until the last sentence. The answer takes the form of a definition. What are the main steps of the discussion leading to his answer? Which is the most important of the words in his definition?*
3. *If you were commissioned to write a history of the semester or of a particular group during the semester, what would be your most important "facts of history"? How would you select those "facts"?*
4. *Write a brief "history" of an event, keeping in mind what Carr says about what the historian does.*

Politics and Government

George Orwell

SHOOTING AN ELEPHANT

In Moulmein, in Lower Burma, I was hated by large numbers of people—the only time in my life that I have been important enough for this to happen to me. I was sub-divisional police officer of the town, and in an aimless, petty kind of way anti-European feeling was very bitter. No one had the guts to raise a riot, but if a European woman went through the bazaars alone somebody would probably spit betel juice over her dress. As a police officer I was an obvious target and was baited whenever it seemed safe to do so. When a nimble Burman tripped me up on the football field and the referee (another Burman) looked the other way, the crowd yelled with hideous laughter. This happened more than once. In the end the sneering yellow faces of young men that met me everywhere, the insults hooted after me when I was at a safe distance, got badly on my nerves. The young Buddhist priests were the worst of all. There were several thousands of them in the town and none of them seemed to have anything to do except stand on street corners and jeer at Europeans.

All this was perplexing and upsetting. For at that time I had already made up my mind that imperialism was an evil thing and the sooner I chucked up my job and got out of it the better. Theoretically—and secretly, of course—I was all for the Burmese and all against their oppressors, the British. As for the job I was doing, I hated it more bitterly than I can perhaps make clear. In a job like that you see the dirty work of Empire at close quarters. The wretched prisoners huddling in the stinking cages of the lock-ups, the grey, cowed faces of the long-term convicts, the scarred buttocks of the men who had been flogged with

First published in *New Writing* (Autumn 1936).

bamboos—all these oppressed me with an intolerable sense of guilt. But I could get nothing into perspective. I was young and ill-educated and I had had to think out my problems in the utter silence that is imposed on every Englishman in the East. I did not even know that the British Empire is dying, still less did I know that it is a great deal better than the younger empires that are going to supplant it. All I knew was that I was stuck between my hatred of the empire I served and my rage against the evil-spirited little beasts who tried to make my job impossible. With one part of my mind I thought of the British Raj[1] as an unbreakable tyranny, as something clamped down, in *saecula saeculorum,*[2] upon the will of prostrate peoples; with another part I thought that the greatest joy in the world would be to drive a bayonet into a Buddhist priest's guts. Feelings like these are the normal by-products of imperialism; ask any Anglo-Indian official, if you can catch him off duty.

One day something happened which in a roundabout way was enlightening. It was a tiny incident in itself, but it gave me a better glimpse than I had had before of the real nature of imperialism—the real motives for which despotic governments act. Early one morning the sub-inspector at a police station the other end of the town rang me up on the 'phone and said that an elephant was ravaging the bazaar. Would I please come and do something about it? I did not know what I could do, but I wanted to see what was happening and I got on to a pony and started out. I took my rifle, an old .44 Winchester and much too small to kill an elephant, but I thought the noise might be useful *in terrorem.* Various Burmans stopped me on the way and told me about the elephant's doings. It was not, of course, a wild elephant, but a tame one which had gone "must."[3] It had been chained up, as tame elephants always are when their attack of "must" is due, but on the previous night it had broken its chain and escaped. Its mahout, the only person who could manage it when it was in that state, had set out in pursuit, but had taken the wrong direction and was now twelve hours' journey away, and in the morning the elephant had suddenly reappeared in the town. The Burmese population had no weapons and were quite helpless against it. It had already destroyed somebody's bamboo hut, killed a cow and raided some fruit-stalls and devoured the stock; also it had met the municipal rubbish van and, when the driver jumped out and took to his heels, had turned the van over and inflicted violences upon it.

The Burmese sub-inspector and some Indian constables were wait-

1. The imperial government of British India and Burma.
2. Forever and ever.
3. Gone into sexual heat.

ing for me in the quarter where the elephant had been seen. It was a very poor quarter, a labyrinth of squalid bamboo huts, thatched with palm-leaf, winding all over a steep hillside. I remember that it was a cloudy, stuffy morning at the beginning of the rains. We began questioning the people as to where the elephant had gone and, as usual, failed to get any definite information. That is invariably the case in the East; a story always sounds clear enough at a distance, but the nearer you get to the scene of events the vaguer it becomes. Some of the people said that the elephant had gone in one direction, some said that he had gone in another, some professed not even to have heard of any elephant. I had almost made up my mind that the whole story was a pack of lies, when we heard yells a little distance away. There was a loud, scandalized cry of "Go away, child! Go away this instant!" and an old woman with a switch in her hand came round the corner of a hut, violently shooing away a crowd of naked children. Some more women followed, clicking their tongues and exclaiming; evidently there was something that the children ought not to have seen. I rounded the hut and saw a man's dead body sprawling in the mud. He was an Indian, a black Dravidian coolie, almost naked, and he could not have been dead many minutes. The people said that the elephant had come suddenly upon him round the corner of the hut, caught him with its trunk, put its foot on his back and ground him into the earth. This was the rainy season and the ground was soft, and his face had scored a trench a foot deep and a couple of yards long. He was lying on his belly with arms crucified and head sharply twisted to one side. His face was coated with mud, the eyes wide open, the teeth bared and grinning with an expression of unendurable agony. (Never tell me, by the way, that the dead look peaceful. Most of the corpses I have seen looked devilish.) The friction of the great beast's foot had stripped the skin from his back as neatly as one skins a rabbit. As soon as I saw the dead man I sent an orderly to a friend's house nearby to borrow an elephant rifle. I had already sent back the pony, not wanting it to go mad with fright and throw me if it smelt the elephant.

The orderly came back in a few minutes with a rifle and five car- 5
tridges, and meanwhile some Burmans had arrived and told us that the elephant was in the paddy fields below, only a few hundred yards away. As I started forward practically the whole population of the quarter flocked out of the houses and followed me. They had seen the rifle and were all shouting excitedly that I was going to shoot the elephant. They had not shown much interest in the elephant when he was merely ravaging their homes, but it was different now that he was going to be shot. It was a bit of fun to them, as it would be to an English crowd; besides they wanted the meat. It made me vaguely uneasy. I had no intention of shooting the elephant—I had merely sent

for the rifle to defend myself if necessary—and it is always unnerving to have a crowd following you. I marched down the hill, looking and feeling a fool, with the rifle over my shoulder and an ever-growing army of people jostling at my heels. At the bottom, when you got away from the huts, there was a metalled road and beyond that a miry waste of paddy fields a thousand yards across, not yet ploughed but soggy from the first rains and dotted with coarse grass. The elephant was standing eight yards from the road, his left side towards us. He took not the slightest notice of the crowd's approach. He was tearing up bunches of grass, beating them against his knees to clean them and stuffing them into his mouth.

I had halted on the road. As soon as I saw the elephant I knew with perfect certainty that I ought not to shoot him. It is a serious matter to shoot a working elephant—it is comparable to destroying a huge and costly piece of machinery—and obviously one ought not to do it if it can possibly be avoided. And at that distance, peacefully eating, the elephant looked no more dangerous than a cow. I thought then and I think now that his attack of "must" was already passing off; in which case he would merely wander harmlessly about until the mahout came back and caught him. Moreover, I did not in the least want to shoot him. I decided that I would watch him for a little while to make sure that he did not turn savage again, and then go home.

But at that moment I glanced round at the crowd that had followed me. It was an immense crowd, two thousand at the least and growing every minute. It blocked the road for a long distance on either side. I looked at the sea of yellow faces above the garish clothes—faces all happy and excited over this bit of fun, all certain that the elephant was going to be shot. They were watching me as they would watch a conjurer about to perform a trick. They did not like me, but with the magical rifle in my hands I was momentarily worth watching. And suddenly I realized that I should have to shoot the elephant after all. The people expected it of me and I had got to do it; I could feel their two thousand wills pressing me forward, irresistibly. And it was at this moment, as I stood there with the rifle in my hands, that I first grasped the hollowness, the futility of the white man's dominion in the East. Here was I, the white man with his gun, standing in front of the unarmed native crowd—seemingly the leading actor of the piece; but in reality I was only an absurd puppet pushed to and fro by the will of those yellow faces behind. I perceived in this moment that when the white man turns tyrant it is his own freedom that he destroys. He becomes a sort of hollow, posing dummy, the conventionalized figure of a sahib. For it is the condition of his rule that he shall spend his life in trying to impress the "natives," and so in every crisis he has got to do what the "natives" expect of him. He wears a mask, and his face grows to fit it. I had got to shoot the elephant. I had committed myself to doing it when I sent for the rifle. A sahib has got to act like a sahib; he has got to appear resolute, to know his own mind and do definite things. To come all that way, rifle in hand, with two thousand people marching at my heels, and then to trail feebly away, having done nothing—no, that was impossible. The crowd would laugh at me. And my whole life, every white man's life in the East, was one long struggle not to be laughed at.

But I did not want to shoot the elephant. I watched him beating his bunch of grass against his knees, with that preoccupied grandmotherly air that elephants have. It seemed to me that it would be murder to shoot him. At that age I was not squeamish about killing animals, but I had never shot an elephant and never wanted to. (Somehow it always seems worse to kill a *large* animal.) Besides, there was the beast's owner to be considered. Alive, the elephant was worth at least a hundred pounds; dead, he would only be worth the value of his tusks, five pounds, possibly. But I had got to act quickly. I turned to some experienced-looking Burmans who had been there when we arrived, and asked them how the elephant had been behaving. They all said the same thing: he took no notice of you if you left him alone, but he might charge if you went too close to him.

It was perfectly clear to me what I ought to do. I ought to walk up to within, say, twenty-five yards of the elephant and test his behavior. If he charged, I could shoot; if he took no notice of me, it would be safe to leave him until the mahout came back. But also I knew that I was going to do no such thing. I was a poor shot with a rifle and the ground was soft mud into which one would sink at every step. If the elephant charged and I missed him, I should have about as much chance as a toad under a steam-roller. But even then I was not thinking particularly of my own skin, only of the watchful yellow faces behind. For at that moment, with the crowd watching me, I was not afraid in the ordinary sense, as I would have been if I had been alone. A white man mustn't be frightened in front of "natives"; and so, in general, he isn't frightened. The sole thought in my mind was that if anything went wrong those two thousand Burmans would see me pursued, caught, trampled on and reduced to a grinning corpse like that Indian up the hill. And if that happened it was quite probable that some of them would laugh. That would never do. There was only one alternative. I shoved the cartridges into the magazine and lay down on the road to get a better aim.

The crowd grew very still, and a deep, low, happy sigh, as of people 10
who see the theatre curtain go up at last, breathed from innumerable throats. They were going to have their bit of fun after all. The rifle was a beautiful German thing with cross-hair sights. I did not then know

that in shooting an elephant one would shoot to cut an imaginary bar running from ear-hole to ear-hole. I ought, therefore, as the elephant was sideways on, to have aimed straight at his ear-hole; actually I aimed several inches in front of this, thinking the brain would be further forward.

When I pulled the trigger I did not hear the bang or feel the kick—one never does when a shot goes home—but I heard the devilish roar of glee that went up from the crowd. In that instant, in too short a time, one would have thought, even for the bullet to get there, a mysterious, terrible change had come over the elephant. He neither stirred nor fell, but every line of his body had altered. He looked suddenly stricken, shrunken, immensely old, as though the frightful impact of the bullet had paralysed him without knocking him down. At last, after what seemed a long time—it might have been five seconds, I dare say—he sagged flabbily to his knees. His mouth slobbered. An enormous senility seemed to have settled upon him. One could have imagined him thousands of years old. I fired again into the same spot. At the second shot he did not collapse but climbed with desperate slowness to his feet and stood weakly upright, with legs sagging and head drooping. I fired a third time. That was the shot that did for him. You could see the agony of it jolt his whole body and knock the last remnant of strength from his legs. But in falling he seemed for a moment to rise, for as his hind legs collapsed beneath him he seemed to tower upward like a huge rock toppling, his trunk reaching skywards like a tree. He trumpeted, for the first and only time. And then down he came, his belly towards me, with a crash that seemed to shake the ground even where I lay.

I got up. The Burmans were already racing past me across the mud. It was obvious that the elephant would never rise again, but he was not dead. He was breathing very rhythmically with long rattling gasps, his great mound of a side painfully rising and falling. His mouth was wide open—I could see far down into caverns of pale pink throat. I waited a long time for him to die, but his breathing did not weaken. Finally I fired my two remaining shots into the spot where I thought his heart must be. The thick blood welled out of him like red velvet, but still he did not die. His body did not even jerk when the shots hit him, the tortured breathing continued without a pause. He was dying, very slowly and in great agony, but in some world remote from me where not even a bullet could damage him further. I felt that I had got to put an end to that dreadful noise. It seemed dreadful to see the great beast lying there, powerless to move and yet powerless to die, and not even to be able to finish him. I sent back for my small rifle and poured shot after shot into his heart and down his throat. They seemed to make no impression. The tortured gasps continued as steadily as the ticking of a clock.

In the end I could not stand it any longer and went away. I heard later that it took him half an hour to die. Burmans were bringing dahs[4] and baskets even before I left, and I was told they had stripped his body almost to the bones by the afternoon.

Afterwards, of course, there were endless discussions about the shooting of the elephant. The owner was furious, but he was only an Indian and could do nothing. Besides, legally I had done the right thing, for a mad elephant has to be killed, like a mad dog, if its owner fails to control it. Among the Europeans opinion was divided. The older men said I was right, the younger men said it was a damn shame to shoot an elephant for killing a coolie, because an elephant was worth more than any damn Coringhee coolie. And afterwards I was very glad that the coolie had been killed; it put me legally in the right and it gave me a sufficient pretext for shooting the elephant. I often wondered whether any of the others grasped that I had done it solely to avoid looking a fool.

4. Butcher knives.

QUESTIONS

1. *Why did Orwell shoot the elephant? Account for the motives that led him to shoot. Then categorize them as, perhaps, personal motives, circumstantial motives, social motives, or political motives. Is it easy to assign his motives to categories? Why or why not?*
2. *In this essay the proportion of narrative to analysis is high. Mark which paragraphs contain which and note, in particular, how much analysis Orwell places in the middle of the essay. What are the advantages and disadvantages of having it there rather than at the beginning and the end of the essay?*
3. *Facts ordinarily do not speak for themselves. How does Orwell present his facts to make them speak in support of his analytic points? Look, for example, at the death of the elephant (paragraphs 11 to 13).*
4. *Write an essay in which you present a personal experience that illuminates a larger issue: schooling, perhaps, or affirmative action, or the homeless, or law enforcement, or taxes, or some other local or national issue.*

Jonathan Swift

A MODEST PROPOSAL

For Preventing the Children of Poor People in Ireland from Being a Burden to Their Parents or Country, and for Making Them Beneficial to the Public

It is a melancholy object to those who walk through this great town[1] or travel in the country, when they see the streets, the roads, and cabin doors, crowded with beggars of the female-sex, followed by three, four, or six children, all in rags and importuning every passenger for an alms. These mothers, instead of being able to work for their honest livelihood, are forced to employ all their time in strolling to beg sustenance for their helpless infants, who, as they grow up, either turn thieves for want of work, or leave their dear native country to fight for the Pretender in Spain, or sell themselves to the Barbadoes.[2]

I think it is agreed by all parties that this prodigious number of children in the arms, or on the backs, or at the heels of their mothers, and frequently of their fathers, is in the present deplorable state of the kingdom a very great additional grievance; and therefore whoever could find out a fair, cheap, and easy method of making these children sound, useful members of the commonwealth would deserve so well of the public as to have his statue set up for a preserver of the nation.

But my intention is very far from being confined to provide only for the children of professed beggars; it is of a much greater extent, and shall take in the whole number of infants at a certain age who are born of parents in effect as little able to support them as those who demand our charity in the streets.

As to my own part, having turned my thoughts for many years upon this important subject, and maturely weighed the several schemes of other projectors,[3] I have always found them grossly mistaken in their computation. It is true, a child just dropped from its dam may be sup-

A pamphlet printed in 1729.

1. Dublin.
2. Many poor Irish sought to escape poverty by emigrating to the Barbadoes and other western English colonies, paying for transport by binding themselves to work for a landowner there for a period of years. The Pretender, claimant to the English throne, was barred from succession after his father, King James II, was deposed in a Protestant revolution; thereafter, many Irish Catholics joined the Pretender in his exile in France and Spain, and in his unsuccessful attempts at counterrevolution.
3. People with projects; schemers.

ported by her milk for a solar year, with little other nourishment; at most not above the value of two shillings,[4] which the mother may certainly get, or the value in scraps, by her lawful occupation of begging; and it is exactly at one year old that I propose to provide for them in such a manner as instead of being a charge upon their parents or the parish, or wanting food and raiment for the rest of their lives, they shall on the contrary contribute to the feeding, and partly to the clothing, of many thousands.

5 There is likewise another great advantage in my scheme, that it will prevent those voluntary abortions, and that horrid practice of women murdering their bastard children, alas, too frequent among us, sacrificing the poor innocent babes, I doubt, more to avoid the expense than the shame, which would move tears and pity in the most savage and inhuman breast.

The number of souls in this kingdom being usually reckoned one million and a half, of these I calculate there may be about two hundred thousand couple whose wives are breeders; from which number I subtract thirty thousand couples who are able to maintain their own children, although I apprehend there cannot be so many under the present distresses of the kingdom; but this being granted, there will remain an hundred and seventy thousand breeders. I again subtract fifty thousand for those women who miscarry, or whose children die by accident or disease within the year. There only remain an hundred and twenty thousand children of poor parents annually born. The question therefore is, how this number shall be reared and provided for, which, as I have already said, under the present situation of affairs, is utterly impossible by all the methods hitherto proposed. For we can neither employ them in handicraft or agriculture; we neither build houses (I mean in the country) nor cultivate land. They can very seldom pick up a livelihood by stealing till they arrive at six years old, except where they are of towardly parts;[5] although I confess they learn the rudiments much earlier, during which time they can however be looked upon only as probationers, as I have been informed by a principal gentleman in the county of Cavan, who protested to me that he never knew above one or two instances under the age of six, even in a part of the kingdom so renowned for the quickest proficiency in that art.

I am assured by our merchants that a boy or a girl before twelve years old is no salable commodity; and even when they come to this age they will not yield above three pounds, or three pounds and half a crown[6] at most on the Exchange; which cannot turn to account either

4. A shilling used to be worth about twenty-five cents.
5. Promising abilities.
6. A pound was twenty shillings; a crown, five shillings.

to the parents or the kingdom, the charge of nutriment and rags having been at least four times that value.

I shall now therefore humbly propose my own thoughts, which I hope will not be liable to the least objection.

I have been assured by a very knowing American of my acquaintance in London, that a young healthy child well nursed is at a year old a most delicious, nourishing, and wholesome food, whether stewed, roasted, baked, or boiled; and I make no doubt that it will equally serve in a fricassee or a ragout.

10 I do therefore humbly offer it to public consideration that of the hundred and twenty thousand children, already computed, twenty thousand may be reserved for breed, whereof only one fourth part to be males, which is more than we allow to sheep, black cattle, or swine; and my reason is that these children are seldom the fruits of marriage, a circumstance not much regarded by our savages, therefore one male will be sufficient to serve four females. That the remaining hundred thousand may at a year old be offered in sale to the persons of quality and fortune through the kingdom, always advising the mother to let them suck plentifully in the last month, so as to render them plump and fat for a good table. A child will make two dishes at an entertainment for friends; and when the family dines alone, the fore or hind quarter will make a reasonable dish, and seasoned with a little pepper or salt will be very good boiled on the fourth day, especially in winter.

I have reckoned upon a medium that a child just born will weigh twelve pounds, and in a solar year if tolerably nursed increaseth to twenty-eight pounds.

I grant this food will be somewhat dear, and therefore very proper for landlords, who, as they have already devoured most of the parents, seem to have the best title to the children.

Infant's flesh will be in season throughout the year, but more plentiful in March, and a little before and after. For we are told by a grave author, an eminent French physician,[7] that fish being a prolific diet, there are more children born in Roman Catholic countries about nine months after Lent than at any other season; therefore, reckoning a year after Lent, the markets will be more glutted than usual, because the number of popish infants is at least three to one in this kingdom; and therefore it will have one other collateral advantage, by lessening the number of Papists among us.[8]

I have already computed the charge of nursing a beggar's child (in which list I reckon all cottagers, laborers, and four fifths of the farm-

7. The comic writer François Rabelais (1483–1553).

8. The speaker is addressing Protestant Anglo-Irish, who were the chief landowners and administrators, and his views of Catholicism in Ireland and abroad echo theirs.

ers) to be about two shillings per annum, rags included; and I believe no gentleman would repine to give ten shillings for the carcass of a good fat child, which, as I have said, will make four dishes of excellent nutritive meat, when he hath only some particular friend or his own family to dine with him. Thus the squire will learn to be a good landlord, and grow popular among the tenants; the mother will have eight shillings net profit, and be fit for work till she produces another child.

Those who are more thrifty (as I must confess the times require) 15
may flay the carcass; the skin of which artificially[9] dressed will make admirable gloves for ladies, and summer boots for fine gentlemen.

As to our city of Dublin, shambles[1] may be appointed for this purpose in the most convenient parts of it, and butchers we may be assured will not be wanting; although I rather recommend buying the children alive, and dressing them hot from the knife as we do roasting pigs.

A very worthy person, a true lover of his country, and whose virtues I highly esteem, was lately pleased in discoursing on this matter to offer a refinement upon my scheme. He said that many gentlemen of this kingdom, having of late destroyed their deer, he conceived that the want of venison might be well supplied by the bodies of young lads and maidens, not exceeding fourteen years of age nor under twelve, so great a number of both sexes in every county being now ready to starve for want of work and service; and these to be disposed of by their parents, if alive, or otherwise by their nearest relations. But with due deference to so excellent a friend and so deserving a patriot, I cannot be altogether in his sentiments; for as to the males, my American acquaintance assured me from frequent experience that their flesh was generally tough and lean, like that of our schoolboys, by continual exercise, and their taste disagreeable; and to fatten them would not answer the charge. Then as to the females, it would, I think with humble submission, be a loss to the public, because they soon would become breeders themselves: and besides, it is not improbable that some scrupulous people might be apt to censure such a practice (although indeed very unjustly) as a little bordering upon cruelty; which, I confess, hath always been with me the strongest objection against any project, how well soever intended.

But in order to justify my friend, he confessed that this expedient was put into his head by the famous Psalmanazar, a native of the island Formosa,[2] who came from thence to London above twenty years

9. Skillfully.
1. Slaughterhouses.
2. Actually a Frenchman, George Psalmanazar had passed himself off as from Formosa (now Taiwan) and had written a fictitious book about his "homeland," with descriptions of human sacrifice and cannibalism.

ago, and in conversation told my friend that in his country when any young person happened to be put to death, the executioner sold the carcass to persons of quality as a prime dainty; and that in his time the body of a plump girl of fifteen, who was crucified for an attempt to poison the emperor, was sold to his Imperial Majesty's prime minister of state, and other great mandarins of the court, in joints from the gibbet, at four hundred crowns. Neither indeed can I deny that if the same use were made of several plump young girls in this town, who without one single groat[3] to their fortunes cannot stir abroad without a chair,[4] and appear at the playhouse and assemblies in foreign fineries which they never will pay for, the kingdom would not be the worse.

Some persons of a desponding spirit are in great concern about that vast number of poor people who are aged, diseased, or maimed, and I have been desired to employ my thoughts what course may be taken to ease the nation of so grievous an encumbrance. But I am not in the least pain upon that matter, because it is very well known that they are every day dying and rotting by cold and famine, and filth and vermin, as fast as can be reasonably expected. And as to the younger laborers, they are now in almost as hopeful a condition. They cannot get work, and consequently pine away for want of nourishment to a degree that if at any time they are accidentally hired to common labor, they have not strength to perform it; and thus the country and themselves are happily delivered from the evils to come.

20 I have too long digressed, and therefore shall return to my subject. I think the advantages by the proposal which I have made are obvious and many, as well as of the highest importance.

For first, as I have already observed, it would greatly lessen the number of Papists, with whom we are yearly overrun, being the principal breeders of the nation as well as our most dangerous enemies; and who stay at home on purpose to deliver the kingdom to the Pretender, hoping to take their advantage by the absence of so many good Protestants, who have chosen rather to leave their country than to stay at home and pay tithes against their conscience to an Episcopal curate.

Secondly, the poorer tenants will have something valuable of their own, which by law may be made liable to distress,[5] and help to pay their landlord's rent, their corn and cattle being already seized and money a thing unknown.

Thirdly, whereas the maintenance of an hundred thousand children, from two years old and upwards, cannot be computed at less than ten shillings a piece per annum, the nation's stock will be thereby

3. An English coin worth about four pennies.
4. A sedan chair.
5. Seizure for the payment of debts.

increased fifty thousand pounds per annum, besides the profit of a new dish introduced to the tables of all gentlemen of fortune in the kingdom who have any refinement in taste. And the money will circulate among ourselves, the goods being entirely of our own growth and manufacture.

Fourthly, the constant breeders, besides the gain of eight shillings sterling per annum by the sale of their children, will be rid of the charge of maintaining them after the first year.

Fifthly, this food would likewise bring great custom to taverns, 25
where the vintners will certainly be so prudent as to procure the best receipts for dressing it to perfection, and consequently have their houses frequented by all the fine gentlemen, who justly value themselves upon their knowledge in good eating; and a skillful cook, who understands how to oblige his guests, will contrive to make it as expensive as they please.

Sixthly, this would be a great inducement to marriage, which all wise nations have either encouraged by rewards or enforced by laws and penalties. It would increase the care and tenderness of mothers toward their children, when they were sure of a settlement for life to the poor babes, provided in some sort by the public, to their annual profit instead of expense. We should see an honest emulation among the married women, which of them could bring the fattest child to the market. Men would become as fond of their wives during the time of their pregnancy as they are now of their mares in foal, their cows in calf, or sows when they are ready to farrow; nor offer to beat or kick them (as is too frequent a practice) for fear of a miscarriage.

Many other advantages might be enumerated. For instance, the addition of some thousand carcasses in our exportation of barreled beef, the propagation of swine's flesh, and improvement in the art of making good bacon, so much wanted among us by the great destruction of pigs, too frequent at our tables, which are no way comparable in taste or magnificence to a well-grown, fat, yearling child, which roasted whole will make a considerable figure at a lord mayor's feast or any other public entertainment. But this and many others I omit, being studious of brevity.

Supposing that one thousand families in this city would be constant customers for infants' flesh, besides others who might have it at merry meetings, particularly weddings and christenings, I compute that Dublin would take off annually about twenty thousand carcasses, and the rest of the kingdom (where probably they will be sold somewhat cheaper) the remaining eighty thousand.

I can think of no one objection that will possibly be raised against this proposal, unless it should be urged that the number of people will be thereby much lessened in the kingdom. This I freely own, and it was indeed one principal design in offering it to the world. I desire the reader will observe, that I calculate my remedy for this one individual kingdom of Ireland and for no other that ever was, is, or I think ever can be upon earth. Therefore let no man talk to me of other expedients: of taxing our absentees at five shillings a pound: of using neither clothes nor household furniture except what is of our own growth and manufacture: of utterly rejecting the materials and instruments that promote foreign luxury: of curing the expensiveness of pride, vanity, idleness, and gaming in our women: of introducing a vein of parsimony, prudence, and temperance: of learning to love our country, in the want of which we differ even from Laplanders and the inhabitants of Topinamboo[6]: of quitting our animosities and factions, nor acting any longer like the Jews, who were murdering one another at the very moment their city was taken: of being a little cautious not to sell our country and conscience for nothing: of teaching landlords to have at least one degree of mercy toward their tenants: lastly, of putting a spirit of honesty, industry, and skill into our shopkeepers; who, if a resolution could now be taken to buy only our native goods, would immediately unite to cheat and exact upon us in the price, the measure, and the goodness, nor could ever yet be brought to make one fair proposal of just dealing, though often and earnestly invited to it.[7]

30 Therefore I repeat, let no man talk to me of these and the like expedients, till he hath at least some glimpse of hope that there will ever be some hearty and sincere attempt to put them in practice.

But as to myself, having been wearied out for many years with offering vain, idle, visionary thoughts, and at length utterly despairing of success, I fortunately fell upon this proposal, which, as it is wholly new, so it hath something solid and real, of no expense and little trouble, full in our own power, and whereby we can incur no danger in disobliging England. For this kind of commodity will not bear exportation, the flesh being of too tender a consistence to admit a long continuance in salt, although perhaps I could name a country[8] which would be glad to eat up our whole nation without it.

After all, I am not so violently bent upon my own opinion as to reject any offer proposed by wise men, which shall be found equally innocent, cheap, easy, and effectual. But before something of that kind shall be advanced in contradiction to my scheme, and offering a better, I desire the author or authors will be pleased maturely to consider two points. First, as things now stand, how they will be able to find food and raiment for an hundred thousand useless mouths and backs. And secondly, there being a round million of creatures in human fig-

6. A district in Brazil.
7. Swift himself had made these proposals seriously in various previous works.
8. England.

ure throughout this kingdom, whose sole subsistence put into a common stock would leave them in debt two millions of pounds sterling, adding those who are beggars by profession to the bulk of farmers, cottagers, and laborers, with their wives and children who are beggars in effect; I desire those politicians who dislike my overture, and may perhaps be so bold to attempt an answer, that they will first ask the parents of these mortals whether they would not at this day think it a great happiness to have been sold for food at a year old in the manner I prescribe, and thereby have avoided such a perpetual scene of misfortunes as they have since gone through by the oppression of landlords, the impossibility of paying rent without money or trade, the want of common sustenance, with neither house nor clothes to cover them from the inclemencies of the weather, and the most inevitable prospect of entailing the like or greater miseries upon their breed forever.

I profess, in the sincerity of my heart, that I have not the least personal interest in endeavoring to promote this necessary work, having no other motive than the public good of my country, by advancing our trade, providing for infants, relieving the poor, and giving some pleasure to the rich. I have no children by which I can propose to get a single penny; the youngest being nine years old, and my wife past childbearing.

QUESTIONS

1. *Identify examples of the reasonable voice of Swift's authorial persona, such as the title of the essay itself.*
2. *Look, in particular, at instances in which Swift's authorial persona proposes shocking things. How does the style of the "Modest Proposal" affect its content?*
3. *Verbal irony consists of saying one thing and meaning another. At what point in this essay do you begin to suspect that Swift is using irony? What additional evidence of irony can you find?*
4. *What does Swift do in paragraphs 29 to 30?*
5. *Write a modest proposal of your own in the manner of Swift to remedy a real problem; that is, propose an outrageous remedy in a reasonable voice.*

Niccolò Machiavelli

THE MORALS OF THE PRINCE

On the Reasons Why Men Are Praised or Blamed—Especially Princes

It remains now to be seen what style and principles a prince ought to adopt in dealing with his subjects and friends. I know the subject has been treated frequently before, and I'm afraid people will think me rash for trying to do so again, especially since I intend to differ in this discussion from what others have said. But since I intend to write something useful to an understanding reader, it seemed better to go after the real truth of the matter than to repeat what people have imagined. A great many men have imagined states and princedoms such as nobody ever saw or knew in the real world, for there's such a difference between the way we really live and the way we ought to live that the man who neglects the real to study the ideal will learn how to accomplish his ruin, not his salvation. Any man who tries to be good all the time is bound to come to ruin among the great number who are not good. Hence a prince who wants to keep his post must learn how not to be good, and use that knowledge, or refrain from using it, as necessity requires.

Putting aside, then, all the imaginary things that are said about princes, and getting down to the truth, let me say that whenever men are discussed (and especially princes because they are prominent), there are certain qualities that bring them either praise or blame. Thus some are considered generous, others stingy (I use a Tuscan term, since "greedy" in our speech means a man who wants to take other people's goods. We call a man "stingy" who clings to his own); some are givers, others grabbers; some cruel, others merciful; one man is treacherous, another faithful; one is feeble and effeminate, another fierce and spirited; one humane, another proud; one lustful, another chaste; one straightforward, another sly; one harsh, another gentle; one serious, another playful; one religious, another skeptical, and so on. I know everyone will agree that among these many qualities a prince certainly ought to have all those that are considered good. But since it is impossible to have and exercise them all, because the conditions of human life simply do not allow it, a prince must be shrewd enough to avoid the public disgrace of those vices that would lose him

From *The Prince* (1513), a book on statecraft written for Giuliano de' Medici (1479–1516), a member of one of the most famous and powerful families of Renaissance Italy. Excerpted from an edition translated and edited by Robert M. Adams (1977).

his state. If he possibly can, he should also guard against vices that will not lose him his state; but if he cannot prevent them, he should not be too worried about indulging them. And furthermore, he should not be too worried about incurring blame for any vice without which he would find it hard to save his state. For if you look at matters carefully, you will see that something resembling virtue, if you follow it, may be your ruin, while something else resembling vice will lead, if you follow it, to your security and well-being.

On Liberality and Stinginess

Let me begin, then, with the first of the qualities mentioned above, by saying that a reputation for liberality is doubtless very fine; but the generosity that earns you that reputation can do you great harm. For if you exercise your generosity in a really virtuous way, as you should, nobody will know of it, and you cannot escape the odium of the opposite vice. Hence if you wish to be widely known as a generous man, you must seize every opportunity to make a big display of your giving. A prince of this character is bound to use up his entire revenue in works of ostentation. Thus, in the end, if he wants to keep a name for generosity, he will have to load his people with exorbitant taxes and squeeze money out of them in every way he can. This is the first step in making him odious to his subjects; for when he is poor, nobody will respect him. Then, when his generosity has angered many and brought rewards to a few, the slightest difficulty will trouble him, and at the first approach of danger, down he goes. If by chance he foresees this, and tries to change his ways, he will immediately be labeled a miser.

Since a prince cannot use this virtue of liberality in such a way as to become known for it unless he harms his own security, he won't mind, if he judges prudently of things, being known as a miser. In due course he will be thought the more liberal man, when people see that his parsimony enables him to live on his income, to defend himself against his enemies, and to undertake major projects without burdening his people with taxes. Thus he will be acting liberally toward all those people from whom he takes nothing (and there are an immense number of them), and in a stingy way toward those people on whom he bestows nothing (and they are very few). In our times, we have seen great things being accomplished only by men who have had the name of misers; all the others have gone under. Pope Julius II, though he used his reputation as a generous man to gain the papacy, sacrificed it in order to be able to make war; the present king of France has waged many wars without levying a single extra tax on his people, simply because he could take care of the extra expenses out of the savings from his long parsimony. If the present king of Spain had a reputation for generosity, he would never have been able to undertake so many campaigns, or win so many of them.

Hence a prince who prefers not to rob his subjects, who wants to be able to defend himself, who wants to avoid poverty and contempt, and who doesn't want to become a plunderer, should not mind in the least if people consider him a miser; this is simply one of the vices that enable him to reign. Someone may object that Caesar used a reputation for generosity to become emperor, and many other people have also risen in the world, because they were generous or were supposed to be so. Well, I answer, either you are a prince already, or you are in the process of becoming one; in the first case, this reputation for generosity is harmful to you, in the second case it is very necessary. Caesar was one of those who wanted to become ruler in Rome; but after he had reached his goal, if he had lived, and had not cut down on his expenses, he would have ruined the empire itself. Someone may say: there have been plenty of princes, very successful in warfare, who have had a reputation for generosity. But I answer: either the prince is spending his own money and that of his subjects, or he is spending someone else's. In the first case, he ought to be sparing; in the second case, he ought to spend money like water. Any prince at the head of his army, which lives on loot, extortion, and plunder, disposes of other people's property, and is bound to be very generous; otherwise, his soldiers would desert him. You can always be a more generous giver when what you give is not yours or your subjects'; Cyrus, Caesar, and Alexander[1] were generous in this way. Spending what belongs to other people does no harm to your reputation, rather it enhances it; only spending your own substance harms you. And there is nothing that wears out faster than generosity; even as you practice it, you lose the means of practicing it, and you become either poor and contemptible or (in the course of escaping poverty) rapacious and hateful. The thing above all against which a prince must protect himself is being contemptible and hateful; generosity leads to both. Thus, it's much wiser to put up with the reputation of being a miser, which brings you shame without hate, than to be forced—just because you want to appear generous—into a reputation for rapacity, which brings shame on you and hate along with it.

On Cruelty and Clemency: Whether It Is Better to Be Loved or Feared

Continuing now with our list of qualities, let me say that every prince should prefer to be considered merciful rather than cruel, yet

1. Persian, Roman, and Macedonian conquerors and rulers in ancient times.

he should be careful not to mismanage this clemency of his. People thought Cesare Borgia[2] was cruel, but that cruelty of his reorganized the Romagna, united it, and established it in peace and loyalty. Anyone who views the matter realistically will see that this prince was much more merciful than the people of Florence, who, to avoid the reputation of cruelty, allowed Pistoia to be destroyed.[3] Thus, no prince should mind being called cruel for what he does to keep his subjects united and loyal; he may make examples of a very few, but he will be more merciful in reality than those who, in their tenderheartedness, allow disorders to occur, with their attendant murders and lootings. Such turbulence brings harm to an entire community, while the executions ordered by a prince affect only one individual at a time. A new prince, above all others, cannot possibly avoid a name for cruelty, since new states are always in danger. And Virgil, speaking through the mouth of Dido,[4] says:

> My cruel fate
> And doubts attending an unsettled state
> Force me to guard my coast from foreign foes.

Yet a prince should be slow to believe rumors and to commit himself to action on the basis of them. He should not be afraid of his own thoughts; he ought to proceed cautiously, moderating his conduct with prudence and humanity, allowing neither overconfidence to make him careless, nor overtimidity to make him intolerable.

Here the question arises: is it better to be loved than feared, or vice versa? I don't doubt that every prince would like to be both; but since it is hard to accommodate these qualities, if you have to make a choice, to be feared is much safer than to be loved. For it is a good general rule about men, that they are ungrateful, fickle, liars and deceivers, fearful of danger and greedy for gain. While you serve their welfare, they are all yours, offering their blood, their belongings, their lives, and their children's lives, as we noted above—so long as the danger is remote. But when the danger is close at hand, they turn against you. Then, any prince who has relied on their words and has made no other preparations will come to grief; because friendships that are bought at a price, and not with greatness and nobility of soul, may be paid for but they are not acquired, and they cannot be used in time of need. People are less concerned with offending a man who makes himself loved than one who makes himself feared: the reason is that love is

2. The son of Pope Alexander VI (referred to later) and duke of Romagna, which he subjugated in 1499–1502.
3. By unchecked rioting between opposing factions (1502).
4. Queen of Carthage and tragic heroine of Virgil's epic, the *Aeneid*.

a link of obligation which men, because they are rotten, will break any time they think doing so serves their advantage; but fear involves dread of punishment, from which they can never escape.

Still, a prince should make himself feared in such a way that, even if he gets no love, he gets no hate either; because it is perfectly possible to be feared and not hated, and this will be the result if only the prince will keep his hands off the property of his subjects or citizens, and off their women. When he does have to shed blood, he should be sure to have a strong justification and manifest cause; but above all, he should not confiscate people's property, because men are quicker to forget the death of a father than the loss of a patrimony. Besides, pretexts for confiscation are always plentiful, it never fails that a prince who starts living by plunder can find reasons to rob someone else. Excuses for proceeding against someone's life are much rarer and more quickly exhausted.

But a prince at the head of his armies and commanding a multitude of soldiers should not care a bit if he is considered cruel; without such a reputation, he could never hold his army together and ready for action. Among the marvelous deeds of Hannibal,[5] this was prime: that, having an immense army, which included men of many different races and nations, and which he led to battle in distant countries, he never allowed them to fight among themselves or to rise against him, whether his fortune was good or bad. The reason for this could only be his inhuman cruelty, which, along with his countless other talents, made him an object of awe and terror to his soldiers; and without the cruelty, his other qualities would never have sufficed. The historians who pass snap judgments on these matters admire his accomplishments and at the same time condemn the cruelty which was their main cause.

10 When I say, "His other qualities would never have sufficed," we can see that this is true from the example of Scipio,[6] an outstanding man not only among those of his own time, but in all recorded history; yet his armies revolted in Spain, for no other reason than his excessive leniency in allowing his soldiers more freedom than military discipline permits. Fabius Maximus rebuked him in the senate for this failing, calling him the corrupter of the Roman armies. When a lieutenant of Scipio's plundered the Locrians,[7] he took no action in behalf of the

5. Carthaginian general who led a massive but unsuccessful invasion of Rome in 218–03 B.C.

6. The Roman general whose successful invasion of Carthage in 203 B.C. caused Hannibal's army to be recalled from Rome. The episode described here occurred in 206 B.C.

7. A people of Sicily, defeated by Scipio in 205 B.C. and placed under Q. Pleminius; *Fabius Maximus:* not only a senator but also a high public official and general who had fought against Hannibal in Italy.

people, and did nothing to discipline that insolent lieutenant; again, this was the result of his easygoing nature. Indeed, when someone in the senate wanted to excuse him on this occasion, he said there are many men who knew better how to avoid error themselves than how to correct error in others. Such a soft temper would in time have tarnished the fame and glory of Scipio, had he brought it to the office of emperor; but as he lived under the control of the senate, this harmful quality of his not only remained hidden but was considered creditable.

Returning to the question of being feared or loved, I conclude that since men love at their own inclination but can be made to fear at the inclination of the prince, a shrewd prince will lay his foundations on what is under his own control, not on what is controlled by others. He should simply take pains not to be hated, as I said.

The Way Princes Should Keep Their Word

How praiseworthy it is for a prince to keep his word and live with integrity rather than by craftiness, everyone understands; yet we see from recent experience that those princes have accomplished most who paid little heed to keeping their promises, but who knew how craftily to manipulate the minds of men. In the end, they won out over those who tried to act honestly.

You should consider then, that there are two ways of fighting, one with laws and the other with force. The first is properly a human method, the second belongs to beasts. But as the first method does not always suffice, you sometimes have to turn to the second. Thus a prince must know how to make good use of both the beast and the man. Ancient writers made subtle note of this fact when they wrote that Achilles and many other princes of antiquity were sent to be reared by Chiron the centaur,[8] who trained them in his discipline. Having a teacher who is half man and half beast can only mean that a prince must know how to use both these two natures, and that one without the other has no lasting effect.

Since a prince must know how to use the character of beasts, he should pick for imitation the fox and the lion. As the lion cannot protect himself from traps, and the fox cannot defend himself from wolves, you have to be a fox in order to be wary of traps, and a lion to overawe the wolves. Those who try to live by the lion alone are badly mistaken. Thus a prudent prince cannot and should not keep his word when to do so would go against his interest, or when the reasons that made him pledge it no longer apply. Doubtless if all men were good,

8. Half man and half horse, the mythical Chiron was said to have taught the arts of war and peace, including hunting, medicine, music, and prophecy. Achilles, foremost among the Greek heroes in the Trojan War.

this rule would be bad; but since they are a sad lot, and keep no faith with you, you in your turn are under no obligation to keep it with them.

Besides, a prince will never lack for legitimate excuses to explain away his breaches of faith. Modern history will furnish innumerable examples of this behavior, showing how many treaties and promises have been made null and void by the faithlessness of princes, and how the man succeeded best who knew best how to play the fox. But it is a necessary part of this nature that you must conceal it carefully; you must be a great liar and hypocrite. Men are so simple of mind, and so much dominated by their immediate needs, that a deceitful man will always find plenty who are ready to be deceived. One of many recent examples calls for mention. Alexander VI[9] never did anything else, never had another thought, except to deceive men, and he always found fresh material to work on. Never was there a man more convincing in his assertions, who sealed his promises with more solemn oaths, and who observed them less. Yet his deceptions were always successful, because he knew exactly how to manage this sort of business.

In actual fact, a prince may not have all the admirable qualities we listed, but it is very necessary that he should seem to have them. Indeed, I will venture to say that when you have them and exercise them all the time, they are harmful to you; when you just seem to have them, they are useful. It is good to appear merciful, truthful, humane, sincere, and religious; it is good to be so in reality. But you must keep your mind so disposed that, in case of need, you can turn to the exact contrary. This has to be understood: a prince, and especially a new prince, cannot possibly exercise all those virtues for which men are called "good." To preserve the state, he often has to do things against his word, against charity, against humanity, against religion. Thus he has to have a mind ready to shift as the winds of fortune and the varying circumstances of life may dictate. And as I said above, he should not depart from the good if he can hold to it, but he should be ready to enter on evil if he has to.

Hence a prince should take great care never to drop a word that does not seem imbued with the five good qualities noted above; to anyone who sees or hears him, he should appear all compassion, all honor, all humanity, all integrity, all religion. Nothing is more necessary than to seem to have this last virtue. Men in general judge more by the sense of sight than by the sense of touch, because everyone can see but only a few can test by feeling. Everyone sees what you seem to be, few know what you really are; and those few do not dare take a stand against the general opinion, supported by the majesty of the government. In the

9. Pope from 1492 to 1503.

actions of all men, and especially of princes who are not subject to a court of appeal, we must always look to the end. Let a prince, therefore, win victories and uphold his state; his methods will always be considered worthy, and everyone will praise them, because the masses are always impressed by the superficial appearance of things, and by the outcome of an enterprise. And the world consists of nothing but the masses; the few who have no influence when the many feel secure. A certain prince of our own time, whom it's just as well not to name,[1] preaches nothing but peace and mutual trust, yet he is the determined enemy of both; and if on several different occasions he had observed either, he would have lost both his reputation and his throne.

1. Probably Ferdinand of Spain, then allied with the house of Medici.

QUESTIONS

1. *This selection contains four sections of* The Prince: *"On the Reasons Why Men Are Praised or Blamed—Especially Princes"; "On Liberality and Stinginess"; "On Cruelty and Clemency: Whether It Is Better to Be Loved or Feared"; and "The Way Princes Should Keep Their Word." How, in each section, does Machiavelli contrast the ideal and the real, what he calls "the way we really live and the way we ought to live" (paragraph 1)? Mark some of the sentences in which he arrestingly expresses these contrasts.*
2. *Rewrite some of Machiavelli's advice to princes less forcibly and shockingly, and more palatably. For example, "Any man who tries to be good all the time is bound to come to ruin among the great number who are not good" (paragraph 1) might be rewritten as "Good men are often taken advantage of and harmed by men who are not good."*
3. *Describe Machiavelli's view of human nature. How do his views of government follow from it?*
4. *Machiavelli might be described as a sixteenth-century spin doctor teaching a ruler how to package himself. Adapt his advice to a current figure in national, state, or local politics.*

Thomas Jefferson

ORIGINAL DRAFT OF THE DECLARATION OF INDEPENDENCE

A Declaration of the Representatives of the UNITED STATES OF AMERICA, in General Congress Assembled.

When in the course of human events it becomes necessary for a people to advance from that subordination in which they have hitherto remained, & to assume among the powers of the earth the equal & independant station to which the laws of nature & of nature's god entitle them, a decent respect to the opinions of mankind requires that they should declare the causes which impel them to the change.

We hold these truths to be sacred & undeniable; that all men are created equal & independant, that from that equal creation they derive rights inherent & inalienable, among which are the preservation of life, & liberty, & the spirit of happiness; that to secure these ends, governments are instituted among men, deriving their just powers from the consent of the governed; that whenever any form of government shall become destructive of these ends, it is the right of the people to alter or to abolish it, & to institute new government, laying its foundation on such principles & organising it's powers in such form, as to them shall seem most likely to effect their safety & happiness. prudence indeed will dictate that governments long established should not be changed for light & transient causes: and accordingly all experience hath shewn that mankind are more disposed to suffer while evils are sufferable, than to right themselves by abolishing the forms to which they are accustomed. but when a long train of abuses & usurpations, begun at a distinguished period, & pursuing invariably the same object, evinces a design to subject them to arbitrary power, it is their right, it is their duty, to throw off such government & to provide new guards for their future security. such has been the patient sufferance of these colonies; & such is now the necessity which constrains them to expunge their former systems of government. The history of his present majesty, is a history of unremitting injuries and usurpations, among which no one fact stands single or solitary to contradict the

On June 11, 1776, Jefferson was elected by the Second Continental Congress to join John Adams, Benjamin Franklin, Roger Sherman, and Robert Livingston in drafting a declaration of independence. The draft presented to Congress on June 28 was primarily the work of Jefferson.

uniform tenor of the rest, all of which have in direct object the establishment of an absolute tyranny over these states. to prove this, let facts be submitted to a candid world, for the truth of which we pledge a faith yet unsullied by falsehood.

he has refused his assent to laws the most wholesome and necessary for the public good:

he has forbidden his governors to pass laws of immediate & pressing importance, unless suspended in their operation till his assent should be obtained; and when so suspended, he has neglected utterly to attend to them.

he has refused to pass other laws for the accommodation of large districts of people unless those people would relinquish the right of representation, a right inestimable to them, & formidable to tyrants alone:[1]

he has dissolved Representative houses repeatedly & continually, for opposing with manly firmness his invasions on the rights of the people:

he has refused for a long space of time to cause others to be elected, whereby the legislative powers, incapable of annihilation, have returned to the people at large for their exercise, the state remaining in the mean time exposed to all the dangers of invasion from without, &, convulsions within:

he has suffered the administration of justice totally to cease in some of these colonies, refusing his assent to laws for establishing judiciary powers:

he has made our judges dependant on his will alone, for the tenure of their offices, and amount of their salaries:

he has erected a multitude of new offices by a self-assumed power, & sent hither swarms of officers to harrass our people & eat out their substance:

he has kept among us in times of peace standing armies & ships of war:

he has affected[2] to render the military, independent of & superior to the civil power:

he has combined with others to subject us to a jurisdiction foreign

1. At this point in the manuscript a strip containing the following clause is inserted: "He called together legislative bodies at places unusual, unco[mfortable, & distant from] the depository of their public records for the sole purpose of fatiguing [them into compliance] with his measures:" Missing parts in the Library of Congress text are supplied from the copy made by Jefferson for George Wythe. This copy is in the New York Public Library. The fact that this passage was omitted from John Adams's transcript suggests that it was not a part of Jefferson's original rough draft.
2. Tried.

to our constitutions and unacknowledged by our laws; giving his assent to their pretended acts of legislation, for quartering large bodies of armed troops among us;
for protecting them by a mock-trial from punishment for any murders they should commit on the inhabitants of these states;
for cutting off our trade with all parts of the world;
for imposing taxes on us without our consent;
for depriving us of the benefits of trial by jury
he has endeavored to prevent the population of these states; for that purpose obstructing the laws for naturalization of foreigners; refusing to pass others to encourage their migrations hither; & raising the conditions of new appropriations of lands;
for transporting us beyond seas to be tried for pretended offences:
for taking away our charters & altering fundamentally the forms of our governments;
for suspending our own legislatures & declaring themselves invested with power to legislate for us in all cases whatsoever:
he has abdicated government here, withdrawing his governors, & declaring us out of his allegiance & protection:
he has plundered our seas, ravaged our coasts, burnt our towns & destroyed the lives of our people:
he is at this time transporting large armies of foreign mercenaries to compleat the works of death, desolation & tyranny, already begun with circumstances of cruelty & perfidy unworthy the head of a civilized nation:
he has endeavored to bring on the inhabitants of our frontiers the merciless Indian savages, whose known rule of warfare is an undistinguished destruction of all ages, sexes, & conditions of existence:
he has incited treasonable insurrections of our fellow-citizens, with the allurements of forfeiture & confiscation of our property:
he has waged cruel war against human nature itself, violating it's most sacred rights of life & liberty in the persons of a distant people who never offended him, captivating & carrying them into slavery in another hemisphere, or to incur miserable death in their transportation thither. this piratical warfare, the opprobrium of *infidel* powers, is the warfare of the CHRISTIAN king of Great Britain. determined to keep open a market where MEN should be bought & sold; he has prostituted his negative for suppressing every legislative attempt to prohibit or to restrain this execrable commerce: and that this assemblage of horrors might want no fact of distinguished die, he is now exciting those very people to rise in arms among us, and to purchase that liberty of which *he* has deprived them, by murdering the people upon

> whom *he* also obtruded them; thus paying off former crimes committed against the *liberties* of one people, with crimes which he urges them to commit against the *lives* of another.

in every stage of these oppressions we have petitioned for redress in the most humble terms; our repeated petitions have been answered by repeated injury. a prince whose character is thus marked by every act which may define a tyrant, is unfit to be the ruler of a people who mean to be free. future ages will scarce believe that the hardiness of one man, adventured within the short compass of twelve years only, on so many acts of tyranny without a mask, over a people fostered & fixed in principles of liberty.

Nor have we been wanting in attentions to our British brethren. we have warned them from time to time of attempts by their legislature to extend a jurisdiction over these our states. we have reminded them of the circumstances of our emigration & settlement here, no one of which could warrant so strange a pretension: that these were effected at the expence of our own blood & treasure, unassisted by the wealth or the strength of Great Britain: that in constituting indeed our several forms of government, we had adopted one common king, thereby laying a foundation for perpetual league & amity with them; but that submission to their [Parliament, was no Part of our Constitution, nor ever in Idea, if History may be] [3] credited: and we appealed to their native justice & magnanimity, as to the ties of our common kindred to disavow these usurpations which were likely to interrupt our correspondence & connection. they too have been deaf to the voice of justice & of consanguinity, & when occasions have been given them, by the regular course of their laws, of removing from their councils the disturbers of our harmony, they have by their free election re-established them in power. at this very time too they are permitting their chief magistrate to send over not only soldiers of our common blood, but Scotch & foreign mercenaries to invade & deluge us in blood. these facts have given the last stab to agonizing affection, and manly spirit bids us to renounce for ever these unfeeling brethren. we must endeavor to forget our former love for them, and to hold them as we hold the rest of mankind, enemies in war, in peace friends. we might have been a free & a great people together; but a communication of grandeur & of freedom it seems is below their dignity. be it so, since they will have it: the road to glory & happiness is open to us too; we will climb it in a separate state, and acquiesce in the necessity which pronounces our everlasting Adieu!

We therefore the representatives of the United States of America in

3. An illegible passage is supplied from John Adams's transcription.

General Congress assembled do, in the name & by authority of the good people of these states, reject and renounce all allegiance & subjection to the kings of Great Britain & all others who may hereafter claim by, through, or under them; we utterly dissolve & break off all political connection which may have heretofore subsisted between us & the people or parliament of Great Britain; and finally we do assert and declare these colonies to be free and independant states, and that as free & independant states they shall hereafter have power to levy war, conclude peace, contract alliances, establish commerce, & to do all other acts and things which independant states may of right do. And for the support of this declaration we mutually pledge to each other our lives, our fortunes, & our sacred honour.

Thomas Jefferson and Others

THE DECLARATION OF INDEPENDENCE

IN CONGRESS, JULY 4, 1776
THE UNANIMOUS DECLARATION OF THE
THIRTEEN UNITED STATES OF AMERICA

When in the Course of human events it becomes necessary for one people to dissolve the political bands which have connected them with another, and to assume among the powers of the earth, the separate and equal station to which the Laws of Nature and of Nature's God entitle them, a decent respect to the opinions of mankind requires that they should declare the causes which impel them to the separation.

We hold these truths to be self-evident, that all men are created equal, that they are endowed by their Creator with certain unalienable Rights, that among these are Life, Liberty and the pursuit of Happiness. That to secure these rights, Governments are instituted among Men, deriving their just powers from the consent of the governed. That whenever any Form of Government becomes destructive of these ends, it is the Right of the People to alter or to abolish it, and to institute new Government, laying its foundation on such principles and organizing its powers in such form, as to them shall seem most likely to effect their Safety and Happiness. Prudence, indeed, will dictate that Governments long established should not be changed for light and transient causes; and accordingly all experience hath shewn that mankind are more disposed to suffer, while evils are sufferable, than to right themselves by abolishing the forms to which they are accustomed. But when a long train of abuses and usurpations, pursuing invariably the same Object evinces a design to reduce them under absolute Despotism, it is their right, it is their duty, to throw off such Government, and to provide new Guards for their future security. Such has been the patient sufferance of these Colonies; and such is now the necessity which constrains them to alter their former Systems of Government. The history of the present King of Great Britain is a history of repeated injuries and usurpations, all having in direct object the establishment of an absolute Tyranny over these States. To prove this, let Facts be submitted to a candid world.

He has refused his Assent to Laws, the most wholesome and necessary for the public good.

He has forbidden his Government to pass laws of immediate and pressing importance, unless suspended in their operation till his Assent should be obtained; and when so suspended, he has utterly neglected to attend to them.

He has refused to pass other Laws for the accommodation of large districts of people, unless those people would relinquish the right of Representation in the Legislature, a right inestimable to them and formidable to tyrants only.

He has called together legislative bodies at places unusual, uncomfortable, and distant from the depository of their Public Records, for the sole purpose of fatiguing them into compliance with his measures.

He has dissolved Representative Houses repeatedly, for opposing with manly firmness his invasions on the rights of the people.

He has refused for a long time, after such dissolutions, to cause others to be elected; whereby the Legislative Powers, incapable of Annihilation, have returned to the People at large for their exercise; the State remaining in the mean time exposed to all the dangers of invasion from without, and convulsions within.

He has endeavored to prevent the population of these States; for that purpose obstructing the Laws for Naturalization of Foreigners; refusing to pass others to encourage their migration hither, and raising the conditions of new Appropriations of Lands.

He has obstructed the Administration of Justice, by refusing his Assent to Laws for establishing Judiciary Powers.

He has made Judges dependent on his Will alone, for the tenure of their offices, and the amount and payment of their salaries.

He has erected a multitude of New Offices, and sent hither swarms of Officers to harass our people, and eat out their substance.

He has kept among us, in times of peace, Standing Armies without the Consent of our legislatures.

He has affected to render the Military independent of and superior to the Civil Power.

He has combined with others to subject us to a jurisdiction foreign to our constitution, and unacknowledged by our laws; giving his Assent to their Acts of pretended Legislation: For quartering large bodies of armed troops among us: For protecting them, by a mock Trial, from punishment for any Murders which they should commit on the Inhabitants of these States: For cutting off our Trade with all parts of the world: For imposing Taxes on us without our Consent: For depriving us in many cases, of the benefits of Trial by Jury; For transporting us beyond Seas to be tried for pretended offenses: for abolishing the free System of English Laws in a neighboring Province, establishing therein an Arbitrary government, and enlarging its Boundaries so as to render it at once an example and fit instrument for introducing the same absolute rule into these Colonies: For taking away our Charters, abolishing our most valuable Laws and altering fundamentally the Forms of our Governments: For suspending our own Legislatures, and declaring themselves invested with power to legislate for us in all cases whatsoever.

He has abdicated Government here, by declaring us out of his Protection and waging War against us.

He has plundered our seas, ravaged our Coasts, burnt our towns, and destroyed the lives of our people.

He is at this time transporting large Armies of foreign Mercenaries to complete the works of death, desolation and tyranny, already begun with circumstances of Cruelty & Perfidy scarcely paralleled in the most barbarous ages, and totally unworthy the Head of a civilized nation.

He has constrained our fellow Citizens taken Captive on the high Seas to bear Arms against their Country, to become the executioners of their friends and Brethren, or to fall themselves by their Hands.

He has excited domestic insurrections amongst us, and has endeavored to bring on the inhabitants of our frontiers, the merciless Indian Savages, whose known rule of warfare, is an undistinguished destruction of all ages, sexes, and conditions.

In every stage of these Oppressions We have Petitioned for Redress in the most humble terms: Our repeated Petitions have been answered only by repeated injury. A Prince, whose character is thus marked by every act which may define a Tyrant, is unfit to be the ruler of a free people.

Nor have We been wanting in attention to our British brethren. We have warned them from time to time of attempts by their legislature to extend an unwarrantable jurisdiction over us. We have reminded them of the circumstances of our emigration and settlement here. We have appealed to their native justice and magnanimity, and we have conjured them by the ties of our common kindred to disavow these usurpations, which would inevitably interrupt our connections and correspondence. They too have been deaf to the voice of justice and of consanguinity. We must, therefore, acquiesce in the necessity, which denounces our Separation, and hold them, as we hold the rest of mankind, Enemies in War, in Peace Friends.

We, THEREFORE the Representatives of the UNITED STATES OF AMERICA, in General Congress, Assembled, appealing to the Supreme Judge of the world for the rectitude of our intentions, do, in the Name, and by Authority of the good People of these Colonies, solemnly publish and declare, That these United Colonies are, and of Right ought to be FREE AND INDEPENDENT STATES; that they are Absolved from all Allegiance to the British Crown, and that all political connection between them and the State of Great Britain, is and ought to be totally dissolved; and that as Free and Independent States, they have full Power to levy War, conclude Peace, contract Alliances, establish Commerce, and to do all other Acts and Things which Independent States may of right do. And for the support of this Declaration, with a firm reliance on the protection of Divine Providence, we mutually pledge to each other our Lives, our Fortunes, and our sacred Honor.

QUESTIONS

1. *The "Declaration of Independence" is an example of deductive argument: Jefferson sets up general principles, details particular instances, and then draws conclusions. Locate the three sections of the "Declaration" in both the original and final drafts. Describe a typical sentence in each section.*
2. *Locate the general principles (or "truths") that Jefferson sets up in the first section of both the original and final drafts. Mark the language he uses to describe them: for example, he calls them "sacred & undeniable" in the original draft, "self-evident" in the final draft. What kinds of authority does his language appeal to?*
3. *Stanton, in the "Declaration of Sentiments" (p. 966), imitates both the argument and style of the "Declaration of Independence." Where does her declaration diverge from Jefferson's? And to what ends?*
4. *Write an essay explaining Jefferson's views on the nature of man, the function of government, and the relationship between morality and political life in the "Declaration of Independence." What assumptions are necessary to make these views, as he says in the final draft, "self-evident"?*

Elizabeth Cady Stanton

DECLARATION OF SENTIMENTS

When, in the course of human events, it becomes necessary for one portion of the family of man to assume among the people of the earth a position different from that which they have hitherto occupied, but one to which the laws of nature and of nature's God entitle them, a decent respect to the opinions of mankind requires that they should declare the causes that impel them to such a course.

We hold these truths to be self-evident: that all men and women are created equal; that they are endowed by their Creator with certain inalienable rights; that among these are life, liberty, and the pursuit of happiness; that to secure these rights governments are instituted, deriving their just powers from the consent of the governed. Whenever any form of government becomes destructive of these ends, it is the right of those who suffer from it to refuse allegiance to it, and to insist upon the institution of a new government, laying its foundation on such principles, and organizing its powers in such form, as to them shall seem most likely to effect their safety and happiness. Prudence indeed, will dictate that governments long established should not be changed for light and transient causes; and accordingly all experience hath shown that mankind are more disposed to suffer, while evils are sufferable, than to right themselves by abolishing the forms to which they were accustomed. But when a long train of abuses and usurpations, pursuing invariably the same object evinces a design to reduce them under absolute despotism, it is their duty to throw off such government, and to provide new guards for their future security. Such has been the patient sufferance of the women under this government, and such is now the necessity which constrains them to demand the equal station to which they are entitled.

The history of mankind is a history of repeated injuries and usurpations on the part of man toward woman, having in direct object the establishment of an absolute tyranny over her. To prove this, let facts be submitted to a candid world.

He has never permitted her to exercise her inalienable right to the elective franchise.

5 He has compelled her to submit to laws, in the formation of which she had no voice.

He has withheld from her rights which are given to the most ignorant and degraded men—both natives and foreigners.

From A *History of Woman Suffrage,* ed. Elizabeth Cady Stanton, Susan B. Anthony, and Matilda Joslyn Gage (1881).

Having deprived her of this first right of a citizen, the elective franchise, thereby leaving her without representation in the halls of legislation, he has oppressed her on all sides.

He has made her, if married, in the eye of the law, civilly dead.

He has taken from her all right in property, even to the wages she earns.

He has made her, morally, an irresponsible being, as she can commit 10
many crimes with impunity, provided they be done in the presence of her husband. In the covenant of marriage, she is compelled to promise obedience to her husband, he becoming, to all intents and purposes, her master—the law giving him power to deprive her of her liberty, and to administer chastisement.

He has so framed the laws of divorce, as to what shall be the proper causes, and in case of separation, to whom the guardianship of the children shall be given, as to be wholly regardless of the happiness of women—the law, in all cases, going upon a false supposition of the supremacy of man, and giving all power into his hands.

After depriving her of all rights as a married woman, if single, and the owner of property, he has taxed her to support a government which recognizes her only when her property can be made profitable to it.

He has monopolized nearly all the profitable employments, and from those she is permitted to follow, she receives but a scanty remuneration. He closes against her all the avenues to wealth and distinction which he considers most honorable to himself. As a teacher of theology, medicine, or law, she is not known.

He has denied her the facilities for obtaining a thorough education, all colleges being closed against her.

He allows her in Church, as well as State, but a subordinate posi- 15
tion, claiming Apostolic authority for her exclusion from the ministry, and, with some exceptions, from any public participation in the affairs of the Church.

He has created a false public sentiment by giving to the world a different code of morals for men and women, by which moral delinquencies which exclude women from society, are not only tolerated, but deemed of little account in man.

He has usurped the prerogative of Jehovah himself, claiming it as his right to assign for her a sphere of action, when that belongs to her conscience and to her God.

He has endeavored, in every way that he could, to destroy her confidence in her own powers, to lessen her self-respect, and to make her willing to lead a dependent and abject life.

Now, in view of this entire disfranchisement of one-half the people of this country, their social and religious degradation—in view of the unjust laws above mentioned, and because women do feel themselves aggrieved, oppressed, and fraudulently deprived of their most sacred rights, we insist that they have immediate admission to all the rights and privileges which belong to them as citizens of the United States.

In entering upon the great work before us, we anticipate no small amount of misconception, misrepresentation, and ridicule; but we shall use every instrumentality within our power to effect our object. We shall employ agents, circulate tracts, petition the State and National legislatures, and endeavor to enlist the pulpit and the press in our behalf. We hope this Convention will be followed by a series of Conventions embracing every part of the country.

Abraham Lincoln

SECOND INAUGURAL ADDRESS

At this second appearing to take the oath of the presidential office, there is less occasion for an extended address than there was at the first. Then a statement, somewhat in detail, of a course to be pursued, seemed fitting and proper. Now, at the expiration of four years, during which public declarations have been constantly called forth on every point and phase of the great contest which still absorbs the attention, and engrosses the energies of the nation, little that is new could be presented. The progress of our arms, upon which all else chiefly depends, is as well known to the public as to myself; and it is, I trust, reasonably satisfactory and encouraging to all. With high hope for the future, no prediction in regard to it is ventured.

On the occasion corresponding to this four years ago, all thoughts were anxiously directed to an impending civil war. All dreaded it—all sought to avert it. While the inaugural address was being delivered from this place, devoted altogether to *saving* the Union without war, insurgent agents were in the city seeking to *destroy* it without war—seeking to dissolve the Union, and divide effects, by negotiation. Both parties deprecated war; but one of them would *make* war rather than let the nation survive; and the other would *accept* war rather than let it perish. And the war came.

One-eighth of the whole population were colored slaves, not distributed generally over the Union, but localized in the Southern part of it. These slaves constituted a peculiar and powerful interest. All knew that this interest was, somehow, the cause of the war. To strengthen, perpetuate, and extend this interest was the object for

Delivered March 4, 1865.

which the insurgents would rend the Union, even by war; while the government claimed no right to do more than to restrict the territorial enlargement of it. Neither party expected for the war, the magnitude, or the duration, which it has already attained. Neither anticipated that the *cause* of the conflict might cease with, or even before, the conflict itself should cease. Each looked for an easier triumph, and a result less fundamental and astounding. Both read the same Bible, and pray to the same God; and each invokes His aid against the other. It may seem strange that any men should dare to ask a just God's assistance in wringing their bread from the sweat of other men's faces; but let us judge not that we be not judged.[1] The prayers of both could not be answered; that of neither has been answered fully. The Almighty has His own purposes. "Woe unto the world because of offenses! for it must needs be that offenses come; but woe to that man by whom the offense cometh!"[2] If we shall suppose that American slavery is one of those offenses which, in the providence of God, must needs come, but which, having continued through His appointed time, He now wills to remove, and that He gives to both North and South, this terrible war, as the woe due to those by whom the offense came, shall we discern therein any departure from those divine attributes which the believers in a Living God always ascribe to Him? Fondly do we hope—fervently do we pray—that this mightly scourge of war may speedily pass away. Yet, if God wills that it continue, until all the wealth piled by the bondman's two hundred and fifty years of unrequited toil shall be sunk, and until every drop of blood drawn with the lash, shall be paid by another drawn with the sword, as was said three thousand years ago, so still it must be said "the judgments of the Lord are true and righteous altogether."[3]

With malice toward none; with charity for all; with firmness in the right, as God gives us to see the right, let us strive on to finish the work we are in; to bind up the nation's wounds; to care for him who shall have borne the battle, and for his widow, and his orphan—to do all which may achieve and cherish a just, and a lasting peace, among ourselves, and with all nations.

1. Lincoln alludes to Jesus' statement in the Sermon on the Mount—"Judge not, that ye be not judged" (Matthew vii.1)—and to God's curse on Adam—"In the sweat of thy face shalt thou eat bread, till thou return unto the ground" (Genesis iii.19).
2. From Jesus' speech to his disciples (Matthew xviii.7).
3. Psalms xix.9.

Carl Becker

DEMOCRACY

Democracy, like liberty or science or progress, is a word with which we are all so familiar that we rarely take the trouble to ask what we mean by it. It is a term, as the devotees of semantics say, which has no "referent"—there is no precise or palpable thing or object which we all think of when the word is pronounced. On the contrary, it is a word which connotes different things to different people, a kind of conceptual Gladstone bag[1] which, with a little manipulation, can be made to accommodate almost any collection of social facts we may wish to carry about in it. In it we can as easily pack a dictatorship as any other form of government. We have only to stretch the concept to include any form of government supported by a majority of the people, for whatever reasons and by whatever means of expressing assent, and before we know it the empire of Napoleon, the Soviet regime of Stalin, and the Fascist systems of Mussolini and Hitler are all safely in the bag. But if this is what we mean by democracy, then virtually all forms of government are democratic, since virtually all governments, except in times of revolution, rest upon the explicit or implicit consent of the people. In order to discuss democracy intelligently it will be necessary, therefore, to define it, to attach to the word a sufficiently precise meaning to avoid the confusion which is not infrequently the chief result of such discussions.

All human institutions, we are told, have their ideal forms laid away in heaven, and we do not need to be told that the actual institutions conform but indifferently to these ideal counterparts. It would be possible then to define democracy either in terms of the ideal or in terms of the real form—to define it as government of the people, by the people, for the people; or to define it as government of the people, by the politicians, for whatever pressure groups can get their interests taken care of. But as a historian I am naturally disposed to be satisfied with the meaning which, in the history of politics, men have commonly attributed to the word—a meaning, needless to say, which derives partly from the experience and partly from the aspirations of mankind. So regarded, the term democracy refers primarily to a form of government, and it has always meant government by the many as opposed to government by the one—government by the people as opposed to

From *Modern Democracy* (1941).

1. A piece of hand luggage with two compartments.

government by a tyrant, a dictator, or an absolute monarch. This is the most general meaning of the word as men have commonly understood it.

In this antithesis there are, however, certain implications, always tacitly understood, which give a more precise meaning to the term. Peisistratus,[2] for example, was supported by a majority of the people, but his government was never regarded as a democracy for all that. Caesar's power derived from a popular mandate, conveyed through established republican forms, but that did not make his government any the less a dictatorship. Napoleon called his government a democratic empire, but no one, least of all Napoleon himself, doubted that he had destroyed the last vestiges of the democratic republic. Since the Greeks first used the term, the essential test of democratic government has always been this: the source of political authority must be and remain in the people and not in the ruler. A democratic government has always meant one in which the citizens, or a sufficient number of them to represent more or less effectively the common will, freely act from time to time, and according to established forms, to appoint or recall the magistrates and to enact or revoke the laws by which the community is governed. This I take to be the meaning which history has impressed upon the term democracy as a form of government.

2. Tyrant of Athens, 561–527 B.C.

QUESTIONS

1. *In this essay Becker carefully defines an abstract term with multiple meanings,* democracy, *using the following strategies: (1) he looks for extreme and paradoxical instances that most people would exclude; (2) he distinguishes between ideal instances "laid away in heaven" (paragraph 2) and real instances; (3) he settles for a common meaning derived "partly from the experience and partly from the aspirations of mankind" (paragraph 2); he looks at additional instances that provide a test for exclusion and inclusion. How, finally, does he define democracy?*
2. *Machiavelli, in "The Morals of the Prince" (p. 950), also draws a contrast between the real and the ideal. What are the particulars of his contrast and Becker's? What is Machiavelli's sense of the relation between the real and the ideal? What is Becker's? What are the differences between them?*
3. *Guinier, in "The Tyranny of the Majority" (p. 973), argues that "majority rule may be perceived as majority tyranny" (paragraph 10). How might Becker include the instances she describes into his definition?*

4. *Consult a standard desk dictionary for the definition of an abstract term with multiple meanings; you might consider terms like* generosity, love, sophistication, tolerance, virtue. *Then write your own definition of the term following the strategy Becker uses to define democracy, supplying your own instances.*

E. B. White

DEMOCRACY

We received a letter from the Writers' War Board the other day asking for a statement on "The Meaning of Democracy." It presumably is our duty to comply with such a request, and it is certainly our pleasure.

Surely the Board knows what democracy is. It is the line that forms on the right. It is the don't in don't shove. It is the hole in the stuffed shirt through which the sawdust slowly trickles; it is the dent in the high hat. Democracy is the recurrent suspicion that more than half of the people are right more than half of the time. It is the feeling of privacy in the voting booths, the feeling of communion in the libraries, the feeling of vitality everywhere. Democracy is a letter to the editor. Democracy is the score at the beginning of the ninth. It is an idea which hasn't been disproved yet, a song the words of which have not gone bad. It's the mustard on the hot dog and the cream in the rationed coffee. Democracy is a request from a War Board, in the middle of a morning in the middle of a war, wanting to know what democracy is.

First appeared in *The New Yorker* (July 3, 1943); later reprinted in *The Wild Flag* (1946).

QUESTIONS

1. *Consult a standard desk dictionary for the definition of* democracy. *Of the several meanings given, which one best encompasses White's definitions? What other meanings do his definitions engage?*
2. *Translate White's examples into nonmetaphorical language. For example, "It is the line that forms on the right" might be translated as "It has no special privileges." Can "It is the don't in don't shove" also be translated as "It has no special privileges"? Consider what is lost in translation or, more important, what is gained by metaphor.*
3. *Using White's technique, write a definition for an abstract term; you might consider terms like* generosity, love, sophistication, tolerance, virtue.

Lani Guinier

THE TYRANNY OF THE MAJORITY

I have always wanted to be a civil rights lawyer. This lifelong ambition is based on a deep-seated commitment to democratic fair play—to playing by the rules as long as the rules are fair. When the rules seem unfair, I have worked to change them, not subvert them. When I was eight years old, I was a brownie. I was especially proud of my uniform, which represented a commitment to good citizenship and good deeds. But one day, when my Brownie group staged a hatmaking contest, I realized that uniforms are only as honorable as the people who wear them. The contest was rigged. The winner was assisted by her milliner mother, who actually made the winning entry in full view of all the participants. At the time, I was too young to be able to change the rules, but I was old enough to resign, which I promptly did.

To me, fair play means that the rules encourage everyone to play. They should reward those who win, but they must be acceptable to those who lose. The central theme of my academic writing is that not all rules lead to elemental fair play. Some even commonplace rules work against it.

The professional milliner competing with amateur Brownies stands as an example of rules that are patently rigged or patently subverted. Yet, sometimes, even when rules are perfectly fair in form, they serve in practice to exclude particular groups from meaningful participation. When they do not encourage everyone to play, or when, over the long haul, they do not make the losers feel as good about the outcomes as the winners, they can seem as unfair as the milliner who makes the winning hat for her daughter.

Sometimes, too, we construct rules that force us to be divided into winners and losers when we might have otherwise joined together. This idea was cogently expressed by my son, Nikolas, when he was four years old, far exceeding the thoughtfulness of his mother when she was an eight-year-old Brownie. While I was writing one of my law journal articles, Nikolas and I had a conversation about voting prompted by a *Sesame Street Magazine* exercise. The magazine pictured six children: four children had raised their hands because they wanted to play tag; two had their hands down because they wanted to play hide-and-seek. The magazine asked its readers to count the number of children whose hands were raised and then decide what game the children would play.

From *The Tyranny of the Majority* (1994).

5 Nikolas quite realistically replied, "They will play both. First they will play tag. Then they will play hide-and-seek." Despite the magazine's "rules," he was right. To children, it is natural to take turns. The winner may get to play first or more often, but even the "loser" gets something. His was a positive-sum solution that many adult rule-makers ignore.

The traditional answer to the magazine's problem would have been a zero-sum solution: "The children—all the children—will play tag, and only tag." As a zero-sum solution, everything is seen in terms of "I win; you lose." The conventional answer relies on winner-take-all majority rule, in which the tag players, as the majority, win the right to decide for all the children what game to play. The hide-and-seek preference becomes irrelevant. The numerically more powerful majority choice simply subsumes minority preferences.

In the conventional case, the majority that rules gains all the power and the minority that loses gets none. For example, two years ago Brother Rice High School in Chicago held two senior proms. It was not planned that way. The prom committee at Brother Rice, a boys' Catholic high school, expected just one prom when it hired a disc jockey, picked a rock band, and selected music for the prom by consulting student preferences. Each senior was asked to list his three favorite songs, and the band would play the songs that appeared most frequently on the lists.

Seems attractively democratic. But Brother Rice is predominantly white, and the prom committee was all white. That's how they got two proms. The black seniors at Brother Rice felt so shut out by the "democratic process" that they organized their own prom. As one black student put it: "For every vote we had, there were eight votes for what they wanted. . . . [W]ith us being in the minority we're always outvoted. It's as if we don't count."

Some embittered white seniors saw things differently. They complained that the black students should have gone along with the majority: "The majority makes a decision. That's the way it works."

10 In a way, both groups were right. From the white students' perspective, this was ordinary decisionmaking. To the black students, majority rule sent the message: "we don't count" is the "way it works" for minorities. In a racially divided society, majority rule may be perceived as majority tyranny.

That is a large claim, and I do not rest my case for it solely on the actions of the prom committee in one Chicago high school. To expand the range of the argument, I first consider the ideal of majority rule itself, particularly as reflected in the writings of James Madison[1]

1. Founding Father (1751–1836) and fourth president of the United States, from 1809–1817.

and other founding members of our Republic. These early democrats explored the relationship between majority rule and democracy. James Madison warned, "If a majority be united by a common interest, the rights of the minority will be insecure." The tyranny of the majority, according to Madison, requires safeguards to protect "one part of the society against the injustice of the other part."

For Madison, majority tyranny represented the great danger to our early constitutional democracy. Although the American revolution was fought against the tyranny of the British monarch, it soon became clear that there was another tyranny to be avoided. The accumulations of all powers in the same hands, Madison warned, "whether of one, a few, or many, and whether hereditary, self-appointed, or elective, may justly be pronounced the very definition of tyranny."

As another colonist suggested in papers published in Philadelphia, "We have been so long habituated to a jealousy of tyranny from monarchy and aristocracy, that we have yet to learn the dangers of it from democracy." Despotism had to be opposed "whether it came from Kings, Lords or the people."

The debate about majority tyranny reflected Madison's concern that the majority may not represent the whole. In a homogeneous society, the interest of the majority would likely be that of the minority also. But in a heterogeneous community, the majority may not represent all competing interests. The majority is likely to be self-interested and ignorant or indifferent to the concerns of the minority. In such case, Madison observed, the assumption that the majority represents the minority is "altogether fictitious."

Yet even a self-interested majority can govern fairly if it cooperates 15
with the minority. One reason for such cooperation is that the self-interested majority values the principle of reciprocity. The self-interested majority worries that the minority may attract defectors from the majority and become the next governing majority. The Golden Rule principle of reciprocity functions to check the tendency of a self-interested majority to act tyrannically.

So the argument for the majority principle connects it with the value of reciprocity: You cooperate when you lose in part because members of the current majority will cooperate when they lose. The conventional case for the fairness of majority rule is that it is not really the rule of a fixed group—The Majority—on all issues; instead it is the rule of shifting majorities, as the losers at one time or on one issue join with others and become part of the governing coalition at another time or on another issue. The result will be a fair system of mutually beneficial cooperation. I call a majority that rules but does not dominate a Madisonian Majority.

The problem of majority tyranny arises, however, when the self-interested majority does not need to worry about defections. When the majority is fixed and permanent, there are no checks on its ability to be overbearing. A majority that does not worry about defectors is a majority with total power.

In such a case, Madison's concern about majority tyranny arises. In a heterogeneous community, any faction with total power might subject "the minority to the caprice and arbitrary decisions of the majority, who instead of consulting the interest of the whole community collectively, attend sometimes to partial and local advantages."

"What remedy can be found in a republican Government, where the majority must ultimately decide," argued Madison, but to ensure "that no one common interest or passion will be likely to unite a majority of the whole number in an unjust pursuit." The answer was to disaggregate the majority to ensure checks and balances or fluid, rotating interests. The minority needed protection against an overbearing majority, so that "a common sentiment is less likely to be felt, and the requisite concert less likely to be formed, by a majority of the whole."

20 Political struggles would not be simply a contest between rulers and people; the political struggles would be among the people themselves. The work of government was not to transcend different interests but to reconcile them. In an ideal democracy, the people would rule, but the minorities would also be protected against the power of majorities. Again, where the rules of decisionmaking protect the minority, the Madisonian Majority rules without dominating.

But if a group is unfairly treated, for example, when it forms a racial minority, *and* if the problems of unfairness are not cured by conventional assumptions about majority rule, then what is to be done? The answer is that we may need an *alternative* to winner-take-all majoritarianism. In this book, a collection of my law review articles, I describe the alternative, which, with Nikolas's help, I now call the "principle of taking turns." In a racially divided society, this principle does better than simple majority rule if it accommodates the values of self-government, fairness, deliberation, compromise, and consensus that lie at the heart of the democratic ideal.

In my legal writing, I follow the caveat of James Madison and other early American democrats. I explore decisionmaking rules that might work in a multi-racial society to ensure that majority rule does not become majority tyranny. I pursue voting systems that might disaggregate The Majority so that it does not exercise power unfairly or tyrannically. I aspire to a more cooperative political style of decisionmaking to enable all of the students at Brother Rice to feel comfortable attending the same prom. In looking to create Madisonian Majorities, I pursue a positive-sum, taking-turns solution.

Structuring decisionmaking to allow the minority "a turn" may be necessary to restore the reciprocity ideal when a fixed majority refuses to cooperate with the minority. If the fixed majority loses its incentive to follow the Golden Rule principle of shifting majorities, the minority never gets to take a turn. Giving the minority a turn does not mean the minority gets to rule; what it does mean is that the minority gets to influence decision making and the majority rules more legitimately.

Instead of automatically rewarding the preferences of the monolithic majority, a taking-turns approach anticipates that the majority rules, but is not overbearing. Because those with 51 percent of the votes are not assured 100 percent of the power, the majority cooperates with, or at least does not tyrannize, the minority.

The sports analogy of "I win; you lose" competition within a political hierarchy makes sense when only one team can win; Nikolas's intuition that it is often possible to take turns suggests an alternative approach. Take family decisionmaking, for example. It utilizes a taking-turns approach. When parents sit around the kitchen table deciding on a vacation destination or activities for a rainy day, often they do not simply rely on a show of hands, especially if that means that the older children always prevail or if affinity groups among the children (those who prefer movies to video games, or those who prefer baseball to playing cards) never get to play their activity of choice. Instead of allowing the majority simply to rule, the parents may propose that everyone take turns, going to the movies one night and playing video games the next. Or as Nikolas proposes, they might do both on a given night.

Taking turns attempts to build consensus while recognizing political or social differences, and it encourages everyone to play. The taking-turns approach gives those with the most support more turns, but it also legitimates the outcome from each individual's perspective, including those whose views are shared only by a minority.

In the end, I do not believe that democracy should encourage rule by the powerful—even a powerful majority. Instead, the idea of democracy promises a fair discussion among self-defined equals about how to achieve our common aspirations. To redeem that promise, we need to put the idea of taking turns and disaggregating the majority at the center of our conception of representation. Particularly as we move into the twenty-first century as a more highly diversified citizenry, it is essential that we consider the ways in which voting and representational systems succeed or fail at encouraging Madisonian Majorities.

To use Nikolas's terminology, "it is no fair" if a fixed, tyrannical majority excludes or alienates the minority. It is no fair if a fixed, tyrannical majority monopolizes all the power all the time. It is no fair if we engage in the periodic ritual of elections, but only the permanent majority gets to choose who is elected. Where we have tyranny by The Majority, we do not have genuine democracy.

Martin Luther King, Jr.

LETTER FROM BIRMINGHAM JAIL[1]

My Dear Fellow Clergymen:

While confined here in the Birmingham city jail, I came across your recent statement calling my present activities "unwise and untimely." Seldom do I pause to answer criticism of my work and ideas. If I sought to answer all the criticisms that cross my desk, my secretaries would have little time for anything other than such correspondence in the course of the day, and I would have no time for constructive work. But since I feel that you are men of genuine good will and that your criticisms are sincerely set forth, I want to try to answer your statement in what I hope will be patient and reasonable terms.

I think I should indicate why I am here in Birmingham, since you have been influenced by the view which argues against "outsiders coming in." I have the honor of serving as president of the Southern Christian Leadership Conference, an organization operating in every southern state, with headquarters in Atlanta, Georgia. We have some eighty-five affiliated organizations across the South, and one of them is the Alabama Christian Movement for Human Rights. Frequently we share staff, educational, and financial resources with our affiliates. Several months ago the affiliate here in Birmingham asked us to be on call to engage in a nonviolent direct-action program if such were deemed necessary. We readily consented, and when the hour came we lived up to our promise. So I, along with several members of my staff, am here because I was invited here. I am here because I have organizational ties here.

But more basically, I am in Birmingham because injustice is here. Just as the prophets of the eighth century B.C. left their villages and carried their "thus saith the Lord" far beyond the boundaries of their

Written April 16, 1963; published in *Why We Can't Wait* (1964).

1. This response to a published statement by eight fellow clergymen from Alabama (Bishop C. C. J. Carpenter, Bishop Joseph A. Durick, Rabbi Milton L. Grafman, Bishop Paul Hardin, Bishop Holan B. Harmon, the Reverend George M. Murray, the Reverend Edward V. Ramage and the Reverend Earl Stallings) was composed under somewhat constricting circumstances. Begun on the margins of the newspaper in which the statement appeared while I was in jail, the letter was continued on scraps of writing paper supplied by a friendly Negro trusty, and concluded on a pad my attorneys were eventually permitted to leave me. Although the text remains in substance unaltered, I have indulged in the author's prerogative of polishing it for publication [King's note].

home towns, and just as the Apostle Paul left his village of Tarsus and carried the gospel of Jesus Christ to the far corners of the Greco-Roman world, so am I compelled to carry the gospel of freedom beyond my own home town. Like Paul, I must constantly respond to the Macedonian call for aid.

Moreover, I am cognizant of the interrelatedness of all communities and states. I cannot sit idly by in Atlanta and not be concerned about what happens in Birmingham. Injustice anywhere is a threat to justice everywhere. We are caught in an inescapable network of mutuality, tied in a single garment of destiny. Whatever affects one directly, affects all indirectly. Never again can we afford to live with the narrow, provincial "outside agitator" idea. Anyone who lives inside the United States can never be considered an outsider anywhere within its bounds.

You deplore the demonstrations taking place in Birmingham. But 5
your statement, I am sorry to say, fails to express a similar concern for the conditions that brought about the demonstrations. I am sure that none of you would want to rest content with the superficial kind of social analysis that deals merely with effects and does not grapple with underlying causes. It is unfortunate that demonstrations are taking place in Birmingham, but it is even more unfortunate that the city's white power structure left the Negro community with no alternative.

In any nonviolent campaign there are four basic steps: collection of the facts to determine whether injustices exist; negotiation; self-purification; and direct action. We have gone through all these steps in Birmingham. There can be no gainsaying the fact that racial injustice engulfs this community. Birmingham is probably the most thoroughly segregated city in the United States. Its ugly record of brutality is widely known. Negroes have experienced grossly unjust treatment in the courts. There have been more unsolved bombings of Negro homes and churches in Birmingham than in any other city in the nation. These are the hard, brutal facts of the case. On the basis of these conditions, Negro leaders sought to negotiate with the city fathers. But the latter consistently refused to engage in good-faith negotiation.

Then, last September, came the opportunity to talk with leaders of Birmingham's economic community. In the course of the negotiations, certain promises were made by the merchants—for example, to remove the stores' humiliating racial signs. On the basis of these promises, the Reverend Fred Shuttlesworth and the leaders of the Alabama Christian Movement for Human Rights agreed to a moratorium on all demonstrations. As the weeks and months went by, we realized that we were the victims of a broken promise. A few signs, briefly removed, returned; the others remained.

As in so many past experiences, our hopes had been blasted, and the shadow of deep disappointment settled upon us. We had no alternative except to prepare for direct action, whereby we would present our very bodies as a means of laying our case before the conscience of the local and the national community. Mindful of the difficulties involved, we decided to undertake a process of self-purification. We began a series of workshops on nonviolence, and we repeatedly asked ourselves: "Are you able to accept blows without retaliating?" "Are you able to endure the ordeal of jail?" We decided to schedule our direct-action program for the Easter season, realizing that except for Christmas, this is the main shopping period of the year. Knowing that a strong economic-withdrawal program would be the by-product of direct action, we felt that this would be the best time to bring pressure to bear on the merchants for the needed change.

Then it occurred to us that Birmingham's mayoral election was coming up in March, and we speedily decided to postpone action until after election day. When we discovered that the Commissioner of Public Safety, Eugene "Bull" Connor, had piled up enough votes to be in the run-off, we decided again to postpone action until the day after the run-off so that the demonstrations could not be used to cloud the issues. Like many others, we wanted to see Mr. Connor defeated, and to this end we endured postponement after postponement. Having aided in this community need, we felt that our direct-action program could be delayed no longer.

10 You may well ask, "Why direct action? Why sit-ins, marches, and so forth? Isn't negotiation a better path?" You are quite right in calling for negotiation. Indeed, this is the very purpose of direct action. Nonviolent direct action seeks to create such a crisis and foster such a tension that a community which has constantly refused to negotiate is forced to confront the issue. It seeks so to dramatize the issue that it can no longer be ignored. My citing the creation of tension as part of the work of the nonviolent-resister may sound rather shocking. But I must confess that I am not afraid of the word "tension." I have earnestly opposed violent tension, but there is a type of constructive, nonviolent tension which is necessary for growth. Just as Socrates felt that it was necessary to create a tension in the mind so that individuals could rise from the bondage of myths and half-truths to the unfettered realm of creative analysis and objective appraisal, so must we see the need for nonviolent gadflies to create the kind of tension in society that will help men rise from the dark depths of prejudice and racism to the majestic heights of understanding and brotherhood.

The purpose of our direct-action program is to create a situation so crisis-packed that it will inevitably open the door to negotiation. I therefore concur with you in your call for negotiation. Too long has our beloved Southland been bogged down in a tragic effort to live in monologue rather than dialogue.

One of the basic points in your statement is that the action that I and my associates have taken in Birmingham is untimely. Some have asked: "Why didn't you give the new city administration time to act?" The only answer that I can give to this query is that the new Birmingham administration must be prodded about as much as the outgoing one, before it will act. We are sadly mistaken if we feel that the election of Albert Boutwell as mayor will bring the millennium to Birmingham. While Mr. Boutwell is a much more gentle person than Mr. Connor, they are both segregationists, dedicated to maintenance of the status quo. I have hoped that Mr. Boutwell will be reasonable enough to see the futility of massive resistance to desegregation. But he will not see this without pressure from devotees of civil rights. My friends, I must say to you that we have not made a single gain in civil rights without determined legal and nonviolent pressure. Lamentably, it is an historical fact that privileged groups seldom give up their privileges voluntarily. Individuals may see the moral light and voluntarily give up their unjust posture; but, as Reinhold Niebuhr[2] has reminded us, groups tend to be more immoral than individuals.

We know through painful experience that freedom is never voluntarily given by the oppressor; it must be demanded by the oppressed. Frankly, I have yet to engage in a direct-action campaign that was "well timed" in the view of those who have not suffered unduly from the disease of segregation. For years now I have heard the word "Wait!" It rings in the ear of every Negro with piercing familiarity. This "Wait" has almost always meant "Never." We must come to see, with one of our distinguished jurists, that "justice too long delayed is justice denied."

We have waited for more than 340 years for our constitutional and God-given rights. The nations of Asia and Africa are moving with jet-like speed toward gaining political independence, but we still creep at horse-and-buggy pace toward gaining a cup of coffee at a lunch counter. Perhaps it is easy for those who have never felt the stinging darts of segregation to say, "Wait." But when you have seen vicious mobs lynch your mothers and fathers at will and drown your sisters and brothers at whim; when you have seen hate-filled policemen curse, kick, and even kill your black brothers and sisters; when you see the vast majority of your twenty million Negro brothers smothering in an airtight cage of poverty in the midst of an affluent society; when you suddenly find your tongue twisted and your speech stammering as you seek to explain to your six-year-old daughter why she can't go to the public amusement park that has just been advertised on television, and see tears welling up in her eyes when she is told that Funtown is closed to colored children, and see ominous clouds of inferiority be-

2. American Protestant theologian (1892–1971).

ginning to form in her little mental sky, and see her beginning to distort her personality by developing an unconscious bitterness toward white people; when you have to concoct an answer for a five-year-old son who is asking, "Daddy, why do white people treat colored people so mean?"; when you take a cross-country drive and find it necessary to sleep night after night in the uncomfortable corners of your automobile because no motel will accept you; when you are humiliated day in and day out by nagging signs reading "white" and "colored"; when your first name becomes "nigger," your middle name becomes "boy" (however old you are) and your last name becomes "John," and your wife and mother are never given the respected title "Mrs."; when you are harried by day and haunted by night by the fact that you are a Negro, living constantly at tiptoe stance, never quite knowing what to expect next, and are plagued with inner fears and outer resentments; when you are forever fighting a degenerating sense of "nobodiness"—then you will understand why we find it difficult to wait. There comes a time when the cup of endurance runs over, and men are no longer willing to be plunged into the abyss of despair. I hope, sirs, you can understand our legitimate and unavoidable impatience.

15 You express a great deal of anxiety over our willingness to break laws. This is certainly a legitimate concern. Since we so diligently urge people to obey the Supreme Court's decision of 1954 outlawing segregation in the public schools, at first glance it may seem rather paradoxical for us consciously to break laws. One may well ask: "How can you advocate breaking some laws and obeying others?" The answer lies in the fact that there are two types of laws: just and unjust. I would be the first to advocate obeying just laws. One has not only a legal but a moral responsibility to obey just laws. Conversely, one has a moral responsibility to disobey unjust laws. I would agree with St. Augustine[3] that "an unjust law is no law at all."

Now, what is the difference between the two? How does one determine whether a law is just or unjust? A just law is a man-made code that squares with the moral law or the law of God. An unjust law is a code that is out of harmony with the moral law. To put it in the terms of St. Thomas Aquinas:[4] An unjust law is a human law that is not rooted in eternal law and natural law. Any law that uplifts human personality is just. Any law that degrades human personality is unjust. All segregation statutes are unjust because segregation distorts the soul and damages the personality. It gives the segregator a false sense of superiority and the segregated a false sense of inferiority. Segregation, to use the terminology of the Jewish philosopher Martin Buber,[5] sub-

3. Early Christian church father (354–430).
4. Christian philosopher and theologian (1225–1274).
5. German-born Israeli (1878–1965).

stitutes an "I-it" relationship for an "I-thou" relationship and ends up relegating persons to the status of things. Hence segregation is not only politically, economically, and sociologically unsound, it is morally wrong and sinful. Paul Tillich[6] has said that sin is separation. Is not segregation an existential expression of man's tragic separation, his awful estrangement, his terrible sinfulness? Thus it is that I can urge men to obey the 1954 decision of the Supreme Court, for it is morally right; and I can urge them to disobey segregation ordinances, for they are morally wrong.

Let us consider a more concrete example of just and unjust laws. An unjust law is a code that a numerical or power majority group compels a minority group to obey but does not make binding on itself. This is *difference* made legal. By the same token, a just law is a code that a majority compels a minority to follow and that it is willing to follow itself. This is *sameness* made legal.

Let me give another explanation. A law is unjust if it is inflicted on a minority that, as a result of being denied the right to vote, had no part in enacting or devising the law. Who can say that the legislature of Alabama which set up that state's segregation laws was democratically elected? Throughout Alabama all sorts of devious methods are used to prevent Negroes from becoming registered voters, and there are some counties in which, even though Negroes constitute a majority of the population, not a single Negro is registered. Can any law enacted under such circumstances be considered democratically structured?

Sometimes a law is just on its face and unjust in its application. For instance, I have been arrested on a charge of parading without a permit. Now, there is nothing wrong in having an ordinance which requires a permit for a parade. But such an ordinance becomes unjust when it is used to maintain segregation and to deny citizens the First-Amendment privilege of peaceful assembly and protest.

I hope you are able to see the distinction I am trying to point out. In 20
no sense do I advocate evading or defying the law, as would the rabid segregationist. That would lead to anarchy. One who breaks an unjust law must do so openly, lovingly, and with a willingness to accept the penalty. I submit that an individual who breaks a law that conscience tells him is unjust, and who willingly accepts the penalty of imprisonment in order to arouse the conscience of the community over its injustice, is in reality expressing the highest respect for law.

Of course, there is nothing new about this kind of civil disobedience. It was evidenced sublimely in the refusal of Shadrach, Meshach, and Abednego to obey the laws of Nebuchadnezzar,[7] on the ground that a higher moral law was at stake. It was practiced superbly by the

6. German-born American Protestant theologian (1886–1965).
7. Daniel 3.

early Christians, who were willing to face hungry lions and the excruciating pain of chopping blocks rather than submit to certain unjust laws of the Roman Empire. To a degree, academic freedom is a reality today because Socrates practiced civil disobedience.[8] In our own nation, the Boston Tea Party represented a massive act of civil disobedience.

We should never forget that everything Adolf Hitler did in Germany was "legal" and everything the Hungarian freedom fighters[9] did in Hungary was "illegal." It was "illegal" to aid and comfort a Jew in Hitler's Germany. Even so, I am sure that, had I lived in Germany at the time, I would have aided and comforted my Jewish brothers. If today I lived in a Communist country where certain principles dear to the Christian faith are suppressed, I would openly advocate disobeying that country's anti-religious laws.

I must make two honest confessions to you, my Christian and Jewish brothers. First, I must confess that over the past few years I have been gravely disappointed with the white moderate. I have almost reached the regrettable conclusion that the Negro's great stumbling block in his stride toward freedom is not the White Citizen's Counciler or the Ku Klux Klanner, but the white moderate, who is more devoted to "order" than to justice; who prefers a negative peace which is the absence of tension to a positive peace which is the presence of justice; who constantly says, "I agree with you in the goal you seek, but I cannot agree with your methods of direct action"; who paternalistically believes he can set the timetable for another man's freedom; who lives by a mythical concept of time and who constantly advises the Negro to wait for a "more convenient season." Shallow understanding from people of good will is more frustrating than absolute misunderstanding from people of ill will. Lukewarm acceptance is much more bewildering than outright rejection.

I had hoped that the white moderate would understand that law and order exist for the purpose of establishing justice and that when they fail in this purpose they become the dangerously structured dams that block the flow of social progress. I had hoped that the white moderate would understand that the present tension in the South is a necessary phase of the transition from an obnoxious negative peace, in which the Negro passively accepted his unjust plight, to a substantive and positive peace, in which all men will respect the dignity and worth of human personality. Actually, we who engage in nonviolent direct

8. The ancient Greek philosopher Socrates was tried by the Athenians for corrupting their youth through his skeptical, questioning manner of teaching. He refused to change his ways and was condemned to death.

9. In the anti-Communist revolution of 1956, which was quickly put down by the Russian army.

action are not the creators of tension. We merely bring to the surface the hidden tension that is already alive. We bring it out in the open, where it can be seen and dealt with. Like a boil that can never be cured so long as it is covered up but must be opened with all its ugliness to the natural medicines of air and light, injustice must be exposed, with all the tension its exposure creates, to the light of human conscience and the air of national opinion, before it can be cured.

In your statement you assert that our actions, even though peaceful, 25
must be condemned because they precipitate violence. But is this a logical assertion? Isn't this like condemning a robbed man because his possession of money precipitated the evil act of robbery? Isn't this like condemning Socrates because his unswerving commitment to truth and his philosophical inquiries precipitated the act by the misguided populace in which they made him drink hemlock? Isn't this like condemning Jesus because his unique God-consciousness and never-ceasing devotion to God's will precipitated the evil act of crucifixion? We must come to see that, as the federal courts have consistently affirmed, it is wrong to urge an individual to cease his efforts to gain his basic constitutional rights because the quest may precipitate violence. Society must protect the robbed and punish the robber.

I had also hoped that the white moderate would reject the myth concerning time in relation to the struggle for freedom. I have just received a letter from a white brother in Texas. He writes: "All Christians know that the colored people will receive equal rights eventually, but it is possible that you are in too great a religious hurry. It has taken Christianity almost two thousand years to accomplish what it has. The teachings of Christ take time to come to earth." Such an attitude stems from a tragic misconception of time, from the strangely irrational notion that there is something in the very flow of time that will inevitably cure all ills. Actually, time itself is neutral; it can be used either destructively or constructively. More and more I feel that the people of ill will have used time much more effectively than have the people of good will. We will have to repent in this generation not merely for the hateful words and actions of the bad people, but for the appalling silence of the good people. Human progress never rolls in on wheels of inevitability; it comes through the tireless efforts of men willing to be co-workers with God, and without this hard work, time itself becomes an ally of the forces of social stagnation. We must use time creatively, in the knowledge that the time is always ripe to do right. Now is the time to make real the promise of democracy and transform our pending national elegy into a creative psalm of brotherhood. Now is the time to lift our national policy from the quicksand of racial injustice to the solid rock of human dignity.

You speak of our activity in Birmingham as extreme. At first I was rather disappointed that fellow clergymen would see my nonviolent efforts as those of an extremist. I began thinking about the fact that I stand in the middle of two opposing forces in the Negro community. One is a force of complacency, made up in part of Negroes who, as a result of long years of oppression, are so drained of self-respect and a sense of "somebodiness" that they have adjusted to segregation; and in part of a few middle-class Negroes who, because of a degree of academic and economic security and because in some ways they profit by segregation, have become insensitive to the problems of the masses. The other force is one of bitterness and hatred, and it comes perilously close to advocating violence. It is expressed in the various black nationalist groups that are springing up across the nation, the largest and best-known being Elijah Muhammad's Muslim movement.[1] Nourished by the Negro's frustration over the continued existence of racial discrimination, this movement is made up of people who have lost faith in America, who have absolutely repudiated Christianity, and who have concluded that the white man is an incorrigible "devil."

I have tried to stand between these two forces, saying that we need emulate neither the "do-nothingism" of the complacent nor the hatred and despair of the black nationalist. For there is the more excellent way of love and nonviolent protest. I am grateful to God that, through the influence of the Negro church, the way of nonviolence became an integral part of our struggle.

If this philosophy had not emerged, by now many streets of the South would, I am convinced, be flowing with blood. And I am further convinced that if our white brothers dismiss as "rabblerousers" and "outside agitators" those of us who employ nonviolent direct action, and if they refuse to support our nonviolent efforts, millions of Negroes will, out of frustration and despair, seek solace and security in black-nationalist ideologies—a development that would inevitably lead to a frightening racial nightmare.

30 Oppressed people cannot remain oppressed forever. The yearning for freedom eventually manifests itself, and that is what has happened to the American Negro. Something within has reminded him of his birthright of freedom, and something without has reminded him that it can be gained. Consciously or unconsciously, he has been caught up by the *Zeitgeist*,[2] and with his black brothers of Africa and his brown and yellow brothers of Asia, South America, and the Caribbean, the United States Negro is moving with a sense of great urgency toward the promised land of racial justice. If one recognizes this vital urge

1. Elijah Muhammed (1897–1975), succeeded to the leadership of the Nation of Islam in 1934.
2. The spirit of the times.

that has engulfed the Negro community, one should readily understand why public demonstrations are taking place. The Negro has many pent-up resentments and latent frustrations, and he must release them. So let him march; let him make prayer pilgrimages to the city hall; let him go on freedom rides—and try to understand why he must do so. If his repressed emotions are not released in nonviolent ways, they will seek expression through violence; this is not a threat but a fact of history. So I have not said to my people, "Get rid of your discontent." Rather, I have tried to say that this normal and healthy discontent can be channeled into the creative outlet of nonviolent direct action. And now this approach is being termed extremist.

But though I was initially disappointed at being categorized as an extremist, as I continued to think about the matter I gradually gained a measure of satisfaction from the label. Was not Jesus an extremist for love: "Love your enemies, bless them that curse you, do good to them that hate you, and pray for them which despitefully use you, and persecute you." Was not Amos an extremist for justice: "Let justice roll down like waters and righteousness like an ever-flowing stream." Was not Paul an extremist for the Christian gospel: "I bear in my body the marks of the Lord Jesus." Was not Martin Luther an extremist: "Here I stand; I cannot do otherwise, so help me God." And John Bunyan:[3] "I will stay in jail to the end of my days before I make a butchery of my conscience." And Abraham Lincoln: "This nation cannot survive half slave and half free." And Thomas Jefferson: "We hold these truths to be self-evident, that all men are created equal. . . ." So the question is not whether we will be extremists, but what kind of extremists we will be. Will we be extremists for hate or for love? Will we be extremists for the preservation of injustice or for the extension of justice? In that dramatic scene on Calvary's hill three men were crucified. We must never forget that all three were crucified for the same crime—the crime of extremism. Two were extremists for immorality, and thus fell below their environment. The other, Jesus Christ, was an extremist for love, truth, and goodness, and thereby rose above his environment. Perhaps the South, the nation, and the world are in dire need of creative extremists.

I had hoped that the white moderate would see this need. Perhaps I was too optimistic; perhaps I expected too much. I suppose I should have realized that few members of the oppressor race can understand the deep groans and passionate yearnings of the oppressed race, and still fewer have the vision to see that injustice must be rooted out by strong, persistent, and determined action. I am thankful, however,

3. English preacher and author (1628–1688); Amos was an Old Testament prophet; Paul a New Testament apostle; Luther (1483–1546), German Protestant reformer.

that some of our white brothers in the South have grasped the meaning of this social revolution and committed themselves to it. They are still all too few in quantity, but they are big in quality. Some—such as Ralph McGill, Lillian Smith, Harry Golden, James McBridge Dabbs, Ann Braden, and Sarah Patton Boyle—have written about our struggle in eloquent and prophetic terms. Others have marched with us down nameless streets of the South. They have languished in filthy, roach-infested jails, suffering the abuse and brutality of policemen who view them as "dirty nigger-lovers." Unlike so many of their moderate brothers and sisters, they have recognized the urgency of the moment and sensed the need for powerful "action" antidotes to combat the disease of segregation.

Let me take note of my other major disappointment. I have been so greatly disappointed with the white church and its leadership. Of course, there are some notable exceptions. I am not unmindful of the fact that each of you has taken some significant stands on this issue. I commend you, Reverend Stallings, for your Christian stand on this past Sunday, in welcoming Negroes to your worship service on a nonsegregated basis. I commend the Catholic leaders of this state for integrating Spring Hill College several years ago.

But despite these notable exceptions, I must honestly reiterate that I have been disappointed with the church. I do not say this as one of those negative critics who can always find something wrong with the church. I say this as a minister of the gospel, who loves the church; who was nurtured in its bosom; who has been sustained by its spiritual blessings and who will remain true to it as long as the cord of life shall lengthen.

35 When I was suddenly catapulted into the leadership of the bus protest in Montgomery, Alabama, a few years ago,[4] I felt we would be supported by the white church. I felt that the white ministers, priests, and rabbis of the South would be among our strongest allies. Instead, some have been outright opponents, refusing to understand the freedom movement and misrepresenting its leaders; all too many others have been more cautious than courageous and have remained silent behind the anesthetizing security of stainedglass windows.

In spite of my shattered dreams, I came to Birmingham with the hope that the white religious leadership of this community would see the justice of our cause and, with deep moral concern, would serve as the channel through which our just grievances could reach the power structure. I had hoped that each of you would understand. But again I have been disappointed.

4. Began in December 1955, when Rosa Parks refused to move to the Negro section of a bus.

I have heard numerous southern religious leaders admonish their worshipers to comply with a desegregation decision because it is the law, but I have longed to hear white ministers declare: "Follow this decree because integration is morally right and because the Negro is your brother." In the midst of blatant injustices inflicted upon the Negro, I have watched white churchmen stand on the sideline and mouth pious irrelevancies and sanctimonious trivialities. In the midst of a mighty struggle to rid our nation of racial and economic injustice, I have heard many ministers say: "Those are social issues, with which the gospel has no real concern." And I have watched many churches commit themselves to a completely otherworldly religion which makes a strange, un-Biblical distinction between body and soul, between the sacred and the secular.

I have traveled the length and breadth of Alabama, Mississippi, and all the other southern states. On sweltering summer days and crisp autumn mornings I have looked at the South's beautiful churches with their lofty spires pointing heavenward. I have beheld the impressive outlines of her massive religious-education buildings. Over and over I have found myself asking: "What kind of people worship here? Who is their God? Where were their voices when the lips of Governor Barnett dripped with words of interposition and nullification? Where were they when Governor Wallace gave a clarion call for defiance and hatred?[5] Where were their voices of support when bruised and weary Negro men and women decided to rise from the dark dungeons of complacency to the bright hills of creative protest?"

Yes, these questions are still in my mind. In deep disappointment I have wept over the laxity of the church. But be assured that my tears have been tears of love. There can be no deep disappointment where there is not deep love. Yes, I love the church. How could I do otherwise? I am in the rather unique position of being the son, the grandson, and the great-grandson of preachers. Yes, I see the church as the body of Christ. But, oh! How we have blemished and scarred that body through social neglect and through fear of being nonconformists.

There was a time when the church was very powerful—in the time 40
when the early Christians rejoiced at being deemed worthy to suffer for what they believed. In those days the church was not merely a thermometer that recorded the ideas and principles of popular opinion; it was a thermostat that transformed the mores of society. Whenever the early Christians entered a town, the people in power became disturbed and immediately sought to convict the Christians for being

5. George Wallace (1919–), governor of Alabama, opposed admission of several black students to the University of Alabama. Ross Barnett (1898–1988), governor of Mississippi, opposed James Meredith's admission to the University of Mississippi.

"disturbers of the peace" and "outside agitators." But the Christians pressed on, in the conviction that they were "a colony of heaven," called to obey God rather than man. Small in number, they were big in commitment. They were too God-intoxicated to be "astronomically intimidated." By their effort and example they brought an end to such ancient evils as infanticide and gladiatorial contests.

Things are different now. So often the contemporary church is a weak, ineffectual voice with an uncertain sound. So often it is an arch-defender of the status quo. Far from being disturbed by the presence of the church, the power structure of the average community is consoled by the church's silent—and often even vocal—sanction of things as they are.

But the judgment of God is upon the church as never before. If today's church does not recapture the sacrificial spirit of the early church, it will lose its authenticity, forfeit the loyalty of millions, and be dismissed as an irrelevant social club with no meaning for the twentieth century. Every day I meet young people whose disappointment with the church has turned into outright disgust.

Perhaps I have once again been too optimistic. Is organized religion too inextricably bound to the status quo to save our nation and the world? Perhaps I must turn my faith to the inner spiritual church, the church within the church, as the true *ekklesia*[6] and the hope of the world. But again I am thankful to God that some noble souls from the ranks of organized religion have broken loose from the paralyzing chains of conformity and joined us as active partners in the struggle for freedom. They have left their secure congregations and walked the streets of Albany, Georgia, with us. They have gone down the highways of the South on tortuous rides for freedom. Yes, they have gone to jail with us. Some have been dismissed from their churches, have lost the support of their bishops and fellow ministers. But they have acted in the faith that right defeated is stronger than evil triumphant. Their witness has been the spiritual salt that has preserved the true meaning of the gospel in these troubled times. They have carved a tunnel of hope through the dark mountain of disappointment.

I hope the church as a whole will meet the challenge of this decisive hour. But even if the church does not come to the aid of justice, I have no despair about the future. I have no fear about the outcome of our struggle in Birmingham, even if our motives are at present misunderstood. We will reach the goal of freedom in Birmingham and all over the nation, because the goal of America is freedom. Abused and scorned though we may be, our destiny is tied up with America's destiny. Before the pilgrims landed at Plymouth, we were here. Before the pen of Jefferson etched the majestic words of the Declaration of Inde-

6. The Greek New Testament word for the early Christian church.

pendence across the pages of history, we were here. For more than two centuries our forebears labored in this country without wages; they made cotton king; they built the homes of their masters while suffering gross injustice and shameful humiliation—and yet out of a bottomless vitality they continued to thrive and develop. If the inexpressible cruelties of slavery could not stop us, the opposition we now face will surely fail. We will win our freedom because the sacred heritage of our nation and the eternal will of God are embodied in our echoing demands.

Before closing I feel impelled to mention one other point in your 45
statement that has troubled me profoundly. You warmly commended the Birmingham police force for keeping "order" and "preventing violence." I doubt that you would have so warmly commended the police force if you had seen its dogs sinking their teeth into unarmed, nonviolent Negroes. I doubt that you would so quickly commend the policemen if you were to observe their ugly and inhumane treatment of Negroes here in the city jail; if you were to watch them push and curse old Negro women and young Negro girls; if you were to see them slap and kick old Negro men and young boys; if you were to observe them, as they did on two occasions, refuse to give us food because we wanted to sing our grace together. I cannot join you in your praise of the Birmingham police department.

It is true that the police have exercised a degree of discipline in handling the demonstrators. In this sense they have conducted themselves rather "nonviolently" in public. But for what purpose? To preserve the evil system of segregation. Over the past few years I have consistently preached that nonviolence demands that the means we use must be as pure as the ends we seek. I have tried to make clear that it is wrong to use immoral means to attain moral ends. But now I must affirm that it is just as wrong, or perhaps even more so, to use moral means to preserve immoral ends. Perhaps Mr. Connor and his policemen have been rather nonviolent in public, as was Chief Pritchett in Albany, Georgia, but they have used the moral means of nonviolence to maintain the immoral end of racial injustice. As T. S. Eliot has said, "The last temptation is the greatest treason: To do the right deed for the wrong reason."[7]

I wish you had commended the Negro sit-inners and demonstrators of Birmingham for their sublime courage, their willingness to suffer, and their amazing discipline in the midst of great provocation. One day the South will recognize its real heroes. They will be the James Merediths,[8] with the noble sense of purpose that enables them to face jeering and hostile mobs, and with the agonizing loneliness that char-

7. Eliot (1888–1965), American-born English poet, in *Murder in the Cathedral.*
8. Meredith was the first black to enroll at the University of Mississippi.

acterizes the life of the pioneer. They will be old, oppressed, battered Negro women, symbolized in a seventy-two-year-old woman in Montgomery, Alabama, who rose up with a sense of dignity and with her people decided not to ride segregated buses, and who responded with ungrammatical profundity to one who inquired about her weariness: "My feets is tired, but my soul is at rest." They will be the young high school and college students, the young ministers of the gospel and a host of their elders, courageously and nonviolently sitting in at lunch counters and willingly going to jail for conscience' sake. One day the South will know that when these disinherited children of God sat down at lunch counters, they were in reality standing up for what is best in the American dream and for the most sacred values in our Judaeo-Christian heritage, thereby bringing our nation back to those great wells of democracy which were dug deep by the founding fathers in their formulation of the Constitution and the Declaration of Independence.

Never before have I written so long a letter. I'm afraid it is much too long to take your precious time. I can assure you that it would have been much shorter if I had been writing from a comfortable desk, but what else can one do when he is alone in a narrow jail cell, other than write long letters, think long thoughts, and pray long prayers?

If I have said anything in this letter that overstates the truth and indicates an unreasonable impatience, I beg you to forgive me. If I have said anything that understates the truth and indicates my having a patience that allows me to settle for anything less than brotherhood, I beg God to forgive me.

50 I hope this letter finds you strong in the faith. I also hope that circumstances will soon make it possible for me to meet each of you, not as an integrationist or a civil-rights leader but as a fellow clergyman and a Christian brother. Let us all hope that the dark clouds of racial prejudice will soon pass away and the deep fog of misunderstanding will be lifted from our fear-drenched communities, and in some not too distant tomorrow the radiant stars of love and brotherhood will shine over our great nation with all their scintillating beauty.

Yours for the cause of Peace and Brotherhood,
MARTIN LUTHER KING, JR.

QUESTIONS

1. *King addressed the "Letter from Birmingham Jail" to eight fellow clergymen (see note 1) who had written a statement criticizing his activities. Where and how, in the course of the "Letter," does he attempt to make common cause with them?*
2. *King was trained in oral composition, that is, in composing and deliv-*

ering sermons. One device he uses as an aid to oral comprehension is prediction: he announces, in advance, the organization of what he is about to say. Locate examples of prediction in the "Letter."

3. *Describe King's theory of nonviolent resistance.*
4. *Imagine an unjust law that, to you, would justify civil disobedience. Describe the law, the form your resistance would take, and the penalties you would expect to incur.*

Stephanie Coontz

A NATION OF WELFARE FAMILIES

The current political debate over family values, personal responsibility, and welfare takes for granted the entrenched American belief that dependence on government assistance is a recent and destructive phenomenon. Conservatives tend to blame this dependence on personal irresponsibility aggravated by a swollen welfare apparatus that saps individual initiative. Liberals are more likely to blame it on personal misfortune magnified by the harsh lot that falls to losers in our competitive market economy. But both sides believe that "winners" in America make it on their own, that dependence reflects some kind of individual or family failure, and that the ideal family is the self-reliant unit of traditional lore—a family that takes care of its own, carves out a future for its children, and never asks for handouts. Politicians at both ends of the ideological spectrum have wrapped themselves in the mantle of these "family values," arguing over *why* the poor have not been able to make do without assistance, or whether aid has exacerbated their situation, but never questioning the assumption that American families traditionally achieve success by establishing their independence from the government.

The myth of family self-reliance is so compelling that our actual national and personal histories often buckle under its emotional weight. "We always stood on our own two feet," my grandfather used to say about his pioneer heritage, whenever he walked me to the top of the hill to survey the property in Washington State that his family had bought for next to nothing after it had been logged off in the early 1900s. Perhaps he didn't know that the land came so cheap because much of it was part of a federal subsidy originally allotted to the railroad companies, which had received 183 million acres of the public domain in the nineteenth century. These federal giveaways were the

From *Harper's Magazine* (Oct. 1992).

original source of most major Western logging companies' land, and when some of these logging companies moved on to virgin stands of timber, federal lands trickled down to a few early settlers who were able to purchase them inexpensively.

Like my grandparents, few families in American history—whatever their "values"—have been able to rely solely on their own resources. Instead, they have depended on the legislative, judicial, and social-support structures set up by governing authorities, whether those authorities were the clan elders of Native American societies, the church courts and city officials of colonial America, or the judicial and legislative bodies established by the Constitution.

At America's inception, this was considered not a dirty little secret but the norm, one that confirmed our social and personal interdependence. The idea that the family should have the sole or even primary responsibility for educating and socializing its members, finding them suitable work, or keeping them from poverty and crime was not only ludicrous to colonial and revolutionary thinkers but dangerously parochial.

5 Historically, one way that government has played a role in the well-being of its citizens is by regulating the way that employers and civic bodies interact with families. In the early twentieth century, for example, as a response to rapid changes ushered in by a mass-production economy, the government promoted a "family wage system." This system was designed to strengthen the ability of the male breadwinner to support a family without having his wife or children work. This family wage system was not a natural outgrowth of the market. It was a *political* response to conditions that the market had produced: child labor, rampant employment insecurity, recurring economic downturns, an earnings structure in which 45 percent of industrial workers fell below the poverty level and another 40 percent hovered barely above it, and a system in which thousands of children had been placed in orphanages or other institutions simply because their parents could not afford their keep. The state policies involved in the establishment of the family wage system included abolition of child labor, government pressure on industrialists to negotiate with unions, federal arbitration, expansion of compulsory schooling—and legislation discriminating against women workers.

But even such extensive regulation of economic and social institutions has never been enough: government has always supported families with direct material aid as well. The two best examples of the government's history of material aid can be found in what many people consider the ideal models of self-reliant families: the Western pioneer family and the 1950s suburban family. In both cases, the ability of these families to establish and sustain themselves required massive underwriting by the government.

Pioneer families, such as my grandparents, could never have moved west without government-funded military mobilizations against the original Indian and Mexican inhabitants or state-sponsored economic investment in transportation systems. In addition, the Homestead Act of 1862 allowed settlers to buy 160 acres for $10—far below the government's cost of acquiring the land—if the homesteader lived on and improved the land for five years. In the twentieth century, a new form of public assistance became crucial to Western families: construction of dams and other federally subsidized irrigation projects. During the 1930s, for example, government electrification projects brought pumps, refrigeration, and household technology to millions of families.

The suburban family of the 1950s is another oft-cited example of familial self-reliance. According to legend, after World War II a new, family-oriented generation settled down, saved their pennies, worked hard, and found well-paying jobs that allowed them to purchase homes in the suburbs. In fact, however, the 1950s suburban family was far more dependent on government assistance than any so-called underclass family of today. Federal GI benefit payments, available to 40 percent of the male population between the ages of twenty and twenty-four, permitted a whole generation of men to expand their education and improve their job prospects without forgoing marriage and children. The National Defense Education Act retooled science education in America, subsidizing both American industry and the education of individual scientists. Government-funded research developed the aluminum clapboards, prefabricated walls and ceilings, and plywood paneling that comprised the technological basis of the postwar housing revolution. Government spending was also largely responsible for the new highways, sewer systems, utility services, and traffic-control programs that opened up suburbia.

In addition, suburban home ownership depended on an unprecedented expansion of federal regulation and financing. Before the war, banks often required a 50 percent down payment on homes and normally issued mortgages for five to ten years. In the postwar period, however, the Federal Housing Authority, supplemented by the GI Bill, put the federal government in the business of insuring and regulating private loans for single-home construction. FHA policy required down payments of only 5 to 10 percent of the purchase price and guaranteed mortgages of up to thirty years at interest rates of just 2 to 3 percent. The Veterans Administration required a mere dollar down from veterans. Almost half the housing in suburbia in the 1950s depended on such federal programs.

10 The drawback of these aid programs was that although they worked well for recipients, nonrecipients—disproportionately poor and urban—were left far behind. While the general public financed the roads that suburbanites used to commute, the streetcars and trolleys that served urban and poor families received almost no tax revenues, and our previously thriving rail system was allowed to decay. In addition, federal loan policies, which were a boon to upwardly mobile white families, tended to systematize the pervasive but informal racism that had previously characterized the housing market. FHA redlining practices, for example, took entire urban areas and declared them ineligible for loans, while the government's two new mortgage institutions, the Federal National Mortgage Association and the Government National Mortgage Association (Fannie Mae and Ginny Mae) made it possible for urban banks to transfer savings out of the cities and into new suburban developments in the South and West.

Despite the devastating effects on families and regions that did not receive such assistance, government aid to suburban residents during the 1950s and 1960s produced in its beneficiaries none of the demoralization usually presumed to afflict recipients of government handouts. Instead, federal subsidies to suburbia encouraged family formation, residential stability, upward occupational mobility, and rising educational aspirations among youth who could look forward to receiving such aid. Seen in this light, the idea that government subsidies intrinsically induce dependence, undermine self-esteem, or break down family ties is exposed as no more than a myth.

I am not suggesting that the way to solve the problems of poverty and urban decay in America is to quadruple our spending on welfare. Certainly there are major reforms needed in our current aid policies to the poor. But the debate over such reform should put welfare in the context of *all* federal assistance programs. As long as we pretend that only poor or single-parent families need outside assistance, while normal families "stand on their own two feet," we will shortchange poor families, overcompensate rich ones, and fail to come up with effective policies for helping out families in the middle. Current government housing policies are a case in point. The richest 20 percent of American households receives three times as much federal housing aid—mostly in tax subsidies—as the poorest 20 percent receives in expenditures for low-income housing.

Historically, the debate over government policies toward families has never been over *whether* to intervene but *how:* to rescue or to warehouse, to prevent or to punish, to moralize about values or mobilize resources for education and job creation. Today's debate, lacking such historical perspective, caricatures the real issues. Our attempt to sustain the myth of family self-reliance in the face of all the historical evidence to the contrary has led policymakers into theoretical contortions and practical miscalculations that are reminiscent of efforts by medieval philosophers to maintain that the earth and not the sun was the center of the planetary system. In the sixteenth century, leading European thinkers insisted that the planets and the sun all revolved around the earth—much as American politicians today insist that our society revolves around family self-reliance. When evidence to the contrary mounted, defenders of the Ptolemaic universe postulated all sorts of elaborate planetary orbits in order to reconcile observed reality with their cherished theory. Similarly, rather than admit that all families need some kind of public support, we have constructed ideological orbits that explain away each instance of middle-class dependence as an "exception," an "abnormality," or even an illusion. We have distributed public aid to families through convoluted bureaucracies that have become impossible to track; in some cases the system has become so cumbersome that it threatens to collapse around our ears. It is time to break through the old paradigm of self-reliance and substitute a new one that recognizes that assisting families is, simply, what government does.

QUESTIONS

1. *Coontz is a historian whose research on the family bears upon politically volatile contemporary issues. This essay from* Harper's Magazine *is based on her testimony before the House Select Committee on Children, Youth, and Families. How does she report fact? How does she signal her interpretation of it? Where and how does she signal where she stands on contemporary issues?*
2. *Why, according to Coontz, does today's debate over government policies toward families resemble debates over the Ptolemaic system (paragraph 13)? What does she mean by "ideological orbits"?*
3. *Coontz describes a conservative position that explains dependence on government assistance as the result of "personal irresponsibility aggravated by a swollen welfare apparatus that saps individual initiative" and a liberal position that explains it as the result of "personal misfortune magnified by the harsh lot that falls to losers in our competitive market economy" (paragraph 1). Write a brief essay in which you argue for one position and against the other or else stake out your own position and argue against both the conservative and the liberal positions as she describes them.*

Stephen L. Carter

THE BEST BLACK

Affirmative action has been with me always. I do not mean to suggest that I have always been the beneficiary of special programs and preferences. I mean, rather, that no matter what my accomplishments, I have had trouble escaping an assumption that often seems to underlie the worst forms of affirmative action: that black people cannot compete intellectually with white people. Certainly I have not escaped it since my teen years, spent mostly in Ithaca, New York, where the presence of Cornell University lends an air of academic intensity to the public schools. At Ithaca High School in the days of my adolescence, we had far more than our share of National Merit Scholars, of students who scored exceptionally well on standardized tests, of students who earned advanced placement credits for college, and of every other commodity by which secondary schools compare their academic quality.

My father taught at Cornell, which made me a Cornell kid, a "fac-brat," and I hung out with a bunch of white Cornell kids in a private little world where we competed fiercely (but only with one another—no one else mattered!) for grades and test scores and solutions to brain teasers. We were the sort of kids other kids hated: the ones who would run around compiling lists of everyone else's test scores and would badger guidance counselors into admitting their errors in arithmetic (no computers then) in order to raise our class ranks a few notches. I held my own in this bunch, although I was forced by the norms of the fac-brat community to retake the Mathematics Level II achievement test to raise a humiliating score of 780 to an acceptable 800. (No one had yet told me that standardized tests were culturally biased against me.) Like the rest of the fac-brats, I yearned for the sobriquet "brilliant," and tried desperately to convince myself and everyone else who would listen that I had the grades and test scores to deserve it.

And yet there were unnerving indications that others did not see me as just another fac-brat, that they saw me instead as that black kid who hung out with the Cornell kids. There was, for example, the recruiter from Harvard College who asked to see those he considered the brightest kids in the school; I was included, so a guidance counselor said, because I was black. And when I decided that I wanted to attend Stanford University, I was told by a teacher that I would surely be ad-

From *Reflections of an Affirmative Action Baby* (1991). Unless marked, all notes to this essay are the author's.

mitted because I was black and I was smart. Not because I was smart and not even because I was smart and black, but because I was black and smart: the skin color always preceding any other observation.

All of this came to a head at National Merit Scholarship time. In those days (this was the early 1970s), the National Merit Scholarship Qualifying Test was a separate examination, not combined with the Preliminary Scholastic Aptitude Test as it later would be. When the qualifying scores came in, I was in heaven. Mine was the third highest in the school. I saw my future then—best fac-brat!—and awaited my National Merit Scholarship. Instead, I won a National Achievement Scholarship, presented, in the awkward usage of the day, to "outstanding Negro students." Well, all right. If one wants more black students to go to college, one had better provide the necessary resources. College is expensive and money is money. Still, at first I was insulted; I saw my "best fac-brat" status slipping away, for what I craved was a National *Merit* Scholarship, the one not for the best black students, but for the *best* students. So I was turned down.

Here it is useful to add some perspective. All through my adolescence, when I failed at some intellectual task (always measuring failure by my distance from the top), I usually, and properly, blamed myself. At times, however, I attributed my inability to reach my goals as a kind of conspiracy to keep me, a black kid, from reaping the rewards I imagined my achievements deserved, and, at times, to keep me from even trying. And sometimes the conspiracy was real.

Particularly vivid is my memory of moving from a mostly black elementary school to a mostly white junior high school, where I was not allowed to enroll in even a basic Spanish class, despite three years' study of the language, because, my mother was told, the limited spaces were all allocated to graduates of a particular elementary school—which happened to be all white. I was assigned to vocational education instead. And when I moved on to high school, carrying with me an A average in mathematics and excellent test scores, not only was I prevented from enrolling in the highest math section—I was not even told that it existed!

Having faced these barriers before, I readily assumed that the National Achievement program was another. (In fact, for nearly twenty years, my memory of the incident was that I was forced to choose between accepting a National Achievement Scholarship and remaining eligible for a National Merit Scholarship.) But when the National Merit people reassured me that I could accept one and remain eligible for the other, I accepted the offered scholarship, and even competed for the cherished National Merit Scholarship—which I didn't get. (That year, like most years, some students won both.) In time, I would come to support racially targeted scholarship programs. As a nervous

17-year-old, however, I worried that such programs were examples of the same old lesson: the smartest students of color were not considered as capable as the smartest white students, and therefore would not be allowed to compete with them, but only with one another.

I call it the "best black" syndrome, and all black people who have done well in school are familiar with it. We are measured by a different yardstick: *first black, only black, best black.* The best black syndrome is cut from the same cloth as the implicit and demeaning tokenism that often accompanies racial preferences: "Oh, we'll tolerate so-and-so at our hospital or in our firm or on our faculty, because she's the best black." Not because she's the best-qualified candidate, but because she's the best-qualified *black* candidate. She can fill the black slot. And then the rest of the slots can be filled in the usual way: with the best-*qualified* candidates.

This dichotomy between "best" and "best black" is not merely something manufactured by racists to denigrate the abilities of professionals who are not white. On the contrary, the durable and demeaning stereotype of black people as unable to compete with white ones is reinforced by advocates of certain forms of affirmative action. It is reinforced, for example, every time employers are urged to set aside test scores (even, in some cases, on tests that are good predictors of job performance) and to hire from separate lists, one of the best white scorers, the other of the best black ones. It is reinforced every time state pension plans are pressed to invest some of their funds with "minority-controlled" money management firms, even if it turns out that the competing "white" firms have superior track records.[1] It is reinforced every time students demand that universities commit to hiring some pre-set number of minority faculty members. What all of these people are really saying is, "There are black folks out there. Go and find the best of them." And the best black syndrome is further reinforced, almost unthinkingly, by politicians or bureaucrats or faculty members who see these demands as nothing more than claims for simple justice.

Successful black students and professionals have repeatedly disproved the proposition that the best black minds are not as good as the best white ones, but the stereotype lingers, even among the most ardent friends of civil rights. In my own area of endeavor, academia, I hear this all the time from people who should know better. It is not at all unusual for white professors, with no thought that they are indulging a demeaning stereotype, to argue for hiring the best available professors of color, whether or not the individuals on whom that double-

1. See, for example, the account of the debate in Maryland in *Bond Buyer,* 31 July 1990, p. 32.

edged mantle is bestowed meet the usual appointment standards. I put aside for the moment the question of the fairness of the standards, for the white people I am describing have few doubts about *that;* I have in mind white people who argue with straight face for the hiring of black people *they themselves* do not believe are good enough to be hired without extra points for race. For example, one prominent law professor, a strong and sincere proponent of racial diversity, sent me a list of scholars in his field who might be considered for appointment to the Yale faculty. The first part of the list set out the names of the best people in the field; the second part, the names of people who were so-so; and the last part, the names of the leading "minorities and women" in the field, none of whom apparently qualified (in his judgment) for even the "so-so" category, let alone the best. I know that my colleague acted with the best of intentions, but the implicit invitation offered by this extraordinary document was to choose between diversity and quality. I suspect that to this day he is unaware of any insult and actually believes he was advancing the cause of racial justice.

"No responsible advocate of affirmative action," argues Ira Glasser, "opposes merit or argues . . . that standards should be reduced in order to meet affirmative action goals."[2] Perhaps not; but the language of standards and merit is slippery at best. I am reminded of a conversation I had some years ago with a veteran civil rights litigator who, concerned at charges that affirmative action sometimes results in hiring unqualified candidates, drew a sharp distinction between *unqualified* and *less qualified.* An employer, he mused, does not have to hire the *best* person for the job, as long as everyone hired is *good enough* to do the job. Consequently, he reasoned, it is perfectly fine to require employers to hire black applicants who are less qualified than some white applicants, as long as the black candidates are capable of doing the job. A tidy argument in its way, but, of course, another example of an almost unconscious acceptance of a situation in which an employer is made to distinguish between the best black candidates and the best ones.

Even our sensible but sometimes overzealous insistence that the rest of the nation respect the achievements of black culture might reinforce the depressing dichotomy: if we insist, as often we must, that others appreciate "our" music and "our" literature, we should not be surprised if those others come to think of the best of our music and the best of our literature as distinct from the best music and the best literature. Indeed, this is the implication of Stanley Crouch's vigorous

2. Ira Glasser, "Affirmative Action and the Legacy of Racial Injustice," in *Eliminating Racism: Profiles in Controversy,* ed. Phyllis A. Katz and Dalmas A. Taylor (New York: Plenum Press, 1988), pp. 341, 350.

argument (on which I here express no view) that white critics accept a level of mediocrity from black artists, filmmakers, and writers that they would never tolerate from creative people who are white.[3]

The best black syndrome creates in those of us who have benefited from racial preferences a peculiar contradiction. We are told over and over that we are among the best black people in our professions. And in part we are flattered, or should be, because, after all, those who call us the best black lawyers or doctors or investment bankers consider it a compliment. But to professionals who have worked hard to succeed, flattery of this kind carries an unsubtle insult, for we yearn to be called what our achievements often deserve: simply the best—no qualifiers needed! In *this* society, however, we sooner or later must accept that being viewed as the best blacks is part of what has led us to where we are; and we must further accept that to some of our colleagues, black as well as white, we will never be anything else.

Despite these rather unsettling pitfalls, many of us resist the best black syndrome less than we should, and one of the reasons is surely that it can bestow considerable benefits. Racial preferences are perhaps the most obvious benefit, but there are others. In high school, for example, I quickly stood out, if only because I was the lone black student in any number of honors and advanced placement courses. Perhaps my intellect was not unusually keen; although I did as well as anyone, I have always thought that with proper training, scoring well on standardized tests is no great trick. Nevertheless, other students and, eventually, teachers as well concluded that I was particularly sharp. These perceptions naturally fed my ego, because all I really wanted from high school was to be considered one of the best and brightest.

What I could not see then, but see clearly now, two decades later, is that while the perceptions others had of my abilities were influenced in part by grades and test scores, they were further influenced by the fact that students and teachers (black and white alike) were unaccustomed to the idea that a black kid could sit among the white kids as an equal, doing as well, learning as much, speaking as ably, arguing with as much force. In their experience, I was so different that I had to be exceptional. But exceptional in a specific and limited sense: the best black.

College was not much different. My college grades were somewhat better than average, but at Stanford in the era of grade inflation, good grades were the norm. Nevertheless, I quickly discovered that black

3. Stanley Crouch, *Notes of a Hanging Judge* (New York: Oxford University Press, 1990).

students with good grades stood out from the crowd. Other students and many of my professors treated me as a member of some odd and fascinating species. I sat among them as an equal in seminars, my papers were as good as anyone else's, so I had to be exceptionally bright. In their experience, it seemed, no merely ordinarily smart black person could possibly sit among them as an equal.

In law school, the trend continued. I was fortunate enough to come early to the attention of my professors, but all I was doing was playing by the rules: talking in class with reasonable intelligence, exhibiting genuine interest in questions at the podium later, and treating papers and examinations as matters of serious scholarship rather than obstacles to be overcome. Lots of students did the same—but, in the stereotyped visions of some of my professors, not lots of black students. Here was the best black syndrome at work once more: I was not just another bright student with an enthusiastic but untrained intellect; I was a bright *black* student, a fact that apparently made a special impression.

The stultifying mythology of racism holds that black people are intellectually inferior. Consistent survey data over the years indicate that this stereotype persists.[4] Such incidents as those I have described, however, make me somewhat skeptical of the familiar complaint that because of this mythology, black people of intellectual talent have a harder time than others in proving their worth. My own experience suggests quite the contrary, that like a flower blooming in winter, intellect is more readily noticed where it is not expected to be found. Or, as a black investment banker has put the point, "Our mistakes are amplified, but so are our successes."[5] And it is the amplification of success that makes the achieving black student or professional into the best black.

When people assign to a smart black person the status of best black, they do so with the purest of motives: the curing of bewilderment. There must be an explanation, the reasoning runs, and the explana-

4. The most recent General Social Survey, a regular report of the widely respected National Opinion Research Center, found that 53 percent of white respondents consider black people generally less intelligent than white people. ("Whites Retain Negative View of Minorities, a Survey Finds," *New York Times*, 10 January 1991, p. B10.) Prior surveys through the late 1960s had shown a decline in the percentage of white respondents who consider black people less intelligent. Historical polling results on the attitudes of white Americans about black Americans are collected in National Research Council, *A Common Destiny: Blacks and American Society* (Washington, D.C.: National Academy Press, 1989), pp. 120–23. For a more detailed discussion of data collected during the 1980s, see Lee Sigelman and Susan Welch, *Black Americans' Views of Racial Inequality* (Cambridge: Cambridge University Press, 1991), esp. pp. 85–100.

5. Quoted in Colin Leinster, "Black Executives: How They're Doing," *Fortune*, 18 January 1988, p. 109.

tion must be that this black person, in order to do as well as white people, is exceptionally bright. What I describe is not racism in the sense of a design to oppress, but it is in its racialist assumption of inferiority every it as insulting and nearly as tragic. The awe and celebration with which our achievements are often greeted (by black and white people alike) suggest a widespread expectation that our achievements will be few. The surprise is greater, perhaps, when our achievements are intellectual, but other achievements, too, seem to astonish. The astonishment, moreover, takes a long time to fade: even, or perhaps especially, in the era of affirmative action, it seems, the need to prove one's professional worth over and over again has not receded.

* * *

My desire to succeed in the professional world without the aid of preferential treatment is hardly a rejection of the unhappy truth that the most important factor retarding the progress of people of color historically has been society's racism. It is, rather, an insistence on the opportunity to do what the National Merit Scholarship people said I would not be allowed to, what I promised at that fateful lunch I would: to show the world that we who are black are not so marked by our history of racist oppression that we are incapable of intellectual achievement on the same terms as anybody else.

In a society less marked by racist history, the intellectual achievements of people of color might be accepted as a matter of course. In *this* society, however, they are either ignored or applauded, but never accepted as a matter of course. As I have said, however, the general astonishment when our achievements are intellectual carries with it certain benefits. Perhaps chief among these is the possibility of entrée to what I call the "star system." The characteristics of the star system are familiar to anyone who has attended college or professional school or has struggled upward on the corporate ladder, and it has analogues in sports, the military, and other arenas. Early in their careers, a handful of individuals are marked by their teachers or supervisors as having the potential for special success, even greatness. Thereafter, the potential stars are closely watched. Not every person marked early as a possible star becomes one, but the vast majority of those who are never marked will never star. Even very talented individuals who lack entrée to the star system may never gain attention in the places that matter: the hushed and private conference rooms (I can testify to their existence, having sat in more than a few) where money is spent and hiring and promotion decisions are made.

Getting into the star system is not easy, and the fact that few people of color scramble to the top of it should scarcely be surprising. The reason is not any failing in our native abilities—although it is true that only in the past decade have we been present as students in numbers sufficient to make entry more plausible—but the social dynamics of the star system itself. Entrée is not simply a matter of smarts, although that helps, or of working hard, although that helps, too. The star system rewards familiarity, comfort, and perseverance. It usually begins on campus, and so do its problems. One must get to know one's professors. Most college and professional school students are far too intimidated by their professors to feel comfortable getting to know them well, and for many students of color, already subject to a variety of discomforts, this barrier may seem especially high. When one feels uneasy about one's status in the classroom to begin with, the task of setting out to get to know the professor personally may seem close to insuperable. The fact that some students of color indeed reap the benefits of the star system does not alter the likelihood that many more would never dream of trying.

Exclusion from the star system is costly. Anyone left out will meet with difficulties in being taken seriously as a candidate for entry-level hiring at any of our most selective firms and institutions, which is why the failure of people of color to get into the star system makes a difference. Still, there is an opportunity here: because so little is expected of students of color, intellectual attainment is sometimes seen as a mark of genuine brilliance. (None of the merely ordinarily smart need apply!) So the best black syndrome can have a salutary side effect: it can help those trapped inside it get through the door of the star system. Certainly it worked that way for me. (Who *is* this character? my professors seemed to want to know.) The star system, in turn, got me in the door of the academy at the entry level. (From the doorway, I would like to think, I made the rest of the journey on my own; my achievements ought to speak for themselves. But in a world in which I have heard my colleagues use the very words *best black* in discussions of faculty hiring, I have no way to tell.) So, yes, I am a beneficiary of both the star system and the best black syndrome. Yet I hope it is clear that I am not a fan of either. The star system is exclusionary and incoherent; the best black syndrome is demeaning and oppressive. Both ought to be abandoned.

Consider the so-called glass ceiling, the asserted reluctance of corporations to promote people of color to top management positions. If indeed the glass ceiling exists, it is very likely a function of the star system. If people of color tend to have trouble getting in good, as the saying goes, with their professors, they are likely to have as much or more trouble getting in good with their employers. And if, once hired, people who are not white face difficulties in finding mentors, powerful institutional figures to smooth their paths, then they will naturally advance more slowly. Oh, there will always be some black participants in the star system, not as tokens but as people who have, as I said, taken to heart the adage that they must be twice as good. (One need but think of Colin Powell or William Coleman.)[6] Still, plenty of people of color who are merely as good as or slightly better than white people who are inside the star system will find themselves outside. The social turns do not work for them, and their advancement on the corporate ladder will be slow or nonexistent.

To be sure, the star system cannot get all of the blame for the dearth of people who are not white in (and, especially, at the top of) the professions. That there is present-day racism, overt and covert, might almost go without saying, except that so many people keep insisting there isn't any. But one should not assume too readily that contemporary discrimination explains all of the observed difference. Groups are complex and no two groups are the same. With cultural and other differences, it would be surprising if all group outcomes were identical. When the nation's odious history of racial oppression is grafted onto any other differences that might exist, the numbers are less surprising still. What would be surprising would be if we as a people had so successfully shrugged off the shackles of that history as to have reached, at this relatively early stage in the nation's evolution, economic and educational parity.

But the star system is not exactly blameless, either. Any system that rewards friendship and comfort rather than merit will burden most heavily those least likely to find the right friends.[7] It is ironic, even awkward, to make this point in an era when the attack on meritocracy is so sharply focused, but the claims pressed by today's critics in that attack—bigotry, unconscious bias, corrupt and malleable standards, social and cultural exclusion—are among the reasons that led other ethnic groups in the past to insist on the establishment of measurable systems for rewarding merit. The star system is a corrupt and biased means for circumventing the meritocratic ideal, but its corruption should not be attributed to the ideal itself.

None of this means that affirmative action is the right answer to the difficulties the star system has spawned. Among the group of intellec-

6. Prominent attorney (1920–); Powell (1937–), retired general, chairman of the Joint Chiefs of Staff, 1987–1989. [Editor's note].

7. My description of the star system might usefully be compared to the French sociologist Pierre Bourdieu's analysis of the role of "cultural capital" and "social capital" in the maintenance of the class structure: Pierre Bourdieu, "Cultural Reproduction and Social Reproduction," in *Power and Ideology in Education,* ed. J. Karabel and A. H. Halsey (New York: Oxford University Press, 1977), p. 487. I am less sure than Bourdieu is that the system works principally to the benefit of the children of those already part of it; my concern with the star system is that it is exclusionary and at the same time a distortion of the meritocratic ideal.

tuals known loosely (and, I believe, often inaccurately) as black conservatives, there is a widely shared view that the removal of artificial barriers to entry into a labor market is the proper goal to be pursued by those who want to increase minority representation. The economist Walter Williams often cites the example of cities like New York that limit the number of individuals permitted to drive taxi-cabs. No wonder, he says, there are so few black cabdrivers: it's too difficult to get into the market. Consequently, says Williams, New York should abolish its limits and, subject only to some basic regulatory needs, open the field to anyone. This, he says, would automatically result in an increase in black drivers—assuming, that is, that there are black people who want to drive cabs.

Other strategies, too, are easy to defend. For example, it is difficult to quarrel with the idea that an employer concerned about diversity—whatever its needs and hiring standards—should be as certain as possible that any candidate search it conducts is designed to yield the names of people of color who fit the search profile. After centuries of exclusion by design, it would be a terrible tragedy were black and other minority professionals excluded through inadvertence. Mari Matsuda has argued that a serious intellectual ought to make an effort to read books by members of groups not a part of his or her familiar experience, and I think she is quite right.[8] It is in the process of that determined reading—that searching—that the people who have been overlooked will, if truly excellent, eventually come to light.

The example can be generalized. Searching is the only way to find outstanding people of color, which is why all professional employers should practice it. Although the cost of a search is not trivial, the potential return in diversity, without any concomitant lowering of standards, is enormous—provided always that the employer is careful to use the search only to turn up candidates, not as a means of bringing racial preferences into the hiring process through the back door. For it is easy, but demeaning, to conflate the goal of searching with the goal of hiring, and to imagine therefore that the reason for the search is to ensure that the optimal number of black people are hired. It isn't. The reason for the search is to find the blacks among the best, not the best among the blacks.

If this distinction is borne firmly in mind, then an obligation to search will of course provide no guarantee that the statistics will improve. But I am not sure that a guarantee is what we should be seeking. People of color do not need special treatment in order to advance in the professional world; we do not need to be considered the best

8. Mari Matsuda, "Affirmative Action and Legal Knowledge: Planting Seeds in Plowed-up Ground," *Harvard Women's Law Journal* 11 (Spring 1988): 5–6.

blacks, competing only with one another for the black slots. On the contrary, our goal ought to be to prove that we can compete with anybody, to demonstrate that the so-called pool problem, the alleged dearth of qualified entry-level candidates who are not white, is at least partly a myth. So if we can gain for ourselves a fair and equal chance to show what we can do—what the affirmative action literature likes to call a level playing field—then it is something of an insult to our intellectual capacities to insist on more.

And of course, although we do not like to discuss it, the insistence on more carries with it certain risks. After all, an employer can hire a candidate because the employer thinks that person is the best one available or for some other reason: pleasing a powerful customer, rewarding an old friend, keeping peace in the family, keeping the work force all white, getting the best black. When the employer hires on one of these other grounds, it should come as no surprise if the employee does not perform as well as the best available candidate would have. There will be times when the performance will be every bit as good, but those will not be the norm unless the employer is a poor judge of talent; and if the employer consistently judges talent poorly, a second, shrewder judge of talent will eventually put the first employer out of business.[9] That is not, I think, a web in which we as a people should want to be entangled.

Racial preferences, in sum, are not the most constructive method for overcoming the barriers that keep people of color out of high-prestige positions. They are often implemented in ways that are insulting, and besides, they can carry considerable costs. Although there are fewer unfair and arbitrary barriers to the hiring and retention of black professionals than there once were, many barriers remain, and the star system, although some few of us benefit from it, is prominent among them. But if the barriers are the problem, then it is the barriers themselves that should be attacked. Should the star system be brushed aside, our opportunities would be considerably enhanced because many of the special advantages from which we are excluded would vanish.

9. Although it is sometimes said that racial discrimination serves the interests of capitalism, the inefficiency of prejudice in the market is well understood in economics. The classic analysis of the market costs of discrimination on the basis of race is Gary S. Becker, *The Economics of Discrimination* (Chicago: University of Chicago Press, 1957). Much of the analysis in Becker's book is mathematical and may be inaccessible to the lay reader. A recent and more accessible treatment of the same issue is Thomas Sowell, *Preferential Policies: An International Perspective* (New York: William Morrow, 1990), esp. pp. 20–40. For a discussion of the way that racial discrimination following the Civil War retarded the growth of the Southern economy, see Roger L. Ransom and Richard Sutch, *One Kind of Freedom: The Economic Consequences of Emancipation* (Cambridge: Cambridge University Press, 1977).

Getting rid of the star system will not be easy. I have discovered through painful experience that many of its most earnest white defenders—as well as many of those who pay lip service to overturning it but meanwhile continue to exploit it—are also among the most ardent advocates of hiring black people who, if white, they would consider second-rate. They are saying, in effect, We have one corrupt system for helping out our friends, and we'll be happy to let you have one for getting the numbers right. Faced with such obduracy, small wonder that racial preferences seem an attractive alternative.

But people of color must resist the urge to join the race to the bottom. The stakes are too high. I am sensitive to Cornell University Professor Isaac Kramnick's comment that even if a school hires some black professors who are not first-rate, "it will take till eternity for the number of second-rate blacks in the university to match the number of second-rate whites."[1] Point taken: one can hardly claim that elite educational institutions have been perfect meritocracies. However, the claim that there are incompetent whites and therefore incompetent blacks should be given a chance is unlikely to resonate with many people's visions of justice. Because of the racial stereotyping that is rampant in our society, moreover, any inadequacies among second-rate white professionals are unlikely to be attributed by those with the power to do something about it to whites as a whole; with black professionals, matters are quite unfairly the other way around, which is why the hiring of second-rate black professionals in any field would be detrimental to the effort to break down barriers.

The corruption of the meritocratic ideal with bias and favoritism offers professionals who are not white an opportunity we should not ignore: the chance to teach the corrupters their own values by making our goal excellence rather than adequacy. Consider this perceptive advice to the black scholar from John Hope Franklin, one of the nation's preeminent historians: "He should know that by maintaining the highest standards of scholarship he not only becomes worthy but also sets an example that many of his contemporaries who claim to be the arbiters in the field do not themselves follow."[2] The need to beat down the star system should spur us not to demand more affirmative action but to exceed the achievements of those who manipulate the system to their advantage.

Besides, the star system does not taint every institution to an equal degree. Some hiring and promotion processes actually make sense. If we rush to graft systems of racial preference onto hiring processes ra-

1. Quoted in Adam Begley, "Black Studies' New Era: Henry Louis Gates Jr.," *New York Times Magazine*, 1 April 1990, p. 24.
2. Franklin, "The Dilemma of the American Negro Scholar," p. 305.

tionally designed to produce the best doctors or lawyers or investment bankers or professors, we might all hope that the professionals hired because of the preferences turn out to be as good as those hired because they are expected to be the best, but no one should be surprised if this hope turns to ashes. Painful though this possibility may seem, it is consistent with a point that many supporters of affirmative action tend to miss, or at least to obscure: racial preferences that make no difference are unimportant.

Racial preferences are founded on the proposition that the achievements of their beneficiaries would be fewer if the preferences did not exist. Supporters of preferences cite a whole catalogue of explanations for the inability of people of color to get along without them: institutional racism, inferior education, overt prejudice, the lingering effects of slavery and oppression, cultural bias in the criteria for admission and employment. All of these arguments are most sincerely pressed, and some of them are true. But like the best black syndrome, they all entail the assumption that people of color cannot at present compete on the same playing field with people who are white. I don't believe this for an instant.

Science

Jacob Bronowski

THE NATURE OF SCIENTIFIC REASONING

What is the insight in which the scientist tries to see into nature? Can it indeed be called either imaginative or creative? To the literary man the question may seem merely silly. He has been taught that science is a large collection of facts; and if this is true, then the only seeing which scientists need to do is, he supposes, seeing the facts. He pictures them, the colorless professionals of science, going off to work in the morning into the universe in a neutral, unexposed state. They then expose themselves like a photographic plate. And then in the darkroom or laboratory they develop the image, so that suddenly and startlingly it appears, printed in capital letters, as a new formula for atomic energy.

Men who have read Balzac and Zola[1] are not deceived by the claims of these writers that they do no more than record the facts. The readers of Christopher Isherwood[2] do not take him literally when he writes "I am a camera." Yet the same readers solemnly carry with them from their schooldays this foolish picture of the scientist fixing by some mechanical process the facts of nature. I have had of all people a historian tell me that science is a collection of facts, and his voice had not even the ironic rasp of one filing cabinet reproving another.

It seems impossible that this historian had ever studied the beginnings of a scientific discovery. The Scientific Revolution can be held to begin in the year 1543 when there was brought to Copernicus, perhaps on his deathbed, the first printed copy of the book he had fin-

First delivered as a lecture at the Massachusetts Institute of Technology in 1953; reprinted as part of Chapter One of *Science and Human Values* (1956).

1. Honoré de Balzac (1799–1850) and Émile Zola (1840–1902), nineteenth-century French novelists.
2. Modern English novelist and playwright (1904–1986).

ished about a dozen years earlier. The thesis of this book is that the earth moves around the sun. When did Copernicus go out and record this fact with his camera? What appearance in nature prompted his outrageous guess? And in what odd sense is this guess to be called a neutral record of fact?

Less than a hundred years after Copernicus, Kepler published (between 1609 and 1619) the three laws which describe the paths of the planets. The work of Newton and with it most of our mechanics spring from these laws. They have a solid, matter-of-fact sound. For example, Kepler says that if one squares the year of a planet, one gets a number which is proportional to the cube of its average distance from the sun. Does anyone think that such a law is found by taking enough readings and then squaring and cubing everything in sight? If he does, then, as a scientist, he is doomed to a wasted life; he has as little prospect of making a scientific discovery as an electronic brain has.

5 It was not this way that Copernicus and Kepler thought, or that scientists think today. Copernicus found that the orbits of the planets would look simpler if they were looked at from the sun and not from the earth. But he did not in the first place find this by routine calculation. His first step was a leap of imagination—to lift himself from the earth, and put himself wildly, speculatively into the sun. "The earth conceives from the sun," he wrote; and "the sun rules the family of stars." We catch in his mind an image, the gesture of the virile man standing in the sun, with arms outstretched, overlooking the planets. Perhaps Copernicus took the picture from the drawings of the youth with outstretched arms which the Renaissance teachers put into their books on the proportions of the body. Perhaps he had seen Leonardo's drawings of his loved pupil Salai. I do not know. To me, the gesture of Copernicus, the shining youth looking outward from the sun, is still vivid in a drawing which William Blake in 1780 based on all these: the drawing which is usually called *Glad Day*.

Kepler's mind, we know, was filled with just such fanciful analogies; and we know what they were. Kepler wanted to relate the speeds of the planets to the musical intervals. He tried to fit the five regular solids into their orbits. None of these likenesses worked, and they have been forgotten; yet they have been and they remain the stepping stones of every creative mind. Kepler felt for his laws by way of metaphors, he searched mystically for likenesses with what he knew in every strange corner of nature. And when among these guesses he hit upon his laws, he did not think of their numbers as the balancing of a cosmic bank account, but as a revelation of the unity in all nature. To us, the analogies by which Kepler listened for the movement of the planets in the music of the spheres are farfetched. Yet are they more so than the wild leap by which Rutherford and Bohr[3] in our own century found a model for the atom in, of all places, the planetary system?

No scientific theory is a collection of facts. It will not even do to call a theory true or false in the simple sense in which every fact is either so or not so. The Epicureans held that matter is made of atoms two thousand years ago and we are now tempted to say that their theory was true. But if we do so we confuse their notion of matter with our own. John Dalton in 1808 first saw the structure of matter as we do today, and what he took from the ancients was not their theory but something richer, their image: the atom. Much of what was in Dalton's mind was as vague as the Greek notion, and quite as mistaken. But he suddenly gave life to the new facts of chemistry and the ancient theory together, by fusing them to give what neither had: a coherent picture of how matter is linked and built up from different kinds of atoms. The act of fusion is the creative act.

All science is the search for unity in hidden likenesses. The search may be on a grand scale, as in the modern theories which try to link the fields of gravitation and electromagnetism. But we do not need to be browbeaten by the scale of science. There are discoveries to be made by snatching a small likeness from the air too, if it is bold enough. In 1935 the Japanese physicist Hideki Yukawa wrote a paper which can still give heart to a young scientist. He took as his starting point the known fact that waves of light can sometimes behave as if they were separate pellets. From this he reasoned that the forces which hold the nucleus of an atom together might sometimes also be observed as if they were solid pellets. A schoolboy can see how thin Yukawa's analogy is, and his teacher would be severe with it. Yet Yukawa without a blush calculated the mass of the pellet he expected to see, and waited. He was right; his meson was found, and a range of other mesons, neither the existence nor the nature of which had been suspected before. The likeness had borne fruit.

The scientist looks for order in the appearances of nature by exploring such likenesses. For order does not display itself of itself; if it can be said to be there at all, it is not there for the mere looking. There is no way of pointing a finger or camera at it; order must be discovered and, in a deep sense, it must be created. What we see, as we see it, is mere disorder.

This point has been put trenchantly in a fable by Karl Popper.[4] Sup- 10

3. Niels Bohr (1885–1962), Danish physicist; Ernest Rutherford (1871–1937), British physicist.

4. Austrian-born British philosopher (1902–1992).

pose that someone wished to give his whole life to science. Suppose that he therefore sat down, pencil in hand, and for the next twenty, thirty, forty years recorded in notebook after notebook everything that he could observe. He may be supposed to leave out nothing: today's humidity, the racing results, the level of cosmic radiation and the stockmarket prices and the look of Mars, all would be there. He would have compiled the most careful record of nature that has ever been made; and, dying in the calm certainty of a life well spent, he would of course leave his notebooks to the Royal Society. Would the Royal Society thank him for the treasure of a lifetime of observation? It would not. The Royal Society would treat his notebooks exactly as the English bishops have treated Joanna Southcott's box.[5] It would refuse to open them at all, because it would know without looking that the notebooks contain only a jumble of disorderly and meaningless items.

Science finds order and meaning in our experience, and sets about this in quite a different way. It sets about it as Newton did in the story which he himself told in his old age, and of which the schoolbooks give only a caricature. In the year 1665, when Newton was twenty-two, the plague broke out in southern England, and the University of Cambridge was closed. Newton therefore spent the next eighteen months at home, removed from traditional learning, at a time when he was impatient for knowledge and, in his own phrase, "I was in the prime of my age for invention." In this eager, boyish mood, sitting one day in the garden of his widowed mother, he saw an apple fall. So far the books have the story right; we think we even know the kind of apple; tradition has it that it was a Flower of Kent. But now they miss the crux of the story. For what struck the young Newton at the sight was not the thought that the apple must be drawn to the earth by gravity; that conception was older than Newton. What struck him was the conjecture that the same force of gravity, which reaches to the top of the tree, might go on reaching out beyond the earth and its air, endlessly into space. Gravity might reach the moon: this was Newton's new thought; and it might be gravity which holds the moon in her orbit. There and then he calculated what force from the earth (falling off as the square of the distance) would hold the moon, and compared it with the known force of gravity at tree height. The forces agreed; Newton says laconically, "I found them answer pretty nearly." Yet they

5. Southcott was a nineteenth-century English farm servant who claimed to be a prophetess. She left behind a box which was to be opened in a time of national emergency in the presence of all the English bishops. In 1927, a bishop agreed to officiate; when the box was opened, it was found to contain only some odds and ends.

agreed only nearly: the likeness and the approximation go together, for no likeness is exact. In Newton's science modern science is full grown.

It grows from a comparison. It has seized a likeness between two unlike appearances; for the apple in the summer garden and the grave moon overhead are surely as unlike in their movements as two things can be. Newton traced in them two expressions of a single concept, gravitation: and the concept (and the unity) are in that sense his free creation. The progress of science is the discovery at each step of a new order which gives unity to what had long seemed unlike.

* * *

QUESTIONS

1. *Mark the generalizations Bronowski makes in the course of "The Nature of Scientific Reasoning" and their location; for example, "No scientific theory is a collection of facts" (paragraph 7). Where is the information that supports them?*
2. *Bronowski tells the well-known story of Newton and the apple (paragraphs 11 to 12). How many of his generalizations does it exemplify, and how?*
3. *"The scientist," Bronowski observes, "looks for order in the appearances of nature" (paragraph 9). Is this operation unique to scientists? Consider the operations of knowers in humanities and social science disciplines such as history, literature, psychology, and sociology.*
4. *Bronowski sets up an adversary, a literary person who believes that scientists observe, collect, and record facts, and writes his essay as a refutation. Adapt his rhetorical strategy in an essay of your own: Explain your beliefs about something by refuting the beliefs of someone who disagrees with them.*

Thomas S. Kuhn

THE ROUTE TO NORMAL SCIENCE

In this essay, "normal science" means research firmly based upon one or more past scientific achievements, achievements that some particular scientific community acknowledges for a time as supplying the foundation for its further practice. Today such achievements are recounted, though seldom in their original form, by science textbooks,

From *The Structure of Scientific Revolutions* (1962).

elementary and advanced. These textbooks expound the body of accepted theory, illustrate many or all of its successful applications, and compare these applications with exemplary observations and experiments. Before such books became popular early in the nineteenth century (and until even more recently in the newly matured sciences), many of the famous classics of science fulfilled a similar function. Aristotle's *Physica*, Ptolemy's *Almagest*, Newton's *Principia* and *Opticks*, Franklin's *Electricity*, Lavoisier's *Chemistry*, and Lyell's *Geology*—these and many other works served for a time implicitly to define the legitimate problems and methods of a research field for succeeding generations of practitioners. They were able to do so because they shared two essential characteristics. Their achievement was sufficiently unprecedented to attract an enduring group of adherents away from competing modes of scientific activity. Simultaneously, it was sufficiently open-ended to leave all sorts of problems for the redefined group of practitioners to resolve.

Achievements that share these two characteristics I shall henceforth refer to as "paradigms," a term that relates closely to "normal science." By choosing it, I mean to suggest that some accepted examples of actual scientific practice—examples which include law, theory, application, and instrumentation together—provide models from which spring particular coherent traditions of scientific research. These are the traditions which the historian describes under such rubrics as "Ptolemaic astronomy" (or "Copernican"), "Aristotelian dynamics" (or "Newtonian"), "corpuscular optics" (or "wave optics"), and so on. The study of paradigms, including many that are far more specialized than those named illustratively above, is what mainly prepares the student for membership in the particular scientific community with which he will later practice. Because he there joins men who learned the bases of their field from the same concrete models, his subsequent practice will seldom evoke overt disagreement over fundamentals. Men whose research is based on shared paradigms are committed to the same rules and standards for scientific practice. That commitment and the apparent consensus it produces are prerequisites for normal science, i.e., for the genesis and continuation of a particular research tradition.

Because in this essay the concept of a paradigm will often substitute for a variety of familiar notions, more will need to be said about the reasons for its introduction. Why is the concrete scientific achievement, as a locus of professional commitment, prior to the various concepts, laws, theories, and points of view that may be abstracted from it? In what sense is the shared paradigm a fundamental unit for the student of scientific development, a unit that cannot be fully reduced to logically atomic components which might function in its stead?

There can be a sort of scientific research without paradigms, or at least without any so unequivocal and so binding as the ones named above. Acquisition of a paradigm and of the more esoteric type of research it permits is a sign of maturity in the development of any given scientific field.

If the historian traces the scientific knowledge of any selected group of related phenomena backward in time, he is likely to encounter some minor variant of a pattern here illustrated from the history of physical optics. Today's physics textbooks tell the student that light is photons, i.e., quantum-mechanical entities that exhibit some characteristics of waves and some of particles. Research proceeds accordingly, or rather according to the more elaborate and mathematical characterization from which this usual verbalization is derived. That characterization of light is, however, scarcely half a century old. Before it was developed by Planck, Einstein, and others early in this century, physics texts taught that light was transverse wave motion, a conception rooted in a paradigm that derived ultimately from the optical writings of Young and Fresnel in the early nineteenth century. Nor was the wave theory the first to be embraced by almost all practitioners of optical science. During the eighteenth century the paradigm for this field was provided by Newton's *Opticks,* which taught that light was material corpuscles. At that time physicists sought evidence, as the early wave theorists had not, of the pressure exerted by light particles impinging on solid bodies.

These transformations of the paradigms of physical optics are scien- 5
tific revolutions, and the successive transition from one paradigm to another via revolution is the usual developmental pattern of mature science. It is not, however, the pattern characteristic of the period before Newton's work, and that is the contrast that concerns us here. No period between remote antiquity and the end of the seventeenth century exhibited a single generally accepted view about the nature of light. Instead there were a number of competing schools and subschools, most of them espousing one variant or another of Epicurean, Aristotelian, or Platonic theory.[1] One group took light to be particles emanating from material bodies; for another it was a modification of the medium that intervened between the body and the eye; still another explained light in terms of an interaction of the medium with an emanation from the eye; and there were other combinations and modifications besides. Each of the corresponding schools derives strength from its relation to some particular metaphysic, and each emphasized, as paradigmatic observations, the particular cluster of optical phenomena that its own theory could do most to explain. Other

1. The reference is to the three principal worldviews of ancient Greek philosophy.

observations were dealt with by *ad hoc* elaborations, or they remained as outstanding problems for further research.

At various times all these schools made significant contributions to the body of concepts, phenomena, and techniques from which Newton drew the first nearly uniformly accepted paradigm for physical optics. Any definition of the scientist that excludes at least the more creative members of these various schools will exclude their modern successors as well. Those men were scientists. Yet anyone examining a survey of physical optics before Newton may well conclude that, though the field's practitioners were scientists, the net result of their activity was something less than science. Being able to take no common body of belief for granted, each writer on physical optics felt forced to build his field anew from its foundations. In doing so, his choice of supporting observation and experiment was relatively free, for there was no standard set of methods or of phenomena that every optical writer felt forced to employ and explain. Under these circumstances, the dialogue of the resulting books was often directed as much to the members of other schools as it was to nature. That pattern is not unfamiliar in a number of creative fields today, nor is it incompatible with significant discovery and invention. It is not, however, the pattern of development that physical optics acquired after Newton and that other natural sciences make familiar today.

The history of electrical research in the first half of the eighteenth century provides a more concrete and better known example of the way a science develops before it acquires its first universally received paradigm. During that period there were almost as many views about the nature of electricity as there were important electrical experimenters, men like Haukshee, Gray, Desaguliers, Du Fay, Nollett, Watson, Franklin, and others. All their numerous concepts of electricity had something in common—they were partially derived from one or another version of the mechanico-corpuscular philosophy that guided all scientific research of the day. In addition, all were components of real scientific theories, of theories that had been drawn in part from experiment and observation and that partially determined the choice and interpretation of additional problems undertaken in research. Yet though all the experiments were electrical and though most of the experimenters read each other's works, their theories had no more than a family resemblance.

One early group of theories, following seventeenth-century practice, regarded attraction and frictional generation as the fundamental electrical phenomena. This group tended to treat repulsion as a secondary effect due to some sort of mechanical rebounding and also to postpone for as long as possible both discussion and systematic research on Gray's newly discovered effect, electrical conduction. Other "electricians" (the term is their own) took attraction and repulsion to be equally elementary manifestations of electricity and modified their theories and research accordingly. (Actually, this group is remarkably small—even Franklin's theory never quite accounted for the mutual repulsion of two negatively charged bodies.) But they had as much difficulty as the first group in accounting simultaneously for any but the simplest conduction effects. Those effects, however, provided the starting point for still a third group, one which tended to speak of electricity as a "fluid" that could run through conductors rather than as an "effluvium" that emanated from non-conductors. This group, in its turn, had difficulty reconciling its theory with a number of attractive and repulsive effects. Only through the work of Franklin and his immediate successors did a theory arise that could account with something like equal facility for very nearly all these effects and that therefore could and did provide a subsequent generation of "electricians" with a common paradigm for its research.

Excluding those fields, like mathematics and astronomy, in which the first firm paradigms date from prehistory and also those, like biochemistry, that arose by division and recombination of specialties already matured, the situations outlined above are historically typical. Though it involves my continuing to employ the unfortunate simplification that tags an extended historical episode with a single and somewhat arbitrarily chosen name (e.g., Newton or Franklin), I suggest that similar fundamental disagreements characterized, for example, the study of motion before Aristotle and of statics before Archimedes, the study of heat before Black, of chemistry before Boyle and Boerhaave, and of historical geology before Hutton. In parts of biology—the study of heredity, for example—the first universally received paradigms are still more recent; and it remains an open question what parts of social science have yet acquired such paradigms at all. History suggests that the road to a firm research consensus is extraordinarily arduous.

History also suggests, however, some reasons for the difficulties en- 10
countered on the road. In the absence of a paradigm or some candidate for paradigm, all of the facts that could possibly pertain to the development of a given science are likely to seem equally relevant. As a result, early fact-gathering is a far more nearly random activity than the one that subsequent scientific development makes familiar. Futhermore, in the absence of a reason for seeking some particular form of more recondite information, early fact-gathering is usually restricted to the wealth of data that lie ready to hand. The resulting pool of facts contains those accessible to casual observation and experiment together with some of the more esoteric data retrievable from established crafts like medicine, calendar making, and metallurgy. Because the crafts are one readily accessible source of facts that could not

have been casually discovered, technology has often played a vital role in the emergence of new sciences.

But though this sort of fact-collecting has been essential to the origin of many significant sciences, anyone who examines, for example, Pliny's encyclopedic writings or the Baconian natural histories of the seventeenth century will discover that it produces a morass. One somehow hesitates to call the literature that results scientific. The Baconian "histories" of heat, color, wind, mining, and so on, are filled with information, some of it recondite. But they juxtapose facts that will later prove revealing (e.g., heating by mixture) with others (e.g., the warmth of dung heaps) that will for some time remain too complex to be integrated with theory at all. In addition, since any description must be partial, the typical natural history often omits from its immensely circumstantial accounts just those details that later scientists will find sources of important illumination. Almost none of the early "histories" of electricity, for example, mention that chaff, attracted to a rubbed glass rod, bounces off again. That effect seemed mechanical, not electrical. Moreover, since the casual fact-gatherer seldom possesses the time or the tools to be critical, the natural histories often juxtapose descriptions like the above with others, say, heating by antiperistasis (or by cooling), that we are now quite unable to confirm.[2] Only very occasionally, as in the cases of ancient statics, dynamics, and geometrical optics, do facts collected with so little guidance from pre-established theory speak with sufficient clarity to permit the emergence of a first paradigm.

This is the situation that creates the schools characteristic of the early stages of a science's development. No natural history can be interpreted in the absence of at least some implicit body of intertwined theoretical and methodological belief that permits selection, evaluation, and criticism. If that body of belief is not already implicit in the collection of facts—in which case more than "mere facts" are at hand—it must be externally supplied, perhaps by a current metaphysic, by another science, or by personal and historical accident. No wonder, then, that in the early stages of the development of any science different men confronting the same range of phenomena, but not usually all the same particular phenomena, describe and interpret them in different ways. What is surprising, and perhaps also unique in its degree to the fields we call science, is that such initial divergences should ever largely disappear.

2. Bacon [in the *Novum Organum*] says, "Water slightly warm is more easily frozen than quite cold" [Kuhn's note]; *antiperistasis:* an old word meaning a reaction caused by the action of an opposite quality or principle—here, heating through cooling.

For they do disappear to a very considerable extent and then apparently once and for all. Furthermore, their disappearance is usually caused by the triumph of one of the pre-paradigm schools, which, because of its own characteristic beliefs and pre-conceptions, emphasized only some special part of the too sizable and inchoate pool of information. Those electricians who thought electricity a fluid and therefore gave particular emphasis to conduction provide an excellent case in point. Led by this belief, which could scarcely cope with the known multiplicity of attractive and repulsive effects, several of them conceived the idea of bottling the electrical fluid. The immediate fruit of their efforts was the Leyden jar, a device which might never have been discovered by a man exploring nature casually or at random, but which was in fact independently developed by at least two investigators in the early 1740's. Almost from the start of his electrical researches, Franklin was particularly concerned to explain that strange and, in the event, particularly revealing piece of special apparatus. His success in doing so provided the most effective of the arguments that made his theory a paradigm, though one that was still unable to account for quite all the known cases of electrical repulsion.[3] To be accepted as a paradigm, a theory must seem better than its competitors, but it need not, and in fact never does, explain all the facts with which it can be confronted.

What the fluid theory of electricity did for the subgroup that held it, the Franklinian paradigm later did for the entire group of electricians. It suggested which experiments would be worth performing and which, because directed to secondary or to overly complex manifestations of electricity, would not. Only the paradigm did the job far more effectively, partly because the end of interschool debate ended the constant reiteration of fundamentals and partly because the confidence that they were on the right track encouraged scientists to undertake more precise, esoteric, and consuming sorts of work.[4] Freed from the concern with any and all electrical phenomena, the united group of electricians could pursue selected phenomena in far more detail, designing much special equipment for the task and employing it more

3. The troublesome case was the mutual repulsion of negatively charged bodies [Kuhn's note].

4. It should be noted that the acceptance of Franklin's theory did not end quite all debate. In 1759 Robert Symmer proposed a two-fluid version of that theory, and for many years thereafter electricians were divided about whether electricity was a single fluid or two. But the debates on this subject only confirm what has been said above about the manner in which a universally recognized achievement unites the profession. Electricians, though they continued divided on this point, rapidly concluded that no experimental tests could distinguish the two versions of the theory and that they were therefore equivalent. After that, both schools could and did exploit all the benefits that the Franklinian theory provided [Kuhn's note].

stubbornly and systematically than electricians had ever done before. Both fact collection and theory articulation became highly directed activities. The effectiveness and efficiency of electrical research increased accordingly, providing evidence for a societal version of Francis Bacon's acute methodological dictum: "Truth emerges more readily from error than from confusion."

We shall be examining the nature of this highly directed or paradigm-based research in the next section, but must first note briefly how the emergence of a paradigm affects the structure of the group that practices the field. When, in the development of a natural science, an individual or group first produces a synthesis able to attract most of the next generation's practitioners, the older schools gradually disappear. In part their disappearance is caused by their members' conversion to the new paradigm. But there are always some men who cling to one or another of the older views, and they are simply read out of the profession, which thereafter ignores their work. The new paradigm implies a new and more rigid definition of the field. Those unwilling or unable to accommodate their work to it must proceed in isolation or attach themselves to some other group.[5] Historically, they have often simply stayed in the departments of philosophy from which so many of the special sciences have been spawned. As these indications hint, it is sometimes just its reception of a paradigm that transforms a group previously interested merely in the study of nature into a profession or, at least, a discipline. In the sciences (though not in fields like medicine, technology, and law, of which the principal *raison d'être* is an external social need), the formation of specialized journals, the foundation of specialists' societies, and the claim for a special place in the curriculum have usually been associated with a group's first reception of a single paradigm. At least this was the case between the time, a century and a half ago, when the institutional pattern of scientific specialization first developed and the very recent time when the paraphernalia of specialization acquired a prestige of their own.

The more rigid definition of the scientific group has other consequences. When the individual scientist can take a paradigm for granted, he need no longer, in his major works, attempt to build his

5. The history of electricity provides an excellent example which could be duplicated from the careers of Priestley, Kelvin, and others. Franklin reports that Nollet, who at mid-century was the most influential of the Continental electricians, "lived to see himself the last of his Sect, except Mr. B.—his *Eleve* [pupil] and immediate Disciple." More interesting, however, is the endurance of whole schools in increasing isolation from professional science. Consider, for example, the case of astrology, which was once an integral part of astronomy. Or consider the continuation in the late eighteenth, and early nineteenth centuries of a previously respected tradition of "romantic" chemistry [Kuhn's note].

field anew, starting from first principles and justifying the use of each concept introduced. That can be left to the writer of textbooks. Given a textbook, however, the creative scientist can begin his research where it leaves off and thus concentrate exclusively upon the subtlest and most esoteric aspects of the natural phenomena that concern his group. And as he does this, his research communiqués will begin to change in ways whose evolution has been too little studied but whose modern end products are obvious to all and oppressive to many. No longer will his researches usually be embodied in books addressed, like Franklin's *Experiments . . . on Electricity* or Darwin's *Origin of Species*, to anyone who might be interested in the subject matter of the field. Instead they will usually appear as brief articles addressed only to professional colleagues, the men whose knowledge of a shared paradigm can be assumed and who prove to be the only ones able to read the papers addressed to them.

Today in the sciences, books are usually either texts or retrospective reflections upon one aspect or another of the scientific life. The scientist who writes one is more likely to find his professional reputation impaired than enhanced. Only in the earlier, pre-paradigm, stages of the development of the various sciences did the book ordinarily possess the same relation to professional achievement that it still retains in other creative fields. And only in those fields that still retain the book, with or without the article, as a vehicle for research communication are the lines of professionalization still so loosely drawn that the layman may hope to follow progress by reading the practitioners' original reports. Both in mathematics and astronomy, research reports had ceased already in antiquity to be intelligible to a generally educated audience. In dynamics, research became similarly esoteric in the latter Middle Ages, and it recaptured general intelligibility only briefly during the early seventeenth century when a new paradigm replaced the one that had guided medieval research. Electrical research began to require translation for the layman before the end of the eighteenth century, and most other fields of physical science ceased to be generally accessible in the nineteenth. During the same two centuries similar transitions can be isolated in the various parts of the biological sciences. In parts of the social sciences they may well be occurring today. Although it has become customary, and is surely proper, to deplore the widening gulf that separates the professional scientist from his collegues in other fields, too little attention is paid to the essential relationship between that gulf and the mechanisms intrinsic to scientific advance.

Ever since prehistoric antiquity one field of study after another has crossed the divide between what the historian might call its prehistory as a science and its history proper. These transitions to maturity have seldom been so sudden or so unequivocal as my necessarily schematic discussion may have implied. But neither have they been historically gradual, coextensive, that is to say, with the entire development of the fields within which they occurred. Writers on electricity during the first four decades of the eighteenth century possessed far more information about electrical phenomena than had their sixteenth-century predecessors. During the half-century after 1740, few new sorts of electrical phenomena were added to their lists. Nevertheless, in important respects, the electrical writings of Cavendish, Coulomb, and Volta in the last third of the eighteenth century seem further removed from those of Gray, Du Fay, and even Franklin than are the writings of these early eighteenth-century electrical discoverers from those of the sixteenth century.[6] Sometime between 1740 and 1780, electricians were for the first time enabled to take the foundations of their field for granted. From that point they pushed on to more concrete and recondite problems, and increasingly they then reported their results in articles addressed to other electricians rather than in books addressed to the learned world at large. As a group they achieved what had been gained by astronomers in antiquity and by students of motion in the Middle Ages, of physical optics in the late seventeenth century, and of historical geology in the early nineteenth. They had, that is, achieved a paradigm that proved able to guide the whole group's research. Except with the advantage of hindsight, it is hard to find another criterion that so clearly proclaims a field a science.

6. The post-Franklinian developments include an immense increase in the sensitivity of charge detectors, the first reliable and generally diffused techniques for measuring charge, the evolution of the concept of capacity and its relation to a newly refined notion of electric tension, and the quantification of electrostatic force [Kuhn's note].

QUESTIONS

1. *Mark the important terms in this selection from* The Structure of Scientific Revolutions *and Kuhn's definitions of them. How many does he illustrate as well as define? Why does he both define and illustrate?*
2. *What are prevailing paradigms in sciences other than those Kuhn discusses? You might consider biology, chemistry, psychology, and sociology. Are you aware of older paradigms in these sciences, or have they and the work based on them, as Kuhn says (paragraph 15), disappeared?*
3. *Without a paradigm, Kuhn writes, "all of the facts that could possibly pertain to the development of a given science are likely to seem equally relevant" (paragraph 10). What, according to Stephen Jay Gould in "Darwin's Middle Road" (p. 1081), was the paradigm*

that enabled Darwin to discriminate among his facts? How can he be said to have made a "scientific revolution"?

Anne Fausto-Sterling

SOCIETY WRITES BIOLOGY[1]

Truth, bias, objectivity, prejudice. In recent years both defenders and critics of the activities of the modern Western scientific community have used these words with a certain abandon as they engage in debate about the role of science and the scientist in our culture. Perhaps the best-known voice in this discussion is that of Thomas Kuhn, whose historical analyses of the "progress" of science threw into sharp relief the uneven nature of the development of scientific ideas.[2] In the past decade feminist analysts of science have joined the discussion. Historians, philosophers, anthropologists, and scientists who write from a feminist perspective have raised varied and complex questions about modern science.[3]

In this essay I propose to examine the process by which cultural understandings of gender become building blocks in supposedly objective understandings of nature. The two case studies (one historical, one contemporary) will illustrate how cultural understandings or beliefs, whether conscious or unconscious, influence the construction of scientific theory. The writings of a famous and highly imaginative Ital-

From *Learning About Women: Gender, Politics, and Power*, ed. Jill K. Conway, Susan C. Bourque, and Joan W. Scott (1987). Unless marked, all notes to this essay are the author's.

1. I would like to thank all the participants in the Conference on Gender, Technology, and Education at Bellagio, Italy, 7–11 October 1985, for their comments, support, and insights into the original draft of this paper. I am grateful to Sandra Harding, Evelyn Fox Keller, and Helen Longino for reading a draft of this paper and offering me their suggestions. I also thank Carol King for typing more than one version of this paper.
2. Thomas W. Kuhn, *The Structure of Scientific Revolutions* (Chicago: University of Chicago Press, 1962).
3. See, for example, Ruth Hershberger, *Adam's Rib* (New York: Pellegrini and Cudahy, 1984); Evelyn Fox Keller, *Reflections on Gender and Science* (New Haven, CT: Yale University Press, 1985); Anne Fausto-Sterling, *Myths of Gender* (New York: Basic Books, 1985); Ruth Bleier, *Science and Gender* (New York: Pergamon Press, 1984); Marian Lowe and Ruth Hubbard, *Women's Nature* (New York: Pergamon Press, 1983); Carolyn Merchant, *The Death of Nature* (San Francisco: Harper & Row, 1980); Janet Sayers, *Biological Politics* (London: Tavistock, 1982); Sandra Harding, *The Science Question in Feminism* (Ithaca, NY: Cornell University Press, 1986).

ian scientist, Abbé Lazzaro Spallanzani (1729–1799), illustrate that the inner workings of the mind of a dedicated experimental scientist are complex and often under subconscious wraps.[4] Although Spallanzani is probably best known for his experimental disproof of the idea of spontaneous generation, he also made an important contribution to eighteenth-century thinking about fertilization and embryonic development. The presence of spermatozoa in the semen had been discovered in Spallanzani's time, but the role of these "vermicelli" (or "spermatozoan worms," as they were often called) remained a subject of considerable debate within the context of a long-lived controversy about the origin of the embryo. Ovists believed that it arose solely from the egg, while spermists maintained that the womb was a passive vessel that offered fertile ground for the growth and development of the semen.

The most famous of early biologists belonged to different camps. The frontispiece of William Harvey's *Concerning the Generation of Living Animals* depicts Zeus sitting on a throne and opening what looks like a bird's egg, out of which hop, fly, and crawl all manner of beasts, mythical and otherwise. On the egg is written *Ex ovo omnia.* On the other side we find Antony van Leeuwenhoek[5] arguing that the animalcules in semen find their way to the womb, where they act as seed; he dismisses eggs as "emunctorys[6] . . . adhering to the bowels of animals."[7]

Spallanzani, an ovist, performed a series of experiments with mating frogs to disprove Carolus Linnaeus's claim that insemination must always be internal. In a classic demonstration of the scientific method, he observed that the male frog, grasping the female frog as she lays eggs, deposits semen on the eggs as they emerge from her uterus. To test the semen's function, he constructed little taffeta breeches for the male frogs (unwittingly presaging Kenneth Grahame's *The Wind in the Willows,* in which toads wear clothes and drive cars) and made the following observations:

> The males, notwithstanding this incumbrance, seek the females with equal eagerness and perform, as well as they can, the act of generation;

4. See also Evelyn Fox Keller, A *Feeling for the Organism* (San Francisco: Freeman, 1983), and June Goodfield, *An Imagined World* (New York: Harper & Row, 1981).
5. Dutch naturalist (1632–1723); Harvey (1578–1657), English physician and anatomist [Editor's note].
6. emunctory; *n, pl* -cries (NL *emunctorium,* far. L. *emunctus,* pp. of *emungere* to clean the nose, fr. e- + *-mungere* (akin to mucus): an organ (as a kidney) or part of the body (as the skin) that carries off body wastes *(Webster's New Collegiate Dictionary).*
7. Albert Tyler, "Comparative Gametology and Syngamy," in *Fertilization: Comparative Morphology, Biochemistry and Immunology,* vol. 1, ed. Charles B. Metz and Alberto Monroy (New York: Academic Press, 1967).

> but the event is such as may be expected: the eggs are never prolific for want of having been bedewed with semen, which sometimes may be seen in the breeches in the form of drops. That these drops are real seed, appeared clearly from the artificial fecondation that was obtained by means of them.[8]

In other words, Spallanzani showed not only that preventing semen deposition prevented egg development, but also that when he spread semen on the eggs, fertilization resulted. A model of good experimentation indeed.

But Spallanzani did not conclude from these or other experiments 5
that the vermicelli were necessary for the embryo to develop. Instead he conducted a series of experiments in an attempt to find out how much semen was needed to achieve fertilization. Observing that even very tiny amounts were sufficient, he concluded that the important factor was something he called the "seminal aura," which he thought to be "nothing but the vapor of the seed exceedingly rarified."[9] Believing that his results proved the ovists's theory, he proceeded to perform a series of experiments on the seminal aura, all of which he designed to disprove the role of the spermatozoan in fertilization. He diluted semen samples until he could see no more sperm and found the diluted fluid still capable of fertilization. He also filtered semen so thoroughly that it could no longer induce development. The former results he took as proof of the existence of a seminal aura; the latter he ignored.[1]

In Spallanzani we have an example of a highly talented eighteenth-century scientist doing careful experiments that prove, to our modern-day eyes, the opposite of what he concluded. Because he interpreted his investigations within a particular theoretical framework—that of ovism—his mind was closed to alternative conclusions that seem obvious to those not so committed. Because Spallanzani was a scientist of considerable authority and influence, his conclusions, rather than his experimental results, dominated biological thought on fertilization. A correct account of the role of the sperm in fertilization and development was not generally accepted for another 100 years. The point here is not that an incompetent scientist made a series of experimental errors, but that an extremely good scientist performed a series of beautifully controlled experiments but did not draw from them the correct conclusions. The process by which cultural categories shape perception and influence reasoning is little studied. The case of Spallanzani and his experiments on spermatozoa and their role in fertilization

8. Ibid.
9. Ibid.
1. Ibid.

would be an excellent starting point for a cultural anthropologist who wished to analyze this process. That this phenomenon holds true for modern scientific activity can be seen in the next, more contemporary example.

During mammalian development all embryos (regardless of their potential sex) pass through a stage that embryologists have dubbed the "indifferent period." Examination of XX and XY embryos during this period shows no evidence of sex differences in either the embryonic gonad or sexually-related somatic structures such as the oviducts or the vas deferens. Present are a single gonad that will later take either a male or female path of development, and two sets of accessory structures known as the mesonephric and paramesonephric ducts. In female development the mesonephric ducts disintegrate while the paramesonephric ducts form the oviducts, uterus, and part of the vagina. In male development the paramesonephric ducts degenerate while the mesonephric ducts develop into the epididymal duct and the vas deferens. In general, then, mammals first develop a single pair of gonads, which subsequently takes either a male or a female direction, and both male and female accessory structures, only one set of which survives while the other degenerates. Baldly stated, up to a certain point all embryos are completely bisexual.

The choice of whether to follow a male or a female path of development is made through the intervention of the sex chromosomes and hormones present in utero. It is at this point in the story that a curious use of language that has set limits on the experimental questions asked about sexual development enters in. I will first recount the tale as it is told in text books, popular literature, and the vast majority of scientific papers, and then underline some of the story's peculiarities, showing how they have resulted in a supposedly general account of the development of the sexes that is in actuality only an account of male development. This example illustrates a case in which the meaning of *man* as a supposedly inclusive universal has slipped unnoticed into its meaning as an exclusive biological category. What biologists turn out to have provided as our account of the development of gender from a mechanistic point of view is really only an account of male differentiation.

The following excerpts come from an up-to-date and heavily used undergraduate embryology text written by Dr. Bruce M. Carlson. My intent is not to attack Carlson, who recounts an almost universally held set of beliefs, but merely to analyze the text to uncover some of the underlying structures of those beliefs. Carlson writes:

> The sex-determining function of the Y chromosome is intimately bound with the activity of the H-Y antigen . . . its major function is to cause the organization of the primitive gonad into the testis. In the *absence* of the

> H-Y antigen the gonad later becomes transformed into the ovary. (Italics added.)

The account continues with a discussion of the formation of non- 10
gonadal (somatic) sex organs such as the uterus and vas deferens.

> The early embryo develops a dual set of potential genital ducts [the mesonephric and paramesonephric ducts]. . . . Under the *influence of testosterone* secreted by the testes, the mesonephric ducts develop into the duct system through which spermatozoa are conveyed from the testes to the urethra. . . . The potentially female paramesonephric ducts regress *under the influence* of another secretion of the embryonic testes, the Mullerian Inhibitory Factor. (Italics added.)
>
> In genetically female embryos neither testosterone nor Mullerian Inhibitory Factor is secreted by the gonads. In the *absence of testosterone* the mesonephric ducts regress and the *lack of Mullerian Inhibitory Factor* permits the paramesonephric ducts to develop into the oviducts, uterus and part of the vagina. The external genitalia also first take form in a morphologically indifferent condition and then develop either in the male direction *under the influence of testosterone* or in the female direction *if the influence of testosterone is lacking.* (Italics added.)[2]

Carlson also writes of "the natural tendency of the body to develop along female lines in the absence of other modifying influences."[3] The presence-or-absence-of-maleness concept is an old one. Simone de Beauvoir quoted Aristotle as saying that "the female is a female by virtue of a certain *lack* of qualities."[4] Psychologist Dr. John Money calls accounts of sexual development similar to Carlson's an example of "the Adam Principle" that something is *added* to an embryo to make it a male.[5] A well-known reproductive biologist, Dr. R.V. Short, concludes an introductory account of sex determination differentiation by spelling out what he sees as the implications of that viewpoint:

> In all systems that we have considered, maleness means mastery; the Y-chromosome over the X, the medulla [of the indifferent gonad] over the cortex, androgen over oestrogen. So physiologically speaking, there is no justification for believing in the equality of the sexes; *vive la différence!*[6]

2. Bruce M. Carlson, *Patten's Foundations of Embryology* (New York: McGraw Hill, 1981), pp. 459–61.
3. Ibid.
4. Simone de Beauvoir, *The Second Sex* (New York: Bantam, 1952), p. xvi.
5. John Money, *Love and Lovesickness* (Baltimore: Johns Hopkins University Press, 1970), p. 5.
6. R. V. Short, "Sex Determination and Differentiation," in *Embryonic and Fetal Development*, ed. C. R. Austin and R. V. Short (London: Cambridge University Press, 1972), p. 70.

The idea that the female represents some natural, fundamental "ground state" is also familiar. Strangely, although biologists emulate physicists by reducing organisms to smaller and smaller parts in order to investigate causes that precede causes ad infinitum, they are generally satisfied to accept the idea that a female direction of development occurs passively in the absence of instructions from so-called male sex hormones.[7] How does it happen? What are the mechanisms? Investigators ask these questions about male development (generically referred to as sexual differentiation), but only a few express interest in applying the same scrutiny to development of the female. This imbalance in levels of intellectual curiosity is reflected in the etymologies of the words that name sex hormones: *androgen* comes from the Greek *andros* and the Latin *generare* (to make a male), *estrogen* from the Latin *oestrus* (gadfly or frenzy). In fact, the word *gynogen*, which would be the etymologically and biologically correct counterpart to *androgen*, cannot be found in biological accounts of sexual development (or, for that matter, in any dictionary).

If we look carefully at the existing biological literature, we can see how we might construct a narrative that treats female sexual differentiation as requiring as much investigation and explanation as male sexual differentiation. We could begin by examining the many studies on hormonal control of sexual development in cold-blooded vertebrates. Some examples: the addition of estrogen to the water of certain XY (potentially male) fish causes them to develop as females rather than males; similarly, the addition of estrogen to the water of amphibian tadpoles before and during their metamorphosis to adults results in all exposed larvae becoming females.[8] Clearly, such research provides evidence that so-called female hormones actively induce female development; that is, they behave as gynogens. But the findings of studies on cold-blooded vertebrates are usually considered inapplicable to mammals. Only rarely does a publication on mammalian development include a consideration of the active role of female hormones.

Estrogen and progesterone (another female hormone) are not absent during female mammalian development. In addition to estrogen synthesis in the fetal ovary, all sexual development, both male and female, takes place in the presence of high concentrations of placentally-produced female hormones, especially the estrogens and progesterones.[9] That sexual development occurs in a sea of female placental

7. In reality, both males and females produce estrogen and androgen, but in differing quantities.
8. Ursula Mittwoch, *Genetics of Sex Differentiation* (New York: Academic Press, 1973).
9. J. D. Wilson et al., "The Hormonal Control of Sexual Development," *Science* 211 (1981), pp. 1278–84.

hormones is recognized and viewed as a "problem" for male development. A variety of hypotheses have been proposed and experiments carried out to explain why the developing male embryo is not feminized by maternal hormones. Yet the scientist who is concerned about the potential feminizing effect of female hormones in male development is often the same one who writes that female development is not directed by hormones at all, but is an event that results from a lack of male hormones. This lopsided logic requires both attention and explanation.

What I've just written is, of course, an oversimplification. In some parts of the scientific literature the idea of a positive role for estrogen has begun to creep in. This is partly due to the discovery that testosterone may be converted into estrogen by certain cells in the body, and that what was long believed to be an effect of testosterone on male behavior in rodents is actually caused by the conversion of testosterone to estrogen by cells in the brain.[1] Nevertheless, the associations of male/presence/active and female/absence/passive still govern our concepts of human development and influence the language used to explain them in the current literature.

There is one other etymological/scientific issue to be teased out of 15
the account of male and female development in vertebrates. It is the designation of the male gamete-transporting ducts as mesonephric (middle kidney) and the female's as paramesonephric (sitting next to the middle kidney). Three different types of kidneys have evolved during the evolution of vertebrates: the pronephros, the mesonephros, and the metanephros. In mammals the pronephros is vestigial in the embryo and completely absent in the adult. The mesonephros functions as a kidney in the embryos of some mammals, and its ducts become part of the adult postembryonic male gonadal duct system (this ancient connection between gamete transport and waste excretion is also seen in vertebrates such as those fish and amphibia whose kidney tubules are the means of transporting both sperm and urine to the outside.) The metanephros becomes the functional kidney at birth.

In female mammals there evolved a separate set of ducts (dubbed the paramesonephric ducts) having nothing to do with the kidneys, apparently designed only for the transport of ova. The prefix *para* has several meanings, including near, beside, adjacent to, closely resembling, almost, beyond, remotely or indirectly relating to, faulty or abnormal condition, and associated in an accessory capacity. The use of

1. See Robert W. Goy and Bruce S. McEwen, eds., *Sexual Differentiation of the Brain* (Cambridge, MA: MIT Press, 1980); Bleier, *Science and Gender;* and *Progress in Brain Research* 61 (1984).

the prefix is common in the language of anatomy and certainly not restricted to structures related to sexual organs. The adrenal glands, for example, are sometimes referred to as the paranephros because of their location atop the kidneys, so the naming of the paramesonephric ducts for their positional relationship to ducts in the male (note that they have no separate name of their own as do the adrenals) could be nothing more than happenstance. It would be easier to sustain that argument, however, if the literature revealed further interest in both the embryonic and evolutionary origins of these ducts. Yet knowledge about them is lacking.

The changing function of an organ such as the embryonic kidney is a well-known evolutionary phenomenon. Front limbs, for example, have evolved into wings, arms, legs, and flippers. Bones that form parts of the jaw in reptiles have become the functional sound-receiving and -transferring bones of the inner ear in mammals. On the other hand, the appearance of a brand new structure is less common and presents a profoundly difficult explanatory problem for evolutionary biologists. Yet the evolutionary and embryological origins of the paramesonephric duct, which might be such a de novo structure, have been little studied; as one author writes, "The phylogenetic origin of paramesonephric ducts is again obscure."[2] As in the case of estrogen's role in governing female development, our lack of understanding of the origin and development of the paramesonephric duct represents a research path not taken. The reasons for this are probably multiple, but at least one of them must be that the road to understanding these ducts has been considered a side path, one lying next to or away from the main road that one must follow in order to understand male development.

Another example of how scientific language betrays a one-sided curiosity can be found in the literature on the study of male and female sexual differentiation of the rat brain, which until very recently has been framed around the idea that testosterone provides an "organizing effect" on the "intrinsic tendency to develop according to a female pattern of body structure and behavior."[3] (Does this phraseology imply that the female brain is disorganized?) Or consider the fact that mutations affecting androgen metabolism in humans and other mammals have been extensively studied and well-cataloged, but that none affecting estrogen metabolism have been isolated. Some authors have suggested that because implantation in the uterus is impossible without estrogen, an ovum affected by a mutation that interferes with es-

2. M. Hildebrand, *Analysis of Vertebrate Structure* (New York: John Wiley & Sons, 1974).
3. Goy and McEwen, *Sexual Differentiation*, p. 3.

trogen metabolism would not survive. In other words, estrogen metabolism may be more poorly understood than androgen metabolism because it is essential for mammalian life. From this perspective, the focus on the role of androgens in sexual development, while not misplaced, certainly seems one-sided. Correcting the imbalance is not technically impossible; estrogen metabolism studies could be conducted with laboratory animals in ways that avoid the problem of lethality. It seems, though, that our considerable scientific and experimental ingenuity has not yet been directed toward solving this particular puzzle.

These cases from the biological literature strongly suggest that broad cultural paradigms about the nature of male and female have had a considerable effect on biological theory. The language used to describe "the facts" has channeled experimental thought along certain lanes, leaving others not only unexplored but unnoticed.

QUESTIONS

1. *What went wrong with the first case study Fausto-Sterling describes, Spallanzani's experiments, and with the second, the collective work of embryologists studying fetal development? How might these flaws have been guarded against?*
2. *"Society Writes Biology," Fausto-Sterling titles her essay. Why is the title provocative? How do we ordinarily conceive of relations between society and biology?*
3. *Consider the passage Fausto-Sterling quotes from Short's introductory account of sex determination differentiation (paragraph 11). If you were assigned Short's text in a biology class, would you object to this passage? On what grounds? If you would not object, can you imagine someone else objecting? Write a brief account of one instance or the other.*

John Henry Sloan et al.*

HANDGUN REGULATIONS, CRIME, ASSAULTS, AND HOMICIDE:

A Tale of Two Cities**

Abstract To investigate the associations among handgun regulations, assault and other crimes, and homicide, we studied robberies, burglaries, assaults, and homicides in Seattle, Washington, and Vancouver, British Columbia, from 1980 through 1986.

Although similar to Seattle in many ways, Vancouver has adopted a more restrictive approach to the regulation of handguns. During the study period, both cities had similar rates of burglary and robbery. In Seattle, the annual rate of assault was modestly higher than that in Vancouver (simple assault: relative risk, 1.18; 95 percent confidence interval, 1.15 to 1.20; aggravated assault: relative risk, 1.16; 95 percent confidence interval, 1.12 to 1.19).*** However, the rate of assaults involving firearms was seven times higher in Seattle than in Vancouver. Despite similar overall rates of criminal activity and assault, the relative risk of death from homicide, adjusted for age and sex, was significantly higher in Seattle than in Vancouver (relative risk, 1.63; 95 percent confidence interval, 1.28 to 2.08). Virtually all of this excess risk was explained by a 4.8-fold higher risk of being murdered with a handgun in Seattle as compared with Vancouver. Rates of homicide by means other than guns were not substantially different in the two study communities.

We conclude that restricting access to handguns may reduce the rate of homicide in a community (*N. Engl. J. Med.* 1988; 319:1256–62).

Approximately 20,000 persons are murdered in the United States each year, making homicide the 11th leading cause of death and the 6th leading cause of the loss of potential years of life before age 65.[1–3] In the United States between 1960 and 1980, the death rate from homicide by means other than firearms increased by 85 percent. In contrast, the death rate from homicide by firearms during this same period increased by 160 percent.[3]

From the *New England Journal of Medicine* (Nov. 10, 1988).

*John Henry Sloan, M.D., M.P.H., Arthur L. Kellermann, M.D., M.P.H., Donald T. Reay, M.D., James A. Ferris, M.D., Thomas Koepsell, M.D., M.P.H., Frederick P. Rivara, M.D., M.P.H., Charles Rice, M.D., Laurel Gray, M.D., and James LoGerfo, M.D., M.P.H.

**The authors' notes are collected at the end as "References," as in the style of *N. Engl. J. Med.* The editors' explanatory footnotes are marked by asterisks (*).

***A statistical method for expressing the likelihood of error; that is, in this instance there is a 95 percent chance that the risk of simple assault in Seattle relative to that in Vancouver, which the authors calculate to be 1.18, will fall between 1.15 and 1.2.

Approximately 60 percent of homicides each year involve firearms. 5
Handguns alone account for three fourths of all gun-related homicides.[4] Most homicides occur as a result of assaults during arguments or altercations; a minority occur during the commission of a robbery or other felony.[2,4] Baker has noted that in cases of assault, people tend to reach for weapons that are readily available.[5] Since attacks with guns more often end in death than attacks with knives, and since handguns are disproportionately involved in intentional shootings, some have argued that restricting access to handguns could substantially reduce our annual rate of homicide.[5–7]

To support this view, advocates of handgun control frequently cite data from countries like Great Britain and Japan, where the rates of both handgun ownership and homicide are substantially lower than those in the United States.[8] Rates of injury due to assault in Denmark are comparable to those in northeastern Ohio, but the Danish rate of homicide is only one fifth as high as Ohio's.[5,6] In Denmark, the private ownership of guns is permitted only for hunting, and access to handguns is tightly restricted.[6]

Opponents of gun control counter with statistics from Israel and Switzerland, where the rates of gun ownership are high but homicides are relatively uncommon.[9] However, the value of comparing data from different countries to support or refute the effectiveness of gun control is severely compromised by the large number of potentially confounding social, behavioral, and economic factors that characterize large national groups. To date, no study has been able to separate the effects of handgun control from differences among populations in terms of socioeconomic status, aggressive behavior, violent crime, and other factors.[7] To clarify the relation between firearm regulations and community rates of homicide, we studied two large cities in the Pacific Northwest: Seattle, Washington, and Vancouver, British Columbia. Although similar in many ways, these two cities have taken decidedly different approaches to handgun control.

METHODS

Study Sites

Seattle and Vancouver are large port cities in the Pacific Northwest. Although on opposite sides of an international border, they are only 140 miles apart, a three-hour drive by freeway. They share a common geography, climate, and history. Citizens in both cities have attained comparable levels of schooling and have almost identical rates of unemployment. When adjusted to U.S. dollars, the median annual income of a household in Vancouver exceeds that in Seattle by less than $500. Similar percentages of households in both cities have incomes of less than $10,000 (U.S.) annually. Both cities have large white majorities. However, Vancouver has a larger Asian population, whereas Seattle has larger black and Hispanic minorities (Table 1).[10,11] The two communities also share many cultural values and interests. Six of the top nine network television programs in Seattle are among the nine most watched programs in Vancouver.[12,13]

Firearm Regulations

Although similar in many ways, Seattle and Vancouver differ markedly in their approaches to the regulation of firearms (Table 2). In Seattle, handguns may be purchased legally for self-defense in the street or at home. After a 30-day waiting period, a permit can be obtained to carry a handgun as a concealed weapon. The recreational use of handguns is minimally restricted.[15]

10 In Vancouver, self-defense is not considered a valid or legal reason to purchase a handgun. Concealed weapons are not permitted. Recreational uses of handguns (such as target shooting and collecting) are regulated by the province, and the purchase of a handgun requires a restricted-weapons permit. A permit to carry a weapon must also be obtained in order to transport a handgun, and these weapons can be discharged only at a licensed shooting club. Handguns can be transported by car, but only if they are stored in the trunk in a locked box.[16,17]

TABLE 1
SOCIOECONOMIC CHARACTERISTICS AND RACIAL AND ETHNIC COMPOSITION OF THE POPULATIONS IN SEATTLE AND VANCOUVER

Index	*Seattle*	*Vancouver*
1980 Population	493,846	415,220
1985–1986 Population estimate	491,400	430,826
Unemployment rate (%)	5.8	6.0
High-school graduates (%)	79.0	66.0
Median household income (U.S. dollars)	16,254	16,681
Households with incomes ≤$10,000 (U.S.) (%)	30.6	28.9
Ethnic and racial groups (%)		
White (non-Hispanic)	79.2	75.6
Asian	7.4	22.1
Black	9.5	0.3
Hispanic	2.6	0.5
Native North American	1.3	1.5

TABLE 2
REGULATION AND OWNERSHIP OF FIREARMS AND LAW-ENFORCEMENT ACTIVITY IN SEATTLE AND VANCOUVER

	Seattle	*Vancouver*
Regulations		
Handguns	Concealed-weapons permit is required to carry a gun for self-defense on the street; none is required for self-defense in the home. Registration of handguns is not mandatory for private sales.	Restricted-weapons permit is required for sporting and collecting purposes. Self-defense in the home or street is not legally recognized as a reason for possession of a handgun. Handguns must be registered.
Long guns (rifles, shotguns)	Long guns are not registered.	Firearm-acquisition certificate is required for purchase. Long guns are not registered.
Law enforcement and sentencing		
Additional sentence for commission of a class A felony with a firearm	Minimum of 2 extra years.	1 to 14 extra years.
Percent of firearm-related homicides that result in police charges (police estimate)	80 to 90%	80 to 90%
Minimum jail sentence for first-degree murder	20 years in prison.	25 years in prison (parole is possible after 15 years).
Status of capital punishment	Legal, though no one has been executed since 1963.	Abolished.
Prevalence of weapons		
Total concealed-weapons permits issued (March 1984 to March 1988)	15,289	—
Total restricted-weapons permits issued (March 1984 to March 1988)	—	4137
Cook's gun prevalence index[14]	41%	12%

Although they differ in their approach to firearm regulations, both cities aggressively enforce existing gun laws and regulations, and convictions for gun-related offenses carry similar penalties. For example, the commission of a class A felony (such as murder or robbery) with a firearm in Washington State adds a minimum of two years of confinement to the sentence for the felony.[18] In the Province of British Columbia, the same offense generally results in 1 to 14 years of imprisonment in addition to the felony sentence.[16] Similar percentages of homicides in both communities eventually lead to arrest and police charges. In Washington, under the Sentencing Reform Act of 1981, murder in the first degree carries a minimum sentence of 20 years of confinement.[19] In British Columbia, first-degree murder carries a minimum sentence of 25 years, with a possible judicial parole review after 15 years.[20] Capital punishment was abolished in Canada during the 1970s.[21] In Washington State, the death penalty may be invoked in cases of aggravated first-degree murder, but no one has been executed since 1963.

Rates of Gun Ownership

Because direct surveys of firearm ownership in Seattle and Vancouver have never been conducted, we assessed the rates of gun ownership indirectly by two independent methods. First, we obtained from the Firearm Permit Office of the Vancouver police department a count of the restricted-weapons permits issued in Vancouver between March 1984 and March 1988 and compared this figure with the total number of concealed-weapons permits issued in Seattle during the same period, obtained from the Office of Business and Profession Administration, Department of Licensing, State of Washington. Second, we used Cook's gun prevalence index, a previously validated measure of intercity differences in the prevalence of gun ownership.[14] This index is based on data from 49 cities in the United States and correlates each city's rates of suicide and assaultive homicide involving firearms with survey-based estimates of gun ownership in each city. Both methods indicate that firearms are far more commonly owned in Seattle than in Vancouver (Table 2).

Identification and Definition of Cases

From police records, we identified all the cases of robbery, burglary, and assault (both simple and aggravated) and all the homicides that occurred in Seattle or Vancouver between January 1, 1980, and December 31, 1986. In defining cases, we followed the guidelines of the U.S. Federal Bureau of Investigation's uniform crime reports (UCR).[22] The UCR guidelines define aggravated assault as an unlawful attack by one person on another for the purpose of inflicting severe or aggravated bodily harm. Usually this type of assault involves the actual or threatened use of a deadly weapon. Simple assault is any case of assault that does not involve the threat or use of a deadly weapon or result in serious or aggravated injuries.

A homicide was defined as the willful killing of one human being by another. This category included cases of premeditated murder, intentional killing, and aggravated assault resulting in death. "Justifiable homicide," as defined by the UCR guidelines, was limited to cases of the killing of a felon by a law-enforcement officer in the line of duty or the killing of a felon by a private citizen during the commission of a felony.[22] Homicides that the police, the prosecuting attorney, or both thought were committed in self-defense were also identified and noted separately.

Statistical Analysis

From both Seattle and Vancouver, we obtained annual and cumula- 15
tive data on the rates of aggravated assault, simple assault, robbery, and burglary. Cases of aggravated assault were categorized according to the weapon used. Data on homicides were obtained from the files of the medical examiner or coroner in each community and were supplemented by police case files. Each homicide was further categorized according to the age, sex, and race or ethnic group of the victim, as well as the weapon used.

Population-based rates of simple assault, aggravated assault, robbery, burglary, and homicide were then calculated and compared. These rates are expressed as the number per 100,000 persons per year and, when possible, are further adjusted for any differences in the age and sex of the victims. Unadjusted estimates of relative risk and 95 percent confidence intervals were calculated with use of the maximum-likelihood method and are based on Seattle's rate relative to Vancouver's.[23] Age-adjusted relative risks were estimated with use of the Mantel-Haenszel summary odds ratio.[24]

Results

During the seven-year study period, the annual rate of robbery in Seattle was found to be only slightly higher than that in Vancouver (relative risk, 1.09; 95 percent confidence interval, 1.08 to 1.12). Burglaries, on the other hand, occurred at nearly identical rates in the two communities (relative risk, 0.99; 95 percent confidence interval, 0.98 to 1.00). During the study period, 18,925 cases of aggravated assault were reported in Seattle, as compared with 12,034 cases in Vancouver. When the annual rates of assault in the two cities were compared for each year of the study, we found that the two communities had similar rates of assault during the first four years of the study. In 1984, however, reported rates of simple and aggravated assault began to climb sharply in Seattle, whereas the rates of simple and aggravated assault remained relatively constant in Vancouver (Fig. 1). This change coincided with the enactment that year of the Domestic Violence Protection Act by the Washington State legislature. Among other provisions, this law required changes in reporting and arrests in cases of domestic violence.[25] It is widely believed that this law and the considerable media attention that followed its passage resulted in dramatic increases in the number of incidents reported and in related enforcement costs in Seattle.[26] Because in Vancouver there was no similar legislative initiative requiring police to change their reporting methods, we restricted our comparison of the data on assaults to the first four years of our study (1980 through 1983) (Fig. 1).

During this four-year period, the risk of being a victim of simple assault in Seattle was found to be only slightly higher than that in Vancouver (relative risk, 1.18; 95 percent confidence interval, 1.15 to 1.20). The risk of aggravated assault in Seattle was also only slightly higher than in Vancouver (relative risk, 1.16; 95 percent confidence

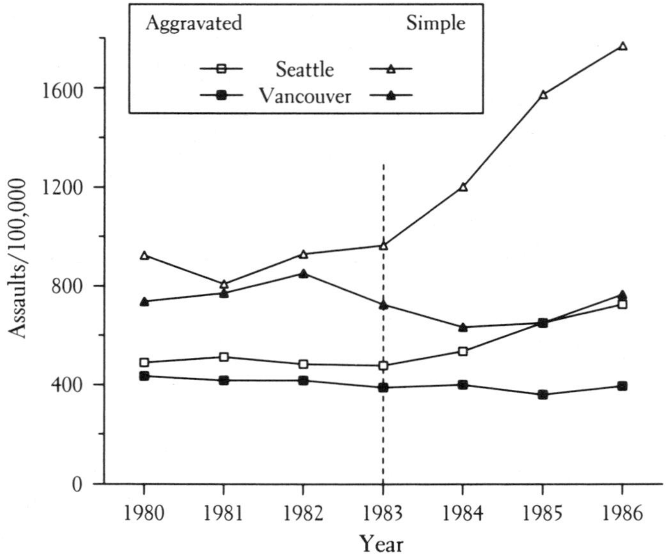

Figure 1. Rates of aggravated and simple assault in Seattle and Vancouver, 1980 through 1986. The dotted line indicates the passage of the Domestic Violence Protection Act in Washington State in 1984.

interval, 1.12 to 1.19). However, when aggravated assaults were subdivided by the type of weapon used and the mechanism of assault, a striking pattern emerged. Although both cities reported almost identical rates of aggravated assault involving knives, other dangerous weapons, or hands, fists, and feet, firearms were far more likely to have been used in cases of assault in Seattle than in Vancouver (Table 3). In fact, all the difference in the relative risk of aggravated assault between these two communities was due to Seattle's 7.7-fold higher rate of assaults involving firearms (Fig. 2).

Over the whole seven-year study period, 388 homicides occurred in Seattle (11.3 per 100,000 person-years). In Vancouver, 204 homicides occurred during the same period (6.9 per 100,000 person-years). After adjustment for differences in age and sex between the populations, the relative risk of being a victim of homicide in Seattle, as compared with Vancouver, was found to be 1.63 (95 percent confidence interval, 1.28 to 2.08). This difference is highly unlikely to have occurred by chance.

When homicides were subdivided by the mechanism of death, the 20
rate of homicide by knives and other weapons (excluding firearms) in Seattle was found to be almost identical to that in Vancouver (relative risk, 1.08; 95 percent confidence interval, 0.89 to 1.32) (Fig. 3). Virtu-

TABLE 3
ANNUAL CRUDE RATES AND RELATIVE RISKS OF AGGRAVATED ASSAULT, SIMPLE ASSAULT, ROBBERY, BURGLARY, AND HOMICIDE IN SEATTLE AND VANCOUVER, 1980 THROUGH 1986[a]

Crime	*Period*	*Seattle*	*Vancouver*	*Relative Risk*	*95% CI*
		no./100,000			
Robbery	1980–1986	492.2	450.9	1.09	1.08–1.12
Burglary	1980–1986	2952.7	2985.7	0.99	0.98–1.00
Simple assault	1980–1983	902	767.7	1.18	1.15–1.20
Aggravated assault	1980–1983	486.5	420.5	1.16	1.12–1.19
Firearms		87.9	11.4	7.70	6.70–8.70
Knives		78.1	78.9	0.99	0.92–1.07
Other		320.6	330.2	0.97	0.94–1.01
Homicides	1980–1986	11.3	6.9	1.63	1.38–1.93
Firearms		4.8	1.0	5.08	3.54–7.27
Knives		3.1	3.5	0.90	0.69–1.18
Other		3.4	2.5	1.33	0.99–1.78

[a]CI denotes confidence interval. The "crude rate" for these crimes is the number of events occurring in a given population over a given time period. The relative risks shown are for Seattle in relation to Vancouver.

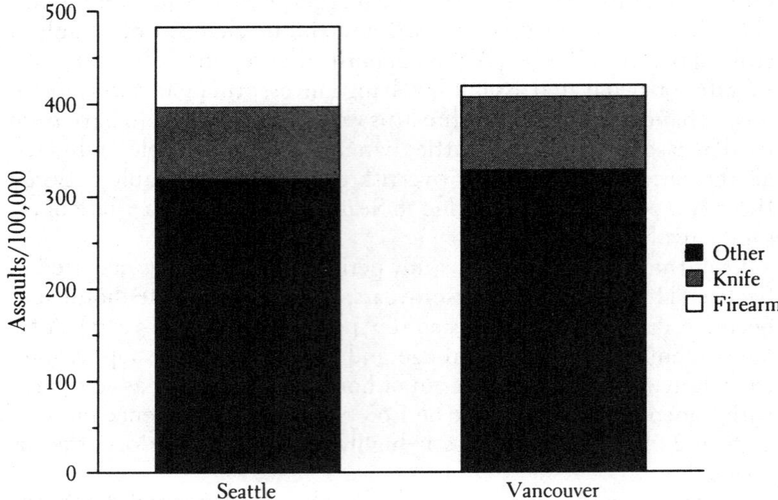

Figure 2. Annual rates of aggravated assault in Seattle and Vancouver, 1980 through 1983, according to the Weapon Used. "Other" includes blunt instruments, other dangerous weapons, and hands, fists, and feet.

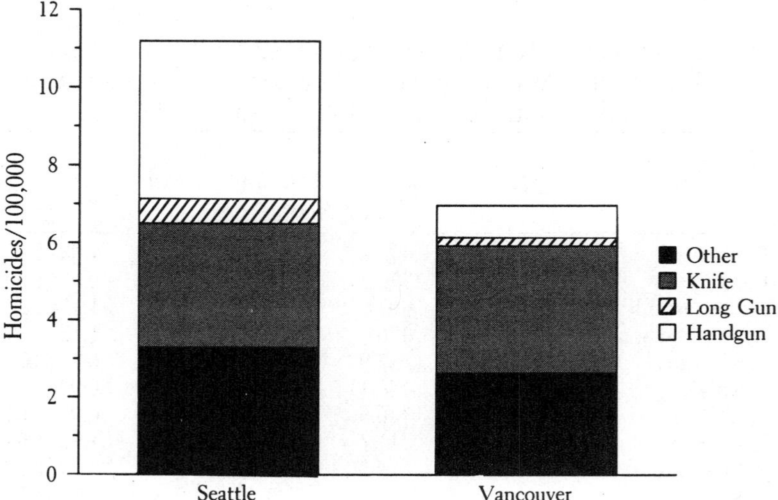

Figure 3. Annual rates of homicide in Seattle and Vancouver, 1980 through 1986, according to the Weapon Used. "Other" includes blunt instruments, other dangerous weapons, and hands, fists, and feet.

ally all of the increased risk of death from homicide in Seattle was due to a more than fivefold higher rate of homicide by firearms (Table 3). Handguns, which accounted for roughly 85 percent of the homicides involving firearms in both communities, were 4.8 times more likely to be used in homicides in Seattle than in Vancouver.

To test the hypothesis that the higher rates of homicide in Seattle might be due to more frequent use of firearms for self-protection, we examined all the homicides in both cities that were ruled "legally justifiable" or were determined to have been committed in self-defense. Thirty-two such homicides occurred during the study period, 11 of which involved police intervention. After the exclusion of justifiable homicide by police, 21 cases of homicide by civilians acting in self-defense or in other legally justifiable ways remained, 17 of which occurred in Seattle and 4 of which occurred in Vancouver (relative risk, 3.64; 95 percent confidence interval, 1.32 to 10.06). Thirteen of these cases (all of which occurred in Seattle) involved firearms. The exclusion of all 21 cases (which accounted for less than 4 percent of the homicides during the study interval) had little overall effect on the relative risk of homicide in the two communities (age and sex-adjusted relative risk, 1.57; 95 percent confidence interval, 1.22 to 2.01).

When homicides were stratified by the race or ethnic group of the victim, a complex picture emerged (Table 4). The homicide rates in Table 4 were adjusted for age to match the 1980 U.S. population. This technique permits fairer comparisons among racial and ethnic groups with differing age compositions in each city. The relative risk for each racial or ethnic group, however, was estimated with use of the Mantel-

TABLE 4
ANNUAL AGE-ADJUSTED HOMICIDE RATES AND RELATIVE RISKS OF DEATH BY HOMICIDE IN SEATTLE AND VANCOUVER, 1980 THROUGH 1986, ACCORDING TO THE RACE OR ETHNIC GROUP OF THE VICTIM[a]

Race or Ethnic Group	*Seattle*	*Vancouver*	*Relative Risk*	*95% CI*
	no./100,000			
White (non-Hispanic)	6.2	6.4	1	0.8–1.2
Asian	15.0	4.1	3.5	2.1–5.7
Excluding Wah Mee murders	9.5	—	2.3	1.4–4.0
Black	36.6	9.5	2.8	0.4–20.4
Hispanic	26.9	7.9	5	0.7–34.3
Native American	64.9	71.3	0.9	0.5–1.5

[a]CI denotes confidence interval. The relative risks shown are for Seattle in relation to Vancouver.

Haenszel summary odds ratio.[24] This method, in effect, uses a different set of weights for the various age strata, depending on the distribution of persons among the age strata for that racial or ethnic group only. Hence, these estimates of relative risk differ slightly from a simple quotient of the age-adjusted rates.

Whereas similar rates of death by homicide were noted for whites in both cities, Asians in Seattle had higher rates of death by homicide than their counterparts in Vancouver. This difference persisted even after the exclusion of the 13 persons who died in the Wah Mee gambling club massacre in Seattle in 1983. Blacks and Hispanics in Seattle had higher relative risks of death by homicide than blacks and Hispanics in Vancouver, but the confidence intervals were very wide, given the relatively small size of both minorities in Vancouver. Only one black and one Hispanic were killed in Vancouver during the study period. Native Americans had the highest rates of death by homicide in both cities.

Discussion

Previous studies of the effectiveness of gun control have generally compared rates of homicide in nations with different approaches to the regulation of firearms.[7] Unfortunately, the validity of these studies has been compromised by the large number of confounding factors that characterize national groups. We sought to circumvent this limitation by focusing our analysis on two demographically comparable and physically proximate cities with markedly different approaches to handgun control. In many ways, these two cities have more in common with each other than they do with other major cities in their respective countries. For example, Seattle's homicide rate is consistently half to two thirds that reported in cities such as Chicago, Los Angeles, New York, and Houston,[4] whereas Vancouver experiences annual rates of homicide two to three times higher than those reported in Ottawa, Toronto, and Calgary (Canadian Centre for Justice Statistics, Homicide Program, Ottawa: unpublished data).

25 In order to exclude the possibility that Seattle's higher homicide rate may be explained by higher levels of criminal activity or aggressiveness in its population, we compared the rates of burglary, robbery, simple assault, and aggravated assault in the two communities. Although we observed a slightly higher rate of simple and aggravated assault in Seattle, these differences were relatively small—the rates in Seattle were 16 to 18 percent higher than those reported in Vancouver during a period of comparable case reporting. Virtually all of the excess risk of aggravated assault in Seattle was explained by a sevenfold higher rate of assaults involving firearms. Despite similar rates of rob-

bery and burglary and only small differences in the rates of simple and aggravated assault, we found that Seattle had substantially higher rates of homicide than Vancouver. Most of the excess mortality was due to an almost fivefold higher rate of murders with handguns in Seattle.

Critics of handgun control have long claimed that limiting access to guns will have little effect on the rates of homicide, because persons who are intent on killing others will only work harder to acquire a gun or will kill by other means.[7,27] If the rate of homicide in a community were influenced more by the strength of intent than by the availability of weapons, we might have expected the rate of homicides with weapons other than guns to have been higher in Vancouver than in Seattle, in direct proportion to any decrease in Vancouver's rate of firearm homicides. This was not the case. During the study interval, Vancouver's rate of homicides with weapons other than guns was not significantly higher than that in Seattle, suggesting that few would-be assailants switched to homicide by other methods.

Ready access to handguns has been advocated by some as an important way to provide law-abiding citizens with an effective means to defend themselves.[27–29] Were this true, we might have expected that much of Seattle's excess rate of homicides, as compared with Vancouver's, would have been explained by a higher rate of justifiable homicides and killings in self-defense by civilians. Although such homicides did occur at a significantly higher rate in Seattle than in Vancouver, these cases accounted for less than 4 percent of the homicides in both cities during the study period. When we excluded cases of justifiable homicide or killings in self-defense by civilians from our calculation of relative risk, our results were almost the same.

It also appears unlikely that differences in law-enforcement activity accounted for the lower homicide rate in Vancouver. Suspected offenders are arrested and cases are cleared at similar rates in both cities. After arrest and conviction, similar crimes carry similar penalties in the courts in Seattle and Vancouver.

We found substantial differences in the risk of death by homicide according to race and ethnic group in both cities. In the United States, blacks and Hispanics are murdered at substantially higher rates than whites.[2] Although the great majority of homicides in the United States involve assailants of the same race or ethnic group, current evidence suggests that socioeconomic status plays a much greater role in explaining racial and ethnic differences in the rate of homicide than any intrinsic tendency toward violence.[2,30,31] For example, Centerwall has shown that when household crowding is taken into account, the rate of domestic homicide among blacks in Atlanta, Georgia, is no higher than that of whites living in similar conditions.[32] Likewise, a recent study of childhood homicide in Ohio found that once cases were stratified by socioeconomic status, there was little difference in race-specific rates of homicide involving children 5 to 14 years of age.[33]

30 Since low-income populations have higher rates of homicide, socioeconomic status is probably an important confounding factor in our comparison of the rates of homicide for racial and ethnic groups. Although the median income and the overall distribution of household incomes in Seattle and Vancouver are similar, the distribution of household incomes by racial and ethnic group may not be the same in Vancouver as in Seattle. For example, blacks in Vancouver had a slightly higher mean income in 1981 than the rest of Vancouver's population (Statistics Canada, 1981 Census Custom Tabulation: unpublished data). In contrast, blacks in Seattle have a substantially lower median income than the rest of Seattle's population.[34] Thus, much of the excess risk of homicide among blacks in Seattle, as compared with blacks in Vancouver, may be explained by their lower socioeconomic status. If, on the other hand, more whites in Vancouver have low incomes than whites in Seattle, the higher risk of homicide expected in this low-income subset may push the rate of homicide among whites in Vancouver higher than that for whites in Seattle. Unfortunately, neither hypothesis can be tested in a quantitative fashion, since detailed information about household incomes according to race is not available for Vancouver.

Three limitations of our study warrant comment. First, our measures of the prevalence of firearm ownership may not precisely reflect the availability of guns in the two communities. Although the two measures we used were derived independently and are consistent with the expected effects of gun control, their validity as indicators of community rates of gun ownership has not been conclusively established. Cook's gun prevalence index has been shown to correlate with data derived from national surveys, but it has not been tested for accuracy in cities outside the United States. Comparisons of concealed-weapons permits in Seattle with restricted-weapons permits in Vancouver are probably of limited validity, since these counts do not include handguns obtained illegally. In fact, the comparison of permit data of this sort probably substantially underestimates the differences between the communities in the rate of handgun ownership, since only a fraction of the handguns in Seattle are purchased for use as concealed weapons, whereas all legal handgun purchases in Vancouver require a restricted-weapons permit. Still, these indirect estimates of gun ownership are consistent with one another, and both agree with prior reports that estimate the rate of handgun ownership in Canada to be about one fourth that in the United States.[35]

Second, although similar in many ways, Seattle and Vancouver may well differ in other aspects that could affect their rates of homicide. For example, differences in the degree of illegal drug-related activity, differences in the rate of illicit gun sales, or other, less readily apparent differences may confound the relation between firearm regulations and the rate of homicide. Although such differences may exist, striking socioeconomic similarities between the cities and the fact that they had similar rates of burglary, robbery, and both simple and aggravated assault during comparable reporting periods make such confounding less likely. Unfortunately, changes in the rules for reporting assault cases in Seattle, mandated by the State of Washington in 1984, precluded a valid comparison of the rates of simple and aggravated assault over the entire seven-year period.

Third, conclusions based on a comparison of two cities in the Pacific Northwest may not be generalizable to other urban areas in North America. Given the complex interaction of individual behavior, environment, and community factors in the pathogenesis of violent death, we cannot predict the precise impact that Canadian-style gun control might have in the United States. Even if such a major change in public policy were to take place, the current high rates of handgun ownership might blunt any effects of tougher handgun regulations for years to come.

Our analysis of the rates of homicide in these two largely similar cities suggests that the modest restriction of citizens' access to firearms (especially handguns) is associated with lower rates of homicide. This association does not appear to be explained by differences between the communities in aggressiveness, criminal behavior, or response to crime. Although our findings should be corroborated in other settings, our results suggest that a more restrictive approach to handgun control may decrease national homicide rates.

REFERENCES

1. Homicide surveillance: 1970–78. Atlanta: Centers for Disease Control, September, 1983.
2. Homicide surveillance: high risk racial and ethnic groups—blacks and Hispanics, 1970 to 1983. Atlanta: Centers for Disease Control, November, 1986.
3. Baker SP, O'Neill B, Karpf RS. The injury fact book. Lexington, Mass.: Lexington Books, 1984.
4. Department of Justice, Federal Bureau of Investigation. Crime in the United States (Uniform Crime Reports). Washington, D.C.: Government Printing Office, 1986.
5. Baker SP. Without guns, do people kill people? Am J Public Health 1985; 75:587–8.
6. Hedeboe J, Charles AV, Nielsen J, et al. Interpersonal violence: patterns in a Danish community. Am J Public Health 1985; 75:651–3.
7. Wright J, Rossi P, Daly K, Weber-Burdin E. Weapons, crime and violence in America: a literature review and research agenda. Washington, D.C.: Department of Justice, National Institute of Justice, 1981.
8. Weiss JMA. Gun control: a question of public/mental health? J Oper Psychiatr 1981; 12:86–8.

9. Bruce-Briggs B. The great American gun war. Public Interest 1976; 45:37–62.
10. Bureau of Census. 1980 Census of population, Washington. Washington, D.C.: Government Printing Office, 1981.
11. Statistics Canada: 1981 census of Canada, Vancouver, British Columbia. Ottawa, Ont.: Minister of Supply and Services, 1983.
12. Seattle local market T.V. ratings, 1985–86. (Based on Arbitron television ratings.) Provided by KING TV, Seattle, Washington.
13. Vancouver local market T.V. ratings, 1985–86. Provided by Bureau of Broadcast Measurement, Toronto.
14. Cook PJ. The role of firearms in violent crime. In: Wolfgang M, ed. Criminal violence. Beverly Hills, Calif.: Sage, 1982:236–90.
15. Revised Code of State of Washington. RCW chapter 9.41.090, 9.41.095, 9.41.070, 1986.
16. Criminal Code of Canada. Firearms and other offensive weapons. Martin's Criminal Code of Canada, 1982. Part II.1 (Sections 81–016.9, 1982).
17. *Idem.* Restricted Weapons and Firearm Control Regulations Sec. 106.2 (11); Amendment Act, July 18, 1977, 1982.
18. Revised Code of State of Washington, Sentence Reform Act Chapter 9 94A.125.1980.
19. Revised Code of State of Washington. Murder I, 9A.32.040.1984.
20. Criminal Code of Canada. Application for judicial review sentence of life imprisonment, 1988 Part XX 669–67, 1(1).
21. *Idem.* Act to Amend Criminal Code B.11 C84, 1976.
22. Department of Justice, Federal Bureau of Investigation. Uniform crime reporting handbook. Washington, D.C.: Government Printing Office, 1984.
23. Rothman KJ, Boice JD Jr. Epidemiologic analysis with a programmable calculator. Boston: Epidemiology Resources, 1982.
24. Armitage P, Berry G. Statistical methods in medical research. 2nd ed. Oxford: Blackwell, 1987.
25. Revised Code of State of Washington. RCW Chapter 10.99.010–.100, 1984.
26. Seattle Police Department. Inspectional service division report, domestic violence arrest costs: 1984–87, Seattle, 1986.
27. Drooz RB. Handguns and hokum: a methodological problem. JAMA 1977; 238:-43–5.
28. Copeland AR. The right to keep and bear arms—a study of civilian homicides committed against those involved in criminal acts in metropolitan Dade County from 1957 to 1982. J Forensic Sci 1984; 29:584–90.
29. Kleck G. Crime control through the private use of armed force. Soc Probl 1988; 35:1–21.
30. Loftin C, Hill RH. Regional subculture and homicide: an examination of the Gastil-Hackney thesis. Am Sociol Rev 1974; 39:714–24.
31. Williams KR. Economic sources of homicide: reestimating the effects of poverty and inequality. Am Sociol Rev 1984; 49:283–9.
32. Centerwall BS. Race, socioeconomic status, and domestic homicide, Atlanta, 1971–72. Am J Public Health 1984; 74:813–5.
33. Muscat JE. Characteristics of childhood homicide in Ohio, 1974–84. Am J Public Health 1988; 78:822–4.
34. Seattle City Government. General social and economic characteristics, city of Seattle: 1970–1980. Planning research bulletin no. 45. Seattle: Department of Community Development, 1983.
35. Newton G, Zimring F. Firearms and violence in American life: a staff report to the National Commission on the Causes and Prevention of Violence. Washington, D.C.: Government Printing Office, 1969.

QUESTIONS

1. *Outline "Handgun Regulations, Crime, Assaults, and Homicide: A Tale of Two Cities" using the authors' section headings: abstract, introduction (unheaded), methods, results, discussion, and references. Explain how the authors fit their information and analysis into this structure.*
2. *Read Stephen Jay Gould's account of induction and prediction in "Darwin's Middle Road" (p. 1081). Is the structure of "Handgun Regulations" primarily inductive or primarily predictive? Do you think that the scientists involved worked inductively, predictively, or, as Gould claims Darwin did, shuttled between induction and prediction?*
3. *"Handgun Regulations, Crime, Assaults, and Homicide: A Tale of Two Cities" contains four tables and three figures. Locate the passages in which the information represented in the tables and figures appears. What kind of information is represented graphically and what are the advantages of such representation?*
4. *Sloan et al., aware that their research is relevant to the controversial issue of gun control, are cautious in their conclusion: "Although our findings should be corroborated in other settings, our results suggest that a more restrictive approach to handgun control may decrease national homicide rates" (paragraph 34). Use their research to argue for or against handgun regulation in an essay written to a general audience.*

Melvin Konner

WHY THE RECKLESS SURVIVE

In a recent election Massachusetts rescinded its seat-belt law.[1] As a result some hundreds of citizens of that commonwealth have in the past year gone slamming into windshields instead of getting a pain in the neck from the shoulder belt. Quite a few are unnecessarily brain-damaged or dead. Such laws in fact make a difference. Americans in general use seat belts at a rate of about 20 percent; but in Texas, where failure to wear one can cost you not only your life but also fifty dollars, nearly seven people in ten wear them habitually—a fivefold increase since the law was passed in 1985. Having lived in Massachusetts for

From *Why the Reckless Survive—and Other Secrets of Human Nature* (1990).

1. Massachusetts rescinded its seat-belt law in 1986, reimposed it in 1994.

fifteen years, I considered it—wrongly, perhaps—the most sensible state in the union, so I was rather amazed by its recent collective decision.

But I shouldn't have been. All I needed to do was to look at my own behavior. I have, while coauthoring a book on health, sat at my word processor at three A.M. guzzling coffee and gobbling Oreo cookies by the dozen, pecking solemnly away about our need to take better care of ourselves. I could almost feel the fat from the cookies sinking into the arteries of my brain, the coffee laying the groundwork for future cardiac arrhythmias.

Why can't we follow our own advice, or others', even when we know it's right? Is it the heedless child in us, or the perverse, destructive teenager, or only the antiauthoritarian, freedom-loving adult that says, *I will do as I please, thank you?* Or could it be that there is something inevitable—even something good—about the taking of all these chances?

People don't think clearly about risk. This is no mere insult, but a conclusion that emerges from attempts by behavioral scientists to understand how people make decisions. In part these studies were sparked by the unprecedented demand for risk reduction that has emerged in recent years. How many cases of cancer do people consider acceptable nationally as a result of the widespread use of a food additive or an industrial chemical? None. How many accidents or near-accidents at nuclear power plants? None. How many airline crashes per decade? Basically, none.

5 We may consider the change good: doesn't it reflect a healthy increase in awareness of real risks? But consider that this is the same American public that, after years of education, wears seat belts at the rate of 20 percent and has reduced its cigarette smoking only somewhat. The widespread success of lotteries alone shows that people do not think or act rationally, even in their own self-interest.

So we ignore some risks and overestimate others. The conundrum for an evolutionist is simple. Natural selection should have relentlessly culled systematic biases in decision making, producing a rational organism that hews to the order of real cost-benefit analysis—an organism that behaves efficiently to minimize those ratios. How can evolution, with its supposedly relentless winnowing out of error, have preserved this bewildering array of dangerous habits?

We are highly sensitive to certain dangers. A Harris poll conducted in 1980 showed that 78 percent of the American public (as opposed to roughly half of business and government leaders) thought that risks in general were greater than they had been twenty years before. The greatest perceived risks were in the areas of crime and personal safety, international and domestic political stability, energy sources, and "the chemicals we use." Comfortable majorities of the general public (but only small minorities of the leadership groups) agreed with the statements "Society has only perceived the tip of the iceberg with regard to the risks associated with modern technology" and "Unless technological development is restrained, the overall safety of society will be jeopardized significantly in the next twenty years."

But the logic of our concerns is problematic. People are willing to pay indirectly large sums of money to reduce the risk of a nuclear accident or a cancer death from a chemical to levels they consider acceptably low. But they will not pay a much smaller amount for air bags in automobiles, that, inflating on impact, will save many more lives; and they will not stop smoking, although this risk-reducing measure would actually save money, both immediately and in the long term.

Apparently, irrational factors are at work. But before we consider them, and why we may be subject to them, it is worth looking at the realities of risk. John Urquhart and Klaus Heilmann, both physicians, have reviewed some of these realities in their book *Riskwatch: The Odds of Life.* There is a genuine hierarchy of danger. For example, the number of deaths linked to cigarette smoking in the United States is equivalent to three jumbo jets full of passengers crashing daily, day in and day out. We have fifty thousand traffic fatalities a year—almost the number of deaths we suffered during our entire involvement in Vietnam. Half involve drunk drivers, and a large proportion would be prevented by seat belts or air bags.

10 Yet neither of these sources of risk evokes the interest—indeed the fear—shown in response to possible nuclear accidents, or to toxic-shock syndrome caused by tampons, or even to homicide, all (for most of us) trivial risks by comparison to smoking or driving. If you tremble when you strap yourself into the seat of an airliner, you ought to really shudder when you climb onto your bicycle, since that is much more dangerous as a regular activity. As for homicide, the people most afraid of it are the ones least likely to be victimized. And the millions of women who stopped taking birth-control pills because of the risk of death from stroke did so in response to an annual probability of dying equal to about one fourth their routine risk of death in an automobile.

Urquhart and Heilmann deal with this quirkiness in our response to risk by developing a Safety-Degree Scale analogous to the Richter scale for earthquake severity. The units are logarithms of the cohort size necessary for one death to occur. Thus lightning, which kills fewer than one person per million exposed, has a safety degree of more than six, while motorcycling, which kills one in a thousand, has a safety degree of three; motorcycling is three orders of magnitude more dangerous. But they aren't perceived in that relation. In general, people will accept one to two orders of magnitude more danger in voluntary risks than they will in involuntary ones. And that is only one aspect of the quirkiness. Risks that result in many deaths at once will be perceived as worse than probabilistically equal risks that kill in a more distributed way. And any bad outcome that is reported unexpectedly—especially if its shock value is exploited—increases fear.

Chronic departures from rationality have been the subject of a major line of thought in economics, in which the most distinguished name is Herbert Simon's. Simon, a winner of the Nobel Memorial prize in economics, has for years criticized and occasionally ridiculed the economic decision theory known as subjective expected utility, or SEU. According to this classic approach, individuals face their life choices with full knowledge of the probability and value of all possible outcomes, and furthermore they possess an unambiguous value scale to measure utility—in plain English, they know a great deal, in advance, about the consequences of their choices, and, more important, they know what they want. In the real world, Simon points out, no such knowledge exists. Whether in the choices of executives or in those of consumers, knowledge is imperfect and values (at least to some extent) indeterminate and mercurial.

A similar point was demonstrated in laboratory experiments by psychologists Amos Tversky and Daniel Kahnemann, in which people are shown to be rather feeble in their abilities to choose among various outcomes. They are readily confused by differences in the language in which a problem is posed. In one study, Tversky and Kahnemann asked physicians to choose among possible programs to combat a hypothetical disease that was on the verge of killing six hundred people. The physicians favored a program guaranteed to save *two hundred lives* over one that had a one-third probability of saving everyone and a two-thirds probability of saving no one. Yet a second group of physicians favored the riskier program over one described as resulting in exactly *four hundred deaths.* They were, of course, rejecting the same alternative the previous group had chosen. The only difference was that it was now being described in terms of victims rather than survivors. Human decision making is rife with such framing errors, and analyzing them has become a cottage industry.

At least equally interesting is a new psychological view—advanced by Lola Lopes among others—that certain "errors" may not be errors at all. Lottery players can be shown to be irrational by multiplying the prize by the probability of winning, and comparing that number to the cost of the ticket. But that does not take into account the subjective value placed on becoming rich, or the fact that this may be someone's only chance for that outcome. Nor, of course, does it consider the thrill of playing.

But another aspect of this behavior clearly is irrational: people—es- 15
pecially, but not only, compulsive gamblers—have unrealistically high expectations of winning. On the average, in the larger game of life, they also have unrealistically high expectations of protection against losing. Linda Perloff and others have shown that people—average people—think that they will live longer than average, that they will have fewer diseases than average, and even that their marriages will last longer than average. Since average people are likely to have average rates of disease, death, and divorce, they are (in these studies) underestimating their risks—a tendency Lionel Tiger has summarized as a ubiquitous, biologically based human propensity to unwarranted optimism.

While these results fit well with the prevalence of risky behavior, they seem to contradict the findings about people's *over*estimate of the risk of violent crime, or terrorist attacks, or airline crashes, or nuclear-plant accidents. Part of this is resolvable by reference to the principle that risks beyond our control are more frightening than those we consider ourselves in charge of. So we drink and drive, and buckle the seat belt behind us, and light up another cigarette, on the strength of the illusion that to *these* risks at least, we are invulnerable; and we cancel the trip to Europe on the one-in-a-million chance of an Arab terrorist attack.

Three patterns, then, emerge in our misestimates. First, we prefer voluntary risks to involuntary ones—or, put another way, risks that we feel we have some control over to those that we feel we don't. By the way we drive and react to cues on the road, we think, we reduce our risk to such a low level that seat belts add little protection. But in the case of the terrorist attack or the nuclear-plant accident, we feel we have no handle on the risks. (We seem especially to resent and fear risks that are imposed on us by others, especially if for their own benefit. If I want to smoke myself to death, we seem to say, it's my own business; but if some company is trying to put something over on me with asbestos or nerve gas, I'll be furious.)

Second, we prefer familiar risks to strange ones. The homicide during a mugging, or the airliner hijacked in Athens, or the nerve gas leaking from an armed forces train, get our attention and so loom much larger in our calculations than they should in terms of real risk. Third, deaths that come in bunches—the jumbo-jet crash of the disaster movie—are more frightening than those that come in a steady trickle, even though the latter may add up to more risk when the counting is done. This principle may be related in some way to the common framing error in which people in Tversky and Kahnemann's studies will act more strongly to prevent two hundred deaths in six hundred people than they will to guarantee four hundred survivors from the same group. Framing the risk in terms of death rather than survival biases judgment.

But there is yet another, more interesting complication. "The general public," "average people," "human" rational or irrational behavior—these categories obscure the simple fact that people differ in these matters.

Average people knowingly push their cholesterol levels upward, but only a third pay essentially no attention to doctors' orders when it comes to modifying their behavior (smoking, or eating a risky diet) in the setting of an established illness worsened by that behavior. Average people leave their seat belts unbuckled, but only some people ride motorcycles, and fewer still race or do stunts with them. Average people play lotteries, friendly poker, and church bingo, but an estimated one to four million Americans are pathological gamblers, relentlessly destroying their lives and the lives of those close to them by compulsively taking outrageous financial risks.

Psychologists have only begun to address these individual differences, but several different lines of research suggest that there is such a thing as a risk-taking or sensation-seeking personality. For example, studies of alcohol, tobacco, and caffeine abuse have found these three forms of excess to be correlated, and also to be related to various other measures of risk taking.

For many years psychologist Marvin Zuckerman, of the University of Delaware, and his colleagues have been using the Sensation Seeking Scale, a questionnaire designed to address these issues directly. Empirically, the questions fall along four dimensions: *thrill and adventure seeking*, related to interest in physical risk taking, as in skydiving and mountain climbing; *experience seeking*, reflecting a wider disposition to try new things, in art, music, travel, friendship, or even drugs; *disinhibition*, the hedonistic pursuit of pleasure through activities like social drinking, partying, sex, and gambling; and *boredom susceptibility*, an aversion to routine work and dull people.

At least the first three of these factors have held up in many samples, of both sexes and various ages, in England and America, but there are systematic differences. Males always exceed females, and sensation seeking in general declines in both sexes with age. There is strongly suggestive evidence of a genetic predisposition: 233 pairs of identical twins had a correlation of 0.60 in sensation seeking, while 138 nonidentical twin pairs had a corresponding correlation of only 0.21.

More interesting than these conventional calculations is a series of studies showing that sensation seeking, as measured by the questionnaire, has significant physiological correlates. For example, heart-rate change in reaction to novelty is greater in sensation-seekers, as is brain-wave response to increasingly intense stimulation. The activity of monoamine oxidase (MAO), an enzyme that breaks down certain neurotransmitters (the chemicals that transmit signals between brain cells), is another correlate. Sensation seekers have less MAO activity, suggesting that neurotransmitters that might be viewed as stimulants may persist longer in their brains. Finally, the sex hormones, testosterone and estrogen, show higher levels in sensation seekers.

But in addition this paper-and-pencil test score correlates with real 25
behavior. High scores engage in more frequent, more promiscuous, and more unusual sex; consume more drugs, alcohol, cigarettes, and even spicy food; volunteer more for experiments and other unusual activities; gamble more; and court more physical danger. In the realm of the abnormal, the measure is correlated with hypomania, and in the realm of the criminal, with psychopathy.

In other words, something measured by this test has both biological and practical significance. Furthermore, independent studies by Frank Farley and his colleagues at the University of Wisconsin, using a different instrument and a somewhat distinct measure they call thrill seeking, have confirmed and extended these findings. For example, in prison populations fighting and escape attempts are higher in those who score high on thrill seeking. But Farley also emphasizes positive outcomes—a well-established correlation between sensation seeking and the extraverted personality underscores the possibility that some such people are well primed for leadership.

We can now return to the main question: how could all this irrationality have been left untouched by natural selection? Herbert Simon, in an accessible, even lyrical, summary of his thought, the 1983 book *Reason in Human Affairs*, surprised some of us in anthropology and biology who are more or less constantly railing against the un-Darwinian musings of social scientists. He shows a quite incisive understanding of Darwin's theories and of very recent significant refinements of them.

But my own anthropological heart was most warmed by passages such as this one: "If this [situation] is not wholly descriptive of the world we live in today . . . it certainly describes the world in which human rationality evolved: the world of the cavemen's ancestors, and of the cavemen themselves. In that world . . . periodically action had to be taken to deal with hunger, or to flee danger, or to secure protection against the coming winter. Rationality could focus on dealing with one or a few problems at a time. . . ." The appeal to the world of our ancestors, the hunters and gatherers, is as explicit as I could wish. As Simon recognizes, this is the world in which our rationality, limited as it is, evolved. It could not be much better now than it needed to be then, because less perfect rationality would not have been selected against; and we, the descendants of those hunters and gatherers, would have inherited their imperfections.

The result is what Simon calls "bounded rationality"—a seat-of-the-pants, day-by-day sort of problem solving that, far from pretending to assess all possible outcomes against a clear spectrum of values, attempts no more than to get by. "Putting out fires" is another way of describing it; and it follows directly from the concept of economic behavior that made Simon famous: "satisficing," the notion that people are just trying to solve the problem at hand in a way that is "good enough"—his practical answer to those too-optimistic constructions of economists, "maximizing" and "optimizing."

30 Simon has perceived that the basic human environment did not call for optimal decision making, in the modern risk-benefit sense of the phrase; thus our imperfection, this "bounded rationality." But this does not explain the systematic departures from rationality—the preference for "controllable" or familiar rather than "uncontrollable" or strange risks, or the particular fear attached to large disasters. And it does not explain, especially, the sense of invulnerability of risk takers. Certain kinds of recklessness are easy to handle by looking at the specific evolutionary provenance of certain motives. Kristin Luker, a sociologist at the University of California at San Diego, studied contraceptive risk taking and uncovered what often seemed an unconscious desire for a baby. It is no challenge to reconcile this with evolutionary theory; a Darwinian couple ought to take such risks right and left. Sexual indiscretions in general could be covered by a similar line of argument: sexy sensation seekers perpetuate their genes. Slightly more interesting are the specific risks involved in certain human culinary preferences. We overdo it on fats and sweets because our ancestors were rewarded for such excesses with that inch of insulation needed to carry them through shortages. Death by atherosclerosis may be a pervasive threat today, but for most of the past three million years it was a consummation devoutly to be wished.

But we are still far from the comprehensive explanation of recklessness we need. For this we must look to the darker side of human nature, as expressed in that same ancestral environment. Martin Daly and Margo Wilson, both psychologists at McMaster University in Ontario, explore this matter directly in a book called *Homicide*. Although their analysis is restricted to only one highly dramatic form of risk taking, it is paradigmatic of the problem.

Homicides occur in all human societies, and a frequent cause is a quarrel over something seemingly trivial—an insult, a misunderstanding, a disagreement about a fact neither combatant cares about. Of course, these conflicts are never *really* trivial; they are about status and honor—which in practical terms means whether and how much you can be pushed around. And on this will depend your access to food, land, women (the participants are almost always male)—in short, most of what matters in life and in natural selection. In societies where heads are hunted or coups counted, the process is more formalized, but the principle is similar.

If you simulate, as Daly and Wilson do, a series of fights in which individuals with different risk propensities—low, medium, and high—encounter each other, the high-risk individuals invariably have the highest mortality. But any assumption that winning increases Darwinian fitness—virtually certain to be correct in most environments—leads to predominance of high- or medium-risk individuals. Their candles burn at both ends, but they leave more genes.

The underlying assumption is that the environment is a dangerous one, but this assumption is sensible. The environments of our ancestors must have been full of danger. "Nothing ventured, nothing gained" must have been a cardinal rule; and yet venturing meant exposure to grave risk: fire, heights, cold, hunger, predators, human enemies. And all this risk has to be seen against a background of mortality from causes outside of human control—especially disease. With an average life expectancy at birth of thirty years, with a constant high probability of dying from pneumonia or malaria—the marginal utility, in economic terms, of strict avoidance of danger would have been much lower than it is now, perhaps negligible. In Oscar Lewis's studies of the Mexican "culture of poverty" and in Eliot Liebow's studies of poor black street-corner men, the point is clearly made: the failure of such people to plan for the future is not irrational—they live for the day because they know that they have no future.

To die, in Darwinian terms, is not to lose the game. Individuals risk 35
or sacrifice their lives for their kin. Sacrifice for offspring is ubiquitous in the animal world, and the examples of maternal defense of the young in mammals and male death in the act of copulation in insects have become familiar. But great risks are taken and sacrifices made for other relatives as well. Consider the evisceration of the worker honeybee in the act of stinging an intruder and the alarm call of a bird or ground squirrel, calling the predator's attention to itself while warning its relatives. During our own evolution small, kin-based groups might have gained much from having a minority of reckless sensation seekers in the ranks—people who wouldn't hesitate to snatch a child from a pack of wild dogs or to fight an approaching grass fire with a counterfire.

In any case, both sensation seekers and people in general should have taken their risks selectively. They may have found it advantageous to take risks with the seemingly controllable and familiar, even while exaggerating the risk of the unknown, and hedging it around with all sorts of taboo and ritual. It is difficult to imagine a successful encounter with a volcano, but an early human would have had at least a fighting chance against a lion. And we, their descendants, fear toxic nuclear waste but leave our seat belts unbuckled.

Why can't we adjust our personal behavior to our modern middle-class spectrum of risks? Because we are just not built to cut it that finely. We are not designed for perfectly rational calculations, or to calibrate such relatively unimpressive risks. For many of us, life seems compromised by such calculations; they too have a cost—in effort, in freedom, in self-image, in fun. And the fun is not incidental. It is evolution's way of telling us what we were designed for.

Sensation seeking fulfills two of the three cardinal criteria for evolution by natural selection: it varies in the population, and the varieties are to some extent inheritable. In any situation in which the varieties give rise in addition to different numbers of offspring, evolution will occur. The notion that riskier types, because they suffer higher mortality, must slowly disappear is certainly wrong for many environments, and it may still be wrong even for ours.

Ideally, of course, one would want a human organism that could take the risks that—despite the dangers—enhance fitness, and leave aside the risks that don't. But life and evolution are not that perfect. The result of the vastly long evolutionary balancing act is a most imperfect organism. The various forms of personal risk taking often hang together; you probably can't be the sort of person who makes sure to maintain perfectly safe and healthy habits, and yet reflexively take the risks needed to ensure survival and reproductive success in the basic human environment. If you are designed, emotionally, for survival and reproduction, then you are not designed for perfect safety.

40 So when my father buckles his seat belt behind him, and my brother keeps on smoking, and my friend rides her motorcycle to work every day, it isn't because, or only because, they somewhat underestimate the risks. My father wants the full sense of competence and freedom that he has always had in driving, since long before seat belts were dreamed of. My brother wants the sense of calm that comes out of the cigarette. My friend wants to hear the roar of the Harley and feel the wind in her hair. And they want the risk, because risk taking, for them, is part of being alive.

As for me, when I avoid those risks, I feel safe and virtuous but perhaps a little cramped. And I suspect that, like many people who watch their diet carefully—despite the lapses—and exercise more or less scrupulously and buckle up religiously, I am a little obsessed with immortality, with the prospect of controlling that which cannot be controlled. I know I am doing the sensible thing—my behavior matches, most of the time, the spectrum of real probabilities. But against what scale of value? I sometimes think that the more reckless among us may have something to teach the careful about the sort of immortality that comes from living fully every day.

QUESTIONS

1. *Mark the research and the researchers' disciplines that Konner relies on. How many kinds of studies does he bring together? What are they?*
2. *Konner is interested in the effects of biology on human behavior. Locate the evidence he draws from biology and explain his uses of it.*
3. *Konner introduces and concludes this essay with autobiographical material; he stations himself with respect to his subject. What does the autobiographical material contribute to this essay?*
4. *Write an essay in which you describe your own or someone else's irrational behavior and speculate about its causes.*

Arthur Koestler

GRAVITY AND THE HOLY GHOST

"If I have been able to see farther than others," said Newton, "it was because I stood on the shoulders of giants." One of the giants was Johannes Kepler (1571–1630) whose three laws of planetary motion provided the foundation on which the Newtonian universe was built. They were the first "natural laws" in the modern sense: precise, verifiable statements expressed in mathematical terms; at the same time, they represent the first attempt at a synthesis of astronomy and physics which, during the preceding two thousand years, had developed on separate lines.

Astronomy before Kepler had been a purely descriptive geometry of the skies. The motion of stars and planets had been represented by the device of epicycles and eccentrics—an imaginary clockwork of circles turning on circles turning on circles. Copernicus, for instance, had used forty-eight wheels to represent the motion of the five known planets around the sun. These wheels were purely fictitious, and meant as such—they enabled astronomers to make more or less precise predictions, but, above all, they satisfied the dogma that all heavenly motion must be uniform and in perfect circles. Though the planets moved neither uniformly nor in perfect circles, the imaginary cogwheels did, and thereby "saved the appearances."

From *The Act of Creation* (1964).

Kepler's discoveries put an end to this state of affairs. He reconciled astronomy with physics, and substituted for the fictitious clockwork a universe of material bodies not unlike the earth, freely floating and turning in space, moved by forces acting on them. His most important book bears the provocative title: *A New Astronomy Based on Causation, or Physics of the Sky* (1609). It contains the first and second of Kepler's three laws. The first says that the planets move around the sun not in circles but in elliptic orbits; the second says that a planet moves in its orbit not at uniform speed but at a speed that varies according to its position, and is defined by a simple and beautiful law: the line connecting planet and sun sweeps over equal areas in equal times. The third law establishes an equally elegant mathematical correlation between the length of a planet's year and its mean distance from the sun.

Kepler did not start his career as an astronomer, but as a student of theology (at the Lutheran University of Thuebingen); yet already as a student he was attracted by the Copernican idea of a sun-centered universe. Now Canon Copernicus's book, *On the Revolutions of the Heavenly Spheres,* had been published in the year of his death, 1543; that is, fifty years before Kepler first heard of him; and during that half century it had attracted very little attention. One of the reasons was its supreme unreadability, which made it into an all-time worst-seller: its first edition of a thousand copies was never sold out. Kepler was the first Continental astronomer to embrace the Copernican theory. His *Mysterium Cosmographicum,* published in 1597 (fifty-four years after Copernicus's death) started the great controversy—Galileo entered the scene fifteen years later.

5 The reason why the idea of a sun-centered universe appealed to Kepler was repeatedly stated by himself: "I often defended the opinions of Copernicus in the disputations of the candidates and I composed a careful disputation on the first motion which consists in the rotation of the earth; then I was adding to this the motion of the earth around the sun *for physical or, if you prefer, metaphysical reasons.*" I have emphasized the last words because they contain the leitmotif of Kepler's quest, and because he used the same expression in various passages in his works. Now what were those "physical or, if you prefer, metaphysical reasons" which made Kepler prefer to put the sun into the center of the universe instead of the earth?

> My ceaseless search concerned primarily three problems, namely, the number, size, and motion of the planets—why they are just as they are and not otherwise arranged. I was encouraged in my daring inquiry by that beautiful analogy between the stationary objects, namely, the sun, the fixed stars, and the space between them, with God the Father, the

> Son, and the Holy Ghost. I shall pursue this analogy in my future cosmographical work.

Twenty-five years later, when he was over fifty, Kepler repeated his credo: "It is by no means permissible to treat this analogy as an empty comparison; it must be considered by its Platonic form and archetypal quality as one of the primary causes."

He believed in this to the end of his life. Yet gradually the analogy underwent a significant change:

> The sun in the middle of the *moving* stars, himself at rest and yet the source of motion, carries the image of God the Father and Creator. He distributes his motive force through a medium which contains the moving bodies, even as the Father creates through the Holy Ghost.

Thus the "moving bodies"—that is, the planets—are now brought into the analogy. The Holy Ghost no longer merely fills the space between the motionless sun and the motionless fixed stars. It has become an active force, a *vis motrix,* which *drives* the planets. Nobody before Kepler had postulated, or even suspected, the existence of a physical force acting between the sun and the planets. Astronomy was not concerned with physical forces, nor with the causes of the heavenly motions, merely with their description. The passages which I have just quoted are the first intimation of the forthcoming marriage between physics and astronomy—the act of betrothal, as it were. By looking at the sky, not through the eyes of the geometrician only, but of the physicist concerned with natural causes, he hit upon a question which nobody had asked before. The question was: "Why do the planets closer to the sun move faster than those which are far away? What is the mathematical relation between a planet's distance from the sun and the length of its year?"

These questions could only occur to one who had conceived the revolutionary hypothesis that the motion of the planet—and therefore its velocity and the duration of its year—was governed by a physical force emanating from the sun. Every astronomer knew, of course, that the greater their distance from the sun the slower the planets moved. But this phenomenon was taken for granted, just as it was taken for granted that boys will be boys and girls will be girls, as an irreducible fact of creation. Nobody asked the cause of it because physical causes were not assumed to enter into the motion of heavenly bodies. The greatness of the philosophers of the scientific revolution consisted not so much in finding the right answers but in asking the right questions; in seeing a problem where nobody saw one before; in substituting a "why" for a "how."

Kepler's answer to the question why the outer planets move slower 10 than the inner ones, and how the speed of their motion is related to their distance from the sun, was as follows:

> There exists only one moving soul in the center of all the orbits that is the sun which drives the planets the more vigorously the closer the planet is, but whose force is quasi-exhausted when acting on the outer planets because of the long distance and the weakening of the force which it entails.

Later on he commented: "If we substitute for the word 'soul' the word 'force,' then we get just the principle which underlies my 'Physics of the Skies.' As I reflected that this cause of motion *diminishes in proportion to distance* just as the light of the sun diminishes in proportion to distance from the sun, I came to the conclusion that this force must be substantial—'substantial' not in the literal sense but . . . in the same manner as we say that light is something substantial, meaning by this an unsubstantial entity emanating from a substantial body."

We notice that Kepler's answer came *before* the question—that it was the answer that begot the question. The answer, the starting point, was the analogy between God the Father and the sun—the former acting through the Holy Ghost, the latter through a physical force. The planets must obey the law of the sun—the law of God—the mathematical law of nature; and the Holy Ghost's action through empty space diminishes, as the light emanating from the sun does, with distance. The degenerate, purely descriptive astronomy which originated in the period of the Greek decline, and continued through the Dark and Middle Ages until Kepler, did not ask for meaning and causes. But Kepler was convinced that physical causes operate between heavenly, just as between earthly, bodies, and more specifically that the sun exerts a physical force on the planets. It was this conviction which enabled him to formulate his laws. Physics became the auxiliary matrix which secured his escape from the blocked situation into which astronomy had maneuvered itself.

The blockage—to cut a very long story short—was due to the fact that Tycho de Brahe[1] had improved the instruments and methods of star-gazing, and produced observational data of a hitherto unequaled abundance and precision; and the new data did not fit into the traditional schemes. Kepler, who served his apprenticeship under Tycho, was given the task of working out the orbit of Mars. He spent six years on the task and covered nine thousand foliosheets with calculations in his small handwriting without getting anywhere. When at last he be-

1. Danish astronomer (1546–1601).

lieved he had succeeded he found to his dismay that certain observed positions of Mars differed from those which his theory demanded by magnitudes up to eight minutes arc.[2] Eight minutes arc is approximately one-quarter of the apparent diameter of the moon.

This was a catastrophe. Ptolemy, and even Copernicus, could afford to neglect a difference of eight minutes, because their observations were accurate only within a margin of ten minutes, anyway. "But," Kepler wrote in the *New Astronomy*, "but for us, who by divine kindness were given an accurate observer such as Tycho Brahe, for us it is fitting that we should acknowledge this divine gift and put it to use. . . . Henceforth I shall lead the way toward that goal according to my ideas. For if I had believed that we could ignore these eight minutes, I would have patched up my hypothesis accordingly. But since it was not permissible to ignore them, those eight minutes point the road to a complete reformation of astronomy. . . ."

Thus a theory, built on years of labor and torment, was instantly thrown away because of a discord of eight miserable minutes arc. Instead of cursing those eight minutes as a stumbling block, he transformed them into the cornerstone of a new science. For those eight minutes arc had at last made him realize that the field of astronomy in its traditional framework was well and truly blocked.

One of the recurrent frustrations and tragedies in the history of thought is caused by the uncertainty whether it is possible to solve a given problem by traditional methods previously applied to problems which seem to be of the same nature. Who can say how many lives were wasted and good minds destroyed in futile attempts to square the circle, or to construct a *perpetuum mobile?*[3] The proof that these problems are *insoluble* was in each case an original discovery in itself (such as Maxwell's second law of thermodynamics);[4] and such proofs could only be found by looking at the problem from a point of view outside its traditional matrix. On the other hand, the mere knowledge that a problem is soluble means that half the game is already won.

The episode of the eight minutes arc had convinced Kepler that his problem—the orbit of Mars—was insoluble so long as he felt bound by the traditional rules of sky-geometry. Implied in those rules was the dogma of "uniform motion in perfect circles." *Uniform* motion he had already discarded before the crisis; now he felt that the even more sa-

2. 8/60ths of a degree; there are 60 minutes of arc in one degree.
3. A hypothetical machine that, once set in motion, would continue in motion forever unless stopped by some external force or by its own wearing out.
4. The second law of thermodynamics, put forward not by James Clerk Maxwell, but by Rudolf Julius Emmanuel Clausius (1822–1888), provides an explanation of why a perpetual-motion machine cannot exist.

cred one of *circular* motion must also go. The impossibility of constructing a circular orbit which would satisfy all existing observations suggested to him that the circle must be replaced by some other curve.

> The conclusion is quite simply that the planet's path is not a circle—it curves inward on both sides and outward again at opposite ends. Such a curve is called an oval. The orbit is not a circle but an oval figure.

This oval orbit was a wild, frightening new departure for him. To be fed up with cycles and epicycles, to mock the slavish imitators of Aristotle was one thing; to assign an entirely new, lopsided, implausible path for the heavenly bodies was quite another. Why indeed an oval? There is something in the perfect symmetry of spheres and circles which has a deep, reassuring appeal to the unconscious mind—otherwise it could not have survived two millennia. The oval lacks that archetypal appeal. It has an arbitrary, distorted form. It destroyed the dream of the "harmony of the spheres," which lay at the origin of the whole quest. At times he felt like a criminal, or worse: a fool. All he had to say in his own defense was: "I have cleared the Augean stables of astronomy of cycles and spirals, and left behind me only a single cartful of dung."

That cartful of dung—nonuniform motion in noncircular orbits—could only be justified and explained by arguments derived not from geometry, but from physics. A phrase kept humming in his ear like a catchy tune, and crops up in his writings over and again: there is a force in the sun which moves the planets, there is a force in the sun. . . . And since there is a force in the sun, there must exist some simple relationship between the planet's distance from the sun, and its speed. A light shines the brighter the nearer one is to its source, and the same must apply to the force of the sun: the closer the planet to it, the quicker it will move. This had been his instinctive conviction; but now he thought that he had found the proof of it. "Ye physicists, prick your ears, for now we are going to invade your territory." The next six chapters in the *Astronomia Nova* are a report on that invasion into celestial physics, which had been out of bounds for astronomy since Plato. He had found the second matrix which would unblock his problem.

20 That excursion was something of a comedy of errors—which nevertheless ended with finding the truth. Since he had no notion of the principle of inertia, which makes a planet persist in its tangential motion under its own momentum, and had only a vague intuition of gravity, he had to invent a force which, emanating from the sun, sweeps the planet round its path like a broom. In the second place, to account for the eccentricity of the orbits he had to postulate that the planets were "huge round magnets" whose poles pointed always in the same direction so that they would alternately be drawn closer to and be re-

pelled by the sun. But although today the whole thing seems cockeyed, his intuition that there are *two antagonistic forces* acting on the planets, guided him in the right direction. A single force, as previously assumed—the divine Prime Mover and its allied hierarchy of angels—would never produce elliptic orbits and periodic changes of speed. These could only be the result of some dynamic tug of war going on in the sky—as indeed there is. The concept of two antagonistic forces provided rules for a new game in which elliptic orbits and velocities depending on solar distance have their legitimate place.

He made many mistakes during that wild flight of thought; but "as if by miracle"—as he himself remarked—the mistakes canceled out. It looks as if at times his conscious critical faculties had been anesthetized by the creative impulse, by the impatience to get to grips with the physical forces in the solar system. The problem of the planetary orbits had been hopelessly bogged down in its purely geometrical frame of reference, and when he realized that he could not get it unstuck he tore it out of that frame and removed it into the field of physics. That there were inconsistencies and impurities in his method did not matter to him in the heat of the moment, hoping that somehow they would right themselves later on—as they did. This inspired cheating—or, rather, borrowing on credit—is a characteristic and recurrent feature in the history of science. The latest example is subatomic physics, which may be said to live on credit—in the pious hope that one day its inner contradictions and paradoxes will somehow resolve themselves.

Kepler's determination of the orbit of Mars became the unifying link between the two formerly separate realisms of physics and astronomy. His was the first serious attempt at explaining the mechanism of the solar system in terms of physical forces; and once the example was set, physics and cosmology could never again be divorced.

Brian Hayes

THE ELECTRONIC PALIMPSEST: DIGITAL DOCUMENTS FOR ALL OCCASIONS

As a writing instrument, the computer is not so much a better pencil as a better eraser. Although it serves well enough to put words on the page, where it really excels is in wiping them out again. Writing

From *The Sciences* (Sept./Oct. 1993).

with a computer affords you the luxury of changing your mind, again and again, without penalty. The excised word leaves no scar; the page never becomes gray or tattered from rubbing; the margins do not fill up with afterthoughts; there is no tangle of arrows showing how sentences are to be rearranged. When you write on the glass screen, the world need never know how you labored to achieve that easygoing prose style. Indeed, this very paragraph conceals the tortured history of its own composition: you the reader cannot see in the space between the lines how I have revised it, a dozen times or more, until hardly a word of the first draft survives.

When I got my first chance to write with a computer, it was an exhilarating experience. I would insert a word into the middle of a paragraph and marvel as all the following words automatically rearranged themselves to make room, cascading from line to line in a kind of domino effect. Or I would hold down the delete key and suck up whole sentences like spaghetti. Suddenly prose became a kind of clay that never hardens, a medium that one can always reshape yet again.

But if the plasticity of electronic text is a great liberation for the author, it can also license the forger, the plagiarist, the swindler, the impostor; and it is not an unmixed blessing for the scholar, the historian or even the ordinary reader. Words stored in electronic form are in certain ways less secure and less permanent than words on paper. When writing is inscribed in the magnetic domains of a spinning disk, can one trust its integrity? Fifty years from now, will anyone even be able to read it? As more of the world's documents migrate from memo pads and filing cabinets and bookshelves into computer memories, those questions are going to take on considerable importance.

One way of exploring the issues is to imagine a world without paper, in which all documents are electronic. Such a world is not far off. True, the "paperless office" has so far turned out to be a bad joke, as office paper consumption doubles every four years. But all those pages spewing out of all those laser printers are coming from computers. In many cases the computer files are already the primary versions of the documents, and the printouts are just a means of distribution or archival storage. In the long run, paper will surely be supplanted in those roles as well.

5 The first thing you notice in a paperless world is that certain awkward situations become even more awkward:

You receive a letter (in the form of a computer file) in which your long-lost sister claims she is being held in a Turkish prison for crimes she didn't commit. Please send her $20,000 to bribe the prosecutor. How do you establish that the letter was written by your sister?

A Washington friend asks you to take a discreet look around someone else's office late one night. In case you get into any trouble, he gives you a letter, stored on a computer disk, that explains the importance of your work to the nation's security. When you are charged with burglary, however, the friend disclaims all knowledge of the letter—and of you. How can you prove the letter is not a forgery? Note that this task is harder than the first one. With the letter from your sister, you need only convince *yourself* of its authenticity; to avoid jail—or at least to take your friend with you—you must convince a judge and a jury of the letter's provenance.

You pick up a hitchhiker in the desert, and in gratitude for that small kindness he gives you a floppy disk bearing a promise of millions of dollars upon his death. How do you prove the bequest is from Howard Hughes? Again, you must demonstrate to others that the document is genuine. Furthermore, you may well have to show not only that Hughes wrote the note but also that you have not altered it (changing "two million" to "two hundred million," say).

In the world of paper documents the primary tool for settling such controversies is the examination of handwriting. You know the letter is from your sister because you recognize her hand; experts compare your cover letter from the White House or your note from Howard Hughes with specimens known to be authentic. But the bits and bytes of a computerized document are all alike, with none of the idiosyncrasies that might identify individual authorship. Anyone could have typed those letters, on almost any computer.

10 The introduction of "pen"-based computers, which substitute a stylus for a keyboard, will not solve the problem. On such a machine one might confect an ornate and quite inimitable signature, ending with the most swashbuckling paragraph, but a document signed in that way offers only a weak warrant of authenticity. The reason is that such a digitized signature—or any other graphic object—can be copied in an instant with the help of a computer. Give me one "signed" electronic document, and I can forge your name to anything I please. As a matter of fact, the widespread availability of high-resolution scanning and printing equipment raises questions about the security of signatures on paper. There is nothing the modern forger might need that can't be found at the local Kinko's.

Digital documents *can* be signed, however; what is needed is not a digitized signature but a truly digital one. A technique for creating such signatures was proposed in 1976 by Whitfield Diffie and Martin E. Hellman, both then at Stanford University, as part of their ingenious public-key cryptosystem; the idea was refined a few years later by Ronald L. Rivest, Adi Shamir and Leonard Adleman (a triumvirate known as RSA), all then at MIT. In the RSA cryptosystem each user has two keys, one of which is made public and the other is held in secret. A message encrypted with the public key can be decrypted with the private key, and vice versa.

When the system is used for secrecy, a message is encrypted with the recipient's public key (which anyone can look up in a directory); then only the recipient can decrypt the message with the corresponding private key. A simple variation on the protocol yields highly secure digital signatures. To sign a document, you encrypt a copy of it with your private key. Anyone can then verify the signature by decrypting it with your public key. The mechanism works like Cinderella's slipper: whoever owns the key that fits must be the author of the document.

A further refinement has since been added to the digital-signature protocol. If you encrypt an entire document in order to sign it, the signature is as large as the document itself. To reduce the bulk, and at the same time avoid a subtle weakness lurking in the original scheme, the document is collapsed to a "digest" of just 160 bits, and then only the digest is signed. The digesting is done in such a way that even the slightest change to the document is almost certain to yield an entirely different digest. The recipient verifies the signature by applying the digesting algorithm to the document and decrypting the digest with the sender's public key; the result should match the supplied signature.

The National Institute of Standards and Technology is at work on a digital-signature standard based on the public-key principle. The standard-setting process has been going on for years, buffeted by much controversy, but it now appears to be nearing a conclusion.

15 Digital signatures would probably deal quite well with the three situations described above. If signatures accompanying the letter from the Turkish prison and the note from Howard Hughes could be decrypted with the appropriate public keys, that would count as strong evidence for the documents' authenticity. Similarly, your Washington friend would have a hard time disowning a letter that had been signed by means of encryption with his own private key. The signatures also protect against after-the-fact tampering. There is no way you could have exaggerated Hughes's generosity in the signed bequest without knowing his private key.

Although digital signatures are dashed clever, they fall short of solving all the problems of the paperless society.

It might seem at first that digital signatures would provide all the security necessary for a system of electronic checks. To pay your rent, you would merely type a note on the computer, or fill in a template, stating the date, the amount and the payee and identifying your bank and your account number; then you would sign the check with your private key and send it off by electronic mail; the recipient would sign it as an endorsement and mail it on to his own bank. You would be confident that your unscrupulous landlord could not alter the amount, because the bank would detect the change when it verified your signature. Unfortunately, you would remain vulnerable to a cruder kind of fraud. The computer is not only a good eraser but also a flawless copier, and your landlord could simply duplicate your check (along with its signature) and deposit multiple copies, all of which would appear equally authentic. Rivest, Shamir and Adleman suggest including a unique serial number in each signed check and requiring banks to accept only one check with a given serial number. But that puts the onus of vigilance and record keeping on the banks, which may be reluctant to accept it.

Another problem arises when readers must verify not only the authorship and the integrity of a document but also its time of composition. In your computerized laboratory notebook you record the discovery of a new comet or a new virus, and you apply a digital signature to the entry. Later, a rival challenges your claim to priority. Naturally you included the date in your signed notebook entry, but your opponent is not much impressed by that evidence. He points out that the digital signature prevents others from tampering with the document, but since you know your own secret key, you could alter the date—or alter other parts of the document—at any time, then resign it. In other words, the signature proves that you wrote the notebook entry, but it cannot establish when you wrote it.

With paper documents there are at least two ways of dealing with the problem. First, important documents are witnessed as well as signed, and the witnesses can later be called to attest to the dating of the material. That practice can be adopted just as easily with digital signatures. Second, laboratory notes are generally kept in a bound volume with numbered pages, so that sheets cannot be inserted or removed. When disputes arise, the notebook will be credible evidence only if it can be read as a complete, continuous and contemporaneous record of laboratory activity. The pages must be filled up in sequence, without leaving gaps where back-dated entries might be inserted. In the recent controversy over the work of Thereza Imanishi-Kari of Tufts University, the U.S. Secret Service was asked to examine certain notebooks in an attempt to verify the chronology of the entries.

A laboratory record kept on a computer is more like a loose-leaf notebook than like a bound volume. New entries can be inserted anywhere in the sequence, or existing entries can be moved around; dates can be misstated or changed after the fact. But a solution is at hand. Inspired by the Imanishi-Kari case, Stuart A. Haber and W. Scott

Stornetta of Bell Communications Research (Bellcore), in Piscataway, New Jersey, have devised a time-stamping service for electronic documents. The scheme is conceptually similar to public-key cryptography. When your notebook needs to be validated, you submit a digest to the time-stamping computer, which returns a "certificate" that encodes the time of receipt and other information.

But what if the time-stamping service itself cannot be trusted? For example, someone might tamper with the time-stamping computer, perhaps resetting the clock for long enough to create a fraudulent certificate, then restoring the clock to the correct current value. As protection against such deceptions, each certificate is combined with others issued at about the same time in a treelike structure; the single certificate at the root of the tree, whose value depends on all the individual certificates, is publicly posted. During preliminary trials of the service, documents are being time-stamped in weekly batches, and the root certificates are being published every Sunday in the Public Notices section of *The New York Times.* A certificate for any document stamped in the past week can be verified by rederiving the published root value. (A question that remains for the future is what will happen when *The New York Times* is published electronically instead of on paper.)

Even documents that no one would dream of having time-stamped or witnessed sometimes come under scrutiny. For example, George Bush has made public some of his private diaries in an attempt to establish what he didn't know (and when he didn't know it) about the sale of arms to Iran during his vice-presidency. Suppose Bush had kept his diary on a computer instead of on paper: he would have had great difficulty convincing his critics that no entries had been altered, deleted or back-dated.

Of course another major cache of documentary evidence in the Iran-Contra affair was in electronic form: the electronic-mail messages of Oliver North. Curiously, those messages were accepted as authentic and unaltered precisely because North had deleted them (or rather had tried to delete them) from the disk memory of his computer. They were recovered through a sector-by-sector examination of the contents of the disk. If North had instead copied all the files onto floppy disks and voluntarily handed them over to congressional investigators, the messages would surely have been viewed with greater skepticism. (The hard-core conspiracy theorist knows that the supposed deletion and subsequent recovery of the messages was all a carefully staged means of increasing the credibility of concocted evidence. That some of the recovered messages were incriminating counts for nothing, apart from demonstrating that the real messages must have been much worse.)

The handling of legal documents is certainly not the only domain in which a conversion to electronic storage and transmission will change the nature of writing. Even personal correspondence is affected. For example, consider the art of the deft postscript. At the end of a chatty letter home, below the signature, you add, "P.S. I've just heard from Stockholm. Good news." Now, it may be that word of your Nobel prize reached you in the moments after the letter was finished but before it was sealed, but it's also possible that you turned the announcement into a casual afterthought purely for rhetorical effect. With a letter on paper, the recipient could never be quite sure. But with an electronic letter, "P.S." is almost certainly an artifice. After all, with a word processor it is no more trouble to add a sentence at the beginning than at the end.

Other rhetorical devices also lose a bit of their impact. In a letter on 25
paper you might write, "Say hi to ~~dreary~~ dear old Dad," where the strike-through is very much a part of the joke. With a computer, since any mistake can be silently and invisibly corrected, the same trick seems more contrived, less spontaneous.

When a manuscript is being prepared for publication, the kind of invisible mending made possible by computers is often a handicap. Traditionally an editor would return to the author a marked-up copy of the original manuscript, showing all the proposed changes and corrections. When the editing is done with a computer, that record of alterations generally disappears. In fact, software solutions are available for that problem; they are just not widely used. Many word-processing programs offer a "red-lining" mode, which displays insertions and deletions explicitly (though seldom as clearly as they can be with a red pencil). There are also special-purpose programs for annotating text, and the contributions of multiple editors are identified by color.

Such tools may capture an editor's changes, but what about the author's transformations of the work during its composition? Few writers have the patience to document every stage in the creation of a novel or a poem (much less a love letter or a business memorandum). Indeed, some authors would cite as an advantage of computerized writing the end of old drafts and scribbled notes; all that remains of those scraps is now seamlessly integrated into the final text. From the scholar's point of view, however, a valuable source of information is being lost.

Take William Wordsworth's long autobiographical poem *The Prelude*. Fragments of the poem are known from as early as 1798; several versions were composed between 1799 and 1804; Wordsworth made sporadic revisions until 1839; various further emendations were introduced by others before a new edition was published soon after the poet's death in 1850. Dozens of manuscript sources survive, and they have enabled scholars to reconstruct the poem's compositional history in detail. There is no consensus among modern readers that the final state of the poem is the best; indeed, the 1805 version has many partisans. Yet if Wordsworth had had a PC, the history of the poem would probably be lost.

Lord Byron is another intriguing case. He presented himself to the world as an aristocrat of letters whose verses were casual, offhand productions, which he would not deign to correct or revise. Had he been writing with a computer (I imagine him toting the latest laptop model across the Alps into Italy), he might have gotten away with that fib. But recently published facsimiles of his manuscripts show just how labored his process of composition was. A reviewer describes the manuscripts as "bristling with added stanzas, overwritten crosswise, with false starts, impatient deletions, emendations, and adjustments of rhymes." A modern Byron can readily conceal all signs of such unseemly labor, and as a result readers of the next century will likely find that manuscript sources for authors of the 1990s are rather scanty. Information that might well have been preserved on paper is being lost on disk.

30 The loss is not inevitable, and the cause is not really technological. As a matter of fact, keeping a complete archive of a life's work is surely easier with a computer than it is with a filing cabinet. One approach—one of many—is the WORM drive: a disk memory that can be written on and read from but never erased. (WORM stands for "write once, read many.") WORM drives have ample storage capacity; a single disk would hold all the versions of all the works of a Wordsworth or a Byron, along with all his journals and correspondence. The trouble is, adopting such a device amounts to a declaration that one's every word is worth preserving—which is even more obnoxious than the pose of the poet who claims he never cancels a line.

Still, somewhere in America today there must be a writer of merit who is either meticulously or absentmindedly saving her complete oeuvre as a series of computer files. Fifty years from now some lucky scholar will sit down in a library carrel to unseal the treasure. There they'll be, packed in a cardboard carton: 600 eight-inch floppy disks from a Radio Shack TRS-80 Model 1. What is the probability anyone will be able to read them? Even supposing the information encoded on the disks has survived, where would one go in the year 2043 to find a working TRS-80? And a copy of the Electric Pencil, the word-processing program the author used to create her works?

It is curious that archival longevity seems to be the last thing anyone worries about when choosing computer hardware and software. In picking a word processor for my own use, for example, I have focused mainly on ease and speed of editing, and the elegance of the on-screen display; I've thought very little about how I will read my own files a few decades from now, when I will have gone on to another computer, another word processor, another disk format (if indeed the very notion of "word processor" or "disk format" is still meaningful). I should know better. I've changed computers five times in ten years. Every few months I need to resurrect a document from some long-gone system, and I spend an exasperating hour puzzling over cryptic formatting commands that were once intimately familiar. What does "@|" mean again? And "«HYØ»"?

I'm not the only one with such a narrowly constrained time horizon. The computer I'm writing on at this moment thinks the world will end in 2040.

Both buyers and sellers of software pay a good deal of attention to the transfer of information between different programs and computer systems, but the emphasis is on synchronic rather than diachronic transfers. We worry about how to move a WordPerfect file on an IBM PC onto an Apple Macintosh equipped with Microsoft Word; we don't pause to ask how our descendants will read any of those files in a century or two, when WordPerfect, IBM, Apple Computer and even Microsoft are only dim memories.

Given all the drawbacks and disadvantages of electronic documents, why not just stick with paper? The best way of answering that question is to look back on the one other occasion in human history when a writing medium was replaced. To societies accustomed to writing on stone or clay, paper must have seemed terribly ephemeral stuff, vulnerable to fire and water, with inscribed marks that all too easily smudged or bleached away. And yet paper prevailed. Moses' tablets were stone, but the story of Moses was told on paper. The economic incentives were just too powerful to be ignored: with paper, information became far cheaper to record, to store and to transport. Exactly the same considerations argue that a transition to paperless, electronic writing is now inevitable.

35 In any case, eternity is too much to ask of any storage medium. Libraries are full of disintegrating paper books; graveyards are full of stone tablets eroded to illegibility; even languages die. Perhaps the best advice, if you must write for the ages, is this: Write very well. In the centuries to come no one will be reading your verses or your novels because they are stored as WordStar files on 1.2 megabyte floppy disks; but maybe someone will preserve the equipment needed to decipher those files and disks if that's the only way to read your deathless works.

Henry Petroski

LITTLE THINGS CAN MEAN A LOT

Many a writer on technology has been struck, in a moment of pause between sentences or an hour of distraction between paragraphs, by the extraordinariness of ordinary things. The push-button telephone, the electronic calculator, the computer on which words such as these are processed are among the more sophisticated things we use, and they can awe into silence those of us who are not electrical engineers. On the other hand, such low-tech objects as pins, thumbtacks, and paper clips are frequently and verbosely praised for their functionality and beauty of line, but are seldom the subject of study, unless it is for the sake of learning how to market something that people use much but consider little. The most common of objects are certainly not generally thought to hold lessons for technological process, prowess, or progress.

But if there are general principles that govern the evolution of technology and artifacts, then the principles must apply equally to the common and to the grand. And how much easier it may be to understand how technology works if we can pursue it in the context of something that is less intimidating than a system that takes teams of engineers years to develop. The individual complexity of supercomputers and skyscrapers, nuclear-power plants and space shuttles, distracts us from the common basic elements of technological development that underlie all things—the great and the small, the seemingly simple and the clearly complex. The individual designer and engineer involved in the creation of large systems is often lost in numerous management shuffles, and the story of the end product is frequently that of a major production with an anonymous if professional cast of thousands, no single one of whom is commonly known to be *the* designer or *the* engineer. But, although the often amateur actors in the little-theater pieces surrounding the design and development of many of our simple objects may also be anonymous as far as myriad consumers are concerned, the plot is usually much easier to follow.

Ironically, the largest and publicly most anonymous engineering structures and systems—like bridges, skyscrapers, airplanes, and power plants—are frequently produced by companies named after people. Thus we have the Burns and Roes, the Brown and Roots, the Bechtels, and the countless regional and local founder-named construction

From *The Evolution of Useful Things* (1992).

companies that ultimately shape so much of our public space and convey a sense of civic pride and achievement. We have the airplanes called Curtiss-Wrights and McDonnell-Douglases, namesakes of inventors and innovators whose pioneering has, directly or indirectly, given us the space shuttles, superjets, and even corporate jets of today. And we have the Westinghouses and the Edisons that have provided us with the electric-power stations and distribution networks that make modern life so comfortable and convenient. We have the Fords, Chryslers, Mercedes-Benzes, Rolls-Royces, and other automobiles invoking with their grilles-cum-headstones the names of long-gone entrepreneurs. Even the giant corporations called General Electric, General Motors, and General Dynamics can invoke the sense of a leader of manufacturing troops more than evoke the culmination of a concatenation of once individual and private companies.

The names commonly associated with some of the most familiar and cherished products on our desks, on the other hand, are obscure if they are known at all. Items like pins and paper clips certainly do not carry nameplates or medallions memorializing their makers. If we do examine the box that paper clips come in, it tells us our clips were made by Acco or Noesting, which hardly sound like the names of inventors or even people. Many a desk stapler reads Bostitch. Is that someone's name, or what? Modest products tend to have at best a pseudonymity that gives little hint of their inventor, but the brand name of a product and that of the company that makes it often do hold clues as to how the product evolved, and thus can give tremendous insight into the evolution of things. And the stories of their names often parallel those of the products that were developed to solve problems with, if not the downright failure of, pre-existing products.

5 On a package of Post-it notes, those little yellow slips of paper that stick to everything from irate correspondence to refrigerator doors, we can find the "Scotch" trademark and a bold "3M," which older thingophiles and trivia buffs may recall was once known as the Minnesota Mining and Manufacturing Company. How did such a seemingly self-explanatory and no-nonsense-sounding company get involved with little sticky notepads? Besides, isn't Minnesota peopled by Scandinavians rather than Scots?

In 1902 five businessmen from Two Harbors, Minnesota, formed the Minnesota Mining and Manufacturing Company to quarry what they thought was a local find of corundum, a mineral just short of diamond in hardness and thus a valuable abrasive for grinding-wheel manufacturers. The mineral proved inferior for that application, however, and so in 1905 the fledgling company turned to making sandpaper in Duluth. Difficult years followed, with new financing staving off bankruptcy, but true success in selling sandpaper could come only with a product at least as good as the other guy's.

In 1916 the company's sales manager insisted that a laboratory be formed to carry out experiments and tests to ensure quality control so that salesmen would not be embarrassed by faulty products. The laboratory in time made possible the research and development necessary to produce new and improved items in response to problems experienced by sandpaper users. Whereas a manufacturer's salesmen might say that, after quality control, the raison d'être for a company laboratory was to respond to customers' needs for new products, engineers might see a laboratory more as a troubleshooting workshop in which to deal with the horror stories of product failures and the general tales of irritating shortcomings brought home by the salesmen. In the course of troubleshooting, new products would naturally evolve to deal with objections to existing products.

In the making of sandpaper, an abrasive material is bonded to a paper backing, and the quality of the product depends not only on the quality of the principal raw materials of grit and paper, but also on how uniformly and securely they can be combined. Hence, to manufacture sandpaper it was necessary to develop an expertise in coating paper with adhesive. Unfortunately, even with good glue, the paper used in early sandpaper fell apart when wet, and so using sandpaper was necessarily a very dry and dusty operation. But in the growing automobile industry, where in the 1920s a considerable amount of sanding was needed to finish the paint on auto bodies, the dust was causing lead poisoning among workers. Making waterproof sandpaper would allow wet sanding, which in turn would cut down on dust, and thus be a great improvement. To remove the failings of existing sandpaper, the Minnesota Mining and Manufacturing Company developed a waterproof paper that one of its young lab technicians, Richard Drew, was asked to take to some St. Paul auto shops, where it might be tested. In doing so, he became aware of another problem.

The new two-tone style of painting automobiles was popular in 1925, but it presented considerable problems for auto manufacturers and body shops alike. In order to get a clean, sharp edge when applying a second paint color, the first had to be masked, of course, and this required that newspaper or butcher paper be fastened to the car body. If shop-brewed glue was used, it would sometimes stick so well that it had to be scraped off, more often than not pulling paint with it. Surgical adhesive tape was sometimes employed, but its cloth backing tended to absorb solvents from the newly sprayed paint and cause the masking materials to stick to the paint they were intended to protect. Clearly, existing means of masking had serious flaws. One day, when he was dropping off a batch of waterproof sandpaper, Drew overheard some body-shop workers cursing two-tone painting. The young technician, who had studied engineering through correspondence-school courses, promised he would make something to solve the problem.

As in the majority of design problems, Drew's objectives were most 10
clearly expressed principally in negative terms: he wished to have a kind of tape whose adhesive would not stick very readily. This not only would allow the tape to be formed in rolls from which it could easily and cleanly be removed, but also should have enabled it to be removed easily from a freshly painted auto body. Stating the problem and finding the right combination of adhesive and paper are two different things, however. The first could have come in a flash at a body shop. The latter took two years of experimenting with oils, resins, and the like, not to mention papers to which they could be applied. After many negative results and suggestions that the problem should be dropped, Drew tried some crepe paper left over from unrelated experiments and found that its crinkled surface proved to be an ideal backing. Samples of the new product were taken by the company's chief chemist to Detroit auto manufacturers, and he returned to Minnesota with orders for three carloads of Drew's masking tape.

According to company lore, the tape came to be called Scotch because on an early batch of two-inch-wide tape the adhesive was applied only to the edges, presumably since this was thought to be sufficient and even perhaps desirable for masking applications. One edge of the tape would hold the paper, the other would adhere to the auto body, and the dry middle would not stick to anything. However, with so little adhesive, the heavy paper pulled the tape off the auto body, and a frustrated painter is said to have told a salesman, "Take this tape back to your stingy Scotch bosses and tell them to put more adhesive on it." Though some company old-timers have labeled the story apocryphal, others give it credence by recalling that the incident "helped spark the inspiration for the name" of the line of pressure-sensitive adhesive tapes that now carry the tartan trademark, presumably not because the manufacturer is stingy with adhesive but, rather, because consumers can use the tape to make economical repairs on so many household items.

Cellophane was another new product in the late 1920s, and its being transparent and waterproof made it ideal for packaging everything from bakery goods to chewing gum. It was even natural to want to package masking tape in cellophane, and so someone in St. Paul was experimenting with it. At the same time, Drew was working on another problem, trying to remove his tape's shortcoming of not being waterproof and thus not being applicable in very moist environments. He got the idea of coating cellophane with his adhesive, which would certainly be a promising new tape to make clear packaging watertight.

But sticking an adhesive that works wonderfully on crepe paper onto cellophane is easier said than done, and using existing machinery to manufacture quantities of a new product made of a new material usually involves considerable experimentation and development. In the case of Scotch cellophane tape, Drew's initial attempt to make it waterproof failed to come up to expectations: "It lacked proper balance of adhesiveness, cohesiveness, elasticity and stretchiness. Furthermore, it had to perform in temperatures of 0 to 110 degrees F in humidity of 2 to 95 percent." Not surprisingly, at first it did not, and so presented some well-defined problems to be solved.

After a year of work, Drew did solve the problems, at least to a satisfactory degree for the time, and shiny-backed cellophane tape was *the* transparent tape for many years. It was used for all sorts of mending and attaching jobs, and its yellowing with age, its curling up and coming off with time, and the notorious stubbornness with which it hid its end and tore diagonally off the roll were accepted by users as just the way the tape was—nothing better was available. But inventors and tinkerers like Drew saw each shortcoming as a challenge for improvement, in part because they and their bosses knew that competitors did also. Difficulties in getting Scotch tape off the roll, for example, prompted the development of a dispenser with a built-in serrated edge to cut off a piece squarely and leave a neat edge handy for the next use. (This provides an excellent example of how the need to dispense a product properly and conveniently can give rise to a highly specialized infrastructure.)

As changes in the tape were made, new and improved versions were offered to users who wondered how they had ever gotten along with the old tape. Indeed, the company's own description of the latest version of its product can be read not only as praise for Scotch Magic Transparent Tape but also as an indictment of cellophane tape: "It unwinds easily. You can write on it. You can machine-copy through it. It's water repellent. And, unlike the earlier tape, it won't yellow or ooze adhesive with age." This list of implicit and explicit faults of the "earlier tape" sure makes it sound disgusting and inadequate, but in its day it was the cat's meow. Our expectations for a technology rise with its advancement.

15 The company that began by making an adequate sandpaper may not have foreseen the nature of its products many years hence, but the accumulation of experience in attaching adhesives of one kind or another to paper and other backings, and a receptivity to new applications of that expertise—and others accumulated along the way—enabled the Minnesota Mining and Manufacturing Company eventually to make tens of thousands of products. Since the old name no longer fully described the diverse output of the giant manufacturer, it came

to be known more and more by the abbreviation "3M," and in a recent annual report to the stockholders the full name appears only in the accounting statement.

The characteristic of 3M that enabled it to attain such diversity in its product line is a policy of what has generally come to be called "intrapreneurship." The basic idea is to allow employees of large corporations to behave within the company as they would as individual entrepreneurs in the outside world. A model intrapreneur is Art Fry, a chemical engineer who in 1974 was working in product development at 3M during the week and singing in his church choir on Sundays. He was accustomed to marking the pages in his hymnal with scraps of paper, so that he could quickly locate the songs during the two services at which he sang. The procedure worked fine for the first service, but often by the second one some of the loose scraps of paper had fallen out of their places. Fry, not having noticed this, was sometimes at a loss for words.

Fry remembered a curious adhesive—a strong and yet easily removed "unglue"—that Spencer Silver, another 3M researcher, had come upon several years earlier in the course of developing very strong and very tacky adhesives. Although it was not suited to solving his immediate problem, Silver felt the unusual adhesive might have some commercial value, and so he demonstrated it to various colleagues, including Fry. At the time, no one had come up with a use for it, and so the formula for the weak adhesive was filed away—until the Monday morning when Fry came to work with the idea of making sticky bookmarks that could also be removed without damaging the book. His initial attempts left some adhesive on the pages, and Fry has surmised that "some of the hymnal pages I tested my first notes on are probably still stuck together." But since it is 3M's policy (and that of other enlightened companies) to allow its engineers to spend a certain percentage of their work time on projects of their own choosing, a practice known as "bootlegging," Fry was able to gain access to the necessary machinery and materials and to spend nearly a year and a half experimenting and refining his idea for sticky—but not-too-sticky—slips of paper that could be used for "temporarily permanent" bookmarks and notes. While Fry wanted bookmarks to stick gently to his pages, he did not want their projecting ends to stick to each other, and so adhesive was applied at one end only. This also served well for repositionable memos and removable notes: with adhesive all over their backs, these would have been as hard to peek under and remove as labels.

When Fry thought the stick-and-remove notes were ready, he took samples to the company's marketing people, "who had to accept the idea as being commercially viable and meeting a market need" before any substantial amount of the company's own time or money was to be invested in the product. There was a general lack of enthusiasm for something that would have to sell at a premium price compared with the scratch paper it was intended to replace. (Its removable-note function was believed to hold greater commercial potential than its sticky-bookmark function.) Fry was committed to his brainchild, however, and he finally convinced an office-supply division of 3M to test-market the product, which "met an unperceived need." Early results were not at all promising, but in those cases where samples were distributed, customers became hooked. Though no prior need for the little sticky notes had been articulated, once they were in the hands of office workers all sorts of uses were found, and suddenly people couldn't do without the things. Post-it notes were generally available by mid-1980 and are now ubiquitous, even coming in long, narrow styles to accommodate the vertical writing of Japanese. It might be argued that they have reduced the recycling of scrap paper as scratch paper and bookmarks, but the removable notes do have the conservatory potential of eliminating the use of unsightly and damaging tape and staples for posting notes and announcements in public places.

Years ago, when I would meet my dean walking across campus to the Engineering School, as we approached the building he would invariably remove the numerous announcements of meetings, parties, and kittens for adoption that had been taped or tacked to the door since his last entrance. He carefully peeled off the tape that made posting notices so easy but maintaining an attractive entrance to a school so difficult. The dean explained on more than one occasion how the tape could become difficult to remove if it stayed up over several days and nights, and how it had ruined some freshly painted walls, which had had to be patched and repainted. The dean was not opposed to notices, but to the damage that their attachment did to the main entrance to his school. How he might have loved Post-it notes and dreamed of them in poster sizes.

20 Post-it notes provide but one example of a technological artifact that has evolved from a perceived failure of existing artifacts to function without frustrating. Again, it is not that form follows function but, rather, that the form of one thing follows from the failure of another thing to function as we would like. Whether it be bookmarks that fail to stay in place or taped-on notes that fail to leave a once-nice surface clean and intact, their failure and perceived failure is what leads to the true evolution of artifacts. That the perception of failure may take centuries to develop, as in the case of loose bookmarks, does not reduce the importance of the principle in shaping our world.

Stephen Jay Gould

DARWIN'S MIDDLE ROAD

"We began to sail up the narrow strait lamenting," narrates Odysseus. "For on the one hand lay Scylla, with twelve feet all dangling down; and six necks exceeding long, and on each a hideous head, and therein three rows of teeth set thick and close, full of black death. And on the other mighty Charybdis sucked down the salt sea water. As often as she belched it forth, like a cauldron on a great fire she would seethe up through all her troubled deeps." Odysseus managed to swerve around Charybdis, but Scylla grabbed six of his finest men and devoured them in his sight—"the most pitiful thing mine eyes have seen of all my travail in searching out the paths of the sea."

False lures and dangers often come in pairs in our legends and metaphors—consider the frying pan and the fire, or the devil and the deep blue sea. Prescriptions for avoidance either emphasize a dogged steadiness—the straight and narrow of Christian evangelists—or an averaging between unpleasant alternatives—the golden mean of Aristotle. The idea of steering a course between undesirable extremes emerges as a central prescription for a sensible life.

The nature of scientific creativity is both a perennial topic of discussion and a prime candidate for seeking a golden mean. The two extreme positions have not been directly competing for allegiance of the unwary. They have, rather, replaced each other sequentially, with one now in the ascendency, the other eclipsed.

The first—inductivism—held that great scientists are primarily great observers and patient accumulators of information. For new and significant theory, the inductivists claimed, can only arise from a firm foundation of facts. In this architectural view, each fact is a brick in a structure built without blueprints. Any talk or thought about theory (the completed building) is fatuous and premature before the bricks are set. Inductivism once commanded great prestige within science, and even represented an "official" position of sorts, for it touted, however falsely, the utter honesty, complete objectivity, and almost automatic nature of scientific progress towards final and incontrovertible truth.

Yet, as its critics so rightly claimed, inductivism also depicted sci- 5
ence as a heartless, almost inhuman discipline offering no legitimate place to quirkiness, intuition, and all the other subjective attributes

From *The Panda's Thumb* (1980).

adhering to our vernacular notion of genius. Great scientists, the critics claimed, are distinguished more by their powers of hunch and synthesis, than their skill in experiment or observation. The criticisms of inductivism are certainly valid and I welcome its dethroning during the past thirty years as a necessary prelude to better understanding. Yet, in attacking it so strongly, some critics have tried to substitute an alternative equally extreme and unproductive in its emphasis on the essential subjectivity of creative thought. In this "eureka" view, creativity is an ineffable something, accessible only to persons of genius. It arises like a bolt of lightning, unanticipated, unpredictable and unanalyzable—but the bolts strike only a few special people. We ordinary mortals must stand in awe and thanks. (The name refers, of course, to the legendary story of Archimedes running naked through the streets of Syracuse shouting eureka [I have discovered it] when water displaced by his bathing body washed the scales abruptly from his eyes and suggested a method for measuring volumes.)

I am equally disenchanted by both these opposing extremes. Inductivism reduces genius to dull, rote operations; eurekaism grants it an inaccessible status more in the domain of intrinsic mystery than in a realm where we might understand and learn from it. Might we not marry the good features of each view, and abandon both the elitism of eurekaism and the pedestrian qualities of inductivism? May we not acknowledge the personal and subjective character of creativity, but still comprehend it as a mode of thinking that emphasizes or exaggerates capacities sufficiently common to all of us that we may at least understand if not hope to imitate?

In the hagiography of science, a few men hold such high positions that all arguments must apply to them if they are to have any validity. Charles Darwin, as the principal saint of evolutionary biology, has therefore been presented both as an inductivist and as a primary example of eurekaism. I will attempt to show that these interpretations are equally inadequate, and that recent scholarship on Darwin's own odyssey towards the theory of natural selection supports an intermediate position.

So great was the prestige of inductivism in his own day, that Darwin himself fell under its sway and, as an old man, falsely depicted his youthful accomplishments in its light. In an autobiography, written as a lesson in morality for his children and not intended for publication, he penned some famous lines that misled historians for nearly a hundred years. Describing his path to the theory of natural selection, he claimed: "I worked on true Baconian principles, and without any theory collected facts on a wholesale scale."[1]

1. Francis Bacon (1561–1626), English philosopher, statesman, and essayist, and the first apostle of inductivism.

The inductivist interpretation focuses on Darwin's five years aboard the *Beagle* and explains his transition from a student for the ministry to the nemesis of preachers as the result of his keen powers of observation applied to the whole world. Thus, the traditional story goes, Darwin's eyes opened wider and wider as he saw, in sequence, the bones of giant South American fossil mammals, the turtles and finches of the Galapagos, and the marsupial fauna of Australia. The truth of evolution and its mechanism of natural selection crept up gradually upon him as he sifted facts in a sieve of utter objectivity.

The inadequacies of this tale are best illustrated by the falsity of its conventional premier example—the so-called Darwin's finches of the Galapagos. We now know that although these birds share a recent and common ancestry on the South American mainland, they have radiated into an impressive array of species on the outlying Galapagos. Few terrestrial species manage to cross the wide oceanic barrier between South America and the Galapagos. But the fortunate migrants often find a sparsely inhabited world devoid of the competitors that limit their opportunities on the crowded mainland. Hence, the finches evolved into roles normally occupied by other birds and developed their famous set of adaptations for feeding—seed crushing, insect eating, even grasping and manipulating a cactus needle to dislodge insects from plants. Isolation—both of the islands from the mainland and among the islands themselves—provided an opportunity for separation, independent adaptation, and speciation.

According to the traditional view, Darwin discovered these finches, correctly inferred their history, and wrote the famous lines in his notebook: "If there is the slightest foundation for these remarks the zoology of Archipelagoes will be worth examining; for such facts would undermine the stability of Species." But, as with so many heroic tales from Washington's cherry tree to the piety of Crusaders, hope rather than truth motivates the common reading. Darwin found the finches to be sure. But he didn't recognize them as variants of a common stock. In fact, he didn't even record the island of discovery for many of them—some of his labels just read "Galapagos Islands." So much for his immediate recognition of the role of isolation in the formation of new species. He reconstructed the evolutionary tale only after his return to London, when a British Museum ornithologist correctly identified all the birds as finches.

The famous quotation from his notebook refers to Galapagos tortoises and to the claim of native inhabitants that they can "at once pronounce from which Island any Tortoise may have been brought" from subtle differences in size and shape of body and scales. This is a statement of different, and much reduced, order from the traditional tale of finches. For the finches are true and separate species—a living example of evolution. The subtle differences among tortoises represent minor geographic variation within a species. It is a jump in reasoning, albeit a valid one as we now know, to argue that such small differences can be amplified to produce a new species. All creationists, after all, acknowledged geographic variation (consider human races), but argued that it could not proceed beyond the rigid limits of a created archetype.

I don't wish to downplay the pivotal influence of the *Beagle* voyage on Darwin's career. It gave him space, freedom and endless time to think in his favored mode of independent self-stimulation. (His ambivalence towards university life, and his middling performance there by conventional standards, reflected his unhappiness with a curriculum of received wisdom.) He writes from South America in 1834: "I have not one clear idea about cleavage, stratification, lines of upheaval. I have no books, which tell me much and what they do I cannot apply to what I see. In consequence I draw my own conclusions, and most gloriously ridiculous ones they are." The rocks and plants and animals that he saw did provoke him to the crucial attitude of doubt—midwife of all creativity. Sydney, Australia—1836. Darwin wonders why a rational God would create so many marsupials on Australia since nothing about its climate or geography suggests any superiority for pouches: "I had been lying on a sunny bank and was reflecting on the strange character of the animals of this country as compared to the rest of the World. An unbeliever in everything beyond his own reason might exclaim, 'Surely two distinct Creators must have been at work.' "

Nonetheless, Darwin returned to London without an evolutionary theory. He suspected the truth of evolution, but had no mechanism to explain it. Natural selection did not arise from any direct reading of the *Beagle*'s facts, but from two subsequent years of thought and struggle as reflected in a series of remarkable notebooks that have been unearthed and published during the past twenty years. In these notebooks, we see Darwin testing and abandoning a number of theories and pursuing a multitude of false leads—so much for his later claim about recording facts with an empty mind. He read philosophers, poets, and economists, always searching for meaning and insight—so much for the notion that natural selection arose inductively from the *Beagle*'s facts. Later, he labelled one notebook as "full of metaphysics on morals."

15 Yet if this tortuous path belies the Scylla of inductivism, it has engendered an equally simplistic myth—the Charybdis of eurekaism. In his maddeningly misleading autobiography, Darwin does record a eureka and suggests that natural selection struck him as a sudden, serendipitous flash after more than a year of groping frustration:

> In October 1838, that is, fifteen months after I had begun my systematic inquiry, I happened to read for amusement Malthus on Population,[2] and being well prepared to appreciate the struggle for existence which everywhere goes on from long-continued observation of the habits of animals and plants, it at once struck me that under these circumstances favorable variations would tend to be preserved, and unfavorable ones to be destroyed. The result of this would be the formation of new species. Here, then, I had at last got a theory by which to work.

Yet, again, the notebooks belie Darwin's later recollections—in this case by their utter failure to record, at the time it happened, any special exultation over his Malthusian insight. He inscribes it as a fairly short and sober entry without a single exclamation point, though he habitually used two or three in moments of excitement. He did not drop everything and reinterpret a confusing world in its light. On the very next day, he wrote an even longer passage on the sexual curiosity of primates.

The theory of natural selection arose neither as a workmanlike induction from nature's facts, nor as a mysterious bolt from Darwin's subconscious, triggered by an accidental reading of Malthus. It emerged instead as the result of a conscious and productive search, proceeding in a ramifying but ordered manner, and utilizing both the facts of natural history and an astonishingly broad range of insights from disparate disciplines far from his own. Darwin trod the middle path between inductivism and eurekaism. His genius is neither pedestrian nor inaccessible.

Darwinian scholarship has exploded since the centennial of the *Origin*[3] in 1959. The publication of Darwin's notebooks and the attention devoted by several scholars to the two crucial years between the *Beagle*'s docking and the demoted Malthusian insight has clinched the argument for a "middle path" theory of Darwin's creativity. Two particularly important works focus on the broadest and narrowest scales. Howard E. Gruber's masterful intellectual and psychological biography of this phase in Darwin's life, *Darwin on Man*, traces all the false leads and turning points in Darwin's search. Gruber shows that Darwin was continually proposing, testing, and abandoning hypotheses, and that he never simply collected facts in a blind way. He began with a fanciful theory involving the idea that new species arise with a prefixed life span, and worked his way gradually, if fitfully, towards an idea of extinction by competition in a world of struggle. He recorded no exultation upon reading Malthus, because the jigsaw puzzle was only missing a piece or two at the time.

2. Thomas Malthus (1766–1834), whose work on population was published under several titles between 1798 and 1817.
3. *The Origin of Species* (1859).

Silvan S. Schweber has reconstructed, in detail as minute as the record will allow, Darwin's activities during the few weeks before Malthus (The Origin of the *Origin* Revisited, *Journal of the History of Biology*, 1977). He argues that the final pieces arose not from new facts in natural history, but from Darwin's intellectual wanderings in distant fields. In particular, he read a long review of social scientist and philosopher Auguste Comte's most famous work, the *Cours de philosophie positive.*[4] He was particularly struck by Comte's insistence that a proper theory be predictive and at least potentially quantitative. He then turned to Dugald Stewart's *On the Life and Writing of Adam Smith*, and imbibed the basic belief of the Scottish economists that theories of overall social structure must begin by analyzing the unconstrained actions of individuals. (Natural selection is, above all, a theory about the struggle of individual organisms for success in reproduction.) Then, searching for quantification, he read a lengthy analysis of work by the most famous statistician of his time—the Belgian Adolphe Quetelet. In the review of Quetelet, he found, among other things, a forceful statement of Malthus's quantitative claim—that population would grow geometrically and food supplies only arithmetically, thus guaranteeing an intense struggle for existence. In fact, Darwin had read the Malthusian statement several times before; but only now was he prepared to appreciate its significance. Thus, he did not turn to Malthus by accident, and he already knew what it contained. His "amusement," we must assume, consisted only in a desire to read in its original formulation the familiar statement that had so impressed him in Quetelet's secondary account.

20 In reading Schweber's detailed account of the moments preceding Darwin's formulation of natural selection, I was particularly struck by the absence of deciding influence from his own field of biology. The immediate precipitators were a social scientist, an economist, and a statistician. If genius has any common denominator, I would propose breadth of interest and the ability to construct fruitful analogies between fields.

In fact, I believe that the theory of natural selection should be viewed as an extended analogy—whether conscious or unconscious on Darwin's part I do not know—to the laissez faire economics of Adam Smith. The essence of Smith's argument is a paradox of sorts: if you want an ordered economy providing maximal benefits to all, then let individuals compete and struggle for their own advantages. The result, after appropriate sorting and elimination of the inefficient, will be a stable and harmonious polity. Apparent order arises naturally from the struggle among individuals, not from predestined principles or higher

4. *Course in Positivist Philosophy* (1830–1842).

control. Dugald Stewart epitomized Smith's system in the book Darwin read:

> The most effective plan for advancing a people . . . is by allowing every man, as long as he observes the rules of justice, to pursue his own interest in his own way, and to bring both his industry and his capital into the freest competition with those of his fellow citizens. Every system of policy which endeavors . . . to draw towards a particular species of industry a greater share of the capital of the society than would naturally go to it . . . is, in reality, subversive of the great purpose which it means to promote.

As Schweber states: "The Scottish analysis of society contends that the combined effect of individual actions results in the institutions upon which society is based, and that such a society is a stable and evolving one and functions without a designing and directing mind."

We know that Darwin's uniqueness does not reside in his support for the idea of evolution—scores of scientists had preceded him in this. His special contribution rests upon his documentation and upon the novel character of his theory about how evolution operates. Previous evolutionists had proposed unworkable schemes based on internal perfecting tendencies and inherent directions. Darwin advocated a natural and testable theory based on immediate interaction among individuals (his opponents considered it heartlessly mechanistic). The theory of natural selection is a creative transfer to biology of Adam Smith's basic argument for a rational economy: the balance and order of nature does not arise from a higher, external (divine) control, or from the existence of laws operating directly upon the whole, but from struggle among individuals for their own benefits (in modern terms, for the transmission of their genes to future generations through differential success in reproduction).

Many people are distressed to hear such an argument. Does it not compromise the integrity of science if some of its primary conclusions originate by analogy from contemporary politics and culture rather than from data of the discipline itself? In a famous letter to Engels, Karl Marx identified the similarities between natural selection and the English social scene:

> It is remarkable how Darwin recognizes among beasts and plants his English society with its division of labor, competition, opening up of new markets, 'invention,' and the Malthusian 'struggle for existence.' It is Hobbes' *bellum omnium contra omnes* (the war of all against all).[5]

Yet Marx was a great admirer of Darwin—and in this apparent paradox lies resolution. For reasons involving all the themes I have empha-

5. From the English philosopher Thomas Hobbes's *Leviathan* (1651).

sized here—that inductivism is inadequate, that creativity demands breadth, and that analogy is a profound source of insight—great thinkers cannot be divorced from their social background. But the source of an idea is one thing; its truth or fruitfulness is another. The psychology and utility of discovery are very different subjects indeed. Darwin may have cribbed the idea of natural selection from economics, but it may still be right. As the German socialist Karl Kautsky wrote in 1902: "The fact that an idea emanates from a particular class, or accords with their interests, of course proves nothing as to its truth or falsity." In this case, it is ironic that Adam Smith's system of laissez faire does not work in his own domain of economics, for it leads to oligopoly and revolution, rather than to order and harmony. Struggle among individuals does, however, seem to be the law of nature.

Many people use such arguments about social context to ascribe great insights primarily to the indefinable phenomenon of good luck. Thus, Darwin was lucky to be born rich, lucky to be on the *Beagle*, lucky to live amidst the ideas of his age, lucky to trip over Parson Malthus—essentially little more than a man in the right place at the right time. Yet, when we read of his personal struggle to understand, the breadth of his concerns and study, and the directedness of his search for a mechanism of evolution, we understand why Pasteur made his famous quip that fortune favors the prepared mind.[6]

6. Louis Pasteur (1822–1895), French chemist.

QUESTIONS

1. *What, according to Gould, constituted Darwin's scientific research? How and why did he falsely depict it in his autobiography (paragraph 8)?*
2. *Rather than isolating scientific research from social and political experience, Darwin, Gould explains, was influenced by a social scientist, an economist, and a statistician (paragraph 20). Identify each one and explain what he contributed to Darwin's theory of natural selection.*
3. *Consider a recent experience of writing an essay. Did you, thinking and writing, shuttle between inductivism and prediction as Gould claims Darwin did? Describe your experience using Gould's analytic vocabulary.*

Evelyn Fox Keller

WOMEN IN SCIENCE: A SOCIAL ANALYSIS

Are women's minds different from men's minds? In spite of the women's movement, the age-old debate centering around this question continues. We are surrounded by evidence of *de facto* differences between men's and women's intellects—in the problems that interest them, in the ways they try to solve those problems, and in the professions they choose. Even though it has become fashionable to view such differences as environmental in origin, the temptation to seek an explanation in terms of innate differences remains a powerful one.

Perhaps the area in which this temptation is strongest is in science. Even those of us who would like to argue for intellectual equality are hard pressed to explain the extraordinarily meager representation of women in science, particularly in the upper echelons. Some would argue that the near absence of great women scientists demonstrates that women don't have the minds for true scientific creativity. While most of us would recognize the patent fallacies of this argument, it nevertheless causes us considerable discomfort. After all, the doors of the scientific establishment appear to have been open to women for some time now—shouldn't we begin to see more women excelling?

In the last fifty years the institutional barriers against women in science have been falling. During most of that time, the percentage of women scientists has declined, although recent years have begun to show an upswing (Table 1). Of those women who do become scientists, few are represented in the higher academic ranks (Table 2). In order to have a proper understanding of these data, it is necessary to review the many influences that operate. I would like to argue that the

First appeared in *Harvard Magazine* (Oct. 1974).

TABLE 1
PERCENTAGE OF PH.D.'S EARNED BY WOMEN, 1920–1970

	1920–29	*1940–49*	*1950–59*	*1960–69*
Physics and Astronomy	5.9	4.2	2.0	2.2
Biological Sciences	19.5	15.7	11.8	15.1
Mathematics	14.5	10.7	5.0	5.7
Psychology	29.4	24.1	14.8	20.7

Source: National Research Council.

TABLE 2
PERCENTAGE REPRESENTATION OF WOMEN, BY RANK, IN 20 LEADING UNIVERSITIES
(1962)

	Instructor	*Assistant Professor*	*Associate Professor*	*Professor*
Physics	5.6	1.2	1.3	0.9
Biological Sciences	16.3	7.1	6.7	1.3
Mathematics	16.7	10.1	7.3	0.4
Psychology	8.3	10.4	11.1	2.7

Source: J. B. Parrish. A.A.U.W. Journal, 55, 99.

convenient explanation that men's minds are intrinsically different from women's is not only unwarranted by the evidence, but in fact reflects a mythology that is in itself a major contribution to the phenomena observed.

As a woman scientist, I have often pondered these questions, particularly at those times when my commitment to science seemed most precarious. Noticing that almost every other woman I had known in science had experienced similar crises of commitment, I sought to explain my ambivalence by concluding that science as a profession is not as gratifying for women as it is for men, and that the reasons for this are to be found in the intrinsic nature of women and science. Several years ago, I endeavored to find out how general my own experiences were. In studying the statistics of success and failure for women in the professions, I indeed found that women fared less well in science than in other professions, although the picture that emerged seemed fairly bleak for all of us.

5 I collected these data during a leave of absence I had taken to accompany my husband to California. At the same time, I was also engaged in completing work I had begun the year before with a (male) colleague—work that seemed less and less compelling as the year wore on. Each week I would receive an enthusiastic telephone call from my colleague, reporting new information and responses he had received from workers he had met while delivering invited lectures on this work. At some point it occurred to me that perhaps there was a relation between my declining interest and isolation on the one hand, and his growing enthusiasm and public recognition on the other. Over the course of the year, he had received a score or more invitations to speak about this work, while I had received none. It began to dawn on me that there were far simpler explanations for both the observations I had made privately and the data I was collecting than that of intrinsic differences between the sexes.

I began to realize, for example, that had I been less isolated and more rewarded, my enthusiasm would have been correspondingly greater—a recognition that has been amply corroborated by my subsequent experience. Upon further reflection, I became aware of how much my own, and other similar, attitudes are influenced by a complex interplay of subtle factors affecting us from birth on. The ways in which we rear our children, train our students, and interact with our colleagues are all so deeply imbued with our expectations and beliefs as to virtually guarantee a fulfillment of these beliefs.

How do men and women develop the characteristics we attribute to them? There are clear differences between the sexes at birth, and there is even some evidence that these differences extend to the brain. Primate studies reveal marked differences in behavior between males and females—differences determined by the prenatal hormonal environment. It seems therefore quite possible that there are even intellectual differences determined prior to birth. For those inclined to believe in such predetermination, such a possibility may appear attractive. It is important to say, however, that there is to date no evidence for biologically determined differences in intelligence or cognitive styles, and that this remains true in spite of a rather considerable desire among many people to find such evidence.

An example of this interest is provided by the great enthusiasm with which a recent study was met. This study purported to show that prenatal injection of progestin, a synthetic male hormone, leads to higher than average I.Q.'s in adolescent girls. Although this result was refuted by the original authors shortly after its original announcement, it nevertheless found its way into a rash of textbooks, where it remains. Similarly, there has been a great deal of interest in the measurement of differences in perceptual modes between girls and boys. Tests designed to measure the degree to which one's perception of a figure is independent of its background, or field, show that girls, by the time they enter school, are more field-dependent than boys. Field independence is positively correlated with mathematical and analytic abilities. While the results of these tests are remarkably culturally invariant (the Eskimos are a notable exception), it is important to point out both that the disparities observed are extremely small (of the order of 2 percent) and that they cannot be discerned before the age of five. While the possibility that these disparities are the result of innate differences between the sexes cannot be excluded, there is evidence relating performance on such tests to the individual's environment. What are the environmental differences that could account for such results?

We treat our sons and daughters differently from birth onward, although the magnitude of our distinction is largely unconscious. A rude awakening to the extent of our differential treatment can come in those rare instances when a fallacious sex assignment is made at birth, usually as a result of ambiguous genitalia, and must be subsequently corrected. The impact of these early cues can be assessed by the fact that such reassignments are considered unduly traumatic to make after the child is eighteen months old, in spite of the fact that failure to do so dooms the child to an apparent sexual identity at odds with his or her genotype. Sex reassignments made before that time result in apparently normal development. From this and related evidence, workers in this area have concluded that gender identity appears to be established, primarily on the basis of parental treatment, by the age of eighteen months.

10 Children acquire the meaning of their sex identity from the models before them. Their concept of female is based largely on the women they see, as their concept of male is based on the men they see. Their immediate perceptions are later expanded by the images they perceive on TV, and in children's literature. It hardly need be pointed out that both of the latter present to our children extraordinarily rigid stereotypes.

It is not surprising, then, that children, even before they enter school, have acquired the belief that certain activities are male and others female. Science is a male activity.

The tenacity of this early view is such as to resist easy change. When my daughter was in nursery school, her class was asked one day about the occupation of their fathers. I objected to this, and, as a result, the next day the teacher asked, "Sarah, what does your mother do?" She replied, "My mother cooks, she sews, she cleans, and she takes care of us." "But Sarah, isn't your mother a scientist?" "Oh, yes," said Sarah—clearly implying that this was not a very relevant piece of information.

The explanation of her response lies not only in her need to define a conventional image of her mother, but also in the reality of her direct perceptions. Indeed it is true that, like many professional women, I do cook, sew, clean, and take care of my children. My professional identity is not brought into my home, although my husband's is. My daughter, therefore, like my son, continues to view mathematics and science as male, in spite of their information to the contrary.

While a child may be concerned with assigning sex labels only to external attributes, such as clothes, mannerisms, and occupations, the adolescent has already begun to designate internal states as male and female. Thus, in particular, clear thinking is characterized as hard thinking (a male image), and fuzzy thinking as soft thinking (a female image). A girl who thinks clearly and well is told she thinks "like a man." What are the implications of such associations for the girl who (for whatever reasons) does transcend social expectation and finds herself interested in science? Confusion in sexual identity is the inevitable concomitant of a self-definition at variance with the surrounding definitions of sexual norm. The girl who can take pride in "thinking like a man" without cost to her integrity as a girl is rare indeed.

15 Nevertheless, a considerable number of women, for whatever reasons, experience enough motivation and have demonstrated enough ability to embark on professional training for a scientific career. Graduate school is a time to prove that one is, in spite of one's aspirations, a woman, and—at one and the same time, because of one's aspirations—"more than" a woman. Social acceptability requires the former, and is considerably facilitated by the acquisition of a husband, while professional respectability requires the latter. The more exclusively male the definition of the profession, the more difficult it is to accomplish these conflicting goals.

My own experience as a graduate student of theoretical physics at Harvard was extreme, but possibly illustrative. I was surrounded by incessant prophecies of failure, independent of my performance. I knew of no counter-examples to draw confidence from, and was led to believe that none existed. (Later, however, I learned that some women in theoretical physics have survived, even at Harvard.) Warned that I would ultimately despair as I came to learn how impossible my ambitions were, I did, though not for the reasons that were then implied. Having denied myself rage, depression was in fact one of the few reasonable responses to the isolation, mockery, and suspicion that I experienced, both within and without my department. Ultimately I did earn my Ph.D. from the Harvard physics department, but only after having adapted my interests and thereby removed myself from the most critical pressures—a course many women have taken before and since.

Hostility, however, was not the only response I received, and not necessarily the usual response experienced by professionally ambitious young women. The necessity of proving one's femininity leaves some women particularly susceptible to another danger—that of accepting, and even seeking, sexual approbation for intellectual and academic performance. There are enough men willing, if not eager, to provide such translated affirmation as to make this a serious problem. The relation between sexuality and intellectuality is an enormously complex subject. I raise it only to point out one perhaps obvious consequence of this confusion for women. Because, unlike men, they are often dependent on sexual and intellectual affirmation from one and the same individual or group, they can never be entirely confident of what is being affirmed. Is it an "A for a Lay" or a "Lay for an A"?

Finally, the female scientist is launched. What are her prospects? Many women choose this point to withdraw for a time in order to have children. Although there is a logic to this choice, it reflects a lack of awareness of the dynamics of normal professional growth. For the male scientist, the period immediately following acquisition of the Ph.D. is perhaps the most critical in his professional development. It is the time that he has, free of all the responsibilities that will later come to plague him, to accomplish enough work to establish his reputation. Often it is a time to affiliate himself with a school of thought, to prove his own independent worth. Although this may have been the original function of the graduate training period, it has in recent times been displaced to the postgraduate years. Awareness of this displacement, of the critical importance of these years, has not permeated to the general public, or even, for the most part, to the science student. Many women therefore take this sometimes fatal step in ignorance. After having been out of a field for a few years, they usually find it next to impossible to return to their field except in the lowest-level positions. Only when it is too late do they learn that it would have been better to have their children first, before completing the Ph.D.

I need hardly enumerate the additional practical difficulties involved in combining a scientific (or any other) career with the raising of children. While the practical drains on one's time and energy are generally recognized, perhaps it is worth pointing out that the drains on one's intellectual energy are not generally recognized by men. Only those men who have spent full time, for an extended period, caring for their children are aware of the extraordinary amount of mental space occupied by the thousand and one details and concerns that mothers routinely juggle. Many have come to the conclusion—beginning with Engels,[1] and more recently including the Swedish government—that equality of the sexes in the work and professional force is not a realistic possibility until the sex roles in the family are radically redefined. Equality must begin at home.

20 Well, one might ask, what about those women in science who have no children, who never marry? Surely they are freed from all of these difficulties. Why don't they perform better?

First of all, to be freed of responsibilities towards others is not equivalent to having your own responsibilities assumed by others. Nowhere among women is to be found the counterpart of the male scientist who has a wife at home to look after his daily needs. The question, however, deserves a more serious answer, although the answer is almost painfully obvious. Our society does not have a place for unmar-

1. Friedrich Engels (1820–1895), German Socialist and, with Karl Marx, author of *The Communist Manifesto.*

ried women. They are among the most isolated, ostracized groups of our culture. When one thinks about the daily social and psychological pressures on the unmarried professional woman, one can hardly be surprised to discover that the data reveal that indeed, on the average, married women in science—even with children—publish more and perform better than unmarried women.

The enumeration of obstacles or handicaps faced by women in science would hardly be complete without at least a reference to the inequalities of reward and approval awarded to work done by men and women. The personal anecdote I began with is more than an anecdote—it is evidence of a rather ubiquitous tendency, neither malicious nor necessarily even conscious, to give more public recognition to a man's accomplishments than to a woman's accomplishments. There are many different reasons for this—not least of which includes the habitually lesser inclination of many women to put themselves forward. There is also a simple, although documented, difference in evaluation of the actual work done by men and women.

While all of the above difficulties are hardly exclusive problems of women in science, the question of identity in what has been defined as an almost exclusively male profession is more serious for women in science than in other fields. Not only is the field defined as male by virtue of its membership, it is also defined as male in relation to its methodology, style of thought, indeed its goals. To the extent that analytic thought is conceived as male thought, to the extent that we characterize the natural sciences as the "hard" sciences, to the extent that the procedure of science is to "attack" problems, and its goal, since Bacon,[2] has been to "conquer" or "master" nature, a woman in science *must* in some way feel alien.

Traditionally, as in other similar situations, women who have succeeded in scientific careers have dealt with this conflict by identifying with the "aggressor"—incorporating its values and ideals, at the cost, inevitably, of separating themselves from their own sex. An alternative resolution, one opted for frequently in other professions, is to attempt to redefine one's subject so as to permit a more comfortable identification with it. It is in this way, and for this reason, that so many professional women root themselves in subjects that are viewed by the profession as peripheral. In science this is not easy to do, but perhaps not impossible. There is another tradition within science that is as replete with female images as the tradition that dominates today is replete with male images. We all know that the most creative science re-

2. Francis Bacon (1561–1626), English thinker who argued for a scientific methodology based on experimentation.

quires, in addition to a hardness of mind, also fertility and receptivity. The best scientists are those who have combined the two sets of images. It may be that a certain degree of intellectual security is necessary in order to permit the expression of both "male" and "female" thought in science. If women have first to prove their "male" qualifications for admission into the profession, they may never achieve the necessary confidence to allow themselves to use their "female" abilities. What is to be done?

25 The central theme of my discussion is that the differential performance of men and women in science, the apparent differences between conceptual styles of men and women everywhere, are the result, not so much of innate differences between the sexes, but rather of the myth that prevails throughout our culture identifying certain kinds of thinking as male and others as female. The consequent compartmentalization of our minds is as effective as if it had been biologically, and not socially, induced.

People conform to the expectations imposed upon them in the evolution of their definition of sexual identity, thus confirming the very myth upon which these expectations are based. Such a process is not easy to change. Myths as deeply rooted and as self-affirming as this one can neither be wished nor willed away. The only hope is to chip away at it everywhere, to make enough small inroads so that future generations may ultimately grow up less hampered. Counter-measures can be effected at every stage of the process. Each may be of only limited effectiveness, but cumulatively they may permit enough women to emerge with intact, fully developed mental capacities—women who can serve as role models for future generations of students.

Specifically, we can begin by exerting a conscious effort to raise our children to less rigid stereotypes. Although the full extent to which we differentiate our treatment of our sons and daughters is hidden from us, being largely unconscious, we can, by attending to what we do, raise our consciousness of our own behavior.

We can specifically encourage and reward interests and abilities that survive social pressures. As teachers, men can consciously refrain from mixing academic with sexual approval. More generally, we can inform women students interested in science about the realities of the external difficulties they will face. It is all too easy for an individual experiencing such obstacles to internalize the responsibility for these obstacles. Specific advice can be given—for instance, to avoid interrupting a career immediately after the Ph.D. High-quality work by professional women can be sought out for recognition and encouragement in order to counteract the normal tendency to grant them less recognition. (The physicist Ernest Courant, a very wise man, responded to the news that one of his most talented students was pregnant by giving her a raise—thus enabling her to hire competent help, and, simultaneously, obligating her to continue. After four such raises, she indeed did go on to become one of the country's better mathematicians.)

Extra care can be taken not to exclude women from professional interaction on any level. Finally, hiring policies must take into account the human and political realities. Women students need role models if they are to mature properly. Providing such a model is an important part of the function of a faculty member and should be considered along with scholarly performance in hiring deliberations. Similarly, marriage is a social reality, and women scientists who marry male scientists need jobs in the same area. Anti-nepotism hiring policies discriminate against women scientists, and even a neutral policy effectively does so as well. Universities might well consider pro-nepotism policies that would recognize the limitations of humans and geographical reality.

Most of the recommendations I have made require the cooperation 30
of the male scientific community to implement. Why should they? Further, one may ask, why should women even be encouraged to become scientists when the list of odds against them is so overwhelming? Is a career in science intrinsically of so much greater value than other options more available to women?

I don't believe it is. Nevertheless, our society has become more and more technologically oriented. As we continue to move in this direction, as we come to attach increasing importance to scientific and technological know-how, women are threatened with a disenfranchisement possibly greater than ever before. The traditional role of the woman becomes increasingly eroded with technology and overpopulation, while the disparity between the more humanly oriented kinds of knowledge thought to be hers and the more technical kinds of knowledge operating in the real world grows larger. This disparity operates not only at the expense of the women who are thus barred from meaningful roles in society, but also at the expense of the society that has been content to relegate to women those more humanistic values we all claim to support.

Finally, myths that compartmentalize our minds by defining certain mental attributes as "male" and others as "female" leave us all functioning with only part of our minds. Though there may well be some innate biological differences between the sexes, there is hardly room for doubt that our preconceptions serve to exaggerate and rigidify any distinctions that might exist. These preconceptions operate as straitjackets for men and women alike. I believe that the best, most creative science, like the most creative human efforts of any kind, can only be achieved with a full, unhampered mind—if you like, an androgynous mind. Therefore, the giving up of the central myth that science is a product of male thought may well lead to a more creative, more imaginative, and, who knows, possibly even a more humanistic science.

QUESTIONS

1. *To what uses does Fox Keller put her own experience in "Women in Science: A Social Analysis"?*
2. *Fox Keller includes two tables. Where and how does she interpret them? Are other interpretations and additional interpretations possible? Should the tables be updated? Why?*
3. *Write an essay in which you contextualize something in your own experience through statistical analysis. Some possibilities: grades, choice of major, choice of career, family composition, income, racial and/or ethnic origins, and gender.*

Literature and the Arts

Eudora Welty

ONE WRITER'S BEGINNINGS

I learned from the age of two or three that any room in our house, at any time of day, was there to read in, or to be read to. My mother read to me. She'd read to me in the big bedroom in the mornings, when we were in her rocker together, which ticked in rhythm as we rocked, as though we had a cricket accompanying the story. She'd read to me in the diningroom on winter afternoons in front of the coal fire, with our cuckoo clock ending the story with "Cuckoo," and at night when I'd got in my own bed. I must have given her no peace. Sometimes she read to me in the kitchen while she sat churning, and the churning sobbed along with *any* story. It was my ambition to have her read to me while *I* churned; once she granted my wish, but she read off my story before I brought her butter. She was an expressive reader. When she was reading "Puss in Boots,"[1] for instance, it was impossible not to know that she distrusted *all* cats.

It had been startling and disappointing to me to find out that story books had been written by *people*, that books were not natural wonders, coming up of themselves like grass. Yet regardless of where they came from, I cannot remember a time when I was not in love with them—with the books themselves, cover and binding and the paper they were printed on, with their smell and their weight and with their possession in my arms, captured and carried off to myself. Still illiterate, I was ready for them, committed to all the reading I could give them.

From a set of three lectures delivered at Harvard University in April 1983, to inaugurate the William E. Massey lecture series; later published as *One Writer's Beginnings* (1984).

1. A fairy tale.

Neither of my parents had come from homes that could afford to buy many books, but though it must have been something of a strain on his salary, as the youngest officer in a young insurance company, my father was all the while carefully selecting and ordering away for what he and Mother thought we children should grow up with. They bought first for the future.

Besides the bookcase in the livingroom, which was always called "the library," there were the encyclopedia tables and dictionary stand under windows in our diningroom. Here to help us grow up arguing around the diningroom table were the Unabridged Webster, the Columbia Encyclopedia, Compton's Pictured Encyclopedia, the Lincoln Library of Information, and later the Book of Knowledge. And the year we moved into our new house, there was room to celebrate it with the new 1925 edition of the Britannica, which my father, his face always deliberately turned toward the future, was of course disposed to think better than any previous edition.

5 In "the library," inside the mission-style bookcase with its three diamond-latticed glass doors, with my father's Morris chair and the glass-shaded lamp on its table beside it, were books I could soon begin on—and I did, reading them all alike and as they came, straight down their rows, top shelf to bottom. There was the set of Stoddard's Lectures, in all its late nineteenth-century vocabulary and vignettes of peasant life and quaint beliefs and customs, with matching halftone illustrations: Vesuvius erupting, Venice by moonlight, gypsies glimpsed by their campfires. I didn't know then the clue they were to my father's longing to see the rest of the world. I read straight through his other love-from-afar: the Victrola Book of the Opera, with opera after opera in synopsis, with portraits in costume of Melba, Caruso, Galli-Curci, and Geraldine Farrar,[2] some of whose voices we could listen to on our Red Seal records.

My mother read secondarily for information; she sank as a hedonist into novels. She read Dickens in the spirit in which she would have eloped with him. The novels of her girlhood that had stayed on in her imagination, besides those of Dickens and Scott and Robert Louis Stevenson,[3] were *Jane Eyre, Trilby, The Woman in White, Green Mansions, King Solomon's Mines.*[4] Marie Corelli's[5] name would crop up but I understood she had gone out of favor with my mother, who had

2. Nellie Melba (1861–1931), Enrico Caruso (1837–1921), Amelita Galli-Curci (1889–1964), Geraldine Farrar (1882–1967).
3. Charles Dickens (1812–1870), Sir Walter Scott (1771–1832), Robert Louis Stevenson (1850–1894). The first was English, the others Scottish.
4. Respectively by Charlotte Brontë (1816–1855), George Du Maurier (1834–1896), Wilkie Collins (1824–1889), William Henry Hudson (1841–1922), Sir H. Rider Haggard (1856–1925). All were English.
5. The pen name of Mary Mackay (1855–1924), a popular and prolific English novelist.

only kept *Ardath* out of loyalty. In time she absorbed herself in Galsworthy, Edith Wharton, above all in Thomas Mann of the *Joseph* volumes.[6]

St. Elmo was not in our house; I saw it often in other houses. This wildly popular Southern novel is where all the Edna Earles in our population started coming from. They're all named for the heroine, who succeeded in bringing a dissolute, sinning roué and atheist of a lover (St. Elmo) to his knees. My mother was able to forgo it. But she remembered the classic advice given to rose growers on how to water their bushes long enough: "Take a chair and *St. Elmo.*"[7]

To both my parents I owe my early acquaintance with a beloved Mark Twain. There was a full set of Mark Twain and a short set of Ring Lardner in our bookcase,[8] and those were the volumes that in time united us all, parents and children.

Reading everything that stood before me was how I came upon a worn old book without a back that had belonged to my father as a child. It was called *Sanford and Merton.* Is there anyone left who recognizes it, I wonder? It is the famous moral tale written by Thomas Day in the 1780s, but of him no mention is made on the title page of *this* book; here it is *Sanford and Merton in Words of One Syllable* by Mary Godolphin. Here are the rich boy and the poor boy and Mr. Barlow, their teacher and interlocutor, in long discourses alternating with dramatic scenes—danger and rescue allotted to the rich and the poor respectively. It may have only words of one syllable, but one of them is "quoth." It ends with not one but two morals, both engraved on rings: "Do what you ought, come what may," and "If we would be great, we must first learn to be good."

This book was lacking its front cover, the back held on by strips of 10
pasted paper, now turned golden, in several layers, and the pages stained, flecked, and tattered around the edges; its garish illustrations had come unattached but were preserved, laid in. I had the feeling even in my heedless childhood that this was the only book my father as a little boy had had of his own. He had held onto it, and might have gone to sleep on its coverless face: he had lost his mother when he was seven. My father had never made any mention to his own children of the book, but he had brought it along with him from Ohio to our house and shelved it in our bookcase.

My mother had brought from West Virginia that set of Dickens; those books looked sad, too—they had been through fire and water

6. John Galsworthy (1867–1933), English; Edith Wharton (1862–1937), American; Thomas Mann (1875–1955), German, whose *Joseph* novels appeared in four parts, from 1933 to 1943.
7. By Augusta Jane Evans (1835–1909).
8. Mark Twain, the pen name of Samuel Langhorne Clemens (1835–1910); Ring (Ringgold Wilmer) Lardner (1885–1933). Both were American.

before I was born, she told me, and there they were, lined up—as I later realized, waiting for *me.*

I was presented, from as early as I can remember, with books of my own, which appeared on my birthday and Christmas morning. Indeed, my parents could not give me books enough. They must have sacrificed to give me on my sixth or seventh birthday—it was after I became a reader for myself—the ten-volume set of Our Wonder World. These were beautifully made, heavy books I would lie down with on the floor in front of the diningroom hearth, and more often than the rest volume 5, *Every Child's Story Book,* was under my eyes. There were the fairy tales—Grimm, Andersen, the English, the French, "Ali Baba and the Forty Thieves"; and there was Aesop and Reynard the Fox; there were the myths and legends, Robin Hood, King Arthur, and St. George and the Dragon, even the history of Joan of Arc; a whack of *Pilgrim's Progress* and a long piece of *Gulliver.*[9] They all carried their classic illustrations. I located myself in these pages and could go straight to the stories and pictures I loved; very often "The Yellow Dwarf" was first choice, with Walter Crane's Yellow Dwarf in full color making his terrifying appearance flanked by turkeys.[1] Now that volume is as worn and backless and hanging apart as my father's poor *Sanford and Merton.* The precious page with Edward Lear's "Jumblies"[2] on it has been in danger of slipping out for all these years. One measure of my love for Our Wonder World was that for a long time I wondered if I would go through fire and water for it as my mother had done for Charles Dickens; and the only comfort was to think I could ask my mother to do it for me.

I believe I'm the only child I know of who grew up with this treasure in the house. I used to ask others, "Did you have Our Wonder World?" I'd have to tell them The Book of Knowledge could not hold a candle to it.

I live in gratitude to my parents for initiating me—and as early as I begged for it, without keeping me waiting—into knowledge of the word, into reading and spelling, by way of the alphabet. They taught it to me at home in time for me to begin to read before starting to school. I believe the alphabet is no longer considered an essential piece of equipment for traveling through life. In my day it was the keystone to knowledge. You learned the alphabet as you learned to count to ten, as you learned "Now I lay me" and the Lord's Prayer and your father's

9. Respectively by John Bunyan (1628–1688) and Jonathan Swift (1667–1745). Both were English.
1. A fairy tale illustrated by Walter Crane (1845–1915), popular illustrator of children's books.
2. A narrative poem about creatures called Jumblies who went to sea in a sieve. Edward Lear (1812–1888), English, wrote nonsense poems for children.

and mother's name and address and telephone number, all in case you were lost.

My love for the alphabet, which endures, grew out of reciting it but, 15
before that, out of seeing the letters on the page. In my own story books, before I could read them for myself, I fell in love with various winding, enchanting-looking initials drawn by Walter Crane at the heads of fairy tales. In "Once upon a time," an "O" had a rabbit running it as a treadmill, his feet upon flowers. When the day came, years later, for me to see the Book of Kells,[3] all the wizardry of letter, initial, and word swept over me a thousand times over, and the illumination, the gold, seemed a part of the word's beauty and holiness that had been there from the start.

Learning stamps you with its moments. Childhood's learning is made up of moments. It isn't steady. It's a pulse.

In a children's art class, we sat in a ring on kindergarten chairs and drew three daffodils that had just been picked out of the yard; and while I was drawing, my sharpened pencil and the cup of the yellow daffodil gave off whiffs just alike. That the pencil doing the drawing should give off the same smell as the flower it drew seemed a part of the art lesson—as shouldn't it be? Children, like animals, use all their senses to discover the world. Then artists come along and discover it the same way, all over again. Here and there, it's the same world. Or now and then we'll hear from an artist who's never lost it.

In my sensory education I include my physical awareness of the *word*. Of a certain word, that is; the connection it has with what it stands for. At around age six, perhaps, I was standing by myself in our front yard waiting for supper, just at that hour in a late summer day when the sun is already below the horizon and the risen full moon in the visible sky stops being chalky and begins to take on light. There comes the moment, and I saw it then, when the moon goes from flat to round. For the first time it met my eyes as a globe. The word "moon" came into my mouth as though fed to me out of a silver spoon. Held in my mouth the moon became a word. It had the roundness of a Concord grape Grandpa took off his vine and gave me to suck out of its skin and swallow whole, in Ohio.

This love did not prevent me from living for years in foolish error about the moon. The new moon just appearing in the west was the rising moon to me. The new should be rising. And in early childhood the sun and moon, those opposite reigning powers, I just as easily assumed rose in east and west respectively in their opposite sides of the sky, and like partners in a reel they advanced, sun from the east, moon

3. An illustrated Irish manuscript of the four Gospels from the eighth or ninth century.

from the west, crossed over (when I wasn't looking) and went down on the other side. My father couldn't have known I believed that when, bending behind me and guiding my shoulder, he positioned me at our telescope in the front yard and, with careful adjustment of the focus, brought the moon close to me.

20 The night sky over my childhood Jackson[4] was velvety black. I could see the full constellations in it and call their names; when I could read, I knew their myths. Though I was always waked for eclipses, and indeed carried to the window as an infant in arms and shown Halley's Comet[5] in my sleep, and though I'd been taught at our diningroom table about the solar system and knew the earth revolved around the sun, and our moon around us, I never found out the moon didn't come up in the west until I was a writer and Herschel Brickell, the literary critic, told me after I misplaced it in a story. He said valuable words to me about my new profession: "Always be sure you get your moon in the right part of the sky."

My mother always sang to her children. Her voice came out just a little bit in the minor key. "Wee Willie Winkie's" song was wonderfully sad when she sang the lullabies.

"Oh, but now there's a record. She could have her own record to listen to," my father would have said. For there came a Victrola record of "Bobby Shafftoe" and "Rock-a-Bye Baby,"[6] all of Mother's lullabies, which could be played to take her place. Soon I was able to play her my own lullabies all day long.

Our Victrola stood in the diningroom. I was allowed to climb onto the seat of a diningroom chair to wind it, start the record turning, and set the needle playing. In a second I'd jumped to the floor, to spin or march around the table as the music called for—now there were all the other records I could play too. I skinned back onto the chair just in time to lift the needle at the end, stop the record and turn it over, then change the needle. That brass receptable with a hole in the lid gave off a metallic smell like human sweat, from all the hot needles that were fed it. Winding up, dancing, being cocked to start and stop the record, was of course all in one the act of *listening*—to "Overture to *Daughter of the Regiment*," "Selections from *The Fortune Teller*," "Kiss Me Again," "Gypsy Dance from *Carmen*," "Stars and Stripes Forever," "When the Midnight Choo-Choo Leaves for Alabam," or whatever came next.[7] Movement must be at the very heart of listening.

4. Jackson, Mississippi, where Welty grew up.
5. A comet named after Edmund Halley (1656–1742), English astronomer.
6. "Wee Willie Winkie," a nursery rhyme of 1841 in which sleep is personified; "Bobby Shafftoe," a traditional sea chantey dating from about 1750; "Rock-a-Bye Baby," words from *Mother Goose's Melodies* (1765) set to music in 1884.

Ever since I was first read to, then started reading to myself, there has never been a line read that I didn't *hear*. As my eyes followed the sentence, a voice was saying it silently to me. It isn't my mother's voice, or the voice of any person I can identify, certainly not my own. It is human, but inward, and it is inwardly that I listen to it. It is to me the voice of the story or the poem itself. The cadence, whatever it is that asks you to believe, the feeling that resides in the printed word, reaches me through the reader-voice. I have supposed, but never found out, that this is the case with all readers—to read as listeners—and with all writers, to write as listeners. It may be part of the desire to write. The sound of what falls on the page begins the process of testing it for truth, for me. Whether I am right to trust so far I don't know. By now I don't know whether I could do either one, reading or writing, without the other.

My own words, when I am at work on a story, I hear too as they go, in 25
the same voice that I hear when I read in books. When I write and the sound of it comes back to my ears, then I act to make my changes. I have always trusted this voice.

7. *Daughter of the Regiment*, an opera (1840) by the Italian composer Gaetano Donizetti; *The Fortune Teller*, an operetta (1898) by the American Victor Herbert; "Kiss Me Again," a song from Herbert's *Mlle. Modiste* (1905); *Carmen*, an opera (1875) by the French composer Georges Bizet; "Stars and Stripes Forever," a march (1897) by the American John Philip Sousa (the "March King"); "When the Midnight Choo-Choo Leaves for Alabam," a popular song (1912) by the American Irving Berlin.

QUESTIONS

1. *In the opening paragraphs Welty speaks of her "sensory education." What does she mean? What examples does she give?*
2. *Throughout the essay Welty lists the names of books she (or her mother) read. What effect does she achieve with such lists? If you have read any of the same books, describe your response to Welty's accounts of her reading experience.*
3. *Welty concludes by talking of* trust *and* truth*—that is, of "trusting this voice" and "testing it for truth." What meaning does she give these key words?*
4. *Welty grew up before the advent of television. How does television affect a child's "sensory education"? Write a brief essay comparing a modern child's "sensory education" with Welty's.*

Cynthia Ozick

THE SEAM OF THE SNAIL

In my Depression childhood,[1] whenever I had a new dress, my cousin Sarah would get suspicious. The nicer the dress was, and especially the more expensive it looked, the more suspicious she would get. Finally she would lift the hem and check the seams. This was to see if the dress had been bought or if my mother had sewed it. Sarah could always tell. My mother's sewing had elegant outsides, but there was something catch-as-catch-can about the insides. Sarah's sewing, by contrast, was as impeccably finished inside as out; not one stray thread dangled.

My uncle Jake built meticulous grandfather clocks out of rosewood; he was a perfectionist, and sent to England for the clockworks. My mother built serviceable radiator covers and a serviceable cabinet, with hinged doors, for the pantry. She built a pair of bookcases for the living room. Once, after I was grown and in a house of my own, she fixed the sewer pipe. She painted ceilings, and also landscapes; she reupholstered chairs. One summer she planted a whole yard of tall corn. She thought herself capable of doing anything, and did everything she imagined. But nothing was perfect. There was always some clear flaw, never visible head-on. You had to look underneath, where the seams were. The corn thrived, though not in rows. The stalks elbowed one another like gossips in a dense little village.

"Miss Brrrroooobaker," my mother used to mock, rolling her Russian *r*'s, whenever I crossed a *t* she had left uncrossed, or corrected a word she had misspelled, or became impatient with a *v* that had tangled itself up with a *w* in her speech. ("*Vvv*entriloquist," I would say. "*Vvv*entriloquist," she would obediently repeat. And the next time it would come out "wiolinist.") Miss Brubaker was my high school English teacher, and my mother invoked her name as an emblem of raging finical obsession. "Miss Brrrroooobaker," my mother's voice hoots at me down the years, as I go on casting and recasting sentences in a tiny handwriting on monomaniacally uniform paper. The loops of my mother's handwriting—it was the Palmer Method[2]—were as big as

Originally published as "Excellence," *Ms.* magazine (Jan. 1985); reprinted in *Metaphor and Memory* (1989).

1. The Great Depression, a period after the crash of the stock market in 1929, characterized by decreasing business activity, falling prices, and widespread unemployment.
2. A method of teaching handwriting; the first exercises included making rows of large, looping O's.

soup bowls, spilling generous splashy ebullience. She could pull off, at five minutes' notice, a satisfying dinner for ten concocted out of nothing more than originality and panache. But the napkin would be folded a little off center, and the spoon might be on the wrong side of the knife. She was an optimist who ignored trifles; for her, God was not in the details but in the intent. And all these culinary and agricultural efflorescences were extracurricular, accomplished in the crevices and niches of a fourteen-hour business day. When she scribbled out her family memoirs, in heaps of dog-eared notebooks, or on the backs of old bills, or on the margins of last year's calendar, I would resist typing them; in the speed of the chase she often omitted words like "the," "and," "will." The same flashing and bountiful hand fashioned and fired ceramic pots, and painted brilliant autumn views and vases of imaginary flowers and ferns, and decorated ordinary Woolworth platters with lavish enameled gardens. But bits of the painted petals would chip away.

Lavish: my mother was as lavish as nature. She woke early and saturated the hours with work and inventiveness, and read late into the night. She was all profusion, abundance, fabrication. Angry at her children, she would run after us whirling the cord of the electric iron, like a lasso or a whip; but she never caught us. When, in seventh grade, I was afraid of failing the Music Appreciation final exam because I could not tell the difference between "To a Wild Rose" and "Barcarole," she got the idea of sending me to school with a gauze sling rigged up on my writing arm, and an explanatory note that was purest fiction. But the sling kept slipping off. My mother gave advice like mad—she boiled over with so much passion for the predicaments of strangers that they turned into permanent cronies. She told intimate stories about people I had never heard of.

Despite the gargantuan Palmer loops (or possibly because of them), 5
I have always known that my mother's was a life of—intricately abashing word!—excellence: insofar as excellence means ripe generosity. She burgeoned, she proliferated; she was endlessly leafy and flowering. She wore red hats, and called herself a gypsy. In her girlhood she marched with the suffragettes and for Margaret Sanger and called herself a Red. She made me laugh, she was so varied: like a tree on which lemons, pomegranates, and prickly pears absurdly all hang together. She had the comedy of prodigality.

My own way is a thousand times more confined. I am a pinched perfectionist, the ultimate fruition of Miss Brubaker; I attend to crabbed minutiae and am self-trammeled through taking pains. I am a kind of human snail, locked in and condemned by my own nature. The ancients believed that the moist track left by the snail as it crept was the snail's own essence, depleting its body little by little; the farther the snail toiled, the smaller it became, until it finally rubbed itself out.

That is how perfectionists are. Say to us Excellence, and we will show you how we use up our substance and wear ourselves away, while making scarcely any progress at all. The fact that I am an exacting perfectionist in a narrow strait only, and nowhere else, is hardly to the point, since nothing matters to me so much as a comely and muscular sentence. It is my narrow strait, this snail's road; the track of the sentence I am writing now; and when I have eked out the wet substance, ink or blood, that is its mark, I will begin the next sentence. Only in treading out sentences am I perfectionist; but then there is nothing else I know how to do, or take much interest in. I miter every pair of abutting sentences as scrupulously as Uncle Jake fitted one strip of rosewood against another. My mother's worldly and bountiful hand has escaped me. The sentence I am writing is my cabin and my shell, compact, self-sufficient. It is the burnished horizon—a merciless planet where flawlessness is the single standard, where even the inmost seams, however hidden from a laxer eye, must meet perfection. Here "excellence" is not strewn casually from a tipped cornucopia, here disorder does not account for charm, here trifles rule like tyrants.

I measure my life in sentences pressed out, line by line, like the lustrous ooze on the underside of the snail, the snail's secret open seam, its wound, leaking attar. My mother was too mettlesome to feel the force of a comma. She scorned minutiae. She measured her life according to what poured from the horn of plenty, which was her own seamless, ample, cascading, elastic, susceptible, inexact heart. My narrower heart rides between the tiny twin horns of the snail, dwindling as it goes.

And out of this thinnest thread, this ink-wet line of words, must rise a visionary fog, a mist, a smoke, forging cities, histories, sorrows, quagmires, entanglements, lives of sinners, even the life of my furnace-hearted mother: so much wilderness, waywardness, plenitude on the head of the precise and impeccable snail, between the horns. (Ah, if this could be!)

Vladimir Nabokov

GOOD READERS AND GOOD WRITERS

"How to be a Good Reader" or "Kindness to Authors"—something of that sort might serve to provide a subtitle for these various discussions of various authors, for my plan is to deal lovingly, in loving and

From *Lectures on Literature* (1980).

lingering detail, with several European masterpieces. A hundred years ago, Flaubert[1] in a letter to his mistress made the following remark: *Comme l'on serait savant si l'on connaissait bien seulement cinq à six livres:* "What a scholar one might be if one knew well only some half a dozen books."

In reading, one should notice and fondle details. There is nothing wrong about the moonshine of generalization when it comes *after* the sunny trifles of the book have been lovingly collected. If one begins with a ready-made generalization, one begins at the wrong end and travels away from the book before one has started to understand it. Nothing is more boring or more unfair to the author than starting to read, say, *Madame Bovary*, with the preconceived notion that it is a denunciation of the bourgeoisie. We should always remember that the work of art is invariably the creation of a new world, so that the first thing we should do is to study that new world as closely as possible, approaching it as something brand new, having no obvious connection with the worlds we already know. When this new world has been closely studied, then and only then let us examine its links with other worlds, other branches of knowledge.

Another question: Can we expect to glean information about places and times from a novel? Can anybody be so naive as to think he or she can learn anything about the past from those buxom best-sellers that are hawked around by book clubs under the heading of historical novels? But what about the masterpieces? Can we rely on Jane Austen's[2] picture of landowning England with baronets and landscaped grounds when all she knew was a clergyman's parlor? And *Bleak House*,[3] that fantastic romance within a fantastic London, can we call it a study of London a hundred years ago? Certainly not. And the same holds for other such novels in this series. The truth is that great novels are great fairy tales—and the novels in this series are supreme fairy tales.

Time and space, the colors of the seasons, the movements of muscles and minds, all these are for writers of genius (as far as we can guess and I trust we guess right) not traditional notions which may be borrowed from the circulating library of public truths but a series of unique surprises which master artists have learned to express in their own unique way. To minor authors is left the ornamentation of the commonplace: these do not bother about any reinventing of the world; they merely try to squeeze the best they can out of a given order of things, out of traditional patterns of fiction. The various combina-

1. Gustave Flaubert (1821–1880), French novelist, author of *Madame Bovary*.
2. English novelist (1775–1817).
3. Novel by Charles Dickens (1812–1870), which alternates scenes in London and the country and includes a satire on the English judicial system.

tions these minor authors are able to produce within these set limits may be quite amusing in a mild ephemeral way because minor readers like to recognize their own ideas in a pleasing disguise. But the real writer, the fellow who sends planets spinning and models a man asleep and eagerly tampers with the sleeper's rib, that kind of author has no given values at his disposal: he must create them himself. The art of writing is a very futile business if it does not imply first of all the art of seeing the world as the potentiality of fiction. The material of this world may be real enough (as far as reality goes) but does not exist at all as an accepted entirety: it is chaos, and to this chaos the author says "go!" allowing the world to flicker and to fuse. It is now recombined in its very atoms, not merely in its visible and superficial parts. The writer is the first man to map it and to name the natural objects it contains. Those berries there are edible. That speckled creature that bolted across my path might be tamed. That lake between those trees will be called Lake Opal or, more artistically, Dishwater Lake. That mist is a mountain—and that mountain must be conquered. Up a trackless slope climbs the master artist, and at the top, on a windy ridge, whom do you think he meets? The panting and happy reader, and there they spontaneously embrace and are linked forever if the book lasts forever.

5 One evening at a remote provincial college through which I happened to be jogging on a protracted lecture tour, I suggested a little quiz—ten definitions of a reader, and from these ten the students had to choose four definitions that would combine to make a good reader. I have mislaid the list, but as far as I remember the definitions went something like this. Select four answers to the question what should a reader be to be a good reader:

1. The reader should belong to a book club.
2. The reader should identify himself or herself with the hero or heroine.
3. The reader should concentrate on the social-economic angle.
4. The reader should prefer a story with action and dialogue to one with none.
5. The reader should have seen the book in a movie.
6. The reader should be a budding author.
7. The reader should have imagination.
8. The reader should have memory.
9. The reader should have a dictionary.
10. The reader should have some artistic sense.

The students leaned heavily on emotional identification, action, and the social-economic or historical angle. Of course, as you have guessed, the good reader is one who has imagination, memory, a dictionary, and some artistic sense—which sense I propose to develop in myself and in others whenever I have the chance.

Incidentally, I use the word *reader* very loosely. Curiously enough, one cannot *read* a book: one can only reread it. A good reader, a major reader, an active and creative reader is a rereader. And I shall tell you why. When we read a book for the first time the very process of laboriously moving our eyes from left to right, line after line, page after page, this complicated physical work upon the book, the very process of learning in terms of space and time what the book is about, this stands between us and artistic appreciation. When we look at a painting we do not have to move our eyes in a special way even if, as in a book, the picture contains elements of depth and development. The element of time does not really enter in a first contact with a painting. In reading a book, we must have time to acquaint ourselves with it. We have no physical organ (as we have the eye in regard to a painting) that takes in the whole picture and then can enjoy its details. But at a second, or third, or fourth reading we do, in a sense, behave towards a book as we do towards a painting. However, let us not confuse the physical eye, that monstrous masterpiece of evolution, with the mind, an even more monstrous achievement. A book, no matter what it is—a work of fiction or a work of science (the boundary line between the two is not as clear as is generally believed)—a book of fiction appeals first of all to the mind. The mind, the brain, the top of the tingling spine, is, or should be, the only instrument used upon a book.

Now, this being so, we should ponder the question how does the mind work when the sullen reader is confronted by the sunny book. First, the sullen mood melts away, and for better or worse the reader enters into the spirit of the game. The effort to begin a book, especially if it is praised by people whom the young reader secretly deems to be too old-fashioned or too serious, this effort is often difficult to make; but once it is made, rewards are various and abundant. Since the master artist used his imagination in creating his book, it is natural and fair that the consumer of a book should use his imagination too.

There are, however, at least two varieties of imagination in the reader's case. So let us see which one of the two is the right one to use in reading a book. First, there is the comparatively lowly kind which turns for support to the simple emotions and is of a definitely personal nature. (There are various subvarieties here, in this first section of emotional reading.) A situation in a book is intensely felt because it reminds us of something that happened to us or to someone we know or knew. Or, again, a reader treasures a book mainly because it evokes a country, a landscape, a mode of living which he nostalgically recalls as part of his own past. Or, and this is the worst thing a reader can do, he identifies himself with a character in the book. This lowly variety is not the kind of imagination I would like readers to use.

So what is the authentic instrument to be used by the reader? It is impersonal imagination and artistic delight. What should be established, I think, is an artistic harmonious balance between the reader's mind and the author's mind. We ought to remain a little aloof and take pleasure in this aloofness while at the same time we keenly enjoy—passionately enjoy, enjoy with tears and shivers—the inner weave of a given masterpiece. To be quite objective in these matters is of course impossible. Everything that is worthwhile is to some extent subjective. For instance, you sitting there may be merely my dream, and I may be your nightmare. But what I mean is that the reader must know when and where to curb his imagination and this he does by trying to get clear the specific world the author places at his disposal. We must see things and hear things, we must visualize the rooms, the clothes, the manners of an author's people. The color of Fanny Price's eyes in *Mansfield Park* and the furnishing of her cold little room are important.

10 We all have different temperaments, and I can tell you right now that the best temperament for a reader to have, or to develop, is a combination of the artistic and the scientific one. The enthusiastic artist alone is apt to be too subjective in his attitude towards a book, and so a scientific coolness of judgment will temper the intuitive heat. If, however, a would-be reader is utterly devoid of passion and patience—of an artist's passion and a scientist's patience—he will hardly enjoy great literature.

Literature was born not the day when a boy crying wolf, wolf came running out of the Neanderthal valley with a big gray wolf at his heels: literature was born on the day when a boy came crying wolf, wolf and there was no wolf behind him. That the poor little fellow because he lied too often was finally eaten up by a real beast is quite incidental. But here is what is important. Between the wolf in the tall grass and the wolf in the tall story there is a shimmering go-between. That go-between, that prism, is the art of literature.

Literature is invention. Fiction is fiction. To call a story a true story is an insult to both art and truth. Every great writer is a great deceiver, but so is that arch-cheat Nature. Nature always deceives. From the simple deception of propagation to the prodigiously sophisticated illusion of protective colors in butterflies or birds, there is in Nature a marvelous system of spells and wiles. The writer of fiction only follows Nature's lead.

Going back for a moment to our wolf-crying woodland little woolly fellow, we may put it this way: the magic of art was in the shadow of the wolf that he deliberately invented, his dream of the wolf; then the story of his tricks made a good story. When he perished at last, the story told about him acquired a good lesson in the dark around the camp fire. But he was the little magician. He was the inventor.

There are three points of view from which a writer can be considered: he may be considered as a storyteller, as a teacher, and as an enchanter. A major writer combines these three—storyteller, teacher, enchanter—but it is the enchanter in him that predominates and makes him a major writer.

To the storyteller we turn for entertainment, for mental excitement 15
of the simplest kind, for emotional participation, for the pleasure of traveling in some remote region in space or time. A slightly different though not necessarily higher mind looks for the teacher in the writer. Propagandist, moralist, prophet—this is the rising sequence. We may go to the teacher not only for moral education but also for direct knowledge, for simple facts. Alas, I have known people whose purpose in reading the French and Russian novelists was to learn something about life in gay Paree or in sad Russia. Finally, and above all, a great writer is always a great enchanter, and it is here that we come to the really exciting part when we try to grasp the individual magic of his genius and to study the style, the imagery, the pattern of his novels or poems.

The three facets of the great writer—magic, story, lesson—are prone to blend in one impression of unified and unique radiance, since the magic of art may be present in the very bones of the story, in the very marrow of thought. There are masterpieces of dry, limpid, organized thought which provoke in us an artistic quiver quite as strongly as a novel like *Mansfield Park* does or as any rich flow of Dickensian sensual imagery. It seems to me that a good formula to test the quality of a novel is, in the long run, a merging of the precision of poetry and the intuition of science. In order to bask in that magic a wise reader reads the book of genius not with his heart, not so much with his brain, but with his spine. It is there that occurs the telltale tingle even though we must keep a little aloof, a little detached when reading. Then with a pleasure which is both sensual and intellectual we shall watch the artist build his castle of cards and watch the castle of cards become a castle of beautiful steel and glass.

QUESTIONS

1. *Make a list of qualities that Nabokov believes "good readers" should have; then make a list for "good writers." Do they correspond? Why or why not?*
2. *Take the "quiz" in paragraph 5: select four answers to Nabokov's question, "What makes a good reader?" Do your answers agree with Nabokov's?*
3. *Write an essay in which you defend some quality of a "good reader" that Nabokov does not credit or in which you discuss some quality of a "good writer" not covered in Nabokov's essay.*

Northrop Frye

THE MOTIVE FOR METAPHOR

For the past twenty-five years I have been teaching and studying English literature in a university. As in any other job, certain questions stick in one's mind, not because people keep asking them, but because they're the questions inspired by the very fact of being in such a place. What good is the study of literature? Does it help us to think more clearly, or feel more sensitively, or live a better life than we could without it? What is the function of the teacher and scholar, or of the person who calls himself, as I do, a literary critic? What difference does the study of literature make in our social or political or religious attitude? In my early days I thought very little about such questions, not because I had any of the answers, but because I assumed that anybody who asked them was naïve. I think now that the simplest questions are not only the hardest to answer, but the most important to ask, so I'm going to raise them and try to suggest what my present answers are. I say try to suggest, because there are only more or less inadequate answers to such questions—there aren't any right answers. The kind of problem that literature raises is not the kind that you ever "solve." Whether my answers are any good or not, they represent a fair amount of thinking about the questions. As I can't see my audience, I have to choose my rhetorical style in the dark, and I'm taking the classroom style, because an audience of students is the one I feel easiest with.

There are two things in particular that I want to discuss with you. In school, and in university, there's a subject called "English" in English-speaking countries. English means, in the first place, the mother tongue. As that, it's the most practical subject in the world: you can't understand anything or take any part in your society without it. Wherever illiteracy is a problem, it's as fundamental a problem as getting enough to eat or a place to sleep. The native language takes precedence over every other subject of study: nothing else can compare with it in its usefulness. But then you find that every mother tongue, in any developed or civilized society, turns into something called literature. If you keep on studying "English," you find yourself trying to read Shakespeare and Milton. Literature, we're told, is one of the arts, along with painting and music, and, after you've looked up all the hard words and the Classical allusions and learned what words like imagery and diction are supposed to mean, what you use in understanding it,

From *The Educated Imagination* (1964).

or so you're told, is your imagination. Here you don't seem to be in quite the same practical and useful area: Shakespeare and Milton, whatever their merits, are not the kind of thing you must know to hold any place in society at all. A person who knows nothing about literature may be an ignoramus, but many people don't mind being that. Every child realizes that literature is taking him in a different direction from the immediately useful, and a good many children complain loudly about this. Two questions I want to deal with, then, are, first: what is the relation of English as the mother tongue to English as a literature? Second: What is the social value of the study of literature, and what is the place of the imagination that literature addresses itself to, in the learning process?

Let's start with the different ways there are of dealing with the world we're living in. Suppose you're shipwrecked on an uninhabited island in the South Seas. The first thing you do is to take a long look at the world around you, a world of sky and sea and earth and stars and trees and hills. You see this world as objective, as something set over against you and not yourself or related to you in any way. And you notice two things about this objective world. In the first place, it doesn't have any conversation. It's full of animals and plants and insects going on with their own business, but there's nothing that responds to you: it has no morals and no intelligence, or at least none that you can grasp. It may have a shape and a meaning, but it doesn't seem to be a human shape or a human meaning. Even if there's enough to eat and no dangerous animals, you feel lonely and frightened and unwanted in such a world.

In the second place, you find that looking at the world, as something set over against you, splits your mind in two. You have an intellect that feels curious about it and wants to study it, and you have feelings or emotions that see it as beautiful or austere or terrible. You know that both these attitudes have some reality, at least for you. If the ship you were wrecked in was a Western ship, you'd probably feel that your intellect tells you more about what's really there in the outer world, and that your emotions tell you more about what's going on inside you. If your background were Oriental, you'd be more likely to reverse this and say that the beauty or terror was what was really there, and that your instinct to count and classify and measure and pull to pieces was what was inside your mind. But whether your point of view is Western or Eastern, intellect and emotion never get together in your mind as long as you're simply looking at the world. They alternate, and keep you divided between them.

The language you use on this level of the mind is the language of 5
consciousness or awareness. It's largely a language of nouns and adjectives. You have to have names for things, and you need qualities like

"wet" or "green" or "beautiful" to describe how things seem to you. This is the speculative or contemplative position of the mind, the position in which the arts and sciences begin, although they don't stay there very long. The sciences begin by accepting the facts and the evidence about an outside world without trying to alter them. Science proceeds by accurate measurement and description, and follows the demands of the reason rather than the emotions. What it deals with is there, whether we like it or not. The emotions are unreasonable: for them it's what they like and don't like that comes first. We'd be naturally inclined to think that the arts follow the path of emotion, in contrast to the sciences. Up to a point they do, but there's a complicating factor.

That complicating factor is the contrast between "I like this" and "I don't like this." In this Robinson Crusoe life I've assigned you, you may have moods of complete peacefulness and joy, moods when you accept your island and everything around you. You wouldn't have such moods very often, and when you had them, they'd be moods of identification, when you felt that the island was a part of you and you a part of it. That is not the feeling of consciousness or awareness, where you feel split off from everything that's not your perceiving self. Your habitual state of mind is the feeling of separation which goes with being conscious, and the feeling "this is not a part of me" soon becomes "this is not what I want." Notice the word "want": we'll be coming back to it.

So you soon realize that there's a difference between the world you're living in and the world you want to live in. The world you want to live in is a human world, not an objective one: it's not an environment but a home; it's not the world you see but the world you build out of what you see. You go to work to build a shelter or plant a garden, and as soon as you start to work you've moved into a different level of human life. You're not separating only yourself from nature now, but constructing a human world and separating it from the rest of the world. Your intellect and emotions are now both engaged in the same activity, so there's no longer any real distinction between them. As soon as you plant a garden or a crop, you develop the conception of a "weed," the plant you don't want in there. But you can't say that "weed" is either an intellectual or an emotional conception, because it's both at once. Further, you go to work because you feel you have to, and because you want something at the end of the work. That means that the important categories of your life are no longer the subject and the object, the watcher and the things being watched: the important categories are what you have to do and what you want to do—in other words, necessity and freedom.

One person by himself is not a complete human being, so I'll provide you with another shipwrecked refugee of the opposite sex and an eventual family. Now you're a member of a human society. This human society after a while will transform the island into something with a human shape. What that human shape is, is revealed in the shape of the work you do: the buildings, such as they are, the paths through the woods, the planted crops fenced off against whatever animals want to eat them. These things, these rudiments of city, highway, garden, and farm, are the human form of nature, or the form of human nature, whichever you like. This is the area of the applied arts and sciences, and it appears in our society as engineering and agriculture and medicine and architecture. In this area we can never say clearly where the art stops and the science begins, or vice versa.

The language you use on this level is the language of practical sense, a language of verbs or words of action and movement. The practical world, however, is a world where actions speak louder than words. In some way it's a higher level of existence than the speculative level, because it's doing something about the world instead of just looking at it, but in itself it's a much more primitive level. It's the process of adapting to the environment, or rather of transforming the environment in the interests of one species, that goes on among animals and plants as well as human beings. The animals have a good many of our practical skills: some insects make pretty fair architects, and beavers know quite a lot about engineering. In this island, probably, and certainly if you were alone, you'd have about the ranking of a second-rate animal. What makes our practical life really human is a third level of the mind, a level where consciousness and practical skill come together.

10 This third level is a vision or model in your mind of what you want to construct. There's that word "want" again. The actions of man are prompted by desire, and some of these desires are needs, like food and warmth and shelter. One of these needs is sexual, the desire to reproduce and bring more human beings into existence. But there's also a desire to bring a social human form into existence: the form of cities and gardens and farms that we call civilization. Many animals and insects have this social form too, but man knows that he has it: he can compare what he does with what he can imagine being done. So we begin to see where the imagination belongs in the scheme of human affairs. It's the power of constructing possible models of human experience. In the world of the imagination, anything goes that's imaginatively possible, but nothing really happens. If it did happen, it would move out of the world of imagination into the world of action.

We have three levels of the mind now, and a language for each of them, which in English-speaking societies means an English for each of them. There's the level of consciousness and awareness, where the most important thing is the difference between me and everything else. The English of this level is the English of ordinary conversation, which is mostly monologue, as you'll soon realize if you do a bit of eavesdropping, or listening to yourself. We can call it the language of self-expression. Then there's the level of social participation, the working or technological language of teachers and preachers and politicians and advertisers and lawyers and journalists and scientists. We've already called this the language of practical sense. Then there's the level of imagination, which produces the literary language of poems and plays and novels. They're not really different languages, of course, but three different reasons for using words.

On this basis, perhaps, we can distinguish the arts from the sciences. Science begins with the world we have to live in, accepting its data and trying to explain its laws. From there, it moves towards the imagination: it becomes a mental construct, a model of a possible way of interpreting experience. The further it goes in this direction, the more it tends to speak the language of mathematics, which is really one of the languages of the imagination, along with literature and music. Art, on the other hand, begins with the world we construct, not with the world we see. It starts with the imagination, and then works towards ordinary experience: that is, it tries to make itself as convincing and recognizable as it can. You can see why we tend to think of the sciences as intellectual and the arts as emotional: one starts with the world as it is, the other with the world we want to have. Up to a point it is true that science gives an intellectual view of reality, and that the arts try to make the emotions as precise and disciplined as sciences do the intellect. But of course it's nonsense to think of the scientist as a cold unemotional reasoner and the artist as somebody who's in a perpetual emotional tizzy. You can't distinguish the arts from the sciences by the mental processes the people in them use: they both operate on a mixture of hunch and common sense. A highly developed science and and a highly developed art are very close together, psychologically and otherwise.

Still, the fact that they start from opposite ends, even if they do meet in the middle, makes for one important difference between them. Science learns more and more about the world as it goes on: it evolves and improves. A physicist today knows more physics than Newton did, even if he's not as great a scientist. But literature begins with the possible model of experience, and what it produces is the literary model we call the classic. Literature doesn't evolve or improve or progress. We may have dramatists in the future who will write plays as good as *King Lear*, though they'll be very different ones, but drama as a whole will never get better than *King Lear*. *King Lear* is it, as far as drama is concerned; so is *Oedipus Rex*, written two thousand years earlier than that, and both will be models of dramatic writing as long as the human race endures. Social conditions may improve: most of us would rather live in nineteenth-century United States than in thirteenth-century Italy, and for most of us Whitman's celebration of democracy makes a lot more sense than Dante's Inferno. But it doesn't follow that Whitman is a better poet than Dante: literature won't line up with that kind of improvement.

So we find that everything that does improve, including science, leaves the literary artist out in the cold. Writers don't seem to benefit much by the advance of science, although they thrive on superstitions of all kinds. And you certainly wouldn't turn to contemporary poets for guidance or leadership in the twentieth-century world. You'd hardly go to Ezra Pound, with his fascism and social credit and Confucianism and anti-semitism. Or to Yeats, with his spiritualism and fairies and astrology. Or to D. H. Lawrence, who'll tell you that it's a good thing for servants to be flogged because that restores the precious current of blood-reciprocity between servant and master. Or to T. S. Eliot, who'll tell you that to have a flourishing culture we should educate an élite, keep most people living in the same spot, and never disestablish the Church of England. The novelists seem to be a little closer to the world they're living in, but not much. When Communists talk about the decadence of bourgeois culture, this is the kind of thing they always bring up. Their own writers don't seem to be any better, though; just duller. So the real question is a bigger one. Is it possible that literature, especially poetry, is something that a scientific civilization like ours will eventually outgrow? Man has always wanted to fly, and thousands of years ago he was making sculptures of winged bulls and telling stories about people who flew so high on artificial wings that the sun melted them off. In an Indian play fifteen hundred years old, *Sakuntala*, there's a god who flies around in a chariot that to a modern reader sounds very much like a private aeroplane. Interesting that the writer had so much imagination, but do we need such stories now that we have private aeroplanes?

This is not a new question: it was raised a hundred and fifty years 15
ago by Thomas Love Peacock, who was a poet and novelist himself, and a very brilliant one. He wrote an essay called *Four Ages of Poetry*, with his tongue of course in his cheek, in which he said that poetry was the mental rattle that awakened the imagination of mankind in its infancy, but that now, in an age of science and technology, the poet has outlived his social function. "A poet in our times," said Peacock, "is a semi-barbarian in a civilized community. He lives in the days that are past. His ideas, thoughts, feelings, associations, are all with barbarous manners, obsolete customs, and exploded superstitions. The march of his intellect is like that of a crab, backwards." Peacock's essay annoyed

his friend Shelley, who wrote another essay called *A Defence of Poetry* to refute it. Shelley's essay is a wonderful piece of writing, but it's not likely to convince anyone who needs convincing. I shall be spending a good deal of my time on this question of the relevance of literature in the world of today, and I can only indicate the general lines my answer will take. There are two points I can make now, one simple, the other more difficult.

The simple point is that literature belongs to the world man constructs, not to the world he sees; to his home, not his environment. Literature's world is a concrete human world of immediate experience. The poet uses images and objects and sensations much more than he uses abstract ideas; the novelist is concerned with telling stories, not with working out arguments. The world of literature is human in shape, a world where the sun rises in the east and sets in the west over the edge of a flat earth in three dimensions, where the primary realities are not atoms or electrons but bodies, and the primary forces not energy or gravitation but love and death and passion and joy. It's not surprising if writers are often rather simple people, not always what we think of as intellectuals, and certainly not always any freer of silliness or perversity than anyone else. What concerns us is what they produce, not what they are, and poetry, according to Milton, who ought to have known, is "more simple, sensuous and passionate" than philosophy or science.

The more difficult point takes us back to what we said when we were on that South Sea island. Our emotional reaction to the world varies from "I like this" to "I don't like this." The first, we said, was a state of identity, a feeling that everything around us was part of us, and the second is the ordinary state of consciousness, or separation, where art and science begin. Art begins as soon as "I don't like this" turns into "this is not the way I could imagine it." We notice in passing that the creative and the neurotic minds have a lot in common. They're both dissatisfied with what they see; they both believe that something else ought to be there, and they try to pretend it is there or to make it be there. The differences are more important, but we're not ready for them yet.

At the level of ordinary consciousness the individual man is the centre of everything, surrounded on all sides by what he isn't. At the level of practical sense, or civilization, there's a human circumference, a little cultivated world with a human shape, fenced off from the jungle and inside the sea and the sky. But in the imagination anything goes that can be imagined, and the limit of the imagination is a totally human world. Here we recapture, in full consciousness, that original lost sense of identity with our surroundings, where there is nothing outside the mind of man, or something identical with the mind of man. Religions present us with visions of eternal and infinite heavens or paradises which have the form of the cities and gardens of human civilization, like the Jerusalem and Eden of the Bible, completely separated from the state of frustration and misery that bulks so large in ordinary life. We're not concerned with these visions as religion, but they indicate what the limits of the imagination are. They indicate too that in the human world the imagination has no limits, if you follow me. We said that the desire to fly produced the aeroplane. But people don't get into planes because they want to fly; they get into planes because they want to get somewhere else faster. What's produced the aeroplane is not so much a desire to fly as a rebellion against the tyranny of time and space. And that's a process that can never stop, no matter how high our Titovs[1] and Glenns[2] may go.

For each of these six talks I've taken a title from some work of literature, and my title for this one is "The Motive for Metaphor," from a poem of Wallace Stevens. Here's the poem:

You like it under the trees in autumn,
Because everything is half dead.
The wind moves like a cripple among the leaves
And repeats words without meaning.

In the same way, you were happy in spring,
With the half colors of quarter-things,
The slightly brighter sky, the melting clouds,
The single bird, the obscure moon—

The obscure moon lighting an obscure world
Of things that would never be quite expressed,
Where you yourself were never quite yourself
And did not want nor have to be,

Desiring the exhilarations of changes:
The motive for metaphor, shrinking from
The weight of primary noon,
The A B C of being,

The ruddy temper, the hammer
Of red and blue, the hard sound—
Steel against intimation—the sharp flash,
The vital, arrogant, fatal, dominant X.

What Stevens calls the weight of primary noon, the A B C of being, and the dominant X is the objective world, the world set over against us. Outside literature, the main motive for writing is to describe this

1. Gherman S. Titov, Russian astronaut and first man to make a multi-orbital flight (Aug. 1961).
2. John H. Glenn, astronaut and first American to make an orbital flight (Feb. 1962).

world. But literature itself uses language in a way which associates our minds with it. As soon as you use associative language, you begin using figures of speech. If you say this talk is dry and dull, you're using figures associating it with bread and breadknives. There are two main kinds of association, analogy and identity, two things that are like each other and two things that are each other. You can say with Burns, "My love's like a red, red rose," or you can say with Shakespeare:

> Thou that art now the world's fresh ornament
> And only herald to the gaudy spring.

One produces the figure of speech called the simile; the other produces the figure called metaphor.

20 In descriptive writing you have to be careful of associative language. You'll find that analogy, or likeness to something else, is very tricky to handle in description, because the differences are as important as the resemblances. As for metaphor, where you're really saying "this *is* that," you're turning your back on logic and reason completely, because logically two things can never be the same thing and still remain two things. The poet, however, uses these two crude, primitive, archaic forms of thought in the most uninhibited way, because his job is not to describe nature, but to show you a world completely absorbed and possessed by the human mind. So he produces what Baudelaire called a "suggestive magic including at the same time object and subject, the world outside the artist and the artist himself." The motive for metaphor, according to Wallace Stevens, is a desire to associate, and finally to identify, the human mind with what goes on outside it, because the only genuine joy you can have is in those rare moments when you feel that although we may know in part, as Paul says, we are also a part of what we know.

QUESTIONS

1. *At what point in his essay does Frye come to the meaning of his title? What does this essay say the motive for metaphor is? Does it seem to you to be a satisfactory motive?*
2. *What are the three kinds of English Frye talks about in his essay? Do we really need three kinds—isn't one enough?*
3. *Does Frye anticipate a possible objection that metaphor distorts the truth and misleads us as to the way things really are? Why, or why not?*
4. *Why doesn't literature get any better, the way science does? Given the fact that it doesn't improve, shouldn't much of it be outdated? Write an answer to these questions in the form of two brief essays, one addressed to an English teacher, one addressed to a fellow student majoring in science. How do your two essays differ?*

Robert Frost

EDUCATION BY POETRY: A MEDITATIVE MONOLOGUE

I am going to urge nothing in my talk. I am not an advocate. I am going to consider a matter, and commit a description. And I am going to describe other colleges than Amherst. Or, rather say all that is good can be taken as about Amherst; all that is bad will be about other colleges.

I know whole colleges where all American poetry is barred—whole colleges. I know whole colleges where all contemporary poetry is barred.

I once heard of a minister who turned his daughter—his poetry-writing daughter—out on the street to earn a living, because he said there should be no more books written; God wrote one book, and that was enough. (My friend George Russell, "Æ", has read no literature, he protests, since just before Chaucer.)

That all seems sufficiently safe, and you can say one thing for it. It takes the onus off the poetry of having to be used to teach children anything. It comes pretty hard on poetry, I sometimes think, what it has to bear in the teaching process.

Then I know whole colleges where, though they let in older poetry, 5
they manage to bar all that is poetical in it by treating it as something other than poetry. It is not so hard to do that. Their reason I have often hunted for. It may be that these people act from a kind of modesty. Who are professors that they should attempt to deal with a thing as high and as fine as poetry? Who are *they?* There is a certain manly modesty in that.

That is the best general way of settling the problem; treat all poetry as if it were something else than poetry, as if it were syntax, language, science. Then you can even come down into the American and into the contemporary without any special risk.

There is another reason they have, and that is that they are, first and foremost in life, markers. They have the marking problem to consider. Now, I stand here a teacher of many years' experience and I have never complained of having had to mark. I had rather mark anyone for anything—for his looks, carriage, his ideas, his correctness, his exactness, anything you please—I would rather give him a mark in terms of letters, A, B, C, D, than have to use adjectives on him. We are all being marked by each other all the time, classified, ranked, put in our place,

An address given at Amherst College in 1930.

and I see no escape from that. I am no sentimentalist. You have got to mark, and you have got to mark, first of all, for accuracy, for correctness. But if I am going to give a mark, that is the least part of my marking. The hard part is the part beyond that, the part where the adventure begins.

One other way to rid the curriculum of the poetry nuisance has been considered. More merciful than the others it would neither abolish nor denature the poetry, but only turn it out to disport itself, with the plays and games—in no wise discredited, though given no credit for. Any one who liked to teach poetically could take his subject, whether English, Latin, Greek or French, out into the nowhere along with the poetry. One side of a sharp line would be left to the rigorous and righteous; the other side would be assigned to the flowery where they would know what could be expected of them. Grade marks were more easily given, of course, in the courses concentrating on correctness and exactness as the only forms of honesty recognized by plain people; a general indefinite mark of X in the courses that scatter brains over taste and opinion. On inquiry I have found no teacher willing to take position on either side of the line, either among the rigors or among the flowers. No one is willing to admit that his discipline is not partly in exactness. No one is willing to admit that his discipline is not partly in taste and enthusiasm.

How shall a man go through college without having been marked for taste and judgment? What will become of him? What will his end be? He will have to take continuation courses for college graduates. He will have to go to night schools. They are having night schools now, you know, for college graduates. Why? Because they have not been educated enough to find their way around in contemporary literature. They don't know what they may safely like in the libraries and galleries. They don't know how to judge an editorial when they see one. They don't know how to judge a political campaign. They don't know when they are being fooled by a metaphor, an analogy, a parable. And metaphor is, of course, what we are talking about. Education by poetry is education by metaphor.

10 Suppose we stop short of imagination, initiative, enthusiasm, inspiration and originality—dread words. Suppose we don't mark in such things at all. There are still two minimal things, that we have got to take care of, taste and judgment. Americans are supposed to have more judgment than taste, but taste is there to be dealt with. That is what poetry, the only art in the colleges of arts, is there for. I for my part would not be afraid to go in for enthusiasm. There is the enthusiasm like a blinding light, or the enthusiasm of the deafening shout, the crude enthusiasm that you get uneducated by poetry, outside of poetry. It is exemplified in what I might call "sunset raving." You look

westward toward the sunset, or if you get up early enough, eastward toward the sunrise, and you rave. It is oh's and ah's with you and no more.

But the enthusiasm I mean is taken through the prism of the intellect and spread on the screen in a color, all the way from hyperbole at one end—or overstatement, at one end—to understatement at the other end. It is a long strip of dark lines and many colors. Such enthusiasm is one object of all teaching in poetry. I heard wonderful things said about Virgil yesterday, and many of them seemed to me crude enthusiasm, more like a deafening shout, many of them. But one speech had range, something of overstatement, something of statement, and something of understatement. It had all the colors of an enthusiasm passed through an idea.

I would be willing to throw away everything else but that: enthusiasm tamed by metaphor. Let me rest the case there. Enthusiasm tamed to metaphor, tamed to that much of it. I do not think anybody ever knows the discreet use of metaphor, his own and other people's, the discreet handling of metaphor, unless he has been properly educated in poetry.

Poetry begins in trivial metaphors, petty metaphors, "grace" metaphors, and goes on to the profoundest thinking that we have. Poetry provides the one permissible way of saying one thing and meaning another. People say, "Why don't you say what you mean?" We never do that, do we, being all of us too much poets. We like to talk in parables and in hints and in indirections—whether from diffidence or some other instinct.

I have wanted in late years to go further and further in making metaphor the whole of thinking. I find some one now and then to agree with me that all thinking, except mathematical thinking, is metaphorical, or all thinking except scientific thinking. The mathematical might be difficult for me to bring in, but the scientific is easy enough.

Once on a time all the Greeks were busy telling each other what the 15
All was—or was like unto. All was three elements, air, earth, and water (we once thought it was ninety elements; now we think it is only one). All was substance, said another. All was change, said a third. But best and most fruitful was Pythagoras' comparison of the universe with number. Number of what? Number of feet, pounds, and seconds was the answer, and we had science and all that has followed in science. The metaphor has held and held, breaking down only when it came to the spiritual and psychological or the out of the way places of the physical.

The other day we had a visitor here, a noted scientist, whose latest word to the world has been that the more accurately you know where a thing is, the less accurately you are able to state how fast it is moving.

You can see why that would be so, without going back to Zeno's problem of the arrow's flight. In carrying numbers into the realm of space and at the same time into the realm of time you are mixing metaphors, that is all, and you are in trouble. They won't mix. The two don't go together.

Let's take two or three more of the metaphors now in use to live by. I have just spoken of one of the new ones, a charming mixed metaphor right in the realm of higher mathematics and higher physics: that the more accurately you state where a thing is, the less accurately you will be able to tell how fast it is moving. And, of course everything is moving. Everything is an event now. Another metaphor. A thing, they say, is an event. Do you believe it is? Not quite. I believe it is almost an event. But I like the comparison of a thing with an event.

I notice another from the same quarter. "In the neighborhood of matter space is something like curved." Isn't that a good one! It seems to me that that is simply and utterly charming—to say that space is something like curved in the neighborhood of matter. "Something like."

Another amusing one is from—what is the book?—I can't say it now; but here is the metaphor. Its aim is to restore you to your ideas of free will. It wants to give you back your freedom of will. All right, here it is on a platter. You know that you can't tell by name what persons in a certain class will be dead ten years after graduation, but you can tell actuarially how many will be dead. Now, just so this scientist says of the particles of matter flying at a screen, striking a screen; you can't tell what individual particles will come, but you can say in general that a certain number will strike in a given time. It shows, you see, that the individual particle can come freely. I asked Bohr about that particularly, and he said, "Yes, it is so. It can come when it wills and as it wills; and the action of the individual particle is unpredictable. But it is not so of the action of the mass. There you can predict." He says, "That gives the individual atom its freedom, but the mass its necessity."

20 Another metaphor that has interested us in our time and has done all our thinking for us is the metaphor of evolution. Never mind going into the Latin word. The metaphor is simply the metaphor of the growing plant or of the growing thing. And somebody very brilliantly, quite a while ago, said that the whole universe, the whole of everything, was like unto a growing thing. That is all. I know the metaphor will break down at some point, but it has not failed everywhere. It is a very brilliant metaphor, I acknowledge, though I myself get too tired of the kind of essay that talks about the evolution of candy, we will say, or the evolution of elevators—the evolution of this, that, and the other. Everything is evolution. I emancipate myself by simply saying that I didn't get up the metaphor and so am not much interested in it.

What I am pointing out is that unless you are at home in the metaphor, unless you have had your proper poetical education in the metaphor, you are not safe anywhere. Because you are not at ease with figurative values: you don't know the metaphor in its strength and its weakness. You don't know how far you may expect to ride it and when it may break down with you. You are not safe in science; you are not safe in history. In history, for instance—to show that is the same in history as elsewhere—I heard somebody say yesterday that Aeneas was to be likened unto (those words, "likened unto"!) George Washington. He was that type of national hero, the middle-class man, not thinking of being a hero at all, bent on building the future, bent on his children, his descendants. A good metaphor, as far as it goes, and you must know how far. And then he added that Odysseus should be likened unto Theodore Roosevelt. I don't think that is so good. Someone visiting Gibbon at the point of death, said he was the same Gibbon as of old; still at his parallels.

Take the way we have been led into our present position morally, the world over. It is by a sort of metaphorical gradient. There is a kind of thinking—to speak metaphorically—there is a kind of thinking you might say was endemic in the brothel. It is always there. And every now and then in some mysterious way it becomes epidemic in the world. And how does it do so? By using all the good words that virtue has invented to maintain virtue. It uses honesty, first—frankness, sincerity—those words; picks them up, uses them. "In the name of honesty, let us see what we are." You know. And then it picks up the word joy. "Let us in the name of joy, which is the enemy of our ancestors, the Puritans . . . Let us in the name of joy, which is the enemy of the kill-joy Puritan . . ." You see. "Let us," and so on. And then, "In the name of health . . ." Health is another good word. And that is the metaphor Freudianism trades on, mental health. And the first thing we know, it has us all in up to the top knot. I suppose we may blame the artists a good deal, because they are great people to spread by metaphor. The stage too—the stage is always a good intermediary between the two worlds, the under and the upper, if I may say so without personal prejudice to the stage.

In all this, I have only been saying that the devil can quote Scripture, which simply means that the good words you have lying around the devil can use for his purposes as well as anybody else. Never mind about my morality. I am not here to urge anything. I don't care whether the world is good or bad—not on any particular day.

Let me ask you to watch a metaphor breaking down here before you.

Somebody said to me a little while ago, "It is easy enough for me to 25
think of the universe as a machine, as a mechanism."

I said, "You mean the universe is like a machine?"

He said, "No. I think it is one . . . Well, it is like . . ."

"I think you mean the universe is like a machine."

"All right. Let it go at that."

30 I asked him, "Did you ever see a machine without a pedal for the foot, or a lever for the hand, or a button for the finger?"

He said "No—no."

I said, "All right. Is the universe like that?"

And he said, "No. I mean it is like a machine, only . . ."

". . . it is different from a machine," I said.

He wanted to go just that far with that metaphor and no further. And so do we all. All metaphor breaks down somewhere. That is the beauty of it. It is touch and go with the metaphor, and until you have lived with it long enough you don't know when it is going. You don't know how much you can get out of it and when it will cease to yield. It is a very living thing. It is as life itself.

35 I have heard this ever since I can remember, and ever since I have taught: the teacher must teach the pupil to think. I saw a teacher once going around in a great school and snapping pupils' heads with thumb and finger and saying, "Think." That was when thinking was becoming the fashion. The fashion hasn't yet quite gone out.

We still ask boys in college to think, as in the nineties, but we seldom tell them what thinking means; we seldom tell them it is just putting this and that together; it is saying one thing in terms of another. To tell them is to set their feet on the first rung of a ladder the top of which sticks through the sky.

Greatest of all attempts to say one thing in terms of another is the philosophical attempt to say matter in terms of spirit, or spirit in terms of matter, to make the final unity. That is the greatest attempt that ever failed. We stop just short there. But it is the height of poetry, the height of all thinking, the height of all poetic thinking, that attempt to say matter in terms of spirit and spirit in terms of matter. It is wrong to call anybody a materialist simply because he tries to say spirit in terms of matter, as if that were a sin. Materialism is not the attempt to say all in terms of matter. The only materialist—be he poet, teacher, scientist, politician, or statesman—is the man who gets lost in his material without a gathering metaphor to throw it into shape and order. He is the lost soul.

We ask people to think, and we don't show them what thinking is. Somebody says we don't need to show them how to think; bye and bye they will think. We will give them the forms of sentences and, if they have any ideas, then they will know how to write them. But that is preposterous. All there is to writing is having ideas. To learn to write is to learn to have ideas.

The first little metaphor . . . Take some of the trivial ones. I would rather have trivial ones of my own to live by than the big ones of other people.

I remember a boy saying, "He is the kind of person that wounds 40
with his shield." That may be a slender one, of course. It goes a good way in character description. It has poetic grace. "He is the kind that wounds with his shield."

The shield reminds me—just to linger a minute—the shield reminds me of the inverted shield spoken of in one of the books of the *Odyssey*, the book that tells about the longest swim on record. I forget how long it lasted—several days, was it?—but at last as Odysseus came near the coast of Phoenicia, he saw it on the horizon "like an inverted shield."

There is a better metaphor in the same book. In the end Odysseus comes ashore and crawls up the beach to spend the night under a double olive tree, and it says, as in a lonely farmhouse where it is hard to get fire—I am not quoting exactly—where it is hard to start the fire again if it goes out, they cover the seeds of fire with ashes to preserve it for the night, so Odysseus covered himself with the leaves around him and went to sleep. There you have something that gives you character, something of Odysseus himself. "Seeds of fire." So Odysseus covered the seeds of fire in himself. You get the greatness of his nature.

But these are slighter metaphors than the ones we live by. They have their charm, their passing charm. They are as it were the first steps toward the great thoughts, grave thoughts, thoughts lasting to the end.

The metaphor whose manage we are best taught in poetry—that is all there is of thinking. It may not seem far for the mind to go but it is the mind's furthest. The richest accumulation of the ages is the noble metaphors we have rolled up.

I want to add one thing more that the experience of poetry is to 45
anyone who comes close to poetry. There are two ways of coming close to poetry. One is by writing poetry. And some people think I want people to write poetry, but I don't; that is, I don't necessarily. I only want people to write poetry if they want to write poetry. I have never encouraged anybody to write poetry that did not want to write it, and I have not always encouraged those who did want to write it. That ought to be one's own funeral. It is a hard, hard life, as they say.

(I have just been to a city in the West, a city full of poets, a city they have made safe for poets. The whole city is so lovely that you do not have to write it up to make it poetry; it is ready-made for you. But, I don't know—the poetry written in that city might not seem like poetry if read outside of the city. It would be like the jokes made when you were drunk; you have to get drunk again to appreciate them.)

But as I say, there is another way to come close to poetry, fortunately, and that is in the reading of it, not as linguistics, not as history, not as anything but poetry. It is one of the hard things for a teacher to know how close a man has come in reading poetry. How do I know whether a man has come close to Keats in reading Keats? It is hard for me to know. I have lived with some boys a whole year over some of the poets and I have not felt sure whether they have come near what it was all about. One remark sometimes told me. One remark was their mark for the year; had to be—it was all I got that told me what I wanted to know. And that is enough, if it was the right remark, if it came close enough. I think a man might make twenty fool remarks if he made one good one some time in the year. His mark would depend on that good remark.

The closeness—everything depends on the closeness with which you come, and you ought to be marked for the closeness, for nothing else. And that will have to be estimated by chance remarks, not by question and answer. It is only by accident that you know some day how near a person has come.

The person who gets close enough to poetry, he is going to know more about the word *belief* than anybody else knows, even in religion nowadays. There are two or three places where we know belief outside of religion. One of them is at the age of fifteen to twenty, in our self-belief. A young man knows more about himself than he is able to prove to anybody. He has no knowledge that anybody else will accept as knowledge. In his foreknowledge he has something that is going to believe itself into fulfilment, into acceptance.

There is another belief like that, the belief in someone else, a relationship of two that is going to be believed into fulfillment. That is what we are talking about in our novels, the belief of love. And disillusionment that the novels are full of is simply the disillusionment from disappointment in that belief. That belief can fail, of course.

Then there is a literary belief. Every time a poem is written, every time a short story is written, it is written not by cunning, but by belief. The beauty, the something, the little charm of the thing to be, is more felt than known. There is a common jest, one that always annoys me, on the writers, that they write the last end first, and then work up to it; that they lay a train toward one sentence that they think is pretty nice and have all fixed up to set like a trap to close with. No, it should not be that way at all. No one who has ever come close to the arts has failed to see the difference between things written that way, with cunning and device, and the kind that are believed into existence, that begin in something more felt than known. This you can realize quite as well—not quite as well, perhaps, but nearly as well—in reading as you can in writing. I would undertake to separate short stories on that principle;

stories that have been believed into existence and stories that have been cunningly devised. And I could separate the poems still more easily.

Now I think—I happen to think—that those three beliefs that I speak of, the self-belief, the love-belief, and the art-belief, are all closely related to the God-belief, that the belief in God is a relationship you enter into with Him to bring about the future.

There is a national belief like that, too. One feels it. I have been where I came near getting up and walking out on the people who thought that they had to talk against nations, against nationalism, in order to curry favor with internationalism. Their metaphors are all mixed up. They think that because a Frenchman and an American and an Englishman can all sit down on the same platform and receive honors together, it must be that there is no such thing as nations. That kind of bad thinking springs from a source we all know. I should want to say to anyone like that: "Look! First I want to be a person. And I want you to be a person, and then we can be as interpersonal as you please. We can pull each other's noses—do all sorts of things. But, first of all, you have got to have the personality. First of all, you have got to have the nations and then they can be as international as they please with each other."

I should like to use another metaphor on them. I want my palette, if I am a painter, I want my palette on my thumb or on my chair, all clean, pure, separate colors. Then I will do the mixing on the canvas. The canvas is where the work of art is, where we make the conquest. But we want the nations all separate, pure, distinct, things as separate as we can make them; and then in our thoughts, in our arts, and so on, we can do what we please about it.

But I go back. There are four beliefs that I know more about from 55
having lived with poetry. One is the personal belief, which is a knowledge that you don't want to tell other people about because you cannot prove that you know. You are saying nothing about it till you see. The love belief, just the same, has that same shyness. It knows it cannot tell; only the outcome can tell. And the national belief we enter into socially with each other, all together, party of the first part, party of the second part, we enter into that to bring the future of the country. We cannot tell some people what it is we believe, partly, because they are too stupid to understand and partly because we are too proudly vague to explain. And anyway it has got to be fulfilled, and we are not talking until we know more, until we have something to show. And then the literary one in every work of art, not of cunning and craft, mind you, but of real art; that believing the thing into existence, saying as you go more than you even hoped you were going to be able to

say, and coming with surprise to an end that you foreknew only with some sort of emotion. And then finally the relationship we enter into with God to believe the future in—to believe the hereafter in.

QUESTIONS

1. *In what way does the subtitle describe this essay? Is it rambling? Is it unified?*
2. *Frost admires a speech that has "range, something of overstatement, something of statement, and something of understatement." Is this spectrum visible in Frost's own speech? Show where and how.*
3. *What does Frost mean when he says "unless you have had your proper poetical education in the metaphor, you are not safe anywhere" (paragraph 21)? Indicate some of the metaphors Frost examines in this essay. From what fields are they drawn? What does he say about each? To what extent are they useful in helping Frost make his point?*
4. *Choose two metaphors from different fields (like literature and science, politics and biology, sports and drama), and write a brief essay comparing the use and usefulness of the metaphors in each field.*

Stephen Greenblatt

STORYTELLING

My earliest recollections of "having an identity" or "being a self" are bound up with storytelling—narrating my own life or having it narrated for me by my mother. I suppose that I usually used the personal pronoun "I" in telling my own stories and that my mother used my name, but the heart of the initial experience of selfhood lay in the stories, not in the unequivocal, unmeditated possession of an identity. Indeed the stories need not have been directly about me for me to experience them as an expression of my identity: my mother was generously fond of telling me long stories I found irresistible about someone named Terrible Stanley, a child whom I superficially resembled but who made a series of disastrous life decisions—running into traffic, playing with matches, climbing out onto the window ledge, or trying to squeeze through the bars on the cast-iron railing that enclosed the back porch where my mother would hang the washing. We lived in Roxbury then—in those days one of Boston's main Jewish neighbor-

From *Hiding in Plain Sight: Essays in Criticism and Autobiography*, ed. Wendy Lesser (1993).

hoods—and Terrible Stanley's worst, and most delicious, misadventures involved the nearby Franklin Park Zoo.

I am presumably one of the few Americans who woke regularly as a child to the sound of lions roaring in the distance. I can still remember pacing back and forth on the porch and imagining that I was a caged lion. My mother has a picture of me holding on to the bars and with my mouth open wide. I suppose I was roaring. Contrary to *his* mother's explicit warnings and his own solemn promises, Terrible Stanley would sneak away from Maple Court (where we also happened to live), walk down Wayne Street past the Garrison Public School (where my brother was caned in the early 1950s for refusing to recite the catechism), cross Blue Hill Avenue, and go to the zoo. On innumerable occasions, he narrowly escaped being eaten by the lions or crushed in the terrible embrace of the pythons. The zoo was hard to resist.

As I grew slightly older, the sense of identity as intertwined with narratives of the self and its doubles was confirmed by my father, who also had a penchant for storytelling—stories not so gratifyingly focused on my small being as my mother's were, but compelling and wonderfully well-told stories of himself and of a cousin, a few years younger than he, by whom he was virtually obsessed. My father and his cousin came from almost identical backgrounds: first-generation Americans born in Boston to poor Jewish immigrants from Lithuania. Like my father, the cousin had become a lawyer, and here began the story. My father was named Harry J. Greenblatt; his cousin, Joseph H. Greenblatt. But when the latter became a lawyer, he moved into the same building in which my father had his office, and he began to call himself J. Harry Greenblatt. He managed, or so my father thought, to siphon off some clients from my father's already established practice. By itself this would have been enough to cause considerable tension, but over the years J. Harry compounded the offense by apparently becoming considerably richer than my father, Harry J.—wealth, as far as I can tell, being measured principally by the amount of money donated annually to local charities, the contributions printed annually in a small but well-perused booklet. There were, as I grew up, endless stories about J. Harry—chance encounters in the street, confusions of identity that always seemed to work to my father's disadvantage, tearful reconciliations that would quickly give way to renewed rancor, great potlatches of charitable contributions. This went on for decades and would, I suppose, have become intolerably boring had my father not possessed considerable comic gifts, along with a vast repertory of other stories.

But a few years before my father's death at eighty-six, the rivalry and doubling took a strange twist: J. Harry Greenblatt was indicted on charges of embezzlement; the charges were prominently reported in the newspapers; and the newspapers mistakenly printed the name of the culprit—convicted and sentenced to prison—as Harry J. Greenblatt. Busybodies phoned our house to offer their commiserations to my mother. The confusion was awkward, but it had at least one benefit: it enabled my father to tell a whole new set of stories about himself and his double. When you are in your eighties, new stories can be a precious commodity.

5 My father's narrative impulse, I can see from this distance, was a strategic way of turning disappointment, anger, rivalry, and a sense of menace into comic pleasure, a way of reestablishing the self on the site of its threatened loss. But there was an underside to this strategy that I have hinted at by calling his stories obsessive. For the stories in some sense *were* the loss of identity which they were meant to ward off—there was something compulsive about them, as if someone were standing outside of my father and insisting that he endlessly recite his tales. Near the end of his life, he would sometimes abandon the pretense of having a conversation, interrupt what was being said, and simply begin to tell one of his stories.

This sense of compulsiveness in the telling of stories is not simply a function of garrulous old age; it is, I think, a quality that attaches to narrative itself, a quality thematized in *The Arabian Nights* and *The Ancient Mariner.*[1] In response to the compulsiveness, there have arisen numerous social and aesthetic regulations—not only the rules that govern civil conversation, but the rules that govern the production and reception of narrative in books, on screen, on the stage. And there have arisen, too, less evident but powerful psychic regulations that govern how much narrative you are meant to experience, as it were, within your identity.

One of the worst times I have ever been through in my life was a period—I cannot recall if it was a matter of days or weeks—when I could not rid my mind of the impulse to narrate my being. I was a student at Cambridge, trying to decide whether to return to America and go to law school or graduate school in English. "He's sitting at his desk, trying to decide what to do with his life," a voice—my voice, I suppose, but also not my voice—spoke within my head. "Now he's putting his head on his hand; now he is furrowing his brow; and now

1. The first (also known as *The Thousand and One Nights*) is a collection of Oriental stories of uncertain date and authorship told by Scheherazade, who each night left unfinished the story she told the king and so postponed her execution indefinitely; the second, a poem by Samuel Taylor Coleridge (1772–1834) in which the narrator, an old mariner, compulsively relates the story of a dreadful voyage.

he is getting up to open the window." And on and on, with a slight tone of derision through it all. I was split off from myself, J. Harry to my Harry J. (or Terrible Stanley to my Stephen), in an unhappy reprise of my early sense of self as story. It was unhappy, I suppose, because by my early twenties my identity had been fashioned as a single being exactly corresponding to the personal pronoun "I," and the unpleasantly ironic "he" sounding inside my head felt like an internal violation of my internal space, an invasion of my privacy, an objectification of what I least wished to objectify. I experienced the compulsive and detached narrativizing voice as something that had seized me, that I could not throw off, for even my attempts to do so were immediately turned into narrative. It occurred to me that I might be going mad. When the voice left me, it did so suddenly, inexplicably, with the sound of something snapping.

If the experience I have just described intensified my interest in narrative, it made me quite literally wish to get the narratives outside myself. Hence the critical distance that I attempt to inscribe in and with the stories I tell, for the narrative impulse in my writing is yoked to the service of literary and cultural criticism; it pulls out and away from myself. Hence too, perhaps, my fascination with figures of estrangement: I could not endure the compulsive estrangement of my life, as if it belonged to someone else, but I could perhaps understand the uncanny otherness of my own voice, make it comprehensible, and bring it under rational control by trying to understand the way in which all voices come to be woven out of strands of alien experience. I am committed to making strange what has become familiar, to demonstrating that what seems an untroubling and untroubled part of ourselves (for example, Shakespeare) is actually part of something else, something different.

We spent last spring in Boston, and I wanted to take my wife to the apartment house in Roxbury. My mother and everyone else in my family told us that we shouldn't go back to the old neighborhood. I had lived in California too long, they said, and didn't know what it was like. There are murders every night, said my cousin Sherman; whites aren't welcome, said my cousin Ann; there is nothing to see, said my cousin Eldon; the animals in the zoo have been killed off one by one, with BB guns and poison, said my brother, and the park is a nightmare, even in broad daylight. Of course, we went anyway. That is, after all, the lesson of the Terrible Stanley stories.

There were lots of animals in the zoo—I don't know if the cages had 10
been restocked or if the story of the killings was merely a grim joke that had eventually, in the tense and racist atmosphere of Boston, been re-

ceived as truth. The park, designed by Olmsted,[2] looked beautiful, easily the loveliest green space in the entire city. But my family was right that the neighborhood looked awful: the streets empty, shops boarded up, trash piled on the sidewalks, windows broken everywhere, graffiti spray-painted on walls. No landlord or bank had put any money into the buildings for years, probably for decades. We found the great old synagogue, Mishkan Tefilah, whose vast neoclassical bulk still dominates the area: it was torched, I don't know when, and stands in massive, burned-out desolation. About half the windows of the apartment house on Maple Court were boarded up, but there were people living there, and I could see washing hanging from the porch where I used to practice my roaring. On the driveway below the porch, a young woman was waxing her car. She heard me say to my wife that that was the apartment we used to live in, and she beckoned to us. "Stand here for a few minutes and let people see that you're talking to me." She spoke in the tone of quiet urgency with which my mother used to enjoin me not to go to the zoo, not to wander off from the haven of the apartment. "Then get out quickly," she added. "It's not safe for you to be here."

2. Frederick Law Olmsted (1822–1903), American landscape architect and notable designer of city parks.

Adrienne Rich

WHEN WE DEAD AWAKEN: WRITING AS RE-VISION

Ibsen's *When We Dead Awaken* is a play about the use that the male artist and thinker—in the process of creating culture as we know it—has made of women, in his life and in his work; and about a woman's slow struggling awakening to the use to which her life has been put. Bernard Shaw wrote in 1900 of this play: "[Ibsen] shows us that no degradation ever devized or permitted is as disastrous as this degradation; that through it women can die into luxuries for men and yet can kill them; that men and women are becoming conscious of this: and that what remains to be seen as perhaps the most interesting of all imminent social developments is what will happen 'when we dead awaken.' "

Written for a forum on "The Woman Writer in the Twentieth Century" in 1971, and later published in *College English* (Vol. 34, No. 1, Oct. 1972); this version is included in *On Lies, Secrets, and Silence: Selected Prose: 1966–1978* (1979).

It's exhilarating to be alive in a time of awakening consciousness; it can also be confusing, disorienting, and painful. This awakening of dead or sleeping consciousness has already affected the lives of millions of women, even those who don't know it yet. It is also affecting the lives of men, even those who deny its claims upon them. The argument will go on whether an oppressive economic class system is responsible for the oppressive nature of male/female relations, or whether, in fact, the sexual class system is the original model on which all the others are based. But in the last few years connections have been drawn between our sexual lives and our political institutions which are inescapable and illuminating. The sleepwalkers are coming awake, and for the first time this awakening has a collective reality; it is no longer such a lonely thing to open one's eyes.

Re-vision—the act of looking back, of seeing with fresh eyes, of entering an old text from a new critical direction—is for us more than a chapter in cultural history: it is an act of survival. Until we can understand the assumptions in which we are drenched we cannot know ourselves. And this drive to self-knowledge, for woman, is more than a search for identity: it is part of her refusal of the destructiveness of male-dominated society. A radical critique of literature, feminist in its impulse, would take the work first of all as a clue to how we live, how we have been living, how we have been led to imagine ourselves, how our language has trapped as well as liberated us; and how we can begin to see—and therefore live—afresh. A change in the concept of sexual identity is essential if we are not going to see the old political order reassert itself in every new revolution. We need to know the writing of the past, and know it differently than we have ever known it; not to pass on a tradition but to break its hold over us.

For writers, and at this moment for women writers in particular, there is the challenge and promise of a whole new psychic geography to be explored. But there is also a difficult and dangerous walking on the ice, as we try to find language and images for a consciousness we are just coming into, and with little in the past to support us. I want to talk about some aspects of this difficulty and this danger.

Jane Harrison, the great classical anthropologist, wrote in 1914 in a 5
letter to her friend Gilbert Murray: "By the by, about 'Women,' it has bothered me often—why do women never want to write poetry about Man as a sex—why is Woman a dream and a terror to man and not the other way around? . . . Is it mere convention and propriety, or something deeper?" I think Jane's question cuts deep into the myth-making tradition, the romantic tradition; deep into what women and men have been to each other; and deep into the psyche of the woman writer. Thinking about that question, I began thinking of the work of two twentieth-century women poets, Sylvia Plath and Diane Wakoski.

It strikes me that in the work of both Man appears as, if not a dream, a fascination, and a terror; and that the source of the fascination and the terror is, simply, Man's power—to dominate, tyrannize, choose or reject the woman. The charisma of Man seems to come purely from his power over her, and his control of the world by force; not from anything fertile or life-giving in him. And, in the work of both these poets, it is finally the woman's sense of *herself*—embattled, possessed—that gives the poetry its dynamic charge, its rhythms of struggle, need, will and female energy. Convention and propriety are perhaps not the right words, but until recently this female anger, this furious awareness of the Man's power over her, were not available materials to the female poet, who tended to write of Love as the source of her suffering, and to view that victimization by Love as an almost inevitable fate. Or, like Marianne Moore and Elizabeth Bishop, she kept human sexual relationships at a measured and chiselled distance in her poems.

One answer to Jane Harrison's question has to be that historically men and women have played very different parts in each others' lives. Where woman has been a luxury for man, and has served as the painter's model and the poet's muse, but also as comforter, nurse, cook, bearer of his seed, secretarial assistant, and copyist of manuscripts, man has played a quite different role for the female artist. Henry James repeats an incident which the writer Prosper Mérimée described, of how, while he was living with George Sand,

> he once opened his eyes, in the raw winter dawn, to see his companion, in a dressing-gown, on her knees before the domestic hearth, a candlestick beside her and a red *madras* round her head, making bravely, with her own hands, the fire that was to enable her to sit down betimes to urgent pen and paper. The story represents him as having felt that the spectacle chilled his ardor and tried his taste; her appearance was unfortunate, her occupation an inconsequence, and her industry a reproof—the result of all of which was a lively irritation and an early rupture.

I am suggesting that the specter of this kind of male judgment, along with the active discouragement and thwarting of her needs by a culture controlled by males, has created problems for the woman writer: problems of contact with herself, problems of language and style, problems of energy and survival.

In rereading Virginia Woolf's *A Room of One's Own* for the first time in some years, I was astonished at the sense of effort, of pains taken, of dogged tentativeness, in the tone of that essay. And I recognized that tone. I had heard it often enough, in myself and in other women. It is the tone of a woman almost in touch with her anger, who is determined not to appear angry, who is *willing* herself to be calm, detached, and even charming in a roomful of men where things have been said which are attacks on her very integrity. Virginia Woolf is addressing an audience of women, but she is acutely conscious—as she always was—of being overheard by men: by Morgan and Lytton and Maynard Keynes[1] and for that matter by her father, Leslie Stephen. She drew the language out into an exacerbated thread in her determination to have her own sensibility yet protect it from those masculine presence. Only at rare moments in that essay do you hear the passion in her voice; she was trying to sound as cool as Jane Austen, as Olympian as Shakespeare, because that is the way the men of the culture thought a writer should sound.

No male writer has written primarily or even largely for women, or with the sense of women's criticism as a consideration when he chooses his materials, his theme, his language. But to a lesser or greater extent, every woman writer has written for men even when, like Virginia Woolf, she was supposed to be addressing women. If we have come to the point when this balance might begin to change, when women can stop being haunted, not only by "convention and propriety" but by internalized fears of being and saying themselves, then it is an extraordinary moment for the woman writer—and reader.

I have hesitated to do what I am going to do now, which is to use myself as an illustration. For one thing, it's a lot easier and less dangerous to talk about other women writers. But there is something else. Like Virginia Woolf, I am aware of the women who are not with us here because they are washing the dishes and looking after the children. Nearly fifty years after she spoke, that fact remains largely unchanged. And I am thinking also of women whom she left out of the picture altogether—women who are washing other people's dishes and caring for other people's children, not to mention women who went on the streets last night in order to feed their children. We seem to be special women here, we have liked to think of ourselves as special, and we have known that men would tolerate, even romanticize us as special, as long as our words and actions didn't threaten their privilege of tolerating or rejecting us according to *their* ideas of what a special woman ought to be. An important insight of the radical women's movement, for me, has been how divisive and how ultimately destructive is this myth of the special woman, who is also the token woman. Every one of us here in this room has had great luck; our own gifts could not have been enough, for we all know women whose gifts are buried or aborted. Our struggles can have meaning only if they can help to change the lives of women whose gifts—and whose very being—continues to be thwarted.

1. E. M. Forster, novelist, and Lytton Strachey, biographer, and John Maynard Keynes, economist—all members of the Bloomsbury group in London during the 1920s and 1930s.

10 My own luck was being born white and middle-class into a house full of books, with a father who encouraged me to read and write. So for about twenty years I wrote for a particular man, who criticized and praised me and made me feel I was indeed "special." The obverse side of this, of course, was that I tried for a long time to please him, or rather, not to displease him. And then of course there were other men—writers, teachers—the Man, who was not a terror or a dream but a literary master and a master in other ways less easy to acknowledge. And there were all those poems about women, written by men: it seemed to be a given that men wrote poems and women frequently inhabited them. These women were almost always beautiful, but threatened with the loss of beauty, the loss of youth—the fate worse than death. Or, they were beautiful and died young, like Lucy and Lenore.[2] Or, the woman was like Maud Gonne,[3] cruel and disastrously mistaken, and the poem reproached her because she had refused to become a luxury for the poet.

A lot is being said today about the influence that the myths and images of women have on all of us who are products of culture. I think it has been a peculiar confusion to the girl or woman who tries to write, because she is peculiarly susceptible to language. She goes to poetry or fiction looking for *her* way of being in the world, since she too has been putting words and images together; she is looking eagerly for guides, maps, possibilities; and over and over in the "words' masculine persuasive force" of literature she comes up against something that negates everything she is about: she meets the image of Woman in books written by men. She finds a terror and a dream, she finds a beautiful pale face, she finds La Belle Dame Sans Merci, she finds Juliet or Tess or Salomé,[4] but precisely what she does not find is that absorbed, drudging, puzzled, sometimes inspired creature, herself, who sits at a desk trying to put words together.

So what does she do? What did I do? I read the older women poets with their peculiar keenness and ambivalence: Sappho, Christina Rossetti, Emily Dickinson, Elinor Wylie, Edna Millay, H.D. I discovered that the woman poet most admired at the time (by men) was Marianne Moore, who was maidenly, elegant, intellectual, discreet. But even in reading these women I was looking in them for the same things I had found in the poetry of men, because I wanted women poets to be the equals of men, and to be equal was still confused with sounding the same.

2. In poems by William Wordsworth and Edgar Allan Poe.
3. Irish revolutionary activist, subject of many love poems by William Butler Yeats.
4. These female figures appear respectively in the poem "La Belle Dame sans Merci" by John Keats, Shakespeare's play *Romeo and Juliet,* Thomas Hardy's novel *Tess of the D'Urbervilles,* and Oscar Wilde's play *Salomé.*

I know that my style was formed first by male poets: by the men I was reading as an undergraduate—Frost, Dylan Thomas, Donne, Auden, MacNiece, Stevens, Yeats. What I chiefly learned from them was craft. But poems are like dreams: in them you put what you don't know you know. Looking back at poems I wrote before I was twenty-one, I'm startled because beneath the conscious craft are glimpses of the split I even then experienced between the girl who wrote poems, who defined herself in writing poems, and the girl who was to define herself by her relationships with men. "Aunt Jennifer's Tigers," written while I was a student, looks with deliberate detachment at this split.

Aunt Jennifer's tigers stride across a screen,
Bright topaz denizens of a world of green.
They do not fear the men beneath the tree,
They pace in sleek chivalric certainty.

Aunt Jennifer's fingers, fluttering through her wool,
Find even the ivory needle hard to pull.
The massive weight of Uncle's wedding-band
Sits heavily upon Aunt Jennifer's hand.

When Aunt is dead, her terrified hands will lie
Still ringed with ordeals she was mastered by.
The tigers in the panel that she made
Will go on striding, proud and unafraid.

In writing this poem, composed and apparently cool as it is, I thought I was creating a portrait of an imaginary woman. But this woman suffers from the opposition of her imagination, worked out in tapestry, and her life-style, "ringed with ordeals she was mastered by." It was important to me that Aunt Jennifer was a person as distinct from myself as possible—distanced by the formalism of the poem; by its objective, observant tone; even by putting the woman in a different generation.

In those years formalism was part of the strategy—like asbestos gloves, it allowed me to handle materials I couldn't pick up barehanded. (A later strategy was to use the persona of a man, as I did in "The Loser.")

A man thinks of the woman he once loved: first, after her wedding, and then nearly a decade later.

I

I kissed you, bride and lost, and went
home from that bourgeois sacrament,
your cheek still tasting cold upon

my lips that gave you benison
with all the swagger that they knew—
as losers somehow learn to do.

Your wedding made my eyes ache; soon
the world would be worse off for one
more golden apple dropped to ground
without the least protesting sound,
and you would windfall lie, and we
forget your shimmer on the tree.

Beauty is always wasted: if
not Mignon's song sung to the deaf,
at all events to the unmoved.
A face like yours cannot be loved
long or seriously enough.
Almost, we seem to hold it off.

II

Well, you are tougher than I thought.
Now when the wash with ice hangs taut
this morning of St. Valentine,
I see you strip the squeaking line,
your body weighed against the load,
and all my groans can do no good.

Because you still are beautiful,
though squared and stiffened by the pull
of what nine windy years have done.
You have three daughters, lost a son.
I see all your intelligence
flung into that unwearied stance.

My envy is of no avail.
I turn my head and wish him well
who chafed your beauty into use
and lives forever in a house
lit by the friction of your mind.
You stagger in against the wind.

1958

15 I finished college, published my first book by a fluke, as it seemed to me, and broke off a love-affair. I took a job, lived alone, went on writing, fell in love. I was young, full of energy, and the book seemed to mean that others agreed I was a poet. Because I was also determined to have a "full" woman's life, I plunged in my early twenties into marriage and had three children before I was thirty. There was nothing overt in the environment to warn me: these were the fifties, and in reaction to the earlier wave of feminism, middle-class women were

making careers of domestic perfection, working to send their husbands through professional schools, then retiring to raise large families. People were moving out to the suburbs, technology was going to be the answer to everything, even sex; the family was in its glory. Life was extremely private; women were isolated from each other by the loyalties of marriage. I have a sense that women didn't talk to each other much in the fifties—not about their secret emptiness, their frustrations. I went on trying to write, my second book and first child appeared in the same month. But by the time that book came out I was already dissatisfied with those poems, which seemed to me mere exercises for poems I hadn't written. The book was praised, however, for its "gracefulness"; I had a marriage and a child. If there were doubts, if there were periods of null depression or active despairing, these could only mean that I was ungrateful, insatiable, perhaps a monster.

About the time my third child was born, I felt that I had either to consider myself a failed woman and a failed poet, or try to find some synthesis by which to understand what was happening to me. What frightened me most was the sense of drift, of being pulled along on a current which called itself my destiny, but in which I seemed to be losing touch with whoever I had been, with the girl who had experienced her own will and energy almost ecstatically at times, walking around a city or riding a train at night or typing in a student room. In a poem about my grandmother, I wrote (of myself): "A young girl, thought sleeping, is certified dead." I was writing very little, partly from fatigue, that female fatigue of suppressed anger and the loss of contact with her own being; partly from the discontinuity of female life with its attention to small chores, errands, work that others constantly undo, small children's constant needs. What I did write was unconvincing to me; my anger and frustration were hard to acknowledge in or out of poem, because in fact I cared a great deal about my husband and my children. Trying to look back and understand that time I have tried to analyze the real nature of the conflict. Most, if not all, human lives are full of fantasy—passive daydreaming which need not be acted on. But to write poetry or fiction, or even to think well, is not to fantasize, or to put fantasies on paper. For a poem to coalesce, for a character or an action to take shape, there has to be an imaginative transformation of reality which is in no way passive. And a certain freedom of the mind is needed—freedom to press on, to enter the currents of your thought like a glider pilot, knowing that your motion can be sustained, that the buoyancy of your attention will not be suddenly snatched away. Moreover, if the imagination is to transcend and transform experience it has to question, to challenge, to conceive of alternatives, perhaps to the very life you are living at that moment. You have to be free to play around with the notion that day might be night, love might be hate; nothing can be too sacred for the imagination to turn into its opposite or to call experimentally by another name. For writing is re-naming. Now, to be maternally with small children all day in the old way, to be with a man in the old way of marriage, requires a holding-back, a putting-aside of that imaginative activity, and seems to demand instead a kind of conservatism. I want to make it clear that I am *not* saying that in order to write well, or think well, it is necessary to become unavailable to others, or to become a devouring ego. This has been the myth of the masculine artist and thinker; and I repeat, I do not accept it. But to be a female human being trying to fulfill traditional female functions in a traditional way *is* in direct conflict with the subversive function of the imagination. The word *traditional* is important here. There must be ways, and we will be finding out more and more about them, in which the energy of creation and the energy of relation can be united. But in those earlier years I always felt the conflict as a failure of love in myself. I had thought I was choosing a full life: the life available to most men, in which sexuality, work and parenthood could coexist. But I felt, at twenty-nine, guilt toward the people closest to me, and guilty toward my own being.

I wanted, then, more than anything, the one thing of which there was never enough: time to think, time to write. The fifties and early sixties were years of rapid revelations: the sit-ins and marches in the South, the Bay of Pigs,[5] the early anti-war movement raised large questions—questions for which the masculine world of the academy around me seemed to have expert and fluent answers. But I needed desperately to think for myself—about pacifism and dissent and violence, about poetry and society and about my own relationship to all these things. For about ten years I was reading in fierce snatches, scribbling in notebooks, writing poetry in fragments; I was looking desperately for clues, because if there were no clues then I thought I might be insane. I wrote in a notebook about this time: "Paralyzed by the sense that there exists a mesh of relationships—e.g. between my anger at the children, my sensual life, pacifism, sex, (I mean sex in its broadest significance, not merely sexual desire)—an interconnectedness which, if I could see it, make it valid, would give me back myself, make it possible to function lucidly and passionately. Yet I grope in and out among these dark webs." I think I began at this point to feel that politics was not something "out there" but something "in here" and of the essence of my condition.

In the late fifties I was able to write, for the first time, directly about experiencing myself as a woman. The poem was jotted in fragments during children's naps, brief hours in a library, or at 3 A.M. after rising

5. Site of a failed American invasion of Cuba, intended to overthrow the Castro regime.

with a wakeful child. I despaired of doing any continuous work at this time. Yet I began to feel that my fragments and scraps had a common consciousness and a common theme, one which I would have been very unwilling to put on paper at an earlier time because I had been taught that poetry should be "universal," which meant, of course, non-female. Until then I had tried very much *not* to identify myself as a female poet. Over two years I wrote a ten-part poem called "Snapshots of A Daughter-in-Law," in a longer, looser mode than I've ever trusted myself with before. It was an extraordinary relief to write that poem. It strikes me now as too literary, too dependent on allusion; I hadn't found the courage yet to do without authorities, or even to use the pronoun *I*—the woman in the poem is *always she.* One section of it, 2, concerns a woman who thinks she is going mad; she is haunted by voices telling her to resist and rebel, voices which she can hear but not obey.

2.

Banging the coffee-pot into the sink
she hears the angels chiding, and looks out
past the raked gardens to the sloppy sky.
Only a week since They said: *Have no patience.*

The next time it was: *Be insatiable.*
Then: *Save yourself; others you cannot save.*
Sometimes she's let the tapstream scald her arm,
a match burn to her thumbnail,

or held her hand above the kettle's spout
right in the woolly steam. They are probably angels,
since nothing hurts her any more, except
each morning's grit blowing into her eyes.

The poem "Orion," written five years later, is a poem of reconnection with a part of myself I had felt I was losing—the active principle, the energetic imagination, the "half-brother" whom I projected, as I had for many years, into the constellation Orion.

Far back when I went zig-zagging
through tamarack pastures
you were my genius, you
my cast-iron Viking, my helmed
lion-heart king in prison.
Years later now you're young

my fierce half-brother, staring
down from that simplified west
your breast open, your belt dragged down
by an oldfashioned thing, a sword

the last bravado you won't give over
though it weighs you down as you stride

and the stars in it are dim
and maybe have stopped burning.
But you burn, and I know it;
as I throw back my head to take you in
an old transfusion happens again:
divine astronomy is nothing to it.

Indoors I bruise and blunder,
break faith, leave ill enough
alone, a dead child born in the dark.
Night cracks up over the chimney,
pieces of time, frozen geodes
come showering down in the grate.

A man reaches behind my eyes
and finds them empty
a woman's head turns away
from my head in the mirror
children are dying my death
and eating crumbs of my life.

Pity is not your forte.
Calmly you ache up there
pinned aloft in your crow's nest,
my speechless pirate!
You take it all for granted
and when I look you back

it's with a starlike eye
shooting its cold and egotistical spear
where it can do least damage.
Breathe deep! No hurt, no pardon
out here in the cold with you
you with your back to the wall.

20 It's no accident that the words *cold and egotistical* appear in this poem, and are applied to myself. The choice still seemed to be between "love"—womanly, maternal love, altruistic love—a love defined and ruled by the weight of an entire culture—and egotism—a force directed by men into creation, achievement, ambition, often at the expense of others, but justifiably so. For weren't they men, and wasn't that their destiny as womanly love was ours? I know now that the alternatives are false ones—that the word *love* is itself in need of re-vision.

There is a companion poem to "Orion," written three years later, in which at last the woman in the poem and the woman writing the poem become the same person. It is called "Planetarium," and it was written after a visit to a real planetarium, where I read an account of the work of Caroline Herschel, the astronomer, who worked with her brother William, but whose name remained obscure, as his did not.

(Thinking of Caroline
Herschel, 1750–1848,
astronomer, sister of
William; and others)

A woman in the shape of a monster
a monster in the shape of a woman
the skies are full of them

a woman 'in the snow
among the Clocks and instruments
or measuring the ground with poles'

in her 98 years to discover
8 comets

she whom the moon ruled
like us
levitating into the night sky
riding the polished lenses

Galaxies of women, there
doing penance for impetuousness
ribs chilled
in those spaces of the mind

An eye,
'virile, precise and absolutely certain'
from the mad webs of Uranisborg
encountering the NOVA

every impulse of light exploding
from the core
as life flies out of us

Tycho whispering at last
'Let me not seem to have lived in vain'

What we see, we see
and seeing is changing

the light that shrivels a mountain
and leaves a man alive

Heartbeat of the pulsar
heart sweating through my body

The radio impulse
pouring in from Taurus

I am bombarded yet   I stand

I have been standing all my life in the
direct path of a battery of signals
the most accurately transmitted most
untranslatable language in the universe
I am a galactic cloud so deep   so invo-
luted that a light wave could take 15
years to travel through me   And has
taken   I am an instrument in the shape
of a woman trying to translate pulsations
into images   for the relief of the body
and the reconstruction of the mind.

In closing I want to tell you about a dream I had last summer. I dreamed I was asked to read my poetry at a mass women's meeting; but when I began to read, what came out were the lyrics of a blues song. I share this dream with you because it seemed to me to say a lot about the problems and the future of the woman writer, and probably of women in general. The awakening of consciousness is not like the crossing of a frontier—one step, and you are in another country. Much of women's poetry has been of the nature of the blues song: a cry of pain, of victimization, or a lyric of seduction. And today, much poetry by women—and prose for that matter—is charged with anger. I think we need to go through that anger, and we will betray our own reality if we try, as Virginia Woolf was trying, for an objectivity, a detachment; that would make us sound more like Jane Austen or Shakespeare. We know more than Jane Austen or Shakespeare knew: more than Jane Austen because our lives are more complex, more than Shakespeare because we know more about the lives of women, Jane Austen and Virginia Woolf included.

Both the victimization and the anger experienced by women are real, and have real sources, everywhere in the environment, built into society. They must go on being tapped and explored by poets, among others. We can neither deny them, nor can we rest there. They are our birth-pains, and we are bearing ourselves. We would be failing each other as writers and as women, if we neglected or denied what is negative, regressive or Sisyphean[5] in our inwardness.

We all know that there is another story to be told. I am curious and expectant about the future of the masculine consciousness. I feel in the work of the men whose poetry I read today a deep pessimism and fatalistic grief; and I wonder if it isn't the masculine side of what

5. The reference is to the Greek myth of Sisyphus. He was condemned to roll a huge rock to the top of a hill, but the rock always rolled back down before the top was reached.

women have experienced, the price of masculine dominance. One thing I am sure of: just as woman is becoming her own midwife, creating herself anew, so man will have to learn to gestate and give birth to his own subjectivity—something he has frequently wanted woman to do for him. We can go on trying to talk to each other, we can sometimes help each other, poetry and fiction can show us what the other is going through; but women can no longer be primarily mothers and muses for men: we have our own work cut out for us.

QUESTIONS

1. *A typical male-chauvinist cliché is that women take everything too personally, that they lack a larger perspective. Does this essay tend to confirm or deny that belief?*
2. *Why does Rich include some of her own poetry? Explain whether you think she is able to make points through it that she couldn't make otherwise.*
3. *Why does Rich use the hyphen in* re-vision? *What does she wish to imply about writing?*
4. *In paragraph 11, Rich refers to "the influence that the myths and images of women have on all of us." Presumably there are also myths and images of men. Write a brief account of either a male or a female myth and its influence upon attitudes and actions of members of the other sex.*

Virginia Woolf

IN SEARCH OF A ROOM OF ONE'S OWN

It was disappointing not to have brought back in the evening some important statement, some authentic fact. Women are poorer than men because—this or that. Perhaps now it would be better to give up seeking for the truth, and receiving on one's head an avalanche of opinion hot as lava, discoloured as dish-water. It would be better to draw the curtains; to shut out distractions; to light the lamp; to narrow the enquiry and to ask the historian, who records not opinions but

From Chapter 3 of Woolf's *A Room of One's Own* (1929), a long essay that began as lectures given at Newnham College and Girton College, women's colleges at Cambridge University, in 1928. In Chapter 1, Woolf advances the proposition that "a woman must have money and a room of her own if she is to write fiction." In Chapter 2, she describes a day spent at the British Museum (now the British Library) looking for information about the lives of women.

facts, to describe under what conditions women lived, not throughout the ages, but in England, say in the time of Elizabeth.

For it is a perennial puzzle why no woman wrote a word of that extraordinary literature when every other man, it seemed, was capable of song or sonnet. What were the conditions in which women lived, I asked myself; for fiction, imaginative work that is, is not dropped like a pebble upon the ground, as science may be; fiction is like a spider's web, attached ever so lightly perhaps, but still attached to life at all four corners. Often the attachment is scarcely perceptible; Shakespeare's plays, for instance, seem to hang there complete by themselves. But when the web is pulled askew, hooked up at the edge, torn in the middle, one remembers that these webs are not spun in midair by incorporeal creatures, but are the work of suffering human beings, and are attached to grossly material things, like health and money and the houses we live in.

I went, therefore, to the shelf where the histories stand and took down one of the latest, Professor Trevelyan's *History of England.* Once more I looked up Women, found "position of," and turned to the pages indicated. "Wife-beating," I read, "was a recognised right of man, and was practised without shame by high as well as low. . . . Similarly," the historian goes on, "the daughter who refused to marry the gentleman of her parents' choice was liable to be locked up, beaten and flung about the room, without any shock being inflicted on public opinion. Marriage was not an affair of personal affection, but of family avarice, particularly in the 'chivalrous' upper classes. . . . Betrothal often took place while one or both of the parties was in the cradle, and marriage when they were scarcely out of the nurses' charge." That was about 1470, soon after Chaucer's time. The next reference to the position of women is some two hundred years later, in the time of the Stuarts. "It was still the exception for women of the upper and middle class to choose their own husbands, and when the husband had been assigned, he was lord and master, so far at least as law and custom could make him. Yet even so," Professor Trevelyan concludes, "neither Shakespeare's women nor those of authentic seventeenth-century memoirs, like the Verneys and the Hutchinsons, seem wanting in personality and character." Certainly, if we consider it, Cleopatra must have had a way with her; Lady Macbeth, one would suppose, had a will of her own; Rosalind, one might conclude, was an attractive girl. Professor Trevelyan is speaking no more than the truth when he remarks that Shakespeare's women do not seem wanting in personality and character. Not being a historian, one might go even further and say that women have burnt like beacons in all the works of all the poets from the beginning of time—Clytemnestra, Antigone, Cleopatra, Lady Macbeth, Phèdre, Cressida, Rosalind, Desdemona, the Duchess of Malfi, among the dramatists; then among the prose writers: Millamant, Clarissa, Becky Sharp, Anna Karenina, Emma Bovary, Madame de Guermantes—the names flock to mind, nor do they recall women "lacking in personality and character." Indeed, if woman had no existence save in the fiction written by men, one would imagine her a person of the utmost importance; very various; heroic and mean; splendid and sordid; infinitely beautiful and hideous in the extreme; as great as a man, some think even greater.[1] But this is woman in fiction. In fact, as Professor Trevelyan points out, she was locked up, beaten and flung about the room.

A very queer, composite being thus emerges. Imaginatively she is of the highest importance; practically she is completely insignificant. She pervades poetry from cover to cover; she is all but absent from history. She dominates the lives of kings and conquerors in fiction; in fact she was the slave of any boy whose parents forced a ring upon her finger. Some of the most inspired words, some of the most profound thoughts in literature fall from her lips; in real life she could hardly read, could scarcely spell, and was the property of her husband.

It was certainly an odd monster that one made up by reading the 5
historians first and the poets afterwards—a worm winged like an eagle; the spirit of life and beauty in a kitchen chopping up suet. But these monsters, however amusing to the imagination, have no existence in fact. What one must do to bring her to life was to think poetically and prosaically at one and the same moment, thus keeping in touch with fact—that she is Mrs. Martin, aged thirty-six, dressed in blue, wearing a black hat and brown shoes; but not losing sight of fiction either—that she is a vessel in which all sorts of spirits and forces are coursing and flashing perpetually. The moment, however, that one tries this method with the Elizabethan woman, one branch of illumination fails; one is held up by the scarcity of facts. One knows nothing

1. "It remains a strange and almost inexplicable fact that in Athena's city, where women were kept in almost Oriental suppression as odalisques or drudges, the stage should yet have produced figures like Clytemnestra and Cassandra, Atossa and Antigone, Phèdre and Medea, and all the other heroines who dominate play after play of the 'misogynist' Euripides. But the paradox of this world where in real life a respectable woman could hardly show her face alone in the street, and yet on the stage woman equals or surpasses man, has never been satisfactorily explained. In modern tragedy the same predominance exists. At all events, a very cursory survey of Shakespeare's work (similarly with Webster, though not with Marlowe or Jonson) suffices to reveal how this dominance, this initiative of women, persists from Rosalind to Lady Macbeth. So too in Racine; six of his tragedies bear their heroines' names; and what male characters of his shall we set against Hermione and Andromaque, Bérénice and Roxane, Phèdre and Athalie? So again with Ibsen; what men shall we match with Solveig and Nora, Hedda and Hilda Wangel and Rebecca West?"—F. L. Lucas, Tragedy, pp. 114–15 [Woolf's note].

detailed, nothing perfectly true and substantial about her. History scarcely mentions her. And I turned to Professor Trevelyan again to see what history meant to him. I found by looking at his chapter headings that it meant—

"The Manor Court and the Methods of Open-field Agriculture . . . The Cistercians and Sheep-farming . . . The Crusades . . . The University . . . The House of Commons . . . The Hundred Years' War . . . The Wars of the Roses . . . The Renaissance Scholars . . . The Dissolution of the Monasteries . . . Agrarian and Religious Strife . . . The Origin of English Sea-power . . . The Armada . . ." and so on. Occasionally an individual woman is mentioned, an Elizabeth, or a Mary; a queen or a great lady. But by no possible means could middle-class women with nothing but brains and character at their command have taken part in any one of the great movements which, brought together, constitute the historian's view of the past. Nor shall we find her in any collection of anecdotes. Aubrey[2] hardly mentions her. She never writes her own life and scarcely keeps a diary; there are only a handful of her letters in existence. She left no plays or poems by which we can judge her. What one wants, I thought—and why does not some brilliant student at Newnham or Girton supply it?—is a mass of information; at what age did she marry; how many children had she as a rule; what was her house like; had she a room to herself; did she do the cooking; would she be likely to have a servant? All these facts lie somewhere, presumably, in parish registers and account books; the life of the average Elizabethan woman must be scattered about somewhere, could one collect it and make a book of it. It would be ambitious beyond my daring, I thought, looking about the shelves for books that were not there, to suggest to the students of those famous colleges that they should rewrite history, though I own that it often seems a little queer as it is, unreal, lop-sided; but why should they not add a supplement to history? calling it, of course, by some inconspicuous name so that women might figure there without impropriety? For one often catches a glimpse of them in the lives of the great, whisking away into the background, concealing, I sometimes think, a wink, a laugh, perhaps a tear. And, after all, we have lives enough of Jane Austen; it scarcely seems necessary to consider again the influence of the tragedies of Joanna Baillie upon the poetry of Edgar Allan Poe; as for myself, I should not mind if the homes and haunts of Mary Russell Mitford were closed to the public for a century at least.[3] But what I find deplorable, I con-

2. John Aubrey (1626–1697), whose biographical writings were published posthumously as *Brief Lives*.
3. Jane Austen (1775–1817), English novelist; Joanna Baillie (1762–1851), Scottish dramatist and poet; Mary Russell Mitford (1787–1855), English novelist and dramatist.

tinued, looking about the bookshelves again, is that nothing is known about women before the eighteenth century. I have no model in my mind to turn about this way and that. Here am I asking why women did not write poetry in the Elizabethan age, and I am not sure how they were educated; whether they were taught to write; whether they had sitting-rooms to themselves; how many women had children before they were twenty-one; what, in short, they did from eight in the morning till eight at night. They had no money evidently; according to Professor Trevelyan they were married whether they liked it or not before they were out of the nursery, at fifteen or sixteen very likely. It would have been extremely odd, even upon this showing, had one of them suddenly written the plays of Shakespeare, I concluded, and I thought of that old gentleman, who is dead now, but was a bishop, I think, who declared that it was impossible for any woman, past, present, or to come, to have the genius of Shakespeare. He wrote to the papers about it. He also told a lady who applied to him for information that cats do not as a matter of fact go to heaven, though they have, he added, souls of a sort. How much thinking those old gentlemen used to save one! How the borders of ignorance shrank back at their approach! Cats do not go to heaven. Women cannot write the plays of Shakespeare.

Be that as it may, I could not help thinking, as I looked at the works of Shakespeare on the shelf, that the bishop was right at least in this; it would have been impossible, completely and entirely, for any woman to have written the plays of Shakespeare in the age of Shakespeare. Let me imagine, since facts are so hard to come by, what would have happened had Shakespeare had a wonderfully gifted sister, called Judith, let us say. Shakespeare himself went, very probably—his mother was an heiress—to the grammar school, where he may have learnt Latin—Ovid, Virgil and Horace—and the elements of grammar and logic. He was, it is well known, a wild boy who poached rabbits, perhaps shot a deer, and had, rather sooner than he should have done, to marry a woman in the neighbourhood, who bore him a child rather quicker than was right. That escapade sent him to seek his fortune in London. He had, it seemed, a taste for the theatre; he began by holding horses at the stage door. Very soon he got work in the theatre, became a successful actor, and lived at the hub of the universe, meeting everybody, knowing everybody, practising his art on the boards, exercising his wits in the streets, and even getting access to the palace of the queen. Meanwhile his extraordinarily gifted sister, let us suppose, remained at home. She was as adventurous, as imaginative, as agog to see the world as he was. But she was not sent to school. She had no chance of learning grammar and logic, let alone of reading Horace and Virgil. She picked up a book now and then, one of her brother's perhaps, and read a few pages. But then her parents came in and told her to mend the stockings or mind the stew and not moon about with books and papers. They would have spoken sharply but kindly, for they were substantial people who knew the conditions of life for a woman and loved their daughter—indeed, more likely than not she was the apple of her father's eye. Perhaps she scribbled some pages up in an apple loft on the sly, but was careful to hide them or set fire to them. Soon, however, before she was out of her teens, she was to be betrothed to the son of a neighbouring wool-stapler. She cried out that marriage was hateful to her, and for that she was severely beaten by her father. Then he ceased to scold her. He begged her instead not to hurt him, not to shame him in this matter of her marriage. He would give her a chain of beads or a fine petticoat, he said; and there were tears in his eyes. How could she disobey him? How could she break his heart? The force of her own gift alone drove her to it. She made up a small parcel of her belongings, let herself down by a rope one summer's night and took the road to London. She was not seventeen. The birds that sang in the hedge were not more musical than she was. She had the quickest fancy, a gift like her brother's, for the tune of words. Like him, she had a taste for the theatre. She stood at the stage door; she wanted to act, she said. Men laughed in her face. The manager—a fat, loose-lipped man—guffawed. He bellowed something about poodles dancing and women acting—no woman, he said, could possibly be an actress.[4] He hinted—you can imagine what. She could get no training in her craft. Could she even seek her dinner in a tavern or roam the streets at midnight? Yet her genius was for fiction and lusted to feed abundantly upon the lives of men and women and the study of their ways. At last—for she was very young, oddly like Shakespeare the poet in her face, with the same grey eyes and rounded brows—at last Nick Greene the actor-manager took pity on her; she found herself with child by that gentleman and so—who shall measure the heat and violence of the poet's heart when caught and tangled in a woman's body?—killed herself one winter's night and lies buried at some cross-roads where the omnibuses now stop outside the Elephant and Castle.

That, more or less, is how the story would run, I think, if a woman in Shakespeare's day had had Shakespeare's genius. But for my part, I agree with the deceased bishop, if such he was—it is unthinkable that any woman in Shakespeare's day should have had Shakespeare's genius. For genius like Shakespeare's is not born among labouring, uneducated, servile people. It was not born in England among the Saxons and the Britons. It is not born today among the working classes. How, then, could it have been born among women whose work began, ac-

4. In the Elizabethan theater boys played women's parts.

cording to Professor Trevelyan, almost before they were out of the nursery, who were forced to it by their parents and held to it by all the power of law and custom? Yet genius of a sort must have existed among women as it must have existed among the working classes. Now and again an Emily Brontë or a Robert Burns blazes out and proves its presence.[5] But certainly it never got itself on to paper. When, however, one reads of a witch being ducked, of a woman possessed by devils, of a wise woman selling herbs, or even of a very remarkable man who had a mother, then I think we are on the track of a lost novelist, a suppressed poet, of some mute and inglorious Jane Austen,[6] some Emily Brontë who dashed her brains out on the moor or mopped and mowed about the highways crazed with the torture that her gift had put her to. Indeed, I would venture to guess that Anon, who wrote so many poems without signing them, was often a woman. It was a woman Edward Fitzgerald,[7] I think, suggested who made the ballads and the folk-songs, crooning them to her children, beguiling her spinning with them, or the length of the winter's night.

This may be true or it may be false—who can say?—but what is true in it, so it seemed to me, reviewing the story of Shakespeare's sister as I had made it, is that any woman born with a great gift in the sixteenth century would certainly have gone crazed, shot herself, or ended her days in some lonely cottage outside the village, half witch, half wizard, feared and mocked at. For it needs little skill in psychology to be sure that a highly gifted girl who had tried to use her gift for poetry would have been so thwarted and hindered by other people, so tortured and pulled asunder by her own contrary instincts, that she must have lost her health and sanity to a certainty. No girl could have walked to London and stood at a stage door and forced her way into the presence of actor-managers without doing herself a violence and suffering an anguish which may have been irrational—for chastity may be a fetish invented by certain societies for unknown reasons—but were none the less inevitable. Chastity had then, it has even now, a religious importance in a woman's life, and has so wrapped itself round with nerves and instincts that to cut it free and bring it to the light of day demands courage of the rarest. To have lived a free life in London in the sixteenth century would have meant for a woman who was poet and playwright a nervous stress and dilemma which might well have killed her. Had she survived, whatever she had written would have

5. Woolf's examples are Emily Brontë (1818–1848), the English novelist, and Robert Burns (1759–96), the Scottish poet.
6. Woolf alludes to Thomas Gray's "Elegy Written in a Country Churchyard": "Some mute inglorious Milton here may rest."
7. Edward Fitzgerald (1809–1883), poet and translator, of the *Rubáiyát of Omar Khayyám*.

been twisted and deformed, issuing from a strained and morbid imagination. And undoubtedly, I thought, looking at the shelf where there are no plays by women, her work would have gone unsigned. That refuge she would have sought certainly. It was the relic of the sense of chastity that dictated anonymity to women even so late as the nineteenth century. Currer Bell, George Eliot, George Sand, all the victims of inner strife as their writings prove, sought ineffectively to veil themselves by using the name of a man.[8] Thus they did homage to the convention, which if not implanted by the other sex was liberally encouraged by them (the chief glory of a woman is not to be talked of, said Pericles,[9] himself a much-talked-of man), that publicity in women is detestable. Anonymity runs in their blood. The desire to be veiled still possesses them. They are not even now as concerned about the health of their fame as men are, and, speaking generally, will pass a tombstone or a signpost without feeling an irresistible desire to cut their names on it, as Alf, Bert or Chas. must do in obedience to their instinct, which murmurs if it sees a fine woman go by, or even a dog, Ce chien est à moi.[1] And, of course, it may not be a dog, I thought, remembering Parliament Square, the Sieges Allee and other avenues; it may be a piece of land or a man with curly black hair. It is one of the great advantages of being a woman that one can pass even a very fine negress without wishing to make an Englishwoman of her.

10 That woman, then, who was born with a gift of poetry in the sixteenth century, was an unhappy woman, a woman at strife against herself. All the conditions of her life, all her own instincts, were hostile to the state of mind which is needed to set free whatever is in the brain. But what is the state of mind that is most propitious to the act of creation, I asked. Can one come by any notion of the state that furthers and makes possible that strange activity? Here I opened the volume containing the Tragedies of Shakespeare. What was Shakespeare's state of mind, for instance, when he wrote *Lear* and *Antony and Cleopatra*? It was certainly the state of mind most favourable to poetry that there has ever existed. But Shakespeare himself said nothing about it. We only know casually and by chance that he "never blotted a line."[2] Nothing indeed was ever said by the artist himself about his state of mind until the eighteenth century perhaps. Rousseau perhaps began

8. The pseudonyms of Charlotte Brontë (1816–1855), English novelist; Mary Ann Evans (1819–1880), English novelist; and Amandine Aurore Lucie Dupin, Baronne Dudevant (1804–1876), French novelist.
9. Pericles (d. 429 B.C.), Athenian statesman.
1. That dog is mine.
2. As recorded by his contemporary Ben Jonson in *Timber: Or Discoveries Made Upon Men and Matter*.

it.[3] At any rate, by the nineteenth century self-consciousness had developed so far that it was the habit for men of letters to describe their minds in confessions and autobiographies. Their lives also were written, and their letters were printed after their deaths. Thus, though we do not know what Shakespeare went through when he wrote *Lear*, we do know what Carlyle went through when he wrote the *French Revolution*; what Flaubert went through when he wrote *Madame Bovary*; what Keats was going through when he tried to write poetry against the coming of death and the indifference of the world.

And one gathers from this enormous modern literature of confession and self-analysis that to write a work of genius is almost always a feat of prodigious difficulty. Everything is against the likelihood that it will come from the writer's mind whole and entire. Generally material circumstances are against it. Dogs will bark; people will interrupt; money must be made; health will break down. Further, accentuating all these difficulties and making them harder to bear is the world's notorious indifference. It does not ask people to write poems and novels and histories; it does not need them. It does not care whether Flaubert finds the right word or whether Carlyle scrupulously verifies this or that fact. Naturally, it will not pay for what it does not want. And so the writer, Keats, Flaubert, Carlyle, suffers, especially in the creative years of youth, every form of distraction and discouragement. A curse, a cry of agony, rises from those books of analysis and confession. "Mighty poets in their misery dead"[4]—that is the burden of their song. If anything comes through in spite of all this, it is a miracle, and probably no book is born entire and uncrippled as it was conceived.

But for women, I thought, looking at the empty shelves, these difficulties were infinitely more formidable. In the first place, to have a room of her own, let alone a quiet room or a sound-proof room, was out of the question, unless her parents were exceptionally rich or very noble, even up to the beginning of the nineteenth century. Since her pin money, which depended on the good will of her father, was only enough to keep her clothed, she was debarred from such alleviations as came even to Keats or Tennyson or Carlyle, all poor men, from a walking tour, a little journey to France, from the separate lodging which, even if it were miserable enough, sheltered them from the claims and tyrannies of their families. Such material difficulties were formidable; but much worse were the immaterial. The indifference of the world which Keats and Flaubert and other men of genius have found so hard

3. Jean-Jacques Rousseau (1712–1778), whose *Confessions* were published posthumously.
4. From William Wordsworth's poem "Resolution and Independence."

to bear was in her case not indifference but hostility. The world did not say to her as it said to them, Write if you choose; it makes no difference to me. The world said with a guffaw, Write? What's the good of your writing? Here the psychologists of Newnham and Girton might come to our help, I thought, looking again at the blank spaces on the shelves. For surely it is time that the effect of discouragement upon the mind of the artist should be measured, as I have seen a dairy company measure the effect of ordinary milk and Grade A milk upon the body of the rat. They set two rats in cages side by side, and of the two one was furtive, timid and small, and the other was glossy, bold and big. Now what food do we feed women as artists upon? I asked, remembering, I suppose, that dinner of prunes and custard.[5] To answer that question I had only to open the evening paper and to read that Lord Birkenhead is of opinion—but really I am not going to trouble to copy out Lord Birkenhead's opinion upon the writing of women. What Dean Inge says I will leave in peace. The Harley Street specialist may be allowed to rouse the echoes of Harley Street with his vociferations without raising a hair on my head. I will quote, however, Mr. Oscar Browning, because Mr. Oscar Browning was a great figure in Cambridge at one time, and used to examine the students at Girton and Newnham.[6] Mr. Oscar Browning was wont to declare "that the impression left on his mind, after looking over any set of examination papers, was that, irrespective of the marks he might give, the best woman was intellectually the inferior of the worst man." After saying that Mr. Browning went back to his rooms—and it is this sequel that endears him and makes him a human figure of some bulk and majesty—he went back to his rooms and found a stable-boy lying on the sofa—"a mere skeleton, his cheeks were cavernous and sallow, his teeth were black, and he did not appear to have the full use of his limbs. . . . 'That's Arthur' [said Mr. Browning]. 'He's a dear boy really and most high-minded.' " The two pictures always seem to me to complete each other. And happily in this age of biography the two pictures often do complete each other, so that we are able to interpret the opinions of great men not only by what they say, but by what they do.

But though this is possible now, such opinions coming from the lips of important people must have been formidable enough even fifty years ago. Let us suppose that a father from the highest motives did

5. In Chapter 1, Woolf contrasts the lavish dinner—partridge and wine—she ate as a guest in a men's college at Cambridge University with the plain fare—prunes and custard—served in a women's college.

6. In Chapter 2, Woolf lists the fruits of her day's research on the lives of women, which include Lord Birkenhead's, Dean Inge's, and Mr. Oscar Browning's opinions of women; she does not, however, quote them. Harley Street is where fashionable medical doctors in London have their offices.

not wish his daughter to leave home and become writer, painter or scholar. "See what Mr. Oscar Browning says," he would say; and there was not only Mr. Oscar Browning; there was the *Saturday Review*; there was Mr. Greg[7]—the "essentials of a woman's being," said Mr. Greg emphatically, "are that *they are supported by, and they minister to, men*"—there was an enormous body of masculine opinion to the effect that nothing could be expected of women intellectually. Even if her father did not read out loud these opinions, any girl could read them for herself; and the reading, even in the nineteenth century, must have lowered her vitality, and told profoundly upon her work. There would always have been that assertion—you cannot do this, you are incapable of doing that—to protest against, to overcome. Probably for a novelist this germ is no longer of much effect; for there have been women novelists of merit. But for painters it must still have some sting in it; and for musicians, I imagine, is even now active and poisonous in the extreme. The women composer stands where the actress stood in the time of Shakespeare. Nick Greene, I thought, remembering the story I had made about Shakespeare's sister, said that a woman acting put him in mind of a dog dancing. Johnson repeated the phrase two hundred years later of women preaching.[8] And here, I said, opening a book about music, we have the very words used again in this year of grace, 1928, of women who try to write music. "Of Mlle. Germaine Tailleferre one can only repeat Dr. Johnson's dictum concerning a woman preacher, transposed into terms of music. 'Sir, a woman's composing is like a dog's walking on his hind legs. It is not done well, but you are surprised to find it done at all.' "[9] So accurately does history repeat itself.

Thus, I concluded, shutting Mr. Oscar Browning's life and pushing away the rest, it is fairly evident that even in the nineteenth century a woman was not encouraged to be an artist. On the contrary, she was snubbed, slapped, lectured and exhorted. Her mind must have been strained and her vitality lowered by the need of opposing this, of disproving that. For here again we come within range of that very interesting and obscure masculine complex which has had so much influence upon the woman's movement; that deep-seated desire, not so much that *she* shall be inferior as that *he* shall be superior, which plants him wherever one looks, not only in front of the arts, but barring the way to politics too, even when the risk to himself seems infinitesimal and the suppliant humble and devoted. Even Lady Bess-

7. Mr. Greg does not appear on Woolf's list (see preceding note).
8. The quotation is from James Boswell's *The Life of Samuel Johnson, L.L.D.* Woolf, in her tale of Judith Shakespeare, imagines the manager bellowing "something about poodles dancing and women acting."
9. *A Survey of Contemporary Music*, Cecil Gray, p. 246 [Woolf's note].

borough, I remembered, with all her passion for politics, must humbly bow herself and write to Lord Granville Leveson-Gower[1]: ". . . notwithstanding all my violence in politics and talking so much on that subject, I perfectly agree with you that no woman has any business to meddle with that or any other serious business, farther than giving her opinion (if she is ask'd)." And so she goes on to spend her enthusiasm where it meets with no obstacle whatsoever upon that immensely important subject, Lord Granville's maiden speech in the House of Commons. The spectacle is certainly a strange one, I thought. The history of men's opposition to women's emancipation is more interesting perhaps than the story of that emancipation itself. An amusing book might be made of it if some young student at Girton or Newnham would collect examples and deduce a theory—but she would need thick gloves on her hands, and bars to protect her of solid gold.

But what is amusing now, I recollected, shutting Lady Bessborough, had to be taken in desperate earnest once. Opinions that one now pastes in a book labelled cock-a-doodle-dum and keeps for reading to select audiences on summer nights once drew tears, I can assure you. Among your grandmothers and great-grandmothers there were many that wept their eyes out. Florence Nightingale[2] shrieked aloud in her agony.[3] Moreover, it is all very well for you, who have got yourselves to college and enjoy sitting-rooms—or is it only bed-sitting-rooms?—of your own to say that genius should disregard such opinions; that genius should be above caring what is said of it. Unfortunately, it is precisely the men or women of genius who mind most what is said of them. Remember Keats. Remember the words he had cut on his tombstone. Think of Tennyson;[4] think—but I need hardly multiply instances of the undeniable, if very unfortunate, fact that it is the nature of the artist to mind excessively what is said about him. Literature is strewn with the wreckage of men who have minded beyond reason the opinions of others.

And this susceptibility of theirs is doubly unfortunate, I thought, returning again to my original enquiry into what state of mind is most propitious for creative work, because the mind of an artist, in order to achieve the prodigious effort of freeing whole and entire the work that

1. Henrietta, Countess of Bessborough (1761–1821) and Lord Granville Leveson Gower, first Earl Granville (1773–1846). Their correspondence, edited by Castalia Countess Granville, was published as his *Private Correspondence, 1781 to 1821,* in 1916.
2. Florence Nightingale (1820–1910), English nurse and philanthropist.
3. See *Cassandra,* by Florence Nightingale, printed in *The Cause,* by R. Strachey [Woolf's note].
4. Keats's epitaph reads "Here lies one whose name was writ in water." Tennyson was notably sensitive to reviews of his poetry.

is in him, must be incandescent, like Shakespeare's mind, I conjectured, looking at the book which lay open at *Antony and Cleopatra*. There must be no obstacle in it, no foreign matter unconsumed.

For though we say that we know nothing about Shakespeare's state of mind, even as we say that, we are saying something about Shakespeare's state of mind. The reason perhaps why we know so little of Shakespeare—compared with Donne or Ben Jonson or Milton—is that his grudges and spites and antipathies are hidden from us. We are not held up by some "revelation" which reminds us of the writer. All desire to protest, to preach, to proclaim an injury, to pay off a score, to make the world the witness of some hardship or grievance was fired out of him and consumed. Therefore his poetry flows from him free and unimpeded. If ever a human being got his work expressed completely, it was Shakespeare. If ever a mind was incandescent, unimpeded, I thought, turning again to the bookcase, it was Shakespeare's mind.

Susan Allen Toth

GOING TO THE MOVIES

I

Aaron takes me only to art films. That's what I call them, anyway: strange movies with vague poetic images I don't always understand, long dreamy movies about a distant Technicolor past, even longer black-and-white movies about the general meaninglessness of life. We do not go unless at least one reputable critic has found the cinematography superb. We went to *The Devil's Eye*, [1] and Aaron turned to me in the middle and said, "My God, this is *funny*." I do not think he was pleased.

When Aaron and I go to the movies, we drive our cars separately and meet by the box office. Inside the theater he sits tentatively in his seat, ready to move if he can't see well, poised to leave if the film is disappointing. He leans away from me, careful not to touch the bare flesh of his arm against the bare flesh of mine. Sometimes he leans so far I am afraid he may be touching the woman on his other side in-

From *How to Prepare for Your High School Reunion and Other Essays* (1988).

1. Swedish film (1960) about seduction directed by Ingmar Bergman.

stead. If the movie is very good, he leans forward too, peering between the heads of the couple in front of us. The light from the screen bounces off his glasses; he gleams with intensity, sitting there on the edge of his seat, watching the screen. Once I tapped him on the arm so I could whisper a comment in his ear. He jumped.

After *Belle de Jour*[2] Aaron said he wanted to ask me if he could stay overnight. "But I can't," he shook his head mournfully before I had a chance to answer, "because I know I never sleep well in strange beds." Then he apologized for asking. "It's just that after a film like that," he said, "I feel the need to assert myself."

II

Bob takes me only to movies that he thinks have a redeeming social conscience. He doesn't call them films. They tend to be about poverty, war, injustice, political corruption, struggling unions in the 1930s, and the military-industrial complex. Bob doesn't like propaganda movies, though, and he doesn't like to be too depressed, either. We stayed away from *The Sorrow and the Pity;*[3] it would be, he said, just too much. Besides, he assured me, things are never that hopeless. So most of the movies we see are made in Hollywood. Because they are always very topical, these movies offer what Bob calls "food for thought." When we saw *Coming Home,*[4] Bob's jaw set so firmly with the first half hour that I knew we would end up at Poppin' Fresh Pies afterward.

When Bob and I go to the movies, we take turns driving so no one owes anyone else anything. We park far away from the theater so we don't have to pay for a space. If it's raining or snowing, Bob offers to let me off at the door, but I can tell he'll feel better if I go with him while he parks, so we share the walk too. Inside the theater Bob will hold my hand when I get scared if I ask him. He puts my hand firmly on his knee and covers it completely with his own hand. His knee never twitches. After a while, when the scary part is past, he loosens his hand slightly and I know that is a signal to take mine away. He sits companionably close, letting his jacket just touch my sweater, but he does not infringe. He thinks I ought to know he is there if I need him.

One night after *The China Syndrome*[5] I asked Bob if he wouldn't like to stay for a second drink, even though it was past midnight. He thought awhile about that, considering my offer from all possible angles, but finally he said no. Relationships today, he said, have a tendency to move too quickly.

2. French film (1967) about erotic fantasies directed by Luis Bunuel.
3. French documentary (1972) about the Nazi occupation of France.
4. American film (1978) about a Vietnam veteran.
5. American film (1979) about a disaster in a nuclear power plant.

III

Sam likes movies that are entertaining. By that he means movies that Will Jones in the *Minneapolis Tribune* loved and either *Time* or *Newsweek* rather liked; also movies that do not have sappy love stories, are not musicals, do not have subtitles, and will not force him to think. He does not go to movies to think. He liked *California Suite* and *The Seduction of Joe Tynan,*[6] though the plots, he said, could have been zippier. He saw it all coming too far in advance, and that took the fun out. He doesn't like to know what is going to happen. "I just want my brain to be tickled," he says. It is very hard for me to pick out movies for Sam.

When Sam takes me to the movies, he pays for everything. He thinks that's what a man ought to do. But I buy my own popcorn, because he doesn't approve of it; the grease might smear his flannel slacks. Inside the theater, Sam makes himself comfortable. He takes off his jacket, puts one arm around me, and all during the movie he plays with my hand, stroking my palm, beating a small tattoo on my wrist. Although he watches the movie intently, his body operates on instinct. Once I inclined my head and kissed him lightly just behind his ear. He beat a faster tattoo on my wrist, quick and musical, but he didn't look away from the screen.

When Sam takes me home from the movies, he stands outside my door and kisses me long and hard. He would like to come in, he says regretfully, but his steady girlfriend in Duluth wouldn't like it. When the *Tribune* gives a movie four stars, he has to save it to see with her. Otherwise her feelings might be hurt.

IV

I go to some movies by myself. On rainy Sunday afternoons I often sneak into a revival house or a college auditorium for old Technicolor musicals, *Kiss Me Kate, Seven Brides for Seven Brothers, Calamity Jane,* even, once, *The Sound of Music.*[7] Wearing saggy jeans so I can prop my feet on the seat in front, I sit toward the rear where no one will see me. I eat large handfuls of popcorn with double butter. Once the movie starts, I feel completely at home. Howard Keel and I are old friends; I grin back at him on the screen, admiring all his teeth. I know the sound tracks by heart. Sometimes when I get really carried away I hum along with Kathryn Grayson, remembering how I once thought I would fill out a formal like that. Skirts whirl, feet tap, acrobatic young men perform impossible feats, and then the camera dissolves into a

6. The first, American film (1978) with a script by Neil Simon; the second, American film (1979) about politics.
7. The first three were made in the 1950s, the fourth in the 1960s.

dream sequence I know I can comfortably follow. It is not, thank God, Bergman.

If I can't find an old musical, I settle for Hepburn and Tracy, vintage Grant or Gable, on adventurous days Claudette Colbert or James Stewart. Before I buy my ticket I make sure it will all end happily. If necessary, I ask the girl at the box office. I have never seen *Stella Dallas* or *Intermezzo*.[8] Over the years I have developed other peccadilloes: I will, for example, see anything that is redeemed by Thelma Ritter. At the end of *Daddy Long Legs*[9] I wait happily for the scene when Fred Clark, no longer angry, at last pours Thelma a convivial drink. They smile at each other, I smile at them, I feel they are smiling at me. In the movies I go to by myself, the men and women always like each other.

8. The first, American film (1937) about a mother's love for her daughter; the second, American film (1939), a love story in which Ingrid Bergman made her American debut.
9. American film (1955) about a May-December romance.

QUESTIONS

1. *Toth describes four kinds of movies by describing the men she sees them with: Aaron, Bob, Sam, and finally no man. Make a list of the adjectives or descriptive phrases she includes for each man. How do such descriptions convey, by implication, her attitudes toward the movies?*
2. *Which kind of movie does Toth like best—or does she like them all equally? How do you know?*
3. *Using Toth as a model, write an account of going to some event or participating in some activity by describing the person(s) you go with. Like Toth, convey your response to the event by means of your description of the person(s).*

S. I. Hayakawa

SEX IS NOT A SPECTATOR SPORT

In current discussions of pornography and obscenity, there is widespread confusion about two matters. First there is sexual behavior and what it means to the participants. Secondly there is the outside observer of sexual behavior and what it means to him. When a man and a woman make love, enjoying themselves and each other unself-con-

From *Through the Communication Barrier* (1979).

sciously, a rich relationship is reaffirmed and made richer by their lovemaking. However beautiful or sacred that love relationship may be to that man and woman, it would have an entirely different significance to a Peeping Tom, secretly watching the proceedings from outside the window. The sexual behavior is not itself obscene. Obscenity is peculiarly the evaluation of the outside observer. Theoretically the actors may themselves be made the observers. If, for example, unknown to the man and woman, a movie were to be made of their lovemaking, and that movie were to be shown to them later, that lovemaking might take on an entirely different significance. What was performed unself-consciously and spontaneously might be viewed later by the actors themselves with giggling or shame or shock. They might even insist that the film be destroyed—which is entirely different from saying that they would stop making love.

What I am saying is that obscenity and pornography can happen only when sexual events are seen from the outside, from a spectator's point of view. This is the crux of the pornography problem. Pornography is sexual behvior made public through symbolization—by representation in literature, by simulation or enactment in a nightclub act or on stage, by arts such as painting, photography, or the movies. To object to pornographic movies or art is not, as some would have us believe, a result of hang-ups about sex. One may be completely healthy and still object to many of the current representations of sexual acts in the movies and on the stage.

Standards of morality are one thing. Standards of decorum are another. There is nothing immoral about changing one's clothes or evacuating one's bowels. But in our culture people as a rule do not change their clothing in the presence of the other sex, excepting their spouses. Men and women have separate public lavatories, and within them each toilet is in a separate compartment for privacy. Love too needs privacy. Human beings normally make love in private, whether that love is socially sanctioned, as in marriage, or unsanctioned, as in a house of prostitution.

The trouble with sexual intercourse as an object of artistic or literary representation is that its meaning is not apparent in the behavior. Hence serious writers have historically been reticent in their description of sex. In Dante's *Divine Comedy* Francesca tells of her tragic love for Paolo. They were reading an ancient romance, and as they read, their passions suddenly overcame them. What happened? Dante simply has Francesca say, "That day we read no further." The rest is left to the reader's imagination—and the reader cannot help feeling the power of that onrushing, fatal passion.

Men and women couple with each other for a wide variety of reasons. Sometimes the sexual encounter is the fulfillment of true love 5 and respect for each other. Sometimes one of the partners is using sex as an instrument of exploitation or aggression against the other. Sometimes sex is a commercial transaction, with either party being the prostitute. Sometimes sex is the expression of neurosis. Sometimes it is evidence of people getting over their neuroses. However, to the movie camera, as to a Peeping Tom, they are all "doing the same thing." To concentrate on the mechanics of sex is to ignore altogether its human significance.

Today movies do not stop at exhibiting copulation. Every kind of aberrant sexual behavior and sadomasochistic perversion is being shown. The advertisements in the newspaper before me announce such titles as *Nude Encounter, Too Hot to Handle, Deep Throat, The Devil in Miss Jones, The Passion Parlor, Hot Kitten,* and *Honeymoon Suite,* as well as "16 hours of hard-core male stag." The only purpose of movies such as these, from all I can tell from advertisements and reviews, is, as D. H. Lawrence expressed it, "to do dirt on sex." Let the American Civil Liberties Union fight for the right of these movies to be shown. I will not.

QUESTIONS

1. *This is a short essay. What is the functional relation of its six paragraphs?*
2. *What is the argumentative function of Hayakawa's distinction between meaning and behavior? Would behavior be obscene if it didn't have the right meaning?*
3. *Rewrite Hayakawa's conclusion so that it asserts a stronger position. Can you do this without changing his argument?*

Michael J. Arlen

THE TYRANNY OF THE VISUAL

I don't think that anyone needs reminding that we are well along in that blessed era when a single picture (sometimes any picture; certainly, any motion picture) is said to be the equal of a thousand words. Of course, words themselves are no longer manufactured or treated with much care, and so the comparison grows more plausible as time goes on. Even so, there have been moments lately when I have had the feeling that—so great has been the spread of visual culture in this cen-

From *The Camera Age* (1981).

tury, and so overwhelming its impact on the tender verbal sensibilities of recent generations—what was not so long ago the liberating, sense-expanding dynamic of a new medium of perception now seems in danger of becoming a new kind of aesthetic tyranny: the tyranny of visual storytelling.

In movies, this tyranny commonly takes the superficially modest form of surface or design effects. This is a fashion of presenting a scene or character which relates not so much to the director's feeling for the scene or character as to his feeling for visual technique. For instance, at the beginning of the 1977 movie *Bobby Deerfield* there occurred a typically striking visual sequence, in which the camera first revealed—sparely and carefully framed—the blacktop surface of a road. Then a man (though only his shoes and trousered legs were visible) walked slowly down the road toward the camera. He stopped, turned around, and with equal deliberation retraced a few steps. Then suddenly and dramatically he bent down and picked up an object from the surface of the blacktop: a key. With key in hand, he now walked briskly back up the road to where a sports car was parked; he climbed into it, started the engine, and sped off. Thus, one assumed that Al Pacino (for he was the man on the road) was driving into an adventure story, whose narrative was already under way and whose substance would soon reveal itself. For example, what was all that business with the key? Was it Pacino's car key? Had it been stolen or mislaid? How stolen, why mislaid? More important, what did his having lost or mislaid and then found the key have to do with the next step in the narrative? Was it the missing clue to a burglary, or even the reason for a missed appointment? In other words, what did the visually striking incident of the key on the road actually mean? Alas, the subsequent action of the movie provided no answer to any of these questions. Indeed, from that moment on, the film seemed totally uninterested in the matter of the key, as if it couldn't really remember having posed any questions with it in the first place. The scene had clearly been a kind of game, a visual non sequitur, though one that had been designed quite deliberately to appeal to our traditional literary orientation through the detective-story ballet of the "search," the "clue," and the "getaway." As such, there had been nothing artistic or even playfully inventive about the sequence, as in a director's or a creative cinematographer's happy conceit. What it had been was merely another example of the disconnected visual effect: a scene invested with the look of narrative importance but which related neither to the character nor the story, only to the filmmaker's apparent wish to persuade the audience that it was watching a stylish and important film. Or to put it less kindly: a minor form of visual bullying.

In numerous recent movies, this tendency to exploit visual language has become increasingly pronounced; and, as in the case of verbal language, what one notices are not so much the always abundant examples of cheap, routine visual effects as the increasing instances of "artistic" fakery and commercialism. Consider the Russian-roulette sequences in *The Deer Hunter.* Here the problem is not disconnected gesture, nor is it a simple question of the screenwriter's or director's right to make up detail and incident. The problem in *The Deer Hunter,* it seems to me, has to do with a film that is not so much composed of sequential parts (one part being set in a small town in Pennsylvania, the other in Vietnam) as rendered on two different, and largely unmixable, levels of imagination. Thus, the small-town American scenes are handled with great naturalism and affection; every effort seems to have been made to show us *how things were.* In other words, even if the energy behind these naturalistic and nostalgic details is the energy of dream, it is clearly a dream that was honestly dreamed. In contrast, the Vietnam scenes aren't just dreamlike in their unreality and contrivance (in their absence of naturalism) but are the dream, one guesses, of a professional dream-maker—a Vietnam fantasist—who has invested his story neither with honest memory nor honest imagination but with the pseudo-energy of visual effects. Part of the movie, then, is "real" (or is at least the product of a real dream), and this reality attempts unsuccessfully to nourish the "unreal" Vietnam part, with its slick, manipulative Russian-roulette sequences. Of course, we hold our breath and wince when a man takes a partly loaded revolver and puts it to his temple. But what has been gained by these automated responses, save for the further dehumanization of a war that was already bad enough without these glib but "powerful" filmmaker's touches?

"But *The Deer Hunter* didn't have to be true to facts. It showed the poetic truth of the war," a young friend said to me as I was making these complaints, the other day.

5 "How do you know, since you weren't there?" I asked.

"Well, I know because of the movie," he said.

It seems self-evident that visual creativity, be it in fine art or in cinematography, might be expected to follow different laws of technique and dynamics from, say, literary or musical creativity. But it seems strange, though perhaps in keeping with a certain defensive self-consciousness about visual matters, that our new visually-oriented crafts should be assumed to possess a morality of their own: a morality that often seems to speak less to the wider, untidy, unframed, undesigned world of men and women (where most morality is forged) than self-servingly back to the smaller, self-isolated province of visual technique as an end in itself.

Of course, there is nowhere that visual manipulation seems more apparent than in television commercials, but I think the role here of visual technique is deceptive. Superficially (and especially if it has been done well, with no expense spared, and so forth), the television commercial appears to be a kind of game: something playful, a thirty-second play period replete with visual tricks such as cars floating in the air, or knights in armor in the laundry room, or talking cats. The television commercial seems to be a classic example of technique for its own sake; though actually, as should be obvious, the technique serves a very definite and forceful master: the selling of a certain product, or of the emotions that are thought to surround that product. As a member of the audience, one may not much care for the product in question, or may find the sales message distasteful, or the interruption irritating, but the fact is that the visual transaction taking place is a fairly straightforward one. Whatever the intricacy or trickiness of the visual effects, the technique in a television commercial rarely speaks only to itself, unless it is a bad commercial, but follows a very clear, other-directed, even at times humanely logical (if not always ennobling) morality of commerce. On the other hand, without this stern logic to guide it, and without art, or pretensions to art, to whet its ambitions, regular television programming seems to flounder happily in a generally harmless morass of what used to be called B-movie special effects. On entertainment TV, nobody seems to have the time, money, or inclination for lighting or for framing shots. Now and then, an adventurous director will borrow a snappy trick or two from a movie or a commercial, but for the most part television cinematography is too caught up with the day-by-day demands of getting through the shooting script to worry about trying anything fancy. Week after week, detectives stalk criminals along catwalks, bodies float in swimming pools, cars spin around intersections and leap across drawbridges: the visual vocabulary of most television dramas is as skimpy as that of a pulp novel.

All the same, video is perhaps the visual language of the future, even more than film, and there is an area where television has started to abuse not so much its skimpy visual skills as its basic visual power. Ironically, it is public television—that relentless bluestocking of broadcasting—that seems to have been leading the way here, by throwing its weight behind a rather different sort of visual tyranny: what might be described as the reconstituting or transforming or overwhelming of works of literature into sequences of moving images, as, for example, in the recent four-part adaptation of Nathaniel Hawthorne's *The Scarlet Letter.*[1] Now, right away, there is a danger of getting tangled up in one of those ancient arguments having to do with

1. Hawthorne (1804–1864), American writer and author of a novel in which the heroine, Hester Prynne, is condemned to wear an embroidered scarlet A on her breast as punishment for committing adultery.

the merits or demerits of transposing books into films, so first let me try to make clear what I am *not* talking about here. I am not, for example, talking about the inviolability of printed matter or suggesting that a story that has been fashioned in one form—be it novel or stage play or Holinshed's *Chronicles*[2]—should always remain in its original form. I am not claiming the inherent or automatic superiority of one form over another: books as "high art" versus film as "low art," as has sometimes been claimed (at least by book people) in the past. After all, the evidence of five or more decades is that some of the most appealing and satisfying movies (perhaps most of the most appealing and satisfying movies) have been adapted from novels or short stories that were often inferior to the filmed version. Indeed, a large proportion of the so-called literary properties that are bought by filmmakers and turned into movies are books of the most routine nature: spy stories or detective stories or the type of popular blockbuster novel that appears to have been written from a movie-oriented perspective, employing "characters" based either on figures in the daily papers or on the personae of movie stars, and, in fact, that is literary only in having made its original appearance as a book.

10 So what am I talking about? For one thing: *The Scarlet Letter* itself. Worthy Hawthorne! Such a nice-looking writer chap, who married one of those Peabody sisters and worked for years with great effort on his short stories, for which he received a certain regional respect but very little cash. He wrote *The Scarlet Letter* fairly quickly, and as soon as his publisher, Mr. Fields, saw the manuscript he knew that it was going to be a big seller, although, being a publisher, he printed a first edition of only two thousand copies, which sold out in ten days. The second edition, of three thousand copies, sold well too, and subsequent editions and printings have kept on selling. (Perhaps there should be some kind of federal law, however, to prevent schoolchildren from being required to read it—or *The House of the Seven Gables* or Melville's *Moby Dick*—[3]at a stage in life when many of them can barely respond to the literary texture of *Car & Driver*.) For *The Scarlet Letter* is not only a marvelous book, surely one of the very great American novels ever written, but also an extraordinarily, profoundly *literary* work. It is actually quite short, and its brevity imparts a feeling of compression. There is scant incident or action in the narrative. Indeed, the "story" is deliberately unrealistic (almost surreal), for Hawthorne was writing two hundred years after the supposed events, and what he was

2. Raphael Holinshed (died c. 1580), English historian famous for the *Chronicles of England, Scotland, and Ireland* (1577), which Shakespeare and other dramatists used as sources for their history plays.
3. Hawthorne wrote *The House of the Seven Gables* (1851); Herman Melville (1819–1891) wrote *Moby Dick* (1851).

attempting to portray often has the flow and density of a dream. Fitzgerald's *The Great Gatsby*[4] is a very different kind of book, but it shares with *The Scarlet Letter*, I think, this same dreamlike energy, as well as a marked absence of action and realistic event. At any rate, Hawthorne's novel is not merely a great work of the imagination but one that owes its strength and presence to the "music" of the soul's interior. So rich is this interior music, in fact, that the reader scarcely notices—or, at least, is not unduly troubled by—some of the more conventional aspects of storytelling which Hawthorne has either not much bothered himself with or simply left out. Not only is there a scarcity of realistic event, but a number of the important characters have surprisingly simplistic surfaces. Dreadful Roger Chillingworth, for instance, is a villain without shading, without redeeming feature. Hester Prynne's child, little Pearl, is hardly believable on any remotely realistic terms—this "lovely and immortal flower" who was "worthy to have been brought forth in Eden; worthy to have been left there, to be the plaything of angels." There is also the matter of the author's deliberately contrived employment of natural background and coloring; or, rather, his failure to employ it. For *The Scarlet Letter* is in the main—and, it is clear, purposely—a novel without colors. There are periodic symbolic appearances of the color red, as in a fire and a red rose, and certainly in Hester's scarlet letter, and there are similarly pointed appearances of the color black, as in the prison ironwork and in the mythic "Black Man" of the forest. But with the exception of Hester's own embroidery on little Pearl's dresses, there is an obviously intentional omission by the author of color, the colors of life, certainly the colors of the New England countryside. Indeed, the countryside itself is noticeably absent from the narrative, save for occasional, equally symbolic allusions to the dark and abstract wilderness that exists on the periphery of the story, and which is made vivid only toward the end of the novel in the important scene that finally brings together Hester, Dimmesdale, little Pearl, and Chillingworth in the forest.

Public television's version of *The Scarlet Letter* wasn't altogether terrible. It had a couple of effective moments, especially in the third episode, when Meg Foster seemed to catch for at least a few seconds some of the transfigured bitterness in Hester Prynne. But it certainly wasn't much good. In theatrical terms, both Foster and John Heard, as Dimmesdale, seemed impossibly burdened by a kind of American high-school stage radiance, while Kevin Conway, as Chillingworth, floundered about in a part that probably only a very bad or a very good actor could have made work. And Rick Hauser's ponderous, "classical"

4. F. Scott Fitzgerald (1896–1940), American novelist and recorder of the "Jazz Age" (the 1920s).

direction propelled Hawthorne's brief and compact narrative forward with the stately lethargy of a becalmed galleon. For the most part, it seemed a misbegotten undertaking, perpetrated by people on the creative or producing end who, if they had read the book at all—at least for the purpose of blocking scenes—couldn't have had much feeling for what they'd read. Indeed, as I watched the series trudge its dutiful and cumbersome course through four consecutive evenings, I thought back to some of those foolish Hollywood re-creations of the "classics" and rather missed them—their foolishness as well as their energy: Mickey Rooney in *A Midsummer Night's Dream*; Gregory Peck as Captain Ahab! At least there had been a sort of loopy fun in these portrayals: a Classics Comics approach to serious literature in which serious literature somehow never really got involved; in which the soul of the original work was left where it was, unreached and undabbled with.

But these new, solemn practitioners of visual storytelling are soul devourers. They're *not* foolish or loopy, inviting us to have a good time and to leave our highfalutin literary notions outside in the coatroom. These are serious and dutiful fellows, bound not merely by a responsibility to "art" but also, in the case of public television, by a responsibility to trustees and educators and government committees and so forth. For example, was poor Hawthorne, scribbling at his desk in the eighteen-forties and trying to work out the novel's formal symbolism, so impeded by a lack of proper archives and research materials that he ignorantly costumed most of the characters in *The Scarlet Letter* in dark colors instead of putting them in the generally colorful robes of the era? Well, then, the research facilities and academic consultants of public television were able to correct Hawthorne's deficiency in this regard by costuming the television performers of his novel in the more historically accurate, colored finery of the period. And did poor Hawthorne, lacking a camera and the creative resources of film with which to tell his tale, give his written version of the story a certain closed-in and claustrophobic atmosphere? Well, then, television's cameras "opened up" the narrative by taking us on little scenic excursions outside the town. There are moody glimpses of the sea breaking on the shore, and cheery views of open meadows and fields of wheat. In fact, by the time the significant scene in the forest finally takes place we feel that we have been in the middle of New England's wild landscape all along. Also, even though this adaptation is by television and for television, it must not be forgotten that the original creator of the literary property was Nathaniel Hawthorne, a celebrated writer, and so the television people have found time to pay respects to Hawthorne's prose. Snatches of Hawthorne's exposition are periodically intoned as scene-setting devices by a generally offscreen actor (playing Hawthorne himself!), while additional bits and pieces of the Master's prose pop up now and then as dialogue, often spliced in with the already "adapted" dialogue. Thus, sometimes the dialogue is genuine Hawthorne and sometimes it is genuine television, but more often than not it is a strange composite of the two, which must have struck the twenty-five consultants who worked on the project as a statesmanly way of solving the problem.

"But let it pass! It is of yonder miserable man that I would speak," says Hawthorne's Hester Prynne, whereas television's Hester says, "I'm here not to talk of myself but of him." Does the difference matter? Does it matter that certain details and points of character have been rearranged, or that information provided by the author in a later chapter of the book turns up as dialogue in an early moment of the television version? Does it matter that childish camera tricks are borrowed from old movies to indicate dreamlike effects or the workings of consciousness, most of them as simple-minded as dissolves on logs blazing in a fireplace? In a certain sense, one would be hard put to say—certainly in a dominantly visual society—what great wrong there was in any of this. One mustn't be too linear or too retentive about such things! But it seems to me, in the end, that all these details do matter, though not necessarily detail by detail (as if we were discussing a blueprint that did or did not match the original specifications), but, instead, in that what is at issue—perhaps carelessly rather than intentionally, in the fashion of our time—is a fundamental question of respect. *The Scarlet Letter* is valuable to us and, indeed, to the literate world, for what it is in essence: a work of literature. It may contain a describable "story"; it may contain historical information, right or wrong; it may contain opportunities for costuming and parts for players. But a great novel is not an engineering model, with interchangeable parts, any more than a great painting (say, a Cézanne still-life) is an accumulation of "graphic information" about nineteenth-century French produce (to be improved, perhaps, by the substitution of a pineapple for a plum), or any more than a great film is an accretion of describable film images. Today nobody, I think, tries to rearrange or restructure a great painting (though sometimes great paintings don't get reproduced very well), and nobody, I think, has plans for putting Chaplin's *City Lights* into book form so that a new audience can get a richer feel for the material. But the abuse of the essence of literature occurs with greater and greater frequency, as the new visual forms attempt to feed their commercial or self-serving appetites for new "artistic" material. And always (to hear the adapters tell it) it is *youth* that is being served. Think of how many young people who have never read *The Scarlet Letter* (or who ran away from school when somebody asked them to read it) will now know about Hester Prynne! Know *what?* is one question. Another question, equally unanswerable, might be: How many of those who saw *The Scarlet Letter* on television will now read the book, and read it as Hawthorne wrote it, communing through his language to the soul of the work, and not merely checking off the incidents as they relate to what they saw, perhaps more vividly, on the screen?

The present time is said not to be a happy one for literature. Good poets are largely unnoticed, few serious novels are read, and the audience for the music of words seems to be drifting away, as if mesmerized by painting, prints, photographs, moving pictures, videotape—by the new power of visual imagery. Perhaps the music of words will never reassert its ancient hold on the popular imagination. Perhaps, as some have suggested, the grip of words has become too strong, too tight, thereby unbalancing the ancient, preliterary equilibrium of the human brain. At any rate, for the moment, one has the impression that the mass media, which are largely visual, are in the process of trying to perpetuate an illusion: the illusion being that culture is somehow neutral as to form and can therefore best be communicated and recommunicated by means of the most popular forms of the day. Thus, some of the great literary spirits of our civilization have been made unwitting participants in a curious sort of visual vs. literary Capture the Flag contest, in which the visual team lately appears to have the upper hand, drawing bigger crowds and winning fatter purses. Will the visual team continue to forge ahead, chewing up Homer and Dante and the Oxford English Dictionary and spitting them out in ten-part installments, each verified for historical accuracy by a battery of academics and scripted so as to be easily comprehensible to a ninth-grade audience? One will have to wait for the twenty-first century to find out. Meanwhile, the crucial issue remains in doubt: respect for man and his art. Will the new communication forms advance this respect, as they sometimes seem to be trying to do? Or will they keep on fudging it, waffling, ducking the serious questions, but talking always of freedom—the new freedoms—and of the splendid gifts they bring us?

QUESTIONS

1. *When you hear the word* tyranny, *what associations do you make? What does Arlen mean in paragraph 1 by "aesthetic tyranny"? What associations does he want the reader to make?*
2. *List the various visual media that Arlen discusses and the possible "tyranny" that each might exercise over the viewer. Which visual medium is most threatening? Why?*
3. *If possible, view the television adaptation of* The Scarlet Letter *that Arlen discusses. With which of Arlen's criticisms do you agree? With which do you disagree?*

Aaron Copland

HOW WE LISTEN

We all listen to music according to our separate capacities. But, for the sake of analysis, the whole listening process may become clearer if we break it up into its component parts, so to speak. In a certain sense we all listen to music on three separate planes. For lack of a better terminology, one might name these: (1) the sensuous plane, (2) the expressive plane, (3) the sheerly musical plane. The only advantage to be gained from mechanically splitting up the listening process into these hypothetical planes is the clearer view to be had of the way in which we listen.

The simplest way of listening to music is to listen for the sheer pleasure of the musical sound itself. That is the sensuous plane. It is the plane on which we hear music without thinking, without considering it in any way. One turns on the radio while doing something else and absentmindedly bathes in the sound. A kind of brainless but attractive state of mind is engendered by the mere sound appeal of the music.

You may be sitting in a room reading this book. Imagine one note struck on the piano. Immediately that one note is enough to change the atmosphere of the room—proving that the sound element in music is a powerful and mysterious agent, which it would be foolish to deride or belittle.

The surprising thing is that many people who consider themselves qualified music lovers abuse that plane in listening. They go to concerts in order to lose themselves. They use music as a consolation or an escape. They enter an ideal world where one doesn't have to think of the realities of everyday life. Of course they aren't thinking about the music either. Music allows them to leave it, and they go off to a place to dream, dreaming because of and apropos of the music yet never quite listening to it.

Yes, the sound appeal of music is a potent and primitive force, but 5
you must not allow it to usurp a disproportionate share of your interest. The sensuous plane is an important one in music, a very important one, but it does not constitute the whole story.

There is no need to digress further on the sensuous plane. Its appeal to every normal human being is self-evident. There is, however, such a thing as becoming more sensitive to the different kinds of sound stuff as used by various composers. For all composers do not use that sound stuff in the same way. Don't get the idea that the value of music is

From *What to Listen for in Music* (1957).

commensurate with its sensuous appeal or that the loveliest sounding music is made by the greatest composer. If that were so, Ravel would be a greater creator than Beethoven. The point is that the sound element varies with each composer, that his usage of sound forms an integral part of his style and must be taken into account when listening. The reader can see, therefore, that a more conscious approach is valuable even on this primary plane of music listening.

The second plane on which music exists is what I have called the expressive one. Here, immediately, we tread on controversial ground. Composers have a way of shying away from any discussion of music's expressive side. Did not Stravinsky himself proclaim that his music was an "object," a "thing," with a life of its own, and with no other meaning than its own purely musical existence? This intransigent attitude of Stravinsky's may be due to the fact that so many people have tried to read different meanings into so many pieces. Heaven knows it is difficult enough to say precisely what it is that a piece of music means, to say it definitely, to say it finally so that everyone is satisfied with your explanation. But that should not lead one to the other extreme of denying to music the right to be "expressive."

My own belief is that all music has an expressive power, some more and some less, but that all music has a certain meaning behind the notes and that that meaning behind the note constitutes, after all, what the piece is saying, what the piece is about. This whole problem can be stated quite simply by asking, "Is there a meaning to music?" My answer to that would be. "Yes." And "Can you state in so many words what the meaning is?" My answer to that would be, "No." Therein lies the difficulty.

Simple-minded souls will never be satisfied with the answer to the second of these questions. They always want music to have a meaning, and the more concrete it is the better they like it. The more the music reminds them of a train, a storm, a funeral, or any other familiar conception the more expressive it appears to be to them. This popular idea of music's meaning—stimulated and abetted by the usual run of musical commentator—should be discouraged wherever and whenever it is met. One timid lady once confessed to me that she suspected something seriously lacking in her appreciation of music because of her inability to connect it with anything definite. That is getting the whole thing backward, of course.

10 Still, the question remains, How close should the intelligent music lover wish to come to pinning a definite meaning to any particular work? No closer than a general concept, I should say. Music expresses, at different moments, serenity or exuberance, regret or triumph, fury or delight. It expresses each of these moods, and many others, in a numberless variety of subtle shadings and differences. It may even ex-

press a state of meaning for which there exists no adequate word in any language. In that case, musicians often like to say that it has only a purely musical meaning. They sometimes go farther and say that *all* music has only a purely musical meaning. What they really mean is that no appropriate word can be found to express the music's meaning and that, even if it could, they do not feel the need of finding it.

But whatever the professional musician may hold, most musical novices still search for specific words with which to pin down their musical reactions. That is why they always find Tchaikovsky easier to "understand" than Beethoven. In the first place, it is easier to pin a meaning-word on a Tchaikovsky piece than on a Beethoven one. Much easier. Moreover, with the Russian composer, every time you come back to a piece of his it almost always says the same thing to you, whereas with Beethoven it is often quite difficult to put your finger right on what he is saying. And any musician will tell you that that is why Beethoven is the greater composer. Because music which always says the same thing to you will necessarily soon become dull music, but music whose meaning is slightly different with each hearing has a greater chance of remaining alive.

Listen, if you can, to the forty-eight fugue themes of Bach's *Well Tempered Clavichord*. Listen to each theme, one after another. You will soon realize that each theme mirrors a different world of feeling. You will also soon realize that the more beautiful a theme seems to you the harder it is to find any word that will describe it to your complete satisfaction. Yes, you will certainly know whether it is a gay theme or a sad one. You will be able, in other words, in your own mind, to draw a frame of emotional feeling around your theme. Now study the sad one a little closer. Try to pin down the exact quality of its sadness. Is it pessimistically sad or resignedly sad; is it fatefully sad or smilingly sad?

Let us suppose that you are fortunate and can describe to your own satisfaction in so many words the exact meaning of your chosen theme. There is still no guarantee that anyone else will be satisfied. Nor need they be. The important thing is that each one feel for himself the specific expressive quality of a theme or, similarly, an entire piece of music. And if it is a great work of art, don't expect it to mean exactly the same thing to you each time you return to it.

Themes or pieces need not express only one emotion, of course. Take such a theme as the first main one of the *Ninth Symphony*, for example. It is clearly made up of different elements. It does not say only one thing. Yet anyone hearing it immediately gets a feeling of strength, a feeling of power. It isn't a power that comes simply because the theme is played loudly. It is a power inherent in the theme itself. The extraordinary strength and vigor of the theme results in the listener's receiving an impression that a forceful statement has been made. But one should never try to boil it down to "the fateful hammer of life," etc. That is where the trouble begins. The musician, in his exasperation, says it means nothing but the notes themselves, whereas the nonprofessional is only too anxious to hang on to any explanation that gives him the illusion of getting closer to the music's meaning.

15 Now, perhaps, the reader will know better what I mean when I say that music does have an expressive meaning but that we cannot say in so many words what that meaning is.

The third plane on which music exists is the sheerly musical plane. Besides the pleasurable sound of music and the expressive feeling that it gives off, music does exist in terms of the notes themselves and of their manipulation. Most listeners are not sufficiently conscious of this third plane. . . .

Professional musicians, on the other hand, are, if anything, too conscious of the mere notes themselves. They often fall into the error of becoming so engrossed with their arpeggios and staccatos that they forget the deeper aspects of the music they are performing. But from the layman's standpoint, it is not so much a matter of getting over bad habits on the sheerly musical plane as of increasing one's awareness of what is going on, in so far as the notes are concerned.

When the man in the street listens to the "notes themselves" with any degree of concentration, he is most likely to make some mention of the melody. Either he hears a pretty melody or he does not, and he generally lets it go at that. Rhythm is likely to gain his attention next, particularly if it seems exciting. But harmony and tone color are generally taken for granted, if they are thought of consciously at all. As for music's having a definite form of some kind, that idea seems never to have occurred to him.

It is very important for all of us to become more alive to music on its sheerly musical plane. After all, an actual musical material is being used. The intelligent listener must be prepared to increase his awareness of the musical material and what happens to it. He must hear the melodies, the rhythms, the harmonies, the tone colors in a more conscious fashion. But above all he must, in order to follow the line of the composer's thought, know something of the principles of musical form. Listening to all of these elements is listening on the sheerly musical plane.

20 Let me repeat that I have split up mechanically the three separate planes on which we listen merely for the sake of greater clarity. Actually, we never listen on one or the other of these planes. What we do is to correlate them—listening in all three ways at the same time. It takes no mental effort, for we do it instinctively.

Perhaps an analogy with what happens to us when we visit the theater will make this instinctive correlation clearer. In the theater, you are aware of the actors and actresses, costumes and sets, sounds and movements. All these give one the sense that the theater is a pleasant place to be in. They constitute the sensuous plane in our theatrical reactions.

The expressive plane in the theater would be derived from the feeling that you get from what is happening on the stage. You are moved to pity, excitement, or gayety. It is this general feeling, generated aside from the particular words being spoken, a certain emotional something which exists on the stage, that is analogous to the expressive quality in music.

The plot and plot development is equivalent to our sheerly musical plane. The playwright creates and develops a character in just the same way that a composer creates and develops a theme. According to the degree of your awareness of the way in which the artist in either field handles his material will you become a more intelligent listener.

It is easy enough to see that the theatergoer never is conscious of any of these elements separately. He is aware of them all at the same time. The same is true of music listening. We simultaneously and without thinking listen on all three planes.

In a sense, the ideal listener is both inside and outside the music at 25
the same moment, judging it and enjoying it, wishing it would go one way and watching it go another—almost like the composer at the moment he composes it; because in order to write his music, the composer must also be inside and outside his music, carried away by it and yet coldly critical of it. A subjective and objective attitude is implied in both creating and listening to music.

What the reader should strive for, then, is a more *active* kind of listening. Whether you listen to Mozart or Duke Ellington, you can deepen your understanding of music only by being a more conscious and aware listener—not someone who is just listening, but someone who is listening *for* something.

Prose Forms: Parables

When we read a short story or a novel, we are less interested in the working out of ideas than in the working out of characters and their destinies. In Dickens' Great Expectations, *for example, Pip, the hero, undergoes many triumphs and defeats in his pursuit of success, only to learn finally that he has expected the wrong things, or the right things for the wrong reasons; that the great values in life are not always to be found in what the world calls success. In realizing this meaning, we consider certain ideas that organize and evaluate the life in the novel and that ultimately we apply to life generally. Ideas are there not to be exploited discursively, but to be understood as the perspective which shapes the direction of the novel and our view of its relation to life.*

When ideas in their own reality are no longer the primary interest in writing, we have obviously moved from expository to other forms of prose. The shift need not be abrupt and complete, however; there is an area where the discursive interest in ideas and the narrative interest in characters and events blend. In allegory, for example, abstract ideas are personified. "Good Will" or "Peace" may be shown as a young woman, strong, confident, and benevolent in her bearing but vulnerable, through her sweet reasonableness, to the single-minded, fierce woman who is "Dissension." Our immediate interest is in their behavior as characters, but our ultimate interest is in the working out, through them, of the ideas they represent. We do not ask that the characters and events be entirely plausible in relation to actual life, as we do for the novel; we are satisfied if they are consistent with the nature of the ideas that define their vitality.

Ideas themselves have vitality, a mobile and dynamic life with a behavior of its own. The title of the familiar Negro spiritual "Sometimes I Feel Like a Motherless Child," for example, has several kinds of "motion" as an idea. The qualitative identity of an adult's feelings and those of a child; the whole burgeoning possibility of all that the phrase "motherless child" can mean; the subtle differences in meaning that occur when it is a black who feels this or when it is a white;

the speculative possibilities of the title as social commentary or psychological analysis—these suggest something of the "life" going on in and around the idea. Definition, analogy, assumption, implication, context, illustration *are some of the familiar terms we use to describe this kind of life.*

There is, of course, another and more obvious kind of vitality that an idea has: its applicability to the affairs of people in everyday life. Both the kind and extent of an idea's relevance are measures of this vitality. When an essayist wishes to exploit both the life in an idea and the life it comprehends, he or she often turns to narration, because there one sees the advantage of lifelike characters and events, and of showing through them the liveliness of ideas in both the senses we have noted. Ideas about life can be illustrated in life. And, besides, people like stories.

The parable and the moral fable are ideal forms for this purpose. In both, the idea is the heart of the composition; in both the ideas usually assume the form of a lesson about life, some moral truth of general consequence; and in both there are characters and actions. Jesus often depended on parables in his teaching. Simple, economical, pointed, the parables developed a "story," but more importantly, applied a moral truth to experience. Peter asked Jesus how often he must forgive the brother who sins against him, and Jesus answered with the parable of the king and his servants, one of whom asked and got forgiveness of the king for his debts but who would not in turn forgive a fellow servant his debt. The king, on hearing of this harshness, retracted his own benevolence and punished the unfeeling servant. Jesus concluded to Peter, "So likewise shall my heavenly Father do also unto you, if ye from your hearts forgive not every one his brother their trespasses." But before this direct drawing of the parallel, the lesson was clear in the outline of the narrative.

Parables usually have human characters; fables often achieve a special liveliness with animals or insects. Swift, in "The Spider and the Bee," narrates the confrontation of a comically humanized spider and bee who debate the merits of their natures and their usefulness in the world of experience. The exchange between the two creatures is brilliantly and characteristically set out, but by its end, the reader realizes that extraordinary implications about the nature of art, of education, of human psychological and intellectual potential have been the governing idea all along.

In writing the parable or fable, the writer will be verging continually on strict prose narrative but through skill and tact he or she can preserve the essayist's essential commitment to the definition and development of ideas in relation to experience.

Aesop: The Frogs Desiring a King

The frogs always had lived a happy life in the marshes. They had jumped and splashed about with never a care in the world. Yet some of them were not satisfied with their easygoing life. They thought they should have a king to rule over them and to watch over their morals. So they decided to send a petition to Jupiter[1] asking him to appoint a king.

Jupiter was amused by the frogs' plea. Good-naturedly he threw down a log into the lake, which landed with such a splash that it sent all the frogs scampering for safety. But after a while, when one venturesome frog saw that the log lay still, he encouraged his friends to approach the fallen monster. In no time at all the frogs, growing bolder and bolder, swarmed over the log Jupiter had sent and treated it with the greatest contempt.

Dissatisfied with so tame a ruler, they petitioned Jupiter a second time, saying: "We want a real king, a king who will really rule over us." Jupiter, by this time, had lost some of his good nature and was tired of the frogs' complaining.

So he sent them a stork, who proceeded to gobble up the frogs right and left. After a few days the survivors sent Mercury[2] with a private message to Jupiter, beseeching him to take pity on them once more.

5 "Tell them," said Jupiter coldly, "that this is their own doing. They wanted a king. Now they will have to make the best of what they asked for."

Moral: Let well enough alone!

3rd century A.D.

1. The king of the gods.

2. The messenger of the gods.

Plato: The Allegory of the Cave

And now, I said, let me show in a figure how far our nature is enlightened or unenlightened: Behold! human beings living in an underground den, which has a mouth open towards the light and reaching all along the den; here they have been from their childhood, and have their

4th century B.C.

legs and necks chained so that they cannot move, and can only see before them, being prevented by the chains from turning round their heads. Above and behind them a fire is blazing at a distance, and between the fire and the prisoners there is a raised way; and you will see, if you look, a low wall built along the way, like the screen which marionette players have in front of them, over which they show the puppets.

I see.

And do you see, I said, men passing along the wall carrying all sorts of vessels, and statues and figures of animals made of wood and stone and various materials, which appear over the wall? Some of them are talking, others silent.

You have shown me a strange image, and they are strange prisoners.

Like ourselves, I replied; and they see only their own shadows, or the shadows of one another, which the fire throws on the opposite wall of the cave?

True, he said; how could they see anything but the shadows if they were never allowed to move their heads?

And of the objects which are being carried in like manner they would only see the shadows?

Yes, he said.

And if they were able to converse with one another, would they not suppose that they were naming what was actually before them?

Very true.

And suppose further that the prison had an echo which came from the other side, would they not be sure to fancy when one of the passers-by spoke that the voice which they heard came from the passing shadow?

No question, he replied.

To them, I said, the truth would be literally nothing but the shadows of the images.

That is certain.

And now look again, and see what will naturally follow if the prisoners are released and disabused of their error. At first, when any of them is liberated and compelled suddenly to stand up and turn his neck round and walk and look towards the light, he will suffer sharp pains; the glare will distress him and he will be unable to see the realities of which in his former state he had seen the shadows; and then conceive some one saying to him, that what he saw before was an illusion, but that now, when he is approaching nearer to being and his eye is turned towards more real existence, he has a clearer vision—what will be his reply? And you may further imagine that his instructor is pointing to the objects as they pass and requiring him to name them—will he not be perplexed? Will he not fancy that the shadows which he formerly saw are truer than the objects which are now shown to him?

Far truer.

And if he is compelled to look straight at the light, will he not have a pain in his eyes which will make him turn away to take refuge in the objects of vision which he can see, and which he will conceive to be in reality clearer than the things which are now being shown to him?

True, he said.

And suppose once more, that he is reluctantly dragged up a steep and rugged ascent, and held fast until he is forced into the presence of the sun himself, is he not likely to be pained and irritated? When he approaches the light his eyes will be dazzled and he will not be able to see anything at all of what are now called realities.

Not all in a moment, he said.

He will require to grow accustomed to the sight of the upper world. And first he will see the shadows best, next the reflections of men and other objects in the water, and then the objects themselves; then he will gaze upon the light of the moon and the stars and the spangled heaven; and he will see the sky and the stars by night better than the sun or the light of the sun by day?

Certainly.

Last of all he will be able to see the sun, and not mere reflections of him in the water, but he will see him in his own proper place, and not in another; and he will contemplate him as he is.

Certainly.

He will then proceed to argue that this is he who gives the season and the years, and is the guardian of all that is in the visible world, and in a certain way the cause of all things which he and his fellows have been accustomed to behold?

Clearly, he said, he would first see the sun and then reason about him.

And when he remembered his old habitation, and the wisdom of the den and his fellow-prisoners, do you not suppose that he would felicitate himself on the change, and pity them?

Certainly, he would.

And if they were in the habit of conferring honors among themselves on those who were quickest to observe the passing shadows and to remark which of them went before, and which followed after, and which were together; and who were therefore best able to draw conclusions as to the future, do you think that he would care for such honors and glories, or envy the possessors of them? Would he not say with Homer,

> Better to be the poor servant of a poor master,

and to endure anything, rather than think as they do and live after their manner?

Yes, he said, I think that he would rather suffer anything than entertain these false notions and live in this miserable manner.

Imagine once more, I said, such an one coming suddenly out of the sun to be replaced in his old situation; would he not be certain to have his eyes full of darkness?

To be sure, he said.

And if there were a contest, and he had to compete in measuring the shadows with the prisoners who had never moved out of the den, while his sight was still weak, and before his eyes had become steady (and the time which would be needed to acquire this new habit of sight might be very considerable) would he not be ridiculous? Men would say of him that up he went and down he came without his eyes; and that it was better not even to think of ascending; and if any one tried to loose another and lead him up to the light, let them only catch the offender, and they would put him to death.

No question, he said.

This entire allegory, I said, you may now append, dear Glaucon, to the previous argument; the prison-house is the world of sight, the light of the fire is the sun, and you will not misapprehend me if you interpret the journey upwards to be the ascent of the soul into the intellectual world according to my poor belief, which, at your desire, I have expressed—whether rightly or wrongly God knows. But, whether true or false, my opinion is that in the world of knowledge the idea of good appears last of all, and is seen only with an effort; and, when seen, is also inferred to be the universal author of all things beautiful and right, parent of light and of the lord of light in this visible world, and the immediate source of reason and truth in the intellectual; and that this is the power upon which he who would act rationally either in public or private life must have his eye fixed.

I agree, he said, as far as I am able to understand you.

Moreover, I said, you must not wonder that those who attain to this beatific vision are unwilling to descend to human affairs; for their souls are ever hastening into the upper world where they desire to dwell; which desire of theirs is very natural, if our allegory may be trusted.

Yes, very natural.

And is there anything surprising in one who passes from divine contemplations to the evil state of man, misbehaving himself in a ridiculous manner; if, while his eyes are blinking and before he has become accustomed to the surrounding darkness, he is compelled to fight in courts of law, or in other places, about the images or the shadows of images of justice, and is endeavouring to meet the conceptions of those who have never yet seen absolute justice?

Anything but surprising, he replied.

Any one who has common sense will remember that bewilderments of the eyes are of two kinds, and arise from two ca either from coming out of the light or from going into the light, wh is true of the mind's eye, quite as much as of the bodily eye; and remembers this when he sees any one whose vision is perple who weak, will not be too ready to laugh; he will first ask whether th d of man has come out of the brighter life, and is unable to see be unaccustomed to the dark, or having turned from darkness to the is dazzled by excess of light. And he will count the one happy in condition and state of being, and he will pity the other; or, if he have mind to laugh at the soul which comes from below into the light, there will be more reason in this than in the laugh which greets him who returns from above out of the light into the den.

That, he said, is a very just distinction.

Jesus: Parables of the Kingdom

The Ten Virgins

Then shall the kingdom of heaven be likened unto ten virgins, which took their lamps, and went forth to meet the bridegroom.

And five of them were wise, and five *were* foolish.

They that *were* foolish took their lamps, and took no oil with them:

But the wise took oil in their vessels with their lamps.

While the bridegroom tarried, they all slumbered and slept.

And at midnight there was a cry made, Behold, the bridegroom cometh; go ye out to meet him.

Then all those virgins arose, and trimmed their lamps.

And the foolish said unto the wise, Give us of your oil; for our lamps are gone out.

But the wise answered, saying *Not so;* lest there be not enough for us and you: but go ye rather to them that sell, and buy for yourselves.

And while they went to buy, the bridgroom came; and they that were ready went in with him to the marriage: and the door was shut.

Afterward came also the other virgins, saying, Lord, Lord, open to us.

But he answered and said, Verily I say unto you, I know you not.

From Jesus' teachings to his disciples on the Mount of Olives, as written in Matthew xxv, King James Bible (1611).

Watch therefore, for ye know neither the day nor the hour wherein the Son of man cometh.

The Ten Talents

For *the kingdom of heaven is* as a man travelling into a far country, *who* called his own servants, and delivered unto them his goods.

And unto one he gave five talents, to another two, and to another one; to every man according to his several ability; and straightway took his journey.

Then he that had received the five talents went and traded with the same, and made *them* other five talents.

And likewise he that *had received* two, he also gained other two.

But he that had received one went and digged in the earth, and hid 5
his lord's money.

After a long time the lord of those servants cometh, and reckoneth with them.

And so he that had received five talents came and brought other five talents, saying, Lord, thou deliveredst unto me five talents: behold, I have gained beside them five talents more.

His lord said unto him, Well done, *thou* good and faithful servant: thou hast been faithful over a few things, I will make thee ruler over many things: enter thou into the joy of thy lord.

He also that had received two talents came and said, Lord, thou deliverdst unto me two talents: behold, I have gained two other talents beside them.

His lord said unto him, Well done, good and faithful servant; thou 10
hast been faithful over a few things, I will make thee ruler over many things: enter thou into the joy of thy lord.

Then he which had received the one talent came and said, Lord, I knew thee that thou art an hard man, reaping where thou hast not sown, and gathering where thou hast not strawed:

And I was afraid, and went and hid thy talent in the earth: lo, *there* thou hast *that is* thine.

His lord answered and said unto him, *Thou* wicked and slothful servant, thou knewest that I reap where I sowed not, and gather where I have not strawed:

Thou oughtest therefore to have put my money to the exchanges, and *then* at my coming I should have received mine own with usury.

Take therefore the talent from him, and give *it* unto him which 15
hath ten talents.

For unto every one that hath shall be given, and he shall have abundance: but from him that hath not shall be taken away even that which he hath.

And cast ye the unprofitable servant into outer darkness: there shall be weeping and gnashing of teeth.

When the Son of man shall come in his glory, and all the holy angels with him, then shall he sit upon the throne of his glory:

And before him shall be gathered all nations: and he shall separate them one from another, as a shepherd divideth *his* sheep from the goats:

And he shall set the sheep on his right hand, but the goats on the left.

Then shall the King say unto them on his right hand, Come, ye blessed of my Father, inherit the kingdom prepared for you from the foundation of the world:

For I was an hungred, and ye gave me meat: I was thirsty, and ye gave me drink: I was a stranger, and ye took me in:

Naked, and ye clothed me: I was sick, and ye visited me: I was in prison, and ye came unto me.

Then shall the righteous answer him, saying, Lord, when saw we thee an hungred, and fed *thee?* or thirsty, and gave *thee* drink?

When saw we thee a stranger, and took *thee* in? or naked, and clothed thee?

Or when saw we thee sick, or in prison, and came unto thee?

And the King shall answer and say unto them, Verily I say unto you, Inasmuch as ye have done *it* unto one of the least of these my brethren, ye have done *it* unto me.

Then shall he say also unto them on the left hand, Depart from me, ye cursed, into everlasting fire, prepared for the devil and his angels:

For I was an hungred, and ye gave me no meat: I was thirsty, and ye gave me no drink.

I was a stranger, and ye took me not in: naked, and ye clothed me not: sick, and in prison, and ye visited me not.

Then shall they also answer him, saying, Lord, when saw we thee an hungred, or athirst, or a stranger, or naked, or sick, or in prison, and did not minister unto thee?

Then shall he answer them, saying, Verily I say unto you, Inasmuch as ye did *it* not to one of the least of these, ye did *it* not to me.

And these shall go away into everlasting punishment: but the righteous into life eternal.

The Prodigal Son

And he said, A certain man had two sons;

And the younger of them said to his father, Father, give me the portion of goods that falleth to me. And he divided unto them his living.

From Luke xv, King James Bible (1611).

And not many days after that, the younger son gathered all together,
and took his journey into a far country, and there wasted his substance
with riotous living.

And when he had spent all, there arose a mighty famine in that land;
and he began to be in want.

And he went and joined himself to a citizen of that country; and he 5
sent him into his fields to feed swine.

And he would fain have filled his belly with the husks that the swine
did eat; and no man gave unto him.

And when he came to himself, he said, How many of my father's
hired servants have bread enough and to spare, and I perish with hunger!

I will arise and go to my father, and will say unto him, Father, I have
sinned against heaven, and before thee,

And am no more worthy to be called thy son; make me as one of thy
hired servants.

And he arose, and came to his father. But when he was yet a great 10
way off, his father saw him, and had compassion, and ran, and fell on
his neck, and kissed him.

And the son said unto him, Father, I have sinned against heaven,
and in thy sight, and am no more worthy to be called thy son.

But the father said to his servants, Bring forth the best robe, and put
it on him; and put a ring on his hand, and shoes on his feet.

And bring the fatted calf, and kill it; and let us eat, and be merry.

For this, my son, was dead, and is alive again; he was lost, and is
found. And they began to be merry.

Now his elder son was in the field; and as he came and drew nigh to 15
the house, he heard music and dancing.

And he called one of the servants, and asked what these things
meant.

And he said unto him, Thy brother is come; and thy father hath
killed the fatted calf, because he hath received him safe and sound.

And he was angry, and would not go in; therefore came his father
out, and entreated him.

And he, answering, said to his father, Lo, these many years do I serve
thee, neither transgressed I at any time thy commandment; and yet
thou never gavest me a kid, that I might make merry with my friends.

But as soon as this, thy son, was come, who hath devoured thy living 20
with harlots, thou hast killed for him the fatted calf.

And he said unto him, Son, thou art ever with me, and all that I
have is thine.

It was meet that we should make merry, and be glad; for this, thy
brother, was dead, and is alive again; and was lost, and is found.

Zen Parables

Muddy Road

Tanzan and Ekido were once traveling together down a muddy road. A heavy rain was still falling.

Coming around a bend, they met a lovely girl in a silk kimono and sash, unable to cross the intersection.

"Come on, girl," said Tanzan at once. Lifting her in his arms, he carried her over the mud.

Ekido did not speak again until that night when they reached a lodging temple. Then he no longer could restrain himself. "We monks don't go near females," he told Tanzan, "especially not young and lovely ones. It is dangerous. Why did you do that?"

"I left the girl there," said Tanzan. "Are you still carrying her?"

A Parable

Buddha told a parable in a sutra:

A man traveling across a field encountered a tiger. He fled, the tiger after him. Coming to a precipice, he caught hold of the root of a wild vine and swung himself down over the edge. The tiger sniffed at him from above. Trembling, the man looked down to where, far below, another tiger was waiting to eat him. Only the vine sustained him.

Two mice, one white and one black, little by little started to gnaw away the vine. The man saw a luscious strawberry near him. Grasping the vine with one hand, he plucked the strawberry with the other. How sweet it tasted!

Learning to Be Silent

The pupils of the Tendai school used to study meditation before Zen entered Japan. Four of them who were intimate friends promised one another to observe seven days of silence.

On the first day all were silent. Their meditation had begun auspiciously, but when night came and the oil lamps were growing dim one of the pupils could not help exclaiming to a servant: "Fix those lamps."

The second pupil was surprised to hear the first one talk. "We are not supposed to say a word," he remarked.

"You two are stupid. Why did you talk?" asked the third.

"I am the only one who has not talked," concluded the fourth pupil.

From *Zen Flesh, Zen Bones* (1957).

Jonathan Swift: The Spider and the Bee

Things were at this crisis, when a material accident fell out. For, upon the highest corner of a large window, there dwelt a certain spider, swollen up to the first magnitude by the destruction of infinite numbers of flies, whose spoils lay scattered before the gates of his palace, like human bones before the cave of some giant. The avenues of his castle were guarded with turnpikes and palisadoes, all after the modern way of fortification. After you had passed several courts, you came to the center, wherein you might behold the constable himself in his own lodgings, which had windows fronting to each avenue, and ports to sally out upon all occasions of prey or defense. In this mansion he had for some time dwelt in peace and plenty, without danger to his person by swallows from above, or to his palace by brooms from below, when it was the pleasure of fortune to conduct thither a wandering bee, to whose curiosity a broken pane in the glass had discovered itself, and in he went; where expatiating a while, he at last happened to alight upon one of the outward walls of the spider's citadel; which, yielding to the unequal weight, sunk down to the very foundation. Thrice he endeavored to force his passage, and thrice the center shook. The spider within, feeling the terrible convulsion, supposed at first that nature was approaching to her final dissolution; or else that Beelzebub,[1] with all his legions, was come to revenge the death of many thousands of his subjects, whom his enemy had slain and devoured. However, he at length valiantly resolved to issue forth, and meet his fate. Meanwhile the bee had acquitted himself of his toils, and posted securely at some distance, was employed in cleansing his wings, and disengaging them from the ragged remnants of the cobweb. By this time the spider was adventured out, when beholding the chasms, and ruins, and dilapidations of his fortress, he was very near at his wit's end; he stormed and swore like a madman, and swelled till he was ready to burst. At length, casting his eye upon the bee, and wisely gathering causes from events (for they knew each other by sight), "A plague split you," said he, "for a giddy son of a whore. Is it you, with a vengeance, that have made this litter here? Could you not look before you, and be d—nd? Do you think I have nothing else to do (in the devil's name) but to mend and repair after your arse?" "Good words, friend," said the bee (having pruned himself, and being disposed to

From *The Battle of the Books* (1704).

1. The Hebrew god of flies.

droll) "I'll give you my hand and word to come near your kennel no more; I was never in such a confounded pickle since I was born." "Sirrah," replied the spider, "if it were not for breaking an old custom in our family, never to stir abroad against an enemy, I should come and teach you better manners." "I pray have patience," said the bee, "or you will spend your substance, and for aught I see, you may stand in need of it all, towards the repair of your house." "Rogue, rogue," replied the spider, "yet methinks you should have more respect to a person, whom all the world allows to be so much your betters." "By my troth," said the bee, "the comparison will amount to a very good jest, and you will do me a favor to let me know the reasons that all the world is pleased to use in so hopeful a dispute." At this the spider, having swelled himself into the size and posture of a disputant, began his argument in the true spirit of controversy, with a resolution to be heartily scurrilous and angry, to urge on his own reasons, without the least regard to the answers or objections of his opposite, and fully predetermined in his mind against all conviction.

"Not to disparage myself," said he, "by the comparison with such a rascal, what art thou but a vagabond without house or home, without stock or inheritance, born to no possession of your own, but a pair of wings and a drone-pipe? Your livelihood is an universal plunder upon nature; a freebooter over fields and gardens; and for the sake of stealing will rob a nettle as easily as a violet. Whereas I am a domestic animal, furnished with a native stock within myself. This large castle (to show my improvements in the mathematics) is all built with my own hands, and the materials extracted altogether out of my own person."

"I am glad," answered the bee, "to hear you grant at least that I am come honestly by my wings and my voice; for then, it seems, I am obliged to Heaven alone for my flights and my music; and Providence would never have bestowed on me two such gifts, without designing them for the noblest ends. I visit indeed all the flowers and blossoms of the field and the garden; but whatever I collect from thence enriches myself, without the least injury to their beauty, their smell, or their taste. Now, for you and your skill in architecture and other mathematics, I have little to say: in that building of yours there might, for aught I know, have been labor and method enough, but by woful experience for us both, 'tis too plain, the materials are naught, and I hope you will henceforth take warning, and consider duration and matter as well as method and art. You boast, indeed, of being obliged to no other creature, but of drawing and spinning out all from yourself; that is to say, if we may judge of the liquor in the vessel by what issues out, you possess a good plentiful store of dirt and poison in your breast; and, tho' I would by no means lessen or disparage your genuine stock of either, yet I doubt you are somewhat obliged for an increase of both, to a little foreign assistance. Your inherent portion of dirt does not fail of acquisitions, by sweepings exhaled from below; and one insert furnishes you with a share of poison to destroy another. So that in short, the question comes all to this—which is the nobler being of the two, that which by a lazy contemplation of four inches round, by an overweening pride, feeding and engendering on itself, turns all into excrement and venom, produces nothing at last, but flybane and a cobweb; or that which, by an universal range, with long search, much study, true judgment, and distinction of things, brings home honey and wax."

Samuel L. Clemens: THE WAR PRAYER

It was a time of great and exalting excitement. The country was up in arms, the war was on, in every breast burned the holy fire of patriotism; the drums were beating, the bands playing, the toy pistols popping, the bunched firecrackers hissing and spluttering; on every hand and far down the receding and fading spread of roofs and balconies a fluttering wilderness of flags flashed in the sun; daily the young volunteers marched down the wide avenue gay and fine in their new uniforms, the proud fathers and mothers and sisters and sweethearts cheering them with voices choked with happy emotion as they swung by; nightly the packed mass meetings listened, panting, to patriot oratory which stirred the deepest deeps of their hearts and which they interrupted at briefest intervals with cyclones of applause, the tears running down their cheeks the while; in the churches the pastors preached devotion to flag and country and invoked the God of Battles, beseeching His aid in our good cause in outpouring of fervid eloquence which moved every listener. It was indeed a glad and gracious time, and the half-dozen rash spirits that ventured to disapprove of the war and cast a doubt upon its righteousness straightway got such a stern and angry warning that for their personal safety's sake they quickly shrank out of sight and offended no more in that way.

Sunday morning came—next day the battalions would leave for the front; the church was filled; the volunteers were there, their young faces alight with martial dreams—visions of the stern advance, the gathering momentum, the rushing charge, the flashing sabers, the flight of the foe, the tumult, the enveloping smoke, the fierce pursuit,

Dictated in 1904 or 1905; published in *Europe and Elsewhere* (1923).

the surrender!—then home from the war, bronzed heroes, welcomed, adored, submerged in golden seas of glory! With the volunteers sat their dear ones, proud, happy, and envied by the neighbors and friends who had no sons and brothers to send forth to the field of honor, there to win for the flag or, failing die the noblest of noble deaths. The service proceeded; a war chapter from the Old Testament was read; the first prayer was said; it was followed by an organ burst that shook the building, and with one impulse the house rose, with glowing eyes and beating hearts, and poured out that tremendous invocation—

> "God the all-terrible! Thou who ordainest,
> Thunder thy clarion and lightning thy sword!"

Then came the "long" prayer. None could remember the like of it for passionate pleading and moving and beautiful language. The burden of its supplication was that an ever-merciful and benignant Father of us all would watch over our noble young soldiers and aid, comfort, and encourage them in their patriotic work; bless them, shield them in the day of battle and the hour of peril, bear them in His mighty hand, make them strong and confident, invincible in the bloody onset; help them to crush the foe, grant to them and to their flag and country imperishable honor and glory—

An aged stranger entered and moved with slow and noiseless step up the main aisle, his eyes fixed upon the minister, his long body clothed in a robe that reached to his feet, his head bare, his white hair descending in a frothy cataract to his shoulders, his seamy face unnaturally pale, pale even to ghastliness. With all eyes following him and wondering, he made his silent way; without pausing, he ascended to the preacher's side and stood there, waiting. With shut lids the preacher, unconscious of his presence, continued his moving prayer, and at last finished it with the words, uttered in fervent appeal, "Bless our arms, grant us the victory, O Lord our God, Father and Protector of our land and flag!"

The stranger touched his arm, motioned him to step aside—which the startled minister did—and took his place. During some moments he surveyed the spellbound audience with solemn eyes in which burned an uncanny light; then in a deep voice he said:

5 "I come from the Throne—bearing a message from Almighty God!" The words smote the house with a shock; if the stranger perceived it he gave no attention. "He has heard the prayer of His servant your shepherd and will grant it if such shall be your desire after I, His Messenger, shall have explained to you its import—that is to say, its full import. For it is like unto many of the prayers of men, in that it asks for more than he who utters it is aware of—except he pause and think.

"God's servant and yours has prayed his prayer. Has he paused and taken thought? Is it one prayer? No, it is two—one uttered, the other not. Both have reached the ear of Him Who heareth all supplications, the spoken and the unspoken. Ponder this—keep it in mind. If you would beseech a blessing upon yourself, beware! lest without intent you invoke a curse upon a neighbor at the same time. If you pray for the blessing of rain upon your crop which needs it, by that act you are possibly praying for a curse upon some neighbor's crop which may not need rain and can be injured by it.

"You have heard your servant's prayer—the uttered part of it. I am commissioned of God to put into words the other part of it—that part which the pastor, and also you in your hearts, fervently prayed silently. And ignorantly and unthinkingly? God grant that it was so! You heard these words: 'Grant us the victory, O Lord our God!' That is sufficient. The *whole* of the uttered prayer is compact into those pregnant words. Elaborations were not necessary. When you have prayed for victory you have prayed for many unmentioned results which follow victory—*must* follow it, cannot help but follow it. Upon the listening spirit of God the Father fell also the unspoken part of the prayer. He commandeth me to put it into words. Listen!

"O Lord our Father, our young patriots, idols of our hearts, go forth to battle—be Thou near them! With them, in spirit, we also go forth from the sweet peace of our beloved firesides to smite the foe. O Lord our God, help us to tear their soldiers to bloody shreds with our shells; help us to cover their smiling fields with the pale forms of their patriot dead; help us to drown the thunder of the guns with the shrieks of their wounded, writhing in pain; help us to lay waste their humble homes with a hurricane of fire; help us to wring the hearts of their unoffending widows with unavailing grief; help us to turn them out roofless with their little children to wander unfriended the wastes of their desolated land in rags and hunger and thirst, sports of the sun flames of summer and the icy winds of winter, broken in spirit, worn with travail, imploring Thee for the refuge of the grave and denied it—for our sakes who adore Thee, Lord, blast their hopes, blight their lives, protract their bitter pilgrimage, make heavy their steps, water their way with their tears, stain the white snow with the blood of their wounded feet! We ask it, in the spirit of love, of Him Who is the Source of Love, and Who is the ever-faithful refuge and friend of all that are sore beset and seek His aid with humble and contrite hearts. Amen.

(*After a pause*) "Ye have prayed it: if ye still desire it, speak! The messenger of the Most High waits."

It was believed afterward that the man was a lunatic, because there 10
was no sense in what he said.

Terry Tempest Williams: The Bowl

There was a woman who left the city, left her husband, and her children, left everything behind to retrieve her soul. She came to the desert after seeing her gaunt face in the mirror, the pallor that comes when everything is going out and nothing is coming in. She had noticed for the first time the furrows under her eyes that had been eroded by tears. She did not know the woman in the mirror. She took off her apron, folded it neatly in the drawer, left a note for her family, and closed the door behind her. She knew that her life and the lives of those she loved depended on it.

The woman returned to the place of her childhood, where she last remembered her true nature. She returned to the intimacy of a small canyon that for years had loomed large in her imagination, and there she set up camp. The walls were as she had recalled them, tall and streaked from rim to floor. The rock appeared as draped fabric as she placed her hand flat against its face. The wall was cold; the sun had not yet reached the wash. She began wading the shallow stream that ran down the center of the canyon, and chose not to be encumbered by anything. She shed her clothing, took out her hairpins, and squeezed the last lemon she had over her body. Running her hands over her breasts and throat and behind her neck, the woman shivered at her own bravery. This is how it should be, she thought. She was free and frightened and beautiful.

For days, the woman wandered in and out of the slick-rock maze. She drank from springs and ate the purple fruit of prickly pears. Her needs were met simply. Because she could not see herself, she was unaware of the changes—how her skin became taut and tan, the way in which her hair relaxed and curled itself. She even seemed to walk differently as her toes spread and gripped the sand.

All along the wash, clay balls had been thrown by a raging river. The woman picked one up, pulled off the pebbles until she had a mound of supple clay. She kneaded it as she walked, rubbed the clay between the palms of her hands, and watched it lengthen. She finally sat down on the moist sand and, with her fingers, continued moving up the string of clay. And then she began to coil it, around and around, pinching shut each rotation. She created a bowl.

The woman found other clay balls and put them inside the bowl. She had an idea of making dolls for her children, small clay figurines that she would let dry in the sun. Once again, she stopped walking and

From *Coyote's Canyon* (1989).

sat in the sand to work. She split each clay ball in two, which meant she had six small pieces to mold out of three balls she had found. One by one, tiny shapes took form. A girl with open arms above her head; three boys—one standing, one sitting, and one lying down (he was growing, she mused); and then a man and a woman facing each other. She had re-created her family. With the few scraps left over she made desert animals: a lizard, a small bird, and a miniature coyote sitting on his haunches. The woman smiled as she looked over her menagerie. She clapped her hands to remove the dried clay and half expected to see them dance. Instead, it began to rain.

Within minutes, the wash began to swell. The woman put the clay creatures into the bowl and sought higher ground up a side canyon, where she found shelter under a large overhang. She was prepared to watch if a flash flood came. And it did. The clear water turned muddy as it began to rise, carrying with it the force of wild horses running with a thunderstorm behind them. The small stream, now a river, rose higher still, gouging into the sandy banks, hurling rocks, roots, and trees down stream. The woman wondered about the animals as she heard stirrings in the grasses and surmised they must be seeking refuge in the side canyons as she was—watching as she was. She pulled her legs in and wrapped her arms around her shins, resting her cheekbones against her knees. She closed her eyes and concentrated on the sound of water bursting through the silence of the canyon.

The roar of the flood gradually softened until it was replaced by birdsong. Swifts and swallows plucked the water for insects as frogs announced their return. The woman raised her head. With the bowl in both hands, she tried to get up, but slipped down the hillside, scraping the backs of her thighs on rabbitbrush and sage. She finally reached the wash with the bowl and its contents intact. And then she found herself with another problem: she sank up to her knees in the wet, red clay, only to find that the more she tried to pull her foot free, the deeper she sank with the other. Finally, letting go of her struggle, she put the bowl and her family aside, and wallowed in it. She fell sideways and rolled onto her stomach, then over onto her back. She was covered in slimy, wet clay, and it was delicious. She stretched her hands above her head, flexed her calves, and pointed her toes. The woman laughed hysterically until she became aware of her own echo.

Her body contracted.

She must get control of herself, she thought; what would her husband think? What kind of example was she setting for her children? And then she remembered—she was alone. She sat up and stared at the coiled bowl full of clay people. The woman took out the figurines and planted them in the wash. She placed the animals around them.

"They're on their own," she said out loud. And she walked back to the spring where she had drunk, filled up her bowl with water, and bathed.

The next morning, when the woman awoke, she noticed that the cottonwood branches swaying above her head had sprouted leaves.

She could go home now.

QUESTIONS ON PARABLES

1. *Many parables end with a moral explicitly stated—as in the conclusion to Aesop's fable, "Let well enough alone!" Which parables in this section include such morals? Which do not? Why might some writers choose not to conclude with an explicit statement of the "moral"?*
2. *For those parables that do not include morals, write your own version of a moral or maxim that might be deduced from the narrative. Is it possible to deduce more than one moral?*
3. *Write a parable that, while using a narrative form, embeds a moral or maxim within it.*

Philosophy and Religion

Langston Hughes

SALVATION

I was saved from sin when I was going on thirteen. But not really saved. It happened like this. There was a big revival at my Auntie Reed's church. Every night for weeks there had been much preaching, singing, praying, and shouting, and some very hardened sinners had been brought to Christ, and the membership of the church had grown by leaps and bounds. Then just before the revival ended, they held a special meeting for children, "to bring the young lambs to the fold." My aunt spoke of it for days ahead. That night I was escorted to the front row and placed on the mourners' bench[1] with all the other young sinners, who had not yet been brought to Jesus.

My aunt told me that when you were saved you saw a light, and something happened to you inside! And Jesus came into your life! And God was with you from then on! She said you could see and hear and feel Jesus in your soul. I believed her. I had heard a great many old people say the same thing and it seemed to me they ought to know. So I sat there calmly in the hot, crowded church, waiting for Jesus to come to me.

The preacher preached a wonderful rhythmical sermon, all moans and shouts and lonely cries and dire pictures of hell, and then he sang a song about the ninety and nine safe in the fold, but one little lamb was left out in the cold.[2] Then he said: "Won't you come? Won't you

From *The Big Sea* (1940).

1. A place in the front where potential converts sat during an evangelical service.
2. "The Ninety and Nine" and "Let the Lower Lights Be Burning," mentioned in the next paragraph, are the titles of famous evangelical hymns collected by Ira Sankey (1840–1908).

come to Jesus? Young lambs, won't you come?" And he held out his arms to all us young sinners there on the mourners' bench. And the little girls cried. And some of them jumped up and went to Jesus right away. But most of us just sat there.

A great many old people came and knelt around us and prayed, old women with jet-black faces and braided hair, old men with work-gnarled hands. And the church sang a song about the lower lights are burning, some poor sinners to be saved. And the whole building rocked with prayer and song.

5 Still I kept waiting to *see* Jesus.

Finally all the young people had gone to the altar and were saved, but one boy and me. He was a rounder's[3] son named Westley. Westley and I were surrounded by sisters and deacons praying. It was very hot in the church, and getting late now. Finally Westley said to me in a whisper: "God damn! I'm tired o' sitting here. Let's get up and be saved." So he got up and was saved.

Then I was left all alone on the mourners' bench. My aunt came and knelt at my knees and cried, while prayers and songs swirled all around me in the little church. The whole congregation prayed for me alone, in a mightly wail of moans and voices. And I kept waiting serenely for Jesus, waiting, waiting—but he didn't come. I wanted to see him, but nothing happened to me. Nothing! I wanted something to happen to me, but nothing happened.

I heard the songs and the minister saying: "Why don't you come? My dear child, why don't you come to Jesus? Jesus is waiting for you. He wants you. Why don't you come? Sister Reed, what is this child's name?"

"Langston," my aunt sobbed.

10 "Langston, why don't you come? Why don't you come and be saved? Oh, Lamb of God! Why don't you come?"

Now it was really getting late. I began to be ashamed of myself, holding everything up so long. I began to wonder what God thought about Westley, who certainly hadn't seen Jesus either, but who was now sitting proudly on the platform, swinging his knickerbockered legs and grinning down at me, surrounded by deacons and old women on their knees praying. God had not struck Westley dead for taking his name in vain or for lying in the temple. So I decided that maybe to save further trouble, I'd better lie, too, and say that Jesus had come, and get up and be saved.

So I got up.

Suddenly the whole room broke into a sea of shouting, as they saw me rise. Waves of rejoicing swept the place. Women leaped in the air.

3. Loafer's, bum's.

My aunt threw her arms around me. The minister took me by the hand and led me to the platform.

When things quieted down, in a hushed silence, punctuated by a few ecstatic "Amens," all the new young lambs were blessed in the name of God. Then joyous singing filled the room.

That night, for the last time in my life but one—for I was a big boy 15
twelve years old—I cried. I cried, in bed alone, and couldn't stop. I buried my head under the quilts, but my aunt heard me. She woke up and told my uncle I was crying because the Holy Ghost had come into my life, and because I had seen Jesus. But I was really crying because I couldn't bear to tell her that I had lied, that I had deceived everybody in the church, and I hadn't seen Jesus, and that now I didn't believe there was a Jesus any more, since he didn't come to help me.

QUESTIONS

1. *Describe what being "saved" means. In particular, note how the word* saved *has one meaning in paragraphs 2, 4, and 10 but takes on different meanings in paragraphs 1, 6, and 11.*
2. *People who really cared about Hughes (his aunt, the preacher, the congregation) were working awfully hard to make him have a particular religious experience. What do you think about the elements of coercion that operate here? What might be said in defense of such encouragement?*
3. *The twelve-year-old Langston obviously took the word* see *literally (paragraphs 2 and 5). Write an explanation to a young person about the difference between actually seeing and how one can "see and hear and feel" a religious experience "in your soul."*

Edward Rivera

FIRST COMMUNION

I spent the first grade of school under Luisa Lugones ("Mees Lugones"), the first-grade teacher of Bautabarro, who never laid a hand on anybody. She might hug one of her thirty-something students for standing out in class, but hit one of her neighbors' children for whatever infraction, never. "That's not what I get paid to do," she used to say. (She earned a couple of dollars a week, maybe less.) She took any complaints against you to your father and mother, or your guardians if

From *Family Installments* (1982).

you were an orphan, and let them handle the situation, which she explained, in front of you, briefly and honestly. If your parents wanted details, she gave them the details, in a serious but not morbid way and without dramatics or sermons. If they wanted to make a big deal out of it, that was their business, and your misfortune, part of the price you had to pay for disturbing her class. It was a well-run class.

* * *

Less than a year after I graduated from Mees Lugones's class, I was enrolled in Saint Misericordia's Academy for Boys and Girls, a parochial school in East Harlem, on the advice of our next-door neighbors, whose daughter and son were in the sixth and seventh grades at "Saint Miseria's," as they called the school. So did I, after a while. It turned out to be a very strict institution. Penalties galore. Maybe that was why our neighbors in apartment 19 had enrolled their kids there: for discipline—*fuetazos*, whiplashings, as the husband called it—and not for a good education and an old-fashioned religious "indoctrination," as our priests and teachers called it. Whatever it was, it was way beyond what my future public-school friends got: next to nothing, except for sports and a way with girls that left us "parochials" in the dust.

Another advantage the "publics" had over us was that their teachers couldn't lay a hand on them. By law. The opposite was true in Saint Miseria's. The law there seemed to be that if your teacher didn't let you have it good from time to time, there was something morally wrong with him or her. It was as if our hands had been made for the Cat's Paw rubber strap that could leave the imprint of a winking, smiling cat on your palm, or the twelve-inch metal-edged ruler (centimeters on one side, inches on the other) that could draw blood from your knuckles if you acted up once your mother delivered you into "their" hands at 8:30 A.M. in front of the church, where you began the day with the Mass.

Just as bad as "corporal punishment"—or worse, because it made you feel like a rat on the run from hell for a long time afterward—was the message they gave you about losing your soul if you persisted in sinning. Meaning you hadn't done your homework by Catholic standards, or had talked out of turn in class; in fact, almost anything they decided wasn't "right" or—as Sister Mary McCullough, our principal, used to put it, with her eyebrows bunched up and her lips pursed—anything that did not "redound to the greater honor and glory of Holy Mother." "Holy Mother" was always *Church*. The other mother, the Mother of our Lord, was usually referred to as "Our Blesséd Mother" or "Blesséd Mary" or "Holy Virgin." She had lots of nicknames. She was seldom called simply Mary. That might encourage vulgar liberties, abusive adjectives.

There was something both cold-hearted and generous about our 5
nuns that gave at least some of us reason to be grateful our parents had signed us up at Saint Miseria's. Sister Mary Felicia, for example. Third grade. The nicest thing Sister Felicia did for me was buy me an unused First Communion outfit in the Marqueta[1] on Park Avenue when she found out I was a Welfare case. She didn't have to do that, because Papi somehow always found a way to scrounge up the funds for whatever we needed. I think he had credit everywhere, though he wasn't one to abuse it. But Sister didn't bother consulting him or Mami about their resources. Maybe my plain, Third Avenue clothes and my apologetic look gave her the impression we were in such bad shape at home that Pap couldn't put out the money for a cheap Communion outfit: a white shirt without a label inside the collar, a pair of Tom McAn shoes (blisters guaranteed) that expanded like John's Bargain Store sponges as soon as it rained, and an even-cheaper Howard Clothes suit with a vest and a big label over the jacket's wallet pocket, so that whenever a man opened up that jacket and reached inside for his wallet, others could see he was moving up in this world. No more Third Avenue cheap stuff for this *elemento*. Unless he had somehow stolen that label and had his wife the seamstress sew it onto the wallet pocket just to impress the kind of people who kept an eye on labels. If Sister Felicia was one of those types, she kept it to herself. All she wanted was for every boy and girl in her class to show up at First Communion ceremonies in a prescribed, presentable outfit: the girls in white, the boys in black, with an oversized red ribbon around the elbow.

"Making your First Communion," Mami told me in private one day when she was in a joking mood, "is almost as important as making your first *caca* all by yourself."

"So why do I have to wear this uniform, then?" I said, confused.

"Because it's a ceremony. The most important of your life so far. Except for Baptism. It's like when you get married for the first time." Meaning what, I didn't know or ask. And what was this about people getting married more than once? Another joke? Sometimes she went over my head and didn't explain the point. Some things I should find out for myself, I guessed. You can't always be depending on your mother to fill you in. She wouldn't even tell me how she felt about Sister Felicia's generosity.

At the time it may have been a nice favor on Sister's part—and on Sister Principal's, because she was the one who dispensed their funds—putting out all that money for a kid on ADC. For one thing,

1. Large market or department store.

they were Irish, all of them, so why should they give a damn for people like me? But they did sometimes. More confusion on my side. And a long time later, when I thought back on it, I was still confused.

* * *

10 You couldn't tell the charity cases from those boys and girls whose parents had paid for their outfits, or signed the credit agreement. Some sixty of us boys sat on the right-hand side of the center pews (best seats in the House); girls, more of them than of us, on the left. A traditional arrangement. Everything was prescribed, nothing left to impulse or accident. We boys were in black, with the red arm ribbon and the red tie. Each one of us had a new black missal and a matching rosary; the Sisters had passed them out to us outside the church, as soon as we lined up in double file. And the girls were wearing the same white dress, the same white imitation-lace mantilla, the same white shoes, knee-length stockings, and gloves that came halfway up their arms. They also had white plastic purses on leashes looped around their arms, white missals, and white rosaries, and instead of an arm ribbon they were holding a bouquet of artificial flowers. I thought they looked better than we did. They always did anyway, even when they were wearing hand-me-downs. Clean human beings—that's what they were—always neat. They took pains with themselves. They had better "characters" than the boys. ("Character" was a big word at our school.)

Every boy had a fresh haircut—standing room only at my barber's the day before, and he had a couple of fast-working assistants, too—slicked-back hair, most of it black except for some of the Irish students, whose genes were different; some of them even had freckles that matched their arm ribbons. I was wearing patent-leather shoes. I wasn't the only one. Papi had insisted on that kind. "So they won't lose their shine, Santos." Fine with me.

"Faggots," I had heard someone call us outside on the sidewalk, while we waited for the order to march inside the church. "Girls," someone else had called us. "Mama's boys," "bunch of punks." And other put-downs of that kind. We knew who it was: the public-school barbarians. They were hiding in the crowd of parents, relatives, next-door neighbors, and people who just happened to be passing by and wanted to see what this was all about.

Under orders from Sister Felicia, we had to ignore the barbarians. "Pretend they don't exist, boys," she told us. That wasn't easy. They were always around somewhere, rubbing it in every chance they got because we were their "betters," we were told, and we believed it; and because they envied us and had to get back at us somehow. The Sisters and our parents and other sympathizers tried to shoo them away but didn't get anywhere. From behind parked cars, from across the street (in front of the Good Neighbor Protestant Church), from the overflow mob gathered on the sidewalk and spilling into the gutter, those P.S. Vandals, as Sister called them, were giving it to us good. And as long as the Sisters had us in their charge, as long as we were in a state of something called "grace," and fasting, too—starving for the Host—there was nothing we could do about it. We were a bunch of "twats" in "pretty" outfits, as our enemies called them. Envy. I couldn't wait to get inside the church, and I hoped the priests would get it over with fast so I could beat it back home in a hurry and change into normal human pants and sneakers. This wasn't my idea of the greatest event in my life since Baptism.

Our parents and guardians felt differently, though. They were actually enjoying this painful event. Otherwise why all the smiles? And those cameras. At least one pair of parents had hired a professional photographer to immortalize the whole thing for their son or daughter and for their old age. This pro, Mr. Taupiero, who had his own storefront studio on Madison Avenue, between Rudi's *butchería* and Al Arentsky's *bodega*,[2] specialized in weddings and funerals. He was always coming in and out of churches and funeral parlors with his equipment. He also made home visits for an extra fee and all the food and drink he could pack in. There was hardly a bride and groom in the neighborhood who hadn't been "shot" by him; he displayed his best portraits in his window, retouched out of recognition, looking embalmed, so that you could be staring at a member of your own family or at yourself and not know it. This Mr. Taupiero was a stout, well-dressed man with a perfect mustache (waxed, I think) and more photographic stuff than a movie set. He had brought his colossal tripod along, and after struggling for an open spot to set it up in, had seen it knocked over, with the camera mounted in place. Now he was almost in tears, cursing the public-school "*bárbaros* and *bandoleros*" in two languages and threatening to call *la policía* on them if they didn't reimburse him for his broken camera. Just let him try catching them. He was still cursing when we marched in twos up the steps.

Another mob scene inside, except less noise and disorder. Every stu- 15
dent's entire family must have been there, and some of those families were pretty big, from suckling babies to weak grandparents who had to be held by the hand and elbow and walked patiently up the high church steps, steered delicately through the mob, and squeezed carefully into the crowded pews. They had come to see their grandsons and granddaughters receive the Host for the first time; nothing would have kept them home. Then there were the next-door neighbors and friends, the curious snoopers and well-wishers, and a few hung-over

2. Neighborhood food store.

crashers who were sneaking into the back pews for a free show and a nap. There was nothing the ushers could do with them.

"It's a free church," one of them told an usher when the usher told him to go home and sleep it off there.

"It's free for sober Christians, Tom," the usher said.

"Who's not sober?" the wino asked. And the usher just walked off disgusted.

Way up at the the top, over the main entrance, was the Saint Misericordia Church Choir: twenty or more parishioners, about equally divided between single men and single women, some of them widows and widowers committed to long-term mourning, maybe addicted to it. The others were still looking around; they had a good view of the prospects from their loft way up there. And they were led by a man who called himself Maestro Padilla (he also rehearsed our entire school in choir practice every Friday). He was an organist, too, and (his real vocation, he insisted) a pianist. He was thin and nervous, a fastidious man with a tic in the right shoulder; it would jump up unexpectedly whenever things weren't going his way. He had been trying for years to make it as a concert pianist so he could quit the church-organ circuit. During choir practice he would tell us in a raised voice, while his right shoulder was ticking away, that the only reason he was "stucked" with us in our basement auditorium (no heat, peeling walls, long benches for chairs) was because the concert halls were discriminating against him on account of his "national origins."

20 "On account of he's cracked, he means," one of the American Christian Brothers had told another ACB one afternoon during practice.

And the other Brother had said, seriously: "Bejesus, will you just listen to the man's playing?"

"What's wrong with it, Mick?" the other Brother had said.

"Arrah, it's not my idea of music, Jerry. I wouldn't pay him to grind me own organ on a street corner. Who does he think he is! Stuck with us in our basement, me foot."

Maestro Padilla, right or wrong, was also outspoken about his wages, which he called indecent. Our pastor, he said, was working him to the bone and paying him nothing for it. As we took our seats in the church pews, he was playing one of the four Puerto Rican national anthems, "La Borinqueña," on the huge organ, blasting the church with it, shaking statues on their pedestals. The pastor had warned him about playing unauthorized secular music there, and about pulling out all the stops except during rehearsals, when Our Lord was locked up in the tabernacle, and the key safe in the sacristan's cabinet. But Padilla couldn't care less about these regulations and threats. He was both an artist and a diehard Puerto Rican patriot, and this organ racket was his way of both proclaiming his loyalty and protesting the wages he received from the "tied-fisted pastor." But Pastor Rooney's budget was so tight that, as he used to say, "all our saints are peeling off of the walls." Not only the painted saints but the statues, too, many of which were missing vital parts. The Christ Child on Saint Christopher's back had lost one of His hands and looked as though He might slip off the saint's back any day now, and another saint, Cecilia, I think, had lost her dulcimer, or harp, or whatever that strange-looking instrument she played was called.

"That's your problem," Maestro Padilla told Father Bardoni one day, when Bardoni, the pastor's right-hand man, tried to reason with him in the matter of wages. "You take care of the peeling saints, Father, I take care of the sacred music, and if I don't get a raise soon, I am going to complain to the Office of the Commonwealth of my country. I have connections with them." His cousin's sister-in-law was a secretary there, he once told Papi. "But keep it to yourself, Don Malánguez."

How could Papi keep it to himself? He told Mami and me right away. "I wish he *would* complain," Mami said. "I wish they'd raise his salary, so we can have some peace in that church."

"I don't think that connection of his is going to do him much good," Papi said. "Even Saint Anthony's better connected than that cousin of nobody."

"What do you mean *even* Saint Anthony?" She was a big fan of Saint Anthony's. Mami and Papi used to sit in one of the pews next to that saint's statue (the bunch of lilies he was holding in one hand needed replastering). That was where they were sitting now, in the back under the balcony, where Padilla's organ was less loud.

They were lost in a mob of well-groomed parents and others who looked as though they'd been put through the same dry-cleaning machine. The two of them had given me a quick kiss on the cheek and a couple of tight hand-squeezes when Sister Mary Principal flounced up to our group in her two-ton uniform and, putting her thumb to one of those metallic hand-crickets that every nun owned, signaled us with hand gestures and eye movements to proceed to our assigned seats. "With all due haste and decorum," she added, as if she needed to. Papi and Mami looked around them, bewildered, when the mob split up and scrambled for the best pews in the House.

I ended up sitting by the aisle, next to a spoiled classmate named Dom Silvestro Grippe, Jr. He was the only one in our class who called himself by three names, plus the Junior, as if his father was someone important. He got the "Dom" from his grandfather, a bricklayer who had come over from somewhere in Europe; and his late father, the original Silvestro, had been into something Grippe called "heavy construction." Dom Silvestro, Jr., was a pretty good example of heavy construction himself. He was so overweight that sometimes, just by looking at him, I'd lose my appetite. In our lunchroom the students called him cruel names, like Dom Grippe Leftovers or the Garbage Machine, and would offer him whatever leftovers they couldn't stomach themselves, preferring to fast till three. Sometimes they collected apple cores, dozens of them, and offered them to him on a platter. He'd throw them back in their faces. For all the heavy doses of religious instruction and discipline we received, we still had a pecking order; and Grippe, with all his weight and compulsive scrounging and scavenging, was our patsy, a martyr to his bottomless stomach.

He was sitting next to me in our packed pew, breathing heavily and staring straight up at the altar festooned with flowers and candles; and from the balcony, right above Mami and Papi and Saint Anthony, his mother was spying him and me out through a pair of heavyweight binoculars, as if this were the opera or the racetrack and we "first-timers" a troupe of overdressed midgets or jockeys. As a one-year widow, she was still dressed in black, head to toe, and the binoculars (also black) were looped around her neck, along with a huge gold medal that looked like a cymbal and flashed like a sunburst when the light caught it.

I don't think the Sisters were crazy about her. She pampered her son, overfed him, made all kinds of excuses for his absences, which were frequent and therefore, in Sister Felicia's opinion, "abusive"; he was always coming down with something, if his mother was telling Sister the truth. "And it can all be blamed on his stomach," I heard Sister tell one of the other nuns one day. "What that boy needs is a gag around his mouth."

"Or a zipper," said the other Sister.

I'd never heard that expression before, and spent a lot of time imagining zippers around Grippe's mouth. None of them fit. It was a capacious mouth, and sad-looking, when you came down to it. After all, he was a half-orphan already, with a mother who would probably go through life wearing those morbid-looking black dresses and dangling those heavyweight binoculars from her three-ring neck. And overfeeding her only son, her only flesh-and-blood possession, it looked like, because I don't think they had any relatives in this country. (Not that Papi and Mami and I had much to brag about on that score.)

35 But I wished she'd take those binoculars off my immediate area. I was feeling self-conscious enough to begin with, a semi-charity case in an outfit that the barbarians outside had called a "faggot fashion show." I didn't need in addition Mrs. Grippe's close-up inspection, or any comparisons with her dolled-up son, who was already sweating away to the left of me, sucking up all the scarce oxygen in our vicinity

and expelling it in the form of what Sister had once labeled halitosis[3] —one of those big words that stuck in my mind. I wrote it down in my spelling notebook as "holytoses." *Tos:* Spanish for cough. I thought she was referring to one of his frequent, "abusive" absences, and spelled it after my own misconception. But why the "holy" before "toses"? Mami and Papi said they hadn't the scarcest idea. They'd never heard of a cough like that; maybe it was some kind of Italian whooping cough, thought Papi. "*Tos ferina,* Santos."

Whatever it was, I didn't want to catch it, but since I was sitting next to the carrier in our assigned First Communion pews, I had no choice but to hold my breath as much as possible and not turn my mouth and nose his way, in the hope that whenever one of those holytoses germs happened to be coming in my direction, I'd be letting out my own breath, or holding it.

Dom Silvestro, Jr., wasn't what my family called a "considerate human being"; he was more like what Sister Felicia had once labeled a "regardless type," talking about another student who had coughed in a girl's face, and to whose parents she had written a special note: "Please buy Francisco a bottle of Father John's Cough Syrup and a jar of Vick's Vapo-Rub. Put two tablespoons of this medicated ointment in a bowl of boiling water and have your son inhale it. (See the jar label for details on this.) It is effective. Otherwise Francisco may cause an epidemic in our class, and there will be many absences. And please teach him not to cough in other students' faces. It is not very polite." It was regardless.

Grippe's mother had received several such notes herself.

"Did Sister Felicia purchase that First Communion outfit for you, Malánguess?" Dom Silvestro asked me, just as I was inhaling. He had turned his mouth right up close to my nose.

I held my breath and kicked his fat foot, and told him, without exhaling, that it was none of his business. "What the hell's it to you, Grippe?"

"Hey, hey," he said, "you can't curse in here. This is the House of God. Now you can't receive, Malánguess."

"What you talking about, Grippe?" I kept my voice down to a whisper, beginning to feel the panic waking up somewhere in the tail of my spine. "Who says I can't receive?"

"I say," he said.

"Why not?"

"Because you just cursed."

"So mind your business."

"If you receive, I'm gonna tell Sister Felicha."

3. Bad breath.

"Yeah? You tell her and I'm gonna get you right after this is over. Me and Almendras. We're gonna jump you outside. Kick your big ass, Grippe."

"Yeah?" he said, swarming my face with germs. "A whole bunch of my father's friends is in here. They're all over the place. And they got a piece in their pockets. With bullets, Malánguess. You and Almendras try anything with me, you ain't gonna receive no more Hosts in your life. You know what I'm talking about?"

Not quite, but I knew better than to mess with more than one Italian at a time, especially grown-up Italians, whose looks were always serious. So I cooled it with Grippe right there.

"Do me a big favor, Dom," I said, pulling out his first name for the first and last time in my life.

"Yeah? What you want now, Malánguess?" He wasn't about to return the familiarity.

"Don't squeal on me and I won't tell Sister you was talking in church."

"You're nobody to talk yourself, Malánguess."

"If I don't receive the Host," I said, "my father and mother's gonna kill me."

"Good," he said, to which I had nothing to add.

I was despising myself for coming on so abjectly, but this menace on my left wasn't giving me anything like a choice. He thought about it, with his face generously turned away from mine, and while his mother kept her binoculars trained on us.

"I'll give you a break this time, Malánguess," he finally told me, turning his germs loose on me again.

I thanked him, and actually felt grateful for a minute or two before going back to despising the "stoolie," as I put it to myself. A holytoses carrier, too. It figured. And now, through this degenerate specimen sitting on my left, they were trying to infect my people with it, through me. On top of committing the sin of cursing in church, I was committing the more serious one of self-righteousness. But I let it slide.

During this exchange, Maestro Padilla had been booming his idea of music down on us: a combination of sacred sounds, the strictly prescribed stuff, with intermezzos of all four Puerto Rican national anthems, which I had no doubt was endangering his immortal soul, and possibly the soul of his number one enemy, Pastor Rooney, who was officiating with two other priests up at the altar and probably cursing the choirmaster under his breath in between snatches of Latin. The choir of men and women who had lost their spouses, or who had still to find them, was doing its best to be heard above his irreligious blitz. But it was an unequal contest. Their own instruments were only vocal cords, many of them damaged from abuses of one sort or another, including, in at least three cases I knew of, chain-smoking.

* * *

With Dom Grippe breathing toses behind me ("Get up, Malánguess—this is it, man. Even though you cursed in church"), and his mother's binoculars trained on me, just in case I was thinking of pulling any "Portorican" stunts on her son, I got to my feet and faced the girl across the aisle—who was biting her lip, either out of nervousness or in expectation—and waited for the next clic-cloc of Sister's grasshopper. Every pew was a platoon of ten, and if you were one of the unluckies who had landed the aisle position, you were automatically the leader of nine others; no backing out. I'd never led anything in my life and I didn't like this, except for being ahead of Grippe, who was probably disliking me for my "luck."

The trouble was that you had to look good in front of all those "foreigners"; otherwise they'd start buzzing to each other about "that little P.R. over there who can't even walk a straight line to the abiding presence. He must have got grogged first thing he gets up this morning . . . can of six-pack in a little brown bag . . . keeps Rheingold and Schaefer[4] in business . . . a sin to receive in that state . . . eighty-proof mouthwash . . . I hear they even wash their hair in it. . . ." And my father and mother, sitting back there next to Saint Anthony and his lilies, would feel horrible about themselves, and about their son, the cause of it all.

So I watched my step; and when Sister let go with her cricket and gave me the nod (along with a menacing squint), I stepped out of my pew on tiptoes, looking (I hoped) like a self-important honors student going up to collect his big golden pin or plaque for straight A's and no absences.

I made it up to the Communion railing without tripping over myself. It was a long slow walk, halting half-steps all the way, as if we'd sprained our ankles to qualify for the You-carry-this-blanket. I hit a bump when I got to where the central aisle of the nave ran into another aisle called the "crossing" (all these symbols of what this House was all about didn't help out my nerves). This happened a few feet from the railing, but it wasn't all my fault; I knew a loose floorboard when I stepped on one, even if it was hidden by a Catholic rug with symbolic designs all over it. A couple of other first-time receivers ahead of me had also stepped on it and had given a start as if the rug had teeth in it. It was like a trap set there to catch daydreamers, or anyone who'd cursed before receiving, or held back a couple of "grievous" sins at Confession, cold-feet types who'd go through life lying to Fathers Confessor about how many pennies they'd really stolen from their mothers, while the poor woman was tied up in the kitchen, tending the pot of this and that with hacked codfish and oregano, unaware

4. Two prominent New York breweries.

that she had given birth to a crook who was depleting the family's tight budget and stealing confiscated magnets from Sister's desk during lunch period: giving our people a bad name.

65 But I was doing it again, daydreaming. I had stopped when I got to the first line of pews at the crossing and waited there, inches from the trap, trying to make myself as stiff as possible so I wouldn't pee in my pants (we had rehearsed all this: "I don't want anyone passing water in his or her pants, whichever applies," Sister had told us during run-throughs), waiting for Sister to give me the go-ahead for the Host. You couldn't just walk up to the railing and kneel there with the others; you had to wait until you were told. Sister had been very strict about that for weeks. "Remember," she had told us, "you're not going up to a cafeteria for a frankfurter. Our church is not a luncheonette and the Host is not a hot dog. So just watch your *deportment*." (I wrote that new one down in my spelling notebook first chance I got, but I misspelled it as "department," and misused it for a long time.)

While I was waiting there, turning to stone, or salt, or liquid, someone grabbed my arm, the same spot where Sister had pinched it. It was still sore. "Don't move." It was her voice again, down low. It sounded like something out of a cowboy movie I'd seen with Papi. "Okay, Mulánguezzz, don't move. This is a chodown."

She was only getting me ready for the walk to the railing. She held me there in a tight grip for about ten seconds, and as soon as one of the kneeling receivers, looking no better than before, had made a stiff about-face and started solemnly back to his pew with the Host in his mouth, Sister pointed a finger at the opening and told me to go get It, before one of Sister Haughney's girls beat me to It. Then she let go my arm, and it was as if she had pressed a button or released a spring I didn't know I had: I took off for that railing like a hungry dog tearing ass for a bowl of chow. But there was a lot of "chow" for everyone. Father Rooney's ciborium[5] was stacked, and there was plenty more Host back in the tabernacle. One of the assisting priests, Father Mooney, had already replaced Father Rooney's empty ciborium with a fresh ciborium, and was standing by in front of the altar, waiting for another nod from the railing.

"Walk, Ssantoss Malánguezzz, don't run!" Sister hizzed behind me. Too late. I was already kneeling at the railing, hands joined under my chin. She'd get me tomorrow morning. Maybe in the auditorium. Special assembly for the execution. Organ music and chorus.

And then Father Rooney and his other assistant were on top of me with the ciborium. The assistant stuck a golden plate with a handle under my chin—a paten, it was called, a metallic bib just in case. Father Rooney was holding the Host between thumb and index and wag-

5. Sacred vessel to hold the Host.

ging It in front of my mouth, which suddenly wouldn't open. Lockjaw from fright. My punishment for cursing in church.

"Open your mouth, young man," Father Rooney suggested. We hadn't rehearsed this part.

I used both hands to do it: one hand under my nose, the other pushing down on my chin. But then my tongue wouldn't come out for the presence. The spit in my mouth had thickened and turned to glue, and my tongue was stuck to my palate.

"Stick out your tongue," the priest with the paten said.

I stuck two fingers in my mouth and unstuck my tongue.

"What's he doing, Matt?" Father Rooney asked his assistant.

"You got me, Mark. What are you doing, kid?"

"I am sorry, Father," I said. "The tongue got stuck to the—"

"Shh! You're not supposed to talk in here during Mass," the pastor said. He wasn't looking too happy.

"I am sorry, Father," I said automatically, trying to get the spit going again.

"Out with the tongue, son," Father Matt repeated. "Or leave the railing."

I closed my eyes and did as he said. Then Father Rooney delivered his Latin lines: "*Corpus Domini nostri Jesu Christi custodiat animam tuam*, etcetera. Amen." Father Matt had his paten under my chin—cold metal—and I felt a familiar warm dribble working its way down my thigh, spoiling my fresh pair of First Communion shorts. The whole place was looking on, except possibly Papi and Mami, who must have been staring down at their hands in embarrassment. Then the worst of all possible things happened: the Host broke in half on my nose. I still had my eyes shut, so I didn't see just how Father Rooney managed to do it but I could figure it out. I must have made him nervous, and instead of slapping It down on the tip of my tongue, he caught the tip of my nose, and the presence broke in two. One half stayed in Father Rooney's fingers, and the other floated past my tongue, bounced off the railing, missing Father Matt's paten altogether, and came to a stop on the symbol-crowded rug on their side of the railing, between Father Matt's shoes, which were barely visible under his alb, as Sister Felicia had called that fancy undergarment.

Both priests gasped at the same time and crossed themselves. Everyone in church, except for the sleeping winos in the back, must have done the same thing. Padilla's organ began playing "*En mi viejo San Juan*," a golden oldie, probably to distract everyone from the horrible accident I'd just caused at the railing. And my bladder was having itself a time with my new shorts. Father Matt stopped quickly, with his paten held tight to his heart, and started looking for the half-Host. I remembered what Sister had said about "His body broken in pieces" is why something-something, and felt horrible. The people who had nailed Him to the Cross couldn't have felt worse afterwards than I did just then.

Father Matt was still down on his knees looking for It. He was getting warm. I could have told him, but I was afraid to open my mouth. He was saying something under his breath, and Father Rooney, all out of patience, said, "Just pick It up, Matt. We'll be here all day at this rate."

"Sorry, Mark," said Father Matt. "Here It is." He used his paten as a dust pan to scoop It up, nudging It with his index finger. It broke again during this delicate recovery, but that didn't matter. You could split It up into a couple of hundred pieces, and It was still one. That was part of the mystery behind It. The "accidents" were one thing, Sister had told us; the "essence" was something else. You couldn't violate *that*. She had told us about an egg named Humpty Dumpty to illustrate the difference between a "material" object, in this case a talking egg, and the mysterious "indivisible Host." Just the same I was having my doubts. One piece was in Father Rooney's chalice (he had slipped it back inside when no one was looking), and the other half was down there, getting scooped up by Father Matt; and I was having trouble understanding how both pieces were one and the same. Sister Felicia would tell me all about it first thing tomorrow morning, in front of everyone. I wanted to go back home. I wanted no part of this business; I was unfit, unworthy, un-everything, but I was frozen there on my knees, terrified.

Father Matt finally got back to his feet, the paten with the two extra pieces held against his chest, and the thumb and index finger of his other hand pinning Them down to prevent another accident. Then Father Rooney held out his ciborium, which looked like a fancy trophy to me—it had jewels in the middle and was made of gold, or something that resembled gold—and Father Matt nudged the two pieces into it. I thought Father Rooney was going to slap a fresh sample on my tongue, but he had nothing like that in mind. I didn't even get the three broken pieces. I had my tongue out again, but all I got was a piece of advice. "Go back to your pew, kid," he told me. "You're not ready to receive."

85 And Father Matt said, "Grow up, son. You're seven already." I was eight, already one year behind, and no end in sight. And then he turned to Father Rooney and said, in a whisper, "This whole neighborhood's going to the—"

But Father Rooney cut him short: "Not here, Matt. Later, in the rectory."

"You're the boss, Mark." And off they went to plant an intact presence on Grippe's tongue. The worst disgrace in my life to date; and once you started in with the disgraces, it was hard to stop. Some types couldn't do a thing right. They talked in church when they should have been praying in silence, they cursed before receiving, they didn't know their own neck size, or the size of their feet, and they conned their parents into paying for half their First Communion outfits, just to insult Sister. And now this. In public, too. Hundreds had seen it. Maybe a thousand. And my own parents sitting in the back, next to Saint Anthony and his lilies, pretending they didn't know who I was. At least I thought they were pretending. I wanted them to.

Sister Felicia helped me up to my feet and turned me around toward the pews. She walked back there with me, slowly, because my knees seemed to have run out of the oil that makes knees work and my shoes felt like something poured from cement. Heavy construction. She led me back to my pew by the arm she'd pinched, and as she was sitting me down she put her mouth to my ear and said, "Ssantoss Málanguezzz, you are a disgrace to our school," bearing down on "disgrace." "You are not fit for First Communion, and maybe never will be. We have a lot to discuss tomorrow morning."

I nodded; but did she think I was going to show up at school next morning? Even as I sat there in my wet shorts, my mind was out in Central Park playing hooky next day. They were going to get me anyway, day after next, no way out of it; but in the meantime I thought I was entitled to a day of rest and I was going to take it. Maybe they'd send me to P.S. Genghis Khan, where I'd have no trouble blending in with the "barbarians," which might not be a bad idea.

Papi and Mami didn't bring it up on the way home—we left in a 90
hurry—or in the house, where they insisted I sit down to eat after I changed out of my outfit, washed the pee off my thighs, and changed into normal clothes and sneakers.

Menu: Fricasseed chicken (boneless), saffron rice, a hot loaf of unconsecrated garlic bread, a bottle of grape juice (full strength), and Humpty Dumpty egg custard. Not exactly my first post-Communion meal, but no reason to throw it out, either. Mami reminded me that in the world at large a lot of people were going hungry right now. I knew she'd say that.

"You was nervous, Santos," Papi said in English while we were living it up in the dining room. I'd been expecting that one too. But he wasn't going to preach at me. "Next time," he added in Spanish, "no more accidents, okay?"

"Okay, Papi." But didn't he know it wasn't up to me?

QUESTIONS

1. *Show how one theme of this narrative is the conflict between Puerto Ricans and "others" who represent authority. Does that theme dominate? Why or why not?*
2. *Describe the conflicts within the young Rivera, who often acts like an*

impulsive eight-year-old but who has also taken on the standards set by the parochial school.

3. *Describe an experience in which someone was unable to live up to the expectations of parents or authority figures like teachers.*

Randall Balmer

ADIRONDACK FUNDAMENTALISM

In the early morning hours, Schroon Lake is gray and placid. Wispy clouds tumble over the pine-covered hillsides that surround the lake. Steam rises from the water. A lone canoe paddles by. For a brief moment, the sun pushes past the clouds but then settles back into exile.

When the receding glaciers carved Schroon Lake into the Adirondack mountains of upstate New York, they left a ninety-acre island at the north end of the lake. There, pine trees sprouted among the glacial rocks, and thus surrounded by frigid mountain water, the island became an ideal location for a youth camp.

Jack Wyrtzen, a fundamentalist Bible teacher from New York City, took possession in 1946, at about the same time that motor travel began to diminish the attractiveness of the resorts dotting the Adirondacks. He has since added an inn, a family campground, a ranch, and a Bible institute—hundreds of acres, all told—to his empire, the Word of Life Fellowship, in and around Schroon Lake. Word of Life also includes radio broadcasts on more than one hundred stations around the world, mission enterprises in places as diverse as Peru, Hungary, Israel, and New Zealand, various traveling evangelists, musicians, and drama troupes, and over a thousand Bible clubs held in churches throughout the country. All of this consumes an annual budget of about $12 million, but the youth camp, "for young people and college-career young adults aged 13 to 30," remains the centerpiece of Word of Life.[1]

I'm not sure there is any way I could document this, but I suspect that the greatest fear that haunts evangelical parents is that their children will not follow in their footsteps, that they will not sustain the same level of piety as their parents—stated baldly, that they are headed for hell rather than heaven. Such themes as waywardness and

From *Mine Eyes Have Seen the Glory* (1989). Unless indicated, all notes to this essay are the author's.

1. *Word of Life 1987 Annual* (Schroon Lake, N.Y.: Word of Life Fellowship, 1986).

redemption provide the grist for countless evangelical sermons; the parable of the prodigal son, I am convinced, is one of the most popular texts in the evangelical subculture. Prayer meetings fairly reverberate with petitions for this or that son or daughter who has wandered from the faith. In recent decades, many churches, reflecting the concerns of parents in the congregation, have hired youth pastors, whose job it is to keep children safely within the evangelical fold, to shield them from the perils of worldliness.

5 Indeed, there is ample cause for concern. What can be harder than passing on religious verve and vitality from one generation to the next, especially within a tradition that defines itself by the conversion process, that transition from darkness to light, from sinfulness to redemption? The Puritans of the seventeenth century faced this problem and never fully resolved it. New England's founding generation had forsaken fortune and family in England in order to carve a godly commonwealth out of the wilderness of Massachusetts. By the time the second generation approached adulthood, the spirituality of the founding generation had taken on heroic proportions, and when this next generation was asked as a requirement for church membership to stand before their elders in the meetinghouse and give an account of their conversions, most of them refused, knowing full well that their piety paled before that of their elders. Before long, the Puritans discerned in their midst a spiritual malaise that they called declension, and by the latter half of the seventeenth century the pulpits of New England resounded with calls to repentance.

In his novel *The Chosen,* Chaim Potok illustrates how this generational problem plays itself out within a different context. Reb Saunders, a pious, learned man venerated by his Hasidic followers, wants desperately to pass along the mantle of religious leadership to his eldest son, Danny, a precocious child who has studied the Talmud exhaustively all of his life and who regularly astounds his father's congregation with his grasp of even the most recondite Jewish sacred writings. Danny Saunders, the elders all agree, would be a worthy spiritual successor to his father.

But Danny Saunders's restless mind leads him in other directions, to intellectual pursuits outside the narrow confines of his father's calling and to friendships outside of his Hasidic community. When it finally becomes clear that Danny will not follow in his father's footsteps, Reb Saunders bids his son an anguished farewell, whereupon Danny Saunders, shorn of his earlocks and no longer dressed in black Hasidic hat and coat, walks down the street and toward a new life very different from the sheltered existence he has known.[2]

2. Chaim Potok, *The Chosen* (New York: Simon & Schuster, 1967).

It doesn't take much imagination to appreciate the quandary of parents who want to pass along to their children the faith that has shaped their lives and solved for them the riddle of eternity. You want to shelter your children from the temptations that assail them at every turn. You want to school them in the Scriptures and in the theology that you know to be correct. And you also want them to be models of godliness, a credit not only to the faith but also to you as wise, godly parents.

Yet at the same time, such sheltering diminishes the drama of their own spiritual conversions when—and if—those conversions do occur. Whereas your embracing of the gospel had delivered you from a life of, say, alcohol or drugs or promiscuity, theirs serves merely as a ratification of the beliefs and lifestyle that you, their parents, have drilled into them since infancy. (The prodigal son's older brother who stayed at home, after all, never knew the contrast between the perils of the world and the security of home, and he envied the lavish party his father threw for his brother's homecoming.) On the other hand, neglecting your children's spiritual nurture will not suffice either, for that entails the considerable risk of trusting them (through God's leading, of course) to come to Christ of their own volition.

10 Ever since the 1925 Scopes Trial convinced fundamentalists that the broader American culture had turned hostile to their interests, fundamentalists have busied themselves devising various institutions to insulate themselves and their children from the depredations of the world. (In fact, the terms *worldly* and *worldliness* are probably the closest most evangelicals come to epithets; these words are often spoken sneeringly, in a tone at the same time condescending and cautionary.) First, the fundamentalists separated out of mainline denominations so that they could maintain a theology untainted by liberalism or, in the argot of the day, "modernism." Evangelicals then established their own mission boards, Christian schools, Bible institutes, colleges, and, eventually, seminaries. For children, Sunday school provided socialization and instruction in the rudiments of evangelical theology. Once the children had grown, you could ship them off to a Bible institute where they might prepare for the pastorate, missionary work, or some other kind of "Christian service."

But by the 1940s many fundamentalist parents recognized a gap in this system. How do you shelter your children from the onslaughts of the world during those critical teenage years when, with hormones swirling furiously, temptations reach their zenith?

About this time Jack Wyrtzen devised a summer Bible camp for teenagers, a sanctuary for fundamentalist parents to send their children, a place where strict parietal rules[3] would be enforced and, more

3. Dormitory regulations about visits by the opposite sex [Editor's note].

important, where some sort of religious commitment would be exacted.

A small pontoon provides ferry service between the western shores of Schroon Lake and Word of Life Island. As you approach, a boathouse with the legend A VERY SPECIAL ISLAND comes into view. Once on the landing, a sign welcomes you to Word of Life Island and, beyond that, a second notice warns: ALL VISITORS MUST REPORT TO THE OFFICE AND SIGN IN! A winding pathway leads to a large frame building called the Pine Pavilion.

The Pine Pavilion is a squarish building constructed on a hillside, with terraces of long, wooden benches sloping down toward the stage. Flags and red-white-and-blue bunting festoon the interior. In the northeast corner, a large wooden sign reads:

> CHRIST WALKS ON THIS ISLAND
> WILL YOU MEET HIM HERE?

Green porcelain warehouse-style lamps hang from the rafters.

The evening service begins at seven, and several announcements 15
over a public-address system warn campers to be on time. Soon, a torrent of energetic campers tumbles into the building. Most of them are white and dressed in standard teenage fashions—tee-shirts, denims, sneakers, large, oversized sweatshirts.

Ten minutes into the meeting, as the sun sets across Schroon Lake, the Pine Pavilion is rocking. It's military week on the island, and the campers have been divided into Army and Navy teams. A series of games, challenges, and good-natured rivalry has been devised by the camp directors to generate spirit, teamwork, and enthusiasm. Apparently they've succeeded. Some of the counselors wear camouflage fatigues, and not infrequently amidst the singing of various evangelical songs and choruses, the pavilion erupts in rival chants of "Army! Army!" and "Navy! Navy!" Each team sings its fight song—"Anchors Aweigh" and "The Caissons Keep Rolling Along"—accompanied by spirited stomping, and soon, amidst all this excitement, the building begins to smell faintly of adolescent sweat.[4]

The crowd reverts to rhythmic clapping and stomping when a middle-aged man in a plaid, open-necked shirt plays "When the Roll Is Called Up Yonder" on his trumpet, triple-tonguing the second verse. When he finishes, more applause, shouting, hooting, and stomping.

4. This is a composite description taken from the observation of several evening rallies at the Pine Pavilion during the summers of 1984 and 1987.

The pavilion quiets somewhat as a pretty blonde woman in her late teens, wearing a khaki skirt and a navy blazer, mounts the stage. She sings several songs to the accompaniment of taped music played over the sound system. After one of the songs, she exhorts the audience in a kind of breathless whisper: "It's so important to keep your standards high. You know, it's a nasty world out there." The next song, "Build on Higher Ground," reiterates that theme:

Build your house above the ocean.
Build your house on higher ground.
Build above the world's commotion
And its mesmerizing sound.

The music finishes with a flourish, and after an announcement encouraging campers to purchase a Ryrie Study Bible and books by Chuck Swindoll at the bookstore, the young soprano joins the trumpet player for a duet, "I've Just Seen Jesus," a fitting complement, I thought, to the sign in the northeast corner of the pavilion.

Jack Wyrtzen, a snowy-haired man in white pants and a floral-print tropical shirt, comes to the podium. He reminds the campers about some of the rules that govern life on the island. Everyone must wear a robe or sweat clothes to the beach. Shorts must be at least fingertip length. Word of Life promotional literature has already spelled out these regulations in some detail. "Please keep modesty in mind regarding all clothing," the literature counsels, adding that campers should bring a Bible and "sportswear for daytime activities, dress-up clothes (dress shirt and slacks for guys, dress for girls) for Sunday and some evening meals, modest one-piece bathing suit (I Tim. 2:9) and beach robe."[5]

Wyrtzen is an old fashioned, unvarnished fundamentalist. An affable, bespeckled man, his photographs in Word of Life promotional materials invariably show him with a large, open-mouthed grin, wearing an expression that suggests he has just told you the funniest joke in the world and is awaiting your reaction. He opens with a prayer asking God that everyone in the building will be "born again by the Word of God." Immediately thereafter, he asks how many in the audience have Bibles. Virtually everyone thrusts a Bible high into the air. As he announces this evening's text, he tells the audience that he hopes "before the night is done you will come to the Lamb of God." For the first nineteen years of his life, he says, "nobody told me about Jesus Christ" in the liberal churches he attended. The United States Army,

5. *Word of Life 1987 Annual.* 1 Tim. 2:9 reads: "women should adorn themselves modestly and sensibly in seemly apparel, not with braided hair or gold or pearls or costly attire" (RSV). These rules apply to all campers in all the Word of Life camps, including the adults at Word of Life Inn.

in fact, is "the greatest denomination in the U.S.," because that's where Wyrtzen became a Christian.

Fundamentalists are fond of belittling the pretensions of mainline, 20
liberal churches, and Wyrtzen is no exception. He uses certain code words or phrases to indicate his derision of theological liberals. The one he employs most often is "First Church." He will tell of some member of "First Church" who came to one of Wyrtzen's rallies, heard the gospel for the first time, and went away born again. Or some worldly woman, also a member of "First Church," who "got saved" at Word of Life and now is "on fire for the Lord." The audience, many of whom have apparently heard this nomenclature before, picks up on this right away, snorting disapprovingly at the reference to theological liberals and the putative name of their churches.

But tonight Wyrtzen is not interested in preaching to the converted; he wants to bring more of the unsaved into the fold. After telling of various sinners—including a woman he refers to as the "blonde bomber"—whose lives have been transformed by Jesus, and after warning of the torments of hell, he asks, "Have you been to Calvary?" He implores the campers to come to Jesus and leads them in a slow, mournful chorus that evokes Jesus's death at Calvary:

Dying there for me,
Dying there for me.
Jesus died, was crucified.
Dying there for me.

"You need to confess you are a sinner and believe Jesus died for you," Wyrtzen says. "Invite Him into your heart right now." Wyrtzen makes it easy, providing a formula prayer for the wavering: "Dear Jesus, I confess that I am a sinner. Thank you for dying on the cross for me. Come into my heart and save me now. Amen."

All heads are bowed. All eyes closed. The meeting's raucous beginning is long forgotten. Wyrtzen asks for a show of hands from those who prayed the prayer. A few timid arms reach upward. Wyrtzen acknowledges each one. "Yes, I see that hand. Is there another?" He pleads a bit longer and then closes the meeting with this stark admonition: "If you leave this building without Jesus, you're guilty of His crucifixion."

The harvest tonight is disappointing, but it's still early in the week. Wyrtzen has a whole stable of speakers, Bible teachers, and counselors who will hammer the message home in the next few days. The entire schedule, in fact, is calculated to produce a maximum yield of converts and rededications, those who publicly reaffirm their conversions and resolve to live holier lives.

The day begins with breakfast at eight, followed by a morning of Bible study. After lunch, the campers have an afternoon of play—swimming, water skiing, basketball, volleyball—before supper and the evening meeting, either a rally in the pavilion or around a campfire. After the meeting, the counselors organize more competitive games between the Army and Navy teams. Even with lights-out at ten-thirty, fatigue sets in, what with all the fresh air, sunshine, and just plain fun. But that's part of the scheme as well, for there is a certain rhythm the organizers are trying to impose. The religious appeals begin early in the week at the rallies and in the morning sessions. By Wednesday evening's campfire, a sense of camaraderie, of shared experience, has set in. Campers are beginning to see their friends profess conversions or rededications, and nothing motivates an adolescent better than the example of his or her peers.

25 Figuring unpredictably into this mix is that confounding, exhilarating phenomenon: the summer romance. The people at Word of Life Island tolerate such courtships and even encourage them with a special dinner on Wednesday night to which boys are encouraged to bring dates. Parents back home, who are praying fervently for their child's spiritual renewal, also tolerate the courting that takes place at teen camp. They figure that their child's chances of meeting a nice Christian girl or boy at Bible camp are certainly greater than back home in a public high school. They trust Jack Wyrtzen and his staff, moreover, to police such romances carefully, lest passions run awry.

I kissed a girl for the first time at Bible camp—and, come to think of it, the second, third, and fourth times—all of it quite innocent, of course. Somewhere along the shores of Rainbow Lake a tree still bears the initials "R.B. + C.S.," chiseled into the bark with a jackknife. Word of Life Island bears the markings of similar romances and infatuations, flames that burn brightly, last through several exchanges of letters, but then generally flicker and die before the leaves fall:

Erika & Howard
I love Dave
Dawn & John
Kyle + Deanna
Leon and Joan

Some have thoughtfully included the date in their memorials, as if establishing a statute of limitations:

85 Denise -n- John
I ♥ Joel Hoffman '86

Adolescent love is a sweet and wonderful thing, and if your beloved is a good Christian girl—"wholesome" is the adjective my parents always favored—then your resistance to the gospel weakens further.

By the time the Friday night campfire comes around, you are tired to the bone. You've never played so hard, swum so far, or slept so little. You are sunburned and mosquito-bitten; you have several proud bruises to show your sister. A sense of melancholy sets in because you know that tomorrow you must say goodbye to all the friends you've made at camp that week: the cabinmates who put corn flakes and shaving cream in the bottom of your sleeping bag and who helped you ambush one of the girls' cabins, the counselor who listened and became a friend, and most of all the lovely girl with the cornflower-blue eyes seated next to you. You have been peppered all week with invitations to receive Christ into your life and warnings about the fate of those who refuse. You may not have another chance, you are told; Jesus may come at any time—before the week is out, before morning, even before the campfire ends. Don't let Him find you unsaved. It's easy. Come to Jesus. Just ask Him into your heart and live for Him.

The counselors at Word of Life Island refer to the Friday campfire as the "say so" meeting, taken from Psalm 107:2: "Let the redeemed of the Lord say so." Other Bible camps have different names. "Testimony service" or "afterglow" are rather common. Some camps used to refer to the final campfire, quite seriously, as a "faggot fire," a reference to the practice of grabbing the unburned end of one of the embers and tossing it into the fire as you begin your testimony about what Jesus has done in your life that past week. There is an illusion of spontaneity in these services, but for anyone who has witnessed more than a couple of them at Bible camps across the country, there is a remarkable uniformity to these gatherings. Having stared into a few fundamentalist campfires myself, I well remember the rhythms, the emotions, the ritualized adolescent behavior that takes place around the fire.

The service at Word of Life Island opens with singing; one of the counselors has supplied a guitar. The purpose of the say so meeting, another counselor informs the gathering, is to provide a chance for campers to tell what the Lord has done in their lives. He continues: "I'd just like to begin by saying that I've grown a lot this week. Pastor Jim's Bible studies have taught me a lot about what it means to be a Christian and to live for the Lord. I don't know about the rest of you, but I just praise the Lord for Pastor Jim and for the insight God has given him into the Scriptures."[6]

A few appreciative murmurs follow and then a short silence as half a

6. This account of the campfire is entirely fictionalized—the only such passage in this book. It is based, nevertheless, on conversations with campers and counselors at Word of Life Island as well as on observations of meetings there. It is also based on personal experience and reminiscences from many summers at several different Bible camps.

dozen people sitting there in the encroaching darkness summon the courage to stand and address the other campers. The fire is still struggling to take hold. The sun has just disappeared beyond the ridge at the west end of the lake, and all eyes are adjusting to the twilight.

There are no takers yet, the Spirit hasn't yet moved, so the guitarist begins strumming the chords for "Cum by Yah," and after the first few bars everyone joins in:

Cum by yah, my Lord, cum by yah.
Cum by yah, my Lord, cum by yah.
Cum by yah, my Lord, cum by yah.
O, Lord, cum by yah.

The plaintive, doleful melody functions as a kind of invocation: Come here, Jesus, and grace this gathering with Your presence.

Once the music dies, Joyce Johnson is ready. She rises confidently to her feet. All eyes move briefly from the fire to see who is talking and then, after a moment, settle back on the flames. There will be no dramatic confession here; Joyce Johnson, everyone at camp knows by now, is too good for that. Instead, this is a kind of homily disguised as self-disclosure. "I've been coming to camp ever since I was eight years old," she begins, "and once again the Lord has really worked in my life. He's shown me some new things out of His Word this week, and I know I'll be a better witness for the Lord during this next year." The tone then shifts from self-congratulatory to admonitory. "If anybody here isn't a Christian, my prayer is that you'll accept Jesus as your savior before tonight is over, before you leave this island tomorrow. You may never have another chance to receive Jesus into your heart."

After a decent interval, Candy Schroeder stands. "I'm not sure what I'm gonna say," she confesses with an uneasy chuckle, "but I wanted to tell you what the Lord has been doing in my life. For a while now I've been seeking the Lord's will for my life, and I've been praying for His guidance—especially to know what to do after I graduate from high school next year." She pauses, then wipes the corners of her eyes with the back of her hand. The length of the silence is uncomfortable for those seated around the fire, and only a few steal a glance at Candy, standing there in denims and a loose, gray sweatshirt. "I'm just so grateful to my parents," she continues between sobs, "and to everyone who has prayed for me. On Tuesday during the missionary hour, the Lord just spoke to my heart. When Reverend Hunt told about the millions of unsaved people down in Argentina, I just knew that the Lord was calling me to be a missionary to all those people who have never heard the gospel, to all those people—" she pauses again, biting her lower lip, "to all those people who are lost without Jesus." A dozen "amens" greet this happy news, and they are repeated sporadically as

Candy Schroeder reveals her plans to attend a Bible institute after high school and then go to South America as a missionary.

Paul Snyder, a big, strapping kid of fourteen, is next. "I didn't grow up in a Christian home," he says. "In fact, my parents are members of the Lutheran church back in Easton, Pennsylvania, and they didn't want me to come. When my friend Mike here invited me to Word of Life, I wasn't sure, either, but then he told me how much fun it was, so I convinced my mom and dad to let me come." The fire was thriving now, shooting flames and sparks upward into the darkness like a kind of offering. The mosquitos have arrived, searching for patches of flesh. A small motorboat trolls by, its green and red lights slicing through the darkness. "I sure am glad I came, though, because on Thursday night after the rally I gave my life to Christ. I had always thought I was a Christian because I went to church with my parents. But when I asked Don, my counselor, if I was going to heaven, he told me that unless I asked Jesus into my heart I would go to hell when I died. Well," Paul continues, halting slightly, "I gave my life to Christ. I'm a new, baby Christian. I'm going to read my Bible every day and tell all my friends at school about the Lord."

The guitarist thinks it's time for another song:

> Seek ye first the kingdom of God
> and His righteousness
> and all these things shall be added unto you.
> Hallelu-hallelujah.

The sweet, soft words echo across the lake. Paul Snyder's testimony has stirred something inside of Amy Durkin, because last year at this time she, too, gave her life to Jesus for the first time. She remembers now the feeling, the euphoria, and also her resolve to live a Christian life.

"I became a Christian here at camp last summer," Amy says, almost apologetically. "But once school started I fell in with the wrong crowd. Many of my friends are worldly, and I thought I was a strong enough Christian to stand up to them—" she begins to cry, "but I wasn't. Pretty soon I was just as worldly as the rest of them—going to movies and dances and stuff like that." Amy stops to regain her composure. The mournful cry of a loon reverberates across the lake. "But this year is going to be different. I've rededicated my life to the Lord this week, and I'm going to live for Him and bring my Bible with me to school every day and witness to my friends."

There are countless subtle variations to this rededication soliloquy, but most of them recount a previous commitment to Christ and a resolve to maintain high standards of godliness in the midst of a sinful and decadent world. But somehow, something went wrong—perhaps the lack of parental support or the absence of a good church youth program. Most often, however, even the most resolute convert from Bible camp caves in to peer pressure. "It's not easy being a Christian in my high school," is a familiar refrain.

Indeed not. If being a Christian as the people here define it means abstaining from drinking, smoking, dancing, movies, and perhaps even bowling and roller-skating (because of their "worldly" connotations), it doesn't take long for an evangelical high school student to become a pariah among his or her peers—or, more frequently, a kind of cipher on the social scene. The options then become either finding a new support network—a church youth group, perhaps—or compromising your fundamentalist scruples in order to fit in with your peers. If your parents are evangelical Christians, they want you to do the former, of course, but doing so exacts a price. It's not easy turning your back on your peers, rejecting the companionship and approval of friends at school for the comparatively unfulfilling friendships of people your own age at church.

No, it's not easy being an evangelical in high school. Carl Watkins, I think, understands that. For some time now I had been watching him shift uneasily on the stony ground; he seemed to be summoning the courage to get up and speak. Now, finally, Carl unfolds his tall, gangly frame, shuffles his feet uneasily, and clears his throat.

40 "My father is a preacher," Carl begins, "so I was raised in a Christian home. But I haven't always lived a good Christian witness. I'm not even sure that the kids at school know I'm a Christian." Carl stares at his shoetops. "I mean, sometimes I go out drinking with my friends. I know that's not right. I know that's not what the Lord wants me to do, but, I don't know, I just do it."

As he continues his halting confession, I begin to see myself in Carl Watkins. I see a Little Leaguer who had to miss all his Wednesday games, even the all-star game, because Wednesday was prayer-meeting night. I see in Carl Watkins an eighth-grader forced to sit on the sidelines during square dances in gym class and a teenager who couldn't wear bluejeans to school because his parents thought they would damage his Christian testimony. I see a high school graduate who never overcame his sense of alienation from his peers.

"I don't mean to hurt my parents," Carl continues, his voice cracking now, "but I guess, I don't know, that I always feel like I'm supposed to be perfect, to be this super-Christian at church and at school. But I'm not." Carl thrusts his hands deep into his pockets and shrugs his shoulders. "I really love my mom and dad. And I'm so grateful to the Lord for allowing me to grow up in a Christian home."

I also see in Carl Watkins a teenager contemplating the consequences of his rebellion, recounting sermon illustrations about eternity—time utterly without end, going on and on and on. If a tiny sparrow flew around the world and took a sip from the ocean at each pass, so the sermon illustration goes, by the time the ocean was dry, eternity would only have begun. Eternity was an awfully long time to be burning in hell, that lake of fire and brimstone.

"I ask you to pray for me this year," Carl concludes, "as I try to live a good Christian life." His gaze rests on the flames for a brief moment, and then he sits down. The fire crackles and spits sparks into the air. Carl Watkins reaches back and turns up the collar of his jacket against the sudden autumn chill that whips across the lake. Off to the east, a new moon hangs in the late-August darkness. Carl shifts once more and squeezes the hand of the girl with the cornflower-blue eyes seated next to him.

45 In another era, in another camp, I sat next to a fire and shifted uneasily on the stony ground. My repeated attempts to appropriate the faith of my parents were desultory and imperfect, as I realized even then. Summer camp was where I tried annually to get it right, to conjure the same piety that my elders showed, to claim the elusive "victory in Christ" that they professed. More often than not, what I felt instead was defeat and inadequacy, a gnawing sense that the persistent doubts I harbored about God and Christianity or my occasional transgressions of the fundamentalist behavioral codes would consign me to damnation.

Therein lay the conundrum. What I did not see then—indeed, *could* not have seen—was that the "gospel" presented to me was really an adumbration of the New Testament "good news." Much of the news I heard was bad—that I deserved damnation for my sinfulness and that if I didn't do something about it quickly I would certainly receive my just deserts. The solution to the predicament, as I understood it, was not to rely utterly on the grace of God, as Martin Luther recognized in the sixteenth century; rather, the way of salvation seemed to lay in subscribing to a set of doctrines and then hewing to strict standards of morality, usually expressed in negative terms: Don't dance, drink, smoke, swear, or attend movies.

That differed, I suspect, from the message that brought my parents into the evangelical fold. They heard about their sinfulness, yes, but the complementary element of the law is God's grace, which saves us in spite of ourselves. Therein, as Luther realized, lies true freedom and liberation—not in the observance of tiresome moralistic schemes, but in the celebration of deliverance from sin in Christ. In time, first-generation evangelical converts learn the canon of evangelical taboos, but only *after* their experience of grace. For their children, however, the sequence often is reversed. As an evangelical parent, if you are concerned (understandably) about the spiritual welfare of your children, you will establish guidelines for them so they will grow up in the faith, or, more accurately, grow up with all the trappings of godliness. Their "conversions" then become adolescent (or pre-adolescent) rites of passage, often accompanied by fabricated emotions in order to convince their peers, their parents, and, most important, themselves of their sincerity.

The difficulty, however, is that Christianity has already been defined for them in behavioral terms—do this, don't do that—rather than in terms that Luther would have approved: We all are sinners by dint of *who we are*, not *what we do*, and therefore we rely abjectly on God's mercy. For a child in a fundamentalist household, a second-generation evangelical who already adheres to most of the standards of "godly" behavior, it is difficult to grasp the significance of any such conversion, since it demands no alteration of behavior. Instead of assurance, very often they feel anger and resentment because their conversions failed to deliver the religious euphoria and freedom from doubt implied in their parents' promises.

What brings Carl Watkins and Amy Durkin back to Word of Life Island year after year, I suspect, is the same mixture of motivations that took me back to Rainbow Lake summer after summer during my teenage years. Our parents want us there, in the first place, not only because Bible camp offers a sheltered, protective environment, but also because of their abiding hope that we will someday, somehow claim their faith as our own. That's easier to do, of course, in the company of those who have professed their own conversions—certainly much easier than in the alien, godless environment of the public schools back home.

50 Aside from the perennial, elusive quest for summer romance, we are at camp, many of us, for the same reason that our parents want us there. We too want to claim the faith, not merely to win our parents' approval, but also because of a deep yearning for a religious experience that will meet our expectations and dispel our anxieties. We seek above all an experience that will yield the spiritual fulfillment we see (or think we see) in our parents. That experience comes to some. Others grasp it for a time and then lose it, year after year. Still others find the standards too high and abandon the quest in frustration or despair.

For people of faith, of course, and for people who want to pass their faith to the next generation, there is no easy solution to this predicament. Abandoning children to their own devices violates everything evangelicals believe about nurture, and yet mapping their children's spiritual pilgrimages may, in the end, deprive them of the kind of forceful, dramatic conversion that shaped the parents' lives.

Will evangelicalism, then, inevitably suffer from a gradual enervation of religious ardor as the faith passes from one generation to the next? Sociologists like Max Weber, who talks about the routinization of religion, insist that the answer is yes. Fervent evangelical parents pray that the answer is no.

QUESTIONS

1. *Why does Balmer make extended comparisons with Puritans and Hasidic Jews in paragraphs 5 to 7? How does this comparison prepare for his reflections at the end?*
2. *Balmer notes (paragraph 20) that Jack Wyrtzen "uses certain code words or phrases." In fact, code words occur throughout this essay. List some code words and see if you can come up with useful definitions.*
3. *At the heart of this essay is the difficulty of passing along a religious tradition from one generation to the next. Write about a family that faced this kind of issue.*

Mary Gordon

GETTING HERE FROM THERE: A WRITER'S REFLECTIONS ON A RELIGIOUS PAST

To begin speaking about the words "spiritual quest" in relation to myself fills me simultaneously with amusement and alarm. Amusement because the words "spiritual" and "quest" conjure up the imagery of the knight consecrate, Galahad after the Holy Grail, dying picturesquely at the very moment he fulfills his goal.[1] I can't see myself in the part. And alarm because the very word "spiritual" suggests to me the twin dangers of the religious life: dualism and abstraction.

Abstraction I define as the error that results from refusing to admit that one has a body and is an inhabitant of the physical world. Dualism, its first cousin, admits that there is a physical world but calls it evil and commands that it be shunned. I'd venture to say that these two "sins"—dualism and abstraction—are the cause of at least as much human misery as pride, covetousness, lust, envy, hatred, glut-

From *Good Boys and Dead Girls and Other Essays* (1991).

1. Galahad, a knight of King Arthur who found the Holy Grail, which was according to medieval legend the cup or platter Christ used at the Last Supper.

tony, and sloth. Those names come very easily to my mind—names learned in childhood, memorized in childhood. They form one of those lists, those catalogues, that made the blood race with the buildup. So many catalogues there were in the church I grew up in, so many lists: seven capital sins, three theological virtues and four moral ones, seven sacraments, seven gifts of the Holy Ghost. A kind of poetry of accumulation, gaining power like an avalanche from its own momentum—perhaps a small influence, but an important one that I grew up hearing every day of my life, for my childhood days were shaped and marked by the religious devotions of my parents, by the rhythmic, repetitive cadences of formal prayer. It bred in me a love for strongly rhythmic prose.

I can never talk about the spiritual or the religious life without talking about early memory, which is anything but disembodied. Whatever religious instincts I have bring their messages to me through the senses—the images of my religious life, its sounds, its odors, the kind of kinesthetic sense I have of prayerfulness. These are much more real to me than anything that takes place in the life of the mind. I want to say that I've never been drawn to any kind of systematic theology except as a kind of curiosity, though as soon as I say this I want to qualify it, because what makes me even more nervous than the word "spiritual" are the words "evangelical" or "charismatic." The religious impulse unmediated by reason terrifies me, and it seems to me that we are always having to mediate between the emotions, the body, the reason. So even though I can't be moved forward in any way by systematic theology, I like it to be there, in the same way that I like modern architecture to be there, even though I don't want to live in it.

And the body must not be left out. I was born into a church shaped and ruled by celibate males who had a history of hatred and fear of the body, which they lived out in their lives and in the rituals they invented. They excluded women from the center of their official and their personal lives. When I tried to think of any rituals that acknowledged the body, except for rituals involving death and in a very oblique way birth, the only one I could think of was what used to be called "the churching of women," which is a blessing for the mother, a kind of purification after the mess of birth. It's a remembrance of the purification of the Virgin Mary; she would have been actually submerged in water, not merely symbolically cleansed, for the reentry into the legitimate world, where body life could once again be hidden.

5 I keep having to backtrack; every time I say something I instantly think that I haven't quite told the truth, because I have to confess and acknowledge my own dualism. Much of what is beautiful to me in my religious experience is its bodylessness. I remember the early-morning Masses of my childhood. In my memory the atmosphere is always gray,

a kind of false dawn, air without heat or light. I'm walking with one of my parents, never both, because these memories are the tête-à-têtes of the anointed "only child," the child of parents who preferred her to each other. The women in my memories are wearing coats of muted colors, kerchiefs, round-toed nunlike shoes. The nuns themselves are disappearing in their habits, faceless. They are only forms. The church is coldish. It is silent. In the sacristy you can hear the mysterious, inexplicable, untraceable noises of the priest and the altar boy—the cruet's tinkle, the vestments' rustle. There are whispered words.

And then there is the Mass. What an excellent training ground the regular attendance at Mass was for an aspiring novelist! First, there's the form of the Mass itself, which popularly has been compared to drama, but the likenesses with the novel are also not at all unapt. The central event of the Mass occurs—interestingly for the novelist, I think—way past its middle. It's the consecration, the turning of bread and wine into the body and blood of Christ. I have to say a word about this, because for orthodox Catholics this is an actual transformation of substance. (The doctrine is called transubstantiation.) That is to say, for an orthodox Catholic the bread and wine are no longer believed to be bread and wine; they have changed in their essence, in what the scholastic philosophers called their substance, so that they are no longer bread and wine but have been actually transformed into the body and blood of Christ. Somewhere there's a conversation I like between Mary McCarthy and Flannery O'Connor[2] in which McCarthy tries to get O'Connor to admit that she really believes that transubstantiation is only a symbolic act. And Flannery O'Connor is reported to have said, "If I thought it were just a symbol I'd say the hell with it."

For the novelist, then, there is a central dramatic event. But interestingly, there is also a regular alternation of levels of language and types of literature within the Mass itself. There's scriptural invocation, reflective prayer, the poetry of the Psalms, the Old Testament and Gospel narratives, and the repetitions: the Sanctus, the Angus Dei, the *Domini non sum dignus,* repeated three times, the first and last time to the accompaniment of bells.[3] Different types of Masses offer to the sensitive ear examples of different kinds of formality and embellishment, from the simple daily Low Mass to the more formal Sunday Low Mass to the High Mass, complete with choirs, chants, and all the liturgical stops pulled out.

I'm not saying that as a child I consciously understood this. Obvi-

2. American novelist (1925–1964); McCarthy (1912–1989), American critic and novelist. Both were raised Roman Catholics; O'Connor remained devout, McCarthy did not.
3. The Sanctus ("Holy, holy, holy"); the Agnus Dei ("O Lamb of God"); the *Domini non sum dignus* ("Lord, I am not worthy").

ously, I didn't. But I absorbed it unconsciously, this elaborate and varied and supple use of language. From a very early age I had it woven into my bones. Once again, Flannery O'Connor says that the writer learns everything important to him or her before the age of six. So every day, for however often I was taken to daily Mass, I was learning lessons in rhetoric.

And I was also learning a lot of other things. If we accept the truism that all writers are voyeurs, then we can say that an hour a day in a confined space like a church, where one has the leisure or the boredom to observe others of one's kind when they imagine themselves to be in private communion with their deepest souls, is as useful for a prospective novelist as a wiretap. Daily Mass was the home ground of the marginal, the underemployed; you always wondered why they weren't at work or getting ready for work. A child at daily Mass got to observe at close range the habits of old women, of housewives at eight-thirty already tired out for the day, of men down on their luck praying for a reversal of their bad fortunes.

10 You also got wonderful lessons in structure. The structure of the Mass, like that of the parish, composed itself around the figure of the priest, the center of all our earthly attentions, the center of parish life, at an observable distance on the altar for an hour of our time. The erotically charged yet unreachable figure of the priest! And around him, theoretically invisible and yet of course the pulse of parish life, the women: jockeying, serving (except on the altar, where they were forbidden to be), dreaming, losing and gaining lives against the backdrop of history. And the single figure of the priest, who could contain in himself the whole world. The priest was theoretically available to all and yet was available to no one, just as the Church was in theory open to all and in theory welcoming of all, but operated in fact on principles of initiation and exclusion. For all that, it has always contained a membership that includes representatives from all of Europe and all the places where the Europeans set down their iron-shod feet.

So to be a Catholic, or even to have been one, is to feel a certain access to a world wider than the vision allowed by the lens of one's own birth. You grew up believing that the parish is the world, and that anyone in the world could be a member of the parish. But of course the parish was a fiercely limited terrain: the perfect size and conformation for the study of the future novelist. Anachronistically limited, its hierarchies clear, its loyalties assumed and stated and then in practice always undermined, it has at its center issues of money. You learned from the parish how the watermarks of class and privilege work. You could see how the impressive personality, the personality of the clergy, can change life.

A novelist builds a fence enclosing a certain area of the world and then calls it his or her subject. To be a Catholic, particularly in Protestant America, made one an expert at building the limiting, excluding fence. Inside the paddock there were shared assumptions about everything from the appropriate postures for kneeling to the nature of human consciousness. But there was always a right way and a wrong way, and you always knew which was which.

One could be, at least in the time when I was growing up, a Catholic in New York and deal only in the most superficial of ways with anyone non-Catholic. Until I went to college I had no genuine contact with anyone who wasn't Catholic. The tailor and the man who ran the candy store were Jews, and the women who worked in the public library were Protestants, but you allowed them only the pleasantries. Real life, the friendships, the feuds, the passions of proximate existence, took place in the sectarian compound, a compound, like any other, with its secrets—a secret language, secret customs, rites, which I now understand must have been very menacing at worst or at the best puzzling to the outside world.

But we never knew that, because we never understood that the rest of the world was looking. We weren't interested in the rest of the world. If some of us did assume that the rest of the world was looking, our response was to be all the more zealous in keeping the secrets secret. One of the greatest treasures a novelist can have is a secret world, which he or she can open up to his or her reader. When I turned from poetry to fiction in my mid-twenties, I had a natural subject—the secrets of the Catholic world. And since the door had not been very widely opened before I got there, I was a natural. I think that accounts to a great extent for the popularity of *Final Payments.*[4]

Now we're going to descend into autobiography. I don't know how 15
successful I can be in conveying the extent to which my family life was shaped by Catholicism. My parents' whole marriage was based on it; it was literally the only thing they had in common. My father was an intellectual Jew, who had had a very wild life. And simply to give you the outlines of it will give you a sense of its wildness. He was born in Lorain, Ohio. He also lied a lot, so it's extremely hard to trace what's the truth. I think this is the truth; at least I'm not consciously passing on lies. But it could also perhaps *not* be the truth. So I possibly have a great-grandfather who was a rabbi, but my father also said that his mother was a concert pianist, and who knows? He told me, for example, that his father ran a saloon; in fact, he ran a dry goods store.

In any case, my father went to Harvard in 1917. At that time there was a rigid quota system for Jews, and I think it must have caused him tremendous pain. Because what I think is that at Harvard he deter-

4. Gordon's best-selling novel (1978) about Catholic life.

mined to "pass" at any cost. And my father, who was endlessly inventive, figured out that the best way for a Jew to pass was to be right-wing. My father became righter-wing than anybody, with a couple of interesting pit stops. For example, he went to Paris and England for a while in the twenties. And one persona that he created for some reason was to pass himself off as a Middle West Presbyterian. He looked a lot like me—I don't know why anybody believed him. Maybe they thought all Americans look alike. He wrote a series of articles in English journals, passing himself off as a Midwest Protestant who understands that Europe is really a superior culture to his own.

His other pit stop was also in the late twenties. He published a girlie magazine called *Hot Dog*. I remember being twelve, and my father had died when I was seven, and I came upon this magazine while looking through his pictures. By today's standards it was exceedingly mild. But I was an exceedingly prudish twelve-year-old, and I took a look at this thing and I saw that my father had been the editor, and I was appalled and I ripped it to shreds and threw it away. So I have no record of it. But I'm pretty sure I didn't make it up.

In any case, my father became a Francoist[5] in the thirties. You rarely meet somebody who can say that sentence—everybody else's father was in the Lincoln Brigade.[6] Not mine. And in the course of several later adventures he met my mother. They met through a priest. My mother is the daughter of very simple Irish and Italian Catholics. I think she embodied for my father a kind of peasant Catholicism that he romanticized. But both of them could say with truthfulness that their faith was the most important thing in the world to them.

From an early age I had to take the measure of myself against their devotedness, and I always found myself wanting. Throughout my childhood I prayed to be spared martyrdom. But then I always felt guilty for the prayer. I was no little Teresa of Ávila[7] setting out in the desert hoping to convert the Moors; the priests in China having bamboo shoved under their fingernails and Cardinal Mindszenty[8] I didn't want that for my fate, but I was told that it was the highest fate. So as a child I had always to be consciously choosing an inferior fate. It was a real burden.

20 But I do remember that, although I didn't want to be a martyr, I did want to be a nun. I remember being taken by my parents to the Con-

5. A supporter of General Francisco Franco (1892–1975), leader of the rightist Nationalists during the Spanish Civil War, 1936–1939.
6. American volunteers who fought with the leftist Loyalists during the Spanish Civil War.
7. Spanish Carmelite nun, reformer, and mystic (1515–1582).
8. The Roman Catholic primate of Hungary (1892–1975), who took refuge from the Communists in the American legation in Budapest for fifteen years (1956–1971).

vent of Mary Reparatrix on Twenty-ninth Street in New York. It's a semicloistered convent—the nuns weren't allowed out, but people could talk to them. And I remember going into the chapel with my parents and a very old nun. I saw a young nun kneeling in a pool of light. I saw her from the back only. The habits of the Sisters of Mary Reparatrix were sky blue. I've never seen a color like that in a nun's habit, and I'm quite sure I didn't invent it. But if I had wanted to invent it, it would have been perfect, because it was a color dreamed up for movie stars. It was the color of Sleeping Beauty's ball gown, and that was what I wanted for myself. I wanted to be beautifully kneeling in light, my young, straight back clothed in the magic garment of the anointed. I knew that was what I wanted, but I knew I didn't want to drink filthy water or walk barefoot in the snow. A few times, though, I did try some local free-lance missionary work.

Once, for instance, I had just finished reading the life of Saint Dominic Savio, who was a Neapolitan orphan. I was six or seven. Saint Dominic walked into a playground and heard his rough playmates—nobody uses the phrase "rough playmates" anymore—using blasphemous language. And he didn't skip a beat. He held up a crucifix, and he said to those boys, "Say it in front of Him." And the boys fell silent. Inspired, I tried the same thing in my neighborhood. I walked into the crowd of boys with my crucifix aloft, and I said, "Say it in front of Him." And they were glad to.

The comedy of Catholic life. It comes, of course, like all other comedy, from the gap between the ideal and the real. In my case the ideal was so high and the real was so real that the collision was bound to be risible. I tried walking with thorns in my shoes for penance, but then I found out that it hurt. So I walked around on the heels of my shoes and put the thorns in the toes, so I could have them in my shoes but not feel them. My heroisms were always compromised and always unsuccessful. I tried to talk the man in our gas station into taking the nude calendar off his wall. He told me never to come into the office again. I tried to make the candy store man, whom I genuinely liked, stop selling dirty magazines. He stopped giving me free egg creams, and our friendship ended. But he went right on selling dirty magazines.

I always tried. The serious part of the ideals that shaped my early life was that they did teach me that life was serious. I think all children believe that. I think parents cheat children by refusing to understand that everything is serious to them and that it is the modulations of the adult world that cause them such confused grief. At a very early age I was taught that happiness was not important; what was important was to save my soul. I was not supposed to be only a good girl or even a lady, although I was supposed to begin there. I was not supposed to even strive to be popular, successful, beloved, or valued by the world. I was supposed to be a saint. The cautionary and inspirational tales of my youth were the lives of the saints.

The lives of the saints. I recently took down a saints' lives book that was mine as a child. I sometimes read it to my children today. To my children, these people—Saint Barnabas who juggled, Saint Nicholas who found children pickled in the basement of an inn and brought them back to life—are fairy-tale characters. They're characters like Ali Baba or Rapunzel. My daughter likes the picture of the boy Saint Hugh kicking the devil downstairs. She asks me if the devil is real. And I tell her, "No, no, he's not real; he's like the banshee or the Loch Ness monster." And as I tell her that, I realize that for me the devil *was* real. And he was feared. My mother cured me of early narcissism by telling me that if I kept looking in the mirror the devil would pop out behind me and that when I was looking at my face it would turn into the face of the devil. I stopped immediately. I was thinking about eternal life, and so was she, and we couldn't afford to take the risk.

25 There's a sentence in the incomparable story "In Dreams Begin Responsibilities," by Delmore Schwartz,[9] in which the boy says, "Everything you do matters too much." Did everything matter too much for me? I'm not sure. But at least it mattered. What you learned with a background like mine was that everything mattered terribly and that you could never do enough.

I remember a friend of mine, a Jew, telling me years later that he felt sorry for Christians because if you took seriously the words of Christ "Greater love hath no man than this, that a man lay down his life for his friends," then as long as you were alive you hadn't done enough. But this is not such a bad thing for an artist. For the life of the working artist is a perpetual reminder that everything you do matters. Nothing is enough.

Speaking of the lives of the saints makes me try to differentiate among the kinds of narratives that a pious Catholic child encountered. There were the Old Testament narratives, which always seemed to me forbidding and harsh and frightening—exciting as war movies were exciting and dangerous, but of no comfort. Abraham and Isaac, Moses left in the bulrushes, Joseph thrown down the well by his brothers, the boy David all alone with a slingshot: you had the vision of children for whom the adult world offered no protection. There were the failing parents and the implacable voice of God. I always felt as if the narratives of the Old Testament were accompanied by a kind of rumble. The colors were dark and vibrant. I was drawn to them, but I wanted to get away. To Jesus and the children.

9. American poet and short-story writer (1913–1966).

I remember a jigsaw puzzle I had of Jesus and the children: the warm, inviting lap, the face of infinite acceptance. And there were the other images—the prodigal son forgiven, the daughter of Gyrus raised, the blind man given his sight, the lame man his nimbleness, the good thief ushered into paradise. But there was also a disturbing underside of New Testament violence. It was disturbing in a way that Old Testament violence was not, because in the old narratives the violence all seemed of a piece with the rest of the vision of the world, whereas in the Gospels it was always a surprise and something of a cheat. It was the terrible massacre of the innocents, the beheading of John the Baptist, the sufferings and death of Christ himself—somehow the triumph always paid for by some ancillary, unwilled or only partially willed carnage. Easter paid for by Lent. How fully I lived my childhood Holy Weeks, the most solemn time of the year, religiously then as now my favorite! The black vestments, the stripped altar, the shocked silence of the congregation, and then the midnight fire and the morning promise of Easter. In my memory Easter was always warm; you could always wear your spring coat and your straw hat, although in my adulthood more than half the Easters have been covered in snow.

The third kind of narrative, the lives of the saints, were magical in ways that the Bible of both Testaments was too austere to permit. Saint Francis talked to birds and wolves. Saint Elizabeth of Hungary, a queen, carried bread to the poor and the plague-ridden, although her husband the king had forbidden it. She hid the bread in her apron to keep it from the eyes of her husband and the palace guards. Her husband the king found out; he confronted her with his soldiers at the castle gate, demanding that she show him what was inside her apron. She opened her apron, and where there had been bread there were roses. He fell on his knees before his wife.

30 It occurs to me that one good fortune in being brought up a Catholic and a woman was that you did have images of heroic women. And that's not so frequently the case in other religious traditions. In the tradition of Catholicism you have a poem spoken by the Virgin Mary that points out her place in the divine order. And she speaks with pride. She says, "My soul doth magnify the Lord and my spirit hath rejoiced in God, my savior. Because He has regarded the loneliness of His handmaid, and behold from henceforth all generations shall call me blessed, for He that is mighty hath done great things to me and holy is His name."[1] That's an example of a woman's speech and a woman acknowledging her importance in the hierarchy, which at least in some subliminal way a girl got to hold on to.

In the lives of the saints you had a lot of examples of women who

1. Mary's song of Thanksgiving (Luke 1.46–55), the *Magnificat* in the Latin Vulgate.

defined themselves not in terms of men but in terms of each other. You had the founders of orders. You had women who defied the Pope, defied the bishops, to go off and do things that women were not supposed to do. You had "doctors of the church"—women saints who were given that title. Did I know at age five what that meant—"doctor of the church"? Not exactly. But there was something there. You had an image of an alternative female world that often had to trick the male world in the same way that Saint Elizabeth had to trick her husband the king. A lot of women have survived through trickery. It was not entirely a bad life, but I hope it's one we can soon forget. Still, it wasn't a bad arrow to have in your quiver.

The saints came in various personality types. There was the meek Little Flower and the fierce Spanish Teresa. There was Saint Jerome in the desert with his blood-red eyes[2] and the Curé of Ars, the friend of everybody in his little village. There were monks and scholars, widows and virgins, popes and ferrymen. I've stopped doing missionary work among the candy store owners of the world, but I do try to remind people of wonderful women writers who are undernoticed and often out of print. Louise Bogan,[3] I think, is an exquisite poet—as good as anybody who has written in this century. Except for one small collection, her work is out of print. I offer you a poem of hers called "Saint Christopher," since we're talking about saints' lives. I think it will give you something of the flavor of those lives, which were so wonderful for a child to hear, getting from them a sense of narrative.

A raw-boned and an ignorant man
Keeps ferry, but a man of nerve,
His freight a Child and a Child's toy.
(Which is our globe, you will observe.)

But what a look of intent love!
This is the look we do not see
In manners or in mimicry.
Strength's a derivative thereof.

The middle class is what we are.
Poised as a brigand or a barber
The tough young saint, Saint Christopher,
Brings the Child into the safe harbor.

Among all these saints, among all the types that were represented and honored, there are no artists, unless you count Saint Francis de

2. Saint Jerome (340?–420), Latin scholar, doctor of the church, translator of the Vulgate; Thérèse de Lisieux (1873–1897), the Little Flower, a French Carmelite nun; Teresa of Ávila (n. 7, p. 1238).
3. American poet (1897–1970).

Sales,[4] who is the patron saint of writers, and he was hardly what we would call a creative writer; he was a composer of meditations. From the way I've described the riches of the Catholic background, you may think it would be almost inevitable that any pious child would grow up to be an artist. But as a group, Catholics—particularly Catholics in America and even ex-Catholics—are scandalously underrepresented in the arts. I'm always surprised by this, but I shouldn't be. The orthodox have no need of consolation, and a closed world has no need of descriptions of itself. For a Catholic who took the teachings of the Church seriously, art for art's sake is as foreign as the idea of a Moslem heaven. Even knowledge was encouraged not for its own sake but in the service of God. I've just gone through an old prayer book of my mother's, which I used to read a lot as a child. And I came across these prayers, which illustrate the notion that the life of the mind was never for itself but always in the service of God.

This first prayer is to Saint Catherine of Siena, who was a doctor of the church. It goes:

> O glorious Saint Catherine, wise and prudent virgin, Thou who didst set the knowledge of Jesus Christ above all other knowledge. Obtain for us the grace to remain inviolably attached to the Catholic faith and to seek in our studies and in our teaching only the extension of the kingdom of Jesus Christ our Lord and of His holy church, both in our selves and in the souls of others. Amen.

The second prayer is to the Virgin Mary, which is supposed to be 35
said by students:

> Under thy patronage, Dear Mother, and invoking the mystery of thine immaculate conception, I desire to pursue my studies and my literary labors. I hereby solemnly declare that I am devoting myself to these studies chiefly to the following end: That I may the better contribute to the glory of God and to the spread of thy veneration among men. I pray thee, therefore, most loving mother, who art the seat of wisdom, to bless my labors in thy loving kindness. Moreover, I promise with true affection and a waking spirit, as it is right that I should do, to ascribe all the good that shall accrue to me therefrom wholly to thine intercession for me in God's holy presence. Amen.

Nobody walking fully under the banner represented by those prayers could create a modern work of art. The artistic ego, a product of the Renaissance, coincided with the loosening of the grip of the Church over the hearts and minds of women and men. The enclosed garden of my childhood was enclosed by a system that said all acts found their

4. Author (1567–1622) of an *Introduction to a Devout Life* (1608–1609) and a *Treatise on the Love of God* (1616).

meaning in the reiteration of the Truth. Capital T. Whereas that might have been a vessel of inspiration for the author of *The Divine Comedy* or the *Pange Lingua*,[5] it could be of no help to a modern artist, particularly a novelist whose origins are in the secular mind of the eighteenth century.

When you're talking about the Catholic Church you always have to go back and forth between the levels of the spiritual, the private, the ideal, and the real. Because the Catholic Church, for better and for worse, is a worldwide church that encompasses races and classes of all sorts. And I think that the silence of American Catholics in relation to the arts is an accident of class, ethnicity, and history as much as it is of spiritual overidealism. I think we have to remember that the Catholic Church in America is the Irish Church. And the Irish Church is a church that is obsessed and committed to the idea of keeping silence. There's a famous Irish expression: "An Irish person will tell you something and then will say, 'Mind you, I've said nothing.' "

In working on my novel *The Other Side*, I had the funny experience of listening to researchers who have done oral histories of the Irish. And I could tell they weren't Irish themselves. They went into nursing homes, where the old people had nothing to do—they're a captive audience—and interviewers ask questions and ask questions and these old people answer with tremendous politeness and a great flurry of language and convey absolutely no information.

People always say, "Well, the Irish are so garrulous. They love to talk." They love to talk, but they don't like to tell you anything. So if you're happy to have a good time and listen to the shape of the language itself, you'll have a wonderful time talking to an Irishman. If you want to know anything about his or her life, forget it. People say, "Well, he'll get drunk and . . ." Nothing. That has nothing to do with it. You will not get at the truth. The Irish are obsessed with concealing the inner life.

I think this is another reason why there has been such a silence, such an absence of the Catholic voice, in America. There's a lot of talk about the Irish Renaissance in Ireland.[6] But those are not Catholic writers; you're talking about English Protestants who happened to set down roots and then get romantic about the auld sod. Nothing made Joyce more crazy than to hear Yeats carrying on about the Celtic twilight. And Yeats, of course, couldn't stand the Irish that he came in contact with. He wanted to fantasize about them heroically, but if he

5. The first was written by Dante Alighieri (1265–1321); the second ("Sing, my tongue") is a medieval Latin hymn attributed to Venantius Fortunatus.

6. The revival of knowledge about and interest in ancient Irish literature in Gaelic; William Butler Yeats (1865–1939) was an Anglo-Irish Protestant, James Joyce (1882–1941) an Irish Catholic.

happened to meet one of his workmen in front of the tower, he'd just as soon send him to jail as invite him in to dinner. So when you're talking about the Catholicism in America and the presence of the arts, you have to talk about the presence of the Irish, which adds a lot of complications.

Well, how did I get from there to here? An easy answer would be that I substituted art for faith, so that I found my new priesthood. That would be an easy answer, but it's not true. I don't believe in the religion of art, although I do believe in the vocation of the artist—altogether a more slogging enterprise. I don't believe that the aesthetic and the religious are one. To my mind, an experience to be properly religious must include three things: an ethical component, the possibility of full participation by the entire human community, and acknowledgment of the existence of a life beyond the human. Art need do none of these things, although it may. Most art does not suggest a life beyond the human, unless you want to say that all inspiration is beyond the human and therefore art acknowledges this tacitly. I think that's fudging the question. There can be all sorts of sources of inspiration. They need not be personal; they need not be suprahuman or extrahuman.

And even the greatest art, even the greatest art when it is the simplest art, requires a certain prior cluing in, a kind of training, however informal, in the rudiments of the art. Great art need have nothing in it of the ethical, although the greatness of some great literature is enhanced by ethical components. But some is not. And certainly it would be absurd to make those claims for painting or music. This is why I say that the aesthetic and the religious are not necessarily one.

So how did I get there from here? How did I get here from there? You may notice that when I speak of religious influences I speak of the memories of childhood. I was fourteen when the Second Vatican Council began.[7] Virginia Woolf tells us that on or about December 1910 the world changed. Well, the great changes in the Church coincided—unfortunately perhaps—with the great changes in my body. I became at puberty properly irreligious, and I say "properly" with great advisement. I think one should beware of the religious adolescent; he may be planning your assassination in the night. I was fourteen when one of the greatest events in the Church's history took place. I'm reminded again—a bit irrelevantly but not unpleasantly, I hope—of a poem, by Stevie Smith,[8] called "The Conventionalist":

> Fourteen-year-old, why must you giggle and dote?
> Fourteen-year-old, why are you such a goat?

7. It began in October 1962, convoked by Pope John XXIII, pope from 1958 to 1963.
8. British poet (1902–1971).

I'm fourteen years old, that is the reason.
I giggle and dote in season.

I'm afraid I was giggling and doting when Pope John was opening the windows of the Church. And the outside world beckoned me with much more force than the confused and angry Church of the early and mid sixties. It's always amusing to me to talk to non-Catholics about their fantasy of what the Second Vatican Council did. They all imagine that we were clapping and singing and shouting "Hallelujah!" Most people were furious. Most people were confused and angry and outraged. They felt that the rug had been taken out from under them, particularly if they grew up, as I did, in a working-class neighborhood. There was no great sense of jubilation. It was a lucky thing for Pope John that he died; he got to look good, like John Kennedy.

45 It was at that point that I began to think of myself as a poet, as an artist. I had no more interest in being a saint. And a good thing too—I stopped trying to get people to not sell magazines, and I stopped putting thorns in my shoes. When I looked back over my shoulder to see what they were doing in the open-windowed Church, the part of me that was learning about great art could only run away. People were playing guitars at Mass now and rewriting Peter, Paul and Mary[9] tunes to express Church dogma.

Take this bread
And take this wine
And take our hearts
And take our minds
At this Eucharistic feast
We are all priests.

I was fourteen. What could I do?

Well, it's fun to make fun of these excesses. I like doing it very much. But I don't think the answer is to turn the clock back. I don't want it turned back, because the people who are plumping for the reintroduction of Gregorian chant into the liturgy are also funding the contras in Nicaragua, and they're doing it for the same reason. But I am grieved every time I enter a parish church and hear an unlovely liturgy, and I often have to leave for my own protection. I'm in a queer position: the Church of my childhood, which was so important for my formation as an artist, is now gone. As Gertrude Stein[1] said of Oakland, "There is no there there."

But there *is* something there, something that formed me and that touches me still: the example of the nuns killed in El Salvador, of liber-

9. A folk-music group of the 1960s.
1. American author (1874–1946).

ation theologians[2] standing up to the Pope, of the nuns—the "Vatican 24"—who signed the statement asserting that it was possible for Catholics to have different positions on abortion and still be Catholics. These sisters, many of them in their sixties and seventies, faced the loss of everything—their sisterhood, their community, their lives, and things we wouldn't think of, like their medical insurance. They had no Social Security; they had no pension plans; they faced literally being thrown out on the street. They are extraordinary women.

These people whom I am moved by and whom I admire are nevertheless people who are very different from me. And what I admire in them is at a very great remove from the world of literature and art. Nevertheless, I can't quite give up what they stand for. I don't want to give it up because I don't want to give it over to John Cardinal O'Connor[3] and his kind.

So what do I do? I write my fictions. And my relation to the "there" that is not there I make up each day, and it changes each day as I go along.

2. Latin-American theologians who focus on the political, economic, and ideological causes of social inequality.
3. A traditionalist (1920–   ) who became archbishop of New York in 1984.

QUESTIONS

1. *Precisely what does Gordon's title refer to?*
2. *How did Gordon structure her piece? There is no conventional argument or story; what, if anything, holds it together?*
3. *As she wrote this essay, Gordon could expect most of her readers to know that her novels were deep explorations of religious life. What in the essay itself shows a reader that this is true?*
4. *Gordon writes of how helpful it was for a novelist to have been raised a Catholic. Write of how "useful" a religious tradition or background has been for yourself or someone you know.*

Arthur M. Schlesinger, Jr.

THE OPENING OF THE AMERICAN MIND

Little is more surprising these days than the revival of blasphemy as a crime. A secular age had presumably relegated blasphemy—irreverence toward things sacred—to the realm of obsolete offenses. No

Adapted from a lecture given at Brown University on the occasion of Vartan Gregorian's inauguration as president. From the *New York Times Book Review* (July 23, 1989).

American has been convicted for blasphemy since Abner Kneeland in Massachusetts a century and a half ago (for what was deemed a "scandalous, impious, obscene, blasphemous and profane libel of and concerning God"); and the last prosecution, in Maryland 20 years ago, was dismissed by an appellate court as a violation of the First Amendment.

But a secular age, when it creates its own absolutes, may well secularize blasphemy too. Consider the deplorable role the Pledge of Allegiance to the flag played in a recent Presidential campaign; or the cries of outrage provoked by the Supreme Court decision in Texas v. Johnson, holding that punishment for the political burning of an American flag breached the Constitution; or the demonstrations protesting the "desecration" of the flag at the Art Institute of Chicago.

The very word "desecration" implies that the American flag is sanctified, an object of worship. We are witnessing the rise of what Charles Fried, Ronald Reagan's Solicitor General, calls the "doctrine of civil blasphemy." Whether religious or secular in guise, all forms of blasphemy have in common that there are things so sacred that they must be protected by the arm of the state from irreverence and challenge—that absolutes of truth and virtue exist and that those who scoff are to be punished.

It is this belief in absolutes, I would hazard, that is the great enemy today of the life of the mind. This may seem a rash proposition. The fashion of the time is to denounce relativism as the root of all evil. But history suggests that the damage done to humanity by the relativist is far less than the damage done by the absolutist—by the fellow who, as Mr. Dooley[1] once put it, "does what he thinks th' Lord wud do if He only knew th' facts in th' case."

5 Let me not be misunderstood lest I be taken for a blasphemer myself and thereby subject to the usual dire penalties. I hold religion in high regard. As Chesterton[2] once said, the trouble when people stop believing in God is not that they thereafter believe in nothing; it is that they thereafter believe in anything. I agree with Tocqueville[3] that religion has an indispensable social function: "How is it possible that society should escape destruction if the moral tie is not strengthened in proportion as the political tie is relaxed?" I also sympathize with Tocqueville who, André Jardin, his most recent biographer, tells us, went to his death an unbeliever.

It would hardly seem necessary to insist on the perils of moral absolutism in our own tawdry age. By their fruits ye shall know them.

1. An imaginary Irish bartender filled with folk wisdom, created by the American humorist Finley Peter Dunne (1867–1936).
2. G. K. Chesterton (1874–1936), conservative Catholic English writer.
3. Count Alexis de Tocqueville (1805–1859), French historian known for his studies of democracy in Europe and America.

It is as illogical to indict organized religion because of Jimmy Swaggart and the Bakkers[4] as Paul Johnson is to indict the intelligentsia because of the messy private lives of selected intellectuals; but the moral absolutists who are presently applauding Paul Johnson's cheap book *Intellectuals* might well be invited to apply the same methodology to their own trade. As the great theologian Reinhold Niebuhr[5] said, "The worst corruption is a corrupt religion"—and organized religion, like all powerful institutions, lends itself to corruption. Absolutism, whether in religious or secular form, becomes a haven for racketeers.

As a historian, I confess to a certain amusement when I hear the Judeo-Christian tradition praised as the source of our concern for human rights. In fact, the great religious ages were notable for their indifference to human rights in the contemporary sense. They were notorious not only for acquiescence in poverty, inequality, exploitation and oppression but for enthusiastic justifications of slavery, persecution, abandonment of small children, torture, genocide.

Religion enshrined and vindicated hierarchy, authority and inequality and had no compunction about murdering heretics and blasphemers. Till the end of the 18th century, torture was normal investigative procedure in the Roman Catholic church as well as in most European states. In Protestant America in the early 19th century, as Larry Tise points out in his book *Pro-Slavery: A History of the Defense of Slavery in America, 1701–1840*, men of the cloth "wrote almost half of all the defenses of slavery published in America"; an appendix lists 275 ministers of the Gospel who piously proclaimed the Christian virtue of a system in which one man owned another as private property to be used as he pleased.

Human rights is not a religious idea. It is a secular idea, the product of the last four centuries of Western history.

It was the age of equality that brought about the disappearance of 10
such religious appurtenances as the auto-da-fé and burning at the stake, the abolition of torture and of public executions, the emancipation of the slaves. Only later, as religion itself began to succumb to the humanitarian ethic and to view the Kingdom of God as attainable within history, could the claim be made that the Judeo-Christian tradition commanded the pursuit of happiness in this world. The basic human rights documents—the American Declaration of Independence and the French Declaration of the Rights of Man—were written by political, not by religious, leaders. And the revival of absolutism in the 20th century, whether in ecclesiastical or secular form, has

4. Jimmy Swaggart and James and Tammy Fay Bakker were popular television evangelists involved in sex and money scandals during the 1980s.

5. American Protestant theologian (1892–1971) who wrote about religion and politics.

brought with it the revival of torture, of slaughter and of other monstrous violations of human rights.

Take a look at the world around us today. Most of the organized killing now going on is the consequence of absolutism: Protestants and Catholics killing each other in Ireland; Muslims and Jews killing each other in the Middle East; Sunnites and Shiites killing each other in the Persian Gulf; Buddhists and Hindus killing each other in Ceylon; Hindus and Sikhs killing each other in India; Christians and Muslims killing each other in Armenia and Azerbaijan; Buddhists and Communists killing each other in Tibet. "We have," as Swift[6] said, "just enough religion to make us hate, but not enough to make us love." The Santa Barbara Peace Resource Center, reporting on the 32 wars in progress around the planet in 1988, found that 25 had "a significant ethnic, racial or religious dimension." And when religious religion is not the cause, then the totalitarian social religions of our age inspire mass slaughter.

It is natural enough, I suppose, if you believe you have privileged access to absolute truth, to want to rid the world of those who insist on divergent truths of their own. But I am not sure that it is a useful principle on which to build a society. Yet, as I noted earlier, the prevailing fashion is, or was a year or two ago, to hold relativism responsible for the ills of our age. A key document, of course, is Allan Bloom's best seller of a couple of years back, *The Closing of the American Mind.* Indeed, one cannot but regard the very popularity of that murky and pretentious book as the best evidence for Mr. Bloom's argument about the degradation of American culture. It is another of those half-read best sellers, like Charles Reich's murky and pretentious *Greening of America* 17 years before, that plucks a momentary nerve, materializes fashionably on coffee tables, is rarely read all the way through and is soon forgotten.

Now one may easily share Mr. Bloom's impatience with many features of higher education in the United States. I too lament the incoherence in the curriculums, the proliferation of idiotic courses, the shameful capitulation to factional demands and requisitions, the decay of intellectual standards. For better or for worse, in my view, we inherit an American experience, as America inherits a Western experience; and solid learning must begin with our own origins and traditions. The bonds of cohesion in our society are sufficiently fragile, or so it seems to me, that we should not strain them by excessive worship at artificial shrines of ethnicity, bilingualism, global cultural base-touching and the like. Let us take pride in our own distinctive inheri-

6. Jonathan Swift (1667–1745), English satirist, poet, political writer, and clergyman.

tance as other countries take pride in their distinctive inheritances; and let us understand that no culture can hope to ingest other cultures all at once, certainly not before it ingests its own.

But a belief in solid learning, rigorous standards, intellectual coherence, the virtue of elites is a different thing from a faith in absolutes. It is odd that Professor Bloom spends 400 pages laying down the law about the American mind and never once mentions the two greatest and most characteristic American thinkers, Emerson and William James.[7] One can see why he declined the confrontation: it is because he would have had to concede the fact that the American mind is by nature and tradition skeptical, irreverent, pluralistic and relativistic.

Nor does relativism necessarily regard all claims to truth as equal or 15
believe that judgment is no more than the expression of personal preference. For our relative values are not matters of whim and happenstance. History has given them to us. They are anchored in our national experience, in our great national documents, in our national heroes, in our folkways, traditions, standards. Some of these values seem to us so self-evident that even relativists think they have, or ought to have, universal application: the right to life, liberty and the pursuit of happiness, for example; the duty to treat persons as ends in themselves; the prohibition of slavery, torture, genocide. People with a different history will have different values. But we believe that our own are better for us. They work for us; and, for that reason, we live and die by them.

At least this is what great Americans have always believed. "Deep-seated preferences," as Justice Holmes put it, "cannot be argued about . . . and therefore, when differences are sufficiently far-reaching, we try to kill the other man rather than let him have his way. But that is perfectly consistent with admitting that, so far as it appears, his grounds are just as good as ours."

Once Justice Holmes and Judge Learned Hand[8] discussed these questions on a long train ride. Learned Hand gave as his view that "opinions are at best provisional hypotheses, incompletely tested. The more they are tested . . . the more assurance we may assume, but they are never absolutes. So we must be tolerant of opposite opinions." Holmes wondered whether Hand might not be carrying his tolerance

7. Harvard professor (1842–1910) famous for his studies in philosophy and psychology; Ralph Waldo Emerson (1803–1882), one of the most famous American philosophers and essayists.

8. Learned Hand (1872–1961), federal judge for fifty-two years, considered by many to be the greatest judge of his day; Oliver Wendell Holmes, Jr. (1841–1935), Supreme Court justice, 1902–1932, whose powerful dissenting opinions helped shape judicial thinking.

to dangerous lengths. "You say," Hand wrote Holmes later, "that I strike at the sacred right to kill the other fellow when he disagrees. The horrible possibility silenced me when you said it. Now, I say, 'Not at all, kill him for the love of Christ and in the name of God, but always remember that he may be the saint and you the devil.' "

These "deep-seated preferences" are what Holmes called his "Can't Helps"—"When I say that a thing is true, I mean that I cannot help believing it. . . . But . . . I do not venture to assume that my inabilities in the way of thought are inabilities of the universe. I therefore define truth as the system of my limitations, and leave absolute truth for those who are better equipped." He adds: "Certitude is not the test of certainty. We have been cock-sure of many things that were not so."

Absolutism is abstract, monistic, deductive, ahistorical, solemn, and it is intimately bound up with deference to authority. Relativism is concrete, pluralistic, inductive, historical, skeptical and intimately bound up with deference to experience. Absolutism teaches by rote; relativism by experiment. "I respect faith," that forgotten wit Wilson Mizener once said, "but doubt is what gets you an education."

20 I would even hazard the proposition that relativism comports far more than absolutism with the deepest and darkest teachings of religion. For what we have learned from Augustine, from Calvin, from Jonathan Edwards[9] is not man's capacity to grasp the absolute but quite the contrary: the frailty of man, the estrangement of man from God, the absolute distance between mortals and divinity—and the arrogance of those who suppose they are doing what the Lord would do if He only knew the facts in the case. That is why Reinhold Niebuhr acknowledged such an affinity with William James—far more, I would warrant, than he would have found with Allan Bloom.

When it came to worldly affairs, Niebuhr was a relativist, not because he disbelieved in the absolute, but precisely because he believed in the absoluteness of the absolute—because he recognized that for finite mortals the infinite thinker was inaccessible, unfathomable, unattainable. Nothing was more dangerous, in Niebuhr's view, than for frail and erring humans to forget the inevitable "contradiction between divine and human purposes." "Religion," he wrote, "is so frequently a source of confusion in political life, and so frequently dangerous to democracy, precisely because it introduces absolutes into the realm of relative values." He particularly detested "the fanaticism of all good men, who do not know that they are not as good as they esteem themselves," and he warned against "the depth of evil to

9. American theologian and preacher (1703–1758); Augustine (354–430), early Christian church father and philosopher; John Calvin (1509–1564), French Protestant reformer.

which individuals and communities may sink . . . when they try to play the role of God to history."

Niebuhr accepted, as James did, "the limits of all human striving, the fragmentariness of all human wisdom, the precariousness of all historic configurations of power, and the mixture of good and evil in all human virtue." His outlook is as far away from Mr. Bloom's simple-minded absolutism as one can imagine. It represents, in my view, the real power of religious insight as well as the far more faithful expression of the American mind.

I would summon one more American, the greatest of them all, as a last witness in the case for relativism against absolutes. In his Second Inaugural, Lincoln noted that both sides in the Civil War "read the same Bible, and pray to the same God; and each invokes His aid against the other. . . . The prayers of both could not be answered; that of neither has been answered fully. The Almighty has His own purposes." Replying thereafter to a congratulatory letter from Thurlow Weed, Lincoln doubted that such sentiments would be "immediately popular. Men are not flattered by being shown that there has been a difference of purpose between the Almighty and them. To deny it, however, in this case, is to deny that there is a God governing the world."

The Almighty has His own purposes: this is the reverberant answer to those who tell us that we must live by absolutes. Relativism is the American way. As that most quintessential of American historians, George Bancroft,[1] wrote in another connection, "The feud between the capitalist and laborer, the house of Have and the house of Want, is as old as social union, and can never be entirely quieted; but he who will act with moderation, prefer fact to theory, and remember that every thing in this world is relative and not absolute, will see that the violence of the contest may be stilled."

The mystic prophets of the absolute cannot save us. Sustained by 25
our history and traditions, we must save ourselves, at whatever risk of heresy or blasphemy. We can find solace in the memorable representation of the human struggle against the absolute in the finest scene in the greatest of American novels. I refer of course to the scene when Huckleberry Finn decides that the "plain hand of Providence" requires him to tell Miss Watson where her runaway slave Jim is to be found. Huck writes his letter of betrayal to Miss Watson and feels "all washed clean of sin for the first time I had ever felt so in my life, and I knowed I could pray now." He sits there for a while thinking "how

1. American historian (1800–1891) famous for his ten-volume *History of the United States.*

good it was all this happened so, and how near I come to being lost and going to hell."

Then Huck begins to think about Jim and the rush of the great river and the talking and the singing and the laughing and friendship. "Then I happened to look around and see that paper. . . . I took it up, and held it in my hand. I was a-trembling because I'd got to decide, forever, betwixt two things, and I knowed it. I studied a minute, sort of holding my breath, and then says to myself: 'All right, then, I'll go to hell'—and tore it up."

That, if I may say so, is what America is all about.

Letters in Response

To the Editor:

In its wealth of quotations and anecdotes drawn from his long experience as an Americanist, Arthur Schlesinger Jr.'s defense of relativism against absolutism is a delight to read ("The Opening of the American Mind," July 23). But his treatment of religion seems to me fundamentally contradictory. Mr. Schlesinger, who holds "religion in high regard," agrees with Tocqueville, an atheist, that religion has "an indispensable social function" where morality is concerned. As a historian, however, he rejects the idea that the Judeo-Christian tradition is the source of our concern for human rights. On the contrary, the great ages of faith were notorious for "enthusiastic justifications of slavery, persecution, abandonment of small children, torture, genocide." Religion "had no compunction about murdering heretics and blasphemers."

But how can the religious morality supposedly necessary for a free democracy derive from such cruelty and injustice? Is it conveyed through the Bible, which Mr. Schlesinger, though favoring religion, does not even mention? The Bible is notoriously inconsistent where moral behavior is concerned, from the Sermon on the Mount, which Christians generally ignore as impractical, to the Ten Commandments, which the patriarchs, Moses and the early leaders of Israel could so flagrantly violate and yet retain God's favor.

Though our political leaders routinely mention God in the last paragraph of campaign speeches, they never, when discussing policy toward other nations, ask seriously how the purposes of a God of Love are being served, whether the Prince of Peace who preached the Sermon on the Mount approves of all those warheads set to explode at the touch of a button. Quoting Reinhold Niebuhr and Abraham Lincoln,

From *The New York Times Book Review* (Aug. 13, 1988).

Mr. Schlesinger says it would be wrong to claim that we know God's will. This would encourage the absolutism that he fears. "Relativism is the American way."

We can agree. But if our God is a God who never speaks to us, whose will we can never know, how is this different from not having any God at all? And how does it provide the basis for a specific morality "indispensable" to a democracy?

Robert Gorham Davis
Cambridge, Mass.

To the Editor:

As usual, Arthur Schlesinger Jr. is so lubricious in making his points 5
that it is very difficult to take hold of anything to refute him. Yet he is speaking nonsense. Mr. Schlesinger's argument, in essence: Whatever promotes authority, hierarchy, torture and wars is wrong and un-American and therefore should not be followed. Absolutism does these things. Therefore, etc.

First, not all of Mr. Schlesinger's evils are on a par. It is typical of the man that he shudders as much in saying that religion has justified authority as in saying that it has justified torture. Second, on his own premises, Mr. Schlesinger has no right to speak authoritatively on what is right and best for America. He does have the right to make a logical argument, which he does not do. Third, "absolutism" means many things. Mr. Schlesinger writes as if anyone who believes in God or any other absolute goes about murdering his neighbors.

Robert B. Nordberg
Fox Point, Wis.

To the Editor:

Though not without merits of its own, Arthur Schlesinger Jr.'s rebuttal to Allan Bloom's *Closing of the American Mind* is exceedingly strange. Nowhere in the book does Mr. Bloom contrast the "relativism" he deplores with religious absolutism; nowhere does he propose a return to any such absolutism. Instead, he goes to great lengths to describe an intellectual groundwork prepared by such secular thinkers as Locke and Rousseau,[2] on which the academic world built solid structures until the ravages of the 1960's.

Howard Kissel
New York

2. French philosopher, author, and political theorist (1712–1778); John Locke (1632–1704), English philosopher and political theorist. Locke and Rousseau represent the liberal thought of their times.

To the Editor:

Arthur Schlesinger Jr.'s call for a more tolerant, pluralistic America is undermined by the author's own intolerance toward those who would disagree with him. Even as Mr. Schlesinger decries the notion of "privileged access to absolute truth," he presents his relativism as a truth in itself: "Relativism is concrete, pluralistic, inductive, historical, skeptical and intimately bound up with deference to experience." The *truth* of relativism is presented as superior to that of absolutism. Mr. Schlesinger's essay does not oppose all absolute standards of social behavior, only those that contradict his own. For instance, the Constitution is not attacked for granting citizens the absolute right to burn their flag if they wish.

Joseph R. Bardin
New York

To the Editor:

Arthur Schlesinger Jr.'s essay is a study in near misses and subtle qualifications that lead to testimony he is not entitled to. To say that today's local wars are a "consequence" of absolutism is the summary technique of the propagandist, not the scholar. To say that human rights are a secular idea is to ignore the efforts of the church through the centuries to advance them. Mr. Schlesinger's offensive effort to portray religion as a willing partner in poverty and cruelty ignores the progress that (at least) Western man has made; equally important, it ignores the influence of time, place and circumstance on these matters, unpardonable for a historian. Mr. Schlesinger fails to mention directly the most unforgiving of all of man's experiences in cruelty, the Nazi and Communist horrors in Europe, and when he does allude to them he identifies them as products of absolutism! Is he embarrassed that these nearly total desecrations of man's essential worth came in an enlightened century almost free of all those God-centered absolutes that he chastises?

G. Roger Cahaney
Cold Spring Harbor, L.I.

To the Editor:

10 I must comment on Arthur Schlesinger Jr.'s muddled and startlingly wrongheaded essay. This urge is fueled by a diametrically opposed view: *ignoring* absolutes has brought us to the sorry state Mr. Schlesinger describes. For instance:

"Thou shalt not kill." That's about as absolute as you can get. It's only when you add exceptions making it a relative prohibition that the slaughter begins.

F. Paul Wilson
Brick, N.J.

To the Editor:

I agree that revealed, dogmatic absolutes such as those that inform modern conservatism and the recent crusade against flag burning do have disastrous consequences. But relativism, the rejection of *any* absolute standards, rational or irrational, is not the answer to dogmatic absolutes. Religion is a rejection of reason, but so is relativism with its spurning of certainty as a legitimate goal of inquiry and its view that any ethics is inherently subjective and undemonstrable or culturally "relative." Can't we be certain that assassinating Salman Rushdie[3] would be evil, even if his assassin were not to agree? In fact, there are universal truths, and we can be certain of them.

David M. Brown
Trenton

3. Indian novelist and critic who lives in hiding in England (1947–). His novel *The Satanic Verses* provoked threats of assassination from Iranian Shiite clerics.

QUESTIONS

1. *Exactly what does Schlesinger want to happen? How much of an argument about such an important topic can fit in the six or seven pages he has available?*
2. *What would American life be like if everyone followed Schlesinger's advice about relativism?*
3. *Describe the effect that Schlesinger's citing of so many names has on you as a reader.*

James Thurber

THE OWL WHO WAS GOD

Once upon a starless midnight there was on owl who sat on the branch of an oak tree. Two ground moles tried to slip quietly by, unnoticed. "You!" said the owl. "Who?" they quavered, in fear and astonishment, for they could not believe it was possible for anyone to see

From *Fables for Our Time* (1940).

them in that thick darkness. "You two!" said the owl. The moles hurried away and told the other creatures of the field and forest that the owl was the greatest and wisest of all animals because he could see in the dark and because he could answer any question. "I'll see about that," said a secretary bird, and he called on the owl one night when it was again very dark. "How many claws am I holding up?" said the secretary bird, "Two," said the owl, and that was right. "Can you give me another expression for 'that is to say' or 'namely'?" asked the secretary bird. "To wit," said the owl. "Why does a lover call on his love?" asked the secretary bird. "To woo," said the owl.

The secretary bird hastened back to the other creatures and reported that the owl was indeed the greatest and wisest animal in the world because he could see in the dark and because he could answer any question. "Can he see in the daytime, too?" asked a red fox. "Yes," echoed a dormouse and a French poodle. "Can he see in the daytime, too?" All the other creatures laughed loudly at this silly question, and they set upon the red fox and his friends and drove them out of the region. Then they sent a messenger to the owl and asked him to be their leader.

When the owl appeared among the animals it was high noon and the sun was shining brightly. He walked very slowly, which gave him an appearance of great dignity, and he peered about him with large, staring eyes, which gave him an air of tremendous importance. "He's God!" screamed a Plymouth Rock hen. And the others took up the cry "He's God!" So they followed him wherever he went and when he began to bump into things they began to bump into things, too. Finally he came to a concrete highway and he started up the middle of it and all the other creatures followed him. Presently a hawk, who was acting as outrider, observed a truck coming toward them at fifty miles an hour, and he reported to the secretary bird and the secretary bird reported to the owl. "There's danger ahead," said the secretary bird. "To wit?" said the owl. The secretary bird told him. "Aren't you afraid?" He asked. "Who?" said the owl calmly, for he could not see the truck. "He's God!" cried all the creatures again, and they were still crying "He's God!" when the truck hit them and ran them down. Some of the animals were merely injured, but most of them, including the owl, were killed.

Moral: You can fool too many of the people too much of the time.

Robert Graves

MYTHOLOGY

Mythology is the study of whatever religious or heroic legends are so foreign to a student's experience that he cannot believe them to be true. Hence the English adjective "mythical," meaning "incredible"; and hence the omission from standard European mythologies of all Biblical narratives even when closely paralleled by myths from Persia, Babylonia, Egypt, and Greece, and of all hagiological legends. * * *

Myth has two main functions. The first is to answer the sort of awkward questions that children ask, such as: "Who made the world? How will it end? Who was the first man? Where do souls go after death?" The answers, necessarily graphic and positive, confer enormous power on the various deities credited with the creation and care of souls—and incidentally on their priesthoods.

The second function of myth is to justify an existing social system and account for traditional rites and customs. The Erechtheid clan of Athens, who used a snake as an amulet, preserved myths of their descent from King Erichthonius, a man-serpent, son of the Smith-god Hephaestus and foster-son of the Goddess Athene. The Ioxids of Caria explained their veneration for rushes and wild asparagus by a story of their ancestress Perigune, whom Theseus the Erechtheid courted in a thicket of these plants; thus incidentally claiming cousinship with the Attic royal house. The real reason may have been that wild asparagus stalks and rushes were woven into sacred baskets, and therefore taboo.

Myths of origin and eventual extinction vary according to the climate. In the cold North, the first human beings were said to have sprung from the licking of frozen stones by a divine cow named Audumla; and the Northern afterworld was a bare, misty, featureless plain where ghosts wandered hungry and shivering. According to a myth from the kinder climate of Greece, a Titan named Prometheus, kneading mud on a flowery riverbank, made human statuettes which Athene—who was once the Libyan Moon-goddess Neith—brought to life, and Greek ghosts went to a sunless, flowerless underground cavern. These afterworlds were destined for serfs or commoners; deserving nobles could count on warm, celestial mead halls in the North, and Elysian Fields in Greece.

Primitive peoples remodel old myths to conform with changes pro- 5

Originally appeared as the introduction to the *Larousse Encyclopedia of Mythology* (1959).

duced by revolutions, or invasions and, as a rule, politely disguise their violence: thus a treacherous usurper will figure as a lost heir to the throne who killed a destructive dragon or other monster and, after marrying the king's daughter, duly succeeded him. Even myths of origin get altered or discarded. Prometheus' creation of men from clay superseded the hatching of all nature from a world-egg laid by the ancient Mediterranean Dove-goddess Eurynome—a myth common also in Polynesia, where the Goddess is called Tangaroa.

A typical case-history of how myths develop as culture spreads: Among the Akan of Ghana, the original social system was a number of queendoms, each containing three or more clans and ruled by a Queen-mother with her council of elder women, descent being reckoned in the female line, and each clan having its own animal deity. The Akan believed that the world was born from the all-powerful Moon-goddess Ngame, who gave human beings souls, as soon as born, by shooting lunar rays into them. At some time or other, perhaps in the early Middle Ages, patriarchal nomads from the Sudan forced the Akans to accept a male Creator, a Sky-god named Odomankoma, but failed to destroy Ngame's dispensation. A compromise myth was agreed upon: Odomankoma created the world with hammer and chisel from inert matter, after which Ngame brought it to life. These Sudanese invaders also worshipped the seven planetary powers ruling the week—a system originating in Babylonia. (It had spread to Northern Euope, bypassing Greece and Rome, which is why the names of pagan deities—Tuisto, Woden, Thor, and Frigg—are still attached to Tuesday, Wednesday, Thursday, and Friday.) This extra cult provided the Akan with seven new deities, and the compromise myth made both them and the clan gods bisexual. Towards the end of the fourteenth century A.D., a social revolution deposed Odomankoma in favor of a Universal Sun-god, and altered the myth accordingly. While Odomankoma ruled, a queendom was still a queendom, the king acting merely as a consort and male representative of the sovereign Queen-mother, and being styled "Son of the Moon": a yearly dying, yearly resurrected, fertility godling. But the gradual welding of small queendoms into city-states, and of city-states into a rich and populous nation, encouraged the High King—the king of the dominant city-state—to borrow a foreign custom. He styled himself "Son of the Sun," as well as "Son of the Moon," and claimed limitless authority. The Sun, which, according to the myth, had hitherto been reborn every morning from Ngame, was now worshipped as an eternal god altogether independent of the Moon's life-giving function. New myths appeared when the Akan accepted the patriarchal principle, which Sun-worship brought in; they began tracing succession through the father, and mothers ceased to be the spiritual heads of households.

This case-history throws light on the complex Egyptian corpus of myth. Egypt, it seems, developed from small matriarchal Moonqueendoms to Pharaonic patriarchal Sun-monarchy. Grotesque animal deities of leading clans in the Delta became city-gods, and the cities were federated under the sovereignty of a High King (once a "Son of the Moon"), who claimed to be the Son of Ra the Sun-god. Opposition by independent-minded city-rulers to the Pharaoh's autocratic sway appears in the undated myth of how Ra grew so old and feeble that he could not even control his spittle; the Moon-goddess Isis plotted against him and Ra retaliated by casting his baleful eye on mankind—they perished in their thousands. Ra nevertheless decided to quit the ungrateful land of Egypt, whereupon Hathor, a loyal Cow-goddess, flew him up to the vault of Heaven. The myth doubtless records a compromise that consigned the High King's absolutist pretensions, supported by his wife, to the vague realm of philosophic theory. He kept the throne, but once more became, for all practical purposes, an incarnation of Osiris, consort of the Moon-goddess Isis—a yearly dying, yearly resurrected fertility godling.

Indian myth is highly complex, and swings from gross physical abandon to rigorous asceticism and fantastic visions of the spirit world. Yet it has much in common with European myth, since Aryan invasions in the second millennium B.C. changed the religious system of both continents. The invaders were nomad herdsmen, and the peoples on whom they imposed themselves as a military aristocracy were peasants. Hesiod, an early Greek poet, preserves a myth of pre-Aryan "Silver Age" heroes: "divinely created eaters of bread, utterly subject to their mothers however long they lived, who never sacrificed to the gods, but at least did not make war against one another." Hesiod put the case well: in primitive agricultural communities, recourse to war is rare, and goddessworship the rule. Herdsmen, on the contrary, tend to make fighting a profession and, perhaps because bulls dominate their herds, as rams do flocks, worship a male Sky-god typified by a bull or a ram. He sends down rain for the pastures, and they take omens from the entrails of the victims sacrificed to him.

When an invading Aryan chieftain, a tribal rainmaker, married the Moon-priestess and Queen of a conquered people, a new myth inevitably celebrated the marriage of the Sky-god and the Moon. But since the Moon-goddess was everywhere worshipped as a triad, in honor of the Moon's three phases—waxing, full, and waning—the god split up into a complementary triad. This accounts for three-bodied Geryon, the first king of Spain; three-headed Cernunnos, the Gallic god; the Irish triad, Brian, Iuchar, and Iucharba, who married the three queenly owners of Ireland; and the invading Greek brothers Zeus, Poseidon, and Hades, who, despite great opposition, married the pre-Greek

Moon-goddess in her three aspects, respectively as Queen of Heaven, Queen of the Sea, and Queen of the Underworld.

The Queen-mother's decline in religious power, and the goddesses' continual struggle to preserve their royal prerogatives, appears in the Homeric myth of how Zeus ill-treated and bullied Hera, and how she continually plotted against him. Zeus remained a Thunder-god, because Greek national sentiment forbad his becoming a Sun-god in Oriental style. But his Irish counterpart, a thunder-god named The Dagda, grew senile at last and surrendered the throne to his son Bodb the Red, a war-god—in Ireland, the magic of rainmaking was not so important as in Greece.

One constant rule of mythology is that whatever happens among the gods above reflects events on earth. Thus a father-god named "The Ancient One of the Jade" (Yu-ti) ruled the pre-revolutionary Chinese Heaven: like Prometheus, he had created human beings from clay. His wife was the Queen-mother, and their court an exact replica of the old Imperial Court at Pekin, with precisely the same functionaries: ministers, soldiers, and a numerous family of the gods' sisters, daughters, and nephews. The two annual sacrifices paid by the Emperor to the August One of the Jade—at the winter solstice when the days first lengthen and at the Spring equinox when they become longer than the nights—show him to have once been a solar god. And the theological value to the number 72 suggests that the cult started as a compromise between Moongoddess worship and Sun-god worship. 72 means three-times-three, the Moon's mystical number, multipled by two-times-two-times-two, the Sun's mystical number, and occurs in solar-lunar divine unions throughout Europe, Asia, and Africa. Chinese conservatism, by the way, kept these gods dressed in ancient court-dress, making no concessions to the new fashions which the invading dynasty from Manchuria had introduced.

In West Africa, whenever the Queen-mother, or King, appointed a new functionary at Court, the same thing happened in Heaven, by royal decree. Presumably this was also the case in China; and if we apply the principle to Greek myth, it seems reasonably certain that the account of Tirynthian Heracles' marriage to Hera's daughter Hebe, and his appointment as Celestial Porter to Zeus, commemorates the appointment of a Tirynthian prince as vizier at the court of the Mycenaean High King, after marriage to a daughter of his Queen, the High Priestess of Argos. Probably the appointment of Ganymede, son of an early Trojan king, as cup-bearer to Zeus, had much the same significance: Zeus, in this context, would be more likely the Hittite king resident at Hattusas.

Myth, then, is a dramatic shorthand record of such matters as invasions, migrations, dynastic changes, admission of foreign cults, and social reforms. When bread was first introduced into Greece—where only beans, poppyseeds, acorns, and asphodel roots had hitherto been known—the myth of Demeter and Triptolemus sanctified its use; the same event in Wales produced a myth of "The Old White One," a Sow-goddess who went around the country with gifts of grain, bees, and her own young; for agriculture, pig breeding and beekeeping were taught to the aborigines by the same wave of neolithic invaders. Other myths sanctified the invention of wine.

A proper study of myth demands a great store of abstruse geographical, historical, and anthropological knowledge, also familiarity with the properties of plants and trees, and the habits of wild birds and beasts. Thus a Central American stone sculpture, a Toad-god sitting beneath a mushroom, means little to mythologists who have not considered the worldwide association of toads with toxic mushrooms or heard of a Mexican Mushroom-god, patron of an oracular cult; for the toxic agent is a drug, similar to that secreted in the sweat glands of frightened toads, which provides magnificent hallucinations of a heavenly kingdom.

Myths are fascinating and easily misread. Readers may smile at the picture of Queen Maya and her prenatal dream of the Buddha descending upon her disguised as a charming white baby elephant—he looks as though he would crush her to pulp—when "at once all nature rejoiced, trees burst into bloom, and musical instruments played of their own accord." In English-speaking countries, "white elephant" denotes something not only useless and unwanted, but expensive to maintain; and the picture could be misread there as indicating the Queen's grave embarrassment at the prospect of bearing a child. In India, however, the elephant symbolizes royalty—the supreme God Indra rides one—and white elephants (which are not albinos, but animals suffering from a vitiliginous skin disease) are sacred to the Sun, as white horses were for the ancient Greeks, and white oxen for the British druids. The elephant, moreover, symbolizes intelligence, and Indian writers traditionally acknowledge the Elephant-god Ganesa as their patron; he is supposed to have dictated the *Mahabharata*.[1]

Again, in English, a scallop shell is associated either with cookery or with medieval pilgrims returning from a visit to the Holy Sepulcher; but Aphrodite the Greek Love-goddess employed a scallop shell for her voyages across the sea, because its two parts were so tightly hinged together as to provide a symbol of passionate sexual love—the hinge of the scallop being a principal ingredient in ancient love-philters. The lotus-flower sacred to Buddha and Osiris has five petals, which symbolize the four limbs and the head; the five senses; the five digits; and,

1. A vast Indian epic of 200,000 lines, written before A.D. 500.

like the pyramid, the four points of the compass and the zenith. Other esoteric meanings abound, for myths are seldom simple, and never irresponsible.

Paul Tillich

THE RIDDLE OF INEQUALITY

> For to him who has will more be given; and from him who has not, even what he has will be taken away.
>
> —MARK iv. 25

One day a learned colleague called me up and said to me with angry excitement: "There is a saying in the New Testament which I consider to be one of the most immoral and unjust statements ever made!" And then he started quoting our text: "To him who has will more be given," and his anger increased when he continued: "and from him who has not, even what he has will be taken away." We all, I think, feel offended with him. And we cannot easily ignore the offense by suggesting what *he* suggested—that the words may be due to a misunderstanding of the disciples. It appears at least four times in the gospels with great emphasis. And even more, we can clearly see that the writers of the gospels felt exactly as we do. For them it was a stumbling block, which they tried to interpret in different ways. Probably none of these explanations satisfied them fully, for with this saying of Jesus, we are confronted immediately with the greatest and perhaps most painful riddle of life, that of the inequality of all beings. We certainly cannot hope to solve it when neither the Bible nor any other of the great religions and philosophies was able to do so. But we can do two things: We can show the breadth and the depth of the riddle of inequality and we can try to find a way to live with it, even if it is unsolved.

I

If we hear the words, "to him who has will more be given," we ask ourselves: What *do* we have? And then we may find that much is given to us in terms of external goods, of friends, of intellectual gifts and even of a comparatively high moral level of action. So we can expect that more will be given to us, while we must expect that those who are

From *The Eternal Now* (1963).

lacking in all that will lose the little they already have. Even further, according to Jesus' parable, the one talent[1] they have will be given to us who have five or ten talents. We shall be richer because they will be poorer. We may cry out against such an injustice. But we cannot deny that life confirms it abundantly. We cannot deny it, but we can ask the question, do we *really* have what we believe we have so that it cannot be taken from us? It is a question full of anxiety, confirmed by a version of our text rendered by Luke. "From him who has not, even what he *thinks* that he has will be taken away." Perhaps our having of those many things is not the kind of having which is increased. Perhaps the having of few things by the poor ones is the kind of having which makes them grow. In the parable of the talents, Jesus confirms this. Those talents which are used, even with a risk of losing them, are those which we really have; those which we try to preserve without using them for growth are those which we do not really have and which are being taken away from us. They slowly disappear, and suddenly we feel that we have lost these talents, perhaps forever.

Let us apply this to our own life, whether it is long or short. In the memory of all of us many things appear which we had without having them and which were taken away from us. Some of them became lost because of the tragic limitations of life; we had to sacrifice them in order to make other things grow. We all were given childish innocence; but innocence cannot be used and increased. The growth of our lives is possible only because we have sacrificed the original gift of innocence. Nevertheless, sometimes there arises in us a melancholy longing for a purity which has been taken from us. We all were given youthful enthusiasm for many things and aims. But this also cannot be used and increased. Most of the objects of our early enthusiasm must be sacrificed for a few, and the few must be approached with soberness. No maturity is possible without this sacrifice. Yet often a melancholy longing for the lost possibilities and enthusiasm takes hold of us. Innocence and youthful enthusiasm: we had them and had them not. Life itself demanded that they were taken from us.

But there are other things which we had and which were taken from us, because we let them go through our own guilt. Some of us had a deep sensitivity for the wonder of life as it is revealed in nature. Slowly under the pressure of work and social life and the lure of cheap pleasures, we lose the wonder of our earlier years when we felt intense joy and the presence of the mystery of life through the freshness of the young day or the glory of the dying day, the majesty of

1. A Middle Eastern coin at the time of Christ (see p. 1263).

the mountains or the infinity of the sea, a flower breaking through the soil or a young animal in the perfection of its movements. Perhaps we try to produce such feelings again, but we are empty and do not succeed. We had it and had it not, and it has been taken from us.

5 Others had the same experience with music, poetry, the great novels and plays. One wanted to devour all of them, one lived in them and created for oneself a life above the daily life. We *had* all this and did not have it; we did not let it grow; our love towards it was not strong enough and so it was taken from us.

Many, especially in this group, remember a time in which the desire to learn to solve the riddles of the universe, to find truth has been the driving force in their lives. They came to college and university, not in order to buy their entrance ticket into the upper middle classes or in order to provide for the preconditions of social and economic success, but they came, driven by the desire for knowledge. They had something and more could have been given to them. But in reality they did not have it. They did not make it grow and so it was taken from them and they finished their academic work in terms of expediency and indifference towards truth. Their love for truth has left them and in some moments they are sick in their hearts because they realize that what they have lost they may never get back.

We all know that any deeper relation to a human being needs watchfulness and growth, otherwise it is taken away from us. And we cannot get it back. This is a form of having and not having which is the root of innumerable human tragedies. We all know about them. And there is another, the most fundamental kind of having and not having—our having and losing God. Perhaps we were rich towards God in our childhood and beyond it. We may remember the moments in which we felt his ultimate presence. We may remember prayers with an overflowing heart, the encounter with the holy in word and music and holy places. We had communication with God; but it was taken from us because we had it and had it not. We did not let it grow, and so it slowly disappeared leaving an empty space. We became unconcerned, cynical, indifferent, not because we doubted about our religious traditions—such doubt belongs to being rich towards God—but because we turned away from that which once concerned us infinitely.

Such thoughts are a first step in approaching the riddle of inequality. Those who have, receive more if they really have it, if they use it and make it grow. And those who have not, lose what they have because they never had it really.

II

But the question of inequality is not yet answered. For one now asks: Why do some receive more than others in the very beginning, before there is even the possibility of using or wasting our talents? Why does the one servant receive five talents and the other two and the third one? Why is the one born in the slums and the other in a well-to-do suburban family? It does not help to answer that of those to whom much is given much is demanded and little of those to whom little is given. For it is just this inequality of original gifts, internal and external, which arouses our question. Why is it given to one human being to gain so much more out of his being human than to another one? Why is so much given to the one that much *can* be asked of him, while to the other one little is given and little *can* be asked? If this question is asked, not only about individual men but also about classes, races and nations, the everlasting question of political inequality arises, and with it the many ways appear in which men have tried to abolish inequality. In every revolution and in every war, the will to solve the riddle of inequality is a driving force. But neither war nor revolution can remove it. Even if we imagine that in an indefinite future most social inequalities are conquered, three things remain: the inequality of talents in body and mind, the inequality created by freedom and destiny, and the fact that all generations before the time of such equality would be excluded from its blessings. This would be the greatest possible inequality! No! In face of one of the deepest and most torturing problems of life, it is unpermittably shallow and foolish to escape into a social dreamland. We have to live now; we have to live this our life, and we must face today the riddle of inequality.

Let us not confuse the riddle of inequality with the fact that each of 10
us is a unique incomparable self. Certainly our being individuals belongs to our dignity as men. It is given to us and must be used and intensified and not drowned in the gray waters of conformity which threaten us today. One should defend every individuality and the uniqueness of every human self. But one should not believe that this is a way of solving the riddle of inequality. Unfortunately, there are social and political reactionaries who use this confusion in order to justify social injustice. They are at least as foolish as the dreamers of a future removal of inequality. Whoever has seen hospitals, prisons, sweatshops, battlefields, houses for the insane, starvation, family tragedies, moral aberrations should be cured from any confusion of the gift of individuality with the riddle of inequality. He should be cured from any feelings of easy consolation.

III

And now we must make the third step in our attempt to penetrate the riddle of inequality and ask: Why do some use and increase what was given to them, while others do not, so that it is taken from them? Why does God say to the prophet in our Old Testament lesson that the ears and eyes of a nation are made insensible for the divine message?

Is it enough to answer: Because some use their freedom responsibly and do what they ought to do while others fail through their own guilt? Is this answer, which seems so obvious, sufficient? Now let me first say that it *is* sufficient if we apply it to ourselves. Each of us must consider the increase or the loss of what is given to him as a matter of his own responsibility. Our conscience tells us that we cannot put the blame for our losses on anybody or anything else than ourselves.

But if we look at others, this answer is not sufficient. On the contrary: If we applied the judgment which we *must* apply to anyone else we would be like the Pharisee in Jesus' parable.[2] You cannot tell somebody who comes to you in distress about himself: Use what has been given to you; for he may come to you just because he is unable to do so! And you cannot tell those who are in despair about what they are: Be something else; for this is just what despair means—the inability of getting rid of oneself. You cannot tell those who did not conquer the destructive influences of their surroundings and were driven into crime and misery that they should have been stronger; for it was just of this strength they had been deprived by heritage or environment. Certainly they all are men, and to all of them freedom is given; but they all are also subject to destiny. It is not up to us to condemn them because they were free, as it is not up to us to excuse them because they were under their destiny. We cannot judge them. And when we judge ourselves, we must be conscious that even this is not the last word, but that we like them are under an ultimate judgment. In it the riddle of inequality is eternally answered. But this answer is not ours. It is our predicament that we must ask. And we ask with an uneasy conscience. Why are they in misery, why not we? Thinking of some who are near to us, we can ask: Are we partly responsible? But even if we are, it does not solve the riddle of inequality. The uneasy conscience asks about the farthest as well as about the nearest: Why they, why not we?

Why has my child, or any of millions and millions of children, died before even having a chance to grow out of infancy? Why is my child, or any child, born feeble-minded or crippled? Why has my friend or

2. Praying in the temple, the Pharisee said, "God, I thank thee, that I am not as other men are, extortioners, unjust, adulterers" (Luke xviii.11).

relative, or anybody's friend or relative, disintegrated in his mind and lost both his freedom and his destiny? Why has my son or daughter, gifted as I believe with many talents, wasted them and been deprived of them? And why does this happen to any parent at all? Why have this boy's or this girl's creative powers been broken by a tyrannical father or by a possessive mother?

In all these questions it is not the question of our own misery which we ask. It is not the question: Why has this happened to *me*?

It is not the question of Job which God answers by humiliating him and then by elevating him into communion with him.[3] It is not the old and urgent question: Where is the divine justice, where is the divine love towards me? But it is almost the opposite question: Why has this *not* happened to me, why has it happened to the other one, to the innumerable other ones to whom not even the power of Job is given to accept the divine answer? Why—and Jesus has asked the same question—are many called and few elected?

He does not answer; he only states that this is the human predicament. Shall we therefore cease to ask and humbly accept the fact of a divine judgment which condemns most human beings away from the community with him into despair and self-destruction? Can we accept the eternal victory of judgment over love? We cannot; and nobody ever could, even if he preached and threatened in these terms. As long as he could not see himself with complete certainty as eternally rejected, his preaching and threatening would be self-deceiving. And who could see himself eternally rejected?

But if this is not the solution of the riddle of inequality at its deepest level, can we trespass the boundaries of the Christian tradition and listen to those who tell us that this life does not decide about our eternal destiny? There will be occasions in other lives, as our present life is determined by previous ones and what we have achieved or wasted in them. It is a serious doctrine and not completely strange to Christianity. But if we don't know and never will know what each of us has been in the previous or future lives, then it is not really *our* destiny which develops from life to life, but in each life it is the destiny of someone else. This answer also does not solve the riddle of inequality.

There is no answer at all if we ask about the temporal and eternal destiny of the single being separated from the destiny of the whole. Only in the unity of all beings in time and eternity can a humanly possible answer to the riddle of inequality be found. *Humanly* possible

3. Job, one of God's favored servants, was stricken with afflictions. His question, very briefly, was "Why?" God's answer was to remind Job of how powerless man was in comparison with God, and to refuse to explain His actions. After accepting this pronouncement, Job was elevated again into God's favor.

does not mean an answer which removes the riddle of inequality, but an answer with which we can live.

20 There is an ultimate unity of all beings, rooted in the divine life from which they come and to which they go. All beings, nonhuman as well as human, participate in it. And therefore they all participate in each other. We participate in each other's having and we participate in each other's not-having. If we become aware of this unity of all beings, something happens. The fact that others have-not changes in every moment the character of my having: It undercuts its security, it drives me beyond myself, to understand, to give, to share, to help. The fact that others fall into sin, crime and misery changes the character of the grace which is given to me: It makes me realize my own hidden guilt, it shows to me that those who suffer for their sin and crime, suffer also for me; for I am guilty of their guilt—at least in the desire of my heart—and ought to suffer as they do. The awareness that others who *could* have become fully developed human beings and never *have*, changes my state of full humanity. Their early death, their early or late disintegration, makes my life and my health a continuous risk, a dying which is not yet death, a disintegration which is not yet destruction. In every death which we encounter, something of us dies; in every disease which we encounter, something of us tends to disintegrate.

Can we live with this answer? We can to the degree in which we are liberated from the seclusion within ourselves. But nobody can be liberated from himself unless he is grasped by the power of that which is present in everyone and everything—the eternal from which we come and to which we go, which gives us to ourselves and which liberates us *from* ourselves. It is the greatness and the heart of the Christian message that God—as manifest in the Cross of the Christ—participates totally in the dying child, in the condemned criminal, in the disintegrating mind, in the starving one and in him who rejects him. There is no extreme human condition into which the divine presence would not reach. This is what the Cross, the most extreme of all human conditions, tells us. The riddle of inequality cannot be solved on the level of our separation from each other. It is eternally solved in the divine participation in all of us and every being. The certainty of the divine participation gives us the courage to stand the riddle of inequality, though finite minds cannot solve it. Amen.

Virginia Woolf

THE DEATH OF THE MOTH

Moths that fly by day are not properly to be called moths; they do not excite that pleasant sense of dark autumn nights and ivy-blossom which the commonest yellow-underwing asleep in the shadow of the curtain never fails to rouse in us. They are hybrid creatures, neither gay like butterflies nor sombre like their own species. Nevertheless the present specimen, with his narrow hay-coloured wings, fringed with a tassel of the same colour, seemed to be content with life. It was a pleasant morning, mid-September, mild, benignant, yet with a keener breath than that of the summer months. The plough was already scoring the field opposite the window, and where the share had been, the earth was pressed flat and gleamed with moisture. Such vigour came rolling in from the fields and the down beyond that it was difficult to keep the eyes strictly turned upon the book. The rooks too were keeping one of their annual festivities; soaring round the tree tops until it looked as if a vast net with thousands of black knots in it had been cast up into the air; which, after a few moments sank slowly down upon the trees until every twig seemed to have a knot at the end of it. Then, suddenly, the net would be thrown into the air again in a wider circle this time, with the utmost clamour and vociferation, as though to be thrown into the air and settle slowly down upon the tree tops were a tremendously exciting experience.

The same energy which inspired the rooks, the ploughmen, the horses, and even, it seemed, the lean bare-backed downs, sent the moth fluttering from side to side of his square of the window-pane. One could not help watching him. One was, indeed, conscious of a queer feeling of pity for him. The possibilities of pleasure seemed that morning so enormous and so various that to have only a moth's part in life, and a day moth's at that, appeared a hard fate, and his zest in enjoying his meagre opportunities to the full, pathetic. He flew vigorously to one corner of his compartment, and, after waiting there a second, flew across to the other. What remained for him but to fly to a third corner and then to a fourth? That was all he could do, in spite of the size of the downs, the width of the sky, the far-off smoke of houses, and the romantic voice, now and then, of a steamer out at sea. What he could do he did. Watching him, it seemed as if a fibre, very thin but pure, of the enormous energy of the world had been thrust into his

From *The Death of the Moth and Other Essays* (1942).

frail and diminutive body. As often as he crossed the pane, I could fancy that a thread of vital light became visible. He was little or nothing but life.

Yet, because he was so small, and so simple a form of the energy that was rolling in at the open window and driving its way through so many narrow and intricate corridors in my own brain and in those of other human beings, there was something marvellous as well as pathetic about him. It was as if someone had taken a tiny bead of pure life and decking it as lightly as possible with down and feathers, had set it dancing and zig-zagging to show us the true nature of life. Thus displayed one could not get over the strangeness of it. One is apt to forget all about life, seeing it humped and bossed and garnished and cumbered so that it has to move with the greatest circumspection and dignity. Again, the thought of all that life might have been had he been born in any other shape caused one to view his simple activities with a kind of pity.

After a time, tired by his dancing apparently, he settled on the window ledge in the sun, and, the queer spectacle being at an end, I forgot about him. Then, looking up, my eye was caught by him. He was trying to resume his dancing, but seemed either so stiff or so awkward that he could only flutter to the bottom of the window-pane; and when he tried to fly across it he failed. Being intent on other matters I watched these futile attempts for a time without thinking, unconsciously waiting for him to resume his flight, as one waits for a machine, that has stopped momentarily, to start again without considering the reason of its failure. After perhaps a seventh attempt he slipped from the wooden ledge and fell, fluttering his wings, on to his back on the window sill. The helplessness of his attitude roused me. It flashed upon me that he was in difficulties; he could no longer raise himself; his legs struggled vainly. But, as I stretched out a pencil, meaning to help him to right himself, it came over me that the failure and awkwardness were the approach of death. I laid the pencil down again.

5 The legs agitated themselves once more. I looked as if for the enemy against which he struggled. I looked out of doors. What had happened there? Presumably it was midday, and work in the fields had stopped. Stillness and quiet had replaced the previous animation. The birds had taken themselves off to feed in the brooks. The horses stood still. Yet the power was there all the same, massed outside indifferent, impersonal, not attending to anything in particular. Somehow it was opposed to the little hay-coloured moth. It was useless to try to do anything. One could only watch the extraordinary efforts made by those tiny legs against an oncoming doom which could, had it chosen, have submerged an entire city, not merely a city, but masses of human beings; nothing, I knew, had any chance against death. Nevertheless after

a pause of exhaustion the legs fluttered again. It was superb this last protest, and so frantic that he succeeded at last in righting himself. One's sympathies, of course, were all on the side of life. Also, when there was nobody to care or to know, this gigantic effort on the part of an insignificant little moth, against a power of such magnitude, to retain what no one else valued or desired to keep, moved one strangely. Again, somehow, one saw life, a pure bead. I lifted the pencil again, useless though I knew it to be. But even as I did so, the unmistakable tokens of death showed themselves. The body relaxed, and instantly grew stiff. The struggle was over. The insignificant little creature now knew death. As I looked at the dead moth, this minute wayside triumph of so great a force over so mean an antagonist filled me with wonder. Just as life had been strange a few minutes before, so death was now as strange. The moth having righted himself now lay most decently and uncomplainingly composed. O yes, he seemed to say, death is stronger than I am.

QUESTIONS

1. *Woolf begins her essay with a description of the scene outside. What seems most striking about that description? What does she not describe in the world outside her window?*
2. *Does Woolf see any resemblances between the moth's struggles and the human condition? How do you know?*
3. *Observe an insect and describe it from two points of view—one objective and one subjective, as a scientist might describe it and as a poet or novelist might describe it.*

Annie Dillard

SIGHT INTO INSIGHT

When I was six or seven years old, growing up in Pittsburgh, I used to take a penny of my own and hide it for someone else to find. It was a curious compulsion; sadly, I've never been seized by it since. For some reason I always "hid" the penny along the same stretch of sidewalk up the street. I'd cradle it at the roots of a maple, say, or in a hole left by a chipped-off piece of sidewalk. Then I'd take a piece of chalk and, starting at either end of the block, draw huge arrows leading up to the penny from both directions. After I learned to write I labeled the

From *Harper's Magazine* (Feb. 1974).

arrows "SURPRISE AHEAD" or "MONEY THIS WAY." I was greatly excited, during all this arrowdrawing, at the thought of the first lucky passerby who would receive in this way, regardless of merit, a free gift from the universe. But I never lurked about. I'd go straight home and not give the matter another thought, until, some months later, I would be gripped by the impulse to hide another penny.

There are lots of things to see, unwrapped gifts and free surprises. The world is fairly studded and strewn with pennies cast broadside from a generous hand. But—and this is the point—who gets excited by a mere penny? If you follow one arrow, if you crouch motionless on a bank to watch a tremulous ripple thrill on the water, and are rewarded by the sight of a muskrat kit paddling from its den, will you count that sight a chip of copper only, and go your rueful way? It is very dire poverty indeed for a man to be so malnourished and fatigued that he won't stoop to pick up a penny. But if you cultivate a healthy poverty and simplicity, so that finding a penny will make your day, then, since the world is in fact planted in pennies, you have with your poverty bought a lifetime of days. What you see is what you get.

Unfortunately, nature is very much a now-you-see-it, now-you-don't affair. A fish flashes, then dissolves in the water before my eyes like so much salt. Deer apparently ascend bodily into heaven; the brightest oriole fades into leaves. These disappearances stun me into stillness and concentration; they say of nature that it conceals with a grand nonchalance, and they say of vision that it is a deliberate gift, the revelation of a dancer who for my eyes only flings away her seven veils.

For nature does reveal as well as conceal: now-you-don't-see-it, now-you-do. For a week this September migrating red-winged blackbirds were feeding heavily down by Tinker Creek at the back of the house. One day I went out to investigate the racket; I walked up to a tree, an Osage orange, and a hundred birds flew away. They simply materialized out of the tree. I saw a tree, then a whisk of color, then a tree again. I walked closer and another hundred blackbirds took flight. Not a branch, not a twig budged: the birds were apparently weightless as well as invisible. Or, it was as if the leaves of the Osage orange had been freed from a spell in the form of redwinged blackbirds; they flew from the tree, caught my eye in the sky, and vanished. When I looked again at the tree, the leaves had reassembled as if nothing had happened. Finally I walked directly to the trunk of the tree and a final hundred, the real diehards, appeared, spread, and vanished. How could so many hide in the tree without my seeing them? The Osage orange, unruffled, looked just as it had looked from the house, when three hundred red-winged blackbirds cried from its crown. I looked upstream where they flew, and they were gone. Searching, I couldn't spot one. I wandered upstream to force them to play their hand, but they'd crossed the creek and scattered. One show to a customer. These appearances catch at my throat; they are the free gifts, the bright coppers at the roots of trees.

It's all a matter of keeping my eyes open. Nature is like one of those 5
line drawings that are puzzles for children: Can you find hidden in the tree a duck, a house, a boy, a bucket, a giraffe, and a boot? Specialists can find the most incredibly hidden things. A book I read when I was young recommended an easy way to find caterpillars: you simply find some fresh caterpillar droppings, look up, and there's your caterpillar. More recently an author advised me to set my mind at ease about those piles of cut stems on the ground in grassy fields. Field mice make them; they cut the grass down by degrees to reach the seeds at the head. It seems that when the grass is tightly packed, as in a field of ripe grain, the blade won't topple at a single cut through the stem; instead, the cut stem simply drops vertically, held in the crush of grain. The mouse severs the bottom again and again, the stem keeps dropping an inch at a time, and finally the head is low enough for the mouse to reach the seeds. Meanwhile the mouse is positively littering the field with its little piles of cut stems into which, presumably, the author is constantly stumbling.

If I can't see these minutiae, I still try to keep my eyes open. I'm always on the lookout for ant lion traps in sandy soil, monarch pupae near milkweed, skipper larvae in locust leaves. These things are utterly common, and I've not seen one. I bang on hollow trees near water, but so far no flying squirrels have appeared. In flat country I watch every sunset in hopes of seeing the green ray. The green ray is a seldom-seen streak of light that rises from the sun like a spurting fountain at the moment of sunset; it throbs into the sky for two seconds and disappears. One more reason to keep my eyes open. A photography professor at the University of Florida just happened to see a bird die in midflight; it jerked, died, dropped, and smashed on the ground.

I squint at the wind because I read Stewart Edward White: "I have always maintained that if you looked closely enough you could *see* the wind—the dim, hardly-made-out, fine débris fleeing high in the air." White was an excellent observer, and devoted an entire chapter of *The Mountains* to the subject of seeing deer: "As soon as you can forget the naturally obvious and construct an artificial obvious, then you too will see deer."

But the artificial obvious is hard to see. My eyes account for less than 1 percent of the weight of my head; I'm bony and dense; I see what I expect. I once spent a full three minutes looking at a bullfrog that was so unexpectedly large I couldn't see it even though a dozen enthusiastic campers were shouting directions. Finally I asked, "What color am I looking for?" and a fellow said, "Green." When at last I picked out the frog, I saw what painters are up against: the thing wasn't green at all, but the color of wet hickory bark.

The lover can see, and the knowledgeable. I visited an aunt and uncle at a quarter-horse ranch in Cody, Wyoming. I couldn't do much of anything useful, but I could, I thought, draw. So, as we all sat around the kitchen table after supper, I produced a sheet of paper and drew a horse. "That's one lame horse," my aunt volunteered. The rest of the family joined in: "Only place to saddle that one is his neck"; "Looks like we better shoot the poor thing, on account of those terrible growths." Meekly, I slid the pencil and paper down the table. Everyone in that family, including my three young cousins, could draw a horse. Beautifully. When the paper came back it looked as though five shining, real quarter horses had been corraled by mistake with a papier-mâché moose; the real horses seemed to gaze at the monster with a steady, puzzled air. I stay away from horses now, but I can do a creditable goldfish. The point is that I just don't know what the lover knows; I just can't see the artificial obvious that those in the know construct. The herpetologist asks the native, "Are there snakes in that ravine?" "Nosir." And the herpetologist comes home with, yessir, three bags full. Are there butterflies on that mountain? Are the bluets in bloom, are there arrowheads here, or fossil shells in the shale?

10 Peeping through my keyhole I see within the range of only about 30 percent of the light that comes from the sun; the rest is infrared and some little ultraviolet, perfectly apparent to many animals, but invisible to me. A nightmare network of ganglia, charged and firing without my knowledge, cuts and splices what I do see, editing it for my brain. Donald E. Carr points out that the sense impressions of one-celled animals are *not* edited for the brain: "This is philosophically interesting in a rather mournful way, since it means that only the simplest animals perceive the universe as it is."

A fog that won't burn away drifts and flows across my field of vision. When you see fog move against a backdrop of deep pines, you don't see the fog itself, but streaks of clearness floating across the air in dark shreds. So I see only tatters of clearness through a pervading obscurity. I can't distinguish the fog from the overcast sky; I can't be sure if the light is direct or reflected. Everywhere darkness and the presence of the unseen appalls. We estimate now that only one atom dances alone in every cubic meter of intergalactic space. I blink and squint. What planet or power yanks Halley's Comet out of orbit? We haven't seen it yet; it's a question of distance, density, and the pallor of reflected light. We rock, cradled in the swaddling band of darkness. Even the simple darkness of night whispers suggestions to the mind. This summer, in August, I stayed at the creek too late.

Where Tinker Creek flows under the sycamore log bridge to the tear-shaped island, it is slow and shallow, fringed thinly in cattail marsh. At this spot an astonishing bloom of life supports vast breeding populations of insects, fish, reptiles, birds, and mammals. On windless summer evenings I stalk along the creek bank or straddle the sycamore log in absolute stillness, watching for muskrats. The night I stayed too late I was hunched on the log staring spellbound at spreading, reflected stains of lilac on the water. A cloud in the sky suddenly lighted as if turned on by a switch; its reflection just as suddenly materialized on the water upstream, flat and floating, so that I couldn't see the creek bottom, or life in the water under the cloud. Downstream, away from the cloud on the water, water turtles smooth as beans were gliding down with the current in a series of easy, weightless push-offs, as men bound on the moon. I didn't know whether to trace the progress of one turtle I was sure of, risking sticking my face in one of the bridge's spider webs made invisible by the gathering dark, or take a chance on seeing the carp, or scan the mudbank in hope of seeing a muskrat, or follow the last of the swallows who caught at my heart and trailed it after them like streamers as they appeared from directly below, under the log, flying upstream with their tails forked, so fast.

But shadows spread and deepened and stayed. After thousands of years we're still strangers to darkness, fearful aliens in an enemy camp with our arms crossed over our chests. I stirred. A land turtle on the bank, startled, hissed the air from its lungs and withdrew to its shell. An uneasy pink here, an unfathomable blue there, gave great suggestion of lurking beings. Things were going on. I couldn't see whether that rustle I heard was a distant rattle-snake, slit-eyed, or a nearby sparrow kicking in the dry flood debris slung at the foot of a willow. Tremendous action roiled the water everywhere I looked, big action, inexplicable. A tremor welled up beside a gaping muskrat burrow in the bank and I caught my breath, but no muskrat appeared. The ripples continued to fan upstream with a steady, powerful thrust. Night was knitting an eyeless mask over my face, and I still sat transfixed. A distant airplane, a delta wing out of nightmare, made a gliding shadow on the creek's bottom that looked like a stingray cruising upstream. At once a black fin slit the pink cloud on the water, shearing it in two. The two halves merged together and seemed to dissolve before my eyes. Darkness pooled in the cleft of the creek and rose, as water collects in a well. Untamed, dreaming lights flickered over the sky. I saw hints of hulking underwater shadows, two pale splashes out of the water, and round ripples rolling close together from a blackened center.

At last I stared upstream where only the deepest violet remained of the cloud, a cloud so high its underbelly still glowed, its feeble color reflected from a hidden sky lighted in turn by a sun halfway to China.

And out of that violet, a sudden enormous black body arced over the water. Head and tail, if there was a head and tail, were both submerged in cloud. I saw only one ebony fling, a headlong dive to darkness; then the waters closed, and the lights went out.

15 I walked home in a shivering daze, up hill and down. Later I lay openmouthed in bed, my arms flung wide at my sides to steady the whirling darkness. At this latitude I'm spinning 836 miles an hour round the earth's axis; I feel my sweeping fall as a breakneck arc like the dive of dolphins, and the hollow rushing of wind raises the hairs on my neck and the side of my face. In orbit around the sun I'm moving 64,800 miles an hour. The solar system as a whole, like a merry-go-round unhinged, spins, bobs, and blinks at the speed of 43,200 miles an hour along a course set east of Hercules. Someone has piped, and we are dancing a tarantella until the sweat pours. I open my eyes and I see dark, muscled forms curl out of water, with flapping gills and flattened eyes. I close my eyes and I see stars, deep stars giving way to deeper stars, deeper stars bowing to deepest stars at the crown of an infinite cone.

"Still," wrote Van Gogh in a letter, "a great deal of light falls on everything." If we are blinded by darkness, we are also blinded by light. Sometimes here in Virginia at sunset low clouds on the southern or northern horizon are completely invisible in the lighted sky. I only know one is there because I can see its reflection in still water. The first time I discovered this mystery I looked from cloud to no-cloud in bewilderment, checking my bearings over and over, thinking maybe the ark of the covenant was just passing by south of Dead Man Mountain. Only much later did I learn the explanation: polarized light from the sky is very much weakened by reflection, but the light in clouds isn't polarized. So invisible clouds pass among visible clouds, till all slide over the mountains; so a greater light extinguishes a lesser as though it didn't exist.

In the great meteor shower of August, the Perseid, I wail all day for the shooting stars I miss. They're out there showering down committing hara-kiri in a flame of fatal attraction, and hissing perhaps at last into the ocean. But at dawn what looks like a blue dome clamps down over me like a lid on a pot. The stars and planets could smash and I'd never know. Only a piece of ashen moon occasionally climbs up or down the inside of the dome, and our local star without surcease explodes on our heads. We have really only that one light, one source for all power, and yet we must turn away from it by universal decree. Nobody here on the planet seems aware of this strange, powerful taboo, that we all walk about carefully averting our faces, this way and that, lest our eyes be blasted forever.

Darkness appalls and light dazzles; the scrap of visible light that doesn't hurt my eyes hurts my brain. What I see sets me swaying. Size and distance and the sudden swelling of meanings confuse me, bowl me over. I straddle the sycamore log bridge over Tinker Creek in the summer. I look at the lighted creek bottom: snail tracks tunnel the mud in quavering curves. A crayfish jerks, but by the time I absorb what has happened, he's gone in a billowing smoke screen of silt. I look at the water; minnows and shiners. If I'm thinking minnows, a carp will fill my brain till I scream. I look at the water's surface: skaters, bubbles, and leaves sliding down. Suddenly, my own face, reflected, startles me witless. Those snails have been tracking my face! Finally, with a shuddering wrench of the will, I see clouds, cirrus clouds. I'm dizzy, I fall in.

This looking business is risky. Once I stood on a humped rock on nearby Purgatory Mountain, watching through binoculars the great autumn hawk migration below, until I discovered that I was in danger of joining the hawks on a vertical migration of my own. I was used to binoculars, but not, apparently, to balancing on humped rocks while looking through them. I reeled. Everything advanced and receded by turns; the world was full of unexplained foreshortenings and depths. A distant huge object, a hawk the size of an elephant, turned out to be the browned bough of a nearby loblolly pine. I followed a sharp-shinned hawk against a featureless sky, rotating my head unawares as it flew, and when I lowered the glass a glimpse of my own looming shoulder sent me staggering. What prevents the men at Palomar[1] from falling, voiceless and blinded, from their tiny, vaulted chairs?

I reel in confusion: I don't understand what I see. With the naked 20
eye I can see two million light-years to the Andromeda galaxy. Often I slop some creek water in a jar, and when I get home I dump it in a white china bowl. After the silt settles I return and see tracings of minute snails on the bottom, a planarian or two winding round the rim of water, roundworms shimmying, frantically, and finally, when my eyes have adjusted to these dimensions, amoebae. At first the amoebae look like *muscae volitantes,* those curled moving spots you seem to see in your eyes when you stare at a distant wall. Then I see the amoebae as drops of water congealed, bluish, translucent, like chips of sky in the bowl. At length I choose one individual and give myself over to its idea of an evening. I see it dribble a grainy foot before it on its wet, unfathomable way. Do its unedited sense impressions include the fierce focus of my eyes? Shall I take it outside and show it Andromeda, and blow its little endoplasm? I stir the water with a finger, in case it's running out of oxygen. Maybe I should get a tropical aquarium with mo-

1. An astronomical observatory in California.

torized bubblers and lights, and keep this one for a pet. Yes, it would tell its fissioned descendants, the universe is two feet by five, and if you listen closely you can hear the buzzing music of the spheres.

Oh, it's mysterious, lamplit evenings here in the galaxy, one after the other. It's one of those nights when I wander from window to window, looking for a sign. But I can't see. Terror and a beauty insoluble are a riband of blue woven into the fringe of garments of things both great and small. No culture explains, no bivouac offers real haven or rest. But it could be that we are not seeing something. Galileo thought comets were an optical illusion. This is fertile ground: since we are certain that they're not, we can look at what our scientists have been saying with fresh hope. What if there are *really* gleaming, castellated cities hung up-side-down over the desert sand? What limpid lakes and cool date palms have our caravans always passed untried? Until, one by one, by the blindest of leaps, we light on the road to these places, we must stumble in darkness and hunger. I turn from the window. I'm blind as a bat, sensing only from every direction the echo of my own thin cries.

I chanced on a wonderful book called *Space and Sight,* by Marius Von Senden. When Western surgeons discovered how to perform safe cataract operations, they ranged across Europe and America operating on dozens of men and women of all ages who had been blinded by cataracts since birth. Von Senden collected accounts of such cases; the histories are fascinating. Many doctors had tested their patients' sense perceptions and ideas of space both before and after the operations. The vast majority of patients, of both sexes and all ages, had, in Von Senden's opinion, no idea of space whatsoever. Form, distance, and size were so many meaningless syllables. A patient "had no idea of depth, confusing it with roundness." Before the operation a doctor would give a blind patient a cube and a sphere; the patient would tongue it or feel it with his hands, and name it correctly. After the operation the doctor would show the same objects to the patient without letting him touch them; now he had no clue whatsoever to what he was seeing. One patient called lemonade "square" because it pricked on his tongue as a square shape pricked on the touch of his hands. Of another post-operative patient the doctor writes, "I have found in her no notion of size, for example, not even within the narrow limits which she might have encompassed with the aid of touch. Thus when I asked her to show me how big her mother was, she did not stretch out her hands, but set her two index fingers a few inches apart."

For the newly sighted, vision is pure sensation unencumbered by meaning. When a newly sighted girl saw photographs and paintings, she asked, " 'Why do they put those dark marks all over them?' 'Those aren't dark marks,' her mother explained, 'those are shadows. That is one of the ways the eye knows that things have shape. If it were not for shadows, many things would look flat.' 'Well, that's how things do look,' Joan answered. 'Everything looks flat with dark patches.' "

In general the newly sighted see the world as a dazzle of "colorpatches." They are pleased by the sensation of color, and learn quickly to name the colors, but the rest of seeing is tormentingly difficult. Soon after his operation a patient "generally bumps into one of these colour-patches and observes them to be substantial, since they resist him as tactual objects do. In walking about it also strikes him—or can if he pays attention—that he is continually passing in between the colours he sees, that he can go past a visual object, that a part of it then steadily disappears from view; and that in spite of this, however he twists and turns—whether entering the room from the door, for example, or returning back to it—he always has a visual space in front of him. Thus he gradually comes to realize that there is also a space behind him, which he does not see."

The mental effort involved in these reasonings proves overwhelm- 25
ing for many patients. It oppresses them to realize that they have been visible to people all along, perhaps unattractively so, without their knowledge or consent. A disheartening number of them refuse to use their new vision, continuing to go over objects with their tongues, and lapsing into apathy and despair.

On the other hand, many newly sighted people speak well of the world, and teach us how dull our own vision is. To one patient, a human hand, unrecognized, is "something bright and then holes." Shown a bunch of grapes, a boy calls out, "It is dark, blue and shiny. . . . It isn't smooth, it has bumps and hollows." A little girl visits a garden. "She is greatly astonished, and can scarcely be persuaded to answer, stands speechless in front of the tree, which she only names on taking hold of it, and then as 'the tree with the lights in it.' " Another patient, a twenty-two-year-old girl, was dazzled by the world's brightness and kept her eyes shut for two weeks. When at the end of that time she opened her eyes again, she did not recognize any objects, but "the more she now directed her gaze upon everything about her, the more it could be seen how an expression of gratification and astonishment overspread her features; she repeatedly exclaimed: 'Oh God! How beautiful!' "

I saw color-patches for weeks after I read this wonderful book. It was summer; the peaches were ripe in the valley orchards. When I woke in the morning, color-patches wrapped round my eyes, intricately, leaving not one unfilled spot. All day long I walked among shifting color-patches that parted before me like the Red Sea and closed again in silence, transfigured, wherever I looked back. Some patches swelled and loomed, while others vanished utterly, and dark marks flitted at random over the whole dazzling sweep. But I couldn't sustain the illusion of flatness. I've been around for too long. Form is condemned to an eternal danse macabre with meaning: I couldn't unpeach the peaches. Nor can I remember ever having seen without understanding; the color-patches of infancy are lost. My brain then must have been smooth as any balloon. I'm told I reached for the moon; many babies do. But the color-patches of infancy swelled as meaning filled them; they arrayed themselves in solemn ranks down distance which unrolled and stretched before me like a plain. The moon rocketed away. I live now in a world of shadows that shape and distance color, a world where space makes a kind of terrible sense. What Gnosticism[2] is this, and what physics? The fluttering patch I saw in my nursery window—silver and green and shape-shifting blue—is gone; a row of Lombardy poplars takes its place, mute, across the distant lawn. That humming oblong creature pale as light that stole along the walls of my room at night, stretching exhilaratingly around the corners, is gone, too, gone the night I ate of the bittersweet fruit, put two and two together and puckered forever my brain. Martin Buber tells this tale: "Rabbi Mendel once boasted to his teacher Rabbi Elimelekh that evenings he saw the angel who rolls away the light before the darkness, and mornings the angel who rolls away the darkness before the light. 'Yes,' said Rabbi Elimelekh, 'in my youth I saw that too. Later on you don't see these things anymore.' "

Why didn't someone hand those newly sighted people paints and brushes from the start, when they still didn't know what anything was? Then maybe we all could see color-patches too, the world unraveled from reason, Eden before Adam gave names. The scales would drop from my eyes; I'd see trees like men walking; I'd run down the road against all orders, hallooing and leaping.

Seeing is of course very much a matter of verbalization. Unless I call my attention to what passes before my eyes, I simply won't see it. If Tinker Mountain erupted, I'd be likely to notice. But if I want to notice the lesser cataclysms of valley life, I have to maintain in my head a running description of the present. It's not that I'm observant; it's just that I talk too much. Otherwise, especially in a strange place, I'll never know what's happening. Like a blind man at the ball game, I need a radio.

30 When I see this way I analyze and pry. I hurl over logs and roll away stones; I study the bank a square foot at a time, probing and tilting my

2. Pretension to esoteric spiritual knowledge.

head. Some days when a mist covers the mountains, when the muskrats won't show and the microscope's mirror shatters, I want to climb up the blank blue dome as a man would storm the inside of a circus tent, wildly, dangling, and with a steel knife claw a rent in the top, peep, and, if I must, fall.

But there is another kind of seeing that involves a letting go. When I see this way I sway transfixed and emptied. The difference between the two ways of seeing is the difference between walking with and without a camera. When I walk with a camera I walk from shot to shot, reading the light on a calibrated meter. When I walk without a camera, my own shutter opens, and the moment's light prints on my own silver gut. When I see this second way I am above all an unscrupulous observer.

It was sunny one evening last summer at Tinker Creek; the sun was low in the sky, upstream. I was sitting on the sycamore log bridge with the sunset at my back, watching the shiners the size of minnows who were feeding over the muddy sand in skittery schools. Again and again, one fish, then another, turned for a split second across the current and flash! the sun shot out from its silver side. I couldn't watch for it. It was always just happening somewhere else, and it drew my vision just as it disappeared: flash! like a sudden dazzle of the thinnest blade, a sparking over a dun and olive ground at chance intervals from every direction. Then I noticed white specks, some sort of pale petals, small, floating from under my feet on the creek's surface, very slow and steady. So I blurred my eyes and gazed toward the brim of my hat and saw a new world. I saw the pale white circles roll up, roll up, like the world's turning, mute and perfect, and I saw the linear flashes, gleaming silver, like stars being born at random down a rolling scroll of time. Something broke and something opened. I filled up like a new wineskin. I breathed an air like light; I saw a light like water. I was the lip of a fountain the creek filled forever; I was ether, the leaf in the zephyr; I was flesh-flake, feather, bone.

When I see this way I see truly. As Thoreau says, I return to my senses. I am the man who watches the baseball game in silence in an empty stadium. I see the game purely; I'm abstracted and dazed. When it's all over and the white-suited players lope off the green field to their shadowed dugouts, I leap to my feet, I cheer and cheer.

But I can't go out and try to see this way. I'll fail, I'll go mad. All I can do is try to gag the commentator, to hush the noise of useless interior babble that keeps me from seeing just as surely as a newspaper dangled before my eyes. The effort is really a discipline requiring a lifetime of dedicated struggle; it marks the literature of saints and monks of every order east and west, under every rule and no rule, discalced and shod. The world's spiritual geniuses seem to discover universally that the mind's muddy river, this ceaseless flow of trivia and trash, cannot be dammed, and that trying to dam it is a waste of effort that might lead to madness. Instead you must allow the muddy river to flow unheeded in the dim channels of consciousness; you raise your sights; you look along it, mildly, acknowledging its presence without interest and gazing beyond it into the realm of the real where subjects and objects act and rest purely, without utterance. "Launch into the deep," says Jacques Ellul,[3] "and you shall see."

35 The secret of seeing, then, is the pearl of great price. If I thought he could teach me to find it and keep it forever I would stagger barefoot across a hundred deserts after any lunatic at all. But although the pearl may be found, it may not be sought. The literature of illumination reveals this above all: although it comes to those who wait for it, it is always, even to the most practiced and adept, a gift and a total surprise. I return from one walk knowing where the killdeer nests in the field by the creek and the hour the laurel blooms. I return from the same walk a day later scarcely knowing my own name. Litanies hum in my ears; my tongue flaps in my mouth, *Alim non,* alleluia! I cannot cause light; the most I can do is try to put myself in the path of its beam. It is possible, in deep space, to sail on solar wind. Light, be it particle or wave, has force: you rig a giant sail and go. The secret of seeing is to sail on solar wind. Hone and spread your spirit till you yourself are a sail, whetted, translucent, broadside to the merest puff.

When her doctor took her bandages off and led her into the garden, the girl who was no longer blind saw "the tree with the lights in it." It was for this tree I searched through the peach orchards of summer, in the forests of fall and down winter and spring for years. Then one day I was walking along Tinker Creek thinking of nothing at all and I saw the tree with the lights in it. I saw the backyard cedar where the mourning doves roost charged and transfigured, each cell buzzing with flame. I stood on the grass with the lights in it, grass that was wholly fire, utterly focused and utterly dreamed. It was less like seeing than like being for the first time seen, knocked breathless by a powerful glance. The flood of fire abated, but I'm still spending the power. Gradually the lights went out in the cedar, the colors died, the cells unflamed and disappeared. I was still ringing. I had been my whole life a bell, and never knew it until at that moment I was lifted and struck. I have since only very rarely seen the tree with the lights in it. The vision comes and goes, mostly goes, but I live for it, for the moment when the mountains open and a new light roars in spate through the crack, and the mountains slam.

3. French social and economic writer.

QUESTIONS

1. *How is the kind of seeing Dillard describes at the end of her essay different from what she talks of at the beginning? Does her title accurately reflect this difference?*
2. *How does Dillard establish her authority during the course of her essay? Why should we be convinced by what she says?*
3. *Dillard says "I see what I expect." Look at an object or scene briefly, then write down what you see. Then look at it longer and more intensely, and write down the additional things you see. Then write a brief comparison of your first and second views.*

Gilbert Highet

THE MYSTERY OF ZEN

The mind need never stop growing. Indeed, one of the few experiences which never pall is the experience of watching one's own mind, and observing how it produces new interests, responds to new stimuli, and develops new thoughts, apparently without effort and almost independently of one's own conscious control. I have seen this happen to myself a hundred times; and every time it happens again, I am equally fascinated and astonished.

Some years ago a publisher sent me a little book for review. I read it, and decided it was too remote from my main interests and too highly specialized. It was a brief account of how a young German philosopher living in Japan had learned how to shoot with a bow and arrow, and how this training had made it possible for him to understand the esoteric doctrines of the Zen sect of Buddhism. Really, what could be more alien to my own life, and to that of everyone I knew, than Zen Buddhism and Japanese archery? So I thought, and put the book away.

Yet I did not forget it. It was well written, and translated into good English. It was delightfully short, and implied much more than it said. Although its theme was extremely odd, it was at least highly individual; I had never read anything like it before or since. It remained in my mind. Its name was *Zen in the Art of Archery,* its author Eugen Herrigel, its publisher Pantheon of New York. One day I took it off the shelf and read it again; this time it seemed even stranger than before and even more unforgettable. Now it began to cohere with other interests of mine. Something I had read of the Japanese art of flower arrange-

From *Talent and Geniuses* (1957).

ment seemed to connect with it; and then, when I wrote an essay on the peculiar Japanese poems called *haiku*, other links began to grow. Finally I had to read the book once more with care, and to go through some other works which illuminated the same subject. I am still grappling with the theme; I have not got anywhere near understanding it fully; but I have learned a good deal, and I am grateful to the little book which refused to be forgotten.

The author, a German philosopher, got a job teaching philosophy at the University of Tokyo (apparently between the wars), and he did what Germans in foreign countries do not usually do: he determined to adapt himself and to learn from his hosts. In particular, he had always been interested in mysticism—which, for every earnest philosopher, poses a problem that is all the more inescapable because it is virtually insoluble. Zen Buddhism is not the only mystical doctrine to be found in the East, but it is one of the most highly developed and certainly one of the most difficult to approach. Herrigel knew that there were scarcely any books which did more than skirt the edge of the subject, and that the best of all books on Zen (those by the philosopher D. T. Suzuki) constantly emphasize that Zen can never be learned from books, can never be studied as we can study other disciplines such as logic or mathematics. Therefore he began to look for a Japanese thinker who could teach him directly.

5 At once he met with embarrassed refusals. His Japanese friends explained that he would gain nothing from trying to discuss Zen as a philosopher, that its theories could not be spread out for analysis by a detached mind, and in fact that the normal relationship of teacher and pupil simply did not exist within the sect, because the Zen masters felt it useless to explain things stage by stage and to argue about the various possible interpretations of their doctrine. Herrigel had read enough to be prepared for this. He replied that he did not want to dissect the teachings of the school, because he knew that would be useless. He wanted to become a Zen mystic himself. (This was highly intelligent of him. No one could really penetrate into Christian mysticism without being a devout Christian; no one could appreciate Hindu mystical doctrine without accepting the Hindu view of the universe.) At this, Herrigel's Japanese friends were more forthcoming. They told him that the best way, indeed the only way, for a European to approach Zen mysticism was to learn one of the arts which exemplified it. He was a fairly good rifle shot, so he determined to learn archery; and his wife co-operated with him by taking lessons in painting and flower arrangement. How any philosopher could investigate a mystical doctrine by learning to shoot with a bow and arrow and watching his wife arrange flowers, Herrigel did not ask. He had good sense.

A Zen master who was a teacher of archery agreed to take him as a pupil. The lessons lasted six years, during which he practiced every single day. There are many difficult courses of instruction in the world: the Jesuits, violin virtuosi, Talmudic scholars, all have long and hard training, which in one sense never comes to an end; but Herrigel's training in archery equaled them all in intensity. If I were trying to learn archery, I should expect to begin by looking at a target and shooting arrows at it. He was not even allowed to aim at a target for the first four years. He had to begin by learning how to hold the bow and arrow, and then how to release the arrow; this took ages. The Japanese bow is not like our sporting bow, and the stance of the archer in Japan is different from ours. We hold the bow at shoulder level, stretch our left arm out ahead, pull the string and the nocked arrow to a point either below the chin or sometimes past the right ear, and then shoot. The Japanese hold the bow above the head, and then pull the hands apart to left and right until the left hand comes down to eye level and the right hand comes to rest above the right shoulder; then there is a pause, during which the bow is held at full stretch, with the tip of the three-foot arrow projecting only a few inches beyond the bow; after that, the arrow is loosed. When Herrigel tried this, even without aiming, he found it was almost impossible. His hands trembled. His legs stiffened and grew cramped. His breathing became labored. And of course he could not possibly aim. Week after week he practiced this, with the Master watching him carefully and correcting his strained attitude; week after week he made no progress whatever. Finally he gave up and told his teacher that he could not learn: it was absolutely impossible for him to draw the bow and loose the arrow.

To his astonishment, the Master agreed. He said, "Certainly you cannot. It is because you are not breathing correctly. You must learn to breathe in a steady rhythm, keeping your lungs full most of the time, and drawing in one rapid inspiration with each stage of the process, as you grasp the bow, fit the arrow, raise the bow, draw, pause, and loose the shot. If you do, you will both grow stronger and be able to relax." To prove this, he himself drew his massive bow and told his pupil to feel the muscles of his arms: they were perfectly relaxed, as though he were doing no work whatever.

Herrigel now started breathing exercises; after some time he combined the new rhythm of breathing with the actions of drawing and shooting; and, much to his astonishment, he found that the whole thing, after this complicated process, had become much easier. Or rather, not easier, but different. At times it became quite unconscious. He says himself that he felt he was not breathing, but being breathed; and in time he felt that the occasional shot was not being dispatched by him, but shooting itself. The bow and arrow were in charge; he had become merely a part of them.

All this time, of course, Herrigel did not even attempt to discuss

Zen doctrine with his Master. No doubt he knew that he was approaching it, but he concentrated solely on learning how to shoot. Every stage which he surmounted appeared to lead to another stage even more difficult. It took him months to learn how to loosen the bowstring. The problem was this. If he gripped the string and arrowhead tightly, either he froze, so that his hands were slowly pulled together and the shot was wasted, or else he jerked, so that the arrow flew up into the air or down into the ground; and if he was relaxed, then the bowstring and arrow simply *leaked* out of his grasp before he could reach full stretch, and the arrow went nowhere. He explained this problem to the Master. The Master understood perfectly well. He replied, "You must hold the drawn bowstring like a child holding a grownup's finger. You know how firmly a child grips; and yet when it lets go, there is not the slightest jerk—because the child does not think of itself, it is not self-conscious, it does not say, 'I will now let go and do something else,' it merely acts instinctively. That is what you must learn to do. Practice, practice, and practice, and then the string will loose itself at the right moment. The shot will come as effortlessly as snow slipping from a leaf." Day after day, week after week, month after month, Herrigel practiced this; and then, after one shot, the Master suddenly bowed and broke off the lesson. He said "Just then it shot. Not you, but *it*." And gradually thereafter more and more right shots achieved themselves; the young philosopher forgot himself, forgot that he was learning archery for some other purpose, forgot even that he was practicing archery, and became part of that unconsciously active complex, the bow, the string, the arrow, and the man.

10 Next came the target. After four years, Herrigel was allowed to shoot at the target. But he was strictly forbidden to aim at it. The Master explained that even he himself did not aim; and indeed, when he shot, he was so absorbed in the act, so selfless and unanxious, that his eyes were almost closed. It was difficult, almost impossible, for Herrigel to believe that such shooting could ever be effective; and he risked insulting the Master by suggesting that he ought to be able to hit the target blindfolded. But the Master accepted the challenge. That night, after a cup of tea and long meditation, he went into the archery hall, put on the lights at one end and left the target perfectly dark, with only a thin taper burning in front of it. Then, with habitual grace and precision, and with that strange, almost sleepwalking, selfless confidence that is the heart of Zen, he shot two arrows into the darkness. Herrigel went out to collect them. He found that the first had gone to the heart of the bull's eye, and that the second had actually hit the first arrow and splintered it. The Master showed no pride. He said, "Perhaps, with unconscious memory of the position of the target, *I* shot the first arrow; but the second arrow? *It* shot the second arrow, and *it* brought it to the center of the target."

At last Herrigel began to understand. His progress became faster and faster; easier, too. Perfect shots (perfect because perfectly unconscious) occurred at almost every lesson; and finally, after six years of incessant training, in a public display he was awarded the diploma. He needed no further instruction: he had himself become a Master. His wife meanwhile had become expert both in painting and in the arrangement of flowers—two of the finest of Japanese arts. (I wish she could be persuaded to write a companion volume, called *Zen in the Art of Flower Arrangement*; it would have a wider general appeal than her husband's work.) I gather also from a hint or two in his book that she had taken part in the archery lessons. During one of the most difficult periods in Herrigel's training, when his Master had practically refused to continue teaching him—because Herrigel had tried to cheat by *consciously* opening his hand at the moment of loosing the arrow—his wife had advised him against that solution, and sympathized with him when it was rejected. She in her own way had learned more quickly than he, and reached the final point together with him. All their effort had not been in vain: Herrigel and his wife had really acquired a new and valuable kind of wisdom. Only at this point, when he was about to abandon his lessons forever, did his Master treat him almost as an equal and hint at the innermost doctrines of Zen Buddhism. Only hints he gave; and yet, for the young philosopher who had now become a mystic, they were enough. Herrigel understood the doctrine, not with his logical mind, but with his entire being. He at any rate had solved the mystery of Zen.

Without going through a course of training as absorbing and as complete as Herrigel's, we can probably never penetrate the mystery. The doctrine of Zen cannot be analyzed from without: it must be lived.

But although it cannot be analyzed, it can be hinted at. All the hints that the adherents of this creed give us are interesting. Many are fantastic; some are practically incomprehensible, and yet unforgettable. Put together, they take us toward a way of life which is utterly impossible for westerners living in a western world, and nevertheless has a deep fascination and contains some values which we must respect.

The word Zen means "meditation." (It is the Japanese word, corresponding to the Chinese Ch'an and the Hindu Dhyana.) It is the central idea of a special sect of Buddhism which flourished in China during the Sung period (between *a.d.* 1000 and 1300) and entered Japan in the twelfth century. Without knowing much about it, we might be certain that the Zen sect was a worthy and noble one, because it produced a quantity of highly distinguished art, specifically painting. And if we knew anything about Buddhism itself, we might say that Zen goes closer than other sects to the heart of Buddha's teaching: because Buddha was trying to found, not a religion with temples and rituals, but a way of life based on meditation. However, there is something eccentric about the Zen life which is hard to trace in Buddha's teaching; there is an active energy which he did not admire, there is a rough grasp on reality which he himself eschewed, there is something like a sense of humor, which he rarely displayed. The gravity and serenity of the Indian preacher are transformed, in Zen, to the earthy liveliness of Chinese and Japanese sages. The lotus brooding calmly on the water has turned into a knotted tree covered with spring blossoms.

In this sense, "meditation" does not mean what we usually think of when we say a philosopher meditates: analysis of reality, a long-sustained effort to solve problems of religion and ethics, the logical dissection of the universe. It means something not divisive, but whole; not schematic, but organic; not long-drawn-out, but immediate. It means something more like our words "intuition" and "realization." It means a way of life in which there is no division between thought and action; none of the painful gulf, so well known to all of us, between the unconscious and the conscious mind; and no absolute distinction between the self and the external world, even between the various parts of the external world and the whole.

When the German philosopher took six years of lessons in archery in order to approach the mystical significance of Zen, he was not given direct philosophical instruction. He was merely shown how to breathe, how to hold and loose the bowstring, and finally how to shoot in such a way that the bow and arrow used him as an instrument. There are many such stories about Zen teachers. The strangest I know is one about a fencing master who undertook to train a young man in the art of the sword. The relationship of teacher and pupil is very important, almost sacred, in the Far East; and the pupil hardly ever thinks of leaving a master or objecting to his methods, however extraordinary they may seem. Therefore this young fellow did not at first object when he was made to act as a servant, drawing water, sweeping floors, gathering wood for the fire, and cooking. But after some time he asked for more direct instruction. The master agreed to give it, but produced no swords. The routine went on just as before, except that every now and then the master would strike the young man with a stick. No matter what he was doing, sweeping the floor or weeding in the garden, a blow would descend on him apparently out of nowhere; he had always to be on the alert, and yet he was constantly receiving unexpected cracks on the head or shoulders. After some months of this, he saw his master stooping over a boiling pot full of vegetables; and he thought he would have his revenge. Silently he lifted a stick and brought it down; but without any effort, without even a glance in his direction, his master parried the blow with the lid of the cooking pot. At last, the pupil began to understand the instinctive alertness, the effortless perception

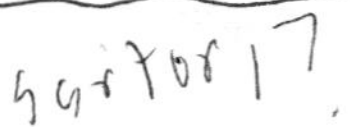

and avoidance of danger, in which his master had been training him. As soon as he had achieved it, it was child's play for him to learn the management of the sword: he could parry every cut and turn every slash without anxiety, until his opponent, exhausted, left an opening for his counterattack. (The same principle was used by the elderly samurai for selecting his comrades in the Japanese motion picture *The Magnificent Seven.*)

These stories show that Zen meditation does not mean sitting and thinking. On the contrary, it means acting with as little thought as possible. The fencing master trained his pupil to guard against every attack with the same immediate, instinctive rapidity with which our eyelid closes over our eye when something threatens it. His work was aimed at breaking down the wall between thought and act, at completely fusing body and senses and mind so that they might all work together rapidly and effortlessly. When a Zen artist draws a picture, he does it in a rhythm almost the exact reverse of that which is followed by a Western artist. We begin by blocking out the design and then filling in the details, usually working more and more slowly as we approach the completion of the picture. The Zen artist sits down very calmly; examines his brush carefully; prepares his own ink; smooths out the paper on which he will work; falls into a profound silent ecstasy of contemplation—during which he does not think anxiously of various details, composition, brushwork, shades of tone, but rather attempts to become the vehicle through which the subject can express itself in painting; and then, very quickly and almost unconsciously, with sure effortless strokes, draws a picture containing the fewest and most effective lines. Most of the paper is left blank; only the essential is depicted, and that not completely. One long curving line will be enough to show a mountainside; seven streaks will become a group of bamboos bending in the wind; and yet, though technically incomplete, such pictures are unforgettably clear. They show the heart of reality.

All this we can sympathize with, because we can see the results. The young swordsman learns how to fence. The intuitional painter produces a fine picture. But the hardest thing for us to appreciate is that the Zen masters refuse to teach philosophy or religion directly, and deny logic. In fact, they despise logic as an artificial distortion of reality. Many philosophical teachers are difficult to understand because they analyze profound problems with subtle intricacy: such is Aristotle in his *Metaphysics.* Many mystical writers are difficult to understand because, as they themselves admit, they are attempting to use words to describe experiences which are too abstruse for words, so that they have to fall back on imagery and analogy, which they themselves recognize to be poor media, far coarser than the realities with which they have been in contact. But the Zen teachers seem to deny the power of language and thought altogether. For example, if you ask a Zen master what is the ultimate reality, he will answer, without the slightest hesitation, "The bamboo grove at the foot of the hill" or "A branch of plum blossom." Apparently he means that these things, which we can see instantly without effort, or imagine in the flash of a second, are real with the ultimate reality; that nothing is more real than these; and that we ought to grasp ultimates as we grasp simple immediates. A Chinese master was once asked the central question, "What is the Buddha?" He said nothing whatever, but held out his index finger. What did he mean? It is hard to explain; but apparently he meant "Here. Now. Look and realize with the effortlessness of seeing. Do not try to use words. Do not think. Make no efforts toward withdrawal from the world. Expect no sublime ecstasies. Live. All *that* is the ultimate reality, and it can be understood from the motion of a finger as well as from the execution of any complex ritual, from any subtle argument, or from the circling of the starry universe."

In making that gesture, the master was copying the Buddha himself, who once delivered a sermon which is famous, but was hardly understood by his pupils at the time. Without saying a word, he held up a flower and showed it to the gathering. One man, one alone, knew what he meant. The gesture became renowned as the Flower Sermon.

20 In the annals of Zen there are many cryptic answers to the final question, "What is the Buddha?"—which in our terms means "What is the meaning of life? What is truly real?" For example, one master, when asked "What is the Buddha?" replied, "Your name is Yecho." Another said, "Even the finest artist cannot paint him." Another said, "No nonsense here." And another answered, "The mouth is the gate of woe." My favorite story is about the monk who said to a Master, "Has a dog Buddha-nature too?" The Master replied, "Wu"—which is what the dog himself would have said.

Now, some critics might attack Zen by saying that this is the creed of a savage or an animal. The adherents of Zen would deny that—or more probably they would ignore the criticism, or make some cryptic remark which meant that it was pointless. Their position—if they could ever be persuaded to put in into words—would be this. An animal is instinctively in touch with reality, and so far is living rightly, but it has never had a mind and so cannot perceive the Whole, only that part with which it is in touch. The philosopher sees both the Whole and the parts, and enjoys them all. As for the savage, he exists only through the group; he feels himself as part of a war party or a ceremonial dance team or a ploughing-and-sowing group or the Snake clan; he is not truly an individual at all, and therefore is less than fully human. Zen has at its heart an inner solitude; its aim is to teach us to live, as in the last resort we do all have to live, alone.

A more dangerous criticism of Zen would be that it is nihilism, that its purpose is to abolish thought altogether. (This criticism is handled, but not fully met, by the great Zen authority Suzuki in his *Introduction to Zen Buddhism.*) It can hardly be completely confuted, for after all the central doctrine of Buddhism is—Nothingness. And many of the sayings of Zen masters are truly nihilistic. The first patriarch of the sect in China was asked by the emperor what was the ultimate and holiest principle of Buddhism. He replied, "Vast emptiness, and nothing holy in it." Another who was asked the searching question "Where is the abiding-place for the mind?" answered, "Not in this dualism of good and evil, being and non-being, thought and matter." In fact, thought is an activity which divides. It analyzes, it makes distinctions, it criticizes, it judges, it breaks reality into groups and classes and individuals. The aim of Zen is to abolish that kind of thinking, and to substitute—not unconsciousness, which would be death, but a consciousness that does not analyze but experiences life directly. Although it has no prescribed prayers, no sacred scriptures, no ceremonial rites, no personal god, and no interest in the soul's future destination, Zen is a religion rather than a philosophy. Jung[1] points out that its aim is to produce a religious conversion, a "transformation": and he adds, "The transformation process is incommensurable with intellect." Thought is always interesting, but often painful; Zen is calm and painless. Thought is incomplete; Zen enlightenment brings a sense of completeness. Thought is a process; Zen illumination is a state. But it is a state which cannot be defined. In the Buddhist scriptures there is a dialogue between a master and a pupil in which the pupil tries to discover the exact meaning of such a state. The master says to him, 'If a fire were blazing in front of you, would you know that it was blazing?'

"Yes, master."

"And would you know the reason for its blazing?"

"Yes, because it had a supply of grass and sticks."

"And would you know if it were to go out?"

"Yes, master."

"And on its going out, would you know where the fire had gone? To the east, to the west, to the north, or to the south?"

"The question does not apply, master. For the fire blazed because it had a supply of grass and sticks. When it had consumed this and had no other fuel, then it went out."

"In the same way," replies the master, "no question will apply to the meaning of Nirvana, and no statement will explain it."

Such, then, neither happy nor unhappy but beyond all divisive de-

1. Carl Gustav Jung (1875–1961), Swiss psychologist, one of Freud's early followers, who explored symbolism and the unconscious.

scription, is the condition which students of Zen strive to attain. Small wonder that they can scarcely explain it to us, the unilluminated.

QUESTIONS

1. *Highet says Zen is "a religion rather than a philosophy" (paragraph 22). How has he led up to this conclusion? What definitions of religion and philosophy does he imply?*
2. *What difficulties does Highet face in discussing Zen? How does he manage to give a definition in spite of his statement that Zen "cannot be analyzed"?*
3. *How does Highet go about defining meditation? Would other means have worked as well? Using an approach similar to Highet's, write a brief definition of a similar term (perhaps intuition or realization).*

Jean-Paul Sartre

EXISTENTIALISM

Man is nothing else but what he makes of himself. Such is the first principle of existentialism. It is also what is called subjectivity, the name we are labeled with when charges are brought against us. But what do we mean by this, if not that man has a greater dignity than a stone or table? For we mean that man first exists, that is, that man first of all is the being who hurls himself toward a future and who is conscious of imagining himself as being in the future. Man is at the start a plan which is aware of itself, rather than a patch of moss, a piece of garbage, or a cauliflower; nothing exists prior to this plan; there is nothing in heaven; man will be what he will have planned to be. Not what he will want to be. Because by the word "will" we generally mean a conscious decision, which is subsequent to what we have already made of ourselves. I may want to belong to a political party, write a book, get married; but all that is only a manifestation of an earlier, more spontaneous choice that is called "will." But if existence really does precede essence, man is responsible for what he is. Thus, existentialism's first move is to make every man aware of what he is and to make the full responsibility of his existence rest on him. And when we say that a man is responsible for himself, we do not only mean that he is responsible for his own individuality, but that he is responsible for all men.

From *Existentialism* (1947).

The word "subjectivism" has two meanings, and our opponents play on the two. Subjectivism means, on the one hand, that an individual chooses and makes himself; and, on the other, that it is impossible for man to transcend human subjectivity. The second of these is the essential meaning of existentialism. When we say that man chooses his own self, we mean that every one of us does likewise; but we also mean by that that in making this choice he also chooses all men. In fact, in creating the man that we want to be, there is not a single one of our acts which does not at the same time create an image of man as we think he ought to be. To choose to be this or that is to affirm at the same time the value of what we choose, because we can never choose evil. We always choose the good, and nothing can be good for us without being good for all.

If, on the other hand, existence precedes essence, and if we grant that we exist and fashion our image at one and the same time, the image is valid for everybody and for our whole age. Thus, our responsibility is much greater than we might have supposed, because it involves all mankind. If I am a workingman and choose to join a Christian trade union rather than be a Communist, and if by being a member, I want to show that the best thing for man is resignation, that the kingdom of man is not of this world, I am not only involving my own case—I want to be resigned for everyone. As a result, my action has involved all humanity. To take a more individual matter, if I want to marry, to have children, even if this marriage depends solely on my own circumstances or passion or wish, I am involving all humanity in monogamy and not merely myself. Therefore, I am responsible for myself and for everyone else. I am creating a certain image of man of my own choosing. In choosing myself, I choose man.

This helps us understand what the actual content is of such rather grandiloquent words as anguish, forlornness, despair. As you will see, it's all quite simple.

First, what is meant by anguish? The existentialists say at once that 5
man is anguish. What that means is this: the man who involves himself and who realizes that he is not only the person he chooses to be, but also a lawmaker who is, at the same time, choosing all mankind as well as himself, cannot help escape the feeling of his total and deep responsibility. Of course, there are many people who are not anxious; but we claim that they are hiding their anxiety, that they are fleeing from it. Certainly, many people believe that when they do something, they themselves are the only ones involved, and when someone says to them, "What if everyone acted that way?" they shrug their shoulders and answer, "Everyone doesn't act that way." But really, one should always ask himself, "What would happen if everybody looked at things that way?" There is no escaping this disturbing thought except by a

kind of double-dealing. A man who lies and makes excuses for himself by saying "not everybody does that," is someone with an uneasy conscience, because the act of lying implies that a universal value is conferred upon the lie.

Anguish is evident even when it conceals itself. This is the anguish that Kierkegaard called the anguish of Abraham. You know the story: an angel has ordered Abraham to sacrifice his son; if it really were an angel who has come and said, "You are Abraham, you shall sacrifice your son," everything would be all right. But everyone might first wonder, "Is it really an angel, and am I really Abraham? What proof do I have?"

There was a madwoman who had hallucinations; someone used to speak to her on the telephone and give her orders. Her doctor asked her, "Who is it who talks to you?" She answered, "He says it's God." What proof did she really have that it was God? If an angel comes to me, what proof is there that it's an angel? And if I hear voices, what proof is there that they come from heaven and not from hell, or from the subconscious, or a pathological condition? What proves that they are addressed to me? What proof is there that I have been appointed to impose my choice and my conception of man on humanity? I'll never find any proof or sign to convince me of that. If a voice addresses me, it is always for me to decide that this is the angel's voice; if I consider that such an act is a good one, it is I who will choose to say that it is good rather than bad.

Now, I'm not being singled out as an Abraham, and yet at every moment I'm obliged to perform exemplary acts. For every man, everything happens as if all mankind had its eyes fixed on him and were guiding itself by what he does. And every man ought to say to himself, "Am I really the kind of man who has the right to act in such a way that humanity might guide itself by my actions?" And if he does not say that to himself, he is masking his anguish.

There is no question here of the kind of anguish which would lead to quietism, to inaction. It is a matter of a simple sort of anguish that anybody who has had responsibilities is familiar with. For example, when a military officer takes the responsibility for an attack and sends a certain number of men to death, he chooses to do so, and in the main he alone makes the choice. Doubtless, orders come from above, but they are too broad; he interprets them, and on this interpretation depend the lives of ten or fourteen or twenty men. In making a decision he cannot help having a certain anguish. All leaders know this anguish. That doesn't keep them from acting; on the contrary, it is the very condition of their action. For it implies that they envisage a number of possibilities, and when they choose one, they realize that it has value only because it is chosen. We shall see that this kind of anguish, which is the kind that existentialism describes, is explained, in addition, by a direct responsibility to the other men whom it involves. It is not a curtain separating us from action, but is part of action itself.

When we speak of forlornness, a term Heidegger was fond of, we mean only that God does not exist and that we have to face all the consequences of this. This existentialist is strongly opposed to a certain kind of secular ethics which would like to abolish God with the least possible expense. About 1880, some French teachers tried to set up a secular ethics which went something like this: God is a useless and costly hypothesis; we are discarding it; but, meanwhile, in order for there to be an ethics, a society, a civilization, it is essential that certain values be taken seriously and that they be considered as having an *a priori* existence. It must be obligatory, *a priori*, to be honest, not to lie, not to beat your wife, to have children, etc., etc. So we're going to try a little device which will make it possible to show that values exist all the same, inscribed in a heaven of ideas, though otherwise God does not exist. In other words—and this, I believe, is the tendency of everything called reformism in France—nothing will be changed if God does not exist. We shall find ourselves with the same norms of honesty, progress, and humanism, and we shall have made of God an outdated hypothesis which will peacefully die off by itself.

The existentialist, on the contrary, thinks it very distressing that God does not exist, because all possibility of finding values in a heaven of ideas disappears along with Him; there can no longer be an *a priori* Good, since there is no infinite and perfect consciousness to think it. Nowhere is it written that the Good exists, that we must be honest, that we must not lie; because the fact is we are on a plane where there are only men. Dostoievsky said, "If God didn't exist, everything would be possible." That is the very starting point of existentialism. Indeed, everything is permissible if God does not exist, and as a result man is forlorn, because neither within him nor without does he find anything to cling to. He can't start making excuses for himself.

If existence really does precede essence, there is no explaining things away by reference to a fixed and given human nature. In other words, there is no determinism, man is free, man is freedom. On the other hand, if God does not exist, we find no values or commands to turn to which legitimize our conduct. So, in the bright realm of values, we have no excuse behind us, nor justification before us. We are alone, with no excuses.

That is the idea I shall try to convey when I say that man is condemned to be free. Condemned, because he did not create himself, yet, in other respects is free; because, once thrown into the world, he is responsible for everything he does. The existentialist does not believe in the power of passion. He will never agree that a sweeping passion is a ravaging torrent which fatally leads a man to certain acts and is therefore an excuse. He thinks that man is responsible for his passion.

The existentialist does not think that man is going to help himself by finding in the world some omen by which to orient himself. Because he thinks that man will interpret the omen to suit himself. Therefore, he thinks that man, with no support and no aid, is condemned every moment to invent man. Ponge, in a very fine article, has said, "Man is the future of man." That's exactly it. But if it is taken to mean that this future is recorded in heaven, that God sees it, then it is false, because it would really no longer be a future. If it is taken to mean that, whatever a man may be, there is a future to be forged, a virgin future before him, then this remark is sound. But then we are forlorn.

15 To give you an example which will enable you to understand forlornness better, I shall cite the case of one of my students who came to see me under the following circumstances: his father was on bad terms with his mother, and, moreover, was inclined to be a collaborationist,[1] his older brother had been killed in the German offensive of 1940, and the young man, with somewhat immature but generous feelings, wanted to avenge him. His mother lived alone with him, very much upset by the half-treason of her husband and the death of her older son; the boy was her only consolation.

The boy was faced with the choice of leaving for England and joining the Free French forces—that is, leaving his mother behind—or remaining with his mother and helping her to carry on. He was fully aware that the woman lived only for him and that his going off—and perhaps his death—would plunge her into despair. He was also aware that every act that he did for his mother's sake was a sure thing, in the sense that it was helping her to carry on, whereas every effort he made toward going off and fighting was an uncertain move which might run aground and prove completely useless; for example, on his way to England he might, while passing through Spain, be detained indefinitely in a Spanish camp; he might reach England or Algiers and be stuck in an office at a desk job. As a result, he was faced with two very different kinds of action: one, concrete, immediate, but concerning only one individual; the other concerned an incomparably vaster group, a national collectivity, but for that very reason was dubious, and might be interrupted en route. And, at the same time, he was wavering between two kinds of ethics. On the one hand, an ethics of sympathy, of personal devotion; on the other, a broader ethics, but one whose efficacy was more dubious. He had to choose between the two.

Who could help him choose? Christian doctrine? No. Christian

1. With the occupying German army, or its puppet government in Vichy.

doctrine says, "Be charitable, love your neighbor, take the more rugged path, etc., etc." But which is the more rugged path? Whom should he love as a brother? The fighting man or his mother? Which does the greater good, the vague act of fighting in a group, or the concrete one of helping a particular human being to go on living? Who can decide *a priori?* Nobody. No book of ethics can tell him. The Kantian ethics says, "Never treat any person as a means, but as an end." Very well, if I stay with my mother, I'll treat her as an end and not as a means; but by virtue of this very fact, I'm running the risk of treating the people around me who are fighting, as means; and, conversely, if I go to join those who are fighting, I'll be treating them as an end, and, by doing that, I run the risk of treating my mother as a means.

If values are vague, and if they are always too broad for the concrete and specific case that we are considering, the only thing left for us is to trust our instincts. That's what this young man tried to do; and when I saw him, he said, "In the end, feeling is what counts. I ought to choose whichever pushes me in one direction. If I feel that I love my mother enough to sacrifice everything else for her—my desire for vengeance, for action, for adventure—then I'll stay with her. If, on the contrary, I feel that my love for my mother isn't enough, I'll leave."

But how is the value of a feeling determined? What gives his feeling for his mother value? Precisely the fact that he remained with her. I may say that I like so-and-so well enough to sacrifice a certain amount of money for him, but I may say so only if I've done it. I may say "I love my mother well enough to remain with her" if I have remained with her. The only way to determine the value of this affection is, precisely, to perform an act which confirms and defines it. But, since I require this affection to justify my act, I find myself caught in a vicious circle.

20 On the other hand, Gide has well said that a mock feeling and a true feeling are almost indistinguishable; to decide that I love my mother and will remain with her, or to remain with her by putting on an act, amount somewhat to the same thing. In other words, the feeling is formed by the acts one performs; so, I cannot refer to it in order to act upon it. Which means that I can neither seek within myself the true condition which will impel me to act, nor apply to a system of ethics for concepts which will permit me to act. You will say, "At least, he did go to a teacher for advice." But if you seek advice from a priest, for example, you have chosen this priest; you already knew, more or less, just about what advice he was going to give you. In other words, choosing your adviser is involving yourself. The proof of this is that if you are a Christian, you will say, "Consult a priest." But some priests are collaborating, some are just marking time, some are resisting. Which to choose? If the young man chooses a priest who is resisting or collaborating, he has already decided on the kind of advice he's going to

get. Therefore, in coming to see me he knew the answer I was going to give him, and I had only one answer to give: "You're free, choose, that is, invent." No general ethics can show you what is to be done; there are no omens in the world. The Catholics will reply, "But there are." Granted—but, in any case, I myself choose the meaning they have.

When I was a prisoner, I knew a rather remarkable young man who was a Jesuit. He had entered the Jesuit order in the following way: he had had a number of very bad breaks; in childhood, his father died, leaving him in poverty, and he was a scholarship student at a religious institution where he was constantly made to feel that he was being kept out of charity; then, he failed to get any of the honors and distinctions that children like; later on, at about eighteen, he bungled a love affair; finally, at twenty-two, he failed in military training, a childish enough matter, but it was the last straw.

This young fellow might well have felt that he had botched everything. It was a sign of something, but of what? He might have taken refuge in bitterness or despair. But he very wisely looked upon all this as a sign that he was not made for secular triumphs, and that only the triumphs of religion, holiness, and faith were open to him. He saw the hand of God in all this, and so he entered the order. Who can help seeing that he alone decided what the sign meant?

Some other interpretation might have been drawn from this series of setbacks; for example, that he might have done better to turn carpenter or revolutionist. Therefore, he is fully responsible for the interpretation. Forlornness implies that we ourselves choose our being. Forlornness and anguish go together.

As for despair, the term has a very simple meaning. It means that we shall confine ourselves to reckoning only with what depends upon our will, or on the ensemble of probabilities which make our action possible. When we want something, we always have to reckon with probabilities. I may be counting on the arrival of a friend. The friend is coming by rail or streetcar; this supposes that the train will arrive on schedule, or that the streetcar will not jump the track. I am left in the realm of possibility; but possibilities are to be reckoned with only to the point where my action comports with the ensemble of these possibilities, and no further. The moment the possibilities I am considering are not rigorously involved by my action, I ought to disengage myself from them, because no God, no scheme, can adapt the world and its possibilities to my will. When Descartes said, "Conquer yourself rather than the world," he meant essentially the same thing.

25 The Marxists to whom I have spoken reply, "You can rely on the support of others in your action, which obviously has certain limits because you're not going to live forever. That means: rely on both what others are doing elsewhere to help you, in China, in Russia, and what

they will do later on, after your death, to carry on the action and lead it to its fulfillment, which will be the revolution. You even *have* to rely upon that, otherwise you're immoral." I reply at once that I will always rely on fellow-fighters insofar as these comrades are involved with me in a common struggle, in the unity of a party or a group in which I can more or less make my weight felt; that is, one whose ranks I am in as a fighter and whose movements I am aware of at every moment. In such a situation, relying on the unity and will of the party is exactly like counting on the fact that the train will arrive on time or that the car won't jump the track. But, given that man is free and that there is no human nature for me to depend on, I cannot count on men whom I do not know by relying on human goodness or man's concern for the good of society. I don't know what will become of the Russian revolution; I may make an example of it to the extent that at the present time it is apparent that the proletariat plays a part in Russia that it plays in no other nation. But I can't swear that this will inevitably lead to a triumph of the proletariat. I've got to limit myself to what I see.

Given that men are free and that tomorrow they will freely decide what man will be, I cannot be sure that, after my death, fellow-fighters will carry on my work to bring it to its maximum perfection. Tomorrow, after my death, some men may decide to set up Fascism, and the others may be cowardly and muddled enough to let them do it. Fascism will then be the human reality, so much the worse for us.

Actually, things will be as man will have decided they are to be. Does that mean that I should abandon myself to quietism? No. First, I should involve myself; then, act on the old saw, "Nothing ventured, nothing gained." Nor does it mean that I shouldn't belong to a party, but rather that I shall have no illusions and shall do what I can. For example, suppose I ask myself, "Will socialization, as such, ever come about?" I know nothing about it. All I know is that I'm going to do everything in my power to bring it about. Beyond that, I can't count on anything. Quietism is the attitude of people who say, "Let others do what I can't do." The doctrine I am presenting is the very opposite of quietism, since it declares, "There is no reality except in action." Moreover, it goes further, since it adds, "Man is nothing else than his plan; he exists only to the extent that he fulfills himself; he is therefore nothing else than the ensemble of his acts, nothing else than his life."

According to this, we can understand why our doctrine horrifies certain people. Because often the only way they can bear their wretchedness is to think, "Circumstances have been against me. What I've been and done doesn't show my true worth. To be sure, I've had no great love, no great friendship, but that's because I haven't met a man or woman who was worthy. The books I've written haven't been very good because I haven't had the proper leisure. I haven't had children to devote myself to because I didn't find a man with whom I could have spent my life. So there remains within me, unused and quite viable, a host of propensities, inclinations, possibilities, that one wouldn't guess from the mere series of things I've done."

Now, for the existentialist there is really no love other than one which manifests itself in a person's being in love. There is no genius other than one which is expressed in works of art; the genius of Proust is the sum of Proust's works; the genius of Racine is his series of tragedies. Outside of that, there is nothing. Why say that Racine could have written another tragedy, when he didn't write it? A man is involved in life, leaves his impress on it, and outside of that there is nothing. To be sure, this may seem a harsh thought to someone whose life hasn't been a success. But, on the other hand, it prompts people to understand that reality alone is what counts, that dreams, expectations, and hopes warrant no more than to define a man as a disappointed dream, as miscarried hopes, as vain expectations. In other words, to define him negatively and not positively. However, when we say, "You are nothing else than your life," that does not imply that the artist will be judged solely on the basis of his works of art; a thousand other things will contribute toward summing him up. What we mean is that a man is nothing else than a series of undertakings, that he is the sum, the organization, the ensemble of the relationships which make up these undertakings.

When all is said and done, what we are accused of, at bottom, is not our pessimism, but an optimistic toughness. If people throw up to us our works of fiction in which we write about people who are soft, weak, cowardly, and sometimes even downright bad, it's not because these people are soft, weak, cowardly, or bad; because if we were to say, as Zola did, that they are that way because of heredity, the workings of environment, society, because of biological or psychological determinism, people would be reassured. They would say, "Well, that's what we're like, no one can do anything about it." But when the existentialist writes about a coward, he says that this coward is responsible for his cowardice. He's not like that because he has a cowardly heart or lung or brain; he's not like that on account of his physiological make-up; but he's like that because he has made himself a coward by his acts. There's no such thing as a cowardly constitution; there are nervous constitutions; there is poor blood, as the common people say, or strong constitutions. But the man whose blood is poor is not a coward on that account, for what makes cowardice is the act of renouncing or yielding. A constitution is not an act; the coward is defined on the basis of the acts he performs. People feel, in a vague sort of way, that this coward we're talking about is guilty of being a coward, and the thought frightens them. What people would like is that a coward or a hero be born that way. . . .

From these few reflections it is evident that nothing is more unjust than the objections that have been raised against us. Existentialism is nothing else than an attempt to draw all the consequences of a coherent atheistic position. It isn't trying to plunge man into despair at all. But if one calls every attitude of unbelief despair, like the Christians, then the word is not being used in its original sense. Existentialism isn't so atheistic that it wears itself out showing that God doesn't exist. Rather, it declares that even if God did exist, that would change nothing. There you've got our point of view. Not that we believe that God exists, but we think that the problem of His existence is not the issue. In this sense existentialism is optimistic, a doctrine of action, and it is plain dishonesty for Christians to make no distinction between their own despair and ours and then to call us despairing.

QUESTIONS

1. *Why does Sartre use three separate terms*—anguish, forlornness, despair? *What, if any, are the differences among them?*
2. *What are some of the methods or devices Sartre uses to define existentialism? Why does he use more than one method or device? Compare the techniques that Sartre uses with those that Highet uses in defining Zen (p. 1281).*
3. *Sartre says that "when we say that a man is responsible for himself, we do not only mean that he is responsible for his own individuality, but that he is responsible for all men" (p. 1290). Write a brief essay explaining how, in the existentialist view, this is possible.*

Authors

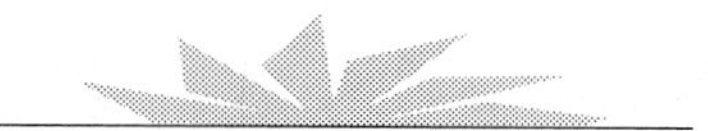

Edward Abbey (1927–1989)
American writer, essayist, and self-described "agrarian anarchist." Born in Pennsylvania, Abbey lived in the Southwest since 1948, when he arrived there to study at the University of New Mexico. A former ranger for the National Park Service, he took as his most pervasive theme the beauty of that region and the ways it has been despoiled by government, business, and tourism. Abbey's books include the novels *Fire on the Mountain* (1963), *The Monkey Wrench Gang* (1975), and *Good News* (1980). He has also published several collections of essays, among them *Desert Solitaire* (1968), *Abbey's Road* (1979), *Beyond the Wall: Essays from the Outside* (1984), and *One Life at a Time, Please* (1988).

Joseph Addison (1672–1719)
Eighteenth-century British essayist, poet, and dramatist. Born to an academic family, Addison was educated at Oxford and eventually became a member of the British Parliament. During a lag in his political career, Addison started writing for popular periodicals such as *The Tatler, The Spectator,* and *The Guardian.* After returning to office, he started his own political newspaper, *The Freeholder.*

Aesop (ca. 620–560 B.C.)
Legendary Greek storyteller. A collection of Greek fables, orally composed and transmitted, was ascribed to Aesop, a Phrygian slave, sometime in the third century A.D., but many are far older, being found on Egyptian papyri of 800 to 1,000 years earlier. Preserved and copied during the Middle Ages, the fables probably made their way into English through the work of the Dutch scholar Erasmus, who translated them into Latin; Erasmus's Latin text was later rendered into English. The fable has proved to be an enduring literary form, practiced in this century by writers as different as Orwell, Golding, and Nabokov.

Woody Allen (b. 1935)
Popular name of Heywood Allen, born Allen Stewart Konigsberg, American comedian, writer, playwright, actor, and film director. Allen began his career as a television comedy writer in the late 1950s. Eventually he became a comedian himself, then a screenwriter, playwright (*Don't Drink the Water,* 1966; *Play It Again, Sam,* 1969), and film director. His films include *Annie Hall* (1977), which won Allen the Academy Award for best director; *Manhattan* (1979), *The Purple Rose of Cairo* (1985), *Hannah and Her Sisters* (1986), *Crimes and Misdemeanors* (1989), *Alice* (1991), and *Bullets over Broadway* (1994). Allen's books include *Getting Even* (1971), *Without Feathers* (1975), and *Side Effects* (1980).

Dorothy Allison (b. 1949)
American poet, feminist, and lesbian activist. Born in Greenville, North Carolina, Allison received a college scholarship, which helped her to escape, in her words, her "family's heritage of poverty, jail, and illegitimate children." She specialized in urban anthropology at the

New School for Social Research, and she went on to teach writing, literature, and anthropology in the San Francisco area. Although her fiction and essays have won several awards, Allison considers herself primarily an autobiographically informed poet. Her books include *The Women Who Hate . . . Me* (1983), *Bastard Out of Carolina* (1992), *Skin: Talking about Sex, Class, and Literature* (1993), and *Cavedwelling* (1995).

Maya Angelou (b. 1928)
American author, playwright, actress, poet, and singer. Born in St. Louis, Angelou attended public schools in Arkansas and California before studying music and dance. In a richly varied career, she has been a cook, streetcar conductor, singer, actress, dancer, and teacher. Author of several volumes of poetry and ten plays (stage, screen, and television), Angelou may be best known for her poem "On the Pulse of Morning," which she read at the inauguration of President Bill Clinton in 1993. *I Know Why the Caged Bird Sings* (1970), the first volume of her autobiography, is one of the fullest accounts of the African-American woman's experience in contemporary literature.

Hannah Arendt (1906–1975)
German-American political scientist and philosopher. Born in Hanover, Germany, and educated at the University of Heidelberg, Arendt began her academic career in Germany but was forced to leave when Hitler came to power. Arriving in the United States in 1940, she became chief editor for a major publisher and a frequent lecturer on college campuses. Arendt taught at a number of American colleges and universities, finishing her career at the New School for Social Research in New York City. Of the dozen or so major books she wrote, three received greatest attention: *Eichmann in Jerusalem: A Report on the Banality of Evil* (1963); *On Revolution* (1963); and *The Origins of Totalitarianism* (1968).

Michael J. Arlen (b. 1930)
Movie and television critic, essayist. Born in London to Armenian parents, Arlen moved to the United States as a child and graduated from Harvard University in 1952. He began his writing career as a reporter for *Life* magazine. In 1966 he became a staff writer and television critic for *The New Yorker*. He has written about his parents in *Exiles* (1970) and about Armenia in the award-winning *Passage to Ararat* (1975). Arlen's books on the media include *The View from Highway 1* (1976) and *Thirty Seconds* (1980). The latter described and critiqued the production of AT&T commercials. His collections of essays include *Living Room War* (1969), which analyzed television coverage of the Vietnam War, and *The Camera Age* (1981).

Isaac Asimov (1920–1992)
American biochemist, science writer, and novelist. Born in Russia, Asimov was educated in the United States and received a Ph.D. in biochemistry from Columbia University. He became a member of the faculty at the School of Medicine, Boston University, in 1949 and he is currently professor of biochemistry there. An extraordinary prolific author, Asimov has published more than 250 books on topics as diverse as mathematics, astronomy, physics, chemistry, biology, mythology, Shakespeare, the Bible, and geography; his science fiction works include some of the most famous and influential in that genre. Among his books: *The Stars, Like the Dust* (1951), *Science, Numbers and I* (1968), *ABC's of the Earth* (1971), *The Road to Infinity* (1979), *The Exploding Suns: The Secrets of Supernovas* (1985), and *The Tyrannosaurus Prescription* (1989).

Margaret Atwood (b. 1939)
Canadian novelist, poet, and literary critic. Born in Ontario, Atwood received her degrees from the University of Toronto, Radcliffe College, and Harvard University. She began writing as a poet in the 1960s; her later fiction builds on many of the themes she began to explore in her poetry. Her novels are well regarded by both critics and the general public, an unusual feat for any writer. Her best-known novels include *The Edible Woman* (1969), *Surfacing* (1972), *Bodily Harm* (1982), *The Handmaid's Tale* (1986), which was made into a movie in 1990, *Cat's Eye* (1988), and *The Robber Bride* (1993).

Francis Bacon (1561–1626)
English civil servant, politician, statesman, and philosopher. Trained as a lawyer, Bacon served as a member of Parliament during the reign of Queen Elizabeth I. After her death, he found favor with King James I and advanced in government service to the position of lord chancellor. His career was cut short in 1621 when he was convicted of accepting bribes. Retired, he married and devoted the rest of his life to study and writing philosophical works. Bacon's only predecessor in the field of the essay was Michel de Montaigne. His books include *The Advancement of Learning* (1605), *Novum Organum* (1620), and *Essays.*

James Baldwin (1924–1987)
American essayist, novelist, and social activist. Baldwin was born in Harlem, became a minister at fourteen, and grew to maturity in an America disfigured by racism and prejudice. Only after moving to Paris in 1948 did he begin to write. Both his first novel, *Go Tell it on the Mountain* (1953), and his first play, *The Amen Corner* (1955), are autobiographical explorations. Although he would write other plays—*Blues for Mister Charlie* (1964) was one of his best—Baldwin concentrated his energies on novels such as *Giovanni's Room* (1956), *Another Country* (1962), and *If Beale Street Could Talk* (1974) as well as on essays. His stories are collected in *Going to Meet the Man* (1965); his essay collections, including *Notes of a Native Son* (1955), *Nobody Knows My Name* (1961), *The Fire Next Time* (1963), and *No Name in the Street* (1972), demonstrate Baldwin's skills as a social critic of insight and passion. A number of his most important essays and reviews have been gathered in *The Price of the Ticket* (1985).

Randall Balmer (b. 1954)
American scholar and educator. Balmer received his Ph.D. from Princeton and now teaches religion at Barnard College. Balmer regularly contributes to *The Christian Century,* and he narrated the PBS documentary *In the Beginning: The Creationist Controversy.* His books include *A Perfect Babel of Confusion* (1989) and *Mine Eyes Have Seen the Glory* (1989).

Benjamin R. Barber (b. 1939)
American scholar and educator. A professor of political science at Rutgers University, Barber also directs the Walt Whitman Center on that campus. His books include *Strong Democracy* (1984), *The Struggle for Democracy* (1988), and *An Aristocracy of Everyone* (1992). Barber's political commentary appears frequently in *Government & Opposition;* he has also published essays in *History Today, The New Republic, The New York Times, PS,* and *World Policy Journal.*

Roland Barthes (1915–1980)
French semiologist and cultural critic. Educated at the Sorbonne, Barthes taught French for many years throughout Rumania and Egypt. His international experience and his background in literary criticism led Barthes to write about everyday experiences, events, and objects with a critical eye towards their hidden meanings. He wrote numerous books which have influenced contemporary literary criticism, including *S/Z* (1974) and *The Pleasure of the Text* (1973).

Carl Becker (1873–1945)
American historian and teacher. Educated at the University of Wisconsin, Becker held several teaching appointments (Dartmouth, University of Kansas, University of Minnesota) before joining the faculty of Cornell University, where he taught from 1917 until 1941. The author of fifteen books, Becker's most important book is the text *Modern Democracy* (1941).

Bruno Bettelheim (1903–1990)
American child psychologist, teacher, and writer. Born and educated in Vienna, Bettelheim came to the United States in 1939 and joined the faculty of the University of Chicago in 1944, beginning a long and distinguished teaching career there (1944–73). He wrote several dozen books, including *Love Is Not Enough: The Treatment of Emotionally Disturbed Children* (1950), *The Informed Heart: Autonomy in a Mass Age* (1960), *The Children of the Dream* (1969), *The Uses of Enchantment: The Meaning and Importance of Fairy Tales* (1976), and *A Good Enough Parent* (1987).

Ambrose Bierce (1842–1914?)
American journalist, poet, and writer. Bierce was born the tenth child of a poor Ohio family. After serving in the Civil War and working as a journalist in San Francisco, he went to England, where he wrote comic and satiric sketches for several publications. In 1876, he returned to San Francisco as a reporter for William Randolph Hearst's *Examiner.* The death of his two sons, along with a divorce, might well have led him to Mexico, where he reportedly rode with Pancho Villa's revolutionaries; he disappeared and is presumed to have died there. Bierce's twelve-volume *Collected Works* (1909–12) include a generous sampling of his tales, essays, verses, and fables. Today, Bierce may be best known for *The Devil's Dictionary* (1906), a collection of ironic definitions compiled while he was a Hearst correspondent in Washington, D.C.

Caroline Bird (b. 1915)
American journalist, public-relations specialist, and writer. Bird attended Vassar College, graduated from the University of Toledo, and received her master's from the University of Wisconsin (1939). She worked as a researcher at *Newsweek* and *Fortune* in the 1940s, then moved into public relations, which she left after twenty years to pursue writing full time. Bird is the author of a number of books focussing on feminist concerns: *Born Female: The High Cost of Keeping Women Down* (1968), *Everything a Woman Needs to Know to Get Paid What She's Worth* (1973; revised edition, 1982), *The Two-Paycheck Marriage* (1979), *The Good Years: Your Life in the Twenty-first Century* (1983), and *The Case Against College* (1975).

William Blake (1757–1827)
English poet, artist, and writer. The son of a London haberdasher, Blake studied drawing at ten and became an engraver and illustrator by trade; he established a printing shop in London, where he engraved and printed his second volume of poems, *Songs of Innocence* (1789). Blake's poems and illuminations, reflecting an independent spirit seeking freedom from repression, take their inspiration from nature and religion, both being transformed into a deeply personal and unorthodox vision. His major works include the *Songs of Experience* (1794), *The Four Zoas* (1803), *Milton* (1804), *Jerusalem* (1809), and *The Marriage of Heaven and Hell* (1793).

Wayne C. Booth (b. 1921)
American writer, literary critic, and teacher. After receiving a Ph.D. from the University of Chicago in 1950, Booth began a teaching career that has taken him to Haverford College, Earlham College, and back to the University of Chicago, where he is now professor of English. Among Booth's books are *The Rhetoric of Fiction* (1961; revised edition, 1983), *Now Don't Try to Reason with Me* (1970), *A Rhetoric of Irony* (1974), *Modern Dogma and the Rhetoric of Assent* (1974), *Critical Understanding: The Powers and Limits of Pluralism* (1979), *The Vocation of a Teacher* (1988), *The Company We Keep: An Ethics of Fiction* (1988), and *The Art of Growing Older* (1992).

Jacob Bronowski (1908–1974)
English mathematician, scientist, and writer. Born in Poland and educated in England, where he received a Ph.D. in mathematics from Cambridge in 1933, Bronowski served as a university lecturer before entering government service during World War II. From 1950 until 1963, he was head of research for Britain's National Coal Board; from 1964 until his death, he was a resident fellow at the Salk Institute, La Jolla, California. The author of many books, among them *Science and Human Values* (1956; 1965), *Nature and Knowledge* (1969), *Magic, Science, and Civilization* (published posthumously, 1978), Bronowski is best known for the thirteen-part television series "The Ascent of Man" (1973–74).

Anthony Burgess (1917–1993)
[John] Anthony Burgess [Wilson], English novelist, playwright, editor, and writer. Born in Manchester, England, and a graduate of Manchester University, Burgess was a lecturer and teacher of English until 1954, when he became an education officer in the Colonial Service, stationed in Malaya. His writing career began there. In 1959, when he was told that he had a year to live, Burgess returned to England and wrote five novels in one year. After that he

wrote several dozen more, including *A Clockwork Orange* (1962), *Enderby Outside* (1968), *Earthly Powers* (1980), *The End of the World News: An Entertainment* (1984), *Any Old Iron* (1989), and *A Dead Man in Deptford* (1993). In addition, Burgess has written critical studies, giving special attention to James Joyce and D. H. Lawrence.

Herbert Butterfield (1900–1979)
British educator and writer. He was educated at Cambridge and has spent his career there, serving in a variety of capacities including professor of modern history (1944–63), vice-chancellor (1959–61), and Regius Professor. A specialist in eighteenth-century English and French history, Butterfield wrote a classic study, *The Whig Interpretation of History* (1931), as well as *Lord North and the People* (1949), *George III and the Historians* (1957), and *Writings on Christianity and History* (1979), a collection of Butterfield's essays edited by C. T. McIntire.

Edward Hallett Carr (1892–1982)
English historian, journalist, and statesman. After studying classics at Trinity College, Cambridge, Carr spent twenty years in the diplomatic service. In 1936, he became professor of international relations at University College in Wales and began to write about diplomatic history. In 1941, he became assistant editor of the *Times* (London). In 1946, he left teaching and journalism to begin work on his major opus, a fourteen-volume study titled *A History of Russia*, which he completed in 1978.

Stephen L. Carter (b. 1954)
African-American essayist and professor of Law. Teaching at Yale and writing on a wide range of public issues, Carter has published in *The New Yorker*, *Esquire*, *Current*, and *Commonweal*. His books include his controversial, autobiographical collection of essays, *Reflections of an Affirmative Action Baby* (1991), the award-winning *The Culture of Disbelief* (1993), which argues for increasing the role of religion in American life and politics, and *Confirmation Mess* (1994), which explores the process of making federal appointments.

Lord Chesterfield (1694–1773)
Philip Dormer Stanhope, fourth earl of Chesterfield, English statesman, diplomat, and writer. Although attracted to the literary world as a youth, Chesterfield entered diplomatic service and held important posts in Holland and Ireland. His literary reputation rests on his *Letters*. Addressed to his son Philip and written with near-daily frequency beginning in 1737, they became a handbook of gentlemanly conduct when they were published in 1774. In a now-famous episode, Samuel Johnson sent the *Plan* for his *Dictionary* to Chesterfield but received no response. Even though Chesterfield published two favorable reviews when the *Dictionary* was printed, Johnson, always sensitive to slights, wrote his "Letter to Lord Chesterfield," scorning the nobleman's praise.

Samuel L. Clemens (1835–1910)
American novelist, journalist, humorist, and writer. First apprenticed as a printer, Clemens was by turns a riverboat pilot, gold prospector, and journalist. Under the pen name Mark Twain, he became famous when his short story "The Celebrated Jumping Frog of Calaveras County" was published in 1867. Clemens wrote a good deal and lectured widely after that. At least two of his novels, *The Adventures of Tom Sawyer* (1876) and *The Adventures of Huckleberry Finn* (1885), rank as American classics.

Judith Ortiz Cofer (b. 1952)
Novelist, poet, and essayist. Born in Hormigueros, Puerto Rico, Cofer spent much of her childhood traveling between her Puerto Rican home and Paterson, New Jersey. Educated at Florida Atlantic University and Oxford, Cofer currently teaches bilingual workshops in nonfiction writing and poetry at the University of Georgia. Her work has appeared in *Callaloo, Southern Review, Prairie Schooner, Appalachee Quarterly, Kansas Quarterly*, and *Kalliope*. Her books include *Peregrina* (1986) and *The Line of the Sun* (1989). *Silent Dancing* (1990) shows her ongoing efforts to combine her bicultural family traditions with the language possibilities of both Spanish and English.

Carl Cohen (b. 1931)
American philosopher and teacher. After taking a Ph.D. in philosophy at the University of California, Los Angeles (1955), Cohen became a member of the Department of Philosophy at the University of Michigan, Ann Arbor, where he has been professor of philosophy since 1960. With special interests in political philosophy, the philosophy of law and medical ethics, Cohen has published widely in a number of journals. His books include *Civil Disobedience: Conscience, Tactics, and the Law* (1971) and *Democracy* (1973).

Jill Ker Conway (b. 1934)
Historian, educator, and women's rights advocate. Born in the Australian outback, Conway has spent her adult life in the United States and Canada. She received her Ph.D. from Harvard, taught history at the University of Toronto, and went on to become the first female president of Smith College. She received popular acclaim for her autobiography *The Road from Coorain* (1989). Her scholarly books include *The Female Experience in Eighteenth- and Nineteenth-Century America: A Guide to the History of Women* (1982) and *The Politics of Women's Education: Perspectives from Asia, Africa, and Latin America* (1993).

Mason Cooley (b. 1927)
American teacher. Born in Tennessee's Blue Ridge Mountains, Cooley moved to San Diego as a child. He studied at San Diego State University and the New School for Social Research before receiving his Ph.D. from the University of California at Berkeley. He now teaches at the College of Staten Island. In writing his aphorisms, he says he follows the example of La Rochefoucauld in getting as much editorial advice as possible from his friends.

Stephanie Coontz (b. 1944)
American social historian. Born in Seattle, Washington, Coontz received degrees from the University of California at Berkeley and the University of Washington. Most of her research exposes common misconceptions about "traditional" American families, and attempts to explain why "nostalgia for a mythical Golden Age will not help the American families of the twenty-first century." Her articles have appeared in *Harper's Magazine, Vogue,* and *Lear's.* Her books include *Women's Work, Men's Property* (1986), *The Social Origins of Private Life* (1988), and *The Way We Never Were* (1992).

Aaron Copland (1900–1990)
American composer, conductor, and writer. Born in New York City, Copland studied music theory and practice in Paris (1921–24), then returned to New York to write, organize concert series, publish American scores, and further the cause of the American composer. After some experimentation with adapting jazz to classical composition, Copland developed a distinctly American style, incorporating American folk songs and legends into three ballet scores: *Billy the Kid* (1938), *Rodeo* (1942), and *Appalachian Spring* (1944; Pulitzer Prize); poetry into *Twelve Poems of Emily Dickinson,* songs for voice and piano (1950); and historical material into *Lincoln Portrait* (1942), for narrator and orchestra. Copland also wrote *about* music.

William Cronon (b. 1954)
American environmental historian. Born in Connecticut and raised in Wisconsin, Cronon was a double major in history and English at the University of Wisconsin. After winning a Rhodes Scholarship and completing a degree at Oxford, Cronon taught at Yale until he returned to his alma mater. He now divides his time between the history department and the environmental studies program there. His books include *Changes in the Land* (1983), *Nature's Metropolis* (1991), and *Under an Open Sky* (1992).

Joan Didion (b. 1934)
American novelist, essayist, and screenwriter. A native Californian, Didion studied at the University of California, Berkeley. After winning *Vogue* magazine's Prix de Paris contest for excellence in writing, she went to work for the magazine. Didion rose from promotional copywriter to associate feature editor before leaving *Vogue* in 1963, the year her first novel, *Run River,* was published. Since then, she has written four more novels (*Play It as It Lays,* 1971, *A Book of Common Prayer,* 1977, *Democracy,* 1984, and *After Henry,* 1992). A

frequent contributor to magazines such as *Vogue* and *Harper's Bazaar,* Didion's essay collections include *Slouching towards Bethlehem,* (1969) and *The White Album* (1979). *Salvador,* a work of reportage based on her visit to El Salvador in 1983, marked Didion's growing concern with politics. *Miami* (1987), another book of reportage, is an attempt to come to terms with the complexities of an American city.

Annie Dillard (b. 1945)
American writer of prose and poetry. Dillard received a B.A. and an M.A. from Hollins College. An observer of the natural world, Dillard published a collection of poems, *Tickets for a Prayer Wheel,* and a Pulitzer Prize-winning nonfiction narrative, *Pilgrim at Tinker Creek,* in 1974. Since then she has written books on a range of subjects, including *Holy the Firm* (1977), a true story, *An American Childhood* (1987), a memoir, and a book of theory, *Living by Fiction* (1982). *The Writing Life* (1989) tells stories from the working life of a writer. Dillard has written one book of essays, *Teaching a Stone to Talk* (1982), and one novel, *The Living* (1992), about pioneers on Puget Sound.

Kildare Dobbs (b. 1923)
Canadian writer. Born in India and educated at Cambridge, Dobbs spent time in the British foreign service before becoming a journalist and an editor; he is now a freelance writer. He has written autobiographical sketches (*Running to Paradise,* 1962), short stories (*Pride and Fall,* 1981), and essays, which have been collected in *Reading the Time* (1968) and *Anatolian Suite* (1989).

John Donne (1572–1631)
English poet, essayist, and cleric. Born into an old Roman Catholic family, Donne attended Oxford and Cambridge, but could not receive a degree because of his religion. He studied, although never practiced, law and, after quietly abandoning Catholicism some time during the 1590s, entered government service. In 1615, he was received into the Anglican Church. One of the greatest religious orators of his age, Donne became dean of St. Paul's Cathedral in 1621. Donne's literary reputation rests on his poetry as well as on his sermons, among them "Let Me Wither," and devotions.

Gerald Early (b. 1952)
African-American scholar and cultural critic. Born in Philadelphia, Early earned degrees from Cornell University and the University of Pennsylvania. Now on the faculty at Washington University, Early continues to write on popular issues for general readers in addition to pursuing his scholarly work; his essays and articles have appeared in *The Kenyon Review, Antioch Review, Black Scholar,* and *American Quarterly.* He has written numerous essays, now collected in *Lure and Loathing* (1993), *The Culture of Bruising* (1994), and *Tuxedo Junction* (1989).

Gretel Ehrlich (b. 1946)
American poet, essayist, journalist, and filmmaker. Born in Santa Barbara, California, Ehrlich studied at Bennington College in Vermont, at the UCLA Film School, and at the New School for Social Research in New York before working as a documentary filmmaker. Arriving in Wyoming to film a documentary on sheep herding for the American Public Broadcasting Service, she fell in love with the place and stayed. In addition to her poetry, Ehrlich has published two collections of essays—*The Solace of Open Spaces* (1985) and *Islands, the Universe, Home* (1987)—as well as a novel, *Heart Mountain* (1988). Her work has appeared in *The New York Times, Harper's Magazine, The Atlantic Monthly,* and *Antaeus.*

Lars Eighner (b. 1948)
American writer. Born in Corpus Christi, Texas, Eighner attended the University of Texas and now lives and works in Austin, Texas, as a freelance writer. Describing himself as a "skeptical Democrat," Eighner has worked in hospitals and drug-crisis programs. His articles have appeared in *Threepenny Review, Utne Reader,* and *Harper's Magazine.* His book, *Travels with Lizbeth* (1993), describes his three years of surviving on the streets with his dog.

Loren Eiseley (1907–1977)
American anthropologist, sociologist, archaeologist, historian of science, and poet. Educated at the University of Ne-

braska and the University of Pennsylvania, Eiseley taught at the University of Kansas, Oberlin, and finally back at the University of Pennsylvania, where he remained for thirty years. A humanist concerned with the whole spectrum of life on earth and our place in it, he established a national reputation with his writings: *The Immense Journey* (1957), *Darwin's Century: Evolution and the Men Who Discovered It* (1958), *The Firmament of Time* (revised edition, 1960), *The Mind as Nature* (1962), *The Night Country* (1971), and *The Unexpected Universe* (1972). A collection of Eiseley's poems, *Another Kind of Autumn*, was published posthumously in 1977.

Ralph Waldo Emerson (1803–1882)
American poet, philosopher, and essayist. One of the most influential writers in the American tradition, Emerson entered Harvard at the age of fourteen. After graduation in 1821, he taught school for several years before beginning theological studies in 1825. In 1829, he was ordained a Unitarian minister. In 1832, he resigned his pastorate, retiring to Concord, Massachusetts, to a life of study and reflection. With the publication of his first book, *Nature* in 1836, Emerson became an important force in the development of American transcendentalism. Emerson's occasional lectures at Harvard and the publication of his *Essays* (1841) enhanced his reputation.

Daniel Mark Epstein (b. 1948)
American poet, playwright, and essayist. Educated at Kenyon College, Epstein is the author of several books of poetry (including *No Vacancies in Hell*, 1973; *The Follies*, 1977; *Young Men's Gold*, 1978; *The Book of Fortune*, (1982), two plays (*Jenny and the Phoenix*, 1977; *The Gayety Burlesque*, 1978), and a collection of essays (*Star of Wonder*, 1986). He is much concerned with myth and ritual, both political and religious, and with the American character as shown in his most recent book *Sister Aimee: The Life of Aimee Semple McPherson* (1993). Epstein is a frequent contributor to *The Atlantic, The New Yorker*, and *The New Criterion*.

William Faulkner (1897–1962)
American novelist. A native of Mississippi, Faulkner lived his whole life there, with the exception of a short time in military service and a period spent in Hollywood as a screenwriter. He attended the University of Mississippi in the town of Oxford. With the help of the author Sherwood Anderson, he published his first novel, *Soldier's Pay*, in 1926. His work, which won him a Nobel Prize in 1949, often depicts life in fictional Yoknapatawpha County, an imaginative reconstruction of the area near Oxford. Faulkner's major novels include *The Sound and the Fury* (1929), *As I Lay Dying* (1930), *Sanctuary* (1931), *Light in August* (1932), and *Absalom! Absalom!* (1936). His short stories are included in the collections *These Thirteen* (1931), *Go Down, Moses and Other Stories* (1942), and *The Collected Stories of William Faulkner* (1950).

Anne Fausto-Sterling (b. 1944)
American developmental geneticist and feminist. Born in New York City, Fausto-Sterling was educated at the University of Wisconsin and Brown University, where she now teaches. Much of her scholarship challenges the tendency of the scientific community to link social categories of gender with biology and genetics. In her book *Myths of Gender* (1992), Fausto-Sterling systematically reveals the methodological flaws and underlying ideology of biological determinist theories. She has published articles in *Dædalus, Discover, Science, Genetics*, and *Women's Studies Quarterly*.

Robert Finch (b. 1943)
American writer. Finch combines a keen interest in the world of the naturalist with a concern for the craft of writing. He has published four books—*Common Ground: A Naturalist's Cape Cod* (1981), *The Primal Place* (1983), *Outlands; Journeys to the Outer Edges of Cape Cod* (1986), and *Cape Cod: Its Natural and Cultural History* (1993)—and co-edited, with John Elder, *The Norton Book of Nature Writing* (1990). Publicity director for the Cape Cod Museum of Natural History, he also serves on the staff of the Bread Loaf Writers' Conference at Middlebury College.

Frances FitzGerald (b. 1940)
American journalist and writer. Coming from a family with a strong interest in politics and international affairs (her father was a deputy director of the CIA, her mother an ambassador to the United Nations), FitzGerald has worked as a free-lance journalist since her graduation from Radcliffe in 1962. She went to Vietnam in 1966 and achieved critical success with her first book, *Fire in the Lake: The Vietnamese and Americans in Vietnam* (1972); it won four major awards, including a Pulitzer Prize and a National Book Award. Her other books include *America Revised: History Schoolbooks in the Twentieth Century* (1979) and *Cities on a Hill: Journeys through American Cultures* (1986). Although FitzGerald regularly contributes to several American periodicals, she is most closely associated with *The New Yorker*.

Benjamin Franklin (1706–1790)
American statesman, inventor, writer, and diplomat. Apprenticed at the age of twelve to his brother, a Philadelphia printer, Franklin learned all aspects of the trade, from setting type to writing editorials. At the age of twenty-four, he was editor and publisher of the *Pennsylvania Gazette.* In 1733, he began writing *Poor Richard's Almanack,* a collection of aphorisms and advice. He retired from business at the age of forty-two to devote himself to study and research but soon found himself involved in colonial politics. From 1757 until 1763, he was diplomatic representative for the colonies in England. He served as a member of the committee appointed to draft the Declaration of Independence and later as minister to France and delegate to the Paris peace conference that officially concluded the Revolutionary War.

H. Bruce Franklin (b. 1934)
Scholar and critic. Born in Brooklyn, New York, Franklin was educated at Amherst College and Stanford University. After a stint as a tugboat deckhand and several years in military service, Franklin returned to Stanford as a scholar, critic, and social activist. This combination caused him to be the first tenured professor to be fired from Stanford after he urged his students to protest secret military testing on college campuses. He now teaches at the Newark campus of Rutgers University. Much of his popular writing explores the connections between modern war and the media. He also writes on science fiction and American literature. His books include *Victim as Criminal and Artist* (1978), *American Prisoners and ex-Prisoners* (1982), *War Stars* (1988), and *Prison Literature in America* (1989). His essays have been published in *Science Fiction Studies, The Nation, The Progressive,* and *The Georgia Review.*

Erich Fromm (1900–1980)
German-American psychoanalyst and social philosopher. Born in Frankfurt, he received a Ph.D. in philosophy from the University of Heidelberg, then trained at the Psychoanalytic Institute in Berlin. He immigrated to the United States in 1934, where he held a succession of academic appointments at Columbia University, Bennington College, Yale University, Michigan State University, and New York University. In establishing a reputation as a gifted and innovative psychoanalyst, Fromm wrote twenty books, among them *Escape from Freedom* (1941), *The Forgotten Language* (1951), *The Sane Society* (1955), and *The Art of Loving* (1956).

Robert Frost (1874–1963)
American poet, teacher, and lecturer. This quintessential "New England" poet was born in California and spent his childhood there. He studied briefly at Dartmouth and Harvard, married, and tried farming for a while. In 1912, he moved to England, where his first book of poems, *A Boy's Will,* was published. In 1914, his second collection, *North of Boston,* received favorable reviews, and the poet returned to the United States. For the next fifty years, Frost was a respected and successful poet, writing about the people and landscape of New England in a voice sometimes lyric, sometimes humorous, sometimes desolate. During the last part of his life, Frost held a number of teaching appointments and lectured widely on poetry and the role of the poet.

Northrop Frye (1912–1991)
Canadian literary critic and teacher. Educated at the University of Toronto

and at Merton College, Oxford, he was a member of the faculty at Victoria College, University of Toronto, since 1939. Although Frye specialized in Renaissance and Romantic literature, he had also written on Milton, the Bible, and Canadian literature. He published more than forty books, including *Fearful Symmetry: A Study of William Blake* (1947), *Anatomy of Criticism* (1957), *The Educated Imagination* (1964), *The Secular Scripture: A Study of the Structure of Romance* (1976), *The Great Code: The Bible and Literature* (1982), *A Natural Perspective: The Development of Shakespearean Comedy and Romance* (1988), *Double Vision* (1991), and *The Eternal Act of Creation* (1993).

Paul Fussell (b. 1924)
American writer and teacher. After distinguished military service in World War II, Fussell earned a Ph.D. at Harvard and became an instructor of English at Connecticut College. In 1955, he was hired by the University of Pennsylvania, where he is professor of English today. Fussell's early books deal with poetic theory (*Poetic Meter and Poetic Form,* 1965) and eighteenth-century literature (*Samuel Johnson and the Life of Writing,* 1971). With the publication of *The Great War and Modern Memory* (1975) and *Abroad: British Literary Traveling between the Wars* (1980), his attention shifted to the twentieth century. In 1983, he published *Class: A Guide through the American Status System.* Two recent essay collections are *The Boy Scout Handbook and Other Observations* (1982) and *Thank God for the Atom Bomb and Other Essays.* Fussell has also edited *The Norton Book of Travel* (1987) and *The Norton Book of Modern War* (1990).

Henry Louis Gates, Jr. (b. 1950)
African-American scholar and literary critic. Born and raised in West Virginia, Gates was educated at Yale and Cambridge. Now a professor at Harvard University, Gates balances his time between editing African-American literature, writing literary criticism, and writing for general audiences. A proponent of multiculturalism and educational reform, Gates has been responsible for collecting thousands of short stories, poems, reviews, and other literary works written by and about African-Americans in the nineteenth and early twentieth centuries. For the general public, he created the television documentary "The Image of the Black in the Western Imagination," and he has also written for *The New Yorker, Newsweek, Sports Illustrated,* and *The New York Times.* His books include *Figures in Black* (1987), *The Signifying Monkey* (1988), *Loose Canons* (1992), and his autobiography, *Colored People* (1994).

Willard Gaylin (b. 1925)
American psychiatrist and psychoanalyst. After receiving an M.D. degree from Case Western Reserve University, Gaylin did advanced work in psychoanalytic medicine at Columbia and opened a private practice in psychiatry. In 1970, he co-founded the Hastings Center, Institute of Society, Ethics and the Life Sciences at Hastings-on-Hudson, New York. His writings reflect a broad range of interests: *In the Service of Their Country: War Resisters in Prison* (1970), *Partial Justice: A Study of Bias in Sentencing* (1974), *Feelings: Our Vital Signs* (1979), and *Rediscovering Love* (1986). Gaylin's study of the use of the insanity defense, *The Killing of Bonnie Garland: A Question of Justice* (1982), received considerable attention.

Herb Goldberg (b. 1937)
American psychologist and nonfiction writer. Born in Berlin, Germany, Goldberg studied at City College (now City College of the City University of New York) and at Adelphi University; since then he has taught psychology at California State University in Los Angeles. Goldberg's books, which interpret and explain for the lay reader the phenomena he deals with as a professional, include *Creative Aggression* (1974), *The Hazards of Being Male* (1976), *The New Male: From Self-Destruction to Self-Care* (1979), and *The New Male-Female Relationship* (1983).

William Golding (1911–1993)
English novelist. Educated at Marlborough Grammar School and Oxford, Golding was a schoolmaster at Bishop Wordsworth's School, Salisbury, before becoming a novelist at the age of forty-three. His novels are characterized by

their darkly poetic tone, dense symbolism, and rejection of societal norms. His most famous work is *Lord of the Flies* (1954), a story of schoolboys marooned on an island who revert to savagery. Other novels include *Pincher Martin* (1956), *The Spire* (1964), *The Pyramid* (1967), *Rites of Passage* (1980), *Close Quarters* (1987), and *Fire Down Below* (1989). In 1983, Golding received the Nobel Prize for literature.

Jewelle Gomez (b. 1948)
Novelist, teacher, and lesbian feminist activist. Born and raised in Boston, Gomez worked as a production assistant and stage manager after her education at Northeastern and the Columbia School of Journalism. She now lives in San Francisco, contributing articles to *Advocate, Village Voice, Ms.*, and *Signs*. She has published two books of poetry, *The Lipstick Papers* (1980) and *Flamingos and Bears* (1987); a novel, *The Gilda Stories* (1991); and a book of essays *Forty-Three Septembers* (1993). Gomez has been strongly influenced by her mixed African-American and Native American heritages and by the grandmother who raised her.

Mary Gordon (b. 1949)
American novelist. Born on Long Island, New York, and educated at Barnard College and Syracuse University, Gordon now teaches at Barnard College. She has contributed to *Salmagundi, South Atlantic Quarterly, America*, and *The Nation*. Her books include *The Company of Women* (1981), *Men and Angels* (1985), *Good Boys and Dead Girls* (1991), and *The Rest of Life* (1993). Much of her writing is autobiographical and revolves around issues of Catholicism.

Stephen Jay Gould (b. 1941)
American paleontologist, writer, and teacher. Gould grew up in New York City, graduated from Antioch College, and received his Ph.D. from Columbia in 1967, joining Harvard the same year. Now professor of geology and zoology at Harvard, Gould teaches paleontology, biology, and history of science. Witty and fluent, Gould demystifies science for lay readers in essays written for a regular column in *Natural History* magazine and collected in *Ever Since Darwin* (1977), *The Panda's Thumb* (1980), *Hen's Teeth and Horse's Toes* (1983), *The Flamingo's Smile* (1985), and *Eight Little Piggies* (1993). His books include *Ontogeny and Phylogeny* (1977), *Time's Arrow, Time's Cycle: Myth and Metaphor in the Discovery of Geological Time* (1987), *Wonderful Life* (1989), and *Between Home and Heaven* (1992).

Robert Graves (1895–1985)
British poet, novelist, and classical scholar. After private education, distinguished service in World War I, and study at St. John's College, Oxford, Graves held a brief appointment at the University of Cairo before becoming a professional writer. In a long and prolific career, he published 130 volumes, ranging from poetry and novels to essays, lectures, and criticism. He is perhaps best known for his classic memoir, *Goodbye to All That* (1929); his historical novels, *I, Claudius* (1934) and *King Jesus* (1946); his work on writing, *The Reader over Your Shoulder* (1943); and his study of poetic myth, *The White Goddess* (1948). Graves's classical scholarship provided much of the material for his fiction and poetry.

Charlotte Gray (b. 1948)
Canadian political journalist. Born in Sheffield, England, and educated at Oxford and the London School of Economics, Gray became a political journalist, in 1978 winning the Pakenham Award for the "most promising young woman journalist." She is now a contributing editor to the Canadian periodical *Saturday Night*, and she appears frequently as a political commentator on CBC radio and CTV television.

Stephen Greenblatt (b. 1943)
Literary critic and scholar. Born in Cambridge, Massachusetts, and educated at Yale University and Cambridge, Greenblatt now teaches at the University of California at Berkeley. He has been credited with coining the term and the methodology of "new historicism," a field of inquiry that considers the traditional arts (like plays, novels, and paintings) alongside the social phenomena of that historical time (like newspapers, cartoons, political tracts, and advertisements). His books include *Renaissance Self-Fashioning* (1980),

Shakespearean Negotiations (1988), and *Marvelous Possessions* (1991).

Lani Guinier (b. 1950)
Law professor and writer. Born of black and Jewish parents in Queens, New York, Guinier attended Yale Law School with the Clintons and now teaches at the University of Pennsylvania. President Clinton nominated her for assistant attorney general but then withdrew the nomination after protests arose over her alleged political views. Guinier has since written a book, *The Tyranny of the Majority* (1994), and numerous articles about the implications of her experience.

David Guterson (b. 1956)
American travel writer. Born in Seattle, Washington, and educated at the University of Washington, Guterson taught high school for many years. Based on his own educational experience and that of his children, he has written numerous essays and a book, *Family Matters* (1993), in favor of homeschooling. His most recent book is a novel, *Snow Falling on Cedars* (1994). Guterson is a contributing editor to *Harper's Magazine* and has also published in *The New York Times Magazine* and *Utne Reader*. Often writing about everyday subjects like sports or shopping malls, Guterson says that he has an "ethical and moral duty . . . to tell stories that inspire readers to consider more deeply who they are."

Nathaniel Hawthorne (1804–1864)
American novelist, short-story writer, and essayist. Educated at Bowdoin College, Hawthorne returned to his home in Salem, Massachusetts, and devoted himself to writing tales. In 1837, *Twice-told Tales* appeared, and Hawthorne became a public literary figure. After his marriage in 1842, he and his wife moved to Concord, where they lived for three years. In 1846, Hawthorne was appointed surveyor of the Port of Salem, the first of a number of political positions that would culminate in his appointment as American consul in Liverpool, England (1853). Although he may be best known for his short stories or novels—*The Scarlet Letter* (1850) and *The House of the Seven Gables* (1851) in particular—Hawthorne also wrote a series of valuable sketches for the *Atlantic Monthly*.

S. I. Hayakawa (1906–1992)
Samuel Ichize Hayakawa, Japanese-American writer, educator, and politician. Before becoming president of San Francisco State College, Hayakawa established himself as a scholar and pioneer in language and semantics with books such as *Language in Action* (1941; revised as *Language in Thought and Action*, 1949), *Our Language and Our World* (1959), and *Symbol, Status and Personality* (1963). His tenure as college president (1969–73) was marked by student demonstrations and protests. Throughout, Hayakawa asserted a firm belief in authority, traditional values, and the rule of law and order. With the same ideas as a campaign platform, he was elected to the United States Senate, where he served from 1977 until 1982.

Brian Hayes (b. 1949)
American science writer. Born in New Jersey and raised in Pennsylvania, Hayes now lives in North Carolina. After a three-year stint as a laboratory technician, Hayes became a staff writer for *Scientific American*, and he wrote a monthly column on the pleasures of computing. He has been a freelance writer since the mid-1980s and contributes regularly to both *American Scientist* and *The Sciences*.

William Hazlitt (1778–1830)
British essayist, journalist, and literary critic. After deciding not to pursue his early training as a Unitarian minister, Hazlitt began writing on art, politics, and society and eventually made a career as a literary critic. His publications include *Characters of Shakespeare's Plays* (1817), *Lectures on the English Poets* (1818), *A View of the English Stage* (1818), *Lectures on the English Comic Writers* (1819), and *The Spirit of the Age* (1825).

Maggie Helwig (b. 1961)
Canadian poet and self-described "radical Christian anarchist." Educated at the University of Trent, Helwig worked as a bookstore clerk and typesetter before founding her own publishing company, Lowlife Publishing. The daughter of prominent Canadian poet

David Helwig, she has published numerous collections of poetry including *Walking Through Fire* (1981), *Tongues of Men and Angels* (1985), *Eden* (1987), and *Talking Prophet Blues* (1989). Helwig's collection of essays is *Desire and the Dead* (1990).

Ernest Hemingway (1899–1961)
American novelist and short-story writer. Hemingway began his professional writing career as a journalist, reporting for newspapers in Kansas City and Toronto. In the 1920s, he lived in Paris, a part of the American expatriate community that included Gertrude Stein and Ezra Pound. Hemingway's literary reputation rests on his short stories, collected in volumes like *In Our Time* (1925) and *Men without Women* (1927), and his novels, including *The Sun Also Rises* (1926), *A Farewell to Arms* (1929), and *For Whom the Bell Tolls* (1940). *The Old Man and the Sea* (1952) was the last work published during his lifetime. Hemingway received the Nobel Prize for literature in 1954.

Gilbert Highet (1906–1978)
American scholar of classical literature, poet, writer, and teacher. Born in Glasgow, Scotland, Highet was educated at the University of Glasgow and Oxford University. From 1932 until 1936, he taught at St. John's College, Oxford, then accepted an appointment at Columbia University, where he taught Greek and Latin literature for thirty years. Considered a master teacher, Highet communicated his enthusiasm for classical literature not only in the classroom, but also in a number of books. Of the fourteen books he wrote, perhaps the most famous are *The Classical Tradition* (1949), *The Art of Teaching* (1950), and *The Anatomy of Satire* (1962).

John Holt (1923–1985)
American theorist of education. Born in New York City, Holt taught for many years in high schools in Colorado and Massachusetts and then at Harvard University and the University of California at Berkeley. His numerous books, based on his teaching experience and all centrally concerned with education, include *How Children Fail* (1964), *How Children Learn* (1967), *The Under-Achieving School* (1967), *Freedom and Beyond* (1972), and *Escape from Childhood* (1984).

Langston Hughes (1902–1967)
American poet, playwright, and writer. An extraordinarily prolific writer, Hughes published in his lifetime seventeen volumes of poetry, two novels, seven collections of short stories, and twenty-six plays. He emerged as a key figure in the Harlem Renaissance of the 1920s and 1930s, an awakening of black artists centered in New York City. Encouraged by his fellow artists, Hughes published his first collection of poems, *The Weary Blues* (1926). Although critical response was mixed, the degree of public acceptance achieved by Hughes with this and subsequent works enabled him to become the first black American writer to support himself from his writing and lecturing.

Zora Neale Hurston (1891–1960)
American writer and folklorist. A central figure of the Harlem Renaissance of the 1920s and 1930s, Hurston was born in Eatonville, Florida, daughter of a Baptist preacher and a seamstress. She attended Howard University and received a B.A. from Barnard in 1928, where she studied anthropology and developed an interest in black folk traditions and in oral history. Hurston's writing, pulled from her knowledge of folklore, reveals a vigorous, rhythmical, direct prose style that has influenced later writers. Rediscovered by the women's movement, Hurston's works include plays (e.g., *Mule Bone: A Comedy of Negro Life in Three Acts*, 1931, with Langston Hughes) as well as novels (*Their Eyes Were Watching God*, 1937; *Moses, Man of the Mountain*, 1939; *Seraph on the Suwanee*, 1948).

Barbara Huttmann (b. 1935)
American nurse and teacher. Actively involved in patient-advocacy, Huttmann has written two books about her experiences as a nurse, *The Patient's Advocate* (1981) and *Code Blue* (1982).

Ada Louise Huxtable (b. 1921)
American architecture critic and social commentator. Born in New York City, Huxtable studied at Hunter College and New York University before working as curator for architecture and design at the Museum of Modern Art.

Later, she studied architecture in Italy, worked as a freelance writer, and was architecture critic for *The New York Times* from 1963 to 1973. Huxtable won the Pulitzer Prize for distinguished criticism in 1970 and recently received the prestigious MacArthur Foundation Award. Her books include *Pier Luigi Nervi* (1960), *Classic New York* (1964), *Will They Ever Finish Bruckner Boulevard?* (1970), and *Kicked a Building Lately?* (1976).

Thomas Jefferson (1743–1826)
Third president of the United States, lawyer, architect, and writer. An educated man of significant accomplishments in many fields, Jefferson entered politics in his native state of Virginia, serving in the House of Burgesses and eventually becoming governor (1779–81). He founded the University of Virginia (1809) and designed both the buildings and curriculum. Jefferson served as secretary of state to Washington (1789–93), vice-president to John Adams (1797–1801), and president (1801–09). A fluent stylist, Jefferson wrote books on science, religion, architecture, even Anglo-Saxon grammar, but is probably best known for writing the final draft of the Declaration of Independence. Preliminary drafts were done by committee, but it was to Jefferson that the members turned for the last revision.

Jesus (c. 6 B.C.–c. A.D. 30)
Jesus of Nazareth, first-century Jewish religious teacher. Acknowledged by Christians as the Son of God, Jesus spent his short public career in Palestine, preaching a message of conversion and repentance. One of his favorite teaching devices was the parable, a literary form with a long history and used extensively in rabbinic tradition.

Samuel Johnson (1709–1784)
English lexicographer, critic, moralist, and journalist. In spite of childhood poverty, poor eyesight, and scant advanced education, Johnson achieved renown in his day as wit, conversationalist, and astute observer of the human experience. In 1737, having failed as a schoolmaster, he sought his fortune in London, where he soon found work contributing essays and poems to *The Gentleman's Magazine*. Johnson's literary career prospered as he wrote and published poems, plays, and essays. In 1750, he founded *The Rambler*, a popular periodical containing essays, fables, and criticism. One of the greatest prose stylists of the English language, Johnson prepared the monumental *Dictionary* (1755) that bears his name, wrote *Rasselas* (1759), a novel, and *Lives of the Poets* (1779–81).

June Jordan (b. 1936)
African-American poet, essayist, and educator. Born in Harlem, New York, Jordan was educated at Barnard College and the University of Chicago. A prolific writer who blends autobiography with what she calls "Black-survivor consciousness," Jordan has published poetry, political essays, and children's books. She now teaches at the University of California at Berkeley, and her writing appears frequently in *Esquire, Ms., New York Newsday, The Nation,* and *The New York Times Magazine*; she also contributes a monthly column to *The Progressive.* Her books include *Who Look at Me* (1969), *Civil Wars* (1981), *On Call* (1985), *Naming Our Destiny* (1989), and *Technical Difficulties* (1992).

Evelyn Fox Keller (b. 1936)
American research scientist, teacher, and social critic. In "The Anomaly of Women in Physics" Keller wrote about her experience of demoralization and neglect as a graduate student in theoretical physics at Harvard in the late 1950s. Her response was an active commitment to equality for women scientists throughout her professional life. Despite persistent discrimination, Keller earned her Ph.D. in physics from Harvard in 1963 and worked in New York as a research scientist in molecular biology before becoming a professor of mathematics at the State University of New York at Purchase in 1972. She currently teaches in interdisciplinary programs at the Massachusetts Institute of Technology. Keller's recent books include *A Feeling for the Organism: The Life and Work of Barbara McClintock* (1984), *Reflections on Gender and Science* (1985), *Body Politics* (1990), *Conflicts in Feminism* (1990), and *Secrets of Life, Secrets of Death* (1992).

Jamaica Kincaid (b. 1949)
Caribbean writer. Born in the West Indies, Kincaid moved to the United States when she was seventeen and became a domestic helper to support herself. Although she had barely the equivalent of a high school diploma, she took classes at the New School for Social Research and eventually became a staff writer for *The New Yorker.* Her books include *At the Bottom of the River* (1988), *A Small Place* (1988), *Lucy* (1990), and *The Autobiography of My Mother* (1995).

Martin Luther King, Jr. (1929–1968)
American clergyman and civil rights leader. By the age of twenty-six, King had completed his undergraduate education, finished divinity school, and received a Ph.D. in religion from Boston University. The Montgomery bus boycott (1956) marked King's entry into public politics; blacks in Montgomery, Alabama, boycotted segregated buses, and King took a public stand in their support. Drawing on the New Testament teachings of Jesus and the principles of passive resistance of Mahatma Gandhi, King advocated nonviolent protest to effect significant social change. In the years following the boycott, he became a major figure in the civil rights movement, uniting disparate groups in their struggle. In 1963, Birmingham, Alabama, the most segregated city in the South, became the focal point for violent confrontations between blacks and whites; 2,400 civil rights workers, King among them, went to jail. It was then that he wrote his now-famous "Letter from Birmingham Jail." In 1964, at the age of thirty-five, Martin Luther King, Jr., became the youngest person ever to receive the Nobel Peace Prize. He was assassinated on April 14, 1968, in Memphis, Tennessee.

Maxine Hong Kingston (b. 1940)
Chinese-American autobiographer and novelist. Born in California, the eldest of six children in a Chinese immigrant family, Kingston grew up in a world where English was a second language and friends and relatives regularly gathered at her family's laundry to tell stories in Chinese and reminisce about their native country. Graduating from the University of California at Berkeley, she taught school in California and Hawaii and began publishing poetry, stories, and articles in a number of magazines, including *The New Yorker, New West, The New York Times Magazine, Ms.,* and *Iowa Review.* Her two acclaimed books of reminiscence are *The Woman Warrior: Memoirs of a Girlhood Among Ghosts* (1973) and *China Men* (1980). Her most recent work is a novel, *Tripmaster Monkey* (1989).

Arthur Koestler (1905–1983)
British writer. Born in Hungary and educated at the University of Vienna, Koestler worked as an editor of a Cairo newspaper, then as foreign correspondent for several other papers before settling in England in 1941, when his novel, *Darkness at Noon,* appeared. That novel, an indictment of the Communist party, mapped the territory for Koestler's next ten years of work. In the 1950s, however, he turned to writing about a wide range of topics: psychology, religion, philosophy, evolution, among others. Koestler wrote over forty books, among them *The God That Failed* (1950), *The Ghost in the Machine* (1967), and *The Lion and the Ostrich* (1973).

Melvin Konner (b. 1946)
Anthropologist, biologist, educator, and physician. Born in Brooklyn, New York, Konner began his teaching career as an anthropologist at Harvard University. He now holds a joint appointment in the departments of anthropology and medicine at Emory University, and his writing focuses on the public debate over healthcare. He frequently writes for *The New York Times* and *Newsweek.* His books include *The Tangled Wing* (1982), *Becoming a Doctor* (1988), *Why the Reckless Survive* (1990), *Dear America* (1993), and *Medicine at the Crossroads* (1993).

Joseph Wood Krutch (1893–1970)
American naturalist, journalist, theater and literary critic. Born in Knoxville, Tennessee, Krutch studied science at the University of Tennessee before taking a Ph.D. in English at Columbia University; he later remarked that he knew "more about botany than any other New York critic, and more about the theater than any other botanist." A frequent contributor to such periodi-

cals as *Atlantic Monthly, Harper's Magazine, Saturday Review,* and *Natural History,* Krutch is best known for two widely read and influential books, *The Desert Year* (1952) and *The Modern Temper* (1956).

Elisabeth Kübler-Ross (b. 1926)
Swiss-American psychologist. Born and educated in Switzerland, Kübler-Ross has come to prominence in the United States, where she has lived since 1958. Her work is largely a response to what she calls "the horrifying experience of the [postwar European] concentration camps." She has given seminars and written about death and dying not only in order to understand the process better, but also to learn how to care for the terminally ill. Books on the subject include Kübler-Ross's best-selling *On Death and Dying* (1969), *On Children and Death* (1983), and *AIDS: The Ultimate Challenge* (1987). Kübler-Ross's most recent book, *On Life after Death* (1995), retracts much of her earlier work.

Thomas S. Kuhn (b. 1922)
American philosopher and historian. Educated at Harvard, where he earned a Ph.D. in physics, Kuhn is a specialist in the history and philosophy of science. The author of *The Copernican Revolution* (1957) and *The Essential Tension: Selected Studies in Scientific Tradition and Change* (1977), he is perhaps best known for *The Structure of Scientific Revolutions* (1962, 1970). Kuhn is currently Laurence S. Rockefeller Professor of Philosophy at the Massachusetts Institute of Technology.

La Rochefoucauld (1613–1680)
François, duc de La Rochefoucauld, French nobleman, soldier, and writer. La Rochefoucauld's literary fame rests on his *Réflexions ou sentences et maximes morales* (1665), better known as *Maxims.* This collection of witty observations about human behavior established him as a moralist of decidedly pragmatic persuasion.

Charles Lamb (1775–1834)
English essayist and poet. A contemporary and colleague of Coleridge and Wordsworth, Lamb was born in London, left school before he was fifteen, and soon thereafter became a clerk in the accounting department of the East India Company, where he remained for thirty-three years. To supplement his salary, he turned early to writing. In 1818, at the age of forty-three, he published his *Works,* consisting of minor verse, a sentimental novel, a blank verse tragedy in the Elizabethan style, and the famous children's book *Tales from Shakespeare,* written in collaboration with his sister Mary. At the time he apparently thought his major writing had already been accomplished, yet not until two years after his *Works* appeared did Lamb begin to contribute essays to *London Magazine,* writing that elevated him to the rank of a major English essayist.

Aldo Leopold (1887–1948)
American conservationist and nature writer. Born in Burlington, Iowa, and educated at Yale University, Leopold was a forester who early understood the value of the wilderness and a professor of wildlife management at the University of Wisconsin who became a champion of the predator's role within a healthy ecosystem. He was one of the founders of the Wilderness Society in the 1930s, but his most important contribution to both the environmental movement and to literature is *A Sand County Almanac* (1949), published after he had died while fighting a forest fire on a neighbor's land.

Michael Levin (b. 1943)
American philosopher. Educated at Michigan State University and Columbia, Levin was a member of the Department of Philosophy at Columbia from 1968 until 1980. He is currently professor of philosophy at City College of the City University of New York. His research interests include ethics, philosophy, and the mind. The author of a number of scholarly articles, Levin has published *Metaphysics and the Mind-Body Problem* (1979).

Abraham Lincoln (1809–1865)
Lawyer, orator, and sixteenth president of the United States (1861–65). Born in Kentucky, Lincoln was a self-made and self-taught man. His family moved to Illinois in 1830, where Lincoln prepared himself for a career in law. In 1834, he was elected to the first of four terms in the Illinois state legislature

and in 1847, to the U.S. Congress. Elected president in 1860, Lincoln sought to preserve the Union amid the strife of the Civil War while he worked for the passage of the Thirteenth Amendment, which would outlaw slavery everywhere and forever in the United States. Lincoln was assassinated by actor John Wilkes Booth on April 15, 1865. During his first term, Lincoln delivered the "Gettysburg Address" (1863) at the site of one of the Civil War's bloodiest battles. Reelected in 1864, he gave his Second Inaugural Address, an eloquent appeal for reconciliation and peace.

Michael Lynch (1944–1991)
American educator and gay rights activist. Born in North Carolina, Lynch was educated at Oberlin College, Goddard College, and the University of Iowa. He taught at the University of Toronto from 1977 until his death. He founded several gay rights groups in Canada, including Gay Fathers of Toronto and AIDS Action Now! He published a collection of poetry, *These Waves of Dying Friends*, in 1989.

Dorothy Gies McGuigan (1914–1982)
American essayist, social critic, and teacher. Born in Ann Arbor, Michigan, McGuigan studied at the University of Michigan, Columbia University, and King's College, London, after which she worked for five years at a publishing company. After another thirteen years as a freelance writer for various magazines, she joined the faculty of the University of Michigan, first as an instructor in English and later as program director and editor at the Center for the Continuing Education of Women. McGuigan's work includes the books *The Hapsburgs* (1966), *A Dangerous Experiment* (1970), and *Metternich and the Duchess* (1975); she has also edited *The Role of Women in Conflict and Peace: Papers* (1977) and *Changing Family, Changing Workplace: New Research* (1986).

Niccolò Machiavelli (1469–1527)
Florentine statesman and political philosopher. An aristocrat who held office while Florence was a republic, Machiavelli fell from favor when the Medicis returned to power in 1512. Briefly imprisoned, he was restored to an office of some influence, but he never regained his former importance. Machiavelli's most famous work, *The Prince* (1513), has exerted considerable literary and political influence within the Western tradition.

Hugh MacLennan (1907–1990)
Canadian novelist, essayist, and educator. Born in a remote coal-mining town of Nova Scotia, MacLennan was educated at Dalhousie University and Princeton University and became a Rhodes Scholar at Oxford University. He fought against British colonialism from an early age and was repeatedly denied jobs and publication in part because of his Canadian heritage. His first published novel, *Barometer Rising* (1941), provided a sense of the Canadian nationalism that had been taking root throughout the early twentieth century. Other novels include *The Precipice* (1948), *The Watch That Ends the Night* (1959), and *Voices in Time* (1980).

John McMurtry (b. 1939)
Canadian writer, teacher, and philosopher. Educated at the University of Toronto, McMurtry became a professional football player before earning his Ph.D. at the University of London. Now professor of philosophy at the University of Guelph he has written four books: *The Dimensions of English* (1970), *The Structure of Marx's World-View* (1978), *Understanding War* (1989), and *Love, War, and Freedom: Covert Structures of Power* (1995).

John McPhee (b. 1931)
American nature writer and journalist. Born in Princeton, New Jersey, McPhee was educated at Princeton and Cambridge universities. After working as a TV scriptwriter and erstwhile poet, McPhee eventually became a staff writer for *The New Yorker*. His books include *A Sense of Where You Are* (1965), *The Pine Barrens* (1968), *Coming into the Country* (1977), *Assembling California* (1993), and *The Ransom of Russian Art* (1994). Many of these books began as essays in *The New Yorker*. It has been said that "sometimes it seems that McPhee deliberately chooses unpromising subjects, just to show what he can do with them."

Nancy Mairs (b. 1943)
American nonfiction writer and essayist. Married at nineteen, Mairs finished college, had a child, and earned an M.F.A. and a Ph.D. from the University of Arizona. The personal difficulties that inform her writing include six months spent in a state mental hospital, suffering from a near-suicidal mixture of agoraphobia and anorexia, and the later discovery that she suffered from multiple sclerosis. She found a dual salvation in writing and in Roman Catholicism, to which she converted in her thirties. Mairs's major works, *Plaintext* (1986), and *Remembering the Bone House* (1989), are both autobiographical.

Joyce Maynard (b. 1953)
Canadian-American journalist and novelist. As an eighteen-year-old Yale freshman, Maynard created a literary sensation when she published a critical appraisal of the jaded youth of the 1960s in *The New York Times.* She expanded that essay into book-length form in *Looking Back: A Chronicle of Growing Old in the Sixties* (1973). Her books, generally about American life and particularly about the lives of women, include the short-story collections *Baby Love* (1981) and *New House* (1987).

Casey Miller (b. 1919) and **Kate Swift** (b. 1923)
American essayists and editors. Miller and Swift have co-written numerous articles on sexism and language for national newspapers and magazines. Born in Toledo, Ohio, Miller graduated from Smith College, studied graphic arts at Yale, and was for ten years an editor at Seabury Press. Swift was born in Yonkers, New York, studied journalism at the University of North Carolina, and later worked as a science writer and editor with the American Museum of Natural History and the Yale School of Medicine. As freelance partners since 1970, they have explored sexual prejudice and language in such books as *Words and Women: New Language in New Times* (1976) and *The Handbook of Nonsexist Writing* (1980).

Jessica Mitford (b. 1917)
Anglo-American writer and social critic. Born into one of England's most famous aristocratic families, Mitford left for the United States shortly after completing her education (1936). A naturalized American citizen (1944), she has established herself as an investigative reporter with a talent for pungent social criticism. Her study of the American funeral industry, *The American Way of Death* (1963), was followed by *The Trial of Dr. Spock* (1969) and *Kind and Unusual Punishment: The Prison Business* (1973). She has also written autobiography: *Faces of Philip* (1984) and *Grace Had an English Heart* (1989). Her most recent work echoes her earliest, *The American Way of Birth* (1992).

Rita Moir (b. 1952)
Canadian journalist, essayist, and playwright. Moir has worked as a waitress, tree planter, secretary, playwright, and reporter for CBC Radio, the *Globe*, and the *Mail.* Three of her plays have been produced professionally. Her most recent book, *Survival Gear* (1994), is the result of her automobile journeys across Canada from her rural home in British Columbia to the fishing community of Freeport, Nova Scotia.

N. Scott Momaday (b. 1934)
Native American poet, writer, and artist. Momaday grew up on reservations in the Southwest, deeply influenced by the example and traditions of the Kiowa people. He studied at the University of New Mexico and Stanford University before beginning a teaching career. Currently, Momaday teaches at Arizona State University. He has published several volumes of poetry, including *Angle of Geese and Other Poems* (1973) and *The Gourd Dancer* (1976); a Pulitzer Prize-winning novel, *House Made of Dawn* (1968); an autobiography, *The Names: A Memoir* (1976); and a collection of Kiowa folktales, *The Way to Rainy Mountain* (1969). His most recent book is *In the Presence of the Sun* (1992).

Susanna Moodie (1803–1885)
British colonial writer. Born in England, Moodie moved to Canada as an adult, where she began to write in order to supplement her household income. Her books of poetry and fiction include *Enthusiasm and Other Poems* (1831), *Mark Hurdlestone and the Gold Wor-*

shipper (1853), *Geoffrey Moncton* (1852), and *Flora Lindsey* (1854). Moodie is now best known for her nonfiction memoirs, *Life in the Clearings Versus the Bush* (1853) and *Roughing It in the Bush or Life in Canada* (1852), both of which are based on her experiences as a woman in nineteenth-century Canada.

Desmond Morris (b. 1928)
British zoologist and writer on human and animal behavior. After receiving a Ph.D. in zoology from Oxford, Morris remained there to do research. In 1959, he became curator of mammals at the London Zoo. During the next eight years, he wrote five books on animals. In 1968, he returned to research at Oxford and began writing books on human and animal behavior: *The Naked Ape* (1967), *The Human Zoo* (1969), *Intimate Behavior* (1971), *Manwatching* (1977), *Bodywatching* (1985), *Catwatching* (1987), *Dogwatching* (1987), *Horsewatching* (1989), *Animal Watching* (1990), and *Body Talk* (1995).

Vladimir Nabokov (1899–1977)
American fiction writer and teacher. Born in Russia and educated at Trinity College, Cambridge, Nabokov came to the United States in 1940 to lecture at Stanford University and stayed for twenty years. While teaching at Wellesley and Cornell, he wrote dozens of novels and contributed essays, stories, and poems to several American magazines. Although he was well known in literary circles, Nabokov did not achieve fame until 1958, when his controversial and explicit novel *Lolita* was published. *Lolita* earned Nabokov enough money so that he could retire to Switzerland and write fiction full time.

Gloria Naylor (b. 1950)
American fiction writer and essayist. Naylor received her B.A. from Brooklyn College, and an M.A. in Afro-American studies from Yale. She has been a writer-in-residence at George Washington University. Naylor has written four books: *The Women of Brewster Place* (1982), *Linden Hills* (1985), *Mama Day* (1988), and *Bailey's Cafe* (1992).

John Henry Newman (1801–1890)
English Roman Catholic prelate, poet, novelist, and religious thinker. Educated at Trinity College, Oxford, Newman became a priest in the Anglican Church. He was a major force in the Oxford movement, an effort to reestablish the authority and traditions of the Church of England. In 1845, Newman became Roman Catholic; in 1846, he was ordained in Rome and then returned to England. From 1852 on, he delivered not only sermons but also a number of influential lectures on education. The latter culminated in one of Newman's finest works, *The Idea of a University Defined and Illustrated* (1852), which ranks with his treatise *An Essay in Aid of a Grammar of Assent* (1870) as a classic statement of belief. Newman wrote two novels (*Loss and Gain,* 1848; *Callista,* 1856), an explanation of his conversion (*Apologia Pro Vita Sua,* 1864), and a visionary poem ("The Dream of Gerontius," 1865). In 1879, he became a cardinal in the Roman Catholic Church.

George Orwell (1903–1950)
Pen name of Eric Blair, English journalist, essayist, novelist, and critic. Born in India and educated in England, Orwell became an officer in the Indian Imperial Police in Burma (1922–27), a part of his life that he later recounted in a novel, *Burmese Days* (1934). In 1927, he went to Europe to develop his writing talents. His first book, *Down and Out in Paris and London* (1933), depicts his years of poverty and struggle while working as a dishwasher and day laborer. Orwell's experiences fighting in the Spanish Civil War are the subject of his memoir, *Homage to Catalonia* (1938). Of his seven novels, *Animal Farm* (1945) and *Nineteen Eighty-Four* (1949), satires directed at totalitarian government, have become twentieth-century classics. Orwell published five collections of essays, including *Shooting an Elephant* (1950).

Cynthia Ozick (b. 1928)
Novelist, essayist, literary critic, and translator. Born in the Bronx, New York, and raised by parents she has described as "unintentional storytellers," Ozick received her degrees from New York University and Ohio State University. She began writing poetry, but it

was her fiction that brought her critical acclaim. Her books include *Trust* (1966), *The Pagan Rabbi, and Other Stories* (1971), *Bloodshed and Three Novellas* (1976), *The Cannibal Galaxy* (1983), *The Messiah of Stockholm* (1987), and *The Shaw* (1989).

Walter Pater (1839–1894)
English novelist, art and literary critic, and essayist. Educated at King's School, Canterbury, and Queen's College, Oxford, Pater devoted his life to study, reflection, and writing. As a prose stylist, he has few equals in the English language. Pater's first book, *Studies in the History of the Renaissance,* appeared in 1873. *Marius the Epicurean* (1885), a novel set in Rome, *Imaginary Portraits* (1887), a collection of fictional sketches, and *Appreciations: With an Essay on Style* (1889) followed.

Noel Perrin (b. 1927)
American nature writer and educator. Born in New York City, Perrin fled to rural New England for his higher education; he was educated at Williams College, Duke University, and Cambridge, and he now teaches at Dartmouth College. His books give accounts of being a part-time farmer as well as an academic, including *First Person Rural* (1978), *Second Person Rural* (1980), and *Third Person Rural* (1983). More recently, Perrin has written about environmental hazards in *Solo: Life with an Electric Car* (1992).

William G. Perry, Jr. (b. 1913)
American educator. Born in Paris and educated at Harvard, Perry taught at Williams College from 1941 to 1945 before moving to Harvard, where he has been director of the Bureau of Study Counsel since 1948 and professor of education since 1964. With C. P. Whitelock, he wrote the *Harvard Reading Course* (1948). His *Forms of Intellectual and Ethical Development in the College Years: A Scheme* was published in 1968.

Henry Petroski (b. 1942)
Educator and writer. Born and raised in New York City, Petroski was educated at Manhattan College and the University of Illinois. Now a professor of civil engineering at Duke University, Petroski describes his subject matter as "the extraordinariness of everyday things." His articles have appeared in *Discover* and *The New Republic,* and he writes the engineering column for *American Scientist.* Petroski's books include *To Engineer is Human* (1985), which examines the role of failure in successful designs; *The Pencil* (1990), which traces the serendipitous history of that common writing implement; *The Evolution of Useful Things* (1992); and *Design Paradigms* (1994), which explores case histories of system failures in engineering projects.

Alexander Petrunkevitch (1875–1964)
Russian-born zoologist and teacher. Petrunkevitch was educated in Russia and Germany before coming to the United States as a lecturer at Harvard in 1904. In 1910, he joined the Department of Zoology at Yale, where he became professor in 1917, and served until 1944. Petrunkevitch was an expert on the behavior of American spiders; his *Index Catalogue of Spiders of North, Central, and South America* (1911) and *An Inquiry into the Natural Classification of Spiders* (1933) are classic studies.

Plato (c. 428–c. 348 B.C.)
Greek philosopher and teacher. When Socrates died in 399 B.C., Plato went into exile. He returned in the 380s and founded a school, the Academy. He adopted the Socratic method of teaching, a technique of asking, rather than answering, questions. Although many of Plato's writings take the form of dialogues, he does occasionally use the parable.

Anna Quindlen (b. 1953)
American journalist. Born in Philadelphia, Quindlen graduated from Barnard College and immediately began writing for the *The New York Post.* Eventually she moved to *The New York Times,* where she was a regular columnist for over twenty years. Her columns allowed her to thrive by "taking things personally for a living," even earning her a Pulitzer Prize. They have been collected in *Living Out Loud* (1988). Quindlen recently resigned from *The New York Times* in order to spend more time writing fiction. She has written two novels, *Object Lessons* (1991) and *One True Thing* (1994).

Santha Rama Rau (b. 1923)
Writer and writing teacher. Born in Madras, India, Santha Rama Rau lived all over the world, from England to South Africa to Japan, until she settled in the United States. After graduating from Wellesley College, she became a freelance writer and writing instructor. She is best known for her travel writing and for her books on India, including her autobiography *Gifts of Passage* (1961) and *Home to India* (1945).

Tom Regan (b. 1938)
American philosopher and teacher. After receiving a Ph.D. in philosophy from the University of Virginia, Regan taught at Sweet Briar College before joining the Department of Philosophy at North Carolina State University. He does research in theoretical and applied ethics.

Adrienne Rich (b. 1929)
American poet. While she was an undergraduate at Radcliffe, Rich's first book of poetry, *A Change in the World,* was chosen by W. H. Auden for the Yale Younger Poet's Prize (1951). Since then, Rich has published nineteen books of poetry and prose, most recently *What Is Found There* (1993), *An Atlas of the Difficult World: Poems 1988–1991* (1991), and *Time's Power: Poems 1985–1988* (1989). In 1994 she was awarded a MacArthur fellowship. Her newest work is *Dark Fields of the Republic* (1995).

Mordecai Richler (b. 1931)
Canadian novelist, screenwriter, and commentator. Born in a Jewish ghetto of Montreal, Richler was educated in Canada, then lived in England for twenty years before returning to his homeland. Much of his writing reflects his traditional Jewish upbringing and his Canadian identity. His books include *The Apprenticeship of Duddy Kravitz* (1959), *St. Urbain's Horsemen* (1971), *Joshua Then and Now* (1980), and *Home Sweet Home* (1984). Richler's most recent work, *Oh Canada! Oh Quebec!* (1992), discusses the secessionist tension that threatens to divide Canada.

Edward Rivera (b. 1945)
Writer and educator. Born in Puerto Rico, Rivera grew up in the Spanish Harlem section of New York City and was educated at The City College of New York and Columbia University. After holding a number of clerical jobs and spending time in the military, he became a neighborhood activist in grassroots causes. He has published a book, *Family Installments* (1982), and now teaches English at City College.

Richard Rodriguez (b. 1944)
American essayist and teacher. The son of Mexican-American immigrants, Rodriguez learned to speak English in a Catholic grammar school. A proficient student, he received a B.A. from Stanford and an M.A. from Columbia. Enrolled in the doctoral program in English literature at the University of California, Berkeley, Rodriguez won a Fulbright and attended the Warburg Institute in London (1972–73). He now works as a lecturer and educational consultant as well as a freelance writer. In *Hunger of Memory: The Education of Richard Rodriguez* (1982), from which "Aria" comes, Rodriguez recounts his assimilation into mainstream American society. His most recent book is *Days of Obligation* (1992).

Betty Rollin (b. 1936)
American journalist, television reporter, and nonfiction writer. Rollin spent several years as a stage and television actress before beginning a career in journalism, first at *Vogue* (1964), then at *Look* (1965–71). Since 1971, she has worked as a network correspondent, chiefly for NBC. Rollin is the author of several books, including *First, You Cry* (1976); *Am I Getting Paid for This?: A Romance about Work* (1982); and *Last Wish* (1985).

Carl Sagan (b. 1934)
American astronomer, science writer, and novelist. Sagan received a Ph.D. in astronomy and astrophysics from the University of Chicago in 1960. He taught at the University of California, Berkeley, and at Harvard before joining the faculty of Cornell, where he is currently professor of astronomy and director of the Laboratory for Planetary Studies. While Sagan's early writing concerns his work as an astronomer, *The Dragons of Eden* (1977) delves into the subject of human intelligence. Like *Broca's Brain* (1979) and his television

series "Cosmos," it extended Sagan's audience considerably. His novel *Contact* (1985) became a best-seller. Sagan's most recent book is *Pale Blue Dot* (1994).

Scott Russell Sanders (b. 1945)
American writer and teacher. Born in Tennessee and educated at Brown and Cambridge, Sanders has spent his entire teaching career in the Department of English at Indiana University, where he is now professor of English. He is best known for his nature writing and his depictions of American places and people including: *Wilderness Plots: Tales about the Settlement of the American Land* (1983), *Audubon's Early Years* (1984), *In Limestone Country* (1985), and *Staying Put* (1993). Another work is *The Paradise of Bombs* (1987), a collection of essays on violence in the United States.

May Sarton (b. 1912)
American novelist, poet, and essayist. Born in Belgium, Sarton came to the United States as a child. The daughter of a Harvard professor, she did not attend college. Instead, she pursued a career in the theater, which she left to become a scriptwriter, then an instructor in writing. She now lives on the coast of Maine. Sarton is the author of seventeen novels, among them *The Bridge of Years* (1946), *Kinds of Love* (1970), and *A Reckoning* (1978), as well as fourteen books of poetry, including *Encounter in April* (1937), *The Land of Silence* (1953), and *A Durable Fire* (1972). She has also published several nonfiction works.

Jean-Paul Sartre (1905–1980)
French playwright, novelist, critic, philosopher, and political activist. After earning an advanced degree in philosophy, Sartre became a provincial schoolmaster, then a playwright and writer of philosophical essays. Described by *The New York Times* as "a rebel of a thousand causes, a modern Don Quixote," Sartre was a major force in the intellectual life of post-World War II France. His philosophy of existentialism influenced generations of artists and thinkers. Steadfastly independent, Sartre refused both the Nobel Prize for Literature (1964) and the Legion of Honor. He died having completed only three volumes of a four-volume study of Gustave Flaubert. A sampling of his major works includes *The Flies* (1943), *Being and Nothingness* (1943), *No Exit* (1944), and *Life Situations* (1977).

Arthur Schlesinger, Jr. (b. 1917)
American historian, teacher, and social critic. Born in Columbus, Ohio, Schlesinger studied at Harvard University and did postgraduate work at Cambridge University. Returning to Harvard in 1946 as a professor of history, he remained there until asked to serve as special assistant to President Kennedy and President Johnson. Since 1966 he has taught at the City University of New York as Schweitzer Professor of the Humanities. Schlesinger has written such influential books as *The Age of Jackson* (1945), which won a Pulitzer Prize, *The Crisis of the Old Order* (1957), *A Thousand Days* (1965), which won a Pulitzer Prize and the National Book Award, *The Imperial Presidency* (1973), and *The Cycles of American History* (1986). His most recent book, *The Disuniting of America* (1992), considers whether multicultural education has increased racial tensions.

Arthur Schopenhauer (1788–1860)
Nineteenth-century German philosopher. Born in Danzig (today Gdansk), Poland, to a businessman and a writer, Schopenhauer was raised in Germany. He traveled extensively during his young life, developing an appreciation for nature that stood in sharp contrast to his strong distaste for human cruelty. He entered the University of Göttingen as a medical student but quickly found philosophical study more to his liking. Eventually he earned his doctorate from the University of Berlin. Influenced by Buddhist thought, Schopenhauer was one of the first Western philosophers to pay close attention to Eastern ideas. Schopenhauer is still noted for his biting sarcasm, pessimism, misogynism, and stinginess. It is well documented how much noise bothered Schopenhauer; once he pushed a woman down the stairs because of her loud chattering, an act for which he was ordered to pay her a monthly stipend for the rest of her life.

Chief Seattle (c. 1786–1866)
Native American leader. A fierce young warrior, Seattle (also Seathl or Sealth)

was chief of the Suquamish, Duwamish, and allied Salish-speaking tribes of the Northwest. In the 1830s, he was converted to Christianity and became an advocate of peace. Local settlers honored him and his work by naming their town Seattle. When the Port Elliott Treaty of 1855 established reservations for Native Americans, Seattle signed it and lived the rest of his life at the Port Madison Reservation. Because of his example, his people did not become involved in the bloody warfare that marked the history of the territory from 1855 until 1870. His "Address" is the reply to a treaty proffered in 1854 by Governor Isaac Stevens, commissioner of Indian Affairs for the Washington Territory. Chief Seattle died on June 7, 1866, and was buried at the Suquamish cemetery near Seattle.

Susan Sontag (b. 1933)
Writer, art critic, social activist, and filmmaker. Born in New York City, Sontag grew up in Tucson, Arizona, and Los Angeles. A young woman with keen intelligence and curiosity, Sontag graduated from high school at the age of fifteen, immediately started classes at the University of California at Berkeley, and received degrees from the University of Chicago and Harvard University. Her collection of essays *Against Interpretation* (1966) established her reputation as a serious intellectual and critic, just as *Trip to Hanoi* (1968) established her reputation as a political and cultural critic. After a near-fatal bout with breast cancer, Sontag wrote *Illness as Metaphor* (1978), followed by *AIDS and Its Metaphors* (1988). She has written several films and plays, and her most recent novel is *Volcano Lover* (1992).

Elizabeth Cady Stanton (1815–1902)
American feminist and women's rights activist. Born in Johnstown, New York, Cady Stanton married the prominent abolitionist Henry B. Stanton, and the two spent their honeymoon at the World's Antislavery Convention. Cady Stanton combined her energies with those of Lucretia Mott and Susan B. Anthony and spent the rest of her life fighting for women's rights. She cofounded the National Women Suffrage Association. She also was one of the first women to try introducing legislation that would make divorce laws more sympathetic to women in abusive marriages. "The Declaration of Sentiments and Resolutions" grew out of the first American convention for women's rights, held in Seneca Falls, New York, in 1848.

Brent Staples (b. 1951)
American journalist and writer. Born in Chester, Pennsylvania, Staples holds a Ph.D. in psychology from the University of Chicago. He is assistant metropolitan editor of *The New York Times*. His memoir, *Parallel Time*, was published in 1994.

Shelby Steele (b. 1946)
American essayist and nonfiction writer. Currently a professor of English at San Jose State University in California, Steele won a National Magazine Award in 1989, and he is a recipient of the 1991 National Book Critics Circle Award for general nonfiction. His work has appeared in such diverse publications as *Harper's Magazine*, *The American Scholar*, the *Washington Post*, *The New Republic*, and *The New York Times Book Review*. Steele's first book, *The Content of Our Character: A New Vision of Race in America* (1990), received wide critical acclaim.

Wallace Stegner (1909–1993)
American essayist, novelist, and teacher. Influenced by Twain, Cather, and Conrad, Stegner writes of the development of individuals within particular landscapes. Stegner's landscapes are often those of the American West, for he is a serious naturalist with special interest in that area. In a long career, he has written and edited more than forty books, among them the novels *Remembering Laughter* (1937), *The Big Rock Candy Mountain* (1943), and *Recapitulation* (1979), as well as historical narratives like *Mormon Country* (1941) and *The Gathering of Zion: The Story of the Mormon Trail* (1964). Near the end of his life, Stegner wrote about the American West and became a spokesman for environmental concerns. Stegner directed the prestigious creative writing program at Stanford University. His last book was *Where the Bluebird Sings to the Lemonade Springs* (1992).

Gloria Steinem (b. 1934)
American essayist, journalist, and editor. After receiving a B.A. from Smith College, Steinem spent two years studying in India. On her return, she held several positions in publishing and worked as a writer for television, film, and political campaigns until 1968, when she and others founded *New York* magazine. Founding editor of *Ms.* magazine (1971), Steinem is an influential spokesperson for the women's movement. "The Good News Is: These Are Not the Best Years of Your Life" first appeared in *Ms.* with the title "Why Young Women Are More Conservative" (Sept. 1979). It was reprinted in *Outrageous Acts and Everyday Rebellions* (1983), a collection of Steinem's essays and articles. Her most recent book, *Moving Beyond Words* (1995), is a collection of essays on women's issues.

Fred Strebeigh (b. 1951)
American nonfiction writer and teacher. Born in New York City and raised in Nonquitt, Massachusetts, Strebeigh attended Yale University and now teaches nonfiction writing there. His work has appeared in *American Heritage, The Atlantic Monthly, Audubon, The New Republic, Reader's Digest, Smithsonian,* and *The New York Times Magazine.*

Jonathan Swift (1667–1745)
Anglo-Irish poet, satirist, and cleric. Born to English parents who resided in Ireland, Swift studied at Trinity College, Dublin, then departed for London (1689). There he became part of the literary and political worlds, beginning his career by writing political pamphlets in support of the Tory cause. Ordained in the Church of Ireland (1695), Swift was appointed dean of St. Patrick's Cathedral, Dublin, in 1713 and held the post until his death. One of the master satirists of the English language, he wrote several scathing attacks on extremism, including *The Tale of a Tub* (1704), *The Battle of the Books* (1704), and *A Modest Proposal* (1729), as well as poetry, but he is probably best known for his novel *Gulliver's Travels* (1726).

Deborah Tannen (b. 1945)
American linguist and educator. Born in Brooklyn, New York, Tannen received her doctorate from the University of California at Berkeley. Because of a childhood illness that left her partially deaf, Tannen grew interested in nonverbal signals and other conversational phenomena. She now teaches linguistics at Georgetown University, and her scholarship bridges both academic and popular audiences. Tannen takes her even-handed descriptions of gender differences in language to the public with frequent appearances on television and with her books, *You Just Don't Understand* (1990) and *Talking 9 to 5* (1994).

Paul Theroux (b. 1941)
American novelist, essayist, and travel writer. Born in Medford, Massachusetts, Theroux took his B.A. at the University of Massachusetts and later taught in Africa and Asia. For some time he has lived in London, at least when he has not been traveling all over the world—by railway whenever possible. Theroux's novels include *The Family Arsenal* (1976), *The Mosquito Coast* (1982), and *O-Zone* (1986). His best-known travel books are *The Great Railway Bazaar: By Train Through Asia* (1975) and *The Old Patagonian Express: By Train Through the Americas* (1979). More recent works include *Chicago Loop* (1990), *The Happy Isles of Oceana* (1992), and *Millroy the Magician* (1994). His essays are collected in *Sunrise with Seamonsters* (1985).

Dylan Thomas (1914–1953)
Welsh poet and writer. Born and raised in the coal-mining district of Wales, Thomas lived a turbulent life marked by chronic alcoholism that helped bring about his early death. His writing, though, particularly his recollections of childhood, reveals an awareness of the sweetness of living that is expressed in bold, inventive, often playful language. Although he is perhaps best known for his poetry, particularly the verse drama *Under Milk Wood* (1954), Thomas also wrote short stories, plays, and film scripts. *Quite Early One Morning* (1954), a collection of his reminiscences of a Welsh childhood, and especially *A Child's Christmas in Wales* (1954) have become classics.

Lewis Thomas (1913–1993)
American physician, teacher, science writer, and humanist. Educated at

Princeton and Harvard Medical School, Thomas has specialized in pediatrics, public health, and cancer research. From 1973 until 1980, he served as president of Memorial Sloan-Kettering Cancer Center in New York City; he is currently emeritus president there. In 1970, Thomas began writing occasional essays for the *New England Journal of Medicine.* A number of these, gathered in *The Lives of a Cell* (1974), established Thomas's reputation as a writer. Other collections are *The Medusa and the Snail* (1979), *The Youngest Science* (1983), *Late Night Thoughts on Listening to Mahler's Ninth Symphony* (1983), *Et Cetera, Et Cetera* (1991), and *The Fragile Species* (1992).

Henry David Thoreau (1817–1862)
American philosopher, essayist, naturalist, and poet. A graduate of Harvard, Thoreau worked at a number of jobs—schoolmaster, house painter, employee in his father's pencil factory—before becoming a writer and political activist. He became a friend of Emerson's and a member of the Transcendental Club, contributing frequently to its journal *The Dial.* Drawn to the world of nature, he wrote his first book, *A Week on the Concord and Merrimac Rivers* (1849), about his impressions. Thoreau's strong stance against slavery led to his arrest for refusing to pay the Massachusetts poll tax (an act of protest against government sanction of the Mexican War, which he viewed as serving the interests of slaveholders). His eloquent essay defending this act, "Civil Disobedience" (1849), his probing meditation on the solitary life, *Walden* (1854), and his speech "A Plea for Captain John Brown" (1859) are classic literary documents in the history of American life and thought.

James Thurber (1894–1961)
American humorist, cartoonist, essayist, and fiction writer. Born in Columbus, Ohio, Thurber attended Ohio State University. He began his career as a professional writer working for the *Columbus Dispatch* (1920–24), then moved on to the *Chicago Tribune* and the *New York Evening Post.* In 1927, encouraged by E. B. White, he became managing editor of and staff writer for *The New Yorker.* Throughout his career he contributed stories, essays, and cartoons to the magazine. Thurber wrote more than thirty books, including *The Owl in the Attic and Other Perplexities* (1931), *The Beast in Me and Other Animals* (1948), and *The Secret Life of Walter Mitty* (1939).

Paul Tillich (1886–1965)
German-American philosopher and theologian. Born into a German Lutheran family and educated at several German universities, Tillich served as an army chaplain in World War I. Afterward, he joined the theology faculty of the University of Berlin. When Hitler came to power, Tillich was dismissed from the Chair of Philosophy at Frankfurt University. He fled to the United States, where he spent over twenty years on the faculty of the Union Theological Seminary in New York City. Upon retirement, he became University Professor at Harvard. Tillich's most important work, the three-volume *Systematic Theology,* was published in 1963. Among other important works are *The Eternal Now* (1963) and *A History of Christian Thought* (revised edition 1968).

Sallie Tisdale (b. 1957)
American nurse and essayist. A writer on a wide range of health and medical issues, Tisdale has contributed to the *Antioch Review, Cosmopolitan, Esquire, Glamour, The New York Times Magazine, The New Republic, Utne Reader,* and *Vogue.* Tisdale is also a contributing editor of *Harper's Magazine.* She has written several books, including *The Sorcerer's Apprentice* (1986), *Harvest Moon* (1987), *Lot's Wife* (1988), and *Talk Dirty to Me* (1994).

Susan Allen Toth (b. 1940)
American writer and educator. Born in Ames, Iowa, Toth was educated at Smith College, the University of California at Berkeley, and the University of Minnesota. She currently teaches English at Macalester College in St. Paul, Minnesota. Although Toth did not begin writing fiction and essays until she was in her midthirties, she has already published several books, including *Blooming* (1981), *Ivy Days* (1984), and *Reading Rooms* (1991). Her essays have appeared in *The New York Times, Utne Reader, Travel & Leisure,* and *Harper's Magazine.*

Barbara Tuchman (1912–1989)
American historian. After graduating from Radcliffe College in 1933, Tuchman worked as a research assistant for the Institute of Pacific Relations, an experience that later found expression in *Stilwell and the American Experience in China,* for which she won a Pulitzer Prize in 1971. During the 1930s and 1940s she wrote on politics for *The Nation,* covered the Spanish Civil War as a journalist in London, and after Pearl Harbor took a job with the Office of War Information in Washington, D.C. Critical and public acclaim followed the publication of *The Zimmerman Telegram* (1958) and *The Guns of August* (1962), both on the origins of World War I. Her other books include *The Proud Tower* (1966), *A Distant Mirror: The Calamitous Fourteenth Century* (1978), *The March of Folly* (1984), and *Practicing History* (1981), a collection of articles, reviews, and talks.

John Updike (b. 1932)
American poet, fiction writer, and critic. After attending Harvard and Oxford, Updike joined the staff of *The New Yorker,* beginning an association that continues today. He has written over thirty books, including collections of poetry (*The Carpentered Hen and Other Tame Creatures,* 1958; *Seventy Poems,* 1972), short stories (some collected in *The Music School,* 1966; *Trust Me,* 1987), and novels (*The Centaur,* 1963; *The Witches of Eastwick,* 1984; *Roger's Version,* 1986; and his quartet of "Rabbit" novels, the most recent *Rabbit at Rest* (1990). He has since written *Memories of the Ford Administration* (1992), *After Life* (1994), and *Brazil* (1994).

Alice Walker (b. 1944)
African-American poet, novelist, and essayist. Born and raised by sharecroppers in rural Georgia, Walker was educated at Spelman College and Sarah Lawrence College. Afterwards, Walker worked as an editor for *Ms.* magazine and became active in the civil rights movement. She received widespread fame for her Pulitzer Prize–winning novel, *The Color Purple* (1982). Other books include *In Search of Our Mothers' Gardens* (1983), *The Temple of My Familiar* (1989), *Possessing the Secret of Joy* (1992), and many volumes of poetry. Walker currently lives in San Francisco, runs a publishing company, Wild Trees Press, and has turned her attention to writing nonfiction.

Eudora Welty (b. 1909)
American writer, critic, amateur painter, and photographer. Born and brought up in Jackson, Mississippi, Welty has retained her deep attachment to the people and places of the South. After graduating from the University of Wisconsin in 1929 and a year's study at Columbia University's School of Business, she returned to Jackson and eventually found work as a publicity agent for the Works Progress Administration, a New Deal social agency. With the help of Robert Penn Warren and Cleanth Brooks, she had several short stories published, and her literary career was launched. Welty has published several collections of short stories, including a *Collected Stories* (1980); novellas, and novels, including *Delta Wedding* (1946), *Losing Battles* (1970), and *The Optimist's Daughter* (Pulitzer, Prize, 1972); two volumes of photographs; and an acclaimed collection of critical essays, *The Eye of the Story* (1978). Three lectures delivered at Harvard in April 1983 have been published as *One Writer's Beginnings* (1984).

E. B. White (1899–1985)
American poet, journalist, editor, and essayist. After graduating from Cornell in 1921, White became a reporter, then an advertising copywriter before beginning a sixty-year career on the staff of *The New Yorker.* With Harold Ross, the magazine's founding editor, and Katharine Angell, its literary editor, White made *The New Yorker* the most important publication of its kind in the United States. He wrote poems and articles for the magazine and served as a discreet and helpful editor. Among his many books, three written for children earned him lasting fame: *Stuart Little* (1945), *Charlotte's Web* (1952), and *The Trumpet of the Swan* (1970). White revised and edited William Strunk's text *The Elements of Style,* a classic guide.

Edmund White (b. 1940)
American writer and gay activist. Born in Cincinnati, Ohio, White was raised

by his mother in Chicago. After graduating from the University of Michigan, White took a job as a staff writer for Time Inc. and wrote fiction in his spare time. His first novel, *Forgetting Elena* (1973), received wide acclaim and allowed him to teach creative writing at a number of academic institutions, including Brown University, where he teaches today. He has published numerous plays, biographies, novels, and social histories. He is a contributing editor to *Vogue,* and his articles frequently appear in *Architectural Digest, Mother Jones, Travel & Leisure,* and *Saturday Review.*

Alfred North Whitehead (1861–1947)
British mathematician, philosopher, and educator. Born in England and educated at Cambridge, Whitehead began his academic career as a mathematics lecturer at Cambridge, where he met Bertrand Russell. The two collaborated on the three-volume *Principia Mathematica* (1910–1913), which connects mathematics and logic with symbolic reasoning. Whitehead eventually moved to Harvard University's philosophy department, where he taught until his death. In *The Aims of Education* (1929), Whitehead criticized prevailing educational practices and suggested a system of reform rooted in the belief that "students are alive, and the purpose of education is to stimulate and guide their self-development."

Walt Whitman (1819–1892)
American poet and writer. Born on Long Island and raised in Brooklyn, New York, Whitman received scant formal education before going to work at age eleven in a newspaper office. Even though he taught school from 1835 to 1840 and worked at several government posts during his lifetime, Whitman considered himself a writer, publishing poetry, stories, and newspaper articles from the age of nineteen. In 1855, he published *Leaves of Grass,* a series of twelve poems that most scholars consider his finest work. As it evolved through a number of editions, *Leaves of Grass* came to include well over 100 poems, including "Calamus," "Crossing Brooklyn Ferry," and "Out of the Cradle Endlessly Rocking." In his poetry and prose, Whitman celebrates the landscape and people of the United States. Although he was an ardent Democrat, he supported Lincoln; indeed, Lincoln was one of the subjects of Whitman's moving elegy "When Lilacs Last in the Dooryard Bloom'd" (1865).

Patricia Williams (b. 1951)
African-American legal scholar and educator. Williams teaches commercial and consumer law at the City University of New York School of Law. She has written on a wide range of public issues in *Ms.* magazine, *The Nation,* and *The Village Voice.* Among her publications is the book *The Alchemy of Race and Rights* (1991).

Terry Tempest Williams (b. 1955)
American naturalist, poet, and nonfiction writer. Currently naturalist-in-residence at the Utah Museum of Natural History in Salt Lake City, Williams grew up surrounded by the vast desert landscape of her native Utah. She says that she writes "through my biases of gender, geography, and culture, that I am a woman whose ideas have been shaped by the Colorado Plateau and the Great Basin, that these ideas are then sorted out through the prism of my culture—and my culture is Mormon." Her first book, *Pieces of White Shell: A Journey to Navajoland* (1984), is a personal exploration of Native American myths. *Coyote's Canyon* (1989) combines personal narratives of southern Utah's desert canyons with photographs by John Telford. "The Clan of One-Breasted Women" is now the final section of *Refuge: An Unnatural History of Family and Place* (1991).

Tom Wolfe (b. 1931)
American journalist, essayist, novelist, and social commentator. After receiving a Ph.D. from Yale, Wolfe began a career in journalism that has taken him from newspapers like the *Washington Post* and *New York Herald Tribune* to magazines like *New York, Esquire,* and *Vanity Fair.* Several of Wolfe's books have established his reputation as a witty social critic and historian of popular culture: *The Kandykolored Tangerine-Flake Streamline Baby* (1965), *Radical Chic and Mau-Mauing the Flak Catchers* (1970), *From Bauhaus to Our House* (1981), and *Bonfire of the Vanities* (1987), his scathing satirical novel.

Wolfe's chronicle of the American space program, *The Right Stuff* (1979), became a successful film.

George Woodcock (1912–1995)
Canadian poet, critic, and essayist. Born in Manitoba, Canada, and educated in England, Woodcock traveled extensively throughout the world before returning to Canada to work as a travel writer, farmer, and railway administrator. After teaching for a few years, he founded Canada's first literary journal, *Canadian Literature*, as well as the anarchist literary journal *Now*. He has published numerous poems, biographies, literary criticism, histories, plays, and travel books, many of which have been translated. He described his motivation for writing as arising from "an immense and zestful and lasting curiosity about the world and the beings who inhabit it."

Virginia Woolf (1882–1941)
English novelist, critic, and essayist. The daughter of respected philosopher and writer Sir Leslie Stephen, Woolf educated herself by unrestricted reading in her father's library. She lived at the center of the "Bloomsbury Group," a celebrated gathering of artists, scholars, and writers. Woolf, together with her husband socialist writer Leonard Woolf, founded the Hogarth Press. Her work, whether it be nonfiction or fiction, is marked by a resonant autobiographical voice. *A Room of One's Own* (1929), an historical investigation of women and creativity; *Mrs. Dalloway* (1925), *To the Lighthouse* (1927), and *The Waves* (1931), novels about artistic consciousness and the development of personality; *The Common Reader* (1925, 1932), collections of essays on topics as diverse as literature and automobiles, reveal penetrating intelligence as well as innovations in narrative technique.

Elizabeth Wurtzel (b. 1968)
American cultural critic. Wurtzel has been the pop music critic for both *The New Yorker* and *New York* magazine; she has also written for *Rolling Stone, Mademoiselle, People,* and *Musician.* Her first book is *Prozac Nation: Young and Depressed in America* (1994).

William Zinsser (b. 1922)
American journalist, writer, and teacher. After graduating from Princeton in 1944 and serving in the army for two years, Zinsser joined the staff of the *New York Herald Tribune* (1946–59), first as a features editor, then as a drama editor and film critic, and finally as an editorial writer. In 1959, he became a freelance writer, joining the English faculty at Yale University from 1971 until 1979. Zinsser is the author of more than a dozen books, among them the well-known *On Writing Well: An Informal Guide to Writing Non-Fiction* (1976; revised edition, 1994), and *Writing with a Word-Processor* (1983).

Acknowledgments

Abbey: "The Serpents of Paradise" from *Desert Solitaire* by Edward Abbey. Reprinted by permission of Don Congdon Associates, Inc. Copyright © 1968 by Edward Abbey.

Allen: "Selections from the Allen Notebooks" from *Without Feathers* by Woody Allen. Copyright © 1975 by Woody Allen. Reprinted by permission of Random House, Inc.

Allison: "Gun Crazy" from *Skin: Talking About Sex, Class, and Literature* by Dorothy Allison. Copyright © 1994 by Dorothy Allison. Reprinted by permission of Firebrand Books.

Angelou: "Graduation" from *I Know Why the Caged Bird Sings* by Maya Angelou. Copyright © 1969 by Maya Angelou. Reprinted by permission of Random House, Inc.

Arendt: "Denmark and the Jews" from *Eichmann in Jerusalem* by Hannah Arendt. Copyright © 1963, 1964 by Hannah Arendt. Used by permission of Viking Penguin, a division of Penguin Books USA Inc.

Arlen: "The Tyranny of the Visual" from *The Camera Age* by Michael Arlen. Copyright © 1979, 1981 by Michael Arlen. Reprinted by permission of Farrar, Straus & Giroux, Inc.

Asimov: "The Eureka Phenomenon." Copyright © 1971 by Mercury Press, Inc. from *The Left Hand of the Electron* by Isaac Asimov. Used by permission of Doubleday, a division of Bantam Doubleday Dell Publishing Group, Inc.

Atwood: "True North" from *Saturday Night* vol. 102, no. 1 (Jan. 1987). Reprinted by permission of the author.

Baldwin: "Stranger in the Village" from *Notes of a Native Son* by James Baldwin. Copyright © 1955, renewed 1983, by James Baldwin. Reprinted by permission of Beacon Press.

Balmer: "Adirondack Fundamentalism" from *Mine Eyes Have Seen the Glory* by Randall Balmer. Copyright © 1989 by Randall Balmer. Reprinted by permission of Oxford University Press, Inc.

Barber: "America Skips School" by Benjamin R. Barber. Originally published in *Harper's Magazine*, Nov. 1993. Reprinted by permission of the author.

Barthes: "Toys" from *Mythologies* by Roland Barthes and translated by Annette Lavers. Translation copyright ©1972 by Jonathan Cape Ltd. Reprinted by permission of Hill and Wang, a division of Farrar, Straus & Giroux, Inc.

Becker: "Democracy" from *Modern Democracy* by Carl L. Becker. Copyright © 1941 by Yale University Press. Reprinted by permission of Yale University Press.

Bettelheim: "A Victim" from *The Informed Heart* by Bruno Bettelheim. Copyright © 1960 by The Free Press, renewed 1988 by Bruno Bettelheim. Reprinted with permission of The Free Press, a division of Simon & Schuster, Inc.

Bird: "College Is a Waste of Time and Money" from *The Case Against College* by Caroline Bird. Reprinted by permission of the author.

Booth: "Boring from Within: The Art of the Freshman Essay" from an address to the Illinois Council of College Teachers in 1963. Copyright © Wayne C. Booth. Reprinted by permission of the author.

Bronowski: "The Nature of Scientific Reasoning" from *Science and Human Values* by Jacob Bronowski. Copyright © 1956 by Oxford University Press, Inc. Reprinted by permission of the publisher. "The Reach of Imagination," delivered as the Blashfield Address, May 1966. Reprinted by permission from the *Proceedings of the American Academy of Arts and Letters and National Institute of Arts and Letters*, 2nd Ser., No. 17, 1967.

Burgess: "Is America Falling Apart?" from *The New York Times Magazine*, Nov. 7, 1971. Copyright © 1971 by The New York Times Company. Reprinted by permission.

Butterfield: "The Originality of the Old Testament" from *Writings on Christianity and History*, edited by C. T. MacIntire. Copyright © 1979 by Oxford University Press, Inc. Reprinted by permission of the publisher.

Carr: "The Historian and His Facts" from *What Is History?* by Edward Hallett Carr. Copyright © 1961 by Edward Hallett Carr. Reprinted by permission of Macmillan Ltd. and Alfred A. Knopf, Inc.

Carter: "The Best Black" from *Reflections of an Affirmative Action Baby* by Stephen L. Carter. Copyright © 1991 by Stephen L. Carter. Reprinted by permission of BasicBooks, a division of HarperCollins Publishers, Inc.

Cofer: "More Room" from *Silent Dancing: A Partial Remembrance of a Puerto Rican Childhood* by Judith Ortiz Cofer. Reprinted by permission of Arte Publico Press, University of Houston.

Cohen: "The Case for the Use of Animals in Biochemical Research," no. 315, Oct. 1986. Copyright © 1986 by the Massachusetts Medical Society. All rights reserved. Reprinted by permission of *The New England Journal of Medicine*.

Conway: "Politics, Pedagogy, and Gender" by Jill K. Conway. Reprinted by permission of *Dædalus*, Journal of the American Academy of Arts and Sciences, from the issue entitled, "Learning About Women: Gender, Politics, and Power," Fall 1987, vol. 116, no. 4.

Cooley: Excerpts from "City Aphorisms" by Mason Cooley. Reprinted by permission of the author.

Coontz: "A Nation of Welfare Families" from *The Way We Never Were* by Stephanie Coontz. Copyright © 1992 by BasicBooks, a division of HarperCollins Publishers, Inc. Reprinted by permission of the publisher. First appeared in *Harper's Magazine*.

Copland: "How We Listen" from *What to Listen for in Music* by Aaron Copland. Copyright © 1957, 1985 by the estate of Aaron Copland. Reprinted by permission.

Cronon: "A Place for Stories: Nature, History, and Narrative," *Journal of American History*, 78 (March 1992). Copyright © 1992 by Organization of American Historians. Reprinted by permission of *Journal of American History*.

Didion: "On Keeping a Notebook," "Marrying Absurd," and "On Going Home" from *Slouching Towards Bethlehem* by Joan Didion. Copyright © 1967, 1968 by Joan Didion. Reprinted by permission of Farrar, Straus & Giroux, Inc.

Dillard: "Sight into Insight" from *Harper's Magazine*, Feb. 1974. Copyright © 1974 by Annie Dillard. Reprinted by permission of the author and Blanche C. Gregory, Inc. "Terwilliger Bunts One" excerpt from *An American Childhood*. Copyright © 1987 by Annie Dillard. Reprinted by permission of HarperCollins Publishers, Inc.

Dobbs: "The Shatterer of Worlds" from *Reading the Time* by Kildare Dobbs. Copyright © Kildare Dobbs 1968. "Gallipoli" from *Anatolian Suite* by Kildare Dobbs. Copyright © Kildare Dobbs 1989. Reprinted by permission of the author.

Early: "Their Malcolm, My Problem." Copyright © 1992 by *Harper's Magazine*. Reprinted from the December issue by special permission. All rights reserved.

Ehrlich: "Spring" originally appeared in *Antaeus*, Spring 1986. Copyright © 1986 by Gretel Ehrlich. Reprinted by permission of the author.

Eighner: "Dumpster Diving" from *Travels with Lizbeth* by Lars Eighner. Reprinted by permission of St. Martin's Press.

Eisley: "The Brown Wasps" from *The Night Country* by Loren Eisley. Copyright © by Loren Eisley. Reprinted by permission of Scribner, an imprint of Simon & Schuster, Inc.

Epstein: "The Case of Harry Houdini" from *Star of Wonder* by Daniel Mark Epstein. Copyright © 1986 by Daniel Mark Epstein. Reprinted by permission of the Overlook Press.

Faulkner: "Nobel Prize Award Speech." From *Essays, Speeches and Public Letters by William Faulkner* by William Faulkner, ed. by James Meriwether. Reprinted by permission of W. W. Norton, Inc.

Fausto-Sterling: Excerpt from "Society Writes Biology / Biology Constructs Gender" by Anne Fausto-Sterling. Reprinted by permission of *Dædalus*, Journal of the American Academy of Arts and Sciences, from the issue entitled, "Learning About Women: Gender, Politics, and Power," Fall 1987, vol. 116, no. 4.

Finch: "Very Like a Whale" from *Common Ground: A Naturalist's Cape Cod* by Robert Finch. Reprinted by permission of the author.

FitzGerald: "Rewriting American History" from *America Revised: History Schoolbooks in the Twentieth Century* by Frances FitzGerald. Copyright © 1979 by Frances FitzGerald. First appeared in *The New Yorker*. Reprinted by permission of Little, Brown and Company.

Franklin: "From Realism to Virtual Reality: Images of America's Wars" by H. Bruce Franklin.

Originally appeared in *The Georgia Review*, Spring 1994. Copyright © 1994 by H. Bruce Franklin. Reprinted by permission of the author.

Fromm: "The Nature of Symbolic Language" from *The Forgotten Language* by Erich Fromm. Copyright © 1951, © 1979 by Erich Fromm. Reprinted by permission of Henry Holt and Company, Inc.

Frost: "Education by Poetry: A Meditative Monologue" from *Selected Prose of Robert Frost* edited by Hyde Cox and Edward Connery Lathem. Copyright © 1966 by Henry Holt and Company, Inc. Reprinted by permission of Henry Holt and Company, Inc.

Frye: "The Motive for Metaphor" from *The Educated Imagination* by Northrop Frye. Reprinted by permission of Stoddart Publishing Co. Limited.

Fussell: "Thank God for the Atom Bomb" by Paul Fussell originally appeared as an article titled "Hiroshima: A Soldier's View" in *The New Republic*, Aug. 22 and 29, 1981. Reprinted by permission of *The New Republic*. Copyright © 1981, The New Republic, Inc.

Gates: "In the Kitchen" from *Colored People* by Henry Louis Gates. Copyright © 1994 by Henry Louis Gates. Reprinted by permission of Alfred A. Knopf, Inc. Originally appeared in *The New Yorker*.

Gaylin: "What You See Is the Real You" from *The New York Times*, Oct. 7, 1977. Copyright © 1977 by The New York Times Company. Reprinted by permission.

Goldberg: "In Harness: The Male Condition" from *The Hazards of Being Male* by Herb Goldberg. Copyright © 1976 by Herb Goldberg. Reprinted by permission of the author.

Golding: "Thinking as a Hobby" first printed in *Holiday Magazine*. Copyright © 1961 by William Golding. Renewed. Reprinted by permission of Curtis Brown, Ltd.

Gomez: "A Swimming Lesson" from *Forty-Three Septembers* by Jewelle Gomez. Copyright © 1993 by Jewelle Gomez. Reprinted by permission of Firebrand Books.

Gordon: "Getting Here from There: A Writer's Reflections on a Religious Past" from *Good Boys and Dead Girls: And Other Essays* by Mary Gordon. Copyright © 1991 by Mary Gordon. Reprinted by permission of Sterling Lord Literistic, Inc.

Gould: "Our Allotted Lifetimes" from *Natural History*, vol. 86, no. 7. Copyright © 1977 by the American Museum of Natural History. Reprinted by permission of *Natural History*. "Darwin's Middle Road" from *The Panda's Thumb* by Stephen Jay Gould. Copyright © 1980 by Stephen Jay Gould. Reprinted by permission of W. W. Norton & Company, Inc. "The Terrifying Normalcy of AIDS" from *The New York Times Magazine*, Apr. 19, 1987. Copyright © 1987 by The New York Times Company. Reprinted by permission.

Graves: "Mythology" by Robert Graves from *The Larousse Encyclopedia of World Mythology*. Reprinted by permission of Reed Consumer Books.

Gray: "The Temple of Hygiene" by Charlotte Gray. Originally appeared in *Saturday Night*, Sept. 1989. Copyright © 1989 by Charlotte Gray. Reprinted by permission of the author.

Greenblatt: "Storytelling" from *Hiding in Plain Sight: Essays in Criticism and Autobiography*. Copyright © 1993 by Wendy Lesser. Reprinted by permission of the author.

Guinier: "from *The Tyranny of the Majority*" by Lani Guinier. Copyright © 1994 by Lani Guinier. Reprinted by permission of The Free Press, a Division of Simon & Schuster, Inc.

Guterson: "Enclosed. Encyclopedic. Endured: The Mall of America" by David Guterson. Copyright © 1993 by David Guterson. Reprinted by permission of Georges Borchardt, Inc. for the author. Originally appeared in *Harper's Magazine*.

Hayakawa: "Sex Is Not a Spectator Sport" from *Through the Communication Barrier* by S. I. Hayakawa. Copyright © 1979 by S. I. Hayakawa. Reprinted by permission of the estate of S. I. Hayakawa.

Hayes: "The Electronic Palimpset" from *The Sciences*, Sept./Oct. 1993. Reprinted by permission of *The Sciences*.

Helwig: "Hunger" from *Apocalypse Jazz* by Maggie Helwig. Reprinted by permission of Oberon Press.

Hemingway: "from *A Farewell to Arms*" by Ernest Hemingway. Copyright © 1929 by Charles Scribner's Sons; renewed copyright © 1957 by Ernest Hemingway. Reprinted with permission of Scribner, an imprint of Simon & Schuster, Inc.

Highet: "The Mystery of Zen" from *Talent and Geniuses* by Gilbert Highet. Copyright © 1957 by Gilbert Highet. Reprinted by permission of Curtis Brown, Ltd.

Holt: "How Teachers Make Children Hate Reading" from *The Under-Achieving School* by John Holt. Copyright © 1994 by Holt Associates, Inc. Reprinted by permission of Holt Associates, Inc.

Hughes: "Salvation" from *The Big Sea* by Langston Hughes. Copyright © 1940 by Langston Hughes. Renewal copyright © 1968 by Arna Bontemps and George Houston Bass. Reprinted by permission of Hill and Wang, a division of Farrar, Straus & Giroux, Inc.

Hurston: "How It Feels to Be Colored Me" from *I Love Myself When I Am Laughing*, edited by

Alice Walker. Published by The Feminist Press, 1979. Reprinted by permission of the estate of Zora Neale Hurston.

Huttmann: "A Crime of Compassion" by Barbara Huttmann. Originally appeared in the *My Turn* column of *Newsweek*, Aug. 3, 1983. Reprinted by permission of the author.

Huxtable: "Modern-Life Battle: Conquering Clutter" from the *New York Times*. Copyright © 1981 by The New York Times Company. Reprinted by permission.

Jordan: "For My American Family" from *Technical Difficulties* by June Jordan. Copyright © 1994 by June Jordan.

Keller: "Women in Science: A Social Analysis" from *Harvard Magazine*, Sept./Oct. 1974. Copyright © 1974 *Harvard Magazine*. Reprinted with permission of the author.

Kincaid: Excerpt from *A Small Place* by Jamaica Kincaid. Copyright © 1988 by Jamaica Kincaid. Reprinted by permission of Farrar, Straus & Giroux, Inc.

King: "Letter from Birmingham Jail" from *Why We Can't Wait* by Martin Luther King, Jr. Copyright © 1963, 1964 by Martin Luther King, Jr.; copyright © renewed 1991, 1992 by Coretta Scott King. Reprinted by arrangement with The Heirs to the Estate of Martin Luther King, Jr., c/o Joan Daves Agency as agent for the proprietor.

Kingston: "Tongue-Tied" from *The Woman Warrior* by Maxine Hong Kingston. Copyright © 1975, 1976, by Maxine Hong Kingston. Reprinted by permission of Alfred A. Knopf, Inc.

Koestler: "Gravity and the Holy Ghost" from *The Act of Creation* by Arthur Koestler. Reprinted with permission of the Peters Fraser & Dunlop Group Limited.

Konner: "Why the Reckless Survive" from *Why the Reckless Survive* by Melvin Konner. Copyright © 1990 by Melvin Konner. Reprinted by permission of Viking Penguin, a division of Penguin Books USA, Inc.

Krutch: "The Most Dangerous Predator" from *The Best Nature Writing of Joseph Wood Krutch*. Copyright © 1969 by Joseph Wood Krutch. Reprinted by permission of William Morrow & Company, Inc.

Kübler-Ross: "On the Fear of Death" from *On Death and Dying* by Elisabeth Kübler-Ross. Copyright © 1969 by Elisabeth Kübler-Ross. Reprinted by permission of Simon & Schuster, Inc.

Kuhn: "The Route to Normal Science" from *The Structure of Scientific Revolutions* by Thomas S. Kuhn. Reprinted by permission of the University of Chicago Press.

Leopold: "Thinking Like a Mountain" from *A Sand County Almanac: And Sketches Here and There* by Aldo Leopold. Copyright © 1949, 1977 by Oxford University Press, Inc. Reprinted by permission of the publisher.

Levin: "The Case for Torture" from *Newsweek*, June 7, 1982. Copyright © 1982 by Michael Levin. Reprinted by permission of the author.

Lynch: "Last Onsets: Teaching with AIDS" from *Profession 90*, 1990. Reprinted by permission of the Modern Language Association of America.

McGuigan: "To Be a Woman and a Scholar" from *LSA*, Fall 1978. Reprinted by permission of The Center for the Education of Women.

Machiavelli: "The Morals of the Prince" from *The Prince* by Niccolò Machiavelli, translated by Robert M. Adams. A Norton Critical Edition. Copyright © 1977 by W. W. Norton & Company, Inc. Reprinted by permission of W. W. Norton & Company, Inc.

MacLennan: "Scotchman's Return" from *Scotchman's Return* by Hugh MacLennan. Reprinted by permission of McGill-Queen's University Press.

McMurtry: "Kill 'Em! Crush 'Em! Eat 'Em Raw!" from *Macleans*, Oct. 1971. Copyright © 1971 John McMurtry. Reprinted by permission of the author.

McPhee: "Duty of Care" from *The New Yorker*, June 28, 1993. Copyright © 1993 by John McPhee. Reprinted by permission of *The New Yorker*.

Mairs: "On Being a Cripple" from *Plaintext* by Nancy Mairs. Copyright © 1986 by Nancy Mairs. Reprinted by permission of the University of Arizona Press.

Maynard: "Four Generations" from *The New York Times Magazine*, "Hers" column, Apr. 12, 1979. Copyright © 1979 by Joyce Maynard. Reprinted by permission of the author.

Miller and Swift: "Who's in Charge of the English Language?" first appeared in *The Exchange*, no. 62. Copyright © 1990 by Casey Miller and Kate Swift. Reprinted by permission of the authors.

Mitford: "Behind the Formaldehyde Curtain" from *The American Way of Death* by Jessica Mitford. Copyright © 1963, 1978 by Jessica Mitford. Reprinted by permission of Jessica Mitford. All rights reserved.

Moir: "Leave Taking" from *Event*. Reprinted by permission of the author.

Momaday: "The Way to Rainy Mountain" from *The Way to Rainy Mountain* by N. Scott Momaday. Copyright © 1969 by The University of New Mexico Press. First published in the *Reporter*, Jan. 26, 1967. Reprinted by permission of The University of New Mexico Press.

Morris: "Territorial Behavior" from *Manwatching: A Field Guide to Human Behavior* (1977) by Desmond Morris. Text copyright © 1977 by Desmond Morris. Published by Harry N. Abrams, Inc. All rights reserved.

Nabokov: "Good Readers and Good Writers" from *Lectures on Literature* by Vladimir Nabokov. Copyright © 1980 by the Estate of Vladimir Nabokov. Reprinted by permission of Harcourt Brace and Company.

Naylor: "Mommy, What Does 'Nigger' Mean?" from *The New York Times Magazine*, Feb. 20, 1986. Copyright © 1986 by Gloria Naylor. Reprinted by permission of Sterling Lord Literistic, Inc.

Orwell: "Politics and the English Language" and "Shooting an Elephant" from *Shooting an Elephant and Other Essays* by George Orwell. Copyright © 1946, 1950, 1974, 1978 by The estate of the late Sonia Brownell Orwell and Martin Secker and Warburg Ltd. Reprinted by permission of A. M. Heath & Company Ltd. and Harcourt Brace & Company.

Ozick: "The Seam of the Snail" from *Metaphor and Memory* by Cynthia Ozick. Copyright © 1989 by Cynthia Ozick. Reprinted by permission of Alfred A. Knopf, Inc.

Perrin: "Forever Virgin: The American View of America" from *Antaeus*, Autumn 1989, no. 57. Reprinted by permission of the author.

Perry: "Examsmanship and the Liberal Arts: A Study in Educational Epistemology" from *Examining in Harvard College: A Collection of Essays*, by members of the Harvard Faculty. Copyright © 1963. Reprinted by permission of Harvard University Press.

Petroski: "Little Things Can Mean a Lot" from *The Evolution of Useful Things* by Henry Petroski. Copyright © 1992 by Henry Petroski. Reprinted by permission of Alfred A. Knopf, Inc.

Petrunkevitch: "The Spider and the Wasp" from *Scientific American*, Aug. 1952. Copyright © 1952 by Scientific American, Inc. Reprinted by permission of the publisher. All rights reserved.

Quindlen: "A Great Divide" from *The New York Times Magazine*, "Hers" column, Feb. 24, 1988. Copyright © 1988 by The New York Times Company. Reprinted by permission.

Rau: "By Any Other Name" from *Gifts of Passage* by Santha Rama Rau. Copyright © 1961 by Santha Rama Rau. Reprinted by permission of the William Morris Agency, Inc. on behalf of the author.

Regan: "The Case for Animal Rights" from *In Defense of Animals* by Tom Regan. Copyright © 1985 by Tom Regan. Reprinted by permission of Basil Blackwell Inc.

Reps: "Zen Parables" from *Zen Flesh, Zen Bones* by Paul Reps. Reprinted by permission of Charles E. Tuttle Co., Inc.

Rich: "Taking Women Students Seriously" and "When We Dead Awaken: Writing as Re-vision" from *On Lies, Secrets, and Silence: Selected Prose, 1966–1978* by Adrienne Rich. Copyright © 1979 by W. W. Norton & Company, Inc. Reprinted by permission of W. W. Norton & Company Inc.

Richler: "St. Urbain Street, Then and Now" from *Home Sweet Home* by Mordecai Richler. Reprinted by permission of the Canadian Publishers, McClelland & Stewart.

Rivera: "First Communion" from *Family Installments* by Edward Rivera. Copyright © 1992 by Edward Rivera. Reprinted by permission of William Morrow & Company, Inc.

Rodriguez: "Aria" from *Hunger of Memory* by Richard Rodriguez. Copyright © 1982 by Richard Rodriguez. Reprinted by permission of David R. Godine, Publisher.

Rollin: "Motherhood: Who Needs It?" from *Look* magazine, Sept. 22, 1970. Reprinted by permission of H & C Communications, Inc.

Sagan: "The Abstraction of Beasts" from *The Dragons of Eden* by Carl Sagan. Copyright © 1979 by Carl Sagan. Reprinted by permission of the author. All rights reserved.

Sanders: "Looking at Women" from *Secrets of the Universe* by Scott Russell Sanders. Copyright © 1991 by Scott Russell Sanders. Reprinted by permission of Beacon Press. "Under the Influence." Copyright © 1989 by *Harper's Magazine*. Reprinted from the November issue by special permission. All rights reserved.

Sarton: Excerpts reprinted from *Journal of a Solitude* by May Sarton. Copyright © 1973 by May Sarton. Reprinted by permission of W. W. Norton & Company, Inc.

Sartre: "Existentialism" from *Existentialism* by Jean-Paul Sartre. Reproduced by permission of Philosophical Library Publishers.

Schlesinger: "The Opening of the American Mind" from *The New York Times Book Review*, Sept. 23, 1989. Copyright © 1989 by The New York Times Company. Reprinted by permission.

Sloan, et al.: "Handgun Regulations, Crime, Assaults, and Homicide: A Tale of Two Cities" from *The New England Journal of Medicine*, vol. 319, 1988. Copyright © 1988 Massachusetts Medical Society. All rights reserved. Reprinted by permission of *The New England Journal of Medicine*.

Sontag: Excerpts from *AIDS and Its Metaphors* by Susan Sontag. Copyright © 1988, 1989 by Susan Sontag. Reprinted by permission of Farrar, Straus & Giroux.

Staples: "Black Men and Public Space" first appeared as "Just Walk on By," in *Ms.* magazine, Sept. 1986. Copyright © 1986 by Brent Staples. Reprinted by permission of the author.

Steele: "The Recoloring of Campus Life." Copyright © 1989 by *Harper's Magazine*. Reprinted from the February issue by special permission. All rights reserved.

Stegner: "The Town Dump" from *Wolf Willow* by Wallace Stegner. Copyright © 1959 by Wallace Stegner. Copyright renewed © 1987 by Wallace Stegner. Reprinted by permission of Brandt & Brandt Literary Agents, Inc.

Steinem: "The Good News Is: These Are Not the Best Years of Your Life" from *Ms.* magazine, Sept. 1979. Copyright ©1979 by Gloria Steinem. Reprinted by permission of the author.

Stevens: "The Motive for Metaphor" from *Collected Poems* by Wallace Stevens. Copyright © 1947 by Wallace Stevens. Reprinted by permission of Alfred A. Knopf, Inc.

Strebeigh: "Bicycles in China" from *Bicycling* magazine, April 1991. Copyright ©1991 by Fred Strebeigh. Reprinted by permission of the author.

Tannen: "Conversational Styles" (Originally "Teachers' Classroom Strategies Should Recognize That Men and Women Use Language Differently') from *The Chronicle of Higher Education*, 37.40 (June 19, 1991). Copyright © 1991 by Deborah Tannen. Reprinted by permission of International Creative Management, Inc.

Theroux: "Being a Man" from *Sunrise with Seamonsters* by Paul Theroux. Copyright © 1985 by Cape Cod Scriveners Co. Reprinted by permission of Houghton Mifflin Company. All rights reserved.

Thomas, Dylan: "Memories of Christmas" from *Quite Early One Morning* by Dylan Thomas. Reprinted by permission of David Higham Associates Limited.

Thomas, Lewis: "Notes on Punctuation" from *The Medusa and the Snail: More Notes of a Biology Watcher* by Lewis Thomas. Copyright © 1979 by Lewis Thomas. Originally published in *The New England Journal of Medicine*. "The Long Habit" from *The Lives of the Cell* by Lewis Thomas. Copyright © 1972 by the Massachusetts Medical Society. Originally published in *The New England Journal of Medicine*. Reprinted by permission of *The New England Journal of Medicine*.

Thurber: "University Days" from *My Life and Hard Times*. Copyright © 1933, 1961 by James Thurber. "The Bear Who Let It Alone" and "The Owl Who Was God" from *Fables for Our Time* by James Thurber. Copyright © 1940 by James Thurber. Copyright © 1968 Helen Thurber. "A Dog's Eye View of Man" from *Thurber's Dogs* by James Thurber. Copyright © 1955 James Thurber. Copyright © 1983 by Helen Thurber and Rosemary A. Thurber. All selections reprinted by permission of Helen Thurber.

Tillich: "The Riddle of Inequality" from *The Eternal Now* by Paul Tillich. Copyright © 1963 by Paul Tillich. Reprinted with permission of Scribner, an imprint of Simon & Schuster, Inc.

Tisdale: "We Do Abortions Here" from *Harper's Magazine*, Oct. 1990. Copyright © 1990 by Sallie Tisdale. Reprinted by permission of the author.

Toth: "Going to the Movies" from *How to Prepare for Your High-School Reunion* by Susan Toth. Copyright © 1988 by Susan Toth. Reprinted by permission of Little, Brown and Company.

Tuchmann: "This Is the End of the World" from *A Distant Mirror* by Barbara Tuchmann. Copyright © 1978 by Barbara Tuchmann. Reprinted by permission of Random House, Inc.

Updike: "Beer Can" from *Assorted Prose* by John Updike. Copyright © 1964 by John Updike. Reprinted by permission of Alfred A. Knopf, Inc. Originally appeared in *The New Yorker*.

Walker: "Beauty: When the Other Dancer is the Self" from *In Search of Our Mothers' Gardens: Womanist Prose* by Alice Walker. Copyright © 1983 by Alice Walker. Reprinted by permission of Harcourt Brace & Company.

Welty: "Clamorous to Learn" and "One Writer's Beginnings" from *One Writer's Beginnings* by Eudora Welty. Copyright © 1983, 1984 by Eudora Welty. Reprinted by permission of Harvard University Press.

White, E. B.: "Once More to the Lake" from *One Man's Meat*. Copyright © 1941 by E. B. White. Reprinted by permission of HarperCollins Publishers, Inc. "Progress and Change" from *One Man's Meat* by E. B. White. Copyright © 1938 by E. B. White. Reprinted by permission of HarperCollins Publishers. "Democracy" from *The Wild Flag* by E. B. White. Copyright © 1943, 1971 by E. B. White. Originally appeared in *The New Yorker*. Reprinted by permission of *The New Yorker*.

White, Edmund: "Sexual Culture" from *The Burning Library* by Edmund White. Copyright © 1994 by Edmund White. Reprinted by permission of Alfred A. Knopf, Inc. Originally appeared in *Vanity Fair.*

Whitehead: "The Rhythmic Claims of Freedom and Discipline" from *The Aims of Education and Other Essays* by Alfred North Whitehead. Copyright © 1929 by Macmillan Publishing Company, renewed 1957 by Evelyn Whitehead. Reprinted by permission of Simon & Schuster, Inc.

Williams, Patricia J.: "Death of the Profane" from *The Alchemy of Race and Rights* by Patricia J. Williams. Copyright © 1991 by the President and Fellows of Harvard College. Reprinted by permission of Harvard University Press.

Williams, Terry Tempest: "The Clan of One-Breasted Women" by Terry Tempest Wiliams. First published in *Witness*, Winter 1989, vol. 3, no. 4. "The Bowl" from *Coyote's Canyon* by Terry Tempest Williams. Copyright © 1989 by Terry Tempest Williams. Reprinted by permission of Gibbs Smith, Publisher.

Wolfe: Excerpt from "Yeager" from *The Right Stuff* by Tom Wolfe. Copyright © 1979 by Tom Wolfe. Reprinted by permission of Farrar, Straus & Giroux.

Woodcock: "The Tyranny of the Clock" by George Woodcock. Reprinted by permission of the author.

Woolf: "My Father: Leslie Stephen," from *The Captain's Death Bed and Other Essays* by Virginia Woolf. Copyright © 1950, 1978 by Harcourt Brace & Company. Reprinted by permission of Random House UK Limited. "The Death of the Moth" from *The Death of the Moth and Other Essays* by Virginia Woolf. Copyright © 1942 by Harcourt Brace and Company, renewed 1970 by Marjorie T. Parsons, Executrix. "What the Novelist Gives Us," from *The Second Common Reader* by Virginia Woolf. Copyright © 1932 by Harcourt Brace & Company and 1960 by Leonard Woolf. "A Room of One's Own" from *A Room of One's Own* by Virginia Woolf. Copyright © 1929 by Harcourt Brace & Company, renewed 1957 by Leonard Woolf. All selections reprinted by permission of Harcourt Brace & Company.

Wurtzel: "Parental Guidance Suggested" from *NEXT: Young Writers on the New Generation,* edited by Eric Liu. Selection copyright © 1994 by Elizabeth Wurtzel. Reprinted by permission of W. W. Norton & Company, Inc.

Zinsser: "College Pressures" from *Blair & Ketchum's Country Journal*, vol. 6, no. 4, Apr. 1979. Copyright © 1979 by William K. Zinsser. Reprinted by permission of the author.

Index